LOEB CLASSICAL LIBRARY
FOUNDED BY JAMES LOEB 1911

EDITED BY
JEFFREY HENDERSON

OPPIAN
COLLUTHUS
TRYPHIODORUS

LCL 219

OPPIAN
COLLUTHUS
TRYPHIODORUS

WITH AN ENGLISH TRANSLATION BY

A. W. MAIR

HARVARD UNIVERSITY PRESS
CAMBRIDGE, MASSACHUSETTS
LONDON, ENGLAND

First published 1928

ISBN 978-0-674-99241-2

*Printed on acid-free paper and bound by
The Maple-Vail Book Manufacturing Group*

CONTENTS

CONTENTS

TRYPHIODORUS

PREFACE

The present volume forms the third instalment of those translations from the Greek poets on which, almost by an accident, I have spent no inconsiderable portion of the little leisure of my life. If now, contemplating that work dispassionately, I am moved by some misgiving and am tempted to consider it as being, however useful,

σπουδῆς γε μέντοι τῆς ἐμῆς οὐκ ἄξιον,

perhaps the same sober reflection occurs to most men in looking upon the finished labour of their hands: *fecine operae pretium?* Be that as it may, if it should occur to any, otherwise approving, to regret that I have selected for my purpose a series of poets who, after all, dwell rather on the lower levels of Parnassus, I am not altogether without hope that I may hereafter find time to do similar homage to some choicer spirits, to Aeschylus, for example, and to Pindar: for which last, indeed, what I have hitherto written was in a sense and in the first instance merely preparatory. But for the immediate future another sort of work suggests itself which cannot wisely be postponed and which one might, when too late, regret to have left unattempted. *Vitae summa brevis spem nos vetat incohare longam.* Even as I write, while the September sea breaks at my feet on the grey stones of Loch Ranza, not the least prominent thought in my mind is the moving memory of the vanished eyes—of Sir William Ridgeway, Sir John Sandys, J. S. Reid, Arthur Platt, J. S. Phillimore, to name but these, and of others nearer and unnamed—which would have looked upon these pages with a kindly interest, and, I would fain think, not wholly without approval :

> ἔστι δὲ καί τι θανόντεσσιν μέρος
> κὰν νόμον ἐρδομένων,
> κατακρύπτει δ᾽ οὐ κόνις
> συγγόνων κεδνὰν χάριν.

Some little inconsistency in minor detail between one part of the book and another will be explained by the fact that Colluthus and Tryphiodorus—apart from the Index—were in type so long ago as 1921, while Oppian is only now completed.

This last, being largely pioneer work, has occupied more time and labour than one would have cared deliberately to contemplate. The identification of the animals mentioned, and of the fishes in particular, is a difficult and perilous task, and while I have done what I could by collation of the statements in ancient authors and by the use of such hints as could be derived from modern nomenclature or from the apparent etymological significance of the old names, I can hardly expect that my identifications, some of them novel, will command complete approval. But the statement of facts as here presented may lighten the labour of any future editor.

It only remains to thank all who have in sundry ways and at divers seasons helped me. Dr. Page, whose interest has been a great encouragement, has not only read my proofs with almost disconcerting vigilance, but has, in his capacity as one of the Editors, done perhaps some violence to his proper judgement in allowing me unusual space for explanatory or illustrative comment: *superest ut nec me consilii nec illum paeniteat obsequii.* Professor D'Arcy Thompson, *ποταvὸς ἀπὸ πατρός*, has given me kindly counsel and—*φίλων ἔλεγχον ἀψευδέστατον*—the loan of books, and, in addition, read and annotated the proofs of the *Cynegetica*: those of the *Halieutica* he was unhappily prevented by circumstances from reading. Conversations at various times with some of my colleagues, Sir Edward Sharpey-Schafer, Emeritus Professor Cossar Ewart, Professor Ashworth, and with my brothers, have been helpful. Dr. James Ritchie of the Royal Scottish Museum has generously placed his knowledge at my service, and in these last days, when I have been beyond the reach of books, Mr. P. H. Grimshaw of that institution has supplemented some gaps in my knowledge of Natural History from Eels to Whales. In the same circumstances, Mr. W. R. Cunningham, Librarian of Glasgow University, has at some personal trouble supplied me with information otherwise inaccessible. My colleagues of the Greek Department in Edinburgh University, Mr. J. A. FitzHerbert, now Professor of Classics in the University of Adelaide, and Mr. P. B. R. Forbes, have rendered me helpful services of the most varied kind—*μάλιστα δέ τ' ἔκλυον αὐτοί*—and in particular have read the bulk of the proofs; in which matter some assistance was given also by Mr. C. J. Fordyce, of Jesus College, Oxford, as by my eldest son, C. G. R., in connexion with the Colluthus and Tryphiodorus Index. Nor must I forget my nameless informants both among landward men and among them that go down to the sea in ships, τοῖσίν τε θαλάσσια ἔργα μέμηλεν, with whom, as occasion served, I have held illuminating converse.

Lastly, I would express my thanks, sincerely but briefly—for gratitude lies not in the much predication of it—to Mr. William Maxwell, Managing Director of Messrs. R. & R. Clark, to their accomplished Reader, and to the rest of their Staff, whose patience I have often tried, but never exhausted; for indeed it seems to be inexhaustible.

A. W. M.

TO OPPIAN, COLLUTHUS, TRYPHIODORUS

Farewell awhile! who somewhile dwelt with me
In sunny days and sullen, good and ill,
Discoursing still your measured minstrelsy,
Legends of lowly daring, craft, and skill,
Lore of dead men which yet hath power to thrill
Spirits attuned to Nature's mystery,
Things secret of the everlasting hill
And precious things of the eternal sea.

In other mood ye sang of him who chose
For Beauty's Crown the Daughter of the Foam,
Mistook for gain what proved his bitter loss
And prelude to an Iliad of woes—
Won Helen from her happy Spartan home
And drenched with blood the soil of Ilios.

A. W. M.

OPPIAN

INTRODUCTION

I. The Authorship of the Poems

The authorship of the *Cynegetica* and the *Halieutica* presents a problem of some perplexity owing to the impossibility of reconciling some of the external evidence regarding Oppian with the internal evidence presented by the poems themselves.

I. External Evidence.—This consists in the ancient *Vitae* (Βίοι) preserved in various mss. of the poems, with a short notice in Suidas, and some references to and quotations from the *Halieutica*—there are no references to or quotations from the *Cynegetica*—in later writers.

Vitae.—Of the ancient Lives, which show at once considerable agreement and considerable discrepancy, Anton. Westermann, in his ΒΙΟΓΡΑΦΟΙ, Brunsvigae, 1845, distinguishes two recensions, which we shall here denote as *Vita* A and *Vita* B respectively.

Vita A, "quae narrationem praebet omnium simplicissimam," as printed by Westermann may be translated as follows:—

"Oppian the poet was the son of Agesilaus and Zenodotè, and his birthplace was Anazarbos in Cilicia. His father, a man of wealth and considered the foremost citizen of his native city, distinguished too for culture and living the life of a philosopher, trained his son on the same lines and educated him in the whole curriculum of education—music and geometry and especially grammar. When Oppian was about thirty years of age, the Roman Emperor Severus[a] visited Anazarbos. And whereas it was the duty of all public men to meet the Emperor, Agesilaus as a philosopher and one who despised all vain-glory neglected to do so. The Emperor was angered and banished him to the island of Melite in the Adriatic. There the son accompanied his father and there he wrote these very notable poems. Coming to Rome in the time of Antoninus,[b] son of Severus—Severus being already dead—he read his poetry and was bidden to ask anything he pleased. He asked and obtained the restoration of his father, and received further for each verse or line of his poetry a golden coin. Returning home with his father and a pestilence coming upon Anazarbos he soon after died. His fellow-citizens gave him a funeral and erected in his honour a splendid monument with the following inscription:

"'I, Oppian, won everlasting fame, but Fate's envious thread carried me off and chilly Hades took me while still young—me the minstrel of sweet song. But had dread Envy allowed me to remain alive long, no man would have won such glory as I.'[c]

"He wrote also certain other poems and he lived for thirty years. He possessed much polish and

[a] Emperor 193-211 A.D.

[b] *i.e.* Caracalla, Emperor 211-217.

[c] *'Οππιανὸς κλέος εἷλον ἀείδιον· ἀλλά με Μοίρης | βάσκανος ἐξήρπαξε μίτος, κρυερός τ' Ἀΐδας με | καὶ νέον ὄντα κατέσχε τὸν εὐεπίης ὑποφήτην. | εἰ δὲ πολύν με χρόνον ζωὸν μίμνειν φθόνος αἰνὸς | εἴασ', οὐκ ἄν τίς μοι ἴσον γέρας ἔλλαχε φωτῶν.*

smoothness coupled with conciseness and nobility—a most difficult combination. He is particularly successful in sententious sayings and similes."

Vita B, which is "referta interpolationibus," is given by Westermann in its most interpolated form. In the main it agrees with *Vita* A and we merely note the discrepancies, apart from those which are only verbal.

1. The birthplace of Oppian is first given as "either Anazarbos or Corycos" and afterward it is referred to as Corycos.

2. The Melite to which his father was banished is described as an island of Italy, whereas in *Vita* A it is said to be in the Adriatic. This points to a confusion of the Adriatic Meleda with Malta—both anciently Melite.

3. While *Vita* A describes the poetry written at Melite quite vaguely as τοιαῦτα τὰ ποιήματα ἀξιολογώτατα ὄντα, *Vita* B says, τὰ ποιήματα τὰ κάλλιστα ταῦτα ἐν ε′ βιβλίοις [*i.e.* the *Halieutica*].

4. While *Vita* A says no more of his other writings than merely: ἔγραψε δὲ καὶ ἄλλα ποιήματά τινα, *Vita* B has; συνέταξε δὲ καὶ ἄλλα ποιήματα θαυμαστὰ παῖς ὢν ἔτι, τά τε Ἰξευτικὰ καὶ Κυνηγετικά, ἑκάτερα ἐν ε′ (sic) βιβλίοις παρὰ μέρος περιλαβών. ἐν τούτοις δὲ [*sc.* the *Halieutica*] μάλιστα διέπρεψεν, ἅτε δὴ περὶ τὴν ἀκμὴν τοῦ φρονεῖν γεγενημένος.

Westermann prints also a Life of Oppian in στίχοι πολιτικοί by Constantinus Manasses which is merely a paraphrase of *Vita* A.

Lastly, we have the notice in Suidas *s.* Ὀππιανός· Κίλιξ ἀπὸ Κωρύκου πόλεως, γραμματικὸς καὶ ἐποποιός, γεγονὼς ἐπὶ Μάρκου Ἀντωνίνου βασιλέως. Ἁλιευτικὰ ἐν βιβλίοις ε′, Κυνηγετικὰ ἐν βιβλίοις τέσσαρσι,

Ἰξευτικὰ βιβλία β′ (*sc.* ἔγραψεν). He adds a single sentence about his being rewarded by the Emperor —as he does not specify what Emperor, doubtless he means Marcus Antoninus as above.

Other references or quotations

Athenaeus 13 b (in a list of verse Ἁλιευτικά): καὶ τὸν ὀλίγῳ πρὸ ἡμῶν γενόμενον Ὀππιανὸν τὸν Κίλικα. The precise date of Athenaeus is not certainly known. Suidas has *s.* Ἀθήναιος Ναυκρατίτης· γραμματικός, γεγονὼς ἐπὶ τῶν χρόνων Μάρκου. The contemptuous reference to the Emperor Commodus in Athen. 537 f τί οὖν θαυμαστὸν εἰ καὶ καθ' ἡμᾶς Κόμμοδος ὁ αὐτοκράτωρ ἐπὶ τῶν ὀχημάτων παρακείμενον εἶχεν τὸ Ἡράκλειον ῥόπαλον ὑπεστρωμένης αὐτῷ λεοντῆς καὶ Ἡρακλῆς καλεῖσθαι ἤθελεν suggests that the *Deipnosophistae* was not finished till after the death of Commodus (A.D. 193).

Suidas [10th cent.] *s.* Ἀσφάλιος Ποσειδῶν· Ἀσφάλιος ῥιζοῦχα θεμείλια νέρθε φυλάσσων· τελευταῖος οὗτος τοῦ ε′ τῶν Ἁλιευτικῶν Ὀππιανοῦ [*Hal.* v. 680].

Geoponica [10th cent.] xx. 2 gives Oppian as the authority for that chapter: Ἰχθῦς εἰς ἕνα τόπον συναγαγεῖν. Ὀππιανοῦ.

Etymologicum Magnum [c. A.D. 1100] *s.* ἀφύη· . . . ἡ μὴ πεφυκυῖα, τοῦ ā κακὸν σημαίνοντος. Ὀππιανός· Ὧδε καὶ ἠπεδανῆς ἀφύης ὀλιγηπελὲς ἔθνος | οὔτινος ἐκγεγάασιν ἀφ' αἵματος οὐδὲ τοκήων [=*Hal.* i. 767 f.]· καὶ μεθ' ἑτέρους ⟨ϛ′⟩[a] ζήτει στίχους· ἐκ δὲ γενέθλης | οὔνομ' ἐπικλήδην ἀφρήτιδες αὐδάωνται [=*Hal.* i. 775 f.]· γράφεται ἀφυήτιδες. *s.* Κωρύκιον· . . . καὶ Ὀππιανὸς ἐν τρίτῳ Ἁλιευτικῶν· Πανὶ δὲ Κωρυκίῳ βυθίην παρα-

[a] Added by Editor.

κάτθεο τέχνην | παιδὶ τεῷ [= *Hal.* iii. 15]. *s.* λάβραξ· . . . ἔστιν οὖν παρὰ τὸ λάβρως ἐσθίειν· ἀδηφάγον γάρ ἐστι τὸ ζῷον, ὡς ἱστορεῖ Ὀππιανὸς ἐν τοῖς Ἁλιευτικοῖς [= *Hal.* ii. 130].

Eustathius [12th cent.] on Dion. P. ii. 270 τοῦ εὐρωποῦ, ὅπερ δηλοῖ τὸν πλατὺν ἢ σκοτεινόν, ἐξ οὗ καὶ σπήλαιον παρὰ τῷ Ὀππιανῷ εὐρωπόν [apparently thinking of *Hal* iii. 19 f. ἔκ τε βερέθρου | δύμεναι εὐρωποῖο]; on 538 οἱ δὲ περὶ Κύζικον καὶ Προκόννησον τὸν Μέλανα κόλπον τιθέμενοι δοκοῦσιν ἀμάρτυρα λαλεῖν, εἰ μὴ ἄρα ἔκ τινος χωρίου βοηθοῦνται κειμένου ἐν τοῖς τοῦ Ὀππιανοῦ Ἁλιευτικοῖς, ὅπου περὶ τῆς τῶν πηλαμύδων ἄγρας ἐκεῖνός φησι [= *Hal.* iv. 115]; on 772 Ὀππιανὸς δὲ καὶ τοὺς περὶ Τίγριν Ἀσσυρίους καλεῖ, οὓς καὶ πολυγύναικας ἱστορεῖ [= *Hal.* iv. 204]; on 803 καὶ τὸ ἀλγινόεις παρὰ τῷ Ὀππιανῷ [= *Hal.* iv 73]; on 916 καὶ Ὀππιανὸς τοῦ ἀλγινόεις ἀπισχνάνας τὴν δίφθογγον εἰς μονόφθογγον διὰ τοῦ ῑ γράφει ὡς προερρέθη τὴν προπαραλήγουσαν [= *Hal.* iv. 73]; on 1055 ὅτι εὕρηται ὧδε τὸ ἀέναος διὰ ἑνὸς ῡ μετὰ ἐκτάσεως τῆς ἀρχούσης. φησὶ γάρ, καὶ πόρον ἀενάων ποταμῶν . . . εἰ μή τις τὴν τῶν ἀντιγράφων αἰτιώμενος φαυλότητα φυλάσσει μὲν τὴν διὰ τῶν δύο ν̄ν̄ γραφήν, θεραπεύει δὲ τὸ πάθος τοῦ μέτρου διὰ συνιζήσεως, ὡς καὶ ἐν τῇ ἀρχῇ τῶν Ἁλιευτικῶν Ὀππιανοῦ [= *Hal.* i. 24].

Eustathius on Hom. quotes Oppian thus: on Hom. *Il.* xxi 337 οὕτω δέ πως καὶ Ὀππιανὸς τὴν λέξιν λαμβάνει, φλέγμα λέγων τὴν θερινὴν φλόγωσιν [= *Hal.* i. 20]; on Hom. *Od.* xxii. 468 διδάσκει δὲ (ὁ Ἀθηναῖος) ἀκολούθως τῷ Ὀππιανῷ καὶ ὅτι ἡ τρίγλη τριγόνοις γοναῖς ἐπώνυμος οὖσα [= *Hal.* i. 590]; on Hom. *Od.* xviii. 367 ἰστέον δὲ καὶ ὅτι Ὀππιανὸς μὲν καὶ τὸ αἷμα ἔαρ ἔφη διὰ μόνου τοῦ ε̄ ψιλοῦ [= *Hal.* ii. 618]; on *Od.* ii. 290 ὁ τρόφις, οὗ αἰτιατικὴ μὲν παρὰ Ὀππιανῷ ἐν τῷ "ἱερὸν τρόφιν (*v.l.* τρόχιν) Ἐννοσιγαίου," εὐθεῖα δὲ πληθυντικὴ παρὰ τῷ Ἡροδότῳ ἐν τῷ ἐπὰν γένωνται τρόφιες (Herod. iv. 9) [= *Hal.* ii. 634]; on *Il.* iv. 20 ὅτι μύξα οὐ μόνον περίττωμα τὸ ζωικὸν ἀλλὰ καί τις ἑτεροία ἡ παρὰ τῷ Ὀππιανῷ γλαγόεσσα (*cf.* Eustath. on *Il.* ii. 637) [= *Hal.* iii. 376]; on *Il.* iii. 367 ἔστι καὶ ὄνομα (*i.e.* adjective) παρὰ τῷ Ὀππιανῷ ὀφέλλιμος, ὅ τινες ὀφέλσιμος ἔγραψαν Αἰολικώτερον [= *Hal.* iii. 429]; on *Il.* iii. 54 Ὀππιανὸς οὖν λατύσσεσθαι πτερυγίοις [= *Hal.* i. 628 λατυσσομένη πτερύγεσσιν] ἰχθύας καὶ ἔλαφον πτώσσειν ἠλέματον [= *Hal.* iv. 590 ἔλαφοι ἠλέματα πτώσσουσι]. Schol. BV on *Il.* xiii. 443 quotes *H.* i. 134 f.

II. Internal Evidence.—*Cynegetica.* 1. The *Cynegetica* is dedicated to Caracalla (more correctly Caracallus), one of the two sons (the other being Geta) of L. Septimius Severus, Roman Emperor, A.D. 193–211, by his second wife, Julia Domna of Emesa in Syria: *Cyn.* i. 3 f. Ἀντωνῖνε· | τὸν μεγάλη μεγάλῳ φιτύσατο Δόμνα Σεβήρῳ. Caracalla (this is only a nickname), born at Lyons in A.D. 188, was first called Bassianus. He was made Caesar in 196, Imperator under the name of M. Aurelius Antoninus in 197, and Augustus with tribunician power in 198. On the death of Severus at York in 211, his two sons shared the imperial throne till the murder of Geta in 212. The most natural date for the *Cynegetica* is after Caracalla became sole Emperor, *i.e.*, after 212.

2. The poem is in any case dated after 198 by the allusion in i. 31 ἐφρασάμην Πάρθων τε δύας καὶ Κτησιφόωντα to the capture of Ctesiphon by Severus in that year, when Caracalla was but ten years of age.

3. The author of the poem belongs to Apamea on

the Orontes in Syria, as is shown by *Cyn.* ii. 125 ff. where, speaking of the Orontes he writes:

αὐτὸς δ' ἐν μεσάτοισιν ἐπαιγίζων πεδίοισιν,
αἰὲν ἀεξόμενος καὶ τείχεος ἐγγὺς ὁδεύων,
χέρσον ὁμοῦ καὶ νῆσον,[a] ἐμὴν πόλιν, ὕδατι χεύων

and just below 156 f. (after mentioning the Syrian tomb of Memnon) he says:

ἀλλὰ τὰ μὲν κατὰ κόσμον ἀείσομεν εὐρέα κάλλη
πάτρης ἡμετέρης ἐρατῇ Πιμπληΐδι μολπῇ.

Halieutica.—1. The author of the *Halieutica* is a Cilician as is proved by two passages:

(*a*) *H.* iii. 7 ff.—

σοὶ δ' ἐμὲ τερπωλήν τε καὶ ὑμνητῆρ' ἀνέηκαν
δαίμονες ἐν Κιλίκεσσιν ὑφ' Ἑρμαίοις ἀδύτοισι.
Ἑρμεία, σὺ δέ μοι πατρώϊε κτλ.

(*b*) *H.* iii. 205 ff.—

Ἀνθιέων δὲ πρῶτα περίφρονα πεύθεο θήρην,
οἵην ἡμετέρης ἐρικυδέος ἐντύνονται
πάτρης ἐνναετῆρες ὑπὲρ Σαρπηδόνος ἀκτῆς

[a] χέρσον ὁμοῦ καὶ νῆσον = Χερσόνησον, "quod versu dicere non est," one of the names of Apamea or Pella on the Orontes. *Cf.* Steph. B. *s.* Ἀπάμεια, Συρίας πόλις, ἀπὸ Ἀπάμας, τῆς Σελεύκου μητρός· ἐκλήθη καὶ Χερρόνησος, ἀπὸ τῆς περιοχῆς τῶν ὑδάτων, καὶ Πέλλα, ἀπὸ τῆς ἐν Μακεδονίᾳ; Strabo 752 ἡ δ' Ἀπάμεια καὶ πόλιν ἔχει τὸ πλέον εὐερκῆ· λόφος γάρ ἐστιν ἐν πεδίῳ κοίλῳ τετειχισμένος καλῶς, ὃν ποιεῖ χερρονησίζοντα ὁ Ὀρόντης καὶ λίμνη περικειμένη μεγάλη καὶ ἕλη πλατέα λειμῶνάς τε βουβότους καὶ ἱπποβότους διαχεομένους ὑπερβάλλοντας τὸ μέγεθος· ἥ τε δὴ πόλις οὕτως ἀσφαλῶς κεῖται (καὶ δὴ καὶ Χερρόνησος ἐκλήθη διὰ τὸ συμβεβηκός) καὶ χώρας εὐπορεῖ παμπόλλης εὐδαίμονος [*cf.* *C.* ii. 150 ff.], δι' ἧς ὁ Ὀρόντης ῥεῖ . . . ἐκαλεῖτο δὲ καὶ Πέλλα ποτὲ ὑπὸ τῶν πρώτων Μακεδόνων διὰ τὸ τοὺς πλείστους τῶν Μακεδόνων ἐνταῦθα οἰκῆσαι τῶν στρατευομένων.

ὅσσοι θ' Ἑρμείαο πόλιν, ναυσίκλυτον ἄστυ
Κωρύκιον, ναίουσι καὶ ἀμφιρύτην Ἐλεοῦσαν.

These passages certainly suggest that the author of the *Halieutica* came from Corycus, but they by no means prove it. The poet is describing a method of fishing, and Anazarbos as an inland town (Ptolem. v. 8. 7 among inland [μεσόγειοι] towns in Cilicia is Καισάρεια πρὸς Ἀναζάρβῳ) would not be in point. Nor is Ἑρμεία, σὺ δέ μοι πατρώϊε conclusive, as Hermes appears on coins of other Cilician towns, *e.g.* Adana and Mallos.

2. The *Halieutica* is dedicated to a Roman Emperor, who is addressed as Antoninus[a] (*H.* i. 3, etc.) without further specification.

3. That Emperor's son, whose name is not indicated, is several times in the poem coupled with his father: *H.* i. 66, the fish in a royal preserve are a ready spoil σοί τε, μάκαρ, καὶ παιδὶ μεγαυχέϊ; i. 77 ff. σὺ δ' ἰθύνειας ἕκαστα, | πότνα Θεά, καὶ πατρὶ καὶ υἱέϊ παμβασιλῆος | θυμήρη τάδε δῶρα τεῆς πόρσυνον ἀοιδῆς; ii. 41 σοί τε, μάκαρ σκηπτοῦχε, καὶ ἀγλαόπαιδι γενέθλῃ; ii. 682 Justice prevails among men ἐξ οὗ μοι κραίνουσι μέγαν θρόνον ἐμβεβαῶτες | ἄμφω θεσπέσιός τε πατὴρ καὶ φαίδιμος ὄρπηξ; iv. 4 ff. ἀλλά σύ μοι, κάρτιστε πολισσούχων βασιλήων, | αὐτός τ', Ἀντωνῖνε, καὶ υἱέος ἠγάθεον κῆρ, | πρόφρονες εἰσαΐοιτε κτλ.

Suidas, as we have seen above, puts the Cilician Oppian ἐπὶ Μάρκου Ἀντωνίνου βασιλέως, which most naturally means Marcus Aurelius Antoninus, Emperor 161–180, in which case the son will be L. Aurelius

[a] The ambiguity is sufficiently great since the name Antoninus was borne by Antoninus Pius 138–161, M. Aurelius Antoninus 161–180, Commodus 180–192, Caracalla 211–217, Opellius 217–218, Elagabalus 218–222, etc.

Commodus,[a] son of Marcus Aurelius and Faustina, Emperor 180–192. Born in 161, he was made a Caesar in 166, and Imperator in 176. As *H.* ii. 682 ff. (quoted above) implies that the son was associated with his father in the imperial power, this would date the *Halieutica* between 176, and the death of Marcus Aurelius in 180. For the sporting proclivities of Commodus *cf.* Herodian i. 15. The schol. in most places, i. 66, i. 77, ii. 41, iv. 4 take the son to be Ἀντωνίνῳ (sic) τῷ Γορδιανῷ, but on ii. 683 the father and son are given as Ἀντωνῖνος καὶ Κώμοδος.

The identification of the Antoninus of the *Halieutica* with Marcus Aurelius has been generally accepted. The date thus assigned to the Cilician Oppian agrees admirably with the external evidence mentioned above. It agrees too with the date given for Oppian by Eusebius (Chron. *ap.* S. Hieron., vol. viii. p. 722, ed. Veron. 1736), and Syncellus (*Chronogr.* pp. 352 f., ed. Paris, 1652), who place Oppian in the year 171 or 173. If there be anything at all in the somewhat suspicious story of the banishment of the father and his restoration through his son, the story would appear to refer to the poet of the *Cynegetica.*

The latest edition (sixth) of W. von Christ's *Geschichte der griechischen Literatur* (ed. W. Schmid and O. Stählin) holds that the *Cynegetica* and the *Halieutica,* although by different authors, are both alike dedicated to Caracalla. von Christ himself held, as we hold, that the *Halieutica* was dedicated to Marcus Aurelius. The reasoning by which the

[a] His imperial name was Marcus Aurelius Commodus Antoninus.

latest editors reach their conclusion is nothing less than astounding:

(1) Assuming *Vita* A to be the most trustworthy, they take the banishment to refer to the father of the Cilician Oppian.

(2) They put the visit of Severus in 194, when he was marching against Pescennius Niger.

(3) The poet of the *Halieutica*, they say, died in the thirtieth year of his age, after the death of Severus in 211. But the *Vita* A—their sole authority—says that the poet was about thirty years of age when his father was banished, and that he died at the age of thirty. In any case the whole story seems to contemplate a short period of banishment. On the showing of Messrs. Schmid-Stählin it extended at least from 194–212, a period of eighteen years.

(4) Caracalla had no son. It was, apparently, only after his death that any hint was made with regard to the paternity of Elagabalus or his cousin; in any case neither youth could possibly have been referred to in the terms in which the poet of the *Halieutica* refers to the son of Antoninus. Messrs. Schmid & Stählin, feeling this difficulty, comfortably say that in *H*. i. 66 "ist wohl πατρί statt παιδί zu schreiben." It is regrettable that their researches in Oppian should not have proceeded a little further, when the other references to the son, as quoted above, would have needed more serious surgery.

Our conclusion, on the whole, is that the *Halieutica* alone is the work of the Cilician Oppian. The *Cynegetica*, which shows knowledge of the *Halieutica* not merely in detail, *e.g.* *Cyn*. i. 82 compared with *Hal*. iii. 35, but in general treatment, is the work of a Syrian imitator, dedicated very naturally to Caracalla, with regard to whom, amid so many uncertainties, nothing about his later years seems certain except his close relations with Syria.

II. Zoology before Oppian

The earliest classification of animals in any detail that we possess occurs in Book II. of the Περὶ Διαίτης, a treatise in the *Corpus Hippocrateum*, the collection of writings which pass under the name of Hippocrates. This particular treatise is assigned to the 5th century and has been by some ascribed to Herodicus of Selymbria, teacher of Hippocrates and father of Greek Medicine (*cf.* Suid. *s.* Ἱπποκράτης, Soranus, *Vit. Hippocr.*, Tzetz. *Chil.* viii. 155). This classification is purely incidental and is confined moreover to animals which are eaten. The author is discussing the qualities of the flesh of various edible animals (περὶ ζῴων τῶν ἐσθιομένων ὧδε χρὴ γινώσκειν) and he divides them according to their habitat, on land, in air, in water, into the three popular genera of Beasts—or as the writer calls them Quadrupeds (τετράποδα)—Birds (ὄρνιθες), Fish (ἰχθύες). Such grouping as there is within these great divisions is based on similarity in quality of flesh—distinguished as light or heavy, firm or flaccid, and so forth. Under the first genus he distinguishes Cattle, Goats, Swine (Wild and Tame), Sheep, Asses, Horses, Dogs, Deer, Hares, Foxes, Hedgehogs. Under the second genus he specifies φάσσα (Ringdove), περιστερά (Domestic Pigeon), Partridge, Cock, Turtle-dove, Goose; then ὅσα σπερμολογέει (no specific bird is mentioned but the reference would be first and foremost to the Rook, *Corvus frugilegus,* L., *cf.* A. 592 b 28, Aristoph. *Av.* 232, 579, etc.), and lastly "the Duck (νῆσσα) and others which live in marshes or in water." Here we have traces of sub-groups based on habit or habitat. Under the third genus (Fishes) we have several such groups. He specifies (1) σκορπίος, δράκων, κόκκυξ, γλαῦκος, πέρκη, θρίσσα; (2) οἱ πετραῖοι (rock-haunting fishes), of which he mentions κίχλη, φυκίς, ἐλεφιτίς (ἀλφηστής?), κωβιός; (3) οἱ πλανῆται[a] (wandering fishes), no example being named; (4) νάρκαι καὶ ῥῖναι καὶ ψῆσσαι καὶ ὅσα τοιαῦτα; (5) fishes which live in muddy and wet places—κέφαλοι, κεστραῖοι, ἐγχέλυες καὶ οἱ λοιποὶ τοιοῦτοι; (6) fishes of River and Lake (οἱ ποτάμιοι καὶ λιμναῖοι); (7) πολύποδες καὶ σηπίαι καὶ τὰ τοιαῦτα; (8) τὰ κογχύλια (*i.e.* Ostracoderms): πίνναι, πορφύραι, λεπάδες, κήρυκες, ὄστρεα, μύες, κτένες, τελλῖναι, κνίδαι, ἐχῖνοι; (9) κάραβος, μύες (μαῖαι?), καρκίνοι (ποτάμιοι καὶ θαλάσσιοι) —*i.e.* Crustaceans.

This enumeration, as we have said, is introduced incidentally and there are indications that the writer was familiar with more detailed classifications. For example, he uses the term *Selachian* (τὰ σελάχεα), although he neither defines the group nor specifies the fishes which belong to it. Again, at the end of the list he makes a series of other distinctions such as Wild and Tame (these latter again being sub-

[a] This should correspond to Aristotle's ῥυάδες or πελάγιοι but there is a curious discrepancy as to the quality of their flesh: Περὶ Δ. οἱ δὲ πλανῆται καὶ κυματόπληγες . . . στερεωτέρην τὴν σάρκα ἔχουσιν, *i.e.* than οἱ πετραῖοι, but A. 598 a 8 αἱ σάρκες συνεστᾶσι μᾶλλον τῶν τοιούτων ἰχθύων [*i.e.* τῶν προσγείων], τῶν δὲ πελαγίων ὑγραὶ εἰσι καὶ κεχυμέναι.

divided into ἑλονόμα καὶ ἀγρονόμα on the one hand and τὰ ἔνδον τρεφόμενα on the other); Carnivorous (ὠμοφάγα) and Vegetarian (ὑλοφάγα); ὀλιγοφάγα and πολυφάγα; καρποφάγα and ποηφάγα; ὀλιγοπότα and πολυπότα; and what suggests more than superficial observation, πολύαιμα, ἄναιμα, ὀλίγαιμα.

The real founder of scientific Zoology is Aristotle (385/4–322/1 B.C.), and for more than eighteen centuries writers on Natural History hardly did more than copy or translate his works or comment upon them. We know but little of his predecessors in this field, as Aristotle is not prone to base his statements upon authority. In his *History of Animals* (αἱ περὶ τὰ ζῷα ἱστορίαι) the writers referred to are Aeschylus,[a] Alcmaeon[b] of Croton, Ctesias[c] of Cnidus, Democritus,[d] Diogenes[e] of Apollonia, Herodorus[f] of Heracleia, Herodotus,[g] Homer,[h] Musaeus,[i] Polybus[j] son-in-law of Hippocrates, Simonides[k] of Ceos, Syennesis[l] of Cyprus. But in any case, so far as scientific Zoology is concerned, the opinion of Cuvier is probably not far from the truth: "Je ne pense pas au reste qu'il ait fait grand tort aux ichtyologistes qui l'ont précédé, s'il y en a eu avant lui; ceux des fragmens conservés par Athénée que l'on pourrait

[a] 633 a 19.
[b] 492 a 14; 581 a 16.
[c] 501 a 25; 523 a 26; 606 a 8.
[d] 623 a 32.
[e] 511 b 30; 512 b 12.
[f] 563 a 7; 615 a 9.
[g] 523 a 17; 579 b 2.
[h] 513 b 27; 519 a 18; 574 b 34; 575 b 5; 578 b 1; 597 a 6; 606 a 20; 615 b 9; 618 b 25; 629 b 22.
[i] 563 a 18.
[j] 512 b 12.
[k] 542 b 7.
[l] 511 b 23; 512 b 12.

leur attribuer, n'annoncent point qu'ils aient traité leur sujet avec méthode ou avec étendue ; et tout nous fait croire que c'est sous la plume d'Aristote seulement que l'ichtyologie, comme toutes les autres branches de la zoologie, a pris pour la première fois la forme d'une véritable science" (Cuv. et Val. i. p. 16).

The chief writings of Aristotle upon Natural History are 1. *History of Animals,* in ten Books. In the best MSS. there are only nine Books and Bk. x. is universally regarded as spurious. Doubt has also been cast upon Bk. ix., and even upon Bk. vii., which in the MSS. follows Bk. ix. and was first put in its present place by Theodorus Gaza (15th cent.). 2. *On the Parts of Animals* (Περὶ ζῴων μορίων), four Books. 3. *On the Generation of Animals* (Περὶ ζῴων γενέσεως), five Books. 4. *On the Locomotion of Animals,* one Book.

With regard to the achievement of Aristotle in the field of Zoology we may conveniently quote—especially as a large part of his work is concerned with Ichthyology—the words of Cuvier in the Introduction to the *Histoire Naturelle de Poissons:* "Ce grand homme, secondé par un grand prince [Alexander the Great], rassembla de toute part des faits, et ils parurent dans ses ouvrages si nombreux et si nouveaux, que pendant plusieurs siècles ils excitèrent la défiance de la postérité. Les personnages d'Athénée se demandent [Athen. 352 d] où Aristote a pu apprendre tout ce qu'il raconte des mœurs des poissons, de leur propagation et des autres détails de leur histoire qui se passent dans les abymes les plus cachés de la mer. Athénée lui-même répond à cette question, puisqu'il nous dit [Athen. 398 ὀκτακόσια γὰρ εἰληφέναι τάλαντα παρ' Ἀλεξάνδρου τὸν Σταγιρίτην λόγος ἔχει εἰς τὴν περὶ τῶν ζῴων ἱστορίαν] qu'Alexandre donna à Aristote, pour recueiller les matériaux de son histoire des animaux, des sommes qui montèrent à neuf [*sic*] cents talens, à quoi Pline [viii. 44] ajoute que le roi mit plusieurs milliers d'hommes à la disposition du philosophe, pour chasser, pêcher et observer tout ce qu'il désirait connaître.

" Ce n'est pas ici le lieu d'exposer en détail le parti qu'Aristote tira de cette munificence, d'analyser ses nombreux ouvrages d'histoire naturelle, et d'énumérer l'immense quantité de faits et de lois qu'il est parvenu à constater; nous ne nous occuperons pas même de montrer avec quel génie il jeta les bases de l'anatomie comparée, et établit dans le règne animal, et dans plusieurs de ses classes, d'après leur organisation, une distribution à laquelle les âges suivans n'ont presque rien eu à changer. C'est uniquement comme ichtyologiste que nous avons à le considérer, et dans cette branche même de la zoologie, n'eût-il traité que celle-là, on devrait encore le reconnaître comme un homme supérieur. Il a parfaitement connu la structure générale des poissons. . . . Quant aux espèces, Aristote en connaît et en nomme jusqu'à cent dix-sept, et il entre, sur leur manière de vivre, leurs voyages, leurs amitiés et leurs haines, les ruses qu'elles emploient, leurs amours, les époques de leur frai et de leur ponte et leur fécondité, la manière de les prendre, les temps où leur chair est meilleure, dans des détails que l'on serait aujourd'hui bien embarrassé, ou de contredire ou de confirmer, tant les modernes soient loin d'avoir observé les poissons comme ce grand naturaliste paraît l'avoir fait par lui-même ou par ses correspondants. Il faudrait passer plusieurs années dans les îles de l'Archipel, et y vivre avec les pêcheurs, pour être en état d'avoir une opinion à ce sujet" (Cuv. et Val. pp. 16 ff.).

Two examples may be quoted to illustrate the accurate observation either of Aristotle himself or of his informants: (1) the assertion (A. 538 a 20; 567 a 27) that the *Erythrinos* and the *Channa* (both belonging to the genus *Serranus*) are hermaphrodite, a fact rediscovered by Cavolini.[a] (2) The assertion (A. 565 b 4) that in the Smooth Dog-fish, γαλεὸς ὁ λεῖος, the embryon is attached to the uterus by a "yolk-sac placenta," rediscovered by Johannes Müller, "Ueber d. glatten Hai d. Aristoteles (Mustelus laevis)," Abh. d. Berlin. Akad. 1840.

As regards the classification of animals we can here notice only the main outlines of Aristotle's system. All animals are distributed into two groups: I. ἔναιμα, blooded animals [= Vertebrates]. II. ἄναιμα, bloodless animals [= Invertebrates].

Group I., ἔναιμα, is subdivided into:

(a) ζῳοτοκοῦντα ἐν αὑτοῖς [= Mammals].
(b) ὄρνιθες [Birds].
(c) τετράποδα ἢ ἄποδα ᾠοτοκοῦντα [Reptiles and Amphibia].
(d) ἰχθύες [Fishes].

Group II., ἄναιμα, is subdivided into:

(a) μαλάκια [Cephalopods].
(b) μαλακόστρακα [Crustaceans].
(c) ἔντομα [Insects, Arachnidae, Worms].
(d) ὀστρακόδερμα [Mussels, Sea-snails, Ascidia, Holothuria, Actinia, Sponges].

[a] *Memoria sulla generazione dei pesci e dei granchi*, Naples, 1787.

INTRODUCTION

Theophrastus of Eresos (*circ.* 372–287), the successor of Aristotle as head of the Peripatetic school, wrote Περὶ ζῴων (Athen. 387 b), Περὶ τῶν δακέτων καὶ βλητικῶν (Athen. 314 c), Περὶ τῶν μεταβαλλόντων τὰς χρόας (Athen. 317 f), Περὶ τῶν φωλευόντων (Athen. 314 b, etc.), Περὶ τῶν ἐν τῷ ξηρῷ διαιτωμένων (Athen. 312 b: διατριβόντων 317 f), Περὶ τῶν κατὰ τόπους διαφορῶν (Athen. 317 f), which are known to us only by quotations.

Aristophanes of Byzantium (*circ.* 257–180 B.C.) made an Epitome of Aristotle's *History of Animals*, which was used by Aelian (*circ* A.D. 200) and Suidas (*circ.* A.D. 950) and is perhaps identical with the pseudo-Aristotelian ζωικά (Athen. 319 d, etc.). This Epitome was extracted by Sopatros of Apameia (4th cent. A.D.), *cf.* Phot. *Bibl.* 104 b 26 ὁ δε ἐνδέκατος ἔχει τὴν συναγωγὴν . . . ἀλλὰ μὴν καὶ ἐκ τῶν Ἀριστοφάνους τοῦ γραμματικοῦ περὶ ζῴων βιβλίου πρώτου καὶ δευτέρου. Extracts were also made from the Epitome for Constantine VII. (Porphyrogennetos), Emperor A.D. 912–959 [ed. Spuridion Lambros, Suppl. Aristot. I. Berlin 1885].

Clearchus of Soli (3rd cent. B.C.) wrote Περὶ ἐνύδρων (Athen. 332 b, *cf.* 317 c]. Nicander of Colophon (b. *circ.* 200 B.C.) wrote the extant *Theriaca* and *Alexipharmaca*, the former on the bites of venomous animals and their remedies, the latter on antidotes to poison. Tryphon of Alexandria (1st cent. B.C.) wrote Περὶ ζῴων (Suid. *s.* Τρύφων, Athen. 324 f). Dorion (for whom see Athen. 337 b, M. Wellmann, *Hermes* 23 [1888]) wrote, in 1st cent. B.C., Περὶ ἰχθύων, frequently cited by Athenaeus. Juba II., king of Mauretania, after the death of his father in 46 B.C., was brought a prisoner (Plut. *Caes.* 55 Ἰόβας υἱὸς ὢν ἐκείνου κομιδῇ νήπιος ἐν τῷ θριάμβῳ παρήχθη, μακαριωτάτην ἁλοὺς ἅλωσιν, ἐκ βαρβάρου καὶ Νομάδος Ἑλλήνων τοῖς πολυμαθεστάτοις ἐναρίθμιος γενέσθαι συγγραφεῦσι) to Rome, where he remained till his restoration by Octavian in 30 B.C. One of the most erudite men of his time (Plut. *Sert.* 9 ἱστορικωτάτου βασιλέων; Athen. 83 b ἄνδρα πολυμαθέστατον; Plin. v. 16 studiorum claritate memorabilior etiam quam regno), he wrote on Assyria, Arabia, and Africa—his work on the latter supplying information on the Elephant (Plin. viii. 7, 14, 35; Plut. *Mor.* 972 b; Ael. ix. 58), the Lion (Ael. vii. 23), the Crocotta (Plin. viii. 107) etc., *cf.* M. Wellmann, *Hermes* 27 (1892) "Iuba eine Quelle d. Aelian" About the same date Metrodorus of Byzantium and his son Leonidas (Athen. 13 c, *cf.* M. Wellmann, *Hermes* 30 [1895] "Leonidas von Byzanz u. Demostratos") and Demostratus wrote on Fishes (Ael. *N.A. epilog.*). Alexander of Myndos (first half of 1st cent. A.D., *cf.* M. Wellmann, *Hermes* 26 [1891], 51 [1916]) wrote Περὶ ζῴων (Athen. 392 c, Bk. II. being on Birds, περὶ πτηνῶν, Athen. 388 d etc.), based mainly on Aristophanes' Epitome of the *H.A.* of Aristotle, as well as a Θηριακός and a Θαυμασίων συναγωγή (Phot. *Bibl.* p. 145 b Bekker λέγει δὲ περί τε ζῴων καὶ φυτῶν καὶ χωρῶν τινῶν καὶ ποταμῶν καὶ κρηνῶν καὶ βοτανῶν καὶ τῶν τοιούτων). He made use of Leonidas of Byzantium and Juba, and was one of the sources of Aelian, Dionysius *De avibus,* and Plut. *De sollert. animalium.* Pamphilos of Alexandria (middle of 1st cent. A.D.) was the author of a lexicon Περὶ γλωσσῶν ἤτοι λέξεων, in ninety-five books. This lexicon, which was at once a glossary and an encyclopaedia of general information, was excerpted in the reign of Hadrian first by Julius Vestinus and then by Diogenianus of Heracleia—the work of the latter being the basis of the extant lexicon of Hesychius. The zoological matter in Pamphilus was utilized by Aelian, Athenaeus, etc.; *cf.* M. Wellmann, *Hermes* 51 (1916). Plutarch of Chaeroneia (*circ.* A.D. 46–120) wrote *De sollertia animalium* (Πότερα τῶν ζῴων φρονιμώτερα, τὰ χερσαῖα ἢ τὰ ἔνυδρα) and *Bruta ratione uti* (Περὶ τοῦ τὰ ἄλογα λόγῳ χρῆσθαι).

More or less contemporary with Oppian (*i.e.*, the author of the *Halieutica*) was Julius Polydeuces (Pollux) of Naucratis in Egypt, whose extant Ὀνομαστικόν (ten books), dedicated to Commodus, Emperor 180–192, contains a good deal of zoological information. Somewhat later Claudius Aelianus of Praeneste (*circ.* A.D. 170–235) wrote *De natura animalium* (Περὶ ζῴων) in seventeen books and *Varia historia* (Ποικίλη ἱστορία) in fourteen books Lastly we may mention here, although we know on his own authority that he was a little later than the author of the *Halieutica* (Athen. 13 b τὸν ὀλίγῳ πρὸ ἡμῶν γενόμενον Ὀππιανὸν τὸν Κίλικα), Athenaeus of Naucratis, whose Δειπνοσοφισταί, in fifteen books, contains an immense amount of undigested information. His zoological information is probably largely based on the Lexicon of Pamphilus and thus indirectly on Alexander of Myndos.

M. Wellmann, who has discussed the sources of Aelian, Oppian, etc, in a series of articles in *Hermes* (23 [1888], 26 [1891], 27 [1892], 30 [1895], 51 [1916]) regards Leonidas of Byzantium and Alexander of Myndos as the chief sources of the *Halieutica* The close agreement in many passages of Aelian and Oppian he attributes to the use of common sources, not to direct borrowing of the one from the other.

III. Hunting, Fishing, Fowling

And God said, Let us make man in our image, after our likeness : and let them have dominion over the fish of the sea, and over the fowl of the air, and over the cattle, and over all the earth, and over every creeping thing that creepeth upon the earth. —Genesis i. 26.

ἰχθύσι μὲν καὶ θηρσὶ καὶ οἰωνοῖς πετεηνοῖς. Hesiod, *W.* 277.

φῦλά θ' ἑρπετὰ τόσσα τρέφει μέλαινα γαῖα
θῆρές τ' ὀρεσκῷοι καὶ γένος μελισσᾶν
καὶ κνώδαλ' ἐν βένθεσσι πορφυρέας ἁλός,
εὕδουσιν δ' οἰωνῶν φῦλα τανυπτερύγων. Alcman fr 65 (10).

κουφονόων τε φῦλον ὀρνίθων ἀμφιβαλὼν ἄγει
καὶ θηρῶν ἀγρίων ἔθνη πόντου τ' εἰναλίαν φύσιν
σπείραισι δικτυοκλώστοις
περιφραδὴς ἀνήρ. Soph. *Antig.* 343 ff.

Tum laqueis captare feras et fallere visco
inventum et magnos canibus circumdare saltus,
atque alius latum funda iam verberat amnem
alta petens pelagoque alius trahit humida lina.
Verg. *Georg.* i. 139 ff.

Corresponding to the popular division of wild life according to habitat—creatures of the land, the water, the air—we find the art of capturing or killing wild creatures divided into Hunting, Fishing, Fowling. Xen. *Hell.* iv. 1. 15 ἔνθα καὶ τὰ βασίλεια ἦν Φαρναβάζῳ . . . καὶ θῆραι αἱ μὲν καὶ ἐν περιειργμένοις παραδείσοις, αἱ δὲ καὶ ἐν ἀναπεπταμένοις τόποις, πάγκαλαι. περιέρρει δὲ καὶ ποταμὸς παντοδαπῶν ἰχθύων πλήρης. ἦν δὲ καὶ τὰ πτηνὰ ἄφθονα τοῖς ὀρνιθεῦσαι δυναμένοις; Cic. *De fin.* ii. 8. 25 piscatu, aucupio, venatione; Plin. viii. 44 Alexandro Magno rege inflammato cupidine animalium naturas noscendi delegataque hac commentatione Aristoteli, summo in omni doctrina viro, aliquot millia hominum in totius Asiae Graeciaeque tractu parere iussa omnium quos venatus, aucupia, piscatusque alebant quibusque vivaria, armenta, alvearia, piscinae, aviaria in cura erant, ne quid usquam genitum ignoraretur ab eo. Pliny's *alebant* reminds us that the capture of wild creatures was at first a practical affair, the provision of food; *cf.* Pind. *I.* i. 47 μισθὸς γὰρ ἄλλοις ἄλλος ἐφ' ἔρμασιν ἀνθρώποις γλυκύς, | μηλοβότᾳ τ' ἀρότᾳ τ' ὀρνιχολόχῳ τε καὶ ὃν πόντος τρέφει· | γαστρὶ δὲ πᾶς τις ἀμύνων λιμὸν αἰανῆ τέταται. And it may be noted that Izaak Walton, *The Compleat Angler,* c. i. makes each of his three disputants, Auceps, Venator, and Piscator, in commending the rival claims of their different arts, refer to this practical aspect: Auceps: "the very birds of the air . . . are both so many and so useful and pleasant to mankind. . . . They both feed and refresh him; feed him with their choice bodies, and refresh him with their heavenly voices." Venator: "the Earth feeds man and all those several beasts that both feed him and afford him recreation." Piscator: "And it may be fit to remember that Moses appointed fish to be the chief diet for the best commonwealth that ever was." Later the three arts are regarded more as forms of healthy recreation or, in the case of Hunting, as useful preparation for the art of war: Xenoph. *Cyn.* 1. 18 *ἐγὼ μὲν οὖν παραινῶ τοῖς νέοις μὴ καταφρονεῖν κυνηγεσίων μηδὲ τῆς ἄλλης παιδείας· ἐκ τούτων γὰρ γίγνονται τὰ εἰς τὸν πόλεμον ἀγαθοί.*

In the Greek Anthology we have a series of epigrams (*A.P.* vi. 11-16 and 179-187) in which three brothers, Damis, a Hunter, Pigres, a Fowler, Cleitor, a Fisher, make dedicatory offerings of the instruments of their several crafts.

1. Fowling (*ὀρνιθευτική, ἰξευτική, aucupium*). The methods of the Fowler are alluded to *C.* i. 64 ff., *H.* i. 31 ff.; iv. 120 ff. (where see notes). The practice of Hawking is mentioned in Aristot. *H.A.* 620 a 32 *ἐν δὲ Θρᾴκῃ τῇ καλουμένῃ ποτὲ Κεδρειπόλει ἐν τῷ ἕλει θηρεύουσιν οἱ ἄνθρωποι τὰ ὀρνίθια κοινῇ μετὰ τῶν ἱεράκων· οἱ μὲν γὰρ ἔχοντες ξύλα σοβοῦσι τὸν κάλαμον καὶ τὴν ὕλην ἵνα πέτωνται τὰ ὀρνίθια, οἱ δ' ἱέρακες ἄνωθεν ὑπερφαινόμενοι καταδιώκουσιν· ταῦτα δὲ φοβούμενα κάτω πέτονται πάλιν πρὸς τὴν γῆν· οἱ δ' ἄνθρωποι τύπτοντες τοῖς ξύλοις λαμβάνουσι, καὶ τῆς θήρας μεταδιδόασιν αὐτοῖς· ῥίπτουσι γὰρ τῶν ὀρνίθων, οἱ δὲ ὑπολαμβάνουσιν.* The same story is told A. *Mirab.* 841 b 15 ff., Antig. 28, Ael. ii. 42, Plin. x. 23. For a different method of employing the Hawk see Dionys. *De av.* iii. 5 and for the employment of the Owl (*γλαῦξ, noctua*) see Dionys. *De av.* iii. 17, Arist. *H.A.* 609 a 13 *τῆς δὲ ἡμέρας καὶ τὰ ἄλλα ὀρνίθια τὴν γλαῦκα περιπέταται, ὃ καλεῖται θαυμάζειν, καὶ προσπετόμενα τίλλουσιν· διὸ οἱ ὀρνιθοθῆραι θηρεύουσιν αὐτῇ παντοδαπὰ ὀρνίθια*; *cf.* 617 b 4. For Doves (*περιστεραί*) as Decoy birds *cf.* Aristoph. *Av.* 1082

τὰς περιστεράς θ' ὁμοίως συλλαβὼν εἵρξας ἔχει, | κἀπαναγκάζει παλεύειν δεδεμένας ἐν δικτύῳ; Arist. *H.A.* 613 a 23, Ael. iv. 16, xiii. 17; for Partridges used in the same way, Arist. *H.A.* 614 a 10, Ael. iv. 16. *Cf.* in general Xen. *Cyrop.* i. 6. 39 σὺ γὰρ ἐπὶ μὲν τὰς ὄρνιθας ἐν τῷ ἰσχυροτάτῳ χειμῶνι ἀνιστάμενος ἐπορεύου νυκτός, καὶ πρὶν κινεῖσθαι τὰς ὄρνιθας ἐπεποίηντό σοι αἱ πάγαι αὐταῖς καὶ τὸ κεκινημένον χωρίον ἐξείκαστο τῷ ἀκινήτῳ· ὄρνιθες δ' ἐξεπεπαίδευντό σοι ὡς σοὶ μὲν τὰ συμφέροντα ὑπηρετεῖν, τὰς δὲ ὁμοφύλους ὄρνιθας ἐξαπατᾶν. Fowling furnishes Homer with a simile *O.* xxii. 468 ὡς δ' ὅταν ἢ κίχλαι τανυσίπτεροι ἠὲ πέλειαι | ἕρκε' ἐνιπλήξωσι, τά θ' ἑστήκῃ ἐνὶ θάμνῳ, | αὖλιν ἐσιέμεναι, στυγερὸς δ' ὑπεδέξατο κοῖτος, | ὣς αἵ γ' ἑξείης κεφαλὰς ἔχον, ἀμφὶ δὲ πάσαις | δειρῇσι βρόχοι ἦσαν. The Fowler's dedications in the *A.P.* vi. include νεφέλαι, ἰχνοπέδη, παγίς, κλωβιοί, στάλικες (stakes to support the nets), limed reeds, ἐπισπαστήρ (= ἐπίδρομος of the Hunter's net), and a net or noose for catching cranes by the neck (ἄρκυν τε κλαγερῶν λαιμοπέδαν γεράνων, *cf.* δεράγχη *A.P.* vi. 109).

Of ancient writings on Fowling we possess, in addition to some fragments of the *De aucupio* of Nemesianus (A.D. 3rd cent.), a prose paraphrase by Eutecnius of a lost poem—sometimes supposed to be the Ἰξευτικά ascribed to Oppian (Suid. *s.* Ὀππιανός), but now generally attributed to Dionysius the Periegete (in time of Hadrian). We quote it as Dionys. *De av.* *i.e.* Διονυσίου περὶ Ὀρνίθων (Cramer *Anec. Par.* i. 22 f.). The treatise (3 Bks.) reminds one of the Oppianic manner. Thus Bk. III. begins, like our *Cynegetica* and *Halieutica*, with a comparison of Hunting, Fishing, and Fowling. While the business of the first two is hazardous, "it suffices the Fowlers to wander with delight in plain and grove and meadow and to hearken to the sweet singing of the birds, using neither sword nor club nor spear, nor employing nets and dogs, but carrying only birdlime and reeds, and fine lines and lightest creels (κύρτους, traps, cages) under the arm. Sometimes too they dress a tree with branches not its own and bring tame birds to share the hunt." Fowling methods are summarized thus: *ἰξῷ χρωμένοις ἢ θριξὶν ἱππείαις ἢ λίνοις ἢ πάγαις ἢ καὶ πηκτίσιν ἢ τροφῇ δελεάζουσιν ἢ τὸν σύμφυλον ὄρνιν ἐπιδεικνῦσιν.* Pliny x. deals with Birds. There are nine lines on Fowling (*Paulini Nolani carmen de aucupio*) in *Poet. Lat. Minores*, ed. N. E. Lemaire, Paris, 1824, vol. i.

2. Hunting (κυνηγέσιον, κυνηγετική, *venatio*). On Hunting we possess the *Cynegeticus* of Xenophon (*c.* 430–*c.* 354 B.C.) and the supplementary *Cynegeticus* of Arrian (*c.* A.D. 150), and in Latin the *Cynegetica* of Grattius (contemporary of Ovid, *cf. Ep. ex Pont.* iv. 16. 34 aptaque venanti Grattius arma daret) in 541 hexameters, and the *Cynegetica* of Nemesianus (A.D. 3rd cent.). Much useful information is to be found in the *Onomasticon* of Pollux (*circ.* A.D. 166 dedicated to Commodus), especially v. 1-94, which is practically a systematic treatise on the subject; in the περὶ Ζῴων of Aelian (in time of Septimius Severus); and in the *Natural History* of Pliny (A.D. 23-79), especially Bk. viii., as well as in the *Res rusticae* of Varro (116-27 B.C.), the *De re rustica* of Columella (A.D 1st cent.), and Palladius (A.D. iv. cent.). Merely incidental references are often instructive, *e.g.* Xen. *Cyr.* i. 6. 40 "Against the Hare, again, because he

feeds in the night and hides by day, you reared dogs which should find him by scent. And because, when found, he fled swiftly, you had other dogs fitted to take him by speed of foot. If again, he escaped these also, you would learn his roads and the sort of places that he is caught fleeing to, and in these you would spread nets difficult to see and the Hare in his impetuous flight would fall into them and entangle himself. And, to prevent him from escaping even from these, you set watchers of what happened (*i.e.* ἀρκυωροί Xen. *Cyn.* 6. 5), who from close at hand might quickly be on the spot; and you behind shouting close upon the Hare frightened him so that he was foolishly taken, while, by instructing those in front to be silent, you caused their ambush not to be perceived." See also "Joannis Caii Britanni *De canibus Britannicis*" and "Hier. Fracastorii *Alcon sive De cura canum Venaticorum*" in Lemaire, *op. cit.* vol. i. pp. 147 ff. The work of Dr. Caius—founder of Caius College, Cambridge—is addressed to Gesner.

3. Fishing (ἁλιευτική, *piscatus*). We possess a fragment—some 132 hexameters—of the *Halieutica* of Ovid (*cf.* Plin. xxxii. 152 his adiciemus ab Ovidio posita nomina quae apud neminem alium reperiuntur, sed fortassis in Ponto nascentium, ubi id volumen supremis suis temporibus inchoavit: *bovem, cercurum* in scopulis viventem, *orphum* rubentemque *erythinum, iulum*, pictas *mormyras* aureique coloris *chrysophryn*, praeterea *sparum, tragum*, et placentem cauda *melanurum, epodas* lati generis. Praeterea haec insignia piscium tradit: *channen* ex se ipsa concipere, *glaucum* aestate nunquam apparere, *pompilum* qui semper comitetur navium cursus, *chromim* qui nidificet in

aquis. *Helopem* dicit nostris incognitum undis, ex quo apparet falli eos qui eundem acipenserem existimaverint. Helopi palmam saporis inter pisces multi dedere), the genuineness of which has been wrongly suspected. But for the most part we must depend on general works, such as Aristot. *H.A.*, Ael. *N.A.*, Pliny (especially ix. and xxxii.) and other works mentioned in the previous section (Hunting).

In Plato's *Sophist* 219 *sq.*, Socrates, wishing to define a sophist and considering that the sophist is a γένος χαλεπὸν καὶ δυσθήρευτον, proposes to practise definition on an easier subject, and he selects the Angler (ἀσπαλιευτής) as "known to everyone and not a person to be taken very seriously." He proceeds as follows:

Angling is an Art and of the two kinds of Art—Creative and Acquisitive—it belongs to the latter. Again the Acquisitive is of two kinds—that which proceeds by voluntary Exchange and that which proceeds by Force—and Angling belongs to the latter. Force may be open, *i.e.* Fighting, or secret, *i.e.* Hunting. Hunting again is of the Lifeless—this sort of Hunting has "no special name except some sorts of diving" (Plato no doubt means σπογγοθηρική [sponge-cutting, Poll. vii. 139 or the like])—or of the Living, *i.e.* Animal Hunting. This again is divided into Hunting of Land Animals and Hunting of Water Animals (Animals which swim). Water animals may be Winged, *i.e.* Birds, and the hunting of these is called Fowling, or they may live in the water, and the hunting of these is called Fishing. Of Fishing there are two kinds, that which proceeds by Enclosures (ἕρκη)—*i.e.* κύρτοι, δίκτυα, βρόχοι, πόρκοι, and the like—and that which proceeds by Striking (πληγή), *i.e.* by Hooks (ἄγκιστρα) and Tridents (τριόδοντες). This again is divided into (1) Night-fishing, done by the light of a fire and called by fishermen πυρευτική; (2) Day-fishing, which may be called as a whole ἀγκιστρευτική, ὡς ἐχόντων ἐν ἄκροις ἄγκιστρα καὶ τῶν τριοδόντων, but is further divided into (1) τριοδοντία or Spearing, in which the blow is downward and the fish is struck in any part of the body; (2) ἀσπαλιευτική or Angling, where the fish is hooked about the head or mouth and drawn upwards from below by rods or reeds (ῥάβδοις καὶ καλάμοις ἀνασπώμενον); *cf.* Plato, *Laws*, 823.

Oppian, *H.* iii. 72 ff., distinguishes four methods of Fishing—by Hook and Line, Nets, Weels, Trident.

With regard to the Hook and Line he distinguishes Rod-fishing from fishing without a Rod, *i.e.* with hand-lines, and in the case of the latter method he distinguishes two sorts of line—the κάθετος, or leaded line (see *H.* iii. 77 n.) and the πολυάγκιστρον, or line with many hooks, for which *cf.* A. 621 a 15 ἁλίσκονται (*sc.* αἱ ἀλώπεκες, Fox Sharks) περὶ ἐνίους τόπους πολυαγκίστροις; 532 b 25 a certain monstrous sea creature is said λαβέσθαι ποτὲ τοῦ πολυαγκίστρου τῷ ἄκρῳ αὐτοῦ, *i.e.* to have seized a night-line with its extremity. Apost. p. 47 is disposed to identify the πολυάγκιστρον with a species of lines used in Greece to-day especially for catching Ἐρυθρίνια (Sea-breams) but also for other fishes. These lines are called παραγάδια, presumably from being mainly used near the land (παρὰ γῆν, παραγάδι). It is a species of line, he says, well known in the N. of France and on all the coasts of England, where it is used for catching Congers and Rays. It consists of a very long and strong line, which, to protect it from the action of the salt water, is dyed red by dipping in an infusion of oak-bark and which carries a large number of hooks attached at intervals by short lines of finer quality (*παράμωλα*). This sort of line is employed at night. One end is anchored, while to the other end a piece of cork or the like is attached to indicate its position. On dark nights, in place of a cork, a triangle is attached, made of wood of the elder-tree, surmounted by a bell, which rings as it is swayed by the waves and so guides the fisherman to the spot. When this engine is withdrawn from the sea, the lines are arranged in a basket, the sides of which are furnished with pieces of cork into which the hooks are stuck. At Paxo, near Corfu, these lines are arranged in such a way that they float and small sails are attached which, driven by the wind, set the whole apparatus in motion.

With regard to Nets the different sorts mentioned by Oppian are not easy to identify with certainty.

1. *δίκτυον* is generic for every sort of Net.

2. *ἀμφίβληστρον* is usually taken to be a "casting-net," which is supported by Hesiod, *Sc.* 213 f. *αὐτὰρ ἐπ' ἀκταῖς | ἧστο ἀνὴρ ἁλιεὺς δεδοκημένος· εἶχε δὲ χερσὶν | ἰχθύσιν ἀμφίβληστρον ἀπορρίψοντι ἐοικώς*, although Theocritus i. 44 in a parallel passage has *μέγα δίκτυον ἐς βόλον ἕλκει*. This sense suits Aesch. *Ag.* 1382, where Clytemnestra, describing how she enveloped Agamemnon in a bath-robe, says: *ἀμφίβληστρον | ὥσπερ ἰχθύων περιστιχίζω, πλοῦτον εἵματος κακόν*. *Cf.* Aesch. *Ch.* 492; Herod. i. 141; ii. 95. Pollux i. 97 mentions together *δίκτυα, ἀμφίβληστρα, γρῖφοι, πάναγρον λίνον*, and so x. 132 where he adds *γάγγαμον*. Plut. *Mor.* 977 F *οἱ δ ἁλιεῖς συνορῶντες . . τὰ πλεῖστα διακρουόμενα τὰς ἀπ' ἀγκίστρου βολὰς*

ἐπὶ βίας ἐτράπησαν, καθάπερ οἱ Πέρσαι σαγηνεύοντες (Herod. iii. 149, vi. 31), ὡς τοῖς ἐνσχεθεῖσιν ἐκ λογισμοῦ καὶ σοφίας διάφευξιν οὖσαν. ἀμφιβλήστροις μὲν γὰρ καὶ ὑποχαῖς κεστρεῖς καὶ ἰουλίδες ἁλίσκονται, μόρμυροί τε καὶ σαργοὶ καὶ κωβιοὶ καὶ λάβρακες· τὰ δὲ βολιστικὰ καλούμενα, τρίγλα καὶ χρυσωπὸν καὶ σκορπίον, γρίποις [i.q. γρίφοις] τε καὶ σαγήναις σύρουσι περιλαμβάνοντες· τῶν δικτύων οὖν τὸ γένος ὀρθῶς Ὅμηρος πάναγρον προσεῖπεν (*Il.* v. 487). The primary meaning of "casting-net" seems pretty well established, but it could easily be extended to any sort of Net (Aesch. *P.V.* 81 of the chains of Prometheus, Soph. *Ant.* 343 φῦλον ὀρνίθων ἀμφιβαλὼν ἄγει σπείραισι δικτυοκλώστοις). In the N.T. Matth. iv. 18 and John xxi. some difficulties are raised which cannot be discussed here. Usually a "casting-net" is understood to be a Net cast by a single person and immediately withdrawn. It is thus the πεζόβολος of modern Greece: Apost. p. 38 "Le πεζόβολος, épervier, est un filet qu'on jette de terre en entrant parfois dans l'eau jusqu'aux genoux. On le tire à la hâte et aussitôt après l'avoir lancé pour ne pas laisser aux poissons avant qu'il ne se renferme le temps de s'échapper entre les mailles et le fond de la mer. Cet engin est, croyons-nous, celui qu'Oppian décrit dans ses Ἁλιευτικά sous le nom de σφαιρών [see below]. La forme même de l'engin autorise cette supposition. Il faut une grande adresse pour se servir de cet filet. Le pêcheur doit le lancer de manière à ce qu'il tombe tout ouvert sur le banc des poissons qu'il a aperçu du rivage."

Those nets which are withdrawn a few moments after being cast are called in M. G. Nets ἀπὸ βολῆς (at Paros ἡμεροβόλια), or ἀφρόδυκτα *i.e.* foam-nets, being designed to catch surface fishes, ἀφρόψαρα, fishes which swim between two waters, such as Mackerel, Horse-Mackerel, etc. Nets, on the other hand, which are shot in the morning and drawn next morning are called ἀπὸ στατοῦ, and are generally "compound," μανώμενα, consisting of a Net with fine meshes between two with larger meshes, as opposed to the simple Nets, ἁπλάδια, Apost. pp. 32 f.

3. γρῖφος (γρῖπος) is the generic name for the draw-net or seine. Plutarch, as we have seen, couples γρῖφος and σαγήνη. *Cf. A.P.* vi. 23. 3 δέξο σαγηναίοιο λίνου τετριμμένον ἅλμῃ | λείψανον, αὐχμρόν, ξανθὲν ἐπ' ἠιόνων, | γρίπους τε; *cf.* Poll. i. 97, x. 32. So the Nets employed in analogous manner for the capture of land animals and bearing the same names are coupled by Plut. *Mor.* 471 D οὐδ' ὁ γρίφοις καὶ σαγήναις ἐλάφους μὴ λαμβάνων. Apostolides p. 35 (who errs in thinking that Oppian identifies γρῖφος and ἀμφίβληστρον) describes the γρῖφος as consisting of two parallel nets, to which is attached another having the form of a sack. These two nets are called at Poros [off coast of Argolis] πτερά, "wings." The parallel Nets are suspended on two cords; the lower having hung on it at equal intervals pieces of lead (μολυβίθρες), the upper, called in some places σαρδοῦνας (*cf.* Xen. *Cyn.* 6. 9 σαρδονίων, Poll. v. 31 σαρδόνες), being hung with corks (φελλοί). The two pieces of wood, at the front ends of the two parallel Nets, to which is attached the cord by which the seine is drawn to land, are called at Paros σταλίκια, the triangular cord being called χαλινός.

Three species of seine are used in modern Greece according to Apostolides, 1. the γρῖπος proper, called in many places *trata*, consisting of two parallel nets with very large meshes and the bag-net with very fine meshes. It is cast by a special boat and drawn to land. It is used especially for Sardines and other surface fish. One of these Nets employs fifteen or more men. 2. The γριπαρόλι or κωλοβρέχτης, a smaller sort, managed by four men, used for catching Grey Mullets and other shore fishes. 3. The ἀνεμό-τρατα, a very large seine In the use of this two boats are always associated. They set out early in the morning, taking advantage of the off-shore wind (ἀπόγι)—which in summer blows during the night from the land—and when they reach the open sea they cast the seine, moor their boats, and remain till mid-day. Then when the landward breeze begins to blow, the two boats proceed, parallel to one another, harbourwards, drawing the seine behind them.

4. γάγγαμον. The name γάγγαμον (γαγγάμιον) is still used round the Black Sea, although in most parts of Greece a slightly altered form—γαγγάβα—is in use. The Net is a dredge-net and is employed in fishing for Sponges, Oysters, and Sea-urchins. It is constructed thus: "autour d'un arc en fer est cousu un filet de forme conique; la corde, très large, de l'arc est aussi en fer; de la corde et de l'arc partent en rayonnant différentes cordes, au point de rencontre desquelles est attachée une grosse corde au moyen de laquelle on tire l'appareil." *Cf.* schol. γάγγαμον· γαγγάμη, λίνος παχὺς δικτυωτός, σιδήρῳ κύκλῳ περι-εχόμενος; Aesch. *Ag.* 361 μέγα δουλείας γάγγαμον ἄτης παναλώτου. Strabo 307, speaking of the cold in the region of the Sea of Azov, says: ὀρυκτοί τέ εἰσιν ἰχθύες οἱ ἀποληφθέντες ἐν τῷ κρυστάλλῳ τῇ προσ-αγορευομένῃ γαγγάμῃ. Poll. ii. 169 τὸ δικτυῶδες ὃ

καλεῖται νῦν γάγγαμον ἤ, ὡς οἱ πολλοί, σαγήνη; x. 132 γρῖφοι καὶ γάγγαμον; Hesych. *s.* γαγγάμη· σαγήνη ἢ δίκτυον ἁλιευτικόν; *E.M. s.* γαγγαμών· . . . σημαίνει δὲ τὸ λαμβάνον δίκτυον. ἔστι κυρίως γαγγάμη σαγήνη ἢ δίκτυον.

5. ὑποχή. The schol. says "κυρίως δίκτυα περιφράττοντα καὶ ἐπέχοντα τόπους ἐν οἷς καὶ τὸ θυννοσκοπεῖον λεγόμενον." It looks as if this note which describes the σαγήνη had got misplaced. All the evidence points to the ὑποχή being a bag-net, much like the modern shrimp-net. In modern Greek the word used is ἀποχή, *cf.* Apost. p. 39 "Les haveneaux, ἀποχαί, sont des filets en forme de poche à mailles très serrées, d'un mètre ou 50 centimètres d'ouverture. Le bord est tendu sur un arc en bois ou en fer dont une corde forme le rayon. Un bâton ou manche, terminé par une fourche en bois, est attaché au milieu de la corde. La partie moyenne de l'arc est solidement fixée un peu plus haut. En se servant de cet engin, pour la pêche des crevettes, le pêcheur entre dans l'eau jusqu'au genou, ratisse le fond en marchant devant lui, d'un mouvement continu, rasant le sable au moyen de la corde tendue. L'autre extrémité du manche est tenue sous le bras ou appuyée contre la poitrine," *cf.* Plut. *Mor.* 977 E ἀμφιβλήστροις μὲν γὰρ καὶ ὑποχαῖς κεστρεῖς καὶ ἰουλίδες ἁλίσκονται, μόρμυροί τε καὶ σαργοὶ καὶ κωβιοὶ καὶ λάβρακες; Ael. xiii. 17 κορακίνους ταῖς ὑποχαῖς πολλοὺς συλλαβόντες.

6. σαγήνη, from which our Seine is ultimately derived (Lat. *sagena,* Fr. *seine*), is a large Seine or Draw-net. It seems to be undistinguishable from the γρῖφος and, like the γρῖφος, is sometimes a Fishing-net (Alciphr. i. 13; 20; 21; Plut. *Mor.*

977 F; Luc. *Pisc.* 51; *Tim.* 22, etc.), sometimes a Hunting-net (Plut. *Mor.* 471 D; Babr. 43. 8).

7. *κάλυμμα.* What sort of Net this is, is very uncertain. The metaphorical use in Aesch. *Ch.* 494 *βουλευτοῖσιν ἐν καλύμμασιν*, referring to the bath-robe which entangled Agamemnon, suggests an *ἀμφίβληστρον*, which is used immediately before (*v.* 492). Otherwise it may be the form of *ὑποχή* used in the Sporades and elsewhere for taking the Sea Crayfish or Spiny Lobster, Apost. p. 41 "C'est un haveneau dont le cercle de fer est disposé de manière à tourner autour d'un demi-cercle également en fer qui se fixe perpendiculairement aux extrémités de son diamètre. Sur ce second demi-cercle est attaché le baton; il y a plus, le sommet de la poche du haveneau est pourvu d'un morceau de liège. Voilà comment on opère: Aussitôt qu'on a aperçu, au fond de la mer, une *Langouste* (*ἀστακός* vulg.), on la couvre avec le cercle sur lequel est tendue la poche, qui, grâce au liège flottant, reste ouverte dans toute sa hauteur. Une fois qu'on est certain que l'animal est dedans, qu'on le voit se cramponner contre les parois du filet, on enlève brusquement l'engin, le pois de l'animal alors, faisant bascule, entraîne la poche de haut en bas et fait tourner les cercles de fer autour de ces points d'appui; ainsi l'animal se prend comme dans un sac et on le sort intact de la mer."

8. *πέζαι* acc. to the schol. are a species of small Net (*εἶδος καὶ τοῦτο δικτύου μικροῦ*), while 9. *σφαιρῶνες* acc. to the schol. are round Nets (*δίκτυα στρογγύλα*). The *σφαιρών* is identified by Apost. p. 38, with the *πεζόβολος* or Casting-net.

10. *πάναγρον* is found already in Hom. *Il.* v. 487

μή πως, ὡς ἀψῖσι λίνου ἁλόντε πανάγρου, | ἀνδράσι δυσμενέεσσιν ἕλωρ καὶ κύρμα γένησθε, where the reference seems to be to a Seine, which also is apparently intended in the only other Homeric reference to Net-fishing (also in a simile), *Od.* xxii. 383 τοὺς δὲ ἴδεν μάλα πάντας ἐν αἵματι καὶ κονίῃσι | πεπτεῶτας πολλούς, ὥς τ' ἰχθύας, οὕς θ' ἁλιῆες | κοιλὸν ἐς αἰγιαλὸν πολιῆς ἔκτοσθε θαλάσσης | δικτύῳ ἐξέρυσαν πολυωπῷ· οἱ δέ τε πάντες | κύμαθ' ἁλὸς ποθέοντες ἐπὶ ψαμάθοισι κέχυνται· | τῶν μέν τ' ἠέλιος φαέθων ἐξείλετο θυμόν.

Next we have fishing by means of Weels (κύρτοι), of which Apost. p. 51, says: "La pêche au moyen de nasses est bien simple, mais toutes n'ont pas la même forme: elle change suivant les poissons qu'on cherche à capturer. Ce sont des paniers, avec un orifice précédé d'une entrée cônique, par laquelle, une fois entrés, les poissons ne peuvent plus sortir. Pour attirer les poissons, on les amorce en mettant à l'intérieur des sardines salées, ou d'autres aliments souvent en putréfaction."

Next we have the use of the Trident, or Fish-spearing, which, according to Tristram, p. 292, is much used in the smaller streams and the northern rivers of the Lebanon; *cf.* Job xli. 7 "Canst thou fill his skin with barbed irons? or his head with fish spears?" This method was practised either by day or at night by the light of a fire. For the former *cf.* Apost. p. 49 "La pêche au harpon est fort simple, elle dépend surtout de l'agilité du pêcheur à viser le poisson. Les habitants de l'île de Spetzia [off S. coast of Argolis] attachent à la hampe du trident une longue corde, lancent ainsi quelquefois le harpon à de grandes profondeurs. Mais les pêcheurs de Missolonghi sont plus adroits que tous les autres pêcheurs grecs. C'est à une véritable chasse aux poissons, surtout contre les daurades, les loups et les anguilles, qu'ils se livrent dans les lagunes qui entourent leur ville. Trente ou quarante bateaux armés de harpons (énormes fourchettes à trois dents) ou tridents se mettent en marche. Un seul pêcheur se tient sur le devant du bateau qu'il gouverne et fait marcher avec le trident en guise d'aviron et avec lequel il transperce les poissons qui se trouvent à sa portée."

Night-fishing by firelight (πυρευτική Plato, *Sophist*, 220 D, πυρίαι A. 537 a 18, Poll. vii. 138) might be either with Trident or Net. The former is referred to in Oppian, *H.* iv. 640-646, Q. Smyrn. vii. 569-576, *cf.* Scott, *Guy Mannering*, c. xxvi.; the latter in Oppian, *C.* iv. 140 ff., *cf.* Apost. p. 40, where he describes the method of fishing for Belone (Gar-fish) in the Sporades: "Pendant les nuits les plus obscures du mois d'Octobre, aussitôt après l'arrivée des poissons, les bateaux quittent leur mouillage le soir et se rendent au large. Arrivés à l'endroit désigné, les pêcheurs amènent les voiles et marchent lentement à la rame en examinant la mer de tous côtés. Il est facile de se rendre compte de la présence du poisson en écoutant le bruit que font les dauphins qui le poursuivent à la surface de l'eau. Alors, les pêcheurs allument un grand feu avec du bois résineux sur une espèce de gril en fer, qu'ils fixent à la proue du navire (πυροφάνι et πυριά vulg.). Les poissons attirés par la lueur accourent vers le bateau comme pour y chercher un abri contre l'ennemi qui ne cesse de les décimer." After rowing about and making the boat turn upon itself some score of times, so as to reflect the light in all directions, they row slowly shorewards, followed by the fish. "On arrive ainsi à la côte. Là on prend des précautions pour que le bateau ne touche terre, le moindre choc faisant déguerpir aussitôt les poissons. On l'arrête à une distance d'un ou de deux mètres, et, laissant les rames, on prend les haveneaux en main, et l'on commence à envelopper le poisson des deux côtés du bateau."

Fishing by poisoning the water, referred to by Oppian, *H.* iv. 647 ff., is said by Tristram, p. 292, to be very commonly practised on the Lake of Galilee by the poorest classes. "Men sit on a rock overhanging the water, on which they scatter crumbs poisoned with vitriol, which are seized by the fish. As soon as they are seen to float on their backs, then men rush into the sea and collect them."

Apost. p. 52 ff. gives an interesting account of fishing by Weirs and Stake-nets as practised in modern Greece; in a great number of river-mouths, the shallower waters of several gulfs, in lakes, pools, and lagoons, "les poissons sont pris exclusivement au moyen des écrilles et des claies de roseau. Tous les endroits sont appelés vulg. Βιβάρια," *i.e.* Lat. *vivaria.* Similar methods are practised in Palestine, Tristram, p. 292, who says "Among the laws of Joshua, the Rabbis relate, was one forbidding the use of stake-nets in the Sea of Chinnereth (Galilee), for fear of damage to the boats." The reader will remember that the use of stake-nets got a fictitious Joshua (Geddes) into trouble (Scott, *Redgauntlet*).

Finally, for the earliest references to Fly-fishing, natural or artificial—Mart. v. 18. 7 f., Ael. xiv. 22, xv. 1, the reader may be referred to the discussion in Radcliffe c. ix.

IV. On the Identification of Certain Fishes

Ce que l'on doit le plus regretter dans cette masse d'instructions si précieuses, c'est que l'auteur [Aristotle] ne se soit pas douté que la nomenclature usitée de son temps pût venir à s'obscurcir, et qu'il n'ait pris aucune précaution pour faire reconnaître les espèces dont il parle. C'est le défaut général des naturalistes anciens ; on est presque obligé de deviner le sens des noms dont ils se sont servis ; la tradition même a changé, et nous induit souvent en erreur : ce n'est que par des combinaisons très pénibles, et le rapprochement des traits épars dans les auteurs, qu'on parvient sur quelques espèces à des résultats un peu positifs ; mais nous sommes condamnés à en ignorer toujours le plus grand nombre.

Cuvier et Valenciennes,
Histoire naturelle de poissons, i. p. 23.

Diese Unzulänglichkeit unsers jetzigen Wissens darf man sicherlich nicht ignoriren—wir sind überzeugt, dass mit der Vermehrung unsrer Kenntnisse in dieser Richtung, der Beobachtung des Haushaltes, der Lebensweise, der Instincte der Thiere Griechenlands eine grosse Anzahl von Angaben des Aristoteles bestätigt und in das rechte Licht gestellt werden wird.

Aubert u. Wimmer, p. 55.

Certains procédés de pêche qui existent chez nous étonnant le voyageur au point qu'il les range parmi les fables, se sont maintenus par la tradition. Ceux qui sont familiers avec les écrits des anciens, Aristote, Athénée, Théophraste, Xénocrate, Oppien, etc. et qui se sont occupés d'histoire naturelle, ne trouveront pas étrange notre assertion. Aucun naturaliste moderne n'a poussé la curiosité de l'observation et de la connaissance des mœurs et habitudes des animaux aussi loin que les anciens.

Apostolides, *La Pêche en Grèce*, p. 44.

Alphestes, Alphesticus, or Cinaedus ; Phycis ; Cirrhis

H. i. 126 f.

καὶ κίχλαι ῥαδιναὶ καὶ φυκίδες οὕς θ' ἁλιῆες
ἀνδρὸς ἐπωνυμίην θηλύφρονος ηὐδάξαντο.

MSS. and schol. ἅς θ'.

1. There can be no doubt that the reference in ἀνδρὸς ἐπωνυμίην θηλύφρονος is to the fish called κίναιδος (*cf.* the synonyms of κίναιδος in Poll. vi. 126 καταπύγων, . . . θηλυδρίας, . . . γυναικίας, . . . ἀνδρόγυνος, . . . θῆλυς τὴν ψυχήν), ἀλφηστής, ἀλφηστικός. The first name occurs Plin. xxxii. 146 Cinaedi soli piscium lutei, and is no doubt intended in Hesych. *s.* κιναουιδες (sic)· ἰχθῦς. For the other names *cf.* Athen. 281 e. Apollodorus of Athens (b. *circ.* 180 B.C.), after quoting Sophron's "καταπυγοτέραν τ' ἀλφηστᾶν," says: "The ἀλφησταί are a species of fish, yellowish (κιρροειδεῖς) as a whole but purplish in parts. It is said that they are taken in couples, one following in the rear of the other. From this following in the rear (κατὰ τὴν πυγήν) of one another the name was applied to the licentious and lewd" (ἀκρατεῖς καὶ καταφερεῖς) [*i.e.* καταπύγονες]. Aristotle ἐν τῷ περὶ Ζῴων says "μονάκανθον (with a single spine) εἶναι καὶ κιρρὸν (yellow) τὸν ἀλφηστικόν." Numenius, of Heracleia, ἐν Ἁλιευτικῷ mentions it thus: ⟨ἄλλοτε δ' αὖ πέρκας, ὅτε δὲ στροφάδας παρὰ πέτρην⟩[a] | φυκίδας ἀλφηστήν τε καὶ ἐν χροιῇσιν ἐρυθρὸν | σκορπίον ⟨ἢ πέρκαισι καθηγητὴν μελάνουρον⟩[a] Also Epicharmus, ἐν Ἥβας γάμῳ· μύες ἀλφησταί τε κορακῖνοί τε κοριοειδέες; *cf.* Eustath. Hom. *Il.* xviii. p. 1166. 42; Athen. 305 b Diocles ἐν πρώτῳ Ὑγιεινῶν· οἱ δὲ πετραῖοι καλούμενοι μαλακόσαρκοι, κόσσυφοι,

[a] Supplied from Athen. 319 b, 320 e.

κίχλαι, πέρκαι, κωβιοί, φυκίδες, ἀλφηστικός. *E.M. s.* ἀλφηστής repeats Apollodorus in Athen. 281 e as quoted above; *cf. E.M. s.* θηλυτεράων· ὅτι τὰ λοιπὰ ζῷα ὅρον ἔχει τῆς μίξεως τὴν σύλληψιν, αὗται δὲ ἀεί· διὸ ἐκ τοῦ ἐναντίου οἱ ἄνδρες ἀλφησταὶ λέγονται οἱ κατωφερεῖς, κατὰ μεταφορὰν ἀπὸ τῶν ἰχθύων· ἀλφησταὶ γὰρ εἶδος ἰχθύος. Hesych. *s.* ἀλφηστίς· ἰχθύος εἶδος. In Homer ἀλφησταί is an obscure epithet of men in general, but in later Greek a bad association seems to have attached to ἀλφάνω and its derivatives, perhaps through an idea that παρθένοι ἀλφεσίβοιαι (Hom. *Il.* xviii 593, *H. Aphr.* 119) meant—to quote Dugald Dalgetty—"such *quae quaestum corporibus faciebant,* as we said of Jean Drochiels at Marischal College"[a]; *cf.* Lycophron 1393 τῆς (Mestra) παντομόρφου βασσάρας λαμπουρίδος | τοκῆος (Erysichthon), ἥ τ' ἀλφαῖσι ταῖς καθ' ἡμέραν | βούπειναν ἀλθαίνεσκεν ἀκμαίαν πατρός.

The fish intended is one of the Wrasses (they had the repute of lasciviousness, *cf.* Epicharm. *ap.* Athen. 305 c [see too 287 b, *E.M. s.* βεμβράς] βαμβραδόνες τε καὶ κίχλαι λαγοὶ δράκοντές τ' ἄλκιμοι, where perhaps λάγνοι should be read: *cf.* κιχλίζω), such as *Crenilabrus melops,* the Gold-sinny or Corkwing.

2. The reading of the MSS. and schol. ἅς θ' would make ἅς refer to φυκίδες. So the Schol. φυκίδες· αἱ λαπίναι. τοῦτο δ' εἶπε σκώπτων τὸν γυναικώδη. φυκίδας εἶπεν ἐνταῦθα ὁ ποιητὴς θέλων λοιδορῆσαί τινα εὐνοῦχον φυκαρίζοντα (*i.e.* rouging) τὰς παρειὰς αὐτοῦ. ἦν δ' ὁ εὐνοῦχος οὗτος ὃν λοιδορῆσαι θέλει ὁ ποιητής, ὡς ἔοικεν, ὁ καταλαλήσας τὸν Ἀγησίλαον τὸν πατέρα τοῦ ποιητοῦ εἰς τὸν βασιλέα Σεβῆρον, ὡς εἴπομεν, ὅτι κατεφρόνησεν ὁ Ἀγησίλαος ἐξελθεῖν εἰς

[a] Scott, *Legend of Montrose,* c. ix.

συνάντησιν τοῦ βασιλέως, ἅτε ζῶν φιλοσόφως καὶ καταφρονῶν τὰ πάντα. All this seems to be pure invention. The fish called φυκίς is mentioned frequently. A. 567 b 18 τίκτουσι δ' οἱ μὲν ἄλλοι τῶν ᾠοτόκων ἰχθύων ἅπαξ τοῦ ἐνιαυτοῦ, πλὴν τῶν μικρῶν φυκίδων, αὗται δὲ δίς. διαφέρει δ' ὁ ἄρρην φύκης τῆς θηλείας τῷ μελάντερος εἶναι καὶ μείζους ἔχειν τὰς λεπίδας; 591 b 10 τὰ δ' ὡς ἐπὶ τὸ πολὺ νέμονται μὲν τὸν πηλὸν καὶ τὸ φῦκος . . . οἷον φυκὶς καὶ κωβιὸς καὶ οἱ πετραῖοι· ἡ δὲ φυκὶς ἄλλης μὲν σαρκὸς οὐχ ἅπτεται, τῶν δὲ καρίδων; 607 b 18 μεταβάλλει δὲ καὶ ἡ φυκὶς τὴν χρόαν· τὸν μὲν γὰρ ἄλλον χρόνον λευκή ἐστι, τοῦ δ' ἔαρος ποικίλη· μόνη δ' αὕτη τῶν θαλαττίων ἰχθύων (builds a nest), ὥς φασι, καὶ τίκτει ἐν τῇ στιβάδι; Plut. *Mor.* 981 F ἰδίᾳ δ' αἱ φυκίδες ἐκ τῶν φυκίων οἷον νεοττιὰν διαπλασάμεναι περιαμπέχουσι τὸν γόνον καὶ σκέπουσιν ἀπὸ τοῦ κλυδῶνος; Ovid, *Hal.* 122 Atque avium phycis (MSS. dulcis, emend. Ulitzius) nidos imitata sub undis; Plin. ix. 81 mutat (colorem) et phycis, reliquo tempore candida, vere varia. Eadem piscium sola nidificat ex alga atque in nido parit; xxxii. 150 phycis saxatilium; Ael. xii. 28 ἰχθῦς δὲ τὴν χρόαν μεταβλητικοὶ οἵδε· κίχλαι τε καὶ κόσσυφοι καὶ φυκίδες τε καὶ μαινίδες; Athen. 305 b Διοκλῆς . . . "οἱ δὲ πετραῖοι," φησίν, "καλούμενοι μαλακόσαρκοι, κόσσυφοι, κίχλαι, πέρκαι, κωβιοί, φυκίδες, ἀλφηστικός"; 319 b Σπεύσιππος ἐν δευτέρῳ Ὁμοίων παοαπλησίας εἶναι λέγων πέρκην, χάνναν, φυκίδα . . . Νουμήνιος δ' ἐν Ἁλιευτικῷ "ἄλλοτε δ' αὖ πέρκας, ὅτε δὲ στροφάδας παρὰ πέτρην | φυκίδας ἀλφηστήν τε καὶ ἐν χροιῇσιν ἐρυθρὸν | σκορπιόν (*cf.* 282 a, 320 e)"; 319 c Ἀριστοτέλης ἐν τῷ περὶ ζωικῶν ἀκανθοστεφῆ φησιν εἶναι καὶ ποικιλόχροα φυκίδα; Marc. S. 19 καὶ σκάροι ἀνθεμόεντες ἐρευθήεσσά τε φυκίς;

A.P. vi. 105 *τρίγλαν ἀπ' ἀνθρακιῆς καὶ φυκίδα σοι, λιμενῖτι* | *Ἄρτεμι, δωρεῦμαι* (= Suid. *s. φυκίδα*). The statement that the *φυκίς* builds a nest led Cuvier to identify it with *Gobius niger,* the Black Goby. But all the other evidence points to one of the Wrasses (*Labridae*), for which *χειλοῦ, φυκόψαρο, πετρόψαρο* are in M.G. generic names, and it is now known that some at least of the Wrasses build nests. The schol. here, as we have seen above, interprets *φυκίδες* by *λαπίναι.* In M G. *Crenilabrus pavo* is *λήπαινα*, at Chalcis *λαπίνα μαύρη* and *λ. μεγάλη* and this identification is in all probability right.

It should be pointed out that, both *φυκίς* and the *κίναιδος* being Wrasses, it is quite possible that Oppian or Oppian's source may have identified them and thus *ἅς θ'* may after all be the correct reading.

3. The Cirrhis (*κίρρις*) of *H.* i. 129, iii. 187, which is not mentioned in Aristotle, seems to be another of the Wrasses, perhaps *Labrus mixtus, cf. E.M. s. κίρρις· ὁ ἰχθύς, ἐπειδὴ κιρρός ἐστι τὴν χροιάν.* In *H.* i. 129 the schol., reading *σκιρρίς,* interprets *λεπιδυταί ἢ ὕσκας.*

Anthias: Aulopias: Callichthys: Callionymus

The chief references may be grouped as follows:

(1) A. 570 b 19 *τίκτει δὲ καὶ ὁ αὐλωπίας, ὃν καλοῦσί τινες ἀνθίαν, τοῦ θέρους.*

(2) A. 610 b 5 the Anthias is one of the gregarious (*ἀγελαῖοι*) fishes.

(3) A. 620 b 33 *ὅπου ἂν ἀνθίας ὁραθῇ, οὐκ ἔστι θηρίον· ᾧ καὶ σημείῳ χρώμενοι κατακολυμβῶσιν οἱ σπογγεῖς, καὶ καλοῦσιν ἱεροὺς ἰχθῦς τούτους; cf.*

Athen. 282 c; Plut. *Mor.* 981 E; Ael. viii. 28; Plin. ix. 153 certissima est securitas vidisse planos [anthias?] pisces, quia nunquam sunt ubi maleficae bestiae, qua de causa urinantes (*i.e.* divers) sacros appellant eos.

(4) Ovid, *Hal.* 45 Anthias his tergo quae non videt utitur armis, Vim spinae novitque suae versoque supinus Corpore lina secat fixumque intercipit hamum; Plin. xxxii. 13 anthias tradit idem [*sc.* Ovidius in eo volumine quod *Halieuticon* inscribitur, *ib.* 11] infixo hamo invertere se, quoniam sit in dorso cultellata spina, eaque lineam praesecare; ix. 182 idem anthiae cum unum hamo teneri viderint, spinis quas in dorso serratas habent lineam secare traduntur, eo qui teneatur extendente ut praecidi possit; Plut. *Mor.* 977 c οἱ δ' ἀνθίαι τῷ συμφύλῳ βοηθοῦσιν ἰταμώτερον· τὴν γὰρ ὁρμιὰν ἀναθέμενοι κατὰ τὴν ῥάχιν καὶ στήσαντες ὀρθὴν τὴν ἄκανθαν ἐπιχειροῦσι διαπρίειν τῇ τραχύτητι καὶ διακόπτειν; Ael. i. 4 ὅταν νοήσωσι τεθηρᾶσθαι τὸν σύννομον, προσνέουσιν ὤκιστα· εἶτα ἐς αὐτὸν τὰ νῶτα ἀπερείδουσιν καὶ ἐμπίπτοντες καὶ ὠθούμενοι τῇ δυνάμει κωλύουσιν ἕλκεσθαι.

(5) Plin. ix. 180 describes the mode of catching the Anthias practised in the Chelidonian islands [ἐν μεθορίῳ τῆς Παμφυλίας καὶ Λυκίας, Strabo 651]: parvo navigio et concolori veste eademque hora per aliquot dies continuos piscator enavigat certo spatio escamque proicit. Quicquid ex eo mittitur, suspecta fraus praedae est cavetque quod timuit. Cum id saepe factum est, unus aliquando consuetudine invitatus anthias escam appetit. Notatur hic intentione diligenti ut auctor spei conciliatorque naturae, neque est difficile cum per aliquot dies solus accedere audeat. Tandem et aliquos invenit paulatimque comitatior

postremo greges adducit innumeros, iam vetustissimis quibusque adsuetis piscatorem agnoscere et e manu cibum rapere. Tum ille paulum ultra digitos in esca iaculatus hamum singulos involat verius quam capit, ab umbra navis brevi conatu rapiens ita ne ceteri sentiant, alio intus excipiente centonibus raptum, ne palpitatio ulla aut sonus ceteros abigat. Conciliatorem nosse ad hoc prodest ne capiatur, fugituro in reliquum grege. This is evidently the method described in Oppian, *H.* iii. 205 ff. and is identical with that which was used for the Aulopias in the Tyrrhenian islands (*i.e.* the *Aeoliae insulae* between Italy and Sicily) according to Ael. xiii. 17: "Having selected in advance places where they suppose the Aulopias to congregate and thereafter having caught in their scoop-nets (ὑποχαί) many Crow-fish (κορακίνους), they anchor their boat and keeping up a continuous din they project the Crow-fish attached to lines (ἅμμασι). The Aulopias, hearing the din and beholding the bait, swim up from all directions and congregate and circle about the boat. And under the influence of the din and the abundance of food they become so tame that even when the fishermen stretch out their hands they remain and suffer the touch of man, enslaved, as I should judge, by the food but, as the experts say, already confident in their valour. And there are among them tame ones whom the fishermen recognize as their benefactors and comrades and towards these they maintain a truce. These leaders are followed by stranger fishes which, as aliens, so to say, the fishermen hunt and kill. But with regard to the tame fishes, the position of which is like that of decoy pigeons, they refrain from hunting them and observe a truce, nor would any pressure of circumstances induce a wise fisherman to catch a tame Aulopias intentionally: for he is grieved even when he catches one accidentally." Ael. xii. 47, on the capture of the Anthias, has nothing which helps identification.

(6) Ananios, *ap.* Athen. 282 b, the Anthias is in prime condition in winter.

(7) The Aulopias is described Ael. xiii. 17: "About the Tyrrhenian islands fishermen catch the huge (κητώδη) fish which is found there and which they call Aulopias. . . . In size the largest Aulopias is inferior to the largest Tunnies, but in strength and prowess it would bear away the palm in comparison with them. . . . It opposes the fisherman as an equal adversary, and for the most part gets the better of him. . . . When caught it is beautiful to behold, having the eyes open and round and large, like the ox-eyes of which Homer sings. The jaw is strong . . . yet adds to the beauty of the fish. The back is of the deepest blue, the belly white; from the head a gold-coloured line extends to the hinder part where it ends in a circle."

(8) Oppian thrice mentions the Anthias. (i) *H.* i. 248-258 the Anthias frequents deep rocks, but ranges everywhere under the impulse of gluttony. The mouth is toothless. There are four species—yellow, white, black, and a fourth called εὐωπός or αὐλωπός,

> οὕνεκα τοῖς καθύπερθεν ἑλισσομένη κατα κύκλον
> ὀφρὺς ἠερόεσσα περίδρομος ἐστεφάνωται (256 f.).

The precise meaning of αὐλωπός is not easy to determine (schol. στενοφθάλμους . . . τοὺς ἔχοντας μεγάλους ὀφθαλμοὺς δίκην αὐλῶν, ὁποῖοί εἰσιν οἱ τῶν παγούρων [Crabs] καὶ ἀστακῶν [Lobsters]; *cf.* Hesych. *s.* αὐλωπίας· κοιλόφθαλμος, *s.* αὐλώπιδι· στενῇ περὶ τοὺς ὀφθαλμούς), whether "hollow-eyed" or "with lobster-like eyes": *cf.* Xen. *Symp.* v. 5 καρκίνον εὐοφθαλμότατον εἶναι τῶν ζῴων. (ii) *H.* iii. 192 the bait for the Anthias is the Basse (λάβραξ). (iii) *H.* iii. 205-334, where he describes modes of fishing for the Anthias, and says its "mouth is unarmed" (στόμα τοῖσιν ἄοπλον), *i.e.* is toothless (328). His account of its struggles to escape—βιώμενος εἰς ἄλλα δῦναι (310)—shows that he means by Anthias what Aelian means by Aulopias, xiii. 17 ὡς πρὸς ἀντίπαλον ἵσταται τὸν ἁλιέα καὶ κρατεῖ τὰ πλεῖστα, ἐπὶ μᾶλλον ἑαυτὸν πιέσας καὶ κάτω νεύσας τὴν κεφαλὴν καὶ ὠθήσας κατὰ τοῦ βυθοῦ.

(9) Archestratus *ap.* Athen. 326 a νεαροῦ μεγάλου τ αὐλωπία ἐν θέρει ὠνοῦ | κρανία also suggests a large fish.

Callichthys. To Oppian *Callichthys* (1) differs from Anthias, (2) is called ἱερὸς ἰχθύς, (3) is comparable in strength to the Anthias, (4) is a deep-sea fish, (5) is called Callichthus, *i.e.* Beauty-fish, on account of its beauty: *H.* i. 179 οἱ δ' ἐν ἀμετρήτοισιν ἄλην πελάγεσσιν ἔχουσι, | τηλοῦ ἀπὸ τραφερῆς οὐδ' ᾐόσιν εἰσὶν ἑταῖροι . . . ἐν τοῖς καὶ κάλλιχθυς ἐπώνυμος, ἱερὸς ἰχθύς; *H.* iii. 191 θύννῳ μὲν κάλλιχθυς ἰαίνεται, αὐτὰρ ὀνίσκοις | ὄρκυνος, λάβρακα δ' ἐπ' ἀνθίῃ ὁπλίζοιο; iii. 335 (after an account of capture of Anthias) τοῖον καὶ κάλλιχθυς ἔχει σθένος ἠδὲ γενέθλη | ὀρκύνων ὅσσοι τε δέμας κητώδεες ἄλλοι | πλάζονται· τοίοις δὲ βραχίοσιν ἀγρώσσονται; v. 627 ff. sponge-cutters are safe if they see a κάλλιχθυς: τῷ καί μιν ἐφήμισαν ἱερὸν ἰχθύν. Bussemaker, identifying it with ἀνθίας εὐωπός, makes it *Serranus gigas*, the Métou, which we identify with ὀρφός.

The epithet ἱερός is used of a fish in Hom. *Il.* xvi. 407 ὡς ὅτε τις φὼς | πέτρῃ ἔπι προβλῆτι καθήμενος ἱερὸν ἰχθὺν | ἐκ πόντοιο θύραζε λίνῳ καὶ ἤνοπι χαλκῷ (*sc.* ἕλκῃ), where acc. to the schol. some interpreted πομπίλος, some κάλλιχθυς, while others took the epithet in a general sense (ἀνετὸν καὶ εὔτραφῆ, ὡς ἱερὸν βοῦν λέγομεν τὸν ἀνειμένον). From Athen. 282 e *sq.* it seems that ἱερός was used of several fishes besides the Anthias (Dolphin, Pilot-fish, Gilthead, etc.) and, while Athenaeus himself seems to identify Anthias and Callichthys, he tells us that Dorion denied the identity: Athen. 282 c μνημονεύει δ' αὐτοῦ καὶ Δωρίων ἐν τῷ περὶ ἰχθύων· "τὸν δ' ἀνθίαν τινὲς καὶ κάλλιχθυν καλοῦσιν, ἔτι δὲ καλλιώνυμον καὶ ἔλοπα". . . . Ἀριστοτέλης δὲ καὶ καρχαρόδοντα εἶναι τὸν κάλλιχθυν σαρκοφάγον τε καὶ συναγελαζόμενον. Ἐπίχαρμος δ' ἐν Μούσαις τὸν μὲν ἔλοπα [*cf.* Ael. viii. 28] καταριθμεῖται, τὸν δὲ κάλλιχθυν ἢ καλλιώνυμον ὡς τὸν αὐτὸν ὄντα σεσίγηκεν. . . . Δωρίων δ' ἐν τῷ περὶ ἰχθύων διαφέρειν φησὶν ἀνθίαν καὶ κάλλιχθυν, ἔτι τε καὶ καλλιώνυμον καὶ ἔλοπα; *cf.* *E.M* *s.* ἄνθεια (*sic*)· εἶδος ἰχθύος· ἀνθίαν τινὲς καὶ κάλλιχθυν καλοῦσι καὶ καλλιώνυμον καὶ ἔλλοπα; Suid. *s.* ἱερὸν ἰχθῶν· . . . οὐ τὸν κάλλιχθυν ἢ τὸν πομπίλον, ὥς τινες.

Callionymus.—The Callionymus is almost certainly *Uranoscopos scaber*, the *Hemerocoetes* or *Nycteris* of Oppian (see note on *H.* ii. 199 ff.). It is an ugly fish and was only euphemistically called καλλιώνυμος: *cf.* *E.M.* *s.* ἁλεσούριος· εἶδος ἰχθύος θαλασσίου ὅν τινες κατ' εὐφημισμὸν καλλιώνυμον καλοῦσιν κτλ.; Hesych. *s.* καλλιώνυμος and *s.* ἁλεσούριον. From its habit of hiding in the sand it was also called ψαμμοδύτης or Sand-diver, Hesych. *s.* ψαμμοδύτης· ἰχθύς, ὃν καὶ καλλιώνυμον ὀνομάζουσιν. The similarity of name might easily lead to confusion with κάλλιχθυς, but we think that in discussing the identity of that fish and of the Anthias the Callionymus may be left out of the question.

The identification of the Anthias and the Callichthys has hitherto proved an insoluble problem. Both are pelagic fishes, comparable in size to the Tunny. The one definite distinction between them, if we can trust it, is that the Anthias is, according to Oppian *H.* i. 253 and iii. 328, toothless, whereas according to Athen. 282 c Aristotle described the Callichthys as καρχαρόδους.

Rondelet,[a] who supposed the name Anthias to be applied to more than one fish, identified his *Anthias primus* with *Serranus anthias*—the *Barbier* of the Mediterranean—*Labrus anthias* L., *Anthias sacer* Bloch, "le plus beau poisson de mer, aux couleurs les plus éclatantes" (Apost. p. 13). "Le barbier est un des plus beaux poissons de la Méditerranée et des plus faciles à caractériser. La longue épine flexible qui s'élève sur son dos, les filets qui prolongent ses

[a] Guillaume Rondelet (b. at Montpellier in 1507), the greatest of the sixteenth-century naturalists who laid the foundations of modern Ichthyology. He had a unique knowledge of the fishes of the Mediterranean. Of his work on fishes the first part, *Libri de piscibus marinis in quibus verae piscium effigies expressae sunt*, appeared at Lyons in 1554; the second, *Universae aquatilium historiae pars altera, cum veris ipsorum imaginibus* in 1555. Almost simultaneously P. Belon (who was murdered by robbers when gathering herbs at a late hour in the Bois de Boulogne, no doubt in connexion with a translation of Dioscorides, on which he was engaged) published his *De aquatilibus libri ii.*, Paris, 1553; H. Salviani his *Aquatilium animalium historia*, 1554–1557; and Conrad Gesner—the correspondent of Dr. John Caius—his *Historiae animalium liber iv., qui est de piscium et aquatilium animantium natura*, Zürich, 1558.

ventrales, et les deux lobes de sa caudale, surtout l'inférieur, suffiraient pour le distinguer de tous les autres poissons ; enfin, l'éclat de l'or et du rubis dont brillent ses écailles, auraient dû attirer de tout temps l'attention des naturalistes" (Cuv. ii. p. 250). Against this identification Cuvier vigorously protests: "rien n'a été hasardé plus légèrement, et même, si quelque chose en cette matière peut être susceptible de preuve, c'est qu'aucun des caractères attribués à des anthias ne convient au barbier." For his own part Cuvier would identify the Anthias with *Thynnus alalonga*, the Albicore: "Pour moi, si j'étais obligé de me prononcer sur le poisson qui a porté ce nom autrefois, je dirais au moins de l'anthias d'Élien que c'est le *germon* (*Scomber alalonga*). Il est un peu moindre que le thon, qu'il accompagne souvent ; il va en grandes troupes. Son dos est bleu ; son ventre blanc. On voit sur ses flancs une ligne argentée. On ne peut pas dire qu'il manque de dents ; mais il les a plus faibles même que le thon. On en prend en abondance près des côtes de Sardaigne, et l'on y en prendrait encore davantage, si l'on faisait les mailles des mandragues un peu plus petites que pour le thon.

"Certainement bien des poissons décrits par les anciens, et que l'on croit avoir reconnus, ne l'ont pas été sur autant de caractères.

"A la vérité, il n'y a point de germons, ni d'espèces voisines, qui soient blancs, jaunes ou rouge-noir, comme Oppien le dit de ses anthias ; mais nous sommes si accoutumés à voir le même nom appliqué chez les anciens aux êtres les plus différens, que nous ne devons pas nous étonner qu'Oppien ait entendu celui d'anthias autrement qu'Élien. Peut-être a-t-il voulu parler du mérou, du cernier, ou de tel autre très-grand acanthoptérygien : toujours est-il certain qu'il n'a point désigné, par l'épithète de μεγακήτεα, le barbier, petit poisson qui passe à peine cinq ou six pouces."

Glaucus

The chief references may be grouped as follows: (1) A. 508 b 20. The Glaucus has few caecal appendages (ἀποφυάδας). (2) A. 598 a 13. It is a pelagic (πελάγιος) fish. *Cf.* gaudent pelago, Ovid, *Hal.* 94. (3) A. 599 b 32 γλαῦκος· οὗτος γὰρ τοῦ θέρους φωλεῖ περὶ ἑξήκονθ' ἡμέρας. *Cf.* Ovid, *Hal.* 117 Ac nunquam aestivo conspectus sidere glaucus; Plin. ix. 58 quidam rursus aestus impatientia mediis fervoribus sexagenis diebus latent, ut glaucus; xxxii. 153 (tradit) (Ovidius) . . . glaucum aestate nunquam apparere. (4) A. 607 b 27 ὅμοιοι δὲ κύοντες καὶ μὴ ὀλίγοι [*i.e.* a few fishes are in the same condition whether with spawn or not], οἷον γλαῦκος. (5) Opp. *C.* iii. 113 οἵην μὲν κομιδὴν τεκέων ἐνὶ κύμασι δελφὶς | αἰὲν ἔχει γλαῦκός τε χάροψ; *H.* i. 749 of all oviparous (ᾠοτοκῆες) fishes it shows most affection for its young. When the young are hatched, it remains with them, and when danger threatens, ἀμφιχανὼν κατέδεκτο διὰ στόμα, μέσφα κε δεῖμα | χάσσηται, τότε δ' αὖτις ἀνέπτυσε λευκανίηθεν. So Ael. i. 16; Phil. 90. (6) Opp. *H.* i. 170 γλαῦκοι, are mentioned among fishes which ἐν πέτρῃσι καὶ ἐν ψαμάθοισι νέμονται. (7) Opp. *H.* iii. 193. The bait for Glaucus is the Grey Mullet (κεστρεύς). (8) Marc. S. 66 σὺν χλοεροῖς λαχάνοις δὲ καθεψομένου γλαύκοιο Σωμὸς ἄγει γάλα λευκὸν ἐελδομένῃσι τιθήναις | πινόμενος, τῆθαι δὲ φίλαι τότε νηπιάχοισι | ἕλκουσιν πόμα λαρὸν εὐγλαγέων ἀπὸ μαστῶν. (9) It was obviously a large fish: Geopon. xx. 7. 2 πρῶτον δὲ πάντων ἐστὶ δέλη πρὸς τὰ μεγάλα ὀψάρια, οἷον . . . γλαύκους; Eupolis *ap.* Athen. 107 b κειμένων ἰχθυδίων | μικρῶν, τρεμόντων τῷ δέει τί πείσεται, | θαρρεῖν κελεύσας ἕνεκ' ἐμοῦ ταῦτ' οὐδὲ ἓν | φήσας ἀδικήσειν ἐπριάμην γλαῦκον μέγαν. Hence special cuts of it are commended: Archestr. *ap.* Athen. 295 c ἀλλά μοι ὀψώνει γλαύκου κεφαλὴν ἐν Ὀλύνθῳ | καὶ Μεγάροις; Anaxandr. *ibid.* E ὁ πρῶτος εὑρὼν πολυτελὲς τμητὸν μέγα | γλαύκου πρόσωπον τοῦ τ' ἀμύμονος δέμας | θύννου; Amphis *ibid.* F γλαῦκοι δ' ὅλοι, ῥαχιστὰ κρανίων μέρη . . . and γλαυκινιδίου κεφάλαια; Antiph. *ibid.* γλαύκου προτομή. (10) Numen. *ap.* Athen. 295 b ὕκην ἢ κάλλιχθυν, ὁτὲ χρόμιν, ἄλλοτε δ' ὀρφὸν | ἢ γλαῦκον περόωντα κατὰ μνία σιγαλόεντα.

The legend that the Glaucus takes in its young would suggest a Dog-fish, but the possession of *caeca* mentioned in A. 508 b 20 is against that supposition, since Selachians have no *caeca*. Cuvier makes the Glaucus *Sciaena aquila*. Bussemaker makes it some species of Cod (*Gadi quaedam species*).

Onos or Assfish: Oniscus: Callarias

1. The ὄνος is mentioned twice in Aristotle: (*a*) A. 599 b 26 "Some fishes hide (φωλεῖ) in the sand, some in the mud, with only the mouth projecting. The majority hide only in winter—Crustaceans and Rock-fishes and Rays and Cartilaginous fishes only during the wintriest days, as is shown by the fact that they are not caught when the weather is cold. But some fishes hide also in summer, for instance the Glaucus, which hides in summer for about 60 days. The Onos and the Gilthead also hide [*i.e.* in summer]. That the Onos hides for the longest time

seems to be proved by the fact that there is the longest interval when it is not caught. And that the fishes hide in summer seems to be indicated by the fact that catches are made only at the rising [a] of the constellations, particularly at the rising of the Dog-star; for at that time the sea is turned up, a thing which is very well known in the Bosporus. For the mud comes to the top and the fishes are brought up. It is said too that often when the sea-bottom is dredged, more fish are caught by the second haul than by the first; and after heavy rains many creatures become visible which previously were not seen at all or only infrequently." *Cf.* Oppian, *H.* i. 151. See below. (*b*) A. 620 b 29 καθαμμίζουσι δ' ἑαυτὰ καὶ ὄνος καὶ βάτος καὶ ψῆττα καὶ ῥίνη, καὶ ὅταν ποιήσῃ ἑαυτὰ ἄδηλα, εἶτα ῥαβδεύεται τοῖς ἐν τῷ στόματι ἃ καλοῦσιν οἱ ἁλιεῖς ῥαβδία· προσέρχονται δ' ὡς πρὸς φυκία ἀφ' ὧν τρέφονται. It may be noted that the ὄνος is absent in the rendering of this passage in Pliny ix. 144 simili modo squatina [=ῥίνη, *cf.* Plin. xxxii. 150 rhine quem squatum vocamus] et rhombus [=ψῆττα] abditi pinnas exsertas movent specie vermiculorum, item quae vocantur raiae [=βάτοι].

Other references to the ὄνος are Athen. 315 e ὄνος καὶ ὀνίσκος. "ὄνος, φησὶν Ἀριστοτέλης ἐν τῷ περὶ ζωικῶν, ἔχει στόμα ἀνερρωγὸς ὁμοίως τοῖς γαλεοῖς· καὶ οὐ συναγελαστικός. καὶ μόνος οὗτος ἰχθύων τὴν καρδίαν ἐν τῇ κοιλίᾳ ἔχει καὶ ἐν τῷ ἐγκεφάλῳ λίθους ἐμφερεῖς μύλαις. φωλεύει τε μόνος ἐν ταῖς ὑπὸ κύνα θερμοτάταις ἡμέραις, τῶν ἄλλων ταῖς χειμεριωτάταις φωλευόντων.

[a] As the Editor has elsewhere shown, references to a star as indicating the time of year are (unless the context very definitely—not merely implies—but explicitly asserts the opposite) always to the rising (heliacal) of a star.

μνημονεύει δ αὐτῶν Ἐπίχαρμος ἐν Ἥβας γάμῳ· "μεγαλοχάσμονάς τε χάννας κηκτραπελογάστορας ὄνους." διαφέρει δ' ὄνος ὀνίσκου, ὥς φησι Δωρίων ἐν τῷ περὶ ἰχθύων γράφων οὕτως· "ὄνος, ὃν καλοῦσί τινες γάδον· γαλλερίας, ὃν καλοῦσί τινες ὀνίσκον τε καὶ μάξεινον." Εὐθύδημος δ' ἐν τῷ περὶ ταρίχων "οἱ μὲν βάκχον, φησί, καλοῦσιν, οἱ δὲ γελαρίην, οἱ δὲ ὀνίσκον." Ἀρχέστρατος δέ φησι· "τὸν δ' ὄνον Ἀνθηδών, τὸν καλλαρίαν καλέουσιν | ἐκτρέφει εὐμεγέθη" κτλ.; Ael. vi. 30 ὁ ἰχθὺς ὁ ὄνος τὰ μὲν ἄλλα, ὅσα ἐντὸς προσπέφυκεν, οὐ πάνυ τι τῶν ἑτέρων διεστῶτα κέκτηται, μονότροπος δέ ἐστι καὶ σὺν ἄλλοις βιοῦν οὐκ ἀνέχεται. ἔχει δὲ ἄρα ἰχθύων μόνος οὗτος ἐν τῇ γαστρὶ τὴν καρδίαν [=Ael. v. 20] καὶ ἐν τῷ ἐγκεφάλῳ λίθους, οἵπερ οὖν ἐοίκασι μύλαις τὸ σχῆμα. Σειρίου δὲ ἐπιτολῇ φωλεύει μόνος, τῶν ἄλλων ἐν ταῖς κρυμωδεστάταις φωλεύειν εἰθισμένων; Oppian, *H.* iii. 138 ff. ἀλλ' ὁπόταν καθέτοισι πελώριοι ἀμφιχάνωσιν | ἰχθύες, οἷα βοῶν τε πέλει προβάτων τε γένεθλα | ἢ βατὶς ἢ καὶ ὄνων νωθρὸν γένος, οὐκ ἐθέλουσιν | ἑσπέσθαι, ψαμάθοισι δ' ἐπὶ πλατὺ σῶμα βαλόντες | ἀθρόοι ἐμβαρύθουσι, μόγον δ' ἁλιεῦσιν ἔθηκαν. | πολλάκι δ ἐξώλισθον ἀπ' ἀγκίστροιο λυθέντες.

2. Dorion, as quoted above, distinguished ὄνος and ὀνίσκος, which we may take to mean that they were not usually distinguished. Oppian thrice mentions the ὀνίσκος, *H.* iii. 191 as bait for the ὄρκυνος; *H.* i. 105 where he says its habitat is in πηλοῖσι καὶ ἐν τενάγεσσι θαλάσσης (102), while the habitat of the ὄνος is ἐν βένθεσσιν *H.* i. 145 ff. Lastly, *H.* i. 593, the mode of propagation of the ὀνίσκος is said to be unknown. To Oppian therefore the ὄνος and ὀνίσκος were different fishes. On the other hand they are identified by Eustath. *Hom.* p. 862 ὄνος, ἰχθὺς ποιός, ὁ καὶ ὀνίσκος καὶ βάκχος.

3. The Latin *asellus* represents ὄνος. Ovid, *Hal.* 131 Et tam deformi non dignus nomine asellus; Plin. xxxii. 145 peculiares autem maris . . . asellus. See below for Plin. ix. 58.

Callarias.—Oppian, *H.* i. 105 mentions καλλαρίαι along with the ὀνίσκος, where incidentally it may be noted that the schol. has ὀνίσκων· ἀειδάρων (γαδαρίων ?). We have seen above that Archestratus *ap.* Athen. 316 a equates ὄνος with καλλαρίας. *Cf.* Athen. 118 c καθάπερ καὶ τὸν χελλαρίην· καὶ γὰρ τοῦτον ἕνα ὄντα ἰχθὺν πολλῶν ὀνομασιῶν τετυχηκέναι· καλεῖσθαι γὰρ καὶ βάκχον καὶ ὀνίσκον καὶ χελλαρίην; Hesych. *s.* γαλαρίας· ἰχθὺς ὁ ὀνικός, and Hesych. *s.* γαλίαι· οἱ ὀνίσκοι; Hesych. *s.* λαζίνης· χαραδρίας· καλαρίας ἰχθύς; Pliny ix. 61 postea praecipuam auctoritatem fuisse lupo et asellis Nepos Cornelius et Laberius poeta mimorum tradidere . . . asellorum duo genera collyri [=callariae] minores et bacchi, qui non nisi in alto capiuntur, ideo praelati prioribus; Plin. xxxii. 146 collyris, asellorum generis, ni minor esset. Plin. xxxii. 145 mentions *bacchus* among the "peculiares maris."

The generally accepted opinion is that those fishes are *Gadidae* or members of the Cod-family. A difficulty is suggested by Athen. 306 e where discussing the Grey Mullets he says καταδεέστεροι δὲ πάντων οἱ χελλῶνες οἱ λεγόμενοι βάκχοι. The ὄνος is traditionally identified with the Hake (*Gadus merluccius* L., *Merluccius vulgaris* Cuv.), *cf.* Ital. *asinello,* Gr. γάδος. A. 620 b 29 (quoted above) would seem to imply that the ὄνος has some sort of oral appendages which it employs in catching smaller fishes. The Hake has nothing of the sort, not even barbels (which the Fork-beard Hake,

Phycis blennioides, and the Mediterranean Hake, *P. mediterranea*, have). But it seems probable that in Aristotle *l.c.* either ὄνος should be omitted, as Plin. ix. 144 omits it, or that ῥαβδεύεται should not be extended to it. Bussemaker makes ὄνος *Gadus mustela* L., ὀνίσκος, *Gadus merlangus* L.

This is a convenient place to explain Oppian, *H.* i. 151 ff. "Among these also is numbered the Hake, which beyond all fishes shrinks from the bitter assault of the Dog-star in summer, and remains retired within his dark recess and comes not forth so long as the breath of the fierce star prevails." The origin of this passage is A. 599 b 33 φωλεῖ δὲ καὶ ὁ ὄνος καὶ ὁ χρύσοφρυς· σημεῖον δὲ δοκεῖ εἶναι τοῦ τὸν ὄνον πλεῖστον φωλεῖν χρόνον τὸ διὰ πλείστου χρόνου ἁλίσκεσθαι. τοῦ δὲ καὶ θέρους τοὺς ἰχθῦς φωλεῖν δοκεῖ σημεῖον εἶναι τὸ ἐπὶ τοῖς ἄστροις γίνεσθαι τὰς ἁλώσεις καὶ μάλιστα ἐπὶ κυνί· τηνικαῦτα γὰρ ἀνατρέπεσθαι τὴν θάλατταν· ὅπερ ἐν τῷ Βοσπόρῳ γνωριμώτατόν ἐστιν· ἡ γὰρ ἰλὺς ἐπάνω γίνεται καὶ ἐπιφέρονται οἱ ἰχθύες. A. and W. understand ἐπὶ τοῖς ἄστροις to mean "at the setting" of certain constellations and the Oxford translation "between the rise and setting of certain constellations" is no improvement. It means "at the *rising* of the constellations" as Pliny ix. 58 rightly understood; Quidam rursus aestus impatientia mediis fervoribus sexagenis diebus latent, ut glaucus, asellus, auratae. Fluviatilium silurus caniculae *exortu* sideratur . . . et alioqui totum mare sentit *exortum* eius sideris, quod maxime in Bosporo apparet. Alga enim et pisces superferuntur omniaque ab imo versa. The meaning is that the hiding of the ὄνος in summer is indicated by the fact that when the sea is turned up by stormy weather catches of this fish occur. *Cf.*

Ael. vi. 30 Σειρίου δὲ ἐπιτολῇ φωλεύει μόνος [ὁ ὄνος], τῶν ἄλλων ἐν ταῖς κρυμωδεστάταις φωλεύειν εἰθισμένων; Ael. ix. 38 ἀριθμοῖτο δ' ἂν ἐν τούτοις [*i.e.* among fishes which hide in summer] καὶ ὁ ὄνος· δέδοικε δὲ μάλιστα ἰχθύων τὴν τοῦ Σειρίου ἐπιτολὴν οὗτος. For the convulsion of the sea at the rising of the Dog-star *cf.* Plin. ii. 107 caniculae exortu accendi solis vapores quis ignorat? cuius sideris effectus amplissimi in terra sentiuntur: fervent maria exoriente eo. And for the association of weather phenomena with the Rising and Setting of certain stars *cf.* Plin. ii. 105 ut solis ergo natura temperando intelligitur anno, sic reliquorum quoque siderum propria est quibusque vis et ad suam cuique naturam fertilis. Alia sunt in liquorem soluti umoris fecunda, alia concreti in pruinas aut coacti in nives aut glaciati in grandines, alia flatus, alia teporis, alia vaporis, alia roris, alia rigoris. . . . Nec meantium modo siderum [*i.e.* Planets] haec vis est sed multorum etiam adhaerentium caelo [*i.e.* Fixed Stars].

Cetus: Phalaena: Physalus

Κήτεα is used in Oppian, *C.* i. 71, *H.* i. 360, v. 46 to denote the larger sea-beasts generally, including not only the Cetaceans (Whales and Dolphins) but also Selachians (*cf. H.* v. 63 where νόσφι κυνῶν implies that the Dog-fish are included among the θῆρες ὑπερφυέες = κήτεα). *Cf.* Strabo 24 τοῖς μείζοσι τῶν ζῴων οἷον δελφίνων καὶ κυνῶν καὶ ἄλλων κητωδῶν. But in *H.* v 71 ff the singular κῆτος seems to indicate a definite animal, and the indications point to the Cachalot or Sperm Whale, *Physeter macrocephalus*, the only large Whale possessing teeth

(v. 140). For the occurrence of the Cachalot in Greek waters *cf. H.* 368 n. With the account of the hunting of the κῆτος *H.* v. 111 ff. the reader may compare the hunting of the Sword-fish (ξιφίας or γαλεώτης) in the Straits of Messina as described in Strabo (after Polybius) 24: "One outlook is set for a large number of men who lie in waiting in two-oared boats, two men in each boat. One man rows, the other stands on the prow armed with a spear, when the outlook indicates the appearance of the Sword-fish—the animal swims with a third of its body projecting above the water. When the boat has come to close quarters, the spearman strikes the fish and then withdraws his spear from its body excepting the point, which is barbed and is purposely attached but loosely to the shaft and has a long rope fastened to it. This rope they pay out to the wounded fish until it is weary of struggling and trying to escape. Then they hale it to land or, if it is not altogether a full-sized fish, they take it on board the boat. Even if the spear-shaft fall into the sea, it is not lost, as it is made of oak and pine, and while the oaken part is submerged by its weight the remainder floats and is easily recoverable. Sometimes the oarsman gets wounded through the boat owing to the size of the animal's sword and because its strength, as also the manner of hunting it, is comparable to that of the Wild Boar."

Phalaena H. i 404 and *Physalus H.* i. 368 are sufficiently discussed in the notes on these passages. If they are not identical, possibly *Phalaena* may be, as A. and W. incline to think, *Delphinus tursio,* and *Physalus* the Cachalot. Bussemaker, identifying

Physalus with the Cachalot, takes *Phalaena* to be *Balaena musculus,* properly *Balaenoptera musculus,* the Common Finner, the average length of the males being about 60 feet, that of the females rather more

V. Some Animal Idiosyncrasies

1. *Narce,* Torpedo, Crampfish, or Electric Ray: *H.* i. 104, ii. 56 ff., *H.* iii. 149 ff. In all the Torpedoes the electric organ consists of a large patch of hexagonal cells, as many as 400 in the larger species. These are placed under the skin on each side of the head, below and behind the eye, and covering the base of the enlarged pectoral fin. They are modified muscle-cells and each is filled with a clear jelly-like substance. The shock which the animal communicates when touched is capable of being carried along a metallic conductor, such as a knife or spear, and is said to render the needle magnetic and to decompose chemical compounds. The exercise of this power soon exhausts its possessor and renders a period of recuperation necessary.

2. *Fox feigning death*: *H.* i. 107 ff. "When a fox is caught in a trap or run down by dogs he fights savagely at first, but by-and-by he relaxes his efforts, drops on the ground, and apparently yields up the ghost. The deception is so well carried out that dogs are constantly taken in by it, and no one, not previously acquainted with this clever trickery of nature, but would at once pronounce the creature dead, and worthy of some praise for having perished in so brave a spirit. Now, when in this condition of feigning

death, I am quite sure that the animal does not altgether lose consciousness. It is exceedingly difficult to discover any evidence of life in the opossum ; but when one withdraws a little way from the feigning fox, and watches him very attentively, a slight opening of the eye may be detected ; and, finally, when left to himself, he does not recover and start up like an animal that has been stunned, but slowly and cautiously raises his head first, and only gets up when his foes are at a safe distance. Yet I have seen gauchos, who are very cruel to animals, practise the most barbarous experiments on a captured fox without being able to rouse it into exhibiting any sign of life. This has greatly puzzled me, since, if death-feigning is simply a cunning habit, the animal could not suffer itself to be mutilated without wincing. I can only believe that the fox, though not insensible, as its behaviour on being left to itself appears to prove, yet has its body thrown by extreme terror into that benumbed condition which simulates death, and during which it is unable to feel the tortures practised on it." W. H. Hudson, *The Naturalist in La Plata* (1903).

3. *Deer and Snakes* : *C.* ii. 233 ff., *H.* ii. 289 ff. " The gauchos of the pampas give a reason for the powerful smell of the male deer. . . . They say that the effluvium of *Cervus campestris* is abhorrent to snakes of all kinds . . . and even go so far as to describe its effect as fatal to them ; according to this, the smell is therefore a protection to the deer. In places where venomous snakes are extremely abundant, as in the Sierra district on the southern pampas of Buenos Ayres, the gaucho frequently ties a strip

of the male deer's skin, which retains its powerful odour for an indefinite time, round the neck of a valuable horse as a protection. . . . Considering then the conditions in which *C. campestris* is placed—and it might also be supposed that venomous snakes have in past times been much more numerous than they are now—it is not impossible to believe that the powerful smell it emits has been made protective. . . . The gaucho also affirms that the deer cherishes a wonderful animosity against snakes ; that it becomes greatly excited when it sees one and proceeds at once to destroy it, they say, by running round and round it in a circle, emitting its violent smell in larger measure, until the snake dies of suffocation. It is hard to believe that the effect can be so great ; but that the deer is a snake hater and killer is certainly true : in North America, Ceylon, and other districts deer have been observed excitedly leaping on serpents, and killing them with their sharp-cutting hoofs." W. H. Hudson, *op. cit.*

4. *The Life-history of the Eel* (*Anguilla vulgaris*) : *H.* i. 513 ff. The propagation of the Eel is referred to several times in Aristotle's *History of Animals* : 538 a 3 " The Eel is neither male nor female and engenders nothing of itself. Those who assert that they are sometimes found with hairy or worm-like attachments speak inconsiderately, not observing the situation of these attachments. For no such animal is viviparous without being oviparous and no Eel has ever been seen with an egg ; and viviparous animals have their young in the womb and closely attached, not in the belly." To the same effect 570 a 3 *sq.* where he adds : " Eels spring from the so-called

earth's entrails' (γῆς ἔντερα, earth-worms), which grow spontaneously in mud and moist ground. Eels have in fact sometimes been seen to emerge from such earth-worms and at other times have been rendered visible when the earth-worms were laid open by scraping or cutting. Such earth-worms are found both in the sea and in rivers, particularly where there is decayed matter." *Cf.* 517 b 8, 567 a 21, 569 a 6, 608 a 5.

Till within the last half-century or so the problem remained in much the same position as it was in the time of Aristotle, but in recent years and in particular through the systematic and elaborate investigations of Dr. J. Schmidt, the life-history of the Eel has been greatly elucidated. The result of these investigations may be briefly summarized:

The Eel is oviparous and its spawning-ground is in the deep waters of the Atlantic Ocean near the Bermudas. Thence the larval "Ribbon-eels" travel eastward, a direction of migration which is instinctive and not due to drift of the current, as is proved by experiments with bottles and the like cast overboard. After a journey which lasts for about two years the young Eels in their third year, when about three inches in length, enter the European rivers, being now known as Elvers or "Glass-Eels." They ascend the rivers in spring, travelling in compact bodies and swimming close to the river-banks. They show remarkable determination in their upward journey, overcoming such obstacles as waterfalls by wriggling through the grass upon the banks. Examination of the growth-rings on the minute scales, on the otoliths ("ear-stones"), and on the centra of the vertebrae, shows that at three years of age, after a year in fresh water, an Eel is about 3½ inches long, at 5 years it is about 6 inches, at 8 years about 1 foot, and at 13 years nearly 2 feet in length.

Eels do not spawn in fresh waters. When the period of maturity approaches and with it the reproductive impulse, at the age of from 6 to 10 years, they become silvery in appearance (" Silver-eels "), their eyes become larger, and they make for the rivers in which they descend to the sea. Having reached the sea they travel oceanwards, at an average rate of more than 9 miles a day, on their final journey —*pour l'amour et pour la mort*—of over 2000 miles to their breeding-ground in the depths of the Atlantic Ocean, where they spawn and die.

The occurrence of Eels in land-locked waters, which seemed to complicate the problem of their origin and mode of propagation, is explained by the ability of the Eel to exist for a considerable time out of the water (A. 592 a 13, Plin. ix. c. 38) and to the agility of the young Eels in travelling for some distance overland (A. *Part. An.* 696 a 5, Theophrast. περὶ ἰχθύων τῶν ἐν τῷ ξηρῷ διατριβόντων fr. 171), and so making their way even into waters from which the adult Eels under the reproductive impulse in vain endeavour to escape. On the other hand there are no Eels in the Danube, nor in the Black Sea or the Caspian Sea, these waters being beyond the reach of the young Eels migrating from the Atlantic Ocean.

Cf. J. Schmidt, " The Breeding-place of the Eel," *Ann. Rep. Smithsonian Inst. Washington*, 1924 [1925], pp. 279-316 ; C. Rabot, " Les Anguilles du Pacifique," *Nature*, Paris, 1926, pp. 113-118 ; K. Marcus, " Über Alter und Wachstum des Aales," *Jahrb. Hamburg wiss. Anst.* xxxvi (1919), pp. 1-70.

VI. Analyses

Analysis of the *Cynegetica*:

Bk. I. 1-46 Prooemium; 47-80 Triple division of the hunting of wild creatures—Fowling, Hunting, Fishing; 81-90 Physical qualities of Hunter; 91-109 The Hunter's equipment; 110-146 Seasons of Hunting; 147-157 The Hunter's weapons; 158-367 Horses; 368-538 Dogs.

Bk. II. 1-42 The Inventors of Hunting; 43-175 Bulls; 176-292 Deer; 293-295 Broad-horn; 296-299 Iorcus; 300-314 Antelope; 315-325 Gazelle; 326-444 Wild Goats and Sheep; 445-488 Oryx; 489-550 Elephant; 551-569 Rhinoceros; 570-585 Panther, Cat, Dormouse; 586-597 Squirrel; 598-604 Hedgehog and Spiny Mouse; 605-611 Ape; 612-628 Blind Rat.

Bk. III. 1-6 Prooemium; 7-62 Lion; 63-83 Leopard; 84-106 Lynx; 107-138 Digression on the affection of animals for their young; 139-182 Bear; 183-250 Wild Ass; 251-261 Wild Horse; 262-339 Wolf and Hyena; 340-363 Tiger; 364-390 Wild Boar; 391-406 Porcupine; 407-448 Ichneumon, Crocodile, and Asp; 449-460 Fox; 461-481 Giraffe; 482-503 Ostrich; 504-525 Hare.

Bk. IV. 1-76 Prooemium; general precepts on Hunting; 77-211 Lion Hunting; 212-229 Hunting of Thos and Leopard; 230-353 Leopards and Dionysus; 354-424 Bear Hunting; 425-438 Hare Hunting; 439-447 Gazelle Hunting; 448-453 Fox Hunting.

Analysis of the *Halieutica*:

Bk. I. 1-79 Prooemium; comparison of Hunting Fishing, and Fowling; 79-92 Depth of the Sea, etc.;

93-445 Habitat and Habit of various Fishes; 446-512 the Mating of various Fishes; 513-553 Mating of Eels, Turtles, Poulpes; 554-579 Mating of Muraena; 580-583 Mating of Dolphin; 584-637 Fish-breeding in general; 638-645 Molluscs, Selachians, etc.; 646-685 Dolphin; 686-701 Seal; 702-733 Love of offspring among animals; 734-741 Dog-fish; 742-746 Angel-shark; 747-755 Glaucus; 756-761 Tunny; 762-797 Oysters and Aphya.

Bk. II. 1-42 Prooemium; 43-55 Fishes prey one on the other; 56-85 the Torpedo; 86-119 the Fishing Frog; 120-127 Cuttle-fish; 128-140 Prawn; 141-166 Ox-ray (Cephalopterus Giorna); 167-180 Crab and Oyster; 181-185 Star-fish and Oyster; 186-198 Pinna and Pinnoteres; 199-224 Uranoscopus scaber; 225-231 Sea-urchins; 232-252 Poulpe (Octopus); 253-421 Spiny Lobster, Muraena, Poulpe; 422-500 Venomous Fishes—Scolopendra, Iulis, Poulpe, Cuttle-fish, Goby, Scorpion, Sea-swallow, Weever, Squalus centrina, Sting-ray; 501-532 Parasites of Tunny and Dog-fish; 533-552 Dolphin; 553-627 Dolphin and Amia (Bonito); 628-641 Dolphin; 642-663 Grey Mullet (*κεστρεύς*); 664-688 Epilogue.

Bk. III. 1-28 Prooemium; 29-49 Attributes of the Fisherman; 50-71 Seasons for Fishing; 72-91 Instruments of Fisherman; 92-97 Wiles of Fish; 98-116 Grey Mullet (*κεστρεύς*); 117-120 Muraena; 121-125 Basse; 126-127 Mormyrus; 128-131 Basse; 132-137 Orcynus (largest size of Tunny); 138-143 Ox-ray, Sea-sheep, Skate, Hake (?); 144-148 Bonito and Fox-shark; 149-155 Torpedo; 156-165 Cuttle-fish; 166-168 Squid; 169-204 Baits for various Fish; 205-337 Anthias; 338-370 Cantharus or Black Sea-bream; 371-413 Admos; 414-431 Saupe; 432-442 Red

Mullet; 443-481 Melanurus; 482-528 Grey Mullet (κεστρεύς); 529-575 Sword-fish; 576-619 Mackerel, Tunny, Needle-fish, Dentex; 620-648 Tunny.

Bk. IV. 1-10 Fishes captured through love of their kind; 11-39 Address to Love (Eros); 40-126 Parrot-wrasse; 127-146 Grey Mullet (κέφαλος); 147-171 Cuttle-fish; 172-241 Merle-wrasse and Thrush-wrasse; 242-263 Dog-fishes; 264-307 Poulpes; 308-403 Sargues; 404-436 Hippurus; 437-438 Pilot-fish; 439-449 Squid; 450-467 Eel; 468-503 Aphya; 504-592 Pelamyds; 593-615 Divers catch Sargue; 616-634 Divers catch Sciaena; 635-646 Weel, Hook, Net, Trident, Burning the water; 647-693 Poisoning the water.

Bk. V. 1-45 Prooemium; 46-357 Sea-monsters; Whale-guide (67-108); Whale-hunting (109 ff.); 358-364 Lamia (Lamna); 365-375 Dog-fishes; 376-391 Seal; 392-415 Turtles; 416-588 Dolphin, Legends of; 589-597 Testaceans; 598-611 Purple-shells; 612-674 Sponge-fishers; 675-680 Epilogue.

VII. Bibliography

1. Editions of Oppian

1. *Editio princeps.* Greek Text of *Hal.* and *Cyn.*, with Lat. verse rendering of *Hal.* by Laurentius Lippius, Ald., Venice, 1517.
2. Oppiani de Venatione libri IV., Parisiis apud Vascosanum, 1549.
3. Oppiani Anazarbei de Piscatu libri V., de Venatione libri IV., Parisiis, 1555, apud Turnebum.
4. Oppiani Poetae Cilicis de Venatione lib. IV., de

Piscatu lib. V., cum interpretatione latina, comment. et indice rerum . . . studio et opera Conradi Rittershusii, Lugduni Bat., 1597.

5. Poet. graec. veteres carm. heroici scriptores qui exstant omnes, apposita est e regione latina interpretatio . . . cura et recensione Iac. Lectii, Aureliae Allobrog., 1606.
6. Opp. Poet. Cilicis de Ven. lib. IV. et de Pisc. lib. V. cum paraphr. gr. librorum de Aucupio, gr. et lat., cur. J. G. Schneider, Argentorati, 1776.
7. Opp. Poem. de Ven. et Pisc. cum interpr. lat. et schol. . . . tom. I. Cynegetica . . . recens. Iac. Nic. Belin de Ballu, Argent., 1786.
8. Opp. *Cyn.* et *Hal.* . . . emend. J. G. Schneider . . . Accedunt versiones lat. metrica et prosaica, plurima anecdota et ind. graecitatis, Lipsiae 1813 [the Lat. metrical version of the *Cyn.* is by David Peifer (1555); there is no metrical version of the *Hal.*, no prose version of either poem, no *anecd.*, no *index graecitatis*].
9. Opp. et Nicandr. quae supersunt . . . gr. et lat. ed. F. S. Lehrs *in* Poet. bucolici et didactici, Didot, Paris., 1846.
10. Oppians des jüngeren Gedicht von der Jagd . . . I. Buch, metrisch übers. u. mit erklärenden Bemerk. versehen von M. Miller, Programm, Amberg, 1885; II. Buch (1-377), München, 1891; IV. Buch, Programm, Amberg, 1886.
11. Opp. *Cyn.* (Oppien d'Apamée *La Chasse*), éd. crit. par P. Boudreaux, Libr. H. Champion, Paris, 1908.

Translations: *Halieutica*, English verse, by Diaper and Jones, Oxford, 1722. *Cynegetica* in French, Limes, Paris, 1817. Both poems in Ita'ian, Salvini, Florence, 1728.

2. Editions of Scholia and Paraphrases

Scholia et Paraphrases in Nicandrum et Oppianum ed. Bussemaker, Didot, Paris, 1849. *Cf.* O. Tüselmann,

Zur handschrift. Überlief. v. Oppians Kyn., Progr., Ilfeld, 1890, and *Abh. d. Königl. Gesellsch. d. Wissensch., Philol.-hist. Klasse, N. Folge*, iv. 1, 1900; A. Ludwich, *Aristarchs homerische Textkritik*, ii. 597 ff.

3. Other Oppianic Literature

Bodinus, J., *Opp. de Ven. lib. IV. I. Bodino . . . interpret. . . . accessit commentarius*, Lutetiae, 1555.

Brodaei, J., *Annotationes in Opp. Cyn. libr. IV.*, Basileae, 1552.

Headlam, W., *Various Conjectures, Journ. of Philol.* xxiii. (1895).

Schmidt, O., *De elocutione Oppiani Apameensis*, Leipzig, 1866.

4. Chief Abbreviations used in quoting Ancient Authors

A. = Aristotle, *History of Animals.* Other works of Aristotle are quoted by A. with abbreviations for particular works as *e.g.* A. *P.A.* = Aristotle, *De Partibus Animalium*, A. *De Gen.* = Arist. *De Generatione*, and so on.

Ael. = Aelian, *De Natura Animalium.* If the *Varia Historia* is referred to, *V.H.* is added.

Antig. = Antigonus of Carystus (3rd cent. B.C.), *Hist. Paradox. Synagoge.*

Arr. *C.*, *Tact.* = Arrianus of Nicomedia (*c.* A.D. 100), *Cynegetica, Tactica.*

Ath. (Athen.) = Athenaeus (*c.* A.D. 200), *Deipnosophistae.*

E.M. = *Etymologicum Magnum* (12th cent. A.D.).

Dion. P. = Dionysius Periegetes (2nd cent. A.D.).

Geop. = *Geoponica* (Cassianus Bassus), 10th cent. A.D.

Gratt. = Grattius, *Cynegetica.*

Marc. S. = Marcellus of Side in Pamphylia (2nd cent. A.D.), author of *Iatrica* (101 lines extant).

Nemes. = Nemesianus (3rd cent. A.D.), *Cynegetica.*

Phil. = Manuel Philes, *De Animalium Proprietate*.
Plin. = Pliny's *Natural History*.
Poll. = Julius Pollux (Πολυδεύκης) of Naucratis (2nd cent. A.D.), Ὀνομαστικόν.
Solin. = C. Iulius Solinus (3rd cent. A.D.), *Collectanea rerum memorabilium*.
Varr. = Varro, *De Re Rustica*.
Xen. *C.* = Xenophon, *Cynegeticus*.

5. Chief Abbreviations used in referring to Modern Authors

A. and W. = Aubert and Wimmer, *Aristotles Thierkunde*, Leipzig, 1868.
Apost. = Apostolides, *La Pêche en Grèce*², Athens, 1907.
Badham = C. D. Badham, *Ancient and Modern Fish Tattle*, London, 1854.
Bik. = Bikélas [*i.e.* Vicelas], *La Faune de Grèce*, Paris, 1879.
Bussemaker = U. C. Bussemaker, *Index Animalium* in edition of *Scholia* to Nicander and Oppian, Paris, 1849.
Cuvier = Cuvier et Valenciennes, *Histoire Naturelle des Poissons*, Paris, 1828–1849.
Day = F. Day, *British Fishes*, 1889.
Erh. = Erhard, *Fauna der Cykladen*, Leipzig, 1858.
Forbes = Edw. Forbes, *Natural History of the European Seas*, 1859.
Gesner = Konrad von Gesner, *Historia Animalium*, 1551–8.
Günther = Günther, *Introduction to the Study of Fishes*, 1880.
Lindermayer = A. Lindermayer, *Die Vögel Griechenlands*, Passau, 1860.
Mommsen = August Mommsen, *Griechische Jahreszeiten*, Hft. III., Schleswig, 1875.
McIntosh = W. C. McIntosh, *British Marine Food Fishes*, 1897.
Mühle = H. von der Mühle, *Beiträge zur Ornithologie Griechenlands*, Leipzig, 1844.

Radcliffe = W. Radcliffe, *Fishing from the Earliest Times*, London, 1921.

Ridg. = Sir W. Ridgeway, *Origin and Influence of the Thoroughbred Horse* [Cambridge Biological Series], Cambridge University Press, 1905.

St. John, *N.H.* = C. St. John, *Natural History and Sport in Moray*, Edin., 1863.

St. John, *Wild Sports.* = C. St. John, *Wild Sports and Natural History of the Highlands*, Lond., 1846.

Sundevall = C. I. Sundevall, *Thierarten des Aristoteles*, Stockholm, 1863.

Thompson, Glossary = D'Arcy W. Thompson, *A Glossary of Greek Birds*, Oxford, 1895.

Tristram = H. B. Tristram, *The Natural History of the Bible*, London, 1880.

Turner = *Turner on Birds* (1544), ed. Evans, Cambridge, 1903.

VIII. Mss. of Oppian

A = Venetus 479, XI. century (*Cyn.* only).
B = Parisinus 2736, XV. cent. (*Cyn.* only).
C = Parisinus 2860, XV. cent. (*Cyn.* only).
D = Neapolitanus II. F. 17, XV. cent. (*Cyn.* and *Hal.*).
E = Laurentianus 31. 27, XVI. cent. (*Cyn.* only).
F = Parisinus Suppl. Gr. 109, XVI. cent. (*Cyn.* only).
G = Parisinus 2723, XIV. cent. (*Cyn.* only).
H = Venetus 468, XIII. cent. (*Hal.* and *Cyn.*, the latter incomplete).
I = Matritensis 4558, XV. cent. (*Hal.* and *Cyn.*).
K = Laurentianus 32. 16, XIII. cent. (*Hal.* and *Cyn.*).
L = Vindobonensis 135, XV. cent. (*Hal.* and *Cyn.*).
M = Laurentianus 31. 3, XIII. cent. (*Hal.* and *Cyn.*).
N = Venetus 480, XV. cent. (*Hal.* and *Cyn.*).
O = Laurentianus 86. 21, XV. cent. (*Hal.* and *Cyn.*).
P = Parisinus 2737, A.D. 1554 (*Cyn.* only).
Q = Salmanticensis 1–1–18, copied 1326 (*Hal.* and *Cyn.*).
R = Vaticanus 118, XV. cent. (*Hal.* and *Cyn.*).

CYNEGETICA AND HALIEUTICA

ΟΠΠΙΑΝΟΥ

ΚΥΝΗΓΕΤΙΚΩΝ ΤΟ Α

Σοί, μάκαρ, ἀείδω, γαίης ἐρικυδὲς ἔρεισμα,
φέγγος ἐνυαλίων πολυήρατον Αἰνεαδάων,
Αὐσονίου Ζηνὸς γλυκερὸν θάλος, Ἀντωνῖνε·
τὸν μεγάλη μεγάλῳ φιτύσατο Δόμνα Σεβήρῳ,
ὀλβίῳ εὐνηθεῖσα καὶ ὄλβιον ὠδίνασα,
νύμφη ἀριστοπόσεια, λεχὼ δέ τε καλλιτόκεια,
Ἀσσυρίη Κυθέρεια καὶ οὐ λείπουσα Σελήνη,
οὐδὲν ἀφαυρότερον Ζηνὸς Κρονίδαο γενέθλης·
(εὐμενέοι Τιτὰν Φαέθων καὶ Φοῖβος Ἀπόλλων.)
τῷ ῥα πατὴρ μεγάλῃσι πονησάμενος παλάμῃσι[1]
δῶκεν ἔχειν πᾶσαν τραφερήν, πᾶσαν δὲ καὶ ὑγρήν.
σοὶ μὲν γὰρ θαλέθουσα κύει πάνδωρος ἄρουρα,
καὶ πάλιν εὐδιόωσα τρέφει κλυτὰ φῦλα θάλασσα·

[1] *v.l.* κρατερῇσι.

---

[a] M. Aurelius Severus Antoninus Augustus (Caracalla), Emperor A.D. 211–217.

[b] Romans. Lucret. i. 1; Verg. *Aen.* viii. 648.

[c] Italian.

[d] = *Divus*, of Roman Emperors; here of L. Septimius Severus Pertinax Augustus, Emperor A.D. 193–211, in which year (4 Feb.) he died at York.

[e] Julia D. of Emesa in Syria, second wife of Severus (Gibbon c. 6); died A.D. 217.

[f] The Syrian (Assyrian) Ashtoreth or Astarte, the

OPPIAN

CYNEGETICA, or THE CHASE

I

To thee,[a] blessed one, I sing: thou glorious bulwark of the earth, lovely light of the warlike sons of Aeneas,[b] sweet scion of Ausonian [c] Zeus,[d] Antoninus, whom Domna [e] bare to Severus, mighty mother to mighty sire. Happy the husband whom she wedded and happy the son to whom she gave birth—bride of the best of men and mother of a noble son, Assyrian Cythereia,[f] the uneclipsed Moon; a son no meaner than the breed of Cronian Zeus (with favour of Titan Phaethon [g] be it spoken and of Phoebus Apollo!); to whom thy sire, by the labour of his mighty hands, gave in keeping all the dry land and all the wet sea.[h] Yea, for thee doth earth, giver of all gifts, conceive and blossom; for thee again the sunny sea rears

"moonèd Ashtoroth" of Milton (*Nativ.* 22), was pictured with horns, representing the crescent moon, and by the Greeks usually identified with Aphrodite, but also with the moon-goddess, Selene: Plut. *Mor.* 357 B; Lucian, *De dea Syr.* For Assyrian = Syrian see *C.* i. 340 n.

[g] The poets often use Phaethon (Verg. *Aen.* v. 105) and Titan (Verg. *Aen.* iv. 119) for the Sun. For this parenthetic apology *cf. H.* v. 339 n.

[h] Lycophr. 1229 γῆς καὶ θαλάσσης σκῆπτρα καὶ μοναρχίαν λαβόντες; Luc. i. 83 populum terrae pelagique potentem.

σοὶ δέ τε πάντα νάουσιν ἀπ' Ὠκεανοῖο ῥέεθρα,
φαιδρά τε μειδιόωσα θέει κλυτὸς Ἠριγένεια.
Τοιγὰρ ἐγὼν ἔραμαι θήρης κλυτὰ δήνε' ἀεῖσαι.
τοῦτό με Καλλιόπη κέλεται, τοῦτ' Ἄρτεμις αὐτή.
ἔκλυον, ᾗ θέμις ἐστί, θεείης ἔκλυον ἠχῆς,
καὶ θεὸν ἠμείφθην· πρώτη δέ με τοιάδ' ἔνισπεν·
Α. Ἔγρεο, καὶ τρηχεῖαν ἐπιστείβωμεν ἀταρπόν,
τὴν μερόπων οὔπω τις ἑῆς ἐπάτησεν ἀοιδαῖς.
Ο. Ἵλαθι, πότνια δῖα, τὰ δ' ἐν φρεσὶ σῇσι μενοινᾷς,
ἄμμες ὑφ' ἡμετέρῃ μεροπηΐδι λέξομεν ἠχῇ·
Α. Οὐκ ἐθέλω τριετῆ σε τὰ νῦν Ὀρίβακχον ἀείδειν,
οὐ χορὸν Ἀονίου παρὰ βένθεσιν Ἀσωποῖο.
Ο. Λείψομεν, ὡς κέλεαι, τὰ Σαβάζια[1] νύκτερα θύσθλα·
δηθάκις ἀμφεχόρευσα Θυωναίῳ Διονύσῳ.
Α. Μὴ γένος ἡρώων εἴπῃς, μὴ ναυτίλον Ἀργώ,
μηδὲ μόθους μερόπων, μή μοι Βροτολοιγὸν ἀείσῃς.
Ο. Οὐκ ἐρέω πολέμους, οὐκ Ἄρεος ἔργα κάκιστα·
ἐφρασάμην Πάρθων τε δύας καὶ Κτησιφόωντα.

[1] τὰ σὰ βάζειν MSS.

---

[a] Lucret. i. 920 avia Pieridum peragro loca nullius ante Trita solo; Nemes. *C.* 8 ducitque per avia qua sola nunquam Trita rotis; Verg. *G.* iii. 291; Hor. *C.* iii. 1. 2; Milton, *P.L.* i. 16.

[b] *Cf.* ὀρίδρομος Nonn. ii. 230.

[c] τριετῆ here = τριετηρικόν. Trieterica (Ov. *R.A.* 593, *M.* vi. 587; Verg. *Aen.* iv. 302; *repetita triennia* Ov. *M.* ix. 641; τριετηρίς Eur. *Bacch.* 133; Diod. iii. 54, etc.) is what we should call a *biennial* festival, recurring in alternate years, παρ' ἔτος (Paus. vi. 26. 2, viii. 23. 1, x. 4. 3). Hence Stat. *A.* i. 595 Alternam renovare piae trieterida matres Consuerant.

[d] r. in Boeotia (Aonia).

[e] Dionysus (Phrygian): Aristoph. *V.* 9. θύσθλα, the *thyrsi* and the like (Hom. *Il.* vi. 134), here perhaps "Bacchic rites."

[f] δηθάκις· πλειστάκις Suid.; δηθάκι· πυκνῶς, πολλάκις Hes. Properly "for a long time"; the transition is seen in Hom.

her splendid broods; for thee flow all the streams from Ocean; for thee with cheerful smile springs up the glorious Dawn.

Fain then am I to sing the glorious devices of the chase. So biddeth me Calliope, so Artemis herself. I hearkened, as is meet, I hearkened to the heavenly voice, and I answered the goddess who first to me spake thus.

ARTEMIS. Arise, let us tread a rugged path, which never yet hath any mortal trodden with his song.[a]

OPPIAN. Be gracious, holy Lady, and whatsoever things thou thinkest in thy mind, these will we declare with our mortal voice.

ART. I would not now have thee sing Mountain-Bacchus[b] of the triennial feast,[c] nor his choir by the deep waters of Aonian Asopus.[d]

OPP. We will leave, as thou biddest, the nightly rites of Sabazius[e]; often[f] have I danced around Dionysus, son of Thyone.[g]

ART. Tell not of the race of heroes, tell not of the seafaring Argo; sing not the battles of men, sing not to me the Destroyer of Men.[h]

OPP. I will not tell of wars, nor of Ares' works most evil; I have remarked the Parthians' woes and Ctesiphon.[i]

Il. xxi. 131 ᾧ δὴ δηθὰ πολεῖς ἱερεύετε ταύρους, where Didymus τὸ "δηθὰ" ὡς οὐχ Ὁμηρικῶς κείμενον αἰτιῶνται, *i.e.* δηθά was taken to be not = ἐπὶ πολὺν χρόνον or ἐκ πολλοῦ χρόνου, as usually in Hom. but = πολλά, συνεχῶς. *Cf. E.M. s.v.*

[g] *i.e.* Semele, d. of Cadmus and m. of Dionysus. *Cf.* Pind. *P.* iii. 99.

[h] Ares (Hom. *Il.* v. 31).

[i] Ctesiphon (Polyb. v. 45. 4; Strabo 743; Tac. *A.* vi. 42; Plin. *N.H.* vi. 122; Amm. Marc. xxiii. 6. 23; T. Simoc. iv. 3. 3) on left bank of Tigris, seat of the Parthian kings in second century, taken by the Emperor Septimius Severus A.D. 198: Herodian iii. 9.

Α. Ἀμφὶ πόθοις[1] ὀλοοῖσιν ἀκὴν ἔχε, λεῖπέ τε κεστούς·
ἐχθαίρω τὰ λέγουσιν ἀθύρματα Ποντογενείης.
Ο. Ἐκλυόμέν σε, μάκαιρα, γάμων ἀμύητον ἐοῦσαν.
Α. Μέλπε μόθους θηρῶν τε καὶ ἀνδρῶν ἀγρευτήρων·
μέλπε γένη σκυλάκων τε καὶ ἵππων αἰόλα φῦλα,
βουλὰς ὠκυνόους, στιβίης εὐκερδέος ἔργα·
ἔχθεά μοι θήρεια λέγειν, φιλότητας ἀείδειν
καὶ θαλάμους ἐν ὄρεσσιν ἀδακρύτοιο Κυθείρης
καὶ τοκετοὺς ἐνὶ θηρσὶν ἀμαιεύτοιο λοχείης.
Τοῖαι συνθεσίαι Ζηνὸς μεγάλοιο θυγατρός.
ἔκλυον, ἀείδω· βάλλοιμι δ' ἐπίσκοπον ἠχήν.
ἀλλὰ σύ γ', ἀντολίηθεν ἐπ' Ὠκεανὸν βασιλεύων,
εὔδιον ἀμβροσίῃσιν ὑπ' ὀφρύσι σῇσι γεγηθώς,
δεξιτερὴν ὀπάσαιο πανίλαον ὀλβοδότειραν
γαίῃ καὶ πολίεσσι καὶ εὐθήροισιν ἀοιδαῖς.
Τριχθαδίην θήρην θεὸς ὤπασεν ἀνθρώποισιν,
ἠερίην χθονίην τε καὶ εἰναλίην ἐρατεινήν·
ἀλλ' οὐκ ἶσος ἄεθλος· ἐπεὶ πόθεν ἶσα τέτυκται,
ἰχθὺν ἀσπαίροντα βυθῶν ἀπομηρύσασθαι,
καὶ ταναοὺς ὄρνιθας ἀπ' ἠέρος εἰρύσασθαι,
ἢ θηρσὶν φονίοισιν ἐν οὔρεσι δηρίσασθαι;
οὐ μὲν ἄρ' οὐδ' ἁλιῆϊ καὶ οὐκ ἐτὸς ἰξευτῆρι

[1] πόθοις Koechly: μόθοις.

---

[a] Hom. *Il.* xiv. 214.

[b] *i.e.* Aphrogeneia, Aphrodite: Hes. *T.* 196.

[c] The epithet (applied to Athena, Colluth. 33) is used of Artemis as the huntress maid, ἰοχέαιρα παρθένος Pind. *P.* ii. 9.

[d] *Cf.* ii. 15; Herod. iii. 35 ἐπίσκοπα τοξεύοντα. For metaphor *cf.* Pind. *O.* ii. 98, xiii. 94; *N.* vi. 27, ix. 25.

ART. Be silent about deadly passion and leave alone the girdles[a] of love: I abhor what men call the toys of the Daughter of the Sea.[b]

OPP. We have heard, O blessed Lady, that thou art uninitiate in marriage.[c]

ART. Sing the battles of wild beasts and hunting men; sing of the breeds of hounds and the varied tribes of horses; the quick-witted counsels, the deeds of skilful tracking; tell me the hates of wild beasts, sing their friendships and their bridal chambers of tearless love upon the hills, and the births which among wild beasts need no midwifery.

Such were the counsels of the daughter of mighty Zeus. I hear, I sing: may my song hit the mark![d] But do thou, who rulest from the East unto the Ocean,[e] with serene joy on thine immortal brows, vouchsafe thy right hand gracious and prosperous to land and cities and to songs of the happy chase.

Triple[f] sorts of hunting hath God bestowed on men—in air and on earth and on the sea delightful. But not equal is the venture: for how can these be equal—to draw the writhing fish from the deeps or hale the winged birds from the air and to contend with deadly wild beasts on the hills? Yet not for the fisherman either and truly not[g] for the fowler

[e] *i.e.* the West.

[f] *Cf.* Walton's Piscator, Venator, Auceps; *Greek Anthol.* vi. 11-16, 179-187. More elaborate division, Plato, *Soph.* 219 E. See Introd. p. xxxviii.

[g] οὐκ ἐτὸς normally means "not for nothing," *haud frustra*, *e.g.* Aristoph. *Pl.* 404, 1166. But the old *Lexica* (Hesych., etc.) confuse this ἐτὸς with ἐτὸς = genuine and ἐτώσιος = vain (the schol. on our passage has ἐτός· ἔστι μάταιος) and, whatever the punctuation and syntax intended, the sense seems to be as we have given it.

ἄγρη νόσφι πόνοιο· πόνῳ δ' ἅμα τέρψις ὀπηδεῖ
μούνη, καὶ φόνος οὔτις· ἀναίμακτοι δὲ πέλονται.
ἤτοι ὁ μὲν πέτρῃσιν ἐφήμενος ἀγχιάλοισι
γυραλέοις δονάκεσσι καὶ ἀγκίστροισι δαφοινοῖς
ἄτρομος ἀσπαλιεὺς ἐπεδήσατο δαίδαλον ἰχθύν·[1]
τερπωλὴ δ', ὅτε χαλκοῦ[2] ὑπαὶ γενύεσσι τορήσας
ὕψι μάλα θρώσκοντα βυθῶν ὕπερ ἀσπαίροντα
εἰνάλιον φορέῃσι δι' ἠέρος ὀρχηστῆρα.
ναὶ μὴν ἰξευτῆρι πόνος γλυκύς· ἢ γὰρ ἐπ' ἄγρην
οὐκ ἄορ, οὐ δρεπάνην, οὐ χάλκεα δοῦρα φέρονται,
ἀλλ' αὐτοῖς ἐπὶ δρυμὰ συνέμπορος ἕσπετο κίρκος
καὶ δολιχαὶ θώμιγγες ὑγρός τε μελίχροος ἰξὸς
οἵ τε διηερίην δόνακες πατέουσιν ἀταρπόν.
τίς τάδε τολμήσειεν ἀείδειν ἰσοτάλαντα;
ἢ βασιλῆϊ λέοντι τίς αἰετὸν ἀντιβάλοιτο;
ἰῷ πορδαλίων δὲ τίς ἂν μύραιναν εἴσκοι,
ἢ θῶας κίρκοις, ἢ ῥινοκέρωτας ἐχίνοις,

[1] l. 58 is omitted in Aldine (Editio princeps), Venice, 1517.
[2] χαλκὸν MSS.

---

[a] κίρκος hawk generically; specifically A. 620 a 17 τῶν ἱεράκων κράτιστος μὲν ὁ τριόρχης (Buzzard?), δεύτερος δ' ὁ αἰσάλων (Merlin?), τρίτος ὁ κίρκος. *Cf.* *Turner on Birds* (Evans), pp. 14 f.; Hawks of English fowlers, Walton, *C.A.* c. 1.

[b] Ps. 140. 5 "The proud have hid a snare (פַּח, LXX παγίδα) for me and cords" (חֲבָלִים, LXX σχοινία). *Cf.* *A.P.* vi. 109 γηραλέον νεφέλας τρῦχος τόδε καὶ τριέλικτον ἰχνοπέδαν καὶ τὰς νευροτενεῖς παγίδας κλωβούς τ' ἀμφίρρωγας ἀνασπαστούς τε δεράγχας; Aristoph. *Av.* 194 and espec. 565 ff. ὀρνιθευτὴς ἵστησι βρόχους, παγίδας, ῥάβδους, ἕρκη, νεφέλας, δίκτυα, πηκτάς.

[c] Made of mistletoe berries: *A.P.* vi. 109 καὶ τὰν εὔκολλον

is their hunting without toil. But their toil only pleasure attends and no bloodshed: unstained of gore are they. The angler sits on the rocks beside the sea and with curving rods and deadly hooks he catches, at his ease, the fish of varied sheen; and joy is his when he strikes home with barbs of bronze and sweeps through the air the writhing dancer of the sea, leaping high above the deeps. Yea and to the fowler his toil is sweet; for to their hunt the fowlers carry nor sword nor bill nor brazen spear, but the Hawk[a] is their attendant when they travel to the woods, and the long cords[b] and the clammy yellow birdlime[c] and the reeds[d] that tread an airy path. Who would dare to sing of these things as of equal weight? Or who would pit the Eagle against the Lion King[e]? And who would liken the Muraena to the venom of the Pard, or Jackal to Hawk, or Rhinoceros to Sea-urchin, or Gull to Wild Goat, or any

δρυὸς ἰκμάδα τόν τε πετεινῶν ἀγρευτὰν ἰξῷ μυδαλέον δόνακα. *Cf.* Athen. 451 D *Ἴων δὲ . . δρυὸς ἱδρῶτα εἴρηκε τὸν ἰξὸν ἐν τούτοις· δρυός μ' ἱδρὼς | καὶ θαμνομήκης ῥάβδος ἤ τ' Αἰγυπτία | βόσκει λινουλκὸς χλαῖνα, θήραγρος πέδη.* It may have been sometimes made, as now, from holly bark.

[d] The limed reeds ("lime-twigs," Milton, *Com.* 646) of the fowler: *ἰξευταῖς καλάμοις* *A.P.* vi. 152. As in the case of the fishing-rod (*δόνακα τριτάνυστον* *A.P.* vi. 192), several reeds might be so joined together as to be capable of extension. *Cf.* Bion, iv. 5 (*ἰξευτὰς*) *τὼς καλάμως ἅμα πάντας ἐπ' ἀλλάλοισι συνάπτων*; *A.P.* ix. 273 *δουνακόεντα Κρίτων συνθεὶς δόλον*; Mart. xiv. 218 Non tantum calamis sed cantu fallitur ales, Callida dum tacita crescit arundo manu; Mart. ix. 54; Sil. vii. 674; Ov. *M.* xv. 474, and especially Val. Fl. *Arg.* vi. 260 Qualem populeae fidentem nexibus umbrae Siquis avem summi deducit ab aere rami, Ante manu tacita cui plurima crevit harundo; Illa dolis viscoque super correpta tenaci Implorat calamos atque inrita concitat alas.

[e] Ael. iii. 1 *λέων . . . ὁ τῶν ζώων βασιλεύς*; Phil. 34 *θηρῶν βασιλεὺς θρασὺς ἄναξ λέων.*

ἢ λάρον αἰγάγροις, ἢ κήτεα πάντ' ἐλέφαντι;
θηρητῆρε λύκους ὄλεσαν, θύννους ἁλιῆες,
ἀγρευτῆρες ὄϊς, τρήρωνας ἕλον δονακῆες,
ἄρκτον ἐπακτῆρες, καὶ μορμύρον ἀσπαλιῆες,
τίγριν δ' ἱππῆες, καὶ τριγλίδας ἰχθυβολῆες,
κάπριον ἰχνευτῆρες, ἀηδόνας ἰξευτῆρες.
ἀλλὰ σὺ μέν, Νηρεῦ, καὶ δαίμονες Ἀμφιτρίτης,
ἠδὲ φιλορνίθων Δρυάδων χορὸς, ἱλήκοιτε·
δὴ γὰρ ἐπιστροφάδην με φίλαι καλέουσιν ἀοιδαί·
δαίμοσι θηροφόνοισι παλίντροπος ἔρχομ' ἀείσων.
Πρῶτα μὲν αἰζηοὶ μή μοι μάλα πίονες ἔστων·
ἦ γάρ τοι σκοπέλοισι θορεῖν μὲν ὑπείροχον ἵππον
χρειὼ ἀναγκαίη, χρειὼ δ' ἄρα τάφρον ἀλέσθαι.
δηθάκι δ' ἐν δρυμοῖσιν ἀνάγκη θῆρα δίεσθαι,
ποσσὶν ἐλαφρίζοντα καὶ εὐφόρτοις μελέεσσι.
τῷ μὴ πιαλέοι θήρης ἐπὶ μῶλον ἴοιεν,
μηδ' ἔτι λεπταλέοι· καὶ γάρ ποτε δηρίσασθαι
θηρσὶν ἐνυαλίοισι χρεὼ πολυαγρέα φῶτα.
τοὔνεκά μοι δέμας ὧδε κερασσάμενοι φορέοιεν,
ἀμφότερον κραιπνόν τε θέειν σθεναρόν τε μάχεσθαι.
καὶ δ' ἄρα δεξιτερῇ μὲν ἐπικραδάοιεν ἄκοντας
ἀμφιδύμους ταναούς, δρεπάνην δ' ἐπὶ μεσσόθι ζώνης·

---

[a] *Cf. H.* i. 100, iii. 126. *Pagellus mormyrus*, one of the sea-breams (*Sparidae*). M.G. μουρμούρι(ον): known in Rome as *mormillo*, Venice as *mormiro*, Genoa as *mormo*. A. 570 b 20; Ov. *H.* 110 (= Plin. xxxii. 152) pictae mormyres; μύρμης Epicharm.; μορμύλος Dorio ap. Ath. 313 e f.

[b] We assume that τριγλίς = τρίγλη. So, in Arist. fr. 189, Porph. v. 45 has τριγλίδος, Diog. L. viii. 19 τρίγλης.

[c] *Cf. C.* ii. 158; Emped. frag. 35 αὐτὰρ ἐγὼ παλίνορσος ἐλεύσομαι ἐς πόρον ὕμνων; Lucr. i. 418.

[d] Poll. v. 18 εἴη δὲ (ὁ κυνηγέτης) νέος, κοῦφος, ἐλαφρός, δρομικός κτλ.

[e] *Cf.* Eutecn. par. πρός τε τάφρων καὶ σκοπέλων ἅλματα.

Sea-monster to the Elephant? Hunters kill Wolves, fishermen kill Tunnies; the hunter with his net takes Sheep, the fowler with his reeds takes Doves; the hunter with his hounds takes the Bear, the angler takes the Mormyrus[a]; the mounted hunter takes the Tiger, the fisher with his trident takes the Red Mullet[b]; the tracker takes the Boar, the fowler with his birdlime takes the Nightingale. But thou, Nereus, and ye gods of Amphitrite and the choir of Dryads who love the birds, grant me your grace! For now dear themes of song invite me earnestly; I, turning back,[c] proceed to sing to the gods of the chase.

First, give me young men who are not over-stout.[d] For the hunter must mount[e] the noble horse amid the rocks and anon must leap a ditch. And often in the woods must he with light feet and nimble limbs pursue the wild beast. Therefore let them not be stout who come to the warfare of the chase, nor yet over-lean; for at times the keen hunter must contend with warlike wild beasts. So I would have them bear a body tempered thus—both swift to run and strong to fight. And in the right hand let them brandish two[f] long javelins and have a hunting-bill[g] at

So of the war-horse Xen. *Eq.* 3. 7 τάφρους διαπηδᾶν, τειχία ὑπερβαίνειν, ἐπ' ὄχθους ἀνορούειν, ἀπ' ὄχθων καθάλλεσθαι; Arr *Tact.* 44. 2 καὶ τάφρον δὲ διαπηδᾶν μελετῶσιν αὐτοῖς οἱ ἵπποι καὶ τειχίον ὑπεράλλεσθαι.

[f] ἀμφιδ.· ἀμφοτέρωθεν κόπτων schol., but δύο Eutecn. rightly. *Cf.* Hom. *Il.* iii. 18 δοῦρε δύω: so x. 76, xii. 298, etc. Verg. *Aen.* i. 313 = xii. 165 Bina manu lato crispans hastilia ferro; *cf.* v. 557, xii. 488; Xen. *Cyr.* i. 2. 9 παλτὰ δύο, ὥστε τὸ μὲν ἀφεῖναι, τῷ δέ, ἂν δέῃ, ἐκ χειρὸς χρῆσθαι.

[g] *Cf.* v. 63; Xen. *C.* 2. 9 καὶ τὰ δρέπανα, ἵνα ᾖ τῆς ὕλης τέμνοντα φράττειν τὰ δεόμενα; Gratt. 343 et curvae rumpant non pervia falces; Poll. v. 19 δρέπανα δὲ ὅπως εἰ δέοι τῆς ὕλης τι κόψαι εἰς τὴν τῶν ἀρκύων ἀκώλυτον στάσιν ὑπάρχοι τὰ δρέπανα.

καὶ γὰρ καὶ θήρεσσι πικρὸν φόνον ἐντύνοιντο,
καί τε κακῶν φορέοιεν ἀλεξητήρια φωτῶν.
λαιῇ δὲ πεζὸς μὲν ἄγοι κύνας, ἱππελάτης δὲ
ἵππων ἰθύνειε κυβερνητῆρα χαλινόν.
εὐσταλέως δὲ χιτῶνα καὶ εἰς ἐπιγουνίδα πήξας
ἑλκέσθω, σφίγγοιτο δ' ἐπημοιβοῖς τελαμῶσιν.
αὐχένος αὖθ' ἑκάτερθε παρήορον ἐκ παλαμάων
εἶμα περιστέλλοιτ' ὀπίσω σθεναρῶν ὑπὲρ ὤμων,
ῥήϊον ἐς κάματον· γυμνοῖσι δὲ ποσσὶν ὁδεύειν
κείνους, τοῖσιν ἴχνη μέλεται δυσδερκέα θηρῶν,
ὄφρα κε μὴ θήρεσσιν ἀπ' ὄμματος ὕπνον ἕλοιτο
ἠχὴ τριβομένων λιπαροῖς ὑπὸ ποσσὶ πεδίλων.
μηδ' ἄρα λῶπος ἔχειν μάλα λώϊον· οὕνεκεν εἶμα
πολλάκι κινύμενον πνοιῇ κελάδοντος ἀήτου
θῆρας ἀνεπτοίησεν, ἀνήϊξαν δὲ φέβεσθαι.
ὧδε μὲν εὖ στέλλοιντο θοὸν δέμας ἀγρευτῆρες·
τοίους γὰρ φιλέει Λητωϊὰς Ἰοχέαιρα.
Ἄλλοτε δ' ἀλλοίην ὥρην ἐπὶ θῆρας ἰόντων,
ἤματος ἱσταμένοιο, καὶ ἤματος ἀνομένοιο,
καὶ μεσάτου, ποτὲ δ' ἑσπερίου· ποτὲ δ' αὖτε καὶ ὄρφνῃ
θῆρας ὑπ' ἀκτίνεσσι σεληναίης ἐδάμασσαν.
Ἠὼς μὲν τέταται περιδέξιος ἀγρευτῆρι
πᾶσα γαληνιόωσα πανηματίοισι δρόμοισιν
εἴαρι φυλλοτόκῳ καὶ φυλλορόῳ φθινοπώρῳ·

[a] Poll. v. 17 χιτὼν εὐσταλὴς πρὸς τὴν ἰγνύαν καθήκων; Hes. *Sc.* 287 ἐπιστολάδην δὲ χιτῶνας ἐστάλατο. εὐσταλής = *succinctus*, in ref. to the high-girt tunic of the hunter: Ov. *Am.* iii. 2. 31 Talia pinguntur succinctae crura Dianae Cum sequitur fortes fortior ipsa feras; *M.* x. 536 Fine genus vestem ritu succincta Dianae; Juv. vi. 446 Crure tenus medio tunicas succingere debet; Philostr. *Im.* 28 (of a hunter) συμμετρεῖται δὲ ὁ χιτὼν εἰς ἥμισυ τοῦ μηροῦ; Ov. *A.A.* iii. 143; *M.* iii. 156, ix. 89.

the midst of their girdle. For they should both array bitter slaughter for wild beasts and also carry defences against evil men. With his left hand the hunter on foot should lead his hounds; with his left the mounted hunter should guide the bridle that steers his horse. Let him wear a tunic well-girt [a] and fastened above the knee and held tight by crossing straps. Again on either side of his neck let his mantle [b] be flung back over his strong shoulders to hang away from the hands, for easy toil. With naked feet should they travel who study the dim tracks of wild beasts, lest the noise of their sandals grating under their sleek feet drive sleep from the eyes of the wild beasts. To have no mantle at all were much better; since many a time a cloak stirred by the breath of the noisy wind alarms the wild beasts and they start up to flee. Thus let hunters well array the agile body; for such doth the archer daughter of Leto love.

Other times [c] at other hour let them go after the wild beasts—at rising morn and when the day wanes and at mid-day and anon at evening; sometimes again even in the dark they slay wild beasts by the rays of the moon.[d] The whole span of day is favourable and fair to the hunter for all-day coursing in leafy spring [e] and in autumn when the leaves fall.

[b] Poll. v. 18 *καὶ χλαμὺς ὁμοία ἣν δεῖ τῇ λαιᾷ χειρὶ περιελίττειν ὁπότε μεταθέοι τὰ θηρία ἢ προσμάχοιτο τούτοις.*

[c] Poll. v. 49 *θηρατέον μὲν τοίνυν ἐν παντὶ καιρῷ*; Xen. *C.* 4. 11 *ἀγέσθωσαν δὲ (αἱ κύνες) θέρους μὲν μέχρι μεσημβρίας, χειμῶνος δὲ δι' ἡμέρας, μετοπώρου δὲ ἔξω μεσημβρίας, ἐντὸς δ' ἡμέρας τὸ ἔαρ.* *Cf. ibid.* c. 5.

[d] "Many a deer is killed during the bright moonlight nights" (St. John, *Wild Sports*, p. 50).

[e] See v. 459 n.

ἔξοχα γὰρ τελέθουσι καὶ ἵπποις καὶ μερόπεσσι
καὶ κυσὶν ὠμηστῇσι θέειν εὐκραέες ὧραι
εἴαρι χρυσείῳ, κρυερῶν νεφέων ἐλατῆρι,
ὁππότε ποντοπόροισι βατὴ πλώουσι θάλασσα,
ἄργυφα τειναμένοισι λινοπτερύγων ὅπλα νηῶν·
ὁππότε γαῖα βροτοῖσι φυτηκομέουσι γέγηθεν·
ὁππότε καὶ καλύκεσσι καὶ ἄνθεσιν ἄμματα λύει·
ἢ πάλιν ἐσχατίῃσιν ὀπωρινῇσι τροπῇσιν,
ἡνίκα δῶμα τέθηλεν ὀπωρολόγοιο γεωργοῦ,
καρπὸς Ἀθηναίης λιπαρὴν ὅτε γαυλίδα πλήθει
καὶ βότρυς ἡμερίδων θλίβων ἐπιλήνια χαίρει,
σίμβλα μελισσάων ὅτε λείρια κηρία βρίθει.
χείματι δ' ἐν μεσάτῳ μέσου ἤματος ἀγρώσσοιεν,
εὖτέ τις ἐν δρυμοῖσιν ὑπὸ σπήλυγγι λιασθείς,
κάρφεα λεξάμενός τε καὶ ὠκύμορον φλόγα νήσας,
ἄγχι πυρὸς κλινθεὶς ὁπλίσσατο δόρπον ἀμορβός.
ἐν δὲ θέρει χρειὼ φυγέειν φλογόεσσαν ἐνιπὴν
ἄζαν τ' ἠελίου· κέλομαι δ' ἐπ' ἄεθλον ἱκάνειν

[a] περὶ φθίνουσαν ὀπώραν Eutecn. τροπαί here, not in its strict sense of the Solstice, but of the Equinox. *Cf.* Sext. Empir. *Adv. M.* v. 11 ἐν Κριῷ μὲν γὰρ ἐαρινὴ γίνεται τροπή, ἐν Αἰγοκέρῳ δὲ χειμερινή, ἐν Καρκίνῳ δὲ θερινή, καὶ ἐν Ζυγῷ φθινοπωρινή. So in Latin *tropicus* of the Equin. as well as the Solst. *Cf.* Auson. *Opusc.* vii. 15. 1 Nonaginta dies et quattuor ac medium Sol Conficit, a tropico in tropicum dum permeat astrum; *ibid.* 15 Scandit Lanigeri (Ram) tropicum Sol aureus astrum; Manil. iii. 621 Quae tropica appellant, quod in illis quattuor anni Tempora vertuntur signis.

[b] The Olive.

[c] γαυλίς pail, basin, tub. *Cf.* κυρτίς Nicand. *A.* 493 with schol.

[d] For θλίβων ἐπιλήνια *cf.* Mart. iv. 44. 2 *Presserat* hic madidos nobilis uva *lacus*. We assume that ἐπιλήνιον is part of the wine-press, whether the press strictly, *cf.* Suid. and *E.M.* s. τριπτήρ . . . πιθάκνη ἐκπέταλος οἷα τὰ ἐπιλήνια,

For excellent well tempered for the running of horses and men and carrion dogs are the seasons in golden spring which puts to rout the chilly clouds; when the sea is navigable for seafaring men, who spread the white rigging of their canvas-winged ships, what time the earth rejoices in them that tend plants; when, too, she looses the bands of bud and flower; or again in late autumn [a] when the year is on the turn, when the house of the rustic vintager flourishes; when the fruit of Athena [b] fills the shining pail [c] and the clusters of the garden vines joyfully straiten [d] the wine-vats; when the lilywhite combs fill the hives of the bees. But in mid-winter let the hunters hunt at mid-day, in the season when in the woods the swain shelters in a cave and gathering dry sticks and piling a swiftly dying flame lies down beside the fire and makes his supper. And in summer the hunter must shun the fiery assault and heat of the sun: at earliest dawn I bid him come to his

or = ὑπολήνιον, Lat. *lacus*, a sense which τριπτήρ also has (πολλὰ σημαίνει τοὔνομα *E.M.*), *cf.* Poll. x. 130 τριπτήρ, ὁ κρατήρ, εἰς ὃν ἀπορρεῖ τοὔλαιον ἀλλὰ καὶ ληνὸς καὶ ὑπολήνιον. Our rendering, reached independently, agrees with the Lat. version of D. Peifer (1555): Cum premit arcta nimis sibi torcularia botrus Gaudens. Schn.'s βότρυν assumes that the subject to χαίρει is γεωργός. If that is right, then the construction of ἐπιλήνια is difficult. Does it go with θλίβων or χαίρει? The schol. taking βότρυς as acc. pl. has ἐπὶ λήνια· ἐπὶ τὰς πίλας (*i.e.* Lat. *pilas*, presses). Eutecn. has ἀμπέλων δὲ βότρυς ἀπαλοῖς ποσὶ θλιβόμενος σκιρτᾶν παρασκευάζει τὰ ἐπιλήνια. We hear of songs of the wine-press: Ath. 199 a ἐπάτουν δὲ ἑξήκοντα Σάτυροι πρὸς αὐλὸν ᾄδοντες μέλος ἐπιλήνιον; Anacreont. 57. 9 (Hiller) ἐπιληνίοισιν ὕμνοις; Poll. iv. 55 (*cf.* *ib.* 53) ἐπιλήνιον αὔλημα ἐπὶ βοτρύων θλιβομένων; and of a dance, Long. *Daph. and Ch.* ii. 36 Δρύας δὲ ἀναστὰς καὶ κελεύσας συρίττειν Διονυσιακὸν μέλος ἐπιλήνιον αὐτοῖς ὄρχησιν ὠρχήσατο. But ἐπιλήνια χαίρειν would be a very bold expression.

πρώτῃ ὑπ' ἀμφιλύκῃ, ὅθ' ἑωθινὸν ἀγροιῶται
ἱστοβοῆος ἔνερθεν ὑπ' εὐποίητον ἐχέτλην
γειοτόμον δαμάλῃσιν ἐπιθύνουσιν ἄροτρον·
ἢ πάλιν ἑσπερίῃσιν ὅτ' ἠέλιος ζυγὰ κλίνει,
ὁππότε σημαίνουσιν ἑαῖς ἀγέλῃσι νομῆες,
εὖτε καταστείχουσι ποτὶ σφετέρους πάλι σηκοὺς
βριθόμεναι μαζούς τε καὶ οὔθατα κυμαίνουσαι·
οἱ δ' ἀπὸ λαϊνέων ἄμοτον προθορόντες ἐναύλων
πάντες ἑαῖσι φίλῃσι περισκαίρουσι τεκούσαις,
ἀμφὶ μὲν εὐγλήνους δαμάλας βλοσυρώπεε μόσχω,
αὐτὰρ ἐϋκραίρους ὄϊας περὶ βληχάδας ἀμνώ,
μηκάδας αὖτ' ἐρίφω, καὶ φορβάδας ὠκέε πώλω.
Καὶ μὴν τόσσα φέροιντο ποτὶ κνημοὺς ξυλόχους τε
ἐργοπόνοι κρατεροὶ θήρης ἐρικυδέος ὅπλα,
ἔντεά τ' εὐθήροιο μέγα πνείοντα φόνοιο,
ἄρκυας εὐστρεφέας τε λύγους ταναόν τε πάναγρον
δίκτυά τε σχαλίδας τε βρόχων τε πολύστονα δεσμά,
αἰχμὴν τριγλώχινα, σιγύνην εὐρυκάρηνον,
ἁρπάλαγον κάμακάς τε καὶ εὔπτερον ὠκὺν ὀϊστόν,

---

[a] *Cf.* Ov. *M.* xi. 257 Pronus erat Titan inclinatoque tenebat Hesperium temone fretum; Hor. *C.* i. 28. 21 devexi Orionis.

[b] *Cf.* Poll. v. 17 ff.; Xen. *C.* 2.

[c] For hunting-nets in general *cf.* Xen. *C.* 2; Arr. *C.* 1; Gratt. 25 ff.; and espec. Poll. v. 4, who says that while all nets may be called δίκτυα, hunting parlance distinguishes (1) δίκτυα = τὰ ἐν τοῖς ὁμαλοῖς καὶ ἰσοπέδοις ἱστάμενα (*i.e.* set up on level ground); (2) ἐνόδια τὰ ἐν ταῖς ὁδοῖς (*i.e.* set up on the "roads" or tracks of wild beasts); (3) αἱ δὲ ἄρκυες τούτων μὲν ἐλάττους εἰσὶ τοῖς μεγέθεσι, κεκρυφάλῳ δὲ ἐοίκασι κατὰ τὸ σχῆμα, εἰς ὀξὺ καταλήγουσαι. Thus δίκτυον = Lat. *rete*, net in general or specifically a large net or haye; ἐνόδιον = Lat. *plaga*, a net placed in a known "road" of the game; ἄρκυς = Lat. *cassis*, a funnel-shaped net, resembling, as Pollux says, a κεκρύφαλος = Lat. *reticulum*, which means (1) a net-work cap for the hair (Hom. *Il.* xxii. 469); (2) any bag-shaped reticule

task, when in the morning the countrymen with well-fashioned stilt guide the earth-cutting plough behind the steers beneath the pole; or again at evening when the sun slopes[a] his team toward the West; when herdsmen command their herds what time they travel homeward to their folds, heavy of breast and swollen of udder: and, bounding incontinently from the stone-built steading, all leap about their beloved mothers—the bright-eyed calves about the large-eyed cows, the lambs about the bleating horned ewes, the kids about the bleating goats, and about the brood mares their swift foals.

And these are the weapons[b] of the glorious chase which the stalwart hunters should carry to hill and wood, these their arms breathing of the blood of beasts: purse-nets[c] and well-twisted withes and long sweep-net[d] and hayes and net-props[e] and grievous fettering nooses, three-pronged spear, broad-headed hunting lance,[f] hare-stick[g] and stakes and swift winged

or purse (the "women's ridicules" of Noah Claypole, *Oliver Twist*, c. 42). *Cf.* Nemes. 299 f. casses venatibus aptos Atque plagas, longoque meantia retia tractu.

[d] *Cf.* Hom. *Il.* v. 487 ἀψῖσι λίνου ἁλόντε πανάγρου; Hesych. πάναγρα, πανάγρια, ἐν οἷς τὰ λεπτὰ θηρεύεται; *E.M.* ἀψίς; Poll. i. 97, ix. 12, x. 132.

[e] Forked sticks for supporting nets = Lat. *varae*, *cf.* Luc. iv. 439 Dum dispositis attollat retia varis; Xen. *C.* 2. 7 ff. (*v.l.* στάλικες, σταλίδες), vi. 7 ff. It is hard to know if σχαλίδες differ from στάλικες (v. 157). Poll. v. 19 has σταλίδες, σταλιδώματα as well as σχαλίδες, σταλίδες, σχαλιδώματα (*cf.* *ib.* 32). Hesych. σχαλίς· τὸ δίκτυον, and σχαλίδες· δι' ὧν σχάζουσι τὰ δίκτυα ὀρθὰ ἑστῶτα, which suggests that σχαλίδες may = Lat. *amites* and have been used with the clap-net. *Cf.* Poll. vii. 114 μυάγρας, ὧν τὸ ἱστάμενόν τε καὶ σχαζόμενον παττάλιον.

[f] Athen. 201 b κυνηγοὶ ἔχοντες σιβύνας ἐπιχρύσους; Verg. *Aen.* iv. 131 lato venabula ferro.

[g] Only here; possibly = λαγωβόλον Theoc. iv. 49, vii. 128.

φάσγανα βουπλῆγάς τε λαγωοφόνον τε τρίαιναν,
ἀγκυλίδας σκολιὰς μολιβοσφιγγέας τε κορώνας,
σπαρτόδετον μήρινθον ἐΰπλεκτόν τε ποδάγρην,
ἅμματά τε στάλικάς τε πολύγληνόν τε σαγήνην.
Ἵππους δ' εἰς θήρην μέγα κυδήεντας ἀγέσθων
ἄρσενας· οὐ μόνον ὅττι χερείονές εἰσι πόδεσσι
θηλύτεραι τελέειν δολιχὸν δρόμον ἐν ξυλόχοισιν,
ἀλλ' ὅτ' ἀλεύασθαι χρειὼ φιλοδέμνιον ἦτορ
ἵππων ὠκυπόδων, ἀπὸ δ' ἱππάδα τηλόσ' ἐρύκειν,
ὄφρα κε μὴ χρεμέθωσι λιλαιόμεναι φιλότητος,
καί τ' ἀΐοντες ἄδην[1] κρυερὴν φύζανδε νέωνται
νεβροὶ δορκαλίδες τε θοαὶ καὶ δειμαλέος πτώξ.
ἵππων δ' αἰόλα φῦλα, τόσ' ἔθνεα μυρία φωτῶν,
ὅσσα βροτοῖσι γένεθλα δεδασμένα σῖτον ἔδουσιν·
ἀλλ' ἔμπης ἐρέω, τόσσοι μετὰ πᾶσι κραταιοὶ
ὅσσοι θ' ἱππαλέοισιν ἀριστεύουσιν ὁμίλοις·

[1] *v.l.* αὐδὴν.

---

[a] Poll. v. 19 mentions ξίφη among the hunter's weapons.

[b] Poll. *l.c.* καὶ ἀξίνας παρασκευαστέον, εἰ καὶ πρέμνα κόψαι δέοι.

[c] Lat. *tridens*, *fuscina*.

[d] The sense of ἀγκυλίδες (only here) and κορῶναι is only to be guessed.

[e] *Stipa tenacissima* L. (or allied species), which grows wild in Spain and Africa, still called *sparto* or *esparto*. Plin. xix. 26 ff.; Cato 3; Varr. *R.R.* i. 23. 6; Colum. xii. 52. 8; Aul. Gell. xvii. 3. 4; Xen. *C.* 9. 13; Ael. *N.A.* xii. 43; Blümner, *Technologie*, i. 294.

[f] *Cf. C.* iv. 43; *A.P.* vi. 296 ἀστεμφῆ ποδάγρην; Xen. *Cyr.* i. 6. 28 ἐλάφους (δολοῦν) ποδάγραις καὶ ἀρπεδόναις. See Xen. *C.* 9. 12 ff. for description of the ποδοστράβη (*pedica dentata*); Gratt. 92 dentatas iligno robore clausit Venator pedicas.

[g] The precise sense of ἅμματα here is uncertain: possibly the same as the ἀρπεδόναι of Xen. *Cyr.* i. 6. 28.

[h] See n. on v. 150. *Cf. A.P.* vi. 152, vi. 187, xii. 146; Theocr. *Ep.* iii. 2; Tryphiod. 222; Poll. v. 19, 31, 80; x. 141; Hesych. *s.* στάλικας and *s.* δοκάναι, who has also σταλίδας· τοὺς κάμακας ἢ χάρακας.

arrow, swords[a] and axes[b] and hare-slaying trident,[c] bent hooks[d] and lead-bound crooks, cord of twisted broom[e] and the well-woven foot-trap,[f] and ropes[g] and net-stays[h] and the many-meshed seine.[i]

As for Horses, let them bring to the hunt proud stallions; not only because mares are inferior in speed for accomplishing a long course in the woods but also because it is needful to avoid the amorous passion of swift-footed horses and to keep mares far away, lest in their amorous desire they neigh and, hearing, the wild beasts incontinently[j] betake them to chilly flight—fawns and swift gazelles[k] and timid hare.[l]

Various are the tribes of horses, even as the countless races of men, the diverse tribes of mortals that live by bread. Nevertheless I will declare which are the best among them all, which are foremost in the companies of horses; to wit, the Tuscan,[m] Sicilian,[n]

[i] Lat. *sagena*, *verriculum*, a large sweep-net; more usually of the fisherman's drag-net (Opp. *H.* iii. 81). *Cf.* σαγηνεύω (Herod. iii. 149, vi. 31; Plato, *Legg.* 698 D) of "rounding up" the inhabitants of a country (procedure described Herod. vi. 31 and Plato *l.c.*).

[j] ἄδην· αὐταρκῶς, δαψιλῶς (schol.); *cf.* Hesych. ἄδην· ἀθρόως, ἐξαίφνης, δαψιλῶς. ἀίοντ' αὐδήν K, Boudreaux, perhaps rightly. Dual for plural is common in late epic.

[k] Assuming that δορκαλίς (*cf.* 441) means the same as δόρκος *C.* ii. 12, 315 ff., 405, 428, iii. 3, iv. 439 ff. (*cf.* πάρδαλις, πάρδος) we may suppose that this is Aristotle's δορκάς (*H.A.* 499 a 9; *De part. an.* 663 a 11, 663 b 27), prob. *Antilope dorcas*, Gazelle.

[l] Hor. *Epod.* ii. 35 pavidumque leporem.

[m] "Down to modern times Tuscany, Ancona, and the region of Bologna have been noted for fine breeds of black horses" (Ridgeway, p. 314).

[n] Gratt. 524 Possent Aetnaeas utinam se ferre per arces, Qui ludus Siculis; Arr. *C.* 23 Scythian and Illyrian horses are not, to look at, comparable ἵππῳ Θεσσαλικῷ ἢ Σικελῷ.

Τυρσηνοί, Σικελοί, Κρῆτες, Μάζικες,[1] Ἀχαιοί,
Καππαδόκαι, Μαῦροι, Σκυθικοί, Μάγνητες, Ἐπειοί,
Ἴονες, Ἀρμένιοι, Λίβυες, Θρήϊκες, Ἐρεμβοί.
ἵππον δ' ἐν πάντεσσι πανέξοχον ἐφράσσαντο
ἴδμονες ἱπποδρόμων καὶ βουκολίων ἐπίουροι,
εἴδεσιν ὃς τοίοισιν ὅλον δέμας ἐστεφάνωται·
βαιὸν ὑπὲρ δειρῆφι μετήορον ὕψι κάρηνον
ἀείροι, μέγας αὐτὸς ἐὼν περιηγέα γυῖα·
ὕψι κάρα, νεάτην δὲ γένυν ποτὶ δειράδα νεύοι·

[1] *v.l.* Μάζηκες.

---

[a] The Mazices (Amm. Marc. xxix. 5. 51) or Mazaces (Suet. *Ner.* 30; Luc. iv. 681; Claud. *Stil.* i. 356; Nemes. 261), Μάζυες (Hecat. *fr.* 304; Steph. Byz. Μάζυες· οἱ Λιβύης νομάδες), Μάξυες (Herod. iv. 191 ἀροτῆρες ἤδη Λίβυες καὶ οἰκίας νομίζοντες ἐκτῆσθαι, τοῖσι οὔνομα κέεται M.) were a people of Mauretania famous for horsemanship. See *C.* iv. 50 n. As Mazaca was an old name for Caesarea in Cappadocia, there is sometimes a doubt as to the reference.

[b] Nemes. 241 Cappadocumque notas referat generosa propago; Mart. x. 76 Nec de Cappadocis eques catastis.

[c] Nemes. 259 Sit tibi praeterea sonipes Maurusia tellus quem mittit; Strabo 828; Paus. viii. 43. 3; Ridg. pp. 242 and 248.

[d] Arr. *C.* 1. 4, 23. 2; Strabo 312 ἴδιον δὲ τοῦ Σκυθικοῦ καὶ τοῦ Σαρματικοῦ παντὸς ἔθνους τὸ τοὺς ἵππους ἐκτέμνειν εὐπειθείας χάριν· μικροὶ μὲν γάρ εἰσιν, ὀξεῖς δὲ σφόδρα καὶ δυσπειθεῖς; Ridg. pp. 125 f.

[e] It is not clear whether this refers to the Thessalian Magnesia or the Lydian, near Mt. Sipylus, or that on the Maeander. For the horses of the first *cf.* Luc. vi. 385 Magnetes equis gens cognita; Pind. *P.* ii. 45; for Lydian horses, Ridg. pp. 194 f.

[f] *i.e.* Eleian (Strabo 340; Steph. Byz. *s.v.*): τοὺς ἐξ Ἤλιδος Eutecn.

[g] Strabo 525 ἱππόβοτος δὲ καὶ αὕτη ἐστὶ διαφερόντως καὶ ἡ Ἀρμενία. *Cf.* Strabo 529 and note on Nesaean v. 312. Togarmah in Ezekiel xxvii. 14, "They of the house of Togarmah traded in thy fairs with horsemen (or war-horses?) and mules" is Armenia or neighbouring country

Cretan, Mazician,[a] Achaean, Cappadocian,[b] Moorish,[c] Scythian,[d] Magnesian,[e] Epeian,[f] Ionian, Armenian,[g] Libyan,[h] Thracian,[i] Erembian.[j] As the best horse of all men skilled in horse-racing and overseers of herds have remarked the horse whose whole body is crowned with these features.[k] He should have a small head [l] rising high above his neck, himself being big [m] and round of limb; the head should be high, the nether jaw curving toward the neck; the brow [n]

(Ridg. p. 193). Armenian mounted archers, Arr. *Tact.* 44. 1.

[h] See *C.* iv. 50 n; Arr. *C.* 1. 4, 24. 1 f.; Ael. *N.A.* iii. 2; Ridg. 238 ff., 470 ff. The horses of Cyrene were specially famous, Strabo 837 ἱπποτρόφος ἐστὶν ἀρίστη (*sc.* Κυρήνη); Pind. *P.* iv. 2 εὐίππου Κ.; *P.* ix. 4 διωξίππου Κ.

[i] Schol. Theocr. xiv. 47 ἵπποι Θρηΐκιοι Λακεδαιμόνιαί τε γυναῖκες. *Cf.* Hom. *Il.* x. 545 ff.; Verg. *Aen.* v. 565 ff.; Ridg. p. 108.

[j] τοὺς ἐκ τῆς Τρωγλοδύτιδος, Eutecn. *Cf.* Hom. *Od.* iv. 84 where Schol. and Eustath. say Aristarchus identified them with the Arabians. Strabo 41; Dionys. Per. 180, 963.

[k] *Cf.* in general Xen. *Eq.* 1; Poll. i. 189 f.; Geopon. xvi. 1; Verg. *G.* iii. 72 ff.; Varro, *R.R.* ii. 7; Columell. vi. 29; Nemes. 240 ff.; Pallad. iv. 13; M. H. Hayes, *Points of the Horse* (London 1904); Goubaux and Barrier, *The Exterior of the Horse* (1892).

[l] Xen. *Eq.* 1. 8 ἡ δὲ κεφαλὴ ὀστώδης οὖσα μικρὰν σιαγόνα ἔχοι; Poll. i. 189 κεφαλὴ ὀστώδης, προτομὴ βραχεῖα (opposed to κεφαλὴν βαρεῖαν σαρκώδη *ib.* 191); Geop. xvi. 1. 9 τὴν κεφαλὴν ἔχει μικράν; Verg. *G.* iii. 79 Illi ardua cervix argutumque caput; Hor. *S.* i. 2. 89 breve quod caput, ardua cervix; Varro, *R.R.* ii. 7. 5 si caput habet non magnum; Colum. vi. 29 Corporis vero forma constabit exiguo capite; Pallad. iv. 13 exiguum caput et siccum. *Cf.* Hayes p. 193, "When the head is large and 'fleshy' we may generally assume that the animal is 'soft' and wanting in 'blood.'"

[m] Geop. *l.c.* τῇ περιοχῇ τοῦ σώματος μέγαν, εὐπαγῆ πᾶσι τοῖς μέρεσι.

[n] "Good width between the eyes is generally regarded as a sign of intelligence and of a generous disposition" (Hayes, p. 196).

εὐρὺ πέλοι φαιδρόν τε μεσόφρυον· ἐκ δ' ἄρα κόρσης
ἀμφὶ μέτωπα τριχῶν πυκινοὶ σείοιντο κόρυμβοι·
ὄμμα τορόν, πυρσωπόν, ἐπισκυνίοισι δαφοινόν·
εὐρεῖαι ῥῖνες, στόμα δ' ἄρκιον, οὔατα βαιά·
γυραλέη δειρὴ τελέθοι λασιαύχενος ἵππου,
ὡς ὅτε χαιτήεσσα λόφον νεύει τρυφάλεια·
πουλὺ πέλοι στέρνον, δολιχὸν δέμας, εὐρέα νῶτα,
καὶ ῥάχις ἀμφίδυμος μέσον ἰσχία πιαίνουσα[1]·

[1] *leg.* πειραίνουσα?

---

[a] Poll. i. 189 προκόμιον (forelock) εὐπρεπές; Xen. *Eq.* 5. 8 δέδοται παρὰ θεῶν καὶ ἀγλαΐας ἕνεκα χαίτη καὶ προκόμιόν τε καὶ οὐρά.

[b] "The eye should be clear and free from tears, the pupil black," Hayes p. 212. *Cf.* G. and B. p. 54 among the beauties of the eye is "the clearness and little abundance of the tears"; Xen. *Eq.* 1. 9 τὸ ἐξόφθαλμον εἶναι ἐγρηγορὸς μᾶλλον φαίνεται τοῦ κοιλοφθάλμου; Poll. i. 189 ὄμμα προπετὲς ὡς ἐξόφθαλμον εἶναι, ὀφθαλμοὶ πυρώδεις, ὕφαιμον βλέποντες (opp. to κοιλόφθαλμος *ib.* 191); Geop. *l.c.* ὄμμα μέλαν; Varr. *l.c.* oculis nigris; so Colum. *l.c.*; Pallad. *l.c.* oculi magni.

[c] "The nostrils should be . . . of ample capacity, so as to suggest the possession of large air-passages," Hayes, p. 214; "The absolute beauty of the nostril resides in its width . . . Small nostrils are an absolute defect and associate themselves with a chest that is narrow," G. and B. p. 60; Xen. *Eq.* 1. 10 καὶ μυκτῆρές γε οἱ ἀναπεπταμένοι τῶν συμπεπτωκότων εὐπνοώτεροί τε ἅμα εἰσὶ καὶ γοργότερον τὸν ἵππον ἀποδεικνύουσι; Poll. i. 190 μυκτῆρες ἀναπεπταμένοι (opp. to μυκτῆρες συμπεπτωκότες *ib.* 191); Geop. *l.c.* ῥῖνας μὴ συμπεπτωκυίας; Varr. *l.c.* naribus non angustis; Colum. *l.c.* naribus apertis; Pallad. *l.c.* nares patulae.

[d] "The old practical rule of finding whether a horse is wide enough between the jaws is to try if the clenched fist can be placed within the hollow," Hayes, p. 216.

[e] "The ear is beautiful when it is short," G. and B. p. 43; Xen. *Eq.* 1. 11 ὦτα μικρότερα; Poll. i. 190 ὦτα βραχέα (opp. to ὦτα μεγάλα *ib.* 191); Geop. *l.c.* ὦτα προσεσταλμένα; Varr. *l.c.* auribus applicatis; Colum. *l.c.* brevibus auriculis et arrectis; Pallad. *l.c.* aures breves et argutae.

should be broad and bright; from the temples the hair should wave in dense curls about the forehead [a]; the eye [b] should be clear and fiery under beetling brows; the nostrils [c] should be wide, the mouth [d] adequate, the ears [e] small; the neck [f] of the shaggy-maned [g] horse should be curved, even as the arched crest of a plumed helmet; the breast [h] should be large, the body long, the back broad, with a double chine [i] running between fat hips [j]; behind should flow

[f] ardua cervix, Verg. *G.* iii. 79; Hor. *S.* i. 2. 89; cervice molli lataque nec longa, Colum. *l.c.*; erecta cervix, Pallad. *l.c.*

[g] Varr. *l.c.* iuba crebra; Verg. *G.* iii. 86 and Colum. *l.c.* densa iuba; Pallad. *l.c.* coma densa; Geop. *l.c.* χαίτην βαθεῖαν; Poll. *l.c.* χαίτη εὔθριξ.

[h] Xen. *Eq.* 1. 7 στέρνα πλατύτερα ὄντα καὶ πρὸς κάλλος καὶ πρὸς ἰσχὺν καὶ πρὸς τὸ μὴ ἐπαλλὰξ ἀλλὰ διὰ πολλοῦ τὰ σκέλη φέρειν εὐφυέστερα; Geop. *l.c.* στῆθος εὐρὺ μεμυωμένον; Poll. *l.c.* στέρνα πλατέα; Varr. *l.c.* pectus latum et plenum; Verg. *G.* iii. 81 Luxuriatque toris animosum pectus; Colum. *l.c.* lato et musculorum toris numeroso pectore; Pallad. *l.c.* pectus late patens.

[i] Xen. *Eq.* 1. 11 ῥάχις ἡ διπλῆ τῆς ἁπλῆς καὶ ἐγκαθῆσθαι μαλακωτέρα καὶ ἰδεῖν ἡδίων; Poll. i. 190 ὀσφὺς διπλῆ· τὸ δὲ αὐτὸ καὶ ῥάχις καὶ ἕδρα (*ib.* 190 the bad horse has ὀσφὺν ὀξεῖαν, *cf.* Gratt. 526 tenuis dorso curvatur spina); Geop. *l.c.* ῥάχιν μάλιστα μὲν διπλῆν, εἰ δὲ μή, μή γε κυρτήν; Verg. *G.* iii. 87 At duplex agitur per lumbos spina; Varr. *l.c.* spina maxime duplici, si minus, non extanti; Colum. *l.c.* spina duplici; Hayes, p. 250 "In many draught animals the upper muscles of the loins and back stand out as distinct ridges of muscle on each side of the backbone. This beauty in the coarser breeds is not confined to them, but may sometimes be seen in well-bred horses. . . . This 'double-backed' condition [well shown in a photograph of a Boulonnais horse in Hayes, p. 251] may come on or disappear according to the amount of 'flesh' which the animal carries." *Cf.* G. and B. p. 119.

[j] Xen. *Eq.* 1. 13 ἰσχία πλατέα . . . καὶ εὔσαρκα. *Cf.* Poll. *l.c.*

ἐκ δὲ θέοι πολλὴ μετόπισθε τανύτριχος οὐρή·
μηροὶ δ' εὐπαγέες, μυώδεες· αὐτὰρ ἔνερθεν
ὀρθοτενεῖς δολιχοί τε ποδῶν περιηγέες αὐλοὶ
καὶ μάλα λεπταλέοι· καὶ σαρκὶ λελειμμένα κῶλα,
οἷα τανυκραίροισιν ἀελλοπόδεσσ' ἐλάφοισι·
καὶ σφυρὸν ἀγκλίνοιτο, θέοι δὲ περίδρομος ὁπλὴ
ὕψι μάλ' ἐκ γαίης, πυκινή, κερόεσσα, κραταιή.
τοῖός μοι βαίνοι κρατερὴν θήρειον ἐνυὼ
θυμαίνων, συνάεθλος, ἀρήϊος, ὄβριμος ἵππος.
Τυρσηνοὶ τοιοίδε καὶ Ἀρμένιοι καὶ Ἀχαιοὶ
Καππαδόκαι τε κλυτοὶ Ταύρου πρόπαρ οἵ τε[1] νέμονται.
θαῦμα δὲ Καππαδόκεσσι μέγ' ἔδρακον ὠκυπόδεσσι·
εἰσόκε μὲν νεογιλὸν ὑπὸ στομάτεσσιν ὀδόντα
καὶ γλαγερὸν φορέουσι δέμας, τελέθουσ' ἀμενηνοί·
κραιπνότεροι δὲ πέλουσιν, ὅσῳ μάλα γηράσκουσι.
κείνους εἰς πόλεμον μεγαλήτορα θωρήσσοιο
αἴθωνάς τ' ἐπὶ θῆρας· ἐπεὶ μάλα θαρσήεντες
ὅπλοις ἀντιάαν, πυκινὴν ῥῆξαί τε φάλαγγα,

[1] πρόπαρ οἵ τε Koechly : προπάροιθε MSS.

---

[a] *Cf.* Xen. *Eq.* 1. 5, 7; Poll. *l.c.* οὐρὰ προμήκης; Geop. *l.c.* οὐρὰν μεγάλην οὐλότριχα; Varr. *l.c.* cauda ampla subcrispa; Colum. *l.c.* cauda longa et saetosa; Pallad. *l.c.* cauda profusior.

[b] "The muscles of the thighs should be well developed" (Hayes p. 311); Geop. *l.c.* μηροὺς μεμυωμένους; Colum. *l.c.* feminibus torosis et numerosis. Xen. *Eq.* 1 distinguishes the μηροὶ οἱ ὑπὸ ταῖς ὠμοπλάταις (§ 7), *i.e.* what are now called the "fore-arms" (extending from elbow to knee), from the μηροὶ οἱ ὑπὸ τῇ οὐρᾷ, *i.e.* thighs + gaskins (the latter term now being used to denote the hind leg from thigh to hock).

[c] *i.e.* the part of the leg between knee and fetlock: the "shanks" (Cossar Ewart *ap.* Hayes p. 16). αὐλοί = tibiae.

an abundant hairy tail[a]; the thighs[b] should be well compact and muscular; the rounded cannons[c] beneath should be straight[d] and long and very thin,[e] and the limbs[f] should be unfleshy, even as in the horned windswift stag; the pastern[g] should be sloping; the rounded hoof[h] should run high above the ground, close-grained, horny, strong. Such would I have the horse to be who goes to the fierce warfare with wild beasts, a spirited helper, warlike and strong. Such are the Tuscan horses and the Armenian and the Achaean and the famous Cappadocian horses which dwell in front of Taurus.[i] A marvel have I seen among the Cappadocian horses; so long as they have their foal teeth in their mouth and are milk-fed, they are weakling, but as they grow older, they become swifter. Those are the horses which thou shouldst array for manly war and against fierce wild beasts; for they are very brave to face arms and break the serried phalanx and contend against

[d] Geop. *l.c.* *σκέλη ὀρθά*; Varr. *l.c.* cruribus rectis; Colum. *l.c.* altis rectisque cruribus.

[e] *i.e.* not fleshy. *Cf.* Xen. *Eq.* 1. 5 *τῶν κνημῶν τὰ ὀστᾶ παχέα χρὴ εἶναι· . . . οὐ μέντοι φλεψί γε οὐδὲ σαρξὶ παχέα*; Poll. *l.c.* *κνῆμαι ἄσαρκοι.*

[f] It seems on the whole better to take the vague term *κῶλα* as continuing the description of the leg from knee to fetlock (as in 408) than to refer it to the "gaskins."

[g] Xen. *Eq.* 1. 4 *δεῖ τὰ ἀνωτέρω μὲν τῶν ὁπλῶν κατωτέρω δὲ τῶν κυνηπόδων* (fetlock) *ὀστᾶ μήτε ἄγαν ὀρθὰ εἶναι ὥσπερ αἰγὸς . . . οὐδὲ μὴν ἄγαν ταπεινά.*

[h] Xen. *Eq.* 1. 3 *οὐδὲ τοῦτο δεῖ λανθάνειν, πότερον αἱ ὁπλαί εἰσιν ὑψηλαὶ ἢ ταπειναί . . . αἱ μὲν γὰρ ὑψηλαὶ πόρρω ἀπὸ τοῦ δαπέδου ἔχουσι τὴν χελιδόνα* (the "frog") *καλουμένην . . . καὶ τῷ ψόφῳ δέ φησι Σίμων δήλους εἶναι τοὺς εὔποδας, καλῶς λέγων· ὥσπερ γὰρ κύμβαλον ψοφεῖ πρὸς τῷ δαπέδῳ ἡ κοίλη ὁπλή.* *Cf.* Poll. *l.c.*

[i] Mountain range in Asia Minor.

θηρσί τ' ἐνυαλίοισιν ἐναντία δηρίσασθαι.
πῶς μὲν γάρ τε μάχαισιν ἀρήϊος ἔκλυεν ἵππος
ἦχον ἐγερσίμοθον δολιχῶν πολεμήϊον αὐλῶν;
ἢ πῶς ἄντα δέδορκεν ἀκαρδαμύτοισιν[1] ὀπωπαῖς
αἰζηοῖσι λόχον πεπυκασμένον ὁπλίτῃσι,
καὶ χαλκὸν σελαγεῦντα, καὶ ἀστράπτοντα σίδηρον,
καὶ μάθεν εὖτε μένειν χρειώ, πότε δ' αὖτις ὀρούειν,
καὶ μάθεν εἰσαΐειν κρατερῶν σύνθημα λοχαγῶν;
πολλάκι καὶ δῆριν[2] ἀνδρῶν ἐπελάσσατο πύργοις
ἤρεμος ἀσπιδόεσσαν ὑπόπτερον, εὖτε βροτοῖσιν
ἀσπὶς ὑπὲρ κεφαλῆς ἐπικάρσιον ἀσπίδ' ἐρείδει,
ὁππότ' ἐέλδονται δηΐων πόλιν ἐξαλαπάξαι,
καὶ πεδίον τεύχουσι μετήορον, ἑπταβόειον,
δαιδαλέον, πυκινόν, πολυόμφαλον, ἀντία δ' αἴγλη
χαλκοῦ ἀποθρώσκει φαεθοντιάς, αἶψα δ' ὀπίσσω
κλινομένης ἀκτῖνος ἀπαστράπτει πολὺς αἰθήρ.
ἵπποις γὰρ περίαλλα φύσις πόρε τεχνήεσσα
ἡμερίων κραδίην καὶ στήθεσιν αἰόλον ἦτορ·
αἰὲν γινώσκουσιν ἑὸν φίλον ἡνιοχῆα
καὶ χρεμέθουσιν ἰδόντες ἀγακλυτὸν ἡγεμονῆα
καὶ πολέμοισι πεσόντα μέγα στενάχουσιν ἑταῖρον.
ἵππος ἐν ὑσμίνῃ ῥῆξεν ποτὲ δεσμὰ σιωπῆς
καὶ φύσιος θεσμοὺς ὑπερέδραμε καὶ λάβεν ἠχὴν

[1] *vv.ll.* ἀσκαρδαμύκτοισιν, ἀσκαρδαμύτοισιν, ἀκαρδαμύκτοισιν.
[2] δηΐων most mss.

[a] The distinction between the rhetorical interrog. and the exclamation disappears in late Greek, so that πῶς, πόσος = ὡς, ὅσος. *Cf.* πόσσῃ 330.

[b] *Cf.* Job xxxix. 19 ff.

[c] Here and in iv. 134 ἀκαρδαμύτοισιν (given by three mss. in the latter place) seems the safest reading. καρδαμύσσω (for ἀσκαρδ-) is recognized by Hesych. and *E.M.* *s.v.* See further iii. 478 n.

[d] The *lect. vulg.* δηΐων necessitates (1) the change of

warlike wild beasts. How [a] in the battle doth the war-horse [b] hearken to the martial note of the long trumpet that makes the din of conflict! How with unwinking [c] eyes doth he look upon the dense array of armed warriors, the gleaming bronze, the flashing sword! He hath learned also when it behoves him to stand and anon to charge; and he hath learned to hearken to the watchword of mighty captains. Often, too, he calmly brings nigh to the towers the warfare [d] of men with soaring shields, when athwart the heads of men shield presses upon shield, what time they are fain to sack the city of the enemy and fashion aloft a plain with their shields of sevenfold hides, daedal and dense and many-bossed; in front the sunlight glances from the bronze and straightway behind great space of sky lightens with rays refracted. To horses beyond all mortal creatures cunning Nature has given a subtle mind and heart. Always they know their own dear charioteer and they neigh when they see their glorious rider and greatly mourn [e] their comrade when he falls in war. Ere now in battle a horse has burst the bonds of silence and overleapt

ὑπόπτερον to ὑπὸ πτερόν; (2) the assumption that Opp. used the fem. termin. -εσσαν with a neuter (for the converse *cf.* Nicand. *T.* 129 ψολόεντος ἐχίδνης, Colluth. 83 πεpόνην θυόεντα); (3) taking πτερόν to be (as in Procop. *De aed.* ii. 8) = Lat. *pinna* but here as denoting not a defensive *propugnaculum* but the *testudo*, χελώνη (for which *cf.* Arr. *Tact.* 11. 4; 36. 1 f.). On the other hand δῆριν, which Boudreaux reads (apparently with some MS. authority), makes δ. ἀσπ. ὑπόπτ. a simple metonomy for the χελώνη. *Cf.* Luc. iii. 474 Ut tamen hostiles densa testudine muros Tecta subit virtus armisque innexa priores Arma ferunt galeamque extensus protegit umbo.

[e] *Cf.* Tryph. 14; Verg. *Aen.* xi. 89 Post bellator equus positis insignibus Aethon It lacrimans guttisque humectat grandibus ora; Solin. xlv. 13.

ἀνδρομέην καὶ γλῶσσαν ὁμοίϊον ἀνθρώποισιν.
ἵππος ἐνυαλίοιο Μακηδονίου βασιλῆος
Βουκεφάλας ὅπλοισιν ἐναντία δηριάασκεν.
ἵππος ἐπ' ἀνθερίκων ἔθεεν κούφοισι πόδεσσιν,
ἄλλος ὑπὲρ πόντοιο, καὶ οὐ στεφάνην ἐδίηνεν.
ἵππος ὑπὲρ νεφέων Χιμαροκτόνον ἤγαγε φῶτα,
καὶ χρεμέθων ποτὲ πῶλος ὑφ' ἡνιόχοιο δόλοισι
θήκατο τῶν Περσῶν Ἀσιηγενέων βασιλῆα.
ἔξοχα δ' αὖ τίουσι φύσιν· τὸ δὲ πάμπαν ἄπυστον
ἐς φιλότητα μολεῖν, τὴν οὐ θέμις· ἀλλὰ μένουσιν
ἄχραντοι μυσέων,[1] καθαρῆς τ' ἐράουσι Κυθείρης.
ἔκλυον ὡς προπάροιθε πολυκτεάνων τις ἀνάκτων
καλὸν ἔχεν πεδίοις ἵππων ἀγελαῖον ὅμιλον·
τοὺς πάντας μετέπειτα δαμασσαμένη προθελύμνους
ἱππαλέη νοῦσος πρόλιπεν δύο, μητέρα μούνην
καὶ μητρὸς φιλίης ὑπομάζιον εἰσέτι πῶλον.
αὐτὰρ ἐπεὶ μέγας ἦν, πειρᾶτο σχέτλιος ἀνὴρ
μητέρα παιδὸς ἑοῖο παρ' ἀγκοίνῃσι βαλέσθαι.
τοὺς δ' ὡς οὖν ἐνόησεν ἀναινομένους φιλότητα
καὶ γάμον ἀμφοτέροισιν ἀπώμοτον, αὐτίκ' ἔπειτα
αἰνὰ τιτυσκόμενος δολίην ἐπὶ μῆτιν ὕφαινεν,
ἐλπόμενος καλέειν γένος ἵπποισιν παλίνορσον.
ἄμφω μὲν πρώτιστα καλύψατο βυσσοδομεύων
ἀλλοισιν ῥινοῖς· μετέπειτα δὲ χρῖσεν ἐλαίῳ
πᾶν δέμας εὐώδει, κηώδει· ἔλπετο γὰρ δὴ
ὀδμὴν ἡγήτειραν ἀμαλδῦναι φιλότητος·

[1] μυσῶν MSS.

[a] Hom. *Il.* xix. 404 Xanthus, the horse of Achilles, prophesies his death.

[b] The charger of Alexander the Great: Ael. vi. 44; Diod. xvii. 76 and 95; Plin. viii. 154; Arr. *Anab.* v. 14. 4 and v. 19. 4.

[c] Hom. *Il.* xx. 226 (of the offspring of Boreas and the

the ordinance of nature and taken a human voice[a] and a tongue like that of man. Bucephalas,[b] the horse of the warrior king of Macedon, fought against armed men. A horse there was which ran with light feet over the corn-ears[c] and brake them not; another ran over the sea and wetted not his coronet.[d] A horse carried above the clouds him that slew the Chimaera[e]; and the neighing[f] of a horse through the craft of his charioteer made one king of the Asian Persians. Above others, again, horses honour nature, and it is utterly unheard of that they should indulge unlawful passion, but they remain unstained of pollution and cherish chaste desire. I have heard[g] how of old a prince of great possessions had in his fields a fair herd of horses. All these a disease of horses utterly destroyed, leaving but two—only a mare and a foal yet at its mother's foot. But when it grew up, the wicked man essayed to mate the foal with its dam. And when he saw a union forsworn of both, immediately he with dreadful design wove a subtle device, hoping to call back his breed of horses. First in his craft he covered both with alien hides, and then he anointed all their bodies with sweet-smelling oil and fragrant; for he hoped to destroy the tell-tale scent.

mares of Erichthonius) *αἱ δ' ὅτε μὲν σκιρτῷεν ἐπὶ ζείδωρον ἄρουραν, ἄκρον ἐπ' ἀνθερίκων καρπὸν θέον οὐδὲ κατέκλων· ἀλλ' ὅτε δὴ σκιρτῷεν ἐπ' εὐρέα νῶτα θαλάσσης, ἄκρον ἐπὶ ῥηγμῖνος ἁλὸς πολιοῖο θέεσκον.*

[d] The portion of the pastern immediately above the hoof.

[e] A monster (Hom. *Il.* vi. 179; Lucr. v. 905) slain by Bellerophon (tetrico domitore Chimaerae, Ov. *Tr.* ii. 397) with the aid of his winged horse Pegasus; Pind. *O.* xiii. 84, *I.* vi. 44.

[f] Darius, s. of Hystaspes, became king of Persia by the craft of his groom Oebares: Herod. iii. 84.

[g] The story is told A. 631 a 1-7; Ael. iv. 7; Antig. 54; Varr. ii. 7. 9; Plin. viii. 156; Hierocl. *Hipp.* p. 173.

καὶ λάθεν, ὦ μάκαρες, ῥέζων κακά· καὶ τετέλεστο
ξεῖνος, ἀπόπτυστος θάλαμος, στυγερώτατος ἵπποις,
οἷος ἐν ἀνθρώποισιν ἐνυμφεύθη προπάροιθε
Καδμεῖος γάμος αἰνὸς ἀλήμονος Οἰδιπόδαο.
οἱ δ' ὅτε γυμνωθέντες ἑὴν ἄτην ἐνόησαν,
λοξῇσίν τ' ἄθρησαν ἀνιάζοντες ὀπωπαῖς
ἡ μὲν ἄρα τλήμων ἄγονον γόνον, αὐτὰρ ὅ γ' αἶψα
αἰνόγαμος κακόλεκτρος ἀμήτορα μητέρα δειλήν,
ὕψι μάλ' ἠέρθησαν, ἀμείλιχα φυσιόωντες,
δεσμά τ' ἀπορρήξαντες ἵτην μεγάλα χρεμέθοντες,
οἷα θεοὺς μάκαρας μαρτυρόμενοι κακότητος,
ἀράς τ' εὐχόμενοι πολυπήμονι νυμφευτῆρι·
ὀψὲ δὲ μυρόμενοί τε καὶ ἄσχετον ἀΐσσοντες,
ἀντιπέρην πέτρῃσιν ἑὰς κεφαλὰς ἐλόωντες,
ὀστὰ συνηλοίησαν, ἑὸν δ' ἀπὸ φέγγος ἄμερσαν
αὐτοφόνοι, κλίναντες ἐπ' ἀλλήλοισι κάρηνα.
ὧδε φάτις προτέροις κλέος ἵπποισιν μέγ' ἀείδει.
ἵππων δ' ὅσσα γένεθλ' ἀτιτήλατο μυρίος αἶα,
ὠκύτατοι Σικελοί, Λιλυβήϊον οἵτε νέμονται
καὶ τρικάρηνον ὄρος ὅθι τοι σκέπας Ἐγκελάδοιο
πυρσοῖς αἰθερίοισιν ἐρευγομένοιο κεραυνοῦ
Σικελικῆς Αἴτνης ἀνεκάχλασεν ἀέναον πῦρ.
κραιπνότεροι Σικελῶν δὲ παρ' Εὐφρήταο ῥέεθρα
Ἀρμένιοι Πάρθοι τε βαθυπλόκαμοι τελέθουσιν.
ἀλλ' ἄρα καὶ Πάρθοισι μέγα προφέρουσιν Ἴβηρες,
ὠκυτέροισι πόδεσσι κροαίνοντες πεδίοιο.
κείνοισιν τάχα μοῦνος ἐναντίον ἰσοφαρίζοι

---

[a] King of Thebes, who unwittingly married his own mother: Soph. *O.T.*

[b] *Cf.* Soph. *El.* 1154 μήτηρ ἀμήτωρ.

[c] Cic. *Verr.* II. ii. 20.

[d] S.W. Sicily.

And, ye blessed Gods, without their knowledge he wrought his wickedness and there was fulfilled a union monstrous and abominable and most abhorred of horses, like that dread marriage that was made of old among men, the Cadmean bridal of the wanderer Oedipus.[a] But when they were made naked and knew their sin, and in sorrow and with eyes askance looked one on the other, the unhappy mother on her dishonoured son, and he anon, victim of a terrible and evil union, upon his poor unmothered[b] mother, they leapt on high, snorting terribly, and brake their bonds and went neighing loudly as if they were calling the blessed gods to witness their evil plight and cursing him who contrived their woeful union; and at last, rushing wildly in their grief, they dashed their foreheads against the rocks and brake the bones and took away their light of life, self-slain, leaning their heads on one another. So report proclaims the fame of the horses of former days. Now of all the breeds of horses that the infinite earth nourishes most swift are the Sicilian,[c] which dwell in Lilybaeum[d] and where the three-peaked hill that covers Enceladus,[e] as the thunderbolt belches forth in beams reaching to the sky, discharges the eternal fire of Sicilian Aetna. Fleeter than the Sicilian are by the streams of Euphrates the Armenian and Parthian[f] horses of flowing mane. Yet the Parthian horses are greatly excelled by the Iberian,[g] which gallop over the plains with swifter feet. With them might vie only the

[e] Giant buried under Aetna: Apollod. i. 6. 2; Callim. *fr.* 117: Luc. vi. 293; Verg. *Aen.* iii. 578; Stat. *T.* iii. 595; Q. Sm. v. 642.

[f] *Cf.* 302 and *C.* iv. 112 f.; Strab. 525; Gratt. 508; Ridg. pp. 189 f.

[g] Ridg. pp. 256 f.

αἰετὸς αἰθερίοισιν ἐπιθύνων γυάλοισιν,
ἢ κίρκος ταναῇσι τινασσόμενος πτερύγεσσιν,
ἢ δελφὶς πολιοῖσιν ὀλισθαίνων ῥοθίοισι.
τόσσον Ἴβηρες ἔασι θοοὶ πόδας ἠνεμόεντας·
ἀλλ' ὀλίγοι βαιοί τε μένος καὶ ἀνάλκιδες ἦτορ,
καὶ δρόμον ἐν παύροισιν ἐλεγχόμενοι σταδίοισιν·
εἴδεα δ' ἀγλαόμορφα κλυτὸν δέμας ἀμφιέσαντο,
ὁπλὴν δ' οὐ κρατερήν, πηλότροφον, εὐρυπέδιλον.
Μαύρων δ' αἰόλα φῦλα πολὺ προφέρουσιν ἁπάντων
ἀμφὶ δρόμους ταναούς τε καὶ ἀμφὶ πόνους ἀλεγεινούς.
καὶ Λίβυες μετὰ τοὺς δολιχὸν δρόμον ἐκτελέουσιν,
ὅσσοι Κυρήνην πουλυψηφῖδα νέμονται.
εἴδεα δ' ἀμφοτέροισιν ὁμοίια, πλὴν ὅσον αὖτε
μείζονες εἰσιδέειν Λίβυες κρατεροὶ γεγάασιν,
ἀλλὰ δέμας δολιχοί· πλευρῇσι γὰρ ἀμφὶς ἔχουσι
τῶν ἄλλων πλέονα σπαθίην κτένα· τοὔνεκέν εἰσι
πάσσονες εἰσιδέειν καὶ κρείσσονες ἰθὺς ὀρούειν,
ἐσθλοὶ δ' ἠελίου φορέειν πυρόεσσαν ἐρωὴν
καί τε μεσημβρινὴν δίψους δριμεῖαν ἐνιπήν.
ἵπποι Τυρσηνοὶ δὲ καὶ ἄπλετα Κρήσια φῦλα
ἀμφότερον κραιπνοί τε θέειν δολιχοί τε πέλονται.
Μαύρων δ' ὠκύτεροι Σικελοί, Σικελῶν δέ τε Πάρθοι[1]
καὶ χαροποὶ τελέθουσι καὶ ἔξοχον αἰγλήεντες,
καὶ μοῦνοι μίμνουσι μέγα βρύχημα λέοντος.
ἦ γάρ τοι θήρεσσιν ἐπ' ἄλλοις ἄλλα γένεθλα
ἵππων ἄρμενα πολλὰ τά τοι φράζουσιν ὀπωπαί.
στικτοπόδεσσ' ἐλάφοις κυανώπεας ὁπλίζοιο,

[1] Πάρθοι Brodaeus (*cf.* iv. 112 ff.): θυμόν mss. Gesner supposed that a line has been lost after v. 302 which mentioned the Πάρθοι.

[a] The eagle (Pind. *P.* ii. 50, v. 112, *N.* iii. 80; Hom. *Il.*

eagle [a] speeding over the vales of air, or the hawk hasting with long pinions spread, or the dolphin gliding over the grey waves. So fleet are the Iberian horses of wind-swift feet; but they are small and weak of spirit and unvaliant of heart and in a few furlongs are found wanting [b] in speed; and though clothed in fair form and glorious shape, yet the hoof is lacking in strength, bred to soft ground and broad. The dappled breed of Moorish horses are far the best of all for extended courses and laborious toil. And next to these for accomplishing a long course come the Libyan horses, even those which dwell in many-pebbled Cyrene. Both are of similar type, save only that the strong Libyan horses are larger to look at; but these latter are long of body, having in their sides more space of broad rib than others, and hence are stouter to look at and superior in a charge and good at enduring the fiery force of the sun and the keen assault of noontide thirst. The Tuscan horses and the immense Cretan breeds are both swift in running and long of body. The Sicilian are swifter than the Moorish horses, while the Parthian are swifter than the Sicilian, grey-eyed [c] also and eminently handsome, and they alone abide [d] the loud roar of the lion. For verily against different wild beasts different breeds of horses are fitting in many cases, as the eyes declare. Against the deer of spotted feet thou shouldst array dark-eyed horses; blue-

xxi. 252); the dolphin (Pind. *P.* ii. 51, *N.* vi. 72); the hawk (Hom. *Il.* xv. 237, *Od.* xiii. 86) are types of swiftness.

[b] But Nemes. 253 says Spanish horses "valent longos intendere cursus"; Mart. i. 49, xiv. 199.

[c] χαροποί may here mean merely "bright-eyed." For the sense of the word when applied to colour see note on 308.

[d] *Cf. C.* iv. 116.

ἄρκτοισι γλαυκούς, καὶ πορδαλίεσσι δαφοινούς,
αἴθωνας δ' ἵππους πυριλαμπέας ἀμφὶ σύεσσιν,
αὐτὰρ ἐριγλήνους χαροποὺς χαροποῖσι λέουσι.
κάλλεϊ δ' ἐν πάντεσσι πέλει πανυπείροχος ἵππος
Νησαῖος,[1] τὸν ἄγουσιν ἐρικτέανοι βασιλῆες·
καλὸς ἰδεῖν, ἀταλός τε φέρειν εὐπειθεῖ δεσμῷ·
βαιὸς μὲν κεφαλήν, πολλὸς δὲ βαθύτριχα δειρήν,
κυδιόων ἑκάτερθε μελιχρύσοισιν ἐθείραις.
Ναὶ μὴν ἄλλο γένεθλον ἐπήρατον ὠπήσαιο
στικτόν, ἀρίζηλον, τοὺς ὤρυγγας καλέουσιν,
ἢ ὅτι καλλικόμοισιν ἐν οὔρεσιν ἀλδήσκουσιν,
ἢ ὅτι πάγχυ θέλουσ' ἐπὶ θηλυτέρῃσιν ὀρούειν.
δοιὰ δ' ἐπ' ὠρύγγων τελέθει πολυανθέα κάλλη·
τοὶ μὲν γὰρ δειρὴν καλλίτριχά τ' εὐρέα νῶτα
γεγράφαται δολιχῇσιν ἐπήτριμα ταινίῃσι,
τίγριες οἷα θοοί, κραιπνοῦ Ζεφύροιο γενέθλη·
τοὶ δ' ἄρ' εὐτροχάλοισι περίδρομα δαιδάλλονται
σφραγῖσιν πυκινῇσιν ὁμοΐα πορδαλίεσσι·
τοὺς ἔτι νηπιάχους γράψαν τεχνήμονες ἄνδρες
αἰθομένῳ χαλκῷ τανaὴν τρίχα πυρσεύοντες.
δηθάκι δ' ἄλλα βροτοὶ πανεπίφρονα μητίσαντο,
πῶλον ἐπιγράψαι καὶ νηδύϊ μητρὸς ἐόντα.

[1] *v.l.* Νισ(σ)αῖος.

---

[a] γλαυκός and χαροπός are not easy to distinguish. *Cf.* A. 491 b 34 ὀφθαλμοῦ δὲ τὸ μὲν λευκὸν ὅμοιον ὡς ἐπὶ τὸ πολὺ πᾶσιν, τὸ δὲ καλούμενον μέλαν διαφέρει· τοῖς μὲν γάρ ἐστι μέλαν, τοῖς δὲ σφόδρα γλαυκόν, τοῖς δὲ χαροπόν, ἐνίοις δὲ αἰγωπόν; Hom. *Od.* xi. 611 χαροποὶ λέοντες but γλαυκιόων of lion *Il.* xx. 172. Perhaps if we call γλ. "greyish-blue" and χαρ. "bluish-grey," we shall be nearly right.

[b] Or Nisaean: famous breed of horses from the Nesaean plain in Media: Steph. B. *s.* Νησαῖον πεδίον, ἀφ' οὗ παρὰ Μήδοις οἱ Νησαῖοι ἵπποι; Herod. iii. 106, vii. 40; Strab.

eyed[a] against bears; tawny-eyed against leopards; fiery and flaming against swine; brilliant and grey of eye against the grey-eyed lion. In beauty the most excellent of all horses is the Nesaean,[b] which wealthy kings drive; beautiful to behold, gentle to ride and obedient to the bit, small of head but shaggy-maned, glorying in the yellow locks on either side his neck.

Yet another lovely breed thou mayst see, the dappled conspicuous breed which men call the Orynx,[c] either because they flourish on the grassy hills (οὔρεσιν), or because they are very eager to mate (ὀρούειν) with their females. In the case of the Orynxes there are two species of many-patterned beauty. One species are inscribed on neck and broad hairy back with a series of long stripes, even as the swift tigers, the offspring of rapid Zephyrus.[d] The others are adorned all about with densely set round spots, like those of leopards; this species while they are still but baby foals, are tattooed by skilful men, who brand their long hair with the flaming bronze. And ofttimes men have contrived other subtle devices for inscribing[e] the foal while yet

525, 530; Athen. 194 e; Amm. Marc. xxiii. 6. 30; Synes. *Ep.* 40; Arr. *Anab.* vii. 13; A. 632 a 30; Lucian, *Hist.* 39; Ridg. pp. 190 ff.

[c] Oppian seems to denote by this name two species of horses: (1) with neck and back striped like tiger, (2) spotted like leopard. The first he regards as a natural breed, the second as an artificial production. *Cf.* Eutecn. τοὺς μὲν πρώτους ἡ φύσις οὕτω διεζωγράφησε, τῶν δευτέρων δ' ἀνδρῶν εὑρήματα τὰ ποικίλματα. The first suggests the zebra.

[d] The West Wind (Lat. *Favonius*) was supposed to have an impregnating influence; Hom. *Il.* xvi. 150; Plin. xvi. 93; Lucr. i. 11; Verg. *G.* iii. 272 ff.; Plin. x. 166; Varr. ii. 1. 19; Colum. vi. 27; A. 560 a 6; *G.A.* 749 b 1. Of other winds: Hom. *Il.* xx. 222; Ael. vii. 27; Solin. xlv. 18.

[e] *Cf.* O.T. Genesis xxx. 37 ff.; Scott, *Red Gauntlet*, c. xviii.

ὦ πόσση κραδίη, πόσση μερόπεσσι πέλει φρήν.
ἔρξαν ὅπως ἐθέλουσι· θέσαν πολυειδέας ἵππους,
μητρὸς ἔτι γλαγερῇσι περισχομένους λαγόνεσσιν.
ὁππότε θηλυτέρην γὰρ ἕλῃ φιλοτήσιος ὁρμὴ
ἵππον τ' ἐγγὺς ἰόντα κλυτὸν μεγαλήτορα μίμνῃ,
δὴ τότε δαιδάλλουσι πόσιν καλόν· ἀμφὶ δὲ πάντῃ
πᾶν δέμας εὐστίκτοισι περὶ χροιῇσι γράφουσι,
καὶ ποτὶ λέκτρον ἄγουσιν ἐπ' ἀγλαΐῃ κομόωντα.
ὡς δέ τις ἠϊθέων ὑπὸ νυμφοκόμοισι γυναιξὶν
εἵμασιν ἀργεννοῖσι καὶ ἄνθεσι πορφυρέοισι
στεψάμενος, πνείων τε Παλαιστίνοιο μύροιο,
ἐς θάλαμον βαίνῃσιν ὑμὴν ὑμέναιον ἀείδων·
ὣς ἵππον σπέρχοντα γαμήλιά τε χρεμέθοντα,
πρόσθεν ἑῆς ἀλόχοιο κλυτὸν πόσιν ἀφριόωντα,
δηρὸν ἐρητύουσι φίλης λελιημένον εὐνῆς·
ὀψέ δέ τοι μεθιᾶσιν ἐπήρατον ἐς φιλότητα·
ἡ δ' ὑποκυσαμένη πολυανθέα γείνατο παῖδα,
νηδύϊ μὲν πόσιος γόνιμον θορὸν ἀείρασα,
δεξαμένη μορφὴν δὲ πολύχροον ὀφθαλμοῖσι.
τοῖά νυ κἀκεῖνοι, τοῖσιν δόνακες μεμέληνται,
μησάσθην πυκινοῖσι νοήμασιν ἰξευτῆρες,
ὁππότε δαιδάλλουσι πελῃϊάδεσσι νεοσσούς·
εὖτε γὰρ ἐς φιλότητα θοαὶ τρήρωνες ἴωσι,
μιγνύμεναι στομάτεσσι βαρυφθόγγοις ἀλόχοισι,
δὴ τότε μῆτιν ὕφαινε κλυτὴν τιθασοτρόφος ἀνήρ,
ἄγχι δὲ θηλυτέρῃσιν ἐθήκατο δαίδαλα πολλὰ
εἵματα πορφύρεα· ταὶ δὲ κλιδὸν ὄσσε βαλοῦσαι
θυμὸν ἰαινόμεναι τίκτουσ' ἁλιπόρφυρα τέκνα.

---

[a] *Cf.* 206 n.

[b] Stat. *S.* v. 1. 213 Palaestini simul Hebraeique liquores. It is not to be assumed that the perfume meant is one native to Palestine (which is not rich in aromatic shrubs). The spices and perfumes of the Far East came to Europe

in his mother's womb. O what[a] a heart, what a mind have mortal men! They do as they list; they make horses of varied colours while yet enveloped in the milky mother's loins. What time the mating impulse seizes the mare and she abides the approach of the glorious high-spirited horse, then they cunningly adorn the beautiful sire. All about they inscribe all his body with spots of colour and to his bride they lead him, glorying in his beauty. Even as some youth, arrayed by the bridal women in white robes and purple flowers and breathing of the perfume of Palestine,[b] steps into the bridal chamber singing the marriage song, so while the hasting horse neighs his bridal song, long time in front of his bride they stay her glorious spouse, foaming in his eagerness; and late and at last they let him go to satisfy his desire. And the mare conceives and bears a many-patterned foal, having received in her womb the fertile seed of her spouse, but in her eyes his many-coloured form. Such devices have they also with cunning wits contrived whose business is with the reed, even the fowlers, when they variegate the young of doves. For when the swift doves mate and mingle mouths[c] with their deep-noted spouses, then the breeder of tame birds contrives a glorious device. Near the hen-birds he puts many vari-coloured purple cloths; and they, beholding them with eyes askant are gladdened in their hearts and produce sea-purple children. Nay, even so also

by way of Palestine and Syria (Diod. iii. 41) and are generally called indifferently Syrian (Propert. iii. 5. 14; Tibull. iii. 4. 28, iii. 6. 63; Hor. *C.* ii. 7. 8; Catull. vi. 8) or Assyrian (Hor. *C.* ii. 11. 16; Catull. lxviii. 143; Verg. *E.* iv. 25; Tibull. i. 3. 7, iii. 2. 23).

[c] A. 560 b 26.

ναὶ μὴν ὧδε Λάκωνες ἐπίφρονα μητίσαντο
αἶσι φίλαις ἀλόχοις, ὅτε γαστέρα κυμαίνουσι·
γράψαντες πινάκεσσι πέλας θέσαν ἀγλαὰ κάλλη,
τοὺς πάρος ἀστράψαντας ἐν ἡμερίοισιν ἐφήβους,
Νιρέα καὶ Νάρκισσον ἐϋμμελίην θ' Ὑάκινθον,
Κάστορά τ' εὐκόρυθον καὶ Ἀμυκοφόνον Πολυδεύκην,
ἠϊθέους τε νέους, τοί τ' ἐν μακάρεσσιν ἀγητοί,
Φοῖβον δαφνοκόμην καὶ κισσοφόρον Διόνυσον·
αἱ δ' ἐπιτέρπονται πολυήρατον εἶδος ἰδοῦσαι,
τίκτουσίν τε καλοὺς ἐπὶ κάλλεϊ πεπτηυῖαι.
Τόσσα μὲν ἀμφ' ἵπποισιν· ἀτὰρ κατάβηθι, φίλη φρήν,
οἶμον ἐπὶ σκυλάκων· τόσσοι δ' ἐπὶ πᾶσι κύνεσσιν
ἔξοχ' ἀρίζηλοι, μάλα τ' ἀγρευτῆρσι μέλονται,
Παίονες, Αὐσόνιοι, Κᾶρες, Θρήϊκες, Ἴβηρες,
Ἀρκάδες, Ἀργεῖοι, Λακεδαιμόνιοι, Τεγεῆται,
Σαυρομάται, Κελτοί, Κρῆτες, Μάγνητες, Ἀμοργοί,

---

[a] Next to Achilles the handsomest Greek at Troy: Hom. *Il.* ii. 671.

[b] A beautiful youth of Thespiae who, for hopeless love of his own reflection, died and was turned into the flower which bears his name: Ov. *M.* iii. 341; Paus. ix. 31. 7.

[c] A beautiful Spartan youth, accidentally slain by Apollo: from his blood sprang the "hyacinth." See n. on Colluthus 248. *Cf.* Apollod. iii. 10. 3; Paus. iii. 1. 3, iii. 19. 5; Nicand. *T.* 902; Ov. *M.* x. 162, xiii. 394 ff.

[d] Castor and Pollux, the Dioscuri, sons of Zeus (Tyndareus) and Leda: Hom. *Il.* iii. 237.

[e] King of the Bebryces, slain by Pollux: Apollod. i. 9. 20; Theocr. xxii. 27; Ap. Rh. ii. 1; Val. Fl. iv. 99.

[f] *Cf.* generally Xen. *C.* 3 ff.; Arr. *C.* 2 ff.; Poll. v. 37 ff.; *Geop.* xix. 1 ff.; A. 574 a 16 ff. and *passim*; Verg. *G.* iii. 404 ff.; Varr. ii. 9; Plin. viii. 142 ff.; Colum. vii. 12; Gratt. 150 ff.; Nemes. 103 ff.

[g] Poll. v. 46 f.

[h] *i.e.* Italian, including the *vividus Umber* of Verg. *Aen.*

the Laconians contrived a subtle device for their dear wives when they are pregnant. Near them they put pictures of beautiful forms, even the youths that aforetime were resplendent among mortal men, Nireus[a] and Narcissus[b] and Hyacinthus[c] of the goodly ashen spear, and Castor[d] with his helmet, and Polydeuces that slew Amycus,[e] and the youthful twain who are admired among the blessed gods, laurel-crowned Phoebus and Dionysus of the ivy wreath. And the women rejoice to behold their lovely form and, fluttered by their beauty, bear beautiful sons.

Thus much about horses; but now descend, my soul, to the lay of Dogs.[f] These among all dogs are the most excellent and greatly possess the mind of hunters: to wit, Paeonian,[g] Ausonian,[h] Carian,[i] Thracian, Iberian,[j] Arcadian,[k] Argive,[l] Lacedaemonian,[m] Tegean, Sauromatian,[n] Celtic,[o] Cretan,[p]

xii. 753 (*cf.* Varr. ii. 9. 6; Gratt. 172 and 194; Senec. *Thy.* 497; Sid. Ap. vii. 191; Sil. iii. 295); the Sallentine, Varr. ii. 9 5; the Tuscan, Nemes. 231.

[i] Poll. v. 37; Arr. *C.* 3. 1 f.; Dio Chr. *Or.* 15.

[j] Poll. *l.c.*; Nemes. 127. There seems no ground for supposing that the Iberians περὶ τὸν Καύκασον (Strab. 118, 499 f.) are meant.

[k] Poll. *l.c.*; Ov. *M.* iii. 210, *A.A.* i. 272 (Maenalius); Gratt. 160 (Lycaones).

[l] Poll. *l.c.* Ἀργολίδες.

[m] Poll. *l.c.*; Soph. *Aj.* 8; Xen. *C.* 3. 1; Luc. iv. 441; Gratt. 212; Varr. ii. 9. 5; Callim. *H.* iii. 94; Ov. *M.* iii. 208; Plin. x. 177 f.; *A.* 574 a 16 ff.; Shakesp. *M.N's.D.* iv. 1. 123 "My hounds are bred out of the Spartan kind."

[n] The Sauromatae or Sarmatae inhabited S. Russia. Herod. iv. 110 ff.; Dion. P. 653.

[o] Poll. *l.c.*; Arr. *C.* 1. 4, 2. 1; Gratt. 156; Plin. viii. 148.

[p] *Cf. H.* iv. 273; Poll. *l.c.*; Xen. *C.* 10. 1; Arr. *C.* 2·3; Ael. iii. 2; Gratt. 212; Ov. *M.* iii. 208; Luc. iv. 441; Senec. *Hipp.* 33; Claud. *Stil.* iii. 300; Shakesp. *M.N's.D.* iv. 1. 130.

ὅσσοι τ' Αἰγύπτοιο πολυψαμάθοισιν ἐπ' ὄχθαις
βουκολίων οὖροι, Λοκροί, χαροποί τε Μολοσσοί.
 Εἰ δέ νύ τοι κεράσαι φίλον ἔπλετο δοιὰ γένεθλα,
εἴαρι μὲν πρώτιστα λέχος πόρσυνε κύνεσσιν·
εἴαρι γὰρ μᾶλλον φιλοτήσια μέμβλεται ἔργα
θηρσί τε καὶ σκυλάκεσσι καὶ οὐλομένοισι δράκουσιν
ἠερίοις τ' ὄρνισι καὶ εἰναλίοις νεπόδεσσιν.
εἴαρι μὲν χολόεντος ἔχις πεφορυγμένος ἰοῦ
ἷκτο λέχος ποτὶ θῖνα θαλασσαίης ἀλόχοιο·
εἴαρι πόντος ὅλος δὲ περισμαραγεῖ Κυθερείῃ
καὶ νέποδες γαμέοντες ἐπιφρίσσουσι γαλήνῃ·
εἴαρι καὶ τρήρωνες ἐπιθύνουσι πελείαις,
ἵπποι δ' ἀγραύλοις ἐπὶ φορβάσιν ὁπλίζονται,
ταῦροι δ' ἀγροτέρας ἐπὶ πόρτιας ὁρμαίνουσι,
καὶ κτίλοι εἰλικόεντες ἐν εἴαρι μηλοβατεῦσι,
καὶ κάπροι πυρόεντες ἐπαιχμάζουσι σύεσσι,
καὶ χίμαροι λασίῃσιν ἐφιππεύουσι χιμαίραις·
καὶ δ' αὐτοῖς μερόπεσσιν ἐν εἴαρι μᾶλλον ἔρωτες·
εἴαρι γὰρ πάνδημος ἐπιβρίθει Κυθέρεια.
 Ἔθνεα σοὶ δὲ κυνῶν θαλαμηπολέοντι μελέσθω
ἄρμενά τ' ἀλλήλοισιν ἐοικότα τ' ἔξοχα φῦλα.
Ἀρκάδας Ἠλείοις ἐπιμίσγεο, Παίοσι Κρῆτας,
Κᾶρας Θρηϊκίοις, Τυρσηνὰ γένεθλα Λάκωσι,
Σαρματικόν τε πόσιν φορέοις πρὸς Ἰβηρίδα νύμφην.
ὧδε μὲν εὖ κεράσειας· ἀτὰρ πολὺ φέρτατα πάντων

---

[a] The dogs of the Carian Magnesia are mentioned Poll. v. 47; Ael. *V.H.* xiv. 46. *Cf. N.A.* vii. 38.

[b] Here prob. = Nile, as in Hom. *Od.* iv. 47 etc. For Egyptian dogs *cf.* A. 606 a 23; Ael. vi. 53, vii. 19; *V.H.* i. 4; Plin. viii. 148; Solin. xv. 12.

[c] Xen. *C.* 10. 1; Poll. v. 37.

[d] Poll. *l.c.*; Ael. iii. 2, xi. 20; Athen. 201 b; Aristoph. *T.* 416; Lucr. v. 1061; Verg. *G.* iii. 404; Hor. *Epod.* vi. 40

Magnesian,[a] Amorgian, and those which on the sandy banks of Egypt[b] watch the herds, and the Locrian[c] and the bright-eyed Molossian.[d]

If thou shouldst desire to mix two breeds, then first of all mate[e] the dogs in spring[f]; for in spring chiefly the works of love possess the hearts of wild beasts and dogs and deadly snakes and the fowls of the air and the finny creatures of the sea. In spring the serpent, foul with angry venom, comes to the shore to meet his sea bride[g]; in spring all the deep rings with love and the calm sea[h] foams with fishes mating; in spring the male pigeon pursues the female; horses assail the pasturing mares and bulls lust after the cows of the field; in spring the rams of crooked horn mount the ewes and fiery wild boars mate with the sows, the he-goats the shaggy females; yes, and mortals also in spring are more prone to desire; for in spring the spell of Love is heavy upon all.

In mating the tribes of dogs take heed that the breeds are fit and right suitable for one another. Mate Arcadian with Elean, Cretan with Paeonian, Carian with Thracian, Tuscan[i] breed with Laconian; put a Sarmatian sire with an Iberian dam. So shall you mix the breeds aright; but far best of all it

5, *S.* ii. 6. 114; Stat. *T.* iii. 203, *S.* ii. 6. 19, *A.* i. 747; Plaut. *Capt.* 86; Luc. iv. 440; Mart. xii. 1; Senec. *Hipp.* 32; Claud. *Stil.* ii. 215, iii. 293; Gratt. 181 ff.; Nemes. 107; A. 608 a 28.

[e] Xen. *C.* 7. 1 ff.; Arr. *C.* 27 ff.; Varr. ii. 9. 11; Gratt. 263 ff.; Nemes. 103 ff.

[f] *Cf.* Lucr. i. 1 ff.; Verg. *G.* ii. 323 ff.

[g] The Muraena. *Cf. H.* i. 559.

[h] This sense of γαλήνη occurs Hom. *Od.* vii. 319. *Cf.* Callim. *E.* vi. 5.

[i] Nemes. 231 ff.

φῦλα μένειν μονόφυλα, τὰ δ' ἔξοχα τεκμήραντο
ἄνδρες ἐπακτῆρες· τὰ δὲ μυρία φῦλα πέλονται,
τῶν ἀμόθεν μορφαί τε καὶ εἴδεα τοῖα πελέσθω.
μηκεδανόν, κρατερὸν δέμας ἄρκιον, ἠδὲ κάρηνον
κοῦφον, ἐΰγληνον· κυαναὶ στίλβοιεν ὀπωπαί·
κάρχαρον ἐκτάδιον τελέθοι στόμα· βαιὰ δ' ὕπερθεν
οὔατα λεπταλέοισι περιστέλλοιθ' ὑμένεσσι·
δειρὴ μηκεδανή, καὶ στήθεα νέρθε κραταιά,
εὐρέα· τὼ πρόσθεν δέ τ' ὀλιζοτέρω πόδες ἔστων·
ὀρθοτενεῖς κώλων ταναοὶ δολιχήρεες ἱστοί·
εὐρέες ὠμοπλάται, πλευρῶν ἐπικάρσια ταρσά·
ὀσφύες εὔσαρκοι, μὴ πίονες· αὐτὰρ ὄπισθε
στρυφνή τ' ἐκτάδιός τε πέλοι δολιχόσκιος οὐρή.
τοῖοι μὲν ταναοῖσιν ἐφοπλίζοιντο δρόμοισι
δόρκοις ἠδ' ἐλάφοισιν ἀελλοπόδῃ τε λαγωῷ.
Θοῦροι δ' αὖθ' ἕτεροι, τοῖσιν μενεδήϊος ἀλκή,
ὅσσοι καὶ ταύροισιν ἐπέχραον ἠϋγενείοις
καὶ σύας ὑβριστῆρας ἐπαΐξαντες ὄλεσσαν·
ὅσσοι μηδὲ λέοντας ἑοὺς τρείουσιν ἄνακτας,

---

[a] Gratt. 154 mille canum patriae.

[b] *τῶν ἀμόθεν* is taken from Hom. *Od.* i. 10, and the meaning seems to be *either* that the "points of the dog" here enumerated are not an exhaustive description of any breed *or* that they do not apply to all breeds. Eutecn. ἀμωσγέπως. *Cf.* Suid. *s.* ἀμηγέπη.

[c] Arr. *C.* 4. 2 f. πρῶτα μὲν δὴ μακραὶ ἔστων ἀπὸ κεφαλῆς ἐπ' οὐράν.

[d] Xen. *C.* 4. 1 κεφαλὰς ἐλαφράς. *Cf.* Arr. *C.* 4. 4; Poll. v. 57.

[e] Xen. *l.c.* ὄμματα μετέωρα [sint celsi vultus, Nemes. 269] μέλανα λαμπρά. *Cf.* Arr. 4. 5; Poll. *l.c.* *Geop.* xix. 2; Varr. ii. 9. 3 oculis nigrantibus aut ravis; Colum. vii. 12 nigris vel glaucis oculis acri lumine radiantibus.

[f] Xen. *l.c.* ὦτα λεπτὰ καὶ ψιλὰ ὄπισθεν. *Cf.* Poll. *l.c.* On

is that the breeds should remain pure, and those all hunters judge best. Those breeds are without number,[a] and the form and type of them should be approximately[b] these. The body[c] should be long and strong and adequate; the head[d] light and with good eyes[e]; the eyes should be dark of sheen; the saw-toothed mouth should be long; the ears[f] that crown the head should be small and furnished with membranes; the neck[g] long and under it the breast[h] strong and broad; the front legs[i] should be shorter than the hinder; the shanks[j] should be straight, thin, and long; the shoulder-blades[k] should be broad; the row of ribs[l] sloping obliquely; the haunches[m] well-fleshed but not fat; and behind the far-shadowing tail[n] should be stiff and prominent. Such are the dogs which should be arrayed for the swift chase of gazelle and deer and swift-footed hare.

Another species there is, impetuous and of steadfast valour, who attack even bearded bulls and rush upon monstrous boars and destroy them, and tremble not even at their lords the lions; a stalwart breed,

the contrary Arr. *C.* 5. 7 *ὦτα μεγάλα ἔστω καὶ μαλθακά*; Varr. ii. 9. 4 auriculis magnis ac flaccis.

[g] Xen. *l.c.* *τραχήλους μακρούς.* *Cf.* Poll. *l.c.*; Arr. *l.c.*

[h] Xen. *l.c.* *στήθη πλατέα μὴ ἄσαρκα.* *Cf.* Poll. *l.c.*; Arr. *C.* 5. 9; Colum. *l.c.* amplo villosoque pectore.

[i] Xen. *l.c.* *σκέλη τὰ πρόσθε μακρά, ὀρθά, στρογγύλα, στιφρά*; Poll. v. 58 *σκέλη ἑκάτερα μὲν ὑψηλὰ μείζω δὲ τὰ ἐξόπισθεν.*

[j] *ἰστοί = αὐλοί* (189) = *tibiae.*

[k] Xen. *l.c.*; Poll. *l.c.*; Arr. *l.c.*; Colum. *l.c.* latis armis; Nemes. 274 validis tum surgat pectus ab armis.

[l] Xen. *l.c.* *πλευρὰς μὴ ἐπὶ γῆν βαθείας ἀλλ' εἰς τὸ πλάγιον παρηκούσας.*

[m] Xen. *l.c.* *ὀσφῦς σαρκώδεις.* *Cf.* Poll. *l.c.*; Arr. *l.c.* *ὀσφὺν πλατεῖαν ἰσχυράν.*

[n] Xen. *l.c.* *οὐρὰς μακράς, ὀρθάς, λιγυράς*; Poll. v. 59; Arr. *l.c.*

ζατρεφέες, πρώνεσσιν ἐοικότες ἀκρολόφοισι·
σιμότεροι μὲν ἔασι προσώπατα, δεινὰ δ' ὕπερθε
νεύει ἐπισκυνίοισι μεσόφρυα, καὶ πυρόεντες
ὀφθαλμοὶ χαροπαῖσιν ὑποστίλβοντες ὀπωπαῖς·
ῥινὸς ἅπας λάσιος· κρατερὸν δέμας· εὐρέα νῶτα·
κραιπνοὶ δ' οὐ τελέθουσιν, ἀτὰρ μένος ἐνδόθι πολλόν,
καὶ σθένος ἄφραστον, καθαρόν, καὶ θυμὸς ἀναιδής.
ἐς μέν νυν θήρην ὁπλίζεο τοῖα γένεθλα
αἰχμητῶν σκυλάκων, τοὶ κνώδαλα πάντα δίενται.
χροιαὶ δ' ἀργενναί τε κακαὶ μάλα κυάνεαί τε·
οὔτε γὰρ ἠελίοιο φέρειν μένος ὦκα δύνανται
οὔτε νιφοβλήτοιο μένος πολυχειμέρου ὥρης.
κεῖνοι δ' ἐν πάντεσσιν ἀριστεύουσι κύνεσσι,
τοῖς ἴκελαι μορφαὶ μάλα θήρεσιν ὠμηστῇσι,
μηλοφόνοισι λύκοις ἢ τίγρεσιν ἠνεμοέσσαις
ἢ καὶ ἀλωπήκεσσι θοαῖσί τε πορδαλίεσσιν
ἢ ὁπόσοι Δήμητρι πανείκελον εἶδος ἔχουσι
σιτόχροοι· μάλα γάρ τε θοοὶ κρατεροί τε πέλονται.
Εἰ δέ νύ τοι πινυτὴ σκυλακοτροφίη μεμέληται,
μήποτ' ἀμέλγεσθαι σκύλακας νεοθηλέϊ μαζῷ
αἰγῶν ἢ προβάτων, μηδ' οἰκιδίῃσι κύνεσσιν·
ἦ γάρ τοι νωθροί τε καὶ οὐτιδανοὶ βαρύθοιεν·
ἀλλ' ἐλάφων ἤ που μαζῷ τιθασοῖο λεαίνης
ἤ που δορκαλίδων ἢ νυκτιπόροιο λυκαίνης·
ὧδε γὰρ ἂν κρατερούς τε καὶ ὠκέας ἔξοχα θείης,
εἰδομένους αὐτῇσι γαλακτοφόροισι τιθήναις.

---

[a] See 308 n.

[b] Xen. *C.* 4. 7 τὰ δὲ χρώματα οὐ χρὴ εἶναι τῶν κυνῶν οὔτε πυρρὰ οὔτε μέλανα οὔτε λευκὰ παντελῶς· ἔστι γὰρ οὐ γενναῖον τοῦτο ἀλλ' ἁπλοῦν καὶ θηριῶδες. So Poll. v. 65. But Arr. *C.* 6 τὰ δὲ χρώματα οὐδὲν διοίσει ὁποῖα ἂν ἔχωσιν, οὐδ' εἰ παντελῶς εἶεν μέλαιναι ἢ πυρραὶ ἢ λευκαί· οὐδὲ τὸ ἁπλοῦν χρὴ ὑποπτεύειν τῆς χρόας ὡς θηριῶδες.

like unto high-crested mountain peaks. Somewhat flat-nosed of face they are, and dread are their bended brows above and fiery their eyes, flashing with grey [a] light; all their hide is shaggy, the body strong, the back broad. They are not swift, but they have abundant spirit and genuine strength unspeakable and dauntless courage. Array then for the hunt such breeds of warlike dogs, which put to flight all manner of beasts. But as to colour,[b] both white and black are bad exceedingly; for they are not readily able to bear the might of the sun nor the rage of the snowy winter season. Among all dogs those are the best whose colour is like that of ravenous wild beasts, sheep-slaying wolves or wind-swift tigers or foxes and swift leopards, or those which have the colour of Demeter's[c] yellow corn; for these are very swift and strong.

If now prudent dog-breeding is thy care, never suckle whelps on the fresh breast of goats or sheep nor domestic dogs[d]—for they will be sluggish and feeble and heavy—but on the breast of deer or tame lioness or gazelle or she-wolf that roams by night; for so shalt thou make them strong and swift exceedingly, like unto their milky foster-mothers themselves.

[c] ξανθὴ Δημήτηρ (Hom. *Il.* v. 500) = flava Ceres (Verg. *G.* i. 96). The name of the goddess is a common metonomy for corn: Verg. *G.* i. 297 At rubicunda Ceres medio succiditur aestu; Mart. iii. 5. 6 Hic farta premitur angulo Ceres omni; Gratt. 398 Blanditur mensis Cereremque efflagibat ore; Nemes. 161 Interdumque cibo Cererem cum lacte ministra. *Cf. H.* iii. 463, 484.

[d] Xen. *C.* 7. 3 advises that puppies should be suckled by their own mothers. *Cf.* Arr. *C.* 30. 1 f. For domestic dogs *cf.* 473 n.

Αὐτὰρ νηπιάχοισιν ἐπ' οὐνόματα σκυλάκεσσι
βαιὰ τίθει, θοὰ πάντα, θοὴν ἵνα βάξιν ἀκούῃ.
ἵπποισι κρατεροῖσι δ' ὁμήθεες ἀγρευτῆρσιν
ἐξέτι νηπιάχων ἔστων, μερόπεσσί τε πᾶσιν
ἠθάδιοι φίλιοί τε, μόνοισι δὲ θήρεσιν ἐχθροί.
μηδ' ὑλάαν ἐθέλοιεν· ἐπεὶ μάλα θηρευτῆρσι
σιγὴ τέθμιός ἐστι, πανέξοχα δ' ἰχνευτῆρσιν.
Εἴδεα δὲ στιβίης δυσδερκέος ἔπλετο δισσά,
ἀνδρῶν ἠδὲ κυνῶν· μέροπες μὲν ἄρ' αἰολόβουλοι
ὄμμασι τεκμήραντο καὶ ἐφράσσαντο κέλευθα·
μυξωτῆρσι κύνες δὲ πανίχνια σημήναντο.
ναὶ μὴν ἀνθρώποισι πέλει περιδέξιος ὥρη
χειμερίη, στείβουσί τ' ἀμοχθήτοισιν ὀπωπαῖς,
οὕνεκα καὶ νιφετοῖσι γεγραμμένα πάνθ' ἅμ' ὁρᾶται
καὶ πηλοῖσι μένει τετυπασμένα εἴκελα ταρσῷ.[1]
ἐχθρὸν ἔαρ δὲ κύνεσσι, φίλον δὲ πέλει φθινόπωρον·
εἴαρι γὰρ βοτάνῃσιν ἅδην ποιητρόφος αἶα
ἄνθεσι πληθύει τε πολύπνοος, ἀμφὶ δὲ πάντῃ
εὐστέφανοι λειμῶνες ἀνήροτα πορφύρουσι,
καὶ πᾶσαν στιβέεσσιν ἐϋρρίνοισι κύνεσσιν
ὀσμὴν πρεσβεύτειραν ἀμαλδύνουσιν ἄρουραι·
αὐτὰρ ἐν εὐκάρπῳ γλυκεροσταφύλῳ φθινοπώρῳ

[1] τετυπωμένα δείκελα ταρσῶν Brunck.

---

[a] Xen. *C.* 7. 5 τὰ ὀνόματα αὐταῖς τίθεσθαι βραχέα ἵνα εὐανάκλητα εἴη (where he gives forty-seven dog names, all dissyllabic). Colum. vii. 12 Nominibus non longissimis appellandi sunt, quo celerius quisque vocatus exaudiat: nec tamen brevioribus quam quae duabus syllabis enuntientur, sicut Graecum est σκύλαξ (ὕλαξ? Verg. *E.* viii. 107), Latinum *ferox*, Graecum λάκων, Latinum *celer*: vel femina, ut sunt Graeca σπουδή, ἀλκή, ῥώμη (these three from Xen.), Latina *lupa* (*cf.* Lycisca: Verg. *E.* viii. 18), *cerva*, *tigris*.

[b] Xenophon, *C.* 8, gives instructions for hunting hares in

To the young whelps give names that are short[a] and swiftly spoken that they may hear a command swiftly. And from their whelphood let them be acquainted with the mighty horses of the hunt and friendly and familiar with all men and hostile only to wild beasts. Neither let them be prone to bark; for silence is the rule for hunters and above all for trackers.

Tracking the dim trail is of two sorts, by men and by dogs. Men, cunning of counsel, divine and mark the trail by the eyes; dogs trace all tracks by the nostrils. Now for men winter[b] is a favourable season and they track the quarry with untroubled eyes, since every mark is written in the snow to see and the likeness of the foot remains imprinted in the mud. For dogs spring[c] is hostile but autumn kindly; for in spring the grassy earth is many-scented and over-full of herbs and flowers, and all around the fair-crowned meadows without tillage are purple, while the tilled fields destroy all the scent which is the ambassadress to the keen-nosed tracking dogs. But in autumn,[d] rich in fruit and sweet with grapes,

winter (*cf.* Bik. p. 14 On en fait la chasse presque toute l'année, mais surtout en hiver): *κύνας μὲν οὖν οὐδὲν δεῖ ἔχοντα ἐξιέναι ἐπὶ τὴν θήραν ταύτην· ἡ γὰρ χιὼν καίει τῶν κυνῶν τὰς ῥῖνας, τοὺς πόδας, τὴν ὀσμὴν τοῦ λαγῶ ἀφανίζει διὰ τὸ ὑπέρπαγες· λαβόντα δὲ τὰ δίκτυα μετ' ἄλλου ἐλθόντα πρὸς τὰ ὄρη παριέναι ἀπὸ τῶν ἔργων, καὶ ἐπειδὰν λάβῃ τὰ ἴχνη, πορεύεσθαι κατὰ ταῦτα.* *Cf. ib.* 5. 1 ff.

[c] Xen. *C.* 5. 5 *τὸ δὲ ἔαρ κεκραμένον τῇ ὥρᾳ καλῶς παρέχει τὰ ἴχνη, λαμπρά, πλὴν εἴ τι ἡ γῆ ἐξανθοῦσα βλάπτει τὰς κύνας εἰς τὸ αὐτὸ συμμιγνύουσα τῶν ἀνθῶν τὰς ὀσμάς.* *Cf.* Poll. v. 49.

[d] Xen. *C.* 5. 5 *τοῦ δὲ μετοπώρου καθαρά* (*sc. τὰ ἴχνη*)*· ὅσα γὰρ ἡ γῆ φέρει, τὰ μὲν ἥμερα συγκεκόμισται, τὰ δὲ ἄγρια γήρᾳ διαλέλυται· ὥστε οὐ παραλυποῦσι τῶν καρπῶν αἱ ὀσμαὶ εἰς ταὐτὰ φερόμεναι.* *Cf.* Poll. v. 49.

ποῖαι καὶ βοτάναι καί τ' ἄνθεα γηράσκουσι,
γυμνὴ δὲ σκυλάκεσσι μένει θήρειος ἀϋτμή.
Ἔστι δέ τι σκυλάκων γένος ἄλκιμον ἰχνευτήρων,
βαιόν, ἀτὰρ μεγάλης ἀντάξιον ἔμμεν' ἀοιδῆς·
τοὺς τράφεν ἄγρια φῦλα Βρετανῶν αἰολονώτων·
αὐτὰρ ἐπικλήδην σφὰς Ἀγασσαίους ὀνόμηναν.
τῶν ἤτοι μέγεθος μὲν ὁμοίϊον οὐτιδανοῖσι
λίχνοις οἰκιδίοισι τραπεζήεσσι κύνεσσι,
γυρόν, ἀσαρκότατον, λασιότριχον, ὄμμασι νωθές,
ἀλλ' ὀνύχεσσι πόδας κεκορυθμένον ἀργαλέοισι
καὶ θαμινοῖς κυνόδουσιν ἀκαχμένον ἰοφόροισι·
ῥίνεσι δ' αὖτε μάλιστα πανέξοχός ἐστιν Ἀγασσεὺς
καὶ στιβίῃ πανάριστος· ἐπεὶ καὶ γαῖαν ἰόντων
ἴχνιον εὑρέμεναι μέγα δὴ σοφός, ἀλλὰ καὶ αὐτὴν
ἴδμων ἠερίην μάλα σημήνασθαι ἀϋτμήν.
Καί τις ἐπακτήρων πειρηθῆναι σκυλακήων
ἱμείρων, προπάροιθε πυλάων αἰπεινάων
ἢ νέκυν ἢ ζώοντα φέρει παλάμῃσι λαγωόν·
ἑρπύζει δὲ πάροιθε παραιβαδὸν ἀτραπιτοῖο,
πρῶτα μὲν ἰθεῖαν, μετέπειτα δὲ δοχμὸν ἐλαύνων,
λαιῇ, δεξιτερῇ, σκολιὴν ὁδὸν ἀμφὶς ἑλίσσων·

---

[a] This epithet (lit. "of particoloured backs") we take to refer to the practice of staining or tattooing. Caes. *B.G.* v. 14 Omnes se Britanni vitro inficiunt. So of Scythians, Verg. *G.* ii. 115 pictos Gelonos ; *A.* iv. 146 picti Agathyrsi ; Amm. Marc. xxxi. 2. 14 ; Herod. v. 6 τὸ μὲν ἐστίχθαι εὐγενὲς κέκριται (among Thracians), τὸ δὲ ἄστικτον ἀγεννές ; Herodian iii. 14 τὰ σώματα στίζονται (οἱ Βρεταννοί) γραφαῖς ποικίλων ζῴων εἰκόσιν, ὅθεν οὐδὲ ἀμφιέννυνται, ἵνα μὴ σκέπωσι τοῦ σώματος τὰς γραφάς.

[b] The chief ancient references to British dogs are Strab. 199 among exports from Britain are κύνες εὐφυεῖς πρὸς τὰς κυνηγεσίας· Κελτοὶ δὲ καὶ πρὸς τοὺς πολέμους χρῶνται καὶ τούτοις καὶ τοῖς ἐπιχωρίοις ; Gratt. 174 ff. Quid freta si Morinum

grass and herbs and flowers wax old and the scent of the wild beasts remains naked for the hounds.

There is one valiant breed of tracking dogs, small indeed but as worthy as large dogs to be the theme of song; bred by the wild tribes of the painted[a] Britons and called by the name of Agassaeus.[b] Their size is like that of the weak and greedy domestic table dog[c]: round, very lean, shaggy of hair, dull of eye, it has its feet armed with grievous claws and its mouth sharp with close-set venomous tusks. With its nose especially the Agassian dog is most excellent and in tracking it is best of all; for it is very clever at finding the track of things that walk the earth but skilful too to mark the airy scent.

When some hunter desires to make trial of his dogs, he carries in his hands before the high gates a hare, dead or alive, and walks forward on a devious path, now pursuing a straight course, now aslant, left and right twining his crooked way; but when

dubio refluentia ponto Veneris atque ipsos libeat penetrare Britannos? O quanta est merces et quantum impendia supra, Si non ad speciem mentiturosque decores Protinus—haec una est iactura Britannis—At magnum cum venit opus promendaque virtus, Et vocat extremo praeceps discrimine Mavors, Non tunc egregios tantum admirere Molossos. Comparet his versuta suas Athamania fraudes Azorusque Pheraeque et clandestinus Acarnan: Sicut Acarnanes subierunt proelio furto, Sic canis illa suos taciturna supervenit hostes; Nemes. 124 f. divisa Britannia mittit Veloces nostrique orbis venatibus aptos; Claud. *Stil.* iii. 301 magnaque taurorum fracturae colla Britannae.

[c] *Cf.* 438; Hom. *Od.* xvii. 309 where the disguised Odysseus on seeing his old dog Argus remarks: *καλὸς μὲν δέμας ἐστίν, ἀτὰρ τόδε γ' οὐ σάφα οἶδα, εἰ δὴ καὶ ταχὺς ἔσκε θέειν ἐπὶ εἴδεϊ τῷδε, ἦ αὔτως οἷοί τε τραπεζῆες κύνες ἀνδρῶν γίγνοντ'· ἀγλαΐης δ' ἕνεκεν κομέουσιν ἄνακτες*; *Il.* xxii. 69; xxiii. 173.

ἀλλ' ὅτε δὴ μάλα πολλὸν ἀπ' ἄστεος ἠδὲ πυλάων
ἔλθῃ, δὴ τότε βόθρον ὀρυξάμενος κατέθαψε·
νοστήσας δ' ἐπὶ ἄστυ παλίσσυτος αὐτίκ' ἀγινεῖ
ἀτραπιτοῖο πέλας κύνα μέρμερον· αὐτὰρ ὅγ' αἶψα
ὠρίνθη, φριμάᾳ τε λαγωείης ὑπ' ἀϋτμῆς·
ἴχνια μαστεύει δὲ κατὰ χθονός, οὐδὲ μάλ' εὑρεῖν
ἱμείρων δύναται· μάλα δ' ἀσχαλόων ἀλάληται.
ὡς δ' ὅτε τις κούρη δέκατον περὶ μῆνα σελήνης
πρωτοτόκος λοχίῃσιν ὑπ' ὠδίνεσσι τυπεῖσα
λύσατο μὲν πλοκάμους, λῦσεν δ' ἀπὸ δαίδαλα μαζῶν,
ἠδ' ἀχίτων δειλή τε καὶ ἀκρήδεμνος ἐοῦσα
στρωφᾶται πάντῃ κατὰ δώματα καὶ μογέουσα
ἄλλοτε μὲν πρόδομον μετανίσσεται, ἄλλοτε δ' αὖτε
ἐς λέχος ἰθύνει, ποτὲ δ' ἐν κονίῃσι ῥιφεῖσα
κωκύει ῥοδαλῇσιν ἐπισμήχουσα παρειαῖς·
ὣς ὅ γε, θυμοβόροισιν ἀνιάζων ὀδύνῃσι,
τῇ καὶ τῇ θύει τε καὶ ἑξείης ἐρεείνει
πάντα λίθον καὶ πάντα λόφον καὶ πᾶσαν ἀταρπὸν
δένδρεά θ' ἡμερίδας τε καὶ αἱμασιὰς καὶ ἀλωάς.
ἀλλ' ὁπότ' ἴχνεος ὀψὲ διηερίοιο τυχήσῃ,
καγχαλάᾳ κνυζεῖ τε κεχαρμένος, οἷά τε τυτθαὶ
σκιρτεῦσιν δαμάλαι περὶ πόρτιας οὐθατοέσσας·
ὣς καὶ τῷ μάλα θυμὸς ἐχήρατο, σευόμενος δὲ
εἱλεῖται σκολιοῖσιν ἐπεμβεβαὼς πεδίοισιν·
οὐδ' ἀπό μιν πλάγξαις, οὐδ' εἰ μάλα τηλόθ' ἐλαύνοις,
ἰθύνει δ' ἀπρὶξ γλυκερῆς δεδραγμένος ὀδμῆς,
εἰσόκε τέρμα πόνοιο καὶ εἰς βαλβῖδα περήσῃ.
εἰ δέ μιν ὁπλίσσειας ἀθηρήτοισι λαγωοῖς,
λάθρῃ μὲν πελάει, κατὰ δ' ἴχνιον ἴχνος ἐρείδει,
βαιὸς ὑφ' ἡμερίσιν κεκαλυμμένος ἢ καλάμῃσιν,
οἷά τε ληϊστὴρ ἐρίφων κλόπος, ὅστε νομῆα
ὑπνώοντα πέλας δεδοκημένος ἤρεμος ἕρπει.

he has come very far from the city and the gates, then he digs a trench and buries the hare. Returning back to the city, he straightway brings nigh the path the cunning dog ; and immediately it is excited and snorts at the scent of the hare, and seeks the track upon the ground, but for all its eagerness is not able to find it and roams about in great distress. Even as when a girl in the tenth lunar month, smitten by the birth-pangs of her first child, undoes her hair and undoes the drapery of her breasts and, poor girl, without tunic and without snood, roams everywhere about the house, and in her anguish now goes to the hall and anon rushes to her bed, and sometimes throws herself in the dust and mars her rosy cheeks ; so the dog, distressed by devouring grief, rushes this way and that and searches every stone in turn and every knoll and every path and trees and garden vines and dykes and threshing-floors. And when at last he hits the airy trail, he gives tongue and whines for joy ; even as the little calves leap about the uddered cows, so the dog rejoices exceedingly, and in haste he winds his way over the mazy fields ; nor couldst thou lead him astray, even if thou shouldst then drive him very far, but he runs straight on, holding steadfastly to the sweet scent, until he reaches the end of his labour and to his goal. But if thou wert to array him against the hare difficult of capture, stealthily he draws nigh, planting step on step, hiding low under vines or stubble, even as the robber thief of kids who, watching near at hand the sleeping shepherd, quietly

ἀλλ᾽ ὅτε δὴ λόχμῃσι λαγωείῃσι πελάσσῃ,
ῥίμφ᾽ ἔθορεν, τόξῳ ἐναλίγκιος ἠὲ δράκοντι
συρικτῇ, τὸν ὄρινεν ἑῆς πάρος ἀτρεμέοντα
ἰοδόκου χειῆς ἀμαλητόμος ἤ τις ἀροτρεύς.
ὣς ὅ γε καγχαλόων ὠκὺς θόρεν· ἣν δὲ τυχήσῃ,
ῥεῖά μιν ὀξυτέροισι δαμασσάμενος ὀνύχεσσι
καὶ γενύεσσιν ἑλὼν φόρτον μέγαν ἀντιάσειεν[1]·
ὦκα φέρει μογέων τε βαρυνόμενός τε πελάζει.
οἵη δ᾽ ἐκ ληΐοιο φέρει θέρος ἀμητοῖο
βριθομένη πυρῷ τε μετ᾽ αὔλιον εἶσιν ἀπήνη,
τὴν δ᾽ ἐσιδόντες ὄρουσαν ἀολλέες ἀγροιῶται,
πρόπροθι δ᾽ ἀντήσαντες ὁ μὲν κύκλοισιν ἐρείδει,
ἄλλος ὑπερτερίην, ὁ δ᾽ ἄρ᾽ ἄξονα βουσὶν ἀρήγων·
εἰς αὖλιν δὲ μολόντες ἐλύσανθ᾽ ἱστοβοῆα,
ταῦροι δ᾽ ἱδρώοντες ἀνέπνευσαν καμάτοιο,
θυμὸς δ᾽ ἠπεδανοῦ μέγ᾽ ἐχήρατο βουπελάταο·
ὣς ὁ μὲν ἱκνεῖται φόρτον γενύεσσιν ἀγινῶν.
αὐτὰρ ὅ γ᾽ ἀντιάᾳ κεχαρημένος ὠκὺς ἐπακτήρ,
ἄμφω δ᾽ ἀείρας ἀπὸ μητέρος ὑψόθι γαίης,
κόλποισιν θέτο θῆρα καὶ αὐτὸν θηροφονῆα.

[1] ἀντία σεῖο Lobeck.

steals upon the fold. But when he approaches the covert of the hare, swiftly he springs, like an arrow from the bow or like the hissing snake which some harvester or ploughman has disturbed when lying quietly in front of his venomous lair. So the dog gives tongue and springs; and if he hit his quarry, easily he will overcome him with his sharp claws and take his great load in his mouth and go to meet his master: swiftly he carries his burden but labouring and heavy-laden he draws near. As the wain brings from the cornfield the fruits of harvest and comes to the steading laden with wheat and the rustics when they see it rush forth together to meet it in front of the yard; one presses on the wheels, another on the frame, another on the axle to help the oxen; and when they come into the yard they unstrap the pole and the sweating steers have respite from their toil, and the heart of the swinked teamster rejoices exceedingly; even so the dog comes bringing his burden in his mouth. And the swift hunter meets him joyfully and lifting both high from mother earth he puts in his bosom[a] both the beast and the dog himself that slew the beast.

[a] Plin. viii. 147 (canes) senecta fessos caecosque ac debiles sinu ferunt.

ΚΥΝΗΓΕΤΙΚΩΝ ΤΟ Β

Εἰ[1] δ᾽ ἄγε μοι, Ζηνὸς θύγατερ, καλλίσφυρε Φοίβη,
παρθένε χρυσομίτρη, δίδυμον γένος Ἀπόλλωνι,
εἰπέμεναι μερόπων τίς ἀγασθενέων θ᾽ ἡρώων
σῆς ἀπὸ χειρὸς ἄειρε μεγακλέα δήνεα θήρης.
Ἀμφὶ πόδας Φολόης ἀνεμώδεος ἄγρια φῦλα
θηρομιγῆ, μερόπων μὲν ἐπ᾽ ἰξύας, ἰξυόφιν δὲ
ἵππων ἡμιβρότων, ἐπιδόρπιον εὕρετο θήρην.
ἐν μερόπεσσι δὲ πρῶτος ὁ Γοργόνος αὐχέν᾽ ἀμέρσας,[2]
Ζηνὸς χρυσείοιο πάϊς κλυτός, εὕρετο Περσεύς·
ἀλλὰ ποδῶν κραιπνῇσιν ἀειρόμενος πτερύγεσσι
καὶ πτῶκας καὶ θῶας ἐλάζυτο καὶ γένος αἰγῶν
ἀγροτέρων δόρκους τε θοοὺς ὀρύγων τε γένεθλα
ἠδ᾽ αὐτῶν ἐλάφων στικτῶν αἰπεινὰ κάρηνα.
ἱππαλέην δ᾽ ἄγρην ὁ φαεσφόρος εὕρετο Κάστωρ·
καὶ τοὺς μὲν κατέπεφνεν ἐπίσκοπον ἰθὺς ἄκοντι
βαλλόμενος, τοὺς δ᾽ αὖτε θοοῖς ἵπποισιν ἐλαύνων
θῆρας ἕλε ξυνοχῇσι μεσημβρινοῖο δρόμοιο.

[1] εἰ] νῦν CFGI.
[2] v.l. αὐχένα κόψας.

---

[a] M. in Arcadia, home of the Centaurs.
[b] For ἐπιδόρπιον cf. μεταδόρπια Plat. *Critias*, 115 B.
[c] S. of Danae whom Zeus visited in a golden rain.
[d] The winged shoes of Perseus. Apollod. ii. 4. 2.
[e] Castor and Pollux became the constellation Gemini, the Twins, and aid those in peril at sea; Claud. *Bell. Gild.* i.

CYNEGETICA, OR THE CHASE

II

Come now, daughter of Zeus, fair-ankled Phoebe, maid of the golden snood, twin birth with Apollo, declare, I pray thee, who among men and mighty heroes received at thy hands the glorious devices of the chase.

By the foot of windy Pholoe [a] did savage tribes, half-beast half-men, human to the waist but from the waist horses, invent the chase for pastime after the banquet.[b] Among men it was invented first by him who cut off the Gorgon's head, even Perseus,[c] the son of golden Zeus; howbeit he soared on the swift wings [d] of his feet to capture Hares and Jackals and the tribe of wild Goats and swift Gazelles and the breeds of Oryx and the high-headed dappled Deer themselves. Hunting on horseback did Castor, bringer of light,[e] discover; and some beasts he slew by straight hurling of his javelin to the mark; others he pursued on swift horses and put them to bay [f] in the noontide chase. Saw-toothed [g] dogs were

221 caeca sub nocte vocati Naufraga Ledaei sustentant vela Lacones. *Cf.* Callim. (Loeb) *H.* v. 24 n. For dogs called καστορίαι *cf.* Xen. *C.* 3. 1; Poll. v. 39.

[f] Lit. "took (slew) in the narrows." *Cf.* Lat. *angustiae.* The phrase is from Hom. *Il.* xxiii. 330 ἐν ξυνοχῇσιν ὁδοῦ.

[g] *C.* iii. 5 n.

πρὸς δὲ μόθους θηρῶν κύνας ὥπλισε καρχαρόδοντας
διογενὴς πρῶτος Λακεδαιμόνιος Πολυδεύκης
καὶ γὰρ πυγμαχίῃσι λυγροὺς ἐναρίξατο φῶτας
καὶ σκυλάκεσσι θοαῖς βαλίους ἐδαμάσσατο θῆρας.
ἔξοχα δ' ἐν σταδίοισιν ὀρειοτέροισι μόθοισιν
Οἰνείδης ἤστραψεν ἐνυάλιος Μελέαγρος.
ἄρκυας αὖτε βρόχους τε καὶ ἀγκύλα δίκτυα πρῶτος
Ἱππόλυτος μερόπεσσιν ἐπακτήρεσσιν ἔφηνε.
Σχοινῆος πρώτη δὲ κλυτὴ θυγάτηρ Ἀταλάντη
θηρσὶ φόνον πτερόεντα συηβόλος εὕρετο κούρη.
νυκτερίους δὲ δόλους, νυχίην πανεπίκλοπον ἄγρην,
Ὠρίων πρώτιστος ἐμήσατο κερδαλεόφρων.
τόσσοι μὲν θήρης κρατεροὶ πάρος ἡγεμονῆες.
πολλοὺς δ' αὖ μετόπισθεν ἔρως ἐδαμάσσατο δριμύς·
οὐ γάρ τις κέντροισι δαμεὶς ἄγρης ἐρατεινῆς
αὖθις ἑκὼν λείψειεν· ἔχει δέ μιν ἄσπετα δεσμά.
οἷος μὲν γλυκὺς ὕπνος ἐπ' ἄνθεσιν εἴαρος ὥρῃ,
οἵη δ' αὖτε θέρευς γλυκερὴ σπήλυγγι χαμεύνη,
οἵη δ' ἐν σκοπέλοισιν ἐπακτήρεσσι πάσασθαι
τερπωλή· πόσση δὲ χάρις κείνοισιν ὀπηδεῖ
δρεπτομένοις αὐτοῖσι μελιχρῆς ἄνθος ὀπώρης·
ψυχρὸν δ' ἐξ ἄντροιο προχεύμενον ἄργυφον ὕδωρ
οἷον κεκμηῶσι ποτὸν γλυκερόν τε λοετρόν·
οἷα δ' ἐνὶ ξυλόχοις κεχαρισμένα δῶρα φέρουσιν
ἐν γλυκεροῖς ταλάροισι παρ' αἰπολίοισι νομῆες.
Ἀλλ' ἄγε δὴ ταύρων ζηλήμονα πάγχυ γενέθλην
πρῶτον ἀείδωμεν καὶ μυρίον ἔξοχα νεῖκος

---

[a] Gratt. 213 assigns this distinction to the Boeotian Hagnon.

first arrayed for battle with wild beasts by Polydeuces[a] of Lacedaemon, son of Zeus; for he both slew baleful men in the battle of the fists and overcame spotted wild beasts with swift hounds. Pre-eminent in close combat on the hills shone the son of Oeneus, warlike Meleager.[b] Nets again and nooses and curving hayes did Hippolytus[c] first reveal to hunting men. Winged death for wild beasts did Atalanta[d] invent, the glorious daughter of Schoeneus, the maiden huntress of the Boar. And snaring by night, the guileful hunting of the dark, crafty Orion[e] first discovered. These were the mighty leaders of the chase in former days. But afterward the keen passion seized many; for none who has once been smitten by the charms of the delightful hunt would ever willingly forsake it again: he is held by wondrous bonds. How sweet the sleep upon the flowers in springtime; how sweet in summer the low couch in some cave; what delight for hunters to break their fast amid the rocks and what joy attends them when they cull for themselves the flower of honied fruit; and the cold clear water flowing from a grotto—what a draft for a weary man and how sweet a bath; and in the woods what grateful gifts in pleasant baskets are brought by shepherds watching by their flocks!

But come now let us sing first the very jealous race of Bulls and tell of the tremendous feud which

[b] S. of Aetolian Oeneus and Althaea, killed the Calydonian boar. Apollod. i. 8. 2.

[c] S. of Theseus and the Amazon Hippolyte, was favourite of Artemis and famous hunter.

[d] D. of Schoeneus (Paus. viii. 35, etc.) or Iasus (Callim. *H.* i i. 216, etc.), was first to shoot the Calydonian boar (Apollod. i. 8. 2; Paus. viii. 45).

[e] Giant hunter of Boeotia: Apollod. i. 4. 3.

οἷον ὑπὲρ θαλάμοιο πανάγρια δηρίσαντο.
εἷς βασιλεὺς ἀγέληφι τυραννεύων ὄχ᾽ ἄριστος
βαιοτέροις ταύροις καὶ θηλυτέρῃσιν ἀνάσσει·
πέφρικεν δ᾽ ἀγέλη κεραὸν μέγαν ἡγεμονῆα·
αἱ δ᾽ αὖτε τρομέουσιν ἑὸν πόσιν ἀγριόωντα,
ὁππότε μυκήσαιτ᾽, ἄγριοι[1] βόες· ἀλλ᾽ ὅτ᾽ ἐπ᾽ ἄλλῳ
ταῦρος ἀποκρινθεὶς ἀγέλης, πλατὺν αὐχένα τείνας,
οἷος ἴῃ,[2] κἀκεῖνος ἄναξ σφετέροισιν ἀνάσσων,
δὴ τότ᾽ ἐπ᾽ ἀμφοτέροισιν ὑπέρβιος ἵστατ᾽ ἐνυώ.
πρῶτα μὲν ἀντίπρωρον ἐς ἀλλήλους ὁρόωντες
ἄγρια θυμαίνοντι χόλῳ μέγα παιφάσσουσι
καὶ πυρόεν πνείουσι καὶ ἀμῶνται ποσὶ γαῖαν,
οἷα κονιόμενοι· προκαλίζονται δ᾽ ἑκάτερθεν,
ὀξέα κεκλήγοντες ἐνυαλίοισιν ἀϋταῖς·
αὐτὰρ ἐπεὶ σάλπιγξαν ἐφ᾽ ὑσμίνην ἀλεγεινήν,
ἄσχετον ἀΐσσουσιν, ἑοῖσι δ᾽ ἄφαρ κεράεσσι
πᾶν δέμας ἀλλήλοισιν ἀμοιβαδὶς οὐτάζουσιν.
οἷα δ᾽ ἐνὶ πτολέμῳ βυθίῳ, ὅτε ναυμάχος Ἄρης
δῆριν ἀείρηται, δοιαὶ πανυπείροχα νῆες,
στράπτουσαι θαμινοῖσιν ἐναντίον ὁπλίτῃσιν,
ἀντίβιον πρώρῃσι μετωπαδὸν ἐγχρίμπτονται,
σπερχόμεναι πνοιῇ τε λάβρῳ παλάμῃφι τε ναυτῶν·
ἔντεσι χαλκείοις δὲ περιβρέμεται κτύπος ἀνδρῶν
νηῶν τ᾽ ἀγνυμένων· στένεται δ᾽ ὅλος οἴδματι Νηρεύς·

[1] ἄγριον GI. [2] ἴῃ Turnebus : ἔῃ mss.

[a] A. 572 b 16 ὁ δὲ ταῦρος, ὅταν ὥρα τῆς ὀχείας ᾖ, τότε γίνεται σύννομος καὶ μάχεται τοῖς ἄλλοις, τὸν δὲ πρότερον χρόνον μετ᾽ ἀλλήλων εἰσίν, ὃ καλεῖται ἀτιμαγελεῖν. πολλάκις γὰρ οἵ γ᾽ ἐν τῇ Ἠπείρῳ οὐ φαίνονται τριῶν μηνῶν; *id.* 611 a 2 ἀπόλλυνται δὲ καὶ οἱ ταῦροι, ὅταν ἀτιμαγελήσαντες ἀποπλανηθῶσιν, ὑπὸ θηρίων.

[b] Plin. viii. 181 Sed (tauro) tota comminatio prioribus in pedibus. Stat ira gliscente alternos replicans spargensque in

above others they wage with utter fury over their mating. One Bull is monarch of a herd and easily supreme, and he rules the lesser Bulls and females; the herd quake before their mighty horned leader, and the cows of the field too tremble at their own lord in his anger when he bellows. But when a Bull separates from the herd [a] and arching his mighty neck comes against another all alone, he too being lord and master of his own, then between the twain arises violent war. First face to face they glare at one another and greatly quiver with wildly seething wrath and breathe fiery breath and tear up the earth [b] with their feet, even as if they were wrestlers dusting themselves [c] for the fray. They challenge from either side, loudly bellowing the cry of battle; and when they have sounded the trumpet for grievous combat, incontinently they charge and straightway with their horns each wounds in turn all the body of the other. Even as in battle upon the deep when the sea War-god raises strife, two ships, splendidly flashing with serried warriors face to face, clash with opposing prows front to front, sped by the violent wind and the hands of the sailors; and amid brazen armour rings the din of men and the noise of crashing ships, and the whole sea seethes and groans;

alvum harenam et solus animalium eo stimulo ardescens. *Cf.* Pind. *P.* iv. 226.

[c] Wrestlers anointed with oil and sprinkled themselves with dust; *E.M. s.* κονίω; Plut. *Mor.* 966 C προθέσεις καὶ παρασκευὰς ταύρων ἐπὶ μάχῃ κονιομένων; *ibid.* 970 F διακονίεσθαι; Lucian, *Anach.* xxxi. etc.; *Anth. Gr.* (App. Pl.) xxv. 8; Luc. iv. 613 Perfundit membra liquore Hospes (Hercules) Olympiacae servato more palaestra, Ille (Antaeus) parum fidens pedibus contingere matrem Auxilium membris calidas nfudit harenas.

τοῖος καὶ ταύροισιν ἐς αἰθέρα δοῦπος ἱκάνει,
θεινόντων ἄμοτον καὶ θεινομένων κεράεσσιν,
εἰσόκε δή τις ἕλῃσι φίλην ἑτεραλκέα νίκην.
αὐτὰρ ὅ γ' οὔτι φέρει δοῦλον ζυγόν· αἰδόμενος δὲ
καὶ βαρέα στενάχων ἐπὶ δάσκιον ἤλυθεν ὕλην·
οἶος δ' ἐν σκοπέλοισι περιπλομένων ἐνιαυτῶν
φέρβετ' ὀρειαύλοισιν ἀποσταδὸν ἐν ξυλόχοισιν,
οἷά τις ἀθλεύων· βριαρὸν δ' ὅτε κάρτος ἴδηται
καὶ σθένος ἀμφήριστον, ἀνέκραγεν αὐτίκ' ὄρεσφιν·
αὐτὰρ ὅγ' ἀντήϋσεν· ἐπεσμαράγησε δὲ δρυμών·
ἀλλ' ὅτε θαρσήσειε κραταιοτέρῃσιν ἀϋταῖς,
δή ῥα τότ' ἐξ ὀρέων ἐπὶ δήϊον εὐθὺς ἱκάνει,
ῥεῖα δ' ἕλεν· φορβαῖς γὰρ ἑὸν δέμας ἐξήσκησε
τηλόθ' ἐνὶ δρυμοῖσι σθενοβλαβέος Κυθερείης.
Εἴδεα πολλὰ πέλει δὲ καὶ ἤθεα μυρία ταύροις.
Αἰγύπτου[1] μὲν ἔασι παρ' ὄχθαις ἀγλαοκάρποις
Νείλου πυροφόροιο πολυσχιδέος ποταμοῖο
χιόνεοι χροιήν, μέγεθος πάντων ὄχ' ἄριστοι·

[1] Αἰγύπτιοι Brunck.

---

[a] Verg. *G.* iii. 224 Nec mos bellantes una stabulare, sed alter Victus abit longeque ignotis exulat oris, Multa gemens ignominiam plagasque superbi Victoris, tum quos amisit inultus amores, Et stabula aspectans regnis excessit avitis; Ael. vi. 1 ταῦρος ἡγεμὼν τῆς ἀγέλης, ὅταν ἡττηθῇ ἡγεμόνος ἄλλου, ἑαυτὸν ἀποκρίνει εἰς χῶρον ἕτερον.

[b] Verg. *G.* iii. 229 Ergo omni cura vires exercet et inter Dura iacet pernox instrato saxa cubili, Frondibus hirsutis et carice pastus acuta, Et tentat sese atque irasci in cornua discit, Arboris obnixus trunco ventosque lacessit Ictibus et sparsa pugnam proludit harena; Ael. *l.c.* ἑαυτῷ γίνεται γυμναστὴς καὶ ἀθλεῖ πᾶσαν ἄθλησιν κονιόμενος καὶ τοῖς δένδροις τὰ κέρατα προσανατρίβων.

[c] Verg. *G.* iii. 235 Post ubi collectum robur viresque refectae, Signa movet praecepsque oblitum fertur in hostem;

even in such wise the din of the Bulls ascends to heaven, as they smite amain and are smitten with their horns, until one wins the dear and doubtful victory. But the vanquished [a] cannot endure the yoke of slavery. Ashamed and groaning heavily he goes unto a shady wood and alone among the rocks as the seasons circle round he pastures, retired among the thickets of the hill, as an athlete in training.[b] And when he beholds his debated power and strength have waxed mighty,[c] he straightway lifts up his voice upon the mountains; and the other answers; and therewith the forest resounds. But when he takes good heart for his mightier cry, then straightway from the hills he comes to meet his foe and easily overcomes him. For he has made his body fit by his pasture in the forest far from that lust of sex which saps the strength.[d]

Many are the forms and countless the characters of Bulls. The Egyptian Bulls there are by the fruitful banks of the Nile which makes the wheat to grow, a many-branched river; white of colour they are and far the greatest of all in size [e]: thou wouldst say

Stat. *T.* ii. 251 Sic ubi regnator post exulis otia tauri Mugitum hostilem summa tulit aure iuvencus Agnovitque minas, magna stat fervidus ira Ante gregem spumisque animos ardentibus efflat, Nunc pede torvus humum, nunc cornibus aera findens; Horret ager trepidaeque expectant proelia valles.

[d] Verg. *G.* iii. 209; A. 575 a 20; Ael. *l.c.*

[e] A. 606 a 21 *ἐν Αἰγύπτῳ τὰ μὲν ἄλλα μείζω ἢ ἐν τῇ Ἑλλάδι, καθάπερ οἱ βόες καὶ τὰ πρόβατα.* Prof. D'Arcy Thompson writes: "The Egyptian bulls were large, but not 'white.' The bulls of Apis were black, with white markings; those mentioned here were probably the light-coloured bulls of Mnevis. Both had long, lyre-shaped horns, the type still surviving at Khartoum, etc. (*Bos Africanus* Brehm)."

φαίης κεν κατὰ γαῖαν ἴμεν βαθυτέρμονα νῆα
ἤπια δὲ φρονέουσι καὶ ἠθάλεοι μερόπεσσιν,
ὅττι βροτοὶ δ' ἐνέπουσιν, ἐνηέες ἐξανέχονται.[1]
Οἱ Φρύγιοι χροιὴν μὲν ἀριπρεπέες τελέθουσι,
ξανθοί τε φλογεροί τε· βαθεῖαι δ' αὐχένι σάρκες·
σφαιρωτὸς δ' ἐφύπερθε μετήορος ὕψι κόρυμβος.
ξείνη δ' ἐν κεράεσσι φύσις κείνοισι τέτυκται·
οὐ γάρ τοι κρατερῇσιν ὑπὲρ κεφαλῆφι πέπηγε,
κλίνουσιν δὲ κέρατα καὶ ἀγκλίνουσ' ἑκάτερθε.
Μώνυχες Ἀόνιοι, στικτὸν γένος, οἰοκέρωτες,
ἔκ τε μέσου κέρας αἰνὸν ἐπαντέλλουσι μετώπου.
Ἀρμενίοις δίδυμον μὲν ἀτὰρ κέρας εἰλικόμορφον
αἰχμῇσιν, μέγα πῆμα, παλίστροφον ἠέρτηται.
Οἱ Σύριοι ταῦροι δέ, Χεροννήσοιο γένεθλα,
αἰπεινὴν τοὶ Πέλλαν ἐΰκτιτον ἀμφινέμονται,
αἴθωνες, κρατεροί, μεγαλήτορες, εὐρυμέτωποι,
ἄγραυλοι, σθεναροί, κερααλκέες, ἀγριόθυμοι,
μυκηταί, βλοσυροί, ζηλήμονες, εὐρυγένειοι·
ἀλλ' οὐ πιαλέοι δέμας ἀμφιλαφὲς βαρύθουσιν,
οὐδὲ πάλιν λιπόσαρκοι ἑὸν δέμας ἀδρανέουσιν·
ὧδε θεῶν κλυτὰ δῶρα κερασσάμενοι φορέουσιν,
ἀμφότερον κραιπνοί τε θέειν σθεναροί τε μάχεσθαι·
κεῖνοι, τοὺς φάτις ἔσκε Διὸς γόνον Ἡρακλῆα

[1] ἐνηέες ἐξανέχονται Editor: νεηνίαι εἰσανέχονται most MSS.: ἐνηῆες εἰσανέχονται M: ἐνηῆες ἀνέχονται K, Schn. Lehrs. Boudr.

---

[a] βαθυτ. only here: ἡ βαθὺ κοῖλον βάθος ἔχουσα schol.

[b] A. 517 a 27 τὰ δὲ κέρατα προσπέφυκε μᾶλλον τῷ δέρματι ἢ τῷ ὀστῷ· διὸ καὶ ἐν Φρυγίᾳ εἰσὶ βόες καὶ ἄλλοθι οἳ κινοῦσι τὰ κέρατα ὥσπερ τὰ ὦτα; Plin. ii. 124 (dedit natura) mobilia eadem (*i.e.* cornua) ut aures Phrygiae armentis. *Cf.* Antig. 75. So of other cattle, Solin. lii. 36; Ael. ii. 20, xvi. 33, xvii. 45; Diod. iii. 34; Agatharch. *ap.* Phot. p. 455 b Benner.

it was a deep-drawing ship [a] that was going upon the land. Yet are they kindly of spirit and familiar with men, and whatsoever mortals bid them, they obey with mildness.

The Phrygian Bulls are notable in colour, yellow and of the hue of fire. The neck is deeply fleshed, and high and lofty are the coiled curls upon their heads. Strange is the nature of their horns; for these are not fast fixed upon the powerful head, but they move them [b] to and fro on either side.

The Aonian [c] Bulls do not divide the hoof; a dappled breed they are and with a single horn—a dread horn which they project aloft from the midst of the forehead.

The Armenian Bulls have two horns, indeed, but these curved of form, a dread bane with their backward-bent points.

The Syrian Bulls, the breed of the Chersonese,[d] pasture about high well-builded Pella; tawny, strong, great-hearted, broad of brow, dwellers of the field, powerful, valiant of horn, wild of spirit, loud-bellowing, fierce, jealous, abundant of beard, yet they are not weighed down with fat and flesh of body, nor again are they lean and weak; so tempered are the gifts they have from heaven—at once swift to run and strong to fight. These are they which report said Heracles, the mighty son of Zeus, when fulfilling

[c] This should mean Boeotian (so the schol.), but it seems clear that there is some error. According to A. 499 b 18 *μονοκέρατα καὶ μώνυχα ὀλίγα οἷον ὁ Ἰνδικος ὄνος*; Plin. viii. 76 In India [Ctesias scribit esse] et boves solidis ungulis unicornes; Solin. lii. 38 sunt praeterea [in India] boves unicornes et tricornes solidis ungulis nec bifissis.

[d] Chersonese and Pella were old names for Apamea on the Orontes in Syria; Strab. 752. See Introd. p. xix.

καρτερὸν ἀθλεύοντ' ἀγέμεν πάρος ἐξ 'Ερυθείης,
ὁππότ' ἐπ' 'Ωκεανῷ δηρίσατο Γηρυονῆϊ
καὶ κτάνεν ἐν σκοπιῇσιν· ἐπεὶ πόνον ἄλλον ἔμελλεν
οὐχ Ἥρῃ τελέειν οὐδ' Εὐρυσθῆος ἐνιπαῖς,
'Αρχίππῳ δ' ἑτάρῳ, Πέλλης ἡγήτορι δίης.
ἦ γάρ τοι προπάροιθε παραὶ πόδας 'Εμβλωνοῖο
πᾶν πεδίον πελάγιζεν· ἐπεὶ πολὺς αἰὲν 'Ορόντης
ἵετ' ἐπειγόμενος, χαροποῦ δ' ἐπελήθετο πόντου,
δαιόμενος Νύμφης κυανώπιδος 'Ωκεανίνης·
δήθυνεν δὲ πάγοισι, κάλυπτε δ' ἐρίσπορον αἶαν
οὔτι θέλων προλιπεῖν δυσέρωτα πόθον Μελιβοίης.
οὔρεσί τ' ἀμφότερωθε περίδρομος ἐστεφάνωτο
τειναμένοις ἑκάτερθεν ἐπ' ἀλλήλοισι κάρηνα·
ἤϊεν ἀντολίηθε Διόκλειον δέμας αἰπύ,
ἐκ δ' ἄρα δυσμάων λαιὸν κέρας 'Εμβλωνοῖο,
αὐτὸς δ' ἐν μεσάτοισιν ἐπαιγίζων πεδίοισιν,
αἰὲν ἀεξόμενος καὶ τείχεος ἐγγὺς ὁδεύων,
χέρσον ὁμοῦ καὶ νῆσον, ἐμὴν πόλιν, ὕδασι χεύων.
τοὔνεκεν αὐτίκ' ἔμελλε Διὸς γόνος ἀμφοτέροισι

---

[a] Apollod. ii. 5. 10 δέκατον ἐπετάγη ἆθλον τὰς Γηρυόνου βόας ἐξ 'Ερυθείας κομίζειν. 'Ερύθεια δὲ ἦν 'Ωκεανοῦ πλησίον κειμένη νῆσος, ἣ νῦν Γάδειρα (=Gades: *cf.* Pind. *N.* iv. 68; Dion. P. 451) καλεῖται. ταύτην κατῴκει Γηρυόνης. . . . τριῶν ἔχων ἀνδρῶν συμφυὲς σῶμα; Herod. iv. 8; Diod. iv. 17; Strab. 148; Aesch. *Ag.* 870.

[b] S. of Sthenelus (s. of Perseus). When Heracles was about to be born Zeus declared that the descendant of Perseus then to be born should rule Mycenae. Hera caused Eurystheus to be born, a seven-month child, while she delayed the birth of Heracles. When Heracles in his madness had slain his children, the Delphic oracle κατοικεῖν αὐτὸν εἶπεν ἐν Τίρυνθι, Εὐρυσθεῖ λατρεύοντα ἔτη δώδεκα καὶ τοὺς ἐπιτασσομένους ἄθλους δέκα ἐπιτελεῖν; Apollod. ii. 4. 5.

[c] See Introd. p. xix. This myth seems to be found only here, and Archippus, Diocleium, and Emblonus are nowhere

his labours drove of old from Erytheia,[a] what time he fought with Geryoneus beside the Ocean and slew him amid the crags; since he was doomed to fulfil yet another labour, not for Hera nor at the behest of Eurystheus,[b] but for his comrade Archippus,[c] lord of holy Pella. For aforetime all the plain by the foot of Emblonus was flooded; since evermore in great volume rushed Orontes in his eagerness, forgetting the sea and burning with desire of the dark-eyed nymph, the daughter of Ocean. He lingered amid the heights and he covered the fertile earth, unwilling to forgo his hopeless love of Meliboea. With mountains on either side was he encircled round, mountains that on either hand leaned their heads together. From the East came the lofty form of Diocleium, and from the West the left horn of Emblonus, and in the midst himself raging in the plains, ever waxing and drawing nigh the walls, flooding with his waters that mainland at once and island,[d] mine own city. Therefore was the son of Zeus destined straightway with club and

else mentioned. The schol. on 109 has: οὓς Ἡρακλῆς ἀθλῶν πρότερον ἐξ Ἐρυθείας ἐκόμισεν, τὸν Γηρυόνα ἀνελών, ὅτε δὴ καὶ Ἀρχίππῳ Πέλλης ἡγεμόνι (φίλος δ' ἄρα οἱ καὶ συνήθης ὁ Ἄρχιππος) ἆθλον ἐκτελεῖν ἔμελλεν οὐδὲν ἀτιμότερον <ἢ> ὁ Εὐρυσθεὺς . . . ἐπέταττεν. ὁ γάρ τοι τὴν Ἀντιόχου παραρρέων Ὀρόντης λίμνην προσεκκαυθεὶς καὶ μεθύων τῆς νύμφης τῷ ἔρωτι (Μελίβοια τῇ νύμφῃ τὸ ὄνομα, Ὠκεανὸς τῇ λίμνῃ πατήρ) τῆς ἐπὶ θάλατταν μὲν ἐπελάθετο, ὄρεσι δὲ καὶ πεδίοις περιελίμναζε, νῦν μὲν τὸν Ἐμβλωνὸν (ὄρος δ' οὗτος) καὶ τοὺς αὐτοῦ καταιγίζων πρόποδας, ἄρτι δὲ πρὸς γῆν ἐκτρεπόμενος, καὶ ταύτην ἐπικαλύπτων τῷ ῥεύματι, ἐνίοτε δὲ καὶ μέσος τῶν ὀρέων συρόμενος ἀμφοῖν Ἐμβλωνοῦ καὶ Διοκλείου, τῶν ἐξ ἕω καὶ δυσμῶν ἐπικεκυφότων ἀλλήλοις, καὶ παντοῖος διὰ τὴν ἐρωμέ ην γινόμενος, ἀνοιδαίνων τε καὶ ἀνακαχλάζων, καὶ πελάζων τοῖς τείχεσι καὶ τὴν εἰς Χερρόνησον διεσχηματισμένην πόλιν ἐμὴν περικλύζων τῷ ὕδατι.

[d] *i.e.* Chersonese; *cf.* 100 n.

νάματα μετρήσειν ῥοπάλῳ καὶ χερσὶ κραταιαῖς,
ὕδατα δ' ἐκ πεδίοιο διακριδὸν ἰθύνεσθαι
εὐπλοκάμου λίμνης ἠδ' εὐτροχάλου ποταμοῖο.
ἔρξε δὲ πουλὺν ἄεθλον, ἐπεὶ στεφάνην διέκερσεν
ἀμφιβόλων ὀρέων, λῦσεν δ' ἄπο λάϊνα δεσμά,
καὶ ποταμὸν προέηκεν ἐρευγόμενον προμολῇσιν,
ἄσχετα κυμαίνοντα καὶ ἄγρια μορμύροντα,
ἴθυνεν δ' ἐπὶ θῖνας· ὁ δ' ἔβραχεν ἠπύτα πόντος
καὶ Συρίου κονάβησε μέγαν δέμας αἰγιαλοῖο.
οὐ τοίω γ' ἑκάτερθε πολυσμαράγοιο θαλάσσης
ἀντιπόρω ποταμὼ καταβαίνετον ὕδατι λάβρῳ·
ἔνθεν μὲν Βορέαο τεμὼν ἀργῆτα χαλινὰ
ἂν Σκυθίην Ἴστρος λέλακεν μέγα πάντοθε πάντῃ,
συρόμενος κρημνοῖσι καὶ ὑδατοπλήγεσιν[1] ἄκραις·
τῇ δ' αὖτ' ἐκ Λιβύης ἱερὸν ῥόον Αἰγύπτοιο
ἀμφί ἑ ῥηγνύμενον τρομέει ταναηχέα πόντος.
ὣς ποταμὸς κελάρυζε μέγας περὶ θῖνας Ὀρόντης
σμερδαλέον μύκημα· πελώρια δ' ἴαχον ἀκταὶ
δεχνύμεναι κόλποισι νεήλυδος οἶδμα θαλάσσης·
γαῖα δ' ἀνέπνευσεν μελανόχροος, οὐθατόεσσα,
κύματος ἐξαναδῦσα, νέον πέδον Ἡρακλῆος.
πάντῃ δ' εἰσέτι νῦν σταχυηκομέουσιν ἄρουραι,
πάντῃ δ' ἔργα βοῶν θαλερὰς βέβριθεν ἀλωὰς
Μεμνόνιον περὶ νηόν, ὅθ' Ἀσσύριοι ναετῆρες
Μέμνονα κωκύουσι, κλυτὸν γόνον Ἠριγενείης,
ὅν ποτε Πριαμίδῃσιν ἀμυνέμεναι πελάσαντα
θαρσαλέος πόσις ὦκα δαμάσσατο[2] Δηϊδαμείης.

[1] ὑδατοπήγεσιν MSS. : corr. Guietus.
[2] v.l. παρέδραμε.

---

[a] Danube.
[b] Apparently here, as in Hom. *Od.* iv. 477 etc., = the Nile.
[c] King of the Ethiopians, s. of Eos (Dawn) and Tithonus, fought against the Greeks at Troy (Hom. *Od.* iv. 188; xi. 522),

mighty hands to apportion their water unto each, and to give separate course from the plain for the waters of the fair-tressed lake and the fair-flowing river. And he wrought his mighty labour, when he cut the girdle of the encircling hills and undid their stony bonds, and sent the river belching to its mouth, surging incontinent and wildly murmuring, and guided it toward the shores. And loudly roared the deep sea, and the mighty body of the Syrian shore echoed to the din. Not with such violent flood descend those contrary-travelling rivers on either side the echoing sea: here Ister,[a] cleaving the white barriers of the North through Scythia, roars loudly everywhere, trailing amid precipices and water-smitten heights; while on the other hand the sounding sea trembles at the holy stream of Egypt[b] when from Libya it breaks about it. So the mighty river Orontes made a noise of dread bellowing about the shores; and mightily roared the headlands when they received within their bosom the swell of the new-come sea; and the black and fertile earth took heart again, arisen from the waves, a new plain of Heracles. And to this day the fields flourish everywhere with corn and everywhere the works of oxen are heavy on the prosperous threshing-floors around the Memnonian shrine, where the Assyrian dwellers mourn for Memnon,[c] the glorious son of the Morning, whom, when he came to help the sons of Priam, the doughty husband of Deidameia[d] swiftly slew. How

where he was slain by Achilles (Pind. *O.* ii. 91; *N.* vi. 56) His tomb was shown in various places, among others at Paltos in Syria (Strab. 728). Assyrian = Syrian, *cf.* *C.* i. 7 n.

[d] D. of Lycomedes of Scyros, m. by Achilles of Neoptolemus.

ἀλλὰ τὰ μὲν κατὰ κόσμον ἀείσομεν εὐρέα κάλλη
πάτρης ἡμετέρης ἐρατῇ Πιμπληΐδι μολπῇ·
νῦν δὲ παλίντροπος εἶμι κλυτὴν θήρειον ἀοιδήν.
Ἔστιν ἀμαιμάκετον φονίοις ταύροισι γένεθλον,
τοὺς καλέουσι Βίσωνας· ἐπεὶ πάτρης τελέθουσι
Βιστονίδος Θρῄκης· ἀτὰρ ἔλλαχον εἴδεα τοῖα·
φρικαλέην χαίτην μὲν ἐπωμαδὸν αἰθύσσουσιν
αὐχέσι πιαλέοισι καὶ ἀμφ' ἀταλοῖσι γενείοις·
οἷά τε λαχνήεντες ἀριπρεπὲς εἶδος ἔχουσι
ξανθοκόμαι, βλοσυροί, θηρῶν μεδέοντε λέοντες·
ὀξεῖαι κεράων δὲ πυριγλώχινες[1] ἀκωκαὶ
χαλκείοις γναμπτοῖσιν ἐπείκελοι ἀγκίστροισιν·
ἀλλ', οὐχ ὡς ἑτέροισιν, ἐναντίον ἀλλήλοισι
νεύουσι στυγερῶν κεράων ἐπικάρσιον αἰχμαί,[2]
ὕπτια δ' εἰσορόωντα πρὸς αἰθέρα φοίνια κέντρα.
τοὔνεκεν, ὁππότε δή τιν' ἐπιχρίμψωσι κιχόντες
ἢ βροτὸν ἤ τινα θῆρα, μετήορον ἀείρουσι.
γλῶσσα δὲ τοῖς στεινὴ μὲν ἀτὰρ τρηχεῖα μάλιστα,
οἷα σιδηροβόροιο πέλει τέχνασμα σιδήρου·
γλώσσῃ δ' αἱμάσσοντες ἀπὸ χρόα λιχμάζουσι.
Ναὶ μὴν ὠκυπόδων ἐλάφων γένος ἔτραφεν αἶα

[1] *v.l.* περιγλώχινες. [2] αἰχμαί Boudr. : αἰχμήν MSS.

---

[a] Fountain in Pieria sacred to the Muses. Callim. *H.* iv. 7.

[b] *Bos bonasus* (*Bison europaeus*), the Wisent or European Bison, now exterminated in Lithuania, where a herd was maintained by the Tsar of Russia, and probably in the Caucasus also. Aristotle describes it under the name βόνασος 630 a 18 ff.; *cf.* 498 b 28; 506 b 30. In 630 a 20 he says it is called by the Paeonians μόναπος. *Cf.* A. *Mirab.* 830 a 5 ἐν τῇ Παιονίᾳ φασὶν . . . εἶναί τι θηρίον τὸ καλούμενον βόλινθον, ὑπὸ δε τῶν Παιόνων μόναιπον; Ael. vii. 3 μόνωψ; Antig. 53 μόνωπος; Plin. viii. 40 Tradunt in Paeonia feram quae bonasus vocetur equina iuba, cetera tauro similem,

beit the spacious glories of our fatherland we shall sing in due order with sweet Pimplean [a] song; now I turn back to sing of glorious hunting.

There is a terrible breed of deadly Bulls which they call Bisons,[b] since they are natives of Bistonian[c] Thrace. And they have forms of this sort. Over their shoulders they have bristling hair on their fleshy necks as also about their tender jaws; conspicuous form they have, even as the king of beasts, the shaggy, tawny, fierce-eyed Lion. Sharp are the curved points of their horns, like unto bent hooks of bronze; but the points of their hateful horns, unlike those of other cattle, incline athwart to face one another,[d] and their deadly daggers are sloped backwards and look up to the sky. Therefore when they come upon and attack any man or wild beast, they lift their victim on high. Their tongue is narrow, but exceeding rough, even as the device of iron for devouring iron; and with the tongue they draw blood from the flesh and lick it.

Moreover the earth breeds the race of swift-footed

cornibus ita in se flexis ut non sint utilia pugnae; *cf.* Solin. xl. 10. Pausan. x. 13 gives an account of the capture of the Paeonian Bison by means of a pit. The Bison with short stout horns is not to be confounded with the Aurochs, *Bos taurus* (*B. primigenius*), the Latin *urus*: Caes. *B.G.* vi. 28; Verg. *G.* ii. 374, iii. 532; Macrob. vi. 4. 23, of which the last was killed in Poland in 1627. *Bison* and *urus* are mentioned together Plin. viii. 38 iubatos bisontes excellentique et vi et velocitate uros; Senec. *Hipp.* 64 f. villosi terga bisontes Latisque feri cornibus uri.

[c] A pseudo-etymology. The Bistones dwelt on S. coast of Thrace near Abdera, Strab. 331 fr. 44.

[d] A. 499 b 31 διχαλὰ δ' ἅμα καὶ χαίτην ἔχοντα καὶ κέρατα δύο κεκαμμένα εἰς αὑτά ἐστιν ἔνια τῶν ζῴων, οἷον ὁ βόνασος, ὃς γίνεται περὶ τὴν Παιονίαν καὶ τὴν Μαιδικήν; Plin. viii. 40 (quoted above).

εὐκέραον, μεγαλωπόν, ἀριπρεπές, αἰολόνωτον,
στικτόν, ἀρίζηλον, ποταμηπόρον, ὑψικάρηνον,
πιαλέον νώτοις καὶ λεπταλέον κώλοισιν·
οὐτιδανὴ δειρὴ καὶ βαιοτάτη πάλιν οὐρή·
τετράδυμοι ῥῖνες, πίσυρες πνοιῇσι δίαυλοι·
ἀβληχρὴ κραδίη καὶ θυμὸς ἔσωθεν ἄναλκις,
καὶ κωφαὶ κεράων αἰχμαὶ τόσον ἀντέλλουσιν·
οὔ ποτε γὰρ κεφαλῆφιν ἐναντία δηρίσαιντο,
οὐ θηρσὶ κρατεροῖς, οὐκ ἀργαλέοισι κύνεσσιν,
οὐδ' αὐτοῖς δειλοῖς λασιοκνήμοισι λαγωοῖς.

---

[a] ἔλαφος is (1) specifically the Red Deer, *Cervus elaphus*, (2) generically Deer, and is used both of Stag and Hind.

[b] "Instances too sometimes occur of a stag being found swimming narrow parts of the Moray Firth; a solitary deer who probably has been driven by dogs from his usual haunts, till frightened and bewildered he has wandered at random and, at last, coming to the shore, has swum boldly out, attracted by the appearance of the woods on the opposite side," St. John, *N. H. and Sport in Moray*, p. 240; *cf. Wild Sports and N. H. of the Highlands*, p. 23; *A.P.* ix. 275 τὴν δὲ ταχεῖαν εἰν ἀλὶ καὶ χαροποῖς κύμασιν εἷλ' ἔλαφον.

[c] *Cf.* G. White, *N. H. of Selborne*, Letter xiv. (March 12, 1768): "If some curious gentleman would procure the head of a fallow-deer, and have it dissected, he would find it furnished with two spiracula, or breathing-places, besides the nostrils; probably analogous to the *puncta lacrimalia* in the human head. When deer are thirsty they plunge their noses, like some horses, very deep under water while in the act of drinking, and continue them in that situation for a considerable time; but to obviate any inconveniency, they can open two vents, one at the inner corner of each eye, having a communication with the nose. Here seems to be an extraordinary provision of nature worthy our attention; and which has not, that I know of, been noticed by any naturalist. For it looks as if these creatures would not be suffocated, though both their mouths and nostrils were stopped. This curious formation of the head may be of singular service to beasts of chase, by

Stags,[a] goodly of horn, large of eye, handsome, of dappled back, spotted, conspicuous, river-swimming,[b] lofty of head, fat of chine and lean of shank; the neck is weak and the tail again is very small; the nostrils are fourfold,[c] four passages for the breath; the heart is weak and the spirit within cowardly[d]; and the pointed horns that rise so high are but dummies; for they will never with their heads contend against strong wild beasts nor fierce dogs, nor even the timid hare of furry legs.

affording them free respiration; and no doubt these additional nostrils are thrown open when they are hard run. . . . Oppian, the Greek poet, by the following line [*i.e.* 181] seems to have had some notion that stags have four spiracula." Dr. James Ritchie, Royal Scottish Museum, Edinburgh, writes: "The spiracula of deer, or, as they are now called, the sub-orbital glands, vary a great deal in their development in different species of deer, but in many cases the glands seem to be of very considerable importance, lying in specially deep depressions in the skull. The glands secrete a waxy material, and I have seen this oozing in masses, even after red deer had been dead for several days. The secretion is most active during the pairing season, and there are a number of observations showing that deer seem deliberately to rub the secretion upon trees and stones. The suggestion has been made that this is in order to convey the scent of their passing, and this might be the effect even if we attribute the rubbing simply to a desire to get rid of the annoyance of surplus secretion. . . . The sub-orbital gland has a sort of contractile lip which, closed at one time, may at another be so pulled back that the inner surface is everted and there is exposed the large cavity of the gland lined with pink mucous membrane. The action and the appearance are quite enough to suggest similarity with the movement and appearance of the nostrils, but of course there is no sort of connexion between the sub-orbital glands and the air-passages."

[d] A. 488 b 15 τὰ δὲ φρόνιμα καὶ δειλά, οἷον ἔλαφος, δασύπους; *cf.* Suid. and *E.M.* *s.* ἐλάφειος.

Τρηχὺς δ' αὖτ' ἐλάφοισιν ἔρως πολλή τ' Ἀφροδίτη
καὶ θυμὸς ποτὶ λέκτρον ἀναιθόμενος πρόπαν ἦμαρ,
οἷον ἀειθούροισιν ἀλεκτρυόνεσσι μαχηταῖς
πᾶσίν τ' ἀνθοκόμοις πτεροείμοσιν οἰωνοῖσι.
κεύθουσιν λαγόνεσσι δ' ὑπ' αὐτὴν ἔνδοθι νηδὺν
ἀμφιδύμους ὁλκούς· τοὺς εἴ κέ τις ἀμήσειεν,
αὐτίκα θῆλυν ἔθηκε, πρόπαν δ' ἀπέρευσε καρήνων
ὀξύκομον κεράων πολυδαίδαλον αἰόλον ἔρνος.
οὐ μὲν ἄρ' εἰς εὐνὴν γάμιος νόμος οἷά τε θηρσὶ
τοῖς ἄλλοις, ξεῖνοι δὲ πόθοι κείνοισι μέλονται·
οὔτε γὰρ ἑσταότες παρὰ τέμπεσιν ἀγρονόμοισιν,
οὔτ' ἄρα κεκλιμένοι χθαμαλοῖσιν ἐπ' ἄνθεσι ποίης
θηλυτέραις ἐλάφοισιν ὁμιλαδὸν εὐνάζονται,
ἀλλὰ ποσὶ κραιπνοῖσι θέων ἐκίχανε θέουσαν·
φεύγουσαν μάρπτει δὲ καὶ ἀγκὰς ἔχει παράκοιτιν·
ἀλλ' οὐδ' ὧς παρέπεισε· φέρουσα πόσιν δ' ἐπὶ νώτου
ἐμμενέως φεύγει, παναμείλιχον ἦτορ ἔχουσα·
αὐτὰρ ὅ γ' ἑσπόμενος δισσοῖς λαιψηρὰ πόδεσσιν
οὐ μεθίησι πόθον, γαμίους δ' ἐτελέσσατο θεσμούς.
ἀλλ' ὅτε δὴ μετόπισθε περιπλομένῃσι σελήναις

---

[a] A. 579 a 4 ταῦτα δὲ ποιεῖ τὸ ζῷον διὰ τὸ φύσει λαγνὸν εἶναι; Solin. xix. 9 mares generis huiusce, cum statum tempus venerem incitavit, saeviunt rabie libidinis.

[b] A. 488 b 3 τὰ μὲν ἀφροδισιαστικά, οἷον τὸ τῶν περδίκων καὶ ἀλεκτρυόνων γένος.

[c] A. 632 a 10 οἱ δ' ἔλαφοι, ἐὰν μὲν μήπω τὰ κέρατα ἔχοντες διὰ τὴν ἡλικίαν ἐκτμηθῶσιν, οὐκέτι φύουσι κέρατα· ἐὰν δ' ἔχοντας ἐκτέμῃ τις, τό τε μέγεθος ταὐτὸν μένει τῶν κεράτων καὶ οὐκ ἀποβάλλουσιν; *cf.* 517 a 25; Plin. viii. 117 Non decidunt

But there is rough passion among Stags and much venery,[a] and a heart that burns for mating all the day, even as have the lustful fighting cocks [b] and all the feathered birds of flowery plumage. They have hidden within their loins under the very belly twin ducts. If one cut these out, straightway he makes the animal effeminate, and from its head falls away all the daedal many-branched growth of sharp horns.[c] But the manner of their mating [d] is not after the custom of other beasts, but strange are the passions that possess them. Not standing in the pastoral valleys nor lying on the flowery grass upon the ground do the Stags consort with the female deer, but the hind runs and the Stag running with swift feet overtakes her and seizes the fugitive and embraces her for his bride. But not even so does he persuade her. Carrying her mate upon her back she flees with all her might, having a heart altogether implacable. But he following swiftly on two feet forgoes not his desire but accomplishes the rites of union. Howbeit, when afterward with the circling of the moons the female brings forth her young, she

castratis cornua nec nascuntur ; Solin. xix. 14. "The horns of the Ruminants are frequently a secondary sexual character ; this is especially the case with the Deer. . . . That they are associated with the reproductive function is shown by their being shed after the period of rut, the destruction of the velvet at that period, and also by the effect upon the horns which any injury to the reproductive glands produces," *Camb. N. H.* x. Mammalia, p. 201.

[d] A. 540 a 5 *οὔτε τοὺς ἄρρενας ἐλάφους αἱ θήλειαι ὑπομένουσιν εἰ μὴ ὀλιγάκις, . . . διὰ τὴν τοῦ αἰδοίου* (*cf.* 500 b 23) *συντονίαν, ἀλλ' ὑπάγοντα τὰ θήλεα δέχονται τὴν γονήν· καὶ γὰρ ἐπὶ τῶν ἐλάφων ὦπται τοῦτο συμβαῖνον, τῶν γε τιθασῶν* ; Plin. x. 174 Taurorum cervorumque feminae vim non tolerant: ea de causa ingrediuntur in conceptu.

θηλυτέρη τίκτει, τρίβον ἀνθρώπων ἀλεείνει,
οὕνεκεν ἀτραπιτοὶ μερόπων θήρεσσι βέβηλοι.
Ἔξοχα δ᾽ ἐν θήρεσσιν ἐπ᾽ ἀγλαΐῃ κομόωσιν
ἄρσενες εὐκέραοι, πολυδαίδαλον ἔρνος ἔχοντες·
ἦ γὰρ ἐϋσχιδέων κεράων ὥρῃσι πεσόντων,
βόθρον μὲν κατὰ γαῖαν ὀρυξάμενοι κατέθαψαν,
ὄφρα κε μή τις ἕλῃσιν ἐπ᾽ αὔλακος ἀντιβολήσας·
κεύθονται δ᾽ αὐτοὶ πυμάτοις λασίοισί τε θάμνοις,
αἰδόμενοι θήρεσσι καρήατα τοῖα φανῆναι,
γυμνά, τά τοι προπάροιθε μετήορον ἀείροντο.
Ἀμφίβιοι δ᾽ ἔλαφοι· καὶ γὰρ τραφερὴν πατέουσι
καὶ πόντον περόωσιν,[1] ὁμόστολον ἀλλήλοισι
ναυτιλίην πλώοντες, ὅτ᾽ ἐξανύουσι θάλασσαν·
πρόσθε μὲν εἷς ἐλάφοισιν ἐπὶ στίχας ἡγεμονεύει,
οἷα κυβερνητὴρ μεθέπων οἰήϊα νηός·

[1] πατέουσι . . περόωσιν IK : other MSS. περόωσι . . πατέουσι.

---

[a] Contrary to the usual doctrine; A. 578 b 16 ποιεῖται τοὺς τόκους παρὰ τὰς ὁδοὺς διὰ τὸν πρὸς τὰ θηρία φόβον; 611 a 15 ἡ ἔλαφος οὐχ ἥκιστα δοκεῖ εἶναι φρόνιμον τῷ τε τίκτειν παρὰ τὰς ὁδούς (τὰ γὰρ θηρία διὰ τοὺς ἀνθρώπους οὐ προσέρχεται); Plin. viii. 112 in pariendo semitas minus cavent humanis vestigiis tritas quam secreta ac feris opportuna. *Cf.* Plut. *Mor.* 971 E; Antig. 29: Ael. vi. 11. Oppian seems to have confused the seclusion of the Hind after the birth of the young (A. 578 b 20; Antig. *l.c.*; Plin. viii. 113; Solin. xix. 10) with her behaviour at their birth, just as Ael. *l.c* καταπιανθεῖσα δὲ οὐκ ἂν ἔτι τέκοι παρὰ τὰς ὁδούς confuses this with the seclusion of the Stags when they have grown fat (A. 579 a 5; Plin. viii. 113).

[b] A. 611 a 25 ἀποβάλλουσι δὲ καὶ τὰ κέρατα ἐν τόποις χαλεποῖς καὶ δυσεξευρέτοις· ὅθεν καὶ ἡ παροιμία γέγονεν "οὗ αἱ ἔλαφοι τὰ κέρατα ἀποβάλλουσιν." ὥσπερ γὰρ τὰ ὅπλα ἀποβεβληκυῖαι φυλάττονται ὁρᾶσθαι; A. *Mirab.* 835 b 27; Antig. 20; Ael. iii. 17; Plin. viii. 115; Theophr. *fr.* 175.

[c] Ael. vi. 5 οἱ ἔλαφοι τὰ κέρατα ἀποβαλόντες εἰσδύνονται

avoids [a] the track of men, because the paths of mortals are profane to wild beasts.

Above all wild beasts the Stags of goodly horn plume themselves upon their beauty, having a rich and various growth of horn. Indeed when their branching horns in due season fall off, they dig a trench in the ground and bury them,[b] lest someone chance upon them in the furrow and take them, and themselves hide [c] in the depths of the dense thickets, ashamed that wild beasts should behold thus naked their heads that aforetime soared so high.

Deer are amphibious.[d] For they tread the solid earth and cross the deep, voyaging together in company when they travel over the sea.[e] One in front leads the Deer in line, even as a pilot handles the

παρελθόντες εἰς τὰς λόχμας . . . ἔρημοι γὰρ τῶν ἀμυντηρίων ὄντες ἀφῃρῆσθαι καὶ τὴν ἀλκὴν πεπιστεύκασιν; Plin. viii. 115 cornua mares habent solique animalium omnibus annis stato veris tempore amittunt, ideo sub ista die quam maxime invia petunt. Latent amissis velut inermes. *Cf.* A. *De Plant.* 818 b 25.

[d] In the popular sense. *Cf.* Plat. *Ax.* 368 c (of sailor) ὁ γὰρ ἐπίγειος ἄνθρωπος ὡς ἀμφίβιος αὑτὸν εἰς τὸ πέλαγος ἔρριψεν; Amm. Marc. xxii. 15. 14 Exuberat Aegyptus pecudibus multis, inter quas terrestres sunt et aquatiles: aliae quae humi et in humoribus vivunt unde ἀμφίβιοι; Colum. viii. 13 eas aves quas Graeci vocant ἀμφιβίους, quia non tantum terrestria sed aquatilia quoque desiderant pabula, nec magis humo quam stagno consueverunt. Eiusque generis anser . . .; G. White, *N. H. of Selborne*, xxix. "Quadrupeds that prey on fish are amphibious. Such is the otter"; Ael. xi. 37 ἀμφίβια δὲ ἵππος ποτάμιος, ἔνυδρος, κάστωρ, κροκόδειλος. In stricter sense Arist. *ap.* Athen. 306 b (Newt); *A.P.* vi. 43 (Frog). See A. 589 a 10; 566 b 27. A. does not use the term ἀμφίβιος (except *ap.* Athen. 306 b) but ἐπαμφοτερίζειν.

[e] Plin. viii. 114 maria trameant gregatim nantes porrecto ordine et capita imponentes praecedentium clunibus vicibusque ad terga redeuntes. *Cf.* Ael. v. 56; Solin. xix. 11.

τῷ δ' ἕτερος κατὰ νῶτον ἐρειδόμενος μετόπισθε
δειρὴν ἠδὲ κάρηνον ὁμαρτεῖ ποντοπορεύων·
ἄλλος δ' ἄλλον ἔπειτα φέρων τέμνουσι θάλασσαν.
ἀλλ' ὅτε νηχόμενον κάματος πρώτιστον ἕλῃσι,[1]
στοῖχον ὁ μὲν προλιπὼν ἔμολεν ποτὶ τέρμα φάλαγγος,
παύσατο δ' ἀγκλινθεὶς ἑτέρῳ βαιὸν καμάτοιο·
ἄλλος δ' αὖτ' οἴηκας ἔχων ἐπὶ πόντον ὁδεύει·
πάντες δὲ πλώοντες, ἀμοιβαδὶς ἡγεμονῆες,
ποσσὶ μὲν οἷα πλάταισιν ἐρέσσουσιν μέλαν ὕδωρ,
ὕψι δ' ἀνίσχονται κεράων πολυήρατον εἶδος,
οἷά τε λαίφεα νηὸς ἐπιτρέψαντες ἀήταις.
"Εχθος δ' ἀλλήλοισιν ἀνάρσιον αἰὲν ἔχουσι
πᾶν ὀφίων ἐλάφων τε γένος, πάντῃ δ' ἐρεείνει
οὔρεος ἐν βήσσῃς ἔλαφος θρασὺν ἑρπηστῆρα.
ἀλλ' ὅτ' ἴδῃ στροφάλιγξιν ὑφαινόμενον δολιχῇσιν
ἴχνος ὀφιόνεον, μέγα καγχαλόων ἀφικάνει
ἆσσον φωλειοῦ, ῥῖνας δ' ἐπεθήκατο χειῇ,
πνοιῇσι λάβρῃσιν ἐφελκόμενος ποτὶ δῆριν
ἑρπετὸν οὐλόμενον· τὸν δ' οὐκ ἐθέλοντα μάχεσθαι
ἆσθμα βιησάμενον μυχάτης ἐξείρυσεν εὐνῆς·
αἶψα γὰρ εἴσιδεν ἐχθρόν, ἐς αἰθέρα θ' ὑψόσ' ἀείρει
λευγαλέην δειρήν· λευκοὺς δ' ὑπέσηρεν ὀδόντας,
ὀξέα πεφρίκοντας· ἐπικροτέει δὲ γένειον
πυκνοῖς φυσιόων συρίγμασιν ἰοφόρος θήρ.
αὐτίκα δ' αὖτ' ἔλαφος, καὶ μειδιόωντι ἐοικώς,
δαιτρεύει στομάτεσσιν ἐτώσια δηριόωντα,
καί μιν ἑλισσόμενον περὶ γούνασιν ἀμφί τε δειρὴν
ἐμμενέως δάπτει· κατὰ δὲ χθονὶ πολλὰ κέχυνται
λείψανα παιφάσσοντα καὶ ἀσπαίροντα φόνοισι.

[1] v.l. ἔχῃσι.

helm of a ship. Another behind rests on his back his neck and head and so travels with him in his seafaring. And so in turn, one supporting another, they plough the sea. But when weariness overtakes the foremost swimmer, he leaves his rank and goes to the end of the line and resting on another takes a little respite from his toil, while another takes the helm and journeys over the deep. And all the swimmers leading in turn, they row the dark water with their feet as with oars, and hold aloft the varied beauty of their horns, submitting them, like the sails of a ship, to the breezes.

All the race of Snakes and Deer wage always bitter feud[a] with one another, and everywhere in the mountain glens the Deer seeks out the bold serpent. But when he sees the snaky trail woven with long coils, greatly exulting he draws nigh to the lair and puts his nostrils to the hole, with violent breath drawing the deadly reptile to battle. And the compelling blast hales him, very loth to fight, from the depth of his lair. For straightway the venomous beast beholds his foe and raises high in the air his baleful neck and bares his white teeth, bristling sharp, and snaps his jaws, blowing and hissing fast. And immediately in his turn the Deer, like one who smiles, rends with his mouth the vainly struggling foe, and, while he writhes about his knees and neck, devours him amain. And on the ground are shed many remains, quivering and writhing in death.

[a] Plin. viii. 118 Et his cum serpente pugna. Vestigant cavernas nariumque spiritu extrahunt renitentes. *Cf.* Ael. ii. 9, ix. 20; Phil. 59; Solin. xix. 15; Plut. *Mor.* 976 D ἐλάφοις δ' ὄφεις ἀγόμενοι ῥᾳδίως ὑπ' αὐτῶν· ᾗ καὶ τοὔνομα πεποίηται παρώνυμον οὐ τῆς ἐλαφρότητος ἀλλὰ τῆς ἕλξεως τοῦ ὄφεως; *E.M.* s. ἔλαφος.

καί κε τάχ᾽ οἰκτείρειας ἀπηνέα περ μάλ᾽ ἐόντα
ὠμηστῆρα ῥιφέντα πολυτμήτοισι φόνοισι.
Ἱπποβότου Λιβύης δ᾽ ἐπὶ τέρμασι πουλὺς ἀλᾶται
ἄσπετος οὐλόμενος στρατὸς αἰόλος ἑρπηστήρων·
ἀλλ᾽ ὅτε δὴ κλινθεὶς ἔλαφος ψαμαθώδεσιν ἄκραις
οἶος ἔῃ, τῷδ᾽ αὐτίκ᾽ ἐπέσσυτο πάντοθεν ἐχθρὸς
ἑσμὸς ἀπειρεσίων ὀφίων στυγεραί τε φάλαγγες
ἰοτόκοι· ῥινῷ δὲ πικροὺς ἐνέρεισαν ὀδόντας,
ἅψεα πάντ᾽ ἐλάφοιο περισταδὸν ἀμφιχυθέντες·
οἱ μὲν γάρ τ᾽, ἐφύπερθεν ἐπιστρέψαντε[1] κάρηνον,
ὀφρύας ἠδὲ μέτωπον ἐνιπρίουσι γένυσσιν,
οἱ δ᾽ ἄρα λεπταλέην δειρὴν καὶ στέρνον ἔνερθε
καὶ λαγόνας νηδύν τε διὰ στόμα δαιτρεύουσιν,
ἄλλοι δ᾽ αὖθ᾽ ἑκάτερθε περὶ πλευρῇσιν ἔχονται,
μηροὺς δ᾽ αὖθ᾽ ἕτεροι καὶ νῶτον ὕπερθε νέμονται,
ἄλλος δ᾽ ἄλλοθεν ἐχθρὰ πεπαρμένος ᾐώρηται.
αὐτὰρ ὁ παντοίῃσι περιπληθὴς ὀδύνῃσι
πρῶτα μὲν ἐκφυγέειν ἐθέλει κραιπνοῖσι πόδεσσιν,
ἀλλ᾽ οὐ κάρτος ἔχει· τοῖός μιν ἀθέσφατος ὄχλος
αἰόλος ἀμφιέπει δυσπαίπαλος ἑρπηστήρων.
δὴ τότε δὴ βαρύθων ἔστη κρατερῆς ὑπ᾽ ἀνάγκης,
δάπτει δὲ στομάτεσσιν ἀπείριτα δήϊα φῦλα
βεβρυχὼς ὀδύνῃσιν· ἐπιστροφάδην δ᾽ ἑκάτερθεν
οὐδὲν ἀλευόμενον γένος ἑρπετόεν κεραΐζει.
κεῖνοι δ᾽ οὐ μεθιᾶσι, διολλύμενοι δὲ μένουσιν,
ἄτροπον ἦτορ ἔχοντες ἀναιδείῃσι νόοιο·
καὶ τοὺς μὲν γενύεσσι διέσχισε, τοὺς δὲ πόδεσσι
καὶ χηλῇσιν ὄλεσσε, ῥέει δ᾽ ἐπὶ γαῖαν ἀτέρμων

[1] *v.l.* ἐπιτρέψαντε.

[a] A. 606 b 9 ἐν τῇ Λιβύῃ τὸ τῶν ὄφεων μέγεθος γίνεται ἄπλατον; Solin. xxvii. 28 Africa serpentibus adeo fecunda

Haply thou wouldst pity, unkindly though he be, the ravenous monster rent piecemeal with deadly wounds.

In the borders of Libya,[a] pasture land of horses, roams a great and countless host of deadly spotted Snakes. When a Stag lies down alone on the sandy hills, straightway upon him from every side rush the hostile swarm of Snakes beyond number and the hateful venomous ranks. In his hide they fix their bitter teeth, swarming around about all the limbs of the Stag. Some devote themselves to his head above and fix their teeth in brow and forehead; others rend with their mouths his slender neck and breast and his flanks and belly; others again cling to his ribs on either side; others feed on his thighs and back above; one here, one there, with deadly impalement they hang about him. And he, full of all manner of pain, first is fain to escape on swift feet, but he has not the strength; such an infinite crowd of cruel spotted snakes besets him. Then, oppressed by grievous constraint, he makes a stand and with his jaws he rends the infinite hostile tribes, bellowing the while for pain; and wheeling this way and that he makes havoc of the reptile race which make no endeavour to escape. Yet they do not let go their hold, but abide steadfast unto death, having a relentless mind and a heart not to be turned. And some he rends with his jaws; others he destroys with foot and hoof, and on the ground flows from the serpents

est ut mali huius merito illi potissimum palma detur. *Cf.* Herod. iv. 191 f. where he says ἔλαφος δὲ καὶ ὗς ἄγριος ἐν Λιβύῃ πάμπαν οὐκ ἔστι; A. 606 a 6 ἐν δὲ Λιβύῃ πάσῃ οὔτε σῦς ἄγριός ἐστιν οὔτ' ἔλαφος οὔτ' αἶξ ἄγριος; Ael. xvii. 10 ἐν Λιβύῃ συῶν ἀγρίων ἀπορία ἐστὶ καὶ ἐλάφων; Plin. viii. 120 Cervos Africa propemodum sola non gignit.

ἰχὼρ αἱματόεις ὀφίων ἄπο· γυῖα δὲ θηρῶν
ἄψεά θ' ἡμίβρωτα κατὰ χθονὸς ἀσπαίρουσιν·
ἄλλα δ' ἐνὶ πλευρῇς θλίβει πάλιν ἡμιδάϊκτα·
καὶ φθίμενοι γὰρ ἔχουσιν ἔτι κρατεροῖσιν ὀδοῦσι,
ῥινῷ δ' ἐμπεφυῶτα καρήατα μοῦνα μέμυκεν.
αὐτὰρ ὁ γινώσκων θεόθεν τόπερ ἔλλαχε δῶρον,
πάντῃ μαστεύει δνοφερὸν ποταμοῖο ῥέεθρον·
κεῖθεν καρκινάδας δὲ φίλαις γενύεσσι δαμάσσας
φάρμακον αὐτοδίδακτον ἔχει πολυπήμονος ἄτης·
αἶψα δὲ πικράων μὲν ἐπὶ χθόνα λείψανα θηρῶν
ἐξέπεσεν ῥινοῖο παραὶ πόδας αὐτοκύλιστα,
ὠτειλαὶ δ' ἑκάτερθεν ἐπιμύουσιν ὀδόντων.
Ζώει δ' αὖτ' ἔλαφος δηρὸν χρόνον· ἀτρεκέως δὲ
ἀνθρώπων γενεή μιν ἐφήμισε τετρακόρωνον.
Ἄλλους δ' αὖ καλέουσι βροτοὶ πάλιν εὐρυκέρωτας·
πάντ' ἔλαφοι τελέθουσι, φύσιν κεράων δ' ἐφύπερθεν,
οἵην τοὔνομα θηρσὶ κατηγορέει, φορέουσι.

---

[a] A. 611 a 18 καὶ ἐπὶ τὴν σέσελιν δὲ τρέχουσι, καὶ φαγοῦσαι οὕτως ἔρχονται πρὸς τὰ τέκνα πάλιν; 611 b 20 ὅταν δὲ δηχθῶσιν αἱ ἔλαφοι ὑπὸ φαλαγγίου ἤ τινος τοιούτου, τοὺς καρκίνους συλλέγουσαι ἐσθίουσιν; Cic. *De nat. deorum* ii. 50; Plin. viii. 112, xx. 37, xxv. 92; Ael. *V.H.* xiii. 35 λέγουσι φυσικοὶ ἄνδρες τὴν ἔλαφον καθάρσεως δεομένην σέσελιν ἐσθίειν, φαλαγγίων δὲ κνήσμασιν ἐχομένην καρκίνους.

[b] "The Highlanders assign a great age to the red deer; indeed they seem to suppose that it has no limit, save a rifle ball," St. John, *N. H., etc., in Moray*, p. 235. *Cf.* A. 578 b 23 περὶ δὲ τῆς ζωῆς μυθολογεῖται μὲν ὡς ὂν μακρόβιον, οὐ φαίνεται δ' οὔτε τῶν μυθολογουμένων οὐθὲν σαφές, ἥ τε κύησις καὶ ἡ αὔξησις τῶν νεβρῶν συμβαίνει οὐχ ὡς μακροβίου τοῦ ζῴου ὄντος; Plin. viii. 119; Solin. xix. 18; *A.P.* xi. 72 ἡ φάος ἀθρήσασ' ἐλάφου πλέον.

[c] Hesiod fr. 171 = Plut. *Mor.* 415 c ἐννέα τοι ζώει γενεὰς λακέρυζα κορώνη (Crow) | ἀνδρῶν ἡβώντων· ἔλαφος δέ τε τετρακόρωνος· | τρεῖς δ' ἐλάφους ὁ κόραξ (Raven) γηράσκεται; Plin. vii. 153; Auson. vii. 5; Arist. *Av.* 609 πέντ' ἀνδρῶν γενεὰς

an endless bloody stream, and the limbs and joints of the beasts half-devoured quiver upon the ground; others again upon his ribs he crushes half-dead; for even in death they still keep hold with their strong teeth and, clinging to his hide, their mere heads still groan. But he, knowing the gift that he hath gotten from Heaven, seeks everywhere for the dark stream of a river. Therefrom he kills crabs[a] with his jaws and so gets a self-taught remedy for his painful woe; and speedily the remnants of the cruel beasts fall from his hide of their own motion beside his feet, and the wounds of their teeth on either side close up.

The Stag, moreover, lives a long time,[b] and of a truth men say that he lives four lives of a crow.[c]

Others again men call Broad-horns.[d] They are altogether deer but they carry aloft such nature of horns as the name of the beast declares.

ζώει λακέρυζα κορώνη; Arat. 290 ἐννεάγηρα κορώνη. For longevity of Crow and Stag *cf.* Babr. xlvi. 8; Cic. *Tusc.* iii. 28. 69; of Crow *cf.* *A.P.* v. 288 ἡ γραῦς ἡ τρικόρωνος; Lucr. v. 1082; Hor. *C.* iii. 17. 13; Mart. x. 67. 5, etc.

[d] Fallow Deer, *Cervus dama*, M.G. πλατῶνι. "Le daim se trouve à l'état sauvage en Acarnanie dans la grande forêt Manina qui s'étend à l'ouest du fleuve Achélous jusqu'à Catouna, Il n'y est pas très-abondant et sa destruction est à craindre" (Bik. p. 18). εὐρύκερως, only here and *C.* iii. 2 (except as epithet Mosch. ii. 153), seems to be the same as πλατύκερως (Poll. v. 76) = *platyceros*, Plin. xi. 123 Nec alibi maior naturae lascivia. Lusit animalium armis; sparsit haec in ramos, ut cervorum; aliis simplicia tribuit, ut in eodem genere subulonibus ex argumento dictis; aliorum fudit in palmas digitosque emisit ex his, unde platycerotas vocant. The last of Pliny's three species points clearly to the palmated antlers of the Fallow Deer; his first species is the Red Deer, *Cervus elaphus*; his second apparently the Roe Deer, *Cervus capreolus*, the πρόξ of A. 506 a 22, 515 b 34, 520 b 24; *P.A.* 650 b 15; 676 b 27.

Τοὺς δ' ἄρα κικλήσκουσιν ἐνὶ ξυλόχοισιν ἰόρκους·
κἀκείνοις ἐλάφοιο δέμας, ῥινὸν δ' ἐπὶ νώτῳ
στικτὸν ἅπαντα φέρουσι παναίολον, οἶά τε θηρῶν
πορδαλίων σφραγῖδες ἐπὶ χροῒ μαρμαίρουσι.
Βούβαλος αὖτε πέλει μείων δέμας εὐρυκέρωτος,
μείων εὐρυκέρωτος, ἀτὰρ δόρκου μέγ' ἀρείων·
ὄμμασιν αἰγλήεις, ἐρατὸς χρόα, φαιδρὸς ἰδέσθαι·
καὶ κεράων ὀρθαὶ μὲν ἀπὸ κρατὸς πεφύασιν
ἀκρέμονες προτενεῖς, ὑψοῦ δ' αὖθις ποτὶ νῶτον
ἄψορρον νεύουσι παλιγνάμπτοισιν ἀκωκαῖς.
ἔξοχα δ' αὖ τόδε φῦλον ἑὸν δόμον ἀμφαγαπάζει
ἠθαλέας τ' εὐνὰς φίλιόν τε νάπεσσι μέλαθρον·
εἰ δέ τέ μιν στρεπτῇσι πεδήσαντες βροχίδεσσιν
ἀγρευτῆρες ἄγοιεν ἐπ' ἄλλους αὐτίκα χώρους,
τηλόθι δ' ἐν βήσσῃσιν ἐλεύθερον αὖθι λίποιεν,
ῥεῖα ποτὶ γλυκερὸν δόμον ἤλυθεν, ἧχι ναίεσκεν,
οὐδ' ἔτλη ξεῖνός τις ἐπ' ἀλλοδαποῖσιν ἀλᾶσθαι.
οὐκ ἄρα τοι μούνοισι φίλη πάτρη μερόπεσσι,
καὶ βαλίων δὲ πόθος τις ἐνέστακται φρεσὶ θηρῶν.
Ναὶ μὴν ὠκυτάτων δόρκων ἀρίδηλα γένεθλα
μορφήν τ' ἴδμεν ἅπαντες ὁμῶς μέγεθός τε καὶ ἀλκήν.

---

[a] The Roe Deer, *C. capreolus*, M.G. ζαρκάδι, "still found in Acarnania and on Parnassus, but not numerous" (Bik. p. 18). The form ἴορκος occurs only here and *C.* iii. 3; *cf.* Hes. *s.* ἴορκες· τῶν δορκάδων ζῴων· ἔνιοι δὲ ἡλικίαν ἐλάφου and *s.* ἴυρκες· αἶγες ἄγριαι. In Herod. iv. 192 ζορκάδες seem to be Gazelles: *cf.* Hesych. ζόρξ· ἡλικία ἐλάφου ἢ δορκός. The evidence is confusing but there seems reason to think that δορκάς was used in two senses, (1) = Gazelle, (2) = Roe Deer; *cf.* Ael. vii. 47 τάς γε μὴν δορκάδας καὶ ζόρκας καὶ πρόκας εἰώθασιν ὀνομάζειν; vii. 19.

[b] *Antilope* (*Alcelaphus*) *bubalis*. A. 515 b 34 and 516 a 5 (βουβαλίς); *P.A.* 663 a 11 (βούβαλος); *cf.* Strab. 827; Diod. ii. 51; Ael. v. 48, x. 25, xiii. 25; Plin. viii. 38 uros quibus

Other beasts in the woods they call Iorcus.[a] These also have the form of a deer, but on their back they have a hide, all various with spots, like the marks that twinkle upon the skin of the wild Leopards.

The Antelope[b] again is less in stature than the Broad-horn: less than the Broad-horn but far mightier than the Gazelle: bright of eye, lovely in colour, cheerful of aspect. Straight from the head spring the long branches of its horns but aloft they bend again toward the back with curved points. Above all others doth this race love its own home and its accustomed lair and its dear dwelling in the glades. Even if hunters bind it with twisted ropes and carry it straightway to other regions and far away in the glens leave it there to its freedom, easily doth it come to the sweet home where it used to dwell and endures not to wander as a stranger amid aliens. Not then to men alone is their native land dear, but even in the hearts of the dappled wild beasts is instilled a desire of home.

Furthermore we all know the conspicuous tribes of the most swift[c] Gazelles,[d] their beauty alike and their stature and their strength. The lustful[e] Part-

imperitum volgus bubalorum nomen imponit, cum id gignat Africa vituli potius cervique quadam similitudine.

[c] A. *P.A.* 663 a 11 (*προστέθεικεν ἡ φύσις*) *τάχος βουβάλοις καὶ δορκάσι*. *Cf.* Ael. xiv. 14.

[d] *Gazella dorcas* "is by far the most abundant of all the large game in Palestine" (Tristr. p. 129); A. 499 a 9 *τὰ δὲ τῶν ἱππελάφων κέρατα παραπλήσια τοῖς τῆς δορκάδος ἐστίν*; *P.A.* 663 b 26 *ἐλάχιστόν ἐστι τῶν γνωριζομένων (κερατοφόρων) δορκάς*.

[e] A. 488 b 3 *τὰ μὲν ἀφροδισιαστικά, οἷον τὸ τῶν περδίκων καὶ ἀλεκτρυόνων γένος*. *Cf.* 564 a 24 f., 613 b 25 f.; *G.A.* 746 b 1 etc.; Athen. 389 a *τὸ δὲ ζῷον ἐπὶ λαγνείας συμβολικῶς παρείληπται*; Ael. iii. 5, etc.; Antig. xxxix. 101; Plin. x. 100; Solin. vii. 30; Phil. 12; Dion. *De av.* i. 9.

πέρδικες θοῦροι δὲ πυρώπεες, αἰολόδειροι,
δόρκοισιν φιλίην παρὰ τέμπεσιν ἐσπείσαντο,
ἠθαλέοι τε πέλουσι καὶ ἀλλήλοισιν ὅμαυλοι,
εὐνάς τ᾽ ἐγγὺς ἔχουσι, καὶ οὐκ ἀπάνευθε νέμονται.
ἦ μάλα δὴ μετόπισθεν ἑταιρείης τάχα πικρῆς
καὶ φιλίης ἀπέλαυσαν ἀμειδέος, ὁππότε φῶτες
κερδαλέοι δειλοῖσιν ἐπίφρονα μητίσαιντο,
πέρδικας δόρκοισι φίλοις ἀπατήλια θέντες,
ἔμπαλι δ᾽ αὖ δόρκους ἑτάροις ἴσα περδίκεσσιν.
Αἰγῶν δ᾽ αὖτε πέλει προβάτων τε πανάγρια φῦλα
οὐ πολλὸν τούτων[1] ὀΐων λασίων τε χιμαιρῶν
μείζονες, ἀλλὰ θέειν κραιπνοὶ σθεναροί τε μάχεσθαι,
στρεπτοῖσιν κεφαλῆφι κορυσσόμενοι κεράεσσι.
κάρτος δ᾽ αὖτ᾽ ὀΐεσσιν ἐν ἀργαλέοισι μετώποις·
πολλάκι δ᾽ ὁρμηθέντες ἐνὶ ξυλόχοισιν ἔθηκαν
καὶ σύας αἰθυκτῆρας ἐπὶ χθονὸς ἀσπαίροντας.
ἔστι δ᾽ ὅτ᾽ ἀλλήλοισιν ἐναντίον ἀΐξαντες
μάρνανται· κρατερὸς δὲ πρὸς αἰθέρα δοῦπος ἱκάνει·
οὐδέ τ᾽ ἀλεύασθαι θέμις ἔπλετο δήϊον αὐτοῖς,
νίκην δ᾽ ἀλλήλοις φορέειν ἀτίνακτος ἀνάγκη
ἠὲ νέκυν κεῖσθαι· τοῖον σφίσι νεῖκος ὄρωρεν.
Αἰγάγροις δέ τίς ἐστι δι᾽ αὐτῶν αὐλὸς ὀδόντων
λεπταλέος πνοιῆς, κεράων μέσον, ἔνθεν ἔπειτα

[1] τούτων, *cf.* Schol. τούτων· ἤγουν τῶν ἡμέρων: τιθασῶν Koechly.

---

[a] "*Perdix graeca*, kettenweise auf allen Bergen der Cycladen, die Insel Syra ausgenommen, häufig. Auf letzterer sind die Steinhühner durch fortwährende Verfolgung der Ausrottung nahe. *Perdix cinerea*, auf den Cycladen gänzlich unbekannt." Erh. p. 60; *cf.* Bik. p. 49. "The commonest Partridge of the Holy Land is the Greek Partridge, a bird somewhat resembling our Red-

ridges,[a] fiery of eye and speckled of neck, make pact of friendship with the Gazelles[b] in the vales and are familiar with them and dwell with them and have their nests near them and do not range apart from them. Verily it may well be that afterward they reap bitter fruit of their companionship and laughterless profit of their friendship, when guileful men contrive a cunning device against the hapless creatures, setting the Partridges to decoy their friends the Gazelles and, in turn, setting the Gazelles in like manner to decoy their comrades the Partridges.

Again there are the wild tribes of Goats and Sheep. These are not much larger than our Sheep and shaggy Goats, but they are swift to run and strong to fight, armed as their heads are with twisted horns. The strength, moreover, of the Sheep lies in their terrible foreheads. Many a time in the woods they charge and lay rushing Boars writhing on the ground. Sometimes also they rush upon one another and do battle, and a mighty din reaches unto heaven. And it is not lawful for them to shun the foe, but unshakable constraint is upon them either to win the victory one over another or to lie dead: such strife arises between them.

And wild Goats have a slender channel for the breath[c] right through the teeth between the horns,

legged Partridge in plumage . . . but much larger" (Tristr. p. 225). *Perdix cinerea* is found in Epirus and Macedonia, Momms. p. 261.

[b] The friendship of Partridge and Deer is mentioned Dion. *De av.* i. 9.

[c] A. 492 a 14 Ἀλκμαίων οὐκ ἀληθῆ λέγει, φάμενος ἀναπνεῖν τὰς αἶγας κατὰ τὰ ὦτα [quoted G. White, *N. H. of Selborne*, Letter xiv.]; Plin. viii. 202 auribus eas spirare, non naribus, . . Archelaus auctor est. *Cf.* Ael. i. 53; Varro ii. 3. 5.

αὐτὴν ἐς κραδίην καὶ πνεύμονας εὐθὺς ἱκάνει·
εἰ δέ τις αἰγάγρου κηρὸν κέρασιν περιχεύοι,
ζωῆς ἐξέκλεισεν ὁδοὺς πνοιῆς τε διαύλους.
Ἔξοχα δ᾽ αὖ μήτηρ ἀταλοὺς ἔτι νηπιάχοντας
οὓς παῖδας κομέει· γήρᾳ δ᾽ ἔνι μητέρα παῖδες.
ὡς δὲ βροτοὶ γενέτην πεπεδημένον ἀργαλέοισι
γήραος ἐν δεσμοῖσι, πόδας βαρύν, ἅψεα ῥικνόν,
ἀβληχρὸν παλάμας, τρομερὸν δέμας, ὄψιν ἀμαυρόν,
ἀμφαγαπαζόμενοι περὶ δὴ περὶ πάμπαν ἔχουσι,
τινύμενοι κομιδὴν παιδοτροφίης ἀλεγεινῆς·
ὣς αἰγῶν κοῦροι φιλίους κομέουσι τοκῆας
γηραλέους, ὅτε δεσμὰ πολύστονα γυῖα πεδήσῃ·
βρώμην μέν τ᾽ ὀρέγουσιν ἐΰδροσον ἀνθεμόεσσαν,
δρεψάμενοι στομάτεσσι· ποτὸν δ᾽ ἄρα χείλεσιν ἄκροις
ἐκ ποταμοῦ φορέουσιν ἀφυσσάμενοι μέλαν ὕδωρ·
γλώσσῃ δ᾽ ἀμφιέποντες ὅλον χρόα φαιδρύνουσιν.
εἰ δέ νύ τοι βροχίδεσσι μόνην γενέτειραν ἀείραις,
αὐτίκα καὶ παλάμηφιν ἕλοις νεοθηλέας ἀμνούς·
τὴν μὲν γὰρ δοκέοις παῖδας μύθοισι δίεσθαι,
λισσομένην τοίοισιν ἀπόπροθι μηκηθμοῖσι·
φεύγετέ μοι, φίλα τέκνα, δυσαντέας ἀγρευτῆρας,
μή με λυγρὴν δμηθέντες ἀμήτορα μητέρα θῆτε.
τοῖα φάμεν δοκέοις· τοὺς δ᾽ ἑσταότας προπάροιθε
πρῶτα μὲν ἀείδειν στονόεν μέλος ἀμφὶ τεκούσῃ,
αὐτὰρ ἔπειτ᾽ ἐνέπειν φαίης μεροπήϊον ἠχήν,
ῥηξαμένους βληχήν, στομάτων τ᾽ ἄπο τοῖον ἀΰτεῖν,
φθεγγομένοις ἰκέλους καὶ λισσομένοισιν ὁμοίους·
πρός σε Διὸς λιτόμεσθα, πρὸς αὐτῆς Ἰοχεαίρης,
λύσεο μητέρα μοι φιλίην, τὰ δ᾽ ἄποινα δέδεξο,

whence again the channel goes straight to the very heart and lungs. If one pours wax about the horns of the wild Goat, he blocks the paths of its life and the channels of its breath.

Notable is the care which the dam among these takes for her tender young and which the children take for their mother in her old age. And even as among men, when a parent is fettered in the grievous bonds of old age—heavy of foot, crooked of limb, feeble of hand, palsied of body, dim of eye—his children cherish and attend him with utmost heed, repaying the care of their laborious rearing: so do the young of the Goats care for their dear parents in their old age, when sorrowful bonds fetter their limbs. They cull with their mouths and proffer them dewy food and flowery, and for drink they bring them dark water which they draw from the river with their lips, while with their tongues they tend and cleanse all their body. Didst thou but take the mother alone in a snare, straightway thou mightst take the young lambs with thy hands. For thou wouldst think that she was driving away her children with her words, entreating them afar with such bleatings as these: "Flee, children dear, the cruel hunters, lest ye be slain and make me your poor mother a mother no more!" Such words thou wouldst think she spoke, while they, standing before her, first sing, thou wouldst imagine, a mournful dirge about their mother, and then, breaking forth in bleating, speak in human accents and as if they used the speech of men and like as if they prayed, utter from their lips such language as this: "In the name of Zeus we pray thee, in the name of the Archer Maid herself, release to us our dear mother,

ὅσσα φέρειν δυνάμεσθα λυγροὶ περὶ μητέρι δειλῇ,
ἡμέας αἰνομόρους· γνάμψον τεὸν ἄγριον ἦτορ
αἰδόμενος μακάρων τε θέμιν γενέταό τε γῆρας,
εἴ ῥά νύ τοι γενέτης λιπαρὸν κατὰ δῶμα λέλειπται.
τοῖά τις ἂν δόξειε λιταζομένους ἀγορεύειν.
ἀλλ' ὅτε τευ κραδίην παναμείλιχον ἀθρήσωσιν,
αἰδὼς ὦ πόσση, πόσσος πόθος ἐστὶ τοκήων,
αὐτόδετοι βαίνουσι καὶ αὐτόμολοι περόωσι.
  Εἰσὶ δ' ὄϊς ξανθοὶ πυμάτης ἐνὶ τέρμασι Κρήτης,
ἐν χθαμαλῇ γαίῃ Γορτυνίδι, τετρακέρωτες·
λάχνη πορφυρόεσσα δ' ἐπὶ χροὸς ἐστεφάνωται
πολλή τ' οὐκ ἁπαλή τε· τάχ' αἰγὸς ἂν[1] ἀντιφερίζοι
τρηχυτάτῃ χαίτῃ δυσπαίπαλος, οὐκ ὀΐεσσι.
  Τοίην που καὶ σοῦβος ἔχει ξανθωπὸν ἰδέσθαι
χροιὴν μαρμαίρων, ἀτὰρ οὐκ ἔτι λαχνήεσσαν,
οὐδὲ πάλιν πισύρεσσιν ἀρηραμένην κεράεσσιν,
ἀλλὰ δυσὶ κρατεροῖς ὑπὲρ εὐρυτάτοιο μετώπου.
ἀμφίβιος καὶ σοῦβος, ἐπεὶ κἀκεῖνος ὁδεύει·
ὁππότε γὰρ ποτὶ βυσσὸν ἴῃ θοὰ κύματα τέμνων,
δὴ τότε πουλὺς ὅμιλος ὁμαρτῇ ποντοπορεύων
ἰχθυόεις ἕπεται, κατὰ δ' ἅψεα λιχμάζονται,
τερπόμενοι κερόεντι φίλῳ, τερενόχροϊ σούβῳ.
ἔξοχα δ' αὖ φάγροι τε καὶ οὐτιδανοὶ μελάνουροι

[1] ἂν αἰγὸς MSS. : corr. Turnebus.

[a] *Cf. Anecd. Ox.* iv. 267 ὁ σοῦβος ὡς πρόβατόν ἐστι ξανθὸν καὶ λεῖον. Unidentified. The name suggests the Hebrew צְבִי (the "roe" or "roebuck" of the A.V. Deut. xv. 22,

and accept a ransom, even all that we unhappy can offer for our poor mother—even our hapless selves. Bend thy cruel heart and have regard unto the law of Heaven and to the old age of a parent, if thou hast thyself an aged parent left in thy bright home." Such prayer might one fancy that they utter. But when they see that thy heart is altogether inexorable,—how great their regard, how great their love for their parents!—they come to bondage of their own accord and of their own motion pass the bourne.

Yellow Sheep there are in the bounds of utmost Crete, in the low land of Gortyn—Sheep with four horns; and bright wool is wreathed about their flesh—abundant wool but not soft: so rugged is it that it might compare with the roughest hair of Goats, not with the wool of Sheep.

Such yellow-coloured form has also the brilliant Subus,[a] but no longer shaggy nor again furnished with four horns but with two strong ones above amplest forehead. Amphibious too is the Subus; for he also walks upon the land; but when he travels to the deep and ploughs the swift waves, then a great company of fishes attends him and travels the sea along with him; and they lick his limbs and rejoice in their horned friend, the Subus of tender body. Above all the Braize[b] and the feeble

etc.) and one is reminded of Aelian's amphibious κεμάς (xiv. 14), where the context suggests some species of Gazelle. But Oppian's "Subus" seems to be a Sheep.

[b] One of the Sea-breams (*Sparidae*): either *Pagrus vulgaris*, M.G. μερτζάνι ("c'est un nom turc équivalent au grec ἐρύθρινος" Apost. p. 17) or *Dentex macrophthalmus*, M.G. φαγγρί. A. 598 a 13; 601 b 30; Athen. 300 e, 327 c; Ael. ix. 7, x. 19; Plin. xxxii. 125; Ov. *Hal.* 107 rutilus pagur.

καὶ ῥαφίδες τρίγλαι τε καὶ ἀστακοὶ ἀμφὶς ἕπονται.
θάμβος ἔφυ τόδε, θάμβος ἀθέσφατον, ὁππότε θῆρας
ἀλλοδαποὶ τείρουσι πόθοι καὶ ὑπείροχα φίλτρα.
οὐ γὰρ ἐπ' ἀλλήλοισι μόνον φιλότητος ἐΐσης
θεσμὸν ἀναγκαῖον δῶκεν θεός, οὐδ' ὅσον αὐτῶν
φῦλον ἀναλδήσκειν αἰειγενέος βιότοιο.
θαῦμα μὲν οὖν κἀκεῖνο δαμήμεναι ἄφρονα φῦλα
ἅμμασιν ἱμερτοῖς καὶ ὁμόγνια φίλτρα δαῆναι
καὶ πόθον οὐ νοέοντα ἐν ἀλλήλοισι κεράσσαι,
οἷάπερ ἀνθρώποισιν ἐπιφροσύνη τε νόος τε
ὀφθαλμοὺς ἐπέτασσεν ἔρον θ' ὑπεδέξατο θυμῷ·
ἀλλὰ καὶ ὀθνείοις ἐπεμήνατο ὑψόθι φίλτροις.
οἷος μὲν πόθος ἐστὶν ἀριζήλοις ἐλάφοισι
ἀτταγέων· ὅσσος δὲ τανυκραίροις ἐπὶ δόρκοις

---

[a] A Sea-bream, *Oblata melanura*, M.G. μελανοῦρι. A. 591 a 15; Athen. 313 d, 319 c, 320 e; Phil. 92; Plin. xxxii. 17 and 149; Colum. viii. 16; Ael. i. 41; Ov. *Hal.* 113 laude insignis caudae melanurus.

[b] The Gar-fish, *Belone acus*, M.G. βελονίδα, ζαργάνα: "très abondante depuis le mois d'août jusqu'à la fin d'Octobre" (Apost. p. 25): *cf. H.* i. 172, iii. 577, 605 f. ῥαφίς = βελόνη, *cf.* Athen. 319 d Δωρίων δ' ἐν τῷ περὶ ἰχθύων "βελόνην," φησίν, "ἣν καλοῦσιν ῥαφίδα." Ἀριστοτέλης δ' ἐν πέμπτῳ ζῴων μορίων βελόνην αὐτὴν καλεῖ. ἐν δὲ τῷ περὶ ζωικῶν ἢ ἰχθύων ῥαφίδα αὐτὴν ὀνομάσας ἀνόδουν φησὶν αὐτὴν εἶναι, καὶ Σπεύσιππος αὐτὴν βελόνην καλεῖ. In A. 506 b 9, 567 b 23, etc. βελόνη is *Syngnathus acus*, the Pipe-fish (Needle-fish), M.G. σακκοράφα, κατουρλίδα (Apost. p. 7), but in 610 b 6 it seems to be the Gar-fish. In *H.* iii. 608 Oppian's ῥαφίς has teeth, which suits the Gar-fish, while Athen. 305 d, 319 d says

Melanurus[a] and the Needle-fish[b] and the Red Mullet[c] and the Lobster[d] are attendant upon him. A marvel is this, a marvel unspeakable, when alien desires and strange loves distress wild beasts. For it is not alone for one another that God has given them the compelling ordinance of mutual love, nor only so far that their race should wax with everlasting life. That is, indeed, a marvel, that the brute tribes should be constrained by the bonds of desire and should know the passions of their own kind and, albeit without understanding should feel mutual desire for one another, even as for men thought and intelligence opens the eye and admits love to the heart; but the wild races are also highly stirred by the frenzy of alien desires. What a passion is that of the lordly Stag for the Francolin[e]! How great that of the Partridge for the long-horned Gazelle!

that Aristotle described the *ῥαφίς* as toothless, which suits *Syngnathus acus*.

[c] M.G. *τρίγλες*, *μπαρμπούνι(α)*, the Roman *mullus*, including *Mullus surmuletus* L. (M.G. *πετρόψαρο*, *τσιγαρόλια*), *M. fuscatus* Rafin. (M.G. *μπαρμπούνι*), *M. barbatus* L. (M.G. *κεφαλάδες*, from shape of head, which presents an almost vertical profile).

[d] *Homarus vulgaris*.

[e] *ἀτταγήν*, *ἀτταγᾶς*, *ἀτταβυγάς* (Hesych.), *ταγηνάριον* (Suid, who says it was abundant in Marathon), prob. *Tetrao francolinus* L. Not now found in Greece but resident in Asia Minor, esp. in the swampy regions (*τὰ λιμνώδη καὶ ἕλεια χωρία καταβόσκεται*, Suid. *s.v.*) of the S. (Momms. p. 261). "In the rich lowland plains, as of Gennesaret, Acre, and Phoenicia, the place of the Partridge is taken by the Francolin, a bird of the same family, . . . formerly found in S. Europe as far as Spain, but now quite extinct on this continent" (Tristr. p. 228); A. 617 b 25 *τὸ χρῶμα* (of the *ἀσκαλώπας*, Woodcock) *ὅμοιον ἀτταγῆνι*; 633 a 30 *ὅσοι μὴ πτητικοὶ ἀλλ' ἐπίγειοι, κονιστικοί, οἷον ἀλεκτορίς, πέρδιξ, ἀτταγήν*; Athen. 387 ff.; Ael. iv. 42, etc.; Plin. x. 133.

περδίκων· πῶς δ' αὖτε θοοῖς χαίρουσιν ἐφ' ἵπποις
ὠτίδες, αἷσι τέθηλεν ἀεὶ λασιώτατον οὖας·
ψιττακὸς αὖτε λύκος τε σὺν ἀλλήλοισι νέμονται·
αἰεὶ γὰρ ποθέουσι λύκοι ποεσίχροον ὄρνιν.
ὄβριμ' Ἔρως, πόσος ἐσσί, πόση σέθεν ἄπλετος ἀλκή,
πόσσα νοεῖς, πόσα κοιρανέεις, πόσα δαῖμον, ἀθύρεις!
γαῖα πέλει σταθερή, βελέεσσι δὲ σοῖσι δονεῖται·
ἄστατος ἔπλετο πόντος, ἀτὰρ σύ γε καὶ τὸν ἔπηξας·
ἦλθες ἐς αἰθέρα ἔδδεισεν δέ σε[1] μακρὸς Ὄλυμπος·
δειμαίνει δέ σε πάντα, καὶ οὐρανὸς εὐρὺς ὕπερθε
γαίης ὅσσα τ' ἔνερθε καὶ ἔθνεα λυγρὰ καμόντων,
οἳ Λήθης μὲν ἄφυσσαν ὑπὸ στόμα νηπαθὲς ὕδωρ
καὶ φύγον ἄλγεα πάντα, σὲ δ' εἰσέτι πεφρίκασι.
σῷ δὲ μένει καὶ τῆλε περᾷς, ὅσον οὔποτε λεύσσει
ἠέλιος φαέθων· σῷ δ' αὖ πυρὶ καὶ φάος εἴκει
δειμαῖνον, καὶ Ζηνὸς ὁμῶς εἴκουσι κεραυνοί.
τοίους, ἄγριε δαῖμον, ἔχεις πυρόεντας ὀϊστούς,
πευκεδανούς, μαλερούς, φθισόφρονας, οἰστρήεντας,
τηκεδόνα πνείοντας, ἀναλθέας, οἷσι καὶ αὐτοὺς
θῆρας ἀνεπτοίησας ἐπ' ἀζεύκτοισι πόθοισι.
θάμβος, ὅταν κερόεσσαν ἀχαϊνέην πτερόεντες

[1] So C_2K: most MSS. ἤλυθες εἰς αἰθῆρ', οἶδεν δέ σε.

[a] *Otis tarda* L., M.G. ἀγριόγαλλος. It seems to be becoming rarer in Greece, Momms. p. 263; Bik. p. 50; A. 509 a 4, 539 b 30, 563 a 29, etc.; Plin. x. 57 Proximae his

How again does the Bustard [a] of the shaggy ear [b] rejoice in the swift Horse! The Parrot [c] again and the Wolf herd together; for Wolves have ever a passion for the grass-hued [d] bird. Mighty Love, how great art thou! how infinite thy might! how many things dost thou devise and ordain, how many, mighty spirit, are thy sports! The earth is steadfast: yet is it shaken by thy shafts. Unstable is the sea: yet thou dost make it fast. Thou comest unto the upper air and high Olympus is afraid before thee. All things fear thee, the wide heaven above and all that is beneath the earth and the lamentable tribes of the dead, who, though they have drained with their lips the oblivious water of Lethe, still tremble before thee. By thy might thou dost pass afar, beyond what the shining sun doth ever behold: to thy fire even the light yields place for fear and the thunderbolts of Zeus likewise give place. Such fiery arrows, fierce spirit, hast thou—sharp, consuming, mind-destroying, maddening, whose melting breath knows no healing—wherewith thou dost stir even the very wild beasts to unmeet desires. A marvel it is when the winged Francolins leap on the spotted back of

(*i.e.* tetraonibus) sunt quas Hispania aves tardas appellat, Graecia ὠτίδας. For Bustard and Horse *cf.* Ael. ii. 28; Plut. *Mor.* 981 B; Athen. 390 f; Dion. *De av.* iii. 8.

[b] In ref. to the etymology ὠτίς from οὖς, ὠτός (ear).

[c] Species unknown; according to Prof. Alfred Newton "the Greeks could not have known *Psittacus Alexandri.*" A. 597 b 27; Arr. *Ind.* i. 15. 8; Paus. ii. 28. 1; Plin. x. 117; Ael. vi. 19, etc.

[d] Plin. *l.c.* viridem toto corpore, torque tantum miniato in cervice distinctam; Stat. *S.* ii. 4. 25 Psittacus ille plagae viridis regnator Eoae; Apul. *Flor.* 12 color psittaco viridis . . . nisi quod sola cervice distinguitur . . . cervicula eius circulo mineo velut aurea torqui . . . cingitur.

ἀτταγέες νώτοισιν ἐπὶ στικτοῖσι θορόντες
ἢ δόρκοις πέρδικες ἐπὶ πτερὰ πυκνὰ βαλόντες
ἱδρῶ ἀποψύχωσι, παρηγορέωσί τε θυμὸν
καύματος ἀζαλέοιο, λατυσσόμενοι πτερύγεσσιν·
ἢ ὁπότε προπάροιθεν ἴῃ καναχήποδος ἵππου
ὠτὶς ὀλισθαίνουσα δι᾽ ἠέρος ἱμερόεσσα,
σαργοὶ δ᾽ αἰπολίοισιν ἐπέχραον· ἀμφὶ δὲ σούβῳ
φῦλον ἅπαν νεπόδων τὸ πολύπλανον ἐπτοίηται,
ἕσπονται δ᾽ ἅμα πάντες, ὅτ᾽ ἄγρια κύματα τέμνει,
στείνονταί θ᾽ ἑκάτερθε γεγηθότες, ἀμφὶ δὲ πόντος
ἀφριάᾳ λευκῇσι τινασσόμενος πτερύγεσσιν·
αὐτὰρ ὅ γ᾽ οὐκ ἀλέγων ξείνης φιλίης πανάθεσμος,
εἰναλίους ἑτάρους δάπτει στομάτεσσι δαφοινοῖς
δαινύμενος· τοὶ δ᾽ αἶσαν ἐν ὀφθαλμοῖσιν ὁρῶντες,
οὐδ᾽ ὧς ἐχθαίρουσι καὶ οὐ λείπουσι φονῆα.
σοῦβε τάλαν, κακοεργέ, καὶ αὐτῷ σοὶ μετόπισθε
πόντιον ἀγρευτῆρες ἐπαρτυνέουσιν ὄλεθρον
καὶ δολερῷ περ ἐόντι καὶ ἰχθυφόνῳ τελέθοντι.
Ἔστι δέ τις δρυμοῖσι παρέστιος ὀξύκερως θήρ,
ἀγριόθυμος ὄρυξ, κρυερὸς θήρεσσι μάλιστα·

---

[a] A. 506 a 24 τῶν δ᾽ ἐλάφων αἱ ἀχαΐναι καλούμενοι δοκοῦσιν ἔχειν ἐν τῇ κέρκῳ χολήν (Antig. 70); 611 b 18 ἤδη δ᾽ εἴληπται ἀχαίνης ἔλαφος ἐπὶ τῶν κεράτων ἔχων κιττὸν πολὺν πεφυκότα χλωρόν, ὡς ἀπαλῶν ὄντων τῶν κεράτων ἐμφύντα ὥσπερ ἐν ξύλῳ χλωρῷ (Athen. 353 a; Antig. 29; Theophr. *C.P.* ii. 17). Apoll. Rh. iv. 174 ἐλάφοιο . . . ἥν τ᾽ ἀγρῶσται ἀχαιινέην καλέουσιν, where schol. Ἀχαία ἐστὶ τῆς Κρήτης πόλις ἐν ᾗ γίνονται ἀχαιίνεαι λεγόμεναι ἔλαφοι· αἳ καὶ σπαθίνειαι καλοῦνται· οἱ δὲ κέρατα μεγάλα ἔχοντες ἔλαφοι κερασταί; Eustath. *Il.* p. 711. 38 εἰ μὴ ἄρα αἱ ἀχαΐναι καὶ οἱ σπαθῖναι λεγόμενοι ἡλικίᾳ τινὶ διαφέρουσιν ἢ εἴδει καὶ κεράτων ἰδιότητι καὶ μεγέθει. Perhaps Brocket, a young male Deer in the spring of the year after its birth, when its antlers are straight and unbranched, may be sufficiently accurate: Latin *subulo*.

[b] *Sargus vulgaris*, M.G. σαργός; *S. Rondeletii*, M.G.

the horned Brocket[a] or Partridges wheel swiftly about the Gazelle and cool their sweat and comfort their hearts in the sweltering heat with the flapping of their wings; or when before a Horse of clattering hoof the Bustard goes, gliding delightful through the air; or when the Sargues[b] approach the herds of Goats. About the Subus, indeed, the whole wandering tribe of fishes is fluttered and all follow with him when he ploughs the wild waves and throng on either side for joy and the sea foams round about, lashed by their white fins. But he, recking not of their strange friendship, all lawlessly devours his companions of the sea and banquets on them with bloody jaws. And they, though seeing doom before their eyes, hate him not even so nor desert their slayer. Wretched Subus, worker of evil, for thine own self hereafter shall the hunters devise death by sea, crafty though thou art and slayer of fishes!

There is a certain sharp-horned beast that dwells in the thickets, even the fierce Oryx,[c] most formidable

σπάρος, etc., a Sea-bream; A. 543 a 7, 591 b 19; Athen. 313 d, 321 a; Plut. *Mor.* 977 F; Plin. ix. 162. For Sargues and Goats *cf. H.* iv. 308 ff.; Ennius *ap.* Apul. *Apol.* 60.

[c] *Oryx leucoryx* (the Sable Antelope) from Kordofan to the Syrian and Arabian deserts; and *O. beisa*, in Somaliland, etc.; both figured on Egyptian monuments. The latter species is distinguished by its black face and cheeks; *cf.* A. Bonnet, *L'Oryx dans l'ancienne Égypte*, Lyon, 1908. Plin. x. 201 orygem perpetuo sitientia Africae generant; *cf.* viii. 214; Iuv. xi. 140 Gaetulus oryx; Mart. xiii. 95 Matutinarum non ultima praeda ferarum Saevus oryx constat quod mihi morte canum? Herod. iv. 192 καὶ ὄρυες, τῶν τὰ κέρεα τοῖσι Φοίνιξι οἱ πήχεες ποιεῦνται (μέγαθος δὲ τὸ θηρίον κατὰ βοῦν ἐστί). We are not here concerned with the fabled Oryx of A. 499 b 20 μονόκερων καὶ διχαλὸν ὄρυξ; *cf. P.A.* 663 a 23; Plin. ii. 107, xi. 255 unicorne et bisulcum oryx; Ael. vii. 8, etc.; Plut. *Mor.* 974 F.

τοῦ δ' ἤτοι χροιὴ μὲν ἅτ' εἰαρινοῖο γάλακτος,
μούναις ἀμφὶ πρόσωπα μελαινομένῃσι παρειαῖς·
διπλὰ δέ οἱ μετόπισθε μετάφρενα πίονα δημῷ·
ὀξεῖαι κεράων δὲ μετήοροι ἀντέλλουσιν
αἰχμαὶ πευκεδαναί, μελανόχροον εἶδος ἔχουσαι,
καὶ χαλκοῦ θηκτοῖο σιδήρου τε κρυεροῖο
πέτρου τ' ὀκριόεντος ἀρειότεραι πεφύασιν·
ἰοφόρον κείνοις δὲ φύσιν κεράεσσι λέγουσι.
θυμὸς δ' αὖτ' ὀρύγεσσιν ὑπερφίαλος καὶ ἀπηνής·
οὔτε γὰρ εὐρίνοιο κυνὸς τρομέουσιν ὕλαγμα,
οὐ συὸς ἀγραύλοιο παρὰ σκοπέλοισι φρύαγμα,
οὐδὲ μὲν οὐ ταύρου κρατερὸν μύκημα φέβονται,
πορδαλίων δ' οὐ γῆρυν ἀμειδέα πεφρίκασιν,
οὐδ' αὐτοῦ φεύγουσι μέγα βρύχημα λέοντος,
οὐδὲ βροτῶν ἀλέγουσιν ἀναιδείῃσι νόοιο·
πολλάκι δ' ἐν κνημοῖσιν ἀπέφθιτο καρτερὸς ἀνὴρ
θηρητὴρ ὀρύγεσσι δαφοινοῖς ἀντιβολήσας.
ὁππότε δ' ἀθρήσειεν ὄρυξ κρατερόφρονα θῆρα,
ἢ σῦν χαυλιόδοντ' ἢ καρχαρόδοντα λέοντα
ἢ κρυερῶν ἄρκτων ὀλοὸν θράσος, αὐτίκ' ἄρ' αἴῃ
νευστάζων κεφαλήν τε μέτωπά τε πάμπαν ἐρείδει
τεινάμενος, πήξας τε παρὰ χθονὶ πικρὰ βέλεμνα
ἐσσύμενον μίμνει, τὸν δ' ὤλεσε πρῶτος ἐναίρων.
δόχμια γὰρ κλίνας βαιὸν κερόεντα μέτωπα,
τεύχεσιν ὀξυτέροις δεδοκημένος ἔμπεσε θηρί·
αὐτὰρ ὅ γ' οὐκ ἀλέγει, κατὰ δ' ἄσχετον ἰθὺς ὀρούει,
ὀξέσι πεφρικὼς συνερειδόμενος σκολόπεσσιν.
ὡς δ' ὅτ' ἐνὶ ξυλόχοισιν ἐπεσσυμένοιο λέοντος,
'Αρτέμιδος δώροισι κεκασμένος ἄλκιμος ἀνήρ,
αἰχμὴν ἀστράπτουσαν ἔχων κρατερῇς παλάμῃσιν,
εὖ διαβὰς μίμνῃ, τὸν δ' ἄγρια θυμαίνοντα

[a] "The horns, often exceeding three feet in length, though

to wild beasts. His colour is even as that of milk in spring, only the cheeks about his face being black. He has a double back, rich in fat. Sharp rise aloft the piercing points of his horns, black of hue, which are mightier than whetted bronze or chilly iron or jagged rock, and men say that those horns have a venomous nature. The spirit of the Oryx is overweening and stern. For they tremble neither at the yelping of the keen-scented Hound nor at the snorting of the wild Boar among the rocks, neither do they fear the mighty bellowing of the Bull nor shudder at the mirthless cry of the Leopard nor the mighty roar of the Lion himself, nor in the dauntlessness of their heart do they care aught for men: many a time a mighty hunter has perished[a] on the hills when he has encountered the deadly Oryxes. When the Oryx descries a valiant wild beast, a tusked Boar or a saw-toothed[b] Lion or chilly Bear of deadly courage, straightway he bows to earth and holds steadfast his outstretched head and brows, and fixing close to the ground his sharp weapons, awaits the onset of the foe and strikes him first and slays. For bending a little aside his horned brows he watches and springs with his sharper weapons on the beast; which, heeding not, rushes incontinently straight on and horribly clashes with the sharp palisade of his horns. As when in the thickets, as a Lion charges, a valiant man, who is skilled in the gifts of Artemis, holding in his hands his flashing spear, with feet set well apart, awaits him, and, as he rages

so recurved are a formidable weapon of offence, and when wounded and brought to bay, it will frequently pierce the hunter by a sudden and well-directed blow" (Tristr. p. 58). Diod. iii. 27 (certain Ethiopians) ὅπλοις ἀμυντηρίοις χρώμενοι τοῖς τῶν ὀρύγων κέρασι.

[b] *C.* iii. 5 n.

δέξηται προβλῆτα φέρων ἀμφήκεα χαλκόν·
ὣς ὄρυγες μίμνουσιν ἐπεσσυμένους τότε θῆρας,
αὐτοφόνους σφετέρῃσιν ἀτασθαλίῃσι δαμέντας·
ῥεῖα γὰρ ἐν στέρνοισιν ὀλισθαίνουσιν ἀκωκαί·
πολλὸν δ' αἷμα κελαινὸν ἀπ' ὠτειλῶν ἑκάτερθεν
ἐκχύμενον γλώσσῃσιν ἑὸν τάχα λιχμάζουσιν·
οὐδὲ μὲν ἐκφυγέειν οὐδ' ἱεμένοισι πάρεστιν·
ἀλλήλους δ' ὀλέκουσιν ἀμοιβαίοισι φόνοισι.
καί κέ τις ἀγρονόμων ἢ βουκόλος ἤ τις ἀροτρεύς,
ἀμφιδύμοις νεκύεσσι παραὶ ποσὶν ἀντιβολήσας,
ἄγρην εὐάντητον ἔχει μεγαθαμβέϊ θυμῷ.
Ἑξείης ἐνὶ θηρσὶ κερατοφόροισι γένεθλα
ἀείδειν ἐπέοικεν ἀπειρεσίων ἐλεφάντων·
κεῖνα γὰρ ἐν γενύεσσιν ὑπέρβια τεύχεα δοιά,
εἴκελα χαυλιόδουσιν ἐπ' οὐρανὸν ἀντέλλοντα,
ἄλλοι μὲν πλήθους ὀλοοὺς ἐνέπουσιν ὀδόντας
πλαζόμενοι, νῶϊν δὲ κεράατα μυθήσασθαι
εὔαδεν· ὧδε γὰρ ἄμμι φύσις κεράων ἀγορεύει.
σήματα δ' οὐκ ἀΐδηλα διακριδὰ τεκμήρασθαι·
θηρσὶ γὰρ ἐκφύσιες γενύων ἀπὸ τῶν ἐφύπερθεν
ὅσσαι μὲν κερόεσσαι ἀνωφερὲς ἀΐσσουσιν·
εἰ δὲ κάτω νεύοιεν, ἀτεχνῶς εἰσὶν ὀδόντες.
κείνοισιν δὲ διπλοῖς ἐλεφαντείοις κεράεσσι
ῥίζαι μὲν πρώτιστον ἀπὸ κρατὸς πεφύασιν

---

[a] Ael. iv. 31 ὁ ἐλέφας, οἱ μὲν αὐτοῦ προκύπτειν χαυλιόδοντάς φασι, οἱ δὲ κέρατα; xi. 37 τὸν ἐλέφαντα οὔ φημι ὀδόντας ἔχειν ἀλλὰ κέρατα; Cramer, *Anec.* iii. 357 οὓς ἐπὶ τῶν ἐλεφάντων οὐκ ὀδόντας ἀλλὰ κέρατα καλοῦσιν; Plin. viii. 7 armis suis quae Iuba cornua appellat, Herodotus (iii. 97 ἐλέφαντος ὀδόντας μεγάλους εἴκοσι) tanto antiquior et consuetudo melius dentes; A. 501 b 30 ὀδόντας μὲν ἔχει τέτταρας ἐφ' ἑκάτερα . . . χωρὶς δὲ τούτων ἄλλους δύο τοὺς μεγάλους; Philostr. *Vit. Apollon.*

wildly, receives him with his two-edged brazen spear advanced: even so the Oryxes in that hour await the charge of the wild beasts, who are self-slain by their own folly. For the points of the horns glide easily into their breasts, and much dark blood, pouring on either side from their wounds—their own blood—they speedily lick with their tongues; nor can they escape if they would, but they slay one another with mutual slaughter. And some countryman, a herdsman or a ploughman, chancing on the two corpses at his feet, with marvelling heart wins a welcome prey.

Next in order among horned wild beasts it is meet to sing the tribes of the Elephant infinite in size. Those two mighty weapons in their jaws, which rise like tusks towards the heavens, others of the vulgar herd call deadly teeth; wherein they err: we are pleased to name them horns[a]; for so the nature of horns declares to us. Not obscure are the signs whereby they may be distinguished. For such growths from the upper jaws of wild beasts as are horny, spring upward: if they incline downward, they are certainly teeth.[b] Of those two horns of the Elephant the roots first of all spring from the head,

ii. 12 *οὗτος ὁ Ἰόβας τοὺς ὀδόντας κέρατα ἡγεῖται τῷ φύεσθαι μὲν αὐτοὺς ὅθενπερ οἱ κρόταφοι, παραθήγεσθαι δὲ μηδενὶ ἑτέρῳ, μένειν δ' ὡς ἔφυσαν καὶ μή, ὅπερ οἱ ὀδόντες, ἐκπίπτειν εἶτ' ἀναφύεσθαι· ἐγὼ δ' οὐ προσδέχομαι τὸν λόγον.* Pausan. *l.c.* says just the reverse: *κέρατα γὰρ κατὰ ἐτῶν περίοδον ἀπογίνεται καὶ αὖθις ἐκβλαστάνει ζῴοις, καὶ τοῦτο ἔλαφοί τε καὶ δορκάδες, ὡσαύτως δὲ καὶ οἱ ἐλέφαντες πεπόνθασιν. ὀδοὺς δὲ οὐκ ἔστιν ὅτῳ δεύτερα παρέσται τῶν γε ἤδη τελείων· εἰ δε ὀδόντες τὰ διὰ τοῦ στόματος ἐξίσχοντα καὶ μὴ κέρατα ἦσαν, πῶς ἂν καὶ ἀνεφύοντο αὖθις;*

[b] Pausan. v. 12 (arguing that the tusks are horns) *ποταμίοις γε μὴν ἵπποις καὶ ὑσὶν ἡ κάτωθεν γένυς τοὺς χαυλιόδοντας φέρει, κέρατα δὲ ἀναφυόμενα ὁρῶμεν ἐκ γενύων.*

ἐκ μεγάλου μεγάλαι, φηγῶν ἅτε· νέρθε δ' ἔπειτα
κρυπτόμεναι ῥινοῖσιν ὁμιλοῦσαι κροτάφοισιν
ἐς γένυν ὠθεῦνται· γενύων δ' ἀπογυμνωθεῖσαι
ψευδέα τοῖς πολλοῖσι δόκησιν ὄπασσαν ὀδόντων.
ναὶ μὴν ἄλλο βροτοῖσιν ἀριφραδὲς ἔπλετο σῆμα·
πάντες γὰρ θήρεσσιν ἀκαμπέες εἰσὶν ὀδόντες,
οὐδὲ τέχναις εἴκουσιν, ἀμείλικτοι δὲ μένουσι·
τοὺς σοφίῃ τεῦξαι κεραοξόος ἣν ἐθέλῃσιν
εὐρέας, ἀντιλέγουσιν ἀπηλεγές· ἢν δὲ βιῶνται,
ἄγνυνται καυληδὸν ἀπειθέες· ἐκ δὲ κεράων
τόξα τε κυκλοτερῆ καὶ μυρία τεύχεται ἔργα·
ὣς δὲ κεράατα κεῖνα, τά τοι καλέουσιν ὀδόντας,
γνάμπτειν εὐρύνειν τ' ἐλεφαντοτόμοις ὑποείκει.
Θηρσὶ δέ τοι μέγεθος μὲν ὅσον μήπω κατὰ γαίης
ἄλλος θὴρ φορέει· φαίης κεν ἰδὼν ἐλέφαντα
ἢ κορυφὴν ὄρεος παναπείριτον ἢ νέφος αἰνὸν
χεῖμα φέρον δειλοῖσι βροτῶν ἐπὶ χέρσον ὁδεύειν.
ἴφθιμον δὲ κάρηνον ἐπ' οὔασι βαιοτέροισι,
κοίλοισι, ξεστοῖς· ἀτὰρ ὀφθαλμοὶ τελέθουσι
μείονες ἢ κατ' ἐκεῖνο δέμας, μεγάλοι περ ἐόντες.
τῶν δ' ἤτοι μεσσηγὺς ὑπεκπροθέει μεγάλη ῥίς,
λεπτή τε σκολιή τε, προβοσκίδα τὴν καλέουσι.
κείνη θηρὸς ἔφυ παλάμη· κείνῃ τὰ θέλουσι
ῥηϊδίως ἔρδουσι. ποδῶν γε μὲν οὐκ ἴσα μέτρα·
ὑψόθι γὰρ οἱ πρόσθε πολὺ πλέον ἀείρονται.
ῥινὸς δ' αὖτε δέμας δυσπαίπαλος ἀμφιβέβηκεν,
ἄσχιστος κρατερός τε, τὸν οὔ κε μάλ' οὐδὲ κραταιὸς

---

[a] Pausan. *ibid.* ἐλέφαντι οὖν τὰ κέρατα ἴστω τις διὰ κροτάφων κατερχόμενα ἄνωθεν καὶ οὕτως ἐς τὸ ἐκτὸς ἐπιστρέφοντα. τοῦτο οὐκ ἀκοὴν γράφω, θεασάμενος δὲ ἐλέφαντος ἐν γῇ τῇ Καμπανῶν κρανίον ἐν Ἀρτέμιδος ἱερῷ.

[b] Pausan. *l.c.* οὐ μὴν οὐδὲ εἴκειν πυρὶ ἔχουσιν ὀδόντες φύσιν·

mighty as the head is mighty, even as the roots of the oak; then below, concealed by skin where they meet the temples, they project into the jaw; and when left bare by the jaws they give to the vulgar the false impression of teeth.[a] Moreover, there is another clear sign for men. All teeth of wild beasts are unbending and do not yield to art but remain intractable, and if a worker in horn wishes by his skill to make them broad, they flatly refuse, and if they are forced, the stubborn teeth break stemwise. From horns on the other hand are fashioned bent bows and countless other works of art. In like manner those elephant horns which men call teeth, yield to the ivory-cutter to bend them or to broaden.[b]

These beasts have a bulk such as on the earth no other wild beast yet hath worn. Seeing an Elephant thou wouldst say that a huge mountain-peak or a dread cloud, fraught with storm for hapless mortals, was travelling on the land. The head is strong with ears small, hollow, and polished. The eyes, though large, are small for that size of beast. Between them projects a great nose, thin and crooked, which men call the proboscis. That is the hand[c] of the beast; with it they easily do whatsoever they will. The legs are not equal[d] in size; for the fore-legs rise to a far greater height. The hide that covers the body is rugged, impenetrable and strong, which not

κέρατα δὲ καὶ βοῶν καὶ ἐλεφάντων ἐς ὁμαλές τε ἐκ περιφεροῦς καὶ ἐς ἄλλα ὑπὸ πυρὸς ἄγεται σχήματα.

[c] A. 497 b 26 *ἔχει μυκτῆρα τοιοῦτον . . . ὥστε ἀντὶ χειρῶν ἔχειν αὐτόν*; Ael. iv. 31 *μυκτῆρα . . . χειρὸς πανχρηστότερον*; *cf.* ii. 11; Plut. *Mor.* 972 D *προβοσκίδα . . . ὥσπερ χεῖρα παραβαλών*; Plin. viii. 29 spirant et bibunt odoranturque haud improprie dicta manu; *ibid.* 34; Phil. 40.

[d] A. 497 b 24 *τὰ πρόσθια σκέλη πολλῷ μείζω*; *cf.* Ael. iv. 31.

θηκτὸς πανδαμάτωρ τε διατμήξειε σίδηρος.
θυμὸς ἀπειρέσιος πέλεται κατὰ δάσκιον ὕλην
ἄγριος· ἐν δὲ βροτοῖς τιθασὸς μερόπεσσι τ' ἐνηής.
ἐν μὲν ἄρα χλοερῇσι πολυκνήμοισί τε βήσσαις
καὶ φηγοὺς κοτίνους τε καὶ ὑψικάρηνα γένεθλα
φοινίκων πρόρριζα κατὰ χθονὸς ἐξετάνυσσεν,
ἐγχρίμψας θηκτῇσιν ἀπειρεσίαις γενύεσσιν·
ὁππότε δ' ἐν μερόπων βριαρῇσι πέλει παλάμῃσι,
λήθετο μὲν θυμοῖο, λίπεν δέ μιν ἄγριον ἦτορ·
ἔτλη καὶ ζεύγλην καὶ χείλεσι δέκτο χαλινὰ
καὶ παῖδας νώτοισι φέρει σημάντορας ἔργων.
Φήμη δ' ὡς ἐλέφαντες ἐπ' ἀλλήλοις λαλέουσι,
φθογγὴν ἐκ στομάτων μεροπηΐδα τονθρύζοντες·
ἀλλ' οὐ πᾶσιν ἀκουστὸς ἔφυ θήρειος αὐτή,
κεῖνοι[1] δ' εἰσαΐουσι μόνον τιθασεύτορες ἄνδρες.
θαῦμα δὲ καὶ τόδ' ἄκουσα, κραταιοτάτους ἐλέφαντας
μαντικὸν ἐν στήθεσσιν ἔχειν κέαρ, ἀμφὶ δὲ θυμῷ
γινώσκειν σφετέροιο μόρου παρεοῦσαν ἀνάγκην.
οὐκ ἄρα τοι μούνοισιν ἐν ὀρνίθεσσιν ἔασι
κύκνοι μαντιπόλοι γόον ὕστατον ἀείδοντες,
ἀλλὰ καὶ ἐν θήρεσσιν ἑὴν θανάτοιο τελευτὴν
φρασσάμενοι τόδε φῦλον ἰήλεμον ἐντύνουσι.
Ῥινοκέρως δ' ὄρυγος μὲν ἔφυ δέμας αἰθυκτῆρος
οὐ πολλὸν μείζων, ὀλίγον δ' ὑπὲρ ἄκρια ῥινὸς
ἀντέλλει κέρας αἰνόν, ἀκαχμένον, ἄγριον ἆορ·
κείνῳ μὲν χαλκόν τε διατρήσειεν ὀρούσας,
οὐτήσας βριαρήν τε διατμήξειε χαράδρην.

[1] κείνης Brodaeus.

even a whetted blade of mighty all-subduing iron would easily cleave. Wild without limit is the temper of the Elephant in the shady wood but among men he is tame and gentle to human kind. In the green glens of many cliffs he stretches root and branch upon the ground, oaks and wild olives and the high-crowned race of palms, assailing them with his sharp tremendous tusks; but when he is in the strong hands of men, he forgets his temper and his fierce spirit leaves him: he endures even the yoke and receives the bit in his mouth and carries upon his back[a] the boys who order his work.

It is said that Elephants talk to one another, mumbling with their mouths the speech of men. But not to all is the speech of the beasts audible, but only the men who tame them hear it. This marvel also have I heard, that the mighty Elephants have a prophetic soul within their breasts and know in their hearts when their inevitable doom is at hand. Not then among birds only are there prophets, even the Swans[b] who sing their last lament, but among wild beasts also this tribe divine the end of death and perform their own dirge.

The Rhinoceros[c] is not much larger than the bounding Oryx. A little above the tip of the nose rises a horn dread and sharp, a cruel sword. Charging therewith he could pierce through bronze and with its stroke could cleave a mighty ravine. He attacks

[a] A. 497 b 28; Ael. vii. 41, xiii. 9.

[b] Plato, *Phaed.* 84 E; Aesch. *Ag.* 1444; Ael. ii. 32, v. 34, x. 36; Phil. 10; Mart. xiii. 77; Stat. *S.* ii. 4. 10.

[c] *Rhinoceros indicus*, *cf.* Agatharch. *ap.* Phot. p. 455 a 29 Bekker; Strab. 774; Diod. iii. 34; Athen. 201 c; Ael. xvii. 44; Plin. viii. 71; Suet. *Aug.* 43; Solin. xxvii. 16, xxx. 21; Mart. *Lib. Spect.* ix. xxii.

κεῖνος καὶ σθεναρῷ περ ἐφορμηθεὶς ἐλέφαντι
πολλάκις ἐν κονίῃσι νέκυν τοιοῦτον ἔθηκεν.
ἠρέμα δὲ ξανθοῖς ἐπὶ καλλικόμοισι μετώποις
καὶ νώτῳ ῥαθάμιγγες ἐπήτριμα πορφύρουσι.
πάντες δ' ἄρρενές εἰσι καὶ οὔποτε θῆλυς ὁρᾶται·
καὶ πόθεν, οὐκ ἐδάην, φράζω δ' οὖν[1] ὡς δεδάηκα,
εἴτ' οὖν ἐκ πέτρης ὀλοὸν τόδε φῦλον ἐπῆλθεν,
εἴτ' αὐτόχθονές εἰσιν, ἐπαντέλλουσι δὲ γαίης,
εἴτε πρὸς ἀλλήλων, τέρας ἄγριον, ἐκφύονται
νόσφι πόθων καὶ νόσφι γάμων καὶ νόσφι τόκοιο.
ἤδη καὶ διεροῖσιν ἐν ὑγροπόροιο θαλάσσης
βένθεσιν αὐτόρρεκτα φύει καὶ ἀμήτορα φῦλα,
ὄστρεά[2] τ'[3] ἠπεδαναί τ' ἀφύαι κόχλων τε γένεθλα
ὄστρακά τε στρόμβοι τε, τά τε ψαμάθοισι φύονται.
Μοῦσα φίλη, βαιῶν οὔ μοι θέμις ἀμφὶς ἀείδειν·
οὐτιδανοὺς λίπε θῆρας, ὅσοις μὴ κάρτος ὀπηδεῖ,
πάνθηρας χαροποὺς ἠδ' αἰλούρους κακοεργούς,

[1] οὐχ most MSS. : corr. Brunck.
[2] ὄστρεον BCDE : ὀστρέων FHM.
[3] τ' after ὄστρεα Schneider, om. MSS.

---

[a] Diod. iii. 34 τοῦτο (the Rhinoceros) περὶ τῆς νομῆς ἀεὶ διαφερόμενον ἐλέφαντι τὸ μὲν κέρας πρός τινας τῶν μειζόνων πετρῶν θήγει, συμπεσὸν δ' εἰς μάχην τῷ προειρημένῳ θηρίῳ καὶ ὑποδῦνον ὑπὸ τὴν κοιλίαν ἀναρρήττει τῷ κέρατι, καθάπερ ξίφει, τὴν σάρκα. τῷ δὲ τοιούτῳ τρόπῳ τῆς μάχης χρώμενον ἔξαιμα ποιεῖ τὰ θηρία καὶ πολλὰ διαφθείρει. ὅταν δὲ ὁ ἐλέφας, φθάσας τὴν ὑπὸ τὴν κοιλίαν ὑπόδυσιν, τῇ προβοσκίδι προκαταλάβηται τὸν ῥινόκερων, περιγίνεται ῥᾳδίως, τύπτων τοῖς ὀδοῦσι (*i.e.* tusks) καὶ τῇ βίᾳ πλέον ἰσχύων. Similar account in Strabo, Plin., Ael., Solin. *ll. cc.* Pausan. v. 12 οἱ δὲ Αἰθιοπικοὶ ταῦροι τὰ κέρατα φύουσιν ἐπὶ τῇ ῥινί seems to mean the Rhinoceros.

[b] Diod. *l.c.* τὴν χροὰν πυξοειδῆ. Plin. *l.c.* and Solin. xxx. 21 color buxeus. On the other hand Strab. *l.c.* οὐδὲ πύξῳ τὸ χρῶμα ἐμφερὲς ἀλλ' ἐλέφαντι μᾶλλον.

[c] *Cf. H.* i. 762 ff. where the examples of spontaneous generation given are ὄστρεα σύμπαντα and ἀφύη. The present

the Elephant[a] strong though it be and many a time lays so mighty a beast dead in the dust. On his yellowish,[b] hairy brows and on his back dense spots show darkly. All the breed are males and a female is never seen. Whence they come I know not, but I speak as I have learnt, whether this deadly race springs from the rock or whether they are children of the soil and spring from the ground, or whether the wild monsters are begotten of one another, without desire and without mating and without birth. Even in the wet depths of the sea with its watery ways there are tribes which come into being self-made and motherless[c]—Oysters and feeble Fry and the races of Sea-snails and Testacea and Spiral-shells and all that grow in the sands.

Dear Muse, it is not meet for me to sing of small creatures. Leave thou the feeble beasts which have no strength in them—the grey-eyed Panthers[d] and

list is unintelligible. If ὄστρακα = ὀστρακόδερμα, then the term is either equivalent to or includes ὄστρεα (according as that word is used in a wider or narrower sense), as it also includes κόχλοι (A. 527 b 35 τὰ ὀστρακόδερμα τῶν ζῴων, οἷον . . . οἱ κόχλοι καὶ πάντα τὰ καλούμενα ὄστρεα) and στρόμβοι, whether that term be specific or generic (*i.e.* = τὰ στρομβώδη)—in which case it includes κόχλοι (A. 528 a 10 ὁ κόχλος καὶ τἆλλα τὰ στρομβώδη; *cf. P.A.* 679 b 14). If we ventured to substitute, for ὄστρεα, κεστρέων or κέστρεα (for the spontaneous generation of which *cf.* A. 543 b 17, 569 a 17 etc.; Athen. 306 F) and, for ὄστρακα, ὄστρεα, we should get a more intelligible text.

[d] See *C.* iii. 63 n. Clearly to Oppian πάνθηρ denotes a smaller animal than πόρδαλις. According to Wiegmann (in Oken's *Isis* (1831), pp. 282 ff.) πάνθηρ = ***Felis uncia***, the Ounce or Snow Leopard. It is confined to the highlands of Central Asia; *cf.* Plin. viii. 63 Nunc varias et pardos, qua mares sunt, appellant in eo omni genere creberrimo in Africa Syriaque. Quidam ab his pantheras candore solo discernunt, nec adhuc aliam differentiam inveni; A. 280 a 25.

τοί τε κατοικιδίῃσιν ἐφωπλίσσαντο καλιαῖς,
καὶ τυτθοὺς ἀταλοὺς ὀλιγοδρανέας τε μυωξούς·
τοὶ δ' ἤτοι σύμπασαν ἐπιμύουσι μένοντες
χειμερίην ὥρην, δέμας ὕπνοισιν μεθύοντες·
δύσμοροι, οὔτε βορὴν ἑλέειν, οὐ φέγγος ἰδέσθαι·
φωλειοῖσι δ' ἑοῖς ὕπνον τοσσοῦτον ἔχουσιν,
ἧς νέκυες κεῖνται, δυσχείμερον οἶτον ἑλόντες.
αὐτὰρ ἐπὴν ἔαρος πρῶται γελάσωσιν ὀπωπαί,
ἄνθεά τ' ἐν λειμῶσι νέον γε μὲν ἡβήσειαν,
νωθρὸν κινήσαντο δέμας μυχάτης ἀπὸ λόχμης,
φάεά τ' ἀμπετάσαντο καὶ ἔδρακον ἠελίου φῶς,
καὶ γλυκερῆς νεοτερπὲς ἐδητύος ἐμνήσαντο,
αὖθις δὲ ζωοί τε πάλιν τ'[1] ἐγένοντο μυωξοί.
Λείπω καὶ λάσιον γένος οὐτιδανοῖο σκιούρου,
ὅς ῥά νύ τοι θέρεος μεσάτου φλογερῇσιν ἐν ὥραις
οὐρὴν ἀντέλλει σκέπας αὐτορόφοιο μελάθρου·
οἷον δή νυ ταῶνες ἑὸν δέμας ἀγλαόμορφον
γραπτὸν ἐπισκιάουσιν ἀριπρεπὲς αἰολόνωτον·
τῶν οὐδὲν μερόπεσσι Διὸς τεχνήσατο μῆτις

[1] πάλιν τ' Turnebus: πάλιν MSS.

---

[a] In Oppian, as in A. 540 a 10; 580 a 23; 612 b 15, αἴλουρος seems to be a general name for the Cat, whether *F. catus*, the Wild Cat, M.G. ἀγριόγατος, or the Domestic Cat, *F. domestica*, M.G. γάτα; *cf.* Callim. *H.* vi. 110; Ael. iv. 44, v. 7, v. 30, v. 50. vi. 27; Plin. x. 174; Plut. *Mor.* 959 F γαλαῖ καὶ αἴλουροι.

[b] *Myoxus glis*, *M. nitela*, *M. dryas* are all found in Greece. Erh., p. 20, mentions *M. nitela* as frequenting the orange-groves in Syra, where it climbs the trees and attacks the young fruit. In A. 600 b 13 φωλεῖ δὲ καὶ ὁ ἐλειὸς ἐν αὐτοῖς τοῖς δένδρεσι καὶ γίνεται τότε παχύτατος the ref. seems to be to *M. glis*, or possibly *M. nitela*, though the Squirrel has been suggested, Bik. p. 12. Tristram found in Palestine "three species of dormouse, the largest of which (*M. glis*) is six inches long without the tail, which is five inches more. The

the villain Cats[a] which attack the nests of domestic fowls; and leave thou the tiny, tender, weakling Dormice.[b] These indeed remain with eyes closed all the winter season, drunk with sleep. Hapless creatures! to take no food! not to behold the light! In their lairs, so deep asleep are they, they lie as dead and a wintry lot is theirs. But when the eyes of spring first smile and the flowers in the meadows newly bloom, they stir their sluggish bodies from their secret lair and open their eyes and behold the light of the sun, and with new delight bethink them of sweet food, and once more become alive and Dormice once again.

I leave too the shaggy race of the feeble Squirrel,[c] who in the fiery season of midsummer erects his tail to shelter his self-roofed dwelling[d]; even as the Peacocks[e] shelter their own beautiful form, their splendid form with many-pictured back: than whom the wisdom of Zeus hath devised for men naught

English dormouse we did not find (p. 122)"; Plin. viii. 224 conditi etiam hi cubant; rursus aestate iuvenescunt; Mart. iii. 58. 36 somniculosos glires; *id.* xiii. 59 Tota mihi dormitur hiemps et pinguior illo Tempore sum quo me nil nisi somnus alit.

[c] *Sciurus vulgaris* L., *var. niger*, M.G. βερβερίτζα. "De l'écureuil il n'a été observé jusqu'à présent en Grèce que la variété au pelage noirâtre. Il habite les forêts de sapins des montagnes du Nord de la Grèce, où il a été trouvé par le Dr. Krüper surtout au mont Parnasse, au mt. Velouchi et au mt. Olympe de Thessalie. Mr. A. de Hoeslin m'a assuré de l'avoir vu dans les forêts de sapins du mt. Ménalos en Arcadie" (Bik. p. 13).

[d] Ael. v. 21 ἐν ὥρᾳ θερείῳ σκέπην οἴκοθεν καὶ οὐκ ᾐτημένην οὐδὲ ὀθνείαν παρέχεται; Plin. viii. 138 Provident tempestatem et sciuri obturatisque qua spiraturus est ventus cavernis ex alia parte aperiunt fores. De cetero ipsis villosior cauda pro tegumento est.

[e] *Pavo cristatus*, M.G. παγῶνι.

τερπνότερον φαιδροῖσιν ἐν ὄμμασιν εἰσοράασθαι,
οὐδ' ὅσα πανδώτειραν ἐπὶ χθόνα μητέρα βαίνει,
οὐδ' ὁπόσα πτερύγεσσιν ἐπ' ἠέρα πουλὺν ὁδεύει,
οὐδὲ μὲν ὅσσα βυθοῖσιν ἐπ' ἄγρια κύματα τέμνει·
τοῖον ἐπ' ὀρνίθεσσιν ἀριζήλοις ἀμαρύσσει
χρυσῷ πορφύροντι μεμιγμένον αἰθόμενον πῦρ.
Οὐκ ἐρέω κρυερὸν γένος ὀκριόεντος ἐχίνου
μείονος· ἀμφίδυμοι γὰρ ἐχίνοις ὀξυκόμοισιν
ἀργαλέαι μορφαὶ κρυερόν τε περίδρομον ἕρκος·
οἱ μὲν γὰρ βαιοί τε καὶ οὐτιδανοὶ τελέθουσι,
τυτθῇσι φρίσσοντες ἐπὶ προβλῆσιν ἀκάνθαις·
οἱ δ' ἄρα καὶ μεγέθει πολὺ μείζονες, ἠδ' ἑκάτερθεν
ὀξέα πεφρίκασιν ἀρειοτέρῃσιν ἀκωκαῖς.
Λείπω τρισσὰ γένεθλα, κακὸν μίμημα, πιθήκων·
τίς γὰρ ἂν οὐ στυγέοι τοῖον γένος, αἰσχρὸν ἰδέσθαι,
ἀβληχρόν, στυγερόν, δυσδέρκετον, αἰολόβουλον;
κεῖνοι καὶ φίλα τέκνα δυσειδέα δοιὰ τεκόντες
οὐκ ἀμφοῖν ἀτάλαντον ἑὴν μερίσαντο ποθητύν,

---

[a] The Common Hedgehog, *Erinaceus europaeus*, M.G. *ἀκανθόχοιρος*, is common in Greece (Erh. p. 12, Bik. p. 8), as it is in Palestine (Trist. p. 101). Oppian's lesser Hedgehog is almost certainly the Spiny Mouse, *M. acomys*, of Syria and Africa, of which at least three species occur in Palestine. "They are most beautiful little creatures of a light sandy colour above and white beneath, and covered all over the back with bristles like a hedgehog" (Tristr. p. 123), from which, when the spines are erected, they are, except for their size, almost indistinguishable. A. 581 a 1 *οἱ δ' ἐν Αἰγύπτῳ μύες σκληρὰν ἔχουσι τὴν τρίχα ὥσπερ οἱ χερσαῖοι ἐχῖνοι*; *Mirab.* 832 a 31 *ἐν Κυρήνῃ δέ φασιν οὐχ ἓν εἶναι μυῶν γένος . . . τινὰς δὲ ἐχινώδεις οὓς καλοῦσιν ἐχῖνας*; Herod. iv. 192

more pleasant to behold with glad eyes, neither amid all that walk mother earth, giver of all gifts, nor amid all that travel on wings the spacious air, nor amid those that in the deep cleave the wild waves : in such wise on the splendid birds twinkles blazing fire mingled with the sheen of gold.

I will not tell of the chilly race of the prickly Hedgehog [a]—the lesser; for two dread forms there are of the sharp-spined Hedgehogs with chilly fence encircling them. The one kind are small and feeble and bristle with small jutting spines ; the other sort are far larger in size and have stronger prickles bristling sharp on either side.

I leave the triple breeds of Apes,[b] those villainous mimics.[c] For who would not abhor such a race, ugly to look on, weak, loathsome, evil of aspect, crafty of counsel ? These, though they bring forth twin children of evil mien, divide not their love equally

μυῶν γένεα τριξὰ αὐτόθι (in Libya) *ἐστί . . . οἱ δὲ ἐχινέες*; Plin. viii. 221 plura eorum genera in Cyrenaica regione, . . . alii irenaceorum genere pungentibus pilis; *id.* x. 186 Aegyptiis muribus durus pilus sicut irenaceis; *cf.* Ael. xv. 26; Hesych. *s. ἐχῖνος.*

[b] The triple breeds are doubtless those of A. 502 a 16 *ἔνια δὲ τῶν ζῴων ἐπαμφοτερίζει τὴν φύσιν τῷ τ' ἀνθρώπῳ καὶ τοῖς τετράποσιν, οἷον πίθηκοι καὶ κῆβοι καὶ κυνοκέφαλοι. ἔστι δ' ὁ μὲν κῆβος πίθηκος ἔχων οὐράν, καὶ οἱ κυνοκέφαλοι δὲ τὴν αὐτὴν ἔχουσι μορφὴν τοῖς πιθήκοις, πλὴν μείζονές τ' εἰσι καὶ ἰσχυρότεροι καὶ τὰ πρόσωπα ἔχοντες κυνοειδέστερα, ἔτι δὲ ἀγριώτερά τε τὰ ἤθη καὶ τοὺς ὀδόντας ἔχουσι κυνοειδεστέρους καὶ ἰσχυροτέρους.* They thus correspond to our Ape, Monkey, Baboon, and *πίθηκος* is prob. the Barbary Ape (Strab. 827), *Macacus Inuus*; the *κῆβος* a *Cercopithecus*; the *κυνοκέφαλος* the *Cynocephalus hamadryas* or Arabian Baboon ; *cf.* Plin. viii. 215, xi. 246; Ael. v. 7, xvii. 25 etc. ; Solin. xxvii. 56.

[c] Ael. v. 26 *μιμηλότατόν ἐστιν ὁ πίθηκος ζῷον*; Solin. *l.c.* non sine ingenio aemulandi.

ἀλλὰ τὸ μὲν φιλέουσι, τὸ δ' ἐχθαίρουσι χόλοισιν[1]·
αὐταῖς δ' ἀγκαλίδεσσιν ἑῶν τέθνηκε[2] τοκήων.
Οὐ μὲν θὴν οὐδ' ἀσπαλάκων αὐτόχθονα φῦλα
ποιοφάγων, ἀλαῶν, μέλπειν ἐθέλουσιν ἀοιδαί,
εἰ καὶ βάξις ἄπιστος ἐπ' ἀνθρώπους ἐπέρησεν
ἀσπάλακας βασιλῆος ἀφ' αἵματος εὐχετάασθαι
Φινέος, ὅν ῥ' ἀτίτηλε κλυτὴ Θρήϊσσα κολώνη·
Φινέϊ γάρ ποτε δὴ Φαέθων ἐκοτέσσατο Τιτάν,
μαντιπόλου Φοίβοιο χολωσάμενος περὶ νίκης,
καί οἱ φέγγος ἄμερσεν, ἀναιδέα φῦλα δ' ἔπεμψεν
ἁρπυίας, πτερόεντα παρέστια πικρὰ γένεθλα.
ἀλλ' ἐπεὶ οὖν περόωντο μετὰ χρύσειον ἄεθλον
Ἀργώης ἐπὶ νηὸς Ἰήσονι συμπονέοντες
παῖδε Βορειόνεω Ζήτης Κάλαΐς τε κλεεννώ,
οἰκτείραντε γέροντα κατέκτειναν τότε φῦλα,
καὶ γλυκερὴν μελέοισι δόσαν στομάτεσσιν ἐδητύν.
ἀλλ' οὐδ' ὧς Φαέθων χόλον εὔνασεν, ἀλλά μιν αἶψα
ἀσπαλάκων ποίησε γένος μὴ πρόσθεν ἐόντων·
τοὔνεκα νῦν ἀλαόν τε μένει καὶ λάβρον ἐδωδαῖς.

[1] λόχοιο A_2 in ras. BGH : πόθοισι CDE.
[2] τέθνηκε Pauw : ἔθανε I : ἔκτεινε.

---

[a] ἀσπάλαξ both in Opp. and in A. 488 a 21, 491 b 28, 533 a 3, 605 b 31, etc., is prob. *Spalax typhlus*, a rodent "with much of the external appearance of our mole but considerably larger, . . . of a silvery grey colour, without any external eyes or tail" (Tristr. p. 121). It is found in the Cyclades, where it is called τυφλοποντικός (*i.e.* blind-rat), Erh. p. 21. Neither our Common Mole, *Talpa europaea*, nor *T. caeca* has been found in the Cyclades (Erh. *l.c.*) or in Palestine (Tristr. p. 100); in continental Greece *T. europaea* is not found and the occurrence of *T. caeca* seems to be doubtful.

between both, but they love the one and hate and are angered at the other; and he perishes in the very arms of his parents.

Neither of a truth will minstrels sing the earth-born tribes of the Moles,[a] eaters of grass[b] and blind,[c] albeit a rumour not to be believed has spread among men that the Moles boast themselves sprung from the blood of a king, even of Phineus,[d] whom a famous Thracian hill nurtured. Against Phineus once on a time was the Titan Phaethon angered, wroth for the victory of prophet Phoebus, and robbed him of his sight and sent the shameless tribes of the Harpies, a winged race to dwell with him to his sorrow. But when the two glorious sons of Boreas, even Zetes and Calais, voyaged on the ship Argo in quest of the golden prize, assisting Jason, then did they take compassion on the old man and slew that tribe and gave his poor lips sweet food. But not even so did Phaethon lull his wrath to rest, but speedily turned him into the race of Moles which were before not; wherefore even now the race remains blind and gluttonous of food.

[b] While *T. europaea* and *T. caeca* are insectivorous, *S. typhlus* is entirely vegetarian.

[c] The eyes of *T. europaea*, though rudimentary, are visible externally; those of *T. caeca* and *S. typhlus* are not. A. 491 b 29 ὅλως μὲν γὰρ οὔθ' ὁρᾷ (ὁ ἀσπάλαξ) οὔτ' ἔχει εἰς τὸ φανερὸν δήλους ὀφθαλμούς. *Cf.* 533 a 3; *De an.* 425 a 10; Plin. xi. 139 quadrupedum talpis visus non est: oculorum effigies inest, siquis praetentam detrahat membranam.

[d] Phineus of Salmydessus in Thrace was blinded of both eyes and afflicted by the Harpies until these were destroyed by Zetes and Calais (Pind. *P.* iv. 182), the sons of Boreas; Apollod. i. 9. 21; Ap. Rh. ii. 176 ff.; Verg. *A.* iii. 225 ff. The connexion of Phineus with the mole seems to be peculiar to Oppian.

ΚΥΝΗΓΕΤΙΚΩΝ ΤΟ Γ

Ἀλλ᾽ ὅτε δὴ κεραῶν ἠείσαμεν ἔθνεα θηρῶν,
ταύρους ἠδ᾽ ἐλάφους ἠδ᾽ εὐρυκέρωτας ἀγαυοὺς
καὶ δόρκους ὄρυγάς τε καὶ αἰγλήεντας ἰορκοὺς
ἄλλα θ᾽ ὅσοισιν ὕπερθε καρήατα τευχήεντα,
νῦν ἄγε καρχαρόδοντα, θεά, φράζωμεν ὅμιλον
σαρκοφάγων θηρῶν καὶ χαυλιόδοντα γένεθλα.
Πρωτίστην δὲ λέοντι κλυτὴν ἀναθώμεθα μολπήν.
Ζηνὸς ἔσαν θρεπτῆρες ὑπερμενέος Κρονίδαο
νηπιάχου Κουρῆτες, ὅτ᾽ ἀρτίγονόν μιν ἐόντα
ἀραμένη γενετῆρος ἀμειλίκτοιο Κρόνοιο
κλεψιτόκος Ῥείη κόλποις ἐνικάτθετο Κρήτης.
Οὐρανίδης δ᾽ ἐσιδὼν κρατερὸν νεοθηλέα παῖδα
πρώτους ἀμφήλλαξε Διὸς ῥυτῆρας ἀγαυοὺς
καὶ θῆρας ποίησεν ἀμειψάμενος Κουρῆτας.

---

[a] A. 501 a 14 καὶ τὰ μὲν χαυλιόδοντας ἔχει, ὥσπερ οἱ ἄρρενες ὕες, τὰ δὲ οὐκ ἔχει. ἔτι δὲ τὰ μέν ἐστι καρχαρόδοντα αὐτῶν, οἷον λέων καὶ πάρδαλις καὶ κύων, τὰ δὲ ἀνεπάλλακτα, οἷον ἵππος καὶ βοῦς· καρχαρόδοντα γάρ ἐστιν ὅσα ἐπαλλάττει τοὺς ὀδόντας τοὺς ὀξεῖς; *P.A.* 661 b 22 οὐδὲν δὲ τῶν ζῴων ἐστὶν ἅμα καρχαρόδουν καὶ χαυλιόδουν, διὰ τὸ μηδὲν μάτην ποιεῖν τὴν φύσιν μηδὲ περιεργόν· ἔστι δὲ τῶν μὲν (*sc.* the tusks) διὰ πληγῆς ἡ βοηθεία, τῶν δὲ (*sc.* the saw-teeth) διὰ δήγματος; Plin. xi. 160 dentium tria genera, serrati aut continui aut exserti; serrati pecti-

CYNEGETICA, OR THE CHASE

III

But now that we have sung the tribes of horned wild beasts, Bulls and Stags and splendid Broad-horns and Gazelles, of the Oryx and beautiful Iorcus and others whose heads are armed above, come now, O goddess, let us tell of the saw-toothed[a] company of flesh-eating[b] beasts and the tusked races.

First of all to the Lion let us dedicate the glorious lay. The Curetes were the nurses of the infant Zeus, the mighty son of Cronus, what time Rhea concealed his birth and carried away the newly-born child from Cronus, his sire implacable, and placed him in the vales of Crete. And when the son[c] of Uranus beheld the lusty young child he transformed the first glorious guardians of Zeus and in vengeance made the Curetes wild beasts. And since by the

natim coeuntes, ne contrario occursu atterantur (A. *P.A.* 661 b 21), ut serpentibus, piscibus, canibus; continui, ut homini, equo; exserti, ut apro, hippopotamo, elephanto. . . . Nulli exserti quibus serrati. The *carcharodonts* are carnivorous and have sharp, saw-like, cutting cheek teeth; the *chauliodonts* have flat-crowned cheek teeth, adapted for crushing or grinding.

[b] A. 594 a 25 τῶν δὲ τετραπόδων καὶ ζῳοτόκων τὰ μὲν ἄγρια καὶ καρχαρόδοντα πάντα σαρκοφάγα.

[c] *i.e.* Cronus. *Cf.* Callim. *H.* i., Diod. v. 65, Verg. *G.* iv. 151.

οἱ δ᾽ ἄρ᾽, ἐπεὶ βουλῇσι θεοῦ μεροπηΐδα μορφὴν
ἀμφεβάλοντο Κρόνοιο καὶ ἀμφιέσαντο λέοντας,
δώροισιν μετόπισθε Διὸς μέγα κοιρανέουσι
θηρσὶν ὀρειαύλοις καὶ ῥιγεδανὸν θοὸν ἅρμα
Ῥείης εὐώδινος ὑπὸ ζεύγλῃσιν ἄγουσιν.
Αἰόλα φῦλα δὲ τοῖσι καὶ εἴδεα θηρσὶν ἑκάστοις.
τοὺς μέν νυν προχοῇσι πολυρραθάγου ποταμοῖο,
Τίγρει[1] ἐπ᾽ εὐρυρέοντι, κυήσατο τοξεύτειρα
Ἀρμενίη Πάρθων τε πολύσπορος εὔβοτος αἶα,
ξανθοκόμαι τελέθουσι καὶ οὐ τόσον ἀλκήεντες.
πάσσονα μὲν φορέουσι δέρην, μεγάλην δέ τε κόρσην,
ὄμματα δ᾽ αἰγλήεντα καὶ ὀφρύας ὕψι βαθείας,
ἀμφιλαφεῖς ἐπὶ ῥῖνα κατηφέας· ἐκ δ᾽ ἄρα δειρῆς
καὶ γενύων ἑκάτερθε θοαὶ κομόωσιν ἔθειραι.
Τοὺς δὲ τρέφει μεγάδωρος Ἐρεμβῶν αὖθις ἄρουρα,
τὴν ἔθνη μερόπων εὐδαίμονα κικλήσκουσι,
δειραὶ κἀκείνοις καὶ στήθεα λαχνήεντα
καὶ πυρὸς ἀστράπτουσιν ἀπ᾽ ὀφθαλμῶν ἀμαρυγαί,
ἔξοχα δ᾽ ἐν πάντεσσιν ἀρίζηλοι τελέθουσιν·
ἀλλ᾽ ὀλίγον τούτων γένος ἔλλαχε μυρίος αἶα.
Πουλὺς δ᾽ ἐν Λιβύῃ ἐριβώλακι διψάδι γαίῃ
ὄχλος ἐπιβρομέει βριαρῶν βρύχημα λεόντων,
οὐκέτι λαχνήεις, ὀλίγη δ᾽ ἐπιδέδρομεν αἴγλη[2]·
σμερδαλέος δὲ πρόσωπα καὶ αὐχένα· πᾶσι δὲ γυίοις
ἦκα μέλαν κυάνοιο φέρει μεμορυγμένον ἄνθος·
ἀλκὴ δ᾽ ἐν μελέεσσιν ἀπείριτος ἠδὲ λεόντων
κοιρανικῶν Λίβυες μέγα κοιρανέουσι λέοντες.

[1] ἴστρῳ (ἴστρου) mss. : corr. Brodaeus.
[2] ἐπιδέδρομε λάχνη F.

---

[a] *Cf. H.* i. 651, Lucian, *Asin.* 14. [b] *C.* i. 172 n.

[c] Arabia Felix; *cf.* Strabo 39 τὴν Ἀραβίαν ἣν εὐδαίμονα προσαγορεύουσιν οἱ νῦν; Dion. P. 927 κεῖθεν δ᾽ ὀλβίστων Ἀράβων παρακέκλιται αἶα; Diod. ii. 49 ἡ δ᾽ ἐχομένη τῆς ἀνύδρου καὶ

devising of the god Cronus they exchanged their human shape and put upon them the form [a] of Lions, thenceforth by the boon of Zeus they greatly lord it over the wild beasts which dwell upon the hills, and under the yoke they draw the terrible swift car of Rhea who lightens the pangs of birth.

Various are the tribes of them and each species has its own form. Those which by the waters of a noisy river, even beside the broad stream of the Tigris, are bred by Armenia, mother of archers, and by the land of the Parthians, rich in tilth and pasture, are yellow-haired and not so valiant. They have a stouter neck and a large head, bright eyes and high and bushy brows, ample and lowering over the nose. From neck and jaws springs on either side luxuriant hair.

Those again which the bountiful land of the Erembi [b] rears—the land which the tribes of mortal men call Fortunate [c]—these also have shaggy neck and breast, and flashes of fire lighten from their eyes, and they are handsome above all; but of these the infinite earth hath but a scanty breed.

But a great throng of mighty Lions roar in the goodly land of thirsty Libya—no longer shaggy these but a thin sheen runs over them. Terrible are they of face and neck, and on all their limbs they bear a blackish hue stained with dark blue. The strength in their limbs is limitless, and the Libyan Lions greatly lord it over the lordly Lions.

ἐρήμου χώρας *'Αραβία τοσοῦτο διαφέρει ταύτης ὥστε διὰ τὸ πλῆθος τῶν ἐν αὐτῇ φυομένων καρπῶν τε καὶ τῶν ἄλλων ἀγαθῶν εὐδαίμονα 'Αραβίαν προσαγορευθῆναι*; Solin. xxxiii. 4 hanc Arabiam Graeci Eudaemonem, nostri Beatam nominaverunt; Amm. M. xxiii. 6. 45 Arabes beati, ideo sic appellati quod frugibus iuxta et fetibus et palmite odorumque suavitate multiplici sunt locupletes.

Ἐκ δέ ποτ' Αἰθιόπων Λιβύην ἠμείψατο γαῖαν,
θαῦμα μέγ' εἰσιδέειν, μελανόχροος ἠΰκομος λῖς,
εὐρὺς ὕπερθε κάρηνα, πόδας δασύς, ὄμμασιν αἶθοψ,
μούνοισι ξανθοῖς φοινισσόμενος στομάτεσσιν.
ἔδρακον, οὐ πυθόμην, κεῖνόν ποτε θῆρα δαφοινόν,
κοιρανικοῖς τ' ἔμολεν διαπόμπιμος ὀφθαλμοῖσιν.

Φορβῆς οὐ χατέει πάντ' ἤματα φῦλα λεόντων,
ἀλλὰ τὸ μὲν δόρποισι μέλει, τὸ δέ τ' αὖτε[1] πόνοισιν·
οὐδ' ὕπνον μυχάτοισιν ἔχει παρὰ τέρμασι πέτρης,
ἀμφαδὸν ὑπνώει δέ, θρασύφρονα θυμὸν ἑλίσσων,
εὕδει δ' ἔνθα κίχῃσιν ὑπείροχος ἑσπερίη νύξ.

Ἔκλυον αὖ κἀκεῖνο λεοντοκόμων αἰζηῶν,
δεξιτερὴν ὑπὸ χεῖρα φέρειν αἴθωνα λέοντα
νάρκα θοήν, τῇ πάντα λυγοῦν[2] ἄπο γούνατα θηρῶν.

Πεντάκι θηλυτέρη δὲ τόκων ἀπελύσατο ζώνην·
βάξις δ' ἀτρεκέως ἀνεμώλιος, ὡς ἕνα τίκτει.
πέντε φέρει πρώτιστον· ἀτὰρ πίσυρας μετέπειτα
ὠδίνει σκύμνους, κατά θ' ἑξείης ὑπένερθε
νηδύος ἐκ τριτάτης τρεῖς ἔκθορον· ἐκ δὲ τετάρτης
ἀμφίδυμοι παῖδες· πύματον δ' ἕνα γείνατο μήτηρ
γαστρὸς ἀριστοτόκοιο κλυτὸν βασιλῆα λέοντα.

[1] τότε δ' αὖτε most MSS.
[2] λυγοῦν Editor: λυγρῶν MSS.

---

[a] A. 594 b 18 τῇ δὲ βρώσει (ὁ λέων) χρῆται λάβρως καὶ καταπίνει πολλὰ ὅλα οὐ διαιρῶν, εἶθ' ἡμέρας δύο ἢ τρεῖς ἀσιτεῖ; Plin. viii. 46; Ael. iv. 34; Solin. xxvii. 13.

[b] O.T. Num. xxiv. 9 He couched, he lay down as a lion, and as a great lion: who shall stir him up?

From the Ethiopians once on a time there came to the land of Libya, a great marvel to behold, a well-maned Lion, black of hue, broad of head above, hairy of foot, bright of eye, reddening only on the yellow mouth. I have seen, not merely heard of, that terrible beast, when it was transported to be a spectacle for royal eyes.

The tribes of Lions do not need food [a] every day but one day they devote to feeding, the next in turn to labour. Neither doth the Lion take his sleep by the inmost bounds of a rock, but he sleeps [b] in the open, revolving a courageous soul, and wheresoever sovran night overtakes him at evening, there he sleeps.

This also have I heard from the keepers of Lions, to wit that under his right paw the tawny Lion has a power of swift benumbing,[c] wherewith he utterly benumbs the knees of wild beasts.

Five times [d] doth the Lioness loose her zone in birth, and idle truly is the report that she bears but one. Five she bears the first time, but next she travails with four cubs; then next in order from her third labour spring three; from her fourth spring twin young; and last from her womb of noble progeny the mother brings forth the glorious Lion King.

[c] Schol. B Hom. *Il.* xx. 170 ἔχει (ὁ λέων) ὑπὸ τῇ οὐρᾷ κέντρον μέλαν, ὡς κεράτιον, δι' οὗ ἑαυτὸν μαστίζει, ὑφ' οὗ νυττόμενος πλέον ἀγριοῦται. A. 630 a 5 mentions the suppuration of wounds inflicted by lions' teeth and claws, but says nothing of numbing.

[d] A. 579 b 9 οἱ δ' ἐν Συρίᾳ λέοντες τίκτουσι πεντάκις, τὸ πρῶτον πέντε, εἶτ' ἀεὶ ἑνὶ ἐλάττονα· μετὰ δὲ ταῦτα οὐκέτι οὐδὲν τίκτουσιν, ἀλλ' ἄγονοι διατελοῦσιν; *De gen.* 750 a 32; Plin. viii. 45; Ael. iv. 34; Phil. xxxv.; Solin. xxvii. 16.

Πορδάλιες δ' ὀλοαὶ δίδυμον γένος· αἱ μὲν ἔασι
μείζους εἰσιδέειν καὶ πάσσονες εὐρέα νῶτα,
αἱ δέ τ' ὀλιζότεραι μὲν ἀτὰρ μένος οὔτι χερείους·
εἴδεα δ' ἀμφοτέρῃσιν ὁμοΐα δαιδάλλονται,
νόσφι μόνης οὐρῆς, τῇ τ' ἔμπαλιν εἰσοράαται·
μείοσι μὲν μείζων τελέθει, μεγάλῃσι δὲ μείων.
εὐπαγέες μηροί, δολιχὸν δέμας, ὄμμα φαεινόν·
γλαυκιόωσι κόραι βλεφάροις ὕπο μαρμαίρουσαι,
γλαυκιόωσιν ὁμοῦ τε καὶ ἔνδοθι φοινίσσονται,
αἰθομέναις ἴκελαι, πυριλαμπέες· αὐτὰρ ἔνερθεν
ὠχροί τ' ἰοτόκοι τε περὶ στομάτεσσιν ὀδόντες.
ῥινὸς δαιδαλέος, χροιῇ τ' ἐπὶ παμφανοώσῃ
ἠερόεις, πυκινῇσι μελαινομένῃσιν ὀπωπαῖς.
ὠκύτατον θείει, καί τ' ἄλκιμον ἰθὺς ὀρούει·
φαίης, ὁππότ' ἴδοιο, διηερίην φορέεσθαι.
ἔμπης καὶ τόδε φῦλον ἐπικλείουσιν ἀοιδοὶ
πρόσθ' ἔμεναι Βάκχοιο φερεσταφύλοιο τιθήνας·
τοὔνεκεν εἰσέτι νῦν οἴνῳ μέγα καγχαλόωσι,
δεχνύμεναι στομάτεσσι Διωνύσου μέγα δῶρον.
τί χρέος ἐκ μερόπων δὲ κλυτὰς ἤμειψε γυναῖκας
ἐς τόδε πορδαλίων γένος ἄγριον, αὖθις ἀείσω.
Ναὶ μὴν ἄλλο θοὸν διφυὲς γένος ὠπήσαιο,

---

[a] πάρδαλις (πόρδαλις), the commoner and older word (Hom. *Il.* xiii. 103, xxi. 573; *Od.* iv. 457), and πάνθηρ (first in Herod. iv. 192) are translated alike by *panthera* in Latin writers,

Next the deadly Leopards [a] are a double race. The one sort are larger to look on and stouter as to their broad backs, while the other sort are smaller but no whit inferior in valiance. The daedal forms of both are alike, apart only from the tail, where a perversity is seen: the lesser Leopards have the larger, the large the lesser tail. The thighs are well knit, the body is long, the eye bright: the shining pupils show grey-green beneath their brows, grey-green at once and red within, flaming as if on fire; but in the mouth beneath the teeth are pale and venomous. The hide is variegated and on a bright ground is dark with close-set black spots. Very swift it is in running and valiant in a straight charge. Seeing it thou wouldst say that it sped through the air. Notwithstanding minstrels celebrate this race of beasts as having been aforetime the nurses of Bacchus, giver of the grape; wherefore even now they greatly exult in wine and receive in their mouths the great gift of Dionysus. What matter it was that changed glorious women from the race of mortals into this wild race of Leopards I shall hereafter sing.

Another swift race, moreover, of twofold nature

as conversely the later Greek writers render the Latin *panthera* by πάρδαλις (Plut. *Cic.* xxxvi. coll. Cic. *Ad fam.* ii. 11). When πάρδαλις and πάνθηρ are distinguished (Xen. *C.* 2. 1; Athen. 201 c; Ael. vii. 47; Poll. v. 88), then, according to Wiegmann, πάρδαλις = *Felis pardus* L. and Cuv. (*F. leopardus* Temminck), while πάνθηρ = *F. uncia.* Of the two Panthers or Leopards in our present passage the larger, according to Wiegmann, is *F. pardus* L. and Cuv. (*F. leopardus* Temm.), the *varia* (Plin. viii. 63) and *pardus* of the Romans, while the smaller is *F. pardus* Temm., *cf.* A. and W. ii. p. 294. See *C.* ii. 572 n.

λύγγας ἀριζήλους· αἱ μὲν γὰρ ἔασιν ἰδέσθαι
τυτθαί, βαιοτέροισί τ' ἐφωπλίσσαντο λαγωοῖς·
ταὶ δ' ἄρα μείζονές εἰσιν, ἐπιθρώσκουσι δὲ ῥεῖα
εὐκεράοις ἐλάφοισι καὶ ὀξυτέροις[1] ὀρύγεσσι.
μορφὴν δ' ἀμφίδυμοι πανομοίϊον ἀμφιέσαντο·
ἶσαι μὲν βλεφάροισιν ὑπ'[2] ὀφθαλμῶν ἀμαρυγαὶ
ἱμερόεν στράπτουσι· προσώπατα δ' ἀμφοτέρῃσι
φαιδρὰ πέλει βαιόν τε κάρη καὶ καμπύλον οὖας·
μούνη δ' εἰσιδέειν ἀνομοίϊος ἔπλετο χροιή·
μείοσι μὲν λυγγῶν ἐπιδέδρομε ῥινὸς ἐρευθής,
μείζοσι δὲ κροκόεν τε θεείῳ τ' εἴκελον ἄνθος.
ἔξοχα δ' αὖ τάδε φῦλα φίλην ἀγάσαντο γενέθλην
εὔγληνοι λύγγες τε πυρίγληνοί[3] τε λέοντες
πορδάλιές τ' ὀλοαὶ καὶ τίγριες ἠνεμόεσσαι.
τῶν δ' ὁπότε σκύμνους νεοθηλέας ἐν ξυλόχοισι
λάθρῃ συλήσωσιν ἀταρβέες ἀγρευτῆρες,
αἱ δ' ἄρ' ἔπειτ' ὀπίσω πάλι νεύμεναι ἀθρήσωσιν
ἐξαπίνης κενεούς τε δόμους καὶ ἔρημα μέλαθρα,
μύρονται λιγέως ἀδινὸν γόον, ἐκ δ' ἄρα τηλοῦ
κωκυτὸν προϊᾶσι πολύστονον, οἷά τε πάτρης
περθομένης ὑπὸ δουρὶ καὶ αἰθομένης πυρὶ λάβρῳ
πεπτάμεναι περὶ τέκνα μέγα κλαίουσι γυναῖκες.
ἦ ῥα τόσον τεκέων τε καὶ ἀρτιγόνοιο γενέθλης
φίλτρον ἐνὶ κραδίῃ στάξεν θεός· οὐδ' ἄρα μούνοις

[1] ὀξυκέροις G. [2] ὑπ' Editor: ἀπ'.
[3] περίγληνοι L.

[a] The two species of Lynx appear to be: 1. *Felis lynx* (A. 499 b 24, 500 b 15, 539 b 22, etc.; Plin. viii. 72), M.G. ῥῆσος: "Le lynx, habitant les gorges des montagnes et surtout la région des bois de sapins, est devenu très rare en Grèce, mais n'en est pas disparu. Son existence a été notamment constaté en Attique par un individu tué le 18 mars 1862 au mont Parnès et conservé empaillé au Musée

thou mayst see, the notable Lynxes.[a] Of these the one sort are small to look on and attack the little Hares; the other sort are larger and easily leap upon the Stags of goodly horns and the swift Oryx. Both are clothed in altogether similar form. Alike are the delightful flashes that lighten from their eyes beneath their brows; both have bright face, small head, and curving ear; only their colour is dissimilar to look on. The smaller Lynxes are covered with a ruddy hide, while the colour of the larger is saffron and like sulphur. Beyond others these tribes love their dear offspring, the keen-eyed Lynxes and the fiery-eyed Lions and the deadly Leopards and the windswift Tigers. When in the thickets fearless hunters secretly steal away their suckling cubs, and they returning afterward behold their empty house and home made desolate, they shrilly wail their loud lament and far they send abroad their doleful dirge; even as, when their fatherland is sacked with the spear and burnt with raging fire, women fall upon their children's necks and loudly weep. Such constraining love of child and new-born babe hath God instilled into the

Zoologique d'Athènes; d'après l'Expédition scientifique de Morée il habite le mont Olenos d'Achaïe et les montagnes de Cynurie; d'après Mr. A. de Hoeslin il a été observé dans la gorge de Phlampouritza au mont Cyllène et un individu a été tué près de Xylocastron par Mr. I. Notaras. D'après les renseignements de Mr. le Dr. Krüper il se trouve aussi au mont Olympe en Thessalie," Bik. pp. 11 f. 2. *F. caracal*, the Caracal, a small animal about 14 inches in height and about 34 inches long without the tail, which is about 10 inches; in colour reddish-brown, paling to white under throat and belly. It is sometimes trained to hunt small mammals, such as hares, and the larger birds such as cranes, kites, etc.

ἀνθρώποις, οἳ πάντα νοήμασι μητίσαντο,
ἀλλὰ καὶ ἑρπηστῆρσι[1] καὶ ἰχθύσιν ἠδὲ καὶ αὐτοῖς
θήρεσιν ὠμηστῇσι καὶ ὑψιπόλοις ἀγέλαισιν
οἰωνῶν· τόσσον ῥα φύσις κρατερώτατον ἄλλων.
οἵην μὲν κομιδὴν τεκέων ἐνὶ κύμασι δελφὶς
αἰὲν ἔχει γλαῦκός τε χάροψ φωκή τε δυσαής.
πῶς δ' ἄρ' ἐν οἰωνοῖσι ποθὴν ἀλίαστον ἔχουσιν
ὧν τεκέων φῆναί τε βαρύφθογγοί τε πέλειαι
αἰετόεντά τε φῦλα πολύζωοί τε κορῶναι.
πῶς δ' ὄρνις κατὰ δῶμα συνέστιος ἀνθρώποισιν,
ἀρτιτόκος, νεαροῖσι περισκαίρουσα νεοσσοῖς,
κίρκον ὑπὲρ τέγεος κατεπάλμενον ἀθρήσασα
ὀξὺ μὲν ἔκλαγεν αἶψα καὶ ἄνθορεν ὀξὺ λακοῦσα,
αὐχένα δ' ὑψόσ' ἄειρεν ἐς ἠέρα γυρώσασα
καὶ πάσαις ἑκάτερθε θοῶς ἔφριξεν ἐθείραις
καὶ πτερὰ πάντα χάλασσε ποτὶ χθόνα· τοὶ δ' ἄρα δειλοὶ
τεῖχος ὑπ' εὐπτέρυγον πρυλέες τρύζουσι νεοσσοί·
ἡ δὲ καὶ ἂψ ἐφόβησε καὶ ἤλασεν ὄρνιν ἀναιδῆ,
εἰρυμένη φίλα τέκνα, τά τ' εἰσέτι νήπια φέρβει,
ἄπτερα λυσιτόκων[2] θαλάμων[3] ἀπολύμενα δεσμοῦ.
ὣς δὲ καὶ ἐν θήρεσσιν ἐρίβρυχοί τε λέαιναι
πορδάλιές τε θοαὶ καὶ τίγριδες αἰολόνωτοι
παισὶ πέρι προβεβᾶσι καὶ ἀγρευτῆρσι μάχονται
καί τε περὶ σφετέρων τεκέων τετλᾶσι δαμῆναι,
ἀντίον αἰχμητῇσι συνιστάμεναι μερόπεσσιν·

[1] ἑρπυστῆρσι K: ἑρπηστῆσι E.
[2] vv. ll. λυσικόμων, λυσιτόμων. [3] πτερύγων suprascr. G.

[a] *Cf. H.* i. 648 ff. [b] *Cf. H.* i. 749 ff.
[c] *Cf. H.* i. 686 ff.
[d] *Cf. H.* i. 727. Prob. *Gypaëtus barbatus*, the Lammer-

heart: not alone in men who devise all things by their wits but even in creeping things and fish and the ravenous wild beasts themselves and the high-ranging flocks of birds: so much is nature mightier than all beside. What care doth the Dolphin[a] amid the waves take evermore of its children, and the bright-eyed Glaucus[b] and the Seal[c] of evil smell! And how among the fowls of air do they cherish unfailing love for their own children—the Giers[d] and the deep-noted Doves and the tribes of the Eagle and the long-lived Crow! And the domestic mother Hen, companion of the homes of men, fluttering about her new-hatched chicks, how, when she sees a Hawk swooping down over the roof, doth she straightway utter a piercing scream and spring up with shrill cry and lift her arching neck high into the air and speedily ruffle all her plumage and droop her wings to the ground, while the poor chickens cheeping cower together beneath the bulwark of her wings; and speedily she routs and drives away the shameless bird, defending her dear children, still infants whom she feeds, unfledged and newly delivered from the bondage of the chambers of birth.[e] So also among wild beasts roaring Lionesses and swift Leopards and Tigers of striped back stand forward to defend their children and fight with hunters and for their young ones are prepared to die, joining issue with the spearmen face to face;

geier, M.G. ὀξυά etc., the פֶּרֶס of Lev. xi. 13; Deut. xiv. 12. *Cf.* A. 563 a 27, 592 b 5, 619 a 13, b 23 ff.; Plin. x. 11 genus aquilae quam barbatam vocant, Tusci vero ossifragam; x. 13; Hom. *Od.* iii. 372; xvi. 217.

[e] The reader will remember St. Matt. xxiii. 37 *ποσάκις ἠθέλησα ἐπισυναγαγεῖν τὰ τέκνα σου, ὃν τρόπον ὄρνις ἐπισυνάγει τὰ νοσσία αὐτῆς ὑπὸ τὰς πτέρυγας, καὶ οὐκ ἠθελήσατε.*

οὐδέ ποτ᾽ ἐρρίγασιν ἑῆς ἐν ἀγῶνι γενέθλης
οὐ πληθὺν ἐπιοῦσαν ἀκοντοβόλων αἰζηῶν,
οὐ χαλκὸν σελαγεῦντα καὶ ἀστράπτοντα σίδηρον,
οὐδὲ βολὰς βελέων τε θοὰς μυλάκων τε θαμειάς,
σπεύδουσιν δ᾽ ἢ πρόσθε θανεῖν ἢ τέκνα σαῶσαι.
Ἄρκτοι δ᾽ ἀγριάδες, φόνιον γένος, αἰολόβουλον,
λάχνην μὲν πυκινὴν δυσπαίπαλον ἀμφιέσαντο,
μορφὴν δ᾽ οὐκ ἀγανὴν παναμειδήτοισι προσώποις·
κάρχαρον, οὐλόμενον, ταναὸν στόμα, κυανέη ῥίς,
ὄμμα θοόν, σφυρὸν ὠκύ, τορὸν δέμας, εὐρὺ κάρηνον,
χεῖρες χερσὶ βροτῶν ἴκελαι, πόδες αὖτε πόδεσσι,
σμερδαλέη βρυχή, δολερὸν κέαρ, ἄγριον ἦτορ,
καὶ πολλὴ Κυθέρεια καὶ οὐ κατὰ κόσμον ἰοῦσα·
ἤματα γὰρ καὶ νύκτας ἐελδόμεναι φιλότητος
αὐταὶ θηλύτεραι μάλ᾽ ἐπ᾽ ἄρσεσιν ὁρμαίνουσι,
παῦρα μεθιέμεναι γαμίης παντερπέος εὐνῆς,
τέκνα κυϊσκόμεναι νηδὺν ὅτε κυμαίνουσι.
οὐ γάρ τοι θήρεσσι νόμος, γαστὴρ ὅτε πλήθει,
ἐς λέχος ἐρχομένοις τελέειν φιλοτήσιον ἔργον,
νόσφι μόνων λυγγῶν ὀλιγοδρανέων τε λαγωῶν.
ἄρκτος δ᾽ ἱμείρουσα γάμου στυγέουσά τε λέκτρον
χῆρον ἔχειν τόσα παισὶ ταλάσσατο μητίσασθαι·
πρὶν τοκετοῖο μολεῖν ὥρην, πρὶν κύριον ἦμαρ,
νηδὺν ἐξέθλιψε, βιάσσατο τ᾽ Εἰλειθυίας.
τόσση μαχλοσύνη, τόσσος δρόμος εἰς Ἀφροδίτην.
τίκτει δ᾽ ἡμιτέλεστα καὶ οὐ μεμελισμένα τέκνα,

and in the battle for their offspring they shudder not at the advancing crowd of javelin-throwers, not at the gleaming bronze and flashing iron, nor at the swift cast of shaft and shower of stones, but they are eager either to die first or save their children.

Wild Bears,[a] a deadly race of crafty wits, are clothed in a close and rugged coat of hair[b] and a form unkindly with unsmiling eyes. Sawtoothed, deadly, and long is their mouth ; nose dark, eye keen, ankle swift, body nimble, head broad, hands[c] like the hands of men, feet like men's feet ; terrible their roar, cunning their wits, fierce their heart ; and they are much given to venery and that not orderly. For evermore by day and night the females lust for mating and themselves pursue the males, seldom intermitting the pleasures of union and conceiving young when already pregnant. For it is not the custom for wild beasts when they are with young to mate and fulfil the work of desire, apart only from the Lynxes and the weakling Hares.[d] But the she Bear in her desire for mating, and abhorring to have her bed widowed, endures to devise for her children thus : ere the season of birth, ere the appointed day arrives, she puts pressure on her womb and does violence to the goddesses of birth : so great her lechery, so great her haste for love. She brings forth her children half formed and not

[a] *Ursus arctos*, the European Brown Bear or the Syrian Bear, *U. Syriacus*, which differs from the other only in its lighter colour.

[b] A. 498 b 27.

[c] A. 498 a 33 ἔχει (ἡ φώκη) τοὺς πόδας ὁμοίους χερσίν, ὥσπερ καὶ οἱ τῆς ἄρκτου.

[d] *Cf.* 515 ff.

σάρκα δ' ἄσημον, ἄναρθρον, ἀείδελον ὠπήσασθαι,
ἀμφότερον δὲ γάμῳ παιδοτροφίῃ τε μέμηλεν·
ἀρτιτόκος δ' ἔτ' ἐοῦσα μετ' ἄρσενος εὐθὺς ἰαύει.
λιχμᾶται γλώσσῃ τε φίλον γόνον, οἷά τε μόσχοι
λιχμῶνται γλώσσῃσιν ἀμοιβαδίς, ἀλλήλοισι
τερπόμενοι· γάνυται δὲ βοὸς χροῒ καλλίκερως βοῦς·
οὐδ' ἀποπλάζονται, πρὶν ἀπὸ γλυκὺν ἵμερον εἶναι·
θυμὸν δ' ἑσπομένοιο συνιαίνουσι νομῆος.
ὣς ἄρκτος λιχμῶσα φίλους ἀνεπλάσσατο παῖδας,
εἰσόκε κνυζηθμοῖσιν ἀναιδέα τονθρύζωσι.

Ναὶ μὴν χειμερίην πανυπείροχα δείδιεν ὁρμὴν
καὶ λασίη περ ἐοῦσα· χιὼν δ' ὅτε πάντα παλύνει,
ἑσπερίου ζεφύρου πανεπήτριμα χευαμένοιο,
κεύθετ' ἐνὶ σπήλυγγι, τόθι σκέπας ἄρκιον εὕρῃ,
καὶ βόσιος χατέουσα πόδας χεῖράς τε λιχμαίνει,
οἷά τ' ἀμελγομένη, καὶ γαστρὸς ἔκλεψεν ἐρωήν.
τοῖά νύ που βένθεσσιν ἐν εὐρυπόροιο θαλάσσης
πουλύποδες σκολιοὶ παρὰ κύμασι μητίσαντο,
χείματος οἳ μεσάτου κρυερὴν τρείοντες ἐνιπὴν

---

[a] A. 579 a 21 ἐλάχιστον δὲ τίκτει (ἡ ἄρκτος) τὸ ἔμβρυον τῷ μεγέθει ὡς κατὰ τὸ σῶμα τὸ ἑαυτῆς . . . καὶ ψιλὸν καὶ τυφλὸν καὶ σχεδὸν ἀδιάρθρωτα τὰ σκέλη καὶ τὰ πλεῖστα τῶν μορίων. *Cf.* 580 a 7; *De gen.* 774 b 14.

[b] Plin. viii. 126 hi (the cubs of the Bear) sunt candida informisque caro, paulo muribus maior, sine oculis, sine pilo, ungues tantum prominent; Ov. *M.* xv. 379 Nec catulus partu quem reddidit ursa recenti, Sed male viva caro est; Ael. vi. 3 ἡ ἄρκτος ὅτι τίκτει σάρκα ἄσημον; ii. 19 τὸ δὲ εἰκῇ κρέας καὶ ἄσημόν τε καὶ ἀτύπωτον καὶ ἄμορφον; Phil. 49 ἄσημον ἄρκτος ἀποτίκτουσα κρέας.

[c] Plin. *l.c.* hanc lambendo paulatim figurant; Ov. *l.c.* lambendo mater in artus Fingit et in formam quantum capit ipsa reducit; Ael. ii. 19 λειαίνει τῇ γλώττῃ καὶ ἐκτυποῖ εἰς ἄρθρα καὶ μέντοι καὶ κατὰ μικρὰ ἐκμορφοῖ; vi. 3 τῇ γλώττῃ

articulate,[a] shapeless flesh,[b] and unjointed and mysterious to behold. At one and the same time she attends to mating and to the rearing of her young and when she has but newly given birth she couches with the male. And she licks[c] with her tongue her dear offspring, even as cattle lick one another in turn with their tongues and take delight in each other; and one of the fair-horned kine rejoices in the other and they do not part till they have put from them sweet desire, and they gladden the heart of their attendant herdsman. So doth the she Bear shape her children by licking, while they whine and mumble incontinently.

Moreover the Bear beyond all others dreads the onset of winter, shaggy of hair though she be. And when the snow besprinkles everything, what time the stormy West Wind sheds it thickly all about, she hides[d] in a cave where there is shelter adequate and spacious, and for lack of food she licks her feet[e] and paws even as if she were milking them and beguiles the craving of the belly. Even such a device have the coiling Poulpes[f] devised in the depths of the wide-wayed sea amid the waves; who dreading the chilly menace of mid-winter hide in the shelving

διαρθροῖ αὐτὴν καὶ οἱονεὶ διαπλάττει; Phil. *l.c.* *λεάνασα δὲ μαλθακῆς γλώττης πόνῳ.* *Cf.* Don. *Vit. Verg.* 22 non absurde carmen se ursae more parere dicens et lambendo demum effingere; Aul. Gell. xvii. 10 dicere eum solitum ferunt parere se versus more ursino. Namque ut illa bestia fetum ederet ineffigiatum informemque, lambendo id postea quod ita edidisset, conformaret et fingeret, etc.

[d] *Cf. H.* ii. 247 ff.; A. 600 a 27 b 12; 611 b 34; Plin. viii. 126; Ael. vi. 3.

[e] *Cf. H.* ii. 250; Plin. viii. 127 priorum pedum suctu vivunt; Ael. vi. 3 *ἀπόχρη δὲ αὐτῇ τὴν δεξιὰν περιλιχμᾶσθαι.*

[f] *Cf. H.* ii. 241 ff.

κεύθονται πλαταμῶσιν ἑὰς πλοκαμῖδας ἔδοντες·
αὐτὰρ ἐπὴν ἔαρ ὑγρὸν ἐΰτροφον ἀνθήσειεν,
ἀκρέμονες σφίσιν ὦκα νέοι πάλιν ἀλδήσκουσι,
καὶ πάλιν εὐπλόκαμοι δολιχὴν πλώουσι θάλασσαν.
  Ἑξείης ἐνέπωμεν ἐΰσφυρον, ἠερόεντα,
κραιπνόν, ἀελλοπόδην, κρατερώνυχον, αἰπὺν ὄναγρον·
ὅσσε[1] πέλει φαιδρός, δέμας ἄρκιος, εὐρὺς ἰδέσθαι,
ἀργύρεος χροιήν, δολιχούατος, ὀξύτατος θεῖν·
ταινίη δὲ μέλαινα μέσην ῥάχιν ἀμφιβέβηκε,
χιονέης ἑκάτερθε περισχομένη στεφάνῃσι.
χιλὸν ἔδει, φέρβει μιν ἄδην ποεσιτρόφος αἶα,
ἀλλ᾽ αὐτὸς κρατεροῖς ἀγαθὴ βόσις ἔπλετο θηρσί.
φῦλα δ᾽ ἀελλοπόδων ζηλήμονα πάμπαν ὀνάγρων
πολλαῖσίν τ᾽ ἀλόχοισιν ἀγαλλόμενοι κομόωσι·
θηλύτεραι δ᾽ ἕσπονθ᾽, ὅθι τοι πόσις ἡγεμονεύει·
πρὸς νομὸν ἰθύνουσιν, ἐπὴν ἐθέλῃσιν ἀνώγειν,
πρὸς πηγὰς ποταμῶν, θηρῶν μέθυ, καὶ πάλιν αἶψα
πρὸς λασίους οἴκους, ὅταν ἕσπερος ὕπνον ἄγῃσι.
ζῆλον δ᾽ ἄρσεσι πᾶσιν ἐπὶ σφετέροισιν ὀρίνει
υἱάσι νηπιάχοισι πανάγριος οἶστρος ἀναιδής·
ὁππότε θηλυτέρη γὰρ ἔχει κόπον[2] Εἰλειθυίης,

[1] ὅσσε B. de Ballu: ὅστε MSS.
[2] κόπον Jacobs: τόκον MSS.

---

[a] *Equus onager*, the Asiatic Wild Ass, or *E. onager hemippus*, the Syrian Wild Ass, which hardly differs from the other. A. 580 b 1 εἰσὶ δ᾽ ἐν Συρίᾳ οἱ καλούμενοι ἡμίονοι, ἕτερον γένος τῶν ἐκ συνδυασμοῦ γενομένων ἵππου καὶ ὄνου, ὅμοιοι δὲ τὴν ὄψιν, ὥσπερ καὶ οἱ ἄγριοι ὄνοι πρὸς τοὺς ἡμέρους, ἀπό τινος ὁμοιότητος λεχθέντες. . . . αὗται αἱ ἡμίονοι γεννῶσιν ἐξ ἀλλήλων. *Cf.* A. 491 a 2, 577 b 23. The fertile ἡμίονοι were of course a species of Wild Ass, which perhaps explains the portent in Herod. iii. 151 f. *Cf.* Plin. viii. 174; Hom. *Il.* ii. 852; Herod. vii. 86; Varro ii. 1. 5; Colum. vi. 37; Ael.

rocks and devour their own tentacles; but when spring blooms, moist and fertile, new arms speedily grow for them again and once again with fair array of suckers they sail the long path of the sea.

Next in order let us tell of the Wild Ass,[a] well-ankled, swift as air, fleet-footed[b] like the wind, strong-hoofed, and tall. Bright is he of eye, strong of body, broad to behold, silvery of colour, long-eared, most swift to run. About the middle of his back is set a black stripe, surrounded on either side by snowy bands. He eats hay[c] and the grass-growing earth feeds him abundantly; but he himself is good food for mighty wild beasts. The tribes of the wind-footed Wild Asses are altogether prone to jealousy and they glory in many wives and plume themselves thereon. The females follow whereso-ever the husband leads: they haste to the pasture when he wills to bid them, and, when he bids, to the river springs, the wild beasts' wine, and anon to their bosky homes when evening brings sleep. A fierce and shameless frenzy stirs jealousy[d] in all the males against their own young sons. For when the female is in the travail of Eileithyia, the male sits

xvi. 29; xiv. 10; xvii. 31; Verg. *G.* iii. 409; Mart. xiii. 97 and 100. Hunting of, Amm. M. xxiii. 4. 7; Poll. v. 84; Ridgeway, pp. 43 f.

[b] A. 580 b 4 *εἰσὶ δ' ὥσπερ οἱ ὄνοι οἱ ἄγριοι καὶ αἱ ἡμίονοι τὴν ταχυτῆτα διαφέροντες.*

[c] Job vi. 5 Doth the wild ass bray when he hath grass? *Cf. ibid.* xxiv. 5.

[d] Solin. xxvii. 27 Inter ea quae dicunt herbatica eadem Africa onagros habet, in quo genere singuli imperitant gregibus feminarum. Aemulos libidinis metuunt. Inde est quod gravidas suas servant, ut in editis maribus si qua facultas fuerit generandi spem morsu detruncent, quod caventes feminae in secessibus partus occulunt.

ἄγχι μάλ' ἑζόμενος σφέτερον γόνον ἄντα δοκεύει·
καί ῥ' ὅτε νηπίαχον μητρὸς παρὰ ποσσὶ πέσῃσιν,
εἰ μὲν θῆλυ πέλει, ποθέει τέκος, ἠδ' ἑκάτερθε
γλώσσῃ λιχμάζων φίλιον γόνον ἀμφαγαπάζει·
ἄρσενα δ' εἴ μιν ἴδοι, τότε δὴ τότε θυμὸν ὀρίνει
λευγαλέῳ ζήλῳ περὶ μητέρι μαινόμενος θήρ·
ἐκ δ' ἔθορεν μεμαὼς παιδὸς γενύεσσι ταμέσθαι
μήδεα, μὴ μετόπισθε νέον γένος[1] ἡβήσειεν.
ἡ δὲ λεχώ περ ἐοῦσα καὶ ἀσθενέουσα τόκοισι
παιδὶ λυγρῷ πολεμιζομένῳ μήτηρ ἐπαμύνει.
ὡς δ' ὁπότ' ἐν πολέμῳ πολυκήδεϊ μητέρος ἄντην
νηπίαχον κτείνωσιν ἀπηνέες αἰχμητῆρες,
αὐτήν τ' αὖ ἐρύωσιν ἔτι σπαίροντι φόνοισιν
υἱέϊ πλεγνυμένην, στονόεν μέγα κωκύουσαν,
δρυπτομένην ἁπαλήν τε παρηΐδα, νέρθε τε μαζῶν
αἵματι δευομένην θερμῷ λιαρῷ τε γάλακτι·
ὣς καὶ θῆλυς ὄναγρος ἐφ' υἱέϊ πάμπαν ἔοικεν
οἰκτρὰ κινυρομένῃ καὶ δύσμορα κωκυούσῃ.
φαίης κεν πανάποτμον, ἑὸν παῖν ἀμφιβεβῶσαν,
μείλιχα μυθεῖσθαι καὶ λισσομένην ἀγορεύειν·
ἆνερ, ἄνερ, τί νυ σεῖο προσώπατα τρηχύνονται,
ὄμματα φοινίχθη δέ, τά τ' ἦν πάρος αἰγλήεντα;
οὐχὶ μέτωπον ἀθρεῖς λιθοεργέος ἄγχι Μεδούσης,
οὐ γόνον ἰοβόρον παναμειλίκτοιο δρακαίνης,
οὐ σκύμνον πανάθεσμον ὀριπλάγκτοιο λεαίνης.
παῖδα λυγρὴ τὸν ἔτικτον, ὃν ἀρώμεσθα θεοῖσι,
παῖδα τεὸν γενύεσσι τεῇς οὐκ ἄρσενα θήσεις;
ἴσχε, φίλος, μὴ τάμνε· τί μοι τάμες; οἷον ἔρεξας;

[1] γένος Schneider: γέ μεν MSS.

[a] A. *Mirab.* 831 a 22.

[b] *Cf. C.* ii. 9 n. Her head turned the gazer to stone:

hard by and watches for his own offspring. And when the infant foal falls at the feet of his mother, if it is a female, the father is fond of his child and licks it on either side with his tongue and caresses his dear offspring; but if he sees that it is a male, then, then the frenzied beast stirs his heart with deadly jealousy about the mother and he leaps forth, eager to rend[a] with his jaws the privy parts of his child, lest afterward a new brood should grow up; while the mother, though but newly delivered and weak from the travail of birth, succours her poor child in the quarrel. As when in grievous war cruel warriors slay a child before the eyes of his mother and hale herself while she clings to her son yet writhing in his blood and wails with loud and lamentable cry and tears her tender cheek and is drenched below with the hot blood and warm milk of her breasts; even so the she Wild Ass is just as if she were piteously lamenting and sorrowfully wailing over her son. Thou wouldst say that all unhappy, bestriding her child, she was speaking honeyed words and uttering this prayer. "O husband, husband, wherefore is thy face hardened and thine eyes red that before were bright? It is not Medusa's[b] brow who turned men to stone that thou beholdest near; not the venomous offspring of Dragoness implacable; not the lawless whelp of mountain-roaming Lioness. The child whom I, unhappy mother, bare, the child for whom we prayed to the gods, even thine own child, wilt thou with thine own jaws mutilate? Stay, dear, mar him not! Ah! why hast thou marred him? What a deed thou hast done! Thou

Ov. *M.* v. 217 saxificae vultus Medusae; Ov. *Ib.* 555; Eur. *Alc.* 1118; Pind. *P.* x. 47; Apollod. ii. 4. 3.

παῖδα τὸ μηδὲν ἔθηκας, ὅλον δέμας ἐξαλαώσας.
δειλὴ ἐγώ, πανάποτμος ἀωροτάτοιο λοχείης,
καὶ σὺ τέκος πάνδειλον ἀλιτροτάτοιο τοκῆος.
δειλὴ ἐγώ, τριτάλαινα, κενὸν τόκον ὠδίνασα,
καὶ σὺ τέκος, τμηθεὶς οὐχὶ στονύχεσσι λεόντων,
ἀλλ' ἐχθραῖς γενύεσσι λεοντείῃσι τοκῆος.
τοῖά τις ἂν πανάποτμον ἐὸν περὶ νήπιον υἷα
μυθεῖσθαι φαίη· τὸν δ' οὐκ ἀλέγοντα δαφοινοῖς
δαίνυσθαι στομάτεσσιν ἀμειδέα παιδὸς ἐδητύν.
Ζεῦ πάτερ, ὅσσον ἔφυ ζήλοιο πανάγριον ἦτορ.
κεῖνον καὶ φύσιος κρατερώτερον εἰσοράασθαι
θῆκας, ἄναξ, δῶκας δὲ πυρὸς δριμεῖαν ἐρωήν,
δεξιτερῇ δὲ φέρειν ἀδαμάντινον ὤπασας ἆορ.
οὐ παῖδας τήρησε φίλους γλυκεροῖσι τοκεῦσιν,
οὐχ ἑτάρους πηούς τε μολών, οὐκ οἶδεν ὁμαίμους,
ὁππόταν ἀργαλέος τε καὶ ἄσπετος ἀντιβολήσῃ.
κεῖνος καὶ προπάροιθεν ἑοῖσιν ἐφώπλισε παισὶν
αὐτοὺς ἡμιθέους καὶ ἀμύμονας ἡμιθεαίνας,
Αἰγείδην Θησῆα καὶ Αἰολίδην Ἀθάμαντα,
Ἀτθίδα καὶ Πρόκνην καὶ Θρηϊκίην Φιλομήλην

---

[a] When Hippolytus was falsely accused by his stepmother Phaedra, his father Theseus pronounced a curse on him which led to his death. Apollod. *Epit.* i. 18; Eur. *Hippol.*

[b] His wife Ino tried to kill her step-children, Phrixus and Helle, who escaped on the Ram of the Golden Fleece. Apollod. i. 9.

[c] Philomela and Procne were daughters of Pandion, king of Athens. Procne married Tereus, king of Thrace. Tereus insulted Philomela and, lest she should reveal his guilt, cut out her tongue. But Philomela depicted her misfortune on a tapestry which she sent to Procne. Procne killed her son Itylus and served him up as food to his father Tereus. Tereus was turned into a Hoopoe, Procne into a Nightingale, Philomela into a Swallow. Apollod. iii. 14; Ov. *M.* vi. 426 ff.

hast turned the child to nothingness and hast made all his body blind. Wretched and unhappy I in my untimely motherhood, and altogether wretched thou, my child, in thy most sinful father. Wretched I, thrice miserable, who have travailed in vain, and wretched thou, marred not by the claws of Lions, but by the cruel lion jaws of thy sire." Thus one would say the unhappy mother speaks over her infant son, while the unheeding father with bloody jaws makes mirthless banquet of his child. O father Zeus, how fierce a heart hath Jealousy! Him hast thou made, O lord, mightier than nature to behold and hast given him the bitter force of fire, and in his right hand hast vouchsafed to him to wear a sword of adamant. He preserves not, when he comes, dear children to their loving parents, he knows nor comrade nor kin nor cousin, when he intervenes grievous and unspeakable. He also in former times arrayed against their own children heroes themselves and noble heroines—Theseus,[a] son of Aegeus, and Athamas,[b] son of Aeolus, and Attic Procne[c] and Thracian[d] Philomela and Colchian Medea[e] and

The Roman writers usually invert the story, making Procne the Swallow (*e.g.* Ov. *F.* ii. 855), Philomela the Nightingale (*e.g.* Verg. *G.* iv. 511, but the Greek version *E.* vi. 79), and this has become traditional in English poetry.

[d] To the Greek poets the Swallow is typically the Thracian bird and its twittering the type of barbaric speech. Aristoph. *Ran.* 679 ff. Κλεοφῶντος ἐφ' οὗ δὴ χείλεσιν ἀμφιλάλοις δεινὸν ἐπιβρέμεται Θρῃκία Χελιδών, ἐπὶ βάρβαρον ἑζομένη πέταλον; Aesch. *Ag.* 1050 χελιδόνος δίκην ἀγνῶτα φωνὴν βάρβαρον κεκτημένη; R. Browning, *Waring* vi. 32 "As pours some pigeon, from the myrrhy lands | Rapt by the whirlwind to fierce Scythian strands | Where breed the swallows, her melodious cry | Amid their barbarous twitter."

[e] Daughter of Aietes, killed her children by Jason through jealousy of Glauce, daughter of king of Corinth.

Κολχίδα τε Μήδειαν ἀρίζηλόν τε Θεμιστώ.
ἀλλ' ἔμπης μετὰ φῦλον ἐφημερίων ἀλεγεινῶν
θηρσὶ Θυεστείην ὀλοὴν παρέθηκε τράπεζαν.
"Εστι δ' ἐϋκρήμνοις ἐπὶ τέρμασιν Αἰθιοπήων
ἱππάγρων πολὺ φῦλον, ἀκαχμένον ἰοφόροισι
δοιοῖς χαυλιόδουσι· ποδῶν γε μὲν οὐ μίαν ὁπλήν,
χηλὴν δ' αὖ φορέουσι διπλῆν, ἰκέλην ἐλάφοισι·
χαίτη δ' αὐχενίη μεσάτην ῥάχιν ἀμφιβεβῶσα
οὐρὴν ἐς νεάτην μετανίσσεται· οὐδὲ βροτείην
δουλοσύνην ἔτλη ποθ' ὑπερφίαλον γένος αἰνόν·
ἀλλ' εἴ καί ποθ' ἕλοιεν ἐϋστρέπτοισι βρόχοισιν
ἵππαγρον δολίοισι λόχοις μελανόχροες Ἰνδοί,
οὔτε βορὴν ἐθέλει μετὰ χείλεσιν αἶψα πάσασθαι
οὔτε πιεῖν, ὀλοὸς δὲ φέρειν ζυγὸν ἔπλετο δοῦλον.
Φράζεο καὶ δύο φῦλα δυσάντεα, καρχαρόδοντα,
μηλοφόνον τε λύκον δυσδερκέα τ' αὖθις ὕαιναν,

---

[a] Wife of Athamas, killed her children through jealousy of Ino, the previous wife of Athamas.

[b] Thyestes, s. of Pelops, had an intrigue with the wife of his brother Atreus, king of Argos, who banished him, but afterwards, pretending to be reconciled, recalled him and at a banquet served up to him his own son.

[c] The ref. is not to what are ordinarily called Wild Horses (A. 488 a 30; *P.A.* 643 b 6: *Probl.* 895 b 24) but to the Hippelaphus; A. 478 b 31 *ἔχει δὲ καὶ ὁ ἱππέλαφος καλούμενος ἐπὶ τῇ ἀκρωμίᾳ χαίτην καὶ τὸ θηρίον τὸ πάρδιον ὀνομαζόμενον· ἀπὸ δὲ τῆς κεφαλῆς ἐπὶ τὴν ἀκρωμίαν λεπτὴν ἑκάτερον· ἰδίᾳ δ' ὁ ἱππέλαφος πώγωνα ἔχει κατὰ τὸν λάρυγγα, ἔστι δ' ἀμφότερα κερατοφόρα καὶ διχαλά· ἡ δὲ θήλεια ἱππέλαφος οὐκ ἔχει κέρατα, τὸ δὲ μέγεθός ἐστι τούτου τοῦ ζῴου ἐλάφῳ προσεμφερές. γίνονται δ' οἱ ἱππέλαφοι ἐν Ἀραχώταις. . . . τὰ δὲ τῶν ἱππελάφων κέρατα παραπλήσια τοῖς τῆς δορκάδος ἐστίν.* The Ethiopians of Oppian are the E. Ethiopians on E. of Persian Gulf in the region of Baluchistan

glorious Themisto.[a] But notwithstanding, after the race of afflicted mortals, to wild beasts also he served up a banquet of Thyestes.[b]

In the precipitous bounds of the Ethiopians there is a great tribe of Wild Horses,[c] armed with two venomous tusks. Their feet, however, have not a single hoof, but double like that of Deer. The mane of the neck covers the middle of the back even to the end of the tail. Never does that dread overweening tribe endure the servitude of man, but even if the dark-skinned Indians by crafty ambush take the Wild Horse in their well-twisted toils, he will not readily taste food with his lips nor drink, but badly bears the yoke of slavery.

Mark also two dread saw-toothed[d] tribes, the sheep-slaying Wolf[e] and again the weak-sighted[f]

and so corresponding to A.'s Arachotae, for whom *cf.* Strabo 513 ff., 721 ff.; Dion. P. 1096; Amm. M. xxiii. 6. 72; Solin. liv. 2. The animal intended seems to be the Nylghau (*Boselaphus tragocamelus*), *cf.* the *tragelaphus* of Plin. viii. 120; Diod. ii. 51. On the other hand, O. Keller, *Die Antike Tierwelt*, i. 274 takes ἵππαγρος to be the Gnu.

[d] *Cf. C.* iii. 5 n.

[e] *Canis lupus*, M.G. λύκος, still pretty common in N. Greece and as far S. as Euboea and Attica, especially in severe winters, and in the Peloponnesus (Bik. p. 10), and "now as of old the dread of the shepherds of Palestine" (Tristr. p. 153).

[f] Of the possible senses of δυσδερκής, δυσδέρκετος, (1) seeing with difficulty, (2) seen with difficulty, (3) ill to see, *i.e.* hideous or terrible, δυσδέρκετος in *C.* ii. 607 of the Ape seems to have sense (3); δυσδερκής has sense (2) in *C.* i. 102 ἴχνη δυσδερκέα and 451 στιβίης δυσδερκέος. In *H.* i. 47 where the κήτεα are called δυσδερκέα δείματα λίμνης (Schol. δυσθέατα, δυσθεώρητα) the sense may be (3) or (1); *H.* v. 64 οὔτε γὰρ εἰσορόωσιν ἀπόπροθεν is in favour of the latter. In the case of the Hyena here and 290 it is not easy to decide between (3) and (1), but the latter is rather favoured by l. 269.

τὸν μὲν ποιμενίων τε καὶ αἰπολίων ὀλετῆρα,
τὴν δ' ἐχθρὴν σκυλάκεσσιν ἀρειοτέροις τε κύνεσσι·
τὸν μὲν νυκτερινὸν διὰ γαστρὸς ἄφυκτον ἐρωὴν
ἀρνειῶν ἐρίφων τε πολυπλόκον ἁρπακτῆρα,
τὴν δ' αὖ νυκτιπόρον καὶ νυκτιπλανῆ τελέθουσαν
οὕνεκά οἱ διὰ νύκτα φάος, σκότος αὖτε μετ' ἠῶ.
εἴδεα δ' ἀμφοτέροις ἀνομοιΐα θηρσὶ δαφοινοῖς·
τὸν μὲν γάρ τε κύνεσσι πανείκελον ὠπήσαιο
μείζοσι ποιμενικοῖς, λασίη δ' ἐπιέσπεται οὐρή·
ἡ δέ τε κυρτοῦται μεσάτην ῥάχιν, ἀμφὶ δὲ πάντῃ
λαχνήεσσα κυρεῖ, κατὰ δ' ἔγραπται δέμας αἰνὸν
κυανέῃς ἑκάτερθεν ἐπήτριμα ταινίῃσι·
στεινὴ τ' ἐκτάδιός τε πέλει καὶ νῶτα καὶ οὐρήν·
ῥινὸν δ' ἀμφοτέροισιν ἐπικλείουσιν ἀοιδοὶ
ῥιγεδανόν· τῆς[1] μέν τε διατμήξας περὶ ποσσὶν
εἰ φορέοις, φορέοις σκυλάκων μέγα δεῖμα κραταιῶν,
καί σε κύνες κείνοισιν ἐπεμβεβαῶτα πεδίλοις
ἀντίον οὐχ ὑλάουσι πάρος γε μὲν ὑλακόωντες.
εἰ δὲ λύκου δείρας ῥινῶν ἄπο τεκτήναιο
τύμπανον εὐκέλαδον Διδυμήϊον, ὠλεσίκαρπον,
μοῦνόν τοι μετὰ πᾶσι βαρύβρομον ἔκλαγεν ἠχὴν
καὶ μοῦνον παταγεῖ, τὰ δ' εὔθροα πρόσθεν ἐόντα
τύμπανα σιγάζει κώφησέ τε πᾶσαν ἰωήν.

[1] τοῦ Brodaeus.

---

[a] *Hyaena striata*, or Striped Hyena, which ranges from India to N. Africa and "is very common in all parts of Palestine" (Tristr. p. 108); A. 594 a 31 ὃν καλοῦσιν οἱ μὲν γλάνον, οἱ δ' ὕαιναν; 579 b 15; *De gen.* 757 a 3; *P.A.* 667 a 20; *Mirab.* 845 a 24; Plin. viii. 105 f.; Herod. iv. 192; Ael. i. 25, iii. 7, vi. 14, etc.; Solin. xxvii. 23 f.; Phil. 51.

[b] Pind. *P.* ii. 84; Plut. *Mor.* 971 A.

[c] A. 579 b 15 ἡ δὲ ὕαινα τῷ μὲν χρώματι λυκώδης ἐστί, δασυτέρα δέ, καὶ λοφιὰν ἔχει δι' ὅλης τῆς ῥάχεως; *cf.* 594 b 1.

Hyena [a]; the first a destroyer of flocks of Sheep and herds of Goats, the other the foe of Dogs and mighty Hounds; the one, through the unescapable impulse of hunger, the crafty [b] harrier by night of Lamb and Kid, the other a night-farer and night-wanderer, since for it there is light by night but darkness by day. The forms of these two bloody beasts are unlike. The Wolf thou wouldst behold like to the larger shepherd Dogs, with bushy tail behind. The Hyena has the midst of the back arched and it is shaggy [c] all about and the dread body is marked on either side with close-set dark stripes. It is narrow and long of back and tail. The hide of both beasts the minstrels celebrate as terrible. If thou wert to cut off a piece of hide of the Hyena and wear it on thy feet, thou wouldst wear a great terror to mighty Dogs, and Dogs bark not at thee wearing those shoes, even if they barked before. And if thou shouldst flay a Wolf and from his hide make a sounding tabor, like the tabor of Dindymus [d] which destroys increase,[e] it alone of all sounds its deep note and it alone makes a din, while all the tabors that had a goodly sound before are

[d] Dindymus, or Didymus *metri gratia*, a mt. in Mysia near Pessinus (Strabo 567), associated with the worship of Cybele, in whose rites the drum and the cymbals played a prominent part; Stat. *T.* viii. 221 gemina aera sonant Idaeaque terga.

[e] Homer uses ὠλεσίκαρπος of the willow, *Od.* x. 510, *cf.* Theophr. *H.P.* iii. 1. 3 τὴν ἰτέαν ταχὺ προκαταβάλλειν πρὸ τοῦ τελείως ἁδρῦναι καὶ πέψαι τὸν καρπόν· δι' ὃ καὶ τὸν ποιητὴν οὐ κακῶς προσαγορεύειν αὐτὴν ὠλεσίκαρπον; *id.* *C.P.* ii. 9. 14; Plin. xvi. 110 ocissime salix amittit semen, antequam omnino maturitatem sentiat, ob id dicta Homero frugiperdia. The ref. is to the self-emasculation practised by the worshippers of Cybele and her eunuch priests (*galli*).

καὶ φθίμενοι γὰρ ὄϊς φθίμενον λύκον ἐρρίγασι.
θαῦμα δὲ καὶ τόδ' ἄκουσα περὶ στικτῇσιν ὑαίναις,
ἄρσενα καὶ θήλειαν ἀμείβεσθαι λυκάβαντι,
καί ῥ' ὁτὲ μὲν τελέθειν δυσδερκέα νυμφευτῆρα,
νωλεμὲς ἱμείροντα γάμων, ποτὲ δ' αὖθις ὁρᾶσθαι
θηλυτέρην νύμφην λοχίην καὶ μητέρα κεδνήν.
Ἀλλὰ λύκων τελέθει πολιότριχα πέντε γένεθλα,
εἴδεα δ' ἀλλήλοις ἀνομοίϊα τεκμήραντο
φῶτες ἀμορβῆες, τοῖσιν μάλα δήϊα φῦλα.
πρῶτα μὲν ὃν καλέουσι θρασύφρονα τοξευτῆρα·
ξουθὸς μὲν πρόπαν εἶδος, ἀτὰρ περιηγέα γυῖα
καὶ κεφαλὴν φορέει πολὺ μείζονα καὶ θοὰ κῶλα·
γαστέρα δ' ἀργαίνουσαν ἔχει πολιῇ ῥαθάμιγγι·
σμερδαλέον δ' ἰάχει τε καὶ ὑψόθι πάμπαν ὀρούει,
αἰὲν ἐπισσείων κεφαλὴν πυρόεν τε δεδορκώς.
Ἄλλος δ' αὖ μέγεθος μὲν ὑπέρτερος, ἅψεα δ' αὖτε
μηκεδανός, πάντεσσι θοώτερος ὦκα λύκοισι·
τὸν μέροπες κίρκον τε καὶ ἅρπαγα κικλήσκουσι.
πολλῷ σὺν ῥοίζῳ δὲ μάλ' ὄρθριος εἶσιν ἐπ' ἄγρην
πρώτῃ ὑπ' ἀμφιλύκῃ· ῥέα γάρ τ' ἐπιδευέτ' ἐδωδῆς·
χροιῇ δ' ἀργυφέῃ σελαγεῖ πλευράς τε καὶ οὐρήν,
ναίει δ' οὔρεα μακρά· τὰ δ' ὁππότε χείματος ὥρῃ
ἐκ νεφέων προχυθεῖσα χιὼν κρυόεσσα καλύψῃ,
δὴ τότε καὶ πόλιος πέλας ἵκετο θὴρ ὀλοόφρων,
πᾶσαν ἀναιδείην ἐπιειμένος εἵνεκ' ἐδωδῆς,
λάθρῃ τ' ἐμπελάει μάλα τ' ἤρεμος, εἰσόκεν ἄγρῃ
ἐγχρίμψῃ· τὴν δ' αἶψα θοοῖς ὀνύχεσσιν ἔμαρψεν.

---

[a] A. 579 b 16 περὶ δὲ τῶν αἰδοίων ὃ λέγεται, ὡς ἔχει ἄρρενος καὶ θηλείας, ψεῦδός ἐστιν; *De gen.* 757 a 3 ff.; Diodor. 32 τὰς λεγομένας ὑαίνας τινὲς μυθολογοῦσιν ἄρρενας ἅμα καὶ θηλείας ὑπάρχειν καὶ παρ' ἐνιαυτὸν ἀλλήλας ὀχεύειν, τῆς ἀληθείας οὐχ οὕτως ἐχούσης; Ael. i. 25; Phil. 51; Plin. viii. 105; Ov. *M.* xv. 409 ff.

silent and hush all their noise. Sheep even when dead shudder at a dead Wolf. This marvel[a] also I have heard about the spotted Hyenas, to wit that the male and female change year by year, and one is now a weak-eyed bridegroom all eager to mate and anon appears as a lady bride, a bearer of children, and a goodly mother.

But five in number are the grey-haired breeds of Wolves, and herdsmen, whose bitter foes the wolf-tribes are, have remarked their different forms. First there is that which they call the bold Archer. Tawny is all his body, and his rounded limbs and head and swift limbs are larger far. The belly is light-coloured with grey spots. Terribly he howls and very high he leaps, ever shaking his head and glaring with fiery eyes.

Another again is superior in size and long of limb, swiftest in speed[b] among all Wolves that are; him men name the Hawk and the Harrier. With much din he fares forth in the early morning to seek his prey at the first glimmering of dawn; for he easily becomes anhungered. Silvery gleams his colour on ribs and tail. He dwells on the high[c] hills; but when in the winter season the chilly snow pours from the clouds and covers the hills, then doth the deadly beast draw nigh even to the city, having clothed himself with utter shamelessness for the sake of food; and stealthily he approaches and very quietly till he comes upon his prey, which speedily he seizes in his sharp claws.

[b] ὦκα may be merely = ὄχα (Hom.).

[c] μακρά = high; *cf.* οὔρεα μακρά (Hom. *Il.* xiii. 18, etc.), δένδρεα μακρά (Hom. *Il.* ix. 541, etc.), μακρὸς Ὄλυμπος (Hom. *Il.* xv. 193). So βραχύς = short of stature, Pind. *I.* vi. 44.

Ἔστι δέ τις Ταύροιο νιφοβλήτους ὑπὲρ ἄκρας
ἐνδιάων Κίλικάς τε πάγους καὶ πρῶνας Ἀμανοῦ,
καλὸς ἰδεῖν, θήρεσσι πανέξοχος, ὅντε καλεῦσι
χρύσεον, ἀστράπτοντα περισσοκόμοισιν ἐθείραις,
οὐ λύκος, ἀλλὰ λύκου προφερέστατος αἰπύτατος θήρ,
χείλεσι χαλκείοισι τεθηγμένος, ἄσπετος ἀλκήν.
πολλάκι τοι καὶ χαλκὸν ἀτειρέα, πολλάκι λᾶαν
ἐμμενέως ἐτόρησε καὶ αἰχμήεντα σίδηρον.
καὶ κύνα Σείριον οἶδε καὶ ἀντέλλοντα φοβεῖται·
αὐτίκα δὴ ῥωχμὸν καταδύεται εὐρέος αἴης
ἠὲ κατὰ σπήλυγγος ἀφεγγέος, εἰσόκεν ἄζης
ἠέλιος παύσαιτο καὶ οὐλομένου κυνὸς ἀστήρ.
Ἄκμονες αὖ δοιοί, φόνιον γένος, αὐχένα βαιοί,
εὐρύτατοι νώτοισιν, ἀτὰρ λασιότριχε μηροὺς
καὶ πόδας ἠδὲ πρόσωπον ὀλίζονες, ὄμμασι βαιοί.
τῶν ὁ μὲν ἀργυρέοις νώτοις καὶ γαστέρι λευκῇ
παμφαίνει, δνοφερὸς δὲ μόνων ἄκρα νείατα ταρσῶν·
ὅν τινες ἰκτῖνον πολιότριχα φῶτες ἔλεξαν.
αὐτὰρ ὅ γε χροιῇσι μελαινομένῃσι πέφανται,
μείων μὲν προτέροιο, τὸ δὲ σθένος οὐκ ἐπιδευής.
θηρεύει δ' ἔκπαγλον ἐπὶ πτώκεσσιν ὀρούων·
πᾶσαί τ' ἐκ μελέων ὀρθαὶ φρίσσουσιν ἔθειραι.
Δηθάκι δ' αὖτε λύκοι καὶ πορδαλίεσσι δαφοιναῖς
εἰς εὐνὴν ἐπέλασσαν, ὅθεν κρατερόφρονα φῦλα,
θῶες· ὁμοῦ δὲ φέρουσι διπλοῦν μεμορυγμένον ἄνθος,
μητέρα μὲν ῥινοῖσι, προσώποις δ' αὖ γενετῆρα.

---

[a] M. between Cilicia and Syria: Strab. 749, etc.

[b] It seems impossible to determine whether ἄκμονες here is merely an epithet (=ἀκμῆτες, ἀκάματοι), or a metaphorical use of ἄκμων=anvil, or a specific name (*cf.* Hesych. *s.v.*

And there is one which beyond the snow-clad heights of Taurus inhabits the Cilician hills and cliffs of Amanus,[a] beautiful of aspect, most excellent among beasts, which they call the Golden Wolf, brilliant with abundant hair: no Wolf but a tall beast more excellent than a Wolf, armed with mouth of bronze, infinite in might. Many a time he pierces amain the enduring bronze, many a time he pierces stone or the iron spear. He knows the Dog-star Sirius and dreads his rising; straightway he creeps into some cleft of the wide earth or into a lightless cave, until the sun and the baleful Dog-star abate their heat.

Again there are two redoubtable[b] Wolves, a deadly race, small of neck, very broad of back, but less of size in shaggy thighs and feet and face and small of eye. Of these one is brilliant with silvery back and white belly, and is dark only on the extremities of his feet. This grey-haired Wolf some men have named the Kite. But the other is dark of hue, smaller than the former yet not wanting in strength. He is a great hunter and makes Hares his prey, leaping upon them while all the hair upon his limbs bristles erect.

Often[c] Wolves mate with the fierce Leopards, and from the union springs the mighty tribe of Jackals.[d] They wear two colours mingled together, the mother's colour on the hide, the father's on the face.

ἄκμων . . . ἔστι δὲ καὶ γένος ἀετοῦ). Bodinus has *crudivori*, Peifer *fortes*, Morel *infatigati*, schol. δυνατοί.

[c] *Cf. C.* i. 27 n.

[d] The description of the θώς here suits the Civet, *Viverra civetta* (Ethiopian and Egyptian) and allied species, rather than the Jackal, and according to some authorities the θώς of Aristotle is not the Jackal but the Civet.

Τίγριδος αὖ μετέπειτα κλυτὸν δέμας ἀείδωμεν,
τῆς οὐ τερπνότερον φύσις ὤπασε τεχνήεσσα
ὀφθαλμοῖσιν ἰδεῖν θηρῶν μετὰ πουλὺν ὅμιλον.
τόσσον δ' ἐν θήρεσσι μέγ' ἔξοχος ἔπλετο τίγρις,
ὅσσον ἐν ἠερίοισι ταὼς καλὸς οἰωνοῖσι.
πάντα μιν ἀθρήσειας ὀρέσβιον οἷα λέαιναν,
νόσφι μόνου ῥινοῖο, τὸν αἰόλον ἐστεφάνωται,
δαίδαλα πορφύροντα καὶ ἄνθεσι μαρμαίροντα.
τοίην μὲν πυρόεσσαν ὑπὸ βλεφάροισιν ὀπωπαὶ
μαρμαρυγὴν στράπτουσιν· ἀτὰρ δέμας ἔπλετο τοῖον,
καρτερόν, εὔσαρκον· τοίη δολιχόσκιος οὐρή·
τοῖα περὶ στομάτεσσι προσώπατα· τοῖον ὕπερθε
νεύει ἐπισκύνιον· τοῖοι σελαγεῦσιν ὀδόντες.
ὠκυτέρη τελέθει δὲ θοῶν πανυπείροχα θηρῶν·
αὐτῷ γάρ τε θέειν ἰκέλη Ζεφύρῳ γενετῆρι·
οὔτι γε μὴν γενετῆρι· τίς ἂν τάδε πιστώσαιτο,
θῆρες ὅτι δμηθεῖεν ὑπ' ἠέρι νυμφευτῆρι;
ἔπλετο γὰρ κείνη κενεὴ φάτις, ὡς τόδε φῦλον
θῆλυ πρόπαν τελέθει καὶ ἀδέμνιον ἄρσενός ἐστι·
δηθάκι γάρ κεν ἴδοις πολυανθέα καλὸν ἀκοίτην·
ῥεῖα γὰρ οὐκ ἂν ἕλοις· δὴ γάρ τε λιπὼν ἐὰ τέκνα
ἐμμενέως φεύγει, θηρήτορας εὖτ' ἂν ἴδηται·
ἡ δ' ἕπεται σκύμνοισιν ἀνιάζουσά τε θυμόν,
χάρμα μέγ' ἀγρευτῆρσι, πρὸς ἄρκυας ἰθὺς ἱκάνει.
Κάπρος ἐνυαλίοις δὲ μέγ' ἔξοχος ἐν θήρεσσιν

---

[a] *F. tigris*, A. 607 a 4; Plin. viii. 66; Ael. viii. 1, xv. 14; Solin. xvii. 4 ff., xxvii. 16, liii. 19.

[b] Plin. *l.c.* animal velocitatis tremendae, *cf.* Solin. xvii. 4; Luc. v. 405; Claud. *In Ruf.* i. 90.

[c] See *C.* i. 323 n.; *cf.* Claud. *De rapt. Proserp.* iii. 262 Arduus Hyrcana quatitur sic matre Niphates, Cuius Achaemenio regi ludibria natos Advexit tremebundus eques: fremit illa *marito* Mobilior *Zephyro*.

Next let us sing the Tiger[a] of glorious form, than which cunning nature has vouchsafed naught more pleasant for the eyes to behold amid the great company of wild beasts. As much doth the Tiger excel among wild beasts as the Peacock doth for beauty among the fowls of air. Every way like a lioness of the hills wouldst thou behold it, apart only from the hide, which is variegated, with darkling stripes and brilliant sheen. Like are the eyes that lighten with fiery flash beneath the brows; like the body, strong and fleshy; like the long and bushy tail; like the face about the mouth; like the frowning brows above; like the gleaming teeth. Swifter[b] is it than all wild beasts that are; for it runs with speed like its sire, the West Wind[c] himself. Yet the West Wind is not its sire; who would believe that wild beasts mated with an airy bridegroom? For that also is an empty tale, that all this tribe is female and mates not with a male; for often mightst thou see its handsome spouse of many colours, but not easily couldst thou capture him; for he leaves his young[d] and flees amain when he descries the hunters; but the female follows her cubs and in the anguish of her heart—to the great joy of the hunters—comes straight to the nets.

Eminent among warlike wild beasts is the Boar.[e]

[d] Plin. *l.c.* ubi vacuum cubile reperit feta, maribus enim subolis cura non est, fertur praeceps odore vestigans.

[e] *Sus scrofa*, M.G. ἀγριόχοιρος, ἀγριογούρουνο. The Wild Boar is still pretty common in the mountainous parts of Attica, Euboea, and N. Greece, and occurs, though it has become rare, in the Peloponnesus (Bik. p. 15). It does not occur in the Cyclades, though feral Swine are found (Erh. p. 26). It is very common in Palestine (Tristr. p. 54); *cf.* A. 571 b 13; 578 a 25; Plin. viii. 212; Ael. v. 45; Xen. *C.* 10.

εὐνὰς μὲν ποθέει πυμάτοις ἐνὶ βένθεσι κρημνῶν,
ἔξοχα δὲ στυγέει δοῦπον πολυηχέα θηρῶν.
θηλυτέρῃ δ' ἀλίαστος ἐφορμαίνων ἀλάληται
καὶ μάλ' ἐρωμανέων σφριγᾷ· κατὰ δ' αὐχένος ὀρθαὶ
φρίσσουσι τρίχες, οἷα περισσολόφων πηλήκων,
ἀφρὸν ἀποσταλάει δὲ κατὰ χθονός· αὐτὰρ ὀδόντων
ἕρκος ἐπικροτέει λευκόχροον ἄσθματι θερμῷ·
καὶ χόλος ἀμφὶ γάμοισι πολὺ πλέον ἠέπερ αἰδώς.
θηλυτέρη δ' εἴ μίν κεν ὑποπτήξασα μένῃσιν,
ἔσβεσε πάντα χόλον, κατὰ δ' εὔνασε θηρὸς ἐρωήν·
εἰ δέ κ' ἀνηναμένη φεύγῃ φιλοτήσιον εὐνήν,
αὐτίκ' ὀρινόμενος θερμῷ πυρόεντι μύωπι
ἢ γάμον ἐξετέλεσσεν ἀνάγκῃ, ἶφι δαμάσσας,
ἢ νέκυν ἐν κονίῃσι βάλεν, γενύεσσιν ὀρούσας.
ἔστι δέ τις κάπροιο φάτις πέρι λευκὸν ὀδόντα
λάθριον ἐντὸς ἔχειν μαλερὴν πυρόεσσαν ἐνιπήν.
σῆμα δ' ἐφημερίοισιν ἀριφραδὲς ἐρρίζωται·
ὁππότε γὰρ πολὺς ὄχλος ἐπήτριμος ἀγρευτήρων
σὺν κυσὶν εὐτόλμοισι ποτὶ χθόνα θῆρα βάλωνται,
αἰχμῇσιν δολιχῇσιν ἐπασσύτερον δαμάσαντες,
δὴ τότ' ἀπ' αὐχένος εἴ τις ἀειράμενος τρίχα λεπτὴν
θηρὸς ἔτ' ἀσθμαίνοντος ἐνιχρίμψειεν ὀδόντι,
αἶψα μάλα σφαιρηδὸν ἀνέδραμεν αἰθομένη θρίξ.
καὶ δ' αὐτοῖσι κύνεσσιν ἐπὶ πλευρῇς ἑκάτερθεν,
ἔνθα συὸς γενύων πέλασαν αἴθωνες ὀδόντες,
ἴχνια πυρσευθέντα διὰ ῥινοῖο τέτανται.
Ὑστρίγγων δ' οὔπω τι πέλει κατὰ δάσκιον ὕλην
ῥίγιον εἰσιδέειν οὔτ' ἀργαλεώτερον ἄλλο·

---

[a] Plin. *l.c.* maribus in coitu plurima asperitas.

[b] Xen. *C.* 10. 17 τεθνεῶτος ἐάν τις ἐπὶ τὸν ὀδόντα ἐπιθῇ τρίχας, συντρέχουσιν· οὕτως εἰσὶ θερμοί· ζῶντι δὲ διάπυροι ὅταν ἐρεθίζηται·

He loves a lair in the farthest depths of the crags and greatly he loathes the noisy din of wild beasts. Unceasingly he roams in pursuit of the female and is greatly excited by the frenzy of desire. On his neck the hair bristles erect, like the crest of a great-plumed helmet. He drops foam upon the ground and gnashes the white hedge of his teeth, panting hotly; and there is much more rage about his mating than modesty.[a] If the female abide his advances, she quenches all his rage and lulls to rest his passion. But if she refuses intercourse and flee, straightway stirred by the hot and fiery goad of desire he either overcomes her and mates with her by force or he attacks her with his jaws and lays her dead in the dust. There is a tale touching the Wild Boar that his white tusk[b] has within it a secret devouring fiery force. A manifest proof of this for men is well founded. For when a great thronging crowd of hunters with their Dogs lay the beast low upon the ground, overcoming him with long spear on spear, then if one take a thin hair from the neck and approach it to the tusk of the still gasping beast, straightway the hair takes fire and curls up. And on either side of the Dogs themselves, where the fierce tusks of the Swine's jaws have touched them, marks of burning are traced upon the hide.

Than the Porcupines[c] there is nothing in the shady wood more terrible to behold nor aught more deadly

οὐ γὰρ ἂν τῶν κυνῶν ἁμαρτάνων τῇ πληγῇ τοῦ σώματος ἄκρα τὰ τριχώματα περιεπίμπρα.

[c] *Hystrix cristata.* "It is very common in all the rocky districts and mountain glens of the Holy Land" (Tristr. p. 125); A. 490 b 29; 579 a 29; 600 a 28; Ael. i. 31, vii. 47, xii. 26; Phil. 71; Herod. iv. 192; Plin. viii. 125; Solin. xxx. 28.

τῶν ἤτοι μέγεθος μὲν ὁποῖα λύκοισι δαφοινοῖς,
βαιόν, ὀλιζότερον, κρατερὸν δέμας, ἀμφὶ δὲ ῥινὸς
τρηχείαις λασίαισι πέριξ πέφρικεν ἐθείραις,
ὁπποίαις θωρήξατ' ἐχίνων αἰόλα φῦλα.
ἀλλ' ὅτε μιν σεύωσιν ἀρείονες ἔξοχα θῆρες,
δὴ τότ' ἐμήσατο τοῖα· θοὰς ἔφριξεν ἐθείρας
καί τ' ὀπίσω νώτοισιν ἀκαχμένον ὠκυπέτησιν
ἰθὺς ἀκοντίζει μαλερὸν βέλος· ἀμφότερον δὲ
φεύγει τ' ἐμμενέως καὶ ἀλευόμενος πολεμίζει.
δηθάκις ἔκτεινεν κύνα κάρχαρον· ὧδέ κε φαίης
αἰζηὸν τόξων δεδαηκότα τοξεύεσθαι.
τοὔνεκεν ὁππότε μιν θηρήτορες ὠπήσωνται,
οὔτι κύνας μεθιᾶσι, δόλον δ' ἐπετεκτήναντο,
τὸν μετέπειτ' ἐρέω, θηρῶν φόνον ὁππότ' ἀείδω.
'Ιχνεύμων βαιὸς μέν, ἀτὰρ μεγάλοισιν ὁμοίως
μέλπεσθαι θήρεσσι πανάξιος εἵνεκα βουλῆς
ἀλκῆς τε κρατερῆς ὑπὸ νηπεδανοῖσι μέλεσσιν.
ἦ γάρ τοι κέρδεσσι κατέκτανε διπλόα φῦλα,
ἑρπηστῆρας[1] ὄφεις καὶ ἀργαλέους κροκοδείλους,
κείνους Νειλῴους, φόνιον γένος· ὁππότε γάρ τις
θηρῶν λευγαλέων εὕδῃ τρίστοιχα πετάσσας

[1] ἑρπυστῆρας KM.

[a] A. 490 b 28 τὰς ἀκανθώδεις τρίχας οἵας οἱ χερσαῖοι ἔχουσιν ἐχῖνοι καὶ οἱ ὕστριχες: Claud. *De hystr.* 17; Calpurn. *Ecl.* vi. 13.

[b] A. 623 a 32 τὰ βάλλοντα ταῖς θριξίν, οἷον αἱ ὕστριχες; Ael. i. 31; Phil. *l.c.*; Solin. *l.c.*; Plin. *l.c.* hystrices generat India et Africa spina contectas ex irenaceorum genere, sed hystrici longiores aculei et, cum intendit cutem, missiles. Ora urguentium figit canum et paulo longius iaculatur. The legend, which arose doubtless from "the rattling of the spines and the occasional falling out of loose ones" (Camb. *N.H.* x. p. 501), is elaborated by Claud. *De hystr.* with the inevitable comparison to the shafts of the flying Parthian

Their size is like that of the bloody Wolves; short, small, and strong is their body, but their hide bristles all about with rough and shaggy quills, such as those with which the cunning tribes of Hedgehogs[a] are armed. But when far mightier beasts pursue him, then he uses this device. He erects his sharp quills and backward hurls[b] straight the dire shaft that bristles on his flying back, and both flees amain and fights as he seeks to escape. Many[c] a time he slays a saw-toothed Dog; even so, one would say, shoots a man well skilled in archery. Therefore when the hunters espy him, they do not slip the Dogs but devise a trick, which I shall tell[d] when I sing of the slaying of wild beasts.

The Ichneumon[e] is small, but as well worthy to be sung as large beasts by reason of the cunning and great valiance which it hides in a feeble body. For indeed by its craft it slays two tribes—the reptile Serpents and the terrible Crocodiles,[f] those creatures of the Nile, a deadly race. When one of the dread beasts sleeps, opening his lips with triple row and

(v. 21), whom he feigns to have learned his art from the Porcupine: Parthosque retro didicisse ferire Prima sagittiferae pecudis documenta secutos (47 f.).

[c] For δηθάκις *cf.* i. 27 n.

[d] This promise is nowhere fulfilled in our extant text.

[e] *Herpestes ichneumon* or Pharaoh's Cat, a species of Mongoose, still domesticated in Egypt as a destroyer of Rats and Mice. It is extremely common in every part of Palestine, "so that it is scarcely possible ever to take a walk soon after sunrise without meeting this little animal trotting away to its hole" (Tristr. p. 151). A. 580 a 23; 612 a 15; Strabo 812; Nemes. 54; Phil. 98; Plin. viii. 88; Cic. *N.D.* i. 36. 101. Also called ἰχνευτής Herod. ii. 67; Nicand. *T.* 195; Hesych. *s.* ἰχνευταί· οἱ νῦν ἰχνεύμονες λεγόμενοι.

[f] A. 487 a 22; 503 a 1, etc.; Plin. viii. 89; Herod. ii. 68; Solin. xxxii. 22; Plut. *Mor.* 976 B, 982 C.

χείλεα καὶ χάος εὐρὺ καὶ ἄσπετον αἰόλον ἕρκος,
δή ῥα τότ᾿ ἰχνεύμων δολίην ἐπὶ μῆτιν ὑφαίνων
λοξοῖς ὀφθαλμοῖσιν ἀπείρονα θῆρα δοκεύει,
εἰσόκε τοι βαθὺν ὕπνον ἐπὶ φρεσὶ πιστώσηται·
αἶψα δ᾿ ἄρ᾿ ἐν ψαμάθοισι καὶ ἐν πηλοῖσιν ἐλυσθεὶς
ῥίμφ᾿ ἔθορεν, πυλεῶνα διαπτάμενος θανάτοιο
τολμηρῇ κραδίῃ, διὰ δ᾿ εὐρέος ἤλυθε λαιμοῦ.
αὐτὰρ ὅ γ᾿ ἐξ ὕπνου βαρυαέος ἔγρετο δειλός,
καὶ κακὸν ἐν λαγόνεσσι φέρων τόσον ἀπροτίελπτον,
πάντῃ μαινόμενος καὶ ἀμήχανος ἀμφαλάληται,
ἄλλοτε μὲν ποτὶ τέρματ᾿ ἰὼν μυχάτου ποταμοῖο,
ἄλλοτε δ᾿ αὖ ψαμάθοισι κυλινδόμενος ποτὶ χέρσον,
ἄγριον ἀσθμαίνων, στρωφώμενος ἀμφ᾿ ὀδύνῃσιν.
αὐτὰρ ὅ γ᾿ οὐκ ἀλέγει, γλυκερῇ δ᾿ ἐπιτέρπετ᾿ ἐδωδῇ·
ἥπατι δ᾿ ἄγχι μάλιστα παρήμενος εἰλαπινάζει·
ὀψὲ δέ τοι προλιπὼν κενεὸν δέμας ἔκθορε θηρός.
ἰχνεῦμον μέγα θαῦμα,[1] μεγασθενές, αἰολόβουλε,
ὅσσην τοι κραδίη τόλμαν χάδεν. ὅσσον ὑπέστης,
ἀγχίμολον θανάτοιο τεὸν δέμας ἀμφὶς ἐρείσας.
Ἀσπίδα δ᾿ ἰοφόρον τοίαις ἐδαμάσσατο βουλαῖς.
πᾶν δέμας ἐν ψαμάθοισι καλύψατο θῆρα δοκεύων,
νόσφι μόνης οὐρῆς τε καὶ ὀφθαλμῶν πυροέντων·
οὐρή οἱ δολιχὴ γὰρ ὀφιονέῃ τε τέτυκται,
ἄκροισιν κεφαληδὸν ἐειδομένοισι κορύμβοις,

[1] *v.l.* μεγάθυμε.

---

[a] Diod. i. 87; Ael. viii. 25, x. 47; Phil. 98; Solin. xxxii. 25; Plin. viii. 90; Plut. *Mor.* 966 D; Amm. M. xxii. 15. 19; Strabo 812.

[b] The *Naja haje*, an African species of Cobra, called ἀσπίς (*i.e.* shield) from its shield or hood. When annoyed, it erects itself on its hinder part, while it spreads out the head and neck to right and left. It is much employed by snake-charmers in Palestine (Tristr. p. 271).

his wide gape and his fence unspeakable of flashing teeth, then the Ichneumon weaves a subtle device.[a] With eyes askance he watches the huge beast until he is confident in his heart that it is deep asleep. Then, having rolled himself in sand and mud he swiftly springs and flies with daring heart through the gate of death and passes through the wide throat. Then the wretched Crocodile wakes from his heavy sleep and carrying in his belly such an evil unlooked for, everywhere he roams in helpless rage, now going to the farthest reaches of the river, now rolling shoreward in the sand, gasping wildly and tossing in his agony. But the Ichneumon heeds not but enjoys his sweet repast; and mostly by the liver he sits to banquet; then late and last he leaps forth and leaves the empty body of the beast. O Ichneumon, marvellous and mighty, cunning in counsel, how great daring thy heart holds! What a task thou dost undertake, advancing thy body to the very jaws of death.

The venomous Asp[b] the Ichneumon overcomes by this device.[c] He lies in wait for the beast, hiding all his body in the sands, save only the tail and the fiery eyes; for the tail is long and snakelike with curling

[c] A. 612 a 15 *ὁ δ' ἰχνεύμων ὁ ἐν Αἰγύπτῳ ὅταν ἴδῃ τὸν ὄφιν τὴν ἀσπίδα καλουμένην, οὐ πρότερον ἐπιτίθεται πρὶν συγκαλέσῃ βοηθοὺς ἄλλους· πρὸς δὲ τὰς πληγὰς καὶ τὰ δήγματα πηλῷ καταπλάττουσιν ἑαυτούς· βρέξαντες γὰρ ἐν τῷ ὕδατι πρῶτον, οὕτω καλινδοῦνται ἐν τῇ γῇ*; Strabo 812; Ael. iii. 22, v. 48; vi. 38, x. 47; Phil. 98; Antig. 32; Nicand. *T.* 190 ff.; Plin. viii. 88; Luc. iv. 724 Aspidas ut Pharias cauda sollertior hostis Ludit et iratas incerta provocat umbra Obliquumque caput vanas serpentis in auras Effusae tuto comprendit guttura morsu Letiferam citra saniem; tunc inrita pestis Exprimitur, faucesque fluunt pereunte veneno.

ἄντα μελαινομένη, θηρῶν φολίδεσσιν ὁμοίη.
τὴν δ' ὅτε φυσιόωσαν ἔχιν ψολόεσσαν ἴδηται,
ἀντία γυρώσας προκαλέσσατο θῆρα δαφοινήν.
ἀσπὶς δ' ἰοφόρον πέλας ἀντήειρε κάρηνον,
στήθεά τ' εὔρυνε, στυφελόν θ' ὑπέσηρεν ὀδόντα,
μαρναμένη γενύεσσιν ἐτώσια λευγαλέῃσιν.
ἀλλ' οὐκ ἰχνεύμων τότ' ἀρήϊος ἐν ψαμάθοισι
δηθύνει, πικρῶν δὲ θορὼν ἐδράξατο λαιμῶν,
δαρδάπτει τε γένυσσιν ἑλισσομένην ἑκάτερθε,
καὶ νέκυν αὐτίκ' ἔθηκ' ἀποφώλιον ἐκπτύουσαν
πευκεδανὸν θανάτοιο φίλον, ζαμενῆ χόλον, ἰόν.
Ναὶ μὴν αἰολόβουλος ἐπ' ἀγραύλοισι μάλιστα
θηρσὶ πέλει κερδώ, μάλ' ἀρήϊος ἐν πραπίδεσσι·
καὶ πινυτὴ ναίει πυμάτοις ἐνὶ φωλειοῖσιν,
ἑπταπύλους οἴξασα δόμους τρητάς τε καλιὰς
τηλόθ' ἀπ' ἀλλήλων, μή μιν θηρήτορες ἄνδρες
ἀμφὶ θύρῃ λοχόωντες ὑπὸ βροχίδεσσιν ἄγωνται·
ἀργαλέη γενύεσσι καὶ ἀντία δηρίσασθαι
θηρσί τ' ἀρειοτέροισι καὶ ἀγρευτῆρσι κύνεσσιν.
εὖτε δὲ χεῖμα πέλει κρυερὸν βόσιός τε χατίζει,
γυμναὶ δ' ἡμερίδες περὶ βότρυσιν ἰνδάλλονται,
δὴ τότε καὶ θηρᾶν[1] πικρὴν ἐπὶ μῆτιν ὑφαίνει,
οἰωνούς τε δόλοισιν ἑλεῖν καὶ τέκνα λαγωῶν.

[1] θήραν or θήρην or θῆρα MSS.

---

[a] "The name Spy-slange [given to it by the Boers], meaning Spitting Snake, refers to the habit which this and other African Cobras have of letting the poison drop from the mouth like saliva when they are excited" (*Camb. N.H.* viii. p. 628).

[b] The cunning of the Fox is of course proverbial: A. 488 b 20 τὰ μὲν πανοῦργα καὶ κακοῦργα οἷον ἀλώπηξ. Hence its name κερδώ (*i.e.* κερδαλεόφρων), a fem. *Kosename* or pet-name

headlike tufts, black to the view, like the scales of serpents. When he seeks the dusky puffing viper, he arches his tail in front of her and challenges the deadly beast. The Asp over against him lifts up her head hard by and expands her breast and bares her stubborn teeth and fights vainly with her deadly jaws. But then the warlike Ichneumon lingers not in the sands, but leaps and seizes her terrible throat and rends her with his jaws as she twists this way and that and straightway lays her dead—vainly spitting[a] forth the bitter deadly venom of her passionate wrath.

Furthermore, most cunning[b] among all the beasts of the field is the Fox.[c] Warlike of heart and wise she dwells in remotest lair, with seven-gated openings to her house and tunnelled earths far from one another, lest hunters set an ambush about her doors and lead her captive with snares. Terrible is she to fight with her teeth against stronger wild beasts and hunting Dogs. And when chilly winter comes and she lacks food, and the vines show bare of grapes, then she weaves a deadly device for hunting, to capture by craft birds[d] and the young of Hares.[e]

(*cf.* Ἐνυώ: Ἐνυάλιος) parallel to the masc. πίθων: πίθηκος. Both occur together in Pind. *P.* ii. 72 καλός τοι πίθων . . . αἰεὶ καλός . . . κερδοῖ δὲ τί μάλα τοῦτο κερδαλέον τελέθει; where καλός alludes not merely to the formula καλός, ναιχὶ καλός (*cf.* Callim. *E.* xxx. 5 (Loeb) n.) but also to καλλίας, a pet-name for the Ape (*cf.* Callim. (Loeb) *Fr. Incert.* 141 n.).

[c] *Canis vulpes*, M.G ἀλεποῦ, still pretty common in Greece, where it is smaller and more greyish in hue than the Fox of N. Europe (Bik. p. 11); very frequent in Palestine where the common Fox of the S. and central country is the Egyptian Fox, greyer and smaller than ours (*cf.* A. 606 a 24), while in the N. is found the larger Syrian Fox (Tristr. p. 85).

[d] *Cf. H.* ii. 107 ff. n.

[e] Ael. xiii. 11.

Ἔννεπέ μοι κἀκεῖνα, πολύθροε Μοῦσα λιγεῖα,
μικτὰ φύσιν θηρῶν, διχόθεν κεκερασμένα, φῦλα,
πόρδαλιν αἰολόνωτον ὁμοῦ ξυνήν τε κάμηλον.
Ζεῦ πάτερ, ὅσσα νόησας, ὅσ᾽ εἴδεα νῶϊ φύτευσας,
ὅσσα βροτοῖσιν ὄπασσας, ὅσ᾽ εἰναλίοις νεπόδεσσιν.
ὃς τόδ᾽ ἐμήσαο πάγχυ καμήλων αἰόλον εἶδος,
ἀμφιέσας ῥινοῖσιν ἀναιδέσι πορδαλέοισι
φαίδιμον, ἱμερόεν, τιθασὸν γένος ἀνθρώποισι.
δειρή οἱ ταναή, στικτὸν δέμας, οὔατα βαιά,
ψιλὸν ὕπερθε κάρη, δολιχοὶ πόδες, εὐρέα ταρσά,
κώλων δ᾽ οὐκ ἴσα μέτρα, πόδες τ᾽ οὐ πάμπαν ὁμοῖοι,
ἀλλ᾽ οἱ πρόσθεν ἔασιν ἀρείονες, ὑστάτιοι δὲ
πολλὸν ὀλιζότεροι, κατά τ᾽ ὀκλάζουσιν ὁμοῖοι.
ἐκ δὲ μέσης κεφαλῆς δίδυμον κέρας ἰθὺς ὀρούει,
οὔ τι κέρας κερόεν, παρὰ δ᾽ οὔατα μεσσόθι κόρσης
ἀβληχραὶ κροτάφοισιν ἐπαντέλλουσι κεραῖαι·
ἄρκιον, ὡς ἐλάφοιο, τέρεν στόμα, λεπταλέοι τε
ἐντὸς ἐρηρέδαται γαλακόχροες[1] ἀμφὶς ὀδόντες·
αἴγλην παμφανόωσαν ἀπαστράπτουσιν ὀπωπαί.
οὐρὴ δ᾽ αὖτ᾽ ἐλαχεῖα, θοαῖς ἅτε δορκαλίδεσσιν,
ἄκραισιν μετόπισθε μελαινομένῃσιν ἐθείραις.

[1] γαλακόχροες Editor coll. Callim. *Hec.* i. 4. 3: γαλακτόχροες (γαλοκτ- DE) MSS.

---

[a] Diod. ii. 50 ζῷα διφυῆ καὶ μεμιγμένα ταῖς ἰδέαις.

[b] The Camelopard or Giraffe, *Giraffe Camelopardalis*, *cf.* Agatharch. *ap.* Phot. 455. 4 παρὰ τοῖς τρωγλοδύταις ἐστὶν ἡ λεγομένη παρ᾽ Ἕλλησι καμηλοπάρδαλις, σύνθετον τρόπον τινὰ κατὰ τὴν κλῆσιν καὶ τὴν φύσιν λαχοῦσα. τὴν μὲν γὰρ ποικιλίαν (*i.e.* spotted hide) ἔχει παρδάλεως, τὸ μέγεθος δὲ καμήλου, τὸ πάχος δὲ ὑπερφυές, τὸν δὲ αὐχένα τοιοῦτον ὥστε ἀπ᾽ ἄκρων ἀμέλγεσθαι τῶν δένδρων τὴν τροφήν; Strabo 827; Diod. ii. 51; Heliod. x. 27; Athen. 201 c; Solin. xxx. 19; Plin. viii. 69 Nabun Aethiopes vocant collo similem equo, pedibus et cruribus bovi, camelo capite, albis maculis rutilum colorem dis-

Tell also, I pray thee, O clear-voiced Muse of diverse tones, of those tribes of wild beasts which are of hybrid [a] nature and mingled of two stocks, even the Pard of spotted back joined and united with the Camel.[b] O Father Zeus, how many things hast thou devised, how many forms hast thou created for us, how many hast thou given to men, how many to the finny creatures of the sea! Even as thou hast devised this very varied form of the Camel, clothing with the hide of the shameless Pard a race splendid and lovely and gentle to men. Long is its neck, its body spotted, the ears small, bare the head above, long the legs, the soles of the feet broad; the limbs are unequal and the legs are not altogether alike, but the fore-legs are greater while the hind-legs are much smaller and look as if they were squatting on their haunches. From the middle of the head two horns rise straight up—not horny horns,[c] but feeble projections on the head which alongside the ears rise up between the temples. The tender mouth is sufficiently large, like that of a Stag and within are set on either side thin milk-white teeth. A bright gleam lightens from the eyes. The tail, again, is short, like that of the swift Gazelles, with dark hair at the hinder end.

tinguentibus, unde appellata camelopardalis, dictatoris Caesaris circensibus ludis primum visa Romae. A. 498 b 32 τὸ θηρίον τὸ πάρδιον (*v.l.* ἱππαρίδιον) ὀνομαζόμενον, described as having a fine mane, horned and cloven-hooved, has been thought to refer to the Giraffe.

[c] The so-called "horns" of the Giraffe, which are possessed both by male and female, though less developed in the latter, "differ from those of all other Ruminants; they are small bony prominences of the frontal bones, which become fused with the Skull, and which are covered with unmodified skin. They are not shed" (*Camb. N.H.* x. p. 302).

Ναὶ μὴν ἄλλο γένεθλον ἐμοῖς ἴδον ὀφθαλμοῖσιν
ἀμφίδυμον, μέγα θαῦμα, μετὰ στρουθοῖο κάμηλον·
τὴν ἔμπης κούφοις μεταρίθμιον οἰωνοῖσι
καὶ πτερόεσσαν ἐοῦσαν ἐμαὶ μέλψουσιν ἀοιδαί,
οὕνεκεν ἡμετέρης μιν ἕλεν νόμος αἰόλος ἄγρης.
οὔτε γὰρ ὀρνίθων σφε δαμάσσατο δήϊος ἰξός,
οὔτε διηερίην δόνακες πατέοντες ἀταρπόν.
ἀλλ' ἵπποι σκύλακές τε θοοὶ καὶ ἀείδελα δεσμά.
τῆς ἤτοι μέγεθος μὲν ὑπέρβιον, ὅσσον ὕπερθε
νώτοις εὐρυτάτοισι φέρειν νεοθηλέα κοῦρον·
καὶ πόδες ὑψιτενεῖς, ἴκελοι νωθροῖσι καμήλοις,
ὁπποῖον θαμινῇσιν ἀρηράμενοι φολίδεσσι
σκληρῇς ἄχρι διπλῆς ἐπιγουνίδος· ὕψι δ' ἀείρει
βαιὴν μὲν κεφαλήν, πολλὴν δὲ τανύτριχα δειρὴν
κυανέην· κείνῃσι πολὺ πτερόν· οὐ μὲν ὕπερθεν[1]
ἠέρος ὑψιπόροισιν ἐπιπλώουσι κελεύθοις,
ἀλλ' ἔμπης θείειν ποσσὶ κραιπνοὶ τελέθουσαι
αὐτοῖσιν φορέουσιν ἴσον τάχος οἰωνοῖσιν.
οὐδὲ μὲν ὀρνίθεσσιν ὁμοίϊος ἀμβαδὸν εὐνή,
Βάκτριον οἷα δὲ φῦλον ἔχουσιν ἀπόστροφα λέκτρα·

[1] After 496 all MSS. insert *C.* iv. 74-76.

---

[a] The Ostrich, *Struthio camelus*; A. 616 b 5 τὸν ἐν Λιβύῃ στρουθόν; *P.A.* 697 b 14 ὁ στρουθὸς ὁ Λιβυκός; *cf. ibid.* 695 a 17; 658 a 13; *De gen.* 749 b 17; Ael. ii. 27 ἡ στρουθὸς ἡ μεγάλη; *cf.* iv. 37, v. 50, ix. 58, xiv. 7; Phil. 4; Herod. iv. 192 στρουθοὶ κατάγαιοι; Diod. ii. 50 αἱ ὀνομαζόμεναι στρουθοκάμηλοι, *cf.* iii. 27; Agatharch. *ap.* Phot. 453 a 25; Plin. x. 1 Sequitur natura avium, quarum grandissimi et paene bestiarum generis struthocameli Africi vel Aethiopici.

[b] This is not a mere form of expression for "the two thighs," "thigh of each leg" but a ref. to the notion that the Camel—and by analogy the Ostrich—is double-jointed. Herod. iii. 103 τὸ μὲν δὴ εἶδος ὁκοῖόν τι ἔχει ἡ κάμηλος, ἐπισταμέ-

Yea and another double breed have I beheld with mine eyes, a mighty marvel, Camel united with Sparrow [a]; which, though it is numbered with the lightsome birds and is winged, notwithstanding my lays shall celebrate, since the varied range of our hunting admits it. For the lime that is the enemy of birds does not prevail over it, nor the reeds that tread an airy path, but Horses and swift Hounds and unseen snares. Its size is huge, so that it can carry on its broad back a young boy. The legs are long, like to those of the sluggish Camels, and are arrayed as it were with close-set hard scales up to the double thigh.[b] Small is the head that it rears on high but long the hairy dusky neck. They have abundant feathers; yet they do not sail aloft on the high paths of air, but notwithstanding, as they run swiftly with their feet, they have a speed equal to the birds themselves. Nor do they mate like birds [c] by mounting but, like the Bactrian tribe,[d] rear to

νοισι τοῖσι Ἕλλησι οὐ συγγράφω· τὸ δὲ μὴ ἐπιστέαται αὐτῆς, τοῦτο φράσω· κάμηλος ἐν τοῖσι ὀπισθίοισι σκέλεσι ἔχει τέσσερας μηροὺς καὶ γούνατα τέσσερα; *cf.* Ael. x. 3. The statement is contradicted A. 499 a 19 καὶ γόνυ δ' ἔχει ἐν ἑκάστῳ τῷ σκέλει ἓν καὶ τὰς καμπὰς οὐ πλείους, ὥσπερ λέγουσί τινες, ἀλλὰ φαίνεται διὰ τὴν ὑπόστασιν τῆς κοιλίας, *i.e.* on account of the way in which the belly is supported (for this use of ὑπόστασις *cf.* A. *P.A.* 659 a 24 ἕνεχ' ὑποστάσεως τοῦ βάρους. Similarly ὑπόστημα *De an. incess.* 708 b 2)—the ref. being to the callosities on the joints which support the belly in the same way that the front part of the body is supported by the breast callosity (A. 499 a 16 ἄλλον δ' ἔχουσιν ὕβον τοιοῦτον οἷον ἄνω ἐν τοῖς κάτω, ἐφ' οὗ, ὅταν κατακλιθῇ εἰς γόνατα, ἐστήρικται τὸ ἄλλο σῶμα).

[c] A. 539 b 25 ποιοῦνται σύνδυασμόν τάτε πλεῖστα τῶν τετραπόδων ἐπιβαίνοντος ἐπὶ τὸ θῆλυ τοῦ ἄρρενος καὶ τὸ τῶν ὀρνίθων ἅπαν γένος οὕτω τε καὶ μοναχῶς; *cf.* Plin. x. 143.

[d] The Bactrian Camel, *Camelus bactrianus*, with two humps: A. 498 b 8; 499 a 14; Plin. viii. 67.

τίκτει δ' ἄπλετον ᾠόν, ὅσον χαδέειν τόσον ὄρνιν,
κυκλόσε λαϊνέοις θωρησσόμενον κελύφεσσι.
Πτῶκας ἀείδωμεν, θήρης ἐρίδωρον ὀπώρην.
σῶμα πέλει τυτθόν, λάσιον, δολιχώτατον οὖας,
βαιὸν ὕπερθε κάρη, βαιοὶ πόδες, οὐκ ἴσα κῶλα·
χροιὴν δ' ἀμφιέσαντ' ἀνομοιΐον· οἱ μὲν ἔασι
κυάνεοι δνοφεροί τε μελάμβωλον κατ' ἄρουραν,
ξανθοὶ δ' αὖθ' ἕτεροι πεδίων ἐπὶ μιλτοπαρῄων·
αὐτὰρ ἐρίγληνοι χαροπὸν στράπτουσιν ὀπωπαὶ
κανθὸν ἀγρυπνίῃ κεκορυθμένον· οὔποτε γὰρ δὴ
ὕπνον ἐπὶ βλεφάροισιν ἀποβρίξαντες ἕλοντο,
δειδιότες θηρῶν τε βίην μερόπων τε θοὸν κῆρ·
νυκτὶ δέ τ' ἐγρήσσουσι καὶ ἐς φιλότητα μέλονται·

---

[a] This idea, entertained about various opisthuretic animals (Solin. xxvii. 16 (Leones) aversi [*i.e.* ἀντίπυγοι, ἀπόστροφοι] coeunt: nec hi tantum sed et lynces et cameli et elephanti et rhinocerotes et tigrides) is contradicted by A. 540 a 13 αἱ δὲ κάμηλοι ὀχεύονται τῆς θηλείας καθημένης· περιβεβηκὼς δὲ ὁ ἄρρην ὀχεύει οὐκ ἀντίπυγος (*cf.* 542 a 16), ἀλλὰ καθάπερ καὶ τὰ ἄλλα τετράποδα with regard to Camels, and of Elephants by Diod. ii. 42 ὀχεύεται δὲ τοῦτο τὸ ζῷον οὐχ, ὥσπερ τινὲς φασίν, ἐξηλλαγμένως, ἀλλ' ὁμοίως ἵπποις καὶ τοῖς ἄλλοις τετραπόδοις ζῴοις.

[b] *Lepus timidus* L. and allied species. M.G. λαγωός. Besides the normal Greek name λαγώς we find (1) the poetical term πτώξ (*cf.* *C.* i. 165), first as an epithet, Hom. *Il.* xxii. 310 πτῶκα λαγωόν, "the cowering Hare," in allusion to its timidity (Poll. v. 72: Ael. vii. 19), but already in Hom. *Il.* xvii. 676 as a substantive; *cf.* Aesch. *Ag.* 137 (2) δασύπους, the Furry-footed, frequent in Aristotle, used also by Plut. *Mor.* 971 A, etc.; Poll. v. 68, and, acc. to Athen. 399 e, f, by some of the Comic Poets; Plin. viii. 219 (quoted on l. 519), where he seems to distinguish *lepus* and *dasypus*, is unintelligible. Similarly in the *Anthol.* x. 11 λασίου ποδὸς ἴχνια = tracks of the Hare.

The Hare is very common in the whole of Greece (Bik. p. 14)—though it would appear that at one time it was rare

rear.[a] It lays a huge egg, of size to hold so great a bird, armed about with stony shell.

Let us sing of Hares,[b] rich harvest of the hunt. The body[c] is small and hairy, the ears are very long, small the head above, small the feet, the limbs unequal The colour with which they are clothed varies ; some are dark and dusky, which inhabit the black-soiled tilth : others are reddish-yellow, which live in red-coloured plains. Brightly flash their goodly orbs, their eyes armed with sleeplessness[d] ; for never do they slumber and admit sleep upon their eyelids, being afraid of the violence of wild beasts and the nimble wit of men, but they are wakeful in the night and indulge their desire. Unceasingly

in Attica, *cf.* Nausicrates (Comic Poet) *ap.* Athen. *l.c.* ἐν τῇ γὰρ Ἀττικῇ τίς εἶδε πώποτε | λέοντας ἢ τοιοῦτον ἕτερον θηρίον ; | οὗ δασύποδ' εὑρεῖν ἐστιν οὐχὶ ῥᾴδιον. In many of the Cyclades the Hare is extremely common and differs in no essential point from the Common Hare of Europe (Erh. p. 22). On the other hand, in some of the Cyclades it is either not found at all or confined to a particular region, its place being taken by the Rabbit, *L. cuniculus.* The curious thing is that Hares and Rabbits in the Cyclades seem to be mutually exclusive. Thus only Hares are found in Ceos, Siphnos, Syros, Tenos, Naxos, Paros, Melos, and the North of Andros; only Rabbits in Gyaros, Cythnos, Seriphos, Aspronisi, Myconos, Delos, Cimolos, Pholegandros, and the South of Andros. There is nothing in the geographical conditions to account for this phenomenon ; all the islands offer exactly similar facilities for life and nurture. Yet Syros has only Hares, while the little island of Aspronisi, six nautical miles S. of Syros, has only Rabbits. A curious parallel is offered by Syria, where the Hare is common, while "No Rabbit is found in Syria or in any of the adjoining countries" (Tristr. p. 99). *Cf.* Plin. viii. 226 f.

[c] A. 519 a 22, etc. ; Xen. *C.* 5. 22 ff. ; Poll. v. 66 ff. ; Ael. xiii. 13 f. ; Phil. 60 f. ; Plin. viii. 217 ff.

[d] Callim. *H.* iii. 95 οὐ μύοντα λαγωόν ; Xen. *C.* 5. 11 and 26 ; Poll. v. 69 and 72 ; Phil. 60 : Ael. ii. 12, xiii. 13.

νωλεμὲς ἱμείρουσι γάμων, ἔτι δ᾽ ἔγκυοι οὖσαι[1]
οὔποτ᾽ ἀναίνονται πόσιος πολύθουρον ἐρωήν,
οὐδ᾽ ὅτε γαστρὶ φέρωσι πολύσπορον ὠκὺν ὀϊστόν·
ἔξοχα γὰρ τόδε φῦλον, ὅσ᾽ ἄπλετος ἔτραφεν αἶα,
πουλυγόνον τελέθει· τὸ μὲν ἄρ ποθι νηδύος ἐκτὸς
ἔμβρυον ἐκθρώσκει τετελεσμένον, ἄλλο δ᾽ ἔσωθεν
νόσφι τριχὸς φορέει, τὸ δ᾽ ἄρ᾽ ἡμιτέλεστον ἀέξει,
ἄλλο δ᾽ ἄναρθρον ἔχει θορόεν βρέφος ὠπήσασθαι·
ἑξείης τίκτει δέ, καὶ οὔποτε θῆλυς ἀναιδὴς
λήθετο μαχλοσύνης· τελέει δ᾽ ὅσα θυμὸς ἀνώγει,
οὐδ᾽ αὐταῖς ὠδῖσιν ἀνηναμένη Κυθέρειαν.

[1] ἐγγὺς ἐοῦσαι MSS. : corr. Turnebus.

---

[a] Strabo 144; Athen. 400; Plin. *l.c.*; A. *Rhet.* 1413 a 16.

[b] Herod. iii. 108 ὁ λάγος ὑπὸ παντὸς θηρεύεται θηρίου καὶ ὄρνιθος καὶ ἀνθρώπου, οὕτω δή τι πολύγονόν ἐστι· ἐπικυίσκεται μοῦνον πάντων θηρίων καὶ τὸ μὲν δασὺ τῶν τέκνων ἐν τῇ γαστρί, τὸ δὲ ψιλόν, τὸ δὲ ἄρτι ἐν τῇσι μήτρῃσι πλάσσεται, τὸ δὲ ἀναιρέεται; A. 579 b 30 οἱ δασύποδες . . . ὀχεύονται καὶ τίκτουσιν πᾶσαν ὥραν καὶ ἐπικυίσκονται ὅταν κύωσι καὶ τίκτουσι κατὰ μῆνα. τίκτουσι δ᾽ οὐκ ἀθρόα ἀλλὰ διαλείπουσιν ἡμέρας ὅσας ἂν τύχωσιν. ἴσχει δ᾽ ἡ θήλεια γάλα πρότερον ἢ τεκεῖν καὶ τεκοῦσα εὐθὺς ὀχεύεται καὶ

they yearn to mate and while the females are still pregnant they do not reject the lustful advances of the male, not even when they carry in the womb the swift arrow of fruitfulness. For this tribe, among all that the infinite earth breeds, is the most prolific.[a] The one embryo[b] comes forth from the mother's womb full-formed, while she carries one within her still hairless, and nourishes another half-formed, and has in her womb yet another—a formless foetus to look on. In succession she brings them forth and the shameless female never forgets her lust but fulfils all her desire and not even in the throes of birth does she refuse her mate.

συλλαμβάνει ἔτι θηλαζομένη; *cf.* 542 b 31; *De gen.* 774 a 31; Xen. *C.* 5. 13 *πολύγονον δ' ἐστὶν οὕτως ὥστε τὰ μὲν τέτοκε, τὰ δὲ τίκτει, τὰ δὲ κυεῖ*; Ael. ii. 12 *φέρει δὲ καὶ ἐν τῇ νηδύι τὰ μὲν ἡμιτελῆ, τὰ δὲ ὠδίνει, τὰ δὲ ἤδη οἱ τέτεκται*; Plin. viii. 219 Lepus omnium praedae nascens solus praeter dasypodem superfetat, aliud educans, aliud in utero pilis vestitum, aliud implume, aliud inchoatum gerens pariter; Poll. v. 73; Eratosth. *Catast.* 34; Athen. 400 e; Phil. 61; Varro iii. 12. 4; Clem. Alex. *Paed.* ii. p. 291.

ΚΥΝΗΓΕΤΙΚΩΝ ΤΟ Δ

Εἴδεα μὲν τόσα θηρσί, τόσαι δ' ἀνὰ δάσκιον ὕλην
νυμφίδιοι φιλότητες ὁμήθειαί τε πέλονται
ἔχθεά τε κρυεροί τε μόθοι νόμιοί τε χαμεῦναι.
τλησιπόνων δ' ἀνδρῶν χρέος ἄπλετον ἀείδωμεν,
ἀμφότερον κρατερόν τε μένος καὶ ἐπίφρονα βουλὴν
κέρδεά τ' αἰολόβουλα πολυφράστοις τε δόλοισι
φραξαμένην κραδίην· ἣ γάρ τε πρὸς ἄγρια φῦλα
μάρναται, οἷσι θεὸς σθένος ὤπασε καὶ μένος ἠῢ
καὶ φρένας οὐδ' αὐτῶν πολὺ μείονας ἀγρευτήρων.
Ἤθεα[1] πολλὰ πέλει κλειτῆς πολυαρκέος[2] ἄγρης,
ἄρμενα καὶ θήρεσσι καὶ ἔθνεσιν ἠδὲ χαράδραις,
μυρία· τίς κεν ἅπαντα μιῇ φρενὶ χωρήσειεν
εἰπέμεναι κατὰ μοῖραν ὑπ' εὐκελάδοισιν ἀοιδαῖς;
τίς δ' ἂν πάντ' ἐσίδοι; τίς δ' ἂν τόσον ὠπήσαιτο
θνητὸς ἐών; μοῦνοι δὲ θεοὶ ῥέα πάνθ' ὁρόωσιν.
αὐτὰρ ἐγὼν ἐρέω τά τ' ἐμοῖς ἴδον ὀφθαλμοῖσι,
θήρην ἀγλαόδωρον ἐπιστείχων ξυλόχοισιν,
ὅσσα τ' ἀπ' ἀνθρώπων ἐδάην, τοῖσιν τὰ μέμηλεν,
αἰόλα παντοίης ἐρατῆς μυστήρια τέχνης,
ἱμείρων τάδε πάντα Σεουήρου Διὸς υἱῷ

[1] εἴδεα Brunck. [2] πολυάρκυος or πολυερκέος Brodaeus.

[a] Dion. P. 1169 μοῦνοι δὲ θεοὶ ῥέα πάντα δύνανται, imitated

CYNEGETICA, OR THE CHASE

IV

So many are the species of wild beasts, so many in the shady wood their nuptial loves and companionships, their hates and deadly feuds, their couches in the wild. Now let us sing the great business of the toilsome hunters, both their valiant might and their prudent counsel, their cunning craft and their heart armed with manifold wiles; for verily that heart wars against wild races to whom God hath given strength and goodly courage and wits not far inferior to the hunters themselves.

Many are the modes of glorious and profitable hunting: modes innumerable, suited to the various beasts and tribes and glens. Who with his single mind should comprehend them all and tell of them in order with euphonious song? Who could behold them all? Who could behold so much, being mortal? Only the Gods easily see all things.[a] But I shall tell what I have seen with my own eyes when following in the woods the chase, splendid of boons, and whatever cunning mysteries of all manner of delightful craft I have learned from them whose business it is; fain as I am to sing of all these things to the son of Divine

from Hom. *Od.* x. 305 χαλεπὸν δέ τ' ὀρύσσειν | ἀνδράσι γε θνητοῖσι θεοὶ δέ τε πάντα δύνανται; *Od.* iv. 379 θεοὶ δέ τε πάντα ἴσασιν.

ἀείδειν· σὺ δέ, πότνα θεά, παγκοίρανε θήρης,
εὐμενέουσα θοῇ βασιληΐδι λέξον ἀκουῇ,
ὄφρα τεῶν ἔργων προμαθὼν ὀαρίσματα πάντα
θηροφονῇ, μακαριστὸς ὁμοῦ παλάμῃ καὶ ἀοιδῇ.
Θηρῶν οἱ μὲν ἔασιν ἐπίφρονες, αἰολόβουλοι,
ἀλλὰ δέμας βαιοί· τοὶ δ' ἔμπαλιν ἀλκήεντες,
βουλὴν δ' ἐν στήθεσσιν ἀνάλκιδες· οἱ δ' ἄρ' ὁμαρτῇ
καὶ κραδίην δειλοὶ καὶ γυῖα πέλουσ' ἀμενηνοί,
ἀλλὰ πόδεσσι θοοί· τοῖσιν δὲ θεὸς πόρε πάντα,
βουλὴν κερδαλέην, κρατερὸν δέμας, ὠκέα γοῦνα.
γιγνώσκουσι δ' ἕκαστος ἑῆς φύσιος κλυτὰ δῶρα,
ἔνθ' ὀλιγοδρανέες τε καὶ ἔνθα πέλουσι δαφοινοί.
οὐκ ἔλαφος κεράεσσι θρασύς, κεράεσσι δὲ ταῦρος·
οὐ γενύεσσιν ὄρυξ κρατερός, γενύεσσι λέοντες·
οὐ ποσὶ ῥινόκερως πίσυνος, πόδες ὅπλα λαγωῶν·
πόρδαλις οἶδ' ὀλοὴ παλαμάων λοίγιον ἰόν,
καὶ σθένος αἰνὸς ὄϊς μέγα λαϊνέοιο μετώπου,
καὶ κάπρος μένος οἶδεν ἑῶν ὑπέροπλον ὀδόντων.
Ὅσσαι μέν νυν ἔασιν ἐπακτήρεσσι δαφοινοῖς
μουναδὸν ἐν σκοπέλοισι προμήθειαί τε πάγαι τε,
κεκριμένας φράσομεν θήρας ἐπὶ θηρσὶν ἑκάστοις·
ξυνὰ δέ θ' ὅσσα πέλουσιν, ὁμοίης ἔλλαχεν ᾠδῆς.
ξυναὶ θηροσύναι τε λίνων ξυναί τε ποδάγραι·

---

[a] A stock theme: A. *P.A.* 662 b 33 δέδωκε γὰρ ἡ φύσις τοῖς μὲν ὄνυχας, τοῖς δ' ὀδόντας μαχητικούς, τοῖς δ' ἄλλο τι μόριον ἱκανὸν ἀμύνειν; Lucr. v. 862 Principio genus acre leonum saevaque saecla Tutata est virtus, volpes dolus et fuga cervos; Cic. *N.D.* ii. 50. 127 Iam illa cernimus, ut contra metum et vim suis se armis quaeque defendat: cornibus tauri, apri dentibus, morsu leones; aliae fuga se, aliae occultatione tutantur; atramenti effusione sepiae, torpore

Severus. And do thou of thy grace, O lady goddess, queen of the chase, declare those things for quick royal ears, so that knowing before all the lore of thy works the king may slay wild beasts, blessed at once in hand and song.

Of wild beasts some are wise [a] and cunning but small of body; others again are valiant in might but weak in the counsel of their breasts; others are both craven of heart and feeble of body, but swift of foot; to others again God hath given all the gifts together—cunning counsel, valorous strength, and nimble knees. But they know each [b] the splendid gifts of his own nature—where they are feeble and where they are deadly.[c] Not with his horns is the Stag bold but with his horns the Bull; not with his teeth is the Oryx strong, but with his teeth the Lion; not in his feet doth the Rhinoceros trust, but feet are the armour of the Hare; the deadly Leopard knows the baleful venom of his claws and the dread Ram the mighty strength of his stony forehead, and the wild Boar knows the exceeding might of his tusks.

Now whatever special arts and snares are used by deadly hunters amid the crags, the particular ways of hunting we shall tell for each sort of beast; but those things which are common to all, are sung in one lay. Common is hunting with nets, common

torpedines: multa etiam infectantes odoris intolerabili foeditate depellunt; *cf.* Ov. *Hal.* 1 ff.

[b] Ael. ix. 40 οἶδε δὲ ἄρα τῶν ζῴων ἕκαστον ἐν ᾧ μέρει κέκτηται τὴν ἀλκήν; Ov. *Hal.* 7 Omnibus ignotae mortis timor, omnibus hostem Praesidiumque datum sentire et noscere teli Vimque modumque sui.

[c] δαφοινός is sometimes definitely of colour = πυρρός, reddish; Hom. *Il.* ii. 308 δράκων ἐπὶ νῶτα δαφοινός; x. 23 δαφοινὸν δέρμα λέοντος, but often merely = φόνιος, φοβερός; *cf.* 37 *infr.*, Hes. and Suid. *s.v.*, *E.M.* *s.* ἀρθρέμβολα.

ξυνὰ δέ τ' ἀνθρώποισι ποδωκέα πάντα γένεθλα
ἵπποις ἠδὲ κύνεσσι διωκέμεν· ἄλλοτε δ' αὖτε
καὶ μούνοις ἵπποισι κυνῶν ἄτερ ἰθὺς ἐλαύνειν·
ἵπποισιν κείνοισιν, ὅσοι περὶ Μαυρίδα γαῖαν
φέρβοντ', ἢ Λιβύεσσιν· ὅσοι μὴ κάρτεϊ χειρῶν
ἄγχονται ψαλίοισι βιαζομένοιο χαλινοῦ,
πείθονται δὲ λύγοισιν, ὅπη βροτὸς ἡγεμονεύει.
τοὔνεκεν ἱππελάται κείνων ἐπιβήτορες ἵππων
ἠδὲ κύνας λείπουσι φίλους πίσυνοί τ' ἐλόωσιν
ἵπποις ἠελίου τε βολῇ καὶ νόσφιν ἀρωγῶν.
ξυνὸν ἀκοντίζειν δὲ καὶ ἀντία τοξάζεσθαι
θῆρας ἀρειοτέρους, τοί τ' ἀνδράσιν ἶφι μάχονται.
'Ες δὲ λίνον χρειὼ στέλλειν οἰήϊα θήρης,
καὶ πνοιὴν ἀνέμου φεύγειν ἄνεμόν τε δοκεύειν.

---

[a] The caltrop, ποδάγρα (*A.P.* vi. 296 ἀστεμφῆ ποδάγρην) or ποδοστράβη (Poll. v. 32 καλοῖτο δ' ἂν καὶ ποδοστράβη), was employed chiefly for Deer, but also for wild Swine (Poll. *l.c.*, Xen. *Cyr.* i. 6. 28). It corresponds to the Lat. *pedica dentata* (Gratt. 92 Quid si dentatas iligno robore clausit Venator pedicas?) and is said to have been invented by Aristaeus (Plut. *Mor.* 757 D εὔχονται δ' Ἀρισταίῳ δολοῦντες ὀρύγμασι καὶ βρόχοις λύκους καὶ ἄρκτους, ὃς πρῶτος θήρεσσιν ἔπηξε ποδάγρας; *cf.* Nonn. v. 234). It is described Poll. *l.c.*, Xen. *C.* 9. 11 ff. It consisted of a wooden hoop (στεφάνη) containing a framework (πλόκανον) in which were set nails of wood and iron alternately (Poll. seems to say that the nails were in the στεφάνη but Xen. describes them as ἐγκαταπεπλεγμένους ἐν τῷ πλοκάνῳ and acc. to Poll. πλόκανον ἐν μέσῳ τῷ πλέγματι πέπλεκται). Inside the frame is set a noose (βρόχος) and attached to it by a rope (σειρίς, ἀρπεδόνη) is a clog (ξύλον): trap, rope, and clog are all sunk in the ground and covered over. When the trap is sprung (ἀνεστραμμένη) by the beast treading on it, the noose entangles the foot or feet of the game while the clog hampers its movements and by its trail on the ground indicates the path of its flight.

[b] Arr. *C.* 24. 3 Λιβύων παῖδες ὀκταέτεις ἔστιν οἳ αὐτῶν, οἱ δὲ

are traps,[a] and common is the chase of all the swift-footed tribes by men with horses and dogs, or sometimes without dogs pursuing the quarry with horses only: those horses which pasture in the land of the Moors, or Libyan horses, which are not constrained by might of hand with the curb of the compelling bridle but obey the riding-switch,[b] wheresoever their rider directs their course. Wherefore the riders who are mounted on those horses leave their beloved dogs at home and ride forth trusting to their horses and the rays of the sun, without other helpers. Common, too, is hurling the javelin and shooting with the bow at the mightier wild beasts which fight amain with men.

With reference to the net one must steer the course of the hunt and avoid the breath of the breeze and

οὐ πολλῷ πρεσβύτεροι, ἐπὶ γυμνῶν τῶν ἵππων ἐλαύνουσιν, ῥάβδῳ χρώμενοι ἐπ' αὐτοῖς ὅσα Ἕλληνες χαλινῷ; Strab. 828 σχεδὸν δέ τι καὶ οὗτοι (οἱ Μαυρούσιοι) καὶ οἱ ἐφεξῆς Μασαισύλιοι καὶ κοινῶς Λίβυες . . . μικροῖς ἵπποις χρώμενοι, ὀξέσι δὲ καὶ εὐπειθέσιν ὥστ' ἀπὸ ῥάβδου οἰακίζεσθαι; Verg. *A.* iv. 41 Numidae infreni; Nemes. 263 ff. Nec pigeat quod turpe caput deformis et alvus Est ollis quodque infrenes . . . Nam flecti facilis lascivaque colla secutus Paret in obsequium lentae moderamine virgae. Verbera sunt praecepta fugae, sunt verbera freni; Auson. *Ad Grat. Imp.* xiv. mirabamur poetam (*sc.* Vergilium) qui infrenos dixerat Numidas et alterum (*sc.* Nemes.) qui ita collegerat ut diceret in equitando verbera et praecepta esse fugae et praecepta sistendi; Luc. iv. 682 Et gens quae nudo residens Massylia dorso Ora levi flectit frenorum nescia virga; Sil. i. 215 Numidae, gens nescia freni; *id.* ii. 64 nullaque levis Gaetulus habena; Liv. xxxv. 11 equi sine frenis; xxi. 46 frenatos equites)(Numidis; Polyb. iii. 65 κεχαλινωμένην ἵππον)(Νομαδικοὺς ἱππεῖς; Claud. *Bell. Gild.* i. 439 sonipes ignarus habenae: Virga regit; Mart. ix. 22. 14 Et Massyla meum virga gubernet equum; Herodian vii. 9 οἱ δὲ Νομάδες . . . ἱππεῖς ἄριστοι ὡς καὶ χαλινῶν ἄνευ ῥάβδῳ μόνῃ τὸν δρόμον τῶν ἵππων κυβερνᾶν.

οἷα δὲ ποντοπόρων ἀκάτων ἐπιβήτορες ἄνδρες
ἑζόμενοι πρύμνῃσι, νεῶν ἐφέποντες ὀχῆας,
ἠέρα παπταίνουσι καὶ ἀργεστῇσι Νότοισι
πειθόμενοι τανύσαντο λινοπτερύγων ὅπλα νηῶν·
ὧδε καὶ ἐν τραφερῇ κέλομαι θηρήτορας ἄνδρας
παπταίνειν ἑκάτερθεν ἐπιπνείοντας ἀήτας,
ὄφρα λινοστατέωσι βοηλατέωσί[1] τε πάντῃ
αὔραις ἀντιάσαντες· ἐπεὶ μάλα θήρεσι πᾶσιν
ὀξύταται ῥινῶν ὀσφρήσιες· εἰ δὲ φράσαιντο
ἢ σταλίκων ὀδμὴν ἢ πεπταμένοιο λίνοιο,
ἔμπαλιν ἰθύνουσιν, ἐπιστροφάδην δὲ φέβονται
αὐτοῖς ἄντα βροτοῖσι, πόνον δ᾽ ἅλιον θέσαν ἄγρης.
τῷ μοι παπταίνοιεν ἐπαιγίζοντας ἀήτας
θηροφόνοι, στάλικάς τε λινοστασίην τ᾽ ἐφέποιεν
ἀντιπέρην ἀνέμοιο βολῆς· ὄπιθεν δ᾽ ἐλάοιεν
ἐς Νότον αἰθρήεντος ἐγειρομένου Βορέαο·
ἐς δὲ Βορῆν σαλαγεῦντος ἐπὶ δροσεροῖο Νότοιο·
Εὔρου δ᾽ ἱσταμένοιο θέειν Ζεφυρίτισιν αὔραις·
κινυμένου Ζεφύρου δὲ θοῶς εἰς Εὖρον ἐλαύνειν.
Ἀλλὰ σύ μοι πρώτιστα λεόντων ἔξοχον ἄγρην
ἐν θυμῷ βάλλοιο καὶ ἀνδρῶν ἄλκιμον ἦτορ.
χῶρον μὲν πρώτιστον ἐπεφράσσαντο κιόντες,
ἔνθα περὶ σπήλυγγας ἐρίβρομος ἠΰκομος λῖς
ἐνδιάει, μέγα δεῖμα βοῶν αὐτῶν τε νομήων·
θηρὸς δ᾽ αὖ μετέπειτα πελώριον ὠπήσαντο
ἴχνεσι τριβομένοισιν ἀταρπιτόν, ᾗ ἔνι πολλὸς
λαρὸν πιόμενος ποταμηπόρος ἰθὺς ὁδεύει.

[1] v.l. βροχηλατέωσι.

watch the wind. And even as men who ride in seafaring ships sit in the stern with the tiller in their hands and scan the sky and obedient to the white South Wind[a] spread the sails of their ships of canvas wings,[b] so on the dry land I bid the hunter scan on either hand the winds that blow, that so they may set up their nets and drive the game ever against the wind; since all wild beasts have keenest sense of smell, and if they perceive the scent either of the net-stakes or the spread net, they rush the other way and flee incontinently even in the very face of the men and make vain the labour of the hunt. Therefore I would have the slayers of wild beasts scan the rushing winds and face the course of the wind when they attend to their stakes and the setting of nets; let them make back to the South when the clear North Wind rises; to the North if the dewy South Wind rages; when the East Wind gets up, let them run with the breezes of the West; when the West Wind stirs, let them speedily make for the East.

But I would have thee first of all lay to heart the excellent lion-hunt and the valiant spirit of the hunters. First they go and mark a place where among the caves a roaring well-maned Lion dwells, a great terror to cattle and to the herdsmen themselves. Next they observe the great path with the worn tracks of the wild beast, whereby he often goes to the river to drink a sweet draught. There

[a] Hom. *Il.* xi. 306; xxi. 334 *ἀργεστᾶο Νότοιο*, where the ancient critics interpreted the epithet either as (1) = λευκός; *cf.* Λευκόνοτος, Hor. *C.* i. 7. 15 Albus ut obscuro deterget nubila caelo Saepe Notus neque parturit imbres Perpetuos; A. *Probl.* 942 a 34 *ὁ νότος, ὅταν μὲν ἐλάττων ᾖ, αἴθριός ἐστιν, ὅταν δὲ μέγας, νεφώδης*; or (2) = *ταχύς*.

[b] Aesch. *P.V.* 468 *λινόπτερα ναυτίλων ὀχήματα*.

ἔνθ' ἤτοι βόθρον μὲν ἐΰδρομον ἀμφὶς ὄρυξαν,
εὐρὺν καὶ περίμετρον· ἀτὰρ μεσάτῃ ἐνὶ τάφρῳ
κίονα δειμάσθην μέγαν, ὄρθιον, ὑψικόλωνον·
τοῦ δ' ἄπο μὲν κρεμάσαντο μετήορον αὖ ἐρύσαντες
ἀρνειὸν νεογιλὸν ὑπ' ἀρτιτόκοιο τεκούσης·
ἔκτοθε δ' αὖ βόθροιο περίτροχον ἐστεφάνωσαν
αἱμασιήν, πυκάσαντες ἐπασσυτέροις μυλάκεσσιν,
ὄφρα κε μὴ πελάσας δολερὸν χάος ἀθρήσειε·
καί ῥ' ὁ μὲν ὑψικρεμὴς ὑπομάζιος ἀμνὸς ἀΰτεῖ·
τοῦ δέ τε πειναλέην κραδίην ἐπάταξεν ἰωή·
μαιόμενος δ' ἴθυσε, φίλον κεχαρημένος ἦτορ,
ἴχνος ἐπισπέρχων βληχῆς ἠδ' ἔνθα καὶ ἔνθα
παπταίνων πυρόεν· τάχα δ' ἤλυθεν ἄγχι δόλοιο,
ἀμφί τε δινεῖται, κρατερὸς δέ ἑ λιμὸς ὀρίνει.
αὐτίκα δ' αἱμασιὴν μὲν ὑπέρθορε γαστρὶ πιθήσας,
δέκτο δέ μιν χάος εὐρὺ περιστεφές, οὐδ' ἐνόησεν,
ὡς ἐπὶ βυσσὸν ἵκανεν ἀνωΐστοιο βερέθρου·
παντόσε δινεῖται δὲ παλίσσυτος αἰὲν ὀρούων,
ὁπποῖος περὶ νύσσαν ἀεθλοφόρος θοὸς ἵππος,
ἀγχόμενος παλάμῃσι καὶ ἡνιόχοιο χαλινῷ.
οἱ δ' ἄρ' ἀπὸ σκοπιῆς τηλαυγέος ἀθρήσαντες
ἀγρευτῆρες ὄρουσαν, ἐριτμήτοισι δ' ἱμᾶσι
δησάμενοι καθιᾶσιν ἐΰστροφα τυκτὰ μέλαθρα,
ὀπταλέον κἀκεῖσε δόλον κρύψαντες ἐδωδῆς·
αὐτὰρ ὅ γ' ἐκ βόθροιο δοκεύμενος αὐτίκ' ἀλύξειν
ἔνθορε καγχαλόων· παρὰ δ' οὐκέτι νόστος ἕτοιμος.
ὧδε μὲν ἀμφὶ χυτὴν Λιβύων πολυδίψιον αἶαν.
 Αὐτὰρ ἐϋρρείταο παρ' ὄχθαις Εὐφρήταο
ἵππους μὲν χαροποὺς μεγαλήτορας ἀρτύνονται

[a] Xen. C. 11. 4 ἔστι δὲ οἷς αὐτῶν καὶ ὀρύγματα ποιοῦσι περιφερῆ μεγάλα βαθέα, ἐν μέσῳ λείποντες κίονα τῆς γῆς, ἐπὶ δὲ τοῦτον εἰς νύκτα ἐπέθεσαν δήσαντες αἶγα καὶ ἔφραξαν κύκλῳ τὸ ὄρυγμα ὕλῃ,

they dig a round pit,[a] wide and large; and in the midst of the trench they build a great pillar, sheer and high. From this they hang aloft a suckling lamb taken from its mother that hath newly yeaned. And outside the pit they wreath a wall around, built with close-set boulders, that the Lion may not see the crafty chasm when he draws near. And the high-hung suckling lamb bleats, and the sound strikes the Lion's hungry heart, and he rushes in search of the lamb, exulting in his heart, hasting in the track of the cry and scanning this side and that with fiery eyes. And anon he comes nigh the snare, and he wheels about and a great hunger urges him, and straightway obeying the impulse of hunger he leaps over the wall, and the wide round chasm receives him, and he comes unwittingly to the gulf of a pit unlooked for. Everywhere he circles about, rushing ever backwards and forwards, even as a swift race-horse round the turning-post, constrained by the hands of his charioteer and by the bridle. And from their far-seen place of outlook the hunters see him and rush up, and with well-cut straps they bind and let down a plaited well-compacted cage, in which also they put a piece of roasted meat. And he, thinking straightway to escape from the pit, leaps in exulting; and for him there is no more any return prepared. Thus they use in the alluvial thirsty[b] land of the Libyans.

But by the banks of the fair-flowing Euphrates they array bright-eyed, great-hearted horses for the

ὥστε μὴ προορᾶν, εἴσοδον οὐ λείποντες. τὰ δὲ ἀκούοντα τῆς φωνῆς ἐν τῇ νυκτὶ κύκλῳ τὸν φραγμὸν περιθέουσι καί, ἐπειδὰν μὴ εὑρίσκῃ δίοδον, ὑπερπηδᾷ καὶ ἁλίσκεται.

[b] Verg. *E.* i. 65 sitientes Afros; Plin. x. 21 perpetuo sitientia Africae.

θήρειον ποτὶ μῶλον· ἐπεὶ χαροποὶ γεγάασι
κραιπνότατοι θείειν καὶ ἀναιδέες ἶφι μάχεσθαι
καὶ μοῦνοι τετλᾶσι λεόντων ἀντία βρυχήν·
οἱ δ' ἄλλοι τρείουσι καὶ ἀγκλίνουσιν ὀπωπάς,
δειμαίνοντες ἄνακτος ἑοῦ πυριλαμπέα κανθόν,
ὣς ἐφάμην καὶ πρόσθεν ἐν ἱππαλέοισιν ἀοιδαῖς.
πεζοὶ δ' ἐκτανύσαντο λίνοιο περίδρομον ἕρκος,
ἄρκυας ἀσσυτέροις ἐπιδειμάμενοι σταλίκεσσι·
τόσσον δ' αὖθ' ἑκάτερθεν ἐπιπρονένευκε κεραίη,
ὅσσον ἐπημύει κέρας ἀρτιτόκοιο σελήνης.
τρισσοὶ δ' αὖ λοχόωσι λίνων ἔπι θηρητῆρες,
εἷς μέσατος, δοιοὶ δ' ἄρ' ἐπ' ἀκροτάτοισι κορύμβοις,
ὁππόσον ἐκ μεσάτοιο γεγωνότος ἀμφοτέροισιν
εἰσαΐειν ἑκάτερθε διπλῶν ἀκρόπτερα φωτῶν.
οἱ δ' ἄλλοι στήσαντο νόμῳ πολέμοιο δαφοινοῦ,
φρυκτοὺς αὐσταλέους πυριλαμπέας ἀμφὶς ἔχοντες·
ἀνδρῶν δ' αὐτὸς ἕκαστος ἔχει σάκος ἐν χερὶ λαιῇ,
(ἀσπίδος ἐν πατάγῳ θηρσὶν μέγα δεῖμα δαφοινοῖς·)
δεξιτερῇ δὲ φέρει πεύκης ἄπο δαιόμενον πῦρ·
ἔξοχα γὰρ δείδοικε πυρὸς μένος ἠΰκομος λῖς,
οὐδ' ἐσιδεῖν τέτληκεν ἀταρμύκτοισιν ὀπωπαῖς.
οἱ δ' ὁπότ' ἀθρήσωσι λεόντων ἄλκιμον ἦτορ,
πάντες ὁμῶς ἱππῆες ἐπέσσυθεν, ἀμφὶ δὲ πεζοὶ
ἕσπονται παταγεῦντες, ἀϋτὴ δ' αἰθέρ' ἱκάνει.
θῆρες δ' οὐ μίμνουσιν, ἐπιστροφάδην δὲ νέονται
θυμὸν ὀδὰξ πρίοντες, ἀμυνέμεν οὐκ ἐθέλοντες.
ὡς δ' ἰχθῦς ἀνὰ νύκτα δολόφρονες ἀσπαλιῆες
πρὸς βόλον ἰθύνουσι θοαῖς ἀκάτοισι φέροντες

---

[a] *i.e. C.* i. 304.

[b] Thackeray, *Timbuctoo* (The Lion Hunt), xi Quick issue out, with musket, torch, and brand, The sturdy blackamoors, a dusky band.

warfare of the hunt; since their bright-eyed horses are swiftest in running and stubborn to fight amain, and they alone endure to face the Lion's roar, while other horses tremble and turn away their eyes, fearing the fiery eye of their lord the Lion: as I said before [a] when I sang of horses. Men on foot spread the circling hedge of flax, building up the nets on close-set stakes. And the wings on either side project forward as much as doth the horn of the new-born moon. Three hunters lie in ambush by the nets, one in the middle, the other two at the extreme corners, at such distance that when the man in the middle calls to them the men on the wings can hear. The others take their station after the manner of bloody war, holding in their hands on either side dry flaming torches. And each man of them holds a shield in his left hand—in the din of the shield there is great terror for deadly beasts—and in his right hand a blazing torch [b] of pine; for, above all, the well-maned Lion dreads the might of fire,[c] and will not look on it with unflinching eyes.[d] And when they see the lions of valiant heart the horsemen all rush on together, and the men on foot follow with them making a din, and the noise goes unto heaven. And the beasts abide them not, but turn and flee, gnashing their teeth with rage but unwilling to fight. And even as in the night crafty fishermen in their swift ships guide the fish toward their nets,

[c] A. 629 b 21 *ἀληθῆ τὰ λεγόμενα, τό τε φοβεῖσθαι μάλιστα τὸ πῦρ, ὥσπερ καὶ Ὅμηρος ἐποίησεν "καιόμεναί τε δεταί, τάς τε τρέει ἐσσύμενός περ"* (Hom. *Il.* xi. 554 = xvii. 663); *cf.* Ael. vi. 22; vii. 6; xii. 7; Plin. viii. 52; Claud. *In Rufin.* ii. 252 vacuo qualis discedit hiatu Impatiens remeare leo quem plurima cuspis Et pastorales pepulerunt igne catervae.

[d] See *C.* i. 208 n.

λαμπομένας δαΐδας· τοὶ δὲ τρείουσιν ἰδόντες
ἔλλοπες, οὐδὲ μένουσιν ἑλισσομένην ἀμαρυγήν·
ὣς καὶ θῆρες ἄνακτες ἐπιμύουσιν ὀπωπάς.
καὶ τότε δειδιότες κτύπον ἀνδρῶν καὶ φλόγα πυρσῶν
αὐτόματοι πλεκτῇσι λίνων λαγόνεσσι πέλασσαν.
Ἔστι δέ τις θήρης τρίτατος νόμος Αἰθιοπήων
ἀκάματος, μέγα θαῦμα· τὸ δ' ἀνέρες ἀλκήεντες
Αἴθοπες ἠνορέῃ πίσυνοι πίσυρες τελέουσι.[1]
πλεκτὰ σάκη τεύχουσιν ἐϋστρέπτοισι λύγοισι
καρτερὰ καὶ πλευρῇσι περίδρομα, κὰδ δὲ βοείας
ἀζαλέας τανύουσιν ἐπ' ἀσπίσιν ὀμφαλοέσσαις
ἄλκαρ ἔμεν τ' ὀνύχων βριαρῶν γενύων τε δαφοινῶν·
αὐτοὶ δ' οἰὸς ἄωτα πρόπαν δέμας ἀμφιέσαντο,
σφιγξάμενοι καθύπερθεν ἐπασσυτέροις τελαμῶσι·
καὶ κόρυθες κρύπτουσι καρήατα· μοῦνα δ' ἀθρήσαις
χείλεά τε ῥῖνάς τε καὶ ὄμματα μαρμαίροντα.
ἄντα δὲ θηρὸς ἴασιν ἀολλέες,[2] εὐκελάδοισι
μάστιξιν θαμινῇσι δι' ἠέρος αἰθύσσοντες·
αὐτὰρ ὅ γε σπήλυγγος ὑπεκπροθορὼν ἀλίαστος
βρυχᾶται πετάσας φόνιον χάος ἀντία φωτῶν,
δερκόμενος χαροποῖσιν ὑπ' ὄμμασιν αἰθόμενον πῦρ,
θυμῷ παφλάζων ἴκελος δίοισι κεραυνοῖς.
οὐ τοῖον Γάγγαο ῥόος πρόσθ' ἠελίοιο
Ἰνδὸν ὑπὲρ δάπεδον Μαρυανδέα[3] λαὸν ἀμείβων
μυκᾶται βρύχημα πελώριον, ὁππότε κρημνῶν
ἐκπροθορὼν ἐκάλυψε μέλαν δέμας αἰγιαλοῖο·
ὥστε καὶ εὐρύτατός περ ἐὼν καί τ' εἴκοσιν ἄλλοις
κυρτοῦται ποταμοῖσι κορυσσόμενος λάβρον ὕδωρ·
οἷον ἐπισμαραγεῖ δρίος ἄσπετον ἠδὲ χαράδραι

[1] τελέθουσι MSS.
[2] ἀολλέες: *vv.ll.* ἅμ' ὁρμαῖς, ἅμα ῥώμαις.
[3] *v.l.* βαρυανθέα.

carrying blazing torches[a]; and the fishes tremble to behold them and do not abide the whirling gleam; so the kings of beasts shut their eyes and then, fearing the din of men and the flame of torches, of their own motion they approach the plaited flanks of the nets.

There is a third manner of hunting among the Ethiopians, untiring, marvellous. And this do four valiant Ethiopians perform, trusting in their valour. They fashion with twisted withes plaited shields, strong and with round sides, and stretch dried ox-hides over the bossy shields to be a defence at once against strong claws and murderous jaws. They themselves array all their bodies in the fleeces of sheep, fastening them above with close-set straps. Helmets cover their heads; only their lips and nostrils and shining eyes could you see. And they go together to chase the beast, flashing in the air many a sounding whip. But the Lion leaps forth from his cave unflinchingly and opens his deadly gape in the face of the men and utters his roar, while with his bright eyes he looks blazing fire, blustering in his wrath like the thunder-bolts of Zeus. Not Ganges' stream, which sunward over the Indian land passes the Maryandean[b] people, bellows with such stupendous roar when it leaps forth from the precipices and covers the dark space of the shore; that stream which, although it is exceeding broad, yet by twenty other rivers is it swollen and arches the crest of its furious flood; not Ganges roars so loud as roar the boundless wood and the ravines with

[a] *Cf. H.* iv. 640 ff.

[b] Possibly the people mentioned in Ptolemy, *Geogr.* vii. 2. 14 ὑπὸ δὲ τούτους (sc. Γαγγανούς) Μαροῦνδαι μέχρι τῶν Γαγγαριδῶν, ἐν οἷς πόλεις πρὸς τῷ Γάγγῃ ποταμῷ κτλ.

βρυχηθμοῖς ὀλοοῖσιν, ἐπιβρέμεται δ' ὅλος αἰθήρ.
καί ῥ' ὁ μὲν αὐτίκ' ὄρουσε λιλαιόμενος χροὸς ἆσαι,
λαίλαπι χειμερίῃ πανομοίϊος· οἱ δὲ μένουσιν
ἀστεμφεῖς πυρόεσσαν ἐπαιγίζουσαν ἐνιπήν.
αὐτὰρ ὅ γ' ἔν τ' ὀνύχεσσι γένυσσί τε λευγαλέῃσιν
ἄσχετος ὅν κεν ἕλῃσιν ἐπαιθύσσων κεραΐζει.
τὸν δ' ἕτερος κατόπισθε μεταθρώσκων αἰζηῶν
κικλήσκει, παταγῶν τε διαπρύσιόν τε γεγωνώς.
αἶψα δ' ἐπιστρεφθεὶς μεγαλήνωρ ἠΰκομος λῖς
ὦρτο λιπὼν ὃν ἔμαρψεν ὑπὸ στόμα· καὶ πάλιν ἄλλος
δόχμιος ἠϋγένειον ὀρίνει θῆρα κελαινόν·
ἄλλοι δ' ἀλλαχόθεν μιν ἐπασσύτεροι κλονέουσι
ῥινοῖσιν πίσυνοι σακέεσσί τε καὶ τελαμῶσι,
τοὺς οὔτε κρατεροὶ γενύων τάμνουσιν ὀδόντες,
οὔτε σιδηρείων ὀνύχων πείρουσιν ἀκωκαί.
αὐτὰρ ὁ μαψίδιον φθινύθει πόνον, ἄκριτα θύων,
τὸν μὲν καλλείπων, τὸν δ' αἰρόμενος χθονὸς αἶψα
αὖ ἐρύων, τῷ δ' αὖτις ἀάσχετος ἰθὺς ὀρούων.
ὡς δ' ὁπότ' ἐν πολέμοισιν ἀρήϊον ἄνδρα κραταιὸν
δήϊος ἀμφιβάλῃ στεφάνη μαλεροῖο μόθοιο,
αὐτὰρ ὅ γε πνείων μένος Ἄρεος ἔνθα καὶ ἔνθα
ἀΐσσει, παλάμῃ κραδάων πεφονωμένον ἔγχος,
ὀψὲ δέ μιν δάμνησιν ἐνυάλιος λόχος ἀνδρῶν,
πάντες ὁμοῦ βρίσαντες· ὁ δ' ὀκλάζει κατὰ γαίης,
βαλλόμενος πυκινῇσι τανυρροίζοισιν ἀκωκαῖς·
ὣς ὅ γ' ἀνηνύστοισιν ἀπειπάμενος καμάτοισιν
ὀψὲ βροτοῖσιν ἔδωκε βραβήϊα πάντα μόθοιο·
ἀφρὸν ἀποσταλάει δὲ ποτὶ σχερὸν αἱματόεντα·

---

[a] αὖ ἐρύων, i.e. αὐερύων, i.e. ἀνϜερύων, from ἀνά + ἐρύω. In Homer the verb occurs (1) with reference to sacrifices (*Il.* i. 459, ii. 422 αὐέρυσαν μὲν πρῶτα), where scholl. interpret it of drawing the victim's head backward and upward, (2) of

the deadly bellowing of the Lion, and all the sky resounds. And he straightway rushes, fain to glut him with flesh, like unto a winter storm, while the hunters steadfastly abide the onset of the fiery tempest. He with claws and deadly jaws incontinently assails and mauls any man that he can seize. Then another of the youths rushes on him from behind and calls his attention with clattering din and loud shout. And swiftly the lordly well-maned Lion turns and charges, leaving the man whom he had seized in his mouth; and again another on the flank provokes the bearded swarthy beast. Others on this side and on that in close succession harass him, trusting in hides and shields and baldricks, which neither the mighty teeth of his jaws can cleave nor the points of his iron claws pierce. And the Lion wears out his strength in vain labour, charging blindly—leaving one man, lifting another straightway from the ground and wrenching his neck,[a] and again incontinently rushing straight upon another. And as when in war a hostile ring of fierce battle surrounds a mighty warrior, and he, breathing the spirit of war, rushes this way and that, brandishing in his hand his gory sword, and at last a warlike company of men overcomes him, all pressing on him together, and he sinks to the ground, smitten by many long whistling arrows; even so the Lion, exhausted by ineffectual efforts, at last yields to the men all the prizes of battle, while he sheds to earth[b] the bloody

drawing a bow (*Il.* viii. 325 αὐερύοντα παρ' ὠμόν), (3) of pulling up the palisade (στῆλαι) of a wall (*Il.* xii. 261). To Oppian it was probably two words.

[b] σχερὸν appears to mean "ground," *cf.* Hesych. σχερός· ἀκτή, αἰγιαλός, which would equate it with ξερὸν ἠπείροιο (Hom. *Od.* v. 402).

εἴκελος αἰδομένῳ δὲ ποτὶ χθόνα κανθὸν ἐρείδει.
ὡς δὲ βροτὸς πολλοῖσιν ἐρεψάμενος κοτίνοισι
πυγμαχίης ἐν ἀγῶσιν, ὑπ' ἀνέρος ἀλκήεντος
ἄντην ἀσσυτέρῃσιν ὑπ' ὠτειλῇσι δαμασθείς,
ἔστη μὲν πρώτιστα λελουμένος αἵματι λάβρῳ,
οἷα μεθυσφαλέων, ἑτεροκλινέων τε κάρηνον·
αὐτὰρ ἔπειτ' ἐπὶ γαῖαν ὑποκλαδὸν ἐξετανύσθη·
ὣς ὅ γ' ἐπὶ ψαμάθου κεκαφηότα γυῖα τάνυσσεν.
οἱ δὲ τότ' ἐγκονέουσι πολὺ πλέον, αἶψα δ' ὕπερθε
πάντες ἐρεισάμενοι κρατεροῖσι δέουσ' ὑπὸ δεσμοῖς
οὐδὲν ἀλευόμενον, μάλα δ' ἤρεμον ἀτρεμέοντα.
ὢ μέγα τολμήεντες, ὅσον χάδον, ὅσσον ἔρεξαν,
αἰνὸν κεῖνο πέλωρον ἅτε κτίλον ἀείρουσιν.
Ἔκλυον ὡς βόθροισιν ὁμοίοισίν τε δόλοισι
θήρασσαν καὶ θῶας ἀναιδέας, ἠδὲ γένεθλα
πορδαλίων ἀπάτησαν, ἀτὰρ πολὺ μείοσι βόθροις·
κίονα δ' οὐχὶ λίθοιο, δρυὸς δ' ἐτάμοντο κεραίην·
οὐδὲ μὲν ὑψικρεμῆ χιμάρου γόνον ἠώρησαν,
ἀλλὰ κυνός· τοῦ δ' αὖτ' ἀπὸ μήδεα δῆσαν ἱμάσθλαις
λεπταλέαις· ὁ δ' ἄρ' ὦκα περισπερχὴς ὀδύνῃσιν
ὠρυθμοῖς ὑλάει καὶ πορδαλίεσσιν ἀΰτεῖ·
ἡ δὲ μάλ' ἰάνθη, διά τε δρίος ἰθὺς ὀρούει.
ὡς δ' ὁπότ' ἰχθυβόλοι κύρτου δόλον ἐστήσαντο,
πλεξάμενοι σπάρτῳ Σαλαμινίδι, καὶ λαγόνεσσι
πούλυπον ἢ κεστρῆα πυρὶ φλεγέθοντες ἔθεντο·
ὀδμὴ δ' ἐς πλαταμῶνας ἀφίκετο, καὶ ποτὶ κύρτον

---

[a] Ael. xiii. 10 describes a somewhat similar method used by the Moors.

[b] *Cf. H.* iii. 388.

[c] *Cf. C.* i. 156, *H.* iii. 341. The ref. of Σαλαμινίδι—whether to the island or to the town in Cyprus—is unexplained, but no plausible emendation has been proposed.

foam and, like one ashamed, fixes his eye upon the ground. As a man who hath won many a crown of wild olive for boxing in the games, when he is overcome with wound on wound by a valiant adversary in close combat, stands at first bathed in torrents of blood, as if reeling with drink, and hanging his head to one side; then his legs give way and he is stretched upon the ground; even so the Lion stretches his exhausted limbs upon the sand. Then the hunters busy themselves much more, and, swiftly pressing all upon him, they bind him with strong bonds, while he makes no attempt to escape but is altogether quiet and motionless. O greatly daring men! what a feat they compass, what a deed they do—they carry off that great monster like a tame sheep!

I have heard that with trenches and like devices men capture also the bold Jackals and deceive the tribes of Leopards [a]: only with much smaller trenches, and they cut not a pillar of stone but a beam of oak. And they do not hang aloft a kid,[b] but a puppy, the privy parts of which they bind with thin straps. In its agony it straightway howls and barks, and its cry is heard by the Leopards. The Leopard rejoices and rushes straight through the wood. As when fishermen set up a weel to ensnare fish, plaiting it of Salaminian broom,[c] and in the inside of it put a Poulpe [d] or Grey Mullet [e] roasted in the fire; the savour thereof comes unto the flat ledges and brings

[d] For the Poulpe or Octopus *cf. H.* i. 306 n.; for broiled Poulpe as bait, *H.* iii. 345.

[e] *Cf. H.* i. 111 n. The schol. here is worth quoting for its absurdity: κεστρῆα· κενὸς λῶρος. Read κεντητὸς λῶρος. The schol. has confused κεστρεύς with κεστός, a girdle; *cf.* Zon. κεστός· ὁ κεντητὸς λῶρος.

ἔλλοπας αὐτομόλους εἰσήγαγεν, οὐδὲ δύνανται
αὖτις ὑπεκδῦναι, δεινοῦ δ' ἤντησαν ὀλέθρου·
ὣς κείνη, σκυλακῆος ἀπόπροθεν εἰσαΐουσα,
ἔδραμε καὶ θόρεν, οὔτιν' ὀϊσσαμένη δόλον εἶναι,
γαστέρι πειθομένη δὲ μυχοὺς ἐπέλασσε βερέθρου.
Πορδάλιας καὶ δῶρα Διωνύσοιο δάμασσαν,
θηροφόνων δολερῶν δολερὴν πόσιν οἰνοχοεύντων,
οὐδὲν ἀλευομένων ζαθέοιο κότον Διονύσου.
πορδάλιες νῦν μὲν θηρῶν γένος, ἀλλὰ πάροιθεν
οὐ θῆρες βλοσυραί, χαροπαὶ δ' ἐπέλοντο γυναῖκες,
οἰνάδες, ὠσχοφόροι, τριετηρίδες, ἀνθοκάρηνοι,
Βάκχου φοιταλιῆος ἐγερσιχόροιο τιθῆναι.
νηπίαχον γὰρ Βακχον[1] 'Αγηνορὶς ἔτραφεν 'Ινώ,
μαζὸν ὀρεξαμένη πρωτόρρυτον υἱέϊ Ζηνός·
σὺν δ' ἄρ' ὁμῶς ἀτίτηλε καὶ Αὐτονόη καὶ 'Αγαύη·
ἀλλ' οὐκ εἰν 'Αθάμαντος ἀταρτηροῖσι δόμοισιν,
οὔρεϊ δ' ὃν τότε Μηρὸν ἐπικλήδην καλέεσκον.

[1] Ἴακχον G.

---

[a] In more restricted sense ὠσχο(ὀσχο-)φόροι were two youths of each tribe chosen from noble families (τῶν γένει καὶ πλούτῳ προεχόντων Suid. *s.v.*), who, dressed in female garb (ἐν γυναικείαις στολαῖς *E.M. s.v.*, Procl. *ap.* Phot. p. 322 n.) led the procession of women at the Oschophoria from temple of Dionysus to temple of Athena Sciras at Phalerum (Hesych. *s.* ὠοχοφόριον), carrying ὦσχοι (ὦσχαι, ὄσχοι), *i.e.* vine-branches laden with grapes; *cf.* schol. Nicand. *A.* 109 ὀσχοφόροι λέγονται 'Αθήνησι παῖδες ἀμφιθαλεῖς (*i.e.* having both parents alive; *cf.* Callim. *Ait.* iii. 1. 3; Poll. iii. 40, etc.) ἁμιλλώμενοι κατὰ φυλάς, οἳ λαμβάνοντες κλήματα ἀμπέλου ἐκ τοῦ ἱεροῦ τοῦ Διονύσου ἔτρεχον εἰς τὸ τῆς Σκιράδος 'Αθηνᾶς ἱερόν. . . . . ὄσχαι κυρίως οἱ κλάδοι τῆς ἀμπέλου.

[b] See *C.* i. 24 n.

[c] Cadmus, s. of Agenor, had by Harmonia four daughters, Autonoë, Ino, Semele, Agave. Semele, m. by Zeus of

the fishes of their own will to the weel, and they are unable to get out again and meet a terrible death; so the Leopard, hearing the puppy from afar, runs and makes his spring, suspecting no guile, and obeying the call of hunger, enters the recesses of the pit.

Leopards are overcome also by the gifts of Dionysus, when crafty hunters pour for them the crafty draught, shunning not the anger of holy Dionysus. Leopards are now a race of wild beasts, but aforetime they were not fierce wild beasts but bright-eyed women, wine-drinking, carriers of the vine branch,[a] celebrators of the triennial festival,[b] flower-crowned, nurses of frenzied Bacchus who rouses the dance. For Ino,[c] scion of Agenor, reared the infant Bacchus and first gave her breast to the son of Zeus, and Autonoe likewise and Agave joined in nursing him, but not in the baleful halls of Athamas,[d] but on the mountain which at that time men called by the name of the Thigh (Μηρός).[e] For greatly fearing

Dionysus (Bacchus), died at his birth and the child was conveyed by Hermes to Ino (Apollod. iii. 4. 3).

[d] Athamas, s. of Aeolus and king of Boeotia, married Ino as his second wife.

[e] When Dionysus was born untimely, Zeus sewed the infant in his thigh (μηρός). After Athamas and Ino, driven mad by Hera, had slain their children, Hermes conveyed the child Dionysus πρὸς νύμφας ἐν Νύσῃ κατοικούσας τῆς Ἀσίας (Apollod. *l.c.*) and the name Meros was given to a hill there. The location of Meros thus depends on the location of Nysa which is usually placed in India; Strabo 687 Νυσαίους δή τινας ἔθνος προσωνόμοσαν καὶ πόλιν παρ' αὐτοῖς Νῦσαν Διονύσου κτίσμα καὶ ὄρος τὸ ὑπὲρ τῆς πόλεως Μηρόν; Plin. vi. 79 Nysam urbem plerique Indiae adscribunt montemque Merum Libero Patri sacrum, unde origo fabulae Iovis femine editum; *cf. id.* xvi. 144; Solin. lii. 16; Dion. P. 1159. But there were other localizations; see note on 251 below.

Ζηνὸς γὰρ μεγάλην ἄλοχον μέγα δειμαίνουσαι
καὶ Πενθῆα τύραννον Ἐχιονίδην τρομέουσαι
εἰλατίνῃ χηλῷ δῖον γένος ἐγκατέθεντο,
νεβρίσι δ' ἀμφεβάλοντο καὶ ἐστέψαντο κορύμβοις
ἐν σπέϊ, καὶ περὶ παῖδα τὸ μυστικὸν ὠρχήσαντο·
τύμπανα δ' ἐκτύπεον καὶ κύμβαλα χερσὶ κρόταινον,
παιδὸς κλαυθμυρισμῶν προκαλύμματα· πρῶτα δ' ἔφαινον
ὄργια κευθομένῃ περὶ λάρνακι· σὺν δ' ἄρα τῇσιν
Ἀόνιαι λάθρῃ τελετῶν ἅπτοντο γυναῖκες·
ἐκ δ' ὄρεος πιστῇσιν ἀγερμοσύνην ἑτάρῃσιν[1]
ἔντυον ἰθῦσαι Βοιωτίδος ἔκτοθε γαίης·
μέλλε γὰρ ἤδη, μέλλεν ἀνήμερος ἡ πρὶν ἐοῦσα
γαῖα φυτηκομέειν ὑπὸ λυσιπόνῳ Διονύσῳ.
χηλὸν δ' ἀρρήτην ἱερὸς χορὸς ἀείρασαι
στεψάμεναι νώτοισιν ἐπεστήριξαν ὄνοιο·
Εὐρίπου δ' ἵκανον ἐπ' ᾐόνας, ἔνθα κίχανον
πρέσβυν ὁμοῦ τεκέεσσιν ἁλίπλανον· ἀμφὶ δὲ πᾶσαι
γριφέας ἐλλίσσοντο βυθοὺς ἀκάτοισι περῆσαι·
αὐτὰρ ὅ γ' αἰδεσθεὶς ἱερὰς ὑπέδεκτο γυναῖκας.

[1] ἀγερμ. mss.: corr. Brodaeus.

---

[a] King of Thebes, s. of Echion and Agave, opposed the worship of Dionysus. Spying upon the Bacchants on Cithaeron he was torn in pieces by his mother who mistook him for a wild beast (Apollod. iii. 5. 2).

[b] The prosody of κλαυθμυρισμῶν is no reason for altering the text. It is no worse than Lucan's "distincta zmaragdo" (x. 121), *cf.* Mart. v. 11. 1, and even Homer has ὑλήεντι Ζακύνθῳ and the like.

[c] *Cf.* the legend of the Curetes and the infant Zeus; Callim. *H.* i. 51 ff.

[d] Boeotian.

[e] *i.e.* Meros (241 n.). As obviously a hill in Boeotia is intended, that implies a Boeotian Nysa. Now though Nysa

the mighty spouse of Zeus and dreading the tyrant Pentheus,[a] son of Echion, they laid the holy child in a coffer of pine and covered it with fawn-skins and wreathed it with clusters of the vine, in a grotto where round the child they danced the mystic dance and beat drums and clashed cymbals in their hands, to veil the cries [b] of the infant.[c] It was around that hidden ark that they first showed forth their mysteries, and with them the Aonian[d] women secretly took part in the rites. And they arrayed a gathering of their faithful companions to journey from that mountain [e] out of the Boeotian land. For now, now was it fated that a land,[f] which before was wild, should cultivate the vine at the instance of Dionysus who delivers from sorrow. Then the holy choir took up the secret coffer and wreathed it and set it on the back of an ass. And they came unto the shores of the Euripus, where they found a seafaring old man with his sons, and all together they besought the fishermen that they might cross the water in their boats. Then the old man had compassion on them and received on board the holy women. And lo! on

is generally put in India, Herodotus puts it in Ethiopia: Herod. ii. 146 *Διόνυσόν τε λέγουσι οἱ Ἕλληνες ὡς αὐτίκα γενόμενον ἐς τὸν μηρὸν ἐνερράψατο Ζεὺς καὶ ἤνεικε ἐς Νύσην τὴν ὑπὲρ Αἰγύπτου ἐοῦσαν ἐν τῇ Αἰθιοπίῃ*; *cf. ibid.* iii. 97. Diod. iv. 2 puts it *μεταξὺ Φοινίκης καὶ Νείλου*; *cf.* iii. 65; Hom. *H.* xxxiii. 8; Steph. Byz. *s.* *Νῦσαι* enumerates ten—on Helicon, in Thrace, in Caria, Arabia, Egypt, Naxos, India, Caucasus, Libya, Euboea. Oppian, we must suppose, is thinking of the Heliconian Nysa: *cf.* Strabo 405 *γράφουσι δὲ καὶ τοῦτο* (*sc.* Hom. *Il.* ii. 508 *Νῖσάν τε ζαθέην*) "*Νῦσάν τε ζαθέην.*" *κώμη δ' ἐστὶ τοῦ Ἑλικῶνος ἡ Νῦσα.* *Cf.* Paus. i. 39.

[f] Euboea. *Cf.* Steph. Byz. *s.* *Νῦσαι . . . δεκάτη ἐν Εὐβοίῃ ἔνθα διὰ μιᾶς ἡμέρας τὴν ἄμπελόν φασιν ἀνθεῖν καὶ τὸν βότρυν πεπαίνεσθαι.*

καὶ δή οἱ χλοερὴ μὲν ἐπήνθεε σέλμασι μῖλαξ,
πρύμνην δ' ὡραίη ἕλινος[1] καὶ κισσὸς ἔρεπτον·
καί κεν ὑπὲρ πόντοιο κυβίστεον ἀσπαλιῆες
δείματι δαιμονίῳ πεπτηότες, ἀλλὰ πάροιθεν
ἐς γαῖαν δόρυ κέλσε· πρὸς Εὐβοίην δὲ γυναῖκες
ἠδ' ἐπ' Ἀρισταίοιο θεὸν κατάγοντο φέρουσαι,
ὅσθ' ὕπατον μὲν ἔναιεν ὄρος[2] Καρύῃσιν[3] ὑπ' ἄντρῳ,[4]
μυρία δ' ἄγραυλον βιοτὴν ἐδιδάξατο φωτῶν·
πρῶτος ποιμένιον[5] ἱδρύσατο, πρῶτος ἐκεῖνος
καρποὺς ἀγριάδος λιπαρῆς ἔθλιψεν ἐλαίης,
καὶ ταμίσῳ πρῶτος γάλα πήξατο, καὶ ποτὶ σίμβλους
ἐκ δρυὸς ἀείρας ἀγανὰς ἐνέκλεισε μελίσσας.

[1] σέλινος (-ον GI) MSS.: corr. Brodaeus.
[2] ὄρος Editor: ὄρει MSS.
[3] Καρύῃσιν Editor: καὶ ῥύησιν CDEF: καὶ ῥοιῆσιν AB: καὶ ῥοῆσιν GLM: κεράεσσιν Turnebus. [4] ἄντρῳ: ἄντρου MSS.
[5] ποιμένιον Schneider: ποιμενίων MSS.

---

[a] Similar miracles take place when Dionysus is carried off by Tyrrhenian pirates; Hom. *H.* vii. 35 ff.; Nonn. xlv. 105 ff.; Apollod. iii. 5. 3; Philostr. *Imag.* i. 19; Ov. *M.* iii. 577 ff. [b] *Smilax aspera.*

[c] No doubt the vine is intended. Nonn. xii. 299, speaking of the vine, has ἀγριὰς ἡβώωσα πολυγνάμπτοισι σελίνοις (*cf.* Dion. P. 1157 ἕλικές τε πολυγνάμπτης ἑλίνοιο), whence it might be argued that Oppian used σέλινος for vine-tendril. But (1) σέλινος (for σέλινον) seems not to occur; (2) the penult of σέλινον is long (except *A.P.* vii. 621. 2).

[d] Pind. *N.* ix. 27 ἐν γὰρ δαιμονίοισι φόβοις φεύγοντι καὶ παῖδες θεῶν.

[e] S. of Apollo and Cyrene, patron of all rural life, of flocks and herds, hunting, bee-keeping, etc. Pind. *P.* ix. 59 ff.; Nonn. v. 229 ff., xiii. 253 ff.; Diod. iv. 81 f.; Verg. *G.* i. 14, iv. 315 ff. When Ceos was suffering from pestilence owing to the heat of the Dog-star, Aristaeus went there and built an altar to Zeus Icmaeus, *i.e.* Zeus as God of Moisture, and established an annual sacrifice to Zeus and Sirius on the hills of the island. Ever after Zeus caused

the benches of his boat flowered [a] the lush bindweed [b] and blooming vine [c] and ivy wreathed the stern. Now would the fishermen, cowering in god-sent terror,[d] have dived into the sea, but ere that the boat came to land. And to Euboea the women came, carrying the god, and to the abode of Aristaeus,[e] who dwelt in a cave on the top of a mountain at Caryae [f] and who instructed the life of country-dwelling men in countless things ; he was the first to establish a flock of sheep [g] ; he first pressed the fruit of the oily wild olive,[h] first curdled milk with rennet,and brought the gentle bees [i] from the oak [j] and shut them up in

the Etesian winds to blow for forty days after the rising of Sirius. Hence Aristaeus was worshipped in Ceos as Zeus Aristaeus (Callim. *Ait.* iii. 1. 33 ff. [Loeb]; Ap. Rh. ii. 516 ff. ; Nonn. v. 269 f. ; xiii. 279 ff.). In the present passage he seems to be conceived as dwelling in Euboea.

[f] *κεράεσσιν ὑπ' ἄντρου* (Schneid. and Lehrs) seems to have no probability. We know no example of *κέρατα* applied to a cave (Claud. *Paneg. Prob. et Ol.* 209 has "curvis Tiberinus in antris") and *ὄρευς κεράεσσιν ὑπ' ἄντρῳ* (suggested by Schneid. in note) would be preferable. We venture to read Καρύῃσιν (practically the reading of the MSS.) and suppose that Caryae = Carystus, founding upon Callim. *Ait.* iii. 1. 56 ff., where we are told that Xenomedes recounted the legendary history of Ceos, *ἄρχμενος ὡς νύμφῃσιν ἐναίετο Κωρυκίῃσι τὰς ἀπὸ Παρνησσοῦ λῖς ἐδίωξε μέγας, | Ὑδροῦσσαν τῷ καί μιν ἐφήμισαν, ὥς τε Κιρω . . . | . ο . . . θυσ . το . . . ᾤκεεν ἐν* Καρύαις, coupled with Heraclid. *Περὶ πολιτειῶν* ix. (Müller, *F.H.G.* ii. p. 214) *ἐκαλεῖτο μὲν Ὑδροῦσα ἡ νῆσος· λέγονται δὲ οἰκῆσαι Νύμφαι πρότερον αὐτήν. φοβήσαντος δὲ αὐτὰς λέοντος εἰς Κάρυστον διαβῆναι.* Also acc to one version (schol. Ap. Rh. ii. 498) Carystus was the father of Aristaeus.

[g] Nonn. v. 261 ff. [h] *Ib.* 258 ff. [i] *Ib.* 242 ff.

[j] Before the invention of the artificial hive, the only honey known was "wild honey" (*μέλι τὸ καλούμενον ἄγριον* Diod. xix. 94 ; *μέλι ἄγριον* N.T. Matt. iii. 4) "deposited in the hollow of old trees and in the cavities of rocks" (Gibbon, c. x.). Claud. *In Ruf* ii. 460 ff.

ὃς τότε καὶ Διόνυσον ἑῷ νεογιλὸν ὑπ' ἄντρῳ
Ἰνώης ἔθρεψε δεδεγμένος ἐκ χηλοῖο,
σὺν Δρυάσιν δ' ἀτίτηλε μελισσοκόμοισί τε Νύμφαις
Εὐβοΐσιν τε κόρῃσι καὶ Ἀονίῃσι γυναιξίν.
ἤδη κουρίζων δ' ἑτέραις μετὰ παισὶν ἄθυρε·
νάρθηκα προταμὼν στυφελὰς οὐτάζετο πέτρας,
αἱ δὲ θεῷ μέθυ λάρον ἀνέβλυσαν ὠτειλάων.
ἄλλοτε δ' ἀρνειοὺς αὐτῆς ἐδάϊξε δορῇσι
καὶ μελεϊστὶ τάμεν νέκυας δ' ἔρριψεν ἔραζε,
αὖτις δ' ἅψεα χερσὶν ἐϋσταλέως συνέβαλλεν,
οἱ δ' ἄφαρ ἔζωον χλοεροῦ θ' ἅπτοντο νομοῖο.
ἤδη καὶ θιάσοισιν ἐμέμβλετο καὶ κατὰ πᾶσαν
γαῖαν ἐκίδνατο δῶρα Θυωναίου Διονύσου.
πάντῃ δὲ θνητοῖς ἀρετὴν πωλέσκετο φαίνων·
ὀψὲ δὲ καὶ Θήβης ἐπεβήσατο καὶ πυρίπαιδι
πᾶσαι ὑπηντίασαν Καδμηΐδες· αὐτὰρ ὁ μάργος
Πενθεὺς οὐχὶ δετὰς παλάμας ἔδεεν Διονύσου,
καὶ θεὸν αὐτοφόνοισιν ἀπείλεε χερσὶ δαΐξαι,
οὐ Τυρίου Κάδμοιο καταιδόμενος τρίχα λευκήν,
οὐδὲ κυλινδομένην οἷσι πρὸ πόδεσσιν Ἀγαύην·
σύρειν δ' αἰνομόροισιν ἐβώστρεεν οἷς ἑτάροισι,
σύρειν τε κλείειν τε, χορόν τ' ἐλάασκε γυναικῶν.
οἱ μέν νυν Βρόμιον Πενθηϊάδαι φυλακῆες
δεσμοῖσιν δοκέοντο σιδηρείοισιν ἄγεσθαι
ἄλλοι Καδμεῖοί τε· θεοῦ δ' οὐχ ἅπτετο δεσμά·
παχνώθη δὲ κέαρ θιασώτισι, πάντα δ' ἔραζε
ῥῖψαν ἀπὸ κροτάφων στεφανώματα θύσθλα τε χειρῶν·

---

[a] *Ferula communis.*

[b] Num. xx. 11 Moses lifted up his hand, and with his rod he smote the rock twice: and the water came out abundantly.

[c] Semele (Pind. *P.* iii. 99; Hom. *H.* xxxiv. 22).

hives. He at that time received the infant Dionysus from the coffer of Ino and reared him in his cave and nursed him with the help of the Dryads and the Nymphs that have the bees in their keeping and the maidens of Euboea and the Aonian women. And, when Dionysus was now come to boyhood, he played with the other children; he would cut a fennel [a] stalk and smite [b] the hard rocks, and from their wounds they poured for the god sweet liquor. Otherwhiles he rent rams, skins and all, and clove them piecemeal and cast the dead bodies on the ground; and again with his hands he neatly put their limbs together, and immediately they were alive and browsed on the green pasture. And now he was attended by holy companies, and over all the earth were spread the gifts of Dionysus, son of Thyone,[c] and everywhere he went about showing forth his excellence to men. Late and at last he set foot in Thebes, and all the daughters of Cadmus came to meet the son of fire. But rash Pentheus bound the hands of Dionysus that should not be bound and threatened with his own murderous hands to rend the god. He had not regard unto the white hair of Tyrian Cadmus nor to Agave grovelling at his feet, but called to his ill-fated companions to hale away the god—to hale him away and shut him up—and he drave away the choir of women. Now the guards of Pentheus thought to carry away Bromius [d] in bonds of iron, and so thought the other Cadmeans; but the bonds touched not the god. And the heart of the women worshippers was chilled, and they cast on the ground all the garlands from their temples and the holy emblems of their hands, and the cheeks

[d] Dionysus (Pind. fr. lxxv. 10; Aesch. *E*. 24.

πάσαις δ' ἐστάλαον Βρομιώτισι δάκρυ παρειαί·
αἶψα δ' ἀνηΰτησαν· ἰὼ μάκαρ, ὦ Διόνυσε,
ἅπτε σέλας φλογερὸν πατρώϊον, ἂν δ' ἐλέλιξον
γαῖαν, ἀταρτηροῦ δ' ὄπασον τίσιν ὦκα τυράννου·
θὲς δὲ παρὰ σκοπιῇσι, πυρίσπορε, Πενθέα ταῦρον,
ταῦρον μὲν Πενθῆα δυσώνυμον, ἄμμε δὲ θῆρας
ὠμοβόρους, ὀλοοῖσι κορυσσομένας ὀνύχεσσιν,
φρα μιν, ὦ Διόνυσε, διὰ στόμα δαιτρεύσωμεν.
ὣς φάσαν εὐχόμεναι· τάχα δ' ἔκλυε Νύσιος ἀρῆς.
Πενθέα μὲν δὴ ταῦρον ἐδείξατο φοίνιον ὄμμα,
αὐχένα τ' ᾐώρησε, κέρας τ' ἀνέτειλε μετώπου·
ταῖσι δὲ γλαυκιόωσαν ἐθήκατο θηρὸς ὀπωπήν,
καὶ γένυας θώρηξε, κατέγραψεν δ' ἐπὶ νώτου
ῥινὸν ὅπως νεβροῖσι, καὶ ἄγρια θήκατο φῦλα.
αἱ δὲ θεοῦ βουλῇσιν ἀμειψάμεναι χρόα καλὸν
πορδάλιες Πενθῆα παρὰ σκοπέλοισι δάσαντο.
τοιάδ' ἀείδοιμεν, τοῖα φρεσὶ πιστεύοιμεν·
ὅσσα Κιθαιρῶνος δὲ κατὰ πτύχας ἔργα γυναικῶν,
ἢ μυσαρὰς κείνας, τὰς ἀλλοτρίας Διονύσου,
μητέρας οὐχ ὁσίως ψευδηγορέουσιν ἀοιδοί.
Θηροφόνος δέ τις ὧδε πάγην ἑτάροισι σὺν ἄλλοις
θηρσὶ φιλακρήτοισιν ἐμήσατο πορδαλίεσσι.
πίδακα λεξάμενοι Λιβύης ἀνὰ διψάδα γαῖαν,
ἥ τ' ὀλίγη μάλα πολλὸν ἀνυδρότατον κατὰ χῶρον
ἀπροφάτως ἀΐδηλον ἀνασταλάει μέλαν ὕδωρ,
οὐδὲ πρόσω χεῖται κελαρύσμασιν, ἀλλὰ μάλ' αἰνῶς
βλύζει τε σταδίη τε μένει ψαμάθοισί τε δύνει·
ἔνθεν πορδαλίων γένος ἄγριον εἶσι μετ' ἠῶ
πιόμενον· τοὶ δ' αἶψα κατὰ κνέφας ὁρμηθέντες
ἀγρευτῆρες ἄγουσιν ἐείκοσιν ἀμφιφορῆας

of all the worshippers of Bromius flowed with tears. And straightway they cried: "Io! blessed one, O Dionysus, kindle thou the flaming lightning of thy father and shake the earth and give us speedy vengeance on the evil tyrant. And, O son of fire, make Pentheus a bull upon the hills, make Pentheus of evil name a bull and make us ravenous wild beasts, armed with deadly claws, that, O Dionysus, we may rend him in our mouths." So spake they praying and the lord of Nysa speedily hearkened to their prayer. Pentheus he made a bull of deadly eye and arched his neck and made the horns spring from his forehead. But to the women he gave the grey eyes of a wild beast and armed their jaws and on their backs put a spotted hide like that of fawns and made them a savage race. And, by the devising of the god having changed their fair flesh, in the form of Leopards they rent Pentheus among the rocks. Such things let us sing, such things let us believe in our hearts! But as for the deeds of the women in the glens of Cithaeron, or the tales told of those wicked mothers, alien to Dionysus, these are the impious falsehoods of minstrels.

In this fashion does some hunter with his comrades devise a snare for the Leopards which love neat wine. They choose a spring in the thirsty land of Libya, a spring which, though small, gives forth in a very waterless place abundant dark water, mysterious and unexpected; nor does it flow onward with murmuring stream, but bubbles marvellously and remains stationary and sinks in the sands. Thereof the race of fierce Leopards come at dawn to drink. And straightway at nightfall the hunters set forth and carry with them twenty jars of sweet wine, which

οἴνου νηδυμίοιο, τὸν ἑνδεκάτῳ λυκάβαντι
θλῖψε τις οἰνοπέδῃσι φυτηκομίῃσι μεμηλώς·
ὕδατι δ' ἐγκέρασαν λαρὸν μέθυ καὶ προλιπόντες
πίδακα πορφυρέην οὐ τηλόθεν εὐνάζονται,
προπροκαλυψάμενοι δέμας ἄλκιμον ἢ σισύρῃσιν
ἢ αὐτοῖσι λίνοισιν· ἐπεὶ σκέπας οὔ τι δύνανται
εὑρέμεν οὔτε λίθων οὔτ' ἠϋκόμων ἀπὸ δένδρων·
πᾶσα γὰρ ἐκτέταται ψαφαρὴ καὶ ἀδένδρεος αἶα.
τὰς δ' ἄρα σειριόεντος ὑπ' ἠελίοιο τυπείσας
ἀμφότερον δίψη τε φίλη τ' ἐκάλεσσεν ἀϋτμή·
πίδακι δ' ἐμπέλασαν Βρομιώτιδι καὶ μέγα χανδὸν
λάπτουσιν Διόνυσον, ἐπ' ἀλλήλῃσι δὲ πᾶσαι
σκιρτεῦσιν μὲν πρῶτα χοροιτυπέουσιν ὁμοῖαι,
εἶτα δέμας βαρύθουσι, προσώπατα δ' ἐς χθόνα δῖαν
ἠρέμα νευστάζουσι κάτω· μετέπειτα δὲ πάσας
κῶμα βιησάμενον χαμάδις βάλεν ἄλλυδις ἄλλην.
ὡς δ' ὁπότ' εἰλαπίνῃσιν ἀφυσσάμενοι κρητήρων
ἥλικες εἰσέτι παῖδες, ἔτι χνοάοντες ἰούλους,
λαρὸν ἀείδωσι, προκαλιζόμενοι μετὰ δεῖπνον
ἀλλήλους ἑκάτερθεν ἀμοιβαδίοισι κυπέλλοις,
ὀψὲ δ' ἐλώφησαν· τοὺς δ' ἔρριφεν ἄλλον ἐπ' ἄλλῳ
καὶ φρεσὶ καὶ βλεφάροισιν ἐπιβρῖσαν μένος οἴνου·
ὣς κεῖναι μάλα θῆρες ἐπ' ἀλλήλῃσι χυθεῖσαι
νόσφι πόνου κρατεροῖσιν[1] ὑπ' ἀγρευτῆρσι γένοντο.
"Αρκτοισιν δὲ πονεῦσι κλυτὴν περιώσιον ἄγρην
Τίγριν ὅσοι ναίουσι καὶ Ἀρμενίην κλυτότοξον.
πουλὺς ὄχλος βαίνουσι τανύσκια βένθεα δρυμῶν,
ἴδριες αὐτολύτοις[2] σὺν εὐρίνεσσι κύνεσσιν,

[1] κρατεροῖο MSS. : corr. G. Hermann.
[2] αὐτολύτοις Schneider : αὐτολύγοις MSS. vulg. : αὖτ' ὀλίγοι Tüselmann coll. *Paraphr.* p. 42. 30 βραχεῖς δὲ αὐτῶν : αὖτ' ὀλίγοις A_2KLM.

someone whose business is the keeping of a vineyard had pressed eleven years before,[a] and they mix the sweet liquor with the water and leave the purple spring and bivouac not far away, making shift to cover their valiant bodies with goat skins or merely with the nets, since they can find no shelter either of rock or leafy tree; for all the land stretches sandy and treeless. The Leopards, smitten by the flaming sun, feel the call both of thirst and of the odour which they love, and they approach the Bromian spring and with widely gaping mouth lap up the wine. First they all leap about one another like dancers; then their limbs become heavy, and they gently nod their heads downwards to the goodly earth; then deep slumber overcomes them all and casts them here and there upon the ground. As when at a banquet youths of an age, still boys, still with the down upon their cheeks, sing sweetly and challenge each other after dinner with cup for cup; and it is late ere they give over, and the strength of the wine is heavy on head and eye and throws them over one upon the other; even so those wild beasts are heaped on one another and become, without toil, the prey of the cruel hunters.

For Bears an exceeding glorious hunt is made by those who dwell on the Tigris and in Armenia famous for archery. A great crowd go to the shady depths of the thickets,[b] skilful men with keen-scented

[a] From Hom. *Od.* iii. 391 *οἴνου ἡδυπότοιο, τὸν ἑνδεκάτῳ ἐνιαυτῷ* (*i.e.* eleven years *after* it was made) | *ὤιξεν ταμίη καὶ ἀπὸ κρήδεμνον ἔλυσε.*

[b] *αὐτολύγοις* of most MSS. seems meaningless. *αὐτολύτοις* (Schneid.) means "on a slip-leash." *Cf.* Hes. *s.* *αὐτόλυσις· δέμα ἐφ' ᾧ ἀγκύλη ἐφῆπται καὶ οὐχ ἅμμα γέγονεν.*

ἴχνια μαστεύσοντ'[1] ὀλοῶν πουλύπλανα[2] θηρῶν.
ἀλλ' ὁπότ' ἀθρήσωσι κύνες σημήϊα ταρσῶν,
ἕσπονται στιβέας τε ποδηγετέουσιν ὁμαρτῇ,
ῥῖνας μὲν ταναὰς σχεδόθεν χέρσοιο τιθέντες·
εἰσοπίσω δ' εἴπέρ τι νεώτερον ἀθρήσειαν
ἴχνος, ἐπειγόμενοι θόρον αὐτίκα καγχαλόωντες
ληθόμενοι τοῦ πρόσθεν· ἐπὴν δ' εἰς ἄκρον ἵκωνται
εὐπλανέος στιβίης θηρός τε παναίολον εὐνήν,
αὐτίχ' ὁ μὲν θρώσκει παλάμης ἄπο θηρητῆρος,
οἰκτρὰ μάλ' ὑλακόων, κεχαρημένος ἔξοχα θυμόν.
ὡς δ' ὅτε παρθενικὴ γλαγόεντος ἐν εἴαρος ὥρῃ
ἀβλαύτοισι πόδεσσιν ἀν' οὔρεα πάντ' ἀλάληται,
ἄνθεα διζομένη· τὸ δέ οἱ μάλα τηλόθ' ἐούσῃ
νηδύμιον προπάροιθεν ἴον μήνυσεν ἀϋτμή·
τῇ δὲ μάλ' ἰάνθη μείδησέ τε θυμὸς ἐλαφρός,
ἀμᾶται δ' ἀκόρητος, ἀναψαμένη δὲ κάρηνον
εἶσιν ἐς ἀγραύλων δόμον ἀείδουσα τοκήων·
ὣς κυνὸς ἰάνθη θυμὸς θρασύς· αὐτὰρ ἐπακτὴρ
καὶ μάλα μιν θύνοντα βιησάμενος τελαμῶσι
καγχαλόων παλίνορσος ἔβη μεθ' ὅμιλον ἑταίρων.
τοῖσι δὲ καὶ δρυμὸν διεπέφραδε, θῆρά τε πικρὴν
αὐτὸς καὶ συνάεθλος ὅπου λοχόωντες ἔλειψαν.
οἱ δ' ἄρ' ἐπειγόμενοι στάλικας στήσαντο κραταιοὺς
δίκτυά τ' ἀμπετάσαντο καὶ ἄρκυας ἀμφεβάλοντο·
ἐν δὲ δύω κλῖναν δοιαῖς ἑκάτερθε κεραίαις
ἀνέρας ἀκρολίνους ὑπὸ[3] μειλινέοισι πάγοισιν.[4]
ἐκ δ' αὐτῶν κεράων τε καὶ αἰζηῶν πυλαωρῶν

[1] μαστεύσοντ'] dual for plural.
[2] πολυπλανέα MSS. : corr. Schneider.
[3] ἐπὶ in lit. BK. [4] πάγαισι B de Ballu.

dogs on leash, to seek the mazy tracks of the deadly beasts. But when the dogs descry the signs of footprints, they follow them up and guide the trackers with them, holding their long noses nigh the ground. And afterwards if they descry any fresher track, straightway they rush eagerly, giving tongue the while exultingly, forgetting the previous track. But when they reach the end of their devious tracking and come to the cunning lair of the beast, straightway the dog bounds from the hand of the hunter, whimpering, rejoicing in his heart exceedingly. As when a maiden in the season of milky spring roams with unsandalled feet over all the hills in search of flowers and while she is yet afar the fragrance tells her of the sweet violet ahead; her lightsome heart is gladdened and smiles, and she gathers the flowers without stint and wreathes her head and goes singing to the house of her country-dwelling parents; even so the stout heart of the dog is gladdened. But the hunter for all his eagerness constrains him with straps and goes back exulting to the company of his comrades. And he shows them the thicket and where himself and his helper ambushed and left the savage beast. And they hasten and set up strong stakes and spread hayes and cast nets around. On either hand in the two wings they put two men at the ends of the net[a] to lie under piles of ashen boughs. From the wings themselves and the men who watch the entrance

[a] The word ἀκρολίνους gives much the same sense as ἀκρωλένια (with which, of course, it has no etymological connexion) or "elbows" of Xen. *C.* 2. 6, which Poll. v. 29 defines as τὰ πέρατα τῶν ἀρκύων. μειλινέοισι πάγοισι—if correct—seems to mean "piles" or "heaps" of ashen boughs.

λαιῇ μὲν μήρινθον ἐΰστροφον ἐκτανύουσι
μηκεδανήν, λινέην, ὀλίγον γαίης ἐφύπερθεν,
ὅσσον ἐπ' ὀμφαλὸν ἀνδρὸς ἱκανέμεναι στροφάλιγγα·
τῆς ἀπὸ μὲν κρέμαται περιδαίδαλα παμφανόωντα
ἄνθεα ταινιῶν πουλύχροα, δείματα θηρῶν,
ἐκ δ' ἄρ' ἀπήρτηται πτίλα μυρία παμφανόωντα,
οἰωνῶν τε διηερίων περικαλλέα ταρσὰ
γυπάων πολιῶν τε κύκνων δολιχῶν τε πελαργῶν.
δεξιτερῇ δὲ λόχους ὑπὸ ῥωγάσιν[1] ἐστήσαντο,
ἢ χλοεροῖς πετάλοισι θοῶς πυκάσαντο μέλαθρα,
τυτθὸν ἀπ' ἀλλήλων, πίσυρας δ' ἐκάλυψαν ἑκάστῳ
ἀνέρας, ὀρπήκεσσι πρόπαν δέμας ἀμφιβαλόντες.
αὐτὰρ ἐπὴν κατὰ κόσμον ἐπαρτέα πάντα πέλωνται,
σάλπιγξ μὲν κελάδησε πελώριον, ἡ δέ τε λόχμης
ὀξὺ λέληκε θοροῦσα καὶ ὀξὺ δέδορκε λακοῦσα·
αἰζηοὶ δ' ἐπόρουσαν ἀολλέες, ἐκ δ' ἑκάτερθεν
ἀντία θηρὸς ἴασι φαλαγγηδὸν κλονέοντες.

[1] ῥωπάσιν A_3, in lit. M.

---

[a] The *formido* of Latin writers, a line hung with feathers and ribbons of various colours by which the game is scared and driven in the desired direction. Verg. *A*. xii. 749 Inclusum veluti si quando flumine nactus Cervum aut puniceae saeptum formidine pennae Venator cursu canis et latratibus instat; *G*. iii. 371 Hos (cervos) non inmissis canibus, non cassibus ullis Puniceaeve agitant pavidos formidine pennae; Senec. *Hipp*. 46 Picta rubenti linea penna Vano claudat terrore feras; *De ira* ii. 11. 5 cum maximos ferarum greges linea pennis distincta contineat et in insidias agat, ab ipso adfectu dicta formido; *De clem*. i. 12. 5 Sic feras lineae et pennae clausas continent. Easdem a tergo eques telis incessat: temptabunt fugam per ipsa quae fugerant procalcabuntque formidinem; Luc. iv. 437 Sic dum pavidos formidine cervos Claudat odoratae metuentes aera pennae.

they stretch on the left hand a well-twined long rope [a] of flax a little above the ground in such wise that the cord would reach to a man's waist. Therefrom are hung many-coloured patterned ribbons, various and bright, a scare to wild beasts, and suspended therefrom are countless bright feathers, the beautiful wings of the fowls of the air, Vultures [b] and white Swans [c] and long Storks.[d] On the right hand they set ambushes in clefts of rock, or with green leaves they swiftly roof huts a little apart from one another, and in each they hide four men, covering all their bodies with branches. Now when all things are ready, the trumpet sounds its tremendous note, and the Bear leaps forth from the thicket with a sharp cry and looks sharply as she cries. And the young men rush on in a body and from either side come in battalions against the beast and drive her before

[b] For the feathers used in the *formido cf.* Gratt. 77 ff. Tantum inter nivei iungantur vellera *cygni*, Et satis armorum est; haec clara luce coruscant Terribiles species; ab *vulture* dirus avaro Turbat odor silvas, meliusque alterna valet res; Nemes. 312 ff. Dat tibi pinnarum terrentia millia *vultur*, Dat Libye, magnarum avium fecunda creatrix, Dantque grues *cygnique* senes et candidus anser, Dant quae fluminibus crassisque paludibus errant Pellitosque pedes stagnanti gurgite tingunt. Of Vultures two species are distinguished: A. 592 b 6 *τῶν δὲ γυπῶν δύο ἐστὶν εἴδη, ὁ μὲν μικρὸς καὶ ἐκλευκότερος, ὁ δὲ μείζων καὶ σποδοειδέστερος.* The former is *Neophron percnopterus* L., which nests in Greece, its arrival about 21st March being reckoned by shepherds as the beginning of Spring (Momms. p. 1); the latter *Vultur fulvus* Briss. and perh. *V. cinereus*.

[c] Both *Cygnus musicus*, the Whistling Swan or Whooper, and *C. olor*, the Mute Swan, are found in Greece, but only the latter appears to nest there (Momms. pp. 286 f.).

[d] *Ciconia nigra* and *C. alba* are both visitors in Greece, the latter being resident in Macedonia (Momms. pp. 285 f.).

ἡ δ' ὅμαδον προλιποῦσα καὶ ἀνέρας ἰθὺς ὀρούει,
γυμνὸν ὅπου λεύσσει πεδίον πολύ· κεῖθεν ἔπειτα
ἑξείης κατὰ νῶτον ἐγειρόμενος λόχος ἀνδρῶν
κλαγγηδὸν παταγοῦσιν, ἐπ' ὀφρύα μηρίνθοιο
σευόμενοι καὶ δεῖμα πολύχροον· ἡ δέ τ' ἀνιγρὴ
ἀμφίβολος μάλα πάμπαν ἀτυζομένη πεφόρηται·
πάντα δ' ὁμοῦ δείδοικε, λόχον, κτύπον, αὐλόν, ἀϋτήν,
δειμαλέην μήρινθον· ἐπεὶ κελάδοντος ἀήτεω
ταινίαι τ' ἐφύπερθε διηέριαι κραδάουσι
κινύμεναι πτέρυγές τε λιγήϊα συρίζουσι.
τοὔνεκα παπταίνουσα κατ' ἄρκυος ἀντίον ἕρπει,
ἐν δ' ἔπεσεν λινέοισι λόχοις· τοὶ δ' ἐγγὺς ἐόντες
ἀκρόλινοι θρώσκουσι καὶ ἐγκονέοντες ὕπερθε
σπαρτόδετον τανύουσι περίδρομον· ἄλλο δ' ἐπ' ἄλλῳ
νηήσαντο λίνον· μάλα γὰρ τότε θυμαίνουσιν
ἄρκτοι καὶ γενύεσσι καὶ ἀργαλέαις παλάμῃσι·
δηθάκι δ' ἐξαυτῆς φύγον ἀνέρας ἀγρευτῆρας
δίκτυά τ' ἐξήλυξαν, ἀΐστωσαν δέ τε θήρην.
ἀλλὰ τότε κρατερός τις ἀνὴρ παλάμην ἐπέδησεν
ἄρκτου δεξιτερήν, χήρωσέ τε πᾶσαν ἐρωήν,
δῆσέ τ' ἐπισταμένως, τάνυσέν τε ποτὶ ξύλα θῆρα,
καὶ πάλιν ἐγκατέκλεισε δρυὸς πεύκης τε μελάθρῳ,
πυκνῇσι στροφάλιγξιν ἑὸν δέμας ἀσκήσασαν.

---

[a] *Cf.* i. 156. The περίδρομος is a rope passing through the meshes along the upper and lower margins of the net, which, when the game is driven in, the ambushed hunter pulls and so closes the mouth of the net. Hes. *s.* περίδρομοι· τοῦ δικτύου τὸ διειρόμενον σχοινίον; Poll. v. 28 ἔστι δὲ περίδρομος τῆς ἄρκυος σχοινίον ἑκατέρωθεν τῶν ἄνω τε καὶ κάτω βρόχων διειρόμενον, ᾧ συνέλκεταί τε τὰ δίκτυα καὶ πάλιν ἀναλύεται·

them. And she, leaving the din and the men, rushes straight where she sees an empty space of open plain. Thereupon in turn an ambush of men arises in her rear and make a clattering din, driving her to the brow of the rope and the many-coloured scare. And the wretched beast is utterly in doubt and flees distraught, fearful of all alike—the ambush of men, the din, the flute, the shouting, the scaring rope; for with the roaring wind the ribands wave aloft in the air and the swinging feathers whistle shrill. So, glancing about her, the Bear draws nigh the net and falls into the flaxen ambush. Then the watchers at the ends of the net near at hand spring forth and speedily draw tight above the skirting cord [a] of broom. Net on net they pile; for at that moment Bears greatly rage with jaws and terrible paws, and many a time they straightway evade the hunters and escape from the nets and make the hunting vain. But at that same moment some strong man fetters the right paw of the Bear and widows her of all her force, and binds her skilfully and ties the beast to planks of wood and encloses her again in a cage of oak and pine, after she has exercised her body in many a twist and turn.

Xen. *C.* 2. 4 ὑφείσθωσαν δὲ οἱ περίδρομοι ἀνάμματοι, ἵνα εὔτροχοι ὦσι. The περίδρομοι might also be attached to the net by loops (τοὺς δὲ περιδρόμους ἀπὸ στροφέων Xen. *C.* 2. 6; *cf.* Poll. v. 29 προβάλλονται δὲ τοῖς δικτύοις ἀπὸ στροφέων): Xen. *C.* 10. 7 τὸν περίδρομον ἐξάπτειν ἀπὸ δένδρου ἰσχυροῦ. Xen. *C.* 6. 9 speaks of fastening the περίδρομοι to the ground (καθάπτων τοὺς περιδρόμους ἐπὶ τὴν γῆν). Here he must be referring to the skirting-rope at the lower margin of the net from which the upper rope was sometimes distinguished as ἐπίδρομος: Poll. v. 29 τινὲς δὲ τούτους ἐπιδρόμους ὠνόμασαν, οἱ δὲ δύο ὄντων τὸν μὲν ἐκ τοῦ κάτω περίδρομον, ἐπίδρομον δὲ τὸν ἄνωθεν.

Χρειὼ δὲ σκοπέλου μὲν ἀνάντεος ἠδὲ πάγοιο
σεύεσθαι προθέοντα ποδώκεα φῦλα λαγωῶν,
πρὸς δὲ κάταντα σοφῇσι προμηθείῃσιν ἐλαύνειν·
αὐτίκα γὰρ σκύλακάς τε καὶ ἀνέρας ἀθρήσαντες
πρὸς λόφον ἰθύνουσιν· ἐπεὶ μάλα γιγνώσκουσιν,
ὅττι πάροιθεν ἔασιν ὀλιζότεροι πόδες αὐτοῖς.
τοὔνεκα ῥηΐδιοι πτώκεσσι πέλουσι κολῶναι,
ῥηΐδιοι πτώκεσσι, δυσάντεες ἱππελάτῃσι.
ναὶ μὴν ἀτραπιτοῖο πολυστιβίην ἀλεείνειν
καὶ πάτον, ἐν δ᾽ ἄρα τῇσι γεωμορίῃσιν ἐλαύνειν·
κουφότεροι γὰρ ἔασι τρίβῳ καὶ ποσσὶν ἐλαφροὶ
ῥεῖά τ᾽ ἐπιθρώσκουσιν· ἀρηρομένῃ δ᾽ ἐνὶ γαίῃ
καὶ θέρεος βαρύθουσι πόδες καὶ χείματος ὥρῃ
ἄχρις ἐπισφυρίων ὀλοὴν κρηπῖδα φέρουσιν.
"Ην ποτ᾽ ἐλῇς δόρκον δέ, φυλάσσεο μὴ μετὰ πολλὸν
ἐκτάδιον δολιχόν τε δρόμον καὶ τέρμα πόνοιο
τυτθὸν ὑποσταίῃ, λαγόνων δ᾽ ἀπὸ μήδεα χεύῃ·
δόρκοι γὰρ περίαλλα δρόμοις ἐνὶ μεσσατίοισι
κυστίδα κυμαίνουσιν, ἀναγκαίοισιν ὑπ᾽ ὄμβροις
βριθόμενοι λαγόνας, ποτὶ δ᾽ ἰσχίον ὀκλάζουσιν·
ἢν δ᾽ ὀλίγον πνεύσωσι πολυσφαράγων ἀπὸ λαιμῶν,
πολλὸν ἀρειότεροι λαιψηρότεροί τε φέβονται,
γούνασιν εὐφόρτοισι καὶ ἔγκασι κουφοτέροισι.
Κερδὼ δ᾽ οὔτε λόχοισιν ἁλώσιμος οὔτε βρόχοισιν

---

[a] Xen. *C.* 5. 17 *θέουσι μάλιστα μὲν τὰ ἀνάντη . . . τὰ δὲ κατάντη ἥκιστα.*

[b] Xen. *C.* 5. 30 *σκέλη τὰ ὄπισθεν μείζω πολὺ τῶν ἔμπροσθεν.*

[c] Xen. *C.* 8. 8 *ταχὺ γὰρ ἀπαγορεύει διὰ τὸ βάθος τῆς χιόνος καὶ διὰ τὸ κάτωθεν τῶν ποδῶν λασίων ὄντων προσέχεσθαι αὐτῷ ὄγκον πολύν.*

[d] *i.e.* their feet are caked with mud. The metaphor is

In hunting the swift-footed tribes of the Hare the hunter should run in front and head them off from upward-sloping rock or hill and with cunning prudence drive them downhill. For the moment that they see hounds and huntsmen they rush uphill [a]; since they well know that their forelegs [b] are shorter. Hence hills are easy for Hares—easy for Hares but difficult for mounted men. Moreover, the hunter should avoid much-trodden ways and the beaten track and pursue them in the tilled fields. For on the trodden way they are nimbler and light of foot and easily rush on. But on the ploughed land their feet are heavy in summer and in the winter [c] season they carry a fatal shoe [d] that reaches to the ankle.

If ever thou art hunting a Gazelle, beware that after a very long and extended course and term of toil it do not halt a moment and relieve [e] nature. For in Gazelles beyond all others the bladder swells in the midst of their course and their flanks are burdened by involuntary waters and they squat upon their haunches. But if they take breath a little with their noisy throats, they flee far more strongly and more swiftly with nimble knees and lighter loins.

The Fox is not to be captured by ambush nor by

illustrated by the use of κρηπίς to mean a species of cake ἐξ ἀλεύρου καὶ μέλιτος Poll. vi. 77.

[e] *Cf.* A. 579 a 12 (of Deer, ἔλαφοι) ἐν δὲ τῷ φεύγειν ἀνάπαυσιν ποιοῦνται τῶν δρόμων καὶ ὑφιστάμενοι μένουσιν ἕως ἂν πλησίον ἔλθῃ ὁ διώκων· τότε δὲ πάλιν φεύγουσιν. τοῦτο δὲ δοκοῦσι ποιεῖν διὰ τὸ πονεῖν τὰ ἐντός· τὸ γὰρ ἔντερον ἔχει λεπτὸν καὶ ἀσθενὲς οὕτως ὥστε ἐὰν ἠρέμα τις πατάξῃ, διακόπτεται τοῦ δέρματος ὑγιοῦς ὄντος; Plin. viii. 113 et alias semper in fuga acquiescunt stantesque respiciunt, cum prope ventum est rursus fugae praesidia repetentes. Hoc fit intestini dolore tam infirmi ut ictu levi rumpatur intus.

οὔτε λίνοις· δεινὴ γὰρ ἐπιφροσύνῃσι νοῆσαι,
δεινὴ δ' αὖτε κάλωα ταμεῖν, ὑπὸ δ' ἅμματα λῦσαι,
καὶ πυκινοῖσι δόλοισιν ὀλισθῆσαι θανάτοιο.
ἀλλὰ κύνες μιν ἄειραν ἀολλέες· οὐδ' ἄρ' ἐκεῖνοι
καὶ κρατεροί περ ἐόντες ἀναιμωτὶ δαμάσαντο.

noose nor by net. For she is clever in her cunning at perceiving them; clever too at severing a rope and loosing knots and by subtle craft escaping from death. But the thronging hounds take her; yet even they for all their strength do not overcome her without bloodshed.

ΑΛΙΕΥΤΙΚΩΝ ΤΟ Α

Ἔθνεά τοι πόντοιο πολυσπερέας τε φάλαγγας
παντοίων νεπόδων, πλωτὸν γένος Ἀμφιτρίτης,
ἐξερέω, γαίης ὕπατον κράτος, Ἀντωνῖνε·
ὅσσα τε κυματόεσσαν ἔχει χύσιν, ᾗχί θ᾽ ἕκαστα
ἐννέμεται, διερούς τε γάμους διεράς τε γενέθλας
καὶ βίον ἰχθυόεντα καὶ ἔχθεα καὶ φιλότητας
καὶ βουλάς, ἁλίης τε πολύτροπα δήνεα τέχνης
κερδαλέης, ὅσα φῶτες ἐπ᾽ ἰχθύσι μητίσαντο
ἀφράστοις· ἀΐδηλον ἐπιπλώουσι θάλασσαν
τολμηρῇ κραδίῃ, κατὰ δ᾽ ἔδρακον οὐκ ἐπίοπτα
βένθεα καὶ τέχνῃσιν ἁλὸς διὰ μέτρα δάσαντο
δαιμόνιοι. χλούνην μὲν ὀρίτροφον ἠδὲ καὶ ἄρκτον
θηρητὴρ ὁράᾳ τε καὶ ἀντιόωντα δοκεύει
ἀμφαδίην, ἕκαθέν τε βαλεῖν σχεδόθεν τε δαμάσσαι·
ἄμφω δ᾽ ἀσφαλέως γαίης ἔπι θήρ τε καὶ ἀνὴρ
μάρνανται, σκύλακες δὲ συνέμποροι ἡγεμονῆες
κνώδαλα σημαίνουσι καὶ ἰθύνουσιν ἄνακτας
εὐνὴν εἰς αὐτὴν καὶ ἀρηγόνες ἐγγὺς ἕπονται.
οὐδ᾽ ἄρα τοῖς οὐ χεῖμα τόσον δέος, οὐ μὲν ὀπώρη
φλέγμα φέρει· πολλαὶ γὰρ ἐπακτήρων ἀλεωραὶ
λόχμαι τε σκιεραὶ καὶ δειράδες ἄντρα τε πέτρης
αὐτορόφου· πολλοὶ δὲ τιταινόμενοι κατ᾽ ὄρεσφιν
ἀργύρεοι ποταμοί, δίψης ἄκος ἠδὲ λοετρῶν

[a] Introduction, p. xx.

HALIEUTICA, or FISHING

I

The tribes of the sea and the far scattered ranks of all manner of fishes, the swimming brood of Amphitrite, will I declare, O Antoninus,[a] sovereign majesty of earth; all that inhabit the watery flood and where each dwells, their mating in the waters and their birth, the life of fishes, their hates, their loves, their wiles,[b] and the crafty devices of the cunning fisher's art—even all that men have devised against the baffling fishes. Over the unknown sea they sail with daring heart and they have beheld the unseen deeps and by their arts have mapped out the measures of the sea, men more than human. The mountain-bred Boar and the Bear the hunter sees, and, when he confronts him watches him openly, whether to shoot him afar or slay him at close quarters. Both beast and man fight securely on the land, and the hounds go with the hunter as guides to mark the quarry and direct their masters to the very lair and attend close at hand as helpers. To them winter brings no great fear, nor summer brings burning heat; for hunters have many shelters—shady thickets and cliffs and caves in the rock self-roofed; many a silvery river, too, stretching through the hills to quench thirst and

[b] Of fishes, *cf. H.* ii. 53 f., iii. 92 ff. Editors, punctuating at φιλότητας, take βουλάς of the devices of fishermen.

ἀέναοι ταμίαι· παρὰ δὲ χλοάουσι ῥέεθροις
ποῖαί τε χθαμαλαί, μαλακὴ κλίσις ὕπνον ἑλέσθαι
εὔδιον ἐκ καμάτοιο, καὶ ὥρια δόρπα πάσασθαι
ὕλης ἀγρονόμοιο, τά τ᾽ οὔρεσι πολλὰ φύονται.
τερπωλὴ δ᾽ ἕπεται θήρῃ πλέον ἠέ περ ἱδρώς.
ὅσσοι δ᾽ οἰωνοῖσιν ἐφοπλίζονται ὄλεθρον,
ῥηϊδίη καὶ τοῖσι πέλει καὶ ὑπόψιος ἄγρη·
τοὺς μὲν γὰρ κνώσσοντας ἐληΐσσαντο καλιῆς
κρύβδην· τοὺς δὲ δόναξιν ὑπέσπασαν ἰξοφόροισιν·
οἱ δὲ τανυπλέκτοισιν ἐν ἕρκεσιν ἤριπον αὐτοὶ
εὐνῆς χρηΐζοντες, ἀτερπέα δ᾽ αὖλιν ἔκυρσαν.
τλησιπόνοις δ᾽ ἁλιεῦσιν ἀτέκμαρτοι μὲν ἄεθλοι,
ἐλπὶς δ᾽ οὐ σταθερὴ σαίνει φρένας ἠΰτ᾽ ὄνειρος·
οὐ γὰρ ἀκινήτου γαίης ὕπερ ἀθλεύουσιν,
ἀλλ᾽ αἰεὶ κρυερῷ τε καὶ ἄσχετα μαργαίνοντι
ὕδατι συμφορέονται, ὃ καὶ γαίηθεν ἰδέσθαι
δεῖμα φέρει καὶ μοῦνον ἐν ὄμμασι πειρήσασθαι·
δούρασι δ᾽ ἐν βαιοῖσιν ἀελλάων θεράποντες
πλαζόμενοι, καὶ θυμὸν ἐν οἴδμασιν αἰὲν ἔχοντες,
αἰεὶ μὲν νεφέλην ἰοειδέα παπταίνουσιν,
αἰεὶ δὲ τρομέουσι μελαινόμενον πόρον ἅλμης·
οὐδέ τι φοιταλέων ἀνέμων σκέπας, οὐδέ τιν᾽ ὄμβρων
ἀλκήν, οὐ πυρὸς ἄλκαρ ὀπωρινοῖο φέρονται.
πρὸς δ᾽ ἔτι καὶ βλοσυρῆς δυσδερκέα δείματα λίμνης
κήτεα πεφρίκασι, τά τε σφίσιν ἀντιόωσιν,
εὖτ᾽ ἂν ὑποβρυχίης ἄδυτον περόωσι θαλάσσης·
οὐ μέν τις σκυλάκων ἁλίην ὁδὸν ἡγεμονεύει

[a] Manil. v. 371 Aut nido captare suo ramove sedentem | Pascentemve super surgentia ducere lina; *cf. C.* i. 64.

[b] *Cf.* Gaelic proverbs: "Precarious is the hunting, unreliable the fishing; place thy trust in the land, it never left man empty"; "Unstable is the point of the fish-hook"; "Good is the help of the fishing, but a bad barn is the fish-

dispense a never-failing bath; and by the green-fringed streams are low beds of grass, a soft couch in sunny weather for sleep after toil, and seasonable repast to eat of woodland fruits which grow abundant on the hills. Pleasure more than sweat attends the hunt. And those who prepare destruction for birds, easy for them too and visible is their prey. For some they capture unawares asleep upon their nests[a]; others they take with limed reeds; others fall of themselves into the fine-plaited nets, seeking for a bed, and a woeful roost they find. But for the toilsome fishermen their labours are uncertain,[b] and unstable as a dream is the hope that flatters their hearts. For not upon the moveless[c] land do they labour, but always they have to encounter the chill and wildly raging water, which even to behold from the land brings terror and to essay it only with the eyes. In tiny barks they wander obsequious to the stormy winds, their minds ever on the surging waves; always they scan the dark clouds and ever tremble at the blackening tract of sea; no shelter have they from the raging winds nor any defence against the rain nor bulwark against summer heat. Moreover, they shudder at the terrors awful to behold of the grim sea, even the Sea-monsters[d] which encounter them when they traverse the secret places of the deep. No hounds guide the fishers on their seaward

ing," Carmichael, *Carmina Gadelica* (Edin. 1900), p. 255. "Plough the sea!" said Triptolemus; "that's a furrow requires small harrowing," Scott, *The Pirate*, c. 5.

[c] Walton, *Compleat Angler*, c. i. Venator: The Earth is a solid, settled element.

[d] κῆτος (*Il.* i. 360 n.) denotes Whales, Dolphins, Seals, Sharks, Tunnies, and the large creatures of the sea generally.

ἰχθυβόλοις· ἴχνη γὰρ ἀείδελα νηχομένοισιν·
οὐδ᾽ οἵ γ᾽ εἰσορόωσιν ὅπῃ σχεδὸν ἵξεται ἄγρης
ἀντιάσας, οὐ γάρ τι μίην ὁδὸν ἔρχεται, ἰχθύς·
θριξὶ δ᾽ ἐν ἠπεδανοῖσι παλιγνάμπτοιό τε χαλκοῦ
χείλεσι καὶ δονάκεσσι λίνοισί τε κάρτος ἔχουσιν.
Οὐ μὴν τερπωλῆς ἀπολείπεαι, αἴ κ᾽ ἐθέλησθα
τέρπεσθαι, γλυκερὴ δὲ πέλει βασιλήϊος ἄγρη.
νῆα μὲν εὐγόμφωτον, ἐΰζυγον, ἔξοχα κούφην,
αἰζηοὶ κώπῃσιν ἐπειγομένης ἐλόωσι,
νῶτον ἁλὸς θείνοντες· ὁ δ᾽ ἐν πρύμνῃσιν ἄριστος
ἰθυντὴρ ἁλίαστον ἄγει καὶ ἀμεμφέα νῆα
χῶρον ἐς εὐρύαλόν τε καὶ εὔδια πορφύροντα·
ἔνθα δὲ δαιτυμόνων νεπόδων ἀπερείσια φῦλα
φέρβεται, οὓς θεράποντες ἀεὶ κομέουσιν, ἐδωδῇ
πολλῇ πιαίνοντες, ἑτοιμότατον χορὸν ἄγρης
σοί τε, μάκαρ, καὶ παιδὶ μεγαυχέϊ, πώεα θήρης.
αὐτίκα γὰρ χειρὸς μὲν ἐΰπλοκον εἰς ἅλα πέμπεις
ὁρμιήν, ὁ δὲ ῥίμφα γένυν κατεδέξατο χαλκοῦ
ἰχθὺς ἀντιάσας, τάχα δ᾽ ἕλκεται ἐκ βασιλῆος
οὐκ ἀέκων, σέο δ᾽ ἦτορ ἰαίνεται, ὄρχαμε γαίης·
πολλὴ γὰρ βλεφάροισι καὶ ἐν φρεσὶ τέρψις ἰδέσθαι
παλλόμενον καὶ ἑλισσόμενον πεπεδημένον ἰχθύν.
Ἀλλά μοι ἰλήκοις μὲν ἁλὸς πόρῳ ἐμβασιλεύων

---

[a] ἐν τῷ βιβαρίῳ schol. The reference is to a royal marine fish-preserve. Such a fish-preserve, which might be either in fresh or salt water, was called by the Romans *piscina* (Varro, iii. 17. 2 cum piscinarum genera sint duo, dulcium et salsarum, alterum apud plebem et non sine fructu, ubi lymphae aquam piscibus nostris villaticis ministrant: illae autem maritimae piscinae nobilium, quibus Neptunus et aquam et pisces ministrat, *cf.* iii. 3. 2 ff., 17. 2; Plin. x. 193; Colum. i. 6. 21, 8. 17) or *vivarium* (M.G. βιβάριον), a more general term, applicable to any preserve for wild creatures

path—for the tracks of the swimming tribes are unseen—nor do they see where the fish will encounter them and come within range of capture; for not by one path does the fish travel. In feeble hairs and bent hooks of bronze and in reeds and nets the fishers have their strength.

Yet not bereft of pleasure art thou, if pleasure thou desirest, but sweet is the royal sport. A ship well-riveted, well-benched, light exceedingly, the young men drive with racing oars smiting the back of the sea; and at the stern the best man as steersman guides the ship, steady and true, to a wide space of gently heaving waves; and there feed[a] infinite tribes of feasting fishes which thy servants ever tend, fattening them with abundant food, a ready choir of spoil for thee, O blessed one, and for thy glorious son, the flock of your capture. For straightway thou lettest from thy hand into the sea the well-woven line, and the fish quickly meets and seizes the hook of bronze and is speedily haled forth—not all unwilling—by our king;[b] and thy heart is gladdened, O Lord of earth. For great delight it is for eye and mind to see the captive fish tossing and turning.

But be thou gracious unto me, thou who art king

(Plin. ix. 168 ostrearum vivaria; *ibid.* 170 reliquorum piscium vivaria, viii. 115 for Deer, viii. 211 vivaria eorum (*sc.* Wild Swine) ceterarumque silvestrium), with its subdivisions, *leporarium* (not confined to Hares, Varro, iii. 3. 1), *aviarium* (Varro, iii. 3. 6) or *ornithon* (Varro, iii. 3. 1), etc. *Cf.* Ael. viii. 4, xii. 30; Juv. iv. 51; Mart. iv. 30; Aul. Gell. ii. 20. 4 f.; Badham, pp. 35 ff.; Radcliffe, pp. 224 ff.

[b] *Cf.* Beaumont and Fletcher, *The False One*, i. 2 "She was used to take delight, with her fair hand | To angle in the Nile, where the glad fish, | As if they knew who 'twas sought to deceive them, | Contended to be taken" (quoted Radcliffe, p. 173); Mart. i. 104 norunt cui serviant leones.

εὐρυμέδων Κρονίδης γαιήοχος, ἠδὲ Θάλασσα
αὐτή, καὶ ναετῆρες ἐριγδούποιο θαλάσσης
δαίμονες, ὑμετέρας τ' ἀγέλας καὶ ἁλίτροφα φῦλα
εἰπέμεν αἰνήσαιτε· σὺ δ' ἰθύνειας ἕκαστα,
πότνα Θεά, καὶ πατρὶ καὶ υἱέϊ παμβασιλῆος
θυμήρη τάδε δῶρα τεῆς πόρσυνον ἀοιδῆς.
Μυρία μὲν δὴ φῦλα καὶ ἄκριτα βένθεσι πόντου
ἐμφέρεται πλώοντα· τὰ δ' οὔ κέ τις ἐξονομῆναι
ἀτρεκέως· οὐ γάρ τις ἐφίκετο τέρμα θαλάσσης·
ἀλλὰ τριηκοσίων ὀργυιῶν ἄχρι μάλιστα
ἀνέρες ἴσασίν τε καὶ ἔδρακον Ἀμφιτρίτην.
πολλὰ δ' (ἀπειρεσίη γὰρ ἀμετροβαθής τε θάλασσα,)
κέκρυπται, τά κεν οὔ τις ἀείδελα μυθήσαιτο
θνητὸς ἐών· ὀλίγος δὲ νόος μερόπεσσι καὶ ἀλκή.
οὐ μὲν γὰρ γαίης πολυμήτορος ἔλπομαι ἅλμην
παυροτέρας ἀγέλας οὔτ' ἔθνεα μείονα φέρβειν.
ἀλλ' εἴτ' ἀμφήριστος ἐν ἀμφοτέρῃσι γενέθλη
εἴθ' ἑτέρη προβέβηκε, θεοὶ σάφα τεκμαίρονται,
ἡμεῖς δ' ἀνδρομέοισι νοήμασι μέτρα φέροιμεν.
Ἰχθύσι μὲν γενεή τε καὶ ἤθεα καὶ πόρος ἅλμης
κέκριται, οὐδέ τι πᾶσι νομαὶ νεπόδεσσιν ὁμοῖαι·
οἱ μὲν γὰρ χθαμαλοῖσι παρ' αἰγιαλοῖσι νέμονται,
ψάμμον ἐρεπτόμενοι καὶ ὅσ' ἐν ψαμάθοισι φύονται,
ἵπποι κόκκυγές τε θοοὶ ξανθοί τ' ἐρυθῖνοι

[a] Ael. ix. 35 εἰς τριακοσίας ὀργυιάς φασιν ἀνθρώποις κάτοπτα εἶναι τὰ ἐν τῇ θαλάττῃ, περαιτέρω γε μὴν οὐκέτι. But Plin. ii. 102 Altissimum mare xv. stadiorum Fabianus tradit.

[b] *Hippocampus brevirostris* Cuv. or *H. guttulatus* Cuv., both M.G. ἀλογάκι (*i.e.* Horse), the latter being commoner in Greek waters (Apost. p. 7). *Cf.* Marc. S. 21; Plin. xxxii. 149; Athen. 304 e.

[c] One of the Gurnards, prob. *Trigla lyra* L., The Piper. It is of a bright red colour (ἐρυθρὸν κόκκυγα Numen. *ap.* Athen. 309 f) and Athen. 324 f quotes Speusippus, etc., for

in the tract of the sea, wide-ruling son of Cronus, Girdler of the earth, and be gracious thyself, O Sea, and ye gods who in the sounding sea have your abode; and grant me to tell of your herds and sea-bred tribes; and do thou, O lady Goddess, direct all and make these gifts of thy song well pleasing to our sovereign lord and to his son.

Infinite and beyond ken are the tribes that move and swim in the depths of the sea, and none could name them certainly; for no man hath reached the limit of the sea, but unto three hundred fathoms[a] less or more men know and have explored the deep. But, since the sea is infinite and of unmeasured depth, many things are hidden, and of these dark things none that is mortal can tell; for small are the understanding and the strength of men. The briny sea feeds not, I ween, fewer herds nor lesser tribes than earth, mother of many. But whether the tale of offspring be debatable between them both, or whether one excels the other, the gods know certainly; but we must make our reckoning by our human wits.

Now fishes differ in breed and habit and in their path in the sea, and not all fishes have like range. For some keep by the low shores, feeding on sand and whatever things grow in the sand; to wit, the Sea-horse,[b] the swift Cuckoo-fish,[c] the yellow

its resemblance to the Red Mullet. Marc. S. 21 ὀξύκομοι κόκκυγες in allusion to the dorsal spines which they erect on being touched (Day i. p. 55); A. 598 a 15 ἐπαμφοτερίζουσιν, *i.e.* found both in deep and shallow water; 535 b 20 "utters a sound like the cuckoo, whence its name." *Cf.* Ael. x. 11. The noise made by Gurnards when taken from the water is due to escape of gas from the air-bladder. Apost. p. 11 (where he identifies Aristotle's κόκκυξ with the allied *Dactylopterus volitans* Mor.) enumerates eight species of *Trigla* found in Greek waters.

καὶ κίθαροι καὶ τρίγλα καὶ ἀδρανέες μελάνουροι
τραχούρων τ' ἀγέλαι βούγλωσσά τε καὶ πλατύουροι
ταινίαι ἀβληχραὶ καὶ μορμύρος, αἰόλος ἰχθύς,
σκόμβροι κυπρῖνοί τε καὶ οἳ φίλοι αἰγιαλοῖσιν.
"Αλλοι δ' αὖ πηλοῖσι καὶ ἐν τενάγεσσι θαλάσσης

---

[a] The hermaphrodite Eryth(r)inus of A. 538 a 20, 567 a 27, etc.; Plin. ix. 56, seems to be a *Serranus* (perhaps *S. anthias*). It is a pelagic fish (A. 598 a 13). As a descriptive term like Erythinus (*i.e.* red) might be applied to different fishes (*cf.* Athen. 300 f), the schol. λιθρινάρια, ῥούσια, which suggests a *Pagrus* or *Pagellus*, perhaps *Pagellus erythrinus*, M.G. λυθρίνι, λυθρινάρι (collectively for all species of *Pagellus*, Apost. p. 17) may be right. Ov. *Hal.* 104 caeruleaque rubens erythinus in unda; Plin. xxxii. 152; Hesych. *s.* ἐρυθῖνοι.

[b] A species of Flatfish. Galen, *De aliment. facult.* iii. 30 περὶ δὲ τῶν κιθάρων καὶ πάνυ θαυμάζω τοῦ Φιλοτίμου· παραπλήσιος γὰρ ὢν ὁ ῥόμβος αὐτῶν μαλακωτέραν ἔχει τὴν σάρκα, τῶν ὀνίσκων ἀπολειπόμενος οὐκ ὀλίγῳ; Plin. xxxii. 146 citharus rhomborum generis pessimus. *Cf.* A. 508 b 17; Athen. 305 f ff.; Poll. vi. 50. Ael. xi. 23 describes the κιθαρῳδός, a Red Sea fish, as πλατὺς τὸ σχῆμα κατὰ τὴν βούγλωττον.

[c] *C.* ii. 392 n.

[d] *C.* ii. 391 n. For habitat, Marc. S. 13 ἀκταῖοι μελάνουροι. The schol. οἱ μοσχῖται οἱ οὐροῦντες μέλαν ἢ τὰ καλαμάρια mistakes the etymology.

[e] *H.* iii. 400 n.

[f] *Solea vulgaris*, M.G. γλῶσσα, at Nauplia and Missolonghi χωματίδα (Apost. p. 22). Marc. S. 18 ἐκτάδιον βούγλωσσον; Athen. 136 b, 288 b, where he says Ἀττικοὶ δὲ ψῆτταν αὐτὴν καλοῦσιν. *Cf.* Galen, *De aliment. facult.* iii. 30 παρέλιπε δ' ἐν τούτοις ὁ Φιλότιμος καὶ τὸ βούγλωττον, . . . εἰ μή τι ἄρα τῷ τῆς ψήττης ὀνόματι καὶ κατὰ τῶν βουγλώττων ἐχρήσατο. παραπλήσια μὲν γάρ πώς ἐστιν, οὐ μὴν ἀκριβῶς ὁμοειδῆ βούγλωττόν τε καὶ ψῆττα· μαλακώτερον γάρ ἐστι καὶ ἥδιον εἰς ἐδωδὴν καὶ παντὶ βέλτιον τὸ βούγλωττον τῆς ψήττης; Plin. ix. 52 soleae (Pontum non intrant), cum rhombi intrent; Hesych. *s.v.* and *s.* ψῆττα;

Erythinus,[a] the Citharus[b] and the Red Mullet[c] and the feeble Melanurus,[d] the shoals of the Trachurus,[e] and the Sole[f] and the Platyurus,[g] the weak Ribbon-fish[h] and the Mormyrus[i] of varied hue and the Mackerel[j] and the Carp[k] and all that love the shores.[l]

Others again feed in the mud and the shallows[m]

Ov. *Hal.* 124 Fulgentes soleae candore et concolor illis | Passer et Adriaco mirandus litore rhombus.

[g] Schol. ψησσία, πλατεῖς. Some species of Flatfish.

[h] Schol. ζαργάναι (a term used to interpret σφύραιναι *H.* i. 172, iii. 117 and ῥαφίδες *H.* i. 172). A. 504 b 32 ἡ καλουμένη ταινία has two fins; Athen. 329 f Σπεύσιππος . . . παραπλήσιά φησιν εἶναι ψῆτταν, βούγλωσσον, ταινίαν. Bussemaker makes it *Monochirus Pegusa* Risso, a species of Sole; A. and W. suggest *Cobitis taenia* L., the Spined Loach, as, though like *Cepola rubescens* Cuv. (*C. taenia* Bloch) it has two pairs of fins, the pectoral are very short.

[i] *C.* i. 74 n. For habitat, Marc. S. = Archestr. *ap.* Athen. 313 f μόρμυρος αἰγιαλεύς; *A.P.* vi. 304 Ἀκτῖτ' ἃ καλαμευτά, ποτὶ ξερὸν ἔλθ' ἀπὸ πέτρας | καί με λάβ' εὐάρχαν πρώιον ἐμπολέα· | αἴτε σύ γ' ἐν κύρτῳ μελανουρίδας αἴτε τιν' ἀγρεῖς μορμύρον ἢ κίχλην ἢ σπάρον ἢ σμαρίδα.

[j] *Scomber scomber* L., M.G. σκουμβρί (Apost. p. 13). A. 571 a 14, 597 a 22, 599 a 2, 610 b 7; Athen. 121 a, 321 a. They are pelagic fishes (Ov. *Hal.* 94 gaudent pelago quales scombri), but "at certain seasons approach the shores in countless multitudes, either prior to, during, or after breeding, or else for predaceous purposes," Day, i. p. 85.

[k] *Cyprinus carpio* L., abundant in lakes of Thessaly and Aetolia, M.G. σαζάνι, καρλόψαρο in Thessaly, τσερούκλα in Aetolia (Apost. p. 23). *Cf.* A. 568 b 26, etc.; Athen. 309 a f. "It mostly frequents ponds, canals, sluggish pieces of water . . . being especially partial to localities possessing soft, marly, or muddy bottoms," Day, ii. p. 159.

[l] A. 488 b 7 τῶν θαλαττίων τὰ μὲν πελάγια, τὰ δὲ αἰγιαλώδη, τὰ δὲ πετραῖα.

[m] τεναγώδης as an epithet of fish is opposed to πελάγιος Hices. *ap.* Athen. 320 d; *cf.* A. 548 a 1, 602 a 9. For τέναγος *cf.* Herod. viii. 129; Pind. *N.* iii. 24.

φέρβονται, βατίδες τε βοῶν θ' ὑπέροπλα γένεθλα
τρυγών τ' ἀργαλέη καὶ ἐτήτυμον οὔνομα νάρκη,
ψῆτται καλλαρίαι καὶ τριγλίδες ἔργα τ' ὀνίσκων
σαῦροί τε σκέπανοί τε καὶ ὅσσ' ἐνιτέτροφε πηλοῖς.
Θῖνα δ' ἀνὰ πρασόεσσαν ὑπὸ χλοεραῖς βοτάνῃσι
βόσκονται μαινῖδες ἰδὲ τράγοι ἠδ' ἀθερῖναι

---

[a] *Raia batis* L., M.G. βατί, and allied species of *Raiidae*, of which five others occur in Greek waters—*R. clavata* Rond., *R. punchata* Risso, *R. chagrinea* Pennant, *R. miraletus* Rond., *R. ondulata* or *Mosaica* (Apost. p. 6). βατίς in A. 565 a 27, etc. seems generic for the oviparous Rays. *Cf.* Athen. 286 b-e; Poll. vi. 50; Plin. xxxii. 145.

[b] *H.* ii. 141 n. [c] *H.* ii. 462 n.

[d] *H.* ii. 56 n. [e] *Cf. H.* i. 169, 371, ii. 460.

[f] The references of Aristotle to the ψῆττα (A. 538 a 20, 543 a 2, 620 b 30) do not enable us to say more than that it is a Pleuronectid. In Graeco-Latin glossaries it is equated with Latin *rhombus*, *cf.* Athen. 330 b Ῥωμαῖοι δὲ καλοῦσι τὴν ψῆτταν ῥόμβον καί ἐστι τὸ ὄνομα Ἑλληνικόν. But Ael. xiv. 3 τοὺς ἰχθῦς τοὺς πλατεῖς . . . ψῆττας τε καὶ ῥόμβους καὶ στρουθοὺς distinguishes them; *cf.* Galen, *Aliment. fac.* iii. 30. It was sometimes identified with the Sole: Hesych. *s.* ψῆττα· ἰχθύδιον τῶν πλατέων ἢ ψῆττα ἥν τινες σανδάλιον ἢ βούγλωσσον; Athen. 288 b Ἀττικοὶ δὲ ψῆτταν αὐτὴν καλοῦσιν; Galen, *l.c.* παρέλιπε δ' ἐν τούτοις ὁ Φιλότιμος καὶ τὸ βούγλωττον, . . . εἰ μή τι ἄρα τῷ τῆς ψήττης ὀνόματι καὶ κατὰ τῶν βουγλώττων ἐχρήσατο. παραπλήσια μὲν γάρ πώς ἐστιν, οὐ μὴν ἀκριβῶς ὁμοειδῆ; *cf.* schol. Plato, *Symp.* 191 D. But Oppian (*H.* i. 99) distinguishes them, as do Archestr. *ap.* Athen. *l.c.* and 330 a, Dorion *ibid.*, Speusipp. *ib.* 329 F, Plin. ix. 57 condi per hiemes torpedinem, psettam, soleam tradunt.

[g] Introd. p. lxv. [h] *C.* i. 75 n., ii. 392 n.

[i] Introd. p. lxiv. Schol. ἔργα τ' ὀνίσκων· ἤγουν οἱ ὀνίσκοι, περίφρασις.

of the sea; to wit, the Skate [a] and the monster tribes of the Ox-ray [b] and the terrible Sting-ray,[c] and the Cramp-fish [d] truly named,[e] the Turbot [f] and the Callarias,[g] the Red Mullet [h] and the works of the Oniscus,[i] and the Horse-mackerel [j] and the Scepanus [k] and whatsoever else feeds in mud.

On the weedy beach under the green grasses feeds the Maenis [l] and the Goat-fish [m] and the Atherine,[n]

[j] Schol. σαῦροι· σαυρίδες. If σαῦρος differs from τραχοῦρος v. 99, iii. 400—they are identified Xenocr. *Aliment.* c. 7 but distinguished Galen, *Aliment. fac.* iii. 30-31—it may be *Caranx suareus* which differs little from *Trachurus trachurus.* It is known in M.G. as σαυρίδι κυνηγός or κοκκάλι (Apost. p. 14); *cf.* A. 610 b 5, Athen. 309 f, 322 c-e, Hesych. *s.* σαῦρα, Marc. S. 33, Plin. xxxii. 89 sauri piscis marini (*cf. ibid.* 151), but in Latin usually *lacertus*, Plin. xxxii. 146, Stat. *S.* iv. 9. 13, Mart. x. 48. 11, etc. From Athen. 305 c it seems that the κίχλη was also called σαῦρος.

[k] Schol. σκεπανοί· κόπανοι. A species of Tunny: "*Thynnus brachypterus*, vulg. ὄρκυνος et κόπανος dans le golfe de Volo (Sinus Pagasaeus)," Apost. p. 14; *cf.* Hesych. *s.* σκεπινός; Athen. 322 e σκεπινός· τούτου μνημονεύων Δωρίων . . . καλεῖσθαί φησιν αὐτὸν ἀτταγεινόν.

[l] *H.* iii. 188 n.

[m] The male Maenis in the breeding season: A. 607 b 9 κύουσα μὲν οὖν ἀγαθὴ μαινίς· . . . συμβαίνει δ' ἀρχομένης κυίσκεσθαι τῆς θηλείας τοὺς ἄρρενας μέλαν τὸ χρῶμα ἴσχειν καὶ ποικιλώτερον καὶ φαγεῖν χειρίστους εἶναι· καλεῖται δ' ὑπ' ἐνίων τράγοι περὶ τοῦτον τὸν χρόνον. *Cf.* Athen. 328 c, 356 b, Ael. xii. 28, Marc. S. 23 τραγίσκος, Ov. *Hal.* 112, Plin. xxxii. 152.

[n] *Atherina hepsetus*, M.G. ἀθερίνα (Apost. p. 21); *cf.* A. 570 b 15, 571 a 6, 610 b 6, Athen. 285 a, 329 a. "The Atherines are littoral fishes, living in large shoals. . . . They rarely exceed a length of six inches, but are nevertheless esteemed as food. . . . The young, for some time after they are hatched, cling together in dense masses and in numbers almost incredible. The inhabitants of the Mediterranean coast of France call these newly hatched Atherines 'Nonnat' (unborn)," Günther, p. 500.

καὶ σμαρίδες καὶ βλέννος ἰδὲ σπάροι ἀμφότεροί τε
βῶκες ὅσοις τ' ἄλλοισι φίλον πράσον ἀμφινέμεσθαι.
Κεστρέες αὖ κέφαλοί τε, δικαιότατον γένος ἅλμης,
λάβρακές τ' ἀμίαι τε θρασύφρονες ἠδὲ χρέμητες
πηλαμύδες γόγγροι τε καὶ ὃν καλέουσιν ὄλισθον
γείτονα ναιετάουσιν ἀεὶ ποταμοῖσι θάλασσαν
ἢ λίμναις, ὅθι λαρὸν ὕδωρ μεταπαύεται ἅλμης,
πολλή τε πρόχυσις συμβάλλεται ἰλυόεσσα,
ἑλκομένη δίνῃσιν ἀπὸ χθονός· ἔνθα νέμονται
φορβὴν ἱμερτὴν γλυκερῇ θ' ἁλὶ πιαίνονται.
λάβραξ δ' οὐδ' αὐτῶν ποταμῶν ἀπολείπεται ἔξω,

---

[a] *Smaris vulgaris*, M.G. σμαρίς, μαρίς (Apost. p. 18), a small Mediterranean fish (Fam. *Maenidae*): A. 607 b 22. Athen. 315 b, 328 f; Ov. *Hal.* 120; Plin. xxxii. 151, etc.

[b] Seven species of Blenny are found in Greek waters: *Blennius pavo* Risso, M.G. σαλιάρες, *B. gattorugine*, M.G. σαλιάρα, *B. palmicornis* Cuv., *B. ocellaris* L., *B. Montagui* Flem., *B. trigloides* Val., *B. pholis* L. (Apost. p. 9). *Cf.* Athen. 288 a.

[c] A Sea-bream, Fam. *Sparidae*, Genus *Sargus*, of which four species occur in Greek waters: *S. vulgaris*, M.G. σαργός, χαρακίδα at Siphnas; *S. Rondeletii*, M.G. σπάρος; *S. vetula*, M.G. σκάρος; *S. annularis*, M.G. σουβλομύτης, at Corfu (Apost. p. 16); A. 508 c 17; Ov. *Hal.* 106 et super aurata sparulus cervice refulgens; Mart. iii. 60. 6 res tibi cum rhombo est, at mihi cum sparulo.

[d] *H.* iii. 186 n. [e] *H.* ii. 642 n., iv. 127 n.

[f] *H.* ii. 643 n. [g] *H.* ii. 130 n. [h] *H.* ii. 554 n.

[i] We assume this to be the fish which is otherwise called χρόμις, χρέμυς, χρέμψ, etc; A. 534 a 8 μάλιστα δ' εἰσὶ τῶν ἰχθύων ὀξυήκοοι κεστρεύς, χρέμψ, λάβραξ, σάλπη, χρόμις, where χρέμψ should probably be omitted as a mere *v.l.* for χρόμις. *Cf.* Plin. x. 193 produntur etiam clarissime audire mugil, lupus, salpa, chromis; A. 535 b 16 ψόφους δέ τινας ἀφιᾶσι καὶ τριγμοὺς οὓς λέγουσι φωνεῖν, οἷον λύρα καὶ χρόμις (οὗτοι γὰρ ἀφιᾶσιν ὥσπερ γρυλισμόν); 543 a 2 χρόμις is one of the shoal-fishes (χυτοί) which spawn once a year; 601 b 29 μάλιστα δὲ

the Smaris [a] and the Blenny [b] and the Sparus [c] and both sorts of Bogue [d] and whatsoever others love to feed on sea-weed.

The Grey Mullets [e]—Cestreus and Cephalus—the most righteous [f] race of the briny sea, and the Basse [g] and the bold Amia,[h] the Chremes,[i] the Pelamyd,[j] the Conger,[k] and the fish which men call Olisthus [l]—these always dwell in the sea where it neighbours rivers or lakes, where the sweet water ceases from the brine, and where much alluvial silt is gathered, drawn from the land by the eddying current. There they feed on pleasant food and fatten on the sweet brine. The Basse does not fail even from the rivers themselves but swims up out

πονοῦσιν ἐν τοῖς χειμῶσιν οἱ ἔχοντες λίθον ἐν τῇ κεφαλῇ, οἷον χρόμις, λάβραξ, σκίαινα, φάγρος. *Cf.* Plin. ix. 57 Praegelidam hiemem omnes sentiunt, sed maxime qui lapidem in capite habere existimantur, ut lupi, chromis, sciaena, phagri; Athen. 305 d Ἀριστοτέλης . . . φησί· . . . τὰ μὲν λιθοκέφαλα ὡς κρέμυς; Plin. xxxii. 153 (among fishes mentioned by Ovid) chromim qui nidificet in aquis; Ov. *Hal.* 121 immunda chromis; Hesych. *s.* χρέμυς· ὁ ὀνίσκος ἰχθύς; *s.* χρόμις· εἶδος ἰχθύος; Ael. xv. 11 incidentally mentions χρέμης as having a large beard (γένειον), while in ix. 7 he mentions the otolith and acute hearing of χρόμις. Aristotle's χρόμις is identified by J. Müller, etc., with *Sciaena aquila* Cuv., which "porte le nom vulg. μυλοκόπι et κρανιός à Chalcis" (Apost. p. 13). Bussemaker takes χρέμης to be one of the Cod-family (*Gadidae*).

[j] *H.* iv. 504 n.

[k] *Conger vulgaris*, M.G. μουγγρί, δρόγγα at Missolonghi (Apost. p. 26).

[l] Schol. ὄλισθον· γλίσχρος γάρ ἐστιν γλανεόν, *i.e.* the γλάνις of A. 621 a 21, etc., *Silurus glanis*, M.G. γλανός (Apost. p. 24). It is a fresh-water fish but is given among marine fishes by Marc. S. 11 and Plin. xxxii. 149, just as Oppian, *H.* i. 101 and 592 includes the Carp among marine fishes. Gesner p. 742 suggests the Lamprey.

ἐκ δ' ἁλὸς ἐς προχοὰς ἀνανήχεται· ἐγχέλυες δὲ
ἐκ ποταμῶν πλαταμῶσιν ἐνιχρίμπτουσι θαλάσσης.
  Πέτραι δ' ἀμφίαλοι πολυειδέες· αἱ μὲν ἔασι
φύκεσι μυδαλέαι, περὶ δὲ μνία πολλὰ πέφυκε·
τὰς ἤτοι πέρκαι καὶ ἰουλίδες ἀμφί τε χάννοι
φέρβονται σάλπαι τε μετὰ σφίσιν αἰολόνωτοι
καὶ κίχλαι ῥαδιναὶ καὶ φυκίδες οὕς θ'[1] ἁλιῆες
ἀνδρὸς ἐπωνυμίην θηλύφρονος ηὐδάξαντο.
  Ἄλλαι δὲ χθαμαλαὶ ψαμαθώδεος ἄγχι θαλάσσης
λεπράδες, ἃς κίρρις τε σύαινά τε καὶ βασιλίσκοι
ἐν δὲ μύλοι τρίγλης τε ῥοδόχροα φῦλα νέμονται.
  Ἄλλαι δ' αὖ ποιῇσιν ἐπίχλοοι ὑγρὰ μέτωπα

[1] ἄς θ' MSS. and schol.

---

[a] *H.* i. 520 n.; *cf.* A. 569 a 6.

[b] Either *Perca fluviatilis*—"on le trouve dans les affluents de l'Alphée" Apost. p. 12—a fresh-water fish (Auson. *Mosell.* 115 Nec te, . . . perca, silebo | Amnigenos inter pisces dignande marinis) which sometimes enters salt water (Plin. xxxii. 145 communes amni tantum ac mari . . . percae)—as generally in Aristotle (A. 568 a 20, etc.), or *Serranus scriba*, M.G. πέρκα (Apost. p. 12), as apparently in A. 599 b 8, where it is classed among "rock fishes," οἱ πετραῖοι, as it is in Galen, *De aliment. facult.* iii. 28, Plin. ix. 57 percae et saxatiles omnes. Marc. S. 16 includes πέρκαι among marine fishes. *Cf.* Ov. *Hal.* 112; Athen. 319 b-c, 450 c.

[c] *H.* ii. 434 n.

[d] Aristotle's χάννη (χάννα) is either *Serranus cabrilla* or *S. scriba* (Fam. *Percidae*, Gen. *Serranus*), the former still known in Greece as χάνος. Marc. S. 33. The genus *Serranus* is hermaphrodite as was known to Aristotle: A. 538 a 21, 567 a 27, *De gen.* 755 b 21, 760 a 9; Plin. ix. 56, xxxii. 153; Ov. *Hal.* 107 et ex se | Concipiens channe, gemino fraudata parente; Athen. 319 b, 327 f.

[e] *H.* iii. 414 n. For "spangled" *cf.* Arist. *ap.* Athen. 321 e πολύγραμμος καὶ ἐρυθρόγραμμος. For habitat *cf.* A. 598 a 19 γίνονται . . . ἐν ταῖς λιμνοθαλαττίαις πολλοὶ τῶν ἰχθύων, οἷον σάλπαι.

of the sea into the estuaries; while the Eels [a] come from the rivers and draw to the flat reefs of the sea.

The sea-girt rocks are of many sorts. Some are wet and covered with seaweed and about them grows abundant moss. About these feed the Perch [b] and the Rainbow-wrasse [c] and the Channus [d] and withal the spangled Saupe [e] and the slender Thrush-wrasse [f] and the Phycis [g] and those which fishermen have nicknamed from the name of an effeminate man.[g]

Other rocks are low-lying beside the sandy sea and rough; about these dwell the Cirrhis [h] and the Sea-swine [i] and the Basiliscus [j] and withal the Mylus [k] and the rosy tribes of the Red Mullet.

Other rocks again whose wet faces are green with

[f] *H.* iv. 173 n.

[g] Introduction, p. l. [h] Introd. p. liii.

[i] Schol. ὕσκαι (used again to interpret ὕαινα *H.* i. 372) ἢ συάκιον ἢ σύαινα, which suggests a Flatfish. Hesych. *s.* συάριον· βούγλωσσον. *Cf.* Du Cange, *Gloss. Gr. s.* σιάκιον and *s.* σύαξ. Epicharm. *ap.* Athen. 326 e couples ὑαινίδες, βούγλωσσοι, κίθαρος.

[j] Schol. βασιλίσκοι· σκιρίδια. On *H.* i. 370 the schol. uses βασιλίσκος to interpret πρῆστις, on *H.* i. 592 to interpret ὀνίσκος. Bussemaker gives *Clupea alosa* L., the Shad.

[k] Schol. μύλοι· μυλοκόπια, μυλοκόποι, which points to one of the *Sciaenidae*, μυλοκόπος being in M.G. *Sciaena aquila* Cuv. (Apost. p. 13). *Corvina nigra* Cuv., Bik. p. 81. Athen. 308 e Εὐθύδημος δ' ἐν τῷ περὶ ταρίχων τὸν κορακῖνόν φησιν ὑπὸ πολλῶν σαπέρδην προσαγορεύεσθαι . . . ὅτι δὲ καὶ πλατίστακος καλεῖται ὁ σαπέρδης [we are not here concerned with the freshwater σαπερδίς of A. 608 a 2], καθάπερ καὶ ὁ κορακῖνος, Παρμένων φησίν; 118 c τοὺς δὲ προσαγορευομένους φησὶ (Δωρίων) μύλλους ὑπὸ μέν τινων καλεῖσθαι ἀγνωτίδια, ὑπὸ δέ τινων πλατιστάκους ὄντας τοὺς αὐτούς. . . . οἱ μὲν οὖν μείζονες αὐτῶν ὀνομάζονται πλατίστακοι, οἱ δὲ μέσην ἔχοντες ἡλικίαν μύλλοι, οἱ δὲ βαιοὶ τοῖς μεγέθεσιν ἀγνωτίδια. Bussemaker makes μύλος *Sciaena cirrhosa.*

πέτραι σαργὸν ἔχουσιν ἐφέστιον ἠδὲ σκίαιναν
χαλκέα καὶ κορακῖνον ἐπώνυμον αἴθοπι χροιῇ,
καὶ σκάρον, ὃς δὴ μοῦνος ἐν ἰχθύσι πᾶσιν ἀναύδοις
φθέγγεται ἰκμαλέην λαλαγὴν καὶ μοῦνος ἐδητὺν
ἄψορρον προΐησιν ἀνὰ στόμα, δεύτερον αὖτις
δαινύμενος, μήλοισιν ἀναπτύσσων ἴσα φορβήν.
Ὅσσαι δ' αὖ χήμῃσι περίπλεοι ἢ λεπάδεσσιν,
ἐν δέ σφιν θαλάμαι τε καὶ αὔλια δύμεναι ἰχθῦς,
τῇσι δὲ καὶ φάγροι καὶ ἀναιδέες ἀγριόφαγροι
κέρκουροί τε μένουσι καὶ ὀψοφάγοι καὶ ἀνιγραὶ

---

[a] *C.* ii. 433 n. *Cf. H.* i. 510.

[b] *H.* iv. 596 n.

[c] *Zeus faber* L., M.G. χριστόψαρο, σανπιέρος etc. (Apost. p. 15): Plin. ix. 68 est et haec natura ut alii alibi pisces principatum obtineant, coracinus in Aegypto, Zeus idem faber appellatus Gadibus (*cf.* xxxii. 148); Colum. vii. 16; Ov. *Hal.* 110 Et rarus faber; Athen. 328 d διαφέρει δὲ τῆς χαλκίδος ὁ χαλκεύς, οὗ μνημονεύει . . . Εὐθύδημος . . . λέγων αὐτοὺς περιφερεῖς τε εἶναι καὶ κυκλοειδεῖς; A. 535 b 18 (among fishes which ψόφους τινὰς ἀφιᾶσι καὶ τριγμούς) ἔτι δὲ χαλκὶς (*i.e.* χαλκεύς) καὶ κόκκυξ· ἡ μὲν γὰρ ψοφεῖ οἷον συριγμόν. The Dory makes a noise on being removed from the water, *cf.* Day i. p. 140.

[d] *H.* iii. 184 n.

[e] *Scarus cretensis* (Fam. *Labridae*), M.G. σκάρος (Bik. p. 84, Erh. p. 91); anciently held in high esteem: Epicharm. *ap.* Athen. 319 f ἀλιεύομεν σπάρους | καὶ σκάρους, τῶν οὐδὲ τὸ σκᾶρ θεμιτὸν ἐκβαλεῖν θεοῖς; Plin. ix. 62 Nunc principatus scaro datur; Hor. *Epod.* ii. 50, *S.* ii. 2. 22; Galen, *De aliment. facult.* iii. 23 ἄριστος δ' ἐν αὐτοῖς (*sc.* τοῖς πετραίοις) ἡδονῆς ἕνεκεν ὁ σκάρος εἶναι πεπίστευται.

[f] Aesch. *Pers.* 577 ἀναύδων παίδων τᾶς ἀμιάντου; Hes. *Sc.* 212: Soph. *Aj.* 1297, *id.* fr. 691; Athen. 277, 308; Ov. *A. A.* iii. 325, *cf.* the jest οὐδεὶς κακὸς μέγας ἰχθύς Athen. 348 a.

[g] Athen. 331 d Μνασέας . . . τοὺς ἐν τῷ Κλείτορι ποταμῷ φησιν ἰχθῦς φθέγγεσθαι (Plin. ix. 70; Pausan. viii. 21. 2), καίτοι μόνους εἰρηκότος Ἀριστοτέλους φθέγγεσθαι σκάρον καὶ τὸν ποτάμιον χοῖρον. The "voice" of fishes is discussed A.

grasses have for tenant the Sargue [a] and the Sciaena,[b] the Dory,[c] and the Crow-fish,[d] named from its dusky colour, and the Parrot-wrasse,[e] which alone among all the voiceless [f] fishes utters a liquid note [g] and alone rejects its food back into its mouth, and feasts [h] on it a second time, throwing up its food even as sheep and goats.[i]

Those rocks again which abound in Clams [j] or Limpets [k] and in which there are chambers and abodes for fish to enter—on these abide the Braize [l] and the shameless Wild Braize [m] and the Cercurus [n] and the gluttonous and baleful Muraena [o] and the

535 b 14 ff., where the σκάρος is not mentioned, *cf.* Ael. x. 11; Plin. xi. 267.

[h] *i.e.* chews the cud: A. 591 b 22 δοκεῖ δὲ τῶν ἰχθύων ὁ καλούμενος σκάρος μηρυκάζειν ὥσπερ τὰ τετράποδα μόνος. *Cf.* A. 508 b 12; *P. A.* 675 a 3; Athen. 319 f; Ael. ii. 54; Antig. 73; Plin. ix. 62 solus piscium dicitur ruminare; Ov. *Hal.* 119 ut scarus epastas solus qui ruminat escas.

[i] μῆλα, *Kleinvieh*, Sheep and Goats (Hom. *Od.* ix. 184 μῆλ', διές τε καὶ αἶγες) as opp. to Kine; Hom. *Il.* xviii. 524 μῆλα . . . καὶ ἕλικας βοῦς, *Il.* v. 556 βόας καὶ ἴφια μῆλα; Pind. *P.* iv. 148 μῆλά τε . . . καὶ βοῶν ξανθὰς ἀγέλας. *Cf.* τὰ βληχητά Ael. ii. 54. Here merely as typical Ruminants.

[j] χήμη is generic for certain species of bivalves: Hices. *ap.* Athen. 87 b; Plin. xxxii. 147; Galen, *op. cit.* iii. 33 ὄστρεά τε καὶ χήμας. From A. 547 b 13 αἱ χῆμαι . . . ἐν τοῖς ἀμμώδεσι λαμβάνουσι τὴν σύστασιν it is suggested that Venus-shells (*Veneraceae*) are especially meant.

[k] *Patella vulgata* and allied species. *Cf.* Athen. 85 c-86 f.

[l] *C.* ii. 391 n.

[m] Only here. Schol. ἀγριόφαγροι· διωξίφαγροι διὰ τὸ κινεῖσθαι ταχέως.

[n] Schol. κέρκουροι· κουτζουρίναι (bob-tailed); Ov. *Hal.* 102 Cercurusque ferox scopulorum fine moratus; Plin. xxxii. 152 cercurum in scopulis viventem; Hesych. *s.* κερκοῦρος· εἶδος πλοίου καὶ ἰχθύς. Not identified.

[o] *Muraena helena* L., the Murry, M.G. σμέρνα, σμῦρνα (Apost. p. 26).

μύραιναι σαῦροί τε καὶ ὀψιμόρων γένος ὀρφῶν,
οἳ πάντων περίαλλα κατὰ χθόνα δηθύνουσι
ζωοὶ καὶ τμηθέντες ἔτι σπαίρουσι σιδήρῳ.
Ἄλλοι δ' ἐν βένθεσσιν ὑπόβρυχα μιμνάζουσι
φωλειοῖς, πρόβατόν τε καὶ ἥπατοι ἠδὲ πρέποντες,
ἴφθιμοι μεγάλοι τε φυήν, νωθροὶ δὲ κέλευθα
εἰλεῦνται· τὸ καὶ οὔποθ' ἑὴν λείπουσι χαράδρην,
ἀλλ' αὐτοῦ λοχόωσι παραὶ μυχόν, ὅς κε πελάσσῃ,
χειροτέροις ἀΐδηλον ἐπ' ἰχθύσι πότμον ἄγοντες·
ἐν καὶ ὄνος κείνοις ἐναρίθμιος, ὃς περὶ πάντων
πτήσσει ὀπωρινοῖο κυνὸς δριμεῖαν ὁμοκλήν,

---

[a] *H.* i. 106 n. The reading σαῦροι involves duplication in view of *v.* 106, but so does the *v.l.* σκόμβροι (read by schol. σκόμβροι· σαῦροι) in view of *v.* 101.

[b] The Great Sea-perch, *Serranus* (*Epinephelus*) *gigas*, M.G. ὀρφώς, ῥοφός, "poisson très estimé pour sa chair blanche, et qui se pêche presque toujours à l'hameçon" (Apost. p. 13): Ov. *Hal.* 104 f. Cantharus . . . tum concolor illi | Orphus; Aristoph. *Vesp.* 493; Marc. S. 33; Plin. ix. 57, xxxii. 152. For habitat, A. 598 a 9 πρόσγειος; *cf.* Athen. 315 a, Ael. v. 18. The epithet "late-dying" refers not to longevity —ζῇ οὐ πλέον δύο ἐτῶν Athen. 315 b—but to tenacity of life: Athen. 315 a ἴδιον δ' ἐν αὐτῷ ἐστι . . . τὸ δύνασθαι πολὺν χρόνον ζῆν μετὰ τὴν ἀνατομήν; Ael. *l.c.* εἰ ἕλοις καὶ ἀνατέμοις, οὐκ ἂν ἴδοις τεθνεῶτα παραχρῆμα αὐτόν, ἀλλ' ἐπιλαμβάνει τῆς κινήσεως καὶ οὐκ ἐπ' ὀλίγον. For spelling and accent *cf.* Athen. 315 c, Poll. vi. 50, *E.M.* *s.v.*

[c] Lines 145-154 are paraphrased by Ael. ix. 38 and, in part, by Suid. *s.* ὕπατοι.

[d] Only here and *H.* iii. 139, Ael. *l.c.*, Suid. *s.* ὕπατοι· εἶδος ἰχθύος κητώδους, οἳ καλοῦνται καὶ πρόβατα καὶ πρέποντες. ἀριθμοῖτο δὲ τούτοις καὶ ὁ ὄνος. "Rondeletius umbram piscem a Graecis huius temporis ovem marinam appellari scribit, Bellonius aselli speciem, quam vulgo Merlangum [*i.e.* *M. poutassou*,

Horse-mackerel[a] and the race of the late-dying Merou,[b] which of all others on the earth remain longest alive and wriggle even when cut in pieces with a knife.

Others[c] in the deeps under the sea abide in their lairs ; to wit, the Sea-sheep[d] and the Hepatus[e] and the Prepon.[f] Strong and large of body are they, but slowly they roll upon their way ; wherefore also they never leave their own cleft, but just there they lie in wait beside their lair for any fish that may approach, and bring sudden doom on lesser fishes. Among these also is numbered the Hake,[g] which beyond all fishes shrinks from the bitter assault of the Dog-star in summer, and remains retired within

M.G. *γαϊδουρόψαρον*] vocitant, ovem facit," Gesner, p. 770. One of the Cod-family (*Gadidae*)?

[e] A. 508 b 19 has few *caeca* ; Ael. xv. 11. *ἡ γαλῆ δέ, φαίης ἂν αὐτὴν εἶναι τὸν καλούμενον ἥπατον· . . . καὶ τὸ μὲν γένειον ἔχει τοῦ ἡπάτου μεῖζον* ; Athen. 108 a *ἐστὶ δὲ καὶ ἰχθύς τις ἥπατος καλούμενος ὃν φησιν Εὔβουλος . . . οὐκ ἔχειν χολήν . . . Ἡγήσανδρος δ' . . . ἐν τῇ κεφαλῇ φησι τὸν ἥπατον δύο λίθους ἔχειν τῇ μὲν αὐγῇ καὶ τῷ χρώματι παραπλησίους τοῖς ὀστρείοις τῷ δὲ σχήματι ῥομβοειδεῖς* ; *id.* 300 e *Σπεύσιππος παραπλήσιά φησιν εἶναι φάγρον ἐρυθῖνον ἥπατον* ; *id.* 301 c *ἥπατος = λεβίας* (for which *cf.* Athen. 118 b, Hesych. *s.* *λέβια*, Poll. vi. 48) ; Marc. S. *ἥπατοι ἀγκυλόδοντες* ; Plin. xxxii. 149 hepar ; Galen, *De aliment. fac.* iii. 30 *τοὺς ἡπάτους καλουμένους καὶ τοὺς ἄλλους, ὅσους ἔμιξε τοῖς πετραίοις τε καὶ τοῖς ὀνίσκοις ὁ Φιλότιμος ἐν τῷ μέσῳ καθεστηκέναι γίνωσκε τῶν θ' ἁπαλοσάρκων καὶ τῶν σκληροσάρκων.* Cuvier ii. p. 232 (who, however, wrongly says "dans un autre endroit [xvi. 11] Élien fait entendre que c'est un poisson court, dont les yeux sont rapprochés," that being said not of the *hepatus* but of the *γαλῆ*) thinks most of the indications point—in spite of the "few caeca"—to *Gadus eglefinus*, the Haddock.

[f] Only here, Ael. *l.c.*, Suid. *l.c.*, Marc. S. 8. One of the Gadidae?

[g] Introduction, p. lxii.

μίμνει δ' ἐγκαταδὺς σκότιον μυχόν, οὐδὲ πάροιθεν
ἔρχεται, ὅσσον ἄησιν ἐπὶ χρόνον ἄγριος ἀστήρ.
Ἔστι δέ τις πέτρῃσιν ἁλικλύστοισι μεμηλώς,
ξανθὸς ἰδεῖν, κεστρεῦσι φυὴν ἐναλίγκιος ἰχθύς,
τὸν μερόπων ἕτεροι μὲν ἐπικλείουσιν ἄδωνιν,
ἄλλοι δ' ἐξώκοιτον ἐφήμισαν, οὕνεκα κοίτας
ἐκτὸς ἁλὸς τίθεται, μοῦνος δ' ἐπὶ χέρσον ἀμείβει,
ὅσσοι γε βράγχη, στόματος πτύχας, ἀμφὶς ἔχουσιν.
εὖτε γὰρ εὐνήσῃ χαροπῆς ἁλὸς ἔργα γαλήνη,
αὐτὰρ ὅ γ' ἐσσυμένοισι συνορμηθεὶς ῥοθίοισι,
πέτραις ἀμφιταθεὶς ἀμπαύεται εὔδιον ὕπνον.
ὀρνίθων δ' ἁλίων τρομέει γένος, οἵ οἱ ἔασι
δυσμενέες· τῶν ἤν τιν' ἐσαθρήσῃ πελάσαντα,
πάλλεται ὀρχηστῆρι πανείκελος, ὄφρα ἑ πόντου
προπροκυλινδόμενον σπιλάδων ἄπο χεῦμα σαώσῃ.
Οἵ δὲ καὶ ἐν πέτρῃσι καὶ ἐν ψαμάθοισι νέμονται,

---

[a] Clearchus *ap.* Athen. 332 d ἐστὶ δ' ὁ ἐξώκοιτος τῶν πετραίων καὶ βιοτεύει περὶ τοὺς πετρώδεις τόπους.

[b] One of the Blennies (*H.* i. 109 n.). The description by Clearch. *ap.* Athen. 332 c ὁ ἐξώκοιτος ἰχθύς, ὃν ἔνιοι καλοῦσιν Ἄδωνιν, τοὔνομα μὲν εἴληφε διὰ τὸ πολλάκις τὰς ἀναπαύσεις ἔξω τοῦ ὑγροῦ ποιεῖσθαι· ἐστὶ δὲ ὑπόπυρρος καὶ ἀπὸ τῶν βραγχίων ἑκατέρωθεν τοῦ σώματος μέχρι τῆς κέρκου μίαν ἔχει διηνεκῆ λευκὴν ῥάβδον suggests Montague's Blenny (*B. Montagui*). For its habit (shared by other species of Blenny) of remaining for hours out of the water *cf.* Day i. p. 201; *cf.* Hesych. *s.* Ἄδωνις· ἰχθὺς θαλάσσιος, οὗ μνημονεύει Κλέαρχος; *s.* ἐξώκοιτος· εἶδος ἰχθύος, καὶ Ἄδωνις. Ael. ix. 36, describing the habits of ἐξώκοιτος or Ἄδωνις, calls it a γένος κεστρέως (so too Phil. 114), a misunderstanding of Oppian's κεστρεῦσι φυὴν ἐναλίγκιος, which appears to be based on Clearch. *l.c.* κατὰ τὸ μέγεθος

his dark recess and comes not forth so long as the breath of the fierce star prevails.

A fish there is which haunts the sea-washed rocks,[a] yellow of aspect and in like build unto the Grey Mullet; some men call him Adonis[b]; others name him the Sleeper-out, because he takes his sleep outside the sea and comes to the land, alone of all them that have gills, those folds of the mouth, on either side. For when calm[c] hushes the works of the glancing sea, he hastes with the hasting tide and, stretched upon the rocks, takes his rest in fine weather. But he fears the race of sea-birds[d] which are hostile to him; if he sees any of them approach, he hops like a dancer until, as he rolls on and on, the sea-wave receives him safe from the rocks.

Others live both among the rocks and in the sands;

ἴσος ἐστὶ τοῖς παραιγιαλίταις κεστρινίσκοις. Plin. ix. 70 Miratur et Arcadia suum exocoetum, appellatum ab eo quod in siccum somni causa exeat. Circa Clitorium vocalis hic traditur et sine branchiis, idem aliquis Adonis dictus. Pliny confuses with Clearchus's account of exocoetus another passage of Clearchus which immediately follows in Athen. 332 f *ἐπεί τινες τῶν ἰχθύων οὐκ ἔχοντες βρόγχον φθέγγονται. τοιοῦτοι δ' εἰσὶν οἱ περὶ Κλείτορα τῆς Ἀρκαδίας ἐν τῷ Λάδωνι καλουμένῳ ποταμῷ· φθέγγονται γὰρ καὶ πολὺν ἦχον ἀποτελοῦσιν* (*cf.* Pausan. viii. 21. 2).

[c] Clearch. *ap.* Athen. 332 d *ὅταν ᾖ γαλήνη, συνεξορούσας τῷ κύματι κεῖται ἐπὶ τῶν πετριδίων πολὺν χρόνον ἀναπαυόμενος ἐν τῷ ξηρῷ καὶ μεταστρέφει μὲν ἑαυτὸν πρὸς τὸν ἥλιον· ὅταν δ' ἱκανῶς αὐτῷ τὰ πρὸς τὴν ἀνάπαυσιν ἔχῃ, προσκυλινδεῖται τῷ ὑγρῷ, μέχρι οὗ ἂν πάλιν ὑπολαβὸν αὐτὸν τὸ κῦμα κατενέγκῃ μετὰ τῆς ἀναρροίας εἰς τὴν θάλασσαν.*

[d] Clearch. *l.c.* *ὅταν δ' ἐγρηγορὼς ἐν τῷ ξηρῷ τύχῃ, φυλάττεται τῶν ὀρνίθων τοὺς παρευδιαστὰς καλουμένους, ὧν ἐστι κηρύλος, τροχίλος, καὶ ὁ τῇ κρεκὶ προσεμφερὴς ἐρωδιός· οὗτοι γὰρ ἐν ταῖς εὐδίαις παρὰ τὸ ξηρὸν νεμόμενοι πολλάκις αὐτῷ περιπίπτουσιν, οὓς ὅταν προΐδηται φεύγει πηδῶν καὶ ἀσπαίρων, ἕως ἂν εἰς τὸ ὕδωρ ἀποκυβιστήσῃ.*

ἀγλαΐῃ χρύσοφρυς ἐπώνυμος ἠδὲ δράκοντες
σῖμοί τε γλαῦκοί τε καὶ ἀλκησταὶ συνόδοντες,
σκορπίος ἀϊκτήρ, δίδυμον γένος, ἀμφότεραί τε
σφύραιναι δολιχαὶ ῥαφίδες θ᾽ ἅμα τῇσιν ἀραιαί·
ἐν δὲ χάραξ κοῦφοί τε κυβιστητῆρες ἔασι
κωβιοί· ἐν δὲ μυῶν χαλεπὸν γένος, οἳ περὶ πάντων
θαρσαλέοι νεπόδων καί τ᾽ ἀνδράσιν ἀντιφέρονται,
οὔτι τόσοι περ ἐόντες· ἐπὶ στερεῇ δὲ μάλιστα
ῥινῷ καὶ πυκινοῖσι πεποιθότες ἔνδον ὀδοῦσι,
ἰχθύσι καὶ μερόπεσσιν ἀρειοτέροισι μάχονται.

---

[a] *Chrysophrys aurata* Cuv., M.G. χρυσόφα (*cf.* χρύσαφοι Marc. S. 12) τσιππούρα, κύτσα at Corfu μαρίδα at Missolonghi (Apost. p. 17). Habitat, A. 598 a 10 πρόσγειος, *cf.* 543 b 3; Day i. p. 33. *Cf.* in general Athen. 284 c, 328 a-c; Plut. *Mor.* 981 D; Ael. xiii. 28; Plin. ix. 58; Mart. xiii. 90.

[b] It gets its name (*cf.* Lat. *aurata* [Plin. *l.c.*, etc.], Fr. *Daurade*, etc.) from its interorbital golden band: Ov. *Hal.* 110 et auri | Chrysophrys imitata decus; Plin. xxxii. 152 auri coloris chrysophryn.

[c] *H.* ii. 459 n. Habitat, A. 598 a 11 πρόσγειος. Plin. ix. 82; Day i. p. 79.

[d] Schol. μικροὶ πατζοὶ τὴν ἡλικίαν· πατζοὶ ἤγουν σιμοσπόνδυλοι. In list of Nile fishes Athen. 312 b, but not Strabo 823. *Cf.* fish called αἰθίοψ, διὰ τὸ καὶ τοῦ προσώπου σιμὸν ἔχειν τὸν τύπον Agatharch. *ap.* Phot. p. 460 Bekker.

[e] Introd. p. lxi.

[f] *H.* iii. 610 n.

[g] *Scorpaena scrofa* L., M.G. σκόρπινα, and *S. porcus* L.: "à cette seconde espèce d'une coloration brune on donne vulg. le nom de σκορπιός et χάφτης" (Apost. p. 12). Hices. *ap.* Athen. 320 d τῶν σκορπίων ὁ μέν ἐστι πελάγιος, ὁ δὲ τεναγώδης. καὶ ὁ μὲν πελάγιος πυρρός, ὁ δ᾽ ἕτερος μελανίζων. διαφέρει δὲ τῇ γεύσει καὶ τῷ τροφίμῳ ὁ πελάγιος; Athen. 355 d σκορπίοι δὲ οἱ πελάγιοι καὶ κιρροὶ τροφιμώτεροι τῶν τεναγωδῶν τῶν ἐν τοῖς αἰγιαλοῖς τῶν μεγάλων (μελάνων Coraes); Numen. *ap.* Athen. 320 e ἐρυθρὸν σκορπίον, Epicharm. *ibid.* σκορπίοι ποικίλοι. Aristotle has σκορπίος 508 b 17, 543 a 7, 598 a 14, σκορπίς only 543 b 5 σκορπίδες (*v.l.* σκομβρίδες) ἐν τῷ πελάγει (τίκτουσιν). *Cf.*

to wit, the Gilt-head,[a] named[b] from its beauty, and the Weever[c] and the Simus[d] and the Glaucus[e] and the strong Dentex,[f] the rushing Scorpion,[g], a double race, and both sorts of the long Sphyraena[h] and therewithal the slender Needle-fish[i]; the Charax[j] likewise is there and the nimble tumbling Goby[k] and the savage tribe of Sea-mice,[l] which are bold beyond all other fishes and contend even with men; not that they are so very large, but trusting chiefly to their hard hide and the serried teeth of their mouth, they fight with fishes and with mightier men.

Athen. 320 f *ἐν δὲ πέμπτῳ ζῴων μορίων ὁ Ἀριστοτέλης σκορπίους καὶ σκορπίδας ἐν διαφόροις τόποις ὀνομάζει ἄδηλον δὲ εἰ τοὺς αὐτοὺς λέγει· ὅτι καὶ σκόρπαιναν καὶ σκορπίους πολλάκις ἡμεῖς ἐφάγομεν καὶ διάφοροι καὶ οἱ χυμοὶ καὶ αἱ χρόαι εἰσίν, οὐδεὶς ἀγνοεῖ*; Plin. xxxii. 70 marini scorpionis rufi; *ibid.* 151 scorpaena, scorpio.

[h] Schol. *σφύραιναι· ζαργάναι* (see *H.* i. 100 n.). Apparently *Sphyraena spet* (*S. vulgaris*), M.G. *λοῦτζος* or *σφύραινα*, "the pike-like Bicuda or spet of the Mediterranean" (Lowe *ap.* E. Forbes p. 122) and some similar species. *σφύραινα* = Attic *κέστρα* Athen. 323 a; Plin. xxxii. 154 Sunt praeterea a nullo auctore nominati sudis Latine appellatus, Graece sphyraena, rostro similis nomini, magnitudine inter amplissimos; Hesych. *s. κέστρα*, *s. σφῦρα*; A. 610 b 5.

[i] *C.* ii. 392 n.

[j] *Sargus vulgaris* is in M.G. *σαργός* but *χαρακίδα* at Siphnos (Apost. p. 16), and such evidence as we have points to a Sea-bream: Athen. 355 e *συνόδους καὶ χάραξ τοῦ μὲν αὐτοῦ γένους εἰσί.* *Cf.* Ael. xii. 25.

[k] *H.* ii. 458 n.

[l] *Balistes capriscus*, M.G. *μονόχοιρος*, Apost. p. 8, the File-fish (Fam. *Sclerodermi*): Athen. 355 f *καπρίσκος καλεῖται μὲν καὶ μῦς*; Plin. ix. 71 exeunt in terram et qui marini mures vocantur; Ov. *Hal.* 130 durique sues; Ael. ix. 41 *τῶν γε μὴν οἰκετῶν (μυῶν) θρασύτεροι οἱ θαλάττιοι. μικρὸν μὲν αὐτῶν τὸ σῶμα, τόλμα δὲ ἄμαχος· καὶ θαρροῦσι δύο ὅπλοις, δορᾷ τε εὐτόνῳ καὶ ὀδόντων κράτει· μάχονται δὲ καὶ τοῖς ἰχθύσι τοῖς ἀδροτέροις καὶ τῶν ἁλιέων τοῖς μάλιστα θωρατικοῖς*; Marc. S. 30 *μύες εὐθώρηκες*; Phil. 112.

Οἱ δ' ἐν ἀμετρήτοισιν ἄλην πελάγεσσιν ἔχουσι,
τηλοῦ ἀπὸ τραφερῆς οὐδ' ἠόσιν εἰσὶν ἑταῖροι,
θύννοι μὲν θύνοντες, ἐν ἰχθύσιν ἔξοχοι ὁρμήν,
κραιπνότατοι, ξιφίαι τε φερώνυμοι ἠδ' ὑπέροπλος
ὀρκύνων γενεὴ καὶ πρημάδες ἠδὲ κυβεῖαι,
καὶ κολίαι σκυτάλαι τε καὶ ἱππούροιο γένεθλα.
ἐν τοῖς καὶ κάλλιχθυς ἐπώνυμος, ἱερὸς ἰχθύς·
ἐν κείνοις νέμεται καὶ πομπίλος, ὃν πέρι ναῦται
ἅζονται, πομπῇ δ' ἐπεφήμισαν οὔνομα νηῶν·
ἔξοχα γὰρ νήεσσι γεγηθότες ὑγρὰ θεούσαις

---

[a] *Thynnus thynnus* (*T. vulgaris*), M.G. μαιάτικο τουνῖνα etc., *T. thynina*, *T. brachypterus*. θύννοι θύνοντες is a punning reference (παρήχησις schol.) to the (popular) derivation from θύ(ν)ω: *E.M. s.v.*; Athen. 302 b, 324 d θύω θύννος, ὁ ὁρμητικός, διὰ τὸ κατὰ τὴν τοῦ κυνὸς ἐπιτολὴν ὑπὸ τοῦ ἐπὶ τῆς κεφαλῆς οἴστρου ἐξελαύνεσθαι (see *H.* ii. 508 n.).

[b] *H.* ii. 462 n.

[c] *H.* iii. 132 n.

[d] Young Tunny in its first year: A. 599 b 17 αἱ πριμάδες κρύπτουσιν ἑαυτὰς ἐν τῷ βορβόρῳ· σημεῖον δὲ τὸ μὴ ἁλίσκεσθαι καὶ ἰλὺν ἐχούσας ἐπὶ τοῦ νώτου φαίνεσθαι πολλὴν καὶ τὰ πτερύγια ἐντεθλιμμένα; Athen. 328 b πρημνάδας τὰς θυννίδας ἔλεγον; Hesych *s.* πρημάδες καὶ πρῆμναι· εἶδος θυννώδους ἰχθύος.

[e] The κύβιον was apparently a small-sized Tunny which was cut into κύβοι and salted: Athen. 116 e τὰ νεώτερα τῶν θυννείων τὴν αὐτὴν ἀναλογίαν ἔχειν τοῖς κυβίοις; 118 a πηλαμύδας κύβια εἶναί φησι (Ἱκέσιος) μεγάλα; 120 e κράτιστα δὲ τῶν μὲν ἀπιόνων (ταριχῶν) κύβια καὶ ὡραῖα καὶ τὰ τούτοις ὅμοια γένη, τῶν δὲ πιόνων τὰ θυννεῖα καὶ κορδύλεια . . . τὸ δὲ θυννεῖον, φησί (Δίφιλος), γίνεται ἐκ τῆς μείζονος πηλαμύδος, ὧν τὸ μικρὸν ἀναλογεῖ τῷ κυβίῳ. *Cf.* 356 f.; Poll. vi. 48; Plin. xxxii. 146 cybium —ita vocatur concisa pelamys quae post xl. dies a Ponto in Maeotim redit; *ibid.* 151 tritomum pelamydum generis magni ex quo terra cybia fiunt; ix. 48 Pelamydes in apolectos particulatimque consectae in genera cybiorum dispertiuntur. For the development of meaning *cf.* ἑψητός (Athen. 301), τμητόν (Athen. 357 a), and our "Kipper," formerly a Salmon, now a Herring. κυβιοσάκτης = dealer in salt-fish, Strabo 796, *cf.* Sueton. *Vesp.* xix.

Others roam in the unmeasured seas far from the dry land and companion not with the shores; to wit, the dashing Tunny,[a] most excellent among fishes for spring and speed, and the Sword-fish, truly named,[b] and the huge race of the Orcynus [c] and the Premas [d] and the Cybeia [e] and the Coly-mackerel [f] and the Scytala [g] and the tribes of the Hippurus.[h] Among these, too, is the Beauty-fish,[i] truly named, a holy fish [j]; and among them dwells the Pilot-fish [k] which sailors revere exceedingly, and they have given him this name for his convoying of ships. For they delight exceedingly in ships that run over the wet

[f] *Scomber colias*, M.G. κολιός. "Ce poisson, salé, est très estimé, on le mange surtout au mois d'août. Un proverbe dit: 'Chaque chose son temps, et le colios au mois d'août'" (Apost. p. 14). A. 543 a 2, 598 a 24, b 27, 610 b 7; Plin. xxxii. 146 colias sive Parianus sive Sexitanus a patria Baetica lacertorum minimi. *Cf.* Athen. 120 f *ἡ δὲ σάρδα προσέοικε τῷ κολίᾳ μεγέθει . . . κρείσσων δὲ ὁ Ἀμυνκλανὸς καὶ Σπανὸς ὁ Σαξιτανὸς λεγόμενος.*

[g] Schol. *σκυτάλαι· αἱ ἀβίναι λεγόμεναι λεπίδαι.* Not mentioned elsewhere.

[h] *H.* iv. 404 n. *Cf.* Ov. *Hal.* 95 (gaudent pelago) hippuri celeres.

[i] *H.* iii. 335 n.

[j] For use of this term *cf.* Athen. 282 c-284 e.

[k] *Naucrates ductor*, one of the Horse-mackerels (*Carangidae*): "ce poisson partage avec certains squales le nom vulg. de κουλαγοῦξος. C'est, d'après les pêcheurs grecs, un conducteur d'autres poissons" (Apost. p. 14). *Cf.* Athen. 282 ff.; Ael. ii. 15, xv. 23; Plin. ix. 51 idem (*sc.* Tunny-fish) saepe navigia velis euntia comitantes mira quadam dulcedine per aliquot horarum spatia et passuum milia a gubernaculis spectantur, ne tridente quidem in eos saepius iacto territi. Quidam eos qui hoc e thynnis faciant pompilos vocant; *id.* xxxii. 153 pompilum qui semper comitetur navium cursus; Ov. *Hal.* 100 Tuque comes ratium tractique per aequora sulci | Qui semper spumas sequeris, pompile, nitentes. See further *H.* v. 70 n.

ἕσπονται πομπῆες ὁμόστολοι, ἄλλοθεν ἄλλος
ἀμφιπερισκαίροντες ἐΰζυγον ἅρμα θαλάσσης
τοίχους τ' ἀμφοτέρους περί τε πρυμναῖα χαλινὰ
οἰήκων, ἄλλοι δὲ περὶ πρώρην ἀγέρονται·
οὐδέ κεν αὐτόμολον κείνων πλόον, ἀλλ' ὑπὸ δεσμῷ
φαίης εὐγόμφοισιν ἐνισχομένους πινάκεσσιν
ἑλκομένους ἀέκοντας ἀναγκαίῃσιν ἄγεσθαι.
τόσσον ἔρως γλαφυρῇσιν ἐφ' ὁλκάσιν ἑσμὸν ἀγείρει.
οἷον δὴ βασιλῆα φερέπτολιν ἠέ τιν' ἄνδρα
ἀθλοφόρον, θαλλοῖσι νεοστέπτοισι κομῶντα,
παῖδές τ' ἠΐθεοί τε καὶ ἀνέρες ἀμφιέποντες
ὃν δόμον εἰσανάγουσι καὶ ἀθρόοι αἰὲν ἕπονται,
εἰσόκεν εὐερκῆ μεγάρων ὑπὲρ οὐδὸν ἀμείψῃ·
ὣς οἵ γ' ὠκυπόροισιν ἀεὶ νήεσσιν ἕπονται,
ὄφρ' οὔτις γαίης ἐλάει φόβος· ἀλλ' ὅτε χέρσον
φράσσωνται, τραφερὴν δὲ μέγ' ἐχθαίρουσιν ἄρουραν,
αὖτις ἀφορμηθέντες ἀολλέες ἠΰτε νύσσης
πάντες ἀποθρώσκουσι καὶ οὐκέτι νηυσὶν ἕπονται.
σῆμα τόδε πλωτῆρσιν ἐτήτυμον ἐγγύθι γαίης
ἔμμεναι, εὖτε λιπόντας ὁμοπλωτῆρας ἴδωνται.
πομπίλε, ναυτιλίῃσι τετιμένε, σοὶ δέ τις ἀνὴρ
εὐκραεῖς ἀνέμων τεκμαίρεται ἐλθέμεν αὔρας·
εὔδια γὰρ στέλλῃ τε καὶ εὔδια σήματα φαίνεις.

Καὶ μὲν δὴ πελάγεσσιν ὁμῶς ἐχενηῒς ἑταίρη·
ἡ δ' ἤτοι ταναὴ μὲν ἰδεῖν, μῆκος δ' ἰσόπηχυς,

---

[a] The ἐχενηΐς of A. 505 b 19 ἰχθύδιόν τι τῶν πετραίων ὃ καλοῦσί τινες ἐχενηΐδα; Plin. ix. 79 parvus admodum piscis adsuetus petris echeneis appellatus, may be *Echeneis remora*

seas, and they attend them as convoyers, voyaging with them on this side and on that, gambolling around and about the well-benched chariot of the sea, about both sides and about the controlling helm at the stern, while others gather round the prow; not of their own motion thou wouldst say that they voyage, but rather entangled in the well-riveted timbers are pulled against their will as in chains and carried along perforce; so great a swarm does their passion for hollow ships collect. Even as a city-saving king or some athlete crowned with fresh garlands is beset by boys and youths and men who lead him to his house and attend him always in troops until he passes the fencing threshold of his halls, even so the Pilot-fishes always attend swift-faring ships, so long as no fear of the earth drives them away. But when they mark the dry land—and greatly do they abhor the solid earth—they all turn back again in a body and rush away as from the starting-post and follow the ships no more. This is a true sign to sailors that they are near land, when they see those companions of their voyage leaving them. O Pilot-fish, honoured of seafarers, by thee doth a man divine the coming of temperate winds; for with fair weather thou dost put to sea and fair weather signs thou showest forth.

Companion of the open seas likewise is the Echeneïs.[a] It is slender of aspect, in length a cubit,

L. (Fam. *Scombridae*), but the fish described by Oppian is the Lamprey, *Petromyzon marinus*, M.G. λάμπρινα. For similar confusion *cf.* Day i. p. 109. For legend of Echeneis detaining ships *cf.* Plut. *Mor.* 641 B; Ael. ix. 17; Phil. 117; Plin. xxxii. 2-6; Ov. *Hal.* 99 Parva echeneis adest, mirum, mora puppibus ingens; Lucan vi. 674 f. puppim retinens Euro tendente rudentes | In mediis echeneis aquis.

χροιὴ δ' αἰθαλόεσσα, φυὴ δέ οἱ ἐγχελύεσσιν
εἴδεται, ὀξὺ δέ οἱ κεφαλῆς στόμα νέρθε νένευκε
καμπύλον, ἀγκίστρου περιηγέος εἴκελον αἰχμῇ.
θαῦμα δ' ὀλισθηρῆς ἐχενηΐδος ἐφράσσαντο
ναυτίλοι· οὐ μὲν δή τις ἐνὶ φρεσὶ πιστώσαιτο
εἰσαΐων· αἰεὶ γὰρ ἀπειρήτων νόος ἀνδρῶν
δύσμαχος, οὐδ' ἐθέλουσι καὶ ἀτρεκέεσσι πιθέσθαι·
νῆα τιταινομένην ἀνέμου ζαχρηέος ὁρμῇ,
λαίφεσι πεπταμένοισιν ἁλὸς διὰ μέτρα θέουσαν,
ἰχθὺς ἀμφιχανὼν ὀλίγον στόμα νέρθεν ἐρύκει,
πᾶσαν ὑποτρόπιος βεβιημένος· οὐδ' ἔτι τέμνει
κῦμα καὶ ἱεμένη, κατὰ δ' ἔμπεδον ἐστήρικται,
ἠΰτ' ἐν ἀκλύστοισιν ἐεργομένη λιμένεσσι.
καὶ τῆς μὲν λίνα πάντα περὶ προτόνοισι μέμυκε,
ῥοχθεῦσιν δὲ κάλωες, ἐπημύει δὲ κεραίη,
ῥιπῇ ἐπειγομένη, πρύμνῃ δ' ἔπι πάντα χαλινὰ
ἰθυντὴρ ἀνίησιν, ἐπισπέρχων ὁδὸν ἅλμης·
ἡ δ' οὔτ' οἰήκων ἐμπάζεται οὔτ' ἀνέμοισι
πείθεται, οὐ ῥοθίοισιν ἐλαύνεται, ἀλλὰ παγεῖσα
μίμνει τ' οὐκ ἐθέλουσα καὶ ἐσσυμένη πεπέδηται,
ἰχθύος οὐτιδανοῖο κατὰ στόμα ῥιζωθεῖσα·
ναῦται δὲ τρομέουσιν, ἀείδελα δεσμὰ θαλάσσης
δερκόμενοι καὶ θάμβος ἴσον λεύσσοντες ὀνείρῳ.
ὡς δ' ὅτ' ἐνὶ ξυλόχοισιν ἀνὴρ λαιψηρὰ θέουσαν
θηρητὴρ ἔλαφον δεδοκημένος ἄκρον ὀϊστῷ
κῶλον ὑπὸ πτερόεντι βαλὼν ἐπέδησεν ἐρωῆς·
ἡ δὲ καὶ ἐσσυμένη περ ἀναγκαίῃς ὀδύνῃσιν
ἀμφιπαγεῖσ' ἀέκουσα μένει θρασὺν ἀγρευτῆρα·
τοίην νηΐ πέδην περιβάλλεται αἰόλος ἰχθὺς
ἀντιάσας· τοίων δὲ φερωνυμίην λάχεν ἔργων.

its colour dusky, its nature like that of the eel; under its head its mouth slopes sharp and crooked, like the barb of a curved hook. A marvellous thing have mariners remarked of the slippery Echeneïs, hearing which a man would refuse to believe it in his heart; for always the mind of inexperienced men is hard to persuade, and they will not believe even the truth. When a ship is straining under stress of a strong wind, running with spread sails over the spaces of the sea, the fish gapes its tiny mouth and stays all the ship underneath, constraining it below the keel; and it cleaves the waves no more for all its haste but is firmly stayed, even as if it were shut up in a tideless harbour. All its canvas groans upon the forestays, the ropes creak, the yard-arm bends under the stress of the breeze, and on the stern the steersman gives every rein to the ship, urging her to her briny path. But she nor heeds the helm nor obeys the winds nor is driven by the waves but, fixed fast, remains against her will and is fettered for all her haste, rooted on the mouth of a feeble fish. And the sailors tremble to see the mysterious bonds of the sea, beholding a marvel like unto a dream. As when in the woods a hunter lies in wait for a swift-running Deer and smites her with winged arrow on the leg and stays her in her course; and she for all her haste, transfixed with compelling pain, unwillingly awaits the bold hunter; even such a fetter doth the spotted fish cast about the ship which it encounters, and from such deeds it gets its name.

Χαλκίδες αὖ θρίσσαι τε καὶ ἀβραμίδες φορέονται
ἀθρόαι, ἄλλοτε δ' ἄλλον ἁλὸς πόρον, ἢ περὶ πέτρας
ἢ πελάγη, δολιχοῖσί τ' ἐπέδραμον αἰγιαλοῖσιν,
αἰὲν ἀμειβόμεναι ξείνην ὁδὸν ἠΰτ' ἀλῆται.
Ἀνθιέων δὲ μάλιστα νομαὶ πέτρῃσι βαθείαις
ἔμφυλοι· ταῖς δ' οὔτι παρέστιοι αἰὲν ἔασι,
πάντῃ δὲ πλάζονται, ὅπῃ γένυς, ἔνθα κελεύει
γαστὴρ καὶ λαίμαργος ἔρως ἀκόρητος ἐδωδῆς·
ἔξοχα γὰρ παρὰ πάντας ἀδηφάγος οἶστρος ἐλαύνει
κείνους καὶ νωδόν περ ὑπὸ στόμα χῶρον ἔχοντας.
τέσσαρα δ' ἀνθιέων μεγακήτεα φῦλα νέμονται,
ξανθοί τ' ἀργεννοί τε τὸ δὲ τρίτον αἷμα[1] κελαινοί·
ἄλλους δ' εὐωπούς τε καὶ αὐλωποὺς καλέουσιν,
οὕνεκα τοῖς καθύπερθεν ἑλισσομένη κατὰ κύκλον
ὀφρὺς ἠερόεσσα περίδρομος ἐστεφάνωται.

[1] αἷμα : εἶμα Koechly.

---

[a] *Clupea sardina* Cuv. (*Alosa sardina* Moreau). The precise identification is uncertain. Aristotle's references to χαλκίς are perplexing, but Oppian's fish is probably intended in A. 543 a 2, 621 b 7, 602 b 28. Plin. ix. 154 adeoque nihil non gignitur in mari ut cauponarum etiam aestiva animalia pernici molesta saltu aut quae capillus maxime celat existant et circumglobatae escae saepe extrahantur . . . quibusdam vero ipsis innascuntur, quo in numero chalcis accipitur; Athen. 328 c χαλκίδες καὶ τὰ ὅμοια, θρίσσαι, τριχίδες, ἐρίτιμοι; *ibid.* 328 f Ἐπαίνετος . . . φησὶ . . . χαλκίδας ἃς καλοῦσι καὶ σαρδίνους. *Cf.* Athen. 329 a 355 f; Ael. i. 58.

[b] A. 621 b 15 οὐ γίνεται δ' ἐν τῷ εὐρίπῳ (of Pyrrha in Lesbos A. 621 b 12: Strabo 617 τὸν Πυρραίων εὔριπον, *cf.* Plin. v. 139) οὔτε σκάρος οὔτε θρίττα οὔτε ἄλλο τῶν ἀκανθηροτέρων οὐθέν; Thritta Plin. xxxii. 151. It is clear from Athen. 328 c-329 b that it is a Clupeid, or member of the Herring family,

The Pilchard[a] again and the Shad[b] and the Abramis[c] move in shoals, now in one path of the sea, now in another, round rocks or in the open sea, and they also run to the long shores, ever changing to a strange path like wanderers.

The range of the Anthias[d] is most familiar to the deep rocks; yet no wise do they always dwell among these, but wander everywhere as they are bidden by their jaws, their belly and their gluttonous desire insatiate of food; for beyond others a voracious passion drives those fishes, albeit the space of their mouth is toothless. Four mighty tribes of the Anthias inhabit the sea, the yellow, the white, and, a third breed, the black; others men call Euopus and Aulopus, because they have a circular dark brow ringed above their eyes.

like *χαλκίς* and *τριχίς*. Athen. 328 b *θρισσῶν δὲ μέμνηται* 'Αριστο*τέλης ἐν τῷ περὶ ζῴων καὶ ἰχθύων ἐν τούτοις· "μόνιμα (? μαῖνα) θρίσσα, ἐγκρασίχολος, μεμβράς, κορακῖνος, ἐρυθρῖνος, τριχίς"*; 328 f *τῶν δὲ λεγομένων ἔσθ' ὅτι ἥδεται ὀρχήσει καὶ ᾠδῇ (ἡ τριχίς) καὶ ἀκούσασα ἀναπηδᾷ ἐκ τῆς θαλάσσης*, *cf.* Plut. *Mor.* 961 e where the same is said of the *θρίσσα*: *καὶ τὴν θρίσσαν ᾀδόντων καὶ κροτούντων ἀναδύεσθαι καὶ προιέναι λέγουσιν.* Perhaps the Shad, *Alosa vulgaris*, which is anadromous (Athen. 328 e *Δωρίων δ' ἐν τῷ περὶ ἰχθύων καὶ τῆς ποταμίας μέμνηται θρίσσης καὶ τὴν τριχίδα τριχίαν ὀνομάζει*; Auson. *Mosell.* 127 Stridentesque focis, obsonia plebis, alausas) or the nearly allied *Sardinella aurita*, M.G. *θρίσσα, φρίσσα* (Apost. p. 24). The schol. *θρίσσαι δύο εἴδη ἐχθύων οἱ τριχαῖοι καὶ ἕτερον ὅμοιον σκόμβρῳ ἢ μικρότερον* rather suggests the Twaite Shad (*Alosa finta*) and the larger Allis Shad (*A. vulgaris*).

[c] Mentioned among Nile fishes Athen. 312 b (along with *θρίσσα*). Salted Abramis (*ἀβραμίδια*) are mentioned Xenocr. *De aliment.* 36. Schemseddin Mohammed, an Arabic writer of XVI. cent., gives *abermis* as the old name for modern *bouri* = *Mugil cephalus* (Grey Mullet) which was salted and exported from Egypt. Schneider's *Artedi Synonymia piscium*, p. 322.

[d] Introduction p. liii.

Δοιοὶ δὲ σκληροῖσιν ἀρηρότα γυῖα χιτῶσι
φραξάμενοι κόλποισιν ἐνιπλώουσι θαλάσσης,
κάραβος ὀξυπαγὴς ἠδ' ἀστακός· οἱ δὲ καὶ ἄμφω
πέτραις ἐνναίουσι καὶ ἐν πέτρῃσι νέμονται.
ἄστακος αὖ πέρι δή τι καὶ οὐ φατὸν οἷον ἔρωτα
οἰκείης θαλάμης κεύθει φρεσίν, οὐδέ ποτ' αὐτῆς
λείπεθ' ἑκών, ἀλλ' εἴ μιν ἀναγκαίῃ τις ἐρύσσας
τῆλε φέρων ἑτέρωσε πάλιν πόντονδε μεθείη,
αὐτὰρ ὅγ' οὐ μετὰ δηρὸν ἑὴν νόστησε χαράδρην
σπεύδων, οὐδ' ἐθέλει ξεῖνον μυχὸν ἄλλον ἑλέσθαι,
οὐδ' ἑτέρης πέτρης ἐπιβάλλεται, ἀλλὰ διώκει
καὶ δόμον ὃν κατέλειπε καὶ ἤθεα καὶ νομὸν ἄλμης
κείνης ᾗ μιν ἔφερβε καὶ οὐκ ἤχθηρε θάλασσαν,
τῆς μιν ἀπεξείνωσαν ἁλίπλοοι ἀγρευτῆρες.
ὣς ἄρα καὶ πλωτοῖσιν ἑὸς δόμος ἠδὲ θάλασσα
πατρῴη καὶ χῶρος ἐφέστιος, ἔνθ' ἐγένοντο,
στάζει ἐνὶ κραδίῃ γλυκερὸν γάνος, οὐδ' ἄρα μούνοις
πατρὶς ἐφημερίοισι πέλει γλυκερώτατον ἄλλων·
οὐδ' ἀλεγεινότερον καὶ κύντερον, ὅς κεν ἀνάγκῃ
φυξίπολιν πάτρης τελέσῃ βίον ἀλγινόεντα,
ξεῖνος ἐν ἀλλοδαποῖσιν ἀτιμίης ζυγὸν ἕλκων.
Ἐν κείνῃ γενεῇ καὶ καρκίνοι εἰσὶν ἀλῆται

---

[a] Here Oppian begins his account of μαλακόστρακα or Crustaceans: *cf.* A. 523 b 5 ἓν δὲ τῶν μαλακοστράκων· ταῦτα δ' ἐστὶν ὅσων ἐκτὸς τὸ στερεόν, ἐντὸς δὲ τὸ μαλακὸν καὶ σαρκῶδες· τὸ δὲ σκληρὸν αὐτῶν ἐστιν οὐ θραυστὸν ἀλλὰ θλαστόν, οἷόν ἐστι τὸ τῶν καράβων καὶ τὸ τῶν καρκίνων. In this class A. includes ἀστακός, κάραβος, καρίς, various species of καρκίνος (πάγουρος, πιννοφύλαξ, etc.) and two species of καρκίνιον or Hermit-crab. Plin. ix. 83 piscium sanguine carent de quibus dicemus. Sunt autem tria genera: in primis quae mollia [=μαλάκια,

Two [a] fishes whose limbs are fenced with hard coats swim in the gulfs of the sea; to wit, the Spiny Crayfish [b] and the Lobster.[c] Both these dwell among the rocks and among the rocks they feed. The Lobster again holds in his heart a love exceeding and unspeakable for his own lair and he never leaves it willingly, but if one drag him away by force and carry him elsewhere far away and let him go again in the sea, in no long time he returns to his own cleft eagerly, and will not choose a strange retreat nor does he heed any other rock but seeks the home that he left and his native haunts and his feeding-ground in the brine which fed him before, and leaves not the sea from which seafaring fishermen estranged him. Thus even to the swimming tribes their own house and their native sea and the home place where they were born instil in their hearts a sweet delight, and it is not to mortal men only that their fatherland is dearest of all; and there is nothing more painful or more terrible then when a man perforce lives the grievous life of an exile from his native land, a stranger among aliens bearing the yoke of dishonour.

In that kind are also the wandering Crab [d] and the

see *H.* i. 638 n.] appellantur, dein contecta crustis tenuibus [=Crustaceans], postremo testis conclusa duris [=Testaceans]. *Cf.* Athen. 106 c; Ael. xi. 37; Galen, *De aliment. fac.* iii. 34; A. 490 b 10 ff.

[b] *Palinurus vulgaris*, the Spiny Lobster or Sea Crayfish: A. 525 a 32 ff.; Athen. 104 c-105 d; Marc. S. 34 κάραβος ὀκριόεις. In Latin writers it is usually *locusta* (Plin. ix. 95 Locustae crusta fragili muniuntur), sometimes *carabus* (Plin. ix. 97).

[c] *Homarus vulgaris*. A. 525 a 32 f.; Athen. *l.c.*; Plin. *l.c.*; Marc. S. 31 ἀστακοὶ ἠυκέρωτες.

[d] *Decapoda brachyura* in general. For different species, A. 525 b 3 ff.; Plin. ix. 97.

καρίδων τε νομαὶ καὶ ἀναιδέα φῦλα παγούρων,
οἵτε καὶ ἀμφιβίοις ἐναρίθμιον αἶσαν ἔχουσι.
Πάντες δ' οἷσί τε κῶλον ὑπ' ὀστράκῳ ἐστήρικται,
ὄστρακον ἐκδύνουσι γεραίτερον, ἄλλο δ' ἔνερθε
σαρκὸς ὑπὲκ νεάτης ἀνατέλλεται· οἱ δὲ πάγουροι,
ἡνίκα ῥηγνυμένοιο βίην φράσσωνται ἐλύτρου,
πάντῃ μαιμώωσιν ἐδητύος ἰσχανόωντες,
ῥηϊτέρη ῥινοῖο διάκρισις ὄφρα γένηται
πλησαμένων· εὖτ' ἂν δὲ διατμαγὲν ἕρκος ὀλίσθῃ,
οἱ δ' ἤτοι πρῶτον μὲν ἐπὶ ψαμάθοισι τέτανται
αὔτως, οὔτε βορῆς μεμνημένοι οὔτε τευ ἄλλου,
ἐλπόμενοι φθιμένοισι μετέμμεναι οὐδ' ἔτι θερμὸν
ἐμπνείειν, ῥινῷ δὲ περιτρομέουσιν ἀραιῇ
ἀρτιφύτῳ· μετὰ δ' αὖτις ἀγειρόμενοι νόον ἤδη
βαιὸν θαρσήσαντες ἀπὸ ψαμάθοιο πάσαντο·
τόφρα δὲ θυμὸν ἔχουσιν ἀμήχανον ἀδρανέοντες,
ὄφρα περὶ μελέεσσι νέον σκέπας ἀμφιπαγείη.
ὡς δέ τις ἰητὴρ νουσαχθέα φῶτα κομίζων
ἤμασι μὲν πρώτοισι βορῆς ἀπόπαστον ἐρύκει,
πήματος ἀμβλύνων μαλερὸν σθένος, αὐτὰρ ἔπειτα
τυτθὰ βορῆς ὤρεξε νοσήλια, μέχρις ἅπασαν
ἄτην γυιοβόρους τε δύας ὀδύνας τε καθήρῃ·
ὣς οἵγ' ἀρτιφύτοισιν ἀναΐσσουσιν ἐλύτροις
δειδιότες νούσοιο κακὰς ὑπὸ κῆρας ἀλύξαι.
Ἄλλοι δ' ἑρπυστῆρες ἁλὸς ναίουσιν ἐναύλους,
πουλύποδες σκολιοὶ καὶ κορδύλος ἠδ' ἁλιεῦσιν

---

[a] *Il.* ii. 128 n.

[b] *Cancer pagurus* L., the Edible Crab, M.G. καβούρι: A. 525 b 5; Athen. 319 a.

[c] *C.* ii. 217 n.

[d] A. 601 a 10 τῶν θαλαττίων οἱ κάραβοι καὶ ἀστακοὶ ἐκδύνουσιν . . . ἐκδύνουσι δὲ καὶ οἱ καρκίνοι τὸ γῆρας . . . ὅταν δ' ἐκδύνωσι, μαλακὰ γίνεται πάμπαν τὰ ὄστρακα καὶ οἵ γε καρκίνοι βαδίζειν οὐ σφόδρα δύνανται; Plin. ix. 95 ambo (*i.e.* locustae and cancri)

herds of the Prawn [a] and the shameless tribes of the Pagurus,[b] whose lot is numbered with the amphibians.[c]

All those whose body is set beneath a shell put off the old shell [d] and another springs up from the nether flesh. The Pagurus, when they feel the violence of the rending shell, rush everywhere in their desire for food, that the separation of the slough may be easier when they have sated themselves. But when the sheath is rent and slips off, then at first they lie idly stretched upon the sands, mindful neither of food nor of aught else, thinking to be numbered with the dead and to breathe warm breath no more, and they tremble for their new-grown tender hide. Afterwards they recover their spirits again and take a little courage and eat of the sand; but they are weak and helpless of heart until a new shelter is compacted about their limbs. Even as when a physician tends a man who is laden with disease, in the first days he keeps him from tasting food, blunting the fierceness of his malady, and then he gives him a little food for the sick, until he has cleared away all his distress and his limb-devouring aches and pains; even so they retire, fearing for their new-grown shells, to escape the evil fates of disease.

Other reptiles dwell in the haunts of the sea, the crooked Poulpe [e] and the Water-newt [f] and the Scolopendra,[g] abhorred by fishermen, and the

veris principio senectutem anguium more exuunt renovatione tergorum; Phil. iii.; Ael. ix. 37. For use of comparative γεραίτερον *cf.* παλαίτερος Callim. *E.* vi. 1. An account of Crab casting shell, St. John, *N.H.*, etc., *in Moray*, p. 208.

[e] *Octopus vulgaris.*

[f] *Triton palustris*, or allied species, *cf.* A. 487 a 28, 490 a 4, 589 b 27; *De resp.* 476 a 6; *Part. an.* 695 b 25; Athen. 306 b.

[g] *H.* ii. 424 n.

ἐχθομένη σκολόπενδρα καὶ ὀσμύλος· οἱ δὲ καὶ αὐτοὶ
ἀμφίβιοι· καί πού τις ἀνὴρ ἴδεν ἀγροιώτης
γηπόνος, ἀγχιάλοισι φυτηκομίῃσι μεμηλώς,
ὀσμύλον εὐκάρποις ἢ πούλυπον ἀμφὶ κράδῃσι
πλεγνύμενον γλυκερόν τε φυτῶν ἀπὸ καρπὸν ἔδοντα.
τοῖς δὲ μεθ' ἑρπυστῆρσιν ἴσον λάχεν οἶμα δολόφρων
σηπίη· ἄλλα δὲ φῦλα μετ' οἴδμασιν ὀστρακόρινα,
πολλὰ μὲν ἐν πέτρῃσι, τὰ δ' ἐν ψαμάθοισι νέμονται,
νηρῖται στρόμβων τε γένος καὶ πορφύραι αὐταὶ
κήρυκές τε μύες τε καὶ ἀτρεκὲς οὔνομα σωλὴν
ὄστρεά θ' ἑρσήεντα καὶ ὀκριόεντες ἐχῖνοι·
τοὺς εἴ τις καὶ τυτθὰ διατμήξας ἐνὶ πόντῳ
ῥίψῃ, συμφυέες τε παλίνζωοί τε νέμονται.

---

[a] Probably *Eledone moschata*, a species of Octopus variously named from its strong smell: A. 525 a 19 ἣν καλοῦσιν οἱ μὲν βολίταιναν [βόλιτος = dung], οἱ δ' ὄζολιν [ὄζειν = smell]; 621 b 17 οὐδὲ πολύποδες οὐδὲ βολίταιναι; Athen. 318 e εἴδη δ' ἐστὶ πολυπόδων ἐλεδώνη, πολυποδίνη, βολβιτίνη, ὀσμύλος, ὡς Ἀριστοτέλης ἱστορεῖ καὶ Σπεύσιππος; Athen. 329 a Καλλίμαχος . . . καταλέγων ἰχθύων ὀνομασίας φησίν· ὄζαινα ὀσμύλιον Θούριοι; Epicharm. *ap.* Athen. 318 e χἀ δυσώδης βολβιτίς; Ael. v. 44, ix. 45 ὀσμίλος; Hesych. *s.* ὀσμύλια· τῶν πολυπόδων αἱ ὄζαιναι λεγόμεναι; *s.* ὀσμύναι· βολβιτῖναι θαλάσσιοι; Plin. ix. 89 Polyporum generis est ozaena dicta a gravi capitis odore, ob hoc maxime murenis eam consectantibus.

[b] This passage is paraphrased Ael. ix. 45 Ἀγροῦ γειτνιῶντος θαλάττῃ καὶ φυτῶν παρεστώτων ἐγκάρπων γεωργοὶ πολλάκις καταλαμβάνουσιν ἐν ὥρᾳ θερείῳ πολύποδάς τε καὶ ὀσμύλους ἐκ τῶν κυμάτων προελθόντας καὶ διὰ τῶν πρέμνων ἀνερπύσαντας κτλ. *Cf.* Phil. 101. 32; A. 622 a 31; Plin. ix. 85 (polypi) soli mollium in siccum exeunt; Athen. 317 b-c.

[c] *H.* ii. 121 n. Its craft, Phil. 105; A. 621 b 28.

[d] *i.e.* Testaceans, A. 523 b 8 ἔτι δὲ τὰ ὀστρακόδερμα· τοιαῦτα δ' ἐστὶν ὧν ἐντὸς μὲν τὸ σαρκῶδές ἐστιν, ἐκτὸς δὲ τὸ στερεόν, θραυστὸν ὂν καὶ κατακτόν, ἀλλ' οὐ θλαστόν. τοιοῦτον δὲ τὸ τῶν κοχλιῶν γένος καὶ τὸ τῶν ὀστρέων ἐστίν; Plin. ix. 40 Aquatilium tegumenta plura sunt. Alia . . . teguntur . . . silicum duritia ut ostreae et conchae; Ael. xi. 37; Galen, *De aliment. fac.* iii. 33.

Osmylus.[a] These also are amphibious; and some rustic tiller of the soil, I ween, who tends a vineyard by the sea, has seen an Osmylus or a Poulpe twining about the fruit-laden branches and devouring the sweet fruit off the trees.[b] The same way as these reptiles have also the crafty Cuttle-fish.[c] But other tribes dwell in the waves which have a hard shell,[d] many among the rocks and many amid the sands;[e] to wit, the Nerites[f] and the race of the Strombus and the Purple-shells themselves and the Trumpet-shells and the Mussel[g] and the truly named Razor-shell[h] and the dewy Oysters[i] and the prickly Sea-urchins,[j] which, if one cut them in small pieces and cast them into the sea, grow together and again become alive.[k]

[e] A. 547 b 33 *φύεται δ' αὐτῶν τὰ μὲν ἐν τοῖς τενάγεσι, τὰ δ' ἐν τοῖς αἰγιαλοῖς, τὰ δ' ἐν τοῖς σπιλώδεσι τόποις, ἔνιοι δ' ἐν τοῖς σκληροῖς καὶ τραχέσι, τὰ δ' ἐν τοῖς ἀμμώδεσιν.*

[f] νηρίτης, στρόμβος, πορφύρα, κῆρυξ all belong to the στρομβώδη (A. 528 a 10, *Part. an.* 679 b 14) or spiral-shaped Testaceans. νηρίτης (A. 530 a 7, 547 b 23, etc.; Ael. xiv. 28; also called ἀναρίτης Athen. 85 d, 86 a) and κῆρυξ (A. 528 a 10 547 b 2, etc.; Athen. 86 c-91 e) may be species of *Buccinum* or *Trochus*. στρόμβος (A. 548 a 17, etc.; Ael. vii. 31, etc.) may be *Cerithium vulgatum*, Ital. *strombolo*. πορφύρα (A. 547 a 4 *εἰσὶ δὲ τῶν πορφυρῶν γένη πλείω*, *cf.* Athen. 88 f ff.; Plin. ix. 130 ff.) probably includes *Murex brandaris*, *M. trunculus*, *Purpura lapillus*, etc.

[g] *Mytilus edulis*, etc., A. 528 a 15, 547 b 11, etc.

[h] A bivalve which burrows in the sand; several species, *Solen siliqua*, *S. ensis*, *S. legumen*, etc., occur in the Mediterranean. A. 547 b 13, etc.; Plin. x. 192, xi. 139. It is "truly named" as σωλήν = pipe, in reference to the long tubular shell. Also called αὐλός, δόναξ, ὄνυξ Athen. 90 d, *cf.* Plin. xxxii. 151.

[i] *H.* i. 764 n.

[j] *H.* ii. 225 n.; E. Forbes, pp. 149 ff.

[k] Ael. ix. 47; Phil. 64.

Καρκινάσιν δ' αὐταῖς μὲν ἐπ' ὄστρακον οὔτι πέφυκεν
ἐκ γενετῆς, γυμναὶ δὲ καὶ ἀσκεπέες καὶ ἀφαυραὶ
τίκτονται, κτητοὺς δὲ δόμους ἐπιμηχανόωνται,
ἀβληχροῖς μελέεσσι νόθον σκέπας ἀμφιβαλοῦσαι·
εὖτε γὰρ ἀθρήσωσι λελειμμένον ὀρφανὸν αὔτως
ὄστρακον, οἰκητῆρος ἀνέστιον οἰχομένοιο,
αἴδ' εἴσω καταδῦσαι ὑπ' ἀλλοτρίοισιν ἐλύτροις
ἑζόμεναι ναίουσι καὶ ὃν κτήσαντο μέλαθρον·
τῷ δὲ συνερπύζουσι καὶ ἔνδοθεν ἕρκος ἄγουσιν,
εἴτε τι νηρίτης ἔλιπε σκέπας εἴτε τι κῆρυξ
ἢ στρόμβος· στρόμβων δὲ δύσεις φιλέουσι μάλιστα,
οὕνεκεν εὐρεῖαί τε μένειν κοῦφαί τε φέρεσθαι.
ἀλλ' ὅτ' ἀεξομένη πλήσῃ μυχὸν ἔνδον ἐοῦσα
καρκινάς, οὐκέτι κεῖνον ἔχει δόμον, ἀλλὰ λιποῦσα
δίζεται εὐρύτερον κόχλου κύτος ἀμφιβαλέσθαι.
πολλάκι δὲ γλαφυρῆς κύμβης πέρι καρκινάδεσσιν
ἀλκὴ καὶ μέγα νεῖκος ἐγείρεται, ἐκ δ' ἐλάσασα
κρείττων χειροτέρην δόμον ἅρμενον ἀμφέθετ' αὐτή.
"Εστι δέ τις γλαφυρῷ κεκαλυμμένος ὀστράκῳ ἰχθύς,
μορφὴν πουλυπόδεσσιν ἀλίγκιος, ὃν καλέουσι
ναυτίλον, οἰκείῃσιν ἐπικλέα ναυτιλίῃσι·
ναίει μὲν ψαμάθοις, ἀνὰ δ' ἔρχεται ἄκρον ἐς ὕδωρ
πρηνής, ὄφρα κε μή μιν ἐνιπλήσειε θάλασσα·

---

[a] A. 548 a 14 *τὸ δὲ καρκίνιον γίνεται μὲν τὴν ἀρχὴν ἐκ τῆς γῆς καὶ ἰλύος, εἶτ' εἰς τὰ κενὰ τῶν ὀστράκων εἰσδύεται*, *cf.* 529 b 19; Ael. vii. 31 *αἱ δὲ καρκινάδες τίκτονται μὲν γυμναί, τὸ δὲ ὄστρακον ἑαυταῖς αἱροῦνται ὡς οἰκίαν οἰκῆσαι τὴν ἀρίστην.*

The Hermit-crabs have no shell of their own from birth, but are born naked[a] and unprotected and weak; yet they devise for themselves an acquired home, covering their feeble bodies with a bastard shelter. For when they see a shell left all desolate, the tenant having left his home, they creep in below the alien mantle and settle there and dwell and take it for their home. And along with it they travel and move their shelter from within—whether[b] it be some Nerites that hath left the shell or a Trumpet or a Strombus. Most of all they love the shelters of the Strombus, because these are wide[c] and light to carry. But when the Hermit-crab within grows[d] and fills the cavity, it keeps that house no longer, but leaves it and seeks a wider shell-vessel to put on. Ofttimes battle arises and great contention among the Hermit-crabs about a hollow shell and the stronger drives out the weaker and herself puts on the fitting house.

One fish there is covered with a hollow shell, like in form to the Poulpe, which men call the Nautilus,[e] so named because it sails of itself. It dwells in the sands and it rises to the surface of the water face downwards, so that the sea may not fill it. But when

[b] A. 548 a 16 *αὐξανόμενον μετεισδύνει πάλιν εἰς ἄλλο μεῖζον ὄστρακον, οἷον εἴς τε τὸ τοῦ νηρείτου καὶ τὸ τοῦ στρόμβου . . . πολλάκις δ' εἰς τοὺς κήρυκας τοὺς μικρούς*; Ael. *l.c.*

[c] A. 530 a 6 *προμηκέστερα δ' ἐστὶ τὰ ἐν τοῖς στρόμβοις τῶν ἐν τοῖς νηρείταις.*

[d] A. 548 a 19 *ὅταν δ' εἰσδύνῃ, συμπεριφέρει τοῦτο καὶ ἐν τούτῳ τρέφεται πάλιν· καὶ αὐξανόμενον πάλιν εἰς ἄλλο μετεισδύνει μεῖζον*; Ael. *l.c.*; Plin. ix. 98.

[e] *Argonauta argo* L., *cf.* A. 622 b 5; Athen. 317 f ff., who preserves the famous epigram of Callimachus (*E.* vi); Ael. ix. 34; Antig. 56; Plin. ix. 88.

ἀλλ' ὅτ' ἀναπλώσῃ ῥοθίων ὕπερ Ἀμφιτρίτης,
αἶψα μεταστρεφθεὶς ναυτίλλεται, ὥστ' ἀκάτοιο
ἴδρις ἀνήρ· δοιοὺς μὲν ἄνω πόδας ὥστε κάλωας
ἀντανύει, μέσσος δὲ διαρρέει ἠΰτε λαῖφος
λεπτὸς ὑμήν, ἀνέμῳ τε τιταίνεται· αὐτὰρ ἔνερθε
δοιοὶ ἁλὸς ψαύοντες, ἐοικότες οἰήκεσσι,
πομποί τ' ἰθύνουσι δόμον καὶ νῆα καὶ ἰχθύν.
ἀλλ' ὅτε ταρβήσῃ σχεδόθεν κακόν, οὐκέτ' ἀήταις
φεύγει ἐπιτρέψας, σὺν δ' ἔσπασε πάντα χαλινά,
ἱστία τ' οἴηκάς τε, τὸ δ' ἀθρόον ἔνδον ἔδεκτο
κῦμα βαρυνόμενός τε καθέλκεται ὕδατος ὁρμῇ.
ὢ πόποι, ὃς πρώτιστος ὄχους ἁλὸς εὕρατο νῆας,
εἴτ' οὖν ἀθανάτων τις ἐπεφράσατ' εἴτε τις ἀνὴρ
τολμήεις πρώτιστος ἐπεύξατο κῦμα περῆσαι,
ἦ που κεῖνον ἰδὼν πλόον ἰχθύος εἴκελον ἔργον
δουροπαγὲς τόρνωσε, τὰ μὲν πνοιῇσι πετάσσας
ἐκ προτόνων, τὰ δ' ὄπισθε χαλινωτήρια νηῶν.
Κήτεα δ' ὀβριμόγυια, πελώρια, θαύματα πόντου,
ἀλκῇ ἀμαιμακέτῳ βεβριθότα, δεῖμα μὲν ὄσσοις
εἰσιδέειν, αἰεὶ δ' ὀλοῇ κεκορυθμένα λύσσῃ,
πολλὰ μὲν εὐρυπόροισιν ἐνιστρέφεται πελάγεσσιν,
ἔνθα Ποσειδάωνος ἀτέκμαρτοι περιωπαί,
παῦρα δὲ ῥηγμίνων σχεδὸν ἔρχεται, ὅσσα φέρουσιν
ἠϊόνες βαρύθοντα καὶ οὐκ ἀπολείπεται ἅλμης·
τῶν ἤτοι κρυερός τε λέων βλοσυρή τε ζύγαινα

[a] The list of κήτη μέγιστα Ael. ix. 49 is λέων, ζύγαινα,

it swims above the waves of Amphitrite, straightway it turns over and sails like a man skilled in sailing a boat. Two feet it stretches aloft by way of rigging and between these runs like a sail a fine membrane which is stretched by the wind; but underneath two feet touching the water, like rudders, guide and direct house and ship and fish. But when it fears some evil hard at hand, no longer does it trust the winds in its flight, but gathers in all its tackle, sails and rudders, and receives the full flood within and is weighed down and sunk by the rush of water. Ah! whosoever first invented ships, the chariots of the sea, whether it was some god that devised them or whether some daring mortal first boasted to have crossed the wave, surely it was when he had seen that voyaging of a fish that he framed a like work in wood, spreading from the forestays those parts to catch the wind and those behind to control the ship.

The Sea-monsters [a] mighty of limb and huge, the wonders of the sea, heavy with strength invincible, a terror for the eyes to behold and ever armed with deadly rage—many of these there be that roam the spacious seas, where are the unmapped prospects of Poseidon, but few of them come nigh the shore, those only whose weight the beaches can bear and whom the salt water does not fail. Among these are the terrible Lion [b] and the truculent Hammer-head [c]

πάρδαλις, φύσαλος, πρῆστις, μάλθη, κριός, ὕαινα. Suid. *s. κῆτος* omits *ὕαινα*; Phil. 85 omits *ὕαινα* and *μάλθη*. *Cf.* Plin. ix. 2 ff.

[b] Not identified. Ael. xvi. 18 (the sea round Taprobane) *ἄμαχόν τι πλῆθος καὶ ἰχθύων καὶ κητῶν τρέφειν φασί, καὶ ταῦτα μέντοι καὶ λεόντων ἔχειν κεφαλὰς καὶ παρδαλέων καὶ λύκων καὶ κριῶν.* The *λέων θαλάσσιος* of Ael. xiv. 9 seems to be a Crustacean.

[c] *H.* v. 37 n.

πορδάλιές τ' ὀλοαὶ καὶ φύσαλοι αἰθυκτῆρες·
ἐν δὲ μέλαν θύννων ζαμενὲς γένος, ἐν δὲ δαφοινὴ
πρῆστις ἀταρτηρῆς τε δυσαντέα χάσματα λάμνης,
μάλθη τ' οὐ[1] μαλακῇσιν ἐπώνυμος ἀδρανίῃσι,
κριοί τ' ἀργαλέοι καὶ ἀπαίσιον ἄχθος ὑαίνης
καὶ κύνες ἁρπακτῆρες ἀναιδέες· ἐν δὲ κύνεσσι
τριχθαδίη γενεή· τὸ μὲν ἄγριον ἐν πελάγεσσι
κήτεσι λευγαλέοις ἐναρίθμιον· ἄλλα δὲ φῦλα
διπλόα καρτίστοισι μετ' ἰχθύσι δινεύονται
πηλοῖς ἐν βαθέεσσι· τὸ μὲν κέντροισι κελαινοῖς
κεντρίναι αὐδώωνται ἐπώνυμοι· ἄλλο δ' ὁμαρτῇ
κλείονται γαλεοί· γαλεῶν δ' ἑτερότροπα φῦλα

[1] *v.l.* μάλθη θ' ἡ.

---

[a] *H.* v. 30 n.

[b] Perhaps *Physeter macrocephalus* L.; the Cachalot or Sperm Whale. Erh. pp. 28 f. tells of one which was stranded at Tenos in 1840, another at Melos, and a young one at Tenos in 1857 (Erh. p. 95). Ael. ix. 49. Strabo 145 (of the sea off Turdetania) ὣς δ' αὔτως ἔχει καὶ περὶ τῶν κητέων ἁπάντων, ὀρύγων τε καὶ φαλαινῶν καὶ φυσητήρων, ὧν ἀναφυσησάντων φαίνεταί τις νεφώδους ὄψις κίονος τοῖς πόρρωθεν ἀφορῶσι; Plin. ix. 8 Maximum animal . . . in Gallico oceano physeter ingentis columnae modo se attollens altiorque navium velis diluviem quandam eructans; Phil. 95; Senec. *Hippol.* 1030.

[c] *Pristis antiquorum* (*Squalus pristis*): A. 566 b 3 ζῳοτοκοῦσιν, ἔτι δὲ πρίστις καὶ βοῦς; Plin. ix. 4 f.; schol. πρῆστις. βασιλίσκος. [d] *H.* v. 36 n.

[e] Unidentified. Ael. ix. 49 (among κήτη μέγιστα) ἡ πρῆστις καὶ ἡ καλουμένη μάλθη· δυσανταγώνιστον δὲ ἄρα τὸ θηρίον τοῦτο καὶ ἄμαχον; Suid. *s.* κῆτος· . . . πρῆστις, ἡ λεγομένη μάλθη, ὃ καὶ δυσανταγώνιστόν ἐστι; *s.* πρῆστις· εἶδος κήτους θαλασσίου, ἡ

and the deadly Leopard [a] and the dashing Physalus [b]; among them also is the impetuous black race of the Tunny and the deadly Saw-fish [c] and the dread gape of the woeful Lamna [d] and the Maltha,[e] named not from soft feebleness, and the terrible Rams [f] and the awful weight of the Hyaena [g] and the ravenous and shameless Dog-fish.[h] Of the Dog-fish there are three races; one fierce race [i] in the deep seas is numbered among the terrible Sea-monsters; two other races among the mightiest fishes dwell in the deep mud; one of these from its black spines is called Centrines,[j] the other by the general name of Galeus [k]; and of the Galeus there are different kinds, to wit, the

λεγομένη μάλθη ὃ καὶ δυσανταγώνιστόν ἐστι. Thus to Suidas πρῆστις = μάλθη.

[f] *H.* v. 34 n.

[g] *H.* v. 32 n.

[h] Apparently, like M.G. σκυλόψαρο, collective name for the Sharks and Dog-fishes. κύων is mentioned once in Aristotle where it is included among the γαλεοειδεῖς: A. 566 a 30 οἱ μὲν οὖν γαλεοὶ καὶ οἱ γαλεοειδεῖς, οἷον ἀλώπηξ καὶ κύων. *Cf.* Ael. i. 55.

[i] If this is not one of the *Cete* just mentioned, it may be *Selache maxima* Cuv., the Basking Shark.

[j] κεντρίνης from κέντρον, spine. *Centrina vulpecula* Mor. (*Squalus centrina* L.), M.G. γουρουνόψαρο, Fr. *La Humantin.*

[k] Aristotle's γαλεοί (γαλεώδεις) are the long cartilaginous fishes, *i.e.* the Sharks as opposed to the Skates and Rays: A. 489 b 6 τὰ σελάχη, γαλεοί τε καὶ βάτοι; 505 a 3 τῶν σελαχῶν τὰ μὲν πλατέα, . . . οἷον νάρκη καὶ βάτος, τὰ δὲ προμήκη . . . οἷον πάντα τὰ γαλεώδη; and the species mentioned are ἀκανθίας A. 565 b 27, ἀστερίας A. 543 a 17, 566 a 17, τὰ σκύλια οὓς καλοῦσί τινες νεβρίας γαλεούς A. 565 a 26, ἀλώπηξ A. 566 a 31, 565 b 1, 621 a 12, γαλοὶ λεῖοι A. 565 b 2, *De gen.* 754 b 33. *Cf.* Athen. 294 d Ἀριστοτέλης δὲ εἴδη αὐτῶν (*sc.* τῶν γαλεῶν) φησιν εἶναι πλείω, ἀκανθίαν, λεῖον, ποικίλον, σκύμνον, ἀλωπεκίαν, ῥίνην (the inclusion of the last being due perhaps to mis understanding of A. 565 b 25. See *H.* i. 381 n.).

σκύμνοι καὶ λεῖοι καὶ ἀκανθίαι· ἐν δ' ἄρα τοῖσι
ῥῖναι ἀλωπεκίαι καὶ ποικίλοι· εἴκελα δ' ἔργα
πᾶσιν ὁμοῦ φορβή τε σὺν ἀλλήλοις τε νέμονται.
Δελφῖνες δ' ἀκταῖς τε πολυρραθάγοισι γάνυνται
καὶ πελάγη ναίουσι, καὶ οὔποθι νόσφι θάλασσα
δελφίνων· περὶ γάρ σφε Ποσειδάων ἀγαπάζει·
οὕνεκά οἱ κούρην κυανώπιδα Νηρηΐνην
μαιομένῳ φεύγουσαν ἑὸν λέχος Ἀμφιτρίτην
φρασσάμενοι δελφῖνες ἐν Ὠκεανοῖο δόμοισι
κευθομένην ἤγγειλαν· ὁ δ' αὐτίκα κυανοχαίτης
παρθένον ἐξήρπαξεν ἀναινομένην τε δάμασσε.
καὶ τὴν μὲν παράκοιτιν, ἁλὸς βασίλειαν, ἔθηκε,
ἀγγελίης δ' ᾔνησεν ἐνηέας οὓς θεράποντας,
κλήρῳ δ' ἐν σφετέρῳ περιώσιον ὤπασε τιμήν.
Ἔστι δ' ἀμειλίκτοις ἐνὶ κήτεσιν ἅσσα καὶ ἅλμης
ἐκτὸς ἐπὶ τραφερῆς φυσίζοον ἔρχεται οὖδας·
δηρὸν δ' ἠϊόνεσσι καὶ ἀγχιάλοισιν ἀρούραις

---

[a] As σκύμνος is given in Athenaeus but not in Aristotle, it is perhaps to be equated with Aristotle's σκύλιον and identified as *Scyllium canicula* Cuv., M.G. σκυλί, σκυλόψαρο, which is very common in Greek waters (Apost. p. 1).

[b] *Mustelus laevis* Risso, M.G. γαληός. In this species the embryo is attached to the uterus by a placenta, as was known to Aristotle; A. 565 b 1 ff.

[c] *Acanthias vulgaris*, commonest of Greek *Plagiostoma*, M.G. σκυλόψαρο (Apost. p. 5). A. 565 a 29, b 27, 621 b 17; Athen. 294 d.

[d] *Rhina squatina* or Monk-fish. One of the σελάχη A. 543 a 14, but not one of the γαλεοί A. 565 b 25. *Cf.* 566 a 20; Plin. ix. 161. Aristotle's references, while rather indefinite, associate the ῥίνη rather with the Rays than the Sharks, and

Scymnus,[a] the Smooth Dog-fish,[b] the Spiny Dog-fish [c]; and among them are the Angel-shark,[d] the Fox-shark [e] and the Spotted Dog-fish.[f] But the works and the feeding of them all is alike and they herd together.

The Dolphins both rejoice in the echoing shores and dwell in the deep seas, and there is no sea without Dolphins; for Poseidon loves them exceedingly, inasmuch as when he was seeking the dark-eyed daughter [g] of Nereus who fled from his embraces, the Dolphin marked her hiding in the halls of Ocean and told Poseidon; and the god of the dark hair straightway carried off the maiden and overcame her against her will. Her he made his bride, queen of the sea, and for their tidings he commended his kindly attendants and bestowed on them exceeding honour for their portion.

There are also those among the stern Sea-monsters which leave the salt water and come forth upon the life-giving soil of the dry land. For a long space do Eels [h] consort with the shores and the fields beside

though it is now classed as a Shark, it is "intermediate between the ordinary Sharks and the Skates and Rays, both in external appearance and internal structure, but is more Ray-like than Shark-like in its habits," *Cambridge N.H.* vii. p. 457. It is viviparous.

[e] *Alopias* (*Alopecias*) *vulpes*, the Thresher Shark, commonest of the larger Sharks on British coasts. It grows to a length of 15 feet or more, the tail forming at least one-half. *Cf.* Apost. p. 4; A. 566 a 31 ἀλώπηξ. Fr. *Le Renard.*

[f] *Scyllium catulus* Cuv., the γαλεὸς νεβρίας of A. 565 a 26.

[g] When Poseidon wished to marry Amphitrite, she hid herself. The Dolphin found her, and for this Poseidon gave him the highest honours in the sea and set in the sky the constellation of the Dolphin. Eratosth. *Catast.* 31; Hygin. *Astr.* ii. 17.

[h] A. 592 a 13; Plin. ix. 74.

μίσγοντ᾽ ἐγχέλυές τε καὶ ἀσπιδόεσσα χελώνη
καστορίδες τ᾽ ὀλοαὶ δυσπενθέες, αἵ τ᾽ ἀλεγεινὴν
ὄσσαν ἐπὶ κροκάλῃσιν ἀπαίσιον ὠρύονται
ἀνδράσιν· ὃς δέ κε γῆρυν ἐν οὔασιν ἀλγινόεσσαν
δέξηται στυγερῆς τ᾽ ἐνοπῆς κωκυτὸν ἀκούσῃ,
οὐ τηλοῦ θανάτοιο τάχ᾽ ἔσσεται, ἀλλά οἱ ἄτην
καὶ μόρον αἰνοτάτη κείνη μαντεύεται αὐδή.
ναὶ μὴν καὶ φάλαιναν ἀναιδέα φασὶ θαλάσσης
ἐκβαίνειν χέρσονδε καὶ ἠελίοιο θέρεσθαι.
φῶκαι δ᾽ ἐννύχιαι μὲν ἀεὶ λείπουσι θάλασσαν,
πολλάκι δ᾽ ἠμάτιαι πέτραις ἐνὶ καὶ ψαμάθοισιν
εὔκηλοι μίμνουσι καὶ ἔξαλον ὕπνον ἔχουσι.
Ζεῦ πάτερ, ἐς δὲ σὲ πάντα καὶ ἐκ σέθεν ἐρρίζωνται·
εἴτ᾽ οὖν αἰθέρος οἶκον ὑπέρτατον εἴτ᾽ ἄρα πάντῃ
ναιετάεις· θνητῷ γὰρ ἀμήχανον ἐξονομῆναι.

---

[a] *Chelonia cephalo* Dussum. "Die Caguana und nicht, wie man sie fälschlich in Handbüchern findet, Carette genannt," Erh. p. 71. M.G. ἀχελῶνα (generic for all Turtles and Tortoises). A. 589 a 26, 558 a 11, etc.; Plin. ix. 36 Ferunt et pastum egressas noctu, etc.; *ibid.* 37 in terram egressae herbis vivunt.

[b] Comparison of A. 594 b 28 ἔνια δὲ τῶν τετραπόδων καὶ ἀγρίων ζῴων ποιεῖται τὴν τροφὴν περὶ λίμνας καὶ ποταμούς, περὶ δὲ τὴν θάλατταν οὐδὲν ἔξω φώκης. τοιαῦτα δ᾽ ἐστὶν ὅ τε καλούμενος κάστωρ καὶ τὸ σαθέριον καὶ τὸ σατύριον καὶ ἐνυδρὶς καὶ ἡ καλουμένη λάταξ· ἔστι δὲ τοῦτο πλατύτερον τῆς ἐνυδρίδος, καὶ ὀδόντας ἔχει ἰσχυρούς· ἐξιοῦσα γὰρ νύκτωρ πολλάκις τὰς περὶ τὸν ποταμὸν κερκίδας ἐκτέμνει τοῖς ὀδοῦσιν, *cf.* A. 487 a 22, leaves no doubt that Oppian's καστορίς = Aristotle's κάστωρ = *Castor fiber*, the Beaver, still found in S. Russia, the various names, acc. to Sundevall, being synonyms for the same animal; *cf.* Herod. iv. 109. Ael. ix. 50 paraphrases *vv.* 398-408.

[c] *Cf.* Ael. *l.c.* This seems to be merely an expansion of A. 589 b 19 (of the Dolphin) καὶ ἔξω δὲ ζῇ πολὺν χρόνον μύζων καὶ στένων. *Cf.* A. 535 b 32.

[d] Ael. *l.c.* καὶ ἡ φάλαινα δὲ τῆς θαλάττης πρόεισι καὶ ἀλεαίνεται τῃ ἀκτῖνι. *Cf.* xvi. 18. The statement is probably based on

the sea ; so too the shielded Turtle [a] and the woeful, lamentable Castorids,[b] which utter on the shores their grievous voice [c] of evil omen. He who receives in his ears their voice of sorrow, shall soon be not far from death, but that dread sound prophesies for him doom and death. Nay, even the shameless Whale,[d] they say, leaves the sea for the dry land and basks in the sun. And Seals [e] in the night-time always leave the sea, and often in the day-time they abide at their ease on the rocks and on the sands and take their sleep outside the sea.

O Father Zeus, in thee and by thee are all things rooted, whether thou dwellest in the highest height of heaven or whether thou dwellest everywhere ; for that is impossible for a mortal to declare. With

such passages as A. 589 a 10-b 11 which deals with amphibious animals (*τὰ ἐπαμφοτερίζοντα*) where both *δελφίς* and *φάλαινα* are mentioned. The *φάλαινα* of Aristotle (*cf.* esp. A. 489 b 4 *ἔχει δὲ ὁ μὲν δελφὶς τὸν αὐλὸν* (blow-hole) *διὰ τοῦ νώτου, ἡ δὲ φάλαινα ἐν τῷ μετώπῳ*) is probably *Physeter macrocephalus* or, according to A. and W., *Delphinus tursio*, which is rarer than the common Dolphin (*Delphinus delphis*) and more frequent in the S. Mediterranean, particularly off Crete (Erh. p. 28).

[e] Ael. *l.c.* *κνεφαῖαι δὲ αἱ φῶκαι ἐξιᾶσι μᾶλλον· ἤδη μέντοι καὶ μεσημβρίας οὔσης καθεύδουσι τῆς θαλάσσης ἔξω. τοῦτό τοι καὶ Ὅμηρος ᾔδει* (Hom. *O.* iv. 448). A. 566 b 27 ; Plin. ix. 41. The only Seal found in the Mediterranean appears to be *Phoca monachus* which is common in the Cyclades : "Es giebt kaum ein Eiland, grösseres oder kleineres im ägäischen Meere, wo nicht ein und mehre Paare dieser Robben ihr Standquartier aufgeschlagen hätten, obwohl man sie nur sehr selten, bei ruhigem Wetter oder Tageslicht wohl nie, zu Gesichte bekömmt. Den Fischern des Archipels ist sie besser bekannt; sie wissen die beinahe unterseeischen Uferschluchten, in denen sie sich verbirgt, wohl zu finden, und bezeichnen sie allgemein mit dem Ausdrucke *φωκότρυπαι* " (Erh. p. 18).

οἴη σὺν φιλότητι διακρίνας ἐκέδασσας
αἰθέρα τ' αἰγλήεντα καὶ ἠέρα καὶ χυτὸν ὕδωρ
καὶ χθόνα παμμήτειραν, ἀπ' ἀλλήλων μὲν ἕκαστα,
πάντα δ' ἐν ἀλλήλοισιν ὁμοφροσύνης ὑπὸ δεσμῷ
ἀρρήκτῳ συνέδησας, ἀναγκαίῃ δ' ἐπέρεισας
ἀστεμφῆ πάγκοινον ὑπὸ ζυγόν· οὔτε γὰρ αἰθὴρ
ἠέρος οὔτ' ἀὴρ ἄτερ ὕδατος, οὐδὲ μὲν ὕδωρ
γαίης νόσφι τέτυκται, ἐν ἀλλήλοις δὲ φύονται,
πάντα δ' ὁδὸν μίαν εἶσι, μίαν δ' ἀνελίσσετ' ἀμοιβήν.
τοὔνεκα καὶ ξυνῇσιν ὁμηρεύουσι γενέθλαις
ἀμφιβίων· καὶ τοὶ μὲν ἀναστείχουσ' ἐπὶ γαῖαν
ποντόθεν, ἄλλοι δ' αὖτε κατ' ἠέρος Ἀμφιτρίτῃ
μίσγονται, κοῦφοί τε λάροι στονόεντά τε φῦλα
ἁλκυόνων κρατεροί θ' ἁλιαίετοι ἁρπακτῆρες
ἄλλα θ' ὅσ' ἰχθυάᾳ διερῆς τ' ἐπιβάλλεται ἄγρης.
ἠέρα δ' αὖ τέμνουσι καὶ εἰνάλιοί περ ἐόντες
τευθίδες ἱρήκων τε γένος βυθίη τε χελιδών·
οἱ δ' ὅτε ταρβήσωσιν ὑπέρτερον ἐγγύθεν ἰχθύν,
ἐξ ἁλὸς ἀνθρώσκουσι καὶ ἠέριοι ποτέονται.
ἀλλ' αἱ μὲν καὶ τῆλε καὶ ὑψόθι ταρσὸν ἱεῖσι
τευθίδες· ἦτε κεν ὄρνιν ὀΐσσεαι οὐδὲ μὲν ἰχθὺν
εἰσοράαν, ἀγεληδὸν ὅθ' ὁρμήσωσι πέτεσθαι·
αἱ δ' ἄρα τῶν ὑπένερθε χελιδόνες οἶμον ἔχουσι·
ἵρηκες δ' αὐτῆς ἅλμης σχεδὸν ἠερέθονται,

---

[a] *C.* ii. 217 n.

[b] λάρος, M.G. γλάρος, generic for Gulls and Terns.

[c] *Alcedo ispida* L., M.G. ψαροφάγος etc.

[d] *Pandion haliaëtus*, the Osprey, or *Aquila naevia*, or *Haliaëtus albicilla*. A. 620 a 1-12 etc.

[e] *Loligo vulgaris* Cuv., the Squid. A. 524 a 30 etc. For their flight *cf.* Epicharm. *ap.* Athen. 323 f ποταναὶ τευθίδες; Plin. ix. 84 Loligo etiam volitat extra aquam se efferens. Oppian's lines 427-437 are paraphrased Ael. ix. 52.

[f] Mentioned along with χελιδών Epainet. *ap.* Athen. 329 a.

what loving-kindness, although thou hast marked out and divided the bright sky and the air and the fluid water and earth, mother of all, and established them apart each from the other, yet hast thou bound them all one to another in a bond of amity that may not be broken and set them perforce under a common yoke not to be removed! For neither is the sky without air nor the air without water nor is the water sundered from the earth, but they inhere each in the other, and all travel one path and revolve in one cycle of change. Therefore also they pledge one another in the common race of the amphibians;[a] of whom some come up from the sea to the land; others again go down from the air to consort with the sea; to wit, the light Gulls[b] and the plaintive tribes of the Kingfisher[c] and the strong rapacious Sea-eagle,[d] and whatsoever others there be that fish and seek their prey in the water. Others again, though they are dwellers in the sea, plough the air; to wit, the Calamaries[e] and the race of Sea-hawks[f] and the Swallow[g] of the deep. These, when they fear a mightier fish at hand, leap from the sea and fly in the air. But while the Calamaries ply the wing high and far—a bird you would think you were seeing, not a fish, when they set themselves in shoals to fly—the Swallows keep a lower path and the Hawks

Probably *Exocoetus volitans* Cuv. (*E. exsiliens* Bloch). Plin. ix. 82 volat hirundo, sane perquam similis volucri hirundini, item milvus; Ov. *Hal.* 95 nigro corpore milvi.

[g] *Dactylopterus volitans*, Cuv. (*Trigla volitans* L.), the Flying Gurnard, M.G. χελιδονόψαρο (Apost. p. 11). A. 535 b 26 οἱ κτένες ὅταν φέρωνται ἀπερειδόμενοι τῷ ὑγρῷ ὃ καλοῦσι πέτεσθαι ῥοιζοῦσι, καὶ αἱ χελιδόνες αἱ θαλάττιαι ὁμοίως· καὶ γὰρ αὗται πέτονται μετέωροι, οὐχ ἁπτόμεναι τῆς θαλάττης; Marc. S. ὠκυπέτεια χελιδών.

ἄκρον ἐπιψαύοντες ἁλὸς πόρον, ὅσσον ἰδέσθαι
ἄμφω νηχομένοισι καὶ ἱπταμένοισιν ὁμοῖοι.
Αἵδε μὲν ὥστε πόληες ἐν ἰχθύσιν, οἵδε θ' ὅμιλοι
κεκριμένοι γεγάασιν ἁλιπλάγκτοιο γενέθλης.
τῶν δ' οἱ μὲν πλάζονται ἀολλέες, αἰόλα φῦλα,
πώεσιν ἢ στρατιῇσιν ἐοικότες, οἵ τ' ἀγελαῖοι
κέκληνται· τοὶ δ' αὖτε κατὰ στίχας· οἱ δὲ λόχοισιν
εἴκελοι ἢ δεκάδεσσιν· ὁ δ' ἔρχεται οἶος ἀπ' ἄλλων
μουναδὸν ὁρμηθείς· περόωσι δὲ δίζυγες ἄλλοι·
οἱ δ' αὐτοῦ θαλάμῃσιν ἐν οἰκείῃσι μένουσι.
Χείματι μὲν δὴ πάντες ἀελλάων στροφάλιγγας
σμερδαλέας αὐτοῦ τε δυσηχέος οἴδματα πόντου
ἔξοχα δειμαίνουσιν· ἐπεὶ περιώσιον ἄλλων
ἰχθυόεντα γένεθλα φίλην πέφρικε θάλασσαν
μαινομένην· τότε δ' οἱ μὲν ἀμησάμενοι πτερύγεσσι
ψάμμον ὑποπτήσσουσιν ἀνάλκιδες· οἱ δ' ὑπὸ πέτραις
εἰλόμενοι δύνουσιν ἀολλέες· οἱ δὲ βάθιστα
ἐς πελάγη φεύγουσι κάτω μυχάτην ὑπὸ βύσσαν·
κεῖνα γὰρ οὔτε λίην προκυλίνδεται οὔθ' ὑπ' ἀήταις
πρυμνόθεν εἱλεῖται, διὰ δ' ἔσσυται οὔτις ἄελλα
ῥίζαν ἁλὸς νεάτην· μέγα δέ σφισι βένθος ἐρύκει

---

[a] A. 610 b 4 (list of ἀγελαῖοι), 488 a 3 ἀγελαῖα . . . καὶ τῶν πλωτῶν πολλὰ γένη τῶν ἰχθύων, οἷον οὓς καλοῦσι δρομάδας. *Cf.* χυτοί 543 a 1, ῥυάδες 534 a 27, etc.; Plin. ix. 56 vagantur gregatim fere cuiusque generis squamosi.

[b] Ael. ix. 53 ἁλῶνται δὲ ἄρα ἰχθῦς καὶ πλανῶνται οἱ μὲν ἀθρόοι, ὥσπερ οὖν ἀγέλαι θρεμμάτων ἢ τάξεις ὁπλιτῶν ἰοῦσαι κατὰ ἴλας καὶ φάλαγγας· οἱ δὲ ἐν κόσμῳ κατὰ στοῖχον ἔρχονται· οἱ δέ, φαίης ἂν αὐτοὺς εἶναι λόχους· ἠρίθμηνται δὲ εἰς δεκάδας ἄλλοι, . . . ἤδη δὲ νήχονται καὶ κατὰ ζεῦγός τινες· ἄλλοι δὲ οἰκουροῦσιν ἐν τοῖς φωλεοῖς καὶ ἐνταυθοῖ καταζῶσιν. μοναδικά A. 488 a 1, etc. μονήρης, used by Athen. (*e.g.* 301 c) in quoting Aristotle, does not occur in our texts.

fly close to the very sea, grazing the surface of the water, seeming, to behold, as if they swam at once and flew.

These are the city-states, as it were, among fishes, these the various communities of the sea-wandering race. And of these some roam all together in their various tribes, like flocks of sheep or like armies, and these are called shoaling fishes[a]; others again move in files; others like platoons or sections of ten[b]; another goes on his own course all alone[c] and apart from others; yet others travel in pairs[c]; while some again remain at home[d] in their own lairs.

In winter[e] all dread exceedingly the terrible eddies of the storm-winds and the billows of the evil-sounding sea itself: for beyond all else the fishy tribes abhor their beloved sea when it rages. Then do some with their fins scrape the sand[f] together and skulk like cowards beneath it, others creep below the rocks[g] where they huddle together, others flee down to the nether depths of the deepest[h] seas; for those seas neither roll overmuch nor are stirred to the bottom by the winds and no blast penetrates the nether foundation of the sea; and

[c] A. 610 b 7 *ἔνιά ἐστιν οὐ μόνον ἀγελαῖα ἀλλὰ καὶ σύζυγα.*

[d] *ἐπιδημητικά* opp. to *ἐκτοπιστικά* A. 488 a 13.

[e] *vv.* 446-462 are paraphrased Ael. ix. 57. *Cf.* A. 599 b 2 *φωλοῦσι δὲ πολλοὶ καὶ τῶν ἰχθύων . . . τοῦ χειμῶνος*; Plin. ix. 57 Praegelidam hiemem omnes sentiunt . . . itaque his mensibus iacent speluncis conditi.

[f] A. 599 b 26 *φωλεῖ δὲ τὰ μὲν ἐν τῇ ἄμμῳ*; 537 a 25 *οἱ δὲ πλατεῖς ἐν τῇ ἄμμῳ.*

[g] A. 537 a 23 *τὰ δὲ πλεῖστα καθεύδουσι τῆς γῆς ἢ τῆς ἄμμου ἢ λίθου τινὸς ἐχόμενοι ἐν τῷ βυθῷ ἢ ἀποκρύψαντες ὑπὸ πέτραν ἢ θῖνα ἑαυτούς.*

[h] A. 599 b 8 *φωλοῦσι δὲ καὶ οἱ θύννοι τοῦ χειμῶνος ἐν τοῖς βαθέσιν.*

ῥιγεδανὰς ὀδύνας καὶ ἀπηνέα χείματος ὁρμήν.
ἀλλ᾽ ὁπότ᾽ ἀνθεμόεσσαι ἐπὶ χθονὸς εἴαρος ὧραι
πορφύρεον γελάσωσιν, ἀναπνεύσῃ δὲ θάλασσα
χείματος εὐδιόωσα γαληναίη τε γένηται
ἤπια κυμαίνουσα, τότ᾽ ἰχθύες ἄλλοθεν ἄλλοι
πανσυδίῃ φοιτῶσι γεγηθότες ἐγγύθι γαίης.
ὡς δὲ πολυρραίσταο νέφος πολέμοιο φυγοῦσα
ὀλβίη ἀθανάτοισι φίλη πόλις, ἥν ῥά τε δηρὸν
δυσμενέων πάγχαλκος ἐπεπλήμμυρε θύελλα,
ὀψὲ δ᾽ ἀπολλήξασα καὶ ἀμπνεύσασα μόθοιο
ἀσπασίως γάνυταί τε καὶ εἰρήνης καμάτοισι
τέρπεται ἁρπαλέοισι καὶ εὔδιος εἰλαπινάζει,
ἀνδρῶν τε πλήθουσα χοροιτυπίης τε γυναικῶν·
ὧς οἵ λευγαλέους τε πόνους καὶ φρῖκα θαλάσσης
ἀσπασίως προφυγόντες, ὑπεὶρ ἅλα καγχαλόωντες,
θρώσκοντες θύνουσι χοροιτυπέουσιν ὁμοῖοι.
εἴαρι δὲ γλυκὺς οἶστρος ἀναγκαίης Ἀφροδίτης
καὶ γάμοι ἡβώωσι καὶ ἀλλήλων φιλότητες
πᾶσιν, ὅσοι γαῖάν τε φερέσβιον οἵ τ᾽ ἀνὰ κόλπους
ἠέρος οἵ τ᾽ ἀνὰ πόντον ἐριβρύχην δονέονται.
εἴαρι δὲ πλεῖστον νεπόδων γένος Εἰλείθυιαι
ᾠοφόρων παύουσι βαρυνομένων ὠδίνων.
αἱ μὲν γὰρ γενεῆς κεχρημέναι ἠδὲ τόκοιο
θήλεες ἐν ψαμάθοισιν ἀποθλίβουσιν ἀραιὰς
γαστέρας· οὐ γὰρ ῥεῖα διΐσταται, ἀλλ᾽ ἐνέχονται
ᾠὰ μετ᾽ ἀλλήλοισιν ἀρηρότα νηδύος εἴσω,
φύρδην συμπεφυῶτα· τὰ δ᾽ ἀθρόα πῶς κε τέκοιεν;
στεινόμεναι δ᾽ ὀδύνῃσι μόγις κρίνουσι γενέθλην.
ὡς οὐ ῥηϊδίην γενεὴν οὐδ᾽ ἰχθύσι Μοῖραι
ὤπασαν, οὐδ᾽ ἄρα μοῦνον ἐπιχθονίῃσι γυναιξὶν
ἄλγεα, πάντῃ δ᾽ εἰσὶν ἐπαχθέες Εἰλείθυιαι.
ἄρσενες αὖτ᾽ ἄλλοι μὲν ἐπ᾽ ἰχθύσι κῆρας ἄγοντες

the great depth protects the fishes from the pangs of cold and the cruel assault of winter. But when the flowery hours of spring smile brightly on the earth and with fine weather the sea has respite from winter and there is calm water with a gentle swell, then from this quarter and from that the fishes come trooping joyfully nigh the land. As when, happily escaped from the cloud of ruinous war, some city dear to the deathless gods, which long time the brazen storm of foemen beset as with a flood, at last ceases gladly from strife and recovers her breath; she rejoices and takes her delight in the eager labours of peace and in calm weather holds festival, full of the dancing of men and women; even so the fishes, gladly escaped from sorrowful affliction and rough seas, rush exultant over the wave, leaping like dancers. And in spring the sweet goad of compelling desire and mating and mutual love are in season among all that move upon the fruitful earth and in the folds of air and in the bellowing sea. In spring[a] the Birth-goddesses deliver most part of the fishes from the heavy travail of spawning. The female, in their desire to give birth and to bring forth, rub their tender bellies in the sand; for the eggs do not part easily but are closely entangled together within the belly, confusedly cohering—how could they bring forth the mass?—and, painfully straitened, they with difficulty pass their spawn. So not even on the fishes have the Fates bestowed easy birth, and not alone to women upon earth are there pains, but everywhere the birth-pangs are grievous. As for the males, on the other hand, some hasten to approach

[a] A. 570 b 11 *οἱ δὲ τόκοι γίνονται τοῖς μὲν ῥυάσιν τοῦ ἔαρος, καὶ τοῖς πλείστοις δὲ περὶ τὴν ἐαρινὴν ἰσημερίαν.* *Cf.* Plin. ix. 162.

δαιτυμόνες ῥηγμῖσιν ἐπειγόμενοι πελάουσιν·
ἄλλοι δ' αὖ μετόπισθε διωκόμενοι προθέουσι
θηλυτέραις ἀγέλῃσιν, ἐπεὶ φιλότητος ἔρωτι
ἑλκόμεναι σπεύδουσι μετ' ἄρσενας ἀσχέτῳ ὁρμῇ.
ἔνθ' οἱ μὲν σφετέρας ἐπὶ γαστέρας ἀλλήλοισι
τριβόμενοι θορὸν ὑγρὸν ἀπορραίνουσιν ὄπισθεν,
αἱ δ' οἴστρῳ μεμαυῖαι ἐπαΐγδην στομάτεσσι
κάπτουσιν· τοίῳ δὲ γάμῳ πλήθουσι γόνοιο.
πλεῖστος μὲν νόμος οὗτος ἐν ἰχθύσιν· οἱ δὲ καὶ εὐνὰς
καὶ θαλάμους ἀλόχους τε διακριδὸν ἀμφὶς ἔχουσι
ζευξάμενοι· πολλὴ γὰρ ἐν ἰχθύσιν ἔστ' Ἀφροδίτη
Οἶστρός τε Ζῆλός τε, βαρὺς θεός, ὅσσα τε τίκτει
θερμὸς Ἔρως, ὅτε λάβρον ἐνὶ φρεσὶ κῶμον ὀρίνει.
πολλοὶ δ' ἀλλήλοισι διασταδὸν εἵνεκεν εὐνῆς
μάρνανται, μνηστῆρσιν ἐοικότες, οἳ περὶ νύμφην
πολλοὶ ἀγειρόμενοι καὶ ὁμοίϊοι ἀντιφέρονται
ὄλβῳ τ' ἀγλαΐῃ τε· τὰ δ' ἰχθύσιν οὐ παρέασιν,
ἀλλ' ἀλκὴ γένυές τε καὶ ἔνδοθι κάρχαρον ἕρκος,
τοῖσιν ἀεθλεύουσι καὶ ἐς γάμον ὁπλίζονται·
τοῖσι δ' ὅ κεν προβάληται, ὁμοῦ γάμον εὕρατο νίκῃ.
καὶ τοὶ μὲν πλεόνεσσιν ὁμευναίαις ἀλόχοισι
τέρπονται, σάργων τε γένος καὶ κόσσυφος αἴθων·
τοὶ δὲ μίαν στέργουσι καὶ ἀμφιέπουσιν ἄκοιτιν,
κάνθαροι αἰτναῖοί τε, καὶ οὐ πλεόνεσσι γάνυνται.

---

[a] A. 541 a 14 *περὶ μὲν γὰρ τὴν τῆς ὀχείας ὥραν αἱ θήλειαι τοῖς ἄρρεσιν ἑπόμεναι . . . κόπτουσιν ὑπὸ τὴν γαστέρα τοῖς στόμασιν, οἱ δὲ θᾶττον προΐενται (τὸν θορὸν) καὶ μᾶλλον*; Plin. ix. 157 femina piscis coitus tempore marem sequitur ventrem eius rostro pulsans.

[b] Plin. *l.c.* pisces attritu ventrium coeunt; A. *De gen.* 717 b 36 *οἱ μὲν γὰρ ἰχθύες ὀχεύουσι παραπίπτοντες.*

the shores, bringing doom to other fishes on which they feast; others again run before the shoals of females by whom they are pursued, since drawn by the passion of desire the females haste after the males [a] with rush incontinent. Then the males, rubbing belly against belly,[b] discharge behind them the moist milt; and the females, goaded by desire, rush to gobble [c] it up with their mouths; by such mating they are filled with roe. This is the most common custom among fishes, but others there are which have separate and apart their own beds and bridal chambers and wedded wives; for there is much Passion among fishes and Desire and Jealousy, that grievous god, and all that hot Love brings forth, when he stirs fierce tumult in the heart. Many quarrel with one another and fight over a mate, like unto wooers who about a bride gather many and well-matched and contend in wealth and beauty. These weapons the fish have not, but strength and jaws and sawlike teeth within: with these they enter the lists and arm themselves to win a mate; and he who excels with these, wins at once both victory and mate. And some delight in more mates than one to share their bed, to wit, the race of the Sargue [d] and the dusky Merle [e]; others love and attend a single mate, as the Black Sea-bream [f] and the Aetnaeus [g] and delight not in more than one.

[c] A. 541 a 11 *ἡ δὲ τῶν ᾠοτόκων ἰχθύων ὀχεία ἧττον γίνεται κατάδηλος· διόπερ οἱ πλεῖστοι νομίζουσι πληροῦσθαι τὰ θήλεα τῶν ἀρρένων ἀνακάπτοντα τὸν θορόν.*

[d] *C.* ii. 433 n. [e] *H.* iv. 173 n. [f] *H.* iii. 338 n.

[g] Ael. i. 13 *ὁ γοῦν αἰτναῖος οὕτω λεγόμενος, ἐπὰν τῇ ἑαυτοῦ συννόμῳ οἱονεὶ γαμέτῃ τινὶ συνδυασθεὶς κληρώσηται τὸ λέχος, ἄλλης οὐχ ἅπτεται*; *cf.* Phil. 53. Not identified.

Ἀλλ' οὐκ ἐγχελύεσσιν ὁμοίϊον οὔτε χελώναις
οὔτ' οὖν πουλυπόδεσσι γάμου τέλος οὔτε κελαινῇ
μυραίνῃ, λεχέων δὲ παράτροπον αἶσαν ἔχουσιν·
αἱ μὲν γὰρ σπειρηδὸν ἐν ἀλλήλῃσι χυθεῖσαι
ἐγχέλυες δέμας ὑγρὸν ἀναστρωφῶσι θαμειαὶ
πλεγνύμεναι, τάων δὲ κατείβεται εἴκελος ἀφρῷ
ἰχώρ, ἐν ψαμάθοις τε καλύπτεται· ἡ δέ μιν ἰλὺς
δεξαμένη κυέει τε καὶ ἐγχελύων τέκεν ὁλκούς.
τοίη καὶ γόγγροισιν ὀλισθηροῖσι γενέθλη.
Αἱ δὲ μέγα τρομέουσι καὶ ἐχθαίρουσι χελῶναι
ὃν γάμον· οὐ γὰρ τῇσιν ἐφίμερος οἷα καὶ ἄλλοις
τερπωλὴ λεχέων, πολὺ δὲ πλέον ἄλγος ἔχουσι·
σκληρὸν γὰρ μάλα κέντρον ἐν ἄρσεσιν εἰς Ἀφροδίτην,
ὀστέον οὐκ ἐπιεικτόν, ἀτερπέϊ θήγεται εὐνῇ.
τοὔνεκα μάρνανταί τε παλιγνάμπτοισί τ' ὀδοῦσιν
ἀλλήλους δάπτουσιν, ὅτε σχεδὸν ἀντιάσωσιν,
αἱ μὲν ἀλευόμεναι τρηχὺν γάμον, οἱ δ' ἀεκουσῶν
εὐνῆς ἱμείροντες ἑκούσιοι, εἰσόκεν ἀλκῇ
νικήσας ζεύξῃ μιν ἀναγκαίῃ φιλότητι,
ἠΰτε ληϊδίην, πολέμου γέρας. εἴκελα δ' εὐνῆς
ἔργα κυσὶ χθονίοισι καὶ εἰναλίῃσι χελώναις·
εἴκελα καὶ φώκῃσιν· ἐπεὶ μάλα δηρὸν ἕκαστοι
ἐξόπιθεν συνέχονται, ἀρηρότες ἠΰτε δεσμῷ.
Πουλύποδος δ' ὀλοοί τε γάμοι καὶ πικρὸς ὄλεθρος
συμφέρεται, ξυνὸν δὲ τέλος θανάτοιο καὶ εὐνῆς·

[a] *Anguilla vulgaris*, M.G. χέλυ. For generation of, A. 570 a 3 ff. αἱ δ' ἐγχέλυς οὔτ' ἐξ ὀχείας γίνονται οὔτ' ᾠοτοκοῦσιν, οὐδ' ἐλήφθη πώποτε οὔτε θορὸν ἔχουσα οὐδεμία οὔτ' ᾠά; Plin. ix. 160 anguillae atterunt se scopulis; ea strigmenta vivescunt, nec alia est earum procreatio.

[b] Plin. ix. 73 longis et lubricis ut anguillis et congris.

[c] Ael. xv. 19; Plin. ix. 37 Quidam oculis spectandoque ova foveri ab his putant, feminas coitum fugere, donec mas

But neither Eels [a] nor Turtles nor Poulpes effect their mating in this fashion, nor the dark Muraena, but they have an unusual mode of union. Eels coil round one another and closely entwined they writhe their moist bodies, and from them a fluid like foam flows and is covered by the sands; and the mud receives it and conceives, and gives birth to the trailing Eel. Such also is the generation of the slippery [b] Conger.

The Turtles greatly fear and hate their mating; [c] for they have no delight or pleasure in union, as other creatures have, but they have far more pain. For the organ of the male is very hard, an unyielding bone, which is whetted in a joyless union. Therefore they fight and rend each other with their bent teeth, when they come together: the females seeking to avoid the rough mating, the males eager to mate, willing bridegrooms of unwilling brides; until the male by his strength prevails and makes her perforce his mate, like a captive bride, the prize of war. The mating of Dogs on land is similar to that of Turtles in the sea: similar also is that of Seals [d]; for all of those remain a long time coupled rearwards, fast bound as by a chain.

For the Poulpe [e] his deadly mating goes with bitter destruction and union consummated is con-

festucam aliquam imponat aversae. For mode of mating, A. 540 a 28 *τὰ μὲν γὰρ ἐπιβαίνοντα . . . οἷον χελώνη καὶ ἡ θαλαττία καὶ ἡ χερσαία*; Plin. ix. 158 Testudines in coitu superveniunt.

[d] A. 540 a 23 *ὀχεύεται δὲ καὶ ἡ φώκη καθάπερ τὰ ὀπισθουρητικὰ τῶν ζῴων καὶ συνέχονται ἐν τῃ ὀχείᾳ πολὺν χρόνον, ὥσπερ καὶ αἱ κύνες· ἔχουσι δὲ τὸ αἰδοῖον μέγα οἱ ἄρρενες*; Plin. ix. 41 (vitulus marinus) in coitu canum modo cohaeret.

[e] This passage is paraphrased Ael. vi. 28. *Cf.* A. 622 a 14 ff.; Athen. 316 c ff.

οὐ γὰρ πρὶν φιλότητος ἀπίσχεται οὐδ' ἀπολήγει,
πρίν μιν ἀπὸ μελέων προλίπῃ σθένος ἀδρανέοντα,
αὐτὸς δ' ἐν ψαμάθοισι πεσὼν ἀμενηνὸς ὄληται·
πάντες γάρ μιν ἔδουσιν, ὅσοι σχεδὸν ἀντιάσωσι,
καρκινάδες δειλαὶ καὶ καρκίνοι ἠδὲ καὶ ἄλλοι
ἰχθύες, οὓς πάρος αὐτὸς ἐδαίνυτο ῥεῖα μεθέρπων·
τοῖς ὑπὸ καὶ ζωός περ ἐὼν ἔτι κείμενος αὔτως,
οὐδὲν ἀμυνόμενος, δαιτρεύεται, ὄφρα θάνῃσι.
τοίῳ δυστερπεῖ φιλοτησίῳ ὄλλυτ' ὀλέθρῳ.
ὣς δ' αὔτως καὶ θῆλυς ὑπ' ὠδίνων μογέουσα
ὄλλυται· οὐ γὰρ τῇσιν ἀποκριδὸν οἷα καὶ ἄλλοις
ὠὰ διαθρώσκουσιν, ἀρηρότα δ' ἀλλήλοισι
βοτρυδὸν στεινοῖο μόγις διανίσσεται αὐλοῦ.
τοὔνεκα καὶ λυκάβαντος ὑπέρτερον οὔποτε μέτρον
πουλύποδες ζώουσιν· ἀποφθινύθουσι γὰρ αἰεὶ
αἰνοτάτοισι γάμοισι καὶ αἰνοτάτοισι τόκοισιν.
Ἀμφὶ δὲ μυραίνης φάτις ἔρχεται οὐκ ἀΐδηλος,
ὥς μιν ὄφις γαμέει τε καὶ ἐξ ἁλὸς ἔρχεται αὐτὴ
πρόφρων, ἱμείρουσα παρ' ἱμείροντα γάμοιο.
ἤτοι ὁ μὲν φλογέῃ τεθοωμένος ἔνδοθι λύσσῃ
μαίνεται εἰς φιλότητα καὶ ἐγγύθι σύρεται ἀκτῆς
πικρὸς ἔχις· τάχα δὲ γλαφυρὴν ἐσκέψατο πέτρην,
τῇ δ' ἔνι λοίγιον ἰὸν ἀπήμεσε, πάντα δ' ὀδόντων

---

[a] A. 622 a 25 ὅταν δὲ τὰ ᾠὰ ἐκτέκωσιν, οὕτω καταγηράσκειν καὶ ἀσθενεῖς γίνεσθαι ἀμφοτέρους φασὶν ὥστε ὑπὸ τῶν ἰχθυδίων κατεσθίεσθαι.

[b] A. 622 a 17 αἱ δὲ θήλειαι μετὰ τὸν τόκον . . . γίνονται μωραί κτλ.

[c] A. 544 a 8 τίκτει τὸ ᾠὸν καθάπερ βοστρύχιον ; 549 b 32 ὅμοιον βοστρυχίοις οἰνάνθης ; Athen. 316 e τίκτει ᾠὰ βοτρυδόν ; Plin. ix. 163 Polypi . . . pariunt vere ova tortili vibrata pampino.

[d] A. 550 b 13 ἔστι δὲ καὶ ὁ τεῦθος καὶ ἡ σηπία βραχύβιον. οὐ γὰρ διετίζουσιν, . . . ὁμοίως δὲ καὶ οἱ πολύποδες. *Cf.* A. 622 a 22 ; Athen. 323 ; Ael. *l.c.* ; Plin. ix. 93.

summated death: for he does not abstain or cease from his desire, until he is spent and strength forsakes his limbs and he himself falls exhausted on the sand and perishes. For all that come nigh devour[a] him—the timid Hermit-crab and the Crabs and other fishes which he himself formerly was wont to banquet on, easily stealing upon them; by these he is now devoured, still alive but lying helplessly, and making no resistance, until he dies. By such a death, the sad fruit of desire, he perishes. And even so the female[b] likewise perishes, exhausted by the travail of birth. For their eggs do not issue forth separately, as with other fishes, but, clustered together like grapes,[c] they pass with difficulty through the narrow channel. Wherefore the Poulpes never live beyond the measure of a year[d]; for always they perish by dreadest mating and dreadest travail of birth.

Touching the Muraena there is a not obscure report[e] that a Serpent mates with her, and that the Muraena herself comes forth from the sea willingly eager mate to eager mate. The bitter Serpent, whetted by the fiery passion within him, is frenzied for mating and drags himself nigh the shore; and anon he espies a hollow rock and therein vomits forth

[e] Plin. ix. 76 (Murenas) in sicca litora elapsas vulgu coitu serpentium impleri putat. Oppian's lines are para phrased Ael. i. 50, ix. 66. *Cf.* Nicand. *T.* 823 ff. (with schol. *ad loc.*), whose lines are quoted by Athen. 312 d, where it is said that the story was rejected by Andreas but accepted by Sostratus; Phil. 81. Hence the point o the lines of Matron the parodist *ap.* Athen. 136 b *μύραιναν δ' ἐπέθηκε φέρων . . . | ζώνην θ' ἣν φορέεσκεν . . . | εἰς λέχος ἡνίκ' ἔβαινε Δρακοντιάδῃ μεγαθύμῳ.* For Murena coming ashore, A. 543 a 28; Plin. ix. 73.

ἔπτυσε πευκεδανόν, ζαμενῆ χόλον, ὄλβον ὀλέθρου,
ὄφρα γάμῳ πρηῢς τε καὶ εὔδιος ἀντιάσειε.
στὰς δ' ἄρ' ἐπὶ ῥηγμῖνος ἑὸν νόμον ἐρροίζησε
κικλήσκων φιλότητα· θοῶς δ' ἐσάκουσε κελαινὴ
ἰϋγὴν μύραινα καὶ ἔσσυτο θᾶσσον ὀϊστοῦ.
ἡ μὲν ἄρ' ἐκ πόντοιο τιταίνεται, αὐτὰρ ὁ πόντου
ἐκ γαίης πολιοῖσιν ἐπεμβαίνει ῥοθίοισιν·
ἄμφω δ' ἀλλήλοισιν ὁμιλῆσαι μεμαῶτε
συμπεσέτην, ἔχιος δὲ κάρη κατέδεκτο χανοῦσα
νύμφη φυσιόωσα· γάμῳ δ' ἐπιγηθήσαντες
ἡ μὲν ἁλὸς πάλιν εἶσι μετ' ἤθεα, τὸν δ' ἐπὶ χέρσον
ὁλκὸς ἄγει, κρυερὸν δὲ πάλιν μεταχεύεται ἰὸν
λάπτων, ὃν πάρος ἧκε καὶ ἐξήφυσσεν ὀδόντων.
ἢν δ' ἄρα μή τι κίχῃ κεῖνον χόλον, ὅνπερ ὁδίτης,
ἀτρεκέως ἐσιδών μιν, ἀπέκλυσεν ὕδατι λάβρῳ,
αὐτὰρ ὅ γ' ἀσχαλόων ῥίπτει δέμας, εἰσόκε μοῖραν
λευγαλέοιο λάβῃσιν ἀνωΐστου θανάτοιο,
αἰδόμενος, ὅτ' ἄναλκις ὅπλων γένεθ' οἷς ἐπεποίθει,
ἔμμεν' ὄφις, πέτρῃ δὲ συνώλεσε καὶ δέμας ἰῷ.
Δελφῖνες δ' ἄνδρεσσιν ὁμῶς γάμον ἐντύνονται
μήδεά τ' ἀνδρομέοισι πανείκελα καρτύνονται·
οὐδ' αἰεὶ προφανὴς πόρος ἄρσενος, ἀλλά οἱ εἴσω
κέκρυπται, λεχέων δὲ κατὰ χρέος ἕλκεται ἔξω.
Τοῖαι μὲν φιλότητες ἐν ἰχθύσιν ἠδὲ καὶ εὐναί.
ἄλλος δ' ἀλλοίῃ λεχέων ἱμείρεται ὥρῃ,
καὶ γενεὴν προφέρει· τοῖς μὲν θέρος, οἷσι δὲ χεῖμα,
τοῖς δ' ἔαρ ἢ φθινύθουσα τόκον προὔφηνεν ὀπώρη.
καὶ τοὶ μὲν λυκάβαντι μίαν μογέουσι γενέθλην

[a] A. 540 b 22; *De gen.* 756 b 1; Plin. ix. 74.
[b] A. 570 a 25, 570 b 11 ff., 543 b 18 ff.; Plin. ix. 162.

his baneful venom, the fierce bile of his teeth, a deadly store, that he may be mild and serene to meet his bride. Standing on the shore he utters his hissing note, his mating call ; and the dusky Muraena quickly hears his cry and speeds swifter than an arrow. She stretches her from the sea, he from the land treads the grey surf, and, eager to mate with one another, the two embrace, and the panting bride receives with open mouth the Serpent's head. Then, exulting over their union, she goes back again to her haunts in the sea, while he makes his trailing way to the land, where he takes in again his venom, lapping up that which before he shed and discharged from his teeth. But if he find not that bile—which some wayfarer, seeing it for what it is, has washed away with torrents of water—then indignant he dashes his body, till he finds the doom of a sad and unthought-of death, ashamed to be a Serpent when he is left defenceless of the weapons in which he trusted, and on the rock with his lost venom he loses his life.

Dolphins [a] mate after the manner of men, and the organs with which they are equipped are quite human-like ; the male organ is not always visible but is hidden within and extended on occasion of mating.

Such are the loves and mating among fishes. And others at other season [b] they desire to mate and bring forth their young ; for some summer, for some winter, for others spring or waning autumn brings birth. And some—the greatest part—are in travail of a single brood a year, but the Basse is twice [c]

[c] A. 542 b 32 *ὁμοίως δὲ καὶ τῶν ἰχθύων οἱ πλεῖστοι ἅπαξ (τίκτουσιν) οἷον οἱ χυτοί . . . πλὴν ὁ λάβραξ· οὗτος δὲ δὶς τούτων μόνος.* *Cf.* 567 b 18 ; Plin. ix. 162 ; Ael. x. 2 ; Athen. 310 f.

οἱ πλεῖστοι, λάβραξ δὲ δὶς ἄχθεται Εἰλειθυίαις·
τρίγλαι δὲ τριγόνοισιν ἐπώνυμοί εἰσι γονῇσι·
σκορπίος αὖ τετόρεσσι φέρει βέλος ὠδίνεσσι·
πέντε δὲ κυπρίνοισι γοναὶ μούνοισιν ἔασιν·
οἵου δ' οὔποτέ φασι γένος φράσσασθαι ὀνίσκου,
ἀλλ' ἔτι τοῦτ' ἀΐδηλον ἐν ἀνθρώποισι τέτυκται.

Εὖτ' ἂν δ' εἰαρινοῖο περιπλήθωσι γόνοιο
ἰχθύες ᾠοτόκοι, τοὶ μὲν κατὰ χῶρον ἕκαστοι
εὔκηλοι μίμνουσιν ἐνὶ σφετέροισι δόμοισι·
πολλοὶ δ' ἀγρόμενοι ξυνὴν ὁδὸν ὁρμώωνται
Εὔξεινον μετὰ πόντον, ἵν' αὐτόθι τέκνα τέκωνται.
κεῖνος γὰρ πάσης γλυκερώτερος Ἀμφιτρίτης
κόλπος, ἀπειρεσίοισι καὶ εὐΰδροις ποταμοῖσιν
ἀρδόμενος, μαλακαὶ δὲ πολυψάμαθοί τ' ἐπιωγαί·
ἐν δέ οἱ εὐφυέες τε νομαὶ καὶ ἀκύμονες ἀκταὶ
πέτραι τε γλαφυραὶ καὶ χηραμοὶ ἰλυόεντες
ἄκραι τε σκιεραὶ καὶ ὅσ' ἰχθύσι φίλτατ' ἔασιν·
ἐν δέ οἱ οὔτε τι κῆτος ἀνάρσιον οὔτε τι πῆμα
ἐντρέφεται νεπόδεσσιν ὀλέθριον οὐδὲ μὲν ὅσσοι
δυσμενέες γεγάασιν ἐπ' ἰχθύσι βαιοτέροισιν

---

[a] A. 543 a 5 ἡ δὲ τρίγλη μόνη τρίς. Oppian derives τρίγλη from τρίς, *cf.* Ael. x. 2 τρίγλην δὲ καὶ τρὶς κύειν κατηγορεῖ, φασί, καὶ τὸ ὄνομα. *Cf.* ix. 51; Phil. 116; Athen. 334 d.

[b] But A. 543 a 7 ὁ σκορπίος τίκτει δίς; Plin. ix. 162 scorpaenae bis (anno pariunt); Athen. 320 e.

[c] A. 568 a 16 τίκτουσι δ' ἐν τῇ καθηκούσῃ ὥρᾳ κυπρῖνος μὲν πεντάκις ἢ ἑξάκις· ποιεῖται δὲ τὸν τόκον μάλιστα ἐπὶ τοῖς ἄστροις.

burdened by the pangs of birth; the Red Mullet gets its name Trigla from its triple brood[a]; the Scorpion again endures the pang of four labours;[b] the Carps alone bear five times;[c] and the Oniscus[d] is the only fish, they say, whose breeding no one has ever remarked, but that is still a mystery among men.

When in spring the oviparous fishes are full of roe, some of them remain quietly in their homes, each tribe in its own place; but many gather together and pursue a common path to the Euxine Sea,[e] that there they may bring forth their brood. For that gulf is the sweetest of all the sea, watered as it is by infinite rivers of abundant water; and it has soft and sandy bays; therein are goodly feeding-grounds and waveless shores and caverned rocks and silty clefts and shady headlands and all that fish most love; but no fierce Sea-monster inhabits there nor any deadly bane of the finny race nor any of those which prey upon the smaller fishes—no coiling

[d] Introd. p. lxiv.

[e] Black Sea. A. 598 a 30 *εἰσπλέουσι δ' εἰς τὸν Πόντον διά τε τὴν τροφήν (ἡ γὰρ νομὴ καὶ πλείων καὶ βελτίων διὰ τὸ πότιμον, καὶ τὰ θηρία δὲ τὰ μεγάλα ἐλάττω· ἔξω γὰρ δελφῖνος καὶ φωκαίνης* [Porpoise] *οὐδέν ἐστιν ἐν τῷ Πόντῳ καὶ ὁ δελφὶς μικρός· ἔξω δ' εὐθὺς προελθόντι μεγάλοι), διά τε δὴ τὴν τροφὴν εἰσπλέουσι καὶ διὰ τὸν τόκον· τόποι γάρ εἰσιν ἐπιτήδειοι ἐντίκτειν καὶ τὸ πότιμον καὶ τὸ γλυκύτερον ὕδωρ ἐκτρέφει τὰ κυήματα.* *Cf.* Ael. iv. 4, ix. 59; Plut. *Mor.* 981 D; Plin. ix. 49 f.; Arr. *Peripl. Eux. Pont.* c. viii.; A. 567 b 15 *ἐν τῷ Πόντῳ περὶ τὸν Θερμώδοντα ποταμὸν οἱ πλεῖστοι τίκτουσιν· νήνεμος γὰρ ὁ τόπος καὶ ἀλεεινὸς καὶ ἔχων ὕδατα γλυκέα*: A. *Meteor.* 354 a 16 *πλείους γὰρ εἰς τὸν Εὔξεινον ῥέουσι ποταμοὶ καὶ τὴν Μαιῶτιν ἢ τὴν πολλαπλασίαν χώραν αὐτῆς.*

ὁλκοὶ πουλυπόδων οὐδ' ἀστακοὶ οὐδὲ πάγουροι·
παῦροι μὲν δελφῖνες, ἀκιδνότεροι δὲ καὶ αὐτοὶ
κητείης γενεῆς καὶ ἀκήδεες ἐννεμέθονται.
τοὔνεκεν ἰχθύσι κεῖνο πέλει κεχαρισμένον ὕδωρ
ἐκπάγλως καὶ πολλὸν ἐπισπεύδουσι νέεσθαι.
στέλλονται δ' ἅμα πάντες ὁμιλαδόν, ἄλλοθεν ἄλλος
εἰς ἓν ἀγειρόμενοι, μία δέ σφισι πᾶσι κέλευθος
πομπή τε ῥιπή τε καὶ αὖ παλινόστιμος ὁρμή.
Θρηΐκιον δ' ἀνύουσι Βοὸς Πόρον αἰολόφυλοι
ἑσμοὶ Βεβρυκίην τε παρὲξ ἅλα καὶ στόμα Πόντου
στεινὸν ἀμειβόμενοι δολιχὸν δρόμον Ἀμφιτρίτης.
ὡς δ' ὅτ' ἀπ' Αἰθιόπων τε καὶ Αἰγύπτοιο ῥοάων
ὑψιπετὴς γεράνων χορὸς ἔρχεται ἠεροφώνων,
Ἄτλαντος νιφόεντα πάγον καὶ χεῖμα φυγοῦσαι

---

[a] A. 606 a 10 ἐν μὲν τῷ Πόντῳ οὔτε τὰ μαλάκια γίνεται οὔτε τὰ ὀστρακόδερμα εἰ μὴ ἔν τισι τόποις ὀλίγα. *Cf.* Plin. ix. 52; Ael. xvii. 10; Athen. 317 f ἐν δὲ τῷ περὶ τῶν κατὰ τόπους διαφορῶν ὁ Θεόφραστος πολύποδας οὐ γίνεσθαί φησιν περὶ Ἑλλήσποντον. ψυχρὰ γὰρ ἡ θάλασσα αὕτη καὶ ἧττον ἁλμυρά, ταῦτα δ' ἀμφότερα πολέμια πολύποδι; E. Forbes, *N.H. of the European Seas*, p. 203, "The deficiencies in the Black Sea fauna are remarkable. All those classes of Mollusca which, as we have seen, are but poorly represented in the Eastern Mediterranean as compared with the Western, are either here altogether wanting, or are of rarest occurrence, such as Cephalopods, Pteropods, and Nudibranchs. Echinoderms and Zoophytes are absent. The composition of the water is inimical to all these forms."

[b] πόρον· ἤγουν τὸν Ἑλλήσποντον schol., but the reference can hardly be other than to the strait of Byzantium (Constantinople) which connects the Propontis (Sea of Marmora) with the Euxine (Black Sea) and is regularly called the Thracian Bosporus: Strabo 125 ἐκδίδωσι δ' αὕτη (ἡ Μαιῶτις λίμνη) μὲν εἰς Πόντον κατὰ τὸν Κιμμερικὸν καλούμενον Βόσπορον (Strait of Kertch), οὗτος δὲ κατὰ τὸν Θρᾴκιον εἰς τὴν Προποντίδα· τὸ γὰρ Βυζαντιακὸν στόμα οὕτω καλοῦσι Θρᾴκιον Βόσπορον, ὃ

Poulpe nor Lobster nor Crab [a]; Dolphins, indeed, dwell there but few, and feebler even these than the Sea-monster breed and harmless. Wherefore to fishes that water is pleasant exceedingly and they greatly haste to come to it. All together they set forth in company, gathering to one place from their several haunts, and all have one path, one voyage, one course, even as again all have the same impulse of return. And the swarms of various tribe make the Thracian Ford of the Cow,[b] past the Bebrycian Sea [c] and the narrow mouth [d] of the Pontus traversing a long course of the ocean. And as when [e] from the Ethiopians and the streams of Egypt there comes the high-flying [f] choir of clanging Cranes,[g] fleeing from winter and the snowy Mount of Atlas [h] and the weak

τετραστάδιόν ἐστιν. *Cf.* Strab. 319, 566; Dion. P. 140 Θρηικίου στόμα Βοσπόρου, ὅν πάρος Ἰὼ | Ἥρης ἐννεσίῃσιν ἐνήξατο πόρτις ἐοῦσα. ἀνύουσι: Stat. *T.* vii. 439 Taurus init *fecitque vadum.*

[c] Sea of Marmora. The Bebryces are located in Mysia or eastward to Chalcedon. Dion. P. 805 Βέβρυκες δ' ἐπὶ τοῖσι καὶ οὔρεα Μυσίδος αἴης; Strab. 541.

[d] Dion. P. 142 στεινότατος δὴ κεῖνος ἁπάντων ἔπλετο πορθμὸς | τῶν ἄλλων οἵ τ' εἰσὶ περικλύστοιο θαλάσσης; Arr. *Peripl. Eux. Pont.* xii. 2 καὶ ἔστι στενότατον ταύτῃ τὸ στόμα τοῦ Πόντου καλούμενον, καθ' ὅτι εἰσβάλλει ἐς τὴν Προποντίδα.

[e] Hom. *Il.* iii. 3 ff. ἠύτε περ κλαγγὴ γεράνων πέλει οὐρανόθι πρό, | οἵ τ' ἐπεὶ οὖν χειμῶνα φύγον καὶ ἀθέσφατον ὄμβρον, | κλαγγῇ ταί γε πέτονται ἐπ' Ὠκεανοῖο ῥοάων | ἀνδράσι Πυγμαίοισι φόνον καὶ κῆρα φέρουσαι. But while Homer refers to the Southward migration about October (A. 599 a 24 τοῦ Μαιμακτηριῶνος, the signal for sowing, Hesiod, *W.* 448, Aristoph. *Av.* 710, Theocr. x. 31), Oppian means the N. migration in beginning of March. Momms. *Jahr.* p. 267; Milton, *P.L.* vii. 425 ff.

[f] ὑψόθεν ἐκ νεφέων Hesiod *l.c.*, σύννομοι νεφέων δρόμου Eur. *Hel.* 1488.

[g] *Grus cinerea*, M.G. γερανός, γεράνι, and γορίλλα in Attica. The much rarer *G. virgo* is mentioned as a summer visitor in the Cyclades, Erh. p. 54. [h] In N.W. Africa. Strabo 825.

Πυγμαίων τ' ὀλιγοδρανέων ἀμενηνὰ γένεθλα·
τῇσι δ' ἄρ' ἱπταμένῃσι κατὰ στίχας εὐρέες ἑσμοὶ
ἠέρα τε σκιάουσι καὶ ἄλλυτον ὄγμον ἔχουσιν·
ὣς τότε μυριόφυλοι ἁλὸς τέμνουσι φάλαγγες
Εὔξεινον μέγα κῦμα· περιπλήθει δὲ θάλασσα
πυκνὸν ὑποφρίσσουσα λατυσσομένη πτερύγεσσιν,
εἰσόκ' ἐπειγόμενοι δολιχὸν στόλον ἀμπαύσωσι
καὶ τόκον. ἀλλ' ὅτε μέτρα παραστείχῃσιν ὀπώρης,
νόστου μιμνήσκονται, ἐπεὶ κρυερώτερον ἄλλων
χεῖμα κατασπέρχει κείνην ἅλα δινήεσσαν·
οὐ γὰρ τηλεβαθής, ῥέα δὲ στυφελίζετ' ἀήταις,
οἵ μιν ἐπιρρήσσουσιν ὑπερφίαλοί τ' ὀλοοί τε.
τοὔνεκ' ἀλυσκάζοντες Ἀμαζονίης ἀπὸ λίμνης
αὖτις ὁμοῦ τεκέεσσιν ὑποτροπάδην φορέονται,
κίδνανται δ' ἀνὰ πόντον, ὅπῃ θρέψονται ἕκαστοι.
Ἀλλ' ὅσα μὲν μαλάκεια φατίζεται, οἷσί τ' ἀναίμων

---

[a] A. 597 a 4 ff.; Strabo 35, etc.; Plin. x. 58.

[b] Their flight was in the form of a triangle (γεράνων τὴν ἐν τριγώνῳ πτῆσιν Plut. *Mor.* 979 B), the apex leading, the older birds in front and rear, the young in the middle. Ael. iii. 13; Plut. *Mor.* 967 C; Eur. *Hel.* 1478 ff.; Plin. x. 58.

[c] A. 598 b 6 ὅταν δὲ τέκωσι καὶ τὰ γενόμενα αὐξηθῇ, ἐκπλέουσιν εὐθὺς μετὰ Πλειάδα, *i.e.* after the heliacal rising of the Pleiades.

[d] E. Forbes, *op. cit.* p. 201 "Some of the rivers which discharge into the Black Sea take their rise in high latitudes, in districts annually covered with snow. These rivers also are annually frozen. Again, the winter temperature of the northern shores of this sea is such that coast ice forms there, as also in the Sea of Azof; and hence the waters of the Black Sea are much colder than those of the rest of the marine province to which it belongs. It is to the combined influence of composition and temperature that the great difference in the assemblage of animals in the Mediterranean and Black Seas must be attributed. The Black Sea is the

race of the feeble Pygmies[a]: as they fly in ordered ranks[b] their broad swarms shadow the air and keep unbroken line; even so in that season those myriad-tribed phalanxes of the sea plough the great waves of the Euxine; and the sea is full to overflowing and rough with the beating of many fins, till eagerly they win rest from their long journey and their spawning. But when the term of autumn[c] passes, they bethink them of their homeward way, since chillier[d] than all other is the winter that rages on that eddying sea; for it is not deep offshore[e] but is easily buffeted about by the winds which beat upon it violent and deadly. Wherefore they slip away from the Amazonian mere[f] and with their young travel home again, and scatter over the sea, each tribe to the place where they are to feed.

Now those which are called Molluscs,[g] whose

great ultimate estuary of the rivers which drain one-half of the European area."

[e] τηλεβαθής seems to be modelled on ἀγχιβαθής. For relative depths of different seas *cf.* A. *Meteor.* 354 a 19 καὶ τῆς μὲν Μαιώτιδος ὁ Πόντος (βαθύτερος), τούτου δὲ ὁ Αἰγαῖος, τοῦ δ' Αἰγαίου ὁ Σικελικός· ὁ δὲ Σαρδονικὸς καὶ ὁ Τυρρηνικὸς βαθύτατοι πάντων.

[f] The schol. hesitate between the Euxine (Black Sea) and the Λίμνη Μαιῶτις (Sea of Azov).

[g] In the Aristotelian sense, *i.e.* Cephalopods or Cuttles: A. 523 b 1 περὶ δὲ τῶν ἀναίμων ζῴων νυνὶ λεκτέον. ἔστι δὲ γένη πλείω, ἓν μὲν τὸ τῶν καλουμένων μαλακίων· ταῦτα δ' ἐστὶν ὅσα ἄναιμα ὄντα ἐκτὸς ἔχει τὸ σαρκῶδες, ἐντὸς δ' εἴ τι ἔχει στερεόν . . . οἷον τὸ τῶν σηπιῶν γένος. Aristotle divides the ἄναιμα or bloodless animals (Invertebrates) into μαλάκια (Cephalopods), μαλακόστρακα (Crustaceans), ἔντομα (Insects, Arachnidae, Worms), ὀστρακόδερμα (Mussels, Snails, Ascidians, Holothurians, Actinia, Sponges). His μαλάκια or "Molluscs" are: βολίταινα or ὄζολις, ἐλεδώνη, ναυτίλος πολύπους (3 species), σηπία, τευθίς, τεῦθος. *Cf.* Ael. xi. 37; Plin. ix. 83 Mollia sunt loligo, sepia, polypus et cetera generis eius.

ἐστὶ φυὴ μελέων καὶ ἀνόστεος, ὅσσα τε φῦλα
ἢ λεπίσιν πυκινῇσι καλύπτεται, ἢ φολίδεσσι
φρακτά, τὰ δ' ᾠοφόροισιν ὁμῶς ὠδῖσι μέλονται·
ἐκ δὲ κυνὸς λάβροιο καὶ αἰετοῦ ὅσσα τε φῦλα
κλῄζονται σελάχεια καὶ ἰχθυνόμων βασιλήων
δελφίνων φώκης τε βοώπιδος αὐτίκα παῖδες
ἐκ γενετῆς ἀνέχουσιν ἐοικότες οἷσι τοκεῦσιν.
Οἵ δ' ἦ τοι πάντες μέν, ὅσοι ναίουσι θάλασσαν
ζωοτόκοι, φιλέουσι καὶ ἀμφιέπουσι γενέθλην,
δελφίνων δ' οὔπω τι θεώτερον ἄλλο τέτυκται·
ὡς ἐτεὸν καὶ φῶτες ἔσαν πάρος ἠδὲ πόληας

---

[a] A. *Part. an.* 654 a 9 τὰ δ' ἔντομα τῶν ζῴων καὶ τὰ μαλάκια . . . οὐδὲν . . . ὀστῶδες ἔχειν ἔοικεν οὐδὲ γεηρὸν ἀποκεκριμένον, ὅτι καὶ ἄξιον εἰπεῖν, ἀλλὰ τὰ μὲν μαλάκια σχεδὸν ὅλα σαρκώδη καὶ μαλακά.

[b] For the distinction between λεπιδωτά and φολιδωτά *cf.* A. 505 a 20 ff. ἔτι δὲ πρὸς τἄλλα ζῷα οἱ ἰχθύες διαφέρουσι . . .· οὔτε γὰρ ὥσπερ τῶν πεζῶν ὅσα ζῳοτόκα ἔχει τρίχας, οὔθ' ὥσπερ ἔνια τῶν ᾠοτοκούντων τετραπόδων φολίδας, οὔθ' ὡς τὸ τῶν ὀρνέων γένος πτερωτόν, ἀλλ' οἱ μὲν πλεῖστοι αὐτῶν λεπιδωτοί εἰσιν, ὀλίγοι δέ τινες τραχεῖς, ἐλάχιστον δ' ἐστὶ πλῆθος αὐτῶν τὸ λεῖον. τῶν μὲν οὖν σελαχῶν τὰ μὲν τραχέα ἐστί, τὰ δὲ λεῖα, γόγγροι δὲ καὶ ἐγχέλυες καὶ θύννοι τῶν λείων. For distinction between λεπίς and φολίς *cf.* A. 490 b 22, etc. The λεπιδωτοί thus include the great majority of fishes, while the φολιδωτοί include Snakes (ἄποδα ᾠοτόκα φολιδωτά)—only the Viper (ἔχις) being viviparous (A. 511 a 16)—Lizards and Tortoises (τετράποδα ᾠοτόκα φολιδωτά). *Cf.* Ael. xi. 37 φολιδωτὰ δὲ σαῦρος, σαλαμάνδρα, χελώνη, κροκόδειλος, ὄφις. ταῦτα δὲ καὶ τὸ γῆρας ἀποδύεται, πλὴν κροκοδείλου καὶ χελώνης.

[c] For μαλάκια *cf.* A. 519 b 27 τὰ δὲ μαλάκια ἐκ τοῦ συνδυασμοῦ καὶ τῆς ὀχείας ᾠὸν ἴσχει λευκόν. For λεπιδωτοί *cf.* A. 505 b 2 εἰσὶ δ' αὐτῶν (*sc.* τῶν ἰχθύων οἱ μὲν ᾠοτόκοι οἱ ζῳοτόκοι, οἱ μὲν λεπιδωτοὶ πάντες ᾠοτόκοι τὰ δὲ σελάχη πάντα ζῳοτόκα πλὴν βατράχου. For φολιδωτά *cf.* A. *Part. an.* 733 a 6 οἱ μὲν γὰρ ὄρνιθες καὶ τὰ φολιδωτὰ . . . ᾠοτοκοῦσι.

limbs are bloodless and boneless,[a] and those tribes that are covered with close-set scales or armed with scutes,[b] are all alike oviparous[c]; but from the fierce Dog-fish[d] and the Eagle-ray[e] and all the tribes that are called Selachians[f] and from the kingly Dolphins[g] which lord it among fishes and from the ox-eyed Seal[h] spring children who straightway from birth are like their parents.

Now all the viviparous denizens of the sea love and cherish their young but diviner than the Dolphin is nothing yet created; for indeed they were aforetime men and lived in cities along with mortals, but

[d] κύων is here either generic, as in *H.* i. 373, or, if specific, is as unidentifiable as in A. 566 a 30 ff. οἱ μὲν οὖν γαλεοὶ καὶ οἱ γαλεοειδεῖς, οἷον ἀλώπηξ καὶ κύων [the only case in Aristotle of κύων in sing. in connexion with Dog-fish] καὶ οἱ πλατεῖς ἰχθύες . . . ζῳοτοκοῦσιν ᾠοτοκήσαντες.

[e] *Myliobatis aquila*, M.G. ἀετός. A. 540 b 18.

[f] *i.e.* cartilaginous fishes, the Sharks and Rays. A. 511 a 5 καλεῖται δὲ σέλαχος ὃ ἂν ἄπουν ὂν καὶ βράγχια ἔχον ζῳοτόκον ᾖ. *Cf.* Hesych. *s.* σελάχιον. Aristotle's Selachians are (1) προμήκη (A. 505 a 5) or γαλεώδη, Sharks and Dog-fishes; ἀκανθίας, ἀλώπηξ ἀστερίας, γαλεὸς ὁ λεῖος, κύων, σκύλια, (2) πλατέα καὶ κερκοφόρα (A. 489 b 31, 540 b 8), the Rays; ἀετός, βατίς, βάτος, βοῦς, λάμια, λειόβατος, νάρκη, ῥινόβατος· τρυγών. Among the Selachians he includes also βάτραχος (see *H.* ii. 86 n.) and ῥίνη (see *H.* i. 742 n.). In saying that the Selachians are viviparous Oppian is following Aristotle, who makes ζῳοτόκον part of his definition of σέλαχος (see above). *Cf.* A. 505 b 3 τὰ δὲ σελάχη πάντα ζῳοτοκεῖ πλὴν βατράχου; 564 b 12 ζῳοτοκεῖ δὲ τὰ σελάχη πρότερον ᾠοτοκήσαντα ἐν αὑτοῖς καὶ ἐκτρέφουσιν ἐν αὑτοῖς πλὴν βατράχου; *De gen.* 754 a 23 τὰ δὲ καλούμενα σελάχη τῶν ἰχθύων ἐν αὑτοῖς μὲν ᾠοτοκεῖ τέλειον ᾠὸν ἔξω δὲ ζῳοτοκεῖ, πλὴν ἑνὸς ὃν καλοῦσι βάτραχον· οὗτος δὲ ᾠοτοκεῖ θύραζε τέλειον ᾠὸν μόνος; Plin. ix. 78 cum ceteri pisces ova pariant, hoc genus (*sc.* cartilaginea = σελάχη) solum ut ea quae cete appellant animal parit excepta quam ranam vocant.

[g] A. 504 b 21, etc.

[h] A. 489 a 35, etc.

ναῖον ὁμοῦ μερόπεσσι, Διωνύσοιο δὲ βουλῇ
πόντον ὑπημείψαντο καὶ ἰχθύας ἀμφεβάλοντο
γυίοις· ἀλλ' ἄρα θυμὸς ἐναίσιμος εἰσέτι φωτῶν
ῥύεται ἀνδρομέην ἠμὲν φρόνιν ἠδὲ καὶ ἔργα.
εὖτε γὰρ ὠδίνων δίδυμον γένος ἐς φάος ἔλθῃ,
αὐτίχ' ὁμοῦ τ' ἐγένοντο περὶ σφετέρην τε τεκοῦσαν
νηχόμενοι σκαίρουσι καὶ ἐνδύνουσιν ὀδόντων
εἴσω καὶ μητρῷον ὑπὸ στόμα δηθύνουσιν·
ἡ δὲ φιλοφροσύνῃσιν ἀνίσχεται ἀμφί τε παισὶ
στρωφᾶται γανόωσα καὶ ἔξοχα καγχαλόωσα.
μαζὸν δ' ἀμφοτέροισι παρίσχεται, οἷον ἑκάστῳ,
θήσασθαι γάλα λαρόν· ἐπεί ῥά οἱ ὤπασε δαίμων
καὶ γάλα καὶ μαζῶν ἰκέλην φύσιν οἷα γυναικῶν.
τόφρα μὲν οὖν τοίῃσι τιθηνείῃσι μέμηλεν·
ἀλλ' ὅτε κουρίζωσιν ἑὸν σθένος, αὐτίκα τοῖσι
μήτηρ ἡγήτειρα κατέρχεται εἰς ὁδὸν ἄγρης
ἱεμένοις θήρην τε διδάσκεται ἰχθυόεσσαν,
οὐδὲ πάρος τεκέων ἑκὰς ἵσταται οὐδ' ἀπολείπει,
πρίν γ' ὅταν ἡβήσωσι τελεσφόρα γυῖα καὶ ἀλκήν,
ἀλλ' αἰεὶ ῥυτῆρες ἐπίσκοποι ἐγγὺς ἕπονται.
οἷον δὴ τότε θαῦμα μετὰ φρεσὶ θηήσαιο
τερπωλήν τ' ἐρόεσσαν, ὅτε πλώων ἐσίδηαι
αὔρῃ ἐν εὐκραεῖ δεδοκημένος ἠὲ γαλήνῃ
δελφίνων ἀγέλας εὐειδέας, ἵμερον ἅλμης·
οἱ μὲν γὰρ προπάροιθεν ἀολλέες ἠΰτε κοῦροι

---

[a] The story is variously told (*cf.* schol.). The version of Apollod. iii. 5 is: Wishing to cross from Icaria to Naxos, Dionysus hired a vessel of some Tyrrhenian pirates. Putting him on board, they sailed past Naxos and made all speed for Asia, with a view to selling him. He then turned mast and sails into snakes and filled the ship with ivy and the

by the devising of Dionysus [a] they exchanged the land for the sea and put on the form of fishes [b]; but even now the righteous spirit of men in them preserves human thought and human deeds. For when the twin [c] offspring of their travail come into the light, straightway, soon as they are born they swim and gambol round their mother and enter within her teeth and linger in the maternal mouth; and she for her love suffers them and circles about her children gaily and exulting with exceeding joy. And she gives them her breasts,[d] one to each, that they may suck the sweet milk; for god has given her milk and breasts of like nature to those of women. Thus for a season she nurses them; but, when they attain the strength of youth, straightway their mother leads them in their eagerness to the way of hunting and teaches them the art of catching fish; nor does she part from her children nor forsake them, until they have attained the fulness of their age in limb and strength, but always the parents attend [e] them to keep watch and ward. What a marvel shalt thou contemplate in thy heart and what sweet delight, when on a voyage, watching when the wind is fair and the sea is calm, thou shalt see the beautiful herds of Dolphins, the desire of the sea; the young go before in a troop like youths unwed, even as if

noise of flutes. The pirates, becoming mad, threw themselves into the sea and became Dolphins. *Cf.* Hom. *H.* vii.

[b] *Cf. C.* iii. 16.

[c] A. 566 b 6 τίκτει δ' ὁ μὲν δελφὶς τὰ μὲν πολλὰ ἕν, ἐνίοτε δὲ καὶ δύο; Plin. ix. 21; Ael. i. 18; Phil. 86.

[d] A. 521 b 23 τὰ κήτη, οἷον δελφὶς καὶ φώκη καὶ φάλαινα· καὶ γὰρ ταῦτα μαστοὺς ἔχει καὶ γάλα. *Cf.* A. 504 b 22, 566 b 16, Ael. v. 4; Plin. ix. 7.

[e] A. 566 b 22 παρακολουθεῖ δὲ τὰ τέκνα πολὺν χρόνον, καὶ ἔστι τὸ ζῷον φιλότεκνον; Plin. *l.c.*

ἠΐθεοι στείχουσι, νέον γένος, ὥστε χοροῖο
κύκλον ἀμειβόμενοι πολυειδέα ποικιλοδίνην·
τοὶ δ' ὄπιθεν μεγάλοι τε καὶ ἔξοχοι οὐδ' ἀπάτερθεν
ἔρχονται τεκέων, φρουρὸς στρατός, ὥσθ' ἁπαλοῖσι
φερβομένοις ἕσπονται ἐν εἴαρι ποιμένες ἀμνοῖς.
ὡς δ' ὅτε μουσοπόλων ἔργων ἄπο παῖδες ἴωσιν
ἀθρόοι, οἱ δ' ἄρ' ὄπισθεν ἐπίσκοποι ἐγγὺς ἕπονται
αἰδοῦς τε πραπίδων τε νόου τ' ἐπιτιμητῆρες
πρεσβύτεροι· γῆρας γὰρ ἐναίσιμον ἄνδρα τίθησιν·
ὣς ἄρα καὶ δελφῖνες ἑοῖς παίδεσσι τοκῆες
ἕσπονται, μή τί σφιν ἀνάρσιον ἀντιβολήσῃ.
Ναὶ μὴν καὶ φώκη κομέει γένος οὔτι χέρειον·
καὶ γὰρ τῇ μαζοί τε καὶ ἐν μαζοῖσι γάλακτος
εἰσὶ ῥοαί· τῇ δ' οὔτι μετ' οἴδμασιν ἀλλ' ἐπὶ χέρσου
λύετ' ἀνερχομένῃ γαστρὸς μόγος, ὥριος ὠδίς·
μίμνει δ' ἤματα πάντα δυώδεκα σὺν τεκέεσσιν
αὐτοῦ ἐνὶ τραφερῇ· τρισκαιδεκάτῃ δὲ σὺν ἠοῖ
σκύμνους ἀγκὰς ἔχουσα νεαλδέας εἰς ἅλα δύνει,
παισὶν ἀγαλλομένη, πάτρην ἅτε σημαίνουσα.
ὡς δὲ γυνὴ ξείνης γαίης ἔπι παῖδα τεκοῦσα
ἀσπασίως πάτρην τε καὶ ὃν δόμον εἰσαφικάνει,
παῖδα δ' ἐν ἀγκοίνῃσι πανημερίῃ φορέουσα,
δώματα δεικνυμένη, μητρὸς νομόν, ἀμφαγαπάζει,
τερπωλὴν ἀκόρεστον· ὁ δ' οὐ φρονέων περ ἕκαστα
παπταίνει, μέγαρόν τε καὶ ἤθεα πάντα τοκήων·
ὣς ἄρα καὶ κείνη σφέτερον γένος εἰναλίη θὴρ

[a] The reference is to children attended from school by their paedagogus. Schol. μουσοπόλων· ἡ σχολῆς, ἀπὸ τῶν σχολείων . . . ἐπίσκοποι· οἱ παιδαγωγοί. *Cf.* Hor. *S.* i. 6. 81 Ipse mihi custos incorruptissimus omnes | Circum doctores aderat.

they were going through the changing circle of a mazy dance; behind and not aloof their children come the parents great and splendid, a guardian host, even as in spring the shepherds attend the tender lambs at pasture. As when from the works of the Muses [a] children come trooping while behind there follow, to watch them and to be censors of modesty and heart and mind, men of older years: for age makes a man discreet; even so also the parent Dolphins attend their children, lest aught untoward encounter them.

Yea and the Seal also tends her young no less well; for she too has breasts, and in the breasts streams of milk.[b] But not amid the waves but when she comes up on the dry land [c] is she delivered of the burden of her womb in seasonable travail. For twelve days in all she remains with her children there upon the dry land; but with the thirteenth [d] dawn she takes in her arms her young cubs and goes down into the sea, glorying in her children and showing them, as it were, their fatherland. Even as a woman that has borne a child in an alien land comes gladly to her fatherland and to her own home; and all day long she carries her child in her arms and hugs him while she shows him the house, his mother's home, with sateless delight; and he, though he does not understand, gazes at each thing, the hall and the haunts of his parents; even so that wild thing of the sea

[b] A. 567 a 2 *μαστοὺς δ' ἔχει δύο καὶ θηλάζεται ὑπὸ τῶν τέκνων καθάπερ τὰ τετράποδα*; Plin. ix. 41.

[c] A. 566 b 28 *τίκτει ἐν τῇ γῇ μέν, πρὸς αἰγιαλοῖς δέ*; Ael. ix. 9; Plin. ix. 41.

[d] A. 567 a 5 *ἄγει δὲ περὶ δωδεκαταῖα ὄντα τὰ τέκνα εἰς τὴν θάλατταν πολλάκις τῆς ἡμέρας, συνεθίζουσα κατὰ μικρόν*; Plin. *l.c.*; Ael. *l.c.*

ἐς πόντον προφέρει καὶ δείκνυται ἔργα θαλάσσης.
Δαίμονες, οὐκ ἄρα μοῦνον ἐν ἀνδράσι τέκνα πέλονται
φίλτατα, καὶ φάεος γλυκερώτερα καὶ βιότοιο,
ἀλλὰ καὶ οἰωνοῖσιν ἀμειλίκτοισί τε θηρσὶν
ἰχθύσι τ' ὠμηστῇσιν ἀμήχανος αὐτοδίδακτος
ἐντρέφεται τεκέων δριμὺς πόθος· ἀμφὶ δὲ παισὶ
καὶ θανέειν καὶ πᾶσαν ὀϊζυρὴν κακότητα
πρόφρονες, οὐκ ἀέκοντες, ἀναπλῆσαι μεμάασιν.
ἤδη τις κατ' ὄρεσφιν ἐριβρύχην ἐνόησε
θηρητὴρ τεκέεσσιν ὑπερβεβαῶτα λέοντα,
μαρνάμενον σφετέρης γενεῆς ὕπερ· οὐδ' ὅ γε πυκνῆς
χερμάδος ἱπταμένης οὐδ' αἰγανέης ἀλεγίζει,
ἀλλ' αὔτως ἄτρεστον ἔχει θάρσος τε μένος τε,
βαλλόμενος καὶ ἐρεικόμενος πάσῃσι βολῇσιν·
οὐδ' ὅ γε πρὶν θανέειν ἀναδύεται, ἀλλ' ἐπὶ παισὶν
ἡμιθανὴς προβέβηκε, μέλει δέ οἱ οὔτι μόροιο
τόσσον, ὅσον μὴ παῖδας ὑπ' ἀγρευτῆρσιν ἰδέσθαι
ἑρχθέντας θήρειον ὑπ' αὐτοκμῆτα καλιήν.
ἤδη δ' ἀρτιτόκοιο κυνὸς σκυλακοτρόφῳ εὐνῇ
ποιμὴν ἐγχρίμψας, εἰ καὶ πάρος ἦεν ἑταῖρος,
χάσσατο, ταρβήσας μητρὸς χόλον ὑλακόεντα,
οἷον ὑπὲρ τεκέων προφυλάσσεται, οὐδέ τιν' αἰδῶ
γιγνώσκει, πᾶσιν δὲ πέλει κρυόεσσα πελάσσαι.
οἷον δ' ἑλκομένας περὶ πόρτιας ἀσχαλόωσαι
μητέρες οὐκ ἀπάτερθε γυναικείων στενάχουσι
κωκυτῶν, αὐτοὺς δὲ συναλγύνουσι νομῆας.
καὶ μέν τις φήνης ἀδινὸν γόον ἔκλυεν ἀνὴρ
ὄρθριον ἀμφὶ τέκεσσ', ἢ ἀηδόνος αἰολοφώνου,

---

[a] Hom. *Il.* xvii. 133 ἑστήκει ὥς τίς τε λέων περὶ οἷσι τέκεσσιν | ᾧ ῥά τε νήπι' ἄγοντι συναντήσωνται ἐν ὕλῃ | ἄνδρες ἐπακτῆρες.

brings her children to the water and shows them all the works of the deep.

Ye gods, not alone then among men are children very dear, sweeter than light or life, but in birds also and in savage beasts and in carrion fishes there is inbred, mysterious and self-taught, a keen passion for their young, and for their children they are not unwilling but heartily eager to die and to endure all manner of woeful ill. Ere now on the hills a hunter has seen a roaring Lion bestriding his young, fighting in defence of his offspring;[a] the thick hurtling stones he heeds not nor recks of the hunter's spear but all undaunted keeps heart and spirit, though hit and torn by all manner of wounds; nor will he shrink from the combat till he die, but even half-dead he stands over his children to defend them, and not so much does he mind death as that he should not see his children in the hands of the hunters, penned in the rude[b] wild-beast den. And ere now a shepherd, approaching the kennel where a bitch nursed her new-born whelps,[c] even if he were acquainted with her before, has drawn back in terror at her yelping wrath; so fiercely she guards her young and has no regard for any but is fearful of approach for all. How, too, around calves when they are dragged away do their grieving mothers make lament, not unlike the mourning of women, causing the very herdsmen to share their pain. Yea and a man hears at morn the shrill plaint for her children of Gier[d] or many-noted Nightingale, or in the spring

[b] Schol. *αὐτοκμῆτα· . . . αὐτοφυῆ ἢ τὸ σπήλαιον λέγει τοῦ λέοντος.* *Cf.* *αὐτόκτιτ' ἄντρα* Aesch. *P.V.* 303.

[c] Hom. *Od.* xx. 14 *ὡς δὲ κύων ἀμαλῇσι περὶ σκυλάκεσσι βεβῶσα | ἄνδρ' ἀγνοιήσασ' ὑλάει μέμονέν τε μάχεσθαι.*

[d] *C.* iii. 116 n.

ἠὲ καὶ εἰαρινῇσι χελιδόσιν ἐγγὺς ἔκυρσε
μυρομέναις ἑὰ τέκνα, τά τε σφίσι ληΐσσαντο
ἐξ εὐνῆς ἢ φῶτες ἀπηνέες ἠὲ δράκοντες.
ἰχθύσι δ' αὖ δελφὶς μὲν ἀριστεύει φιλότητι
παίδων, ὣς δὲ καὶ ἄλλοι ἑὸν γένος ἀμφιέπουσι.
Θαῦμα δ' ἁλιπλάγκτοιο κυνὸς τόδε· τῇ γὰρ ἕπονται
τέκνα νεοβλαστῆ καί σφιν σάκος ἔπλετο μήτηρ·
ἀλλ' ὅτε ταρβήσωσι τά τ' ἄσπετα δείματ' ἔασιν
ἐν πόντῳ, τότε παῖδας ἔσω λαγόνεσσιν ἔδεκτο
αὐτὴν εἰσίθμην, αὐτὴν ὁδόν, ἔνθεν ὄλισθον
γεινόμενοι· τοῖον δὲ πόνον μογέουσά περ ἔμπης
ἀσπασίως τέτληκε, πάλιν δ' ὑπεχεύατο παῖδας
σπλάγχνοις, ἂψ δ' ἀνέηκεν, ὅτ' ἀμπνεύσωσι φόβοιο.
Τοίην καὶ ῥίνη τεκέων πορσύνεται ἀλκήν,
ἀλλ' οὐκ εἰς νηδὺν κείνῃ δύσις, οἷα κύνεσσιν,
ἀλλά οἱ ἐν πλευρῇσι διασφάγες ἀμφοτέρωθεν
εἰσὶν ὑπὸ πτερύγων, οἵη γένυς ἰχθύσιν ἄλλοις,
τῇσιν ἀτυζομένων τέκνων φόβον ἀμφικαλύπτει.
Ἄλλοι δ' αὖθ' ἑὰ τέκνα διὰ στόμα ταρβήσαντα
δεξάμενοι ῥύονται ἅτ' ἐς δόμον ἠὲ καλιήν·
οἷον δὴ καὶ γλαῦκος, ὃς ἔξοχα τέκν' ἀγαπάζει
πάντων, ὅσσοι ἔασιν ἐν ἰχθύσιν ᾠοτοκῆες·
κεῖνος γὰρ μίμνει τε παρήμενος, ὄφρα γένωνται

---

[a] Ael. i. 17 *κύων δὲ θαλαττία τεκοῦσα ἔχει συννέοντα τὰ σκυλάκια ἤδη καὶ οὐκ εἰς ἀναβολάς· ἐὰν δὲ δείσῃ τι τούτων, εἰς τὴν μητέρα εἰσέδυ αὖθις κατὰ τὸ ἄρθρον· εἶτα, τοῦ δέους παραδραμόντος, τὸ δὲ πρόεισιν, ὥσπερ οὖν ἀνατικτόμενον αὖθις*; A. 565 b 23 *οἱ μὲν οὖν ἄλλοι γαλεοὶ καὶ ἐξαφιᾶσι καὶ δέχονται εἰς ἑαυτοὺς τοὺς νεοττούς, . . . ὁ δ' ἀκανθίας οὐκ εἰσδέχεται μόνος τῶν γαλεῶν διὰ τὴν ἄκανθαν*. *Cf.* Athen. 294 e; Plut. *Mor.* 982 a; Antig. 21; Phil. 91. In A. *l.c.* the *ῥίνη* and the *νάρκη* are said to take in their young, while the *τρυγών* and the *βάτος* among the

chances on the Swallows wailing for their young, which cruel men or snakes have harried from the nest. Among fishes again the Dolphin is first in love for its children, but others likewise care for their young.

Here is the marvel of the sea-roaming Dog-fish.[a] Her new-born brood keep her company and their mother is their shield ; but when they are affrighted by any of the infinite terrors of the sea, then she receives her children within her loins by the same entry,[b] the same path, by which they glided forth when they were born. And this labour, despite her pain, she endures gladly, taking her children back within her body and putting them forth again when they have recovered from their fear.

A like defence also does the Angel-shark [c] furnish for her young ; but it is not into her womb that her children enter, as with the Dog-fish, but on either side below her fins she has slits, like the jaws of other fishes, wherewith she covers the terror of her frightened children.

Others again protect their children by taking them into the mouth as it were into a house or nest ; as, for example, the Glaucus [d] which loves its children beyond all other fishes that are oviparous. For it both remains sitting by until the young come forth

Rays (*τῶν πλατέων*) do not *διὰ τὴν τραχύτητα τῆς κέρκου*, as neither does the *βάτραχος, διὰ τὸ μέγεθος τῆς κεφαλῆς καὶ τὰς ἀκάνθας* (*cf. De gen.* 754 a 29). Even the Dolphin and the Porpoise *εἰσδέχονται τὰ τέκνα μικρὰ ὄντα* A. 566 b 17.

[b] Ael. i. 17 ; but Aristotle doubtless meant "by the mouth," *cf.* Athen. *l.c.* *εἰς τὸ στόμα* ; Plut. *l.c.* *διὰ τοῦ στόματος* ; Antig. *l.c.* *κατὰ τὸ στόμα*.

[c] *H.* i. 381 n. : A. 565 b 25 says the *ῥίνη* takes in its young, mode not indicated.

[d] Introduction, p. lxi.

παῖδες ὑπωάδιοι, καί σφιν παρανήχεται αἰεί·
τοὺς δ᾽ ὅτε κεν τρομέοντας ἴδῃ κρατερώτερον ἰχθύν,
ἀμφιχανὼν κατέδεκτο διὰ στόμα, μέσφα κε δεῖμα
χάσσηται, τότε δ᾽ αὖτις ἀνέπτυσε λευκανίηθεν.
Θύννης δ᾽ οὔτιν᾽ ἔγωγ᾽ ἀθεμίστερον ἔλπομαι ἰχθὺν
οὐδὲ κακοφροσύνῃ προβεβηκότα ναιέμεν ἅλμην·
ὠὰ γὰρ εὖτε τέκῃσι, φύγῃ δ᾽ ὠδῖνα βαρεῖαν,
αὐτὴ γειναμένη καταδαίνυται ὅσσα κίχῃσι,
νηλής, ἥ θ᾽ ἑὰ τέκνα φυγῆς ἔτι νήϊδ᾽ ἐόντα
ἐσθίει, οὐδέ μιν οἶκτος ἐσέρχεται οἷο τόκοιο.
Ἔστι δ᾽ ὅσ᾽ οὔτε γάμοισι φυτεύεται οὔτε γονῇσι
τίκτεται, αὐτοτέλεστα καὶ αὐτόρρεκτα γένεθλα,
ὄστρεα δὴ σύμπαντα, τά γ᾽ ἰλύϊ τίκτεται αὐτῇ·
κείνων δ᾽ οὔτε τι θῆλυ πέλει γένος, οὔτ᾽ ἐπ᾽ ἀμοιβῆς
ἄρσενες, ἀλλ᾽ ὁμόφυλα καὶ εἴκελα πάντα τέτυκται.
Ὡς δὲ καὶ ἠπεδανῆς ἀφύης ὀλιγηπελὲς ἔθνος
οὔτινος ἐκγεγάασιν ἀφ᾽ αἵματος οὐδὲ τοκήων·
εὖτε γὰρ ἐκ νεφέων Ζηνὸς νόος ὄμβρον ἀφύξῃ
λάβρον ὑπὲρ πόντοιο καὶ ἄσχετον, αὐτίκα πᾶσα
μισγομένη δίνῃσι παλιμπνοίῃσι θάλασσα
σίζει τ᾽ ἀφριάᾳ τε καὶ ἵσταται οἰδαίνουσα,

---

[a] Here generic = *ὀστρακόδερμα*, Testaceans. *Cf.* A. 490 b 9 *ἄλλο δὲ γένος ἐστὶ τὸ τῶν ὀστρακοδέρμων, ὃ καλεῖται ὄστρεον.* *Cf.* Nicandr. *ap.* Athen. 92 d. For their spontaneous generation, A. 547 b 18 *ὅλως δὲ πάντα τὰ ὀστρακώδη γίνεται καὶ αὐτόματα ἐν τῇ ἰλύι, κατὰ τὴν διαφορὰν τῆς ἰλύος ἕτερα, ἐν μὲν τῇ βορβορώδει τὰ ὄστρεα* (here = bivalve Testaceans), *ἐν δὲ τῇ ἀμμώδει κόγχαι καὶ τὰ εἰρημένα, περὶ δὲ τὰς σήραγγας τῶν πετριδίων τήθυα καὶ βάλανοι καὶ τὰ ἐπιπολάζοντα, οἷον αἱ λεπάδες καὶ οἱ νηρεῖται.*

[b] *ἀφύη* (*ἀ-* neg. and *φύω*, *cf.* Athen. 324 d) is generic for various tiny fishes and fish-fry. Some *ἀφύαι* are said by Aristotle to be spontaneously generated, others are merely the young of various fishes (*cf.* *ἑψητός* or Eng. *Whitebait*);

from the eggs and always swims beside them; and when it sees them afraid of a strange fish it opens its gape and takes them into its mouth until the terror has withdrawn, and then again ejects them from its throat.

Than the Tunny I deem there is no fish that dwells in the brine more lawless or which exceeds it in wickedness of heart; for when she has laid her eggs and escaped from the grievous travail of birth, the very mother that bare them devours all that she can overtake: pitiless mother who devours her own children while yet they are ignorant of flight and hath no compassion on her brood.

There are also those which are not produced by bridal or birth—races self-created and self-made: even all the Oysters,[a] which are produced by the slime itself. Of these there is no female sex nor, in turn, are there any males, but all are of one nature and alike.

So also the weak race of the feeble Fry[b] are born of no blood and of no parents. For when from the clouds the wisdom of Zeus draws rain, fierce and incontinent, upon the deep, straightway all the sea, confounded by the eddying winds, hisses and foams

A. 569 a 25 *ὅτι μὲν οὖν γίνεται αὐτόματα ἔνια οὔτ' ἐκ ζῴων οὔτ' ἐξ ὀχείας, φανερὸν ἐκ τούτων. ὅσα δὲ μήτ' ᾠοτοκεῖ μήτε ζῳοτοκεῖ, πάντα γίνεται τὰ μὲν ἐκ τῆς ἰλύος τὰ δ' ἐκ τῆς ἄμμου καὶ τῆς ἐπιπολαζούσης σήψεως, οἷον καὶ τῆς ἀφύης ὁ καλούμενος ἀφρὸς γίνεται ἐκ τῆς ἀμμώδους γῆς*; 569 b 22 *ἡ ἄλλη ἀφύη γόνος ἰχθύων ἐστίν, e.g., κωβῖτις, Φαληρική*, etc.; *cf.* Athen. 284 f ff., Badham, *Fish Tattle*, p. 330 "This Greek epithet, *aphya*, 'unborn,' translated into the Italian equivalent *non-nati*, is that employed by the lazzaroni of Naples to designate young anchovies, and a variety of other *piccoli pesci* of whose origin and parentage they are uncertain"; *cf.* Ael. ii. 22; Phil. 115; Poll. vi. 51; Hesych. *s.v.* and *s.* *τριχθάδες*.

αἱ δ' ἐν ἀτεκμάρτοισι καὶ ἀσκέπτοισι γάμοισιν
ἀθρόαι ἔκ τ' ἐγένοντο καὶ ἔτραφον ἔκ τ' ἐφάνησαν
μυρίαι, ἀβληχραί, πολιὸν γένος· ἐκ δὲ γενέθλης
οὔνομ' ἐπικλήδην ἀφρίτιδες αὐδώωνται.
ἄλλαι δ' ἰλυόεντος ὑπὲκ φλοίσβοιο φύονται·
εὖτε γὰρ ἐν δίνῃσι παλιρροίῃς τε θαλάσσης
βράσσηται πάμφυρτος ἀφυσγετὸς ἐξ ἀνέμοιο
σπερχομένου, τότε πᾶσα συνίσταται εἰς ἓν ἰοῦσα
ἰλὺς εὐρώεσσα, γαληναίης δὲ ταθείσης
ἐξαυτῆς ψάμαθός τε καὶ ἄσπετα φύρματα πόντου
πύθεται, ἐκ δὲ φύονται ἀθέσφατοι, εἴκελοι εὐλαῖς.
οὐ μέν πού τι τέτυκται ἀκιδνότερον γένος ἄλλο
δειλαίης ἀφύης· νεπόδεσσι δὲ πᾶσιν ἔασι
δαὶς ἀγαθή· κεῖναι δὲ δέμας περιλιχμάζουσιν
ἀλλήλων· τό γε δέ σφι βορὴ βίοτός τε τέτυκται·
κεῖναι δ' εὖτε θάλασσαν ἀολλήδην ἐφέπωσιν,
ἠέ νύ που πέτρην ἀμφίσκιον ἠὲ θαλάσσης
διζόμεναι κευθμῶνας ὑποβρυχίην τ' ἀλεωρήν,
πᾶσα τότε γλαυκὴ λευκαίνεται Ἀμφιτρίτη.
ὡς δ' ὁπότ' εὐρύπεδον σκιάσῃ νιφάδεσσιν ἀλωὴν
ἑσπερίου Ζεφύροιο θοὸν μένος, οὐδέ τι γαίης
κυανέης ἰδέειν ὑποφαίνεται, ἀλλ' ἄρα πᾶσα
ἀργεννὴ χιόνεσσιν ἐπασσυτέραις κεκάλυπται·
ὣς τότ' ἀπειρεσίῃσι περιπληθὴς ἀγέλῃσι
φαίνεται ἀργινόεσσα Ποσειδάωνος ἀλωή.

---

[a] Athen. 285 a πάντων δὲ τούτων ἡ ἀφρῖτις ἀρίστη. *Cf.* A. 569 b 9 γίνονται δ' ἐν τοῖς ἐπισκίοις καὶ ἑλώδεσι τόποις, ὅταν

and swells up and, by what manner of mating is beyond ken or guess, the Fry in shoals are born and bred and come to light, numberless and feeble, a hoary brood; and from the manner of their birth they are nicknamed the Daughters of the Foam.[a] And others of the Fry spring from the alluvial slime; for when in the eddies and tides of the sea a medley mass of scum is washed up by the driving wind, then all the slimy silt comes together and when calm is spread abroad, straightway the sand and the infinite refuse of the sea ferment and therefrom spring the Fry innumerable like worms. There is not surely any other race more feeble than the poor Fry; for all fishes they are a goodly feast, but themselves they lick each the body of the other: that is their food and livelihood. And when in their shoals they beset the sea, seeking haply a shady rock or covert of the sea and watery shelter, then all the grey deep shows white. As when the swift might of Zephyrus from the West shadows with snow-flakes a spacious garden and nothing of the dark earth appears to the eye, but all is white and covered with snow on snow; even so in that season, full to overflowing with the infinite shoals of Fry, white shines the garden of Poseidon.

εὐημερίας γενομένης ἀναθερμαίνεται ἡ γῆ, οἷον περὶ Ἀθήνας ἐν Σαλαμῖνι . . . καὶ ἐν Μαραθῶνι· ἐν γὰρ τούτοις τοῖς τόποις γίνεται ὁ ἀφρός. . . . γίνεται δ' ἐνιαχοῦ καὶ ὁπόταν ὕδωρ πολὺ ἐξ οὐρανοῦ γένηται, ἐν τῷ ἀφρῷ τῷ γιγνομένῳ ὑπὸ τοῦ ὀμβρίου ὕδατος, διὸ καὶ καλεῖται ἀφρός· καὶ ἐπιφέρεται ἐνίοτε ἐπιπολῆς τῆς θαλάττης, ὅταν εὐημερία ᾖ, ἐν ᾧ συστρέφεται, οἷον ἐν τῇ κόπρῳ τὰ σκωλήκια, οὕτως ἐν τούτῳ ὁ ἀφρός, ὅπου ἂν συστῇ ἐπιπολῆς.

ΑΛΙΕΥΤΙΚΩΝ ΤΟ Β

Ὧδε μὲν ἰχθύβοτοί τε νομαὶ καὶ φῦλα θαλάσσης
πλάζονται· τοιῷδε γάμῳ, τοιῇδε γενέθλῃ
τέρπονται· τὰ δέ πού τις ἐπιχθονίοισιν ἅπαντα
ἀθανάτων σήμηνε· τί γὰρ μερόπεσσιν ἀνυστὸν
νόσφι θεῶν; οὐδ᾿ ὅσσον ὑπὲκ ποδὸς ἴχνος ἀεῖραι,
οὐδ᾿ ὅσον ἀμπετάσαι βλεφάρων περιφαέα κύκλα·
ἀλλ᾿ αὐτοὶ κρατέουσι καὶ ἰθύνουσιν ἕκαστα,
τηλόθεν ἐγγὺς ἐόντες· ἀναγκαίη δ᾿ ἀτίνακτος
πείθεσθαι· τὴν δ᾿ οὔτι πέλει σθένος οὐδέ τις ἀλκὴ
τρηχείαις γενύεσσιν ὑπερφιάλως ἐρύσαντα
ἐκφυγέειν, ἅτε πῶλον ἀποπτυστῆρα χαλινῶν·
ἀλλ᾿ αἰεὶ μάκαρες πανυπέρτατοι ἡνία πάντῃ
κλίνουσ᾿, ᾗ κ᾿ ἐθέλωσιν, ὁ δ᾿ ἕσπεται ὅστε σαόφρων,
πρὶν χαλεπῇ μάστιγι καὶ οὐκ ἐθέλων ἐλάηται.
κεῖνοι καὶ τέχνας πολυκερδέας ἀνθρώποισιν
δῶκαν ἔχειν καὶ πᾶσαν ἐπιφροσύνην ἐνέηκαν.
ἄλλος δ᾿ ἀλλοίοισιν ἐπώνυμος ἔπλετο δαίμων
ἔργοις, οἷσιν ἕκαστος ἐπίσκοπον ἤρατο τιμήν.
Δηὼ μὲν ζεύγλης τε βοῶν ἀρότοιό τε γαίης

---

[a] ποδὸς ἴχνος is so common a periphrasis for πούς (Eur. *I. in T.* 752 etc.), and αἴρω (Eur. *Tr.* 342 μὴ κοῦφον αἴρῃ βῆμ᾿ ἐς Ἀργείων στρατόν) so naturally refers to "lifting" the foot, that this seems the safer rendering. Nor does ὑπέκ cause any difficulty (Soph. *Ant.* 224 κοῦφον ἐξάρας πόδα, Anonym. Poet. *ap.* Suid. *s.* Ταῦρος . . . τὸν αὐχένα | κυρτῶς ὑπεξαίροντι).

HALIEUTICA, OR FISHING

II

Thus do fishes range and feed, thus roam the tribes of the sea; in such mating, in such breeding they delight. All these things, I ween, someone of the immortals hath showed to men. For what can mortals accomplish without the gods? Nay, not even so much as lift a foot from the ground [a] or open the bright orbs of the eyes. The gods themselves rule and direct everything, being far, yet very near. And doom unshakable constrains men to obey, and there is no strength nor might whereby one may haughtily wrench [b] with stubborn jaws and escape that doom, as a colt that spurns the bit. But evermore the gods who are above all turn the reins all ways even as they will, and he who is wise obeys before he is driven by the cruel lash unwillingly. The gods also have given to men cunning arts and have put in them all wisdom. Other god is namesake of other craft, even that whereof he hath got the honourable keeping. Deo [c] hath the privilege of

[a] The Schol. has τὸν πόδα ἐκ τοῦ ἴχνους, and a possible rendering would be "to move one foot past another." *Cf.* Hom. *Il.* ix. 547 ὀλίγον γόνυ γουνὸς ἀμείβων.

[b] For the behaviour of the ἄστομος πῶλος or "unmouthed" colt *cf.* Aesch. *Pers.* 195 συναρπάζει βίᾳ, Soph. *El.* 723, Eur. *Hipp.* 1224 βίᾳ φέρουσιν, Aesch. *Ag.* 1066, Xen. *Eq.* 3. 5.

[c] Demeter.

πυρῶν τ᾽ εὐκάρποιο φέρει γέρας ἀμητοῖο.
δοῦρα δὲ τεκτήνασθαι ἀναστῆσαί τε μέλαθρα,
φάρεά τ᾽ ἀσκῆσαι μήλων εὐανθέϊ καρπῷ
Παλλὰς ἐπιχθονίους ἐδιδάξατο· δῶρα δ᾽ Ἄρηος
φάσγανα χάλκειοί τε περὶ μελέεσσι χιτῶνες
καὶ κόρυθες καὶ δοῦρα καὶ οἷς ἐπιτέρπετ᾽ Ἐνυώ.
δῶρα δὲ Μουσάων τε καὶ Ἀπόλλωνος ἀοιδαί.
Ἑρμείης δ᾽ ἀγορήν τε καὶ ἀλκήεντας ἀέθλους
ὤπασεν. Ἡφαίστῳ δὲ μέλει ῥαιστήριος ἱδρώς.
καὶ τάδε τις πόντοιο νοήματα καὶ τέλος ἄγρης
πληθύν θ᾽ ὑγροπόρων θεὸς ὤπασε τεκμήρασθαι
ἀνδράσιν, ὃς καὶ πρῶτα μεσορραγέας κενεῶνας
γαίης ἀγρομένοισιν ἐνιπλήσας ποταμοῖσι
πευκεδανὴν ἀνέχευε καὶ ἐξέστεψε θάλασσαν,
ὀφρύσι καὶ ῥηγμῖσι περίδρομον ἀμφιπεδήσας,
εἴτε μιν εὐρυμέδοντα Ποσειδάωνα καλέσσαι,
εἴτ᾽ ἄρα καὶ Νηρῆα παλαίφατον, εἴτ᾽ ἄρα Φόρκυν
βέλτερον, εἴτε τιν᾽ ἄλλον ἁλὸς θεὸν ἰθυντῆρα.
ἀλλ᾽ οἱ μὲν μάλα πάντες, ὅσοι τ᾽ Οὔλυμπον ἔχουσι
δαίμονες οἵ τε θάλασσαν ὅσοι τ᾽ ἐΰδωρον ἄρουραν
ἠέρα τ᾽ ἐνναίουσι, πανίλαον ἦτορ ἔχοιεν
σοί τε, μάκαρ σκηπτοῦχε, καὶ ἀγλαόπαιδι γενέθλῃ
καὶ λαοῖς σύμπασι καὶ ἡμετέρῃσιν ἀοιδαῖς.

Ἰχθύσι δ᾽ οὔτε δίκη μεταρίθμιος οὔτε τις αἰδώς,
οὐ φιλότης· πάντες γὰρ ἀνάρσιοι ἀλλήλοισι
δυσμενέες πλώουσιν· ὁ δὲ κρατερώτερος αἰεὶ
δαίνυτ᾽ ἀφαυροτέρους, ἄλλῳ δ᾽ ἐπινήχεται ἄλλος

---

[a] Goddess of War.

[b] Hor. *C.* i. 10. 1 Mercuri facunde nepos Atlantis.

[c] Pind. *I.* i. 60 ἀγώνιος Ἑρμᾶς.

[d] Hesiod, *W.* 276 τόνδε γὰρ ἀνθρώποισι νόμον διέταξε Κρονίων, | ἰχθυσὶ μὲν καὶ θηρσὶ καὶ οἰωνοῖς πετεηνοῖς | ἐσθέμεν ἀλλήλους,

yoking oxen and ploughing the fields and reaping the fruitful harvest of wheat. Carpentry of wood and building of houses and weaving of cloth with the goodly wool of sheep—these hath Pallas taught to men. The gifts of Ares are swords and brazen tunics to array the limbs and helmets and spears and whatsoever things Enyo [a] delights in. The gifts of the Muses and Apollo are songs. Hermes hath bestowed eloquence [b] and doughty feats of strength.[c] Hephaestus hath in his charge the sweaty toil of the hammer. These devices also of the sea and the business of fishing and the power to mark the multitude of fishes that travel in the water—these hath some god given to men; even he who also first filled the rent bowels of earth with the gathered rivers and poured forth the bitter sea and wreathed it as a garland, confining it about with crags and beaches; whether one should more fitly call him wide-ruling Poseidon or ancient Nereus or Phorcys, or other god that rules the sea. But may all the gods that keep Olympus, and they that dwell in the sea, or on the bounteous earth, or in the air, have a gracious heart toward thee, O blessed wielder of the sceptre, and toward thy glorious offspring and to all thy people and to our song.

Among fishes neither justice [d] is of any account nor is there any mercy nor love; for all the fish that swim are bitter foes to one another. The stronger [e] ever devours the weaker; this against that swims

ἐπεὶ οὐ δίκη ἐστὶν ἐν αὐτοῖς; Plut. *Mor.* 964 B and *ibid.* 970 B *ἄμικτα γὰρ ἐκεῖνα (τὰ ἔναλα ζῷα) κομιδῇ πρὸς χάριν καὶ ἄστοργα;* Ael. vi. 50.

[e] Shakesp. *Per.* ii. 1, Fisherman iii. Master, I marvel how the fishes live in the sea. Fisherman i. Why, as men do a-land; the great ones eat up the little ones.

πότμον ἄγων, ἕτερος δ' ἑτέρῳ πόρσυνεν ἐδωδήν.
οἱ μὲν γὰρ γενύεσσι καὶ ἠνορέῃ βιόωνται
χειροτέρους· τοῖς δ' ἰὸν ἔχει στόμα· τοῖσι δ' ἄκανθαι
τύμμασι λευγαλέοισιν ἀμυνέμεναι πεφύασι,
πικραί τ' ὀξεῖαί τε χόλου πυρόεντος ἀκωκαί.
ὅσσοις δ' οὔτε βίην θεὸς ὤπασεν οὔτε τι κέντρον
θήγεται ἐκ μελέων, τοῖς δ' ἐκ φρενὸς ὅπλον ἔφυσε
βουλὴν κερδαλέην, πολυμήχανον, οἵ τε δόλοισι
πολλάκι καὶ κρατερὸν καὶ ὑπέρτερον ὤλεσαν ἰχθύν.
Οἷον καὶ νάρκῃ τερενόχροϊ φάρμακον ἀλκῆς
ἕσπεται αὐτοδίδακτον ἐν οἰκείοισι μέλεσσιν.
ἡ μὲν γὰρ μαλακή τε δέμας καὶ πᾶσ' ἀμενηνὴ
νωθής τε βραδυτῆτι βαρύνεται, οὐδέ κε φαίης
νηχομένην ὁράαν· μάλα γὰρ δύσφραστα κέλευθα
εἰλεῖται πολιοῖο δι' ὕδατος ἑρπύζουσα·
ἀλλά οἱ ἐν λαγόνεσσιν ἀναλκείης δόλος ἀλκή·
κερκίδες ἐμπεφύασι παρὰ πλευραῖς ἑκάτερθεν
ἀμφίδυμοι· τῶν εἴ τις ἐπιψαύσειε πελάσσας,
αὐτίκα οἱ μελέων σθένος ἔσβεσεν, ἐν δέ οἱ αἷμα
πήγνυται, οὐδ' ἔτι γυῖα φέρειν δύνατ', ἀλλά οἱ ἀλκὴ
ἧκα μαραινομένοιο παρίεται ἄφρονι νάρκῃ.
ἡ δ' εὖ γινώσκουσα θεοῦ γέρας οἷον ἔδεκτο,
ὕπτιον ἀγκλίνασα μένει δέμας ἐν ψαμάθοισι·
κεῖται δ' ἀστεμφὴς οἵη νέκυς· ὃς δέ κεν ἰχθὺς

---

[a] *C.* iv. 25 ff.; A. *P.A.* 662 b 33 ff.; A. 591 b 14 πολλάκις δὲ καὶ ἀλλήλων ἅπτονται . . . καὶ τῶν ἐλαττόνων οἱ μείζους.

[b] The Torpedo or Electric Ray. Three species occur in Mediterranean—*Torpedo marmorata* Risso, M.G. μουδιάστρα (Apost. p. 6), *T. narce*, *T. hebetans*; A. 505 a-506 b, 540 b 18, etc.; Ael. ix. 14, i. 36, etc.; Antig. 53; Phil. 36; Athen. 314; Plut. *Mor.* 978 B; Plin. ix. 143; Claudian, xlix. (xlvi. Gesner). The Torpedo has a pair of large electric organs between the pectoral fin and the head.

fraught with doom and one for another furnishes food. Some[a] overpower the weaker by force of jaws and strength; others have venomous mouth; others have spines wherewith to defend them with deadly blows—bitter, sharp points of fiery wrath. And those to whom God hath not given strength, and who have no sharp sting springing from the body, to these he hath given a weapon of the mind, even crafty counsel of many devices; these by guile ofttimes destroy a strong and mightier fish.

Thus the Cramp-fish[b] of tender flesh is endowed with a specific of valour, self-taught in its own limbs. For soft of body and altogether weak and sluggish it is weighed down with slowness,[c] and you could not say you see it swimming; hard to mark is its path as it crawls and creeps through the grey water. But in its loins it hath a piece of craft, its strength in weakness: even two rays planted in its sides, one on either hand. If one approach and touch these, straightway it quenches the strength of his body and his blood is frozen within him and his limbs can no longer carry him but he quietly pines away and his strength is drained by stupid torpor. Knowing well[d] what a gift it hath received from God, the Cramp-fish lays itself supine among the sands and so remains, lying unmoving as a corpse. But any fish that touches its

[c] A. 620 b 25 *ἁλίσκονται (βάτραχος, νάρκη, τρυγών) γὰρ ἔχοντες κεστρέας πολλάκις ὄντες αὐτοὶ βραδύτατοι τὸν τάχιστον τῶν ἰχθύων*; Claudian, *l.c.* 3 Illa quidem mollis segnique obnixa natatu | Reptat.

[d] Plin. ix. 143 novit torpedo vim suam ipsa non torpens mersaque in limo se occultat piscium qui supernantes obtorpuere corripiens; Claudian, *l.c.* 8 Conscia sortis | Utitur ingenio longeque extenta per algas | Attactu confisa subit. Immobilis haeret: | Qui tetigere iacent. Successu laeta resurgit | Et vivos impune ferox depascitur artus.

ἐγχρίμψῃ λαγόνεσσιν, ὁ μὲν λύτο, κάππεσε δ' αὔτως
ἀδρανίης βαθὺν ὕπνον, ἀμηχανίῃσι πεδηθείς·
ἡ δὲ θοῶς ἀνόρουσε καὶ οὐ κραιπνή περ ἐοῦσα,
γηθοσύνῃ, ζωὸν δὲ κατεσθίει ἶσα θανόντι.
πολλάκι καὶ κατὰ λαῖτμα μετ' ἰχθύσιν ἀντιάσασα
νηχομένοις κραιπνὴν μὲν ἐπειγομένων σβέσεν ὁρμὴν
ἐγγὺς ἐπιψαύσασα καὶ ἐσσυμένους ἐπέδησεν·
ἔσταν δ' αὐαλέοι καὶ ἀμήχανοι, οὔτε κελεύθων
δύσμοροι οὔτε φυγῆς μεμνημένοι· ἡ δὲ μένουσα
οὐδὲν ἀμυνομένους καταδαίνυται οὐδ' ἀΐοντας.
οἷον δ' ὀρφναίοισιν ἐν εἰδώλοισιν ὀνείρων
ἀνδρὸς ἀτυζομένοιο καὶ ἱεμένοιο φέβεσθαι
θρώσκει μὲν κραδίη, τὰ δὲ γούνατα παλλομένοιο
ἀστεμφὴς ἅτε δεσμὸς ἐπειγομένοιο βαρύνει,
τοίην γυιοπέδην τεχνάζεται ἰχθύσι νάρκη.
Βάτραχος αὖ νωθὴς μὲν ὁμῶς καὶ μαλθακὸς ἰχθύς,

[a] Hom. *Il.* xxii. 199 (of Achilles and Hector) ὡς δ' ἐν ὀνείρῳ οὐ δύναται φεύγοντα διώκειν· οὔτ' ἄρ' ὁ τὸν δύναται ὑποφεύγειν οὔθ' ὁ διώκειν; *cf.* Verg. *A.* xii. 908 Ac velut in somnis, oculos ubi languida pressit | Nocte quies, nequidquam avidos extendere cursus | Velle videmur et in mediis conatibus aegri | Succidimus.

[b] *Lophius piscatorius* L., M.G. φλάσκα at Chalcis, σκλεμποῦ and βατραχόψαρο at Patras (Apost. p. 10). Fr. Loup de mer, Diable, Crapaud de mer, etc. In this country *Angler*, *Sea-devil*, etc. It is not infrequently cast ashore in Scotland, especially on the E. coast. The attention of the present writer was called (by his son J. L. R. M.) to a fine specimen near Largo in Fife, April 1927, where it lay amid a crowd of Lump-fish, *Cyclopterus lumpus*, hen-paidle and cock-paidle (Scott, *Antiquary* c. xi.); *cf.* St. John, *N.H. in Moray*, p. 210; A. 540 b 18, 620 b 11 ff. βάτραχον τὸν ἁλιέα; *De gen.* 749 a 23, etc.; Ael. ix. 24; Athen. 286 b, 330 a; Plin. ix. 78 ranae, 143 nec minor sollertia ranae quae in mari piscatrix vocatur. Eminentia sub oculis cornicula turbato limo exerit, adsultantibus pisciculis retrahens, donec tam prope accedant ut adsiliat; Ov. *Hal.* 126 molles tergore

loins is paralysed and falls even so into the deep sleep of weakness, fettered by helplessness. And the Cramp-fish, albeit not swift, speedily leaps up in joy and devours the living fish as if it were dead. Many times also when it meets with fishes swimming in the gulf of the sea, it quenches with its touch their swift career for all their haste and checks them in mid course. And they stay, blasted and helpless, thinking not, poor wretches, either of going on or of flight. But the Cramp-fish stays by and devours them, while they make no defence nor are conscious of their fate. Even as in the darkling phantoms of a dream,[a] when a man is terrified and fain to flee, his heart leaps, but, struggle as he may, a steadfast bond as it were weighs down his eager knees: even such a fetter doth the Cramp-fish devise for fishes.

The Fishing-frog [b] again is likewise a sluggish and

ranae; Cicero *N.D.* ii. 125 Ranae autem marinae dicuntur obruere sese arena solere et moveri prope aquam: ad quas quasi ad escam pisces cum accesserint confici a ranis atque consumi. "The first dorsal ray, inserted on the snout, is very long, movable in every direction, and terminates in a dermal flap, which is supposed to be used by the 'Angler' as a bait, attracting other fishes, which are soon ingulfed in the enormous gape" *C.N.H.* vii. p. 718; Aristotle, classifying it as a Selachian and holding all Selachians to be viviparous, notes the *βάτραχος* as the one exception (A. 505 b 3 *τὰ δὲ σελάχη πάντα ζῳοτόκα πλὴν βατράχου*: *cf.* 564 b 18, etc., *De gen.* 749 a 23). In *De gen.* 754 a 26 he gives as the reason for this the immense size of its head—*πολλαπλασίαν τοῦ λοιποῦ σώματος καὶ ταύτην ἀκανθώδη καὶ σφόδρα τραχεῖαν. διόπερ οὐδ' ὕστερον εἰσδέχεται τοὺς νεοττοὺς οὐδ' ἐξ ἀρχῆς ζῳοτοκεῖ.* "Il y avait une bien meilleure réponse à faire, c'est que la baudroie n'est pas un cartilagineux et d'ailleurs il s'en faut beaucoup que les autres cartilagineux soient tous vivipares; enfin, ni les poissons cartilagineux ni les autres ne font rentrer leurs petits dans leur corps" Cuvier, xii. p. 363.

αἴσχιστος δ' ἰδέειν· στόμα δ' οἴγεται εὐρὺ μάλιστα·
ἀλλ' ἄρα καὶ τῷ μῆτις ἀνεύρατο γαστέρι φορβήν.
αὐτὸς μὲν πηλοῖο κατ' εὐρώεντος ἐλυσθεὶς
κέκλιται ἀτρεμέων, ὀλίγην δ' ἀνὰ σάρκα τιταίνει,
ἥ ῥά οἱ ἐκ γένυος νεάτης ὑπένερθε πέφυκε
λεπτή τ' ἀργεννή τε, κακὴ δέ οἱ ἐστὶν ἀϋτμή·
τὴν θαμὰ δινεύει, δόλον ἰχθύσι βαιοτέροισιν·
οἵ ῥά μιν εἰσορόωντες ἐφορμώωσι λαβέσθαι.
αὐτὰρ ὁ τὴν ἂψ αὖτις ἐφέλκεται ἀτρέμας εἴσω,
ἦκα μάλ' ἀσπαίρουσαν ὑπὸ στόμα, τοὶ δ' ἐφέπονται
οὐδὲν ὀϊόμενοι κρυπτὸν δόλον, ὄφρα λάθωσι
βατράχου εὐρείῃσιν ἔσω γενύεσσι μιγέντες.
ὡς δ' ὅτε τις κούφοισι πάγην ὄρνισι τιτύσκων,
πυροὺς τοὺς μὲν ἔρηνε δόλου προπάροιθε πυλάων,
ἄλλους δ' ἔνδον ἔθηκεν, ὑπεστήριξε δὲ τέχνην·
τοὺς δὲ λιλαιομένους ἕλκει πόθος ὀξὺς ἐδωδῆς,
εἴσω δὲ προγένοντο, καὶ οὐκέτι νόστος ἑτοῖμος
ἐκδῦναι, δαιτὸς δὲ κακὴν εὕραντο τελευτήν·
ὣς κείνους ἀμενηνὸς ἐπέσπασεν ἠπεροπεύσας
βάτραχος, οὐδ' ἐνόησαν ἑὸν σπεύδοντες ὄλεθρον.
τοῖα καὶ ἀγκυλόμητιν ἐπέκλυον ἐντύνασθαι
κερδώ· ὅτ' οἰωνῶν ἀγέλην πλήθουσαν ἴδηται,
δοχμίη ἀγκλινθεῖσα, τανυσσαμένη θοὰ κῶλα,
ὄμματ' ἐπιμύει, σὺν δὲ στόμα πάμπαν ἐρείδει·
φαίης κ' εἰσορόων ἤ μιν βαθὺν ὕπνον ἰαύειν,
ἠὲ καὶ ἀτρεκέως κεῖσθαι νέκυν· ὧδε γὰρ ἄπνους
αἰόλα βουλεύουσα παραβλήδην τετάνυσται·
οἱ δέ μιν εἰσορόωντες ἀολλέες ἰθὺς ἵενται
ὄρνιθες, λάχνην δὲ διαψαίρουσι πόδεσσιν,
ἠΰτε κερτομέοντες· ἐπὴν δέ οἱ ἐγγὺς ὀδόντων

---

[a] Pind. *I.* iii. 65 μῆτιν δ' ἀλώπηξ, αἰετοῦ ἅτ' ἀναπιτναμένα

soft fish and most hideous to behold, with mouth that opens exceeding wide. But for him also craft devises food for his belly. Wrapt himself in the slimy mud he lies motionless, while he extends aloft a little bit of flesh which grows from the bottom of his jaw below, fine and bright, and it has an evil breath. This he waves incessantly, a snare for lesser fishes which, seeing it, are fain to seize it. But the Fishing-frog quietly draws it again gently quivering within his mouth, and the fishes follow, not suspecting any hidden guile until, ere they know it, they are caught within the wide jaws of the Fishing-frog. As when a man, devising a snare for lightsome birds, sprinkles some grains of wheat before the gates of guile while others he puts inside, and props up the trap; the keen desire of food draws the eager birds and they pass within and no more is return or escape prepared for them, but they win an evil end to their banquet; even so the weak Fishing-frog deceives and attracts the fishes and they perceive not that they are hastening their own destruction. A like device, I have heard, the cunning Fox [a] contrives. When she sees a dense flight of birds, she lies down on her side and stretches out her swift limbs and closes her eyes and shuts fast her mouth. Seeing her you would say that she was deep asleep or even lying quite dead: so breathless she lies stretched out, contriving guile. The birds, beholding, rush straightway upon her in a crowd and tear her fur with their feet, as if in mockery. But when they come nigh her teeth, then

ῥόμβον ἴσχει; Ael. vi. 24 τὰς δὲ ὠτίδας (Bustards) ἐν τῷ Πόντῳ θηρεύουσιν οὕτως· ἀποστραφεῖσαι αὑταὶ καὶ εἰς γῆν κύψασαι τὴν κέρκον ἀνατείνουσιν . . . αἱ δὲ ἀπατηθεῖσαι προσίασιν ὡς πρὸς ὄρνιν ὁμόφυλον, εἶτα πλησίον γενόμεναι τῆς ἀλώπεκος ἁλίσκονται ῥᾷστα, ἐπιστραφείσης καὶ ἐπιθεμένης.

ἔλθωσιν, τότ' ἔπειτα δόλου πετάσασα θύρετρα,
ἐξαπίνης συνέμαρψε καὶ ἔσπασεν εὐρὺ χανοῦσα
ἄγρην κερδαλέην, ὅσσην ἕλεν οἰμήσασα.
Καὶ μὲν δὴ δολόμητις ἐπίκλοπον εὕρατο θήρην
σηπίη· ἐκ γάρ οἱ κεφαλῆς πεφύασιν ἀραιοὶ
ἀκρέμονες προτενεῖς, ὥστε πλόκοι, οἷσι καὶ αὐτὴ
ὥστε περ ὁρμιῇσιν ἐφέλκεται ἰχθύας ἄγρῃ,
πρηνὴς ἐν ψαμάθοισιν ὑπ' ὀστράκῳ εἰλυθεῖσα.
κείναις δὲ πλοκαμῖσι καὶ ἡνίκα κύματα θύει
χείματι πετράων ἀντίσχεται, ἠΰτε τις νηῦς
πείσματ' ἐπ' ἀκταίῃσιν ἀναψαμένη σπιλάδεσσι.
Καρῖδες δ' ὀλίγαι μὲν ἰδεῖν, ἴση δὲ καὶ ἀλκὴ
γυίοις, ἀλλὰ δόλοισι καὶ ἄλκιμον ὤλεσαν ἰχθύν,
λάβρακα, σφετέρῃσιν ἐπικλέα λαβροσύνῃσιν.
οἱ μὲν γὰρ σπεύδουσι καὶ ἰθύουσι λαβέσθαι
καρίδων, ταῖς δ' οὔτε φυγεῖν σθένος οὔτε μάχεσθαι,
ὀλλύμεναι δ' ὀλέκουσι καὶ οὓς πέφνουσι φονῆας.
εὖτε γὰρ ἀμφιχανόντες ἔσω μάρψωσιν ὀδόντων,

---

[a] *Sepia officinalis* L., the Common Cuttle.

[b] A. 523 b 21 τῶν μὲν οὖν μαλακίων καλουμένων τὰ μὲν ἔξω μόρια τάδ' ἐστίν, ἓν μὲν οἱ ὀνομαζόμενοι πόδες, δεύτερον δὲ τούτων ἐχομένη ἡ κεφαλή.

[c] *i.e.* tentacles, προβοσκίδες, πλεκτάναι. *Cf.* A. 523 b 29 ἰδίᾳ τ' ἔχουσιν αἵ τε σηπίαι καὶ αἱ τευθίδες καὶ οἱ τεῦθοι δύο προβοσκίδας μακράς, ἐπ' ἄκρων τραχύτητα ἐχούσας δικότυλον, αἷς προσάγονταί τε καὶ λαμβάνουσιν εἰς τὸ στόμα τὴν τροφήν, καὶ ὅταν χειμὼν ᾖ, βαλλόμεναι πρός τινα πέτραν ὥσπερ ἀγκύρας ἀποσαλεύειν; Plin. ix. 83 sepiae et loligini pedes duo ex his longissimi et asperi quibus ad ora admovent cibos et in fluctibus se velut ancoris stabiliunt, cetera cirri quibus venantur; Athen. 323 d τρέφονται δ' αἱ μικραὶ σηπίαι τοῖς λεπτοῖς ἰχθυδίοις, ἀποτείνουσαι τὰς προβοσκίδας ὥσπερ ὁρμιὰς καὶ ταύταις θηρεύουσαι. λέγεται δ' ὡς ὅταν ὁ χειμὼν γένηται τῶν πετριδίων ὥσπερ ἀγκύραις ταῖς προβοσκίσι λαμβανόμεναι ὁρμοῦσι; Ael. v. 41; Plut. *Mor.* 978 D.

[d] The Cuttle-fish has no shell. But the σηπίον, or hard

she opens the doors of guile and suddenly seizes them, and with wide gape cunningly catches her prey, even all that she takes at a swoop.

Yea, the crafty Cuttle-fish[a] also has found a cunning manner of hunting. From her head[b] grow long slender branches,[c] like locks of hair, wherewith as with lines she draws and captures fish, prone in the sand and coiled beneath her shell.[d] With those locks, too, when the waves rage in wintry weather, she clings to the rocks even as a ship fastens her cables to the rocks upon the shore.

Prawns[e] are small to look at and small too is the strength of their limbs, yet by their craft they destroy a valiant fish, even the Basse[f] named[g] for its gluttony. For the Basse are eager and keen to seize the Prawns; and these have no strength either to flee or to fight, yet as they are destroyed they destroy and slay their slayers. When the gaping[h] Basse have caught them within their teeth, they leap oftentimes

(internal) part, towards the back of the body, which is described A. 524 b 22 τῇ μὲν οὖν σηπίᾳ καὶ τῇ τευθίδι καὶ τῷ τεύθῳ ἐντός ἐστι τὰ στερεὰ ἐν τῷ πρανεῖ τοῦ σώματος, ἃ καλοῦσι τὸ μὲν σηπίον τὸ δὲ ξίφος, *cf.* *P.A.* 654 a 20, was apparently sometimes called ὄστρακον, *cf.* Athen. 323 c τὴν σηπίαν δὲ Ἀριστοτέλης (φησὶ) πόδας ἔχειν ὀκτώ . . ., ἔχει δὲ καὶ ὀδόντας δύο . . . καὶ τὸ λεγόμενον ὄστρακον ἐν τῷ νώτῳ. Oppian may have misunderstood this, or, equating ὄστρακον with νῶτον, he may have meant ὑπ' ὀστράκῳ εἰλυθεῖσα as = "hunched up." It seems then not advisable to alter the text.

[e] A. 525 a 34 γένη δὲ πλείω τῶν καρίδων . . . αἵ τε κυφαὶ καὶ αἱ κράγγονες καὶ τὸ μικρὸν γένος (A. *P.A.* 684 a 14), probably *Palaemon squilla*, *Squilla mantis*, and *Crangon vulgaris* (shrimps). Ael. i. 30 gives a similar account of their fight with the Basse, and classes them as ἕλειοι, ἐκ φυκίων, πετραῖαι.

[f] *Labrax lupus* Cuv., M.G. λαυράκι; Apost. p. 12.

[g] *i.e.* λάβραξ from λάβρος: ἰχθύων ὀψοφαγίστατος, Ael. *l.c.*

[h] Ael. *l.c.* κέχηνε δὲ ὁ λάβραξ καὶ μέγα.

αἵδε θαμὰ θρώσκουσι καὶ ἐς μεσάτην ὑπερῴην
ὀξὺ κέρας χρίμπτουσι, τό τε σφίσι τέλλεται ἄκρης
ἐκ κεφαλῆς· λάβραξ δὲ φίλης κεκορημένος ἄγρης
νύγματος οὐκ ἀλέγει· τὸ δέ μιν νέμεταί τε καὶ ἕρπει,
εἰσόκε τρυχόμενόν μιν ἕλῃ μόρος ἐξ ὀδυνάων·
ὀψὲ δὲ γινώσκει νέκυος δεδαϊγμένος αἰχμῇ.
Ἔστι δέ τις πηλοῖσιν ἐφέστιος ὠμοφάγος βοῦς,
εὐρύτατος πάντεσσι μετ᾽ ἰχθύσιν· ἦ γάρ οἱ εὖρος
πολλάκις ἑνδεκάπηχυ δυωδεκάπηχύ τ᾽ ἐτύχθη·
οὐτιδανὸς δὲ βίην καί οἱ δέμας ἄμμορον ἀλκῆς,
μαλθακόν· ἐν δέ οἱ εἰσὶν ἀείδελοι ἔνδον ὀδόντες
βαιοί τ᾽ οὐ κρατεροί τε· βίῃ δέ κεν οὔτι δαμάσσαι,
ἀλλὰ δόλῳ καὶ φῶτας ἐπίφρονας εἷλε πεδήσας·
δαιτὶ γὰρ ἀνδρομέῃ ἐπιτέρπεται, ἔξοχα δ᾽ αὐτῷ
ἀνθρώπων κρέα τερπνὰ καὶ εὐάντητος ἐδωδή.
εὖτέ τιν᾽ ἀθρήσῃ νεάτην ὑπὸ βύσσαν ἰόντα
ἀνθρώπων, ὅσσοισιν ὑποβρύχιος πόνος ἅλμης
μέμβλεται, αὐτὰρ ὁ κοῦφος ὑπὲρ κεφαλῆφιν ἀερθεὶς
νήχεται ἀστεμφής, μεγάρων ὀρόφοισιν ἐοικώς,
ἄτροπος ἀμφιταθείς, σὺν δ᾽ ἔρχεται, ᾗ κεν ἵῃσι
δειλὸς ἀνήρ, μίμνοντι δ᾽ ἐφίσταται ἠΰτε πῶμα.
ὡς δὲ πάϊς δολόεντα μόρον λίχνοισι μύεσσιν
ἔστησεν· τὸν δ᾽ οὔτι πάγης λόχον ὁρμαίνοντα

---

[a] Ael. *l.c.* τὸ ἔξοχον τῆς κεφαλῆς, ἔοικε δὲ τριήρους ἐμβόλῳ καὶ μάλα γε ὀξεῖ, καὶ ἄλλως ἔχει δίκην πριόνων.

[b] Ael. *l.c.* καὶ καινότατα δήπου ἀποκτείνασα ἀνῄρηται.

[c] A. 540 b 17 σελάχη δ᾽ ἐστὶ τά τε εἰρημένα καὶ βοῦς καὶ λάμια καὶ ἀετὸς καὶ νάρκη καὶ βάτραχος καὶ πάντα τὰ γαλεώδη; 566 b 2 δελφὶς καὶ φάλαινα καὶ τὰ ἄλλα κήτη, ὅσα μὴ ἔχει βράγχια ἀλλὰ φυσητῆρα ζῳοτοκοῦσιν, ἔτι δὲ πρίστις καὶ βοῦς; Plin. ix. 78 Planorum piscium alterum est genus quod pro spina cartilaginem habet, ut raiae, pastinacae, squatinae, torpedo, et quos bovis, lamiae, aquilae, ranae nominibus Graeci

and fix in the midst of the palate of the Basse the sharp horn[a] which springs from the top of their heads. The Basse, glutted with the prey which he loves, heeds not the prick. But it spreads and creeps apace, until, worn out with pain, doom overtakes him; and too late he knows that he is stricken by the spear of the dead.[b]

There is a fish which is at home in the mud, even the ravenous Ox-ray,[c] broadest among all fishes; for indeed his breadth is often eleven cubits or twelve. But in might he is a weakling, and his body is devoid of strength and soft. The teeth within his mouth are inconspicuous, small and not strong. By might he could not overpower anything, but by craft he ensnares and overcomes even cunning men. For he greatly delights to banquet upon man and human flesh above all is to him pleasing and a welcome food. When he beholds anyone of those men who have their business in the deep waters of the brine descending to the nether depths, he rises lightly above his head and swims steadfastly, like the roof of a house, stretched about him inexorably. Where the wretched man goes, he goes, and when the man halts, he stands over him like a lid. As a boy sets a guileful doom for greedy mice; and the mouse, not dreaming of the ambush of the trap, is driven within by the desire of the belly;

appellant. . . . Omnia autem carnivora sunt talia . . . et cum ceteri pisces ova pariant, hoc genus solum, ut ea quae cete appellant, animal pariat, excepta quam ranam vocant. *Cf.* Athen. 330 a; Ael. i. 19, xi. 37; Phil. 100; Ov. *Hal.* 94 Nam gaudent pelago quales scombrique bovesque (Plin. xxxii. 152). Clearly one of the Rays—probably *Cephaloptera Giorna* = Couch's Ox-ray. Some members of this family (*Cephalopteridae*) attain an incredible size—one taken at Messina weighing more than half a ton.

γαστὴρ ἔνδον ἔλασσε, θοῶς δέ οἱ ἄγγος ὕπερθε
κοῖλον ἐπεσμαράγησεν, ὁ δ' οὐκέτι πολλὰ μενοινῶν·
ἐκφυγέειν δύναται στιβαρὸν σκέπας, ὄφρα ἑ κοῦρος
μάρψῃ τε κτείνῃ τε, γέλων δ' ἐπιθήσεται ἄγρῃ·
ὣς ὅ γ' ὑπὲρ κεφαλῆς βροτέης ὀλοφώϊος ἰχθὺς
πέπτατ' ἐρητύων ἀναδύμεναι, εἰσόκ' ἀϋτμὴ
φῶτα λίπῃ, ψυχὴν δὲ μετεκπνεύσῃ ῥοθίοισιν·
ἔνθα ἑ τεθνηῶτα δυσώνυμος ἀμφιέπει βοῦς
δαινύμενος, τέχνῃσιν ἑλὼν δυσμήχανον ἄγρην.

Καὶ μέν τις μνιαροῖσιν ἐπὶ πλαταμῶσι νοήσας
καρκίνον αἰνήσει καὶ ἀγάσσεται εἵνεκα τέχνης
κερδαλέης· καὶ τῷ γὰρ ἐπιφροσύνην πόρε δαίμων
ὄστρεα φέρβεσθαι, γλυκερὴν καὶ ἄμοχθον ἐδωδήν.
ὄστρεα μὲν κληῖδας ἀναπτύξαντα θυρέτρων
ἰλὺν λιχμάζουσι καὶ ὕδατος ἰσχανόωντα
πέπταται, ἀγκοίνῃσιν ἐφήμενα πετραίῃσι·
καρκίνος αὖ ψηφῖδα παρὰ ῥηγμῖνος ἀείρας
λέχριος ὀξείῃσι φέρει χηλῇσι μεμαρπώς,
λάθρη δ' ἐμπελάει, μέσσῳ δ' ἐνεθήκατο λᾶαν
ὀστρέῳ· ἔνθεν ἔπειτα παρήμενος εἰλαπινάζει
δαῖτα φίλην· τὸ δ' ἄρ' οὔτι καὶ ἱέμενόν περ ἐρεῖσαι
ἀμφιδύμους πλάστιγγας ἔχει σθένος, ἀλλ' ὑπ' ἀνάγκης
οἴγεται, ὄφρα θάνῃ τε καὶ ἀγρευτῆρα κορέσσῃ.

Τῷ δ' ἴσα τεχνάζουσι καὶ ἀστέρες ἑρπυστῆρες

and swiftly the hollow vessel claps to above him and, for all his endeavour, he can no more escape from the strong cover, till the boy seizes and kills him, mocking the while his prey ; even so over the man's head the deadly fish extends, preventing him from rising to the surface, until breath leaves him and he gasps out his life amid the waves ; where the Ox-ray of evil name sets about him and feasts upon him, having by his wiles captured a difficult prey.

And one who observes a Crab among the mossy ledges will praise and admire him for his cunning art. For to him also hath Heaven given wisdom to feed on Oysters, a sweet and unlaborious food. The Oysters open the bars of their doors and lick the mud, and, in their desire for water, sit wide open in the arms of the rocks. The Crab [a] on the other hand takes a pebble from the beach and, moving sideways, carries it clutched in his sharp claws. Stealthily he draws near and puts the stone in the middle of the Oyster. Then he sits by and makes a pleasant feast. And the Oyster, though fain, is unable to shut his two valves, but gapes perforce until he dies and gluts his captor.

A like craft is practised also by the reptile Star-

[a] *Cambridge N.H.* iii. p. 111 "Crabs crush the young shells with their claws, and are said to gather in bands and scratch sand or mud over the larger specimens, which makes them open their shells."

εἰνάλιοι· καὶ τοῖς γὰρ ἐπ᾽ ὄστρεα μῆτις ὀπηδεῖ·
ἀλλ᾽ οὐ λᾶαν ἄγουσι συνέμπορον οὐδ᾽ ἐπίκουρον
κεῖνοι, τρηχὺ δὲ κῶλον ἐνηρείσαντο μέσοισι
πεπταμένοις· τὰ μὲν ὧδε πιέζεται, οἱ δὲ νέμονται.
  Ὄστρακον αὖ βυθίας μὲν ἔχει πλάκας, ἐν δέ οἱ ἰχθὺς
πίννη ναιετάει κεκλημένος· ἡ μὲν ἄναλκις
οὔτε τι μητίσασθαι ἐπίσταται οὔτε τι ῥέξαι,
ἀλλ᾽ ἄρα οἱ ξυνόν τε δόμον ξυνήν τε καλύπτρην
καρκίνος ἐνναίει, φέρβει δέ μιν ἠδὲ φυλάσσει·
τῷ καὶ πιννοφύλαξ κικλήσκεται· ἀλλ᾽ ὅτε κόχλου
ἰχθὺς ἔνδον ἵκηται, ὁ δ᾽ οὐ φρονέουσαν ἀμύξας
δήγματι κερδαλέῳ πίννην ἔλεν· ἡ δ᾽ ὀδύνῃσιν
ὄστρακα συμπλατάγησε καὶ ἔνδον ἐφράσσατο ἄγρην
αὐτῇ τ᾽ ἠδ᾽ ἑτάρῳ, ξυνόν θ᾽ ἅμα δεῖπνον ἕλοντο.

---

[a] A. *P.A.* 681 b 8 καὶ τὸ τῶν ἀστέρων ἐστὶ γένος· καὶ γὰρ τοῦτο προσπῖπτον ἐγχυμίζει πολλὰ τῶν ὀστρέων; Ael. ix. 22 τὰ μὲν κέχηνε πολλάκις ψύχους δεόμενα καὶ ἄλλως εἴ τί σφισιν ἐμπέσοι τούτῳ τραφησόμενα· οἱ τοίνυν ἀστέρες μέσον τῶν ὀστράκων διείρουσιν ἓν κοῦλον τῶν σφετέρων ἕκαστος καὶ ἐμπίμπλανται τῶν σαρκῶν, διειργομένων συνελθεῖν τῶν ὀστράκων αὖθις. *Cf.* *C.N.H. l.c.* "Sometimes in a single night a whole bed of oysters will be destroyed by an invasion of Star-fish," where different accounts of the procedure of Star-fish are given: 1. The Star-fish wraps its turned-out stomach round the Oyster, enclosing the mouth of the shell so that the Oyster sickens, the hinge-spring relaxes its hold, and the shell opening permits the Star-fish to suck the gelatinous contents. 2. The Star-fish seizes the Oyster with two of his fingers, while with the other three he files away the edge

fishes [a] of the sea; for these too have a device against Oysters. Howbeit they bring no stone as comrade nor ally, but insert in the middle of the open Oyster a rough limb. Thus the Oysters are overcome, while the Starfish feed.

A shell again keeps the plains of the deep, wherein dwells a fish called Pinna.[b] The Pinna herself is weak and can of herself devise nothing nor do aught, but in one house and one shelter with her dwells a Crab which feeds and guards her; wherefore it is called the Pinna-guard. Now when a fish comes within the shell, the Crab seizes the unheeding Pinna and wounds her with crafty bite. Then in her pain she claps her shells together and so contrives to catch within a prey for herself and her companion, and

of the flat valve until he can introduce an arm. 3. The Star-fish suffocates the Oyster by applying two of its fingers so closely to the edge of the valves that the Oyster is unable to open them; after a while the vital powers relax and the shell gapes. 4. The Star-fish pours a secretion from its mouth, which paralyses the hinge-muscle and causes the shell to open. *Cf.* Plin. ix. 183; Plut. *Mor.* 978 B.

[b] A genus of bivalve Molluscs. A. 547 b 15 *αἱ δὲ πίνναι ὀρθαὶ φύονται ἐκ τοῦ βυσσοῦ ἐν τοῖς ἀμμώδεσι καὶ βορβορωδέσιν. ἔχουσι δ' ἐν αὑταῖς πιννοφύλακα, αἱ μὲν καρίδιον* [prob. *Pontonia Tyrrhena* Latr.], *αἱ δὲ καρκίνιον* [*Pinnotheres veterum* Bosc.] *οὗ στερισκόμεναι διαφθείρονται θᾶττον*; *ibid.* b 28 *ἐν ταῖς πίνναις οἱ καλούμενοι πιννοτῆραι.* *Cf.* Athen. 83 d-e; Ael. iii. 29; Phil. 110; Plut. *Mor.* 980 B; Plin. ix. 115, xxxii, 150; Cic. *N.D.* ii. 48.123; *De fin.* iii. 19. 63; Soph. *fr.* 116; Aristoph. *Vesp.* 1510 (of Xenocles, son of Carcinus) *ὁ πιννοτήρης οὗτός ἐστι τοῦ γένους*; *Camb. N.H.* iii. p. 62 "Several of the Crustacea live associated with certain molluscs. *Pinnoteres* lives within the shell of *Pinna*, *Ostrea*, *Astarte*, *Petunculus*, and others. Apparently the females alone reside within the shell of their host, while the males seize favourable opportunities to visit them there."

ὣς ἄρα καὶ πλωτῆρσιν ἐν ὑγροπόροισιν ἔασι
τοὶ μὲν κερδαλέοι, τοὶ δ' ἄφρονες, οἷα καὶ ἡμῖν
ἀνδράσιν, οὐδέ τι πᾶσιν ἐναίσιμόν ἐστι νόημα.
Φράζεο δ' ἀφραδίῃ προφερέστατον ἡμεροκοίτην
ἰχθύν, ὃν παρὰ πάντας ἀεργότατον τέκεν ἅλμη.
τοῦ δ' ἤτοι κεφαλῆς μὲν ἄνω τέτραπται ὕπερθεν
ὄμματα, καὶ στόμα λάβρον ἐν ὀφθαλμοῖσι μέσοισιν·
αἰεὶ δ' ἐν ψαμάθοισι πανημέριος τετάνυσται
εὕδων, νυκτὶ δὲ μοῦνον ἀνέγρεται ἠδ' ἀλάληται·
τοὔνεκα κέκληται καὶ νυκτερίς· ἀλλά μιν ἄτη
γαστρὸς ἀτεκμάρτοιο κακὴ λάχεν· οὐ γὰρ ἐδωδῆς
ἢ κόρον ἠέ τι μέτρον ἐπίσταται, ἀλλ' ἀτέλεστον
λυσσομανῆ βούβρωστιν ἀναιδέϊ γαστρὶ φυλάσσει·
οὐδέ ποτ' ἂν λήξειεν ἐδητύος ἐγγὺς ἐούσης,
εἰσόκεν οἱ νηδύς τε μέση διὰ πᾶσα ῥαγείη,
αὐτός τε προταθεὶς πέσῃ ὕπτιος, ἠέ τις ἄλλος
πέφνῃ μιν νεπόδων πυμάτης ἔμφορτον ἐδωδῆς.
σῆμα δέ τοι τόδε γαστρὸς ἀειμάργοιο πιφαύσκω·

---

[a] Chrysippus *ap.* Athen. 83 d *ἡ πίννη καὶ ὁ πιννοτήρης συνεργὰ ἀλλήλοις, κατ' ἴδια οὐ δυνάμενα συμμένειν. ἡ μὲν οὖν πίννη ὄστρεόν ἐστιν, ὁ δὲ πιννοτήρης καρκίνος μικρός. καὶ ἡ πίννη διαστήσασα τὸ ὄστρακον ἡσυχάζει τηροῦσα τὰ ἐπεισιόντα ἰχθύδια, ὁ δὲ πιννοτήρης παρεστὼς ὅταν εἰσέλθῃ τι δάκνει αὐτὴν ὥσπερ σημαίνων, ἡ δὲ δηχθεῖσα συμμύει. καὶ οὕτως τὸ ἀποληφθὲν ἔνδον κατεσθίουσι κοινῇ*; Theophrast. *C. P.* ii. 17. 8 (in a discussion of Parasitism in general) *ζῷα ἐν ζῴοις οἷον τά τε ἐν ταῖς πίνναις ἐστὶ καὶ ὅσα ἄλλα ζῳοτροφεῖ*; *ibid.* 9 *οὔτε γὰρ ἴσως ταῖς πίνναις βίος εἰ μὴ διὰ τὸν κάρκινον*.

[b] *Uranoscopus scaber*, M.G. λύχνος (Bik. p. 81, λῦχνος Erh. p. 81, while Apost. p. 9 would write λίχνος = gourmand). The name *οὐρανοσκόπος*, referring to the upward direction of the eyes, and *καλλιώνυμος*, euphemistically referring to ugliness (*cf.* *καλλίας* = ape), might be applied to various fishes, *e.g.* ***Lophius piscatorius***, but the identification of the

they take a common meal together.[a] Thus even among the swimming tribes that travel in the water some are crafty and some are stupid, as among us men, and not all have a right understanding.

Mark now a fish that exceeds all in stupidity, even the Day-sleeper,[b] lazy beyond all that the sea breeds. The eyes in his head are turned upward and the ravenous mouth between his eyes. Always he lies all day stretched in the sands asleep and only at night does he awake and wander abroad; wherefore he is also called the Bat. But an evil doom is his for his limitless appetite. For he knows no satiety of food nor any measure, but in his shameless belly he nurses gluttony, rabid and endless, nor would he cease from feeding if food were at hand, till his belly itself burst utterly in the midst and himself fall flat upon his back or some other fish kill him, gorged with his latest meal. This sign I tell you of his ravenous

καλλιώνυμος of Aristotle with *Uranoscopus scaber* is proved by A. 506 b 10 ἔχει δὲ καὶ ὁ καλλιώνυμος (τὴν χολήν, the gall-bladder) ἐπὶ τῷ ἥπατι, ὅσπερ ἔχει μεγίστην τῶν ἰχθύων ὡς κατὰ μέγεθος, which is true of the *Uranoscopus*, but not of the *Callionymus* of Linnaeus (Cuv. et Val. xii. p. 262). *Cf.* Ael. xiii. 4 who quotes Aristotle, Menander, and Anaxippus for this peculiarity; Plin. xxxii. 69 Callionymi fel cicatrices sanat et carnes oculorum supervacuas consumit. Nulli hoc piscium copiosius ut existimavit Menander quoque in comoedis [=Menand. *ap.* Ael. *l.c.* τίθημ' ἔχειν χολήν σε καλλιωνύμου πλείω]. Idem piscis et uranoscopus vocatur ab oculo quem in capite habet; *ibid.* 146 callionymus sive uranoscopus; Athen. 356 a οὐρανοσκόπος δὲ καὶ ὁ ἁγνὸς καλούμενος ἢ καὶ καλλιώνυμος βαρεῖς. *Cf.* 282 d-e, A. 598 a 11 πρόσγειος, which suits *Uranoscopus* as well as the *Callionymus* of Linnaeus. For the gall-bladder of *Uranoscopus cf.* Cuv. iii. 296 La vésicule du fiel est énorme et a la forme d'une fiole à long cou, suspendu à un canal cholédoque aussi gros que le duodénum.

εἰ γάρ τίς μιν ἑλὼν θήρης ἀποπειρήσαιτο
χειρὶ βορὴν ὀρέγων, ὁ δὲ δέξεται, εἰσόκεν αὐτοῦ
λαβροτάτου στόματος νηήσεται ἄχρις ἐδωδή.
κλῦτε, γοναὶ μερόπων, οἷον τέλος ἀφραδίῃσι
λαιμάργοις, ὅσον ἄλγος ἀδηφαγίῃσιν ὀπηδεῖ·
τῷ τις ἀεργίην δυστερπέα τῆλε διώκοι
καὶ κραδίης καὶ χειρός, ἔχοι δέ τι μέτρον ἐδωδῆς·
μηδ' ἐπὶ πανθοίνοισι νόον τέρποιτο τραπέζαις·
πολλοὶ γὰρ τοῖοι καὶ ἐν ἀνδράσιν, οἷσι λέλυνται
ἡνία, γαστρὶ δὲ πάντας ἐπιτρωπῶσι κάλωας·
ἀλλά τις εἰσορόων φεύγοι τέλος ἡμεροκοίτου.
Ἔστι καὶ ὀξυκόμοισι νόος καὶ μῆτις ἐχίνοις,
οἵ τ' ἀνέμων ἴσασι βίας ζαμενεῖς τε θυέλλας
ὀρνυμένας, νώτοισι δ' ἀνοχλίζουσιν ἕκαστος
λᾶαν, ὅσον βαρύθοντα περὶ σφετέρῃσιν ἀκάνθαις
ῥηϊδίως φορέοιεν, ἵν' ἀντία κύματος ὁρμῇ
βριθόμενοι μίμνωσι· τὸ γὰρ τρομέουσι μάλιστα,
μὴ σφὰς ἐπ' ἠιόνεσσι κυκώμενον οἶδμα κυλίσῃ.
Πουλυπόδων δ' οὔπω τιν' ὀΐομαι ἔμμεν' ἄπυστον

---

[a] We take αὐτοῦ, not as = "of him," but as qualifying στόματος, "his *very* jaws," *cf.* Hom. *Il.* xiii. 615 ὑπὸ λόφον αὐτόν.

[b] Sea-urchins generically, *Echinus esculentus*, etc. A. 530 a 34 ἔστι δὲ γένη πλείω τῶν ἐχίνων, ἓν μὲν τὸ ἐσθιόμενον; Hesych. *s.* ἐχῖνοι . . . καὶ ζῷον θαλάσσιον ἐδώδιμον; *cf.* Athen. 91 b.

gluttony. If a man capture him and tempt his prey by offering him food with his hand, he will take it until the food shall be heaped up even[a] unto the most gluttonous jaws of him. Hear, ye generations of men, what manner of issue there is to gluttonous folly, what pain follows upon excessive eating. Let a man therefore drive far from heart and hand idleness that delights in evil pleasure, and observe measure in eating nor delight in luxurious tables. For many such there be among men who hold the reins loose and allow all rope to their belly. But let a man behold and avoid the end of the Day-sleeper.

Wit and cunning belong also to the prickly Urchins,[b] which know[c] when the violence of the wind and the fierce storms are rising, and lift each of them upon their backs a stone of such weight as they can easily carry on their spines, that thus weighted they may withstand the driving of the wave. For that is what they most dread—lest the swelling wave roll them on the shore.

No one, I think, is ignorant of the craft of the

[c] Plut. *Mor.* 979 A *ἐχίνου γέ τινα χερσαίου διηγήσατο πρόγνωσιν* 'Αριστοτέλης *πνευμάτων* (A. 612 b 4; *Mirab.* 831 a 15; Plin. viii. 133) . . . *ἐγὼ δ' ἐχῖνον μὲν οὐδένα* Κυζικηνὸν *ἢ* Βυζάντιον *ἀλλὰ πάντας ὁμοῦ παρέχομαι τοὺς θαλαττίους, ὅταν αἴσθωνται μέλλοντα χειμῶνα καὶ σάλον, ἑρματιζομένους λιθιδίοις, ὅπως μὴ περιτρέπωνται διὰ κουφότητα μηδ' ἀποσύρωνται γενομένου κλυδῶνος, ἀλλ' ἐπιμένωσιν ἀραρότως τοῖς πετριδίοις*; Plin. ix. 100 Ex eodem genere sunt echini . . . tradunt saevitiam maris praesagire eos correptisque opperiri lapillis mobilitatem pondere stabilientes. *Cf.* Ael. vii. 33; Phil. 64.

τέχνης, οἳ πέτρῃσιν ὁμοίϊοι ἰνδάλλονται,
τήν κε ποτιπτύξωσι περὶ σπείρῃς τε βάλωνται.
ἄνδρας δ' ἀγρευτῆρας ὁμῶς καὶ κρέσσονας ἰχθῦς
ῥηϊδίως ἀπάτῃσι παραπλάγξαντες ἄλυξαν.
ἀλλ' ὅτε χειρότερός τις ἐπισχεδὸν ἀντιβολήσῃ,
αὐτίκα πουλύποδές τε καὶ ἰχθύες ἐξεφάνησαν,
μορφῆς πετραίης ἐξάλμενοι, ἐκ δὲ δόλοιο
φορβήν τ' ἐφράσσαντο καὶ ἐξήλυξαν ὄλεθρον.
χείματι δ' οὔποτε φασὶν ἐπιστείχειν ἁλὸς ὕδωρ
πουλύποδας· ζαμενεῖς γὰρ ὑποτρομέουσιν ἀέλλας·
ἀλλ' οἵ γε γλαφυρῇσιν ἐνιζόμενοι θαλάμῃσι
πτήξαντες δαίνυνται ἑοὺς πόδας, ἠΰτε σάρκας
ἀλλοτρίας· οἱ δ' αὖτις ἑοὺς κορέσαντες ἄνακτας
φύονται· τόδε πού σφι Ποσειδάων ἐπένευσε.
τοῖον καὶ βλοσυρῇσιν ἀειμάργοισι νόημα
ἄρκτοις· χειμερίην γὰρ ἀλυσκάζουσαι ὁμοκλήν,
δῦσαι φωλειοῖο μυχὸν κατὰ πετρήεντα
ὃν πόδα λιχμάζουσιν, ἐδητύος ἔργον ἄπαστον,

[a] A. 622 a 8 θηρεύει τοὺς ἰχθῦς τὸ χρῶμα μεταβάλλων καὶ ποιῶν ὅμοιον οἷς ἂν πλησιάζῃ λίθοις; *P.A.* 679 a 12, *Mirab.* 832 b 14; Plut. *Mor.* 978 D τῶν πολυπόδων τῆς χρόας τὴν ἄμειψιν ὅ τε Πίνδαρος περιβόητον πεποίηκεν εἰπών "ποντίου θηρὸς χρωτὶ μάλιστα νόον προσφέρων πάσαις πολίεσσιν ὁμιλεῖ" (*fr.* 43) καὶ Θέογνις (215) ὁμοίως "πουλύποδος νόον ἴσχε πολυχρόου, ὃς ποτὶ πέτρῃ τῇπερ ὁμιλήσῃ, τοῖος ἰδεῖν ἐφάνη"; Athen. 316 f, 513 d; Lucian, *De salt.* c. 67; Ael. *V.H.* i. 1; Dionys. *De A.* i. 9; Phil. 102. 13; Antig. 25 and 30; Plin. ix. 29; Ov. *Hal.* 30 At contra scopelis crinali corpore segnis | Polypus haeret et hac eludit retia fraude | Et sub lege loci sumit mutatque colorem, | Semper ei similis quem contigit. Charles Darwin, in his *Journal of Researches* (H.M.S. Beagle), c. i. tells how in 1832 at St. Iago in the Cape de Verd archipelago he was interested in observing the habits of an Octopus: "These

Poulpes, which make themselves like [a] in appearance to the rocks, even whatsoever rock they embrace and entwine with their tentacles. By their deceits they easily mislead and escape fishers alike and stronger fishes. When a weaker fish meets them near at hand, straightway they leap forth from their stony form and appear as veritable Poulpes and fishes, and by their craft contrive food and escape destruction. But in winter, they say, the Poulpes never travel over the waters of the sea ; for they fear the fierce storms. But sitting in their hollow chambers they cower, and devour their own feet [b] as if they were alien flesh. These feet, when they have glutted their owners, grow again : this gift, I ween, Poseidon has given them. Such a device is used also by the fierce and gluttonous Bears.[c] For they, shunning winter's threat, retreat into the rocky covert of their lair, where they lick their own feet, a fasting feast,

animals also escape detection by a very extraordinary chameleon-like power of changing their colour. They appear to vary their tints according to the nature of the ground over which they pass; when in deep water their general shade was brownish-purple, but when placed on the land, or in shallow water, this dark tint changed into one of a yellowish-green," etc.

[b] *Cf. C.* iii. 176 ff.; Hesiod, *W.* 524 *ἤματι χειμερίῳ ὅτ' ἀνόστεος* [*i.e.* "the Boneless," Hesiod's allusive way of referring to the Poulpe, which has no bony skeleton: A. 524 b 28 *οἱ δὲ πολύποδες οὐκ ἔχουσιν ἔσω στερεὸν τοιοῦτον οὐδέν.* For such allusive expressions, in place of the ordinary name, see *Hesiod*, A. W. Mair, Oxford, 1908, Introd. pp. xv. ff.] *ὃν πόδα τένδει | ἔν τ' ἀπύρῳ οἴκῳ καὶ ἤθεσι λευγαλέοισι*; Plut. *Mor.* 965 F; Ael. i. 27, xiv. 26; Antig. 21; Phil. 102. 5 ff.; Athen. 316 (who quotes allusions to the belief by Alcaeus, Pherecrat., and Diphilus); Plin. ix. 87; A. 591 a 4 *ὃ δὲ λέγουσί τινες, ὡς αὐτὸς αὑτὸν ἐσθίει, ψεῦδός ἐστιν ἀλλ' ἀπεδηδεμένας ἔχουσιν ἔνιοι τὰς πλεκτάνας ὑπὸ τῶν γόγγρων.*

[c] *C.* iii. 174 n.

μαιόμεναι δαίτην ἀνεμώλιον, οὐδ᾽ ἐθέλουσι
προβλώσκειν, εὐκραὲς ἕως ἔαρ ἡβήσειεν.
Ἔξοχα δ᾽ ἀλλήλοισιν ἀνάρσιον ἔχθος ἔχουσι
κάραβος ἀϊκτὴρ μύραινά τε πουλύποδές τε,
ἀλλήλους δ᾽ ὀλέκουσιν ἀμοιβαίοισι φόνοισιν.
αἰεὶ δ᾽ ἰχθυόεσσα μετὰ σφίσιν ἵστατ᾽ ἐνυὼ
καὶ μόθος, ἄλλου δ᾽ ἄλλος ἑὴν ἐνεπλήσατο νηδύν.
ἡ μὲν ὑπὲκ πέτρης ἁλιμυρέος ὁρμηθεῖσα
φοιταλέη μύραινα διέσσυται οἴδματα πόντου,
φορβὴν μαιομένη, τάχα δ᾽ εἴσιδε πούλυπον ἀκτῆς
ἄκρα διερπύζοντα καὶ ἀσπασίην ἐπὶ θήρην
ἔσσυτο γηθομένη· τὸν δ᾽ οὐ λάθεν ἐγγὺς ἐοῦσα·
ἀλλ᾽ ἤτοι πρῶτον μὲν ἀτυζόμενος δεδόνηται
ἐς φόβον, οὐδ᾽ ἄρα μῆχος ἔχει μύραιναν ἀλύξαι
ἕρπων νηχομένην τε καὶ ἄσχετα μαιμώωσαν.
αἶψα δέ μιν κατέμαρψε γένυν τ᾽ ἐνέρεισε δαφοινήν·
πούλυπος αὖτ᾽ ἀέκων ὀλοῆς ὑπὸ μάρνατ᾽ ἀνάγκης,
ἀμφὶ δέ οἱ μελέεσσιν ἑλίσσεται, ἄλλοτε ἄλλας
παντοίας στροφάλιγγας ὑπὸ σκολιοῖσιν ἱμᾶσι
τεχνάζων, εἴ πώς μιν ἐρητύσειε βρόχοισιν
ἀμφιβαλών· ἀλλ᾽ οὔτι κακῶν ἄκος οὔτ᾽ ἀλεωρή·
ῥεῖα γὰρ ἀμφιπεσόντος ὀλισθηροῖς μελέεσσιν
ὀτραλέη μύραινα διαρρέει οἷάπερ ὕδωρ·
αὐτὰρ ὅ γ᾽ ἄλλοτε νῶτα παναίολα, ἄλλοτε δειρὴν
οὐρήν τ᾽ ἀκροτάτην περιβάλλεται, ἄλλοτε δ᾽ αὖτε
ἐμπίπτει στόματός τε πύλαις γενύων τε μυχοῖσιν.
ὡς δὲ παλαισμοσύνης γυιαλκέος ἴδμονες ἄνδρες
δηρὸν ἐπ᾽ ἀλλήλοισιν ἑὴν ἀναφαίνετον ἀλκήν,

---

[a] *i.e.* the Sea Crayfish or Spiny Lobster: *H.* i. 261 n.

[b] *H.* i. 142 n.

[c] Ael. i. 32 (where the hostilities of Poulpe, Muraena, are described) μύραινα μὲν γὰρ ταῖς ἀκμαῖς τῶν ὀδόντων τὰς

seeking an unsubstantial food, and come not forth, until the mild spring be in its prime.

Above all other the dashing Crayfish [a] and the Muraena [b] and the Poulpes have a bitter feud with each other and destroy one another with mutual slaughter. Always there is fishy war and strife between them, and one fills his maw with the other. The raging Muraena comes forth [c] from her sea-washed rock and speeds through the waves of the deep in quest of food. Anon it descries a Poulpe crawling on the edge of the shore and rushes gladly on a welcome prey. The Poulpe is not unaware that the Muraena is at hand. First in terror he turns to flee, but he has no means to escape the Muraena, he crawling while she swims and rushes incontinently. Speedily she catches the Poulpe and fixes her deadly teeth in him. The Poulpe, on the other hand, albeit unwilling, fights under deadly compulsion and twines around her limbs, contriving all manner of twists, now this, now that, with his crooked whips, if haply, embracing her in his nooses, he may stay her onset. But for his evil plight there is no cure nor escape. When the Poulpe enfolds her, the nimble Muraena with her slippery limbs easily escapes through his embrace like water. But the Poulpe twines now round her spotted back, now round her neck, now round her very tail, and anon rushes into the gates of her mouth and the recesses of her jaws. Even as two men skilled in valiant wrestling long time display their might against each other; already from the

πλεκτάνας τῷ πολύποδι διακόπτει, εἶτα μέντοι καὶ ἐς τὴν γαστέρα εἰσδῦσα αὐτῷ τὰ αὐτὰ δρᾷ καὶ εἰκότως· ἡ μὲν γὰρ νηκτική, ὁ δὲ ἔοικεν ἕρποντι· εἰ δὲ καὶ τρέποιτο τὴν χρόαν τὰς πέτρας, ἔοικεν αὐτῷ τὸ σόφισμα αἱρεῖν οὐδὲ ἓν τοῦτο· ἔστι γὰρ συνιδεῖν ἐκείνῃ δεινὴ τοῦ ζῴου τὸ παλάμημα.

ἤδη δ᾿ ἐκ μελέων λιαρὸς καὶ ἀθέσφατος ἱδρὼς
χεύεται ἀμφοτέροισι· τὰ δ᾿ αἰόλα κέρδεα τέχνης
πλάζονται, χεῖρές τε περὶ χροῒ κυμαίνονται·
ὣς καὶ πουλύποδος κοτυληδόνες οὐ κατὰ κόσμον
πλαζόμεναι κενεῇσι παλαισμοσύναις μογέουσιν.
ἡ δέ μιν ὀξυτόμοισιν ὑπὸ ῥιπῇσιν ὀδόντων
δαρδάπτει· μελέων δὲ τὰ μὲν κατεδέξατο γαστήρ,
ἄλλα δ᾿ ἔτ᾿ ἐν γενύεσσι θοοὶ τρίβουσιν ὀδόντες,
ἄλλα δέ τ᾿ ἀσπαίρει καὶ ἑλίσσεται ἡμιδάϊκτα,
εἰσέτι παιφάσσοντα καὶ ἐκφυγέειν ἐθέλοντα.
ὡς δ᾿ ὅτ᾿ ἀνὰ ξυλόχους ὀφίων στίβον ἐξερεείνων
βριθόκερως ἔλαφος ῥινήλατον ἴχνος ἀνεῦρε,
χειὴν δ᾿ εἰσαφίκανε καὶ ἑρπετὸν εἴρυσεν ἔξω
δάπτει τ᾿ ἐμμενέως· ὁ δ᾿ ἑλίσσεται ἀμφί τε γοῦνα,
δειρήν τε στέρνον τε· τὰ δ᾿ ἡμίβρωτα κέχυνται
ἄψεα, πολλὰ δ᾿ ὀδόντες ὑπὸ στόμα δαιτρεύουσιν·
ὣς καὶ πουλύποδος δνοπαλίζεται αἰόλα γυῖα
δυσμόρου· οὐδέ ἑ μῆτις ἐπιφροσύνης ἐσάωσε
πετραίης· εἰ γάρ ποτ᾿ ἀλευόμενος περὶ πέτρην
πλέξηται, χροιήν τε πανείκελον ἀμφιέσηται,
ἀλλ᾿ οὐ μυραίνης ἔλαθεν κέαρ, ἀλλά ἑ μούνη
φράζεται, ἄπρηκτον δὲ πέλει κείνοιο νόημα.
ἔνθα μιν οἰκτείρειας ἀκοσμοτάτοιο μόροιο,
ὡς ὁ μὲν ἐν πέτρῃσιν ὑφέζεται, ἡ δέ οἱ ἄγχι
ἠΰτ᾿ ἐπεγγελόωσα παρίσταται· ὧδέ κε φαίης
μυθεῖσθαι μύραιναν ἀπηνέα κερτομέουσαν·
τί πτώσσεις δολομῆτα; τίν᾿ ἔλπεαι ἠπεροπεύειν;

---

[a] Ael. ii. 9 ἔλαφος ὄφιν νικᾷ κατά τινα φύσεως δωρεὰν θαυμαστήν· καὶ οὐκ ἂν αὐτὸν διαλάθοι ἐν τῷ φωλεῷ ὢν ὁ ἔχθιστος, ἀλλὰ προσερείσας τῇ καταδρομῇ τοῦ δακέτου τοὺς ἑαυτοῦ μυκτῆρας, βιαιότατα εἰσπνεῖ, καὶ ἕλκει ὡς ἴυγγι τῷ πνεύματι, καὶ ἄκοντα προάγει, καὶ προκύπτοντα αὐτὸν ἐσθίειν ἄρχεται; Lucan vi. 673 cervi pastae serpente medullae; Plin. viii. 118 Et his (cervis)

limbs of both pours the sweat warm and abundant and the varied wiles of their art are all abroad and their hands wave about their bodies: even so the suckers of the Poulpe, at random plied, are all abroad, and labour in vain wrestling. But the Muraena with sharp assault of teeth rends the Poulpe; some of his limbs her belly receives, while other parts the sharp teeth still grind in her jaws, others are still quivering and twisting, half consumed, struggling still and fain to escape. As when in the woods the Stag [a] of heavy horns, seeking out the path of serpents, discovers the track by scent and comes to the lair and hales the reptile out and devours it amain, while the serpent twines about knees and neck and breast, and some of its limbs lie half-eaten, much yet in the Stag's jaws the teeth devour: even so the coiling limbs of the hapless Poulpe writhe, nor does his device of stony craft save him. For even if perchance in his endeavours to escape he twine about a rock and clothe him in a colour like to it, yet he escapes not the wit of the Muraena, but she alone remarks him and his cunning is in vain. Then thou wouldst pity him for his unseemly doom, as he crouches on the rocks, while she stands by, as it were mocking him. Thou wouldst say the cruel Muraena spoke and mocked him thus. "Why dost thou skulk, crafty one? Whom hopest thou to

cum serpente pugna. Vestigant cavernas nariumque spiritu extrahunt renitentes; Nicand. *Th.* 139 ff. *ἢ ὁπότε σκαρθμοὺς ἐλάφων ὀχεῇσιν ἀλύξας | ἀνδρὸς ἐνισκίμψῃ χολόων γυιοφθόρον ἰόν· | ἔξοχα γὰρ δολιχοῖσι κινωπησταῖς κοτέουσι | νεβροτόκοι καὶ ζόρκες· ἀνιχνεύουσι δὲ πάντῃ | τρόχμαλα θ' αἱμασιάς τε καὶ ἰλύους ἐρέοντες, | σμερδαλέῃ μυκτῆρος ἐπισπέρχοντες αὐτμῇ.* *Cf.* Phil. 59, *E.M. s.* *ἔλαφος*. It is a common notion in Scotland that Goats destroy Adders.

ἢ τάχα καὶ πέτρης πειρήσομαι, ἥν σε καὶ εἴσω
δέξηται σπιλὰς ἠδὲ καὶ ἠμύσασα καλύψῃ.
αὐτίκα δ' ἀγκύλον ἕρκος ἐνιπλήξασα λαφύσσει,
χοιράδος αὖ ἐρύουσα περίτρομον· αὐτὰρ ὅ γ' οὔτι,
οὐδὲ δαϊζόμενος, λείπει πάγον οὐδ' ἀνίησιν,
ἀλλ' ἔχεται πέτρης εἰλιγμένος, εἰσόκεν αὐταὶ
λείπωνται μοῦναι κοτυληδόνες ἐμπεφυυῖαι.
ὡς δ' ὅτε περθομένης δηΐων ὑπὸ χερσὶ πόληος,
ἑλκομένων παίδων τε δορυκτήτων τε γυναικῶν,
κοῦρον ἀνὴρ δειρῇ τε καὶ ἀγκάσιν ἐμπεφυῶτα
γειναμένης ἐρύσῃ πολέμου νόμῳ, αὐτὰρ ὁ χεῖρας
πλέγδην οὐκ ἀνίησιν ἀπ' αὐχένος, οὐδέ ἑ μήτηρ
κωκυτῷ προΐησιν, ὁμοῦ δέ οἱ ἕλκεται αὐτή·
ὣς καὶ πουλύποδος δειλὸν δέμας ἑλκομένοιο
λισσάδι μυδαλέῃ περιφύεται, οὐδ' ἀνίησι.
 Κάραβος αὖ μύραιναν ἀπηνέα περ μάλ' ἐοῦσαν
ἐσθίει, αὐτοφόνοισιν ἀγηνορίῃσι δαμεῖσαν.
ἣ γὰρ ὁ μὲν πέτρης σχεδὸν ἵσταται, ᾗ ἔνι ναίει
ὀτραλέη μύραινα· δύω δ' ἀνὰ κέντρα τιτήνας
δήϊα φυσιόων προκαλίζεται ἐς μόθον ἐλθεῖν,
ἶσος ἀριστῆϊ προμάχῳ στρατοῦ, ὅς ῥά τε χειρῶν
ἠνορέῃ πολέμου τε δαημοσύνῃσι πεποιθὼς
ἔντεσι καρτύνας βριαρὸν δέμας, ὀξέα πάλλων
ἔγχεα, δυσμενέων προκαλίζεται ὅς κ' ἐθέλῃσιν
ἀντιάαν· τάχα δ' ἄλλον ἀριστήων ὀροθύνει·
ὣς ὅ γε μυραίνης θήγει φρένας, οὐδ' ἐπὶ μῶλον
δηθύνει, θαλάμης δὲ διαΐξασα κελαινή,
αὐχένα γυρώσασα, χόλῳ μέγα παιφάσσουσα
ἀντιάᾳ· τὸν δ' οὔτι περισπέρχουσά περ αἰνῶς
βλάπτει τρηχὺν ἐόντα, γένυν δ' ἀνεμώλιον αὔτως
ἐγχρίμπτει, στερεοῖσι δ' ἐτώσια μαίνετ' ὀδοῦσιν·
οἱ δὲ πάλιν γενύεσσιν ἀπηνέος ὡς ἀπὸ πέτρης

deceive? Soon shall I assault the rock, if this cliff receive thee within it and close and cover thee." And straightway she fixes in him the curved hedge of her teeth and devours him, pulling him all trembling from the rock. But he, even while he is rent, does not leave the rock nor let go. Coiling he clings to it till only his suckers remain fast. As when a city is sacked by the hands of the foemen, and children and women are haled away as the prize of the spear, a man drags away a boy who clings to the neck and arms of his mother; the boy relaxes not his arms that are twined about her neck, nor does the wailing mother let him go, but is dragged with him herself; even so the poor body of the Poulpe, as he is dragged away, clings to the wet rock and lets not go.

The Crayfish [a] again destroys the Muraena,[b] savage though she be, overcome by her valour fatal to herself. He stands near the rock in which dwells the nimble Muraena and extends his two feelers and, breathing hostile breath, challenges the Muraena to battle: even as a chieftain, the champion of an army, who, trusting in the prowess of his hands and his skill in war, arrays in arms his strong body and brandishing his sharp spears challenges any foeman who will to meet him, and presently provokes another chieftain. Even so the Crayfish whets the spirit of the Muraena, and no laggard for battle is the dusky fish, but rushing from her lair with arched neck and quivering with wrath she goes to meet him. Yet for all her terrible rage she hurts not the prickly Crayfish; vainly and idly she fixes in him her jaw and rages with her hard teeth, which in her jaws rebound as from a hard rock and grow weary and

[a] Ael. ix. 25.

[b] Ael. i. 32, ix. 25.

παλλόμενοι κάμνουσι καὶ ἀμβλύνονται ἐρωῆς.
τῆς δὲ μέγα φλεγέθει καὶ ὀρίνεται ἄγριον ἦτορ,
εἰσόκε μιν χηλῇσιν ἐπαΐξας δολιχῇσιν
κάραβος αὐχενίοιο λάβῃ μέσσοιο τένοντος·
ἴσχει δ' ἐμπεφυὼς χαλκείῃ ὥστε πυράγρῃ,
νωλεμές, οὐδ' ἀνίησι καὶ ἐσσυμένην περ ἀλύξαι·
ἡ δὲ βίῃ μογέουσα καὶ ἀσχαλόωσ' ὀδύνῃσι,
πάντῃ δινεύει σκολιὸν δέμας, αἶψα δὲ νῶτα
καράβου ὀξυβελῆ περιβάλλεται ἀμφιχυθεῖσα,
ἐν δ' ἐπάγῃ σκώλοισι καὶ ὀξείῃσιν ἀκωκαῖς
ὀστράκου, ὠτειλαῖς δὲ περιπλήθουσα θαμειαῖς
ὄλλυται αὐτοδάϊκτος, ὑπ' ἀφραδίῃσι θανοῦσα.
ὡς δ' ὅτε θηροφόνων τις ἀνὴρ δεδαημένος ἔργων,
λαῶν ἀμφιδόμοισιν ἐναγρομένων ἀγορῇσι,
πόρδαλιν οἰστρηθεῖσαν ἐνὶ ῥοίζοισιν ἱμάσθλης
ἐγχείῃ δέχεται ταναήκεϊ δοχμὸς ὑποστάς·
ἡ δὲ καὶ εἰσορόωσα γένυν θηκτοῖο σιδήρου
ἄγρια κυμαίνουσα κορύσσεται, ἐν δ' ἄρα λαιμῷ
ἠΰτε δουροδόκῃ χαλκήλατον ἔσπασεν αἰχμήν·
ὣς ἄρα καὶ μύραιναν ἕλεν χόλος ἀφραδίῃσι
δύσμορον, αὐτοτύποισιν ὑπ' ὠτειλῇσι δαμεῖσαν.
τοίην που τραφερῆς γαίης ἔπι δῆριν ἔθεντο
ἄμφω ἐνὶ ξυλόχοισιν ὄφις καὶ τρηχὺς ἐχῖνος
ἀντόμενοι· καὶ τοῖς γὰρ ἀνάρσιος αἶσα μέμηλεν.
ἤτοι ὁ μὲν προϊδὼν ὀλοφώϊον ἑρπυστῆρα,
φραξάμενος πυκινῇσιν ὑπὸ προβλῆσιν ἀκάνθαις
εἱλεῖται σφαιρηδόν, ὑφ' ἕρκεϊ γυῖα φυλάσσων,
ἔνδοθεν ἑρπύζων· ὁ δέ οἱ σχεδὸν αὐτίκα θύνων
πρῶτα μὲν ἰοτόκοισιν ἐπισπέρχει γενύεσσιν,

---

[a] The reference is to a *ludus bestiarius* (Senec. *Ep.* viii.

are blunted by their force. Greatly her fierce heart burns and is stirred, until the Crayfish rushes on her with his long claws and seizes her by the tendon in the midst of her throat, and clings and holds her firm as with brazen tongs, and lets her not go though eager to escape. She, distressed by his violence and vexed by pain, wheels every way her crooked body, and speedily she throws herself about the prickly back of the Crayfish and enfolds him and impales herself on the spine and sharp points of his shell, and, full of many wounds, perishes self-destroyed, dead by her own folly. As when a man skilled in the work of slaying wild beasts,[a] when the people are gathered in the house-encircled market-place,[b] awaits the Leopard [c] maddened by the cracking of the whip and with long-edged spear stands athwart her path; she, though she beholds the edge of sharp iron, mantles in swelling fury and receives in her throat, as it were in a spear-stand, the brazen lance; even so wrath slays the unhappy Muraena in her folly, overcome by self-dealt wounds. Such strife, I ween, upon the dry land a Serpent and a prickly Hedgehog wage, when they meet in the woods; for enmity is their lot also. The Hedgehog, seeing in front of him the deadly reptile, fences himself with his close-set bristling spines and rolls himself into a ball, protecting his limbs under his fence within which he crawls. The Serpent, rushing upon him, first assails him with his venomous

i. 22), in which men, *bestiarii* (Cic. *Pro Sext.* 64), opposed wild beasts in the arena. Plin. viii. 18 ff. 131; Juv. iv. 100.

[b] In the amphitheatre: schol., ἐν ἀγορᾷ κύκλωθεν οἰκήματα ἐχούσῃ. *Cf.* Poll. vii. 125; Claud. *In Ruf.* ii. 394.

[c] Dio Cass. lxxviii. 21 Λούκιος Πρισκιλλιανός . . . ποτε καὶ ἄρκτῳ καὶ παρδάλει λεαίνῃ τε καὶ λέοντι ἅμα μόνος συνηνέχθη.

ἀλλ' αὔτως μογέει κενεὸν πόνον· οὐ γὰρ ἱκάνει
χρωτὸς ἔσω μαλεροῖσι καὶ ἱέμενός περ ὀδοῦσι·
τοίη μιν λάχνη δυσπαίπαλος ἀμφιβέβηκεν·
αὐτὰρ ὁ κυκλοτερὴς ὁλοότροχος αἰόλα γυῖα
δινεύων, πυκινῇσι κυλινδόμενος στροφάλιγξιν,
ἐμπίπτει σπείρῃσι καὶ οὐτάζει βελέεσσι
χαίτης ὀξυτόμοισιν· ὁ δ' ἄλλοθεν εἴβεται ἄλλος
ἰχὼρ αἱματόεις, τὸν δ' ἕλκεα πόλλ' ἀνιάζει.
ἔνθα μιν ἀμφιβαλὼν περιηγέϊ πάντοθεν ὁλκῷ
ὑγρὸς ὄφις χαλεποῖσι περιπλέγδην ὑπὸ δεσμοῖς
ἴσχει τ' ἐμπρίει τε χόλῳ τ' ἐνερείδεται ἀλκήν.
τοῦ δ' εἴσω τάχα πᾶσαι ὀλισθαίνουσιν ἄκανθαι
ὀξέα πεφρικυῖαι· ὁ δ' ἐν σκολόπεσσι πεπηγὼς
οὔτε βίην ἀνίησι καὶ οὐκ ἐθέλων πεπέδηται,
ἀλλὰ μένει γόμφοισιν ἅτε κρατεροῖσιν ἀρηρώς,
ὄφρα θάνῃ, σὺν δ' αὐτὸν ἀπέφθισε θῆρα πιέζων
πολλάκις, ἀλλήλοις δὲ μόρος καὶ πῆμα γένοντο·
πολλάκι δ' ἐξήλυξε καὶ ἔκφυγε δεινὸς ἐχῖνος,
ἐκδὺς ἑρπυστῆρος ἀλυκτοπέδης τε κελαινῆς,
εἰσέτι τεθνηῶτος ἔχων περὶ σάρκας ἀκάνθαις.
τοίη καὶ μύραινα κακόφρονι δάμναται ἄτῃ,
καράβῳ ἁρπαλέη τε καὶ εὐάντητος ἐδωδή.
Κάραβον αὖ καὶ τρηχὺν ὁμῶς καὶ κραιπνὸν ἐόντα
δαίνυτ' ἀφαυρότερός περ ἐὼν καὶ νωθρὸς ἐρωὴν
πούλυπος· ἡνίκα γάρ μιν ὑπὸ σπιλάδεσσι νοήσῃ
αὔτως ἀτρεμέοντα καὶ ἥμενον, αὐτὰρ ὁ λάθρῃ

[a] In Hom. *Il.* v. 340 and 416 *ichor* means the blood of the gods; later the serous or watery part of the blood (A. *P.A.* 651 a 17 τὸ ὑδατῶδες τοῦ αἵματος), the discharge from a wound, etc. *Cf.* Milton, *Par. Lost*, vi. 331 of Satan's wound: "from the gash | A stream of nectarous humour issuing flow'd | Sanguine, such as celestial Spirits may bleed;" Byron, *Vision of Judgement*, 25 of St. Peter, "Of course his

jaws, but his labour is all in vain. For despite his eagerness he cannot reach the flesh within with his devouring teeth; so rough a pile surrounds the Hedgehog; who, like a round boulder, wheels his shifty limbs, rolling turn on turn, and falls upon the coils of the Serpent and wounds him with the sharp arrows of his bristles; and here and there flows the bloody ichor[a] and many wounds torment the Serpent. Then the clammy Snake girds the Hedgehog all about with his circling coil and in the embrace of his grievous bonds holds him and bites and puts therein the strength of anger. Then swiftly all the sharp-bristling spines of the Hedgehog glide into him; yet, impaled upon the prickles, he abates not his effort though fettered against his will, but remains fast as if held by strong dowels, until he dies; and often by his pressure he destroys the beast as well, and they become doom and bane to one another. But often, too, the dread Hedgehog gets away and escapes, slipping from the reptile and his darksome fetter, bearing still upon his spines the flesh of the dead Serpent. In like fashion also the Muraena perishes by a foolish doom, to the Crayfish an eager and welcome feast.

The Crayfish again, prickly though he be and swift, is devoured by the Poulpe,[b] albeit he is weaker and sluggish of motion. For when the Poulpe remarks him under the rocks sitting all motionless, stealthily

perspiration was but ichor | Or some such other spiritual liquor."

[b] Ael. ix. 25 κάραβος πολύποδι ἐχθρός· τὸ δὲ αἴτιον, ὅταν αὐτῷ τὰς πλεκτάνας περιβάλῃ, τῶν μὲν ἐπὶ τοῦ νώτου ἐκπεφυκότων αὐτῷ κέντρων ποιεῖται οὐδεμίαν ὤραν, ἑαυτὸν δὲ περιχέας αὐτῷ ἐς πνῖγμα ἄγχει· ταῦτα ὁ κάραβος σαφῶς οἶδεν καὶ ἀποδιδράσκει αὐτόν.

νῶτον ἐπαΐξας περιβάλλεται αἰόλα δεσμά,
ἰφθίμων δολιχῇσι ποδῶν σειρῇσι πιέζων,
σὺν δέ οἱ ἀκραίης κοτυληδόσι θερμὸν ἐρείδει
αὐλὸν ἐπισφίγγων στόματος μέσον, οὐδ' ἀνίησι
πνοιὴν ἠερίην οὔτ' ἔνδοθεν οὔθ' ἑτέρωθεν·
καὶ γὰρ καὶ νεπόδεσσι παλίρροος ἕλκεται ἀήρ·
ἀλλ' ἔχει ἀμφιπεσών· ὁ δὲ νήχεται, ἄλλοτε μίμνει,
ἄλλοτε δ' ἀσπαίρει, ποτὲ δὲ προβλῆσιν ὑπ' ἄκραις
ῥήγνυται· αὐτὰρ ὅ γ' οὔτι βίης μεθίησιν ἄεθλον,
ὄφρα ἑ τεθνηῶτα λίπῃ ψυχή τε καὶ ἀλκή.
δὴ τότε μιν προπεσόντα παρήμενος ἐν ψαμάθοισι
δαίνυται, ἠΰτε κοῦρος ὑπὲκ μαζοῖο τιθήνης
χείλεσιν αὖ ἐρύει λαρὸν γλάγος· ὣς ὅ γε σάρκας
λάπτων ὀξυπόροιο κατέσπασεν ἄγγεος ἔξω
μυζήσας, γλυκερῆς δὲ βορῆς ἐνεπλήσατο νηδύν.
ὡς δέ τις ἡμερόκοιτος ἀνὴρ ληΐστορι τέχνῃ
ὁρμαίνων ἀΐδηλα, δίκης σέβας οὔποτ' ἀέξων,
ἑσπέριος στεινῇσι καταπτήξας ἐν ἀγυιαῖς,
ἄνδρα παραστείχοντα μετ' εἰλαπίνην ἐλόχησε·
καί ῥ' ὁ μὲν οἰνοβαρὴς ἕρπει πάρος, ὑγρὸν ἀείδων,
οὐ μάλα νηφάλιον κλάζων μέλος· αὐτὰρ ὁ λάθρῃ

---

[a] παλίρροος (Eur. *I. in T.* 1397, Aesch. *Ag.* 191), παλιρροία (Soph. *fr.* 716, Herod. ii. 23, Diodor. i. 32) are constantly used of the ebb and flow of the tide and hence of any ebb and flow, *e.g.* of fortune (παλιρροία τῆς τύχης Diodor. xviii. 59). Especially natural is the application to air or breath (Tryphiod. 76 παλίρροον ἆσθμα; *cf.* Theophrast. *De vent.* 10, A. *De spir.* 482 b 3, *Probl.* 940 b 25). As to the breathing of Fishes, Aristotle classes them among τὰ μὴ ἀναπνέοντα (*De sens.* 444 b 7); but the contrary opinion is maintained by Pliny, ix. 16 ff. "They . . . suppose likewise that no fishes having guils do draw in and deliver their wind againe too and fro . . . Among others I see that Aristotle was of that mind . . . For mine owne part . . I professe that I

he springs upon his back and casts his various bonds about him, oppressing him with the long chains of his strong feet and with the ends of his tentacles withal he constricts and strangles the warm channel in the midst of his mouth and suffers not his airy breath to pass either out or in (for fishes too draw the tide of air),[a] but holds him in his embrace. And the Crayfish now swims, now halts, and again struggles, and anon dashes against the jutting crags. But the Poulpe relaxes not the contest of might, until life and strength forsake the other in death. Then when the Crayfish falls prone, the Poulpe sits by him on the sands and feasts, even as a child draws with his lips the sweet milk from the breast of his nurse; even so the Poulpe laps the flesh of the Crayfish, sucking and drawing it forth from its prickly vessel, and fills his belly with sweet food. Even as a day-sleeping[b] man, with predatory craft devising dark counsels, never honouring the majesty of justice, skulks at evening in the narrow streets and lies in wait for one passing by after a banquet; the banqueter, heavy with wine, goes forward, singing drunkenly, bawling no very sober melody; and the other

am not of their judgement. For why? Nature if she be so disposed, may give insteed of lights [*i.e.* lungs] some other organs and instruments of breath" (Holland's trans.), principally on the ground that (1) they are seen to pant in hot weather, (2) they sleep—"quis enim sine respiratione somno locus?" (3) they have the senses of hearing and of smell—"ex aeris utrumque materia. Odorem quidem non aliud quam infectum aera intelligi potest."

[b] From Hesiod, *W.* 60 *μή ποτέ σ' ἡμερόκοιτος ἀνὴρ ἀπὸ χρήμαθ' ἕληται.* *Cf.* *E.M.* *s.* *ἡμερόκοιτος· Ἡσίοδος, Μήποτέ δ' . . . ἕληται· ὁ τὴν ἡμέραν καθεύδων, τὴν δὲ νύκτα ἀγρυπνῶν, τουτέστιν ὁ κλέπτης.* *Cf.* Suid. and Hesych. *s.v.* *ἡμερόκοιτος· ὁ κλέπτης.*

ἐξόπιθε προὔτυψε καὶ αὐχένα χερσὶ δαφοιναῖς
εἷλεν ἐπιβρίσας, κλῖνέν τέ μιν ἄγριον ὕπνον
οὐ τηλοῦ θανάτοιο καὶ εἵματα πάντ' ἐναρίξας
ᾤχετο, δυσκερδῆ τε φέρων καὶ ἀνέστιον ἄγρην·
τοιάδε καὶ πινυτοῖσι νοήματα πουλυπόδεσσιν.

Οἵδε μὲν ἀντίβιοι καὶ ἀνάρσιοι ἔξοχ' ἔασιν
εἰναλίων· μοῦνοι δὲ μετ' ἰχθύσιν αἰολοφύλοις
ποινητῆρες ἔασι καὶ ἀλλήλων ὀλετῆρες.

Ἄλλοι δ' ἰοφόροι νεπόδων, στομάτεσσι δ' ἀεικὴς
ἰὸς ἐνιτρέφεται στυγερός τ' ἐπὶ δήγμασιν ἕρπει.
τοῖον καὶ σκολόπενδρα, δυσώνυμον ἑρπετὸν ἅλμης,
ἶσον ἐπιχθονίῳ δέμας ἑρπετῷ· ἀλλὰ τό γ' ἄτην
κύντερον· εἰ γάρ οἵ τις ἐπιψαύσειε πελάσσας,
αὐτίκα οἱ κνῆστις μὲν ἐπὶ χροΐ θερμὸν ἔρευθος
φοινίσσει, σμώδιξ δὲ διατρέχει ἠΰτε ποίης,
τὴν κνίδα κικλήσκουσιν, ἐπωνυμίην ὀδυνάων.
ἐχθρὴ δὲ σκολόπενδρα πανέξοχον ἀσπαλιεῦσι
ἐμπελάαν· εἰ γάρ ποτ' ἐπιψαύσειε δελέτρου,
οὐκ ἄν τις νεπόδων κείνου πέλας ἀγκίστροιο
ἔλθοι· τοῖον γάρ οἱ ἀπεχθέα μίσγεται ἰόν.

Τοίη καὶ βαλιῇσιν ἰουλίσι τέτροφεν ἄτη

---

[a] Ael. ii. 50 κωβιός, δράκων, χελιδών, τρυγών are venomous, the last fatally.

[b] A. 505 b 13 εἰσὶ δὲ καὶ σκολόπενδραι θαλάττιαι, παραπλήσιαι τὸ εἶδος ταῖς χερσαίαις, τὸ δὲ μέγεθος μικρῷ ἐλάττους· γίγνονται δὲ περὶ τοὺς πετρώδεις τόπους; 621 a 6 ἣν δὲ καλοῦσι σκολόπενδραν, ὅταν καταπίῃ τὸ ἄγκιστρον, ἐκτρέπεται τὰ ἐντὸς ἐκτός, ἕως ἂν ἐκβάλῃ τὸ ἄγκιστρον· εἶθ' οὕτως εἰστρέπεται πάλιν ἐντός. βαδίζουσι δ' αἱ σκολόπενδραι πρὸς τὰ κνισώδη, ὥσπερ καὶ αἱ χερσαῖαι. τῷ μὲν οὖν στόματι οὐ δάκνουσι, τῇ δὲ ἅψει καθ' ὅλον τὸ σῶμα,

darts forth stealthily behind and seizes his neck with murderous hands and overpowers and lays him low in a cruel sleep not far from death and despoils him of all his raiment and goes his way with his booty, ill-gotten and unlawful: even such are the devices of the cunning Poulpes.

These above all creatures of the sea are hostile and unfriendly and alone among the fishes of varied tribe are avengers and slayers one of the other.

Others of the fishes are venomous[a] and an ugly venom is bred in their mouths and creeps hateful into their bite. Such is the Scolopendra,[b] an ominous reptile of the brine, like in form to the reptile of the land, but deadlier in its hurt. For if one approach and touch it, straightway itch makes a hot redness on his flesh and a weal runs over him as from the grass which, from the pains which it causes, men call the nettle. Most hateful of all is the Scolopendra for fishermen to encounter; for if it touch the bait, not a fish will come near that hook; with such a hateful venom does the Scolopendra infect it.

A like bane also is bred in the mouth of the spotted

ὥσπερ αἱ καλούμεναι κνῖδαι; Ael. vii. 35. Generally supposed to be an annelid worm, *e.g. Nereis*. *Cf.* Plin. ix. 145 Scolopendrae terrestribus similes, quas centipedes vocant, hamo devorato omnia interanea evomunt, donec hamum egerant, deinde resorbent; Plut. *Mor.* 567 B *ὅσοι δὲ πρόσχημα καὶ δόξαν ἀρετῆς περιβαλόμενοι διεβίωσαν κακίᾳ λανθανούσῃ, τούτους ἐπιπόνως καὶ ὀδυνηρῶς ἠνάγκαζον ἕτεροι περιεστῶτες ἐκτρέπεσθαι τὰ ἐντὸς ἔξω τῆς ψυχῆς, ἰλυσπωμένους παρὰ φύσιν καὶ ἀνακαμπτομένους, ὥσπερ αἱ θαλάττιαι σκολόπενδραι καταπιοῦσαι τὸ ἄγκιστρον ἐκτρέπουσιν ἑαυτάς.* The name *σκολόπενδρα* was also given to an unknown sea-monster (*κῆτος θαλάττιον*) described by Ael. xiii. 23, to which the reference must be in *A.P.* vi. 222, vi. 223.

ἂν στόμα· τὰς δὲ μάλιστα βυθῶν διφήτορες ἄνδρες
δύπται σπογγοτόμοι τε δυηπαθέες στυγέουσιν·
εὖτε γὰρ ἀθρήσωσιν ἐρευνητῆρα θαλάσσης
σπερχόμενον ποτὶ βυσσὸν ὑποβρυχίοισι πόνοισιν,
αἵ δ' ἀπὸ πετράων μάλα μυρίαι ὁρμηθεῖσαι
ἄνδρα περιπροθέουσι καὶ ἀθρόαι ἀμφιχέονται
καί μιν ὁδοῦ βλάπτουσι πονεύμενον, ἄλλοθεν ἄλλαι
κνίζουσαι στομάτεσσιν ἀναιδέσιν· αὐτὰρ ὁ κάμνει
ὕδατι καὶ στυγερῇσιν ἰουλίσιν ἀντιβολήσας,
χερσὶ δ', ὅσον σθένος ἐστίν, ἐπειγομένοις τε πόδεσσι
σεύει ἀμυνόμενος διερὸν στρατόν· αἱ δ' ἐφέπονται
ἀστεμφεῖς, μυίαις ἐναλίγκιοι, αἵ ῥά τ' ἐπ' ἔργοις
ἀνέρας ἀμητῆρας ὀπωρινὸν μογέοντας
πάντοσ' ἀνιηραὶ θέρεος στίχες ἀμφιπέτονται.
οἱ δ' ἅμα μὲν καμάτῳ τε καὶ ἀκρήτοισι βολῇσιν
ἠέρος ἱδρώουσιν, ἀνιάζουσί τε μυίαις
ἐκπάγλως· αἱ δ' οὐδὲν ἀναιδείης χαλόωσι,
πρὶν θανέειν ἢ ξουθὸν ἀπ' ἀνέρος αἷμα πάσασθαι.
τόσσος ἔρως καὶ τοῖσιν ἐν ἰχθύσιν αἵματος ἀνδρῶν.
Οὐ μὴν θὴν ἀβληχρὸν ἔχει δάκος εὖτε χαράξῃ

---

[a] *Coris iulis*, M.G. γύλος (ἰύλος), "poisson rusé, d'où le proverbe: γύλος εἶμαι σὲ γελῶ, καὶ χάνος εἶμαι χάνομαι" *i.e.* "I am γύλος (as if = 'the mocker') and I laugh at you: I am χάνος (as if = 'the gaper') and I scoff at you;" *cf.* ἐγχάσκω = mock, Aristoph. *Wasps*, 721 etc. (Apost. p. 20).

Rainbow-wrasses[a]; them do men who explore the depths of the sea chiefly abhor—divers and toilsome sponge-cutters.[b] For when they behold the searcher of the sea hasting to the depths for his labour under the water, in tens of thousands they spring from the rocks and rush around the man and throng in swarms about him and stay him in his course as he labours, on this side and on that stinging him with relentless mouths. He is wearied by his conflict with the water and the hateful Wrasses. With hands and hasting feet he does all he can to ward off and drive away the watery host. But they pursue him stubbornly, like unto flies, the grievous hosts of harvest, which on every side fly about the reapers at their work when they toil in autumn; and the reapers sweat at once with their toil and the intemperate shafts of the air and they are vexed exceedingly by the flies; but these abate nothing of their shamelessness until they die or have tasted the reaper's dusky blood. Even such lust have these fishes also for the blood of men.

No feeble bite verily hath the reptile Poulpe[c] when

[a] "Equally and even more vivid are the Wrasses, of which many gorgeous sorts are common among the rocks close to the shore. The *Iulis Mediterranea* [= *Coris iulis*] is the brightest of these painted beauties, exceeding all fishes of the Mediterranean for splendour of colour" ("Beacon" Report on E. Mediterranean Fishes *ap.* E. Forbes, p. 196).

[b] Ael. ii. 44 *αἱ ἰουλίδες ἰχθῦς εἰσι πέτραις ἔντροφοι καὶ ἔχουσιν ἰοῦ τὸ στόμα ἔμπλεων . . . λυποῦσι δὲ καὶ τοὺς ἐν ταῖς ὑδροθηρίαις ὑποδυομένους τε καὶ νηχομένους, πολλαὶ καὶ δηκτικαὶ προσπίπτουσαι, ὡς αὐτόχρημα ἐπὶ τῆς γῆς αἱ μυῖαι.*

[c] Ael. v. 144 *ἦν δὲ ἄρα δηκτικὸν καὶ ὁ ὀσμύλος καὶ ὁ πολύπους. καὶ δάκοι μὲν ἂν οὗτος σηπίας βιαιότερον, τοῦ δὲ ἰοῦ μεθίησιν ἧττον.*

πούλυπος ἑρπυστὴρ ἢ σηπίη, ἀλλὰ καὶ αὐτοῖς
ἐντρέφεται βαιὸς μὲν ἀτὰρ βλαπτήριος ἰχώρ.
κέντρα δὲ πευκήεντα μετ' ἰχθύσιν ὡπλίσσαντο
κωβιός, ὃς ψαμάθοισι, καὶ ὃς πέτρῃσι γέγηθε
σκορπίος, ὠκεῖαί τε χελιδόνες ἠδὲ δράκοντες
καὶ κύνες οἳ κέντροισιν ἐπώνυμοι ἀργαλέοισι,
πάντες ἀταρτηροῖς ὑπὸ νύγμασιν ἰὸν ἱέντες.

---

[a] Ael. *l.c.* ἔχει δὲ δῆγμα ἡ σηπία ἰῶδες καὶ τοὺς ὀδόντας ἰσχυρῶς ὑπολανθάνοντας.

[b] M.G. κωβιός (γωβιός) is generic for the various species of Goby, of which *Gobius niger* is the commonest in Greek waters (Apost. p. 10). A. 598 a 11, 610 b 4, etc. The identification rests mainly on the use of κωβιός in M.G. Cuvier, xii. 4 ff., argues against the identification on two grounds: 1. A. 508 b 15 οἱ δ' ἰχθύες (ἀποφυάδας ἔχουσιν, have *caeca*) ἄνωθεν περὶ τὴν κοιλίαν, καὶ ἔνιοι πολλάς, οἷον κωβιός, γαλεός. . . . Now the Goby has no *caeca*. But the reading is suspect as the γαλεός also is without *caeca*. 2. Whereas Oppian and Aelian speak of the formidable spines of the κωβιός, "the simple rays of the Gobies are flexible and cannot wound." Cuvier, basing on Athen. 309 c, where we read that the κωβιός was also called κῶθος, or κώθων, identifies the κωβιός with *Cottus gobio* L., the Bull-head or Miller's Thumb. It is possible that κωβιός was also applied to the fresh-water Gudgeon, *Gobio fluviatilis*, which may be the fish referred to Athen. 309 e ποταμίων δὲ κωβιῶν μνημονεύει Δωρίων ἐν τῷ περὶ ἰχθύων, although the Goby also enters rivers and lakes, A. 601 b 21 γίνονται δὲ καὶ οἱ κωβιοὶ πίονες ἐν τοῖς ποταμοῖς, as in Latin writers certainly *gobio* or *gobius* sometimes means Goby, Plin. xxxii. 146 *cobio* (*i.e.* gobio) among "peculiares maris," sometimes Gudgeon, Auson. *Mosell.* 131 Tu quoque flumineas inter memorande cohortes, Gobio, non geminis maior sine pollice palmis, Praepinguis (an epithet which suggests that even A. 601 b 21 may refer to the Gudgeon).

he wounds, nor the Cuttle-fish,[a] but in them also is bred an ichor scanty but noxious. Among fishes armed with sharp stings are the Goby [b] which rejoices in the sands and the Scorpion [c] which rejoices in the rocks, and the swift Swallows and the Weevers [d] and those Dog-fish [e] which are named from their grievous spines — all discharging poison with their deadly pricks.

The Goby is probably intended in Ov. *Hal.* 128 Spina nocuus non gobius ulla.

[c] *H.* i. 171 n.; Ov. *Hal.* 116 Et capitis duro nociturus scorpius ictu.

[d] *Trachinus draco* L., the Greater Weever, and allied species, *T. vipera*, the Lesser Weever, *T. radiatus*, *T. araneus*, the first two found in British waters: all in M.G. *δράκαινα*. *Cf.* Ael. ii. 50, v. 37, xiv. 12; A. 598 a 11; Phil. 94; Plin. ix. 82 rursus draco marinus captus atque immissus in harenam cavernam sibi rostro mira celeritate excavat; xxxii. 148 draco—quidam aliud volunt esse dracunculum [prob. *T. vipera*], est autem gerriculae [= Gr. *μαινίς*] amplae, aculeum in branchiis habet ad caudam spectantem, sicut scorpio laedit dum manu tollitur. Also called *araneus*, Plin. xxxii. 145 Peculiares autem maris . . . araneus, ix. 155 Aeque pestiferum animal araneus spinae in dorso aculeo noxius. "Ils sont très redoutés par les pêcheurs, leurs blessures déterminant quelquefois de graves accidents. Il est généralement admis que les arêtes de ces poissons sont vénéneuses. Aussi les pêcheurs les saisissent-ils avec la plus grande précaution; on les apporte rarement intacts au marché; le plus souvent, pour éviter tout danger, on les mutile aussitôt après les avoir capturés" (Apost. p. 9). Drayton, *Polyolbion* xxv. 167 The Weaver, which although his prickles venom bee, By Fishers cut away which Buyers seldom see. *Cf.* Day i. 78 ff. It is generally thought that the correct spelling of the English name is Weever, O.F. *wivre*, Lat. *vipera*, *cf.* the heraldic *Wyvern*, though the Lat. *araneus* = spider suggests some doubt, Weaver (Wyver) being in some places, *e.g.* Banffshire, in familiar use as a name for a species of spider.

[e] *Squalus centrina* L.; *cf. H.* i. 378 n.

Τρυγόνι δὲ ξιφίῃ τε θεὸς κρατερώτατα δῶρα
γυίοις ἐγκατέθηκεν, ὑπέρβιον ὅπλον ἑκάστῳ
καρτύνας· καὶ τῷ μὲν ὑπὲρ γένυν ἐστήριξεν
ὄρθιον, αὐτόρριζον, ἀκάχμενον, οὔτι σιδήρου
φάσγανον, ἀλλ' ἀδάμαντος ἰσόσθενες ὄβριμον ἆορ.
οὐ κείνου κρυόεσσαν ἐπιβρίσαντος ἀκωκὴν
οὐδὲ μάλα στερεὴ τλαίη λίθος οὐτηθεῖσα·
τοίη οἱ ζαμενής τε πέλει πυρόεσσά τ' ἐρωή.
Τρυγόνι δ' ἐκ νεάτης ἀνατέλλεται ἄγριον οὐρῆς
κέντρον ὁμοῦ χαλεπόν τε βίῃ καὶ ὀλέθριον ἰῷ.
οὐδέ κεν οὐ ξιφίαι, οὐ τρυγόνες ἐν γενύεσσι
φορβὴν πρόσθε πάσαιντο, πάρος βελέεσσι δαφοινοῖς
οὐτῆσαι ζωόν τε καὶ ἄπνοον ὅττι παρείη.
ἀλλ' ἤτοι ξιφίην μὲν ἐπὴν προλίπῃσιν ἀϋτμή,
αὐτίκα οἱ κἀκεῖνο συνέφθιτο καρτερὸν ἆορ,
αὐτῷ δ' ὅπλον ἄνακτι συνέσβετο, καδδὲ λέλειπται
ὀστέον οὐδενόσωρον, ἀμήχανον ὅσσον ἰδέσθαι
φάσγανον· οὐδέ κεν ἄν τι καὶ ἱέμενος τελέσειας.
τρυγονίου δ' οὔπω τι κακώτερον ἔπλετο πῆμα
τρώματος, οὐδ' ὅσα χεῖρες ἀρήϊα τεχνήσαντο
χαλκήων, οὐδ' ὅσσα φερεπτερύγων ἐπ' ὀϊστῶν
Πέρσαι φαρμακτῆρες ὀλέθρια μητίσαντο·
τρυγόνι γὰρ ζωῇ τε βέλος ῥίγιστον ὀπηδεῖ
ζαφλεγές, οἷόν πού τις ἀνὴρ πέφρικεν ἀκούων,
ζώει τε φθιμένης καὶ ἀτειρέα ῥύεται ἀλκὴν

---

[a] *Trygon vulgaris* Risso (*T. pastinaca* Cuv.), M.G. τρυγών at Paros, μούτρουβα at Chalcis (Apost. p. 6). A long spine on the tail represents the dorsal fin. It is sometimes as much as eight inches long and is capable of causing a serious wound. It is used by the savages of the South Sea Islands to tip their spears. *Cf.* A. 598 a 12, etc.; Athen. 330 a; Phil. 106; Plin. ix. 155 Sed nullum usquam execrabilius quam radius super caudam eminens trygonis, quam nostri

For the Sting-ray [a] and the Swordfish [b] God has put in their bodies most powerful gifts, equipping each with a weapon of exceeding might. Above the jaw of the Swordfish he has set a natural sword, upright and sharp, no sabre of iron but a mighty sword with the strength of adamant. When he puts his weight behind his terrible spear not even the hardest rock may endure the wound; so fierce and fiery is the onset.

In the Sting-ray there springs from below the tail a fierce sting, at once grievous in its power and deadly with its venom. Neither the Sword-fishes nor the Sting-rays will taste any food with their jaws, until they have first wounded with their deadly darts whatever prey is at hand whether it be alive or lifeless. But when the breath of life forsakes the Sword-fish, his mighty sword straightway perishes with him and his weapon is quenched with its master and there is left a bone of no account, a great sword only to behold and thou couldst do nothing with it if thou wouldst. But than the wound of the Sting-ray there is no more evil hurt, neither in the warlike weapons which the hands of the smith contrive nor in the deadly drugs which Persian pharmacists have devised upon their winged arrows. While the Sting-ray lives, a terrible and fiery weapon attends it, such, I ween, as a man trembles to hear of, and it lives when the Sting-ray itself has perished and preserves its un-

pastinacam appellant, quincunciali magnitudine. Arbores infixus radici necat, arma ut telum perforat vi ferri et veneni malo letalis trygon; Auson. *Ep.* xiv. 60; Ael. i. 56, ii. 36, ii. 50, viii. 26, xi. 37, xvii. 18.

[b] *Xiphias gladius*, M.G. ξιφίας (Bik. p. 82). A. 505 b 18, 506 b 16, 602 a 26; Athen. 314 e; Ael. ix. 40, xiv. 23 and 26, xv. 6; Plin. iv. 3, 54, and 145.

ἄτροπον· οὐδ᾽ ἄρα μοῦνον ἐνὶ ζῴοις ἀΐδηλον
ἄτην, ὅσσα βάλῃσιν, ἐρεύγεται, ἀλλὰ καὶ ἔρνος
καὶ πέτρην ἐκάκωσε, καὶ εἴ ποθι κεῖνο πελάσσῃ.
εἰ γάρ τίς κ᾽ ἐριθηλὲς ἀεξόμενον φυτὸν ὥραις,
θαλλοῖς τ᾽ εὐφυέεσσι καὶ εὐκάρποισι γονῇσι,
νέρθεν ὑπὸ ῥίζῃσιν ἀναιδέϊ τύμματι κείνῳ
οὐτήσῃ, τόδ᾽ ἔπειτα κακῇ βεβολημένον ἄτῃ
λήγει μὲν πετάλων, κατὰ δὲ ῥέει ἠΰτε νούσῳ·
πρῶτον ἀπ᾽ ἀγλαΐης δὲ μαραίνεται, οὐδέ τι τηλοῦ
αὖόν τ᾽ οὐτιδανόν τε καὶ ἄχλοον ὄψεαι ἔρνος.
Κεῖνό ποτ᾽ αἰγανέῃ δολιχήρεϊ κωπηέσσῃ
Κίρκη Τηλεγόνῳ πολυφάρμακος ὤπασε μήτηρ,
αἰχμάζειν δηΐοις ἅλιον μόρον· αὐτὰρ ὁ νήσῳ
αἰγιβότῳ προσέκελσε, καὶ οὐ μάθε πώεα πέρθων
πατρὸς ἑοῦ, γεραρῷ δὲ βοηδρομέοντι τοκῆϊ
αὐτῷ, τὸν μάστευε, κακὴν ἐνεμάξατο κῆρα.
ἔνθα τὸν αἰολόμητιν Ὀδυσσέα, μυρία πόντου
ἄλγεα μετρήσαντα πολυκμήτοισιν ἀέθλοις,
τρυγὼν ἀλγινόεσσα μιῇ κατενήρατο ῥιπῇ.
Θύννῳ δὲ ξιφίῃ τε συνέμπορον αἰὲν ὀπηδεῖ
πῆμα· τὸ δ᾽ οὔποτ᾽ ἔχουσιν ἀπότροπον οὔτε μεθέσθαι

wearied strength unchanged; and not only on the living creatures which it strikes does it belch mysterious bane but it hurts even tree and rock and wherever it comes nigh. For if one take a lusty tree that flourishes in its season, with goodly foliage and fruitful crop, and wound it in the roots below with that relentless stroke, then, smitten by an evil bane, it ceases to put forth leaves and first droops as if by disease and its beauty fades away; and at no distant date thou shalt behold the tree withered and worthless and its greenery gone.

That sting it was which his mother Circe,[a] skilled in many drugs, gave of old to Telegonus for his long hilted spear, that he might array for his foes death from the sea. And he beached his ship on the island that pastured goats; and he knew not that he was harrying the flocks of his own father, and on his aged sire who came to the rescue, even on him whom he was seeking, he brought an evil fate. There the cunning Odysseus, who had passed through countless woes of the sea in his laborious adventures, the grievous Sting-ray slew with one blow.

The Tunny and the Sword-fish are ever attended and companioned by a plague, which they can never

[a] The story was told in the *Telegony* (Kinkel, p. 57). *Cf.* Apollod. epit. vii. 36 Τηλέγονος [son of Odysseus and Circe] *παρὰ Κίρκης μαθὼν ὅτι παῖς Ὀδυσσέως ἐστίν, ἐπὶ τὴν τούτου ζήτησιν ἐκπλεῖ. παραγενόμενος δὲ εἰς Ἰθάκην τὴν νῆσον ἀπελαύνει τινὰ τῶν βοσκημάτων, καὶ Ὀδυσσέα βοηθοῦντα τῷ μετὰ χεῖρας δόρατι Τηλέγονος* <*τρυγόνος*> *κέντρον τὴν αἰχμὴν ἔχοντι τιτρώσκει, καὶ Ὀδυσσεὺς θνήσκει*; Lycophr. *Alex.* 795 *κτενεῖ δὲ τύψας πλευρὰ λοίγιος στόνυξ | κέντρῳ δυσαλθὴς ἔλλοπος Σαρδωνικῆς.* According to one interpretation this is the reference of the prophecy of Teiresias, Hom. *Od.* xi. 134 *θάνατος δέ τοι ἐξ ἁλὸς αὐτῷ | ἀβληχρὸς μάλα τοῖος ἐλεύσεται, ὅς κέ σε πέφνῃ κτλ.*

οὔτε φυγεῖν, πτερύγεσσιν ἐνήμενον ἄγριον οἶστρον,
ὅς σφισι, καυστηροῖο κυνὸς νέον ἱσταμένοιο,
κέντρου πευκεδανοῖο θοὴν ἐνερείδεται ἀλκήν,
ὀξὺ μάλ' ἐγχρίμπτων, χαλεπὴν δ' ἐπὶ λύσσαν ὀρίνει,
θωρήξας ὀδύνῃσιν· ἐπισπέρχει δ' ἀέκοντας
φοιταλέῃ μάστιγι χορευέμεν· οἱ δὲ κελαινῷ
τύμματι παιφάσσουσι μεμηνότες, ἄλλοτε δ' ἄλλῃ
κῦμα καθιππεύουσιν, ἀνήνυτον ἄλγος ἔχοντες.
πολλάκι καὶ νήεσσιν ἐϋκραίροις ἐνόρουσαν
ῥιπῇ ἐλαυνόμενοι δυσκραέϊ· πολλάκι δ' ἅλμης
ἔκθορον ἐς γαῖάν τε κατέδραμον ἀσπαίροντες
καὶ μόρον ἠμείψαντο πολυκμήτων ὀδυνάων·
τοῖον γὰρ δάκος αἰνὸν ἐπιρρέπει οὐδ' ἀνίησι.
καὶ γάρ τοι καὶ βουσὶν ἀνάρσιος εὖτε πελάσσῃ
οἶστρος, ἐνιχρίμψῃ δὲ βέλος λαγόνεσσιν ἀραιαῖς,
οὔτε τι βουφόρβων μέλεται σέβας οὔτε νομοῖο,
οὔτ' ἀγέλης ποίην δὲ καὶ αὔλια πάντα λιπόντες
σεύονται λύσσῃ τεθοωμένοι· οὐδέ τις αὐτοῖς
οὐ ποταμῶν, οὐ πόντος ἀνέμβατος, οὐδὲ χαράδραι
ῥωγάδες, οὐ πέτρη τις ἀφοίτητος κατερύκει
ῥιπὴν ταυρείην, ὅτ' ἐπιζέσῃ ὀξὺ κελεύων
βουτύπος, ὀτρηρῇσιν ἐπισπέρχων ὀδύνῃσι·
πάντῃ δὲ βρυχή, πάντῃ δέ οἱ ἅλματα χηλῆς
εἱλεῖται· τοίη μιν ἄγει δριμεῖα θύελλα.
καὶ τὸ μὲν ἰχθύσιν ἄλγος ὁμοίϊον ἠδὲ βόεσσι.
Δελφῖνες δ' ἀγέλῃσιν ἁλὸς μέγα κοιρανέουσιν,

---

[a] 602 a 25 οἱ δὲ θύννοι καὶ οἱ ξιφίαι οἰστρῶσι περὶ κυνὸς ἐπιτολήν· ἔχουσι γὰρ ἀμφότεροι τηνικαῦτα περὶ τὰ πτερύγια οἷον σκωλήκιον τὸν καλούμενον οἶστρον, ὅμοιον μὲν σκορπίῳ, μέγεθος δ' ἡλίκον ἀράχνης. ποιοῦσι δὲ ταῦτα πόνον τοσοῦτον ὥστ' ἐξάλλεσθαι οὐκ ἔλαττον ἐνίοτε τὸν ξιφίαν τοῦ δελφῖνος, διὸ καὶ τοῖς πλοίοις πολλάκις ἐμπίπτουσιν. *Cf.* 557 a 27; Plin. ix. 54 Animal est parvum scorpionis effigie, aranei magnitudine. Hoc se et

turn away or escape: a fierce gadfly[a] which infests their fins and which, when the burning Dog-star is newly risen, fixes in them the swift might of its bitter sting, and with sharp assault stirs them to grievous madness, making them drunk with pain. With the lash of frenzy it drives them to dance against their will; maddened by the cruel blow they rush and now here, now there ride over the waves, possessed by pain unending. Often also they leap into well-beaked ships, driven by the stress of their distemper; and often they leap forth from the sea and rush writhing upon the land, and exchange their weary agonies for death; so dire pain is heavy upon them and abates not. Yea, for oxen[b] also, when the cruel gadfly attacks them and plunges its arrow in their tender flanks, have no more regard for the herdsmen nor for the pasture nor for the herd, but leaving the grass and all the folds they rush, whetted by frenzy; no river nor untrodden sea nor rugged ravine nor pathless rock stays the course of the bulls, when the gadfly hot and sharp impels, urging them with keen pains. Everywhere there is bellowing, everywhere range their bounding hoofs: such bitter tempest drives. This pain the fishes suffer even as do the cattle.

The Dolphins lord it greatly among the herds of the

thynno et ei qui gladius vocatur crebro delphini magnitudinem excedenti sub pinna affigit aculeo, tantoque infestat dolore, ut in naves saepenumero exsiliant; Athen. 302 b-c. The characteristic parasite of the Tunny is *Brachiella thynni* Cuv., that of the Sword-fish *Pennatula filosa* Gmelin.

[b] Apoll. Rh. i. 1265 *ὡς δ' ὅτε τίς τε μύωπι τετυμμένος ἔσσυτο ταῦρος | πίσεά τε προλιπὼν καὶ ἑλεσπίδας, οὐδὲ νομήων | οὐδ' ἀγέλης ὄθεται, πρήσσει δ' ὁδὸν ἄλλοτ' ἄπαυστος, | ἄλλοτε δ' ἱστάμενος καὶ ἀνὰ πλατὺν αὐχέν' ἀείρων | ἵησιν μύκημα κακῷ βεβολημένος οἴστρῳ.* *Cf.* Hom. *Od.* xxii. 299; Verg. *G.* iii. 146 ff.

ἔξοχον ἠνορέῃ τε καὶ ἀγλαΐῃ κομόωντες
ῥιπῇ τ' ὠκυάλῳ· διὰ γὰρ βέλος ὥστε θάλασσαν
ἵπτανται· φλογόεν δὲ σέλας πέμπουσιν ὀπωπαῖς
ὀξύτατον· καί πού τιν' ὑποπτήσσοντα χαράδραις
καί τιν' ὑπὸ ψαμάθοις εἰλυμένον ἔδρακον ἰχθύν.
ὅσσον γὰρ κούφοισι μετ' οἰωνοῖσιν ἄνακτες
αἰετοὶ ἢ θήρεσσι μετ' ὠμηστῇσι λέοντες,
ὅσσον ἀριστεύουσιν ἐν ἑρπυστῆρσι δράκοντες,
τόσσον καὶ δελφῖνες ἐν ἰχθύσιν ἡγεμονῆες.
τοῖς δ' οὔτ' ἐρχομένοις πελάσαι σχεδὸν οὔτε τις ἄντην
ὄσσε βαλεῖν τέτληκεν, ὑποπτώσσουσι δ' ἄνακτος
τηλόθεν ἅλματα δεινὰ καὶ ἄσθματα φυσιόωντος.
οἱ δ' ὁπότ' ἰθύσωσι λιλαιόμενοι μετὰ φορβήν,
πάντ' ἄμυδις κλονέουσιν ἀθέσφατα πώεα λίμνης,
παμφύγδην ἐλόωντες· ἐνέπλησαν δὲ φόβοιο
πάντα πόρον· σκιεροὶ δὲ μυχοὶ χθαμαλαί τε χαράδραι
στείνονται λιμένες τε καὶ ἠϊόνων ἐπιωγαὶ
πάντοθεν εἰλομένων· ὁ δὲ δαίνυται ὅν κ' ἐθέλῃσι,
κρινάμενος τὸν ἄριστον ἀπειρεσίων παρεόντων.
'Αλλ' ἔμπης καὶ τοῖσιν ἀνάρσιοι ἀντιφέρονται
ἰχθύες, οὓς ἀμίας κικλήσκομεν· οὐδ' ἀλέγουσι
δελφίνων, μοῦναι δὲ κατ' ἀντία δηριόωνται.
ταῖς μὲν ἀφαυρότερον θύννων δέμας, ἀμφὶ δὲ σάρκες

[a] As the Eagle (ὤκιστος πετεηνῶν Hom. *Il.* xxi. 253, ἔστι δ' αἰετὸς ὠκὺς ἐν ποτανοῖς Pind. *N.* iii. 80) is the type of swiftness in the air, so is the Dolphin (Pind. *N.* vi. 64 δελφῖνί κεν τάχος δι' ἅλμας εἰκάζοιμι Μελησίαν) the type of swiftness in the sea: Pind. P. ii. 50 θεός, ὃ καὶ πτερόεντ' αἰετὸν κίχε καὶ θαλασσαῖον παραμείβεται δελφῖνα.

[b] Hom. *Il.* xxi. 22 ὡς δ' ὑπὸ δελφῖνος μεγακήτεος ἰχθύες ἄλλοι |

sea, pluming themselves eminently on their valiance and beauty and their swift speed in the water; for like an arrow they fly through the sea, and fiery and keen is the light which they flash from their eyes, and they descry, I ween, any fish that cowers in a cleft or wraps itself beneath the sands. Even as the Eagles [a] are lords among the lightsome birds or Lions amid ravenous wild beasts, as Serpents are most excellent among reptiles, so are Dolphins leaders among fishes. Them as they come no fish dares to approach nor any to look them in the face, but they tremble from afar at the dread leaps and snorting breath of the lord of fishes. When the Dolphins set out in quest of food, they huddle [b] before them all the infinite flocks of the sea together, driving them in utter rout; they fill with terror every path of the sea, and shady covert and low ravine, and the havens and the bays of the shore are straitened with fishes huddling from every side; and the Dolphin devours whichsoever he will, choosing the best of the infinite fishes at hand.

But, notwithstanding, even the Dolphins have foes who meet their encounter, the fish called Amia,[c] which care not for the Dolphin but alone fight them face to face. These have a weaker body than the

φεύγοντες πιμπλᾶσι μυχοὺς λιμένος εὐόρμου, | δειδιότες· μάλα γάρ τε κατεσθίει ὃν κε λάβῃσιν; Hesiod, *Sc.* 211 *δοιοὶ δ' ἀναφυσιόωντες | ἀργύρεοι δελφῖνες ἐφοίτων ἔλλοπας ἰχθῦς | τῶν δ' ὕπο χάλκειοι τρέον ἰχθύες*; Apost. p. 40 "il est facile de se rendre compte de la présence du poisson en écoutant le bruit que font les dauphins qui le poursuivent à la surface de l'eau."

[c] *Pelamys sarda*, M.G. *παλαμύδα* (Apost. p. 14), the Bonito. *Cf.* A. 598 a 22, 601 b 21, etc.; Athen. 277 e–278 d, 324 d; Plin. ix. 49 Amiam vocant cuius incrementum singulis diebus intelligitur.

ἀβληχραί, θαμέες δὲ διὰ στόμα λάβρον ὀδόντες
ὀξέα πεφρίκασι· τὸ καὶ μέγα θάρσος ἔχουσιν,
οὐδὲ καταπτώσσουσιν ὑπέρβιον ἡγητῆρα.
εὖτε γὰρ ἀθρήσωσιν ἀπόσσυτον οἶον ἀπ' ἄλλων
δελφίνων ἀγέλης, αἱ δ' ἀθρόαι ἄλλοθεν ἄλλαι,
ἠΰθ' ὑπ' ἀγγελίης στρατὸς ἄσπετος, εἰς ἕν ἰοῦσαι
στέλλονται ποτὶ μῶλον ἀθαμβέες, ὥστ' ἐπὶ πύργον
δυσμενέων θύνοντες ἀρήϊοι ἀσπιστῆρες.
δελφὶς δ' ἠϋγένειος ὑπαντιόωντος ὁμίλου
πρῶτα μὲν οὐκ ἀλέγει, μετὰ δ' ἔσσυται, ἄλλοτε ἄλλην
ἁρπάγδην ἐρύων, μενοεικέα δαῖτα κιχήσας.
ἀλλ' ὅτε μιν πολέμοιο περιστέψωσι φάλαγγες
πάντοθεν, ἀμφὶ δέ μιν στῖφος μέγα κυκλώσωνται,
δὴ τότε οἱ καὶ μόχθος ὑπὸ φρένα δύεται ἤδη·
ἔγνω δ' αἰπὺν ὄλεθρον ἀπειρεσίοις ἔνι μοῦνος
ἑρχθεὶς δυσμενέεσσι· πόνος δ' ἀναφαίνεται ἀλκῆς.
αἱ μὲν γὰρ λυσσηδὸν ἀολλέες ἀμφιχυθεῖσαι
δελφῖνος μελέεσσι βίην ἐνέρεισαν ὀδόντων·
πάντῃ δὲ πρίουσι καὶ ἄτροποι ἐμπεφύασι,
πολλαὶ μὲν κεφαλῆς δεδραγμέναι, αἱ δὲ γενείων
γλαυκῶν, αἱ δ' αὐτῇσιν ἐνὶ πτερύγεσσιν ἔχονται,
πολλαὶ δ' ἐν λαγόνεσσι γένυν πήξαντο δαφοινήν,
ἄλλαι δ' ἀκροτάτην οὐρὴν ἕλον, αἱ δ' ὑπένερθε
νηδύν, αἱ δ' ἄρ' ὕπερθεν ὑπὲρ νώτοιο νέμονται,
ἄλλαι δ' ἐκ λοφιῆς, αἱ δ' αὐχένος ᾐώρηνται.
αὐτὰρ ὁ παντοίοισι περιπληθὴς καμάτοισι
πόντον ἐπαιγίζει, σφακέλῳ δέ οἱ ἔνδον ὀρεχθεῖ
μαινομένη κραδίη, φλεγέθει δέ οἱ ἦτορ ἀνίῃ,
πάντῃ δὲ θρώσκει καὶ ἑλίσσεται ἄκριτα θύων,
παφλάζων ὀδύνῃσι· κυβιστητῆρι δ' ἐοικὼς
ἄλλοτε μὲν βαθὺ κῦμα διατρέχει ἠΰτε λαίλαψ,
ἄλλοτε δ' ἐς νεάτην φέρεται βρύχα, πολλάκι δ' ἅλμης

Tunny and are clothed in feeble flesh, but in their ravenous mouth bristles sharp a dense array of teeth ; wherefore also they have great courage and do not cower before the mighty lord of fishes. For when they see one that has wandered away alone from the rest of the herd of Dolphins, then from this quarter and from that, as a great army at command, they gather in a body together and set forth to battle dauntlessly, like shielded warriors against the tower of the foe. And the bearded Dolphin, when the crowd meets him, at first recks not of them but rushes among them, seizing and rending now one and now another, finding a banquet after his heart. But when the ranks of war surround him on every side and encircle him with their great and dense array, then trouble at length enters his heart and he knows that sheer destruction is upon him, hemmed about as he is, alone among countless foes ; and the toil of battle appears. For furiously they fall in a body about the limbs of the Dolphin and fix in him the might of their teeth ; everywhere they bite him and cling to him relentlessly, many clutching his head, others his grey jaws, while yet others cleave to his very fins ; many in his flanks fix their deadly teeth, others seize the end of his tail, others his belly beneath, others feed upon his back above, others hang from his mane, others from his neck. And, full of manifold distress, he rushes over the sea and his frenzied heart within him is racked with agony and his spirit is afire with pain. Every way he leaps and turns, rushing blindly in the spasms of agony. Like a diver, now he runs over the deep waves like a whirlwind, now he plunges to the nether deeps ; and often he springs up and

ἀφρὸν ὑπερθρώσκων ἀναπάλλεται, εἴ ἑ μεθείη
ἐσμὸς ὑπερφιάλων νεπόδων θρασύς· αἱ δ' ἀλίαστοι
οὔτι βίης μεθιᾶσιν, ὁμῶς δέ οἱ ἐμπεφύασι,
καί οἱ δυομένῳ τε μίαν δύνουσι κέλευθον,
αὖτις δ' ἀνθρώσκοντι σὺν ἔξαλοι ἀΐσσουσιν
ἑλκόμεναι· φαίης κε νέον τέρας Ἐννοσιγαίῳ
τίκτεσθαι δελφῖσι μεμιγμένον ἠδ' ἀμίῃσιν·
ὧδε γὰρ ἀργαλέῃ ξυνοχῇ πεπέδηται ὀδόντων.
ὡς δ' ὅταν ἰητὴρ πολυμήχανος, ἕλκος ἀφύσσων
οἰδαλέον, τῷ πολλὸν ἀνάρσιον ἔνδοθεν αἷμα
ἐντρέφεται, διεράς τε γονάς, κυανόχροα λίμνης
ἑρπετά, τειρομένοιο κατὰ χροὸς ἐστήριξε,
δαίνυσθαι μέλαν αἷμα· τὰ δ' αὐτίκα γυρωθέντα
κυρτοῦται καὶ λύθρον ἐφέλκεται οὐδ' ἀνίησιν,
εἰσόκεν αἱμοβαρῆ ζωρὸν πότον αὖ ἐρύσαντα
ἐκ χροὸς αὐτοκύλιστα πέσῃ μεθύουσιν ὁμοῖα·
ὣς ἀμίαις οὐ πρόσθε χαλᾷ μένος, εἰσόκε σάρκα
κείνην, ἥν ποτ' ἔμαρψαν, ὑπὸ στόμα δαιτρεύσωνται.
ἀλλ' ὅτε μιν προλίπωσιν, ἀναπνεύσῃ δὲ πόνοιο
δελφίς, δὴ τότε λύσσαν ἐσόψεαι ἡγητῆρος
χωομένου· κρυερὴ δ' ἀμίαις ἀναφαίνεται ἄτη.
αἱ μὲν γὰρ φεύγουσιν, ὁ δ' ἐξόπιθεν κεραΐζων,
εἰδόμενος πρηστῆρι δυσηχέϊ, πάντ' ἀμαθύνει,
δάπτων ἐμμενέως, κατὰ δ' αἵματι πόντον ἐρεύθει
αἰχμάζων γενύεσσι, παθὼν δ' ἀπετίσατο λώβην.

---

[a] The reference is to the Leech, βδέλλα, *Hirudo medicinalis*. *Cf.* Theocr. ii. 55 τί μευ μέλαν ἐκ χροὸς αἷμα | ἐμφὺς ὡς λιμνᾶτις ἅπαν ἐκ βδέλλα πέπωκας; Herod. ii. 68; A. *De incess.* 709 a 29; Ael. iii. 11, viii. 25, xii. 15; Plaut. *Epid.* 188;

leaps above the foam of the sea, if haply the bold swarm of overweening fishes may let him go. But they, relentless, no wise abate their violence but cling to him all the same; when he dives, they dive along with him; when he leaps up again, they likewise spring forth from the sea in his train. You would say that the Shaker of the Earth had gotten a new and monstrous birth, half Dolphin and half Amia; so grievous the bond of teeth wherewith he is bound. As when a cunning physician drains a swollen wound, within which is gathered much unwholesome blood, and he applies to the flesh of the sufferer the watery brood, the dark-hued reptiles of the marsh,[a] to feast on his black blood; and straightway they become arched and rounded and draw the filth and abate not until having drained the strong drink of blood they roll of themselves from the flesh and fall like drunken men; even so the fury of the Amia abates not until they have devoured with the mouth the flesh which they once seized. But when they leave him and the Dolphin gets a breathing-space from toil, then shalt thou behold the rage of the angry lord of fishes and deadly doom appears for the Amia. They flee; and he behind working havoc, like hurricane of evil noise, lays all waste, devouring them incontinently, and with ravening jaws reddens the sea with blood; and he avenges the despite that he suffered. Even so in

Plin. viii. 29 hirudine quam sanguisugam vulgo coepisse appellari adverto. For the Leech in medical use *cf.* Plin. xxxii. 123 Diversus hirudinum, quas sanguisugas vocant, ad extrahendum sanguinem usus est. Quippe eadem ratio earum quae cucurbitularum medicinalium ad corpora levanda sanguine, spiramenta laxanda iudicatur; multi podagris quoque admittendas censuere. Decidunt sat[i]atae et pondere ipso sanguinis detractae aut sale aspersae.

ὧδε καὶ ἐν ξυλόχοισιν ἔχει φάτις ἀγρευτήρων
θῶας ὑπερφιάλους ἔλαφον πέρι ποιπνύεσθαι
ἀγρομένους· οἱ μὲν γὰρ ἐπαΐγδην γενύεσσι
σάρκας ἀφαρπάζουσι καὶ ἀρτιχύτοιο φόνοιο
θερμὸν ἔαρ λάπτουσιν· ὁ δ᾽ αἱμάσσων ὀδύνῃσι,
βεβρυχὼς ὀλοῇσι περίπλεος ὠτειλῇσιν,
ἄλλοτ᾽ ἐπ᾽ ἀλλοίων ὀρέων διαπάλλεται ἄκρας·
οἱ δέ μιν οὐ λείπουσιν, ἀεὶ δέ οἱ ἐγγὺς ἕπονται
ὠμησταί, ζωὸν δὲ διαρταμέοντες ὀδοῦσι
ῥινὸν ἀποσχίζουσι, πάρος θανάτοιο κυρῆσαι,
δαῖτα κελαινοτάτην τε καὶ ἀλγίστην πονέοντες.
ἀλλ᾽ ἤ τοι θῶες μὲν ἀναιδέες οὔτιν᾽ ἔτισαν
ποινήν, ἐκ δ᾽ ἐγέλασσαν ἐπὶ φθιμένοις ἐλάφοισιν,
θαρσαλέαι δ᾽ ἀμίαι τάχα κύντερα δηρίσαντο.
Δελφίνων κἀκεῖνο πανέξοχον ἔργον ἀκούων
ἠγασάμην· τοῖς εὖτ᾽ ἂν ὀλέθριος ἐγγὺς ἵκηται
νοῦσος ἀταρτηρή, τοὺς δ᾽ οὐ λάθεν, ἀλλ᾽ ἐδάησαν
τέρμα βίου· πέλαγος δὲ καὶ εὐρέα βένθεα λίμνης
φεύγοντες κούφοισιν ἐπ᾽ αἰγιαλοῖσιν ἔκελσαν·
ἔνθα δ᾽ ἀποπνείουσι καὶ ἐν χθονὶ μοῖραν ἕλοντο,
ὄφρα τις ἢ μερόπων ἱερὸν τρόχιν Ἐννοσιγαίου
κείμενον αἰδέσσαιτο χυτῇ τ᾽ ἐπὶ θινὶ καλύψαι,
μνησάμενος φιλότητος ἐνηέος, ἠὲ καὶ αὐτὴ
βρασσομένη ψαμάθοισι δέμας κρύψειε θάλασσα,
μηδέ τις εἰναλίων ἐσίδοι νέκυν ἡγητῆρα,
μηδέ τις οἰχομένῳ περ ἐνὶ χροῒ λωβήσαιτο
δυσμενέων· ἀρετὴ δὲ καὶ ὀλλυμένοισιν ὀπηδεῖ
καὶ κράτος, οὐδ᾽ ᾔσχυναν ἑὸν κλέος οὐδὲ θανόντες.

the woods, as hunters tell, the terrible Jackals[a] gather and busy themselves about a Stag; they rush upon him and rend his flesh with their jaws and lap the warm gore of new-shed blood: the Stag bellowing in his bloody pain, full of deadly wounds, bounds now to this mountain-crag, now to that, but the ravenous beasts leave him not but always follow him close, and rend him alive and tear off his hide before he finds death, making a black and woeful banquet. But while the shameless Jackals pay no requital but laugh loud over the dead Stags, the bold Amia soon fight a less happy fight.

This other excellent deed of the Dolphins have I heard and admire. When fell disease and fatal draws nigh to them, they fail not to know it but are aware of the end of life. Then they flee the sea and the wide waters of the deep and come aground[b] on the shallow shores. And there they give up their breath and receive their doom upon the land; that so perchance some mortal man may take pity on the holy messenger[c] of the Shaker of the Earth when he lies low, and cover him with mound of shingle, remembering his gentle friendship; or haply the seething sea herself may hide his body in the sands; nor any of the brood of the sea behold the corse of their lord, nor any foe do despite to his body even in death. Excellence and majesty attend them even when they perish, nor do they shame their glory even when they die.

[a] *C.* iii. 338 n.

[b] A. 631 b 2 *διαπορεῖται δὲ περὶ αὐτῶν διὰ τί ἐξοκέλλουσιν εἰς τὴν γῆν· ποιεῖν γάρ φασι τοῦτ' αὐτοὺς ἐνίοτε, ὅταν τύχωσι, δι' οὐδεμίαν αἰτίαν.*

[c] For *τρόχις* *cf.* Aesch. *P.V.* 941 *τὸν Διὸς τρόχιν* = Hermes.

Κεστρέα δ' ἐν πάντεσσιν ἁλὸς νεπόδεσσιν ἀκούω
φέρβειν πρηΰτατόν τε δικαιότατόν τε νόημα·
μοῦνοι γὰρ κεστρῆες ἐνηέες οὔθ' ὁμόφυλον
οὔτέ τιν' ἀλλοίης γενεῆς ἄπο πημαίνουσιν·
οὐδέ ποτε ψαύουσιν ὑπὸ στόμα σαρκὸς ἐδωδῆς,
οὐδὲ φόνου λάπτουσιν, ἀπημοσύνῃ δὲ νέμονται,
αἵματος ἄχραντοι καὶ ἀκηδέες, ἁγνὰ γένεθλα·
φέρβονται δ' ἢ χλωρὸν ἁλὸς μνίον ἠὲ καὶ αὐτὴν
ἰλύν, ἀλλήλων τε δέμας περιλιχμάζουσι.
τοὔνεκα καί τιν' ἔχουσι μετ' ἰχθύσι τίμιον αἰδῶ·
οὐ γάρ τις κείνων νεαρὸν τόκον οἷα καὶ ἄλλων
σίνεται, ὠμοφάγων δὲ βίην ἀπέχουσιν ὀδόντων.
ὧς αἰεὶ μετὰ πᾶσι Δίκης πρεσβήϊα κεῖται
αἰδοίης, πάντῃ δὲ γεράσμιον ἤρατο τιμήν.

---

[a] In Aristotle *κεστρεύς* is sometimes generic for the Grey Mullets (*Mugilidae*), including *κέφαλος*: A. 534 b 14 *ἄρχονται δὲ κύειν τῶν κεστρέων οἱ μὲν χελῶνες τοῦ Ποσειδεῶνος καὶ ὁ σάργος καὶ ὁ σμύξων καλούμενος καὶ ὁ κεφαλος*; sometimes specific and contrasted with *κέφαλος*: A. 570 b 14 *τίκτει δὲ πρῶτον τῶν τοιούτων ἀθερίνη . . . κέφαλος δὲ ὕστατος· . . . τίκτει δὲ καὶ κεστρεὺς ἐν τοῖς πρώτοις*. As a specific name *κέφαλος* is perhaps *Mugil cephalus*, M.G. *κέφαλος*, *γομβύλι* at Chalcis; *στειράδια* the males and *μπάφες* the females at Missolonghi: they spawn about the month of May, "de leurs œufs on fait la boutargue" (Apost. p. 20). *κεστρεύς* is perhaps *M. capito*, M.G. *λαγιάδες* at Chalcis, *βελάνισες* at Aitolico (Apost. *l.c.*). But whatever the original distinction, *κέφαλος* as a name seems to have usurped the place of *κεστρεύς* (Suid. *s. κεστρεύς· ὁ νῦν λεγόμενος κέφαλος*) and in the Cyclades is now the generic name for all species of Grey Mullet (Erh. p. 89). The making of "boutargue" (Sp. *botargo*)—"produit excessivement recherché"—is described by Apostolides, p. 66: "La boutargue n'est autre chose que les ovaires des poissons, arrivés à l'état de maturité regorgeant déjà d'œufs prêts à être pondus et qui sont préparés par salaison. Une fois que le poisson sorti de l'eau, étant encore frais, on incise son ventre et on enlève

The Grey Mullet,[a] I hear, among all the fishes of the sea nurses the gentlest and most righteous[b] mind. For only the kindly Grey Mullets harm neither one of their own kind nor any of another race. Nor do they touch with their lips fleshly food nor drink blood, but feed harmlessly, unstained of blood and doing no hurt, a holy race. Either upon the green seaweed they feed or on mere mud, and lick the bodies one of the other. Wherefore also among fishes they have honourable regard and none harms their young brood, as they do that of others, but refrain the violence of their ravenous teeth. Thus always and among all reverend Justice hath her privilege appointed and everywhere she wins her meed of honour. But all

les ovaires entiers, en tâchant de ne pas produire la moindre coupure à leur mince enveloppe. On les laisse pendant quatre heures dans du sel. Après, on les lave, on les place entre deux planches pour leur donner la forme sous laquelle on les voit habituellement dans le commerce, et on les laisse exposés au soleil pendant 4 à 8 jours. Une fois complètement secs, ils sont prêts à être vendus; mais si on veut les conserver pendant longtemps, on les entoure d'une couche de cire en les plaçant pendant un instant dans la cire jaune fondue, d'où on les retire brusquement."

[b] *Cf. H.* i. 111; A. 591 a 17 ἀλληλοφαγοῦσι δὲ πάντες μὲν πλὴν κεστρέως . . . ὁ δὲ κέφαλος καὶ ὁ κεστρεὺς ὅλως μόνοι οὐ σαρκοφαγοῦσιν· σημεῖον δέ, οὔτε γὰρ ἐν τῇ κοιλίᾳ πώποτ' ἔχοντες εἰλημμένοι εἰσὶ τοιοῦτον οὐδὲν οὔτε δελέατι χρῶνται πρὸς αὐτοὺς ζῴων σαρξὶν ἀλλὰ μάζῃ. τρέφεται δὲ πᾶς κεστρεὺς φυκίοις καὶ ἄμμῳ; Athen. 307; Plut. *Mor.* 965 E; Ael. i. 3; Suid. *s.* κεστρεῖς. The teeth in these fishes are either entirely absent or very fine. "In an aquarium it is most interesting to observe them suck in the sand, the coarser portion of which they almost immediately afterwards expel from their mouths. A sifting or filtering apparatus exists in the pharynx, which precludes large and hard substances from passing into the stomach, or sand from obtaining access to the gills" Day i. p. 229.

οἱ δ' ἄλλοι μάλα πάντες ὀλέθριοι ἀλλήλοισιν
ἔρχονται· τὸ καὶ οὔποτ' ἐσόψεαι ὑπνώοντας
ἔλλοπας, ἀλλ' ἄρα τοῖσι καὶ ὄμματα καὶ νόος αἰὲν
ἐγρήσσει πανάϋπνος· ἐπεὶ τρομέουσι μὲν αἰεὶ
φέρτερον ἀντιόωντα, χερειότερον δ' ὀλέκουσι.
μοῦνον δ' οὔποτε φασὶν ἀνὰ κνέφας ἀσπαλιῆες
εἰς ἄγρην πεσέειν ἁπαλὸν σκάρον, ἀλλά που ὕπνον
ἐννύχιον κοίλοισιν ὑπὸ κευθμῶσιν ἰαύειν.
Οὐ μέντοι τό γε θαῦμα Δίκην ἀπάτερθε θαλάσσης
ναιετάειν· οὐ γάρ τι πάλαι πρέσβειρα θεάων
οὐδὲ μετὰ θνητοῖσιν ἔχε θρόνον, ἀλλὰ κυδοιμοὶ
δυσκέλαδοι καὶ θοῦρος Ἄρευς φθισήνορος ἄτη
μαῖά τ' ἐρικλαύστων πολέμων Ἔρις ἀλγεσίδωρος
ἔφλεγον ἡμερίων δειλὸν γένος· οὐδέ τι θηρῶν
κεκριμένοι πολέες μερόπων ἔσαν, ἀλλὰ λεόντων
αἰνότεροι πύργους τ' εὐτείχεας ἠδὲ μέλαθρα
νηούς τ' ἀθανάτων εὐώδεας αἵματι φωτῶν
καπνῷ τ' αἰθαλόεντι κατείνυον Ἡφαίστοιο,
εἰσόκε ῥαιομένην γενεὴν ᾤκτειρε Κρονίων,
ὑμῖν δ' Αἰνεάδῃσιν ἐπέτραπε γαῖαν ἀνάψας.
ἀλλ' ἔτι καὶ προτέροισιν ἐν Αὐσονίων βασιλεῦσι
θῦνεν Ἄρης, Κελτούς τε καὶ αὐχήεντας Ἴβηρας
θωρήσσων Λιβύης τε πολὺν πόρον ἔργα τε Ῥήνου
Ἴστρον τ' Εὐφρήτην τε· τί μοι τάδε δούρατος ἔργα
μεμνῆσθαι; νῦν γάρ σε, Δίκη θρέπτειρα πολήων,
γινώσκω μερόπεσσι συνέστιον ἠδὲ σύνοικον,
ἐξ οὗ μοι κραίνουσι μέγαν θρόνον ἐμβεβαῶτες

---

[a] On the contrary A. 536 b 32 ὁμοίως δὲ καὶ τὰ ἔνυδρα, οἷον οἵ τε ἰχθύες καὶ τὰ μαλάκια καὶ τὰ μαλακόστρακα, κάραβοί τε καὶ τὰ τοιαῦτα· βραχύυπνα μὲν οὖν ἐστι ταῦτα πάντα, φαίνεται δὲ καθεύδοντα.

[b] *H*. i. 134 n.

other fishes come fraught with destruction to one another; wherefore also thou shalt never see fishes sleeping [a] but evermore awake and sleepless are their eyes and wits, since always they dread the encounter of a stronger and slay the weaker. Only the tender Parrot-wrasse,[b] as fishermen say, never falls into their nets in the darkness but doubtless sleeps [c] by night in the hollow ocean caves.

Yet it is no marvel that Justice should dwell apart from the sea. For not long since that first of goddesses had no throne even among men, but noisy riots and raging ruin of destroying Wars and Strife, giver of pain, nurse of tearful wars, consumed the unhappy race of the creatures of a day. Nor different at all from wild beasts were many among men; but, more terrible than Lions, well-builded towers and halls and fragrant temples of the deathless gods they clothed with the blood of men and dark smoke of Hephaestus: until the Son of Cronus took pity on the afflicted race and bestowed upon you, the Sons of Aeneas, the earth for keeping. Yet even among the earlier kings of the Ausonians War still raged, arming Celts and proud Iberians and the great space [d] of Libya and the lands of the Rhine [e] and Ister and Euphrates. Wherefore need I mention those works of the spear? For now, O Justice, nurse of cities, I know thee to share the hearth and home of men, ever since they hold sway together, mounted on their mighty throne—the

[c] Athen. 320 a Σέλευκος δ' ὁ Ταρσεὺς ἐν τῷ Ἁλιευτικῷ μόνον φησὶ τῶν ἰχθύων τὸν σκάρον καθεύδειν· ὅθεν οὐδὲ νύκτωρ ποτὲ ἁλῶναι. τοῦτο δ' ἴσως διὰ φόβον αὐτῷ συμβαίνει.

[d] For use of πόρον *cf.* Dion. P. 331 Εὐρώπης λοιπὸν πόρον.

[e] For periphrasis *cf. H.* i. 105 ἔργα τ' ὀνίσκων; Dion. P. 916 Ποσιδήια ἔργα.

ἄμφω θεσπέσιός τε πατὴρ καὶ φαίδιμος ὄρπηξ·
ἐκ τῶν μοι γλυκὺς ὅρμος ἀνακτορίης πεπέτασται.
τούς μοι καὶ ῥύοισθε καὶ ἔμπεδον ἰθύνοιτε
πολλαῖς ἐν δεκάδεσσιν ἑλισσομένων ἐνιαυτῶν,
Ζεῦ τε καὶ Οὐρανίδαι, Ζηνὸς χορός, εἴ τις ἀμοιβὴ
εὐσεβίης· σκήπτρῳ δὲ τελεσφόρον ὄλβον ἄγοιτε.

wondrous Sire and his splendid scion[a]: by whose rule a sweet haven is opened for me. Them, I pray, O Zeus and ye Sons of Heaven, the choir of Zeus, may ye keep and direct unfailingly through many tens of the revolving years, if there be any reward of piety, and to their sceptre bring the fulness of felicity.

[a] Schol. Ἀντωνῖνος καὶ Κώμοδος.

ΑΛΙΕΥΤΙΚΩΝ ΤΟ Γ

Νῦν δ' ἄγε μοι, σκηπτοῦχε, παναίολα δήνεα τέχνης
ἰχθυβόλου φράζοιο καὶ ἀγρευτῆρας ἀέθλους,
θεσμόν τ' εἰνάλιον ξυμβάλλεο, τέρπεο δ' οἴμῃ
ἡμετέρῃ· σοῖς μὲν γὰρ ὑπὸ σκήπτροισι θάλασσα
εἰλεῖται καὶ φῦλα Ποσειδάωνος ἐναύλων,
ἔργα δέ τοι ξύμπαντα μετ' ἀνδράσι πορσύνονται,
σοὶ δ' ἐμὲ τερπωλήν τε καὶ ὑμνητῆρ' ἀνέηκαν
δαίμονες ἐν Κιλίκεσσιν ὑφ' Ἑρμαίοις ἀδύτοισι.
Ἑρμεία, σὺ δέ μοι πατρώϊε, φέρτατε παίδων
Αἰγιόχου, κέρδιστον ἐν ἀθανάτοισι νόημα,
φαῖνέ τε καὶ σήμαινε καὶ ἄρχεο, νύσσαν ἀοιδῆς
ἰθύνων· βουλὰς δὲ περισσονόων ἁλιήων
αὐτός, ἄναξ, πρώτιστος ἐμήσαο καὶ τέλος ἄγρης
παντοίης ἀνέφηνας, ἐπ' ἰχθύσι κῆρας ὑφαίνων.
Πανὶ δὲ Κωρυκίῳ βυθίην παρακάτθεο τέχνην,
παιδὶ τεῷ, τὸν φασὶ Διὸς ῥυτῆρα γενέσθαι,

---

[a] Schol. Κίλιξ γὰρ ὁ ποιητὴς ἀπὸ τῆς Ἀναζάρβου (Amm. Marc xiv. 8. 3; Suid. *s.v.*; Plin. v. 93; Steph. Byz. *s.* Ἀναζαρβά) ὅπου ἦν Ἑρμοῦ ἱερόν.

[b] Introd. p. xix.

[c] The craft of Hermes is proverbial; Hom. *H.* (*Herm.*) iii. 413 κλεψίφρονος, 514 ποικιλομῆτα. φαῖνε seems to be used absolutely as in Theocr. ii. 11, Hom. *Od.* vii. 102, etc., or it may govern νύσσαν, *cf.* Theocr. ix. 28 βουκολικαὶ Μοῖσαι μάλα χαίρετε, φαίνετε δ' ᾠδάν. The order of the words is against taking νόημα as object to φαῖνε. For νόημα *cf.* Pind. *O.* vii.

HALIEUTICA, OR FISHING

III

Come now, O Wielder of the Sceptre, mark thou the cunning devices of the fisher's art and his adventures in the hunting of his prey, and learn the law of the sea and take delight in my lay. For under thy sceptre rolls the sea and the tribes of the haunts of Poseidon, and for thee are all deeds done among men. For thee the gods have raised me up to be thy joy and thy minstrel among the Cilicians beside the shrine of Hermes. And, O Hermes,[a] god of my fathers,[b] most excellent of the children of the Aegis-bearer, subtlest mind [c] among the deathless gods, do thou enlighten and guide and lead, directing me to the goal of my song. The counsels of fishermen excellent in wit thou didst thyself, O Lord, first devise and didst reveal the sum of all manner of hunting, weaving doom for fishes. And thou didst deliver the art of the deep for keeping to Pan of Corycus,[d] thy son,[e] who, they say, was the saviour

71 *ἔνθα* 'Ρόδῳ *ποτὲ μιχθεὶς τέκεν* | *ἑπτὰ σοφώτατα νοήματ' ἐπὶ προτέρων ἀνδρῶν παραδεξαμένους παῖδας*; *P.* vi. 28 *ἔγεντο καὶ πρότερον* 'Αντίλοχος *βιατὰς* | *νόημα τοῦτο φέρων*; Hom. *Od.* viii. 548 *νοήμασι κερδαλέοισιν.*

[d] *H.* iii. 209 n.

[e] Schol. 'Ερμοῦ *γὰρ καὶ* Πηνελόπης *ὁ* Πᾶν; Hom. *H.* xix. 1. 'Ερμείαο *φίλον γόνον*; Plin. vii. 204 Pan Mercuri (filius).

Ζηνὸς μὲν ῥυτῆρα, Τυφαόνιον δ᾽ ὀλετῆρα.
κεῖνος γὰρ δείπνοισιν ἐπ᾽ ἰχθυβόλοισι δολώσας
σμερδαλέον Τυφῶνα παρήπαφεν, ἔκ τε βερέθρου
δύμεναι εὐρωποῖο καὶ εἰς ἁλὸς ἐλθέμεν ἀκτήν·
ἔνθα μιν ὀξεῖαι στεροπαὶ ῥιπαί τε κεραυνῶν
ζαφλεγέες πρήνιξαν· ὁ δ᾽ αἰθόμενος πυρὸς ὄμβροις
κρᾶθ᾽ ἑκατὸν πέτρῃσι περιστυφελίζετο πάντῃ
ξαινόμενος· ξανθαὶ δὲ παρ᾽ ἠϊόνεσσιν ἔτ᾽ ὄχθαι
λύθρῳ ἐρευθιόωσι Τυφαονίων ἀλαλητῶν.
Ἑρμεία κλυτόβουλε, σὲ δ᾽ ἔξοχον ἱλάσκονται
ἰχθυβόλοι· τῷ καί σε σὺν ἀγροίοισιν ἀΰσας
δαίμοσιν εὐθήροιο μετὰ κλέος ἔρχομαι οἴμης.
Πρῶτα μὲν ἀσπαλιῆϊ δέμας καὶ γυῖα παρείη
ἀμφότερον καὶ κραιπνὰ καὶ ἄλκιμα, μήτε τι λίην
πίονα μήτε τι σαρκὶ λελειμμένα· δὴ γὰρ ἀνάγκη
πολλάκι μιν κρατεροῖσιν ἀνελκομένοισι μάχεσθαι
ἰχθύσιν, οἷς ὑπέροπλον ἔνι σθένος, εἰσόκεν ἅλμης
μητρὸς ἐν ἀγκοίνῃσιν ἑλισσόμενοι δονέονται.
χρειὼ δ᾽ ἐκ πέτρης τε θορεῖν πέτρην τ᾽ ἀνοροῦσαι
ῥηϊδίως· χρειὼ δὲ πόνου βυθίοιο ταθέντος
ῥίμφα διϊχνεῦσαι δολιχὸν πόρον ἔς τε βάθιστα
δῦναι καὶ μίμνοντα μετ᾽ οἴδμασιν ὡς ἐπὶ γαίης
δηθύνειν ἔργοισι πονεύμενον, οἷς ἐνὶ πόντῳ
ἄνδρες ἀεθλεύουσι ταλάφρονα θυμὸν ἔχοντες.

---

[a] *i.q.* Typhos (Aesch. *P.V.* 370; Pind. *P.* i. 16, viii. 16), Typhoeus (Hes. *Th.* 821), son of Tartarus and Gaia (Hes. *l.c.*). In mythology his birth and life is mostly associated with Cilicia (Pind. *P.* i. 16 Τυφὼς ἑκατοντακάρανος τόν ποτε | Κιλίκιον θρέψεν πολυώνυμον ἄντρον, viii. 16 Τυφὼς Κίλιξ, Aesch. *P.V.* 351 τὸν γηγενῆ τε Κιλικίων οἰκήτορα | ἄντρων, Hom. *Il.* ii. 784), his

of Zeus—the saviour of Zeus but the slayer of Typhon.[a] For he tricked terrible Typhon with promise of a banquet of fish and beguiled him to issue forth from his spacious pit and come to the shore of the sea, where the swift lightning and the rushing fiery thunderbolts laid him low; and, blazing in the rain of fire, he beat his hundred heads upon the rocks whereon he was carded all about like wool. And even now the yellow banks by the sea are red with the blood of the Typhonian battle. O Hermes, glorious in counsel, thee especially do fishermen worship.[b] Therefore invoking thee with the gods who aid their hunt I pursue the glorious song of their chase.

First of all the fisher should have body and limbs both swift and strong, neither over fat nor lacking in flesh. For often he must fight with mighty fish in landing them—which have exceeding strength so long as they circle and wheel in the arms of their mother sea. And lightly he must leap from a rock; and, when the toil of the sea is at its height, he must swiftly travel a long way and dive into the deepest depths and abide amongst the waves and remain labouring at such works as men upon the sea toil at with enduring heart. Cunning of wit too and wise

death with Sicily (Aesch. *P.V.* 365 *ἰπούμενος ῥίζαισιν Αἰτναίαις ὕπο*; Pind. *P.* i. 18 *ταί θ' ὑπὲρ Κύμας ἁλιερκέες ὄχθαι Σικελία τ' αὐτοῦ πιέζει στέρνα λαχνάεντα*).

[b] Pan father of Hermes as a *νόμιος θεός* (Hom. *H.* xix. 5) is patron alike of Hunting, Fishing, *cf.* *A.P.* vi. 167 (a dedication to Pan) *ὦ δισσᾶς ἀγέτα θηροσύνας· | σοὶ γὰρ καστορίδων ὑλακὰ καὶ τρίστομος αἰχμὴ | εὔαδε καὶ ταχινῆς ἔργα λαγωσφαγίης | δίκτυά τ' ἐν ῥοθίοις ἀπλούμενα καὶ καλαμευτὰς | κάμνων καὶ μογερῶν πεῖσμα σαγηνοβόλων*, and Fowling, *cf.* *A.P.* vi. 180 *ταῦτά σοι ἔκ τ' ὀρέων ἔκ τ' αἰθέρος ἔκ τε θαλάσσας | τρεῖς γνωτοὶ τέχνας σύμβολα, Πάν, ἔθεσαν.* *Cf. ibid.* 11-16, 179, 181-187.

ψυχὴν δ' ἀσπαλιεὺς πολυπαίπαλος ἠδὲ νοήμων
εἴη· ἐπεὶ μάλα πολλὰ καὶ αἰόλα μηχανόωνται
ἰχθύες ἐγκύρσαντες ἀνωΐστοισι δόλοισι.
τολμήεις δὲ μάλιστα καὶ ἄτρομος ἠδὲ σαόφρων
εἴη, μηδ' ὕπνου φιλέοι κόρον· ὀξὺ δὲ λεύσσοι
ἐγρήσσων κραδίῃ τε καὶ ὄμμασι πεπταμένοισιν.
εὖ δὲ φέροι καὶ χεῖμα Διὸς καὶ δίψιον ὥρην
Σειρίου· ἱμείροι δὲ πόνων, ἐράοι δὲ θαλάσσης·
ὧδε γὰρ εὐάγρης τε καὶ Ἑρμείᾳ φίλος εἴη.
Θήρη δ' ἑσπερίη μὲν ὀπωρινῇσιν ἐν ὥραις
καρτίστη τελέθει καὶ ἑωσφόρος εὖτ' ἀνατέλλῃ·
χείματι δ' ἠελίοιο βολαῖς ἅμα κιδναμένῃσι
στέλλεσθαι· πᾶν δ' ἦμαρ ἐν εἴαρι τηλεθόωντι
ἄγραις παντοίῃσιν ὀφέλλεται, ἦμος ἅπαντες
ἔλλοπες ἠϊόνεσσιν ἐφέστιοι ἐγγύθι γαίης
ἕλκονται τοκετῶν τε μόγῳ δίψῃ τ' Ἀφροδίτης.
αἰεὶ δ' εἰς ἄνεμον παπταινέμεν, ὅς κεν ἄῃσιν
ἤπιος, εὐδιόων, μαλακὴν ἅλα κοῦφα κυλίνδων·
λάβρους γὰρ τρομέουσι καὶ ἐχθαίρουσιν ἀήτας
ἰχθύες, οὐδ' ἐθέλουσιν ὑπεὶρ ἅλα δινεύεσθαι·
εὐκραεῖ δ' ἀνέμῳ περιδέξιος ἵσταται ἄγρη.
πάντες δὲ πνοιῇσιν ἐναντία καὶ ῥοθίοισι
πλῶτες ἁλὸς θύνουσιν, ἐπεὶ σφίσιν ὧδε κέλευθος
ῥηϊτέρη στείχουσιν ἐπ' ἠόνας, οὐδ' ὑπ' ἀνάγκης
ἐξόπιθε ῥιπῇσιν ἐλαυνόμενοι μογέουσιν.

---

[a] *H.* v. 616 ὕπνῳ τ' οὐχ ἁλιεῦσιν ἐοικότι.

[b] Hom. *H.* xix. 14 (Pan) ὀξέα δερκόμενος.

[c] *Cf. C.* iii. 322 κύνα Σείριον; *H.* i. 152 ὀπωρινοῖο κυνός. Sirius, or the Dog-star, the heliacal (morning) rising of which in July was associated with extreme heat: Hesiod, *S.* 397 ἴδει ἐν ἀκροτάτῳ ὅτε τε χρόα Σείριος ἄζει, *cf. ibid.* 153; *W.* 417, 587, 609: the *dies caniculares* or dog-days; *cf.* Calverley, *Lines on Hearing the Organ*: Neath the baleful star of Sirius,

should the fisher be, since many and various are the devices that fishes contrive, when they chance upon unthought-of snares. Daring also should he be and dauntless and temperate and he must not love satiety [a] of sleep but must be keen of sight,[b] wakeful of heart and open-eyed. He must bear well the wintry weather and the thirsty season of Sirius [c]; he must be fond of labour and must love the sea. So shall he be successful in his fishing and dear to Hermes.

In the autumn season fishing is best in the evening and when the morning-star rises. In winter the fisher should set out with the spreading rays of the sun. In bloomy spring the whole day is prosperous in all manner of fishing, what time all fishes are drawn to haunt the coasts near the land by the travail of birth and the thirst of desire. Look always for a wind that blows gentle and fair, lightly rolling a tranquil sea. For fishes fear and loathe violent winds and will not wheel over the sea, but with a temperate wind fishing is exceedingly favourable. All the fishes that swim the sea speed against wind and wave, since this is the easier way for them in their march toward the shores, and they do not suffer through being driven forcefully by the current. But when the

When the postmen slowlier jog, And the ox becomes delirious, And the muzzle decks the dog. Alcaeus *fr.* 39 τέγγε πλεύμονα οἴνῳ· τὸ γὰρ ἄστρον περιτέλλεται, | ἁ δ' ὥρα χαλέπα, πάντα δὲ δίψαισ' ὑπὰ καύματος. The name Sirius does not occur in Homer, but the star is referred to *Il.* v. 4 ἀστέρ' ὀπωρινῷ ἐναλίγκιον ὅς τε μάλιστα | λαμπρὸν παμφαίνῃσι λελουμένος Ὠκεανοῖο; xxii. 26 παμφαίνονθ' ὥς τ' ἀστέρ' ἐπεσσύμενον πεδίοιο | ὅς ῥά τ' ὀπώρης εἶσιν ἀρίζηλοι δέ οἱ αὐγαὶ | φαίνονται πολλοῖσι μετ' ἀστράσι νυκτὸς ἀμολγῷ, | ὅν τε κύν' Ὠρίωνος ἐπίκλησιν καλέουσι· | λαμπρότατος μὲν ὅ γ' ἐστί κακὸν δέ τε σῆμα τέτυκται, | καί τε φέρει πολλὸν πυρετὸν δειλοῖσι βροτοῖσιν.

ἀλλ' ἁλιεὺς στέλλοιτο λίνον πνοιῇσι πετάσσας
οὔριον, ἐς Βορέην μέν, ἐπὴν Νότος ὑγρὸς ἄῃσιν·
ἐς Νοτίην δὲ θάλασσαν ἐπειγομένου Βορέαο·
Εὔρου δ' ἱσταμένοιο ποτὶ Ζεφύροιο κέλευθα·
πρὸς δ' Εὖρον Ζέφυρος φορέοι σκάφος· ὧδε γὰρ ἐσμοὶ
ἄσπετοι ἀντήσουσι καὶ εὔβολος ἔσσεται ἄγρη.
Τέτραχα δ' εἰναλίης θήρης νόμον ἐφράσσαντο
ἰχθυβόλοι· καὶ τοὶ μὲν ἐπ' ἀγκίστροισι γάνυνται,
τῶν δ' οἱ μὲν δονάκεσσιν ἀναψάμενοι δολιχοῖσιν
ὁρμιὴν ἵππειον ἐΰπλοκον ἀγρώσσουσιν·
οἱ δ' αὔτως θώμιγγα λινόστροφον ἐκ παλαμάων
δησάμενοι πέμπουσιν· ὁ δ' ἢ καθέτοισι γέγηθεν
ἢ πολυαγκίστροισιν ἀγάλλεται ὁρμιῇσι.
δίκτυα δ' αὖτ' ἄλλοισι μέλει πλέον ἐντύνεσθαι·
τῶν τὰ μὲν ἀμφίβληστρα, τὰ δὲ γρῖφοι καλέονται,
γάγγαμά τ' ἠδ' ὑποχαὶ περιηγέες ἠδὲ σαγῆναι·
ἄλλα δὲ κικλήσκουσι καλύμματα, σὺν δὲ σαγήναις

---

[a] Introd. p. xxxix.

[b] Hom. *Od.* iv. 368 αἰεὶ γὰρ νῆσον ἀλώμενοι ἰχθυάασκον | γναμπτοῖς ἀγκίστροισιν, xii. 330 καὶ δὴ ἄγρην ἐφέπεσκον ἀλητεύοντες ἀνάγκῃ, | ἰχθῦς ὄρνιθάς τε, φίλας ὅτι χεῖρας ἵκοιτο, | γναμπτοῖς ἀγκίστροισιν; *A.P.* vi. 4. 1 εὐκαμπὲς ἄγκιστρον; vi. 5. 2 γυρῶν ἀγκίστρων λαιμοδακεῖς ἀκίδας (barbs); *ibid.* 27. 6; 28. 2, etc.; Theocr. xxi. 10.

[c] *A.P.* vi. 4. 2 ὁρμειήν; *E.M.* *s.* ὅρμος . . . παρὰ τὸ εἴρω, ἐξ οὗ καὶ ὁρμιά, ἡ σειρὰ πρὸς ἣν τὸ ἄγκιστρον ἐπησφάλισται δεδεμένον; Hesych. *s.* ὁρμιά· σχοινίον λεπτόν; *s.* ὁρμιευτής· ἁλιεύς; Eur. *Hel.* 1615 ὁρμιατόνοι = fishermen.

[d] *A.P.* vi. 23. 7 καὶ βαθὺν ἱππείης πεπεδημένον ἅμματι χαίτης, | οὐκ ἄτερ ἀγκίστρων, λιμνοφυῆ δόνακα; vi. 192. 3 γαμψὸν χαίτῃσιν ἐφ' ἱππείῃσι πεδηθὲν ἄγκιστρον.

[e] *A.P.* vi. 4. 1 δούρατα δουλιχόεντα; vi. 27. 2 ἀγκίστρων συζυγίην δονάκων; vi. 28. 1 καμπτομένους δόνακας, *cf.* vi. 29. 4. Also called κάλαμοι: Theocr. xxi. 10, and 43, κάλαμος sing. *ibid.* 47. Lat. *arundo.*

[f] Hom. *Il.* xvi. 406 ἕλκε δὲ δουρὸς ἑλὼν ὑπὲρ ἄντυγος ὡς ὅτε

fisher puts to sea let him set his sail with the wind—Northward when the wet South Wind blows; Southward when the North Wind drives the sea; when the East Wind rises, towards the paths of the West Wind; towards the East let the West Wind bear his vessel; for so will infinite shoals meet him and his fishing will be blest with luck.

Fourfold [a] modes of hunting their prey in the sea have fishermen devised. Some delight in Hooks [b]; and of these some fish with a well-twisted line [c] of horse-hair [d] fastened to long reeds,[e] others simply cast a flaxen cord [f] attached to their hands, another rejoices in leaded lines [g] or in lines with many hooks.[h] Others prefer to array Nets [i]; and of these there are those called casting-nets, and those called draw-nets—drag-nets and round bag-nets and seines. Others they call cover-nets, and, with the seines,

τις φὼς | πέτρῃ ἐπὶ προβλῆτι καθήμενος ἱερὸν ἰχθὺν | ἐκ πόντοιο θύραζε λίνῳ καὶ ἤνοπι χαλκῷ. The reference is to what is now called "hand-lines."

[g] *κάθετος* is properly a plummet, Lat. *perpendiculum.* Here of a fishing-line weighted at the end. *A.P.* vii. 637 *Πύρρος ὁ μουνερέτης ὀλίγῃ νεὶ λεπτὰ ματεύων | φυκία καὶ τριχίνης μαινίδας ἐκ καθέτης*; *cf.* Apost. p. 48 "Pour la pêche des serrans (*χάνους*) et celle des pagels on emploie une ligne appelée *χανικό, καθετή*. . . Cet engin porte à son extrémité libre un morceau cônique de plomb (*μολυβίθρα*) à la partie supérieure duquel sont attachés sur des avancées 4 ou 8 hameçons. Il est totalement en crins de cheval tordus; il est employé surtout par les amateurs de pêche, dans leurs moments de loisir. On se rende sur de petites embarcations dans les endroits rocheux, on mouille le bateau et l'on commence la pêche en jetant la ligne, à laquelle le poids du plomb fait prendre, dans l'eau, une direction perpendiculaire; une fois qu'elle a touché le fond, on la soulève un peu et on la tient ainsi disposée pour la pêche."

[h] Introd. p. xxxix.

[i] For the varieties of net mentioned here see Introd. p. xl.

πέζας καὶ σφαιρῶνας ὁμοῦ σκολιόν τε πάναγρον·
μυρία δ' αἰόλα τοῖα δολορραφέων λίνα κόλπων.
ἄλλοι δ' αὖ κύρτοισιν ἐπὶ φρένα μᾶλλον ἔχουσι,
κύρτοις, οἳ κνώσσοντας ἑοὺς ηὔφρηναν ἄνακτας
εὐκήλους· βαιῷ δὲ πόνῳ μέγα κέρδος ὀπηδεῖ.
ἄλλοι δ' οὐτάζουσι τανυγλώχινι τριαίνῃ
ἔλλοπας ἐκ χέρσου τε καὶ ἐκ νεός, ὡς ἐθέλουσι.
τῶν πάντων καὶ μέτρον ὅσον καὶ κόσμον ἑκάστου
ἀτρεκέως ἴσασιν, ὅσοι τάδε τεκταίνονται.
Ἰχθύσι δ' οὐκ ἄρα μοῦνον ἐπ' ἀλλήλοισι νόημα
πυκνὸν ἔην καὶ μῆτις ἐπίκλοπος, ἀλλὰ καὶ αὐτοὺς
πολλάκις ἐξεπάφησαν ἐπίφρονας ἀγρευτῆρας
καὶ φύγον ἀγκίστρων τε βίας λαγόνας τε πανάγρων,
ἤδη ἐνισχόμενοι, παρὰ δὲ φρένας ἔδραμον ἀνδρῶν,
βουλῇ νικήσαντες, ἄχος δ' ἁλιεῦσι γένοντο.
Κεστρεὺς μὲν πλεκτῇσιν ἐν ἀγκοίνῃσι λίνοιο
ἑλκόμενος δόλον οὔτι περίδρομον ἠγνοίησεν,
ὕψι δ' ἀναθρώσκει, λελιημένος ὕδατος ἄκρου,
ὀρθὸς ἄνω σπεύδων ὅσσον σθένος ἅλματι κούφῳ
ὁρμῆσαι, βουλῆς δὲ σαόφρονος οὐκ ἐμάτησε·
πολλάκι γὰρ ῥιπῇσι καὶ ὕστατα πείσματα φελλῶν

---

[a] Lat. *nassa*, Sil. Ital. v. 47, Plin. ix. 132, etc.; a long basket of wickerwork (σχοινίδι κύρτῃ Nicand. *A*. 625, Plat. *Tim.* 79 D κύρτου πλέγματι, *cf.* Plin. xxi. 114) with wide funnel-shaped mouth and narrow throat, so constructed that once the fish has entered, it cannot get out again, Theocr. xxi. 11; Poll. x. 132, *A.P.* vi. 23 πλωτῶν τε πάγην περιδινέα κύρτον; *cf.* vi. 192.

[b] Plato, *Laws* 823 E εὕδουσι κύρτοις ἀργὸν θήραν διαπονουμένοις.

[c] A three-pronged fork for spearing fish: Poll. x. 133 τριόδους, τρίαινα, ἰχθύκεντρον; Plat. *Soph.* 220 C; Athen. 323 E; *A.P.* vi. 30; Hom. *Od.* x. 124 ἰχθῦς δ' ὣς πείροντες, where Eustath. τριαίναις ἤ τισιν ἑτέροις ἀπωξυμμένοις ὀργάνοις; Plin. ix. 51, 84, 92.

there are those called ground-nets and ball-nets and the crooked trawl: innumerable are the various sorts of such crafty-bosomed Nets. Others again have their minds set rather upon Weels [a] which bring joy to their masters while they sleep [b] at ease, and great gain attends on little toil. Others with the long pronged Trident [c] wound the fish from the land or from a ship as they will. The due measure and right ordering of all these they know certainly who contrive these things.

Fishes, it seems, not only against one another employ cunning wit and deceitful craft but often also they deceive even the wise fishermen themselves and escape from the might of hooks and from the belly of the trawl when already caught in them, and outrun the wits of men, outdoing them in craft, and become a grief to fishermen.

The Grey Mullet,[d] when caught in the plaited arms of the net, is not ignorant of the encircling snare, but leaps up, eager to reach the surface of the water, hasting with all his might to spring straight up with nimble leap, and fails not of his wise purpose. For often he lightly overleaps [e] in his rush the utmost

[d] *H.* ii. 642 n.

[e] The leaping powers of the Grey Mullet (τὸν τάχιστον τῶν ἰχθύων A. 620 b 26) necessitate a special arrangement of nets; Apost. p. 34 "Les filets, simples ou compliqués, servent à capturer tous les poissons, excepté les muges, qui, sauteurs par excellence, peuvent d'un bond passer par-dessus le piège tendu. Pour attraper ce poisson, on ajoute aux filets simples et placés perpendiculairement à la surface des eaux d'autres filets compliqués, lesquels, convenablement tendus par des roseaux, se tiennent sur une ligne horizontale à celle de la surface même de l'eau; ainsi le muge en sautant pour échapper au piège tombe sur ces autres filets aux mailles desquels il se prend en se débattant."

ῥηϊδίως ὑπερᾶλτο καὶ ἐξήλυξε μόροιο.
ἢν δ' ὅ γ' ἀνορμηθεὶς πρῶτον στόλον αὖτις ὀλίσθῃ
ἐς βρόχον, οὐκέτ' ἔπειτα βιάζεται οὐδ' ἀνορούει
ἀχνύμενος, πείρῃ δὲ μαθὼν ἀποπαύεται ὁρμῆς.
ὡς δ' ὅτε τις νούσῳ πολυκηδέϊ δηρὸν ἀλύων
πρῶτα μὲν ἱμείρων τε καὶ ἱέμενος βιότοιο
πάντα μάλ' ἰητῆρσιν ἐφέσπεται, ὅσσα κέλονται
ῥέζων· ἀλλ' ὅτε κῆρες ἐπικρατέωσιν ἄφυκτοι
Ἄϊδος, οὐκέτ' ἔπειτα μέλει βίου, ἀλλὰ τανυσθεὶς
κεῖται ἐπιτρέψας θανάτῳ κεκαφηότα γυῖα,
ἤδη λοίσθιον ἦμαρ ὁρώμενος ἐγγύθι πότμου·
ὣς ἄρα καὶ κεστρεὺς ἐδάῃ τέλος οἷον ἱκάνει,
κεῖται δὲ προπεσών, μίμνων μόρον ἀγρευτῆρος.
Μύραιναι δ' ὅτε κέν ποτ' ἐνιπλήξωσι λίνοισι,
διζόμεναι βρόχον εὐρὺν ἐν ἕρκεϊ δινεύονται,
τοῦ δὲ διαΐγδην ὀφίων νόμον ὁρμηθεῖσαι
πᾶσαι ὀλισθηροῖσι διεξέπεσον μελέεσσι.
Λάβραξ δὲ πτερύγεσσι διὰ ψαμάθοιο λαχήνας
βόθρον ὅσον δέξασθαι ἑὸν δέμας ἦΰτ' ἐς εὐνὴν
ἐκλίνθη· καὶ τοὶ μὲν ἐπ' ἠϊόνας κατάγουσι
δίκτυον ἀσπαλιῆες, ὁ δ' ἰλύϊ κείμενος αὔτως
ἀσπασίως ἤλυξε καὶ ἔκφυγεν ἄρκυν ὀλέθρου.

---

[a] The corks which both support the net and mark its position. Pind. *P.* ii. 79 ἅτε γὰρ εἰνάλιον πόνον ἐχοίσας βαθὺ σκευᾶς ἑτέρας ἀβάπτιστός εἰμι φελλὸς ὣς ὑπὲρ ἕρκος ἅλμας; Aesch. *Ch.* 505 παῖδες γὰρ ἀνδρὶ κληδόνες σωτήριοι | θανόντι· φελλοὶ δ' ὣς ἄγουσι δίκτυον, | τὸν ἐκ βυθοῦ κλωστῆρα σῴζοντες λίνου; *A.P.* vi. 192. 5 ἀβάπτιστόν τε καθ' ὕδωρ | φελλὸν ἀεὶ κρυφίων σῆμα λαχόντα βόλων; Alciphr. *Ep.* i. 1. 4 μικρὸν δὲ ἄπωθεν τῆς ἀκτῆς χαλάσαντες, φεῦ τῆς εὐοψίας, ὅσον ἰχθύων ἐξειλκύσαμεν· μικροῦ καὶ τοὺς φελλοὺς ἐδέησε κατασῦραι ὑφάλους τὸ δίκτυον ἐξωγκωμένον; Pausan. viii. 12 Ἀρκάδων δὲ ἐν τοῖς δρυμοῖς εἰσιν αἱ δρῦς διάφοροι, καὶ τὰς μὲν πλατυφύλλους αὐτῶν, τὰς δὲ φηγοὺς καλοῦσιν, αἱ τρίται δὲ ἀραιὸν τὸν φλοιὸν καὶ οὕτω δή τι παρέχονται κοῦφον, ὥστε ἀπ' αὐτοῦ καὶ ἐν θαλάσσῃ ποιοῦνται

bounds of the corks[a] and escapes from doom. But if at his first upward rush he slips back again into the net, he makes no further effort and leaps no more in his grief but taught by trial, ceases from his endeavours. As when a man, long distressed by painful disease, at first, in his yearning and desire for life, obeys the physicians and does all things that they bid him; but when the unescapable fates of death prevail, he cares no more for life but lies stretched out, giving over to death his exhausted limbs, beholding already at hand the final day of fate; even so the Grey Mullet knows what manner of end is come upon him and lies prone, awaiting doom from his captor.

The Muraena,[b] when they are caught in the net, circle about in the enclosure seeking for a wide mesh and through it making their way, after the manner of snakes, with slippery limbs they all escape.

The Basse[c] digs with its fins in the sand a trench large enough to admit its body and lays itself therein as in a bed. And the fishermen bring down to the shore a net but the Basse by simply lying in the mud gladly avoids them and escapes the net of destruction.

σημεῖα ἀγκύραις καὶ δικτύοις· ταύτης τῆς δρυὸς [*Quercus suber*] *τὸν φλοιὸν ἄλλοι τε Ἰώνων καὶ Ἑρμησιάναξ ὁ τὰ ἐλεγεῖα ποιήσας φελλὸν ὀνομάζουσιν*; Plut. *Mor.* 127 D *ὅπως, κἂν πιεσθῇ ποτε, φελλοῦ δίκην ὑπὸ κουφότητος ἀναφέρηται*: Poll. i. 97; x. 133.

[b] Ael. i. 33 *ὅταν δὲ αὐτὴν τὸ δίκτυον περιβάλῃ, διανήχεται καὶ ζητεῖ ἢ βρόχον ἀραῖον ἢ ῥῆγμα τοῦ δικτύου πάνυ σοφῶς· καὶ ἐντυχοῦσα τοιούτων τινὶ καὶ διεκδῦσα ἐλευθέρα νήχεται αὖθις· εἰ δὲ τύχοι μία τῆσδε τῆς εὐερμίας, καὶ αἱ λοιπαὶ ὅσαι τοῦ αὐτοῦ γένους συνεαλώκασι κατὰ τὴν ἐκείνης φυγὴν ἐξίασιν, ὡς ὁδόν τινα λαβοῦσαι παρ' ἡγεμόνος.*

[c] Plut. *Mor.* 977 F *ὥσπερ τῷ λάβρακι· συρομένην (τὴν σαγήνην) γὰρ αἰσθανόμενος βίᾳ διίστησι καὶ τύπτει κοιλαίνων τοὔδαφος· ὅταν δὲ ποιήσῃ ταῖς ἐπιδρομαῖς τοῦ δικτύου χώραν, ἔωσεν ἑαυτὸν καὶ προσέχεται, μέχρι ἂν παρέλθῃ.*

Τοῖα δὲ τεχνάζει καὶ μορμύρος· εὖτ' ἂν ἐς ἄγρην
φράσσηται προπεσών, ὁ δὲ δύεται ἐν ψαμάθοισι.
Λάβραξ δ' ἀγκίστροιο τυπεὶς εὐκαμπέος αἰχμῇ
ὑψόσ' ἀναθρώσκων κεφαλὴν ἀζηχὲς ἐρείδει
αὐτῇ ἐν ὁρμιῇ βεβιημένος, ὄφρα οἱ ἕλκος
εὐρύτερόν τε γένοιτο καὶ ἐκφυγέῃσιν ὄλεθρον.
Τοῖα καὶ ὄρκυνοι μεγακήτεες ἐφράσσαντο·
εὖτε γὰρ ἁρπάξωσι γένυν γναμπτοῖο δόλοιο,
ῥίμφα τιταινόμενοι νεάτην ὑπὸ βύσσαν ἵενται,
χεῖρα βιαζόμενοι θηρήτορος· ἢν δ' ἀνύσωσιν
ἐς πέδον, αὐτίκ' ἔπειτα κάρη θείνοντες ἐς οὖδας
ὠτειλὴν ἔρρηξαν, ἀποπτύουσι δ' ἀκωκήν.
'Αλλ' ὁπόταν καθέτοισι πελώριοι ἀμφιχάνωσιν
ἰχθύες, οἷα βοῶν τε πέλει προβάτων τε γένεθλα
ἢ βατὶς ἢ καὶ ὄνων νωθρὸν γένος, οὐκ ἐθέλουσιν
ἕσπεσθαι, ψαμάθοισι δ' ἐπὶ πλατὺ σῶμα βαλόντες
ἀθρόοι ἐμβαρύθουσι, μόγον θ' ἁλιεῦσιν ἔθηκαν.
πολλάκι δ' ἐξώλισθον ἀπ' ἀγκίστροιο λυθέντες.

---

[a] *C.* i. 74 n.; *H.* i. 100 n.; Plut. *Mor.* 977 F ἀμφιβλήστροις μὲν γὰρ καὶ ὑποχαῖς . . . ἁλίσκονται μόρμυροι κτλ.

[b] Plut. *Mor.* 977 B ὁ δὲ λάβραξ ἀνδρικώτερον τοῦ ἐλέφαντος οὐχ ἕτερον ἀλλ' αὐτὸς ἑαυτόν, ὅταν περιπέσῃ τῷ ἀγκίστρῳ, βελουλκεῖ, τῇ δεῦρο κἀκεῖ παραλλάξει τῆς κεφαλῆς ἀνευρύνων τὸ τραῦμα καὶ τὸν ἐκ τοῦ σπαραγμοῦ πόνον ὑπομένων, ἄχρι ἂν ἐκβάλῃ τὸ ἄγκιστρον.

[c] A large-sized Tunny. In M.G. ὀρκύνος = *Thynnus brachypterus* (Apost. p. 14). *Cf.* Athen. 303 b Ἡρακλέων δ'

A like device is practised by the Mormyrus[a]: when it perceives that it has fallen into the net, it hides in the sands.

The Basse,[b] when smitten by the point of the bent hook, leaps on high and incessantly presses its head violently on the line itself, till the wound becomes wider and it escapes destruction.

The mighty Orcynus[c] employ a similar device. For when they have seized the jaw of the guileful hook, swiftly they strain and rush to the nether depths, putting pressure on the hand of the fisher; and if they reach the bottom, straightway they beat their head against the ground and tear open the wound and spit out the barb.[d]

But when giant fishes swallow the leaded hooks—such as the tribes of the Ox-ray[e] and the Sea-sheep[f] and the Skate[g] or the sluggish race of the Hake[h]—they will not yield to it but throwing their flat bodies in the sands they put all their weight upon the line and cause trouble to the fishermen, and often they get free from the hook and escape.

ὁ Ἐφέσιος <θύννον> τὸν ὄρκυνόν φησι λέγειν τοὺς Ἀττικούς. Σώστρατος δ' ἐν δευτέρῳ περὶ ζῴων τὴν πηλαμύδα θυννίδα καλεῖσθαι λέγει, μείζω δὲ γινομένην θύννον, ἔτι δὲ μείζονα ὄρκυνον, ὑπερβαλλόντως δὲ αὐξανόμενον γίνεσθαι κῆτος. *Cf.* Hesych. *s.* θύννον and *s.* ὄρκυνος; A. 543 b 4 οἱ δ' ὄρκυνες (τίκτουσιν) ἐν τῷ πελάγει. For the form ὄρκυνες *cf.* Anaxandr. *ap.* Athen. 131 e; Plin. xxxii. 149 orcynus—hic est pelamydum generis maximus neque ipse redit in Maeotim, similis tritomi, vetustate melior. *Cf.* P. Rhode, *Thynnorum Captura*, p. 10.

[d] Ael. i. 40 ὅταν γοῦν περιπαρῇ τῷ ἀγκίστρῳ, καταδύει αὐτὸν εἰς βυθὸν καὶ ὠθεῖ καὶ προσαράττει τῷ δαπέδῳ καὶ κρούει τὸ στόμα, ἐκβαλεῖν τὸ ἄγκιστρον ἐθέλων· εἰ δὲ ἀδύνατον τοῦτο εἴη, εὐρύνει τὸ τραῦμα καὶ ἐκπτύεται τὸ λυποῦν αὐτὸν καὶ ἐξάλλεται.

[e] *H.* ii. 141 n. [f] *H.* i. 146 n.

[g] *H.* i. 103 n. [h] *H.* i. 151 n.

Λαιψηραὶ δ' ἀμίαι καὶ ἀλώπεκες εὖτ' ἂν ἔχωνται,
εὐθὺς ἄνω σπεύδουσιν ὑποφθαδόν, αἶψα δὲ μέσσην
ὁρμιὴν ὑπ' ὀδοῦσι διέτμαγον ἠὲ καὶ ἄκρας
χαίτας· τοὔνεκα τῇσιν ἐχαλκεύσανθ' ἁλιῆες
καυλὸν ἐπ' ἀγκίστρῳ δολιχώτερον, ἄρκος ὀδόντων.
Ναὶ μὴν καὶ νάρκη σφέτερον νόον οὐκ ἀπολείπει
πληγῇ ἀνιάζουσα· τιταινομένη δ' ὀδύνῃσιν
ὁρμιῇ λαγόνας προσπτύσσεται· αἶψα δὲ χαίτης
ἱππείης δόνακός τε διέδραμεν ἔς θ' ἁλιῆος
δεξιτερὴν ἔσκηψε φερώνυμον ἰχθύος ἄλγος·
πολλάκι δ' ἐκ παλάμης κάλαμος φύγεν ὅπλα τε θήρης.
τοῖος γὰρ κρύσταλλος ἐνίζεται αὐτίκα χειρί.

---

[a] *H.* ii. 554 n. A. 621 a 16, immediately after the allusion to the Fox-shark quoted in next note, adds συστρέφονται δὲ καὶ αἱ ἄμιαι, ὅταν τι θηρίον ἴδωσι, καὶ κύκλῳ αὐτῶν περινέουσιν αἱ μέγισται, κἂν ἅπτηταί τινος ἀμύνουσιν· ἔχουσι δ' ὀδόντας ἰσχυρούς, καὶ ἤδη ὦπται καὶ ἄλλα καὶ λάμια ἐμπεσοῦσα καὶ καθελκωθεῖσα. Ael. i. 5 describes ὁ ἰχθὺς ὁ τρώκτης, by which he clearly means the Amia: ἁλοὺς ἀγκίστρῳ μόνος ἰχθύων ἐς τὸ ἔμπαλιν ἑαυτὸν οὐκ ἐπανάγει ἀλλ' ὠθεῖται, τὴν ὁρμιὰν ἀποθερίσαι διψῶν, οἱ δὲ ἁλιεῖς σοφίζονται τὰ ἐναντία· τὰς γάρ τοι τῶν ἀγκίστρων λαβὰς χαλκεύονται μακράς κτλ.; Plut. *Mor.* 977 A τῶν δ' ἀγκίστρων τοῖς μὲν στρογγύλοις ἐπὶ κεστρέας καὶ ἀμίας χρῶνται μικροστόμους ὄντας· τὸ γὰρ εὐθύτερον εὐλαβοῦνται.

[b] *H.* i. 381 n. *Cf.* A. 621 a 6 ἣν δὲ καλοῦσι σκολόπενδραν, ὅταν καταπίῃ τὸ ἄγκιστρον, ἐκτρέπεται τὰ ἐντὸς ἐκτός, ἕως ἂν ἐκβάλῃ τὸ ἄγκιστρον· εἶθ' οὕτως εἰστρέπεται πάλιν ἐντός. . . . τῶν δ' ἰχθύων αἱ ὀνομαζόμεναι ἀλώπεκες ὅταν αἴσθωνται ὅτι τὸ ἄγκιστρον καταπεπώκασιν, βοηθοῦσι πρὸς τοῦτο ὥσπερ καὶ ἡ σκολόπενδρα· ἀναδραμοῦσα γὰρ ἐπὶ πολὺ πρὸς τὴν ὁρμιὰν ἀποτρώγουσιν αὐτῆς· ἁλίσκονται γὰρ περὶ ἐνίους τόπους πολυαγκίστροις ἐν ῥοώδεσι καὶ βαθέσι τόποις; Plin. ix. 145 Scolopendrae . . . hamo devorato omnia interanea evomunt, donec hamum

The swift Amia[a] and the Fox-sharks,[b] when they are hooked, straightway hasten upward to forestall the fisher and speedily bite through with their teeth the middle of the line or the extreme hairs. Therefore for them the fishermen forge a longer shank on the hook, as a protection against their teeth.

The Cramp-fish,[c] moreover, forgets not its cunning in the pain of being struck, but straining in its agony it puts its flanks against the line, and straightway through the horse-hair and through the rod[d] runs the pain which gives the fish its name[e] and lights in the right hand of the fisher; and often the rod and the fishing-tackle escape from his palm. Such icy numbness straightway settles in his hand.

egerant, deinde resorbent. At vulpes marinae simili in periculo gluttiunt amplius usque ad infirma lineae qua facile praerodant; Ael. *V.H.* i. 5 (*ἡ ἀλώπηξ ἡ θαλαττία*) *ἀνέθορε καὶ ἀπέκειρε τὴν ὁρμιὰν καὶ νήχεται αὖθις*; Antig. 49 *τὰς δὲ καλουμένας ἀλώπεκας, ὅταν αἴσθωνται ὅτι τὸ ἄγκιστρον καταπεπώκασιν, ἀναδραμούσας ἄνωθεν τῆς ὁρμιᾶς ἀποτρώγειν.* But Ael. *N.A.* ix. 12 *ἢ γὰρ οὐ πρόσεισι τῷ ἀγκίστρῳ τὴν ἀρχὴν ἢ καταπιοῦσα παραχρῆμα ἑαυτῆς τὸ ἐντὸς μετεκδῦσα ἔστρεψεν ἔξω, ὥσπερ οὖν χιτῶνα τὸ σῶμα ἀνελίξασα, καὶ τοῦτον δήπου τὸν τρόπον ἐξεώσατο τὸ ἄγκιστρον*; Plut. *Mor.* 977 B *ἡ δ' ἀλώπηξ οὐ πολλάκις μὲν ἀγκίστρῳ πρόσεισιν ἀλλὰ φεύγει τὸν δόλον, ἁλοῦσα δ' εὐθὺς ἐκτρέπεται· πέφυκε γὰρ δι' εὐτονίαν καὶ ὑγρότητα μεταβάλλειν τὸ σῶμα καὶ στρέφειν, ὥστε τῶν ἐντὸς ἐκτὸς γενομένων ἀποπίπτειν τὸ ἄγκιστρον.*

[c] *H.* ii. 56 n.

[d] Ael. ix. 14 *εἴ τις προσάψαιτο τῆς νάρκης ὅτι τὸ ἐκ τοῦ ὀνόματος πάθος τὴν χεῖρα αὐτοῦ καταλαμβάνει, τοῦτο καὶ παιδάριον ὢν ἤκουσα τῆς μητρὸς λεγούσης πολλάκις, σοφῶν δὲ ἀνδρῶν ἐπυθόμην ὅτι καὶ τοῦ δικτύου ἐν ᾧ τεθήραται εἴ τις προσάψαιτο ναρκᾷ πάντως.* *Cf.* Plut. *Mor.* 978 B-C; Athen. 314 C.

[e] *i.e.* *νάρκη*, cramp: *cf.* Ael. *l.c.* and i. 36 *ὁ ἰχθὺς ἡ νάρκη ὅτου ἂν καὶ προσάψηται τὸ ἐξ αὑτῆς ὄνομα ἔδωκέ τε καὶ ναρκᾶν ἐποίησεν*; Athen. 314 b *ἡ δὲ κλῆσις αὐτῆς καὶ παρ' Ὁμήρῳ* [*Il.* viii. 328] "*νάρκησε δὲ χεὶρ ἐπὶ καρπῷ.*"

Σηπίαι αὖ τοίῃσι δολοφροσύνῃσι μέλονται.
ἔστι τις ἐν μήκωσι θολὸς κείνῃσι πεπηγὼς
κυάνεος, πίσσης δνοφερώτερος, ἀχλύος ὑγρῆς
φάρμακον ἀπροτίοπτον, ὅ τε σφίσιν ἄλκαρ ὀλέθρου
ἐντρέφεται· τὰς δ᾽ εὖτ᾽ ἂν ἕλῃ φόβος, αὐτίκα κείνου
ὀρφναίας ῥαθάμιγγας ἀνήμεσαν, ἀμφὶ δὲ πόντου
πάντα πέριξ ἐμίηνε καὶ ἠμάλδυνε κέλευθα
ἰχὼρ ἀχλυόεις, ἀνὰ δ᾽ ἔτραπε πᾶσαν ὀπωπήν·
αἱ δὲ διὰ θολόεντος ἄφαρ φεύγουσι πόροιο
ῥηϊδίως καὶ φῶτα καὶ εἴ ποθι φέρτερον ἰχθύν.
Ταῖς δ᾽ ἶσα τεχνάζουσι καὶ ἠερόφοιτα γένεθλα
τευθίδος· οὐ δ᾽ ἄρα τῇσι μέλας θολὸς ἀλλ᾽ ὑπερευθὴς
ἐντρέφεται, μῆτιν δὲ πανείκελον ἐντύνονται.
Τοίοις μὲν φρονέουσι νοήμασιν· ἀλλὰ καὶ ἔμπης
ὄλλυνται πυκινῇσιν ἐπιφροσύναις ἁλιήων.
τοὺς μὲν δὴ πελάγεσσιν ἐν ἠλιβάτοισι θέοντας
ῥηϊδίως ἐρύουσιν· ἐπεὶ σφίσιν οὔτι νόημα
ποικίλον· ἤδη γάρ τις ἐπέσπασε καὶ κρομύοισι
γυμνοῖς τ᾽ ἀγκίστροισιν ἑλὼν πελαγοστρόφον ἰχθύν.
ὅσσοι δ᾽ αὖ γαίης ἁλιερκέος ἄγχι νέμονται,
τοῖσι μὲν ὀξύτερος πέλεται νόος, ἀλλὰ καὶ αὐτῶν

---

[a] *H.* ii. 121 n.

[b] A. 524 b 15 *τοῦτον (sc. τὸν θόλον) δὲ πλεῖστον αὐτῶν (sc. τῶν μαλακίων) καὶ μέγιστον ἡ σηπία ἔχει· ἀφίησι μὲν οὖν ἅπαντα, ὅταν φοβηθῇ, μάλιστα δὲ ἡ σηπία*; *cf. P.A.* 679 a 4 ff. But it is not only through fear that it employs this artifice: A. 621 b 28 *τῶν δὲ μαλακίων πανουργότατον μὲν ἡ σηπία καὶ μόνον χρῆται τῷ θόλῳ κρύψεως χάριν καὶ οὐ μόνον φοβουμένη· ὁ δὲ πολύπους καὶ ἡ τευθὶς διὰ φόβον ἀφίησι τὸν θόλον*; Plut. *Mor.* 978 A; Ael. i. 34; Phil. 105; Plin. ix. 84; Cic. *N.D.* ii. 50, 127; Ov. *Hal.* 18 Sepia tarda fugae, tenui cum forte sub unda | Deprensa est iam iamque manus timet illa rapaces,— Inficiens aequor nigrum vomit ore cruorem | Avertitque vias, oculos frustrata sequentes.

The Cuttle-fishes[a] again practise this craft.[b] They have seated in their heads a dark muddy fluid blacker than pitch, a mysterious drug causing a watery cloud, which is their natural defence against destruction. When fear seizes them, immediately they discharge the dusky drops thereof and the cloudy fluid stains and obscures all around the paths of the sea and ruins all the view ; and they straightway through the turbid waters easily escape man or haply mightier fish.

A like craft is practised also by the air-travelling[c] tribes of the Calamary.[d] Only their fluid is not black but reddish,[e] but the device which they employ is altogether similar.

Such are the cunning devices[f] of fishes ; yet notwithstanding they perish by the subtle wiles of fishermen. Those which run in the sheer depths of the sea the fishers capture easily, since they possess no subtle craft. For ere now one has caught and landed a deep-sea fish with onions[g] or with bare hooks. Those on the other hand which range near the sea-girding land have sharper wits ; yet even of these

[c] Schol. *ἠερόφοιτα· ἀέρι πετόμενα· τὰς τευθίδας φησὶν ἠερόφοιτα γένεθλα ὡς ἐν τῷ ἀέρι φοιτῶντα· πέτονται γὰρ καὶ διὰ τοῦ ἀέρος φέρονται ὡς ὑπόπτερα· τευθίδες δ' εἰσὶ τὰ κοινῶς λεγόμενα καλαμάρια.* One might be tempted to take the sense to be "travelling in darkness" like Homer's *ἠερόφοιτος Ἐρινύς* (*Il.* ix. 571), but the reference is no doubt, as the schol. takes it, to its flying habits ; *cf. H.* i. 427 ff. ; Epicharm. *ap.* Athen. 318 e *ποταναὶ τευθίδες.*

[d] *H.* i. 428 n. *Cf.* note on v. 156 above.

[e] Athen. 326 b *ἔχει δὲ (ἡ τευθίς) καὶ θόλον . . . οὐ μέλανα ἀλλ' ὠχρόν.* But Ov. *Hal.* 129 Et nigrum niveo portans in corpore virus | Loligo.

[f] *Cf. H.* i. 7.

[g] On baits in general see A. 534 a 11–534 b 10 ; 591 a-b.

βαιοὶ μὲν καρῖσιν ἀφαυροτέραις ἐρύονται,
πουλυπόδων θυσάνοις ἢ καρκίνῳ ἀμφιχανόντες
καρκινάσιν τ᾽ ὀλίγῃσι καὶ εἰ κρέας ἁλμυρὸν ἅπτοις
πετραίαις θ᾽ ἑλμῖσι καὶ ὅττι τοι ἄγχι παρείη
ἰχθυόεν· βαιοὺς δ᾽ ἐπὶ μείζοσιν ὁπλίζοιο·
δείπνοις γὰρ γελόωντες ἐπισπεύδουσιν ὄλεθρον·
ἦ γὰρ ἀεὶ πλωτῶν σιφλὸν γένος ὑγρὰ θεόντων.
θύννον μὲν κορακῖνος ἄγει, λάβρακα δὲ καρὶς
πιαλέη, χάννος δὲ φίλον φάγροισι δέλετρον
καὶ βῶκες συνόδοντι καὶ ἱππούροισιν ἴουλοι·
τρίγλη δ᾽ ὀρφὸν ἔπεφνε καὶ ἔσπασε κιρρίδα πέρκη,
μαινίδι δὲ χρύσοφρυς ἀνέλκεται· αὐτὰρ ἀνιγραὶ
μύραιναι μετὰ σάρκας ἐπειγόμεναι φορέονται
πουλυπόδων· ὅσσοι δὲ δέμας περίμετρον ἔχουσι,
θύννῳ μὲν κάλλιχθυς ἰαίνεται, αὐτὰρ ὀνίσκοις
ὄρκυνος, λάβρακα δ᾽ ἐπ᾽ ἀνθίῃ ὁπλίζοιο,
ἵππουρον ξιφίῃ, γλαύκῳ δ᾽ ἔπι κεστρέα πείροις·

---

[a] *H.* i. 320 ff.

[b] A. 534 a 16 ἔτι δὲ πολλοὶ τῶν ἰχθύων διατρίβουσιν ἐν σπηλαίοις, οὓς ἐπειδὰν βούλωνται προκαλέσασθαι πρὸς τὴν θήραν οἱ ἁλιεῖς, τὸ στόμα τοῦ σπηλαίου παραλείφουσι ταριχηραῖς ὀσμαῖς, πρὸς ἃς ἐξέρχονται ταχέως; Ael. xiii. 2 περιπείρει τῷ ἀγκίστρῳ γλυκόστομον ὄντα ἡμιτάριχον.

[c] A. 534 a 23 ff.

[d] One of the *Sciaenidae*, perhaps *Corvina nigra* Cuv.; "à Chalcis un vieux pêcheur m'a dit qu'on l'appelle Σκιὸς καλιακούδα, c'est-à-dire Corv. corneille," Apost. p. 13.

[e] *H.* ii. 130 n.

[f] *H.* i. 124 n.

[g] *C.* ii. 391 n.

[h] *Cf. H.* i. 110 where ἀμφότεροι βῶκες refers to the two species *Box boops* (*Box vulgaris*), M.G. βῶπα or γοῦπα, and *Box salpa*, M.G. σάλπα (Apost. p. 17). They belong to the *Sparidae* or Sea-breams.

[i] *H.* iii. 610 n.

[k] *H.* ii. 434 n. For ἴουλος = ἰουλίς *cf.* Eratosth. *ap.* Athen. 284 d ἔτι ζώοντας ἰούλους.

the small fishes are caught with the feeble Prawn: they swallow tentacled Poulpe or Crab or tiny Hermit-crabs [a] or bait of salted flesh [b] or rock-haunting Worms or anything of the fishy kind [c] that may be at hand. The small fish thou shouldst use as bait for the larger; for rejoicing in the banquet they speed their own destruction; gluttonous verily always is the race of the swimming tribes that roam the water. The Crow-fish [d] attracts the Tunny, the fat Prawn attracts the Basse,[e] the Channus [f] is a bait beloved of the Braize,[g] as the Bogue [h] is to the Dentex [i] and the Rainbow-wrasse [k] to the Hippurus [l]; the Red Mullet [m] slays the Merou,[n] the Perch [o] catches the Cirrhis,[p] the Gilt-head [q] is landed by the Maenis [r]; while the baleful Muraena [s] haste after the flesh of the Poulpe.[t] As for those fishes which are of enormous size, the Beauty-fish [u] delights in the Tunny, the Orcynus [v] in the Oniscus [w]; while for the Anthias [x] thou shouldst array the Basse,[y] the Hippurus [z] for the Swordfish,[2a] and for the Glaucus [2b] thou shouldst impale the Grey Mullet.[2c] To entràp

[l] *H.* 404 n.

[m] *C.* ii. 392 n.

[n] *H.* i. 142 n.

[o] *H.* i. 124 n.

[p] *H.* i. 129.

[q] *H.* i. 169 n.

[r] Three species of the genus *Maena* occur in the Mediterranean: *M. vulgaris*, *M. osbeckii*, *M. jusculum*. *σμαρίς* (*ἰσμαρίς*), by which the schol. glosses *μαινίς* here and *H.* i. 108, is an allied genus (M.G. *σμαρίς*, *μαρίς*) of the same family *Maenidae* (Apost. p. 18). *Cf.* Ov. *Hal.* 120 Fecundumque genus maenae.

[s] *H.* i. 142 n.

[t] *H.* i. 306 n.

[u] Introd. p. lvii.

[v] *H.* iii. 132 n.

[w] *H.* i. 593 n.

[x] Introd. p. liii.

[y] *H.* ii. 130 n.

[z] *H.* iv. 404 n.

[2a] *H.* ii. 462 n.

[2b] Introd. p. lxi.

[2c] *H.* ii. 642 n.

ἄλλῳ δ᾽ ἀλλοίην γενεὴν ἐπιτεχνάζοιο,
κρέσσονι χειροτέρην· ἐπεὶ ἦ μάλα πάντες ἔασιν
ἀλλήλοις φορβή τε φίλη καὶ λίχνος ὄλεθρος.
ὣς οὐδὲν λιμοῖο κακώτερον οὐδὲ βαρείης
γαστέρος, ἣ κρατέει μὲν ἐν ἀνθρώποισιν ἀπηνὴς
καὶ χαλεπὴ δέσποινα συνέστιος, οὔποτε δασμῶν
ληθομένη, πολλοὺς δὲ παρασφήλασα νόοιο
εἰς ἄτην ἐνέηκε καὶ αἴσχεσιν ἐγκατέδησε·
γαστὴρ δὲ θήρεσσι καὶ ἑρπυστῆρσιν ἀνάσσει
ἠερίῃς τ᾽ ἀγέλῃσι, τὸ δὲ πλέον ἐν νεπόδεσσι
κάρτος ἔχει· κείνοις γὰρ ἀεὶ μόρος ἔπλετο γαστήρ.
Ἀνθιέων δὲ πρῶτα περίφρονα πεύθεο θήρην,
οἵην ἡμετέρης ἐρικυδέος ἐντύνονται
πάτρης ἐνναετῆρες ὑπὲρ Σαρπηδόνος ἀκτῆς
ὅσσοι θ᾽ Ἑρμείαο πόλιν, ναυσίκλυτον ἄστυ
Κωρύκιον, ναίουσι καὶ ἀμφιρύτην Ἐλεοῦσαν.
πέτρας μὲν κείνας τεκμαίρεται ἐγγύθι γαίης
ἴδρις ἀνήρ, οἵῃσιν ὑπ᾽ ἀνθίαι αὐλίζονται,
ἀντροφυεῖς, κευθμῶσι διαρρῶγας θαμέεσσι·
δουρὶ δ᾽ ἀναπλώσας πινάκων ἐριηχέα τεύχει
δοῦπον ἐπικροτέων· πατάγῳ θ᾽ ἐπιτέρπεται ἦτορ
ἀνθιέων· καί πού τις ἀνέδραμεν αὐτίκα λίμνης,
παπταίνων ἄκατόν τε καὶ ἀνέρα· τῷ δ᾽ ἄρ᾽ ἑτοίμας
πέρκας εὐθὺς ἵησιν ἐν οἴδμασιν ἢ κορακίνους

---

[a] Hom. *Od.* vii. 216 οὐ γάρ τι στυγερῇ ἐπὶ γαστέρι κύντερον ἄλλο | ἔπλετο.

[b] Introd. p. liii.

[c] Introd. p. xix.

[d] Promontory of Cilicia: Strabo 627 Καλλισθένης δ᾽ ἐγγὺς τοῦ Καλυκάδνου καὶ τῆς Σαρπηδόνος ἄκρας παρ᾽ αὐτὸ τὸ Κωρύκιον ἄντρον (φησὶν) εἶναι τοὺς Ἀρίμους. *Cf.* 670, 682; Ptolem. v. 8. 3; Plin. v. 92 mox flumen Calycadnus, promunturium Sarpedon.

[e] *A.P.* ix. 91 Ἑρμῇ Κωρύκιον ναίων πόλιν. *Cf.* Hicks,

other fish employ other breeds, the weaker as bait for the stronger; since verily all fishes are welcome food to one another and gluttonous destruction. So true it is that naught is deadlier than hunger and the grievous belly,[a] which bears harsh sway among men and is a stern mistress to dwell with: who never forgets her tribute and who misleads the wits of many and casts them into ruin and binds them fast to shame. The belly bears sway over wild beasts and over reptiles and over the flocks of the air, but it has its greatest power among fishes; for them evermore the belly proves their doom.

Hear first the cunning mode of taking the Anthias[b] which is practised by the inhabitants of our glorious fatherland[c] above the promontory of Sarpedon,[d] those who dwell in the city of Hermes,[e] the town of Corycus,[f] famous for ships, and in sea-girt Eleusa.[g] A skilful man observes those rocks near the land, under which the Anthias dwell: caverned rocks, cleft with many a covert. Sailing up in his boat he makes a loud noise by striking planks together; and the heart of the Anthias rejoices in the din, and one haply rises presently from the sea, gazing at the boat and the man. Then the fisher straightway lets down into the waves the ready bait of Perch or Crowfish,

I.H.S. xii. p. 240 (metrical dedication of statues of Hermes and Pan from the Corycian cave). Hermes appears on coins of Corycus, Adana, Mallos.

[f] Seaport in Cilicia, N.-E. of Sarpedon, Strabo 670 *Κώρυκος ἄκρα, ὑπὲρ ἧς ἐν εἴκοσι σταδίοις ἐστὶ τὸ Κωρύκιον ἄντρον*; Plin. v. 92 iuxtaque mare Corycos, eodem nomine oppidum et portus et specus; Strabo 671 mentions *τὴν εὐπορίαν τῆς τε ναυπηγησίμου ὕλης καὶ τῶν λιμένων* in this region.

[g] Island off Cilicia: Strabo 671 *εἶθ' ἡ Ἐλαιοῦσσα νῆσος μετὰ τὴν Κώρυκον, προσκειμένη τῇ ἠπείρῳ*; 537 *τὴν Ἐλαιοῦσσαν νήσιον εὔκαρπον*. *Cf. ibid.* 535; Plin. v. 130.

ἀσπαλιεύς, πρώτης ὀρέγων ξεινήϊα φορβῆς.
αὐτὰρ ὅ γ' ἁρπάγδην κεχαρημένος εἰλαπινάζει
δαῖτα φίλην σαίνει τε δολόφρονα θηρητῆρα.
ὡς δὲ φιλοξείνοιο μετ' ἀνέρος οἰκία κέλσῃ
κλεινὸς ἀνὴρ ἢ χειρὸς ἐν ἔργμασιν ἠὲ νόοιο,
ἀσπασίως δ' ὅ μιν εἶδεν ἐφέστιον, εὖ δέ ἑ δώροις
εὖ τέ μιν εἰλαπίναις τε φιλοφροσύναις τ' ἀγαπάζει
παντοίαις· ἄμφω δὲ γεγηθότες ἀμφὶ τραπέζῃ
τέρπονται κρητῆρος ἀμοιβαίοις δεπάεσσιν·
ὣς ὁ μὲν ἀσπαλιεὺς κεχαρημένος ἐλπωρῇσι
μειδιάᾳ, δείπνοις δὲ νέοις ἐπιτέρπεται ἰχθύς.
ἔνθεν ἔπειθ' ὁ μὲν αἰὲν ἐπημάτιος ποτὶ πέτρην
στέλλεται, οὐδ' ἀνίησιν ἑὸν πόνον οὐδ' ἀπολείπει
δαῖτα φέρων· οἱ δ' αὐτίκ' ἀολλέες ἀμφαγέρονται
δαιτυμόνες κατὰ χῶρον, ἅτε κλητῆρος ἄγοντος.
αἰεὶ δὲ πλεόνεσσιν ἑτοιμοτέροις τε παρίσχει
φορβὴν ἁρπαλέην· οὐδέ σφισιν ἄλλα κέλευθα
οὐδ' ἄλλοι κεεθμῶνες ἐνὶ φρεσίν, ἀλλὰ μένοντες
αὐτοῦ δηθύνουσιν, ἅτε σταθμοῖσι νομήων
πώεα χειμερίοισιν ἐν ἤμασιν αὐλίζονται,
οὐδ' ὀλίγον σηκοῖο λιλαιόμενα προνέεσθαι.
οἱ δ' ὅτ' ἐσαθρήσωσιν ἀειρομένην ἀπὸ χέρσου
σπερχομένην τ' ἐλάταις ἄκατον τρόφον, αὐτίκα πάντες
ὀρθοὶ καγχαλόωντες ὑπεὶρ ἅλα δινεύοντες
ἱμερόεν παίζουσι καὶ ἀντιόωσι τιθήνῃ.
ὡς δ' ὁπότ' ἀπτήνεσσι φέρῃ βόσιν ὀρταλίχοισι
μήτηρ, εἰαρινοῦ ζεφύρου πρωτάγγελος ὄρνις,
οἱ δ' ἁπαλὸν τρύζοντες ἐπιθρώσκουσι καλιῇ
γηθόσυνοι περὶ μητρὶ καὶ ἱμείροντες ἐδωδῆς

[a] Ov. *F.* ii. 853 Fallimur, an veris praenuntia venit hirundo. The Swallow as herald of Spring is proverbial: Hes. *W.* 568; Aristoph. *Pax* 800, *Eq.* 419 σκέψασθε παῖδες· οὐχ ὁρᾶθ'; ὥρα νέα χελιδών.

offering a first meal of hospitality. The fish rejoices and greedily feasts on the welcome banquet and fawns upon the crafty fisherman. As to the house of a hospitable man there comes one famous for deeds of hand or head, and his host is glad to see him at his hearth and entreats him well with gifts and feast and all manner of loving-kindness; and at the table both rejoice and take their pleasure in pledging cup for cup; even so the fisher rejoices in hope and smiles while the fish delights in new banquets. Thenceforward the fisherman journeys to the rock every day and relaxes not his labour and ceases not to bring food. And straightway the Anthias gather all together in the place to feast, as if a summoner brought them. Always for more and readier fishes he provides the coveted food, and they have no thought of other paths or other retreats, but there they remain and linger, even as in the winter days the flocks abide in the steadings of the shepherds and care not to go forth even a little from the fold. And when the fishes descry the boat that feeds them starting from the land and speeding with the oars, immediately they are all alert and gaily they wheel over the sea, sporting delightfully, and go to meet their nurse. As when the mother Swallow, the bird that first heralds [a] the West Wind [b] of Spring, brings food to her unfledged nestlings and they with soft cheeping leap for joy about their mother in the nest

[b] The "genitabilis aura Favoni" Lucret. i. 11; *cf.* v. 735 It ver et Venus et Veneris praenuntius ante | Pennatus graditur Zephyrus; Plin. ii. 122 Favonium quidam a.d. viii kalendas Martii chelidoniam vocant ab hirundinis visu. The Swallow (*Hirundo rustica*) arrives in Attica about the second week of March, Mommsen, *Griechische Jahreszeiten*, p. 254.

χεῖλος ἀναπτύσσουσιν, ἅπαν δ' ἐπὶ δῶμα λέληκεν
ἀνδρὸς ξεινοδόκοιο λίγα κλάζουσα νεοσσοῖς·
ὣς οἵ γε θρεπτῆρος ἐναντίον ἐρχομένοιο
γηθόσυνοι θρώσκουσι, χοροιτύπον ὥστ' ἀνὰ κύκλον.
τοὺς δ' ἁλιεὺς βρώμησιν ἐπασσυτέρῃσι λιπαίνων
χειρί τ' ἐπιψαύων χειρός τ' ἄπο δῶρα τιταίνων
πρηΰνει φίλον ἦτορ· ἄφαρ δέ οἱ ἠΰτ' ἄνακτι
πείθονται, καὶ χειρὸς ὅπῃ νεύσειε μύωπι
ῥίμφα διαΐσσουσιν· ὁ δ' ἄλλοτε νηὸς ὄπισθεν
ἄλλοτε δὲ πρόσσω, ποτὲ δὲ σχεδὸν ἠπείροιο
πέμπει δεξιτερήν· τοὺς δ' ὄψεαι ἠΰτε παῖδας
ἀνδρὸς ἐπιφροσύνῃσι παλαισμοσύνης ἀνὰ χῶρον
τῇ καὶ τῇ θύνοντας, ἐπίσκοπος ἔνθα κελεύει.
ἀλλ' ὅτε οἱ κομιδῆς μὲν ἅλις, θήρῃ δὲ μέληται,
δή ῥα τόθ' ὁρμιὴν μὲν ἀναψάμενος χερὶ λαιῇ
ἕζεται, ἀγκίστρου δὲ βέλος κρατερόν τε θοόν τε
ὁπλίζει, καὶ τοὺς μὲν ἀπέτραπε χειρὶ κελεύων
πάντας ὁμῶς ἢ λᾶαν ἑλὼν ἔρριψε καθ' ὕδωρ·
οἱ δ' ἐπὶ τῷ δύνουσιν, ὀϊόμενοι βόσιν εἶναι·
τῶν δ' ἕνα μοῦνον ἔλειπεν ἀπόκριτον, ὅν κ' ἐθέλῃσι,
δύσμορον, ὑστατίοισι κεχαρμένον ἐν δείπνοισι·
ἄγκιστρον μὲν ὄρεξεν ὑπεὶρ ἁλός· αὐτὰρ ὅ γ' ἄτην
καρπαλίμως ἥρπαξεν, ὁ δ' ἔσπασεν ἀμφοτέρῃσι
θερμὸς ἀνήρ, ὠκεῖαν ἑλὼν καὶ ἐπίκλοπον ἄγρην·
λήθει δ' ἀνθιέων ἄλλον χορόν· ἢν γὰρ ἴδωνται
ἢ σμαραγὴν ἀΐωσι δυσαγρέος ἑλκομένοιο,
οὐκέτι οἱ τόσα δεῖπνα παρέσσεται, ὥς κεν ἵκοιντο
αὖτις ὑποτροπάδην, ἀπὸ δ' ἔπτυσαν ἐχθήραντες
καὶ κομιδὴν καὶ χῶρον ὀλέθριον· ἀλλά τις εἴη

---

[a] Apost. p. 39 " Pour faire tomber les Athérines dans le piège le pêcheur promène sur l'eau un morceau d'étoffe noire

and open their beaks in their desire for food, and all the house of some hospitable man resounds with the shrill crying of the mother bird ; even so the fishes leap joyfully to meet their feeder as he comes, even as in the circle of a dance. And the fisherman fattening them with dainty after dainty and with his hand stroking them and proffering them his gifts from his hand, tames their friendly heart, and anon they obey him like a master, and wheresoever he indicates with his finger,[a] there they swiftly rush. Now behind the boat, now in front, now landward he points his hand ; and thou shalt see them, like boys in a place of wrestling, according to the wisdom of a man, rushing this way or that as their master bids. But when he has tended them enough and bethinks him of taking them, then he seats himself with a line in his left hand and fits thereto a hook, strong and sharp. Then all the fishes alike he turns away, commanding them with his hand, or he takes a stone and casts it in the water, and they dive after it, thinking it to be food. One picked fish alone he leaves, whichsoever he will—unhappy fish, rejoicing in a banquet which is to be its last. Then he reaches down the hook over the sea and the fish swiftly seizes its doom ; and the bold fisher draws it in with both hands, winning a speedy prey by his cunning. And he avoids the notice of the rest of the company of Anthias ; for if they see or hear the din of the unhappy victim being landed, then the fisher will never more have banquets enough to tempt the fishes to return, but they spurn with loathing both his attentions and the place of destruction.

attaché au bout d'un long roseau, qu'il tient de la main droite. Les poissons le suivent en grand nombre, et de la main le pêcheur leur montre en quelque sorte le chemin à prendre."

ἴφθιμος, κρατερῶς δὲ βιησάμενός μιν ἀνέλκοι,
ἢ καὶ δεύτερος ἄλλος ἐφαπτέσθω καμάτοιο·
ὧδε γὰρ οὐ φρονέοντες ἑὴν δολομήχανον ἄτην
αὐτοὶ πιανθέντες ἐοικότα πιαίνουσιν·
αἰεὶ δ', εὖτ' ἐθέλησθα, παρέσσεται εὔστοχος ἄγρη.
"Αλλοι δ' ἰφθίμῳ τε βίῃ καὶ κάρτεϊ γυίων
πειθόμενοι μέγαν ἆθλον ἐπ' ἀνθίῃ ὁπλίζονται,
οὐ φιλίην, οὐ σῖτα πονεύμενοι, ἀλλ' ἐς ἀκωκὴν
ἀγκίστρου σπεύδουσι καὶ ἠνορέῃ βιόωνται.
χαλκοῦ μὲν σκληροῖο τετυγμένον ἠὲ σιδήρου
ἄγκιστρον πέλεται, δίχα δὲ γλωχῖνες ἔχουσιν
ἀμφίδυμοι μέγα πεῖσμα λινόστροφον· ἀμφὶ δ' ἄρ' αὐτῷ
λάβρακα ζώοντα παρήλασαν, εἴ σφι παρείη·
εἰ δὲ θάνοι, τάχα οἵ τις ὑπὸ στόμα θῆκε μόλιβδον,
δελφῖν' ὃν καλέουσιν· ὁ δὲ βρίθοντι μολίβδῳ
κλίνει τ' ἀγκλίνει τε κάρη ζώοντι ἐοικώς.
θῶμιξ δὲ κρατερή τε καὶ εὔπλοκος· ἀλλ' ὅτε δοῦπον
ἀνθίαι εἰσαΐοντες ἀναθρώξωσι θαλάσσης,
ἄλλοις μὲν μέλεται κώπης πόνος, αὐτὰρ ὅ γ' ἄκρης
ἐκ πρύμνης ἁλιεὺς δόλον ἀγκύλον εἰς ἅλα πέμπει,
ἧκ' ἀναδινεύων· οἱ δ' αὐτίκα πάντες ἕπονται
νηΐ τε καὶ φεύγοντι δεδορκότες εἴκελον ἰχθὺν
σπεύδοντες μετὰ δαῖτα παραφθαδὸν ἀΐσσουσιν
ἀλλήλων· φαίης κεν ἐπ' ἀνέρα δήϊον ἄνδρα
γούνατ' ἐλαφρίζειν πεφοβημένον· οἱ δ' ἄρα νίκης
ἐσθλῆς ἱμείρουσιν· ὁ δ' ἔξοχον ὅν κεν ἴδηται
ἀσπαλιεύς, τῷ δαῖτα παρέσχεθεν· αὐτὰρ ὁ λάβρως
δῶρα χανὼν δύσδωρα μετέδραμεν· ἔνθεν ἔπειτα
ἀλκὴν ἀμφοτέρων θηήσεαι, οἷος ἄεθλος
μαρναμένων ἀνδρός τε καὶ ἰχθύος ἑλκομένοιο·
τοῦ μὲν γὰρ σθεναροί τε βραχίονες ἠδὲ μέτωπα

But the fisher should be a powerful man and land his fish by force of strength or else a second man should lend a hand in his labour. For so, unwitting of their crafty doom, fattened themselves they fitly fatten others ; and always when thou wilt, successful fishing shall be thine.

Others trust in their valiant might and strength of limb when they array the great adventure against the Anthias, not cultivating friendship nor proffering food but having recourse at once to the pointed hook and overcoming the fish by their valour. The hook is fashioned of hard bronze or iron, and two separate barbs are attached to the great rope of twisted flax. On it they fix a live Basse—if a live one be at hand ; but if it be a dead one, speedily one puts in its mouth a piece of lead, which they call a dolphin [a] ; and the fish, under the weight of the lead, moves his head to and fro, as if alive. The line is strong and well-woven. When the Anthias hear the noise and leap from the sea, then some attend to the labour of the oar, while the fisherman from the stern-end lets down the crooked snare into the sea, gently waving it about. And the fishes all straightway follow the ship and seeing before their eyes what seems to be a fleeing fish, they rush in haste after the banquet, each striving to outstrip the other : thou wouldst say it was a foeman plying swift knees in pursuit of a routed foe : and they are eager for goodly victory. Now whichever fish the fisher sees to be best, to it he offers the banquet, and with eager gape it rushes after the gift that is no gift. Thereupon thou shalt see the valour of both, such a struggle there is as man and captive fish contend. His strong arms and

[a] *H.* iv. 81 n.

ὦμοί τ' αὐχένιοί τε παρασφύριοί τε τένοντες
ἀλκῇ κυμαίνουσι καὶ ἠνορέῃ τανύονται·
αὐτὰρ ὅ γ' ἀσχαλόων ὀδύνης ὕπο μάρναται ἰχθύς,
ἕλκων αὖ ἐρύοντα, βιώμενος εἰς ἅλα δῦναι,
ἄσχετα μαιμώων· ὁ δὲ κέκλεται ἄνδρας ἑταίρους
ἐμπίπτειν ἐλάτῃσι· διωκομένης δ' ἀκάτοιο
ἔμπαλιν ἐκ πρύμνης ὅλος ἕλκεται ἰχθύος ὁρμῇ·
κλάζει δ' ὁρμιή, χειρὸς δ' ἀπολείβεται αἷμα
πριομένης· ὁ δ' ἄρ' οὔτι βαρὺν μεθίησιν ἀγῶνα.
ὡς δὲ δύω μεμαῶτες ὑπέρβιοι ἀνέρες ἀλκὴν
ἅμματ' ἐπ' ἀλλήλοισι τιταινόμενοι βιόωνται
ἑλκῦσαι, ῥιπῇσιν ὀπισθοφόροις ἐρύοντες,
δηρόν τ' ἀμφότεροι καμάτων ἴσα μέτρα φέροντες
ἐμμενέως ἕλκουσι καὶ ἐμμενέως ἐρύονται·
ὣς τοῖς, ἰχθυβόλῳ τε καὶ ἰχθύϊ, νεῖκος ὄρωρε,
τοῦ μὲν ἀπαΐξαι, τοῦ δ' ἑλκέμεν ἱμείροντος.
οὐ μέν μιν λείπουσιν ἐν ἄλγεσιν ἰχθύες ἄλλοι
ἀνθίαι ἀλλ' ἐθέλουσιν ἀμυνέμεν, ἐν δέ οἱ αὐτῷ
νῶτα βίῃ χρίμπτουσι καὶ ἐμπίπτουσιν ἕκαστος,
ἄφρονες, οὐδ' ἐνόησαν ἑὸν τείροντες ἑταῖρον.
πολλάκι καὶ θώμιγγα λιλαιόμενοι γενύεσσι
ῥῆξαι ἀμηχανόωσιν, ἐπεὶ στόμα τοῖσιν ἄοπλον.
ὀψὲ δέ μιν καμάτῳ τε καὶ ἄλγεσι μοχθίζοντα
πυκναῖς τ' εἰρεσίῃσι βιώμενος ἔσπασεν ἀνήρ·

---

[a] So of a fisherman Theocr. i. 42 f. φαίης κα γυίων νιν ὅσον σθένος ἐλλοπιεύειν· | ὧδέ οἱ ᾠδήκαντι κατ' αὐχένα πάντοθεν ἶνες.

[b] ἅμματα is not = σχοινία (ropes), as the schol. interprets, but the hold or grasp of the wrestler. *Cf.* Plut. *Alcib.* ii. ἐν μὲν γὰρ τῷ παλαίειν πιεζούμενος ὑπὲρ τοῦ μὴ πεσεῖν ἀναγαγὼν πρὸς τὸ στόμα τὰ ἅμματα τοῦ πιεζοῦντος οἷος ἦν διαφαγεῖν τὰς χεῖρας. ἀφέντος δὲ τὴν λαβὴν ἐκείνου καὶ εἰπόντος· "Δάκνεις, ὦ 'Αλκιβιάδη, καθάπερ αἱ γυναῖκες," "Οὐκ ἔγωγε," εἶπεν, "ἀλλ' ὡς οἱ λέοντες"; *Fab.* xxiii. ὥσπερ ἀθλητὴς ἀγαθὸς ἐπαγωνι-

brows and shoulders and the sinews of his neck and ankles swell [a] with might and strain with valour; while the fish, chafing with pain, makes a fight, pulling against the pulling fisher, striving to dive into the sea, raging incontinently. Then the fisher bids his comrades to fall to at their oars; and as the ship speeds forward, he on the stern is dragged bodily backward by the rush of the fish, and the line whistles, and the blood drips from his torn hand. But he relaxes not the grievous contest. As two keen men of mighty valour stretch their grasp [b] about one another and endeavour each to pull the other, hauling with backward strain; and long time both, enduring equal measure of toil, pull might and main and are pulled; even so between those, the fisher and the fish, strife arises, the one eager to rush away, the other eager to pull him in. Nor do the other Anthias fishes desert the captive in his agony but are fain to help him [c] and violently hurl their backs against him and fall each one upon him, foolishly, and know not that they are afflicting their comrade. Often also when they are fain to tear through the line with their jaws, they are helpless, since their mouth is unarmed.[d] At last when the fish is weary with labour and pain and the quick rowing, the man overpowers him and pulls him in.

ζόμενος τῷ Ἀννίβᾳ καὶ ῥᾳδίως ἀπολυόμενος αὐτοῦ τὰς πράξεις, ὥσπερ ἅμματα καὶ λαβὰς οὐκέτι τὸν αὐτὸν ἐχούσας τόνον.

[c] Ael. i. 4 τούτων (τῶν ἀνθιῶν) γοῦν ἕκαστοι, ὅταν νοήσωσι τεθηρᾶσθαι τὸν σύννομον, προσνέουσιν ὤκιστα· εἶτα ἐς αὐτὸν τὰ νῶτα ἀπερείδουσιν καὶ ἐμπίπτοντες καὶ ὠθούμενοι τῇ δυνάμει κωλύουσιν ἕλκεσθαι; Plut. *Mor.* 977 c οἱ δ' ἀνθίαι τῷ συμφύλῳ βοηθοῦσιν ἰταμώτερον· τὴν γὰρ ὁρμιὰν ἀναθέμενοι κατὰ τὴν ῥάχιν καὶ στήσαντες ὀρθὴν τὴν ἄκανθαν ἐπιχειροῦσι διαπρίειν τῇ τραχύτητι καὶ διακόπτειν.

[d] *i.e.*, toothless.

εἰ δ' ἄρα οἱ καὶ τυτθὸν ὑπείξεται, οὔ μιν ἔπειτα
ἑλκύσει· τοῖον γὰρ ὑπερφίαλον σθένος αὐτῷ.
πολλάκι δ' ὀξύπρωρον ὑπὲρ ῥάχιν ἔτμαγε δάψας
ὁρμιήν, ἀπὸ δ' ἦξε λιπὼν κενὸν ἀγρευτῆρα.
τοῖον καὶ κάλλιχθυς ἔχει σθένος ἠδὲ γενέθλη
ὀρκύνων ὅσσοι τε δέμας κητώδεες ἄλλοι
πλάζονται· τοίοις δὲ βραχίοσιν ἀγρώσσονται.
Ἄλλους δ' αὖ βρώμῃσι καὶ εἰλαπίνῃσι δολώσας
ἀγρώσσει ἁλιεύς· ἀγαθὸς δέ οἱ ἔσσεται ἰχθὺς
κάνθαρος, ὃς πέτρῃσιν ἀεὶ λεπρῇσι γέγηθε.
κύρτον δὲ πλέξαιο περίδρομον ὅττι μέγιστον,
τεύχων ἢ σπάρτοισιν Ἰβηρίσιν ἠὲ λύγοισι,
ῥάβδους ἀμφιβαλών· λευρὴ δέ οἱ εἴσοδος ἔστω
γαστήρ τ' εὐρυχανής· δέλεαρ δέ οἱ ἔνδον ἐνείης
πούλυπον ἑρπυστὴν ἢ κάραβον, ἐκ πυρὸς ἄμφω
ὀπταλέους· κνίσσῃ γὰρ ἐφέλκεται ἰχθύας εἴσω.
ὧδε μὲν ἐντύνας πλεκτὸν δόλον ἐγγύθι πέτρης
δόχμιον ἀγκλίνοις, ὕφαλον λόχον· αὐτίκα δ' ὀδμὴ
κάνθαρον ὀτρυνέει τε καὶ ἵξεται ἔνδοθι κύρτου,
οὐ μάλα θαρσαλέος πρώτην ὁδόν, ἀλλὰ τάχιστα
δαισάμενος παλίνορσος ἀπέδραμεν· ἔνθεν ἔπειτα
κυρτεὺς μὲν κείνοισιν ἀεὶ νεοτερπέα φορβὴν
ἐντίθεται· τοὺς δ' αἶψα δυσώνυμος ἐντὸς ἀγείρει
γαστήρ, ἄλλον δ' ἄλλος ἄγει σύνδορπον ἑταῖρον.
ἤδη δ' ἀτρομέοντες ἀολλέες ἔνδοθι κύρτου
ἀγρόμενοι πρόπαν ἦμαρ ἐνήμενοι, ὥστε μέλαθρον

---

[a] Introd. p. lvii. [b] *H.* iii. 132 n.

[c] *Cantharus griseus* (*Cantharus lineatus*), M.G. ἀσκάθαρος, βαγιοῦνο at Corfu (Apost. p. 18).

[d] Day i. p. 26 "Prefers rocky ground, feeding on the finer kinds of seaweeds. It is found in bays and harbours, and frequently captured by anglers fishing from the shore, rocks, or piers."

But if the fisher yield to him even a little, he cannot pull him in—so tremendous is his strength. Often he tears and cuts the line on his sharp spine and rushes away, leaving the fisherman empty-handed. A like strength is possessed by the Beauty-fish [a] and the race of the Orcynus [b] and others of monstrous body that roam the deep ; and even by such arms are they captured.

Others the fisherman catches with the wile of food and feast. A good fish will be the Black Sea-bream,[c] which ever rejoices in rough rocks.[d] Plait a round weel [e] as large as may be, fashioning it with Iberian broom [f] or withes and putting staves round it. Let the entrance be smooth and the belly yawning wide. As bait, put within it reptile Poulpe or Crayfish, in either case broiled [g] on the fire ; for the savour entices the fishes within. Having thus prepared the plaited deceit, lean it obliquely beside a rock, to be an ambush under the sea. And immediately the odour will rouse the Black Sea-bream and he will come within the weel, not very confident on his first journey, but with all haste he makes his meal and speeds away again. Thereafter the weel-fisher puts in the weel ever fresh pleasant food for them and ill-omened gluttony speedily gathers them within, and one fish brings another comrade to share the banquet. At length without fear they gather all together within the weel and remain sitting therein

[e] *H.* iii. 86 n.

[f] *C.* i. 156 n.

[g] A. 534 a 22 καὶ ὅλως δὲ πρὸς τὰ κνισώδη πάντες φέρονται μᾶλλον. καὶ τῶν σηπιῶν δὲ τὰ σαρκία σταθεύσαντες ἕνεκα τῆς ὀσμῆς δελεάζουσι τούτοις· προσέρχονται γὰρ μᾶλλον. τοὺς δὲ πολύπους φασὶν ὀπτήσαντες εἰς τοὺς κύρτους ἐντιθέναι οὐδενὸς ἄλλου χάριν ἢ τῆς κνίσης.

κτησάμενοι, μίμνουσι, κακὴν δ' εὕροντο καλιήν.
ὡς δ' ὁπότ' ὀρφανικοῖο μετ' ἠιθέοιο μέλαθρον
οὔτι σαοφροσύνῃσι μεμηλότες ἥλικες ἄλλοι
κλητοί τ' αὐτόμολοί τε πανήμεροι ἀγερέθωνται,
κτῆσιν ἀεὶ κείροντες ἀσημάντοιο δόμοιο,
οἷα νέους ἀνίησι χαλίφρονας ἄκριτος ἥβη,
ἐν δὲ κακοφροσύνῃσι κακὴν εὕραντο τελευτήν·
ὣς τοῖς ἀγρομένοισι παρασχεδὸν ἵσταται ἄτη.
ἡνίκα γὰρ πολλοί τε καὶ εὐλιπέες τελέθωσι,
δὴ τότ' ἀνὴρ κύρτοιο περὶ στόμα πῶμα καλύπτει
εὖ ἀραρός· τοὺς δ' ἔνδον ἐν ἕρκεϊ πεπτηῶτας
ὑστάτιον κνώσσοντας ἀνείρυσεν· ὀψὲ δ' ὄλεθρον
φρασσάμενοι σπαίρουσι καὶ ἐκδῦναι μεμάασι,
νήπιοι, οὐδ' ἔτι κύρτον ὁμῶς εὔοικον ἔχουσιν.
  Ἄδμωσιν δ' ἐπὶ κύρτον ὀπωρινὸν ὁπλίζονται
οἴσυνον, μέσσοισι δ' ἐν οἴδμασιν ὁρμίζουσι,
νέρθεν ἀναψάμενοι τρητὸν λίθον εὐναστῆρα·
φελλοὶ δ' ὀχμάζουσιν ἄνω δόλον· ἐν δέ οἱ αἰεὶ
τέσσαρας ἀκταίους διεροὺς κάχληκας ἱεῖσι·
τοῖς δὲ διαινομένοισι περιτρέφεται γλαγόεσσα
μύξα θαλασσαίη, τῆς ἵμερος ἰχθύας ἕλκει
βαιούς, οὐτιδανούς, λίχνον γένος· οἱ δ' ἀγέρονται
κύρτον ἐπιπροθέοντες ἐν ἀγκοίνῃς τε μένουσιν.
ἄδμωες δ' ὁρόωντες ἔσω κοίλοιο μυχοῖο
ἀγρομένους τάχα πάντες ἐπί σφισιν ὡρμήθησαν,
δαιτὸς ἐελδόμενοι· τοὺς δ' οὐ κίχον, ἀλλ' ὑπόλισθον
ῥηϊδίως· οἱ δ' οὔτι καὶ ἱέμενοί περ ἔχουσιν
αὖτις ὑπεκδῦναι πλεκτὸν λόχον, ἀλλ' ἑτέροισι

---

[a] Admon or Admos, only here. Schol. ἄδμωσι· συακίοις, κατὰ τῶν ἀδμώνων· ἄδμωνες ειδος ἰχθύος τῶν λεγομένων συακίων. This points to some species of Flat-fish, as in late Greek

all the day, as if they had acquired a house, and an evil nest they find it. As when to the house of a fatherless youth his age-fellows, who study not sobriety, gather all day bidden and unbidden, wasting evermore the possessions of the masterless house, in such practices as foolish young men are incited to by the waywardness of youth, and in their folly find an evil end; even so for the gathered fishes doom stands nigh at hand. For when they become many and fat, then the man puts a well-fitting cover on the mouth of the weel and takes captive the fishes huddling within the enclosure and sleeping their last sleep. Too late they perceive their doom and struggle and strive to get out—foolish fishes who find the weel no longer so pleasant a home.

Against the Admon [a] they prepare in autumn a weel of osiers and moor it in the midst of the waves, fastening to the bottom a bored stone [b] by way of anchor, while corks [c] support the trap above. In it they always put four wet stones from the beach. On the wet stones grows a milky slime of the sea, desire for which attracts the wretched little fishes, a greedy race, which gather and rush to the weel and remain in its embrace. The Admon, seeing them gathered within the hollow retreat, all speedily rush upon them, eager for a feast. But them they do not overtake: they easily slip away: but the Admon are nowise able, for all their endeavour, to escape again from the plaited ambush, but, preparing woe

σύαξ, συάκιον=ψῆττα. *Cf.* Du Cange *s.* *σιάκιον* and *s.* *σύαξ.*

[b] Hom. *Od.* xiii. 77 *πεῖσμα δ' ἔλυσαν ἀπὸ τρητοῖο λίθοιο*=*γρώνης χερμάδος* Lycophr. 20. *Cf.* Hesych. *s.* *γρώνους.* With *εὐναστῆρα* *cf.* *εὐναί*=anchors, Hom. *Il.* i. 436, etc.

[c] *H.* iii. 103 n.

πήματα πορσύνοντες ἐπί σφισιν εὗρον ὄλεθρον.
ὡς δέ τις ἐν ξυλόχοισιν ὀρέστερος ἀγροιώτης
θηρὶ πάγην ἤρτυνεν, ἀπηνέϊ δ' ἔνδοθι θυμῷ
δῆσε κυνὸς σφίγγων ἄπο μήδεα· τοῦ δ' ὀδύνῃσιν
ἠχήεις ὀρυμαγδὸς ἀπόπροθι τειρομένοιο
ἔρχεται, ἀμφὶ δέ οἱ στένεται δρίος· ἡ δ' ἀΐουσα
πόρδαλις ἰάνθη τε καὶ ἔσσυται, ἴχνος αὐτῆς
μαιομένη· τάχα δ' ἶξε καὶ ἔνθορε· τὸν μὲν ἔπειτα
ὑψόσ' ἀναρπάζει κρυπτὸς δόλος, ἡ δ' ἐνὶ βόθρῳ
εἰλεῖται προπεσοῦσα, μέλει δέ οἱ οὐκέτι δαιτός,
ἀλλὰ φόβου· τῇ δ' οὔτις ὑπέκδυσίς ἐστιν ἑτοίμη·
τοῖα καὶ ἄδμωες δειλοὶ πάθον, ἀντὶ δὲ φορβῆς
πότμον ἐφωρμήσαντο καὶ Ἄϊδος ἕρκος ἄφυκτον.
Καὶ μέν τις θρίσσῃσιν ὁμῶς καὶ χαλκίσιν ἄγρην
φράσσατ' ὀπωρινήν, καὶ λαρινὸν εἷλε καὶ ἔθνη
τραχούρων, κύρτον μὲν ὑπὸ σπάρτοισιν ὑφήνας
εὐπαγέως, φρυκτῶν δ' ὀρόβων ἐνεθήκατο μάζαν,
οἴνῳ μυδαλέην εὐώδεϊ, μίξε δὲ κούρης
δάκρυον Ἀσσυρίης Θειαντίδος, ἥν ποτέ φασι
πατρὸς ἐρασσαμένην δυσμήχανον ἔργον ἀνύσσαι
ἐλθεῖν τ' ἐς φιλότητα χολωσαμένης Ἀφροδίτης·

---

[a] *Cf. C.* iv. 217.

[b] *H.* i. 244 n.

[c] Schol. λαρινόν· τὸ λεγόμενον κύλας, εἶδος ἰχθύος; Hesych. *s.* λαρινός· ἰχθὺς ποιός. Not identified.

[d] Schol. τραχούρων· τρίχων and on *H.* i. 99 τραχούρων· ὅμοια πηλαμύσιν καὶ τῶν τριχαίων. Probably *Trachurus trachurus* Mor. (*Scomber trachurus* L.), M.G. σαυρίδι: "poisson très abondant et qui se pêche à partir des derniers jours du mois de mai jusqu' à la fin du mois de juin" (Apost. p. 14). Athen. 326 a; Ael. xiii. 27; Hesych. *s.* σισόρβακος, *s.* σκίθακος, *s.* σκίθαρκος; Galen, *De aliment. fac.* iii. 31; *cf.* σαῦροι *H.* i. 106 n.

[e] *Vicia ervilia.*

[f] *i.e.*, myrrh, the resinous exudation of *Balsamodendron myrrha.* "δάκρυ" is the regular expression in Greek for

for others, they find destruction for themselves. As when some hunter on the hills prepares a trap in the woods for a wild beast and with hard heart ties up a dog,[a] fastening him by a cord about his private parts; the loud howling of the dog in pain travels afar and the wood resounds about him; the Leopard hears and is glad and hastes to track the cry; swiftly she arrives and leaps upon the dog; then a hidden device snatches the dog aloft, while the Leopard rolls headlong in the pit, and has no more thought of feasting but of flight; but for it there is no escape prepared: even such is the fate of the hapless Admon and in place of food they rush upon their fate and the unescapable net of Hades.

In like fashion for the Shad [b] also and the Pilchard [b] one devises capture in the autumn and so one takes the Larinus [c] and the tribes of the Trachurus.[d] The fisherman weaves compactly a weel of broom and therein puts a cake of parched vetches,[e] moistened with fragrant wine, and mixes therewith the tear [f] of the Assyrian daughter of Theias [g]: who, they say, did a deed of ill contrivance for love of her father and came into his bed, through the anger of

such exudation: Herod. ii. 96 *τὸ δὲ δάκρυον κόμμι ἐστίν*. *Cf.* A. 553 b 28; 623 b 29; *Meteor.* 388 b 19 *τὸ ἤλεκτρον καὶ ὅσα λέγεται ὡς δάκρυα . . . οἷον σμύρνα, λιβανωτός, κόμμι*; Theophrast. *H. P.* ix. 1. 2 *ὁ λίβανος καὶ ἡ σμύρνα, δάκρυα καὶ ταῦτα.*

[g] Apollodor. iii. 14. 4 *Θείαντος βασιλέως' Ἀσσυρίων, ὃς ἔσχε θυγατέρα Σμύρναν. αὕτη κατὰ μῆνιν Ἀφροδίτης . . . ἴσχει τοῦ πατρὸς ἔρωτα καὶ ἀγνοοῦντι τῷ πατρὶ . . . συνευνάσθη. ὁ δὲ ὡς ᾔσθετο, σπασάμενος ξίφος ἐδίωκεν αὐτήν· ἡ δὲ περικαταλαμβανομένη θεοῖς εὔξατο ἀφανὴς γενέσθαι. θεοὶ δὲ κατοικτείραντες αὐτὴν εἰς δένδρον μετήλλαξαν, ὃ καλοῦσι σμύρναν.* In some versions the father is called Cinyras, the daughter Myrrha: Ov. *M.* x. 298 ff. She became mother of Adonis: Lycophr. 829 *Μύρρας ἐρυμνὸν ἄστυ, τῆς μογοστόκους | ὠδῖνας ἐξέλυσε δενδρώδης κλάδος.*

ἀλλ᾽ ὅτε μιν καὶ δένδρον ἐπώνυμον ἐρρίζωσεν
αἶσα θεῶν, γοάει τε καὶ ἣν ὀλοφύρεται ἄτην,
δάκρυσι δευομένη λέκτρου χάριν· ἧς ἐνιμίσγων
θεῖον ὀπὸν κύρτον μὲν ἐνορμίζει ῥοθίοισιν,
ὀδμὴ δ᾽ αἶψα θάλασσαν ἐπέδραμε λειριόεσσα,
κικλήσκουσ᾽ ἀγέλας πολυειδέας· οἱ δ᾽ ἐφέπονται
πνοιῇ νηδυμίῃ δεδονημένοι, ὦκα δὲ κύρτος
πίμπλαται, ἀγρευτῆρι φέρων εὔθηρον ἀμοιβήν.
Σάλπαι δ᾽ ἰκμαλέοις μὲν ἀεὶ φύκεσσι μάλιστα
τέρπονται, κείνῃ δὲ καὶ ἀγρώσσονται ἐδωδῇ.
πλώει μὲν προτέροισιν ἐν ἤμασιν εἰς ἕνα χῶρον
ἀσπαλιεύς, αἰεὶ δὲ μετ᾽ οἴδμασι λᾶας ἵησι
χερμάδας, ἁψάμενος πέρι φύκια τηλεθόωντα.
ἀλλ᾽ ὅτε δὴ πέμπτη μὲν ἴδῃ πόνον ἠριγένεια
σάλπαι δ᾽ ἀγρόμεναι κεῖνον πόρον ἀμφινέμωνται,
τῆμος ἐπεντύνει κύρτου δόλον· ἐν δέ οἱ εἴσω
φύκεσιν εἰλομένους λᾶας βάλεν, ἀμφὶ δὲ ποίας
εἰναλίας στομίοισιν ἐδήσατο, τῇσι γάνυνται
σάλπαι τ᾽ ἠδ᾽ ὅσσοι βοτανηφάγοι ἰχθύες ἄλλοι·
οἳ τότ᾽ ἀγειρόμενοι ποίας φάγον, αὐτὰρ ἔπειτα
ἐς μυχὸν ἠΐχθησαν· ὁ δ᾽ αὐτίκα κύρτον ἀνέλκει
ῥίμφα μεταπλώσας· σιγῇ δέ οἱ ἄνυται ἔργον,
ἀνδράσι τ᾽ ἀφθόγγοισι καὶ ἀσμαράγοις ἐλάτῃσι·
σιγὴ γὰρ πάσαις μὲν ὀφέλσιμος ἔπλετο θήραις,

---

[a] *Box salpa* (*Gen.* Box, *Fam.* Sparidae), M.G. σάλπα: Apost. p. 17; Plin. ix. 68.

[b] A. 591 a 15 ἡ δὲ σάλπη (τρέφεται) τῇ κόπρῳ καὶ φυκίοις· βόσκεται δὲ καὶ τὸ πράσιον, θηρεύεται δὲ καὶ κολοκύνθῃ [gourd, *Cucurbita maxima*] μόνη τῶν ἰχθύων; 534 a 15 ἔνια γὰρ δελεάζεται τοῖς δυσώδεσιν, ὥσπερ ἡ σάλπη τῇ κόπρῳ.

[c] A. 533 b 15 ἔτι δὲ ἐν ταῖς θήραις τῶν ἰχθύων ὅτι μάλιστα εὐλαβοῦνται ψόφον ποιεῖν ἢ κώπης ἢ δικτύων οἱ περὶ τὴν θήραν ταύτην ὄντες, ἀλλ᾽ ὅταν κατανοήσωσιν ἔν τινι τόπῳ πολλοὺς

Aphrodite ; but since the doom of the gods rooted her and the tree that bears her name, she wails and mourns her woeful fate, wetted with tears for the sake of her bed : her holy sap the fisher mingles with the rest and moors his weel in the waves ; and swiftly the lily fragrance runs over the sea and summons the herds of various kind ; and the fishes moved by the sweet breath obey the call and speedily the weel is filled, bringing to the fisherman a recompense of goodly spoil.

The Saupes [a] always delight above all things in moist seaweed [b] and by that bait also they are taken. On previous days the fisherman sails to one place and always casts in the waves stones of a handy size, to which he has fastened fresh seaweed. But when the fifth morn sees his toil and the gathered Saupes feed about that place, then he arrays his crafty weel. Within it he casts stones wrapped in seaweed and about the mouth he binds such grasses of the sea as Saupes and other plant-eating fishes delight in. Then the fishes gather and eat the grasses and thereafter speed inside the weel. Straightway the fisher sails swiftly to the spot and pulls up the weel. His work is done silently, the men not speaking and the oars hushed. For silence [c] is profitable in all fishing but above all [d] in the case

ἀθρόους ὄντας, ἐκ τοσούτου τόπου τεκμαιρόμενοι καθιᾶσι τὰ δίκτυα, ὅπως μήτε κώπης μήτε τῆς ῥύμης τῆς ἁλιάδος ἀφίκηται πρὸς τὸν τόπον ἐκεῖνον ὁ ψόφος· παραγγέλλουσί τε πᾶσι τοῖς ναύταις ὅτι μάλιστα σιγῇ πλεῖν, μέχρι περ ἂν συγκυκλώσωνται.

[d] The acuteness of hearing of the Saupe is mentioned A. 534 a 8 *μάλιστα δ' εἰσὶ τῶν ἰχθύων ὀξυήκοοι κεστρεύς, χρέμψ, λάβραξ, σάλπη, χρόμις.* *Cf.* Ael. ix.7 ; Plin. x. 193 produntur etiam clarissime audire mugil, lupus, salpa, chromis, et ideo in vado vivere.

ἔξοχα δ' ἐν σάλπῃσιν· ἐπεὶ μάλα τῇσι νόημα
πτοιαλέον· πτοίη δὲ πόνον δύσθηρον ἔθηκε.
  Τρίγλης δ' οὔτινα, φημί, χερειοτέρῃσιν ἐδωδαῖς
τέρπεσθαι· πᾶσαν γὰρ ἄσιν ἁλός, ἥν κε κίχῃσι,
φέρβεται· ἱμείρει δὲ δυσαέος ἔξοχα δαιτός·
σώμασι δ' ἐκπάγλως ἐπιτέρπεται ἀνδρομέοισι
πυθομένοις, εὖτ' ἄν τιν' ἕλῃ στονόεσσα θάλασσα.
τῷ καί μιν δελέασσιν ἀποπνείουσιν ἀϋτμὴν
ῥηϊδίως ἕλκουσιν, ὅσα πνέει ἐχθρὸν ἄημα.
εἴκελα δὲ τρίγλῃσιν ὕεσσί τε, φημί, τετύχθαι
ἤθεα, φυρομένοισιν ἀεὶ περὶ γαστέρος ὁρμήν·
ἄμφω δ' αἱ μὲν ἔασι διάκριτοι ἐν νεπόδεσσιν,
οἱ δ' ἐνὶ χερσαίῃσιν ἀριστεύουσ' ἀγέλῃσιν.
  Οὐ μὲν δὴ μελάνουρον ἀποίσεαι οὔτ' ἐνὶ κύρτῳ
ῥηϊδίως ἀπαφῶν οὔτ' ἐν λινοεργέϊ κύκλῳ·
ἔξοχα γὰρ μελάνουρος ἐν ἰχθύσιν ἠμὲν ἄναλκις
ἠδὲ σαοφρονέων, λίχνη δέ οἱ οὔποτ' ἐδωδὴ
θυμήρης· αἰεὶ δὲ γαληναίης μὲν ἐούσης
κέκλιται ἐν ψαμάθοισι καὶ οὐκ ἀναδύεται ἅλμης·
ἀλλ' ὅτε κυμαίνουσα περισπέρχῃσι θάλασσα
λάβρων ἐξ ἀνέμων, τότε δὴ μοῦνοι μελάνουροι
κῦμα διαΐσσουσιν ἀολλέες, οὔτε τιν' ἀνδρῶν
οὔτε τιν' εἰναλίων πεφρικότες· οἱ μὲν ἅπαντες
ἐς νεάτην κρηπῖδα φόβῳ δύνουσι θαλάσσης,
οἱ δὲ τότ' ἠϊόνας τε πολυφλοίσβους ἐφέπουσι
πέτραις τ' ἐμπελάουσιν ἀλήμονες, εἴ τιν' ἐδητὺν
κοπτομένη δείξειεν ὑπὸ ῥιπῇσι θάλασσα·
νήπιοι, οὐδ' ἐδάησαν ὅσον πινυτώτεροι ἄνδρες,
οἳ κείνους καὶ πάμπαν ἀλευομένους ἕλον ἄγρῃ.

[a] *C.* ii. 392 n.

[b] 591 a 12 αἱ δὲ τρίγλαι καὶ φυκίοις τρέφονται καὶ ὀστρέοις καὶ βορβόρῳ καὶ σαρκοφαγοῦσιν.

of the Saupes; since their wits are easily scared and a scare renders vain the labour of the fisher.

No fish, I declare, delights in meaner bait than doth the Red Mullet[a]; for it feeds on all the silt[b] of the sea that it can find and it loves especially evil-smelling food. It delights exceedingly in the rotting bodies of men, when the dolorous sea makes any man its prey. Wherefore fishers easily take them with smelly baits which have a hateful breath. Red Mullets and Swine,[c] I declare, have like habits, wallowing always in filth for the desire of the belly: and the Red Mullets have the same distinction among the finny tribes as Swine have among the herds of the land.

The Melanurus[d] thou shalt not easily beguile and carry away either with weel or with the encircling net. For the Melanurus among all fishes is eminent at once for cowardice and for prudence, and gluttonous bait[e] is never pleasing to it. Always when the sea is calm it lies in the sands and rises not from the brine. But when under stress of violent winds the sea rages and billows, then do the Melanurus alone speed over the sea together, fearing not any man nor any creature of the sea. While all the rest for fear dive to the nether foundations of the sea, the Melanurus haunt the sounding shores or draw to the rocks as they roam in search of any food that the wind-beaten sea may show them. Foolish fishes! which know not how much more cunning are men, who take them captive despite all their endeavour

[c] A. 595 a 18 *εὐχερέστατον πρὸς πᾶσαν τροφὴν τῶν ζῴων ἐστίν* (*ἡ ὗς*).

[d] *C.* ii. 391 n. Oppian's account of the habits of the Melanurus is paraphrased by Ael. i. 41.

[e] A. 591 a 15 *μελάνουρος φυκίοις* (*τρέφεται*).

χειμερίη πλημμυρὶς ὅταν ζέῃ Ἀμφιτρίτης,
ἵστατ᾽ ἐπὶ προὔχουσαν ἀνὴρ ἁλιηγέα πέτρην,
ὀξύτατον τόθι κῦμα περὶ σπιλάδεσσι μέμυκεν·
εἴδατα δ᾽ ἀγνυμένοισιν ἐπισπείρει ῥοθίοισι,
τυρὸν ὁμοῦ Δήμητρι μεμιγμένον· οἱ δ᾽ ἐπὶ φορβὴν
ἀσπασίην θρώσκουσιν ἐπειγόμενοι μελάνουροι.
ἀλλ᾽ ὅτε οἱ παρέασιν ἀολλέες ἐς βόλον ἄγρης,
αὐτὸς μὲν τρέπεται λοξὸν δέμας, ὄφρα οἱ ὕδωρ
μήτι κατασκιάοιτο καὶ ἰχθύσι τάρβος ἐνείη·
ἔστι δέ οἱ λεπτός τε δόναξ μετὰ χερσὶν ἑτοῖμος
λεπτή θ᾽ ὁρμιὴ κούφης τριχός, ἄπλοκος αὔτως·
λεπτοῖς δ᾽ ἀγκίστροισιν ἀναπλέκεται θαμέεσσι·
τοῖς ἐπέθηκε δέλετρον, ὃ καὶ πάρος ἧκε καθ᾽ ὕδωρ,
πέμπει δ᾽ ἐς βαθὺ κῦμα κυκώμενον· οἱ δ᾽ ὁρόωντες
αὐτίκ᾽ ἐπιθρώσκουσι καὶ ἁρπάζουσιν ὄλεθρον.
οὐδ᾽ ἁλιεὺς εὔκηλον ἔχει χέρα, πυκνὰ δ᾽ ἀνέλκει
ἐκ δίνης ἄγκιστρα, καὶ εἰ κενὰ πολλάκις εἴη·
οὐ γὰρ βρασσομένης κεν ἐπιφράσσαιτο θαλάσσης
ἀτρεκέως, εἴτ᾽ οὖν τις ἐνίσχεται εἴτε μιν αὔτως
κύματ᾽ ἀνακλονέουσιν· ἐπὴν δέ τις ἀμφιχάνῃσι,
ῥίμφα μιν ἐξείρυσσε πάρος δόλον ἐν φρεσὶ θέσθαι,
πρὶν φόβον οὐτιδανοῖσιν ἐνιπλῆξαι μελανούροις.
τοίην χειμερίην πανεπίκλοπον ἤνυσεν ἄγρην.

---

[a] Hom. *Il.* xv. 406 ὡς ὅτε τις φὼς | πέτρῃ ἔπι προβλῆτι καθήμενος ἱερὸν ἰχθὺν | ἐκ πόντοιο θύραζε λίνῳ καὶ ἤνοπι χαλκῷ (*sc.* ἕλκει).

[b] The mode of capture here described seems to be identical with the modern method as described by Apost. p. 49: "Pendant l'été on pêche, dans les Sporades, les oblades [M.G. μελανούρια] et les daurades avec des bouchons de liège (φελλάρια). L'appareil est ainsi disposé : on pierce le liège et on fait passer une racine anglaise [sheep-gut] à l'un des bouts. On attache un hameçon, à l'autre bout un morceau de bois pour empêcher la racine de sortir. On retire la racine et quand le hameçon vient toucher le liège, on le couvre de pâte

to escape. When the sea boils with stormy flood, a man stands upon a jutting sea-beaten cliff,[a] where the wave bellows loudly on the rocks, and scatters dainties [b] in the breaking waves, even cheese mixed with flour [c]; and the Melanurus rush eagerly upon the welcome food. But when they are gathered together within range of his cast, he himself turns his body aside, that he may not cast his shadow on the water, and the fish be frightened. In his hands he holds ready a thin rod and a thin line of light hair all untwined, whereon are strung numerous light hooks. On these he puts the same bait as before he cast in the water, and lets it down into the deep turmoil of the waves. Seeing it the Melanurus immediately rush upon it and snatch—their own destruction. Nor does the fisher hold his hand at rest, but ever and again draws up his hooks from the eddying waters, even if they be often empty. For in the seething sea he cannot mark for certain whether a fish is hooked or whether it is but the waves that shake the line. But when a fish swallows the hook, swiftly he pulls him forth, ere he thinks of guile, ere he cause fright to the feeble Melanurus. In such wise he accomplishes his treacherous fishing in stormy weather.

de farine mêlée de fromage [*cf.* τῦρον ὁμοῦ Δήμητρι μεμιγμένον 463] et on laisse le liège, amorcé, libre dans la mer. Les poissons en venant manger l'appât avalent aussi l hameçon. Lorsqu'ils se déplacent ils entraînent avec eux le liège, ce qu'avertit le pêcheur qui vient les ramasser. Cette pêche est excessivement amusante. Quand on emploie une grande quantité de lièges et que le poisson mord, c'est un perpétuel va-et-vient pour décrocher les poissons qui s'y sont pris et amorcer de nouveau les engins."

[c] Δήμητρι: for the metonymy for bread or flour *cf.* *C.* i. 434 n. and 484 below.

Ναὶ μὴν καὶ κεστρῆα, καὶ οὐ λίχνον περ ἐόντα,
ἤπαφον, ἀγκίστροισι περὶ στεινοῖσιν ἕσαντες
εἶδαρ ὁμοῦ Δήμητρι μεμιγμένον ἠδὲ γάλακτος
πηκτοῖσι δώροισιν· ἐφυρήσαντο δὲ ποίην
τοῖσιν ὁμοῦ μίνθην εὐώδεα, τήν ποτε κούρην
φασὶν ὑπουδαίην ἔμεναι, Κωκυτίδα Νύμφην·
κλίνατο δ' εἰς εὐνὴν 'Αϊδωνέος· ἀλλ' ὅτε κούρην
Περσεφόνην ἥρπαξεν ἀπ' Αἰτναίοιο πάγοιο,
δὴ τότε μιν κλάζουσαν ὑπερφιάλοις ἐπέεσσι,
ζήλῳ μαργαίνουσαν ἀτάσθαλα, μηνίσασα
Δημήτηρ ἀμάθυνεν ἐπεμβαίνουσα πεδίλοις·
φῆ γὰρ ἀγαυοτέρη τε φυὴν καὶ κάλλος ἀμείνων
Περσεφόνης ἔμεναι κυανώπιδος, ἐς δέ μιν αὐτὴν
εὔξατο νοστήσειν 'Αϊδωνέα, τὴν δὲ μελάθρων
ἐξελάσειν· τοίη οἱ ἐπὶ γλώσσης θόρεν ἄτη.
ποίη δ' οὐτιδανὴ καὶ ἐπώνυμος ἔκθορε γαίης,
τὴν ἐνιφυρήσαντες ἐπ' ἀγκίστροισι βάλοντο.
κεστρεὺς δ' οὐ μετὰ δηρόν, ἐπεί ῥά μιν ἷξεν ἀϋτμή,
ἀντιάσας πρῶτον μὲν ἀποσταδὸν ἀγκίστροιο
λοξὸν ὑπ' ὀφθαλμοῖς ὁράᾳ δόλον, εἴκελος ἀνδρὶ

---

[a] *H.* ii. 642 n.

[b] *H.* ii. 643 n. On the other hand A. 591 b 1 λαίμαργος δὲ μάλιστα τῶν ἰχθύων ὁ κεστρεύς ἐστι καὶ ἄπληστος, where, however, the word κεστρεύς is suspect.

[c] *i.e.*, cheese, as in v. 463. Speaking of fishing for, amongst others, Grey Mullets (κεφαλόπουλα), Apost. p. 43

Yea, and the Grey Mullet,[a] albeit he is no glutton,[b] they yet deceive by clothing narrow hooks with bait mixed with flour and gifts of curdled milk.[c] Therewith they knead also the sweet-smelling herb of mint. Mint, men say, was once a maid[d] beneath the earth, a Nymph of Cocytus, and she lay in the bed of Aidoneus; but when he raped the maid Persephone from the Aetnaean hill, then she complained loudly with overweening words and raved foolishly for jealousy, and Demeter in anger trampled upon her with her feet and destroyed her. For she had said that she was nobler of form and more excellent in beauty than dark-eyed Persephone and she boasted that Aidoneus would return to her and banish the other from his halls: such infatuation leapt upon her tongue. And from the earth sprang the weak herb that bears her name. Mint, then, the fishers mingle with the bait which they put upon their hooks. And in no long time the Grey Mullet, when the odour reaches him, first approaches the hook distantly and regards with eyes askance the snare; like to a stranger who, chancing upon

says: "On amorce aussi simplement avec de la pâte de pain mêlée avec du fromage pour lui donner un peu d'odeur." *Cf.* A. 591 a 18 ὁ δὲ κέφαλος καὶ ὁ κεστρεὺς ὅλως μόνοι οὐ σαρκοφαγοῦσιν· σημεῖον δέ, οὔτε γὰρ ἐν τῇ κοιλίᾳ πώποτ' ἔχοντες εἰλημμένοι εἰσὶ τοιοῦτον οὐδέν, οὔτε δελέατι χρῶνται πρὸς αὐτοὺς ζῴων σαρξὶν ἀλλὰ μάζῃ.

[d] Strabo 344 πρὸς ἕω δ' ἐστιν ὄρος τοῦ Πύλου πλησίον ἐπώνυμον Μίνθης, ἣν μυθεύουσι παλλακὴν τοῦ Αἵδου γενομένην πατηθεῖσαν ὑπὸ τῆς Κόρης εἰς τὴν κηπαίαν μίνθην μεταβαλεῖν, ἥν τινες ἡδύοσμον [*Mentha viridis*, spearmint, Theophrast. *H.P.* vii. 7. 1] καλοῦσι; schol. Nicandr. *Alex.* 375 Μινθη Αἵδου παλλακὴ οὕτω καλουμένη, ἣν διεσπάραξεν ἡ Περσεφόνη. ἐφ' ᾗ τὴν ὁμώνυμον πόαν ἀνέδωκεν ὁ Αἵδης; Ov. *M.* x. 728 an tibi quondam | Femineos artus in olentes vertere menthas, | Persephone, licuit?

ξείνῳ, ὃς ἐν τριόδοισι πολυτρίπτοισι κυρήσας
ἔστη ἐφορμαίνων, κραδίη τέ οἱ ἄλλοτε λαιήν,
ἄλλοτε δεξιτερὴν ἐπιβάλλεται ἀτραπὸν ἐλθεῖν·
παπταίνει δ' ἑκάτερθε, νόος δέ οἱ ἠΰτε κῦμα
εἱλεῖται, μάλα δ' ὀψὲ μιῆς ὠρέξατο βουλῆς·
ὣς ἄρα καὶ κεστρῆϊ παναίολα μερμηρίζει
θυμὸς ὀϊομένῳ τε δόλον καὶ ἀπήμονα φορβήν·
ὀψὲ δέ μιν νόος ὦρσε καὶ ἤγαγεν ἐγγύθι πότμου·
αὐτίκα δὲ τρέσσας ἀνεχάσσατο· πολλάκι δ' ἤδη
εἷλε φόβος ψαύοντα καὶ ἔμπαλιν ἔτραπεν ὁρμήν.
ὡς δ' ὅτε νηπίαχος κούρη πάϊς, ἐκτὸς ἐούσης
μητέρος, ἢ βρώμης λελιημένη ἠέ τευ ἄλλου,
ψαῦσαι μὲν τρομέει μητρὸς χόλον, οὐδ' ἀναδῦναι
ἐλδομένη τέτληκεν· ἐφερπύζουσα δὲ λάθρῃ
αὖτις ὑποτρέπεται, κραδίῃ δέ οἱ ἄλλοτε θάρσος,
ἄλλοτε δ' ἐμπίπτει δεινὸς φόβος· ὄμματα δ' αἰὲν
ὀξέα παπταίνοντα ποτὶ προθύροισι τέτανται·
ὣς τότ' ἐπεμβαίνων ἀνελίσσεται ἤπιος ἰχθύς.
ἀλλ' ὅτε θαρσήσας πελάσῃ σχεδόν, οὐ μάλ' ἑτοίμως
ψαῦσε βορῆς, οὐρῇ δὲ πάρος μάστιξεν ἐγείρων
ἄγκιστρον, μή πού τις ἐνὶ χροῒ θέρμετ' ἀϋτμή·
ζωοῦ γὰρ κεστρεῦσιν ἀπώμοτόν ἐστι πάσασθαι.
ἔνθεν ἔπειτ' ἄκροισι διακνίζει στομάτεσσι
δαῖτα περιξύων· ἁλιεὺς δέ μιν αὐτίκα χαλκῷ
πεῖρεν ἀνακρούων, ὥστε θρασὺν ἵππον ἐέργων
ἡνίοχος σκληρῇσιν ἀναγκαίῃσι χαλινοῦ,
ἂν δ' ἔρυσε, σπαίροντα δ' ἐπὶ χθονὶ κάββαλεν ἐχθρῇ.

---

[a] Cic. *De div.* i. 54. 123 Idem etiam Socrates cum apud Delium male pugnatum esset, Lachete praetore, fugeretque cum ipso Lachete, ut ventum est in trivium, eadem qua ceteri fugere noluit. Quibus quaerentibus cur non eadem via pergeret, deterreri se a deo dixit. Tum quidem ii qui alia via fugerant, in hostium equitatum inciderunt ; Theogn.

much trodden cross-ways,[a] stands pondering, and at one moment his heart is set on going by the left road, at another by the right, and he looks on this side and on that and his mind fluctuates like the wave and only at long last he reaches a single purpose ; even so also the spirit of the Grey Mullet ponders variously, now thinking of a snare and now of harmless food. At last his mind impels him and brings him nigh his doom. And immediately he starts back in fear and many times as he touches it, terror seizes him and checks his impulse. As when a little maiden girl, when her mother is abroad, is faint for some eatable or whatever it may be ; and to touch it she is afraid for the anger of her mother, yet, unwilling to withdraw, she dares the deed : stealthily she creeps to it and again turns away ; now courage, now fear enters her heart ; and always her keen eyes are strained watchfully upon the door : even so then the gentle fish approaches and retires. But when he takes heart and draws nigh, not readily does he touch the bait but first lashes with his tail and stirs the hook to see whether haply there is any warm breath in its body ; for to eat of aught living is for the Grey Mullet a thing forsworn. Then he nibbles and plucks at the bait with the tip of his mouth ; and straightway the fisher strikes and pierces him with the bronze, even as a charioteer constrains a gallant horse by the stern compulsion of the bit, and pulls him up and casts him struggling on the loathed earth.

911 *ἐν τριόδῳ δ' ἕστηκα· δύ' εἰσὶ τὸ πρόσθεν ὁδοί μοι· | φροντίζω τούτων ἥντιν' ἴω προτέρην* ; Pind. *P.* x. 38 *ἦ ῥ', ὦ φίλοι, κατ' ἀμευσίπορον τρίοδον ἐδινήθην, | ὀρθὰν ὁδὸν ἰὼν τὸ πρίν* ; Plato, *Laws*, 799 c *στὰς δ' ἄν, καθάπερ ἐν τριόδῳ γενόμενος καὶ μὴ σφόδρα κατειδὼς ὁδόν, εἴτε μόνος εἴτε μετ' ἄλλων τύχοι πορευόμενος, ἀνέροιτ' ἂν αὑτὸν καὶ τοὺς ἄλλους τὸ ἀπορούμενον.*

Καὶ ξιφίην ὀλοοῖσι παρήπαφον ἀγκίστροισιν.
ἀλλ' οὐ μὲν ξιφίῃ τοῖος μόρος, οὐδ' ἴσος ἄλλοις·
οὐ γὰρ ἐπ' ἀγκίστροισι κατεντύνουσιν ἐδωδήν,
ἀλλὰ τὸ μὲν γυμνόν τε καὶ ἄκλοπον ᾐώρηται,
μηρίνθου διπλῇσιν ἀκαχμένου ἔμπαλιν αἰχμαῖς·
τοῦ δ' ὅσσον τριπάλαιστον ἀναψάμενοι καθύπερθε
μαλθακὸν ἀργεννῶν νεπόδων ἕνα χείλεος ἄκρου
δῆσαν ἐπισταμένως· ξιφίης δ' ὅτε θοῦρος ἵκηται,
αὐτίκα δαιτρεύει δέμας ἰχθύος ἄορι λάβρῳ·
τοῦ δὲ δαϊζομένοιο καταρρέει ἅψεα δεσμοῦ,
αὐταῖς δ' ἀγκίστροιο περιστρέφεται γενύεσσιν·
αὐτὰρ ὅ γ' οὐκ ἐδάη γναμπτὸν δόλον, ἀλλὰ βαρεῖαν
δαῖτα χανὼν ἀγρευτὸς ἀνέλκεται ἀνέρος ἀλκῇ.
Πολλὰ δ' ἐπὶ ξιφίῃ θηρήτορες ὁπλίζονται,
ἔξοχα δ' οἳ Τυρσηνὸν ἁλὸς πόρον ἀγρώσσουσιν
ἀμφί τε Μασσαλίην, ἱερὴν πόλιν, ἀμφί τε Κελτούς·
κεῖθι γὰρ ἔκπαγλοί τε καὶ ἰχθύσιν οὐδὲν ὁμοῖοι

---

[a] *Il.* ii. 462 n.

[b] The *Mare Tyrrhenum*, bounded on E. by Italy, S. by Sicily, W. by Sardinia and Corsica, N. by Gaul. Dion. P. 83 Τυρσηνίδος οἶδμα θαλάσσης; Strabo 55 Τυρρηνικοῦ πελάγους; Plin. iii. 75 ab eo (*sc.* mari Ligustico) ad Siciliam insulam Tuscum, quod ex Graecis alii Notium alii Tyrrenum, e nostris plurimi inferum vocant.

[c] Marseilles, 27 miles E. of the mouth of the Rhone, founded about 600 B.C. by colonists from Phocaea (*cf.* v. 626 below) in Asia Minor: Strabo 179; Plin. iii. 34. The epithet "holy" is taken by the schol. as a mere colourless epithet (ἱερήν· μεγάλην), but we rather imagine it to refer to the position of Massalia (Massilia) as the great outpost of Hellenic culture in the West. Under the Empire especially it was, as it were, a great University town: Strabo 181 πάντες γὰρ οἱ χαρίεντες πρὸς τὸ λέγειν τρέπονται καὶ φιλοσοφεῖν, ὥσθ' ἡ πόλις μικρὸν μὲν πρότερον τοῖς βαρβάροις ἀνεῖτο παιδευτήριον καὶ φιλέλληνας κατεσκεύαζε τοὺς Γαλάτας ὥστε καὶ τὰ συμβόλαια

The Swordfish [a] also men deceive by deadly hooks. But the doom of the Swordfish is not such as that of the Grey Mullet nor like that of other fishes. For the fishermen do not put bait upon their hooks, but the hook hangs from the line naked and without deceit, furnished with two recurved barbs, while some three palms above it they tie a soft white fish, fastening it skilfully by the tip of its mouth. When the furious Swordfish comes, straightway he rends the body of the fish with his fierce sword, and as the fish is rent, its members slip down from the fastening and are entangled right about the barbs of the hook. But the fish perceives not the crooked guile but swallows the grievous bait and is caught and hauled up by the might of the man.

Many are the devices which fishers contrive against the Swordfish, and those above all who fish the Tyrrhenian [b] tract of sea and about the holy city of Massalia [c] and in the region of the Celts.[d] For there, wondrous and not at all like fishes, range

ἑλληνιστὶ γράφειν, ἐν δὲ τῷ παρόντι [Strabo's date is *c.* 63 B.C.–23 A.D.] καὶ τοὺς γνωριμωτάτους Ῥωμαίων πέπεικεν ἀντὶ τῆς εἰς Ἀθήνας ἀποδημίας ἐκεῖσε φοιτᾶν φιλομαθεῖς; Tacitus, *Agr.* 4 statim parvulus sedem ac magistram studiorum Massiliam habuit, locum Graeca comitate et provinciali parsimonia mixtum et bene compositum; *id. Ann.* iv. 44 (L. Antonium) seposuit Augustus in civitatem Massiliensem, ubi specie studiorum nomen exilii tegeretur. This on the whole seems more likely than that the reference is to the foundation of Massalia under the direct guidance of Ἄρτεμις Ἐφεσία (Diana of the Ephesians) whose temple was a conspicuous feature of the city (Strabo 179). *Cf.* Ammian. Marc. xv. 9. 7.

[d] *i.e.*, the Gauls of Gallia Narbonensis, in which Massalia was situated. The reference is to the *Mare Gallicum*: Plin. iii. 74 τὸ Γαλατικὸν καλούμενον (πέλαγος); A. *De mundo* 393 a 27. *Cf.* Dion. P. 74 Γαλάτης ῥόος, ἔνθα τε γαῖα | Μασσαλίη τετάνυσται, ἐπίστροφον ὅρμον ἔχουσα.

ἄπλατοι ξιφίαι μεγακήτεες ἐννεμέθονται.
οἱ δ᾽ ἀκάτους αὐτοῖσιν ἐϊσκομένας ξιφίῃσι
καὶ δέμας ἰχθυόεν καὶ φάσγανα τεκτήναντες
ἀντίον ἰθύνουσι· ὁ δ᾽ οὐκ ἀναδύεται ἄγρην,
ἐλπόμενος μὴ νῆας ἐϋσέλμους ὁράασθαι,
ἀλλ᾽ ἑτέρους ξιφίας, ξυνὸν γένος, ὄφρα μιν ἄνδρες
πάντῃ κυκλώσωνται· ὁ δ᾽ ἐφράσαθ᾽ ὕστερον ἄτην,
αἰχμῇ τριγλώχινι πεπαρμένος, οὐδέ οἱ ἀλκὴ
φεύγειν ἱεμένῳ περ, ἀναγκαίῃ δὲ δαμῆναι.
πολλάκι μὲν καὶ νηὸς ἀμυνόμενος κενεῶνα
φασγάνῳ ἀντετόρησε διαμπερὲς ἄλκιμος ἰχθύς,
οἱ δὲ θοῶς βουπλῆγος ὑπ᾽ εὐχάλκοιο τυπῇσιν
ἐκ γενύων ἤραξαν ἅπαν ξίφος· ἐν δ᾽ ἄρα νηὸς
ἕλκεϊ γόμφος ἄρηρεν· ὁ δ᾽ ἕλκεται ὀρφανὸς ἀλκῆς.
ὡς δ᾽ ὅτε δυσμενέεσσι δόλον τεύχοντες ἄρηος,
ἱέμενοι πύργων τε καὶ ἄστεος ἔνδον ἱκέσθαι,
ἔντεα συλήσαντες ἀρηϊφάτων ἀπὸ νεκρῶν
αὐτοὶ θωρήξαντο καὶ ἔδραμον ἄγχι πυλάων·
οἱ δ᾽ ὥστε σφετέροισιν ἐπειγομένοις πολιήταις
ἀγκλίνουσι θύρετρα καὶ οὐ γήθησαν ἑταίροις·
ὣς ἄρα καὶ ξιφίην ἴκελον δέμας ἥπαφε νηῶν.
Καὶ μὲν δὴ σκολιῇσιν ἐν ἀγκοίνῃσι λίνοιο
κυκλωθεὶς ξιφίης μέγα νήπιος ἀφροσύνῃσιν
ὄλλυται, ὃς θρώσκει μὲν ὑπεκδῦναι μενεαίνων,
ἐγγύθι δὲ τρομέων πλεκτὸν δόλον αὖτις ὀπίσσω
χάζεται· οὐδέ οἱ ὅπλον ἐνὶ φρεσίν, οἷον ἄρηρεν
ἐκ γενύων, δειλὸς δὲ μένει κεκαφηότι θυμῷ,
ὄφρα μιν ἐξερύσωσιν ἐπ᾽ ἠόνας· ἔνθα δὲ δούροις
ἄνδρες ἐπασσυτέροισι καταΐγδην ἐλόωντες
κρᾶτα συνηλοίησαν, ὁ δ᾽ ὄλλυται ἄφρονι πότμῳ.
Ἀφροσύνη καὶ σκόμβρον ἕλεν καὶ πίονα θύννον

[a] *Il.* i. 101 n.

monster Swordfishes unapproachable. The fishermen fashion boats in the likeness of the Swordfishes themselves, with fishlike body and swords, and steer to meet the fish. The Swordfish shrinks not from the chase, believing that what he sees are not benched ships but other Swordfishes, the same race as himself, until the men encircle him on every side. Afterwards he perceives his folly when pierced by the three-pronged spear; and he has no strength to escape for all his desire but perforce is overcome. Many a time as he fights the valiant fish with his sword pierces in his turn right through the belly of the ship; and the fishers with blows of brazen axe swiftly strike all his sword from his jaws, and it remains fast in the ship's wound like a rivet, while the fish, orphaned of his strength, is hauled in. As when men devising a trick of war against their foes, being eager to come within their towers and city, strip the armour from the bodies of the slain and arm themselves therewith and rush nigh the gates; and the others fling open their gates as for their own townsmen in their haste, and have no joy of their friends; even so do boats in his own likeness deceive the Swordfish.

Moreover, when encircled in the crooked arms of the net the greatly stupid Swordfish perishes by his own folly. He leaps in his desire to escape but near at hand he is afraid of the plaited snare and shrinks back again; there is no weapon in his wits such as is set in his jaws, and like a coward he remains aghast till they hale him forth upon the beach, where with downward-sweeping blow of many spears men crush his head, and he perishes by a foolish doom.

Folly slays also the Mackerel [a] and the fat Tunny

καὶ ῥαφίδας καὶ φῦλα πολυσπερέων συνοδόντων.
σκόμβροι μὲν λεύσσοντες ἐν ἕρκεϊ πεπτηῶτας
ἄλλους ἠράσσαντο λίνου πολύωπον ὄλεθρον
ἐσδῦναι· τοίη τις ἐσέρχεται εἰσορόωντας
τερπωλή· παίδεσσιν ἀπειρήτοισιν ὁμοῖοι,
οἵ τε πυρὸς λεύσσοντες ἀναιθομένοιο φαεινὴν
μαρμαρυγὴν ἀκτῖσιν ἰαινόμενοι γελόωσι
ψαῦσαί θ' ἱμείρουσι καὶ ἐς φλόγα χεῖρ' ὀρέγουσι
νηπιέην· τάχα δέ σφιν ἀνάρσιον ἐξεφάνη πῦρ·
ὣς οἵ γ' ἱμείρουσιν ἀνοστήτοιο λόχοιο
ἐσπεσέειν κευθμῶνα, κακοῦ δ' ἤντησαν ἔρωτος.
ἔνθ' οἱ μὲν κέλσαντες ἐν εὐρυτέροισι βρόχοισι
ἔκθορον, οἱ δ' ἑρχθέντες ἐνὶ στεινοῖσι πόροισι
πικρὸν ἀνέτλησαν σφιγκτὸν μόρον ἐξανύσαντες.
πολλοὺς δ' ἠϊόνεσσιν ἐφελκομένοιο λίνοιο
ὄψεαι ἀμφοτέρωθεν ἀρηρότας ἠΰτε γόμφοις,
τοὺς μὲν ἔτι φρονέοντας ἐσελθέμεν ἄρκυν ὀλέθρου,
τοὺς δ' ἤδη μεμαῶτας ὑπεκδῦναι κακότητος,
ἔνδοθεν ἰκμαλέῃσιν ἐνισχομένους βροχίδεσσι.

Θύννοι δ' αὖ σκόμβροις μὲν ἴσον πόνον ἀθλεύουσιν
ἀφροσύνῃ· καὶ τοῖς γὰρ ὁμοίιος ἵμερος ἄτης
ἐμπίπτει δολίοιο λίνου λαγόνεσσι μιγῆναι·
ἀλλ' οὐ μὲν κείνοισιν ὑπόβρυχα γαστέρος εἴσω
ἐσδύνειν, σκολιοῖσι δ' ἐπαΐσσουσιν ὀδοῦσι,
σώματι μηδόμενοι πόρον ἄρκιον· ἐν δ' ἄρ' ὀδοῦσιν
ὑγρὸν ἐρειδομένοις τέταται λίνον· οὐδέ τι μῆχος
ἐκφυγέειν, δεσμῷ δὲ περιστομίῳ μογέοντες
ἕλκονται ποτὶ χέρσον ὑπ' ἀφραδίῃσιν ἁλόντες.

Καὶ μὲν δὴ ῥαφίδων τοῖος νόος· αἱ δ' ὅτε κόλπον
δικτύου ἐκπροφύγωσι, πόνου δ' ἔκτοσθε γένωνται,

and the Needle-fishes and the tribes of the wide-spread Dentex. The Mackerels, when they see others crouching in the net, are fain to enter the many-meshed snare of destruction—such delight possesses them when they behold: like untried children who, when they see the bright flashing of blazing fire, rejoice in its rays and are fain to touch it and stretch a childish hand into the flame, and speedily the fire proves unkind; even so the Mackerels are fain to rush within the covert of the ambush whence there is no return and find their fondness fatal. Then some land in the wider meshes and leap out, but others, penned in the narrower openings, suffer a bitter fate by strangling. When the net is hauled ashore, thou shalt see them in multitudes on either side fixed as with nails, some still minded to enter the net of destruction, others already eager to escape from their evil plight, held fast within the dripping nets.

The Tunnies again suffer like affliction with the Mackerel by their foolishness. For they also are possessed by a similar fatal desire to come within the loins of the crafty net; they do not however essay to enter the belly of the net under water but assail it with their crooked teeth, devising to make a passage sufficient for their body. The wet net becomes stretched about their infixed teeth and they have no means of escape, but labouring under the entanglement about their mouth they are haled to the land, taken by their own witlessness.

Such also is the counsel of the Needle-fishes.[a] These when they have escaped the bosom of the net

[a] The Gar-fish, *Belone acus*, M.G. *βελονίδα, ζαργάνα*. *Cf.* *C.* ii. 392 n.

αὖτις ἐπιστρωφῶσι, λίνῳ δ' ἐπιμηνίουσαι
δήγματ' ἐνιπρίουσι· τὸ δέ σφισι δύεται εἴσω
ἴσχει τ' ἐμμενέως πυκινοὺς ἔντοσθεν ὀδόντας.
Αὐτὰρ τοὶ συνόδοντες ἴσοι στείχουσι λόχοισι
κεκριμένοι· τοῖς δ' εὖτ' ἂν ἀνὴρ ἄγκιστρον ἐφείη,
οἱ μὲν ἀποτροπάδην λοξὸν φάος ἀλλήλοισι
πάντες ἐπικλίνουσι καὶ οὐκ ἐθέλουσι πελάσσαι·
ἀλλ' ὅτε τις προθορὼν ἑτέρης στιχὸς αἶψα δέλετρον
ἁρπάξῃ, τότε καί τις ἐνὶ φρεσὶ θάρσος ἔδεκτο
ἀγκίστρῳ τ' ἐπέλασσε καὶ ἕλκεται· οἱ δ' ὁρόωντες
ἀλλήλους, περὶ δαιτὶ γεγηθότες, ἰαίνονται
ἑλκόμενοι, σπεύδουσι δ' ὑποφθαδόν, ὅς κε θάνῃσι
πρῶτος ἁλούς, ἅτε παῖδες ἀθύρμασι καγχαλόωντες.
Θύννων δ' αὖ γενεὴ μὲν ἀπ' εὐρυπόροιο τέτυκται
'Ωκεανοῦ· στείχουσι δ' ἐς ἡμετέρης ἁλὸς ἔργα
εἰαρινοῦ μετὰ λύσσαν ὅτ' οἰστρήσωσι γάμοιο.
τοὺς δ' ἤτοι πρῶτον μὲν 'Ιβηρίδος ἔνδοθεν ἅλμης

---

[a] A curious parallel to this is mentioned in his account of the present-day fishing for the Belone by Apost. p. 41: "quelques-uns effrayés, au début, fuient au large, mais ils reviennent aussitôt rejoindre la grande bande qui n'a pas bougé."

[b] *Dentex vulgaris* Cuv., one of the Sea-breams (*Sparidae*), M.G. *συναγρίδα* (Apost. p. 18). *Cf.* A. 591 a 11, b 5, 10; 598 a 13; 610 b 5; Epicharm. *ap.* Athen. 322 b *συνόδοντάς τ' ἐρυθροποικίλους*; Marc. S. 29 *κρεῖοι (κιρροί?) συνόδοντες*; Ov. *Hal.* 107 fulvi synodontes.

[c] A. 543 a 9 *ἡ θυννὶς ἅπαξ τίκτει, ἀλλὰ διὰ τὸ τὰ μὲν πρώια τὰ δὲ ὄψια προίεσθαι δὶς δοκεῖ τίκτειν· ἔστι δ' ὁ μὲν πρῶτος τόκος περὶ τὸν Ποσειδεῶνα* [November-December] *πρὸ τροπῶν* [before the Winter Solstice, 22 December], *ὁ δ' ὕστερος τοῦ ἔαρος*; 543 b 2 *αἱ δὲ πηλαμύδες καὶ οἱ θύννοι τίκτουσιν ἐν τῷ Πόντῳ* [Black Sea], *ἄλλοθι δ' οὔ*. *Cf.* Plin. ix. 47 (Thynni) intrant e magno mari Pontum verno tempore gregatim, nec alibi fetificant; A. 543 b 11 *(τίκτει) θέρους περὶ τὸν 'Εκατομβαιῶνα* [June-July] *θυννίς, περὶ τροπὰς θερινάς* [Summer Solstice, 21 June]; A.

and are gotten free from trouble, turn again [a] and in their anger fix their teeth in the net; and it enters into their mouths and holds fast the close-set teeth within.

The Dentex [b] travel in separate bands, like companies of soldiers. When a man lets down a hook for them, they stand aloof and all bend sidelong looks on one another and are unwilling to approach. But when one leaps forth from another rank and swiftly seizes the bait, then also one of them takes courage in his heart and draws nigh to the hook and is haled in. The Dentex, eyeing one another and delighting in their banquet, rejoice even while they are being caught, and they vie with one another as to which shall die first, like children exulting in their sports.

The breed of Tunnies [c] comes from the spacious Ocean, and they travel into the regions of our sea [d] when they lust after the frenzy of mating in spring. First the Iberians who plume themselves upon their

571 a 11 *ὀχεύονται δ' οἱ θύννοι . . . περὶ τὸν Ἐλαφηβολιῶνα φθίνοντα* [about middle of March], *τίκτουσι δὲ περὶ τὸν Ἑκατομβαιῶνα ἀρχόμενον* [about middle of June]; 598 a 26 *θυννίδες καὶ πηλαμύδες καὶ ἅμιαι εἰς τὸν Πόντον ἐμβάλλουσι τοῦ ἔαρος καὶ θερίζουσιν.*

[d] *i.e.*, they come from the Atlantic into the Mediterranean on the way to their spawning-grounds in the Euxine. *Cf.* Theodorid. *ap.* Athen. 302 c *θύννοι τε διοιστρήσοντι Γαδείρων δρόμον*, *i.e.* the Straits of Gibraltar, *τὸν Γαδειραῖον πορθμόν* Plut. *Sert.* viii.; *cf.* Plin. iii. 74 in eo maria nuncupantur, unde inrumpit, Atlanticum, ab aliis magnum, qua intrat. Porthmos a Graecis, a nobis Gaditanum fretum. For Gadeira = Gades *cf.* Plin. iv. 120 Poeni Gadir (appellant); Strabo 169 ff; Pind. *N.* iv. 69; *fr.* 256; Dion. P. 63 *ἀφ' ἑσπέρου Ὠκεανοῖο | ἔνθα τε καὶ στῆλαι* [Pillars of Hercules] *περὶ τέρμασιν Ἡρακλῆος | ἑστᾶσιν, μέγα θαῦμα, παρ' ἐσχατόωντα Γάδειρα*; *ibid.* 11; 451 ff.

ἀνέρες ἀγρώσσουσι βίῃ κομόωντες Ἴβηρες·
δεύτερα δὲ Ῥοδανοῖο παρὰ στόμα θηρητῆρες
Κελτοὶ Φωκαίης τε παλαίφατοι ἐνναετῆρες·
τὸ τρίτον ἀγρώσσουσιν ὅσοι Τρινακρίδι νήσῳ
ἐνναέται πόντου τε παρ' οἴδμασι Τυρσηνοῖο.
ἔνθεν ἀπειρεσίοις ἐνὶ βένθεσιν ἄλλοθεν ἄλλος
κίδνανται καὶ πᾶσαν ἐπιπλώουσι θάλασσαν.
πολλὴ δ' ἔκπαγλός τε παρίσταται ἰχθυβόλοισιν
ἄγρη, ὅτ' εἰαρινὸς θύννων στρατὸς ὁρμήσωνται.
χῶρον μὲν πάμπρωτον ἐπεφράσσαντο θαλάσσης
οὔτε λίην στεινωπὸν ἐπηρεφέεσσιν ὑπ' ὄχθαις
οὔτε λίην ἀνέμοισιν ἐπίδρομον, ἀλλὰ καὶ αἴθρῃ
καὶ σκεπανοῖς κευθμῶσιν ἐναίσιμα μέτρα φέροντα.
ἔνθ' ἤτοι πρῶτον μὲν ἐπ' ὄρθιον ὕψι κολωνὸν
ἴδρις ἐπαμβαίνει θυννοσκόπος, ὅστε κιούσας
παντοίας ἀγέλας τεκμαίρεται, αἵ τε καὶ ὅσσαι,

---

[a] *i.e.*, the sea off the south of Spain (Iberia). Strabo 122 καλοῦσι δὲ . . . τὸ μὲν (πέλαγος) Ἰβηρικόν, τὸ δὲ Λιγυστικόν, τὸ δὲ Σαρδόνιον, τελευταῖον δὲ μέχρι τῆς Σικελίας τὸ Τυρρηνικόν; Plin. iii. 74 cum intravit, Hispanum (mare nuncupatur) quatenus Hispanias adluit, ab aliis Ibericum aut Baliaricum.

[b] The people of Massilia, *cf.* note on 544 above. *Cf.* Ael. xiii. 16 ἀκούω δὲ Κελτοὺς καὶ Μασσαλιώτας . . . ἀγκίστροις τοὺς θύννους θηρᾶν.

[c] Sicily. For Tunnies in Sicilian seas *cf.* Archestr. *ap.* Athen. 302 a ἐν Σικελῶν δὲ κλυτῇ νήσῳ Κεφαλοιδὶς [on N. coast of Sicily, Strabo 266 Κεφαλοίδιον, Plin. iii. 90 Cephaloedis] ἀμείνους | πολλῷ τῶνδε τρέφει θύννους καὶ Τυνδαρὶς ἀκτή [also on N. coast, Strabo *l.c.*, Plin. *l.c.*]. *Cf.* Hices. *ap.* Athen. 315 d; Ael. xv. 6.

[d] Dorio *ap.* Athen. 315 b Δωρίων . . . τοὺς ὀρκύνους (large Tunnies) ἐκ τῆς περὶ Ἡρακλέους στήλας θαλάσσης περαιουμένους εἰς τὴν καθ' ἡμᾶς ἔρχεσθαι θάλασσαν· διὸ καὶ πλείστους ἁλίσκεσθαι ἐν τῷ Ἰβηρικῷ καὶ Τυρρηνικῷ πελάγει· κἀντεῦθεν κατὰ τὴν ἄλλην θάλασσαν διασκίδνασθαι.

might capture them within the Iberian brine[a]; next by the mouth of the Rhone the Celts and the ancient inhabitants of Phocaea[b] hunt them; and thirdly those who are dwellers in the Trinacrian isle[c] and by the waves of the Tyrrhenian sea. Thence in the unmeasured deeps they scatter[d] this way or that and travel over all the sea. Abundant and wondrous is the spoil for fishermen when the host of Tunnies set forth in spring. First of all the fishers mark a place in the sea which is neither too straitened under beetling banks nor too open to the winds, but has due measure of open sky and shady coverts. There first a skilful Tunny-watcher[e] ascends a steep high hill,[f] who remarks the various shoals, their kind and size,[g] and informs[h] his comrades.

[e] Analogous to the "Hooer" in the Cornish Pilchard fishing: A. 537 a 19 *πολλάκις δὲ καὶ οἱ θυννοσκόποι περιβάλλονται καθεύδοντας*; Theocr. iii. 25 f. *ἐς κύματα τηνῶ ἁλεῦμαι | ὧπερ τὼς θύννως σκοπιάζεται Ὄλπις ὁ γριπεύς*. Hence metaphorically Aristoph. *Eq.* 312 f. *ὅστις* [*i.e.* Cleon] *ἡμῶν τὰς Ἀθήνας ἐκκεκώφωκας βοῶν, | κἀπὸ τῶν πετρῶν ἄνωθεν τοὺς φόρους θυννοσκοπῶν*. *Cf.* Suid. *s.v.* Alciphr. i. 20 *ὁ σκοπιωρός* in same sense.

[f] The outlook, *θυννοσκοπεῖον*, Strabo 223; 225; 834, etc., was sometimes a high mast (Varr. *ap.* Non. i. p. 49; *cf.* Philostr. *Imag.* i. 13 *σκοπιωρεῖται γάρ τις ἀφ' ὑψηλοῦ ξύλου*), sometimes a more elaborate platform (Ael. xv. 5).

[g] According to Plut. *Mor.* 980 A he was helped in his computation by the cubical formation of the shoal: *ὁ γοῦν θυννοσκόπος, ἂν ἀκριβῶς λάβῃ τὸν ἀριθμὸν τῆς ἐπιφανείας, εὐθὺς ἀποφαίνεται πόσον καὶ ἅπαν τὸ πλῆθός ἐστιν, εἰδὼς ὅτι καὶ τὸ βάθος αὐτῶν ἐν ἴσῳ τεταγμένον στοιχείῳ πρός τε τὸ πλάτος ἐστὶ καὶ τὸ μῆκος.*

[h] Philostr. *Imag.* *l.c.* *κἂν ἐμβάλλοντας τοὺς ἰχθῦς ἴδῃ, βοῆς τε ὡς μεγίστης* [hence the point of *βοῶν* in Aristoph. *Eq.* 312 quoted on 638 above] *δεῖ αὐτῷ πρὸς τοὺς ἐν τοῖς ἀκατίοις καὶ τὸν ἀριθμὸν λέγει καὶ τὰς μυριάδας αὐτῶν*; Ael. xv. 5 *ὁ σκοπὸς ἰδὼν . . . λέγει μὲν τοῖς θηραταῖς ὁπόθεν ἀφικνοῦνται· . . . ἐρεῖ γε μὴν πολλάκις καὶ τὸν πάντα ἀριθμόν.*

πιφαύσκει δ' ἑτάροισι· τὰ δ' αὐτίκα δίκτυα πάντα
ὥστε πόλις προβέβηκεν ἐν οἴδμασιν· ἐν δὲ πυλωροὶ
δικτύῳ, ἐν δὲ πύλαι, μύχατοί τ' αὐλῶνες ἔασιν.
οἱ δὲ θοῶς σεύονται ἐπὶ στίχας, ὥστε φάλαγγες
ἀνδρῶν ἐρχομένων καταφυλαδόν· οἱ μὲν ἔασιν
ὁπλότεροι, τοὶ δ' εἰσὶ γεραίτεροι, οἱ δ' ἐνὶ μέσσῃ
ὥρῃ· ἀπειρέσιοι δὲ λίνων ἔντοσθε ῥέουσιν,
εἰσόκεν ἱμείρωσι καὶ ἀγρομένους ἀνέληται
δίκτυον· ἀφνειὴ δὲ καὶ ἔξοχος ἵσταται ἄγρη.

---

[a] The comparison is easily understood when one reads the account in Ael. xv. 5 ὁ τὴν σκοπιὰν φυλάττων μάλα ὀξὺ ἐκβοήσας λέγει διώκειν ἐκεῖθι καὶ τοῦ πελάγους ἐρέττειν εὐθύ. οἱ δὲ ἐξαρτήσαντες ἐλάτης τῶν τὸν σκοπὸν ἀνεχουσῶν τῆς ἑτέρας [*i.e.* one of the two πρέμνα ἐλάτης ὑψηλά which support the platform of the θυννοσκοπεῖον] σχοῖνον εὖ μάλα μακρὰν τῶν δικτύων ἐχομένην, εἶτα ἐπαλλήλοις ταῖς ναυσὶν ἐρέττουσι κατὰ στοῖχον ἔχονταί τε ἀλλήλων, ἐπεί τοι καὶ τὸ δίκτυον ἐφ' ἑκάστῃ διῄρηται, καὶ ἥ γε πρώτη τὴν ἑαυτῆς ἐκβαλοῦσα μοῖραν τοῦ δικτύου ἀναχωρεῖ, εἶτα ἡ δευτέρα δρᾷ τοῦτο, καὶ ἡ τρίτη, καὶ δεῖ καθεῖναι τὴν τετάρτην, οἱ δὲ τὴν πέμπτην ἐρέττοντες ἔτι μέλλουσι, τοὺς δὲ ἐπὶ ταύτῃ οὐ χρὴ καθεῖναί πω· εἶτα ἐρέττουσιν ἄλλοι ἄλλῃ καὶ ἄγουσι τοῦ δικτύου τὴν μοῖραν, εἶτα ἡσυχάζουσι. *Cf.* Apost. p. 31 "Au mois de mai plus de 20 bateaux de Spetzia, quelques-uns de Skiathos se livrent . . . à la pêche des thons. Quand l'arrivée des thons dans les parages de ces îles est annoncée, les pêcheurs font leurs préparatifs de

Then straightway all the nets are set forth in the waves like a city,[a] and the net has its gate-warders and gates withal and inner courts. And swiftly the Tunnies speed on in line,[b] like ranks of men marching tribe by tribe—these younger, those older, those in the mid season of their age. Without end they pour within the nets, so long as they desire and as the net can receive the throng of them ; and rich and excellent is the spoil.[c]

campagne. Tous les bateaux . . . se placent à l'entrée du golfe d'Argolide, que les poissons traversent toujours pour pénétrer dans l'intérieur de ce golfe ; les pêcheurs approchent de la côte, y jettent l'une des extrémités du filet, et, en avançant vers le large, ils y jettent le reste. Cela fait, ils enfoncent dans l'eau une poutre et y laissent un gardien [the *θυννοσκόπος*]. Le bateau revient à terre en décrivant une courbe et traînant après lui une corde, avec laquelle, en tirant l'extrémité placée du côté de la mer, ils font décrire au filet une ligne circulaire. Aussitôt que le gardien annonce, par des signaux, à ses camarades qu'un nombre assez considérable de thons se trouve à leur portée, ceux-ci tirent de la terre le filet où ils englobent les poissons."

[b] Philostr. *Imag. l.c.* νέουσι δὲ οἷον στρατιωτῶν φάλαγξ ἐπὶ ὀκτὼ καὶ ἐφ' ἑκκαίδεκα καὶ δὶς τόσοι, . . . ἄλλος ἄλλῳ ἐπινέοντες, τοσοῦτον βάθος ὅσον αὐτῶν τὸ εὖρος.

[c] Philostr. *Imag. l.c.* οἱ δὲ ἀποφράξαντες αὐτοὺς βαθεῖ καὶ κλειστῷ δικτύῳ δέχονται λαμπρὰν ἄγραν.

ΑΛΙΕΥΤΙΚΩΝ ΤΟ Δ

Ἄλλους δ᾽ ἀγρευτῆρσιν ὑπήγαγε ληΐδα θήρης
ὑγρὸς ἔρως· ὀλοῶν δὲ γάμων, ὀλοῆς τ᾽ Ἀφροδίτης
ἠντίασαν, σπεύδοντες ἑὴν φιλοτήσιον ἄτην.
ἀλλὰ σύ μοι, κάρτιστε πολισσούχων βασιλήων,
αὐτός τ᾽, Ἀντωνῖνε, καὶ υἱέος ἠγάθεον κῆρ,
πρόφρονες εἰσαΐοιτε καὶ εἰναλίῃσι γάνυσθε
τερπωλαῖς, οἵῃσιν ἐμὸν νόον ἠπιόδωροι
Μοῦσαι κοσμήσαντο καὶ ἐξέστεψαν ἀοιδῆς
δώρῳ θεσπεσίῳ καί μοι πόρον ὑμετέροισι
κίρνασθαι γλυκὺ νᾶμα καὶ οὔασι καὶ πραπίδεσσι.
Σχέτλι᾽ Ἔρως, δολομῆτα, θεῶν κάλλιστε μὲν ὄσσοις
εἰσιδέειν, ἄλγιστε δ᾽ ὅτε κραδίην ὀροθύνεις,
ἐμπίπτων ἀδόκητος, ὑπὸ φρένα δ᾽ ὥστε θύελλα
μίσγεαι, ἀσθμαίνεις δὲ πυρὸς δριμεῖαν ὁμοκλήν,
παφλάζων ὀδύνῃσι καὶ ἀκρήτοισιν ἀνίαις·
δάκρυ δέ σοι προβαλεῖν λαρὸν γάνος ἠδ᾽ ἐσακοῦσαι
βυσσόθεν οἰμωγὴν σπλάγχνοις θ᾽ ὑπὸ θερμὸν ἔρευθος
φοινίξαι χρωτός τε παράτροπον ἄνθος ἀμέρσαι
ὄσσε τε κοιλῆναι παρά τε φρένα πᾶσαν ἀεῖραι
μαινομένην· πολλοὺς δὲ καὶ ἐς μόρον ἐξεκύλισας,
ὅσσοις χειμέριός τε καὶ ἄγριος ἀντεβόλησας
λύσσαν ἄγων· τοίαις γὰρ ἀγάλλεαι εἰλαπίνῃσιν.

---

[a] Introd. p. xx.

[b] So, in the famous address to Eros, Soph. *Antig.* 790 ὁ δ᾽ ἔχων μέμηνεν.

HALIEUTICA, OR FISHING

IV

OTHER fishes doth tender love make for fishermen the spoil of their chase, and fatal mating they find and fatal their passion, hastening their own ruin through desire. But do thou, I pray thee, mightiest of kings who have cities in their keeping, both thyself, O Antoninus [a] and thy son of noble heart, graciously give ear and take pleasure in these delights of the sea wherewith the kindly Muses have furnished forth my mind and have crowned me with the gift divine of song and given me to mix a sweet draught for your ears and for your mind.

O cruel Love, crafty of counsel, of all gods fairest to behold with the eyes, of all most grievous when thou dost vex the heart with unforeseen assault, entering the soul like a storm-wind and breathing the bitter menace of fire, with hurricane of anguish and untempered pain. The shedding of tears is for thee a sweet delight and to hear the deep-wrung groan; to inflame a burning redness in the heart and to blight and wither the bloom upon the cheek, to make the eyes hollow and to wrest all the mind to madness.[b] Many thou dost even roll to doom, even those whom thou meetest in wild and wintry sort, fraught with frenzy; for in such festivals is thy

εἴτ᾽ οὖν ἐν μακάρεσσι παλαίτατος ἐσσὶ γενέθλῃ,
ἐκ Χάεος δ᾽ ἀνέτειλας ἀμειδέος, ὀξέϊ πυρσῷ
λαμπόμενος, πρῶτος δὲ γάμων ἐζεύξαο θεσμούς,
πρῶτος δ᾽ εὐναίοις ἀρότοις ἐπεθήκαο τέκμωρ·
εἴτε σε καὶ πτερύγεσσιν ἀειρόμενον θεὸν ὄρνιν
τίκτε Πάφου μεδέουσα πολυφράδμων Ἀφροδίτη,
εὐμενέοις, πρηΰς τε καὶ εὔδιος ἄμμιν ἱκάνοις
μέτρον ἄγων· οὐ γάρ τις ἀναίνεται ἔργον ἔρωτος.
πάντῃ μὲν κρατέεις, πάντῃ δέ σε καὶ ποθέουσι
καὶ μέγα πεφρίκασιν· ὁ δ᾽ ὄλβιος, ὅστις ἔρωτα
εὐκραῆ κομέει τε καὶ ἐν στέρνοισι φυλάσσει·
σοὶ δ᾽ οὔτ᾽ οὐρανίης γενεῆς ἅλις οὔτε τι φύτλης
ἀνδρομέης· οὐ θῆρας ἀναίνεαι οὐδ᾽ ὅσα βόσκει
ἀὴρ ἀτρύγετος, νεάτης δ᾽ ὑπὸ κεύθεσι λίμνης
δύνεις, ὁπλίζῃ δὲ καὶ ἐν νεπόδεσσι κελαινοὺς
ἀτράκτους, ὡς μή τι τεῆς ἀδίδακτον ἀνάγκης
λείπηται, μηδ᾽ ὅστις ὑπόβρυχα νήχεται ἰχθύς.
Οἵην μὲν φιλότητα μετ᾽ ἀλλήλοισι ῥύονται
καὶ πόθον ὀξυβελῆ στικτοὶ σκάροι, οὐδ᾽ ἐνὶ μόχθοις
ἀλλήλους λείπουσιν, ἀλεξητῆρι δὲ θυμῷ
πολλάκι μὲν πληγέντος ὑπ᾽ ἀγκίστροιο δαφοινοῦ

[a] Hesiod, *Th.* 116 ff. *ἤτοι μὲν πρώτιστα Χάος γένετ᾽, αὐτὰρ ἔπειτα | Γαῖ᾽ εὐρύστερνος, πάντων ἕδος ἀσφαλὲς αἰεὶ | ἀθανάτων, οἳ ἔχουσι κάρη νιφόεντος Ὀλύμπου, Τάρταρά τ᾽ ἠερόεντα μυχῷ χθονὸς εὐρυοδείης, | ἠδ᾽ Ἔρος, ὃς κάλλιστος ἐν ἀθανάτοισι θεοῖσι, | λυσιμελής, πάντων δὲ θεῶν πάντων τ᾽ ἀνθρώπων | δάμναται ἐν στήθεσσι νόον καὶ ἐπίφρονα βουλήν*; Aristoph. *Av.* 693 ff. *Χάος ἦν καὶ Νύξ, Ἔρεβός τε μέλαν πρῶτον καὶ Τάρταρος εὐρύς· | γῆ δ᾽ οὐδ᾽ ἀὴρ οὐδ᾽ οὐρανὸς ἦν· Ἐρέβους δ᾽ ἐν ἀπείροσι κόλποις | τίκτει πρώτιστον ὑπηνέμιον Νὺξ ἡ μελανόπτερος ᾠόν, | ἐξ οὗ περιτελλομέναις ὥραις ἔβλαστεν Ἔρως ὁ ποθεινός, | στίλβων νῶτον*

delight. Whether then thou art the eldest-born[a] among the blessed gods and from unsmiling Chaos didst arise with fierce and flaming torch and didst first establish the ordinances of wedded love and order the rites of the marriage-bed; or whether Aphrodite of many counsels, queen of Paphos,[b] bare thee a winged god on soaring pinions, be thou gracious and to us come gentle and with fair weather and in tempered measure; for none refuses the work of Love. Everywhere thou bearest sway and everywhere thou art desired at once and greatly feared; and happy is he who cherishes and guards in his breast a temperate Love. Nor doth the race of Heaven suffice thee nor the breed of men[c]; thou rejectest not the wild beasts nor all the brood of the barren air; under the coverts of the nether deep dost thou descend and even among the finny tribes thou dost array thy darkling shafts; that naught may be left ignorant of thy compelling power, not even the fish that swims beneath the waters.

Behold what love for one another and keen desire do the spotted Parrot-wrasses[d] entertain and in trouble forsake not one another but in a spirit of helpfulness, many a time, when one Parrot-wrasse is struck by the deadly hook, another rushes to his

πτερύγοιν χρυσαῖν, εἰκὼς ἀνεμώκεσι δίναις. *Cf.* Plato, *Symp.* 178 A, Xen. *Symp.* 8. 1. Otherwise Eros is son of Aphrodite and Ares: Simonid. *fr.* 72 σχέτλιε παῖ δολόμηδες Ἀφροδίτας, | τὸν Ἄρει κακομαχάνῳ τέκεν.

[b] In Cyprus.

[c] Soph. *Antig.* 785 φοιτᾷς δ' ὑπερπόντιος ἔν τ' ἀγρονόμοις αὐλαῖς· | καί σ' οὔτ' ἀθανάτων φύξιμος οὐδεὶς | οὔθ' ἁμερίων ἐπ' ἀνθρώπων. *Cf.* Soph. *fr.* 856 εἰσέρχεται μὲν ἰχθύων πλωτῷ γένει, | ἔνεστι δ' ἐν χέρσου τετρασκελεῖ γονῇ; Lucret. i. 1-23.

[d] *H.* i. 134 n.

ἄλλος ἐπαΐξας πρόμαχος σκάρος ἰχθὺς ὀδοῦσιν
ὁρμιὴν ἀπέκερσε καὶ ἐξεσάωσεν ἑταῖρον
καὶ δόλον ἠμάλθυνε καὶ ἀσπαλιῆ' ἀκάχησεν.
ἤδη δ' ἐν κύρτοισι παλιμπλεκέεσσιν ἁλόντα
ἄλλος ὑπεξέκλεψε καὶ ἐξείρυσσεν ὀλέθρου·
εὖτε γὰρ ἐς κύρτοιο πέσῃ λόχον αἰόλος ἰχθύς,
αὐτίκ' ἐπεφράσθη τε καὶ ἐκδῦναι κακότητος
πειρᾶται, τρέψας δὲ κάτω κεφαλήν τε καὶ ὄσσε
ἔμπαλιν εἰς οὐρὴν ἀνανήχεται ἕρκος ἀμείβων·
ταρβεῖ γὰρ σχοίνους ταναηκέας, αἳ πυλεῶνι
ἀμφιπεριφρίσσουσι καὶ οὐτάζουσιν ὀπωπὰς
ἀντίον ἐρχομένοιο, φυλακτήρεσσιν ὁμοῖαι.
οἱ δέ μιν εἰσορόωντες ἀμήχανα δινεύοντα
ἔκτοθεν ἀντιόωσιν ἀρηγόνες, οὐδ' ἐλίποντο
τειρόμενον· καί πού τις ἑὴν ὤρεξε διασχὼν
οὐρὴν ἠΰτε χεῖρα λαβεῖν ἔντοσθεν ἑταίρῳ·
αὐτὰρ ὀδὰξ μὲν ἔρεισεν, ὁ δ' ἔσπασεν ἄϊδος ἔξω
οὐρὴν ἡγήτειραν ὑπὸ στόμα δεσμὸν ἔχοντα.
πολλάκι δὲ προβαλόντος ἑὴν ἔντοσθεν ἁλόντος
οὐρὴν ἄλλος ἔμαρψε καὶ ἐξείρυσσε θύραζε
ἑσπόμενον· τοιοῖσδε νοήμασι πότμον ἄλυξαν.
ὡς δ' ὅτε παιπαλόεσσαν ἀναστείχωσι κολώνην
φῶτες ὑπὸ σκιερῆς νυκτὸς κνέφας, ἡνίκα μήνη
κέκρυπται, νεφέων δὲ κελαινιόωσι καλύπτραι,

---

[a] Plut. *Mor*. 977 c ἄλλα δ' ἐπιδείκνυται μετὰ τοῦ συνετοῦ τὸ κοινωνικὸν καὶ φιλάλληλον, ὥσπερ ἀνθίαι καὶ σκάροι. σκάρου μὲν γὰρ ἄγκιστρον καταπιόντος οἱ παρόντες σκάροι προσαλλόμενοι τὴν ὁρμιὰν ἀποτρώγουσιν; Ael. i. 4 οἱ σκάροι δὲ εἰς τὴν οἰκείαν ἀγέλην εἰσὶν ἀγαθοὶ τιμωροί· προίασι γοῦν καὶ τὴν ὁρμιὰν ἀποτραγεῖν σπεύδουσιν, ἵνα σώσωσι τὸν ᾑρημένον. *Cf*. Phil. 88. 11.

[b] Plut. *Mor*. 977 c οὗτοι δὲ καὶ τοῖς εἰς κύρτον ἐμπεσοῦσι τὰς οὐρὰς παραδόντες ἔξωθεν ἕλκουσι δάκνοντας προθύμως καὶ συνεξ-

defence and cutting through the line with his teeth[a] rescues his comrade and destroys the snare and grieves the fisherman. And ere now, when a Parrot-wrasse has been taken in the plaited weel,[b] another has stolen him away and saved him from destruction. For when the dappled fish falls into the ambush of the weel, immediately he perceives it and tries to escape from his evil plight. Turning down his head and eyes he swims back tailwards along the barrier, for he dreads the sharp rushes which bristle around the entrance and as he comes against them wound his eyes, even as if they were warders of the gate. The others, seeing him wheeling about helplessly, come from the outside to his aid and leave him not in his distress. And someone of them, I ween, reaches his tail through the weel like a hand for his comrade inside to grasp; and he seizes it in his teeth and the other pulls him forth from death, while he holds in his mouth the guiding tail as a chain. Often too the fish that is caught in the weel puts forth his own tail and another grasps it and pulls him forth in its train. By such devices do they escape doom. As when under the darkness of shadowy night men climb a rugged hill, when the moon is hidden and the curtains of the clouds are

ἄγουσιν; Ael. i. 4 ἤδη δὲ καὶ εἰς τὸν κύρτον τὸν σκάρον ἐμπεσεῖν φασιν καὶ τὸ οὐραῖον μέρος ἐκβαλεῖν, τοὺς δὲ ἀθηράτους καὶ περινέοντας ἐνδακεῖν καὶ εἰς τὸ ἔξω τὸν ἑταῖρον προαγαγεῖν. εἰ δὲ ἔξίοι κατὰ τὸ στόμα τῶν τις ἔξω τὴν οὐρὰν παρώρεξεν, ὁ δὲ περιχανὼν ἠκολούθησεν; Ov. *Hal.* 9 sic et scarus arte sub undis | Incidit adsumptamque dolo tandem pavet escam. | Non audet radiis obnixa occurrere fronte, | Aversus crebro vimen sed verbere caudae | Laxans subsequitur tutumque evadit in aequor. | Quin etiam si forte aliquis dum pone nataret, | Mitis luctantem scarus hunc in vimine vidit, | Aversam caudam morsu tenet.

οἱ δ' ὄρφνῃ μογέουσι καὶ ἀτρίπτοισι κελεύθοις
πλαζόμενοι, χεῖράς τε μετ' ἀλλήλοισιν ἔχουσιν,
ἑλκόμενοί θ' ἕλκουσι, πόνων ἐπίκουρον ἀμοιβήν·
ὣς οἵ γ' ἀλλήλοισιν ἀμοιβαίῃ φιλότητι
ἀλκτῆρες γεγάασι· τὸ δέ σφισι μήσατ' ὄλεθρον
δειλαίοις, ὀλοοῦ δὲ καὶ ἀλγινόεντος ἔρωτος
ἠντίασαν, βλαφθέντες ἐπιφροσύναις ἁλιήων.
τέσσαρες ἐμβεβάασι θοὸν σκάφος ἀγρευτῆρες,
τῶν ἤτοι δοιοὶ μὲν ἐπηρέτμοισι πόνοισι
μέμβλονται, τρίτατος δὲ δολόφρονα μῆτιν ὑφαίνει.
θῆλυν ἀναψάμενος σύρει σκάρον ἀκροτάτοιο
χείλεος ἐν δίνῃσι λινοζεύκτῳ ὑπὸ δεσμῷ·
ζωὴν μὲν κέρδιστον ἀνελκέμεν· ἢν δὲ θάνῃσι,
δελφῖνος μολίβοιο μετὰ στόμα δέξατο τέχνην.
μηρίνθου δ' ἑτέρωθεν ἐλήλαται ἄλλος ὄπισθεν
δινωτὸς μολίβοιο βαρὺς κύβος ἅμματος ἄκρου·
καί ῥ' ἡ μὲν ζωῇ ἐναλίγκιος ἐν ῥοθίοισιν
ἑλκομένη θήλεια τιταίνεται ἐξ ἁλιῆος.
τέτρατος αὖ κύρτοιο βαθὺν δόλον ἀντίον ἕλκει
ἐγγύθεν· οἱ δ' ὁρόωντες ἀολλέες ἰθὺς ἵενται
κραιπνὸν ἐπειγόμενοι βαλιοὶ σκάροι, ὄφρα ῥύωνται
ἑλκομένην, ἀπάτην δὲ περιπροθέουσιν ἁπάντῃ,
οἴστρῳ θηλυμανεῖ βεβιημένοι· οἱ δ' ἐλάτῃσι
νῆα κατασπέρχουσιν ὅσον σθένος· οἱ δ' ἐφέπονται
ἐσσυμένως· τάχα δέ σφι πανύστατος ἔπλετ' ἀρωγή.

---

[a] *Cf.* Polyb. v. 104, Diod. xvii. 55.

[b] Ael. i. 2 λαγνίστατος δ' ἄρα ἰχθύων ἁπάντων ἦν (ὁ σκάρος) καὶ ἥ γε πρὸς τὸ θῆλυ ἀκόρεστος ἐπιθυμία αὐτῷ ἁλώσεως αἰτία γίνεται. *Cf.* Phil. 88.

[c] This method is still in use: "La pêche du scare, dans certaines îles des Cyclades, telles que Amorgos, Pholégandre, etc. dans les parages desquels sont confinés ces poissons, se fait absolument de la même manière aujourd'hui. Ainsi on tâche, avant tout, de pêcher une femelle du scare. Cela fait,

dark: they labour sorely, wandering in gloom and untrodden ways, and hold each the other's hands[a] and pull and are pulled, a helpful exchange of toil; even so those fishes help each other in mutual love. But just this devises destruction[b] for the poor fishes and fatal and sorrowful they find their love when they are destroyed by the craft of fishermen. Four fishers embark on a swift boat, of whom two attend to the labour of the oar while the third weaves a crafty device. Fastening a female[c] Parrot-wrasse by the tip of the mouth he drags it along in the waves by a flaxen cord. A live fish it is best to tow: but if she be dead, then she receives in her mouth the contrivance of a leaden dolphin.[d] On the other side of the line another rounded heavy cube of lead is hung at the end of the cord. The dead female trailing in the waves like a living fish is haled along by the fisherman. A fourth fisher tows near at hand a deep ensnaring weel facing towards the fish. The spotted Parrot-wrasses when they see the trailing female rush all together in eager haste to rescue her and throng all about the decoy, impelled by the goad of frenzied desire. The men with their oars urge on the boat with all their might, while the fishes follow eagerly: and soon it proves their last attempt to

on l'attache, en lui perçant l'extrémité du museau, avec une ligne portée par un long bâton que l'on traîne sur l'eau, en procédant d'après la même manière décrite par Oppien" (Apost. p. 45).

[d] A dolphin-shaped piece of lead. This use of the word is best known in connexion with warships: Thuc. vii. 41 *αἱ κεραῖαι . . . αἱ ἀπὸ τῶν ὁλκάδων δελφινοφόροι*; Pherecr. *Ἄγριοι* *fr.* 12 *ὅδε δὴ δελφίς ἐστι μολυβδοῦς δελφινοφόρος τε κεροῦχος*; Aristoph. *Eq.* 762 *τοὺς δελφῖνας μετεωρίζου*; Suid. *s.* *δελφίς· . . . σιδηροῦν κατασκεύασμα ἢ μολύβδινον εἰς δελφῖνα ἐσχηματισμένον.* *Cf.* Hesych. *s.* *δελφῖνες*; Poll. i. 85.

εὖτε γὰρ ἀγρομένους τε καὶ ἄσχετα μαιμώοντας
θηλείης ἐπὶ λύσσαν ἴδῃ νόος ἀσπαλιῆος,
ἐν κύρτῳ κατέθηκεν ὁμοῦ λίνον ἠδὲ μόλιβδον,
ὃς σκάρον ἐμβαρύθων εἴσω σπάσεν· οἱ δ᾽ ἄρ᾽ ὁμαρτῇ,
ὡς ἴδον, ὡς ἐκέχυντο παραφθαδόν, Ἄϊδος ἕρκος
πλεκτὸν ἐπισπεύδοντες, ἐπειγομένοις δὲ λόχοισι
στείνονται προβολαί τε λύγων καὶ χάσμα πυλάων
ἀργαλέον· τοῖοι γὰρ ἐπισπέρχουσι μύωπες.
ὡς δὲ ποδωκείης μεμελημένοι ἄνδρες ἀέθλων,
στάθμης ὁρμηθέντες ἀπόσσυτοι, ὠκέα γυῖα
προπροτιταινόμενοι, δολιχὸν τέλος ἐγκονέουσιν
ἐξανύσαι· πᾶσιν δὲ πόθος νύσσῃ τε πελάσσαι
νίκης τε γλυκύδωρον ἑλεῖν κράτος ἔς τε θύρετρα
ἀΐξαι καὶ κάρτος ἀέθλιον ἀμφιβαλέσθαι·
τόσσος ἔρως καὶ τοῖσιν ἐς Ἄϊδος ἡγεμονεύει
ἐσθορέειν κευθμῶνας ἀνοστήτοιο λόχοιο.
κύντατα δ᾽ ἐς φιλότητα καὶ ὕστατον οἶστρον ἔχοντες
αὐτόμολοι πιμπλᾶσιν ἐφίμερον ἀνδράσιν ἄγρην.
Ἄλλοι δ᾽ αὖ θήλειαν ἔσω κύρτοιο κελαινοῦ
ζωὴν ἐγκαθιέντες ὑπὸ σπιλάδεσσι τίθενται
κείναις, ᾗσι μέλει γλαγόεις σκάρος· οἱ δ᾽ ὑπ᾽ ἔρωτος
αὔρῃ θελγόμενοι φιλοτησίῃ ἀμφαγέρονται,
ἀμφί τε λιχμάζουσι καὶ ἐξερέουσιν ἁπάντῃ
μαιόμενοι κύρτοιο κατήλυσιν· αἶψα δ᾽ ἵκοντο
εἰσίθμην εὐρεῖαν ἀνέκβατον ἕρκος ἔχουσαν,
ἐς δ᾽ ἔπεσον ἅμα πάντες ὁμιλαδόν, οὐδέ τι μῆχος
ἐκδῦναι, στυγερὴν δὲ πόθων εὕροντο τελευτήν.
ὡς δέ τις οἰωνοῖσι μόρον δολόεντα φυτεύων

---

[a] Schol. θύρετρα· τέλη. *Cf.* Poll. iii. 147 ἵνα δὲ παύονται, τέλος καὶ τέρμα καὶ βατήρ. θύρετρα in this sense seems unique. But it is exactly paralleled by the use of *fores* of the doors of the *carcer* or *carceres* at the end (usually starting end) of the

aid. For when the wit of the fisher perceives them thronging and raging incontinently in their lust after the female, he puts in the weel line and lead together and the weight of the lead pulls the female Parrot-wrasse within. Then the males together, soon as they see it, so soon they rush in emulous haste, speeding to the plaited net of death and with their eager troops the withy vestibule and grievous mouth of the gates are straitened: such goads of passion urge them on. As men who engage in the contest of the footrace dart swiftly from the line and forward and ever forward strain their speedy limbs and haste to accomplish the long course; and the desire of every man is to reach the goal and to win the sweet triumph of victory and dash within the lists [a] and crown them with the athletic prize: even so doth like passion lead those fishes to the house of Hades—to rush within the coverts of an ambush whence there is no return. And, with their fatal and final madness of desire, of their own motion they fulfil the fishermen's desire of spoil.

Others again put a living female within the dark weel and place it under those rocks which the milky Parrot-wrasse affects. Beguiled by the amorous breath of love the Wrasses gather around and lick about and search everywhere to find the entrance of the weel. And speedily they come upon the entry—wide, but with a fence beyond escape—and they rush in altogether in a crowd and there is no means of getting out, but they find a hateful issue to their desires. Even as one who devises a

racecourse: Lucan, i. 293 quantum clamore iuvatur | Eleus sonipes, quamvis iam carcere clauso | immineat foribus pronusque repagula laxet.

θήλειαν θάμνοισι κατακρύπτει λασίοισιν
ὄρνιν, ὁμογλώσσοιο συνέμπορον ἠθάδα θήρης·
ἡ δὲ λίγα κλάζει ξουθὸν μέλος, οἱ δ' ἀΐοντες
πάντες ἐπισπέρχουσι, καὶ ἐς βρόχον αὐτοὶ ἵενται,
θηλυτέρης ἐνοπῇσι παραπλαγχθέντες ἰωῆς·
τοῖς κεῖνοι κύρτοιο πέσον λαγόνεσσιν ὁμοῖοι.
Τοίην δ' αὖ κεφάλοισιν ἔρως περιβάλλεται ἄτην·
καὶ γὰρ τοὺς θήλεια παρήπαφεν ἐν ῥοθίοισιν
ἑλκομένη· θαλερὴ δὲ πέλοι λιπόωσά τε γυῖα·
ὧδε γὰρ εἰσορόωντες ἀπείρονες ἀμφαγέρονται·
κάλλεϊ δ' ἐκπάγλως βεβιημένοι οὐκ ἐθέλουσι
λείπεσθαι, πάντῃ δὲ πόθων ἴϋγγες ἄγουσι
θαλπομένους, εἰ καί σφιν ἀνάρσιον ἡγεμονεύοις
χέρσον ὑπεξερύων θῆλυν δόλον· οἱ δ' ἐφέπονται
ἀθρόοι, οὔτε δόλων μεμνημένοι οὔθ' ἁλιήων·
ἀλλ' ὥστ' ἠΐθεοι περικαλλέος ὄμμα γυναικὸς
φρασσάμενοι πρῶτον μὲν ἀποσταδὸν αὐγάζονται,
εἶδος ἀγαιόμενοι πολυήρατον, ἄγχι δ' ἔπειτα

---

[a] The decoy bird, παλεύτρια A. 613 a 23 and 28, Introd. p. xxxiv, *avis illex* (*cf.* Plaut. *Asin.* i. 3. 66 aedis nobis areast, auceps sum ego, | Escast meretrix, lectus inlex est, amatores aves); σύμφυλος ὄρνις Dion. *De av.* iii. 4; χειροήθεις ὄρνιθες *ib.* iii. 1. *Cf.* iii. 9; Mart. xiv. 216 (on a Hawk captured and trained as a decoy); Praedo fuit volucrum; famulus nunc aucupis idem | Decipit et captas non sibi maeret aves; Pallad. x. 12 noctuae ceteraque instrumenta capturae.

[b] ξουθός, when used of colour, is pretty nearly = ξανθός: when it is used of sound, it is not possible to give more than an approximate rendering.

[c] *H.* ii. 462 n.

[d] A. 541 a 19 περὶ δὲ τὴν Φοινίκην καὶ θήραν ποιοῦνται δι' ἀλλήλων· ἄρρενας μὲν γὰρ ὑπάγοντες κεστρέας τὰς θηλείας περιβάλλονται συνάγοντες, θηλείας δὲ τοὺς ἄρρενας; Plin. ix. 59 isdem (mugilibus) tam incauta salacitas ut in Phoenice et in Narbonensi provincia coitus tempore e vivariis marem

guileful doom for birds hides in a dense thicket a female bird,[a] his tame companion in hunting birds of the same cry; and she shrilly pipes her sweet[b] song, and the birds, hearing, all hasten towards her and rush of themselves into the snare, misled by the call of the female cry: like unto them the Parrot-wrasses rush into the belly of the weel.

A like doom does love bring upon the Grey Mullets[c] (Cephalus); for they also are beguiled by a female[d] trailed in the waves. She should be in good condition and fat of limb. For so, when they behold her, they gather around in countless numbers and wondrously overcome by her beauty they will not leave her but everywhere the spells of desire lead them charmed, yea even wert thou to draw forth the female snare from the water and lead them to the unfriendly dry land: they follow in a body, and heed neither fraud nor fishermen. But even as youths when they remark the face of a woman exceeding fair first gaze at her from afar, admiring her lovely form, and thereafter they draw near and,

linea longinqua per os ad branchias religata emissum in mare eademque linea retractum feminae sequantur ad litus rursusque feminam mares partus tempore. The method is still practised: Apost. p. 45 "Ce n'est pas le scare seulement qui se pêche ainsi, mais aussi les muges, surtout l'espèce *Capito* dans les côtes de Péloponnèse, sur les côtes du département d'Élide. . . . On opère ainsi: On tâche d'abord d'attraper soit aux filets, soit à la ligne, une femelle de muge, qu'on désigne sous le nom vulgaire de Μπάφα. On l'attache ensuite par l'opercule sur une ligne portée par un long roseau, au moyen duquel on la tire sur l'eau; les autres muges, les mâles surtout, la suivent, toujours en quantité, un second pêcheur, posté derrière celui qui traîne le poisson sur l'eau, jette sur eux son filet circulaire (πεζόβολον), épervier, . . . et en capture le plus grand nombre possible." This fishing is pursued from April to the end of June.

ἤλυθον, ἐκ δ' ἐλάθοντο καὶ οὐκέτι κεῖνα κέλευθα
ἔρχονται τὰ πάροιθεν, ἐφεσπόμενοι δὲ γάνυνται
θελγόμενοι λιαρῇσιν ὑπὸ ῥιπῆς Ἀφροδίτης·
ὣς κείνων οἰστρηδὸν ἐπόψεαι ὑγρὸν ὅμιλον
εἰλομένων· τάχα δέ σφιν ἀπεχθέες ἦλθον ἔρωτες·
αἶψα γὰρ ἀμφίβληστρον ἀνὴρ εὐεργὲς ἀείρας
κόλπον ἐπιπροέηκε καὶ ἄσπετον ἔσπασε θήρην,
ῥηϊδίως ἁψῖσι περίσχετον ἀμφικαλύψας.
Σηπίαι αὖ δυσέρωτες ἐπὶ πλέον ἔδραμον ἄτης·
οὐ γὰρ τοῖς οὐ κύρτον ὀλέθριον οὔτε λίνοιο
ἀμφιβολὰς ἐφέηκαν ἁλίστονοι ἀγρευτῆρες,
ἀλλ' αὔτως ἐρύουσιν ἀναψάμενοι μίαν οἴην
ἐν ῥοθίοις· αἱ δ' εὖτ' ἂν ἀπόπροθεν ἀθρήσωσιν,
αἶψα μάλ' ἀντιόωσι, περιπλέγδην δ' ἐνέχονται
ἐμφύμεναι σπείρῃσιν, ἅτε ξείνηθεν ἰδοῦσαι
παρθενικαὶ δηναιὸν ἀδελφεὸν ἢ γενετῆρα
ἤπιον ἐν μεγάροισιν ἀπήμονα νοστήσαντα·
ἠὲ νέον ζεύγλῃσιν ὑπ' εὐναίης Ἀφροδίτης
κούρη ληϊσθεῖσα γάμων εὐαγρέϊ δεσμῷ
νυμφίον ἀμφέπλεξεν, ἐπ' αὐχένι πάννυχα δεσμὰ
ἀργεννοῖς ἑκάτερθε βραχίοσι γυρώσασα·
ὣς τότε κερδαλέαι περὶ σηπίαι εἱλίσσονται
ἀλλήλαις· οὐδέ σφι μεθίεται ἔργον ἔρωτος,
εἰσόκεν ἐξερύσωσιν ἐπὶ σκάφος ἀσπαλιῆες·
αἱ δ' ἔτι συμπεφύασι, πόθῳ δ' ἅμα πότμον ἕλοντο.
Τὰς μὲν καὶ κύρτοισι παρήπαφον εἴαρος ὥρῃ·

[a] *H.* ii. 121 n. For the method of fishing here mentioned *cf.* Apost. p. 51 "Oppien dit que, quand on tire derrière le bateau une femelle de seiche, les mâles, en grand nombre, se mettent à la suivre. Les pêcheurs grecs modernes

forgetting all, walk no more in their former ways but follow her with delight, beguiled by the sweet spells of Aphrodite: even so shalt thou behold the humid crowd of the Mullets passionately thronging. But swiftly with them love turns to hate; for speedily the fisher lifts the well-wrought net and spreads its lap and takes spoil unspeakable, easily enveloping the fishes in the embrace of the meshes.

The Cuttle-fishes,[a] again, of unhappy passion run to a greater height of infatuation. For them neither deadly weel nor encircling net do the toilsome fishers of the sea set but merely trail in the waves a single female attached to a line. The Cuttle-fishes, when they behold it from afar, speedily come to meet it and twine about it and cling to it with their arms: even as maidens cling about brother or kindly father whom after many days they see returned safe to his own halls from a foreign land, or as a maid that is newly taken captive in the yoke of wedded love, the pleasant bond of marriage, embraces her bridegroom and all night long twines about his neck the bondage of her snowy arms: even so in that hour the crafty Cuttle-fishes twine about one another and the work of their passion abates not until the fishermen draw them forth upon the boat. And still they cling and with desire take death.

The Cuttle-fishes, indeed, men also beguile with weels in the spring season. The weels they cover

emploient souvent le même procédé mais quelquefois ils remplacent la femelle, que l'on a peine à se procurer, par un mannequin de seiche, si je puis m'exprimer ainsi, appareil en bois ayant la forme d'une seiche. Sur sa partie convexe sont incrustés des morceaux de miroir. On tire cette seiche en bois, nommée ξυλόσουπια, σπιγιάλλι, derrière le bateau. Les poissons qui la suivent se pêchent au haveneau."

κύρτους γὰρ σκιάσαντες ὑπὸ πτόρθοισι μυρίκης
ἢ κομάρου πετάλοισι τεθηλόσιν ἠὲ καὶ ἄλλῃ
λάχνῃ, ἐπ' ἠϊόνεσσι πολυψαμάθοισιν ἔθηκαν·
αἱ δ' ἅμα μὲν γενεῆς κεχρημέναι ἠδὲ καὶ εὐνῆς
κύρτον ἔσω σπεύδουσι καὶ ἥμεναι ἐν πετάλοισιν
αὐτοῦ μὲν παύσαντο πόθου, παύσαντο δὲ δειλῆς
ζωῆς, ἀγρευτῆρσιν ἀνελκόμεναι πινυτοῖσιν.
Ἔξοχα δ' ἐκ πάντων νεπόδων ἀλγεινὸν ἔρωτα
κόσσυφος ἀθλεύει, κίχλης δ' ἐπιδαίεται ἦτορ,
οἴστρῳ τε ζήλῳ τε, βαρύφρονι δαίμονι, θύων.
κοσσύφῳ οὔτ' εὐνὴ μία σύννομος, οὐ δάμαρ οἴη,
οὐ θάλαμος, πολλαὶ δ' ἄλοχοι, πολλαὶ δὲ χαράδραι
κεκριμέναι κεύθουσιν ἐφέστια λέκτρα γυναικῶν·
τῇσιν ἀεὶ πᾶν ἦμαρ ὑπὸ γλαφυροῖσι μυχοῖσι
κίχλαι ναιετάουσιν, ἀλίγκιαι ἀρτιγάμοισι
νύμφαις, ἃς οὐκ ἄν τις ἴδοι θαλάμοιο πάροιθεν
ἐρχομένας· ἐν δέ σφι γαμήλιος αἴθεται αἰδώς·
ὣς αἵ γ' ἐνδόμυχοι θαλάμων ἔντοσθεν ἑκάστη
αἰεὶ δηθύνουσιν, ὅπῃ πόσις αὐτὸς ἀνώγει.
κόσσυφος αὖ πέτρῃσι παρήμενος οὔποτε λείπει,
αἰὲν ἔχων φυλακὴν λεχέων ὕπερ, οὐδέ ποτ' ἄλλῃ
τέτραπται, πᾶν δ' ἦμαρ ἑλίσσεται, ἄλλοτε δ' ἄλλους

---

[a] *Tamarix tetrandra.* This and κόμαρος, *Arbutus unedo*, are mentioned among evergreens, Theophrast. *H.P.* i. 9.

[b] The κόσσυφος and the κίχλη are mostly mentioned together: A. 599 b 6 κατὰ συζυγίας δ' οἱ πετραῖοι φωλοῦσιν οἱ ἄρρενες τοῖς θήλεσιν, ὥσπερ καὶ νεοττεύουσιν, οἷον κίχλαι, κόττυφοι; 607 b 14 μεταβάλλουσι δὲ καὶ οὓς καλοῦσι κοττύφους καὶ κίχλας . . . τὸ χρῶμα κατὰ τὰς ὥρας, . . . τοῦ μὲν γὰρ ἔαρος μέλανες γίνονται, εἶτα ἐκ τοῦ ἔαρος λευκοὶ πάλιν. *Cf.* Ael. xii. 28; Diocl. *ap.* Athen. 305 b οἱ δὲ πετραῖοι καλούμενοι . . . κόσσυφοι, κίχλαι; Numen. *ibid.* μελάγχρων κόσσυφον ἢ κίχλας ἁλιειδέας; Aristot. *ibid.* τὰ μὲν μελανοστικτα, ὥσπερ κόσσυφος, τὰ δὲ ποικιλόστικτα,

with branches of tamarisk[a] or green leaves of arbutus or other foliage and place them on the sandy beaches. And the Cuttle-fishes in their desire for breeding and mating hasten within the weel and settle amid the foliage and there cease from their desire and cease also from their wretched life, being haled up by the cunning fishermen.

Beyond all the finny brood the Merle-wrasse[b] endures a sorrowful love and it is for the Thrush-wrasse that he burns his heart, raging with frenzy and with jealousy, that grievous god. The Merle has neither one marriage-bed nor one bride nor one bridal chamber, but many are his spouses and many separate clefts hide the home and bed of his wives. Therein evermore the Thrushes dwell all day in their hollow retreats, like newly wedded brides, whom one would never see coming forth from their chamber; but nuptial shame burns in their hearts; even so the Thrushes always abide retired each one within her chamber, wherever her husband himself commands. The Merle, on the other hand, sits by upon the rocks and never leaves them, ever keeping watch over his bed, and he never turns otherwhere but all day wheels about, now looking to this chamber,

ὥσπερ κίχλη. The κίχλη is mentioned separately Nicandr. *ap.* Athen. 305 d as πολυώνυμος, *cf.* Pancrat. *ibid.* 305 c; also Epicharm. *ibid.*, A. 605 a 17, 598 a 11; Plin. xxxii. 9 turdus inter saxatiles nobilis. The κόσσυφος is mentioned separately, Phil. 99; Plin. xxx. 11 merula inter saxatiles laudata; Ov. *Hal.* 114 merulaeque virentes; Ael. i. 14 and 15. They are clearly closely allied species of Wrasse (*Labridae*, M.G. πετρόψαρο, χεῖλος). In M.G. κοτσύφι is *Crenilabrus pavo*; κίχλα is *Coricus rostratus.* Oppian seems to take κόσσυφος and κίχλη to be merely the male and female of the same species, and Aelian, *ll. cc.*, in paraphrasing Oppian, mentions the κόσσυφος only.

παπταίνει θαλάμους καί οἱ νόος οὔτ᾽ ἐπὶ φορβὴν
στέλλεται οὔτε τιν᾽ ἄλλον ἔχει πόνον, ἀλλ᾽ ἐπὶ νύμφαις
μοχθίζει δύσζηλος ἀειφρούροισι πόνοισι·
νυκτὶ δέ οἱ βρώμης τε μέλει καὶ παύεται ἔργων
τυτθὸν ὅσον φυλακῆς ἀζηχέος· ἀλλ᾽ ὅτε κίχλαι
ὃν τόκον ὠδίνωσιν, ὃ δ᾽ ἄσχετα τῆμος ἀΐσσει
ἀμφιπεριτρομέων, ἐπὶ δ᾽ ἔρχεται ἄλλοτε ἄλλην
εἰς ἄλοχον, μέγα δή τι περιτρομέοντι ἐοικὼς
ὠδίνων. οἷον δὲ μετὰ φρεσὶν ἄχθος ἀλύει
μήτηρ, τηλυγέτοιο θοὴν ὠδῖνα θυγατρὸς
πρωτολεχοῦς φρίσσουσα· τὸ γὰρ μέγα δεῖμα γυναικῶν·
αὐτὴν δ᾽ οὔτι χέρειον ἱκάνεται Εἰλειθυίης
κῦμα πόνων, πάντῃ δὲ διὲκ θαλάμων δεδόνηται
εὐχομένη, στενάχουσα, μετήορον ἦτορ ἔχουσα,
εἰσόκε λυσιπόνοιο βοῆς ἔντοσθεν ἀκούσῃ·
ὣς ὁ περιτρομέων ἀλόχοις μέγα δαίεται ἦτορ.
τοῖόν που λεχέων ἀΐω νόμον ἐντύνεσθαι
Ἀσσυρίους, οἳ Τίγριν ὑπὲρ πόρον ἄστε᾽ ἔχουσι,
Βάκτρων τ᾽ ἐνναετῆρας, ἑκηβόλον ἔθνος ὀϊστῶν·
καὶ γὰρ τοῖς πλεονές τε γαμήλια λέκτρα γυναῖκες
κεκριμέναι μεθέπουσι καὶ εὐνάζονται ἅπασαι
νύκτας ἀμειβόμεναι· μετὰ δέ σφισι κέντρον ὀπηδεῖ
ζήλου ἀνιαροῖο, περὶ ζήλῳ δ᾽ ὀλέκονται,
αἰὲν ἐπ᾽ ἀλλήλοισι βαρὺν θήγοντες ἄρηα.
ὣς οὐδὲν ζήλοιο κακώτερον ἀνδράσιν ἄλγος
ἐντρέφεται, πολλοὺς δὲ γόους, πολλὰς δὲ τίθησιν
οἰμωγάς· λύσσης γὰρ ἀναιδέος ἐστὶν ἑταῖρος·
λύσσῃ δ᾽ ἀσπασίως ἐπιμίσγεται, ἐς δὲ βαρεῖαν
ἄτην ἐξεχόρευσε, τέλος δέ οἱ ἔπλετ᾽ ὄλεθρος.
ὃς καὶ τὸν δύστηνον ὑπήγαγε κόσσυφον ἄτῃ

now to that. And his mind is not set upon foraging nor has he any other business, but in unhappy jealousy keeps his tedious and eternal vigil over his brides: only at night he takes thought of food and rests for as short a space as may be from the labour of his ceaseless watch. But when the Thrushes are in the travail of birth, then incontinently he rushes fluttering around and visits now one wife, now another, as if he were greatly anxious for the issue of their travail. Even as a mother is distraught with the burden of her heart when she trembles for the sharp pain of her only daughter in travail of her first child: for that is the great dread of women: and on herself no less comes the wave of the pangs of Eileithyia,[a] and she roams everywhere throughout the halls, praying and groaning in suspense of heart, until she hears from within the cry that delivers from pain: even so the Merle, trembling for his wives, burns greatly in his heart. Such a custom methinks of marriage I hear that the Assyrians practise, who have their cities beyond the Tigris stream and the inhabitants of Bactra, a nation of archers. For them also several different wives deal with the marriage-bed and night about all share the nuptial couch. And the goad of grievous jealousy haunts them and by jealousy they perish, ever one against another whetting bitter war. So true it is that no more evil bane waxes among men than jealousy, which causes much groaning and much lamentation. Jealousy is the companion of shameless madness and with madness it gladly consorts and dances into grievous infatuation; and the end thereof is destruction. Jealousy too it is that leads

[a] Goddess of Birth.

δμηθῆναι, χαλεπῆς δὲ γάμων ἤντησεν ἀμοιβῆς.
εὖτε γὰρ ἀθρήσῃ σπιλάδων ἔπι δινεύοντα
ἰχθὺν ἀσπαλιεύς, ἀλόχοις πέρι μόχθον ἔχοντα,
ἀγκίστρῳ κρατερῷ περιβάλλεται ὅττι τάχιστα
καρῖδα ζώουσαν, ἐπ᾽ ἀγκίστροιο δ᾽ ὕπερθε
βριθὺς ἀνήρτηται μολίβου κύβος· αὐτὰρ ὁ λάθρῃ
πρὸς πέτραις ἀφέηκε βαρὺν δόλον, ἐγγύθι δ᾽ αὐτῶν
δινεύει θαλάμων· ὁ δ᾽ ἐσέδρακεν, αἶψα δ᾽ ὀρινθεὶς
ὡρμήθη, καρῖδα δόμων ἔντοσθεν ἱκάνειν
ἐλπόμενος λεχέεσσιν ἀνάρσιον ἠδ᾽ ἀλόχοισιν·
αἶψα δ᾽ ἐπιθύσας ὁ μὲν ἔλπεται ἐν γενύεσσι
τίνυσθαι καρῖδος ἐπήλυσιν, οὐδ᾽ ἐνόησεν
ὃν μόρον ἀμφιχανών· ἁλιεὺς δέ μιν αἶψα δοκεύσας
χαλκείαις ξυνέπειρεν ἀνακρούων γενύεσσιν
εἴρυσέ τ᾽ ἀσχαλόωντα καὶ ὕστατον ἀσπαίροντα,
καί πού μιν τοίοισιν ἐνίπαπε κερτομίοισι·
νῦν δή, νῦν ἀλόχους τε περιφρούρευε φυλάσσων,
ὦ τάλαν, ἐν θαλάμοις τε μένων ἐπιτέρπεο νύμφαις·
οὐ γάρ τοι μία Κύπρις ἐφήνδανεν οὐδὲ μί᾽ εὐνή,
ἀλλὰ μάλ᾽ ἐν τόσσῃσιν ἀγάλλεο μοῦνος ἀκοίτης
εὐναῖς· ἀλλ᾽ ἴθι δεῦρο, γάμος δέ τοί ἐστιν ἑτοῖμος,
νυμφίε, χερσαίοιο πυρὸς λευκάμπυκος αὐγή.
τοιάδε που νείκεσσε καὶ οὐκ ἀΐοντι πιφαύσκων.
κίχλαι δ᾽, εὖτε θάνῃ φρουρὸς πόσις, ἐκτὸς ἰοῦσαι
πλάζονται θαλάμων, ξυνὸν δ᾽ ἕλον ἀνέρι πότμον.

Καὶ μὴν δὴ φιλότητι καὶ ἀλλήλων ἐπαρωγῇ
ὄλλυνται γαλεοί τε κύνες καὶ φῦλα κελαινῶν
κεντροφόρων· λευκὸς μὲν ἐπ᾽ ἀγκίστρῳ πεπέδηται
ἰχθύς, ἀσπαλιεὺς δὲ κιών, ὅθι πηλὸς ἀϊδνὴς
ἐμβύθιος δολιχῇσιν ὑφίζεται ὀργυιῇσιν,

---

[a] *H.* ii. 128 n. [b] *H.* i. 379 n.

the unhappy Merle to be the victim of infatuation and a bitter requital he finds for his many brides. For when the fisherman perceives him wheeling upon the rocks in trouble about his wives, with all speed he puts upon a strong hook a live Prawn [a] and above the hook is hung a heavy cube of lead. And stealthily he launches his deadly snare beside the rocks and dangles it near the very bridal chambers of the Merle. He espies it and is straightway roused and charges, thinking that the Prawn is coming within his halls with hostile intent to beds and brides. Straightway rushing he thinks to avenge with his jaws the invasion of the Prawn, and perceives not that he is swallowing his own doom. The fisher watching him straightway strikes home and transfixes him with his barbs of bronze, and hales him forth indignant and writhing in his last struggle, and haply he chides with such mocking words as these : "Now then, now watch and guard thy wives, wretched fish, and abide at home rejoicing in thy brides ! for one love and one bed did not content thee, but thou didst glory, a single husband, in so many. Nay, come hither, bridegroom, thy bride is ready—the blaze of landward fire wreathed with white." So haply he rebukes him, albeit speaking to deaf ears. But the Thrushes, when their guardian husband dies, wander forth from their chambers and share his doom.

Moreover, through love and mutual help perish also the Galeus [b] Dog-fishes and the tribes of the dark Spiny Dog-fishes [c]; a white fish [d] is bound upon the hook and the fisherman goes where the dark mud lies long fathoms deep and lets down his

[c] *H.* i. 380 n. [d] Ael. i. 55.

ἄγκιστρον καθέηκε, θοῶς δέ τις ἔσπασεν ἄτην
ἀντιάσας· ὁ μὲν αὐτίκ' ἀνέλκεται, οἱ δέ μιν ἄλλοι
φρασσάμενοι μάλα πάντες ἀολλέες ἐγγὺς ἕπονται,
ὄφρ' αὐτὴν ἐπὶ νῆα καὶ ἀγρευτῆρας ἵκωνται.
δὴ τότε τοὺς μὲν ἕλοις ὑποχῆς περιηγέϊ κύκλῳ,
τοὺς δὲ σιδηρείοισι καταΐγδην στυφελίζων
αἰχμαῖς τριγλώχισι καὶ ἀλλοίοισι δόλοισιν·
οὐ γὰρ πρὶν φεύγουσιν ἀπότροποι, εἰσόχ' ἑταῖρον
ἑλκόμενον λεύσσωσιν, ὁμοῦ δ' ἐθέλουσιν ὀλέσθαι.
οἷον δ' ἀρτιφάτου παιδὸς νέκυν ἐκ μεγάροιο
τύμβον ἐς ἀμφίκλαυτον ἑοὶ στέλλουσι τοκῆες
τηλυγέτου, τῷ πολλὰ μάτην περιμοχθήσωσι·
δρυπτόμενοι δ' ὀδύνῃσι τέκος περικωκύοντες
ἠρίῳ ἐμπεφύασι καὶ οὐκ ἐθέλουσι μέλαθρα
νοστῆσαι, ξυνῇ δὲ θανεῖν δυσπενθέϊ νεκρῷ·
ὣς οἵ γ' οὐκ ἐθέλουσιν ἀνελκομένοιο λιπέσθαι,
εἰσόκεν αὐτὸν ὄλεθρον ὑπ' ἀγρευτῆρσιν ὄλωνται.
Ἄλλους δὲ ξεῖνός τε καὶ οὐκ ἐνδήμιος ἅλμης
εἷλεν ἔρως, χερσαῖον ἐπ' ἰχθύσιν οἶστρον ἐγείρων
ἔξαλον· ἀλλοδαπῆς φιλίης βέλος οἷον ἱκάνει
πουλύποδας σαργῶν τε γένος πέτρῃσιν ἑταῖρον.
ἤτοι πουλύποδες μὲν Ἀθηναίης φιλέουσιν
ἔρνεα καὶ θαλλοῖσιν ἐπὶ γλαυκοῖσιν ἔρωτα
ἔσπασαν· ἦ μέγα θαῦμα πόθῳ φρένα δενδρήεντι
ἕλκεσθαι λιπαροῦ τε φυτοῦ πτόρθοισι γάνυσθαι.

---

[a] *Cf. H.* iii. 81.

[b] Plato, *Soph.* 220 E τοῦ τοίνυν ἀγκιστρευτικοῦ τῆς πληκτικῆς τὸ μὲν ἄνωθεν εἰς τὸ κάτω γιγνόμενον διὰ τὸ τοῖς τριόδουσιν οὕτω μάλιστα χρῆσθαι τριοδοντία τις, οἶμαι, κέκληται.

[c] *H.* i. 306 n.

[d] *C.* ii. 433 n.

[e] Ael. i. 23 οἰκία τῷ σαργῷ τῷ ἰχθύι πέτρα τε καὶ σήραγγες.

[f] *i.e.*, olive-trees which were sacred to Athena. *Cf.* Ael.

hook and swiftly some fish meets it and seizes his doom. And he is straightway pulled in and the others perceiving it all follow close in a body, until they come right to the boat and the fishermen. Then one may take them—some with the curving circle of the bag-net,[a] some with downward-sweeping[b] blows of the iron trident or by other devices. For they do not turn to flee while they see their comrade being haled, but wish to perish with him. Even as when parents convey from the house to the tearful tomb the body of their newly slain boy—their only son for whom they have laboured much and vainly—and tearing their cheeks for grief they bewail their child and cling to the grave and are unwilling to return home but rather would die with the lamented dead: even so the fishes will not leave the captured fish till they die the same death at the hands of the fishers.

Others are taken by a passion strange and not native to the brine, which wakes in fishes a landward frenzy foreign to the sea: such as the alien love whose shaft smites the Poulpes[c] and the race of the Sargues[d] which companion with the rocks.[e] The Poulpes indeed love the trees of Athena[f] and have caught a passion for the grey-green[g] foliage. Verily it is a great marvel that their mind should be drawn by desire for a tree and delight in the

i. 37 λέγουσι δὲ ἁλιεῖς καὶ πολύποδας εἰς τὴν γῆν προιέναι, ἐλαίας θαλλοῦ ἐπὶ τῆς ᾐόνος κειμένου; ix. 45 ἀγροῦ γειτνιῶντος θαλάττῃ καὶ φυτῶν παρεστώτων ἐγκάρπων γεωργοὶ πολλάκις καταλαμβάνουσιν ἐν ὥρᾳ θερείῳ πολύποδάς τε καὶ ὀσμύλους ἐκ τῶν κυμάτων προελθόντας καὶ διὰ τῶν πρέμνων ἀνερπύσαντας καὶ τοῖς κλάδοις περιπεσόντας καὶ ὀπωρίζοντας κτλ. *Cf.* Phil. 102. 26 ff.

[g] Pind. *O.* iii. 13 γλαυκόχροα κόσμον ἐλαίας; Soph. *O.C.* γλαυκᾶς παιδοτρόφου φύλλον ἐλαίας.

ἔνθα γὰρ ἀγλαόκαρπος ἁλὸς σχεδόν ἐστιν ἐλαίη,
γείτοσιν ἐν γουνοῖσιν ἐπακταίη τεθαλυῖα,
κεῖθι δὲ πουλύποδος νόος ἕλκεται, ἠΰτ᾽ ἐπ᾽ ἴχνος
Κνωσίου εὐρίνοιο κυνὸς μένος, ὅστ᾽ ἐν ὄρεσσι
θηρὸς ἀνιχνεύει σκολιὴν βάσιν ἐξερεείνων
ῥινὸς ὑπ᾽ ἀγγελίῃ νημερτέϊ καί τέ μιν ὦκα
μάρψε καὶ οὐκ ἐμάτησεν ἑὸν δ᾽ ἐπέλασσεν ἄνακτα·
ὣς καὶ τηλεθόωσαν ἄφαρ μάθεν ἐγγὺς ἐλαίην
πούλυπος, ἐκδύνει δὲ βυθῶν καὶ γαῖαν ἀνέρπει
καγχαλόων, πρέμνοισι δ᾽ Ἀθηναίης ἐπέλασσεν·
ἔνθ᾽ ἤτοι πρῶτον μὲν ἀγαλλόμενος περὶ ῥίζης
πυθμένας εἰλεῖται στρωφώμενος, ἠΰτε κοῦρος,
ὅστε νέον προμολοῦσαν ἑὴν τροφὸν ἀμφαγαπάζει,
ἀμφὶ δέ οἱ πλέκεται, κόλποις δ᾽ ἐπὶ χεῖρας ἀείρει,
ἱμείρων δειρήν τε καὶ αὐχένα πηχύνασθαι·
ὣς ὅ περὶ πρέμνοισιν ἑλίσσεται ἔρνεϊ χαίρων.
ἔνθεν ἔπειτ᾽ ἄκρῃσιν ἐρειδόμενος κοτύλῃσιν
ὑψόσ᾽ ἀνερπύζει λελιημένος, ἀμφὶ δὲ χαίτας
πτύσσεται, ἄλλοτε ἄλλον ἔχων κλάδον, οἷά τις ἀνὴρ
νοστήσας ξείνηθεν ἑοὺς ἀσπάζεθ᾽ ἑταίρους
ἀθρόον ἀντιόωντας ἑλισσόμενος περὶ δειρήν·
ἢ ὥστε βλωθρῇσιν ἑλίσσεται ἀμφ᾽ ἐλάτῃσιν
ὑγρὸς ἕλιξ κισσοῖο, τιταινόμενος δ᾽ ἀπὸ ῥίζης
ἑρπύζει, πάντῃ δὲ περιρρέει ἀκρεμόνεσσιν·
ὣς ὅ γε γηθόσυνος λιπαροὺς περιβάλλετ᾽ ἐλαίης
ὄρπηκας, κυνέοντι πανείκελος· ἀλλ᾽ ὅτ᾽ ἔρωτος
λωφήσῃ, πάλιν αὖτις ἁλὸς μετὰ κόλπον ἀφέρπει,
πλησάμενος φιλότητος ἐλαιηροῦ τε πόθοιο.
τοῦ δή μιν καὶ ἔρωτος ἕλεν δόλος, ὡς ἐδάησαν
ἰχθυβόλοι· θαλλοὺς γὰρ ὁμοῦ δήσαντες ἐλαίης

---

[a] *i.e.*, Cretan (*C.* i. 373), from Cnos(s)us, town in Crete.

branches of the oily plant. For wherever there is near the sea an olive of splendid fruit, which flourishes on a shoreward slope neighbouring the sea, thither is the mind of the Poulpe drawn, even as to the track the spirit of the keen-scented Cnosian[a] dog, which on the hills searches out the crooked path of the wild beast and tracks it by the unerring guidance of the nose and swiftly seizes it and fails not of its prey but brings it to its master: even so the Poulpe straightway knows that a blooming olive is near at hand, and he comes forth from the deep and crawls upon the land exulting and draws nigh to the trunk of Athena's tree. Then first he coils and twines about the base of the trunk exulting, even as a boy who welcomes his nurse when she is newly come forth and clings about her and lifts his hands to her bosom, fain to put his arms about her neck and shoulders; even so the Poulpe twines about the trunk, rejoicing in the tree. Thereafter he lays hold with the tips of his suckers and crawls up eagerly and clings about the foliage, grasping now one branch, now another, even as a man who has come home from a foreign land greets his friends who throng to meet him and falls upon their necks; or as the twining ivy tendril clings about the tall fir-trees and, reaching forth from the root, climbs upwards and overruns the branches everywhere: so does the Poulpe joyfully embrace the sleek branches of the olive and seems to kiss them. But when he has relieved his desire, he crawls back again to the bosom of the sea, having satisfied his love and longing for the olive. The snare of this same love is his undoing, as fishermen know. For they bind together branches of the olive as goodly as may be

ὅττι μάλ' εὐφυέας μόλιβον μέσον ἐγκατέθηκαν,
ἐκ δ' ἀκάτου σύρουσιν· ὁ δ' οὐκ ἀμέλησε νοήσας
πούλυπος ἀλλ' ἤϊξε καὶ ἀμφέπλεξεν ἑταίρους
πτόρθους· οὐδ' ἔτ' ἔπειτα καὶ ἑλκόμενός περ ἐς ἄγρην
δεσμὰ πόθων ἀνίησιν, ἕως ἔντοσθε γένηται
νηός· ὁ δ' οὐκ ἤχθηρε καὶ ὀλλύμενός περ ἐλαίην.
Σαργοὶ δ' αἰγείοισι πόθοις ἐπὶ θυμὸν ἔχουσιν,
αἰγῶν δ' ἱμείρουσιν, ὀρειαύλοις δὲ βοτοῖσιν
ἐκπάγλως χαίρουσι καὶ εἰνάλιοί περ ἐόντες.
ἦ σέβας οὐκ ἐπίελπτον, ὁμόφρονα φῦλα τεκέσθαι
ἀλλήλοις ὀρέων τε πάγους χαροπήν τε θάλασσαν.
εὖτε γὰρ αἰγονομῆες ἐπὶ ῥηγμῖνος ἄγωσι
μηκάδας, ἐν δίνῃσι λοεσσομένας ἁλίῃσιν
ἐνδίους, ὅτε θερμὸς Ὀλύμπιος ἵσταται ἀστήρ,
οἳ δὲ τότε βληχήν τε παρακταίην ἀΐοντες
αὐδήν τ' αἰπολίων βαρυηχέα πάντες ὁμαρτῇ
καὶ νωθεῖς περ ἐόντες ἐπειγόμενοι φορέονται
σαργοὶ καὶ θρώσκουσιν ἐπ' ἀνδήροισι θαλάσσης,
γηθόσυνοι, κεραὸν δὲ περισαίνουσιν ὅμιλον
ἀμφί τε λιχμάζουσι καὶ ἀθρόοι ἀμφιχέονται,
πυκνὰ κατασκαίροντες· ἔχει δ' ἄρα θαῦμα νομῆας
πρωτοδαεῖς· αἶγες δὲ φίλον χορὸν οὐκ ἀέκουσαι

---

[a] The line is a κάθετος or weighted line (*H.* iii. 77 n.). The modern practice is entirely analogous: Apost. p. 48 "Pour la pêche du poulpe on fixe au plomb [μόλιβος, μόλυβδος] de l'engin quatre hameçons, dont les pointes sont dirigées en dehors; autour d'eux on met un morceau d'étoffe blanche, pour attirer l'animal qu'on veut capturer. Le poulpe, croyant avoir faire à une bonne proie, allonge ses tentacules pour la saisir, mais il s'y raccroche et périt." *Cf. H.* iv. 439 n.

[b] *Cf.* Apost. p. 49 "On ne pêche ainsi que les mâles de ce genre de céphalopodes. Cela nous induit à supposer que l'animal, poussé par l'instinct de la reproduction, se colle à cet engin qu'il prend pour une femelle de son espèce."

and put in the midst thereof the lead,[a] and tow them from the boat. The Poulpe, when he remarks it, is not unheeding but rushes to embrace his branchy comrades. And not even when he is being haled to capture does he relax the bonds of desire,[b] till he is within the boat, nor even while he perishes does he hate the olive.

The Sargues have their hearts possessed by affection for Goats.[c] Goats they yearn for and they rejoice exceedingly in the mountain-dwelling beasts, even though they belong themselves to the sea. Surely it is a marvel beyond expectation that mountain-crags and the flashing sea should give birth to tribes that are of one mind together. For when the goatherds bring their bleating flocks to the shore, to bathe in the eddying waves at noontide, at the season when the hot Olympian star [d] arises, then the Sargues, hearing the bleating on the shore and the deep murmur of the herds, rush all together in haste, sluggish though they be, and leap joyfully on the terraces by the sea and fawn upon the horned company and lick them and crowd about them with many a gambol; and amazement seizes the herdsmen that learn it for the first time. The goats receive the friendly choir not unwillingly and the

[c] Ael. i. 23 *φιλοῦσι δέ πως τῶν ἀλόγων αἶγας ἰσχυρῶς, ἐὰν γοῦν πλησίον τῆς ᾐόνος νεμομένων ἡ σκιὰ μιᾶς ἢ δευτέρας ἐν τῇ θαλάττῃ φανῇ, οἱ δὲ ἀσμένως προσνέουσι καὶ ἀναπηδῶσιν ὡς ἡδόμενοι, καὶ προσάψασθαι τῶν αἰγῶν ποθοῦσιν ἐξαλλόμενοι κτλ.*

[d] Sirius. Olympian = in Olympus = in the sky. Schol. *ὀλύμπιος οὐράνιος.* A common use in late, especially Latin poets: Verg. *E.* v. 56 Candidus insuetum miratur limen Olympi | Sub pedibusque videt nubes et sidera Daphnis; *G.* i. 450 (sol) emenso cum iam decedit Olympo; *Aen.* i. 374 Ante diem clauso componet Vesper Olympo; vi. 579 Quantus ad aetherium caeli suspectus Olympum.

δέχνυνται· τοὺς δ᾿ οὔτις ἔχει κόρος εὐφροσυνάων.
οὐ τόσον ἐν σταθμοῖσι κατηρεφέεσσι νομήων
μητέρας ἐκ βοτάνης ἔριφοι περικαγχαλόωντες
πολλῇ γηθοσύνῃ τε φιλοφροσύνῃ τε δέχονται,
ἦμος ἅπας περὶ χῶρος ἀγαλλομένῃσιν ἰωῇς
νηπιάχων κέκληγε, νόος δ᾿ ἐγέλασσε βοτήρων,
ὡς κεῖνοι κεραῇσι περισπέρχουσ᾿ ἀγέλῃσιν.
εὖτ᾿ ἂν δ᾿ εἰναλίων ἅδδην ἴσχωσι λοετρῶν,
αἱ δὲ πάλιν στείχωσιν ἐς αὔλια, δὴ τότε σαργοὶ
ἀχνύμενοι μάλα πάντες ἀολλέες ἐγγὺς ἕπονται,
κύματος ἀκροτάτοιο γέλως ὅθι χέρσον ἀμείβει.
ὡς δ᾿ ὅτε τηλύγετον μήτηρ γόνον ἢ καὶ ἀκοίτην
εὐνέτις ἀλλοδαπὴν τηλέχθονα γαῖαν ἰόντα
ἀχνυμένη στέλλῃσι, νόος δέ οἱ ἔνδον ἀλύει,
ὅσση οἱ μεσσηγὺς ἁλὸς χύσις, ὅσσα τε κύκλα
μηνῶν· ἀκροτάτοισι δ᾿ ἐπεμβαίνουσα θαλάσσης
κύμασι δακρυόεσσαν ὑπὸ στόμα γῆρυν ἵησι,
σπεύδειν λισσομένη καί μιν πόδες οὐκέτ᾿ ὀπίσσω
ἱεμένην φορέουσιν, ἔχει δ᾿ ἐπὶ πόντον ὀπωπάς·
ὣς κείνους καί κέν τις ὑπ᾿ ὄμμασι δάκρυα φαίη
στάζειν οἰωθέντας ἐλαυνομένων πάλιν αἰγῶν.
σαργὲ τάλαν· τάχα γάρ σε κακὸν πόθον αἰπολίοισι
φημὶ συνοίσεσθαι· τοῖος νόος ἀσπαλιήων
εἰς ἀπάτην καὶ κῆρα τεοὺς ἔτρεψεν ἔρωτας.
πέτρας μὲν κείνας τεκμαίρεται ἐγγύθι γαίης
πρῶτον ἀνὴρ διδύμοισιν ἀνισταμένας κροτάφοισιν
ἐγγύθεν, αἳ στεινωπὸν ἁλὸς διὰ χῶρον ἔχουσιν,

---

[a] This account of the capture of the Sargues is paraphrased Ael. i. 23. Captain Cook, *Last Voyage*, describes a similar method used by the natives of Nootka Sound: "They sometimes decoy animals by covering themselves

Sargues know no satiety of joy. No, not so much in the roofed steadings of the herdsmen do the kids exult about their mothers when they receive them home from pasture with great and joyful welcome, while all the place around rings with the glad cries of the little things, and the heart of the herdsmen smiles, as those Sargues fuss about the horned herds. And when these have had their fill of bathing in the sea, and go back to their folds, then in sorrow do all the Sargues together attend them closely to where the laughter of the utmost wave skirts the land. As when a sorrowing mother speeds her only son, or wife her husband, on his journey to a foreign land afar, and her heart is distraught within her: so wide the waters of the sea that shall lie between, so many the circles of the moons; standing in the utmost waves of the sea she utters from her lips tearful words, praying him to haste; and her feet carry her no more eagerly homeward but she has her eyes upon the sea; even so the Sargues, one would say, shed tears from their eyes, left desolate, when the Goats are driven away. Poor Sargue! anon methinks thou shalt find thy companioning with the herds of Goats a fatal passion. In such wise does the wit of the fishermen turn thy love into a snare and destruction. First[a] of all a man marks those rocks near the land which rise in twin peaks near together with a narrow space of sea between and

with a skin, and running about on all-fours, which they do very nimbly, as appeared from the specimens of their skill which they exhibited to us—making a kind of noise or neighing at the same time; and on these occasions the masks, or carved heads, as well as the real dried heads of the different animals, are put on." Another method used by the Carians, Ael. xiii. 2.

αἰθέρος ἀκτίνεσσι διαυγέας, αἷς ἔνι σαργοὶ
πολλοὶ ναιετάουσιν, ὁμόκτιτον αὖλιν ἔχοντες·
ἔξοχα γὰρ πυρσοῖσιν ἐπ' ἠελίοιο γάνυνται.
ἐνθάδ' ἀνὴρ μελέεσσιν ἐφεσσάμενος δέρος αἰγός,
δοιὰ κέρα κροτάφοισι περὶ σφετέροισιν ἀνάψας,
στέλλεται ὁρμαίνων νόμιον δόλον, ἐς δ' ἅλα βάλλει
κρείασιν αἰγείοισιν ὁμοῦ κνίσσῃ τε λιπήνας
ἄλφιτα· τοὺς δ' ὀδμή τε φίλη δολόεσσά τ' ἐσωπὴ
φορβή τ' εὐδώρητος ἐφέλκεται, οὐδέ τιν' ἄτην
ἐν φρεσὶν ὁρμαίνουσιν, ἀγαλλόμενοι δὲ μένουσιν
αἰγὶ περισαίνοντες ἐοικότα δήϊον ἄνδρα·
δύσμοροι, ὡς ὀλοοῖο τάχ' ἀντιόωσιν ἑταίρου,
οὐ φρεσὶν αἰγείῃσιν ἀρηρότος· αὐτίκα γάρ σφιν
ῥάβδον τε κραναὴν ὁπλίζεται ἠδὲ λίνοιο
ὁρμιὴν πολιοῖο, βάλεν δ' ὕπερ ἀγκίστροιο
χηλῆς αἰγείης κρέας ἔμφυτον· οἱ μὲν ἐδωδὴν
ἐσσυμένως ἥρπαξαν, ὁ δ' ἔσπασε χειρὶ παχείῃ
αὖ ἐρύων· εἰ γάρ τις οἴσεται ἔργα δόλοιο,
οὐκ ἂν ἔτ' ἐμπελάσειε καὶ εἰ λασιότριχας αὐτὰς
αἶγας ἄγοι, φεύγουσι δ' ἀποστύξαντες ὁμαρτῇ
καὶ μορφὴν καὶ δαῖτα καὶ αὐτῆς ἔνδια πέτρης·
εἰ δὲ λάθοι καὶ κραιπνὸν ἔχοι πόνον, οὔ κέ τις ἄγρης
λειφθείη, πάντας δὲ δαμάσσεται αἰγὸς ὀπωπή.
῎Αλλος δ' αὖ σαργοῖσι μέλει πόθος εἴαρος ὥρῃ
ἀλλήλων, εὐνῆς δὲ γάμων πέρι δηριόωνται·
πολλαῖς δ' εἷς ἀλόχοις πέρι μάρναται· ὃς δέ κεν ἀλκῇ
νικήσῃ, πάσῃσιν ἐπάρκιος ἔπλετ' ἀκοίτης,
πέτρας δ' εἰσελάει θῆλυν στόλον· ἔνθ' ἁλιῆες
κύρτον ἐτεχνήσαντο βαθύν, περιηγέα πάντῃ·

are open to the rays of the sun: wherein dwell many Sargues which have their habitation together; for the Sargues delight exceedingly in the beams of the sun. Here the man betakes himself, his limbs clothed in the skin of a goat and two horns fastened to his temples, meditating a rustic trick: and he casts into the sea a bait of barley-meal enriched with goatflesh and roasted meat together. The welcome savour, the deceiving aspect of the man, and the goodly boon of food entice the Sargues, and they think not in their minds of any harm but delighted they remain, fawning round their foeman in the guise of a goat. Unhappy fishes! how fatal a friend they presently find him, whose mind is nowise goatlike. For straightway he arrays against them a rough rod and a line of grey flax and puts on the hook the natural flesh of a goat's hoof. They greedily seize the bait and he with stout hand pulls and lands them. For if any of them suspect the work of guile, no more will he come near, even were the fishermen to bring the shaggy goats themselves, but together they take to flight, loathing alike the form of the man and the feast and the sunny spaces of the rock itself. But if the fisher escape their notice and do his work swiftly, none will be left uncaptured, but the goatlike aspect will overcome them all.

Another passion employs the Sargues in the season of spring, even their passion for one another, and they contend about the bridal bed. One male fights for many wives and he who prevails by his valour is sufficient mate for all; and he drives his female company among the rocks, where the fishermen contrive a deep weel, rounded on all sides, and

τὸν δὲ φυτῶν λάχνῃσι περὶ στόμα πάντα πύκασσαν,
μύρτων ἢ δάφνης εὐώδεος ἠέ τευ ἄλλου
πτόρθοισιν θαλεροῖσιν ἐπισταμένως σκιάσαντες.
τοὺς δ' οἶστρος ποτὶ μῶλον ἐπώρορεν εὐνητῆρας
μάρνασθαι, πολλὴ δὲ γαμήλιος ἵστατ' Ἐνυώ.
ἀλλ' ὅτ' ἀριστεύσας τις ἕλῃ κράτος, αὐτίκα πέτρην
παπταίνει γλαφυρήν, ἀλόχοις δόμον, ἐς δ' ἴδε κύρτον
κείμενον, εὐφύλλοισιν ἐπηρεφὲ ἀκρεμόνεσσιν,
ἔνθ' ἐλάει νυμφεῖον ἑὸν χορόν· αἱ μὲν ἔπειτα
κύρτον ἔσω δύνουσιν, ὁ δ' ἔκτοθι πάντας ἐρύκει
ἄρσενας, οὐδέ τιν' ἄλλον ἐᾷ νύμφῃσι πελάσσαι.
ἀλλ' ὅταν ἐμπλήσῃ πλεκτὸν δόλον, ὕστατος αὐτὸς
ἐς θάλαμον προὔτυψεν, ἀνέκβατον Ἄϊδος εὐνήν.
ὡς δ' ὅτε μηλονόμος τις ἀνὴρ βοτάνηθεν ἐλαύνων
εἰροπόκους ἀγέλας ἀνάγει πάλιν, ἐν δὲ θυρέτροις
ἱστάμενος σταθμοῖο νόῳ πεμπάζεται οἰῶν
πληθὺν εὖ διέπων, εἴ οἱ σόα πάντα πέλονται,
πώεσι δ' εἰλομένοισι περιπλήθουσα μὲν αὐλὴ
στείνεται, ὑστάτιος δὲ μετά σφισιν ἔσσυτο ποιμήν·
ὣς αἱ μὲν προπάροιθεν ἔσω κοίλοιο μυχοῖο
θηλύτεραι κατέδυσαν, ὁ δ' ὕστερος ἔνθορ' ἀκοίτης,
δειλαίῃς ἅμα δειλὸς ἐπισπεύδων ἀλόχοισι.
τοῖα μὲν ἐν νεπόδεσσιν ἔρως ἐστήσατ' ἄεθλα,
τοίαις δ' ἐξαπάτῃσιν ἐρωμανέεσσιν ὄλοντο.

Ἵππουροι δ' ὅτε κέν τι μετ' οἴδμασιν ἀθρήσωσι
πλαζόμενον, τῷ πάντες ἀολλέες ἐγγὺς ἕπονται·
ἔξοχα δ', ὁππότε νῆα διαραισθεῖσαν ἀέλλαις,
αἰνὰ Ποσειδάωνος ἀμειλίκτοιο τυχοῦσαν,
δασσάμενον μέγα κῦμα διακριδὸν ἄλλοθεν ἄλλα

[a] *Cf. H.* i. 184. Probably *Coryphaena hippurus*, M.G. λαμπούγα, μανάλια: A. 543 a 23; 599 b 3; Plin. ix. 57;

cover it all about the mouth with foliage of plants, shadowing it cunningly with green branches of myrtle or fragrant bay or some other tree. Now the goad of desire rouses the males to the moil of battle and the war for brides waxes keen. But when one by his prowess wins the victory, straightway he looks for a hollow rock as a dwelling for his wives, and he espies the weel lying, roofed with leafy boughs and therein he drives his choir of brides. They then enter within the weel, while he outside keeps away all the males nor suffers any other to approach his brides. But when he has filled the plaited snare, last, he himself advances into the bridal chamber, a bed of Hades without escape. As when some shepherd drives from the pasture his fleecy flocks and leads them home, and standing in the entrance of the steading reckons in his mind the number of his sheep, reviewing them well to see if all are safe, and the courtyard, full to overflowing, is straitened with the huddling sheep, and last the shepherd himself enters among them; even so the female Sargues enter first within the hollow retreat, and after them their spouse leaps in himself, hasting unhappy bridegroom with unhappy brides. Such contests does love array among the finny tribe and by such snares of amorous madness they perish.

The Hippurus,[a] when they behold anything floating in the waves, all follow it, closely in a body, but especially when a ship is wrecked by the stormy winds, finding Poseidon terribly unkind, and the great waves break her up and carry hither and

xxxii. 149; Ov. *Hal.* 95. Called also κορύφαινα Athen. 304 c-d, ἀρνευτὴν ἵππουρον Numenius, *ibid.* *Cf.* 319 D. These fishes are popularly, but erroneously, called "Dolphins."

δοῦρα φέρῃ λώβῃσι πολυσχιδέεσσι λυθέντα.
τῆμος δ' ἱππούρων ἀγέλαι πινάκεσσι θεούσαις
ἑσπόμεναι μεθέπουσιν· ὁ δ' ἐγκύρσας ἁλιήων
πολλὴν ῥηϊδίως ἄγρην ἕλεν ἠδ' ἀμέγαρτον.
ἀλλὰ τὸ μὲν ναύτῃσιν ἀλεξήσειε Κρονίων
ἐμβύθιος, νῆες δὲ διὰ πλατὺ κῦμα θέοιεν
αὔραις εὐκήλοισιν ἀπήμονες ἠδ' ἀτίνακτοι,
φόρτον ἀμοιβαίοισι μετερχόμεναι καμάτοισιν,
ἱππούροις δ' ἀλλοῖα νοήματα τεχνήσασθαι
ἐστίν, ἀπημοσύνῃ δὲ νεῶν μεταβαινέμεν ἄγρην.
Συμφερτοὺς δονάκων φακέλους ἅμα γυρώσαντες
δίναις ἐγκατέθηκαν, ἔνερθε δὲ λᾶαν ἔδησαν
βριθὺν ὑφορμιστῆρα· τὰ μὲν μάλα πάντα καθ' ὕδωρ
ἀτρέμα δινεύουσι· φιλόσκια δ' αὐτίκα φῦλα
ἱππούρων ἀγεληδὸν ἀγείρεται, ἀμφὶ δὲ νῶτα
τερπόμενοι δονάκεσσιν ἀνατρίβουσι μένοντες·
τοῖς δὲ τότ' ἀσπαλιῆες ἐπιπλώουσιν ἑτοίμην
εἰς ἄγρην, ἄγκιστρα δ' ὑπ' εἴδασιν ὁπλίσσαντες
πέμπουσ', οἱ δ' ἐρύουσιν ἅμα σπεύδοντες ὄλεθρον.
ὡς δὲ κύνας βρώμῃσιν ἀνὴρ ἐπὶ μῶλον ὀρίνει
δινεύων μέσσοισιν ἑλώρια, τοὶ δ' ἐπὶ γαστρὶ
ἔξοχα μαργαίνοντες ὑποφθαδὸν ἅρπαγι λύσσῃ
ἀλλήλους προθέουσι καὶ ἐς χέρα παπταίνουσιν
ἀνδρός, ὅπῃ ῥίψειεν, ἔρις δ' ἀναφαίνετ' ὀδόντων·
ὣς οἵ γ' ἀγκίστροισιν ἐπαΐσσουσιν ἑτοίμως.
ῥηϊδίως δ' ἀγρευτὸν ἐρύσσεαι ἄλλον ἐπ' ἄλλῳ
κραιπνὸς ἐών· αὐτοὶ γὰρ ἐπισπεύδουσ' ἁλιήων
μᾶλλον, ὑπ' ἀφραδίῃσιν ἑὸν μόρον ἐγκονέοντες.
Τοίῃ ἐπιφροσύνῃ καὶ πομπίλον ἀγρώσσονται·
καὶ γὰρ τοῖς ἴσον ἦτορ ἐπὶ σκιεροῖσι πόθοισι.
Τευθίσι δ' ἄτρακτόν τις ἀνὴρ ἐπιμηχανόῳτο,

[a] *Il.* i. 186 n. [b] *Il.* i. 428 n.

thither her scattered timbers, loosened by the rending assaults of the sea. Then the shoals of the Hippurus follow in the train of the drifting planks, and the fisherman who chances upon them wins easily great and unstinted spoil. But that may the Son of Cronus, the lord of the deep, avert from our sailors, and may their ships speed over the broad waves with gentle breezes, unhurt and unshaken, while they ply to and fro for cargo! And for the Hippurus men may contrive other devices and without the wreck of ships pursue their prey.

The fishermen gather reeds and tie them together in bundles which they let down into the waves and underneath they tie a heavy stone by way of ballast. All this they let sway gently in the water; and straightway the shade-loving tribes of the Hippurus gather in shoals and linger about delightedly rubbing their backs against the reeds. Then the fishers row to them to find a ready prey, and bait their hooks and cast them, and the fish seize them, hastening therewith their own destruction. Even as a hunter excites with meat his dogs to the warfare of the chase, waving among them a piece of game, and the dogs in a frenzy of appetite with ravenous rage run emulous one before the other and look to the man's hand to see where he will throw it, and strife of teeth arises: so the fishes rush readily upon the hooks. And easily, if active, thou shalt catch and land them one after the other; for they are more eager than the fishermen themselves and by their own folly hasten their doom.

By like craft are the Pilot-fishes [a] also taken; for their heart equally is set upon desire for shade.

Against the Calamaries [b] a man should devise a

ἐντύνων κλωστῆρι πανείκελον· ἀμφὶ δ᾽ ἄρ᾽ αὐτῷ
πυκνὰ καταζεύξειεν ἀνακλίνων γενύεσσιν
ἄγκιστρ᾽ ἀλλήλοισι παρασχεδόν, οἷς ἔπι σῶμα
ποικίλον ἐμπείρειεν ἰουλίδος, ὕπτια χαλκοῦ
δήγματ᾽ ἐπικρύπτων, γλαυκοῖς δ᾽ ἐνὶ βένθεσι λίμνης
τοῖον ἀναψάμενος σύροι δόλον· ἡ δ᾽ ἐσιδοῦσα
τευθὶς ἐφωρμήθη τε καὶ ἀμφιέπουσα πιέζει
ἰκμαλέοις θυσάνοις, ἐπάγη δ᾽ ἐνὶ χείλεσι χαλκοῦ·
οὐδ᾽ ἔτι καὶ μεμαυῖα λιπεῖν δύνατ᾽, ἀλλ᾽ ἀέκουσα
ἕλκεται, αὐτόπλεκτον ἐὸν δέμας ἀμφιβαλοῦσα.

Καὶ μέν τις λιμένεσσι παρ᾽ ἀκλύστοισι θαλάσσης
ἄγρην ἐγχελύων τεχνήσατο κοῦρος ἀθύρων.
ἔντερον οἰὸς ἑλὼν περιμήκετον ἧκε καθ᾽ ὕδωρ
ἐκτάδιον, δολιχῇσιν ἀλίγκιον ὁρμιῇσιν·
ἡ δ᾽ ἐσιδοῦσ᾽ ἐπόρουσε καὶ ἔσπασε· τὴν δὲ χανοῦσαν
ἔγνω καὶ μήλειον ἄφαρ κύρτωσεν ἀϋτμῇ
ἔγκατον ἐμπνείων· τὸ δ᾽ ἀνίσταται ἄσθματι λάβρῳ
οἰδαλέον, πλῆσεν δὲ τιταινόμενον στόμα δειλῆς
ἐγχέλυος· πνοιῇ δὲ περιστένεται μογέουσα
ἀνδρομέῃ, δέδεται δὲ καὶ ἱεμένη περ ἀλύξαι,
εἰσόκεν οἰδαίνουσα καὶ ἄσχετον ἀσθμαίνουσα
ὑψόσ᾽ ἀναπλώσῃ καὶ ὑπ᾽ ἀγρευτῆρι γένηται.
ὡς δ᾽ ὅτε τις πλείου πειρώμενος ἀμφιφορῆος
αὐλὸν ἔχων ἤρεισεν ὑπὸ στόμα φυσητῆρα,
ἄσθματι δ᾽ αὖ ἐρύει μέθυος ποτὸν ἔμπαλιν ἕλκων
χείλεσιν ἀκροτάτοις, τὸ δ᾽ ἀνατρέχει ἀνδρὸς ἀϋτμῇ·

[a] It is amazing to read in Apost. p. 48 " Pour les calmars (Loligo) qui pénètrent dans l'intérieur des ports, on donne au plomb la forme d'un fuseau et l'on dispose, à sa partie inférieure, en couronne, un grand nombre d'aiguilles à coudre. Quand, au contraire, on veut pêcher les sepioteuthis,

rod fashioned after the manner of a spindle.[a] And about it let him fasten close to one another many hooks with recurving barbs, and on these let him impale the striped body of a Rainbow-wrasse to hide the bent teeth of bronze, and in the green depths of the sea let him trail such snare upon a cord. The Calamary when it sees it, darts up and grasps it in the embrace of its moist tentacles and becomes impaled upon the lips of bronze. And no more can it leave them for all its endeavour but is haled against its will, having of itself entangled its body.

In havens of the sea beyond the wash of the waves some youth in sport contrives a mode of catching Eels.[b] He takes a long sheep-gut and lets it trail its length in the water, like a long line. The Eel espies it and rushes up and seizes it. The youth perceives that the Eel has swallowed the bait and straightway blows in the sheep-gut and inflates it with his breath. By his vehement blowing the gut swells up and fills the straining mouth of the wretched Eel; which is straitened and distressed by the human breath, but is held a fast prisoner for all its endeavour to escape, until, swollen and wildly gasping, it swims to the surface and becomes the prey of the fisher. Even as one who makes essay of a full jar, takes a blow-pipe and puts it in his mouth and by drawing in his breath draws with the tip of his lips draught of wine, which streams up under the force of his breathing: so the

τεύθους, θράψαλα vulg., les grands calmars du large, on remplace les aiguilles par des hameçons."

[b] Ael. xiv. 8 describes this method of catching Eels as used at Vicetia in Cisalpine Gaul. For Eel-catching in general *cf.* A. 592 a 6; Athen. 298 b; Aristoph. *Eq.* 864 ff.; Plin. ix. 74; Walton, *Compleat Angler*, c. xiii.; Radcliffe, p. 246 ff.; Badham, c. xvii.

ὥς αἵ γ᾽ ἐγχέλυες πνοιῆς ὕπο κυμαίνουσαι
ἕλκονται δολίοιο ποτὶ στόμα φυσητῆρος.
Ἔστι δέ τις νεπόδων δειλὸς καὶ ἄκικυς ὅμιλος,
ἀβληχρῆς ἀφύης ἀδινὸν γένος, αἳ καλέονται
ἐγγραύλεις· ἀγαθὴ δὲ βόσις πάντεσσιν ἔασιν
ἰχθύσιν· αἰεὶ δέ σφιν ἐνὶ φρεσὶ φῦζα δέδηε,
πάντα δ᾽ ὑποτρομέουσι, σὺν ἀλλήλαις δὲ χυθεῖσαι
σωρηδὸν μίμνουσι καὶ ἀθρόαι ἐμπεφύασιν,
ἠΰτ᾽ ἀναγκαίοιο βίην δεσμοῖο φέρουσαι·
οὐδέ κε μητίσαιο διάκρισιν εὐρέος ἐσμοῦ
οὐδὲ λύσιν· τοῖον γὰρ ἐν ἀλλήλῃσιν ἔχονται.
πολλάκι μὲν καὶ νῆες ἐν ἕρμασιν ἠΰτ᾽ ἔκελσαν
κείναις, πολλάκι δέ σφιν ἐνιπλήσσουσιν ἐρετμοῖς
κληΐδων ἐλατῆρες, ἐνέσχετο δ᾽ ἱεμένη περ
κώπη, πετραίης ἅτε χοιράδος ἀντιτυχοῦσα·
καί πού τις βουπλῆγα βαρύστομον ἰθὺς ἀείρας
ἐγγραύλεις ἐτίναξε καὶ οὐ διέκερσε σιδήρῳ
στῖφος ἅπαν, βαιὴν δ᾽ ἀγέλης ἀπεδάσσατο μοῖραν·
καὶ τῆς μὲν κεφαλὴν πέλεκυς τάμε, τὴν δ᾽ ἐκόλουσεν
οὐρῆς, τὴν δ᾽ ἤμησε μέσην, τὴν δ᾽ εἷλεν ἅπασαν.
οἰκτρὸν ἰδεῖν μογεροῖσιν ἐοικότα σώματα νεκροῖς.
αἱ δ᾽ οὐδ᾽ ὧς ἐλάθοντο καὶ οὐκ ἀνέηκαν ἔχουσαι
δεσμὸν ἑόν· τοῖός τις ἐπί σφισι γόμφος ἄρηρε.

---

[a] *H*. i. 767 n.

[b] *Engraulis encrasicholus*, M.G. χαψί, a tiny member of the Herring family (*Clupeidae*): A. 569 b 26 ἐκ δὲ μιᾶς ἀφύης, οἷον τῆς ἐν τῷ Ἀθηναίων λιμένι, (γίνονται) οἱ ἐγκρασίχολοι καλούμενοι. *Cf*. Athen. 285 a, 300 f, 329 a; Ael. viii. 18 ἐγγραύλεις, οἱ δὲ ἐγκρασιχόλους καλοῦσιν αὐτάς, προσακήκοά γε μὴν καὶ τρίτον ὄνομα αὐτῶν, εἰσὶ γὰρ οἳ καὶ λυκοστόμους αὐτὰς ὀνομάζουσιν· ἔστι δὲ μικρὰ ἰχθύδια καὶ πολύγονα φύσει, λευκότατα ἰδεῖν κτλ.

[c] Ael. *l.c.* καθεὶς δὲ τὴν χεῖρα ὡς ἐκ σωροῦ πυρῶν ἢ κυάμων

Eels, swollen by the breath of the youth, are drawn toward the mouth of the crafty blower.

There is a certain timid and strengthless company of fishes, the thronging race of the feeble Fry [a] which are called Anchovies.[b] They are a goodly food for all manner of fishes and flight is evermore the burning thought of their minds. They are afraid of all things and they remain huddled with one another in heaps [c] and cling in crowds together, as if they were under the stress of a compelling chain. And thou couldst not contrive to separate the broad swarm of them or loose them each from each: in such sort do they cling to one another. Many a time even ships [d] run aground on them as upon a reef and many a time the rowers on the benches entangle their oars in them and the hasting blade is stayed as if it struck a stony rock. And haply someone lifts straight a heavy-bladed axe and smites the Anchovies, yet does not cleave with the iron the whole mass in twain but cuts off only a tiny portion of the shoal. And the hatchet cuts off the head [e] of one and maims another of its tail and another it cleaves in the midst of the body and yet another it utterly destroys. Pitiful it is to behold their bodies like wretched corpses. Yet not even so do they forget themselves, and they do not relax the chain that binds them: so fast a rivet holds them together. Encountering those fishes a

λάβοις ἂν βιαίως ἀποσπάσας, ὡς καὶ διασπᾶσθαι πολλάκις καὶ τὰ μὲν ἡμίτομα τῶν ἰχθυδίων λαμβάνεσθαι, τὰ δὲ ὑπολείπεσθαι.

[d] Ael. *l.c.* τοσαύτη ἡ ἕνωσις γίνεται συνδραμόντων ὡς καὶ πορθμίδας ἐπιθεούσας μὴ διασχίζειν αὐτά, καὶ μέντοι καὶ κώπην ἢ κόντον εἰ δὶς αὐτῶν διεῖναι θελήσειεν, τὰ δὲ οὐ διαξαίνεται ἀλλ' ἔχεται ἀλλήλων ὡς συνυφασμένα.

[e] Ael. *l.c.* τὸ μὲν οὐραῖον καθέξεις, μενεῖ δὲ σὺν τοῖς ἄλλοις ἡ κεφαλή· ἢ κεφαλὴν κομιεῖς οἴκαδε, μένει δ' ἐν τῇ θαλάττῃ τὸ λοιπόν.

καί κέν τις παλάμῃσιν ἅτε ψαμάθοιο βαθείης
ἀντιάσας κείνῃσιν ἐπ᾽ ἰχθύσιν ἀμήσαιτο.
τὰς δ᾽ ὁπότε φράσσωνται ἐπὶ σφίσι πεπτηυίας
ἰχθυβόλοι, κοίλῃσι περιπτύσσουσι σαγήναις
ἀσπασίως, πολλὴν δὲ ποτὶ ῥηγμῖνας ἄγουσιν
ἄγρην νόσφι πόνοιο καὶ ἄγγεα πάντ᾽ ἀφύῃσιν
ἔν τ᾽ ἀκάτους ἔπλησαν, ἐπ᾽ ἠϊόσι δὲ βαθείαις
θημῶνας νήησαν, ἀπειρεσίην χύσιν ἄγρης.
οἷον δ᾽ ἐργατῖναι Δηοῦς πόνον ἐκτελέσαντες,
πνοιῇς χερσαίοις τε διακρίναντες ἐρετμοῖς
καρπόν, ἐϋτροχάλοιο μέσον κατὰ χῶρον ἀλωῆς
πολλὸν ἐνηήσαντο, περιπλήθουσα δὲ πάντῃ
πυροδόκος στεφάνη λευκαίνεται ἔνδον ἀλωῆς·
ὣς τότ᾽ ἀπειρεσίῃσι περιπληθὴς ἀφύῃσιν
ὀφρὺς ἀγχιάλου λευκαίνεται αἰγιαλοῖο.

Φῦλα δὲ πηλαμύδων ἐκ μὲν γένος εἰσὶ θαλάσσης
Εὐξείνου, θύννης δὲ βαρύφρονος εἰλείθυιαι·
κεῖναι γάρ, Μαιῶτις ὅπῃ ξυμβάλλεται ἅλμῃ,
ἀγρόμεναι λιμναῖον ὑπὸ στόμα καὶ δονακῆας
ὑδρηλοὺς ὠδῖνος ἐπαλγέος ἐμνήσαντο·
καὶ τὰ μὲν ὅσσα κίχωσι μεταδρομάδην κατέδουσιν
ᾠά, τὰ δ᾽ ἐν δονάκεσσι καὶ ἐν σχοίνοισι μένοντα
πηλαμύδων ἀγέλας ὥρῃ τέκεν· αἱ δ᾽ ὅτε κῦμα
πρῶτον ἐπιψαίρωσι πόροιο τε πειρήσωνται,
ξεῖνον ἁλὸς σπεύδουσι μετὰ πλόον, οὐδ᾽ ἐθέλουσι

[a] Demeter. [b] *i.e.* winnowing fans, *cf.* Hom. *Od.* xi. 128.

[c] One-year-old Tunnies; A. 488 a 6 among gregarious fishes are *οὓς καλοῦσι δρομάδας, θύννοι, πηλαμύδες*, 543 a 2 the *θύννος* and the *πηλαμύς* breed once a year; 543 b 2 *αἱ δὲ πηλαμύδες καὶ οἱ θύννοι τίκτουσιν ἐν τῷ Πόντῳ, ἄλλοθι δ᾽ οὔ*; 571 a 15 *ὅταν γὰρ τέκωσιν οἱ ἰχθύες ἐν τῷ Πόντῳ, γίγνονται ἐκ τοῦ ᾠοῦ ἃς καλοῦσιν οἱ μὲν σκορδύλας, Βυζάντιοι δ᾽ αὐξίδας διὰ τὸ ἐν ὀλίγαις αὐξάνεσθαι ἡμέραις· καὶ ἐξέρχονται μὲν τοῦ φθινοπώρου ἅμα ταῖς θυννίσιν, εἰσπλέουσι δὲ τοῦ ἔαρος ἤδη οὖσαι πηλαμύδες.*

man might gather of them with his hands as if he gathered deep sand. Now when the fishermen behold them huddled together, they gladly enclose them with their hollow seine-nets and without trouble bring ashore abundant booty and fill with the Fry all their vessels and their boats and on the deep beaches pile up heaps, an infinite abundance of spoil. As when the harvesters have finished the work of Deo [a] and with help of the winds and the landsman's oars [b] have separated the grain, they pile it abundant in the mid space of the round threshing-floor and, full everywhere to overflowing, the ring that receives the wheat shows white within the floor: even so then, filled with the infinite Fry, the brow of the beach beside the sea shows white.

The tribes of the Pelamyds [c] are by birth from the Euxine sea and are the offspring of the female Tunny. For these gather by the mouth of the Maeotian Lake [d] where it meets the sea, and there amid the wet reedbeds they bethink them of the painful travail of birth. And such of their eggs as they find they eat as they hurry along, but such as remain among the reeds and rushes give birth in due season to the shoals of the Pelamyds. These when first they skim the waves and make essay of travelling hasten to voyage in alien

Cf. Plin. ix. 47 Thynni . . . intrant e magno mari Pontum verno tempore gregatim, nec alibi fetificant. Cordyla appellatur partus qui fetas redeuntes in mare autumno comitatur, limosae vere aut e luto pelamydes incipiunt vocari et, cum annuum excessere tempus, thynni; A. 598 a 26 *θυννίδες δὲ καὶ πηλαμύδες . . . εἰς τὸν Πόντον ἐμβάλλουσι τοῦ ἔαρος καὶ θερίζουσιν*; 571 a 11 *δοκοῦσι δ' ἐνιαυτῷ εἶναι (οἱ θύννοι) πρεσβύτεροι τῶν πηλαμύδων.*

[d] The Sea of Azov: Μαιῶτις λίμνη Aesch. *P.V.* 419; Palus Maeotica Plin. ii. 168; Maeotis lacus Plin. iv. 78; Maeotius lacus Plin. iv. 76.

μίμνειν ἔνθ' ἐγένοντο καὶ ἡβαιαί περ ἐοῦσαι.
Θρηΐκιος δέ τίς ἐστιν ἁλὸς πόρος, ὅντε βάθιστον
φασὶ Ποσειδάωνος ἐνὶ κλήροισι τετύχθαι·
ἐκ τοῦ καί τε Μέλας κικλήσκεται, οὐδέ ἑ λάβροι
λίην οὐδ' ὑπέροπλοι ἐπιθρώσκουσιν ἀῆται·
ἐν δ' ἄρα οἱ κευθμῶνες ὑποβρύχιοι πεφύασι
κοῖλοι, πηλώεντες, ἀθέσφατοι, οἷς ἔνι πολλὰ
τίκτεται, ἡβαιοῖσιν ὅσ' ἰχθύσι δαῖτας ὀφέλλει.
ἔνθα καὶ ἀρτιγόνοισι πέλει πρώτιστα κέλευθα
πηλαμύδων ἑσμοῖσιν, ἐπεὶ περιώσιον ἄλλων
εἰναλίων φρίσσουσι δυσαέα χείματος ὁρμήν·
χεῖμα δὲ πηλαμύδεσσιν ἀπαμβλύνει φάος ὄσσων.
ἔνθα δ' ἐν εὐρωποῖσιν ἁλὸς λαγόνεσσι πεσοῦσαι
αὔτως δηθύνουσιν, ἀεξόμεναι δὲ μένουσι
λαρὸν ἔαρ· τῇ δέ σφι καὶ ἵμερος ἄνεται εὐνῆς·
πλησάμεναι δὲ τόκοιο παλίμποροι αὖτις ἵενται
πατρῷον μετὰ κῦμα, μόγον δ' ἀπὸ γαστρὸς ἔθεντο.
Τὰς δ' ἤτοι Μέλανος μὲν ὑπὲρ βαθὺ λαῖτμα πόροιο
Θρήϊκες ἀγρώσσουσιν ἀπηνεϊ χείματος ὥρῃ,
θήρην ἀργαλέην καὶ ἀτερπέα, δηϊοτῆτος
θεσμὸν ὑφ' αἱματόεντα καὶ ἄγριον αἶσαν ὀλέθρου.
ἔστι τις οὐ δολιχὴ μὲν ἀτὰρ πάχος ὅττι μεγίστη,
μῆκος ὅσον πῆχυς, στιβαρὴ δοκίς· ἐν δέ οἱ ἄκρῃ
πολλὴ μὲν μολίβοιο χύσις, πολλαὶ δὲ σιδήρου
αἰχμαὶ τριγλώχινες ἐπασσύτεραι πεφύασι·
πεῖσμα δέ μιν περίμηκες ἐΰπλοκον ἀμφιβέβηκε.

---

[a] The Gulf on which Ainos is situated, lying to the W. of the Thracian Chersonese: Strabo, *fr.* 52 εἰθ' ἡ Χερρόνησος ἡ Θρᾳκία καλουμένη, ποιοῦσα τήν τε Προποντίδα καὶ τὸν Μέλανα κόλπον καὶ τὸν Ἑλλήσποντον· ἄκρα γὰρ ἔκκειται πρὸς εὐρόνοτον, συνάπτουσα τὴν Εὐρώπην πρὸς τὴν Ἀσίαν ἑπτασταδίῳ πορθμῷ τῷ κατὰ Ἄβυδον καὶ Σηστόν, ἐν ἀριστερᾷ μὲν τὴν Προποντίδα ἔχουσα,

seas and, tiny though they be, will not abide where they were born. There is a tract of the Thracian sea which, as men say, is the deepest in all the demesne of Poseidon: wherefore also it is called the Black Gulf.[a] Thereon no over-fierce or violent winds make assault, and in it are coverts under water, cavernous, muddy, beyond thought, in which grow abundantly such things as provide food for tiny fishes. There are the first paths of the new-born swarms of Pelamyds; since beyond all other creatures of the sea they dread the stormy onset of winter—for winter dulls the light of their eyes. And there in the spacious loins of the sea they linger idly and grow in size while they await the sweet spring; and there also they mate and fulfil their desire. But when they are full of roe they hasten to travel back to their native wave where they put from them the travail of their belly.

These the Thracians who dwell above[b] the deep expanse of the Black Gulf capture in the unkindly season of winter by a cruel and unpleasant form of fishing under the bloody law of war and savage doom of death.[c] They have a stout log, not long but as thick as may be, about a cubit in length. On the end of it are put abundant lead and many three-pronged spears set close together; and about it runs a well-twisted cable exceeding long. Sailing up in a boat

ἐν δεξιᾷ δὲ τὸν Μέλανα κόλπον, καλούμενον οὕτως ἀπὸ τοῦ Μέλανος ἐκδιδόντος εἰς αὐτόν. *Cf.* Strab. 28, 92, 124, 323, 331, etc.; Plin. iv. 43 A Dorisco incurvatur ora ad Macron tichos cxii. passus, circa quem locum fluvius Melas a quo sinus appellatur. Oppida . . . Macron tichos [Μακρὸν τεῖχος] dictum quia a Propontide ad Melanem sinum inter duo maria porrectus murus procurrentem excludit Cherronesum.

[b] *i.e.*, N. of.

[c] Ael. xv. 10 describes a method of catching Pelamyds which is not identical with either of Oppian's methods.

δουρὶ δ' ἀναπλώσαντες, ἁλὸς πόρος ἔνθα βάθιστος,
ἐς βυθὸν ἠερόεντα περικρατὲς ἧκαν ἔνερθε
πυθμένος εἰλατίνου κρατερὸν σθένος· αἶψα δὲ ῥιπῇ
σπερχόμενον, μολίβῳ τε καταρρεπὲς ἠδὲ σιδήρῳ,
σεύεται ἐς νεάτας ῥίζας ἁλός, ἔνθ' ἀμενηναῖς
πηλαμύσι προὔτυψεν ἐν ἰλύσι πεπτηυίαις·
σὺν δ' ἕλε σύν τ' ἐτόρησεν ὅσον κίχε δειλὸν ὅμιλον.
οἱ δὲ θοῶς ἀνέρυσσαν ἐληλαμένας περὶ χαλκῷ
παλλομένας ἐλεεινὰ σιδηρείῃς ὀδύνῃσι.
τὰς δέ τις εἰσορόων καί κεν θρασυκάρδιος ἀνὴρ
οἰκτείραι θήρης τε δυσαγρέος ἠδὲ μόροιο·
τῆς μὲν γὰρ λαγόνεσσιν ἐλήλατο δουρὸς ἀκωκή,
τῆς δὲ κάρη ξυνέπειρε θοὸν βέλος, ἡ δ' ὑπὲρ οὐρὴν
οὔτασται, νηδὺν δ' ἑτέρης, ἄλλης δ' ἕλε νῶτα
δριμὺς ἄρης, ἄλλη δὲ μέσον κενεῶνα πέπαρται.
ὡς δ' ὁπότε, κρινθέντος ἐνυαλίοιο κυδοιμοῦ,
δουριφάτους κονίης τε καὶ αἵματος ἐξανελόντες
εὐνὴν ἐς πυρόεσσαν ἑοὶ στέλλωσιν ἑταῖροι
μυρόμενοι· τὰ δὲ πολλὰ καὶ αἰόλα σώμασι νεκρῶν
ἕλκεα παντοῖαί τε βολαὶ πλήθουσιν Ἄρηος·
ὣς καὶ πηλαμύδεσσιν ἐπιπρέπει ἕλκεα πάντῃ,
εἴδωλον πολέμοιο, φίλον γε μὲν ἀσπαλιεῦσιν.
Ἄλλοι δ' αὖ κούφοισι λίνοις ἕλον ἔθνε' ἀφαυρῶν
πηλαμύδων· αἰεὶ γὰρ ἀνὰ κνέφας, ὅττι κεν ἅλμῃ
ἐμπίπτῃ, τρομέουσι, φόβον δ' ὀρφναῖον ἔχουσιν·
ὄρφνῃ δ' ἀγρώσσονται, ἀτυζόμεναι κατὰ βένθος.
δίκτυα γὰρ μάλα κοῦφα λίνων στήσαντες ἐλαφρῶν
κυκλόσε δινεύουσι, βίῃ θείνοντες ἐρετμοῖς
νῶτον ἁλός, κοντοῖς τε καταΐγδην κτυπέουσιν·
αἱ δ' ὑπὸ μαρμαρυγῆς ταχυήρεος ἠδ' ὁμάδοιο
φυζαλέαι θρώσκουσι, λίνου δ' εἰς κόλπον ἵενται

to where the gulf is deepest, mightily they launch into the murky deep the pine-log's stubborn strength. Straightway with swift rush, weighed down by lead and iron, it speeds to the nether foundations of the sea, where it strikes upon the weak Pelamyds huddling in the mud and kills and transfixes as many as it reaches of the hapless crowd. And the fishermen swiftly draw them up, impaled upon the bronze and struggling pitifully under the iron torture. Beholding them even a stone-hearted man would pity them for their unhappy capture and death. For the spear-point has entered the flanks of one, the swift shaft has transfixed the head of another; one is wounded over the tail, the groin of this, the back of that is victim of the bitter warfare, and yet another is pierced in the midst of the belly. As, when the mellay of battle is decided, their comrades take up the slain out of the dust and blood, and array them for the fiery bed, lamenting; and many and various are the wounds on the bodies of the dead and every sort of warlike stroke is there: even so on the Pelamyds wounds show everywhere—an image of war but welcome to the fishers.

Others again take the tribes of the feeble Pelamyds with light nets. For always in the darkness, whatever falls upon the sea, they are afraid and they have a horror of the night and in the night they are captured as they flee in terror through the deep. The fishers set up very light nets of buoyant flax and wheel in a circle round about while they violently strike the surface of the sea with their oars and make a din with sweeping blow of poles. At the flashing of the swift oars and the noise the fishes bound in terror and rush into the bosom of the net which stands at

ἀτρέμας ἑστηῶτος, ὀιόμεναι σκέπας εἶναι,
νήπιαι, αἳ δούποιο φόβῳ μόρον εἰσεπέρησαν.
ἔνθ' οἱ μὲν σχοίνοισιν ἐπισπέρχουσ' ἑκάτερθε,
δίκτυον ἐξερύοντες ἐπ' ᾐόνας· αἱ δ' ὀρόωσαι
σχοίνους κινυμένας, ἀνεμώλια δείματ' ἔχουσαι,
εἰλόμεναι πτήσσουσι καὶ ἀθρόαι ἑσπείρηνται.
πολλά κεν ἀγραίοισι τότ' ἀρήσαιτο θεοῖσι
δικτυβόλος, μήτ' οὖν τι θορεῖν ἔκτοσθε λίνοιο,
μήτε τι κινύμενον δεῖξαι πόρον· ἢν γὰρ ἴδωνται
πηλαμύδες, τάχα πᾶσαι ὑπὲρ κούφοιο λίνοιο
ἐς βυθὸν ἀΐσσουσι καὶ ἄπρηκτον λίπον ἄγρην.
εἰ δ' οὔ σφι μακάρων τις ἀλιπλάγκτων νεμεσήσει,
πολλάκι καὶ τραφερῆς ὑπὲρ ᾐόνος ἑλκυσθεῖσαι
ἔξαλοι οὐκ ἐθέλουσι λιπεῖν λίνον, ἀλλ' ἐνέχονται,
αὐτὴν μήρινθον πολυδινέα πεφρικυῖαι.
ὧδε καὶ ἐν ξυλόχοισιν ὀρέστεροι ἀγρευτῆρες
εἷλον ἀναλκείην ἐλάφων εὐαγρέϊ τέχνῃ,
μηρίνθῳ στέψαντες ἅπαν δρίος· ἀμφὶ δὲ κούφων
ὀρνίθων δήσαντο θοὰ πτερά· ταὶ δ' ἐσορῶσαι
ἠλέματα πτώσσουσι κενὸν φόβον, οὐδὲ πελάσσαι
μαψιδίως πτερύγεσσιν ἀτυζόμεναι μεμάασιν,
εἰσόκε θηρητῆρες ἐπαΐξαντες ἕλωσι.

Καὶ μέν τις δύπτης ἁλίων εὐμήχανος ἔργων
νόσφι δόλου παλάμῃσιν ἐπαΐξας ἕλεν αὐταῖς
ἰχθῦς, ἠΰτε χέρσον ἀμειβόμενος πόρον ἅλμης,
σαργόν τε τρέσσαντα φόβῳ δειλήν τε σκίαιναν.
σαργοὶ μὲν δείσαντες ἀολλέες ἐς μυχὸν ἅλμης
εἰλόμενοι πτήσσουσιν, ἐπ' ἀλλήλαις δὲ κέχυνται,
δόχμιαι ἀμφιπεσόντες, ἀναφρίσσουσι δ' ἀκάνθαις

---

[a] The ref. is to the *Formido*, *C.* iv. 385 n.

rest, thinking it to be a shelter: foolish fishes which, frightened by a noise, enter the gates of doom. Then the fishers on either side hasten with the ropes to draw the net ashore. And, when they see the moving rope, the fish, in vain terror, huddle and cower together and are coiled in a mass. Then would the fisher offer many prayers to the gods of hunting that nothing may leap out of the net nor anything make a move and show the way; for if the Pelamyds see such a thing, speedily they all bound over the light net into the deep and leave the fishing fruitless. But if none of the sea-roaming gods be angry with the fishermen, then often even when the fishes are haled out of the sea upon the solid shore they will not leave the net but cling to it, afraid even of the eddying rope itself. Even so in the woods the hunters of the hill take the timorous deer by happy hunting-craft. Encircling all the wood with a rope, they bind about it the swift wings [a] of buoyant birds; and the deer, when they behold it, shrink in vain and empty terror and, idly affrighted by the wings, they will not approach, until the hunters rush upon them and make them their prey.

Moreover, a diver, skilled in the works of the sea, without any snare attacks and captures some fishes with his hands alone, traversing the path of the sea as if it were dry land: to wit, the Sargue [b] which trembles with terror and the craven Sciaena.[c] The Sargues in their fear cower and crowd together in the depths of the sea and they lie in piles athwart one another, while their backs bristle with spines

[b] *C.* ii. 433 n.

[c] Probably *Umbrina cirrhosa*, M.G. σκιός: Apost. p. 13; Ov. *Hal.* 111 corporis umbrae | Liventis; Hesych. *s.* σκιαδεύς.

νῶτα μετακλίνοντες, ἅτε σκολόπεσσιν ἁπάντῃ
φραξάμενοι πυκινῇσι περίδρομον ἕρκος ἀλωῆς
ἀγρονόμοι, σίντῃσι μέγαν πόνον· οὐδέ κεν ἄν τις
ἐσβαίῃ· σκῶλοι γὰρ ἐρητύουσι κέλευθα·
ὣς κείνοις οὐκ ἄν τις ἐνιχρίμψειεν ἑτοίμως,
οὐδ' ἐπὶ χεῖρα βάλοι· περὶ γὰρ φρίσσουσι κελαιναὶ
πρόκροσσαι πυκινῇσιν ὑπὸ σταλίκεσσιν ἄκανθαι.
ἀλλά τις ἰδμοσύνῃσιν ἀνὴρ ὑπὸ κεύθεα πόντου
ἐσσυμένως δύοιτο, περιφράζοιτο δὲ πάντῃ
σαργούς, ἔνθα κάρη τε καὶ οὐραίη κλίσις αὐτῶν·
χεῖρα δ' ὑπὲρ κεφαλῇσι βαλὼν καθύπερθεν ἀκάνθας
ἦκα καταρρέξειεν ἐπικλίνοι τε πιέζων·
οἱ δ' αὔτως μίμνουσιν ἀρηρότες ἀλλήλοισιν
ἀστεμφεῖς, προβολῇσι πεποιθότες ὀξείῃσιν·
ἔνθα δύω παλάμῃσιν ἀνὴρ ἑκάτερθεν ἀείρας
αὖτις ἀναπλώει τελέσας πανεπίκλοπον ἔργον.

Πετραίην δὲ σκίαιναν ἐπὴν φόβος ἦτορ ἵκηται,
ἐσσυμένως σπιλάδεσσιν ἐπέσσυτο καί τινα κοίλην
χειὴν εἰσεπέρησε περίδρομον ἠὲ χαράδρην,
ἢ ποίαις ἁλίῃσιν ὑπέδραμεν, ἠὲ καὶ ὑγροῖς
φύκεσιν· οὐ γάρ οἵ τι μέλει σκέπας, οἷον ἅπασαν
δεξάμενον ῥύσαιτο, κάρη δ' ἄρα δίζεται οἷον
φράξασθαι, κεφαλὴν δὲ κατακρύψασα καὶ ὄσσε
ἔλπεται οὐχ ὁρόωσα λαθεῖν ὁρόωντος ἐφορμήν.
ὡς δέ τις ὠμηστῆρος ἐπεσσυμένοιο λέοντος
βουβαλὶς ἐν λόχμῃσι κάτω τρέψασα κάρηνον
μαψιδίην φυλακὴν προτιβάλλεται, οὐθ' ὁράασθαι
ἔλπεται, εἰσόκε δή μιν ἐπαΐξας ὀλοὸς θὴρ
δαρδάψῃ· τῆς δ' ἦτορ ὁμοίϊον, οὐδὲ κάρηνον

erect, even as farmers fence all round with close-set stakes the hedge that runs about a vineyard: a great trouble for robbers; and none could enter in, since the stakes bar the way. Even so no one would readily touch the Sargues nor lay a hand upon them, for their dark spines bristle about them with close-set jutting points. But the skilful man should dive speedily under the hidden places of the sea and observe the Sargues all round—where lies the head and where the tail—and putting his hand over their heads he should gently stroke[a] their spines above and press and bend them down. The Sargues remain just as they were, clustered together and unmoving, trusting in their sharp defences. Then the man takes two of them, one in either hand, and comes to the surface again, having accomplished a deed of utmost cunning.

The rock-haunting Sciaena, when fear comes upon its heart, rushes eagerly to the reefs and enters some hollow round hole or cleft, or creeps under the sea grasses or the wet weeds; for it does not study to find such shelter as might admit its whole body and protect it, but seeks only to defend its head, and hiding head and eyes hopes because it does not see to escape the attack of one who sees. Even so in the woods the Antelope, when the ravenous Lion attacks it, turning down its head protects itself with a vain defence and hopes itself unseen, till the deadly beast rushes upon it and rends it, while it remains of like mind as before nor lifts its head, but even while

[a] Ael. i. 23 *θηρῶνται δὲ (οἱ σαργοί) καὶ ἀπὸ χειρός, ἐάν τις τὰς ἀκάνθας, ἃς ἐγείρουσιν εἰς τὸ ἑαυτοῖς ἀμύνειν, εἰς τὸ κάτω μέρος ἀπό γε τῆς κεφαλῆς ἡσυχῇ κατάγων εἶτα κλίνῃ, καὶ πιέσας τῶν πετρῶν ἐκσπάσῃ, εἰς ἃς ἑαυτοὺς ὑπὲρ τοῦ λαθεῖν ὠθοῦσιν.*

ἀγκλινει, δοκέει δὲ καὶ ὀλλυμένη περ ἀλύξαι.
τοῖα δὲ καὶ Λιβύης πτερόεν βοτὸν ἀγκυλόδειρον
νήπια τεχνάζει· μελέη δέ οἱ ἔπλετο τέχνη·
ὣς ἀταλὴ μελέῃσιν ὑπ᾽ ἐλπωρῇσι σκίαινα
κέκρυπται· τάχα γάρ μιν ἐρυσσάμενος παλάμῃσιν
ἀγρευτὴρ ἀνέδυ τε καὶ ἀφραίνουσαν ἔφηνε.
Τόσσα μὲν ἰχθυβόλων ἐδάην ἁλιεργέα τέχνης
δήνεα, καὶ τόσσοισιν ἐπ᾽ ἰχθύσι πικρὸν ὄλεθρον·
τοὺς δ᾽ ἄλλους ξύμπαντας ὁμοίιος αἶσα κιχάνει
κύρτων τ᾽ ἀγκίστρων τε βαθυπλεκέος τε λίνοιο
ῥιπῆς τε τριόδοντος, ὅσ᾽ ἀνδράσιν ἔντεα τέχνης.
τοὺς μὲν ὑπηματίους, τοὺς δ᾽ ἕσπερος εἷλε δαμέντας,
εὖτ᾽ ἂν ὑπὸ πρῶτον νυκτὸς κνέφας ἀσπαλιῆες
πυρσὸν ἀναψάμενοι, γλαφυρὸν σκάφος ἰθύνοντες,
ἰχθύσιν ἀτρεμέουσιν ἀείδελον αἶσαν ἄγωσιν.
ἔνθ᾽ οἱ μὲν πεύκης λιπαρῇ φλογὶ καγχαλόωντες
ἀμφ᾽ ἀκάτῳ θύνουσι, κακὸν δ᾽ ἴδον ἑσπέριον πῦρ,
ῥιπῆς τριγλώχινος ἀμειλίκτοιο τυχόντες.
Ἔστι δέ τις θήρης ἕτερος νόμος ἰχθυβόλοισι

---

[a] Ostrich, *cf. C.* iii. 483 n.

[b] This is what is known in Scotland and on the Scottish Borders (Solway Firth, etc.) as "burning the water," the harpoon being a three-pronged or five-pronged spear, called *leister* or *waster* (some say that leister = 3-pronged, waster = 5-pronged spear): Scott, *Guy Mannering*, c. xxvi. "This

it perishes thinks to escape. Such foolish device also doth the winged bent-necked beast [a] of Libya practise: but its craft is vain. Even so with vain hopes the tender Sciaena hides, for speedily the fisher pulls it forth with his hand and comes to the surface and shows its foolishness.

Even so many devices I know of the fishermen's craft in the sea and bitter destruction for so many fishes. And all the others a like fate overtakes, by weels and hooks and deep-woven net and sweeping trident—some in the day-time, but others evening takes and slays, when at earliest dusk of night with lighted torch [b] the fishers steer their hollow boat, bringing to the resting fishes a darkling doom. Then do the fishes exulting in the oily flame of pine rush about the boat and, to their sorrow seeing the fire at even, meet the stern blow of the trident.

There is another manner of fishing practised by

chase in which the fish is pursued and struck with barbed spears, or a long-shafted trident, called a *waster*, is much practised at the mouth of the Esk and in the other salmon rivers of Scotland. The sport is followed by day and night, but most commonly in the latter, when the fish are discovered by means of torches or fire-grates, filled with blazing fragments of tar-barrels, which shed a strong though partial light upon the water." Burns, *Death and Dr. Hornbook*, v. 31 "I there wi' Something did forgither | That pat me in an eerie swither; | An awfu' scythe, outowre ae shouther, | Clear-dangling, hang; | A three-taed leister on the ither | Lay large and lang." It furnishes a simile to Q. Smyrn. vii. 569 *ὣς δ' ἁλιεὺς κατὰ πόντον ἀνὴρ λελιημένος ἄγρης | τεύχων ἰχθύσι πῆμα φέρει μένος Ἡφαίστοιο | νηὸς ἑῆς ἔντοσθε, διεγρομένη δ' ὑπ' ἀυτμῇ | μαρμαίρει περὶ νῆα πυρὸς σέλας, οἱ δὲ κελαινῆς | ἐξ ἁλὸς ἀίσσουσι μεμαότες ὕστατον αἴγλην | εἰσιδέειν· τοὺς γάρ ῥα τανυγλώχινι τριαίνῃ | κτείνει ἐπεσσυμένους, γάνυται δέ οἱ ἦτορ ἐπ' ἄγρῃ· | ὣς κτλ.* *Cf. C.* iv. 140; Neilson, *Annals of the Solway* (1899), p. 52; Introd. p. xlvii.

φαρμάκταις, οἳ λυγρὸν ἐπ' ἰχθύσι μητίσαντο
φάρμακον, ὠκύμορον δὲ τέλος νεπόδεσσιν ἔθηκαν.
οἱ δ' ἤτοι πρῶτον μὲν ἐπασσυτέραις βολίδεσσι
κοντῶν τε ῥιπῇσι καὶ αἰκίῃσιν ἐρετμῶν
εἰλεῦσιν νεπόδων δειλὰς στίχας εἰς ἕνα χῶρον
κοιλοφυῆ, κευθμῶσιν ὑπαγνύμενον θαμέεσσιν·
ἔνθ' οἱ μὲν δύνουσιν ὑπὸ γλαφυρῆς σπιλάδεσσι,
τοὶ δὲ περιστήσαντο λίνων εὐερκέα πάντῃ
δίκτυα κυκλώσαντες, ἅτ' ἀνδράσι δυσμενέεσσι
διπλὰ περιπροβαλόντες ἀνάρσια τείχεα πέτρης.
καὶ τότ' ἀνὴρ ἄργιλον ὁμοῦ πίειραν ἀείρας
ῥίζαν θ', ἣν κυκλάμινον ἐφήμισαν ἰητῆρες,
μίξας ἐν παλάμῃσι δύω φυρήσατο μάζας·
πόντῳ δ' ἐγκατέπαλτο λίνων ὕπερ, ἀμφὶ δ' ἄρ' αὐταῖς
κοιλάσι καὶ θαλάμῃσι δυσαέα φάρμακ' ἄλειψε

[a] Philostr. *Imag.* i. 13 (speaking of Tunnies): *ἰδέαι μὲν οὖν καθ' ἃς ἁλίσκονται μυρίαι· καὶ γὰρ σίδηρον* (*i.e.* the trident) *ἔστιν ἐπ' αὐτοὺς θήξασθαι καὶ φάρμακα ἐπιπάσαι καὶ μικρὸν ἤρκεσε δίκτυον ὅτῳ ἀπόχρη καὶ σμικρόν τι τῆς ἀγέλης.* Besides Cyclamen (659 below) we read of the use of *φλόμος* (*πλόμος*), Mullein, Lat. *verbascum* (Plin. xxv. 120): A. 602 b 31 *ἀποθνήσκουσι δὲ οἱ ἰχθῦς τῷ πλόμῳ· διὸ καὶ θηρεύουσιν οἱ μὲν ἄλλοι τοὺς ἐν τοῖς ποταμοῖς καὶ λίμναις πλομίζοντες, οἱ δὲ Φοίνικες καὶ τοὺς ἐν τῇ θαλάττῃ*, *cf.* Ael. i. 58; of *Ἀριστολοχία*, Birth-wort, *Aristolochia rotunda*: Plin. xxv. 98 Piscatores Campania radicem (aristolochiae) eam quae rotunda est venenum terrae vocant, coramque nobis contusam mixta calce in mare sparsere. Advolant pisces cupiditate mira statimque exanimati fluitant; of *κόνυζα*, Fleabane, used to induce the Poulpe to relax hold of the rocks: A. 534 b 26 *καὶ οἵ γε πολύποδες οὕτω μὲν προσέχονται ὥστε μὴ ἀποσπᾶσθαι ἀλλ' ὑπομένειν τεμνόμενοι, ἐὰν δέ τις κόνυζαν προσενέγκῃ, ἀφιᾶσιν εὐθὺς ὀσμώμενοι.* *Cf.* Apost. p. 50 "A côté des harpons se place une espèce de crochet construit expressément pour la pêche des poulpes, dont la chair est, comme on sait, très

fishermen who use poison;[a] who devise baleful poison for fishes and bring to the finny race swift doom. First with many missiles and sweep of poles and assault of oars the fishermen drive the wretched ranks of the finny creatures into one place, some bay broken with many hiding-places. There the fishes creep below the hollow rocks and the fishermen set goodly nets of flax around, encircling them all about, even as if they threw threatening double walls of stone around the foemen. Then a man takes rich white clay together with the root which mediciners call cyclamen[b] and mixes them in his hands and kneads two cakes.[c] And he leaps over the nets into the sea and about the very caves and chambers of the fishes he smears

estimée par les Grecs. C'est un gros hameçon porté par une très longue hampe. Aux détritus de crabes, aux coquilles vides, le pêcheur reconnaît le nid (*θαλάμι*) du céphalopode. Il cherche, en faisant pénétrer son appareil, à décrocher l'animal, qui, fort souvent, sentant le danger, se fixe, par ses ventouses, très solidement contre les parois de son nid. Pour le faire lâcher prise, on attache alors à une hampe un morceau d'étoffe blanche ou des feuilles de tabac ou de *κονυζό*, que l'on approche du trou. L'animal sort aussitôt et cherche à s'échapper, mais le pêcheur le saisit avec son crochet."

[b] *C. hederaefolium* or *C. neapolitanum*, Sowbread: Plin. xxv. 116 Mihi et tertia cyclaminos demonstrata est cognomine chamaecissos, uno omnino folio, radiae ramosa, qua pisces necantur. The root is still used in preparing a paste which the Neapolitan fishermen call *lateragna*, and which is either thrown in lumps from a boat or enclosed in a bag and then thrust by means of a long pole among the rocks. The fish—particularly Grey Mullets and other low swimming fish—becoming intoxicated come to the surface and are easily taken. Badham, p. 21; Radcliffe, p. 239.

[c] *Cf.* A. 591 a 18 *ὁ δὲ κέφαλος καὶ ὁ κεστρεὺς ὅλως μόνοι οὐ σαρκοφαγοῦσιν· σημεῖον δέ, οὔτε γὰρ ἐν τῇ κοιλίᾳ πώποτ' ἔχοντες εἰλημμένοι εἰσὶ τοιοῦτον οὐδέν, οὔτε δελέατι χρῶνται πρὸς αὐτοὺς ζῴων σαρξὶν ἀλλὰ μάζῃ.*

χρίσματος ἐχθοδοποῖο καὶ ἐξεμίηνε θάλασσαν.
καὶ τὸν μὲν παλίνορσον ὀλέθρια φαρμάξαντα
δέξατο ναῦς· τοὺς δ' αἶψα κακὴ καὶ ἀνάρσιος ὀδμὴ
πρῶτα μὲν ἐν θαλάμῃσιν ἱκάνεται· ἀχλύϊ δ' ὄσσε
καὶ κεφαλὴ καὶ γυῖα βαρύνεται, οὐδὲ δύνανται
μίμνειν ἐν κευθμῶσιν, ἀτυζόμενοι δὲ χέονται
ἐκτὸς ἀπὸ σπιλάδων· ἡ δέ σφισι πουλὺ θάλασσα
πικροτέρη· τοῖον γὰρ ἐν οἴδμασι πῆμα πέφυρται.
οἱ δ' ὥστ' οἰνοβαρεῖς, ὀλοῇ μεθύοντες ἀϋτμῇ,
πάντῃ δινεύουσι καὶ οὔποθι χῶρον ἔχουσι
λειπόμενον κακότητος, ἐπαΐγδην δὲ λίνοισι
σπερχόμενοι πίπτουσι, διεκθορέειν μεμαῶτες·
ἀλλ' οὔ τις χαλεπῆς ἄτης λύσις οὐδ' ἀλεωρή·
πολλῇ δὲ ῥιπῇ τε καὶ ἅλματι κυμαίνονται
τειρόμενοι· τὸ δὲ πολλὸν ἐπιτρέχει Ἀμφιτρίτῃ
ὀλλυμένων φύσημα, τό τ' ἰχθύσιν ἔπλετο δειλοῖς
οἰμωγή· τοὶ δ' ἐκτὸς ἐπ' ἄλγεσιν ἀσπαλιῆες
τερπόμενοι μίμνουσιν ἀκηδέες, εἰσόκε σιγὴ
πόντον ἕλῃ, φλοίσβου τε καὶ ἀργαλέοιο κυδοιμοῦ
παύσωνται, στονόεσσαν ἀποπνεύσαντες ἀϋτμήν.
καὶ τότ' ἀπειρέσιον νεκύων ἐρύουσιν ὅμιλον
ξυνῷ τεθνηῶτας ὁμοῦ λωβήτορι πότμῳ.
ὡς δ' ὅτε δυσμενέεσσιν ἐπιστήσωνται Ἄρηα,
φροῦδον ἐελδόμενοι ῥαῖσαι πόλιν, οὐδ' ἀνιεῖσι
πήματα βουλεύοντες ἐπί σφισιν, ἀλλὰ καὶ ὕδωρ
κρηνάων φάρμαξαν ὀλέθριον· οἱ δ' ἐπὶ πύργοις

[a] κρήνη is properly a spring from which the water has a free out-flow (Hom. *Od.* xvii. 205 ἐπὶ κρήνην ἀφίκοντο | τυκτὴν καλλίροον, ὅθεν ὑδρεύοντο πολῖται ; x. 107 κρήνην καλλιρρέεθρον ; Hesiod, *W.* 595 κρήνης ἀενάου καὶ ἀπορρύτου, ἥ τ' ἀθόλωτος) as opposed to a standing well, but the distinction is not very accurately observed. For poisoning or making undrinkable

the evil-smelling poison of the hateful unguent and pollutes the sea. Him when he has done his deadly poison the ship takes on board again. But speedily the evil and unkindly odour first reaches the fishes in their chambers and their eyes are clouded and their head and limbs are heavy and they cannot remain in their hiding-places but rush in terror from the rocks. But the sea is yet more bitter for them: such bane is mingled with its waves. And heavy as it were with wine, drunk with the deadly fumes, they wheel every way but nowhere find a place free from the plague, and they rush furiously upon the nets, eager to break through. But there is no deliverance from their cruel doom nor any escape. With much rushing and leaping they toss in their agony and as they perish there runs over the sea a great panting —which for the wretched fishes is their way of lamentation. But the fishermen, rejoicing in their agonies, remain callously apart until silence reigns upon the sea and the fishes cease from their noise and grievous tumult, having breathed away their lamentable breath. And then the fishers draw forth an infinite crowd of dead, slain together by a common doom of destruction. As when men bring war upon their foes, eager to destroy and raze their city, and cease not to devise evil in their hearts but even poison with deadly poison the water of their wells:[a] and

wells in enemy country *cf.* Aeneas Tact. viii. 4 *τὰ κατὰ τὴν χώραν στάσιμα ὕδατα ὡς ἄποτα δεῖ ποιεῖν*; Herod. iv. 120 the Scythians resolved not to fight a pitched battle, but to retire and, as they retired, *τὰ φρέατα, τὰ παρεξίοιεν αὐτοί, καὶ τὰς κρήνας συγχοῦν*; Thuc. ii. 48 the plague attacked the people in the Peiraeus *ὥστε καὶ ἐλέχθη ὑπ' αὐτῶν ὡς οἱ Πελοποννήσιοι φάρμακα ἐσβεβλήκοιεν ἐς τὰ φρέατα· κρῆναι γὰρ οὔπω ἦσαν αὐτόθι.*

λιμῷ τ' ἀργαλέῳ καὶ ὀϊζύϊ μοχθίζοντες
ὕδατί τ' ἐχθοδοπῷ στυγερὸν καὶ ἀεικέα πότμον
ὄλλυνται, νεκύων δὲ πόλις πέπληθεν ἅπασα·
ὣς οἱ λευγαλέῳ τε μόρῳ καὶ ἀδευκέϊ πότμῳ
ἀνδράσι φαρμάκτῃσιν ὑποδμηθέντες ὄλοντο.

the others within their towers, afflicted by grievous hunger and distress and hateful water, perish by a sorrowful and unseemly doom, and the whole city is full of dead; so by a sad death and untoward doom, overcome by the poison of men, the fishes perish.

ΑΛΙΕΥΤΙΚΩΝ ΤΟ Ε

Ἔνθεν ἔπειτ᾽ ἀΐων τεκμαίρεο, κοίρανε γαίης,
ὡς οὐδὲν μερόπεσσιν ἀμήχανον, οὐκ ἐνὶ γαίῃ
μητρὶ καμεῖν, οὐ κόλπον ἀν᾽ εὐρώεντα θαλάσσης·
ἀλλά τις ἀτρεκέως ἰκέλην μακάρεσσι γενέθλην
ἀνθρώπους ἀνέφυσε, χερείονα δ᾽ ὤπασεν ἀλκήν,
εἴτ᾽ οὖν Ἰαπετοῖο γένος, πολυμῆτα Προμηθεύς,
ἀντωπὸν μακάρεσσι κάμεν γένος, ὕδατι γαῖαν
ξυνώσας, κραδίην δὲ θεῶν ἔχρισεν ἀλοιφῇ,
εἴτ᾽ ἄρα καὶ λύθροιο θεορρύτου ἐκγενόμεσθα
Τιτήνων· οὐ γάρ τι πέλει καθυπέρτερον ἀνδρῶν
νόσφι θεῶν· μούνοισι δ᾽ ὑπείξομεν ἀθανάτοισιν.
ὅσσους μὲν κατ᾽ ὄρεσφι βίην ἄτρεστον ἔχοντας
θῆρας ὑπερφιάλους βροτὸς ἔσβεσεν· ὅσσα δὲ φῦλα
οἰωνῶν νεφέλῃσι καὶ ἠέρι δινεύοντα
εἷλε, χαμαίζηλόν περ ἔχων δέμας· οὐδὲ λέοντα
ῥύσατ᾽ ἀγηνορίη δμηθήμεναι, οὐδ᾽ ἐσάωσεν

---

[a] Pind. *N.* vi. 1 ff. ἓν ἀνδρῶν, ἓν θεῶν γένος· ἐκ μιᾶς δὲ πνέομεν | ματρὸς ἀμφότεροι· διείργει δὲ πᾶσα κεκριμένα | δύναμις, ὡς τὸ μὲν οὐδέν, ὁ δὲ χάλκεος ἀσφαλὲς αἰὲν ἕδος | μένει οὐρανός. ἀλλά τι προσφέρομεν ἔμπαν ἢ μέγαν | νόον ἤτοι φύσιν ἀθανάτοις.

[b] Apollod. i. 7. 45 Προμηθεὺς δὲ ἐξ ὕδατος καὶ γῆς ἀνθρώπους πλάσας; Callim. *fr.* 24 (133) εἴ σε Προμηθεὺς | ἔπλασε καὶ πηλοῦ μὴ 'ξ ἑτέρου γέγονας; Lucian, *Prom. in v.* 2.

HALIEUTICA, or FISHING

V

Next hear and mark, O lord of earth, that there is nothing impossible for men to do, either on mother earth or in the vasty gulf of the sea, but of a truth someone created men to be a race like unto the blessed gods, albeit he gave them inferior strength : [a] whether it was the son of Iapetus, Prometheus [b] of many devices, who made man in the likeness of the blessed ones, mingling earth with water, and anointed his heart with the anointing of the gods ; or whether we are born of the blood divine that flowed from the Titans ; [c] for there is nothing more excellent than men, apart from the gods : only to the immortals shall we give place. How many monster wild beasts of dauntless might doth man quench upon the mountains, how many tribes of birds that wheel in cloud and air doth he take captive,[d] though he be of lowly stature ! His valour prevents not the Lion from defeat, nor doth the windswift sweep of his

[c] Schol. *τινὲς δέ φασιν ἐκ τοῦ αἵματος τῶν Τιτάνων πολεμούντων μετὰ τῶν οὐρανίων θεῶν, μάλιστα δὲ τοῦ Διός, καὶ ἡττηθέντων, ὅθεν καί, φασί, βροτὸς ὁ ἄνθρωπος λέγεται ὡς ἀπὸ βρότου ἢ τοῦ αἱματηροῦ μολυσμοῦ τῶν Τιτάνων.*

[d] Soph. *Ant.* 342 *κουφονόων τε φῦλον ὀρνίθων ἀμφιβαλὼν ἄγει | καὶ θηρῶν ἀγρίων ἔθνη | πόντου τ' εἰναλίαν φύσιν | σπείραισι δικτυοκλώστοις | περιφραδὴς ἀνήρ.*

αἰετὸν ἠνεμόεις πτερύγων ῥόθος, ἀλλὰ καὶ Ἰνδὸν
θῆρα κελαινόρινον ὑπέρβιον ἄχθος ἀνάγκῃ
κλῖναν ἐπιβρίσαντες, ὑπὸ ζεύγλῃσι δ' ἔθηκαν
οὐρήων ταλαεργὸν ἔχειν πόνον ἑλκυστῆρα.
κήτεα δ' ὅσσα πέλωρα Ποσειδάωνος ἐναύλοις
ἐντρέφεται, τὰ μὲν οὔτι χερείονα φημὶ θάλασσαν
τίκτειν ὠμοφάγων τεκέων χθονός, ἀλλὰ καὶ ἀλκὴν
καὶ μέγεθος προβέβηκεν ἀναιδέα δείματα πόντου.
ἔστιν ἐν ἠπείρῳ χελύων γένος, οὐδέ τιν' ἀλκὴν
οὐδ' ἄτην ἴσασι· θαλασσαίῃ δὲ χελώνῃ
οὐ μάλα θαρσαλέος τις ἐν οἴδμασιν ἀντιβολήσει.
εἰσὶ δ' ἐνὶ τραφερῇ λάβροι κύνες, ἀλλὰ κύνεσσιν
εἰναλίοις οὐκ ἄν τις ἀναιδείην ἐρίσειε.
πορδαλίων γαίης ὀλοὸν δάκος, ἀλλὰ θαλάσσης
αἰνότερον. χέρσον μὲν ἐπιστείχουσιν ὕαιναι,
πολλῷ δ' ἐν ῥοθίοις κρυερώτεραι. οἱ μὲν ἔασι
κριοὶ μηλονόμων τιθασὸν βοτόν, οὐ δὲ θαλάσσης
κριοῖς μειλιχίοισι συνοίσεται, ὅς κε πελάσσῃ.

---

[a] Elephant: *cf.* Ov. *Tr.* iv. 6. 7 Quaeque sui monitis obtemperat Inda magistri | Bellua; Mart. v. 37. 5 pecudis Indicae dentem. Called *bos Luca* by the Romans (Lucret. v. 1300, 1337) because first seen by them in Lucania with Pyrrhus: Plin. viii. 16 Elephantos Italia primum vidit Pyrrhi regis bello et boves Lucas appellavit in Lucanis visos.

[b] χελώνη ἡ χερσαία A. 540 a 29. *Testudo graeca* L. ("Auf allen Cykladen, selbst das von Tieren beinahe entblösste Syra nicht ausgenommen, sehr gemein. Man hält sie häufig im Hause gezähmt" Erh. p. 71), and *T. marginata* Dumeril, which, unlike the other, prefers wet places to dry and is fairly common in the fresh-water pools of Naxos (Erh. *l.c.*). Both are found in Syria, *T. graeca* being found everywhere in great abundance (Tristram, p. 256).

[c] χελώνη ἡ θαλαττία A. 540 a 29, the marine Tortoise or Turtle. See *H.* i. 397 n.

wings save the Eagle. Even the Indian Beast,[a] dark of hide and of tremendous weight, men make to bow to overwhelming force and under the yoke set him to do the patient hauling labour of the mule. And the huge Sea-monsters that are bred in the habitations of Poseidon are, I declare, no whit meaner than the ravening children of the land, but both in strength and size the dauntless terrors of the sea excel. There is upon the mainland the breed of Tortoises [b] which know no valour nor hurt : but the Tortoise [c] of the sea no man shall confidently confront amid the waves. There are fierce Dogs upon the dry land : but not one could vie in shamelessness with the Dogs of the sea.[d] Dread is the bite of the Leopard of the land [e] but that of the sea Leopard [f] is more terrible. Hyenas [g] walk upon the dry land, but those amid the waves [h] are deadlier far. The Ram of the shepherds is a gentle beast, but he who approaches the Rams of the sea [i] shall not find them kindly to encounter. What Boar [k] wields such

[d] Dog-fishes, *H.* i. 373 n.

[e] *C.* iii. 63 n.

[f] Not certainly identified.

[g] *C.* iii. 263 n.

[h] What animal is intended is not known.

[i] Generally identified with *Orca gladiator*, the Grampus or Killer Whale, the *aries* of Plin. ix. 10 arietes candore tantum cornibus adsimulatis; *ibid.* 145 grassatur aries ut latro, et nunc grandiorum navium in salo stantium occultatus umbra si quem nandi voluptas invitet expectat, nunc elato extra aquam capite piscantium cumbas speculatur occultusque adnatans mergit. *Cf.* xxxii. 144; Ael. xv. 2 ὁ ἄρρην κριὸς λευκὴν τὸ μέτωπον ταινίαν ἔχει περιθέουσαν . . . κριὸς δὲ θῆλυς, ὡς οἱ ἀλεκτρυόνες τὰ κάλλαια, οὕτω τοι καὶ οὗτος ὑπὸ τῇ δέρῃ ἠρτημένους πλοκάμους ἔχει.

[k] *C.* iii. 364. For χλούνης (here = κάπρος) *cf.* Hom. *Il.* ix. 539 χλούνην σῦν ἄγριον ἀγριόδοντα.

τίς δὲ τόσον χλούνης φορέει σθένος, ὅσσον ἄαπτοι
λάμναι; τίς δὲ λέοντος ἐνὶ φρεσὶν αἴθεται ἀλκή,
ὅσση ῥιγεδανῇσιν ἀνισώσαιτο ζυγαίναις;
φώκην δὲ βλοσυρὴν καὶ ἐπὶ χθονὶ χαιτήεσσαι
ἄρκτοι πεφρίκασι καὶ ἐς μόθον ἀντιόωσαι
δάμνανται· τοίοισι μέλει θήρεσσι θάλασσα.
ἀλλ' ἔμπης καὶ τοῖσιν ἐπεφράσσαντο βαρεῖαν
ἄτην ἡμερίων ἄμαχον γένος, ἐκ δ' ἁλιήων
ὄλλυνται, κήτειον ὅτ' ἐς μόθον ὁρμήσωνται.
τῶν ἐρέω θήρης βριθὺν πόνον· ἀλλ' ἀΐοιτε
εὐμενέται βασιλῆες, Ὀλύμπια τείχεα γαίης.
  Κήτεα μεσσοπόροις μὲν ἐνιτρέφεται πελάγεσσι
πλεῖστά τε καὶ περίμετρα· τὰ δ' οὐκ ἀναδύεται ἅλμης
δηθάκις, ἀλλ' ὑπένερθεν ἔχει κρηπῖδα θαλάσσης
βριθοσύνῃ, μαιμᾷ δὲ βορῆς ἀζηχέϊ λύσσῃ
αἰεὶ πεινώοντα καὶ οὔποτε νηδύος αἰνῆς
μαργοσύνην ἀνιέντα· τί γὰρ τόσον ἔσσεται εἶδαρ,
ὅσσον ἐνιπλῆσαι γαστρὸς χάος, ὅσσον ἄαπτον
ἐς κόρον ἀμπαῦσαι κείνων γένυν; οἱ δὲ καὶ αὐτοὶ
ἀλλήλους ὀλέκουσι, χερείονα φέρτερος ἀλκῇ
πέφνων, ἀλλήλοις δὲ βορὴ καὶ δαῖτες ἔασι.
πολλάκι καὶ νήεσσιν ἄγει δέος ἀντιόωντα
ἑσπέριον κατὰ πόντον Ἰβηρικόν, ἔνθα μάλιστα
γείτονος Ὠκεανοῖο λελοιπότ' ἀθέσφατον ὕδωρ

[a] The λάμια of A. 540 b 17 σελάχη δ' ἐστὶ τά τε εἰρημένα καὶ βοῦς καὶ λάμια; 621 a 20 ἔχουσι δ' ὀδόντας ἰσχυρούς (αἱ ἄμιαι), καὶ ἤδη ὦπται καὶ ἄλλα καὶ λάμια ἐμπεσοῦσα καὶ καθελκωθεῖσα; Athen. 306 d Νίκανδρος . . . τὸν καρχαρίαν καλεῖσθαί φησι καὶ λάμιαν καὶ σκύλλαν; *cf.* Plin. ix. 78. One of the larger Sharks, perhaps *Lamna cornubica* Cuv. or *Carcharodon lamia* Bp., M.G. λάμια, καρχαρίας: "rare et excessivement dangereux; quelques individus de cette espèce atteignent des proportions énormes" (Apost. p. 4).

strength as doth the invincible Lamna[a]? What valour burns in the heart of the Lion to be likened to that of the dread Hammer-head?[b] Before the dread-eyed Seal[c] the maned Bears[d] on the land tremble and, when they meet them in battle, they are vanquished. Such are the beasts which have their business in the sea. But notwithstanding even for them the dauntless race of men has devised grievous woe, and they perish at the hands of fishermen, when these set themselves to do battle with the Sea-monsters. The manner of hunting these with its heavy labour I will tell. And do ye hearken graciously, O kings, Olympian bulwarks of the earth.

The Sea-monsters that are nurtured in the midst of the seas are very many in number and of exceeding size. And not often do they come up out of the brine, but by reason of their heaviness they keep the bottom of the sea below. And they rave for food with unceasing frenzy, being always anhungered and never abating the gluttony of their terrible maw: for what food shall be sufficient to fill the void of their belly or enough to satisfy and give a respite to their insatiable jaws? Moreover, they themselves also destroy one another, the mightier in valour slaying the weaker, and one for the other is food and feast. Often too they bring terror to ships when they meet them in the Iberian sea[e] in the West, where chiefly, leaving the infinite water of the neighbouring Ocean,[f] they roll upon their way,

[b] *Zygaena malleus*, M.G. ζύγαινα, a large and fierce Shark, common in the Gulf of Messenia (Apost. p. 4). *Cf.* A. 566 b 9 τῶν μακρῶν . . . ζύγαινα.

[c] *H.* i. 686 ff.

[d] *C.* iii. 139 n.

[e] *H.* iii. 623 n.

[f] Atlantic.

εἰλεῖται, νήεσσιν ἐεικοσόροισιν ὁμοῖα.
πολλάκι δὲ πλαγχθέντα καὶ ᾐόνος ἐγγὺς ἱκάνει
ἀγχιβαθοῦς, ὅτε κέν τις ἐπί σφισιν ὁπλίζοιτο.

Πᾶσι δ' ὑπερφυέεσσι πέλει θήρεσσι θαλάσσης
νόσφι κυνῶν βαρύγυια καὶ οὐκ εὔπρηκτα κέλευθα·
οὔτε γὰρ εἰσορόωσιν ἀπόπροθεν οὔτε θάλασσαν
πᾶσαν ἐπιστείχουσι βαρυνόμενοι μελέεσσιν
ἠλιβάτοις, μάλα δ' ὀψὲ κυλινδόμενοι φορέονται.
τοὔνεκα καὶ πάντεσσιν ὁμόστολος ἔρχεται ἰχθὺς
φαιὸς ἰδεῖν δολιχός τε δέμας, λεπτὴ δέ οἱ οὐρή,
ἔξοχος ὃς προπάροιθεν ἁλὸς πόρον ἡγεμονεύει
σημαίνων· τῷ καί μιν ἐφήμισαν Ἡγητῆρα.
κήτει δ' ἐκπάγλως κεχαρισμένος ἐστὶν ἑταῖρος
πομπός τε φρουρός τε· φέρει δέ μιν ᾗ κ' ἐθέλῃσι
ῥηϊδίως· κείνῳ γὰρ ἐφέσπεται ἰχθύϊ μούνῳ
πιστῷ πιστὸν ἔχων αἰεὶ νόον· ἐγγύθι δ' αὐτοῦ
στρωφᾶται, τανύει δὲ παρασχεδὸν ὀφθαλμοῖσιν
οὐρήν, ᾗ οἱ ἕκαστα πιφαύσκεται, εἴτε τιν' ἄγρην
ἐστὶν ἑλεῖν, εἴτ' οὖν τι κορύσσεται ἐγγύθι πῆμα,

---

[a] For this mode of expressing size *cf.* Hom. *Od.* ix. 321 f. τὸ [the club of Polyphemus] μὲν ἄμμες ἐίσκομεν εἰσορόωντες | ὅσσον θ' ἱστὸν νηὸς ἐεικοσόροιο μελαίνης; Pind. *P*, iv. 245 [the Dragon guarding the Golden Fleece] ὃς πάχει μάκει τε πεντηκόντορον ναῦν κράτει.

[b] ἀγχιβαθής, here applied to ᾐόνος, is properly applied to the sea and the meaning is that even close to the shore the water is deep: Hom. *Od.* v. 413 ἀγχιβαθὴς δὲ θάλασσα καὶ οὔπως ἔστι πόδεσσι | στήμεναι ἀμφοτέροισι, where schol. PV rightly ἡ ἐγγὺς τῆς γῆς βάθος ἔχουσα. *Cf.* τηλεβαθής *H.* i. 633.

like unto ships of twenty oars.[a] Often also they stray and come nigh the beach where the water is deep inshore [b]: and there one may attack them.

For all the great beasts of the sea, save the Dog-fishes, travelling is heavy-limbed and not easy. For they neither see far nor do they travel over all the sea, burdened as they are with their vast limbs, but very tardily they roll upon their way. Wherefore also with all of them there travels a companion fish, dusky to the eye and long of body and with a thin tail: which conspicuously goes before to guide them and show them their path in the sea; for which cause men call it the Guide.[c] But to the Whale [d] it is a companion that hath found wondrous favour, as guide at once and guard; and it easily bringeth him whither he will. For that is the only fish that he follows, the ever-loyal comrade of a loyal friend. And it wheels about near him and close by the eyes of the Whale it extends its tail, which tells the monster everything—whether there is some prey to seize or whether some evil threatens nigh,

[c] *Naucrates ductor* = *πομπίλος* *H.* i. 186 n. *H.* iv. 437 ff., the Pilot-fish or Whale-guide, from its habit of attending on Ships and "Whales" or *κήτη*. It is thought also to be the fish referred to in A. 557 a 29 *ἐν δὲ τῇ θαλάττῃ τῇ ἀπὸ Κυρήνης πρὸς Αἴγυπτόν ἐστι περὶ τὸν δελφῖνα ἰχθὺς ὃν καλοῦσι φθεῖρα* [Plin. xxxii. 150 phthir: "Louse"]· *ὃς γίνεται πάντων πιότατος διὰ τὸ ἀπολαύειν τροφῆς ἀφθόνου θηρεύοντος τοῦ δελφῖνος*, paraphrased Ael. ix. 7. Our present passage is paraphrased Ael. ii. 13 *τὰ κήτη τὰ μεγάλα ὀλίγου πάντα ἄνευ κυνῶν δεῖται τοῦ ἡγεμόνος καὶ τοῖς ὀφθαλμοῖς ἐκείνου ἄγεται. ἔστι δὲ ἰχθὺς μικρὸς καὶ λεπτός, τὴν κεφαλὴν προμηκής, στενὸν δὲ αὐτῷ τὸ οὐραῖον συμπέφυκεν κτλ.*, and there is a picturesque account in Plut. *Mor.* 980 F *sq.* *ὁ δὲ καλούμενος ἡγεμὼν μεγέθει μέν ἐστι καὶ σχήματι κωβιῶδες ἰχθύδιον, τὴν δ' ἐπιφάνειαν ὄρνιθι φρίσσοντι διὰ τὴν τραχυτῆτα τῆς λεπίδος ἐοικέναι λέγεται.*

[d] Introduction, p. lxvii.

εἴτ᾽ ὀλίγη πόντοιο πέλει χύσις, ἣν ἀλεείνειν
βέλτερον· αὐδήεσσα δ᾽ ὅπως ἐνδείκνυται οὐρὴ
πάντα μάλ᾽ ἀτρεκέως· τὸ δὲ πείθεται ὕδατος ἄχθος·
κεῖνος γὰρ πρόμαχός τε καὶ οὔατα καὶ φάος ἰχθὺς
θηρὶ πέλει· κείνῳ δ᾽ ἀΐει, κείνῳ δὲ δέδορκεν,
ἡνί᾽ ἐπιτρέψας σφετέρου βιότοιο φυλάσσειν.
ὡς δὲ πάϊς γενετῆρα παλαίτερον ἀμφαγαπάζει,
φροντίσι γηροκόμοισιν ἀπὸ θρεπτήρια τίνων,
τὸν δ᾽ ἤδη μελέεσσι καὶ ὄμμασιν ἀδρανέοντα
ἐνδυκέως μεθέπων προσπτύσσεται, ἔν τε κελεύθοις
χεῖρ᾽ ὀρέγων καὶ πᾶσιν ἐν ἔργμασιν αὐτὸς ἀμύνων·
πατρὶ δὲ γηράσκοντι νέον σθένος υἱες ἔασιν·
ὣς κεῖνος φιλότητι περιπτύσσει δάκος ἅλμης
ἰχθύς, ἠΰτε νῆα νέμων οἴηκι χαλινῷ.
ἤ πού οἱ γενεῆς πρώτης ἄπο σύμφυτον αἷμα
ἔλλαχεν, ἠέ μιν αὐτὸς ἑλὼν ἑταρίσσατο θυμῷ.
ὣς οὔτ᾽ ἠνορίης οὔτ᾽ εἴδεος ἔπλετ᾽ ὄνειαρ
τόσσον, ὅσον πραπίδων· ἀλκὴ δ᾽ ἀνεμώλιος ἄφρων·
καί τε μέγα βριάοντα κατέσβεσεν ἠδ᾽ ἐσάωσε
βαιὸς ἀνὴρ εὔμητις· ἐπεὶ καὶ κῆτος ἄαπτον
ἀπλάτων μελέων ὀλίγον προτιβάλλεται ἰχθύν.
τοὔνεκά τις πάμπρωτον ἕλοι σκοπὸν Ἡγητῆρα

[a] Plut. *Mor.* 980 F καὶ προνήχεται, τὸν δρόμον ἐπευθύνων, ὅπως οὐκ ἐνσχεθήσεται βραχέσιν οὐδ᾽ εἰς τέναγος ἤ τινα πορθμὸν ἐκπεσεῖται δυσέξοδον. For stranded Whales in Greece *cf.* *H.* i. 368 n. In Scotland a remarkable case occurred in 1927, when a vast number of Whales (*Pseudorca crassidens* or False Killer) were stranded at Dornoch. The species had not been seen alive for 80 years. *Scottish Naturalist*, 1927, pp. 161 f.

[b] Epic θρεπτήρια (Hom. *H. Dem.* 168 ἀπὸ θρεπτήρια δοίη; *ibid.* 223; Hesiod, *W.* 188) or θρέπτρα (Hom. *Il.* iv. 477 = xvii. 301 οὐδὲ τοκεῦσι | θρέπτρα φίλοις ἀπέδωκε), Tragedy and Prose τροφεῖα (Eur. *Ion* 852 τροφεῖα δεσπόταις | ἀποδούς.

or if there is a shallow depth[a] of sea which it were better to avoid. Even as if it had a voice, the tail declares all things to him truly, and the burden of the water obeys. For that fish is to the beast champion at once and ears and eye: by it the Whale hears, by it he sees, to it he entrusts the reins of his life for keeping. Even as a son lovingly entreats his aged father, by anxious care of his years repaying the price of his nurture,[b] and zealously attends and cherishes him, weak now of limb and dim of eye, reaching him his arm in the street and himself in all works succouring him—sons[c] are a new strength to an aged sire: so that fish for love cherishes the monster of the brine, steering as it were a ship by the guiding helm.[d] Surely it had blood akin to his from earliest birth or he took it of his own will and made it his companion. Thus neither valour nor beauty hath such profit as wisdom, and strength with unwisdom is vain. A little man of good counsel sinks or saves the man of might; for even the invincible Whale with its unapproachable limbs takes for its friend a tiny fish. Therefore one should first capture that scouting Guide, entrapping it with

Lycurg. 53 *οὐκ ἀπέδωκε τὰ τροφεῖα τῇ πατρίδι*). *Cf.* Eur. *I. in Aul.* 1230 *πόνων τιθηνοὺς ἀποδιδοῦσά σοι τροφάς.*

[c] Pind. *O.* viii. 70 *πατρὶ δὲ πατρὸς ἐνέπνευσεν μένος | γήραος ἀντίπαλον*; *O.* x. 86 *ὥτε παῖς ἐξ ἀλόχου πατρὶ | ποθεινὸς ἵκοντι νεότατος τὸ πάλιν ἤδη*; Nem. vii. 100 *παίδων δὲ παῖδες ἔχοιεν αἰεὶ | γέρας τό περ νῦν καὶ ἄρειον ὄπιθεν*; Proverbs xvii. 6 Children's children are the crown of old men; Psalm cxxvii. 4 As arrows in the hand of a mighty man, so are the children of youth. Happy is the man that hath his quiver full of them; they shall not be ashamed when they speak with their enemies in the gate.

[d] Plut. *Mor.* 981 A *ἕπεται γὰρ αὐτῷ τὸ κῆτος, ὥσπερ οἴακι ναῦς.*

κεῖνον, ὑπ' ἀγκίστροιο βίῃ καὶ δαιτὶ δολώσας·
οὐ γάρ κε ζώοντος ἐπιβρίσας δαμάσαιο
κνώδαλον, οἰχομένου δὲ θοώτερος ἔσσετ' ὄλεθρος.
οὐ γὰρ ἔτ' οὔθ' ἅλμης ἰοειδέος οἶδε κέλευθα
ἀτρεκέως, οὐ πῆμα παρασχεδὸν ἐξαλέασθαι,
ἀλλ' αὔτως, ἅτε φορτὶς ὀλωλότος ἰθυντῆρος,
πλάζεται ἀπροφύλακτον, ἀμήχανον, ᾗ κεν ἄγῃσι
γλαυκὸν ὕδωρ, σκοτίοις δὲ καὶ ἀφράστοισι πόροισιν
ἐμφέρεται, χηρωθὲν ἀρηγόνος ἡνιόχοιο.
πολλάκι καὶ πέτρῃσι καὶ ἠϊόνεσσιν ἔκελσε
πλαζόμενον· τοίη οἱ ἐπ' ὄμμασι πέπταται ἀχλύς.
δή ῥα τότ' ὀτρηροῖσι νοήμασιν ἐς πόνον ἄγρης
ἰχθυβόλοι σπεύδουσιν, ἐπευξάμενοι μακάρεσσι
κητοφόνοις ἀλεγεινὸν ἑλεῖν τέρας Ἀμφιτρίτης.
ὡς δ' ὅτε δυσμενέων βριαρὸς λόχος ἀντιβίοισι
λάθριος ἐμπελάσῃ, μεσάτην ἐπὶ νύκτα δοκεύσας,
εὕδοντας δ' ἐκίχησε φυλακτῆρας πρὸ πυλάων,
Ἄρεος εὐμενέοντος, ἐνιπλήξας δ' ἐδάμασσεν·
ἔνθεν ἔπειτ' ἄκρην τε πόλιν καὶ τύρσιν ἐπ' αὐτὴν
θαρσαλέοι σπεύδουσι, πυρὸς βέλος, ἄστεος ἄτην,
δαλὸν ἐϋδμήτων μεγάρων ῥαιστῆρα φέροντες·
ὣς τότε θαρσαλέως ἁλιεὺς στρατὸς ἐγκονέουσιν
ἄφρακτον μετὰ θῆρα, πεφασμένου ἰθυντῆρος.
τοῦ δ' ἤτοι πρῶτον μὲν ἐνὶ φρεσὶ τεκμαίρονται
ἄχθος ὅσον μέγεθός τε· τὰ δ' ἔπλετο σήματα γυίων·
εἰ μὲν γὰρ πόντοιο κυλινδόμενον μετὰ δίναις
βαιὸν ὑπερτέλλοιτο ῥάχιν λοφιήν τε φαεινὸν
ἄκρην, ἦ μέγα κεῖνο καὶ ἔξοχον· οὐδὲ γὰρ αὐτὴ
ῥηϊδίως φορέει μιν ἀνοχλίζουσα θάλασσα·
εἰ δέ τι καὶ νώτοιο φαείνεται, οὐ τόσον ἄχθος

might of hook and bait; for while it lives thou shalt never overpower and conquer the monster, but when it is gone, his destruction will be swifter. For he no longer knows surely the paths of the violet brine nor knows to shun the evil that is at hand, but, even as a merchant vessel whose steersman has perished, he wanders idly, defenceless and helpless, wherever the grey water carries him, and is borne in darkling and unguessed ways, widowed of his helpful charioteer. Many a time in his wandering he runs aground on rock or beach: such darkness is spread upon his eyes. Thereupon with eager thoughts the fishers hasten to the labour of the hunt, praying to the blessed gods of whale-killing that they may capture the dread monster of Amphitrite.[a] As when a strong company of foemen, having waited for midnight, stealthily approach their enemy and find by favour of Ares the sentinels asleep before the gates and fall upon them and overcome them: thereupon they haste confidently to the high city and the very citadel, carrying the weapon of fire, the doom of the city, even the brand that wrecks the well-builded walls: even so confidently do the fisher host haste after the beast, unguarded now that his pilot is slain. First they conjecture in their minds his weight and size; and these are the signs that tell the measure of his limbs. If, as he rolls amid the waves of the sea, he rise a little above it, showing the top of his spine and the ridge of his neck, then verily he is a mighty beast and excellent: for not even the sea itself can easily support and carry him. But if some portion of his back also appears, that

[a] Spouse of Poseidon (Apollod. i. 4): hence metonomy for Sea.

ἀγγέλλει· κοῦφαι γὰρ ἀφαυροτέροισι κέλευθοι.
τοῖσιν δ᾽ ὁρμιὴ μὲν ἐπασσυτέραις ἀραρυῖα
θωμίγγων ξυνοχῇσι πολυστρεφέεσσι τέτυκται,
ὅσσος τε πρότονος νηὸς πέλει οὔτε βαθείης
οὔτ᾽ ὀλίγης· μῆκος δὲ τιταίνεται ἄρκιον ἄγρῃ·
ἄγκιστρον δ᾽ εὐεργὲς ἐπημοιβαῖς κεχάρακται
γλωχίνων προβολῇσιν ἀκαχμένον ἀμφοτέρωθεν,
οἷον καὶ πέτρην ἑλέειν καὶ ῥωγάδα πεῖραι,
τόσσον ἴτυν κρυερήν, ὅσσον περὶ χάσμα καλύψαι.
δινωτὴ δ᾽ ἅλυσις περιβάλλεται ἄκρα κελαινοῦ
ἀγκίστρου, στιβαρή, χαλκήλατος, ἥ κεν ὀδόντων
λευγαλέην ἀνέχοιτο βίην καὶ χάσματος αἰχμάς·
δεσμῷ δ᾽ ἐν μεσάτῳ τροχοειδέα κύκλα τέτυκται
πυκνὰ παρ᾽ ἀλλήλοισιν, ἅ κεν στροφάλιγγας ἐρύκοι
φοιταλέας, μηδ᾽ ἰθὺς ἀπορρήξειε σίδηρον
αἱμάσσων, ὀλοῇσι περισπερχὴς ὀδύνῃσιν,
ἀλλὰ περιστροφάδην πλαγκτὸν δρόμον εἱλίσσοιτο.
δαῖτα δ᾽ ἐπ᾽ ἀγκίστρῳ δυστερπέα πορσύνουσι
ταύρειον μέλαν ἧπαρ ἀπόκριτον ἠὲ καὶ ὦμὸν
ταύρειον γενύεσσιν ἐοικότα δαινυμένοιο.
πολλαὶ δ᾽ ἀγρευτῆρσιν ὁμόστολοι ὥστ᾽ ἐς Ἄρηα
θήγονται κρατεραί τ᾽ ἀκίδες στιβαραί τε τρίαιναι,
ἅρπαι, βουπλῆγές τε βαρύστομοι, ὅσσα τε τοῖα
ἄκμοσι δυσκελάδοις ῥαιστήρια χαλκεύονται·
ἐσσυμένως δ᾽ ἀκάτοισιν ἐϋσέλμοις ἐπιβάντες,
σιγῇ νευστάζοντες ὅ τι χρέος ἀλλήλοισι,
στέλλονται, κώπῃσι δ᾽ ὑπ᾽ εὐκήλοισι θάλασσαν
ἀτρέμα λευκαίνουσι, φυλασσόμενοι μάλα δοῦπον,
μή τι μάθοι μέγα κῆτος ἀλευόμενόν τε νέοιτο
βυσσὸν ὑποβρυχίην, ἅλιον δέ κε μόχθον ἄροιντο.
ἀλλ᾽ ὅτε οἱ πελάσωσιν ὁμαιχμήσωσί τ᾽ ἀέθλῳ,
δὴ τότε θαρσαλέως πρώρης ἄπο θηρὶ πελώρῳ

does not announce so great a weight: for feebler beasts travel a more buoyant path. For these monsters the line is fashioned of many strands of well-woven cord, as thick as the forestay of a ship, neither very large nor very small, and in length suitable to the prey. The well-wrought hook is rough and sharp with barbs projecting alternately on either side, strong enough to take a rock and pierce a cliff and with deadly curve as great as the gape of the beast can cover. A coiled chain is cast about the butt of the dark hook—a stout chain of beaten bronze to withstand the deadly violence of his teeth and the spears of his mouth. In the midst of the chain are set round wheels close together, to stay his wild struggles and prevent him from straightway breaking the iron in his bloody agony, as he tosses in deadly pain, but let him roll and wheel in his fitful course. For fatal banquet they put upon the hook a portion of the black liver of a bull or a bull's shoulder suited to the jaws of the banqueter. To accompany the hunters, as it were for war, are sharpened many strong harpoons [a] and stout tridents and bills and axes of heavy blade and other such weapons as are forged upon the noisy anvil. Swiftly they go on board their well-benched ships, silently nodding to one another as need may be, and set forth. With quiet oars they gently make white the sea, carefully avoiding any noise, lest the great Whale remark aught and dive into the depths for refuge, and the task of the fishers be undertaken in vain. But when they draw nigh to him and close with their task, then boldly from the prow they

[a] See Ael. i. 18 (quoted on 416 *infra*).

πῆμα δόλου προὔθηκαν· ὁ δ' ὡς ἴδε δαῖτα βαρεῖαν,
ἆλτο καὶ οὐκ ἀμέλησεν ἀναιδέϊ γαστρὶ πιθήσας·
μάρψε δ' ἐπιθύσας γναμπτὸν μόρον, αὐτίκα δ' εἴσω
ἄγκιστρον κατέδυ τεθοωμένον εὐρέϊ λαιμῷ,
ἐν δ' ἐπάγη γλωχῖσιν· ὁ δ' ἕλκεϊ θυμὸν ὀρινθεὶς
πρῶτα μὲν ἀσχαλόων ὁλοὴν γένυν ἀντία πάλλει,
χαλκείην θώμιγγα διαρραῖσαι μενεαίνων·
ἀλλ' ἄρα οἱ κενεὸς τέταται πόνος· ἔνθεν ἔπειτα
σπερχόμενος φλογέῃσιν ἐποχθίζων ὀδύνῃσι
δύεται ἐν κόλποισιν ὑποβρυχίοισι θαλάσσης·
τῷ δὲ τάχ' ἀσπαλιῆες ἐπιτρωπῶσιν ἅπασαν
ὁρμιήν· οὐ μὲν γὰρ ἔνι σθένος ἀνθρώποισιν
ὅσσον τ' αὖ ἐρύσαι καὶ ἀναινόμενον δαμάσασθαι
βριθὺ πέλωρ· ῥέα γάρ σφε σὺν αὐτοῖς σέλμασι νηῶν
ἑλκύσει ποτὶ βυσσόν, ὅθ' ὁρμήσειε φέρεσθαι.
οἱ δέ οἱ ὁρμιῇ προσαρηρότας εὐρέας ἀσκοὺς
πνοιῆς ἀνδρομέης πεπληθότας εὐθὺς ἐς ὕδωρ
δυομένῳ πέμπουσιν· ὁ δ' ὀχθίζων ὀδύνῃσι
ῥινῶν οὐκ ἀλέγει, κατὰ δ' ἔσπασεν οὐκ ἐθέλοντας
ῥηϊδίως ἄκροιο λιλαιομένους ἁλὸς ἀφροῦ.
ἀλλ' ὁπότ' ἐς δάπεδον πελάσῃ μεμογηότι θυμῷ,
στῆ ῥα μέγ' ἀφριόων, τετιημένος· ὡς δέ τις ἵππος
ἱδρῶτ' ἐξανύσας καματώδεα τέρματος ἄκρου
ἀφρῷ ὑφ' αἱματόεντι γένυν σκολιοῖσι χαλινοῖς
ἐμπρίει, θερμὸν δὲ διὰ στόμα κίδναται ἆσθμα,

---

[a] Hom. *Od.* vii. 216 οὐ γάρ τι στυγερῇ ἐπὶ γαστέρι κύντερον ἄλλο | ἔπλετο, ἥ τ' ἐκέλευσεν ἕο μνήσασθαι ἀνάγκῃ.

[b] *Cf. Relation of a Voyage in the North Sea, . . . made in the years 1767 and 1768 by M. de Kerguelen Tremarec* (Pinkerton's Voyages, vol. i. p. 790): "As these poor people [the Greenlanders] have but little wood and iron, they make use of the precaution of fastening to the middle

launch for the giant beast the fatal snare. And when he espies the grievous banquet, he springs and disregards it not, obedient to his shameless belly,[a] and rushing upon the hookèd death he seizes it; and immediately the whetted hook enters within his wide throat and he is impaled upon the barbs. Then, roused by the wound, first, indignant, he shakes his deadly jaw against them and strives to break the brazen cord; but his labour is vain. Then, next, in the anguish of fiery pain he dives swiftly into the nether gulfs of the sea. And speedily the fishers allow him all the length of the line; for there is not in men strength enough to pull him up and to overcome the heavy monster against his will. For easily could he drag them to the bottom, benched ship and all together, when he set himself to rush. Straightway as he dives they let go with him into the water large skins[b] filled with human breath and fastened to the line. And he, in the agony of his pain, heeds not the hides but lightly drags them down, all unwilling and fain for the surface of the foamy sea. But when he comes to the bottom with labouring heart, he halts, greatly foaming in his distress. As some horse when it has accomplished its sweaty labour to the utmost goal, in a bloody foam grinds his teeth in the crooked bit, while the hot panting breath comes through his

of every harpoon which they throw the bladder of a sea-dog, that if the harpoon should not strike the fish or detach itself from it, it may float on the water, and be readily found again. This experiment was known to the fishermen of the Atlantic [*sic*] Ocean, for Opien in his *Halieuticon* speaks of it: lib. v. 177: 'They dart,' says he, 'large sacks blown up by the breath, and fastened to a cord, immediately at the fish, as it is about to plunge.'"

ὧς ὁ μέγ' ἀσθμαίνων ἀμπαύεται, οὐδέ οἱ ἀσκοὶ
μίμνειν ἱεμένῳ περ ἐπιτρωπῶσιν ἔνερθεν,
αἶψα δ' ἄνω σπεύδουσι καὶ ἔξαλοι ἀΐσσουσι
πνοιῇ ἀειρόμενοι· τῷ δ' ἵσταται ἄλλος ἄεθλος.
ἔνθ' ἤτοι πρῶτον μὲν ἐπαΐσσει γενύεσσι
ῥιπὴν μαψιδίην, λελιημένος αὖ ἐρύοντα
δέρματ' ἀμύνεσθαι· τὰ δ' ἀνίπταται οὐδέ ἑ μίμνει,
φεύγει δὲ ζωοῖσιν ἀλευομένοισιν ὁμοῖα·
αὐτὰρ ὅ γ' ἀσχαλόων μυχάτην πάλιν ἵεται ἅλμην,
πολλὰς δὲ στροφάλιγγας ἑλίσσεται, ἄλλοτ' ἀνάγκῃ,
ἄλλοθ' ἑκών, ἕλκων τε καὶ ἑλκόμενος παλίνορσος.
ὡς δ' ὅτε δουροτόμοι ξυνὸν πόνον ἀθλεύωσι
πρίονος ἐγκονέοντες, ὅτε τρόπιν ἠέ τιν' ἄλλην
χρειὼ πλωτήρεσσιν ἐπισπεύδουσι τελέσσαι,
ἄμφω δὲ τρηχεῖαν ἐρειδομένοιο σιδήρου
ἀλκὴν αὖ ἐρύουσι καὶ οὔποτε ταρσὸς ὀδόντων
τέτραπται μίαν οἶμον, ἐπειγόμενος δ' ἑκάτερθεν
κλάζει τε πρίει τε καὶ ἔμπαλιν ἕλκεται αἰεί,
τοῖον καὶ ῥινοῖσι πέλει καὶ θηρὶ δαφοινῷ
νεῖκος ἀνελκομένῳ τε βιαζομένοις θ' ἑτέρωθεν.
πολλὴν δ' αἱματόεσσαν ὑπεὶρ ἁλὸς ἔπτυσεν ἄχνην
παφλάζων ὀδύνῃσιν, ὑποβρύχιον δὲ μέμυκε
μαινομένου φύσημα, περιστένεται δέ οἱ ὕδωρ
ἀμβολάδην· φαίης κεν ὑπ' οἴδμασι πᾶσαν ἀϋτμὴν
κευθομένην Βορέαο δυσαέος αὐλίζεσθαι.
τόσσον ἀνασθμαίνει λάβρον μένος, ἀμφὶ δὲ πυκναὶ
δίναις οἰδαλέῃσιν ἑλισσόμεναι στροφάλιγγες
οἴδματα κοιλαίνουσι διϊσταμένοιο πόροιο.

---

[a] Hom. *Od.* ix. 384 ὡς ὅτε τις τρυπῷ δόρυ νήιον ἀνὴρ | τρυπάνῳ, οἱ δέ τ' ἔνερθεν ὑποσσείουσιν ἱμάντι | ἁψάμενοι ἑκάτερθε, τὸ δὲ τρέχει ἐμμενὲς αἰεί. For simile of "saw" to express reciprocal

mouth: so, breathing hard, the Whale rests. But the skins allow him not, even if he would, to remain below but swiftly speed upward and leap forth from the sea, buoyed by the breath within them; and a new contest arises for the Whale. Then first he makes a vain rush with his jaws, eager to defend himself against the hides which pull him up. But these fly upward and await him not, but flee like living things seeking escape. And he indignant rushes again to the innermost deep of the brine, and many a twist and turn he makes, now perforce, now of his own will, pulling and being pulled in turn. As when woodcutters [a] labour busily at the joint labour of the saw, when they haste to make a keel or other needful matter for mariners: both men in turn draw to them the rough edge of iron pressing on the wood and the row of its teeth is never turned in one path, but urged from either side it sings loudly as it saws and evermore is drawn the other way: even such is the contest between the hides and the deadly beast—he being dragged up, while they are urged the other way. Much bloody spume he discharges over the sea as he struggles in his pain, and his panting breath as he rages resounds under the sea, and the water bubbles and roars around; thou wouldst say that all the blasts of Boreas were housed and hidden beneath the waves: so violently he pants in his fury. And round about many a swirling eddy the swelling waves make a hollow in the waters and the sea is divided in twain. As by the mouth of the

action (*cf.* Eng. "see-saw") *cf.* Aristoph. *Vesp.* 694 *ὡς πρίονθ' ὁ μὲν ἕλκει, ὁ δ' ἀντενέδωκε*; Hippocr. Περὶ Διαίτης, i. p. 634 Kühn *πρίουσιν ἄνθρωποι ξύλον, ὁ μὲν ἕλκει, ὁ δὲ ὠθέει*; *ibid.* p. 635 *ὥσπερ οἱ τέκτονες τὸ ξύλον πρίουσι, καὶ ὁ μὲν ἕλκει, ὁ δὲ ὠθέει.*

οἷον δ' Ἰονίοιο παρὰ στόμα καὶ κελάδοντος
Τυρσηνοῦ πόντοιο μέση πορθμοῖο διαρρὼξ
εἰλεῖται, λάβροισιν ὑπ' ἄσθμασι Τυφάωνος
μαινομένη, δειναὶ δὲ τιταινόμεναι στροφάλιγγες
κῦμα θοὸν κάμπτουσι, περιστρέφεται δὲ κελαινὴ
ἑλκομένη δίνῃσι παλιρροίβδοισι Χάρυβδις,
ὣς τότε κητείοισιν ὑπ' ἄσθμασι χῶρος ἁπάντη
ξαινόμενος βέμβικας ἑλίσσεται Ἀμφιτρίτης.
ἔνθα τις ἰχθυβόλων γλαφυρὸν σκάφος ὠκὺς ἐρέσσων
ἐς χέρσον κατάγοιτο καὶ ἀκταίης ἀπὸ πέτρης
ὁρμιὴν ἅψαιτο καὶ αὐτίκα νοστήσειε,
πρυμναίοις ἅτε νῆα κατοχμάσσας ὑπὸ δεσμοῖς.
τὸν δ' ὅτε παιφάσσοντα λάβῃ κόρος, ἐκ δ' ὀδυνάων
θὴρ ὀλοὸς μεθύῃ, καμάτῳ δέ οἱ ἄγριον ἦτορ
κλίνηται, ῥέψῃ δὲ μόρου στυγεροῖο τάλαντα,
ἀσκὸς μὲν πρώτιστος ἀνέδραμε πείρατα νίκης
ἀγγέλλων, μέγα δ' ἦτορ ἐν ἀγρευτῆρσιν ἄειρεν.
οἷον δ' ἀλγινόεντος ἀνερχόμενον πολέμοιο
κήρυκ' ἀργυφέοισιν ἐν εἵμασιν ἠδὲ προσώπῳ
φαιδρῷ καγχαλόωντες ἑοὶ μεθέπουσιν ἑταῖροι,
αἴσιον ἀγγελίην ποτιδεγμένοι αὐτίκ' ἀκοῦσαι,
ὣς οἱ καγχαλόωσιν ἐσαθρήσαντες ἔνερθε
ῥινὸν ἀνερχομένην εὐάγγελον· αὐτίκα δ' ἄλλοι

---

[a] The Strait of Messina, Σικελικὸς πορθμός (Strabo 43), *Siculum fretum* (Plin. iii. 92), between Italy and Sicily, dividing the Tyrrhenian Sea on the N. from the Ionian Sea on the S. Here were localized the Scylla and Charybdis of Hom. *Od.* xii. 104 ff. *Cf.* Thuc. iv. 24; Strabo 268; Plin. iii. 87 In eo freto est scopulus Scylla, item Charybdis, mare verticosum, ambo clara saevitia.

[b] Strabo 248 ταῦτ' οὖν διανοηθεὶς (Πίνδαρος) τῷ παντὶ τόπῳ τούτῳ φησὶν ὑποκεῖσθαι τὸν Τυφῶνα· νῦν γε μὰν ταί θ' ὑπὲρ Κύμας ἁλιερκέες ὄχθαι Σικελία τ' αὐτοῦ πιέζει στέρνα λαχνάεντα [= Pind. *P.* i. 17 ff.].

Ionian and Tyrrhenian seas the dividing waters of the Strait [a] roll raging under the violent panting of Typhaon [b] and dread straining swirls curve the swift wave and dark Charybdis circles round, drawn by her eddying tides: even so by the panting blasts of the Whale the space of the sea around is lashed and whirled about. Then should one of the whalers row his hollow skiff and come to land and make fast the line to a rock upon the shore and straightway return—even as a man makes fast a ship by cables from the stern.[c] Now when the deadly beast is tired with his struggles and drunk with pain and his fierce heart is bent with weariness and the balance of hateful doom inclines, then first of all a skin comes to the surface, announcing the issue of victory and greatly uplifts the hearts of the fishers. Even as, when a herald [d] returns from dolorous war in white [e] raiment and with cheerful face, his friends exulting follow him, expecting straightway to hear favourable tidings, so do the fishers exult when they behold the hide, the messenger of good news, rising from below. And immediately other skins rise up

[c] By means of the stern-cables (πρυμνήσια) attached to a rock on shore. Hence the Homeric formulae (1) when a ship comes to land: ἐκ δ' εὐνὰς (anchors) ἔβαλον, κατὰ δὲ πρυμνήσι' ἔδησαν (Hom. *Il.* i. 436); (2) when a ship puts to sea: πεῖσμα (cable) δ' ἔλυσαν ἀπὸ τρητοῖο λίθοιο (Hom. *Od.* xiii. 77); *cf.* Poll. x. 134.

[d] Aesch. *Ag.* 638 ff. contrasts the messenger of bad news (ὅταν δ' ἀπευκτὰ πήματ' ἄγγελος πόλει | στυγνῷ προσώπῳ πτωσίμου στρατοῦ φέρῃ) with the bringer of glad tidings (σωτηρίων δὲ πραγμάτων εὐάγγελον | ἥκοντα πρὸς χαίρουσαν εὐεστοῖ πόλιν).

[e] The Greeks, like ourselves, associated white with gladness, black with mourning. Hence the boast of Pericles upon his death-bed: "Οὐδεὶς γάρ," ἔφη, "δι' ἐμὲ τῶν ὄντων Ἀθηναίων μέλαν ἱμάτιον περιεβάλετο" (Plut. *Per.* xxxviii.).

ἀσκοὶ ἐπαντέλλουσι καὶ ἀνδύνουσι θαλάσσης,
βριθὺ πέλωρ σύροντες· ὁ δ' ἕλκεται οὐλόμενος θὴρ
οὐκ ἐθέλων, μόχθῳ τε καὶ ἕλκεϊ θυμὸν ἀλύων.
ἔνθα τότ' ἰχθυβόλων θράσος ἔγρεται, ἄγχι δὲ νῆας
εὐκώπους ἐλόωσιν ἐπειγομένοισιν ἐρετμοῖς·
πολλὴ δὲ σμαραγή, πολλὴ δ' ἀνὰ πόντον ἀϋτὴ
σπερχομένων τέτρηχε καὶ ἀλλήλους ἐς ἄεθλον
κεκλομένων· φαίης κεν ἐνυάλιον πόνον ἀνδρῶν
δέρκεσθαι· τοίη γὰρ ἐνὶ φρεσὶν ἵσταται ἀλκή,
τόσσος δὲ φλοῖσβός τε καὶ ἵμερος ἰωχμοῖο.
τῶν μέν τις καὶ τῆλε δυσηχέα δοῦπον ἀκούσας
αἰπόλος ἢ βαθύμαλλον ἐν ἄγκεσι πῶϋ κομίζων,
ἢ δρυτόμος πεύκης ὀλετὴρ ἢ θῆρας ἐναίρων
θαμβήσας πόντου τε καὶ ᾐόνος ἐγγὺς ἱκάνει,
στὰς δὲ κατὰ προβλῆτος ὑπερφίαλον πόνον ἀνδρῶν
φυλόπιδος βυθίης θηήσατο καὶ τέλος ἄγρης
εὐπάγλου· τοὺς δ' ὑγρὸς Ἄρης ἄσβεστος ὀρίνει.
ἔνθ' ὁ μὲν ἐν παλάμῃσι τανυγλώχινα τρίαιναν
πάλλει, ὁ δ' ὀξείης ἀκίδος βέλος, οἱ δὲ φέρουσιν
εὐκαμπῆ δρεπάνην, ὁ δέ τις βουπλῆγα τιταίνει
ἀμφιτόμον· πᾶσιν δὲ πόνος, πᾶσιν δὲ σιδήρου
χεῖρας ἐφοπλίζει βριαρὴ γένυς, ἄγχι δὲ θῆρα
βάλλουσ', οὐτάζουσι, καταΐγδην ἐλόωντες.
αὐτὰρ ὅ γ' ἠνορέης μὲν ὑπερφιάλοιο λέλησται,
οὐδ' ἔτ' ἔχει γενύεσσι καὶ ἱέμενός περ ἐρύκειν
νῆας ἐπεσσυμένας, πτερύγων δ' ὑπεραχθέϊ ῥιπῇ
ἄκρῃ τ' ἀλκαίῃ βύθιον διὰ κῦμα λαχαίνων
ἔμπαλιν ἐς πρύμνας ὠθεῖ νέας, ἔργα δ' ἐρετμῶν
ἀνδρῶν τ' ἠνορέην γνάμπτει πάλιν, ἠΰτ' ἀήτης
ἀντίβιος πρῴρῃσιν ἐναντία κῦμα κυλίνδων·
τῶν δ' ἐνοπὴ κέκληγεν ἐφιεμένων πονέεσθαι,
κῦμα δ' ἅπαν λύθροιο φορύσσεται ἐκχυμένοιο

and emerge from the sea, dragging in their train the huge monster, and the deadly beast is hauled up all unwillingly, distraught in spirit with labour and wounds. Then the courage of the fishers is roused and with hasting blades they row their well-oared boats near. And much noise and much shouting resound upon the sea as they haste and exhort one another to the struggle. Thou wouldst say thou wert beholding the toil of men in war; such valour rises in their hearts and there is such din and such desire for battle. Far away some goatherd hears their horrid noise, or some shepherd tending his woolly flock in the glens, or woodcutter felling the pine, or hunter slaying wild beasts, and astonished he draws near to sea and shore and standing on a cliff beholds the tremendous toil of the men in this warfare of the sea and the issue of the wondrous hunt, while quenchless lust of war in the water stirs the men. Then one brandishes in his hands the long-barbed trident, another the sharp-pointed lance, others carry the well-bent bill, another wields the two-edged axe. All toil, the hands of all are armed with mighty blade of iron, and close at hand they smite and wound the beast with sweeping blows. And he forgets his mighty valour and is no more able, for all his endeavour, to stay the hasting ships with his jaws, but with heavy sweep of flippers and with the end of his tail he ploughs up the waves of the deep and drives back the ships sternward and turns to naught the work of the oars and the valour of the men, even as a contrary wind that rolls the waves against the prow. The cries of the men resound as they set themselves to work, and all the sea is stained with the gory filth poured forth by

ὠτειλαῖς ὀλοῇσι· τὸ δὲ ζέει ἄπλετον ὕδωρ
αἵματι κητείῳ, γλαυκὴ δ' ἐρυθαίνεται ἅλμη.
ὡς δ' ὅτε χειμερίοιο κατερχομένου ποταμοῖο
κόλπον ἐς οἰδματόεντα λόφων ἄπο μιλτοκαρήνων
ἰλὺς αἱματόεσσα κυλίνδεται ὕδατος ὁρμῇ,
κιρναμένη δίνῃσιν· ἑκὰς δ' ἐρυθαίνεται ὕδωρ
ξανθῆς ἐκ κονίης, λύθρος δ' ἔχει ὥστε θάλασσαν,
ὣς τότε κητείοιο πόρος λύθροιο πέφυρται
φοίνιος ἐν προχοῇσι δαϊζομένου βελέεσσιν.
ἐν δέ οἱ ὠτειλῇσιν ἀφυσσάμενοι ῥόον ἄντλου
πευκεδανὸν στάζουσ'· ἡ δ' ἕλκεσι μισγομένη ἅλς
ἠΰτε πυρκαϊὴ ὀλοώτατον ἧψεν ὄλεθρον.
ὡς δὲ Διὸς μάστιγι βαλεῖ τρόπιν αἰθέριον πῦρ
πόντον ἀμειβομένην, νέμεται δέ μιν αἰθαλόεσσα
ῥιπή, τὴν δ' ἔτι μᾶλλον ἐποτρύνουσα κορύσσει
μισγομένη δίοισιν ὁμοῦ πυρσοῖσι θάλασσα,
ὣς κείνου χαλεπάς τε βολὰς ὀδύνας τε κορύσσει
ἄντλου πυθομένοιο δυσαέος ἄγριον ὕδωρ.
ἀλλ' ὅτε μιν δμηθέντα πολυτμήτοις ὀδύνῃσιν
ἤδη λευγαλέοιο παρὰ προθύροις θανάτοιο
μοῖρα φέρῃ, τότε δή μιν ἀναψάμενοι ποτὶ χέρσον
γηθόσυνοι σύρουσιν· ὁ δ' ἕλκεται οὐκ ἐθέλων περ,
πολλῇσι γλωχῖσι πεπαρμένος ἠΰτε γόμφοις,
νευστάζων ὀλοοῖο μόρου τέλος οἰνοβαρείων·
οἱ δὲ μέγαν νίκης παιήονα κυδαίνοντες,
εἰρεσίῃ σπέρχοντες ἐπικλάζουσι θαλάσσῃ,
ὀξὺν ἐπειγομέναις ἐλάταις νόμον ἀείδοντες.
ὡς δ' ὁπότ' εἰναλίοιο διακρινθέντος Ἄρηος
νῆας ἀναψάμενοι νηῶν ἐπιβήτορας ἄνδρας
δυσμενέας ποτὶ χέρσον ἐπειγόμενοι κατάγωσι

---

[a] Herod. v. 1 νικώντων δὲ τὰ δύο τῶν Περινθίων, ὡς ἐπαιώ-

his deadly wounds. The infinite water boils with the blood of the beast and the grey sea is reddened. As when in winter a river comes down from the hills of red earth into a billowy gulf and the blood-coloured mud is rolled down by the rush of the water, mingling with the eddying waves; and afar the water is reddened by the ruddy dust and the sea is as if covered with blood: even so in that hour the gory waters are stained with the blood of the beast, rent amid the waves by the shafts of the fishermen. Then they draw and drop into his wounds a bitter stream of bilge-water; and the salt mingling in his sores like fire kindles for him deadliest destruction. As when the fire of heaven smites with the lash of Zeus a bark that is traversing the sea, and the flaming onset that devours the ship is stirred and made yet fiercer by the sea mingling with the torches of heaven: even so his cruel wounds and pains are made more fierce by the cruel water of the putrid evil-smelling bilge. But when, overcome by the pains of many gashes, fate brings him at last to the gates of dismal death, then they take him in tow and joyfully haul him to the land; and he is dragged all unwilling, pierced with many barbs as with nails and nodding as if heavy with wine in the issue of deathly doom. And the fishers, raising the loud paean of victory,[a] while they speed the boat with their oars, make the sea resound, singing their shrill song to hasting blades. As when after the decision of a battle at sea the victors take in tow the ships of the vanquished and haste joyfully to bring to land the foemen who man the ships,

νιζον κεχαρηκότες; Thuc. ii. 91 *ἐπαιάνιζόν τε ἅμα πλέοντες ὡς νενικηκότες.*

γηθόσυνοι, νίκης δὲ διαπρύσιον βοόωσι
ναυμάχον εἰρεσίης[1] παιήονα· τοὶ δ' ἀέκοντες
ἀχνύμενοι δηΐοισιν ἀναγκαίῃ ξυνέπονται,
ὥς οἵ γ' αἰνοπέλωρον ἀναψάμενοι δάκος ἅλμης
γηθόσυνοι κατάγουσιν ἐπ' ᾐόνας· ἀλλ' ὅτε χέρσῳ
ἐμπελάσῃ, τότε δή μιν ἐτήτυμος ὦρσεν ὄλεθρος
λοίσθιος ἀσπαίρει τε διαξαίνει τε θάλασσαν
σμερδαλέαις πτερύγεσσιν, ἅτ' εὐτύκτῳ περὶ βωμῷ
ὄρνις ἑλισσομένη θανάτου στροφάλιγγι κελαινῇ,
δύσμορος· ἦ μάλα πολλὰ λιλαίεται οἶδμαθ' ἱκέσθαι,
ἀλλά οἱ ἠνορέης λέλυται σθένος, οὐδέ τι γυῖα
πείθεται, ἐς χέρσον δὲ καθέλκεται αἰνὸν ἄϊσθων,
φορτὶς ὅπως εὐρεῖα πολύζυγος, ἥν τε θαλάσσης
ἀνέρες ἐξερύουσιν ἐπὶ τραφερὴν ἀνάγοντες
χείματος ἱσταμένοιο μεταπνεῦσαι καμάτοιο
ποντοπόρου· βριθὺς δὲ πόνος ναύτῃσι μέμηλεν·
ὥς οἵ γ' ὀβριμόγυιον ἐπὶ χθόνα κῆτος ἄγουσι·
πλῆσεν δ' ᾐόνα πᾶσαν ὑπ' ἀπλάτοις μελέεσσι
κεκλιμένοις, τέταται δὲ νέκυς ῥίγιστος ἰδέσθαι.
τοῦ μέν τις φθιμένοιο καὶ ἐν χθονὶ πεπταμένοιο
εἰσέτι δειμαίνει πελάσαι δυσδερκέϊ νεκρῷ
ταρβεῖ τ' οὐκέτ' ἐόντα καὶ οἰχομένοιό περ ἔμπης
πεφρικὼς αὐτοῖσιν ἐνὶ γναθμοῖσιν ὀδόντας.
ὀψὲ δὲ θαρσήσαντες ἀολλέες ἀμφαγέρονται,
θάμβεϊ παπταίνοντες ἐρείπιον ὠμηστῆρος.
ἔνθ' οἱ μὲν γενύων ὀλοὰς στίχας ἠγάσσαντο,
δεινοὺς χαυλιόδοντας, ἀναιδέας, ἠΰτ' ἄκοντας

[1] *v.l.* εἰρεσίῃς.

[a] Hesiod, *W.* 624 (when winter comes, marked by the setting of the Pleiades) νῆα δ' ἐπ' ἠπείρου ἐρύσαι, πυκάσαι τε

shouting loud to the oarsmen the paean of victory in a fight at sea, while the others against their will sorrowfully follow their foe perforce: even so the fishers take in tow the dread monster of the brine and joyfully bring him ashore. But when he comes nigh the land, then destruction real and final rouses him, and he struggles and lashes the sea with his terrible fins, like a bird upon the well-built altar tossing in the dark struggle of death. Unhappy beast! verily many an effort he makes to reach the waves but the strength of his valour is undone and his limbs obey him not and panting terribly he is dragged to land: even as a merchant ship, broad and many-benched, which men draw forth from the sea and haul up [a] on the dry land when winter comes, to rest from its seafaring toil, and heavy is the labour of the sailors: so they bring the mighty-limbed whale to land. And he fills all the beach with his unapproachable limbs as they lie, and he is stretched out dead, terrible to behold. Even when he is killed and laid upon the land one still dreads to approach his corpse of dread aspect and fears him when he is no more, shuddering even when he is gone at the mere teeth in his jaws. At last they take courage and gather [b] about him in a body, gazing in astonishment at the ruins of the savage beast. Then some marvel at the deadly ranks of his jaws, even the dread and stubborn tusks, like

λίθοισι πάντοθεν, ὄφρ' ἴσχωσ' ἀνέμων μένος ὑγρὸν ἀέντων, | χείμαρον ἐξερύσας, ἵνα μὴ πύθῃ Διὸς ὄμβρος.

[b] So when Achilles slays Hector, Hom. *Il.* xxii. 369 *ἄλλοι δὲ περίδραμον υἷες Ἀχαιῶν, | οἳ καὶ θηήσαντο φυὴν καὶ εἶδος ἀγητὸν | Ἕκτορος· οὐδ' ἄρα οἵ τις ἀνουτητί γε παρέστη. | ὧδε δέ τις εἴπεσκεν ἰδὼν ἐς πλησίον ἄλλον· | "ὢ πόποι, ἦ μάλα δὴ μαλακώτερος ἀμφαφάασθαι | Ἕκτωρ ἢ ὅτε νῆας ἐνέπρηθεν πυρὶ κηλέῳ."*

τριστοιχεὶ πεφυῶτας ἐπασσυτέρῃσιν ἀκωκαῖς·
ἄλλοι δ' ὠτειλὰς πολυδηρίτοιο πελώρου
χαλκοτόρους ἀφόωσιν· ὁ δ' ὀξύπρωρον ἄκανθαν
θηεῖται σμερδνοῖσιν ἀνισταμένην σκολόπεσσιν·
ἄλλοι δ' ἀλκαίην, ἕτεροι πολυχανδέα νηδὺν
καὶ κεφαλὴν ἀπέλεθρον ὁρώμενοι ἠγάσσαντο.
καί τις ἀνὴρ ὁρόων βλοσυρὸν δάκος Ἀμφιτρίτης
ἤθεσιν ἐν τραφεροῖσι πολὺ πλέον ἠὲ νέεσσι
δηθύνων ἑτάροισι μετέννεπεν ἐγγὺς ἐοῦσι·
Γαῖα, φίλη θρέπτειρα, σὺ μὲν τέκες ἠδ' ἐκόμισσας
φορβῇ χερσαίῃ· κόλποις δ' ἐνὶ σεῖο θάνοιμι,
ἦμαρ ὅτ' ἀντήσειε τὸ μόρσιμον· ἔργα δὲ πόντου
εὐμενέοι, χέρσῳ δὲ Ποσειδάωνα σέβοιμι·
μηδέ μ' ἐν ἀργαλέοις ὀλίγον δόρυ κύμασι πέμποι,
μηδ' ἀνέμους νεφέλας τε κατ' ἠέρα παπταίνοιμι·
οὐ γὰρ ἁλὸς ῥοθίων τόσσος φόβος οὐδ' ἀλεγεινῆς
ἀνδράσι ναυτιλίης καὶ ὀϊζύος ἣν μογέουσιν,
αἰεὶ δυσκελάδοισι συνιππεύοντες ἀέλλαις,
οὐδ' ἅλις ὀλλυμένοις διερὸς μόρος, ἀλλ' ἔτι τοίους
δαιτυμόνας μίμνουσιν, ἀτυμβεύτου δὲ τάφοιο
θηρείου λαιμοῖο μυχοὺς πλήσαντο τυχόντες·

javelins, arrayed in triple row with close-set points. Others feel the bronze-pierced wounds of the monster of many battles; another gazes at his sharp spine bristling with terrible points; others behold with wonder his tail, others his capacious belly and measureless head. And, looking on the fierce beast of the sea, one who has lingered more in landward haunts than among ships says among his comrades by his side: O Earth, dear mother, thou didst bear me and hast fed me with landward food, and in thy bosom let me die, when my destined day arrives! (Be the Sea and the works thereof gracious[a] unto me and on the dry land let me worship Poseidon!) And may no tiny bark speed me among the grievous waves nor let me scan the winds and the clouds in the air! Not enough is the so great terror of the waves, not enough for men the terror of distressful seafaring and the woe that they endure, ever riding with the storm-winds of evil noise, nor enough for them to perish by a watery doom: beyond all these they still await such banqueters as these, and find burial without a tomb, glutting the cavern of a wild beast's throat. I fear her who breeds such woes.

[a] This is a parenthetical apology, an appeal to the Sea and the Sea-god not to be offended by the poet's preference for the land. *Cf. C.* i. 9, where the poet deprecates the offence of Phaethon and Apollo at his comparing Antoninus to the sons of Zeus. So in prose, Herod. ii. 45 *καὶ περὶ μὲν τούτων τοσαῦτα ἡμῖν εἰποῦσι καὶ παρὰ τῶν θεῶν καὶ παρὰ τῶν ἡρώων εὐμενείη εἴη*. So Tennyson, *In Memoriam* lxxix. 1 f. "'More than my brothers are to me' [ix. 20]. Let this not vex thee, noble heart!" etc. A good example of the parenthetic apology is Pind. *I.* i. 1 ff. *Μᾶτερ ἐμά, τὸ τεόν, χρύσασπι Θήβα, | πρᾶγμα καὶ ἀσχολίας ὑπέρτερον | θήσομαι—μή μοι κραναὰ νεμεσάσαι | Δᾶλος—ἐν ᾇ κέχυμαι*, where editors amazingly continue to punctuate with a full stop after *θήσομαι*.

δειμαίνω τοίων ἀχέων τροφόν· ἀλλά, θάλασσα,
χαῖρέ μοι ἐκ γαίης, ἕκαθεν δ᾽ ἐμοὶ ἤπιος εἴης.
Κήτεα μὲν τοίοισιν ἐδηώσαντο πόνοισιν
ὅσσα δέμας προβέβηκεν ὑπερφυές, ἄχθεα πόντου.
ὅσσα δὲ βαιοτέρων μελέων λάχε, τοῖσι καὶ ἄγρη
βαιοτέρη, θήρεσσι δ᾽ ἐοικότα τεύχε᾽ ἔασι,
μείονες ὁρμιαί, μείων γένυς ἀγκίστροιο,
φορβὴ παυροτέρη, γενύων δόλος, ἀντὶ δὲ ῥινῶν
αἰγοδόρων ἁψῖδες ἀναπτόμεναι κολοκύντης
ἀζαλέης θήρειον ἄνω δέμας αὖ ἐρύουσι.
Λάμνης δὲ σκύμνοισιν ὅτ᾽ ἀντήσωσ᾽ ἁλιῆες,
πολλάκι καὶ τροπὸν αὐτόν, ἐπαρτέα δεσμὸν ἐρετμοῦ,

---

[a] The sense is exactly that of 339 *supra* χέρσῳ δὲ Ποσειδάωνα σέβοιμι and of ἕκαθεν δέ μοι ἤπιος εἴης here. He is willing to pay his homage to the Sea, but he wishes no closer acquaintance. *Cf.* Plato, *Rep.* 499 A τὰ δὲ κομψά τε καὶ ἐριστικὰ . . . πόρρωθεν ἀσπαζομένων, *i.e.* ordinary men look distantly upon the subtleties and quibbles of the sophist. One is reminded of C. S. Calverley's famous reply to Dr. Jenkyns, when, as C. S. Blayds, he was an undergraduate at Balliol. *Dr. Jenkyns*: "And with what feelings, Mr. Blayds, ought we to regard the Decalogue?" *Blayds*: "Master, with feelings of devotion mingled with awe!" *Cf.* Eurip. *Hipp.* 102 πρόσωθεν αὐτὴν (*sc.* Ἀφροδίτην) ἁγνὸς ὢν ἀσπάζομαι.

[b] *Cf.* Hom. *Il.* xviii. 104 ἐτώσιον ἄχθος ἀρούρης; *Od.* xx. 379 αὔτως ἄχθος ἀρούρης.

[c] The use of a gourd as a float is mentioned by Apostolides in his account, p. 45 f., of fishing for the Great Sea-perch (*H.* i. 142 n.). A strong line with a large hook is employed. Baited with small fishes, especially Saupes, this is cast in front of the Perch's retreat among the rocks. When the fish is hooked, it withdraws into its hole and, dilating its gill-covers, presses against the walls of its retreat in such a way that the fisher cannot pull it out. But "il mouille, le plus loin possible, en ligne droite, l'autre extrémité libre de la ligne au moyen d'une pierre et attache au milieu une gourde (κολοκύνθη) ou un grand morceau de liège, qui, tiré

Nay, O Sea, I greet thee—from the land,[a] and—from afar—mayst thou be kind to me!

Such are the labours by which they slay those Sea-monsters which exceed in monstrous bulk of body, burdens[b] of the sea. But those which are endowed with lesser limbs are caught by lesser sort of hunting and the weapons are suited to the prey: smaller the lines, smaller the jaw of the hook, scantier the food that baits the barbs, and in place of the skins of goats globes of dried gourds[c] fastened to the line pull the body of the beast to the surface.

When fishermen encounter the whelps of the Lamna,[d] many a time they merely undo the oar-thong,[e] the strap which fastens the oar, and project

par les deux bouts, se tire au dessous du niveau de la mer. Un ou deux jours après, si le cernier, pressé par la faim et fatigué de se tenir appuyé contre les parois de son nid, se relâche un peu, il est aussitôt tiré par la ligne qui tend à flotter. N'étant pas assez fort pour entraîner de nouveau le liège, il reste en dehors de son nid, et le pêcheur, avisé par la ligne qui flotte, vient le ramasser" (Apost. *l.c.*).

[d] *H.* v. 36 n.

[e] This refers to the simplest form of rowlock, a pin or thole (σκαλμός) in the gunwale to which the oar was fastened by a leathern thong (τροπός, τροπωτήρ): Poll. i. 87 *ὅθεν μὲν αἱ κῶπαι ἐκδέδενται, σκαλμός· ᾧ δὲ ἐκδέδενται, τροπωτήρ· καὶ τροπώσασθαι ναῦν.* *Cf.* Hom. *Od.* iv. 782 = viii. 53 *ἠρτύναντο δ' ἐρετμὰ τροποῖς ἐν δερματίνοισι*; Aesch. *Pers.* 375 f. *ναυβάτης τ' ἀνὴρ | τροποῦτο κώπην σκαλμὸν ἀμφ' εὐήρετμον.* See further Aristoph. *Ach.* 549, 553; Eur. *Hel.* 1598; *I.T.* 1347; Thuc. ii. 93; Hom. *Hy.* vi. 42; Lucian, *Catapl.* 1; Poll. i. 85 ff., x. 134; *E. M. s. ἐπίκωπος, s. εὔσκαρθμοι, s. σκαλμός, s. τράφηξ, s. τροπωτῆρες*; Hesych. *s. τροποί, s. τροπώσασθαι*; Suid. *s. τροπωτῆρες.* For the dynamics of the arrangement *cf.* [A.] *Mechan.* 850 b 10 ff. In Lat. the thong is *struppus*, Liv. Andr. *ap.* Isidor. *Orig.* xix. 4. 9. The pin is *scalmus*, Cic. *Brut.* 197; *De or.* i. 174; *De offic.* iii. 59; Vell. Pat. ii. 43. 1. In Shetland, where the arrangement is still in use, the pin is called *kabe*, the thong *humlaband.*

λυσάμενοι προὔτειναν ἐν οἴδμασιν· ἡ δ' ἐσιδοῦσα
ἔσσυτο καὶ γενύων προΐει μένος, αἶψα δὲ σειρῇ
ἐνσχόμενοι μίμνουσιν ἅτ' ἐν δεσμοῖσιν ὀδόντες
ἀγκύλοι· ἔνθεν ἔπειτα πόνος ῥήϊστος ὀλέσσαι
λάμνην τριγλώχινος ὑπὸ ῥιπῇσι σιδήρου.
  Ἔξοχα δ' ἐχθοδοποῖς ἐνὶ κήτεσι μαργαίνουσι
λαιμῷ λαβροσύνῃ τε κυνῶν ὑπέροπλα γένεθλα·
ἔξοχα δ' ὑβρισταὶ καὶ ἀγήνορες, οὐδέ κεν ἄν τι
ἀντόμενοι τρέσσειαν, ἀναιδείην ἀχάλινον
αἰεὶ κυμαίνουσαν ἐπὶ φρεσὶ λύσσαν ἔχοντες·
πολλάκι δ' ἰχθυβόλοισι καὶ ἐς λίνον ἀΐξαντες
κύρτοις τ' ἐμπελάσαντες ἐδηλήσανθ' ἁλιεῦσιν
ἄγρην ἰχθυόεσσαν, ἑὴν φρένα πιαίνοντες.
τοὺς δέ τις ἀσπαλιεὺς δεδοκημένος ἰχθύσιν αὐτοῖς,
πείρας ἀγκίστρῳ, μενοεικέα ληΐδα θήρης,
ῥηϊδίως ἐρύσει περὶ γαστέρα μαιμώοντας.
  Φώκῃ δ' οὐκ ἄγκιστρα τετεύχαται οὔτε τις αἰχμὴ
τρίγλυφος ἥ κεν ἕλοι κείνης δέμας· ἔξοχα γάρ μιν
ῥινὸς ὑπὲρ μελέων στερεὴ λάχεν, ὄβριμον ἕρκος·
ἀλλ' ὅτ' ἐϋπλεκέεσσι λίνοις περικυκλώσωνται
φώκην ἀσπαλιῆες ἐν ἰχθύσιν οὐκ ἐθέλοντες,
δὴ τότε τοῖς κραιπνοί τε πόνοι σπουδή τε καθέλκειν
δίκτυον ἐς ῥηγμῖνας, ἐπεὶ φώκην μεμαυῖαν
οὐκ ἂν ἐρητύσειε καὶ εἰ μάλα πολλὰ παρείη
δίκτυα, ῥηϊδίως δὲ βίῃ τ' ὀνύχων θ' ὑπ' ἀκωκαῖς
ῥήξει τ' ἀΐξει τε καὶ ἔσσεται ἰχθύσιν ἄλκαρ
εἰλομένοις, μέγα δ' ἄλγος ἐνὶ φρεσὶν ἀσπαλιήων.
ἀλλ' ἤν μιν καθέλωσιν ὑποφθαδὸν ἐγγύθι γαίης,
ἔνθα δὲ καὶ τριόδοντι καὶ ἰφθίμοις ῥοπάλοισι
δούρασί τε στιβαροῖσι καταΐγδην ἐλόωντες

[a] *H.* i. 373 n.; Ael. i. 55 describes a different mode of capture.

it in the waves. And when the Lamna espies it, she rushes and puts forth the strength of her jaws, and straightway her crooked teeth are entangled in the strap and are held fast as if in chains. Thereafter it is an easy task to kill the Lamna with blows of the iron trident.

Ravenous pre-eminently among the hateful Sea-monsters and gluttonous are the monster tribes of the Dog-fishes [a]; and they are pre-eminently insolent and proud and will fear nothing that they meet, having unbridled shamelessness ever swelling like a frenzy in their hearts. Often they rush upon the nets of the fishermen or attack their weels and destroy their fishy spoil, while fattening their own hearts. And a watchful fisherman may pierce them with the hook in the frenzy of their gluttony and land them along with the fishes, a pleasant spoil of his fishing.

For the Seal no hooks are fashioned nor any three-pronged spear which could capture it: for exceeding hard is the hide which it has upon its limbs as a mighty hedge. But when the fishermen have unwittingly enclosed a seal among the fishes in their well-woven nets, then there is swift labour and haste to pull the nets ashore. For no nets, even if there are very many at hand, would stay the raging seal, but with its violence and sharp claws it will easily break them and rush away and prove a succour to the pent-up fishes but a great grief to the hearts of the fishermen. But if betimes they bring it near the land, there with trident and mighty clubs and stout spears they smite it on the temples [b] and kill

[b] A. 567 a 10 *ἀποκτεῖναι δὲ φώκην χαλεπὸν βιαίως, ἐὰν μή τις πατάξῃ παρὰ τὸν κρόταφον· τὸ γὰρ σῶμα σαρκῶδες αὐτῆς.*

ἐς κροτάφους πέφνουσιν· ἐπεὶ φώκῃσιν ὄλεθρος
ὀξύτατος κεφαλῆφιν ἱκάνεται οὐταμένῃσι.
Ναὶ μὴν καὶ χέλυες μάλα πολλάκις ἀντιόωσαι
θήρην λωβήσαντο καὶ ἀνδράσι πῆμα γένοντο.
τάων δ' ἔπλετο μόχθος ἑλεῖν ῥήϊστος ἁπάντων
ἀνέρι θαρσαλέῳ καὶ ἀταρβέα θυμὸν ἔχοντι·
εἰ γάρ τις καταδὺς κραναὴν χέλυν ἐν ῥοθίοισιν
ὕπτιον ἀνστρέψειεν ἐπ' ὄστρακον, οὐκέτι κείνη
πολλὰ καὶ ἱεμένη δύναται μόρον ἐξαλεείνειν·
ὕψι δ' ἀναπλώει κοῦφον πλόον ἀσπαίρουσα
ποσσίν, ἁλὸς μεμαυῖα· γέλως δ' ἔχει ἀγρευτῆρας.
τὴν δ' ὁτὲ μὲν θείνουσι σιδηρείῃσι βολῇσιν,
ἄλλοτε δ' ἐν βροχίδεσσιν ἀναψάμενοι μεθέπουσιν.
ὡς δ' ὅτε νηπίαχα φρονέων πάϊς οὐρεσίφοιτον
ἀνστρέψῃ τρηχεῖαν ἑλὼν χέλυν, ἡ δ' ἐπὶ νῶτα
κεκλιμένη μάλα πολλὰ λιλαίεται οὖδας ἱκέσθαι,
ῥικνὰ ποδῶν σείουσα καὶ ἀγκύλα γούνατα, μόχθῳ
πυκνὸν ἐπασπαίρουσα, γέλως δ' ἔχει ὅς κεν ἴδηται,
ὣς κείνης ὁμόφυλον ἁλὸς δάκος ὕπτιον ἅλμῃ
ἐμφέρεται λωβητὸν ὑπ' ἀνδράσιν ἰχθυβόλοισι.
Πολλάκι δ' ἐς τραφερὴν ἀνανίσσεται, ἐκ δὲ βολάων

---

[a] *H.* i. 397 n.

[b] The main points of vv. 394-415, but rather differently combined, are found in two accounts: (1) Plin. ix. 35 f. Capiuntur multis quidem modis sed maxime evectae in summa pelagi antemeridiano tempore blandito, eminente toto dorso per tranquilla fluitantes, quae voluptas libere spirandi in tantum fallit oblitas sui ut solis vapore siccato cortice non queant mergi invitaeque fluitent opportunae venantium praedae. Ferunt et pastum egressas noctu avideque saturatas lassari atque, ut remeaverint matutino, summa in aqua obdormiscere. Id prodi stertentium sonitu. Tum adnatare leviter singulis ternos. A duobus in dorsum verti, a tertio laqueum inici supinae atque ita e terra a

it: since destruction comes most swiftly upon seals when they are smitten on the head.

Moreover, the Turtles[a] also very often destroy the spoil of the fishermen when they fall in with it and become a plague to the men. To capture[b] it is the easiest task of all for a man who is courageous and of fearless soul. For if he leap into the waves and turn the stony turtle on its back upon its shell, no more can it avoid doom, however much it try, but it floats on the surface buoyantly, struggling with its feet in its desire for the sea; and laughter seizes the fishermen. And sometimes they smite it with blows of iron, otherwhiles they deal with it by towing it with ropes. And as when a boy in childish frolic takes a rough mountain-roaming Tortoise and turns it over and it lies upon its back and is very eager to reach the ground, waving its wrinkled feet and wriggling furiously its crooked knees in its distress, and laughter seizes all who behold: even so its kindred beast of the sea floats on its back in the brine, the sport of the fishermen.

And often it comes up to the dry land and by the

pluribustrahi; (2) Diodor. iii. 20, speaking of the Aethiopian Chelonophagi (Turtle-eaters), says the Turtles spend the night in deep water feeding, but by day they seek the sheltered waters among the islands near the shore, where they sleep on the surface with carapace towards the sun, presenting the appearanee of overturned boats: *οἱ δὲ τὰς νήσους κατοικοῦντες βάρβαροι κατὰ τοῦτον τὸν καιρὸν ἠρέμα προσνήχονται ταῖς χελώναις· πρὸς ἑκάτερον δὲ μέρος πλησιάσαντες οἱ μὲν πιέζουσιν, οἱ δὲ ἐξαίρουσιν, ἕως ὕπτιον γένηται τὸ ζῷον· ἔπειθ' οἱ μὲν ἐξ ἑκατέρου μέρους οἰακίζουσι τὸν ὅλον ὄγκον, ἵνα μὴ στραφὲν τὸ ζῷον καὶ νηξάμενον τῷ τῆς φύσεως βοηθήματι φύγῃ κατὰ βάθους· εἷς δ' ἔχων μήρινθον μακρὰν καὶ δήσας τῆς οὐρᾶς νήχεται πρὸς τὴν γῆν καὶ προσέλκεται μετάγων τὸ ζῷον ἐπὶ τὴν χέρσον.*

ἠελίου φολίδας περιδαίεται, αὖα δὲ γυῖα
ἐς πόντον φορέει, τὴν δ᾽ οὐκέτι καὶ μεμαυῖαν
κῦμα μέλαν δέχεται, φορέει δέ μιν ἠδὲ κυλίνδει
ὕψι μάλ᾽ ἱεμένην νεάτης ἁλός· οἱ δ᾽ ἐσιδόντες
ἰχθυβόλοι μάλα ῥεῖα καὶ ἀσπασίως ἐδάμασσαν.
Δελφίνων δ᾽ ἄγρη μὲν ἀπότροπος, οὐδὲ θεοῖσι
κεῖνος ἔτ᾽ ἐμπελάσειε θυτὴρ φίλος οὐδέ κε βωμῶν
εὐαγέως ψαύσειεν, ὁμωροφίους δὲ μιαίνει,
ὅς κεν ἑκὼν δελφῖσιν ἐπιφράσσηται ὄλεθρον.
ἶσα γὰρ ἀνδρομέοισιν ἀπεχθαίρουσι φόνοισι
δαίμονες εἰναλίων ὀλοὸν μόρον ἡγητήρων·
ἶσα γὰρ ἀνθρώποισι νοήματα καὶ προπόλοισι
Ζηνὸς ἁλιγδούποιο· τὸ καὶ φιλότητι γενέθλης
κέχρηνται, μέγα δ᾽ εἰσὶ συνάρθμιοι ἀλλήλοισιν.
ἤδη γὰρ δελφῖνες ἐνηέες ἀνδράσιν οἵην
ἄγρην εὐθήρητον ἐπ᾽ ἰχθύσιν ὡπλίσσαντο
νήσῳ ἐν Εὐβοίῃ μετὰ κύμασιν Αἰγαίοισιν·
εὖτε γὰρ ἑσπερίης θήρης πόνον ἐγκονέωσιν

---

[a] For the Dolphin in Greek religion and mythology see Hermann Usener, *Die Sintflutsagen* (Bonn, 1899), chap. v.

[b] We take the sense of ἀπότροπος here to be ἀπὸ τρόπου, "contra morem consuetudinemque civilem" (Cic. *De offic.* i. 41. 148); *cf.* [Phocylic.] 182 μηδὲ κασιγνήτης ἐς ἀπότροπον ἐλθέμεν εὐνήν. So εὐναὶ παράτροποι Pind. *P.* ii. 35. Otherwise it may mean "abominable." But the word needs more careful consideration than it has yet received. It is curious that Aristotle speaks of hunting the Dolphin without a hint of anything unusual: A. 533 b 9 ὃ συμβαίνει καὶ ἐπὶ τῆς τῶν δελφίνων θήρας· ὅταν γὰρ ἀθρόως περικυκλώσωσι τοῖς μονοξύλοις (canoes), ψοφοῦντες ἐξ αὐτῶν ἐν τῇ θαλάττῃ ἀθρόους ποιοῦσιν ἐξοκέλλειν φεύγοντας εἰς τὴν γῆν καὶ λαμβάνουσιν

rays of the sun its scales are burnt about it and it carries but withered limbs back to the sea and the dark wave receives it no more for all its eagerness but carries and rolls it aloft while it yearns for the bottom of the sea. And fishermen espying it very easily and gladly overcome it.

The hunting of Dolphins [a] is immoral [b] and that man can no more draw nigh the gods as a welcome sacrificer nor touch their altars with clean hands but pollutes those who share the same roof with him, whoso willingly devises destruction for Dolphins. For equally with human slaughter the gods abhor the deathly doom of the monarchs of the deep [c]; for like thoughts with men have the attendants of the god of the booming sea: wherefore also they practise love of their offspring [d] and are very friendly one to another. Behold now what manner of happy hunting the Dolphins kindly to men array against the fishes in the island of Euboea [e] amid the Aegean waves. For when the fishers hasten to the toil of

ὑπὸ τοῦ ψόφου καρηβαροῦντας. So Ael. i. 18 *ὅταν δὲ ἁλιεὺς ἢ τρώσῃ τὸν παῖδα αὐτῆς τῇ τριαίνῃ ἢ τῇ ἀκίδι βάλῃ—ἡ μὲν ἀκὶς τὰ ἄνω τέτρηται, καὶ ἐνῆπται σχοῖνος μακρὰ αὐτῇ, οἱ δὲ ὄγκοι εἰσδύντες ἔχονται τοῦ θηρός—καὶ ἕως μὲν ἀλγῶν ἔτι ῥώμης ὁ δελφὶς ὁ τραυματίας μετείληχεν, χαλᾷ ὁ θηρατὴς τὴν σχοῖνον, . . . ὅταν δὲ αἴσθηται καμόντα καί πως παρειμένον ἐκ τοῦ τραύματος, ἡσυχῇ παρ' αὐτὴν ἄγει τὴν ναῦν καὶ ἔχει τὴν ἄγραν.*

[c] *Cf. infra* 441 n. *ἡγητήρ*, like Latin *dux*, a poetical synonym for king or emperor.

[d] Ael. i. 18 *δελφὶς δὲ ἄρα θῆλυς φιλοτεκνότατος ἐς τὰ ἔσχατα ζῴων ἐστί.* *Cf.* v. 6, x. 8; Phil. 86; Plin. ix. 21 gestant fetus infantia infirmos. Quin et adultos diu comitantur magna erga partum caritate.

[e] Oppian's story is paraphrased by Ael. ii. 8. A similar story is told by Plin. ix. 29 ff. who also refers to a similar practice "in Iasio sinu" (in Caria). The fish captured is in Pliny the Grey Mullet (mugil).

ἰχθυβόλοι, νεπόδεσσι πυρὸς φορέοντες ὁμοκλήν,
ἵπνου χαλκείοιο θοὸν σέλας, οἱ δ' ἐφέπονται
δελφῖνες, σύνθηρον ἐπισπεύδοντες ὄλεθρον.
ἔνθ' οἱ μὲν τρομέοντες ἀποτροπάδην ἀλέονται
ἰχθύες, οἱ δ' ἔκτοσθεν ἐπαΐσσοντες ὁμαρτῇ
δελφῖνες φοβέουσι καὶ ἱεμένους ἐπὶ βύσσαν
τρωπᾶσθαι ποτὶ χέρσον ἀνάρσιον ἐξελόωσι,
πυκνὸν ἐπιθρώσκοντες, ἅτ' ἀνδράσι θηρητῆρσι
θῆρα κύνες σεύοντες ἀμοιβαίῃς ὑλακῇσι.
τοὺς δ' ἀγχοῦ ποτὶ χέρσον ἀτυζομένους ἁλιῆες
ῥηϊδίως βάλλουσιν ἐϋγλώχινι τριαίνῃ.
τοῖσι δ' ἄφυκτα κέλευθα, διορχεῦνται δ' ἐνὶ πόντῳ,
καὶ πυρὶ καὶ δελφῖσιν ἐλαυνόμενοι βασιλεῦσιν.
ἀλλ' ὁπόταν θήρης εὐαγρέος ἔργον ἄνηται,

---

[a] The word ὁμοκλή, "call," is used in the vaguest way. The schol. here interprets ἀπειλήν, λαμπηδόνα: in *H.* i. 152 ἀπειλήν, in *H.* iv. 14 ἀπειλήν, ὀργήν. Oppian misunderstands, as does Aelian, the use of the lantern (not mentioned by Pliny) which is not to frighten, but to attract. Apostolides, p. 40, gives the following account of the mode of fishing for the Gar-fish (*Belone acus*) practised in the Sporades N. of Euboea: "Pendant les nuits les plus obscures du mois d'Octobre, aussitôt après l'arrivée des poissons, les bateaux quittent leur mouillage le soir et se rendent au large. Arrivés à l'endroit désigné les pêcheurs amènent les voiles et marchent lentement à la rame en examinant la mer de tous côtés. *Il est facile de se rendre compte de la présence du poisson en écoutant le bruit que font les dauphins qui le poursuivent à la surface de l'eau. Alors, les pêcheurs allument un grand feu avec du bois résineux sur une espèce de gril en fer, qu'ils fixent à la proue du navire* (πυροφάνι *et* πυριά *vulg.*). *Les poissons attirés par la lueur accourent vers le bateau comme pour y chercher un abri contre l'ennemi* [*i.e.*, the Dolphins] *qui ne cesse de les décimer.* Les

evening fishing, carrying to the fishes the menace[a] of fire, even the swift gleam of the brazen lantern,[b] the Dolphins attend them, speeding the slaughter of their common prey. Then the fishes in terror turn away and seek escape, but the Dolphins from the outer sea rush together upon them and frighten them and, when they would fain turn to the deep sea, they drive them forth towards the unfriendly land, leaping at them ever and again, even as dogs chasing the wild beast for the hunters and answering bark with bark. And when the fishes flee close to the land, the fishermen easily smite them with the well-pronged trident. And there is no way of escape for them, but they dance about in the sea, driven by the fire and by the Dolphins, the kings of the sea.[c] But when the work of capture is

pêcheurs ne commencent pas aussitôt la pêche, mais ils continuent à ramer lentement, sans bruit, de manière à faire tourner, sur place, le bateau quinze ou vingt fois sur lui-même. Cette opération . . . a pour but, je crois, de refléter la lumière de tous les côtés de l'horizon, pour attirer les poissons qui se trouveraient à l'arrière du bateau, et qui, par conséquent, ne l'auraient pas vue. Les poissons réunis autour du bateau ne le quittent presque plus, ils y restent, tournant même avec lui quand les pêcheurs le font tourner. Cela fait, on dirige le bateau lentement, à l'aviron, vers la terre, où il est suivi par les nombreuses bandes de Bélones. On arrive ainsi à la côte. Là on prend des précautions pour que le bateau ne touche terre, le moindre choc faisant déguerpir aussitôt les poissons. On l'arrête à une distance d'un ou de deux mètres, et, laissant les rames, on prend les haveneaux en main, et l'on commence à envelopper les poissons des deux côtés du bateau."

[b] Ael. ii. 8 *τῆς πρῴρας τῶν ἀκατίων κοίλας τινὰς ἐξαρτῶσιν ἐσχαρίδας πυρὸς ἐνακμάζοντος· καὶ εἰσὶ διαφανεῖς ὡς καὶ στέγειν τὸ πῦρ καὶ μὴ κρύπτειν τὸ φῶς· ἰπνοὺς καλοῦσιν αὐτάς.*

[c] *Cf.* 421 *supra*; Gregor. Nyss. *Or.* i. *ὁ δελφὶς ἐστι τῶν νηκτῶν βασιλικώτατος.*

δὴ τότ᾽ ἀπαιτίζουσι παρασχεδὸν ἐμπελάσαντες
μισθὸν ὁμοφροσύνης, θήρης ἀποδάσμιον αἶσαν·
οἱ δ᾽ οὐκ ἠνήναντο, πόρον δ᾽ εὐαγρέα μοῖραν
ἀσπασίως· ἢν γάρ τις ὑπερφιάλως ἀλίτηται,
οὐκέτι οἱ δελφῖνες ἀρηγόνες εἰσὶν ἐπ᾽ ἄγρην.

Καὶ μέν τις Λέσβοιο παλαίφατον ἔργον ἀοιδοῦ
ἔκλυεν, ὡς δελφῖνος ὀχησάμενος περὶ νώτῳ
κῦμα μέλαν περάασκε καθήμενος, ἄτρομος ἦτορ,
ἀείδων, καὶ πότμον ὑπέκφυγε ληϊστήρων
Ταιναρίῃ τ᾽ ἐπέλασσεν ἐπὶ προβολῇσι Λακώνων.
καί πού τις Λίβυος κούρου πόθον οἶδεν ἀκούων,
τοῦ ποτε ποιμαίνοντος ἐράσσατο θερμὸν ἔρωτα
δελφίς, σὺν δ᾽ ἤθυρε παρ᾽ ᾐόσι, καὶ κελαδεινῇ
τερπόμενος σύριγγι λιλαίετο πώεσιν αὐτοῖς
μίσγεσθαι πόντον τε λιπεῖν ξυλόχους τ᾽ ἀφικέσθαι.

---

[a] So Plin. ix. 32 (we give Philemon Holland's engaging version) "But after this service perfourmed, the Dolphins retire not presently into the deepe again, from whence they were called, but stay untill the morrow, as if they knew verie well that they had so carried themselves as that they deserved a better reward than one daies refection and victuals: and therefore contented they are not and satisfied, unlesse to their fish they have some sope and crummes of bread given them soaked in wine, and that their bellies full."

[b] Arion of Methymna in Lesbos lived at the court of Periander tyrant of Corinth (625–585 B.C.). Having amassed great wealth in Italy and Sicily he wished to return to Corinth. At Tarentum he hired a boat from some Corinthians. On the voyage the men, wishing to get his money, conspired to throw him overboard. Arion offered them all his wealth if they would spare his life. They gave

happily accomplished, then the Dolphins draw near and ask the guerdon of their friendship, even their allotted portion of the spoil.[a] And the fishers deny them not, but gladly give them a share of their successful fishing; for if a man sin against them in his arrogance, no more are the Dolphins his helpers in fishing.

One has heard, moreover, of the feat famous of old of the Lesbian minstrel,[b] how riding on the back of a Dolphin he crossed the black waves while he sat fearless of heart and singing, and so escaped death from the pirates, and reached the land of Taenarus on the shores of the Laconians. And one knows, methinks, by hearsay the love of the Libyan boy[c] whom as he herded his sheep a Dolphin loved with a burning love and played with him beside the shores and for delight in his shrill pipe[d] was fain to live among the very sheep and to forsake the sea and

him the choice either to kill himself or to jump into the sea. He asked to be allowed to don his minstrel's dress and sing to them. This granted, he stood on the deck and sang, and then jumped into the sea, when a Dolphin took him on its back and carried him ashore at Taenarus in Laconia. Herod. i. 24; Pausan. iii. 25. 7 ἀναθήματα δὲ ἄλλα τέ ἐστιν ἐπὶ Ταινάρῳ καὶ Ἀρίων ὁ κιθαρῳδὸς χαλκοῦς ἐπὶ δελφῖνος; Plut. *Mor.* 160 E ff.; Ael. ii. 6; vi. 15; xii. 45, where he quotes the distich inscribed on the memorial at Taenarus and a hymn purporting to have been written by Arion as a thank-offering to Poseidon; Plin. ix. 28; Philostr. *Imag.* i. 19; Aul. Gell. xvi. 19; Propert. iii. 26. 17; Ov. *Fast.* ii. 83 ff., etc.; K. Klement, *Arion*, Wien, 1898.

[c] This probably refers to the Dolphin of Hippo(n) Diarrytus, now Bizerta (38 m. N. of Tunis), the story of which is told by Pliny ix. 26, and more ornately by the younger Pliny, *Ep.* ix. 33.

[d] For the Dolphin's love of music: Ael. xi. 12; Plin. ix. 24, etc.

ἀλλ᾽ οὐδ᾽ ἠϊθέοιο πόθους ἐπὶ πᾶσα λέλησται
Αἰολίς· οὔτι παλαιόν, ἐφ᾽ ἡμετέρῃ δὲ γενέθλῃ·
δελφὶς ὥς ποτε παιδὸς ἐράσσατο νησαίοιο·
νήσῳ δ᾽ ἐνναίεσκεν, ἀεὶ δ᾽ ἔχε ναύλοχον ὅρμον,
ἀστὸς ὅπως, ἕταρον δὲ λιπεῖν ἠναίνετο θυμῷ,
ἀλλ᾽ αὐτοῦ μίμναζε παρέστιος ἐξέτι τυτθοῦ,
σκύμνος ἀεξηθείς, ὀλίγον βρέφος, ἤθεσι παιδὸς
σύντροφος· ἀλλ᾽ ὅθ᾽ ἵκοντο τέλος γυιαλκέος ἥβης,
καί ῥ᾽ ὁ μὲν ἠϊθέοισι μετέπρεπεν, αὐτὰρ ὁ πόντῳ
ὠκύτατος δελφὶς ἑτέρων προφερέστατος ἦεν,
δή ῥα τότ᾽ ἔκπαγλόν τε καὶ οὐ φατὸν οὐδ᾽ ἐπίελπτον
θάμβος ἔην ξείνοισι καὶ ἐνναέτῃσιν ἰδέσθαι·
πολλοὺς δ᾽ ὦρορε φῆμις ἰδεῖν σέβας ὁρμηθέντας,
ἠΐθεον δελφῖνι συνηβώοντας ἑταίρους·
πολλαὶ δ᾽ ἠϊόνων ἀγοραὶ πέλας ἦμαρ ἐπ᾽ ἦμαρ
ἱεμένων ἵσταντο σέβας μέγα θηήσασθαι.
ἔνθ᾽ ὁ μὲν ἐμβεβαὼς ἄκατον κοίλοιο πάροιθεν
ὅρμου ἀναπλώεσκε, κάλει δέ μιν οὔνομ᾽ ἀΰσας
κεῖνο, τό μιν φήμιξεν ἔτι πρώτης ἀπὸ φύτλης·
δελφὶς δ᾽ ἠΰτ᾽ ὀϊστός, ἐπεὶ κλύε παιδὸς ἰωήν,
κραιπνὰ θέων ἀκάτοιο φίλης ἄγχιστος ἵκανε,
σαίνων τ᾽ οὐραίῃ κεφαλήν τ᾽ ἀνὰ γαῦρος ἀείρων,
παιδὸς ἐπιψαῦσαι λελιημένος· αὐτὰρ ὁ χερσὶν
ἦκα καταρρέζεσκε, φιλοφροσύνῃσιν ἑταῖρον
ἀμφαγαπαζόμενος, τοῦ δ᾽ ἵετο θυμὸς ἱκέσθαι

[a] The reference is to Por(d)oselene on an island of the same name near Lesbos (Strabo 618). Ael. ii. 6 tells the story somewhat differently from Oppian, and omitting the death of the boy and the Dolphin (see note on 518 *infra*): λέγει δὲ καὶ Βυζάντιος ἀνήρ, Λεωνίδης ὄνομα, ἰδεῖν αὐτὸς παρὰ τὴν Αἰολίδα πλέων ἐν τῇ καλουμένῃ Ποροσελήνῃ πόλει δελφῖνα ἠθάδα καὶ ἐν λιμένι τῷ ἐκείνων οἰκοῦντα κτλ.; *cf.* Pausan. iii. 25. 7 τὰ μὲν οὖν ἐς αὐτὸν Ἀρίονα καὶ τὰ ἐπὶ τῷ δελφῖνι Ἡρόδοτος εἶπεν ἀκοὴν ἐν τῇ Λυδίᾳ συγγραφῇ· τὸν δὲ ἐν Ποροσελήνῃ δελφῖνα τῷ

come to the woods. Nay, nor has all Aeolis[a] forgotten the love of a youth—not long ago but in our own generation—how a Dolphin once loved an island boy and in the island it dwelt and ever haunted the haven where ships lay at anchor, even as if it were a townsman and refused to leave its comrade, but abode there and made that its house from the time that it was little till it was a grown cub, like a little child nurtured in the ways of the boy. But when they came to the fullness of vigorous youth, then the boy excelled among the youths and the Dolphin in the sea was more excellent in swiftness than all others. Then there was a marvel strange beyond speech or thought for strangers and indwellers to behold. And report stirred many to hasten to see the wondrous sight, a youth and a Dolphin growing up in comradeship, and day by day beside the shore were many gatherings of those who rushed to gaze upon the mighty marvel. Then the youth would embark in his boat and row in front of the embayed haven and would call it, shouting the name whereby he had named it even from earliest birth. And the Dolphin, like an arrow, when it heard the call of the boy, would speed swiftly and come close to the beloved boat, fawning with its tail and proudly lifting up its head fain to touch the boy. And he would gently caress it with his hands, lovingly greeting his comrade, while it would be eager to come right into the boat beside the boy.

παιδὶ σῶστρα ἀποδιδόντα ὅτι συγκοπέντα ὑπὸ ἁλιέων αὐτὸν ἰάσατο, τοῦτον τὸν δελφῖνα εἶδον [*cf.* Oppian's "not long ago"] *καὶ καλοῦντι τῷ παιδὶ ὑπακούοντα καὶ φέροντα, ὁπότε ἐποχεῖσθαί οἱ βούλοιτο.* For other similar stories *cf.* A. 631 a 8 ff.; Ael. ii. 6, vi. 15, viii. 11; Athen. 606 c; Plin. i. 24 ff.; Antig. 55; Aul. Gell. vi. 8.

αὐτὴν εἰς ἄκατον παιδὸς πέλας· ἀλλ᾽ ὅτ᾽ ἐς ἅλμην
κοῦφα κυβιστήσειεν, ὃ δ᾽ ἐγγύθι νήχετο κούρου,
αὐτῇσι πλευρῇσιν ἀνὰ πλευρὰς παρενείρων,
αὐτῇσι γενύεσσι πέλας γένυν, ἠδὲ καρήνῳ
ἐγχρίμπτων κεφαλήν· φαίης κέ μιν ἱμείροντα
κῦσσαι καὶ στέρνοισι περιπτύξαι μενεαίνειν
ἠΐθεον· τοίῃ γὰρ ὀπάονι νήχετο ῥιπῇ.
ἀλλ᾽ ὅτε καὶ πελάσειε παρ᾽ ἠόσιν, αὐτίκα κοῦρος
ἀψάμενος λοφιῆς διερῶν ἐπεβήσατο νώτων·
αὐτὰρ ὅ γ᾽ ἀσπασίως παιδὸς δέμας ἔμφρονι θυμῷ
δεξάμενος φοίτασκεν, ὅπῃ νόος ἠϊθέοιο
ἤλαεν, εἴτ᾽ ἄρα πόντον ἐπ᾽ εὐρέα τῆλε κελεύοι
στέλλεσθ᾽, εἴθ᾽ αὔτως λιμένος διὰ χῶρον ἀμείβειν,
ἢ χέρσῳ πελάειν, ὁ δ᾽ ἐπείθετο πᾶσαν ἐφετμήν.
οὔτε τις ἡνιόχῳ πῶλος τόσον ἐν γενύεσσι
μαλθακὸς εὐγνάμπτοισιν ἐφέσπεται ὧδε χαλινοῖς,
οὔτε τις ἀγρευτῆρι κύων ἐθὰς ὀτρύνοντι
τόσσον ὑπεικαθέων ἐπιπείθεται, ᾗ κεν ἄγῃσιν,
οὔτ᾽ ἔτι κεκλομένοιο τόσον θεράποντες ἄνακτος
πειθόμενοι ῥέζουσιν ἑκούσιον ἔργον ἑκόντες,
ὅσσον ὑπ᾽ ἠϊθέῳ δελφὶς φίλος ὀτρύνοντι
πείθετ᾽ ἄνευ ζεύγλης τε βιαζομένων τε χαλινῶν.
οὐ μέν μιν μοῦνον φορέειν θέλεν, ἀλλὰ καὶ ἄλλῳ
πείθετο, τῷ μιν ἄνωγεν ἄναξ ἑός, ἂν δ᾽ ἐκόμιζε
νώτοις, οὔτινα μόχθον ἀναινόμενος φιλότητι.
τοίη μὲν ζωῷ φιλίη πέλεν· ἀλλ᾽ ὅτε παῖδα
πότμος ἕλε, πρῶτον μὲν ὀδυρομένῳ ἀτάλαντος
δελφὶς ἠϊόνεσσιν ἐπέδραμεν, ἥλικα κοῦρον
μαστεύων· φαίης κεν ἐτήτυμον ὄσσαν ἀκούειν
μυρομένου· τοῖόν μιν ἀμήχανον ἄμπεχε πένθος·
οὐδ᾽ ἔτι κικλήσκουσιν ἐπείθετο πολλάκις ἀστοῖς
νησαίοις, οὐ βρῶσιν ὀρεγνυμένην ἐθέλεσκε

But when he dived lightly into the brine, it would swim near the youth, its side right by his side and its cheek close by his and touching head with head. Thou wouldst have said that in its love the Dolphin was fain to kiss and embrace the youth: in such close companionship it swam. But when he came near the shore, straightway the youth would lay his hand upon its neck and mount on its wet back. And gladly and with understanding it would receive the boy upon its back and would go where the will of the youth drave it, whether over the wide sea afar he commanded it to travel or merely to traverse the space of the haven or to approach the land: it obeyed every behest. No colt for its rider is so tender of mouth and so obedient to the curved bit; no dog trained to the bidding of the hunter is so obedient to follow where he leads; nay, nor any servants are so obedient, when their master bids, to do his will willingly, as that friendly Dolphin was obedient to the bidding of the youth, without yoke-strap or constraining bridle. And not himself alone would it carry but it would obey any other whom his master bade it and carry him on its back, refusing no labour in its love. Such was its friendship for the boy while he lived; but when death took him, first like one sorrowing the Dolphin visited the shores in quest of the companion of its youth: you would have said you heard the veritable voice of a mourner—such helpless grief was upon it. And no more, though they called it often, would it hearken to the island townsmen nor would it accept food when

δέχνυσθαι, μάλα δ' αἶψα καὶ ἐξ ἁλὸς ἔπλετ' ἄϊστος
κείνης, οὐδέ τις αὐτὸν ἐπεφράσατ', οὐδ' ἔτι χῶρον
ἵκετο· τὸν μέν που παιδὸς πόθος οἰχομένοιο
ἔσβεσε, σὺν δὲ θανόντι θανεῖν ἔσπευσεν ἑταίρῳ.
'Αλλ' ἔμπης καὶ τόσσον ἐνηείῃ προφέροντας
καὶ τόσον ἀνθρώποισιν ὁμόφρονα θυμὸν ἔχοντας
Θρήϊκες ὑβρισταὶ καὶ ὅσοι Βύζαντος ἔχουσιν
ἄστυ σιδηρείοισι νοήμασιν ἀγρώσσουσιν·
ἦ μέγ' ἀταρτηροὶ καὶ ἀτάσθαλοι· οὐδέ κε παίδων,
οὐ πατέρων φείσαιντο, κασιγνήτους τ' ὀλέκοιεν
ῥηϊδίως· τοῖος δὲ νόμος δυστερπέος ἄγρης.
μητρὶ μὲν αἰνοτόκῳ δίδυμον γένος ἐγγὺς ὀπηδεῖ
δελφίνων, ἀταλοῖσιν ἀλίγκιον ἠϊθέοισι·
Θρήϊκες αὖ ἐπὶ τοῖσιν ἀπηνέες ἐντύνονται,
στειλάμενοι δόρυ κοῦφον ἀτάσθαλον ἐς πόνον ἄγρης.
οἱ μὲν δὴ λεύσσοντες ἐπειγόμενον σκάφος ἄντην
ἀτρεμέες μίμνουσι καὶ ἐς φόβον οὐχ ὁρόωσιν,
οὔ τιν' ὀϊόμενοι μερόπων δόλον, οὐδέ τιν' ἄτην
ἵξεσθαι, σαίνουσι δ' ἐνηέας ἠΰθ' ἑταίρους
γηθόσυνοι, χρίμπτοντες ἑὸν χαίροντες ὄλεθρον.
οἱ δὲ θοῶς ἐλάσαντες ἀκοντιστῆρι τριαίνῃ
τήν τ' ἀκίδα κλείουσι, βέλος κρυερώτατον ἄγρης,
δελφίνων ἕνα κοῦρον ἀνωΐστῳ βάλον ἄτῃ·
αὐτὰρ ὅ γ' ἰδνωθείς, ὀδύνης ὕπο πικρὸν ἀχεύων,
αὐτίχ' ὑποβρυχίης εἴσω καταδύεται ἅλμης,
ὀχθίζων σφακέλῳ τε καὶ ἀργαλέῃσιν ἀνίαις·
οἱ δέ μιν οὐκ ἐρύουσι βιώμενοι· ἦ γὰρ ἂν ἄγρης
μαψιδίως ἅλιον καὶ ἐτώσιον ἔργον ἄροιντο·

---

[a] Byzantium, of which Byzas was the legendary founder: Steph. Byz. *s.v.*; Diodor. iv. 49.

offered it, and very soon it vanished from that sea and none marked it any more and it no more visited the place. Doubtless sorrow for the youth that was gone killed it, and with its dead comrade it had been fain to die.

But notwithstanding, although the Dolphins so excel in gentleness and though they have a heart so much at one with men, the overweening Thracians and those who dwell in the city of Byzas [a] hunt them with iron-hearted devices—surely wicked men and sinful! who would not spare their children or their fathers and would lightly slay their brothers born. And this is the manner of their unpleasant hunting. The mother Dolphin—a mother to her sorrow—is closely attended by her twin brood,[b] like unto boys of tender age. Now against these the cruel Thracians array their attack, equipping a light boat for the sinful labour of their hunt. The young Dolphins, when they see the speeding bark before them, remain still and look not to flight, not dreaming that any guile or ill would come upon them from men, but fawn on them as on kindly comrades with delight, rejoicing as they meet their own destruction. Then the fishers strike swiftly the hurled trident which they call a harpoon, most deadly weapon of the hunt, and smite one of the young Dolphins with unthought of woe. And shrinking back in the bitter anguish of its pain, it straightway dives within the nether brine, racked with torture and grievous agony. And the fishers do not hale it up by force—else would they be undertaking to no purpose a vain and empty work of hunting—but as it rushes, they

[b] A. 566 b 6 *τίκτει δ' ὁ μὲν δελφὶς τὰ μὲν πολλά, ἓν ἐνίοτε δὲ καὶ δύο*; Ael. i. 18 *τίκτει δύο.*

ἀλλά οἱ ἱεμένῳ δολιχὴν ἐφιᾶσιν ἄγεσθαι
μήρινθον καὶ νῆα κατασπέρχουσιν ἐρετμοῖς,
ἑσπόμενοι δελφῖνος ἀτυζομένοιο κελεύθοις.
ἀλλ᾽ ὅτε λευγαλέῃσι κακηπελέων ὀδύνῃσι
κάμνῃ καὶ γλωχῖσι περισκαίρῃσι σιδήρου,
δή ῥα τότ᾽ ἀδρανέων ἀναδύεται, ἄλκιμα γυῖα
κεκμηκώς, κούφοισιν ἀειρόμενος ῥοθίοισιν,
ὕστατα φυσιόων· μήτηρ δέ μιν οὔποτε λείπει,
ἀλλ᾽ αἰεὶ μογέοντι συνέσπεται, ἔκ τ᾽ ἀνιόντι
βυσσόθεν, ἀχνυμένῃ τε καὶ αἰνότατον στεναχούσῃ
εἰδομένη· φαίης κεν ὀδυρομένην ὁράασθαι
μητέρα περθομένης πόλιος περὶ δυσμενέεσσι
παίδων θ᾽ ἑλκομένων ὑπὸ ληΐδα δουρὸς ἀνάγκῃ·
ὣς ἥ γ᾽ αἰν᾽ ἀχέουσα δαϊζομένῳ περὶ παιδί,
ὥστ᾽ αὐτὴ μογέουσα καὶ οὐτηθεῖσα σιδήρῳ,
δινεύει· τὸν δ᾽ ἄλλον ἑῆς ἀπὸ παῖδα κελεύθου
στέλλει ἐπεμπίπτουσα καὶ ὀτρύνουσα διώκει·
φεῦγε, τέκος· μέροπες γὰρ ἀνάρσιοι, οὐκέθ᾽ ἑταῖροι
ἡμῖν, ἀλλὰ σίδηρον ἐφοπλίζουσι καὶ ἄγρην·
ἤδη καὶ δελφῖσιν ἐπεντύνουσιν Ἄρηα,
σπονδάς τ᾽ ἀθανάτων καὶ ὁμοφροσύνην ἀλιτόντες
ἡμετέρην, τὴν πρόσθεν ἐπ᾽ ἀλλήλοις ἐθέμεσθα.
τοῖα καὶ ἄφθογγός περ ὅμως τεκέεσσιν ἑοῖσι
μυθεῖται· καὶ τὸν μὲν ἀπέτρεπε τῆλε φέβεσθαι,
τῷ δ᾽ ἑτέρῳ κρυερῶς μεμογηότι συμμογέουσα
αὐτῆς ἄγχ᾽ ἀκάτοιο συνέσπεται, οὐδ᾽ ἀπολείπει·
οὐδέ τις ἱέμενός περ ἀποτρέψειε τεκοῦσαν
οὔτε βαλὼν οὔτ᾽ ἄλλο φέρων δέος· ἀλλ᾽ ἅμα παιδὶ
ἑλκομένῳ δύστηνος ἀνέλκεται, ὄφρα πελάσσῃ
δυσμενέων ὑπὸ χεῖρας· ἀνάρσιοι, ἦ μέγ᾽ ἀλιτροὶ
οἵδ᾽, οὔτ᾽ οἰκτείρουσιν ἀτυζομένην ὁρόωντες
οὔτε νόον γνάμπτουσι σιδήρεον, ἀλλὰ καὶ αὐτὴν

let the long line go with it and urge on the boat with their oars, following the path of the fleeing Dolphin. But when it is weary and in evil case with grievous pains and struggles on the barbs of iron, then being faint it comes to the surface, its strong limbs weary, raised by the buoyant waves, gasping its last. And the mother never leaves it but always follows with it in its distress and when it rises from the depths, like one who grieves and mourns terribly. You would say you were beholding the mourning of a mother when her city is sacked by the foe and her children are haled away perforce as the spoil of the spear. Even so she in sore grief circles about her wounded child as if she herself were suffering and wounded by the iron. Her other child she falls upon to send it from her path and urgently drives it away: "Flee, my child! for men are foes, no longer friends to us, but they prepare against us iron and capture: now even against the Dolphins they array war, sinning against the truce of the immortal gods and against the concord which formerly we made with one another." So, voiceless though she be, she speaks to her children. And one she turns away to flee afar; but the other, suffering with it in its cruel suffering, she attends close to the very boat and forsakes it not; nor could one drive away the mother if he tried either by striking her or by any other form of terror, but along with the child, when it is haled up the unhappy mother is haled up also, till she comes into the hands of the foe. Unkind and surely greatly sinful, these neither have pity upon her when they see her distress nor bend their heart of iron, but, smiting her also with

χαλκείαις ἀκίδεσσι καταΐγδην ἐλάσαντες
παῖδά τε καὶ γενέτειραν ὁμῇ συναπέφθισαν ἄτῃ·
ἔφθισαν οὐκ ἀέκουσαν, ἐπεὶ περὶ παιδὶ θανόντι
μήτηρ καὶ φρονέουσα καὶ ἱεμένη δεδάϊκται.
ὡς δ' ὁπότ' ὀρταλίχοισι χελιδόσι νηπιάχοισι
νέρθεν ὑπὲξ ὀρόφοιο τυχὼν ὄφις ἄγχι πελάσσῃ,
καὶ τοὺς μὲν κατέπεφνε καὶ ἔσπασεν ἔνδον ὀδόντων,
μήτηρ δὲ πρῶτον μὲν ἀτυζομένη δεδόνηται
λοίγια τετριγυῖα φόνου γόον· ἀλλ' ὅτε παῖδας
ἀθρήσῃ φθιμένους, ἣ δ' οὐκέτι φύξιν ὀλέθρου
δίζεται, ἀλλ' αὐτῇσιν ὑπαὶ γενύεσσι δράκοντος
εἰλεῖται, μέσφ' ὄρνιν ἕλῃ παιδοκτόνος ἄτη·
ὣς ἄρα καὶ δελφῖνι νέῳ συναπέφθιτο μήτηρ,
χεῖρας ἐς ἰχθυβόλων αὐτάγρετος ἀντήσασα.
 Ἔθνεα δ' ὀστρακόρινα, τά θ' ἑρπύζουσι θαλάσσῃ,
πάντα φάτις μήνης μὲν ἀεξομένης κατὰ κύκλον
σαρκὶ περιπλήθειν καὶ πίονα ναιέμεν οἶκον·
φθινούσης δ' ἐξαῦτις ἀφαυροτέροις μελέεσσι
ῥικνοῦσθαι· τοίη τις ἐνί σφισιν ἐστὶν ἀνάγκη.
τῶν δὲ τὰ μὲν δύνοντες ὑπόβρυχα χερσὶ λέγονται
ἀνέρες ἐκ ψαμάθοιο, τὰ δ' ἐκ σπιλάδων ἐρύουσι
νωλεμὲς ἐμπεφυῶτα, τὰ δ' ᾐόσιν ἔπτυσαν αὐταῖς
κύματα καὶ βόθροισι λαχαινομένης ψαμάθοιο.
 Πορφύραι αὖ πέρι δή τι μετ' ὀστρείοισιν ἔασι
λίχναι· τοίη δέ σφιν ἐτήτυμος ἵσταται ἄγρη.
κυρτίδες ἠβαιαὶ ταλάροις γεγάασιν ὁμοῖαι,

---

[a] Hom. *Il.* ii. 308 ff.

[b] *H.* i. 313 n.

[c] Ael. ix. 6 *τῶν ὀστρακονώτων τε καὶ ὀστρακοδέρμων καὶ τοῦτο ἴδιον· κενώτερά πως ταῦτα καὶ κουφότερα ὑποληγούσης τῆς σελήνης φιλεῖ γίνεσθαι.*

[d] *H.* i. 315 n.

[e] Ael. vii. 34 *ἡ πορφύρα λίχνον ἐστὶν ἰσχυρῶς*; Athen. 89 a

stroke of brazen harpoons, they slay child and mother together in a common doom : slay her not unwilling to be slain, since over her dead child the mother wittingly and willingly meets her death. As when a snake [a] chances upon the young brood of a swallow under the eaves and approaches them : and them he slays and seizes within his teeth, and the mother first circles about distraught, pitifully crying her lament for their slaying ; but when she sees her children perished, no more she seeks escape from destruction but flutters under the very jaws of the serpent, until the doom that slew the children overtakes the mother bird : even so also with the young Dolphin perishes the mother, coming a willing prey into the hands of the fishermen.

As for the Testacean [b] tribes which crawl in the sea, report tells that all these in due cycle are full of flesh when the moon [c] is waxing and inhabit a rich dwelling, but when she wanes, again they become more meagre and wrinkled of limb : such compelling force resides in them. Of these men gather some from the sand with their hands, diving under the sea ; others they pull from the rocks to which they stubbornlv cling ; yet others the waves cast up on the very shores or in trenches digged in the sand.

The Purple-shells [d] again among Shell-fish are eminently gluttonous,[e] and by gluttony is the true manner of their capture. Small weels [f] like baskets

Ἀπολλόδωρος . . . ἐν τοῖς περὶ Σώφρονος προθεὶς τὰ "λιχνότερα τᾶν πορφυρᾶν" φησὶν ὅτι παροιμία ἐστὶν καὶ λέγει, ὡς μέν τινες, ἀπὸ τοῦ βάμματος· οὗ γὰρ ἂν προσψαύσῃ ἕλκει ἐφ' ἑαυτὸ καὶ τοῖς προσπαρατεθειμένοις ἐμποιεῖ χρώματος αὐγήν· ἄλλοι δ' ἀπὸ τοῦ ζῴου.

[f] Oppian's account is paraphrased Ael. vii. 34.

πυκνῇσι σχοίνοισι τετυγμέναι· ἐν δ' ἄρα τῇσι
στρόμβους συγκέλσαντες ὁμοῦ χήμῃσι τίθενται·
αἱ δ' ὅταν ἐμπελάσωσι βορῆς μεθύουσαι ἔρωτι,
γλῶσσαν ὑπὲκ θαλάμης δολιχὴν βάλον· ἡ δὲ τέτυκται
λεπτή τ' ὀξείη τε, διὰ σχοίνων δ' ἐτάνυσσαν
φορβῆς ἱέμεναι, χαλεπῆς δ' ἤντησαν ἐδωδῆς·
γλῶσσα γὰρ ἐν σχοίνοισιν ἐρειδομένη πυκινῇσιν
οἰδάνεται, στείνει δὲ λύγων βρόχος, οὐδ' ἔτ' ὀπίσσω
ἀνδύνει μεμαυῖα, μένει δ' ὀδύνῃσι ταθεῖσα,
εἰσόκεν αὖ ἐρύσωσι περὶ γλώσσῃ μεμαυίας,
πορφυρέοις κάλλιστον ὑφάσμασιν ἄνθος ἄγοντες.
Σπογγοτόμων δ' οὔ φημι κακώτερον ἄλλον ἄεθλον
ἔμμεναι, οὐδ' ἄνδρεσσιν ὀϊζυρώτερον ἔργον.
οἱ δ' ἤτοι πρῶτον μέν, ὅτ' ἐς πόνον ὁπλίζωνται,
βρώμῃ τ' ἠδὲ ποτοῖσιν ἀφαυροτέροισι μέλονται,
ὕπνῳ τ' οὐχ ἁλιεῦσιν ἐοικότι μαλθάσσονται.
ὡς δ' ὅτ' ἀνὴρ εὔγηρυν ἐφοπλίζητ' ἐς ἀγῶνα,
μολπῆς εὐφόρμιγγος ἔχων Φοιβήϊον εὖχος,
πᾶσα δέ οἱ μέλεται κομιδή, πάντῃ δὲ φυλάσσει,
πιαίνων ἐς ἄεθλα λιγυφθόγγου μέλος αὐδῆς,
ὧς οἵ γ' ἐνδυκέως κομιδὴν εὔφρουρον ἔχουσι,
ὄφρα σφι πνοιή τε μένῃ ποτὶ βυσσὸν ἰοῦσιν
ἀσκηθής, προτέροιο δ' ἀναψύξωσι πόνοιο.

---

[a] *Camb. N. H.* iii. p. 111 "Another dreaded enemy [of the Oyster] is the 'whelk,' a term which includes *Purpura lapillus*, *Murex erinaceus*, *Buccinum undatum*, and probably also *Nassa reticulata*. All these species perforate the shell with the end of their radula, and then suck out the contents through the neatly-drilled hole"; *ibid.* p. 60 "Besides the dangers to which they are exposed from other enemies, many of the weaker forms of Mollusca fall a prey to their own brethren. . . . *Purpura lapillus* prefers *Mytilus edulis* to any other food, piercing the shell in about two days' time by its powerful radula, which it appears to employ

are made with close-set rushes, and the fishers gather and place in them Spiral-shells and Clams together. Now when the Purple-fishes draw near, drunk with the lust of food, they put forth from within their chamber their long tongue,[a] which is thin and sharp, and stretch it through the rushes, in quest of food and fatal feast they find. For the tongue, fixed in the close-set rushes, swells and is straitened by the mesh of withes and cannot any more draw back if it try but remains stretched in pain, until the fishers land the shell-fish while intent upon their tongue, bringing a colour most beautiful for purple cloths.

Than the task of the Sponge-cutters[b] I declare that there is none worse nor any work more woeful for men. These, when they prepare themselves for their labour, use more meagre food and drink and indulge themselves with sleep[c] unfitting fishermen. As when a man prepares himself for the tuneful contest—one who hath Phoebus' boast of lyric song—and he studies all care and every way takes heed, nursing for the games the melody of his clear voice: so do they zealously take all watchful care that their breath may abide unscathed when they go down into the depths and that they may recover from

somewhat in gimlet fashion." *Cf.* A. 547 b 4 *νέμονται δὲ ἐξείροντα τὴν καλουμένην γλῶτταν ὑπὸ τὸ κάλυμμα* (operculum). *τὸ δὲ μέγεθος τῆς γλώττης ἔχει ἡ πορφύρα μεῖζον δακτύλου, ᾧ νέμεται καὶ διατρυπᾷ τὰ κογχύλια καὶ τὸ αὑτῆς ὄστρακον*; *P.A.* 661 a 21 *ταῖς γὰρ πορφύραις τοσαύτην ἔχει δύναμιν τοῦτο τὸ μόριον ὥστε καὶ τῶν κογχυλίων διατρυπῶσι τὸ ὄστρακον, οἷον τῶν στρόμβων οἷς δελεάζουσιν αὐτάς*; Athen. 89 c; Plin. ix. 128 Lingua purpurae longitudine digitali, qua pascitur perforando reliqua conchylia.

[b] For the Sponge-cutter (*σπογγεύς, σπογγοθήρας, σπογγοτόμος*, etc.) in general *cf. H.* ii. 435 ff.; Plin. ix. 151 ff.

[c] *Cf. H.* iii. 45.

ἀλλ᾽ ὅτ᾽ ἀεθλεύωσι μέγαν πόνον ἐξανύοντες,
εὐχόμενοι μακάρεσσιν ἁλὸς μεδέουσι βαθείης
ἀρῶνται κήτειον ἀλεξῆσαί σφισι πῆμα,
μήτε τιν᾽ ἀντιάσαι λώβην ἁλός· ἣν δ᾽ ἐσίδωνται
κάλλιχθυν, τότε δή σφι νόον μέγα θάρσος ἱκάνει·
οὐ γάρ πω κείνῃσι νομαῖς ἔνι κῆτος ἄαπτον,
οὐ δάκος, οὐδέ τι πῆμα θαλάσσιον ἄλλο φαάνθη,
ἀλλ᾽ αἰεὶ καθαροῖσιν ἀπημάντοις τε πόροισι
τέρπονται· τῷ καί μιν ἐφήμισαν ἱερὸν ἰχθύν.
τῷ δ᾽ ἐπιγηθήσαντες ἐπισπεύδουσι πόνοισι.
πείσματι μηκεδανῷ μεσάτης ὑπὲρ ἰξύος ἀνὴρ
ἔζωσται, παλάμῃσι δ᾽ ἐν ἀμφοτέρῃσιν ἀείρει
τῇ μὲν ἐριβριθῆ μολίβου χύσιν ἀμφιμεμαρπώς,
δεξιτερῇ δ᾽ ἅρπην εὐήκεα χειρὶ τιταίνει·
φρουρεῖ δ᾽ ἐν γενύεσσιν ὑπὸ στόμα λευκὸν ἄλειφαρ·
στὰς δ᾽ ἄρ᾽ ὑπὲρ πρώρης ἐσκέψατο πόντιον οἶδμα
ὁρμαίνων βριθύν τε πόνον καὶ ἀθέσφατον ὕδωρ.
οἱ δέ μιν ὀτρύνουσιν ἐπισπέρχουσί τε μύθοις
θαρσαλέοις ἐπὶ μόχθον, ἅτ᾽ ἐν νύσσῃ βεβαῶτα
ἄνδρα ποδωκείης δεδαημένον· ἀλλ᾽ ὅτε θυμῷ
θαρσήσῃ, δίναις μὲν ἐνήλατο, τὸν δὲ καθέλκει
ἱέμενον πολιοῦ μολίβου βεβριθότος ὁρμή.
αὐτὰρ ὅ γ᾽ ἐς βυσσὸν προμολὼν ἐξέπτυσ᾽ ἀλοιφήν·
ἡ δὲ μέγα στίλβει τε καὶ ὕδατι μίσγεται αὐγή,
ὄρφνης ἠΰτε πυρσὸς ἀνὰ κνέφας ὄμμα φαείνων·
πέτραις δ᾽ ἐμπελάσας σπόγγους ἴδεν· οἱ δὲ φύονται

---

[a] Introduction, p. lvii.

[b] *i.e.*, olive-oil: Plut. *Mor.* 950 B τῶν δ᾽ ἄλλων ὑγρῶν διαφανὲς μάλιστα τοὔλαιόν ἐστι, πλείστῳ χρώμενον ἀέρι· τούτου δὲ τεκμήριον ἡ κουφότης, δι᾽ ἣν ἐπιπολάζει πᾶσιν ὑπὸ τοῦ ἀέρος ἄνω φερόμενον. ποιεῖ δὲ καὶ τὴν γαλήνην ἐν τῇ θαλάττῃ τοῖς κύμασιν ἐπιρραινόμενον, οὐ διὰ τὴν λειότητα τῶν ἀνέμων ἀπολι-

past toil. But when they adventure to accomplish their mighty task, they make their vows to the blessed gods who rule the deep sea and pray that they ward from them all hurt from the monsters of the deep and that no harm may meet them in the sea. And if they see a Beauty-fish,[a] then great courage comes into their hearts; for where these range there never yet hath any dread Sea-monster appeared nor noxious beast nor hurtful thing of the sea but always they delight in clean and harmless paths: wherefore also men have named it the Holy Fish. Rejoicing in it they hasten to their labours. A man is girt with a long rope above his waist and, using both hands, in one he grasps a heavy mass of lead and in his right hand he holds a sharp bill, while in the jaws of his mouth he keeps white oil.[b] Standing upon the prow he scans the waves of the sea, pondering his heavy task and the infinite water. His comrades incite and stir him to his work with encouraging words, even as a man skilled in foot-racing when he stands upon his mark. But when he takes heart of courage, he leaps into the eddying waves and as he springs the force of the heavy grey lead drags him down. Now when he arrives at the bottom, he spits out the oil, and it shines brightly and the gleam mingles with the water, even as a beacon showing its eye in the darkness of the night. Approaching the rocks[c] he sees the Sponges which

σθανόντων, ὡς Ἀριστοτέλης ἔλεγεν· ἀλλὰ παντὶ μὲν ὑγρῷ τὸ κῦμα διαχεῖται πληττόμενον, ἰδίως δὲ τοὔλαιον αὐγὴν καὶ καταφάνειαν ἐν βυθῷ παρέχει, διαστελλομένων τῷ ἀέρι τῶν ὑγρῶν· οὐ γὰρ μόνον ἐπιπολῆς τοῖς διανυκτερεύουσιν ἀλλὰ καὶ κάτω τοῖς σπογγοθήραις διαφυσώμενον ἐκ τοῦ στόματος ἐν τῇ θαλάττῃ φέγγος ἐνδίδωσιν.

[c] A. 548 a 23 (γίνονται) οἱ σπόγγοι ἐν ταῖς σήραγξι τῶν πετρῶν; Plin. ix.

ἐν νεάτοις πλαταμῶσιν, ἀρηρότες ἐν σπιλάδεσσι·
καί σφισι καὶ πνοιὴν φάτις ἔμμεναι, οἷα καὶ ἄλλοις,
ὅσσα πολυρραθάγοισιν ἐνὶ σπιλάδεσσι φύονται.
αἶψα δ' ἐπαΐξας δρεπάνῃ τάμε χειρὶ παχείῃ
ὥστε τις ἀμητὴρ σπόγγων δέμας, οὐδέ τι μέλλει
δηθύνων, σχοῖνον δὲ θοῶς κίνησεν, ἑταίροις
σημαίνων κραιπνῶς μιν ἀνελκέμεν· αἷμα γὰρ ἐχθρὸν
αὐτίκ' ἀπὸ σπόγγων ῥαθαμίζεται, ἀμφὶ δ' ἄρ' ἀνδρὶ
εἱλεῖται, πνοιῇ δὲ δυσαέϊ πολλάκι φῶτα
ἔσβεσε μυκτήρεσσιν ἐνισχόμενος βαρὺς ἰχώρ.
τοὔνεκα λαιψηρῶς ἀναδύεται ὥστε νόημα
ἑλκόμενος· τὸν μέν τις ἰδὼν προφυγόντα θαλάσσης
ἄμφω γηθήσειε καὶ οἰκτείρων ἀκάχοιτο·
ὧδε γὰρ ἠπεδανοῖσι παριεμένου μελέεσσι
δείματι καὶ καμάτῳ θυμαλγέϊ γυῖα λέλυνται.
πολλάκι δ' ἐχθίστης τε τυχὼν καὶ ἀπηνέος ἄγρης
ἅλμενος ἐς πόντοιο βαθὺν πόρον οὐκέτ' ἀνέσχε,
δύσμορος, ἀντιάσας δυσδερκέϊ θηρὶ πελώρῳ·
καί ῥ' ὁ μὲν οἷς ἑτάροισιν ἐπισείων θαμὰ δεσμὸν
κέκλεται αὖ ἐρύειν, τὸ δέ οἱ δέμας ἡμιδάϊκτον

---

[a] Oppian is thinking of the sensibility of the Sponge: A. 487 b 9 *δοκεῖ δὲ καὶ ὁ σπόγγος ἔχειν τινὰ αἴσθησιν· σημεῖον δὲ ὅτι χαλεπώτερον ἀποσπᾶται, ἂν μὴ γένηται λαθραίως ἡ κίνησις, ὥς φασιν*; *cf.* Plut. *Mor.* 980 c; Plin. ix. 148 intellectum inesse his apparet quia, ubi avulsorem sensere, contractae multo difficilius abstrahuntur.

[b] The best commentary on all this passage is Plin. ix. 152 f. Cum caniculis (Dog-fishes) atrox dimicatio. Inguina et calces omnemque candorem corporum [Ael. xv. 11 says that for this reason divers blacken the soles of their feet and the palms of their hands] appetunt. Salus una in adversas eundi ultroque terrendi. Pavet enim hominem aeque ac terret, et sors aequa in gurgite. Ut ad summa aquae ventum est, ibi periculum anceps adempta ratione contra eundi dum conetur emergere, et salus omnis in sociis. Funem illi religatum ab

grow on the ledges of the bottom, fixed fast to the rocks; and report tells that they have breath[a] in them, even as other things that grow upon the sounding rocks. Straightway rushing upon them with the bill in his stout hand, like a mower, he cuts the body of the Sponges, and he loiters not, but quickly shakes the rope,[b] signalling to his comrades to pull him up swiftly. For hateful blood[c] is sprinkled straightway from the Sponges and rolls about the man, and many a times the grievous fluid, clinging to his nostrils, chokes the man with its noisome breath. Therefore swift as thought he is pulled to the surface; and beholding him escaped from the sea one would rejoice at once and grieve and pity: so much are his weak members relaxed and his limbs unstrung with fear and distressful labour. Often when the sponge-cutter has leapt into the deep waters of the sea and won his loathly and unkindly spoil, he comes up no more, unhappy man, having encountered some huge and hideous beast.[d] Shaking repeatedly the rope he bids his comrades pull him up. And the mighty Sea-monster

umeris eius trahunt. Hunc dimicans, ut sit periculi signum, laeva quatit, dextera apprehenso stilo in pugna est. Modicus alias tractatus: ut prope carinam ventum est, nisi praeceleri vi repente rapiunt, absumi spectant. Ac saepe iam subducti e manibus auferuntur, si non trahentium opem conglobato corpore in pilae modum ipsi adiuvere. Protendunt quidem tridentes alii, sed monstro sollertia est navigium subeundi atque ita e tuto proeliandi. Omnis ergo cura ad speculandum hoc malum insumitur.

[c] Plut. *Mor.* 980 B οὐ γὰρ ἄψυχον οὐδ' ἀναίσθητον οὐδ' ἄναιμον ὁ σπόγγος ἐστίν; Ael. viii. 16; Phil. 93; Plin. ix. 149; xxxi. 124 aliqui narrant et auditu regi eas contrahique ad sonum . . . nec avelli petris posse, ideo abscindi ac saniem emittere.

[d] Such as the Ox-ray described *H.* ii. 141 ff. and obviously meant in Plin. ix. 151.

κητείῃ τε βίῃ καὶ ὁμόστολοι ἔσπασαν ἄνδρες,
οἰκτρὸν ἰδεῖν, ἔτι νηὸς ἐφιέμενον καὶ ἑταίρων·
οἱ δὲ θοῶς κεῖνόν τε πόρον καὶ λυγρὸν ἄεθλον
ἀχνύμενοι λείπουσι καὶ ἐς χέρσον κατάγονται
λείψανα δυστήνοιο περικλαίοντες ἑταίρου.
Τόσσ' ἐδάην, σκηπτοῦχε διοτρεφές, ἔργα θαλάσσης.
σοὶ δ' αἰεὶ νῆες μὲν ἀπήμονες ἰθύνοιντο,
πεμπόμεναι λιαροῖσι καὶ ἰθυπόροισιν ἀήταις,
αἰεὶ δ' ἰχθυόεσσα περιπλήθοιτο θάλασσα,
γαίης δ' ἀστυφέλικτα Ποσειδάων ἐρύοιτο
'Ασφάλιος ῥιζοῦχα θεμείλια νέρθε φυλάσσων.

[a] For Ποσειδῶν 'Ασφάλειος ('Ασφάλιος) *cf.* Plut. *Thes.* xxxvi. καὶ γὰρ Ποσειδῶνα ταῖς ὀγδόαις τιμῶσιν. ἡ γὰρ ὀγδοὰς κύβος, ἀπ' ἀρτίου πρῶτος οὖσα καὶ τοῦ πρώτου τετραγώνου διπλασία, τὸ μόνιμον καὶ δυσκίνητον οἰκεῖον ἔχει τῆς τοῦ θεοῦ δυνάμεως ὃν 'Ασφάλειον καὶ Γαιήοχον προσονομάζομεν; Pausan. vii. 21 7. Πελάγιος καὶ 'Ασφάλιός τε καὶ "Ιππιος; Heliodor. vi. 7 'Ερμῆς

and the companions of the fisher pull at his body rent in twain, a pitiful sight to see, still yearning for ship and shipmates. And they in sorrow speedily leave those waters and their mournful labour and return to land, weeping over the remains of their unhappy comrade.

So much I know, O Wielder of the Sceptre, nursling of the gods, of the works of the sea. But for thee may thy ships be steered free from harm, sped by gentle winds and fair; and always for thee may the sea teem with fish; and may Poseidon, Lord of Safety,[a] guard and keep unshaken the nether foundations which hold the roots of Earth.

μὲν κερδῷος Ποσειδῶν δὲ Ἀσφάλειος; Aristoph. *Ach.* 682 *οἷς Ποσειδῶν Ἀσφάλειός ἐστιν ἡ βακτηρία*; Suid. *s. Ταίναρον· . . . ἔνθα καὶ Ποσειδῶνος ἱερὸν Ἀσφαλείου* and *s. Ἀσφάλιος· Ποσειδῶν Ἀσφάλιος ῥιζοῦχα θεμείλια νέρθε φυλάσσων· τελευταῖος οὗτος τοῦ ε′ τῶν Ἁλιευτικῶν Ὀππιανοῦ.*

CLASSIFIED ZOOLOGICAL CATALOGUE

1. Mammals

Αἴγαγρος, Wild Goat, *Aegoceros pictus*, etc.
Αἴλουρος, Wild Cat, *Felis catus*, and Domestic Cat, *F. domestica.*
Αἴξ, Goat, *Capra hircus.*
Ἀλώπηξ, Fox, *Canis vulpes.*
Ἄρκτος, Brown Bear, *Ursus arctos.*
Ἅρπαξ, Harrier, species of Wolf (= Κίρκος), *C.* iii. 304.
Ἀσπάλαξ, Mole-rat (Blind Rat), *Spalax typhlus.*
Ἀχαινέη (ἔλαφος), Brocket, *C.* ii. 426 n.
Βίσων, European Bison (Wisent), *Bos bonasus* (*Bison Europaeus*).
Βούβαλος, Cow Antelope, *Antilope* (*Alcelaphus*) *bubalis.*
Βοῦς (Ταῦρος), Ox, Bull, *Bos taurus.*
Δελφίς, Dolphin, *Delphinus delphis.*
Δορκαλίς (Δόρκος), Gazelle, *Gazella dorcas.*
Ἔλαφος, Red Deer, *Cervus elaphus.*
Ἐλέφας, Elephant, *Elephas indicus* and *E. africanus.*
Εὐρυκέρως, Fallow Deer, *Cervus dama.*
Ἐχῖνος χερσαῖος, (1) the Common Hedgehog, *Erinaceus europaeus*; (2) in *C.* ii. 598 the Spiny Mouse, *Mus acomys.*
Θώς, either the Jackal, *Canis aureus*, or the Civet, *Viverra civetta.*
Ἰκτῖνος, Kite, species of Wolf, *C.* iii. 331.
Ἴορκος, Roe Deer, *Cervus capreolus.*
Ἵππαγρος, the Nylghau, *Boselaphus tragocamelus.*
Ἵππος, Horse, *Equus caballus.*
Ἰχνεύμων, Ichneumon, *Herpestes ichneumon.*
Καμηλοπάρδαλις, Giraffe, *Camelopardalis giraffa.*
Κάμηλος, Camel, *Camelus bactrianus* and *C. dromedarius.*
Κάπρος, Wild Boar, *Sus scrofa.*
Καστορίς, Beaver, *Castor fiber*, *H.* i. 398 n.
Κίρκος, Hawk, species of Wolf (= Ἅρπαξ), *C.* iii. 304.
Κριός, Grampus, Killer Whale, *Orca gladiator.*
Κύων, Dog, *Canis familiaris.*
Λαγώς, Hare, *Lepus timidus.*
Λέων, Lion, *Felis leo.*
Λύγξ, (1) Lynx, *Felis lynx*, (2) the Caracal, *F. caracal.*
Λύκος, Wolf, *Canis lupus.*
Μυοξός, Dormouse, *Myoxus glis, M. nitela, M. dryas.*

Μῦς, Mouse, *Mus musculus* (Common Mouse).
Ὄις, Sheep, *Ovis aries.*
Ὄναγρος, Wild Ass, *Equus onager.*
Ὄνος, Ass, *Equus asinus.*
Ὄρυξ, Sable Antelope, *Oryx leucoryx.*
Πάνθηρ, Panther, perhaps the Ounce, *C.* ii. 572 n.
Πάρδαλις (Πόρδαλις), Leopard (Panther), two species, *C.* iii. 63 n.
Πίθηκος, Ape, three species, (1) Ape, *Macacus inuus*; (2) Monkey, *Cercopithecus*; (3) Baboon, *Cynocephalus hamadryas*, *C.* ii. 605 n.
Πτώξ = Λαγώς.
Ῥινοκέρως, Rhinoceros, *Rhinoceros indicus.*
Σκιοῦρος, Squirrel, *Sciurus vulgaris.*
Σοῦβος, species of Sheep? *C.* ii. 382 n.
Σῦς = Κάπρος.
Τοξευτήρ, the Archer, species of Wolf, *C.* iii. 296.
Τίγρις, Tiger, *Felis tigris.*
Ὕαινα, Striped Hyena, *Hyaena striata.*
Ὕστριξ, Porcupine, *Hystrix cristata.*
Φάλαινα, *H.* i. 404 } Whales, *Cetacea.*
Φύσαλος, *H.* i. 368 }
Φώκη, Seal, *Phoca vitulina* (Common Seal), *Ph. monachus* (Monk Seal).
Χρύσεος, Golden, species of Wolf, *C.* iii. 317.

2. Birds

Ἀετός, Eagle, generic for species of *Aquila* and *Falco.*
Ἀηδών, Nightingale, *Daulias luscinia* (Common N.) and *Motacilla luscinia.*
Ἀλεκτρυών, Domestic Cock, *Gallus gallinaceus.*
Ἁλιαίετος, Sea-eagle, perhaps *Pandion haliaëtus*, the Osprey, *H.* i. 425 n.
Ἀλκυών, Kingfisher, *Alcedo ispida.*
Ἀτταγήν, Francolin, *Tetrao francolinus.*
Γέρανος, Common Crane, *Grus cinerea.*
Γύψ, Vulture, (1) *Gypaetus barbatus*, the Lämmergeier; (2) *Vultur fulvus*, Griffon Vulture; (3) *V. cinereus*, Black Vulture; (4) *Neophron percnopterus.*
Κίρκος, generic for smaller Hawks and Falcons.
Κορώνη, Crow, *Corvus corone* L. and *C. cornix*, the Hooded Crow.
Κύκνος, Swan, (1) Whooper, *Cygnus musicus*; (2) Mute, *C. olor.*
Λάρος, Sea-gull, including Gulls (*Larus*) and Terns (*Sterna*).
Πελαργός, Stork, *Ciconia alba* and *C. nigra.*
Πελειάς (Πέλεια), Τρήρων, Stock-dove, *Columba oenas*, and perhaps the Ring-dove, *C. palumbus.*
Πέρδιξ, Partridge, *Perdix graeca* (*P. saxatilis*) and Common Partridge, *P. cinerea.*
Στρουθοκάμηλος, Ostrich, *Struthio camelus*, L.
Ταώς, Peacock, *Pavo cristatus.*
Φήνη, Lämmergeier, *Gypaetus barbatus.*
Χελιδών, Swallow, (1) the Chimney Swallow, *Hirundo rustica*; (2) House Martin, *H. urbica.*
Ψιττακός, Parrot, *Psittacus cubicularis* (?).
Ὠτίς, Bustard, *Otis tarda*, L.

ZOOLOGICAL CATALOGUE

3. Reptiles

Ἀσπίς, Asp or Egyptian Cobra, *Naja haje.*
Δράκων, generic for Serpents, *Ophidia.*
Ἔχις = Ὄφις, *C.* i. 381, *H.* i. 569.
Κροκόδειλος, Crocodile, *Crocodilus vulgaris* Cuv.
Ὄφις, generic for Serpents.
Χελώνη θαλασσία, Turtle, *Chelonia cephalo.*
Χελώνη χερσαία, Tortoise, *Testudo graeca* and *T. marginata.*

4. Fishes

Ἀβραμίς, species of Grey Mullet (*Mugil*), found in the Nile.
Ἀγριόφαγρος. Not identified, *H.* i. 140.
Ἄδμων. Not identified, *H.* iii. 371 n.
Ἄδωνις = Ἐξώκοιτος, a Blenny, perhaps *Blennius Montagui.*
Αετός, Eagle-ray, perhaps *Myliobatis aquila.*
Αἰτναῖος. Not identified, *H.* i. 512.
Ἀκανθίας, Spiny Dog-fish, *Acanthias vulgaris.*
Ἀλώπηξ (Ἀλωπεκίας), Thresher or Fox-shark, *Alopecias vulpes*
Ἀλφηστικός = Κίναιδος, a Wrasse, Introd. p. l.
Ἀμία, Bonito, *Pelamys sarda.*
Ἀνθίας. Introd. p. liii.
Ἀφρῖτις = Ἀφύη.
Ἀφύη, generic for various small fish and fish-fry, *H.* i. 767 n.
Βασιλίσκος. Not identified, *H.* i. 129 n.
Βατίς, Ray, including the Common Skate, *Raia batis*, etc.
Βάτραχος, Fishing-frog or Angler, *Lophius pis atorius.*
Βλέννος, Blenny, *Blennius*; for various species *cf. H.* i. 109 n.
Βούγλωσσος, Sole, *Solea vulgaris.*
Βοῦς, Ox-ray, perhaps *Cephaloptera giorna.*
Βώξ, Bogue, *Box boops* (*B. vulgaris*) and *B. salpa.*
Γαλεός, generic for smaller Sharks (*Squalus*), *H.* i. 379 n.
Γλαῦκος, Introd. p. lxi.
Γόγγρος, Conger, *Conger vulgaris.*
Δράκων, the Weever, *Trachinus draco.*
Ἐγγραυλις, Anchovy, *Engraulis encrasicholus.*
Ἔγχελυς, Eel, *Anguilla vulgaris.*
Ἐξώκοιτος = Ἄδωνις, *q.v.*
Ἐρυθῖνος, a Sea-perch, *Serranus anthias* or *S. cabrilla.*
Ἐχενηίς, in *H.* i. 212 Lamprey, *Petromyzon marinus*, not *Echeneis remora.*
Ζύγαινα, Hammer-head or Balance Shark, *Zygaena malleus.*
Ἡγητήρ, Whale-guide or Pilot-fish, *Naucrates ductor.*
Ἡμεροκοίτης = Νυκτερίς, Day-sleeper or "Bat," *Uranoscopus scaber.*
Ἥπατος. Not identified, perhaps one of the Cod family (*Gadidae*), *H.* i. 146 n.
Θρίσσα, Shad, *Alosa vulgaris.*
Θύννος, Tunny, *Thynnus thynnus.*
Ἱέραξ, Sea-hawk, *Exocoetus volitans* Cuv.
Ἰουλίς (Ἴουλος, *H.* iii. 186), Rainbow-wrasse, *Coris iulis*
Ἵππος, Sea-horse, *Hippocampus brevirostris* Cuv.
Ἵππουρος, Hippurus, *Coryphaena hippurus.*

Καλλαρίας, perhaps one of the *Gadidae* (Cod family), Introd. p. lxv.
Κάλλιχθυς, Introd. p. lvii.
Κάνθαρος, Black Sea-bream, *Cantharus griseus.*
Κεντρίνη (Κεντροφόρος), a Shark, *Squalus centrina* L.
Κερκοῦρος. Not identified, *H.* i. 141.
Κεστρεύς } generic for Grey Mullet (*Mugil*); specifically, perhaps Κεστρεύς
Κέφαλος } = *M. capito*, Κέφαλος = *M. cephalus*, *H.* ii. 642 n.
Κίθαρος, a Flat-fish (*Pleuronectia*); possibly *Rhombus luteus* Risso.
Κίναιδος = Ἀλφηστικός, *q.v.*
Κιρρίς, a Wrasse, perhaps *Labrus mixtus*, Introd. p. liii.
Κίχλη, Thrush-wrasse, *Coricus rostratus.*
Κόκκυξ, Cuckoo-fish, a Gurnard, probably the Piper, *Trigla lyra.*
Κολίας, Coly Mackerel, *Scomber colias.*
Κορακῖνος, Crow-fish, one of the *Sciaenidae*, perhaps *Corvina nigra* Cuv.
Κόσσυφος, Merle-wrasse, *Crenilabrus pavo.*
Κυβεία(ς), a Tunny, *H.* i. 183 n.
Κυπρῖνος, Carp, *Cyprinus carpis.*
Κύων, generic for smaller Sharks and Dog-fishes (*Squalus*), *H.* i. 373 n.
Κωβιός, Goby, *Gobius niger* being commonest in Greek waters.
Λάβραξ, Basse, *Labrax lupus.*
Λάμνη, a large Shark, perhaps *Lamna cornubica.*
Λαρινός. Not identified, *H.* iii. 399.
Λεῖος, the Smooth Dog-fish, *Mustelus laevis* Risso.
Λέων, perhaps a large Shark. Not identified.
Μαινίς, *Maena vulgaris* and allied species.
Μάλθη, perhaps a large Shark. Not identified, *H.* i. 371 n.
Μελάνουρος, a Sea-bream, *Oblata melanura.*
Μορμύρος (Μορμύλος), Mormyrus, a Sea-bream, *Pagellus mormyrus.*
Μύλος, perhaps *Sciaena cirrhosa*, *H.* i. 130 n.
Μύραινα, the Murry, *Muraena helena.*
Μῦς θαλάσσιος, Sea-mouse, *i.e.* File Fish, *Balistes capriscus*, *H.* i. 174.
Νάρκη, Cramp-fish, Torpedo, or Electric Ray, *Torpedo marmorata*, etc.
Νυκτερίς = Ἡμεροκοίτης, *q.v.*
Ξιφίας, Sword-fish, *Xiphias gladius.*
Ὄλισθος, possibly the Sheat-fish, *Silurus glanis*, *H.* i. 113 n.
Ὀνίσκος and Ὄνος, perhaps *Gadidae* (Cod family), Introd. p. lxii.
Ὄρκυνος, large Tunny, *Thynnus brachypterus.*
Ὀρφός, Great Sea-perch, the Merou, *Serranus* (*Epinephelus*) *gigas.*
Πόρδαλις (Πάρδαλις), perhaps a large Shark. Not identified.
Πέρκη, Perch, either freshwater Perch, *Perca fluviatilis*, or a Sea-perch, *e.g. Serranus scriba.*
Πηλαμύς, one-year-old Tunny, *H.* iv. 504 n.
Πλατύουρος, unidentified Flat-fish (?), *H.* i. 99.
Ποικίλος, Spotted Dog-fish, *Scyllium catulus.*
Πομπίλος = Ἡγητήρ, *q.v.*
Πρέπων. Not identified. One of the Gadidae? *H.* i. 146.
Πρημάς, young Tunny in its first year, *H.* i. 183 n.
Πρῆστις, Sawfish, *Pristis antiquorum.*
Πρόβατον. Not identified, *H.* i. 146 n.
Ῥαφίς, Gar-fish (Needle-fish), *Belone acus*, *C.* ii. 392 n.
Ῥίνη, Monkfish or Angel-shark, *Rhina squatina.*
Σάλπη, Saupe, *Box salpa.*
Σαργός, Sargue, *Sargus vulgaris.*
Σαῦρος, Horse-mackerel, *Caranx saureus.*
Σῖμος. Not identified, *H.* i. 170 n.

Σκάρος, Parrot-wrasse, *Scarus cretensis.*
Σκέπανος, species of Tunny? *H* i. 106 n.
Σκίαινα, Sciaena, perhaps *Umbrina cirrhosa.*
Σκόμβρος, Mackerel, *Scomber scomber* L.
Σκορπίος, Scorpion-fish, two species, *Scorpaena scrofa* and *S. porcus, H.* i. 171 n.
Σκύμνος, a Dog-fish, perhaps *Scyllium canicula* Cuv.
Σκυτάλη. Not identified, *H.* i. 184.
Σμαρίς, *Smaris vulgaris, H.* i. 109 n.
Σπάρος, a Sea-bream, *Sargus Rondeletii* or allied species.
Σύαινα, *H.* i. 129 n., unidentified Flat-fish (?).
Συνόδους, a Sea-bream, *Dentex vulgaris* Cuv.
Σφύραινα, *H.* i. 172, two species, (1) *Sphyraena spet (S. vulgaris),* the Bicuda; (2) *Esox belone?*
Ταινία, Ribbon-fish, *Cobitis taenia? H.* i. 100 n.
Τράγος, the male *Maenis, H.* i. 108 n.
Τράχουρος, species of Mackerel, *Trachurus trachurus* Mor. (*Scomber trachurus* L.).
Τρίγλα. Red Mullet, *Mullus barbatus, M. surmuletus,* etc.
Τριγλίς = Τρίγλα, *C.* i. 75 n.
Τρυγών, Sting-ray, *Trygon vulgaris* Risso (*T. pastinaca* Cuv.).
Ὕαινα, an unidentified Sea-monster.
Φάγρος, a Sea-bream, perhaps *Pagrus vulgaris.*
Φυκίς, a Wrasse, perhaps *Crenilabrus pavo,* Introd. p. li.
Χαλκεύς, the Dory, *Zeus faber.*
Χαλκίς, Pilchard, *Clupea sardina* Cuv. (*Alosa sardina* Mor.).
Χάννος one of the Sea-perches, perhaps *Serranus cabrilla.*
Χάραξ, perhaps one of the Genus *Sargus, H.* i. 173 n.
Χελιδών the Flying Gurnard, *Dactylopterus volitans* Cuv. (*Trigla volitans* L.).
Χρέμης. one of the *Sciaenidae,* perhaps *Sciaena aquila.*
Χρύσοφρυς, *Chrysophrys aurata,* Gilt-head.
Ψῆττα, a Pleuronectid, possibly the Turbot, *Rhombus maximus.*

5. Molluscs

Κῆρυξ, Trumpet-shell, *Buccinum* in general.
Κόχλος, Sea-snail, undefinable, *C.* ii. 568.
Λεπάς, Limpet, *Patella vulgata,* etc.
Μῦς, Mussel, *Mytilus edulis.*
Ναυτίλος, Nautilus, *Argonauta argo.*
Νηρίτης, perhaps species of *Trochus* and *Buccinum.*
Ὀσμύλος, species of Octopus, perhaps *Eledone moschata.*
Οστρακον, generic for *Testacea.*
Ὄστρεον, generic for *Testacea,* or specifically the Oyster, *Ostrea edulis* L.
Πίννη, Pinna, a genus of bivalve Molluscs.
Πολύπους, Poulpe or Octopus, *Octopus vulgaris.*
Πορφύρα, Purple-shell, *Murex brandaris, M. trunculus,* etc.
Σηπία, the Common Cuttlefish, *Sepia officinalis,* L.
Στρόμβος, spiral shells generally, or specifically *Cerithium vulgatum.*
Σωλήν, Razor-shell, *Solen siliqua,* etc.
Τευθίς, Squid or Calamary, *Loligo vulgaris* Cuv.
Χήμη, Clam, generic for certain species of bivalves, *e.g. Veneraccae.*

6. Crustacea

Ἀστακός, Lobster, *Homarus vulgaris.*
Κάραβος, Spiny Lobster or Sea Crayfish, *Palinurus vulgaris.*
Καρίς, Prawn, *Palaemon squilla.*
Καρκινάς, Hermit Crab, *Pagurus Bernhardus* or *P. Diogenes.*
Καρκίνος, Crab, *Decapoda brachyura* in general.
Πάγουρος, the common edible Crab, *Cancer pagurus* L.
Πιννοφύλαξ, *Pinnoteres veterum.*

7. Vermes

Βδέλλα, Leech, *Hirudo medicinalis.*
Ἑλμίς, Worm, unidentified, *H.* iii 180.
Σκολόπενδρα θαλασσία. Not identified, *H.* i. 307, ii. 424 ff.

8. Insects

Μέλισσα, Bee generically, *Apis mellifica* L.
Μυῖα, Fly generically, *Musca domestica*, etc.

9. Echinoderms

Ἀστὴρ θαλάσσιος, Starfish generically, *Asterias.*
Ἐχῖνος θαλάσσιος, Sea-urchin, *Echinus esculentus.*

10. Porifera

Σπόγγος Sponge, *Spongia autorum.*

GENERAL INDEX TO OPPIAN

C. = *Cynegetica*. *H.* = *Halieutica*.

GENERAL INDEX

GENERAL INDEX

GENERAL INDEX

GENERAL INDEX

COLLUTHUS

INTRODUCTION

I. The Life of Colluthus

For the life of Colluthus we have the following authorities:

1. Suidas *s.v.* Κόλουθος "of Lycopolis in the Thebais [in Egypt: Ptolemy iv. 5. 62, Strabo 812], epic poet, who lived [or 'flourished,' γεγονώς] in the times of the emperor Anastasius [i.e. Anastasius I., emperor 491–518], wrote *Calydoniaca* in six books, and *Encomia* in epic verse, and *Persica.*" So Eudocia (Villoisin, *Anecd. Gr.* i. p. 271).

2. A Life of Colluthus in cod. Ambrosianus Q 5 *sup.*: "Coluthus of Lycopolis in the Thebais, epic poet, lived, according to Suidas, in the time of Anastasius, surnamed Brachinûs, who succeeded Zeno as emperor in Constantinople, and after whom reigned Justinus the Thracian, after whom again the emperor was *divus* (ὁ θεῖος) Justinianus, who delivered Italy from the servitude of the Goths through Belisarius—Justinian being the nephew of Justinus—a little over a thousand years ago. He wrote *Calydoniaca* in epic verse in six books and *Encomia* and *Persica.* To him is ascribed also the present poem, the *Rape of Helen,* a poem familiar and well known in Apulia, where also the poetry of the Homeric Quintus [the *Post-Homerica*—τῶν μεθ' Ὅμηρον λόγοι of Q. Smyrnaeus or Calaber] was first discovered in the temple

of St. Nicolas of Cassuli [Casoli] outside Hydrumtum [Otranto] and which its recoverer, the sainted Bessarion, archbishop of Nicaea, cardinal-bishop of Tusculum [Frascati], communicated to all concerned. And this also which was hidden, shall now be public property."

Notes.—(1) Zeno was emperor of the East at Constantinople from A.D. 474 to 491. He was succeeded by Anastasius I. who reigned 491–518. He in turn was succeeded by Justinus I. who reigned 518–527. He is called "the Thracian" because he was a native of Thrace. He again was succeeded by his nephew Justinian who reigned 527–565. For Belisarius see Gibbon, chap. xli.

(2) Bessarion (1395 ?–1472), a native of Trapezus (Trebizond), was a pupil of Plethon in the Peloponnese, became Cardinal and Patriarch of Constantinople, died in 1472 at Ravenna. In 1446 the Pope committed to him the oversight of the Greek monasteries of the Basilian Order to which, before leaving the East, Bessarion belonged.[1] The Italian monasteries of this Order were in the South of Italy. This circumstance led in 1450 to the discovery by Bessarion in the monastery of St. Nicola di Casoli (close to Otranto in Calabria), destroyed by the Turks in 1480, of various MSS. including Quintus Smyrnaeus (hence called Calaber) and Colluthus. He bequeathed his MSS. to Venice, where they now form part of the library of St. Mark, founded by Bessarion in 1468.

(3) The *Hypothesis* preserved in Parisinus 2764 adds nothing to (2).

[1] *Cf. Ecthesis Chronica* ed. Lambros, London 1902, p. 6 ἦλθον ἅπαντες ἐν Κωνσταντινουπόλει . . . ὁ Νικαίας Βησσαρίων . . . ὁ φιλόσοφος Γεμιστὸς καὶ ἄλλοι ἐκ τῶν ἀρχιερέων οὐκ ὀλίγοι. *Ibid.* p. 7 ὁ γὰρ Βησσαρίων ἦν πολὺς ἐνὶ τῷ λέγειν καὶ ἄκρος φιλόσοφος· γέγονε γὰρ καὶ γαρδινάλιος, ἔχων τιμὴν καὶ δόξαν οὐ τὴν τυχοῦσαν· ἠγάπησε γὰρ τὴν δόξαν τῶν ἀνθρώπων ἢ τοῦ θεοῦ.

II.—The Text

The best ms. of Colluthus is—

M = codex Mutinensis, now Parisinus suppl. graec. 388. Hall, *Companion to Classical Texts*, p. 278, says it "was never at Modena but was brought by the French in the Napoleonic wars at the beginning of the 19th century from somewhere in North Italy."

It is dated Xth or XIth century.

This ms. was first used by I. Bekker in his edition of Colluthus, impensis G. Reimeri, Berlin 1816.

The only critical edition before that of Bekker was that of John Daniel van Lennep, Leovardiae 1747, which was founded on collations (given him by D'Orville, Ruhnken, Valckenaer) of six mss.

V = Vossianus, a collation of which is in the library at Leyden; probably to be identified with Palatinus 319.

P = Parisinus 2764.

Q = Parisinus 2600.

A = Ambrosianus Q 5 sup.

L = Laurentianus xxxi. 27.

R = Hauniensis 60 (once belonging to Elias Putsch, then to J. A. Fabricius, then to H. S. Reimar).

All these are probably derived from Bessarion's ms.

Other late mss. are:

Neapolitanus ii. F 17.

Paris. suppl. 109.

Marcianus viiii. 1.

BIBLOGRAPHY

Editions

Editio Princeps :—Aldine, Venice, no date (probably about 1521), along with Quintus Calaber and Tryphiodorus.

Coluthi Lycopolitae Thebani de Raptu Helenae ac Judicio Paridis Poema nunc primum ab Helio Eobano Hesso [1488–1540] latino carmine redditum. Erphurdiae (Erfurt), 1533.

Coluthi Theb. Rapt. Hel., Iodoco Velaraeo interprete [Latin prose], Antuerpiae ap. Jo. Steelsium, 1539. Brodaei [Io.] Annotationes in Col. Theb. de Rapt. Hel. librum, Basel, 1552.

Col. Rapt. Hel. per Renatum Perdrierium ad verbum translatus, c. brevibus Bernardi Bertrandi annotationibus. Ex off. I. Oporini, Basel 1555. H. Stephanus (in *Poet. Graec. principes her. carm.*), Paris 1566. Col. Rapt. Hel. graece, per Sixtum Henricpetri, Basel, 1569 (along with Q. Calaber and Tryphiod. "Saepius autem mendas, quae Aldinae inerant, fideliter exhibet non tantum, sed ubique fere prioribus novas accumulat" van Lennep). Michael Neander in *Opus Aureum* Part ii., Basel 1559 (preff. to Coluthus and Tryph. are dated March 5th 1559).

Founded on Neander was the edition with short notes of Stephanus Ubelus, Franequerae (Franeker), ap. Aegid. Radaeum, 1600. Col. Rapt. Hel. in the *Corpus Poet. Graec.* of Jacobus Lectius, Collon. Allobr. (Cologne), 1606, founded on Stephanus. Col. Rapt. Hel., Aemil. Portus, Geneva, 1609, with short extracts from Neander's notes. Claud. Dausqueii

Annot. in Col., Frankfort, 1614. V. E. Loescheri Lect. Coluth. Liber singularis, Wittenberg, 1724. Col. Hel. Rapt. graece, ap. Janss. Waesbergios, Amsterdam, 1735. Col. Rapt. Hel. recens. ad fidem codd. MSS. ac variantes lectiones et notas adjecit Io. Dan. a Lennep, Leovardiae (Leeuwarden), 1747.

Col. Rapt. Hel. gr. et lat. Accedit metrica interpretatio italica Ant. Mar. Salvini, nunc primum edita. Recens. var. codd., MSS. lect. et select. annotat. adjec. Ang. Mar. Bandinius, Florence 1765. Apart from the translation in Italian this is simply van Lennep. Bandinius not merely reprints Lennep's text, but, without acknowledgement, reproduces his Latin version, his notes, and even his preface (translated into Italian). Cf. Buhle's remarks on Bandini's Aratus.

Another ed. entirely founded on Lennep is Col. Lycop. Theb. de Rapt. Hel. libellus: ex graec. in latina carmina conversus, versionibus, variantibus, et animadversionibus illustratus opera et studio Philippi Scio a S[to] Michaele. Madrid 1770, which however, contains, besides a trans. in Latin verse, a rendering in Spanish verse by Antonio Garcia (see below—Translations).

Col. Rapt. Hel., curante Theoph. Christ. Harles, Nuremberg, 1776, likewise entirely founded on Lennep.

In 1816 appeared Col. Rapt. Hel. ex recensione Immanuel. Bekkeri, Berlin 1816. In addition to the MSS. of Lennep, Bekker had a collation of the Mutinensis (containing seven hitherto unpublished lines) and cod. Gothanus.

In 1823 appeared the elaborate edition of A. Stanislas Julien, Paris 1823. This handsome volume contains a revised text, translation in French prose, a new Latin prose trans., a commentary, index verborum, etc., translations in English verse, Italian verse, Spanish verse, and German prose (see below Translations) and facsimiles of two MSS., Parisinus 2764 and Parisinus 2600.

New ed. of Lennep by G. H. Schaefer, Leipzig 1825. Lehrs, Didot, Paris 1839. Crit. ed. E. Abel, Berlin 1880. W. Weinberger, Leipzig, 1896 (with Tryphiod.), crit. notes and ind. verb.

Translations

French :—Charles Dumolard, Paris 1747. Simon de Troyes, London, 1790. Cournand, Paris, 1807 (verse). The author describes his work as an imitation, not a translation.

German :—K. A. Kütner, Mietau and Leipzig, 1772, reprinted in Julien ; Alzinger, Weimar, 1785 (verse) —superior, according to Julien, to that of Kütner.

Spanish :—Phil. Scio a S[to] Michaele, Madrid, 1770 (verse).

Italian :—Corradino dall' Aglio, Venice, 1741 ; Ang. Teodoro Villa, Milan, 1753 ; Ant. Maria Salvini in Bandini's edition, Florence, 1765, reprinted in Julien. C. Lanza, Naples, 1881. P. Ambrogio Curti, Milan, 1882. E. R. Tur, Leghorn, 1886. A. G. Danesi, Corleone, 1893.

English :—The Rape of Helen by Edward Sherburne, London, 1651 (rhymed verse), reprinted in Julien.

Other Literature

A. Ludwich, *Rh. Mus.* xlii. (1887). M. Schneider, *Philologus* xlix. (1890). W. Weinberger, *Wiener Studien* xviii. (1896).

THE RAPE OF HELEN

ΚΟΛΛΟΥΘΟΥ ΠΟΙΗΤΟΥ ΛΥΚΟΠΟΛΙΤΟΥ

ΑΡΠΑΓΗ ΤΗΣ ΕΛΕΝΗΣ

Νύμφαι Τρωιάδες, ποταμοῦ Ξάνθοιο γενέθλη,
αἳ πλοκάμων κρήδεμνα καὶ ἱερὰ παίγνια χειρῶν
πολλάκι πατρῴῃσιν ἐπὶ ψαμάθοισι λιποῦσαι
ἐς χορὸν Ἰδαίῃσιν ἐπεντύνασθε χορείαις,
δεῦτε, θεμιστοπόλοιο νοήματα μηλοβοτῆρος
εἴπατέ μοι, κελάδοντος ἀπορνύμεναι ποταμοῖο,
ἐξ ὀρέων πόθεν ἦλθεν ἀήθεα πόντον ἐλαύνων
ἀγνώσσων ἁλὸς ἔργα; τί δὲ χρέος ἔπλετο νηῶν
ἀρχεκάκων, ἵνα πόντον ὁμοῦ καὶ γαῖαν ὀρίνῃ
βουκόλος; ὠγυγίη δὲ τίς ἔπλετο νείκεος ἀρχή,
ὄφρα καὶ ἀθανάτοισι θεμιστεύσωσι νομῆες;
τίς δὲ δικασπολίη; πόθεν ἔκλυεν οὔνομα νύμφης
Ἀργείης; αὐταὶ γὰρ ἐθηήσασθε μολοῦσαι
Ἰδαίης τρικάρηνον ὑπὸ πρηῶνα Φαλάκρης
καὶ Πάριν οἰοπόλοισιν ἐφεδριόωντα θοώκοις
καὶ Χαρίτων βασίλειαν ἀγαλλομένην Ἀφροδίτην.
ὣς ὁ μὲν ὑψιλόφοισιν ἐν οὔρεσιν Αἱμονιήων
νυμφιδίων Πηλῆος ἀειδομένων ὑμεναίων
Ζηνὸς ἐφημοσύνῃσιν ἐῳνοχόει Γανυμήδης·
πᾶσα δὲ κυδαίνουσα θεῶν ἔσπευδε γενέθλη

[a] Scamander, a river in the Troad.
[b] A mountain in the Troad.

THE RAPE OF HELEN

Ye Nymphs of Troy, children of the river Xanthus,[a] who oft-times leave on your father's sands the snoods that bind your tresses and the sacred toys of your hands, and array you for the dance on Ida,[b] come hither, leaving the sounding river, and declare to me the counsel of the herdsman judge[c]: say whence from the hills he came, sailing the unaccustomed deep, albeit ignorant of the business of the sea; and what was the occasion of the ships that were the spring of woe, that a cowherd should stir ocean and earth together; and what was the primeval beginning of the feud, that herdsmen should deal judgement to immortals: what was the suit: whence heard he the name of the Argive nymph[d]? For ye came yourselves and beheld, beneath the three-peaked cliff of Idaean Phalacra,[e] Paris sitting on his shepherd seat and the queen of the Graces, even Aphrodite, glorying. So among the high-peaked hills of the Haemonians,[f] the marriage song of Peleus was being sung while, at the bidding of Zeus, Ganymede[g] poured the wine. And all the race of the gods hasted to do honour to the white-

[c] Paris. [d] Helen.

[e] Peak of Ida, *cf.* Lyc. 24. [f] Thessalians.

[g] Son of Tros, for his beauty carried away and made cup-bearer to Zeus (Hom. *Il.* xx. 232).

αὐτοκασιγνήτην λευκώλενον Ἀμφιτρίτης,
Ζεὺς μὲν ἀπ' Οὐλύμποιο, Ποσειδάων δὲ θαλάσσης·
ἐκ δὲ Μελισσήεντος ἀπ' εὐόδμου Ἑλικῶνος
Μουσάων λιγύφωνον ἄγων χορὸν ἦλθεν Ἀπόλλων·
39 χρυσείοις[1] δ' ἑκάτερθε τινασσόμενος πλοκάμοισι
40 βότρυς ἀκερσεκόμης ζεφύρῳ στυφελίζετο χαίτης.
τὸν δὲ μεθ' ὡμάρτησε κασιγνήτη Διὸς Ἥρη.
οὐδ' αὐτὴ βασίλεια καὶ ἁρμονίης Ἀφροδίτη
ἐρχομένη δήθυνεν ἐς ἄλσεα Κενταύροιο.
καὶ στέφος ἀσκήσασα γαμήλιον ἤλυθε Πειθώ,
τοξευτῆρος Ἔρωτος ἐλαφρίζουσα φαρέτρην.
καὶ βριαρὴν τρυφάλειαν ἀπὸ κροτάφοιο μεθεῖσα
ἐς γάμον ὡμάρτησε γάμων ἀδίδακτος Ἀθήνη.
οὐδὲ κασιγνήτη Λητωιὰς Ἀπόλλωνος
Ἄρτεμις ἠτίμησε καὶ ἀγροτέρη περ ἐοῦσα.
οἷος δ' οὐ κυνέην, οὐ δήιον ἔγχος ἀείρων
ἐς δόμον Ἡφαίστοιο σιδήρεος ἔρχεται Ἄρης,
τοῖος ἄτερ θώρηκος, ἄτερ θηκτοῖο σιδήρου
μειδιόων ἐχόρευεν. Ἔριν δ' ἀγέραστον ἐάσας
οὐ Χείρων ἀλέγιζε καὶ οὐκ ἐμπάζετο Πηλεύς.
ἡ δ' ἅτε βησσήεντος ἀποπλαγχθεῖσα νομοῖο
πόρτις ἐρημαίῃσιν ἐνὶ ξυλόχοισιν ἀλᾶται
φοινήεντι μύωπι, βοῶν ἐλατῆρι, τυπεῖσα·
τοῖα βαρυζήλοισιν Ἔρις πληγῇσι δαμεῖσα
πλάζετο μαστεύουσα, θεῶν πῶς δαῖτας ὀρίνοι.
πολλάκι δ' εὐλάιγγος ἀπὸ κλισμοῖο θοροῦσα
ἵστατο καὶ παλίνορσος ἐφέζετο· χειρὶ δὲ γαίης
οὔδεϊ κόλπον ἄραξε καὶ οὐκ ἐφράσσατο πέτρην·

[1] ll. 39, 40 were transposed to precede 25 by Graefe.

[a] Thetis. [b] Daughter of Nereus and Doris (Hes. *Th.* 243).

[c] Legendary king of the district of Helicon (schol. Nicand. *Ther.* ii.).

armed bride,[a] own sister of Amphitrite[b]: Zeus from Olympus and Poseidon from the sea. Out of the land of Melisseus,[c] from fragrant Helicon, Apollo came leading the clear-voiced choir of the Muses. On either side, fluttering with golden locks, the unshorn cluster of his hair was buffeted by the west wind. And after him followed Hera, sister of Zeus; nor did the queen of harmony herself, even Aphrodite, loiter in coming to the groves of the Centaur.[d] Came also Persuasion,[e] having fashioned a bridal wreath, carrying the quiver of archer Eros. And Athena put off her mighty helmet from her brow and followed to the marriage, albeit of marriage she was untaught. Nor did Leto's daughter Artemis, sister of Apollo, disdain to come, goddess of the wilds though she was. And iron Ares, even as, helmetless nor lifting warlike spear, he comes into the house of Hephaestus, in such wise without breastplate and without whetted sword danced smilingly. But Strife did Cheiron leave unhonoured: Cheiron did not regard her and Peleus heeded her not.

And as some heifer wanders from the pasture in the glen and roams in the lonely brush, smitten by the bloody gadfly, the goad of kine: so Strife,[f] overcome by the pangs of angry jealousy, wandered in search of a way to disturb the banquet of the gods. And often would she leap up from her chair, set with precious stones, and anon sit down again. She smote with her hand the bosom of the earth and heeded not the rock. Fain would she unbar the

[d] Cheiron, who had his cave on Pelion.

[e] Peitho, an attendant goddess of Aphrodite; *cf.* Paus. i. 22. 3, Hes. *W.* 73.

[f] Eris, daughter of Night (Hes. *Th.* 225 ff.).

ἤθελεν ὀρφναίων γνάλων κληῖδας ἀνεῖσα,
ἐκ χθονίων Τιτῆνας ἀναστήσασα βερέθρων
οὐρανὸν ὑψιμέδοντος ἀιστῶσαι Διὸς ἕδρην.
ἤθελεν ἠχήεντα πυρὸς πρηστῆρα τινάσσειν,
Ἡφαίστῳ δ' ὑπόεικεν ἀμαιμακέτη περ ἐοῦσα,
καὶ πυρὸς ἀσβέστοιο καὶ ὀπτευτῆρι σιδήρου.
καὶ σακέων βαρύδουπον ἐμήσατο κόμπον ἀράσσειν,
εἴ ποτε δειμαίνοντες ἀναθρῴσκοιεν ἰωήν·
ἀλλὰ καὶ ὁπλοτέρης δολίης ἀνεχάσσατο βουλῆς
Ἄρεα δειμαίνουσα, σιδήρεον ἀσπιδιώτην.
ἤδη δ' Ἑσπερίδων χρυσέων ἐμνήσατο μήλων·
ἔνθεν Ἔρις, πολέμοιο προάγγελον ἔρνος ἑλοῦσα
μῆλον, ἀριζήλων ἐφράσσατο δήνεα μόχθων.
χειρὶ δὲ δινήσασα μόθου πρωτόσπορον ἀρχὴν
ἐς θαλίην ἔρριψε, χορὸν δ' ὤρινε θεάων.
Ἥρη μὲν παράκοιτις ἀγαλλομένη Διὸς εὐνῇ
ἵστατο θαμβήσασα καὶ ἤθελε ληΐζεσθαι·
πασάων δ' ἅτε Κύπρις ἀρειοτέρη γεγαυῖα
μῆλον ἔχειν ἐπόθησεν, ὅτι κτέρας ἐστὶν Ἐρώτων·
Ἥρη δ' οὐ μεθέηκε καὶ οὐχ ὑπόεικεν Ἀθήνη.
Ζεὺς δὲ θεῶν καὶ νεῖκος ἰδὼν καὶ παῖδα καλέσσας
τοῖον ὑφεδρήσσοντα προσέννεπεν Ἑρμάωνα·
εἴ τινά που Ξάνθοιο παρ' Ἰδαίοιο ῥεέθροις
παῖδα Πάριν Πριάμοιο, τὸν ἀγλαὸν ἡβητῆρα,
Τροίης βουκολέοντα κατ' οὔρεα, τέκνον, ἀκούεις,
κείνῳ μῆλον ὄπαζε· διακρίνειν δὲ θεάων

---

[a] Sons of Uranus and Ge.

[b] The Garden of the Hesperides lay in the far West. There the Hesperides, daughters of Night, guard the golden apple along with a dragon, son of Phorkys and Ceto; *cf.* Hes. *Th.* 215 ff.

[c] The apple was a love-symbol and the presentation or throwing of an apple (μηλοβολεῖν) was a declaration of love

bolts of the darksome hollows and rouse the Titans[a] from the nether pit and destroy the heaven the seat of Zeus, who rules on high. Fain would she brandish the roaring thunderbolt of fire, yet gave way, for all her age, to Hephaestus, keeper of quenchless fire and of iron. And she thought to rouse the heavy-clashing din of shields, if haply they might leap up in terror at the noise. But from her later crafty counsel, too, she withdrew in fear of iron Ares, the shielded warrior.

And now she bethought her of the golden apples of the Hesperides.[b] Thence Strife took the fruit that should be the harbinger of war, even the apple,[c] and devised the scheme of signal woes. Whirling her arm she hurled into the banquet the primal seed of turmoil and disturbed the choir of goddesses. Hera, glorying to be the spouse and to share the bed of Zeus, rose up amazed, and would fain have seized it. And Cypris,[d] as being more excellent than all, desired to have the apple, for that it is the treasure of the Loves. But Hera would not give it up and Athena would not yield. And Zeus, seeing the quarrel of the goddesses, and calling his son Hermaon,[e] who sat below his throne, addressed him thus:

"If haply, my son, thou hast heard[f] of a son of Priam, one Paris, the splendid youth, who tends his herds on the hills of Troy, give to him the apple;

(schol. Arist. *Nub.* 997, Lucian, *Dial. Mer.* xii. 1, Theocr. v. 88). *Cf.* the story of Acontius and Cydippe and Solon's enactment—ὁ Σόλων ἐκέλευε τὴν νύμφην τῷ νυμφίῳ συγκατακλίνεσθαι μήλου Κυδωνίου κατατραγοῦσαν (Plut. *Praec. Coni.* 138 d).

[d] Aphrodite. [e] =Hermes (Hesiod fr. 46).

[f] For the type of expression *cf.* Ap. Rh. iv. 1560, iii. 362.

κέκλεο καὶ βλεφάρων ξυνοχὴν καὶ κύκλα προσώπων.
ἡ δὲ διακρινθεῖσα φέρειν περίπυστον ὀπώρην
κάρτος ἀρειοτέρης ἐχέτω καὶ κόσμον Ἐρώτων.
ὣς ὁ μὲν Ἑρμάωνι πατὴρ ἐπέτελλε Κρονίων·
αὐτὰρ ὁ πατρῴῃσιν ἐφημοσύνῃσι πιθήσας
εἰς ὁδὸν ἡγεμόνευε καὶ οὐκ ἀμέλησε θεάων.
πᾶσα δὲ λωιτέρην καὶ ἀμείνονα δίζετο μορφήν.
Κύπρις μὲν δολόμητις ἀναπτύξασα καλύπτρην
καὶ περόνην θυόεντα[1] διαστήσασα κομάων
χρυσῷ μὲν πλοκάμους, χρυσῷ δ' ἐστέψατο χαίτην.
τοῖα δὲ παῖδας Ἔρωτας ἀνηΰτησεν ἰδοῦσα·
ἐγγὺς ἀγών, φίλα τέκνα· περιπτύξασθε τιθήνην.
σήμερον ἀγλαΐαι με διακρίνουσι προσώπων·
δειμαίνω, τίνι μῆλον ὁ βουκόλος οὗτος ὀπάσσει.
Ἥρην μὲν Χαρίτων ἱερὴν ἐνέπουσι τιθήνην,
φασὶ δὲ κοιρανίην μεθέπειν καὶ σκῆπτρα φυλάσσειν·
καὶ πολέμων βασίλειαν ἀεὶ καλέουσιν Ἀθήνην·
μούνη Κύπρις ἄναλκις ἔην θεός. οὐ βασιλήων
κοιρανίην, οὐκ ἔγχος ἀρήιον, οὐ βέλος ἕλκω.
ἀλλὰ τί δειμαίνω περιώσιον ἀντὶ μὲν αἰχμῆς
ὡς θοὸν ἔγχος ἔχουσα μελίφρονα δεσμὸν ἐρώτων;
κεστὸν ἔχω καὶ κέντρον ἄγω καὶ τόξον ἀείρω,
κεστόν, ὅθεν φιλότητος ἐμῆς ἐμὸν οἶστρον ἑλοῦσαι
πολλάκις ὠδίνουσι καὶ οὐ θνῄσκουσι γυναῖκες.
τοῖον ἐφεσπομένη ῥοδοδάκτυλος ἔννεπε Κύπρις.
οἱ δ' ἄρα μητρῴης ἐρατῆς ἀίοντες ἐφετμῆς
φοιτητῆρες Ἔρωτες ἐπερρώοντο τιθήνῃ.
ἄρτι μὲν Ἰδαίην ὑπερέδραμον οὔρεος ἄκρην,
ἔνθα λιθοκρήδεμνον ὑπὸ πρηῶνος ἐρίπνην
κουρίζων ἐνόμευε Πάρις πατρώια μῆλα.

[1] So inferior MSS., making θυόεντα feminine; πτερὸν ἰθυνθέντα M.

and bid him judge the goddesses' meeting brows and orbèd eyes. And let her that is preferred have the famous fruit to carry away as the prize of the fairer and ornament of the Loves."

So the father, the son of Cronus, commanded Hermaon. And he hearkened to the bidding of his father and led the goddesses upon the way and failed not to heed. And every goddess sought to make her beauty more desirable and fair. Cypris of crafty counsels unfolded her snood and undid the fragrant clasp of her hair and wreathed with gold her locks, with gold her flowing tresses. And she saw her children the Loves and called to them.

"The contest is at hand, dear children! embrace your mother that nursed you. To-day it is beauty of face that judges me. I fear to whom this herdsman will award the apple. Hera they call the holy nurse of the Graces, and they say that she wields sovereignty aud holds the sceptre. And Athena they ever call the queen of battles. I only, Cypris, am an unwarlike goddess. I have no queenship of the gods, wield no warlike spear, nor draw the bow. But wherefore am I so sore afraid, when for spear I have, as it were, a swift lance, the honeyed girdle of the Loves! I have my girdle, I ply my goad, I raise my bow: even that girdle, whence women catch the sting of my desire, and travail often-times, but not unto death."

So spake Cypris of the rosy fingers and followed. And the wandering Loves heard the dear bidding of their mother and hasted after their nurse.

Now they had just passed over the summit of the hill of Ida, where under a rock-crowned cliff's height young Paris herded his father's flocks. On either

ποιμαίνων δ' ἑκάτερθεν ἐπὶ προχοῇσιν ἀναύρου
νόσφι μὲν ἀγρομένων ἀγέλην πεμπάζετο ταύρων,
νόσφι δὲ βοσκομένων διεμέτρεε πώεα μήλων·
καί τις ὀρεσσαύλοιο δορὴ μετόπισθε χιμαίρης
ἐκκρεμὲς ἠώρητο καὶ αὐτῶν ἥπτετο μηρῶν,
ποιμενίη δ' ἀπέκειτο, βοῶν ἐλάτειρα, καλαῦροψ,
τοῖος ἐπεὶ σύριγγος, ἐς ἤθεα βαιὸν ὁδεύων,
ἀγροτέρων καλάμων λιγυρὴν ἐδίωκεν ἀοιδήν·
πολλάκι δ' οἰοπόλοισιν ἐνὶ σταθμοῖσιν ἀείδων
καὶ ταύρων ἀμέλησε καὶ οὐκ ἐμπάζετο μήλων·
ἔνθεν ἔχων σύριγγα κατ' ἤθεα καλὰ νομήων
Πανὶ καὶ Ἑρμάωνι φίλην ἀνεβάλλετο μολπήν·
οὐ κύνες ὠρύοντο καὶ οὐ μυκήσατο ταῦρος,
μούνη δ' ἠνεμόεσσα, βοῆς ἀδίδακτος ἐοῦσα,
Ἰδαίων ὀρέων ἀντίθροος ἴαχεν Ἠχώ.
ταῦροι δὲ χλοερῆς κεκορηότες ὑψόθι ποίης,
κεκλιμένοι βαρύγουνον ἐπ' ἰσχίον εὐνάζοντο.
ὣς ὁ μὲν ὑψορόφοιο φυτῶν ὑπένερθε καλύπτρης
τηλόθεν Ἑρμάωνα διάκτορον εἶδε λιγαίνων.
δειμαίνων δ' ἀνόρουσε, θεῶν δ' ἀλέεινεν ὀπωπήν·
καὶ χορὸν εὐκελάδων δονάκων ἐπὶ φηγὸν ἐρείσας
μήπω πολλὰ καμοῦσαν ἑὴν ἀνέκοπτεν ἀοιδήν.
τοῖα δὲ δειμαίνοντα προσέννεπε θέσκελος Ἑρμῆς·
γαῦλον ἀπορρίψας καὶ πώεα καλὰ μεθήσας
δεῦρο θεμιστεύσειας ἐπουρανίῃσι δικάζων·
δεῦρο διακρίνων προφερέστερον εἶδος ὀπωπῆς
φαιδροτέρῃ τόδε μῆλον, ἐπήρατον ἔρνος, ὀπάσσαις.
τοῖον ἀνηΰτησεν· ὁ δ' ἤπιον ὄμμα τανύσσας
ἦκα διακρίνειν πειρήσατο κάλλος ἑκάστης.
δέρκετο μὲν γλαυκῶν βλεφάρων σέλας, ἔδρακε δειρὴν
χρυσῷ δαιδαλέην, ἐφράσσατο κόσμον ἑκάστης

side the streams of the mountain torrent he tended his herds, numbering apart the herd of thronging bulls, apart measuring the droves of feeding flocks. And behind him hung floating the hide of a mountain goat, that reached right to his thighs. But his herdsman's crook, driver of kine, was laid aside: for so, walking mincingly in his accustomed ways, he pursued the shrill minstrelsy of his pipe's rustic reeds. Often as he sang in his shepherd's shieling he would forget his bulls and heed no more his sheep. Hence with his pipe, in the fair haunts of shepherds, he was making dear music to Pan and to Hermaon. The dogs bayed not, and the bull did not bellow. Only windy Echo[a] with her untutored cry, answered his voice from Ida's hills; and the bulls upon the green grass, when they had eaten their fill, lay down and rested on their heavy flanks.

So as he made shrill music under the high-roofed canopy of trees, he beheld from afar the messenger Hermaon. And in fear he leapt up and sought to shun the eye of the gods. He leaned against an oak his choir of musical reeds and checked his lay that had not yet laboured much. And to him in his fear wondrous Hermes spake thus:

"Fling away thy milking-pail and leave thy fair flocks and come hither and give decision as judge of the goddesses of heaven. Come hither and decide which is the more excellent beauty of face, and to the fairer give this apple's lovely fruit."

So he cried. And Paris bent a gentle eye and quietly essayed to judge the beauty of each. He looked at the light of the grey eyes, he looked on the neck arrayed with gold, he marked the bravery

[a] Nymph beloved of Pan (Mosch. 6, Long. 3. 23).

καὶ πτέρνης μετόπισθε καὶ αὐτῶν ἴχνια ταρσῶν.
χειρῶν μειδιόωντα δίκης προπάροιθεν ἑλοῦσα
τοῖον Ἀλεξάνδρῳ μυθήσατο μῦθον Ἀθήνη·
δεῦρο, τέκος Πριάμοιο, Διὸς παράκοιτιν ἐάσας
καὶ θαλάμων βασίλειαν ἀτιμήσας Ἀφροδίτην
ἠνορέης ἐπίκουρον ἐπαινήσειας Ἀθήνην.
φασί σε κοιρανέειν καὶ Τρώιον ἄστυ φυλάσσειν·
δεῦρό σε τειρομένοισι σαόπτολιν ἀνδράσι θήσω,
μή ποτέ σοι βαρύμηνις ἐπιβρίσειεν Ἐνυώ.
πείθεο, καὶ πολέμους τε καὶ ἠνορέην σε διδάξω.
ὣς ἡ μὲν πολύμητις ἀνηΰτησεν Ἀθήνη.
τοῖα δ' ὑποβλήδην λευκώλενος ἔννεπεν Ἥρη·
εἴ με διακρίνων προφερέστερον ἔρνος ὀπάσσῃς,
πάσης ἡμετέρης Ἀσίης ἡγήτορα θήσω.
ἔργα μόθων ἀθέριζε· τί γὰρ πολέμων βασιλῆι;
κοίρανος ἰφθίμοισι καὶ ἀπτολέμοισι κελεύει.
οὐκ αἰεὶ θεράποντες ἀριστεύουσιν Ἀθήνης·
ὠκύμοροι θνῄσκουσιν ὑποδρηστῆρες Ἐνυοῦς.
τοίην κοιρανίην πρωτόθρονος ὤπασεν Ἥρη.
ἡ δ' ἑανὸν βαθύκολπον, ἐς ἠέρα γυμνώσασα
κόλπον, ἀνῃώρησε καὶ οὐκ ᾐδέσσατο Κύπρις.
χειρὶ δ' ἐλαφρίζουσα μελίφρονα δεσμὸν ἐρώτων
στῆθος ἅπαν γύμνωσε καὶ οὐκ ἐμνήσατο μαζῶν.
τοῖα δὲ μειδιόωσα προσέννεπε μηλοβοτῆρα·
δέξό με καὶ πολέμων ἐπιλήθεο, δέχνυσο μορφὴν
ἡμετέρην καὶ σκῆπτρα καὶ Ἀσίδα κάλλιπε γαῖαν.
ἔργα μόθων οὐκ οἶδα· τί γὰρ σακέων Ἀφροδίτῃ;
ἀγλαΐῃ πολὺ μᾶλλον ἀριστεύουσι γυναῖκες.
ἀντὶ μὲν ἠνορέης ἐρατὴν παράκοιτιν ὀπάσσω,

[a] Paris. [b] Goddess of War (Hom. *Il.* v. 592).

of each; the shape of the heel behind, yea and the soles of their feet. But, before he gave judgement, Athena took him, smiling, by the hand and spake to Alexander[a] thus:

"Come hither, son of Priam! leave the spouse of Zeus and heed not Aphrodite, queen of the bridal bower, but praise thou Athena who aids the prowess of men. They say that thou art a king and keepest the city of Troy. Come hither, and I will make thee the saviour of their city to men hard pressed: lest ever Enyo[b] of grievous wrath weigh heavily upon thee. Hearken to me and I will teach thee war and prowess."

So cried Athena of many counsels, and white-armed Hera thus took up the tale:

"If thou wilt elect me and bestow on me the fruit of the fairer, I will make thee lord of all mine Asia. Scorn thou the works of battle. What has a king to do with war? A prince gives command both to the valiant and to the unwarlike. Not always are the squires of Athena foremost. Swift is the doom and death of the servants of Enyo!"

Such lordship did Hera, who hath the foremost throne, offer to bestow. But Cypris lifted up her deep-bosomed robe and bared her breast to the air and had no shame. And lifting with her hands the honeyed girdle of the Loves she bared all her bosom and heeded not her breasts. And smilingly she thus spake to the herdsman:

"Accept me and forget wars: take my beauty and leave the sceptre and the land of Asia. I know not the works of battle. What has Aphrodite to do with shields? By beauty much more do women excel. In place of manly prowess I will give thee a

ἀντὶ δὲ κοιρανίης Ἑλένης ἐπιβήσεο λέκτρων·
νυμφίον ἀθρήσει σε μετὰ Τροίην Λακεδαίμων.
οὔπω μῦθος ἔληγεν, ὁ δ' ἀγλαὸν ὤπασε μῆλον,
ἀγλαΐης ἀνάθημα, μέγα κτέρας Ἀφρογενείῃ,
φυταλιὴν πολέμοιο, κακὴν πολέμοιο γενέθλην.
χειρὶ δὲ μῆλον ἔχουσα τόσην ἀνενείκατο φωνὴν
Ἥρην κερτομέουσα καὶ ἀντιάνειραν Ἀθήνην·
εἴξατέ μοι πολέμοιο συνήθεες, εἴξατε νίκης.
ἀγλαΐην ἐφίλησα, καὶ ἀγλαΐη με διώκει.
φασί σε, μῆτερ Ἄρηος, ὑπ' ὠδίνεσσιν ἀέξειν
ἠυκόμων Χαρίτων ἱερὸν χορόν· ἀλλά σε πᾶσαι
σήμερον ἠρνήσαντο, καὶ οὐ μίαν εὗρες ἀρωγόν.
οὐ σακέων βασίλεια καὶ οὐ πυρός ἐσσι τιθήνη·
οὔ σοι Ἄρης ἐπάρηξε, καὶ εἰ δορὶ μαίνεται Ἄρης,
οὐ φλόγες Ἡφαίστοιο, καὶ εἰ φλογὸς ἆσθμα λοχεύει.
οἷα δὲ κυδιάεις ἀνεμώλιος, Ἀτρυτώνη,
ἣν γάμος οὐκ ἔσπειρε καὶ οὐ μαιώσατο μήτηρ,
ἀλλὰ σιδηρείη σε τομὴ καὶ ῥίζα σιδήρου
πατρῴων ἀλόχευτον ἀνεβλάστησε καρήνων.
οἷα δὲ χαλκείοισι καλυψαμένη χρόα πέπλοις
καὶ φεύγεις φιλότητα καὶ Ἄρεος ἔργα διώκεις,
ἁρμονίης ἀδίδακτος, ὁμοφροσύνης ἀδαήμων.
ἀγνώσσεις, ὅτι μᾶλλον ἀνάλκιδές εἰσιν Ἀθῆναι
τοῖαι, κυδαλίμοισιν ἀγαλλόμεναι πολέμοισι,
κεκριμένων μελέων οὔτ' ἄρσενες οὔτε γυναῖκες;
τοῖον ἐφυβρίζουσα προσέννεπε Κύπρις Ἀθήνην.
ὣς ἡ μὲν πτολίπορθον ἀέθλιον ἔλλαχε μορφῆς

[a] Aphrodite.

[b] The Graces are generally said to be daughters of Zeus and Eurynome (Hes. *Th.* 907), but the names of the parents are variously given. Here their mother is Hera.

[c] *i.e.* Athena sprang from the head of Zeus (who before

lovely bride, and, instead of kingship, enter thou the bed of Helen. Lacedaemon, after Troy, shall see thee a bridegroom."

Not yet had she ceased speaking and he gave her the splendid apple, beauty's offering, the great treasure of Aphrogeneia,[a] a plant of war, of war an evil seed. And she, holding the apple in her hand, uttered her voice and spake in mockery of Hera and manly Athena:

"Yield to me, accustomed as ye be to war, yield me the victory. Beauty have I loved and beauty follows me. They say that thou, mother of Ares, didst with travail bear the holy choir of the fair-tressed Graces.[b] But to-day they have all denied thee and not one hast thou found to help thee. Queen but not of shields and nurse but not of fire, Ares hath not holpen thee, though Ares rages with the spear: the flames of Hephaestus have not holpen thee, though he brings to birth the breath of fire. And how vain is thy vaunting, Atrytone[c]! whom marriage sowed not nor mother bare, but cleaving of iron and root of iron made thee spring without bed of birth from the head of thy sire. And how, covering thy body in brazen robes, thou dost flee from love and pursuest the works of Ares, untaught of harmony and wotting not of concord. Knowest thou not that such Athenas as thou are the more unvaliant—exulting in glorious wars, with limbs at feud, neither men nor women?"[d]

Thus spake Cypris and mocked Athena. So she got the prize of beauty that should work the ruin of

her birth had swallowed her mother Metis) when it was cleft by the axe of Hephaestus or Prometheus (Hes. *Th.* 924, Hom. *H.* 28, Pind. *O.* vii. 35, Apollod. i. 3. 6).

[d] *Cf.* 302 ff.

Ἥρην ἐξελάσασα καὶ ἀσχαλόωσαν Ἀθήνην·
ἱμείρων δ' ὑπ' ἔρωτι καὶ ἣν οὐκ εἶδε διώκων,
Δύσπαρις ἀθροίσας ἐπὶ δάσκιον ἤγαγεν ὕλην
ἀνέρας ἐργοπόνοιο δαήμονας Ἀτρυτώνης.
ἔνθα πολυπρέμνοιο δαϊζόμεναι δρύες Ἴδης
ἤριπον ἀρχεκάκοιο περιφροσύνῃσι Φερέκλου,
ὃς τότε μαργαίνοντι χαριζόμενος βασιλῆι
νῆας Ἀλεξάνδρῳ δρυτόμῳ τεκτήνατο χαλκῷ.
αὐτῆμαρ προβέβουλε καὶ αὐτῆμαρ κάμε νῆας,
νῆας δ' οὐκ ἐνόησε καὶ οὐκ ἤσκησεν Ἀθήνη.
  ἄρτι μὲν Ἰδαίων ὀρέων ἠλλάξατο πόντον
καὶ λεχέων ἐπίκουρον ἐφεσπομένην Ἀφροδίτην
πολλάκις ἀκταίοισιν ἱλασσάμενος θυέεσσιν
ἔπλεεν Ἑλλήσποντον ἐπ' εὐρέα νῶτα θαλάσσης,
τῷ δὲ πολυτλήτων σημήια φαίνετο μόχθων.
κυανέη μὲν ὕπερθεν ἀναθρῴσκουσα θάλασσα
οὐρανὸν ὀρφναίων ἑλίκων ἐζώσατο δεσμῷ
εἶθαρ ἀμιχθαλόεντος ἀπ' ἠέρος ὄμβρον ἱεῖσα,
ἐκλύσθη δέ τε πόντος ἐρεσσομένων ἐρετάων.
τόφρα δὲ Δαρδανίην καὶ Τρώιον οὖδας ἀμείψας
Ἰσμαρίδος μεθέηκε παραπλώων στόμα λίμνης,
αἶψα δὲ Θρηικίοιο μετ' οὔρεα Παγγαίοιο
Φυλλίδος ἀντέλλοντα φιλήνορος ἔδρακε τύμβον

[a] Athena.

[b] The Trojan who built the ship which brought back Paris to his country (*Il.* v. 59 ff.).

[c] Athena was patron of all carpentry, but in this case she withheld her blessing.

[d] In Thrace, between Maroneia and Stryma (Herod. vii. 109).

[e] Strabo 331 and 680; famous for its mines of gold and silver.

[f] Phyllis was daughter of the king of Thrace. When Demophoon son of Theseus (the same story is told of his

a city, repelling Hera and indignant Athena. And unhappy Paris, yearning with love and pursuing one whom he had not seen, gathered men that were skilled of Atrytone,[a] queen of handicraft, and led them to a shady wood. There the oaks from Ida of many tree-trunks were cut and felled by the excellent skill of Phereclus,[b] source of woe; who at that time, doing pleasure to his frenzied king, fashioned with the wood-cutting bronze ships for Alexander. On the same day he willed and on the same made the ships: ships which Athena[c] neither planned nor wrought.

And now he had just left the hills of Ida for the deep, and, after with many a sacrifice upon the shore he had besought the favour of Aphrodite that attended him to aid his marriage, he was sailing the Hellespont over the broad back of the sea, when to him there appeared a token of his laborious toils. The dark sea leapt aloft and girdled the heaven with a chain of dusky coils and straightway poured forth rain from the murky air, and the sea was turmoiled as the oarsmen rowed. Then when he had passed Dardania and the land of Troy and, coasting along, left behind the mouth of the Ismarian lake,[d] speedily, after the mountains of Thracian Pangaeon,[e] he saw rising into view the tomb of Phyllis[f] that loved her husband and the

brother Acamas) was on his way home from Troy to Athens he married Phyllis. When he left for Athens he promised to return for her soon. As he failed to return, she went nine journeys to the shore to look for his returning ship. Hence the place was called Ἐννέα Ὁδοί, the site of the later colony of Amphipolis (cf. Aeschin. *De fals. leg.* 31). Phyllis cursed Demophoon and hanged herself; *cf.* Ov. *Her.* 2, *Rem. Am.* 605.

καὶ δρόμον ἐννεάκυκλον ἀλήμονος εἶδε κελεύθου,
ἔνθα διαστείχουσα κινύρεο, Φυλλίς, ἀκοίτην
δεχνυμένη παλίνορσον ἀπήμονα Δημοφόωντα,
ὁππότε νοστήσειεν Ἀθηναίης ἀπὸ δήμων.
τῷ δὲ βαθυκλήροιο διὰ χθονὸς Αἱμονιήων
ἐξαπίνης ἀνέτελλεν Ἀχαιίδος ἄνθεα γαίης,
Φθίη βωτιάνειρα καὶ εὐρυάγυια Μυκήνη.
ἔνθεν ἀνερχομένοιο παρ᾽ εἰαμενὰς Ἐρυμάνθου
Σπάρτην καλλιγύναικα, φίλην πόλιν Ἀτρείωνος,
κεκλιμένην ἐνόησεν ἐπ᾽ Εὐρώταο ῥεέθροις.
ἄγχι δὲ ναιομένην ὑπὸ δάσκιον οὔρεος ὕλην
γείτονα παπταίνων ἐρατὴν θηεῖτο Θεράπνην.
οὔπω κεῖθεν ἔην δολιχὸς πλόος, οὐδὲ γαλήνης
δηρὸν ἐρεσσομένων ἠκούετο δοῦπος ἐρετμῶν,
καὶ χθονὸς εὐκόλποισιν ἐπ᾽ ἠιόνεσσι βαλόντες
πείσματα νηὸς ἔδησαν, ὅσοις ἁλὸς ἔργα μεμήλει.
αὐτὰρ ὁ χιονέοιο λοεσσάμενος ποταμοῖο
ᾤχετο φειδομένοισιν ἐπ᾽ ἴχνεσιν ἴχνος ἐρείδων,
μὴ πόδες ἱμερόεντες ὑποχραίνοιντο κονίης,
μὴ πλοκάμων κυνέῃσιν ἐπιβρίσαντες ἐθείρας
ὀξύτερον σπεύδοντος ἀναστέλλοιεν ἀῆται.
ἄρτι μὲν αἰπύδμητα φιλοξείνων ναετήρων
δώματα παπταίνων καὶ γείτονας ἐγγύθι νηοὺς
ἄστεος ἀγλαΐην διεμέτρεεν, ἔνθα μὲν αὐτῆς
χρύσεον ἐνδαπίης θηεύμενος εἶδος Ἀθήνης,
ἔνθα δὲ Καρνείοιο φίλον κτέρας Ἀπόλλωνος
οἶκον Ἀμυκλαίοιο παραγνάμψας Ὑακίνθου,
ὅν ποτε κουρίζοντα σὺν Ἀπόλλωνι νοήσας
δῆμος Ἀμυκλαίων ἠγάσσατο, μὴ Διὶ Λητὼ

[a] Thessalians. [b] A river in Arcadia.

nine-circled course of her wandering path, where thou didst range and cry, Phyllis, waiting the safe return of thy husband Demophoon, when he should come back from the land of Athena. Then across the rich land of the Haemonians [a] there suddenly arose upon his eyes the flowery Achaean land, Phthia, feeder of men, and Mycene of wide streets. Then past the marshes where Erymanthus [b] rises he marked Sparta of fair women, the dear city of the son of Atreus, lying on the banks of the Eurotas. And hard by, established under a hill's shady wood, he gazed upon her neighbour, lovely Therapne. Thence they had not far to sail, nor was the noise of the oars rowing in the calm sea heard for long, when they cast the hawsers of the ship upon the shores of a fair gulf and made them fast, even they whose business was the works of the sea.

And he washed him in the snowy river and went his way, stepping with careful steps, lest his lovely feet should be defiled of the dust; lest, if he hastened more quickly, the winds should blow heavily on his helmet and stir up the locks of his hair.

And now he scanned the high-built houses of the hospitable inhabitants and the neighbouring temples hard by, and surveyed the splendour of the city; here gazing on the golden image of native [c] Athena herself, and there passing the dear treasure of Carneian Apollo, even the shrine of Hyacinthus of Amyclae, whom once while he played as a boy with Apollo the people of Amyclae marked and marvelled whether he too had not been conceived and borne

[c] See Pausan. iii. 13. 3–4. With "native" (ἐνδαπία) Athena we may compare Carneios Oiketes.

κυσαμένη καὶ τοῦτον ἀνήγαγεν· αὐτὰρ Ἀπόλλων
οὐκ ἐδάη Ζεφύρῳ ζηλήμονι παῖδα φυλάσσων.
γαῖα δὲ δακρύσαντι χαριζομένη βασιλῆι
ἄνθος ἀνηέξησε, παραίφασιν Ἀπόλλωνος,
ἄνθος ἀριζήλοιο φερώνυμον ἡβητῆρος.
ἤδη δ᾽ ἀγχιδόμοισιν ἐπ᾽ Ἀτρείδαο μελάθροις
ἵστατο θεσπεσίῃσιν ἀγαλλόμενος χαρίτεσσιν.
οὐ Διὶ τοῖον ἔτικτεν ἐπήρατον υἷα Θυώνη·
ἱλήκοις, Διόνυσε· καὶ εἰ Διός ἐσσι γενέθλης,
καλὸς ἔην καὶ κεῖνος ἐπ᾽ ἀγλαΐῃσι προσώπων.
ἡ δὲ φιλοξείνων θαλάμων κληῖδας ἀνεῖσα
ἐξαπίνης Ἑλένη μετεκίαθε δώματος αὐλὴν
καὶ θαλερῶν προπάροιθεν ὀπιπεύουσα θυράων
ὡς ἴδεν, ὣς ἐκάλεσσε καὶ ἐς μυχὸν ἤγαγεν οἴκου
καί μιν ἐφεδρήσσειν νεοπηγέος ὑψόθεν ἕδρης
ἀργυρέης ἐπέτελλε· κόρον δ᾽ οὐκ εἶχεν ὀπωπῆς
ἄλλοτε δὴ χρύσειον ὀισαμένη Κυθερείης
κοῦρον ὀπιπεύειν θαλαμηπόλον—ὀψὲ δ᾽ ἀνέγνω,
ὡς οὐκ ἔστιν Ἔρως· βελέων δ᾽ οὐκ εἶδε φαρέτρην—
πολλάκι δ᾽ ἀγλαΐῃσιν ἐυγλήνοισι προσώπων
παπταίνειν ἐδόκευε τὸν ἡμερίδων βασιλῆα·
ἀλλ᾽ οὐχ ἡμερίδων θαλερὴν ἐδόκευεν ὀπώρην
πεπταμένην χαρίεντος ἐπὶ ξυνοχῇσι καρήνου.
ὀψὲ δὲ θαμβήσασα τόσην ἀνενείκατο φωνήν·
ξεῖνε, πόθεν τελέθεις; ἐρατὸν γένος εἰπὲ καὶ ἡμῖν.
ἀγλαΐην μὲν ἔοικας ἀριζήλῳ βασιλῆι,

---

[a] The hyacinth was feigned to have sprung from the blood of Hyacinthus or of Aias, and to bear on its petals either Υ, *i.e.* the initial of Ὑάκινθος, or the letters ΑΙ, *i.e.* the initials of ΑΙΑΙ = Alas! or of Aias; Ovid, *Met.* xiii. 394 f.:

rubefactaque sanguine tellus
purpureum viridi genuit de caespite florem,
qui prius Oebalio fuerat de vulnere natus.

by Leto to Zeus. But Apollo knew not that he was keeping the youth for envious Zephyrus. And the earth, doing a pleasure to the weeping king, brought forth a flower to console Apollo, even that flower[a] which bears the name of the splendid youth.

And at last by the halls of the son[b] of Atreus, builded near, he stood, glorying in his marvellous graces. Not so fair was the lovely son[c] whom Thyone[d] bare to Zeus: forgive me, Dionysus! even if thou art of the seed of Zeus, he, too, was fair as his face was beautiful. And Helen unbarred the bolts of her hospitable bower and suddenly went to the court of the house, and, looking in front of the goodly doors, soon as she saw, so soon she called him and led him within the house, and bade him sit on a new-wrought chair of silver. And she could not satisfy her eyes with gazing, now deeming that she looked on the golden youth that attends on Cythereia[e]—and late she recognized that it was not Eros; she saw no quiver of arrows—and often in the beauty of his face and eyes she looked to see the king[f] of the vine: but no blooming fruit of the vine did she behold spread upon the meeting of his gracious brows. And after long time, amazed, she uttered her voice and said:

"Stranger, whence art thou? declare thy fair lineage even unto us. In beauty thou art like unto

> littera communis [=A] mediis pueroque viroque
> inscripta est foliis, haec nominis [Aias], illa querellae [Αἰαῖ].

It is the "lettered hyacinth" of Theocr. x. 28 and Milton's "sanguine flower inscribed with woe," *Lycid.* 106. The flower seems to be not our hyacinth but a species of larkspur, *Delphinium Ajacis.* For the myth see Frazer, *Adonis, Attis, Osiris* i. p. 313 ff.

[b] Menelaus.

[c] Dionysus. [d] Semele. [e] Aphrodite. [f] Dionysus.

ἀλλὰ τεὴν οὐκ οἶδα παρ' Ἀργείοισι γενέθλην.
πᾶσαν Δευκαλίωνος ἀμύμονος οἶδα γενέθλην·
οὐ Πύλον ἠμαθόεσσαν ἔχεις, Νηλήιον οὖδας,
—Ἀντίλοχον δεδάηκα, τεὴν δ' οὐκ εἶδον ὀπωπὴν
οὐ Φθίην χαρίεσσαν, ἀριστήων τροφὸν ἀνδρῶν·
οἶδα περικλήιστον ὅλον γένος Αἰακιδάων,
ἀγλαΐην Πηλῆος, ἐυκλείην Τελαμῶνος,
ἤθεα Πατρόκλοιο καὶ ἠνορέην Ἀχιλῆος.
τοῖα Πάριν ποθέουσα λιγύθροος ἔννεπε νύμφη·
αὐτὰρ ὁ μειλιχίην ἠμείβετο γῆρυν ἀνοίξας·
εἴ τινά που Φρυγίης ἐνὶ πείρασι γαῖαν ἀκούεις,
Ἴλιον, ἣν πύργωσε Ποσειδάων καὶ Ἀπόλλων·
εἴ τινά που πολύολβον ἐνὶ Τροίῃ βασιλῆα
ἔκλυες εὐώδινος ἀπὸ Κρονίδαο γενέθλης·
ἔνθεν ἀριστεύων ἐμφύλια πάντα διώκω.
εἰμί, γύναι, Πριάμοιο πολυχρύσου φίλος υἱός,
εἰμὶ δὲ Δαρδανίδης· ὁ δὲ Δάρδανος ἐκ Διὸς ἦεν,
ᾧ καὶ ἀπ' Οὐλύμποιο θεοὶ ξυνήονες ἀνδρῶν
πολλάκι θητεύουσι καὶ ἀθάνατοί περ ἐόντες·
ὧν ὁ μὲν ἡμετέρης δωμήσατο τείχεα πάτρης,
τείχεα μαρμαίροντα, Ποσειδάων καὶ Ἀπόλλων.
αὐτὰρ ἐγώ, βασίλεια, δικασπόλος εἰμὶ θεάων·
καὶ γὰρ ἀκηχεμένῃσιν ἐπουρανίῃσι δικάζων
Κύπριδος ἀγλαΐην καὶ ἐπήρατον ᾔνεσα μορφήν,
ἡ δὲ περικλήιστον, ἐμῶν ἀντάξιον ἔργων,
νύμφην ἱμερόεσσαν ἐμοὶ κατένευσεν ὀπάσσαι,
ἣν Ἑλένην ἐνέπουσι, κασιγνήτην Ἀφροδίτης,
ἧς ἕνεκεν τέτληκα καὶ οἴδματα τόσσα περῆσαι.
δεῦρο γάμον κεράσωμεν, ἐπεὶ Κυθέρεια κελεύει·
μή με καταισχύνειας, ἐμὴν <μὴ> Κύπριν ἐλέγξῃς.

---

[a] Apollo and Poseidon served Laomedon for a year and built for him the walls of Troy (Apollod. ii. 103, *Il.* vii. 452).

a glorious king, but thy family I know not among the Argives. I know all the family of blameless Deucalion. Not in sandy Pylus, the land of Neleus, hast thou thy dwelling: Antilochus I know, but thy face I have not seen; not in gracious Phthia, nurse of chieftains; I know the whole renowned race of the sons of Aeacus, the beauty of Peleus, the fair fame of Telamon, the gentleness of Patroclus and the prowess of Achilles."

So, yearning for Paris, spake the lady of sweet voice. And he opened honeyed speech and answered her:

"If haply thou hast heard of a town in the bounds of Phrygia, even Ilios, whereof Poseidon built the towers and Apollo: if thou hast haply heard of a very wealthy king in Troy, sprung from the fruitful race of Cronus: thence am I a prince and pursue all the works of my race. I, lady, am the dear son of Priam rich in gold, of the lineage of Dardanus am I, and Dardanus was the son of Zeus. And the gods from Olympus, companioning with men, oft-times became his servants,[a] albeit they were immortal: of whom Poseidon with Apollo built the shining walls of our fatherland. And I, O Queen, am the judge of goddesses. For, deciding a suit for the aggrieved daughters of heaven, I praised the beauty of Cypris and her lovely form. And she vowed that she would give me a worthy recompense of my labour, even a glorious and a lovely bride, whom they call Helen, sister of Aphrodite; and it is for her sake that I have endured to cross such seas. Come, let us join wedlock, since Cythereia bids. Despise me not, put not my love to shame. I will not say—why should

οὐκ ἐρέω· τί δὲ τόσσον ἐπισταμένην σε διδάξω;
οἶσθα γάρ, ὡς Μενέλαος ἀνάλκιδός ἐστι γενέθλης·
οὐ τοῖαι γεγάασιν ἐν Ἀργείοισι γυναῖκες,
καὶ γὰρ ἀκιδνοτέροισιν ἀεξόμεναι μελέεσσιν
ἀνδρῶν εἶδος ἔχουσι, νόθοι δ' ἐγένοντο γυναῖκες.
ἔννεπεν· ἡ δ' ἐρόεσσαν ἐπὶ χθονὶ πῆξεν ὀπωπὴν
δηρὸν ἀμηχανέουσα καὶ οὐκ ἠμείβετο νύμφη.
ὀψὲ δὲ θαμβήσασα τόσην ἀνενείκατο φωνήν·
ἀτρεκέως, ὦ ξεῖνε, τεῆς ποτε πυθμένα πάτρης
τὸ πρὶν ἐδωμήσαντο Ποσειδάων καὶ Ἀπόλλων;
ἤθελον ἀθανάτων δαιδάλματα κεῖνα νοῆσαι
καὶ νομὸν οἰοπόλοιο λιγύπνοον Ἀπόλλωνος,
ἔνθα θεοδμήτοισι παρὰ προθύροισι πυλάων
πολλάκις εἰλιπόδεσσιν ἐφέσπετο βουσὶν Ἀπόλλων.
ἀγρέο νῦν Σπάρτηθεν ἐπὶ Τροίην με κομίζων.
ἕψομαι, ὡς Κυθέρεια γάμων βασίλεια κελεύει.
οὐ τρομέω Μενέλαον, ὅταν Τροίῃ με νοήσῃ.
τοίην συνθεσίην καλλίσφυρος ἔννεπε νύμφη.
νὺξ δέ, πόνων ἄμπαυμα μετ' ἠελίοιο κελεύθους,
ὕπνον ἐλαφρίζουσα, παρήορον ὤπασεν ἠῶ
ἀρχομένην· δοιὰς δὲ πύλας ὤιξεν ὀνείρων,
τὴν μὲν ἀληθείης—κεράων ἀπελάμπετο κόσμος—
ἔνθεν ἀναθρῴσκουσι θεῶν νημερτέες ὀμφαί,
τὴν δὲ δολοφροσύνης, κενεῶν θρέπτειραν ὀνείρων.
αὐτὰρ ὁ ποντοπόρων Ἑλένην ἐπὶ σέλματα νηῶν
ἐκ θαλάμων ἐκόμισσε φιλοξείνου Μενελάου,
κυδιόων δ' ὑπέροπλον ὑποσχεσίῃ Κυθερείης
φόρτον ἄγων ἔσπευδεν ἐς Ἴλιον ἰωχμοῖο.
Ἑρμιόνη δ' ἀνέμοισιν ἀπορρίψασα καλύπτρην
ἱσταμένης πολύδακρυς ἀνέστενεν ἠριγενείης,

[a] *Cf.* 187 ff.

[b] Gates of Horn and of Ivory (Hom. *Od.* xix. 562 ff.).

I tell thee who knowest so much? for thou knowest that Menelaus is of an unvaliant race. Not such as thou are women born among the Argives; for they wax with meaner limbs and have the look of men and are but bastard women." [a]

So he spake. And the lady fixed her lovely eyes upon the ground, and long time perplexed replied not. But at last amazed she uttered her voice and said:

"Of a surety, O stranger, did Poseidon and Apollo in days of old build the foundation of thy fatherland? Fain would I have seen those cunning works of the immortals and the shrill-blowing pasture of shepherd Apollo, where by the god-built vestibules of the gates Apollo often-times followed the kine of shuffling gait. Come now, carry me from Sparta unto Troy. I will follow, as Cythereia, queen of wedlock, bids. I do not fear Menelaus, when Troy shall have known me."

So the fair-ankled lady plighted her troth. And night, respite from labour after the journey of the sun, lightened sleep and brought the beginning of wandering morn; and opened the two gates [b] of dreams: one the gate of truth—it shone with the sheen of horn—whence leap forth the unerring messages of the gods; the other the gate of deceit, nurse of empty dreams. And he carried Helen from the bowers of hospitable Menelaus to the benches of his sea-faring ships; and exulting exceedingly in the promise of Cythereia he hastened to carry to Ilios his freight of war.

And Hermione [c] cast to the winds her veil and, as morning rose, wailed with many tears. And often

[c] Daughter of Menelaus and Helen.

πολλάκι δ' ἀμφιπόλους θαλάμων ἔκτοσθε λαβοῦσα,
ὀξύτατον βοόωσα τόσην ἀνενείκατο φωνήν·
παῖδες, πῆ με λιποῦσα πολύστονον ᾤχετο μήτηρ,
ἢ χθιζὸν σὺν ἐμοὶ θαλάμων κληῖδας ἑλοῦσα
ἔδραθεν ὑπνώουσα καὶ ἐς μίαν ἤλυθεν εὐνήν;
ἔννεπε δακρυχέουσα, συνωδύροντο δὲ παῖδες.
ἀγρόμεναι δ' ἑκάτερθεν ἐπὶ προθύροισιν ἐρύκειν
Ἑρμιόνην στενάχουσαν ἐπειρήσαντο γυναῖκες·
τέκνον ὀδυρομένη, γόον εὔνασον. ᾤχετο μήτηρ,
νοστήσει παλίνορσος· ἔτι κλαίουσα νοήσεις.
οὐχ ὁράᾳς; γοεραὶ μὲν ἐπιμύουσιν ὀπωπαί,
πυκνὰ δὲ μυρομένης θαλεραὶ μινύθουσι παρειαί.
ἢ τάχα νυμφάων ἐς ὁμήγυριν ἀγρομενάων
ἤλυθεν, ἰθείης δὲ παραπλάζουσα κελεύθου
ἵσταται ἀσχαλόωσα, καὶ ἐς λειμῶνα μολοῦσα
Ὡράων δροσόεντος ὑπὲρ πεδίοιο θαάσσει,
ἢ χρόα πατρῴοιο λοεσσομένη ποταμοῖο
ᾤχετο καὶ δήθυνεν ἐπ' Εὐρώταο ῥεέθροις.
τοῖα δὲ δακρύσασα πολύστονος ἔννεπε κούρη·
οἶδεν ὄρος, ποταμῶν ἐδάη ῥόον, οἶδε κελεύθους
ἐς ῥόδον, ἐς λειμῶνα· τί μοι φθέγγεσθε, γυναῖκες;
ἀστέρες ὑπνώουσι, καὶ ἐν σκοπέλοισιν ἰαύει·
ἀστέρες ἀντέλλουσι, καὶ οὐ παλίνορσος ἱκάνει.
μῆτερ ἐμή, τίνα χῶρον ἔχεις; τίνα δ' οὔρεα ναίεις;
πλαζομένην θῆρές σε κατέκτανον; ἀλλὰ καὶ αὐτοὶ
θῆρες ἀριζήλοιο Διὸς τρομέουσι γενέθλην.
ἤριπες ἐξ ὀχέων χθαμαλῆς ἐπὶ νῶτα κονίης
σὸν δέμας οἰοπόλοισιν ἐνὶ δρυμοῖσι λιποῦσα;
ἀλλὰ πολυπρέμνων ξυλόχων ὑπὸ δάσκιον ὕλην
δένδρεα παπτήνασα καὶ αὐτῶν μέχρι πετήλων
σὸν δέμας οὐκ ἐνόησα· καὶ οὐ νεμεσίζομαι ὕλῃ.

taking her handmaidens outside her chamber, with shrillest cries she uttered her voice and said:

"Girls, whither hath my mother gone and left me in grievous sorrow, she that yester-even with me took the keys of the chamber and entered one bed with me and fell asleep?"

So spake she weeping and the girls wailed with her. And the women gathered by the vestibule on either side and sought to stay Hermione in her lamentation:

"Sorrowing child, stay thy lamentation; thy mother has gone, yet shall she come back again. While still thou weepest, thou shalt see her. Seest not? thine eyes are blinded with tears and thy blooming cheeks are marred with much weeping. Haply she hath gone to a meeting of women in assembly and, wandering from the straight path, stands distressed, or she hath gone to the meadow and sits on the dewy plain of the Hours, or she hath gone to wash her body in the river of her fathers and lingered by the streams of Eurotas."

Then spake the sorrowful maiden weeping: "She knows the hill, she hath skill of the rivers' flow, she knows the paths to the roses, to the meadow. What say ye to me, women? The stars sleep and she rests among the rocks; the stars rise, and she comes not home. My mother, where art thou? in what hills dost thou dwell? Have wild beasts slain thee in thy wandering? but even the wild beasts tremble before the offspring of high Zeus. Hast thou fallen from thy car on the levels of the dusty ground, and left thy body in the lonely thickets? but I have scanned the trees of the many-trunked copses in the shady wood, yea, even to the very leaves, yet thy form have I not seen; and the wood I do

μὴ διεροῖς στονόεντος ἐπ' Εὐρώταο ῥεέθροις
νηχομένην ἐκάλυψεν ὑποβρυχίην σε γαλήνη;
ἀλλὰ καὶ ἐν ποταμοῖσι καὶ ἐν πελάγεσσι θαλάσσης
Νηιάδες ζώουσι καὶ οὐ κτείνουσι γυναῖκας.
ὣς ἡ μὲν στενάχιζεν· ἀνακλίνουσα δὲ δειρὴν
ὕπνον ἔπνει, θανάτοιο συνέμπορον· ἦ γὰρ ἐτύχθη
ἄμφω ἀναγκαίη ξυνήια πάντα λαχόντε
ἔργα παλαιοτέροιο κασιγνήτοιο διώκειν.
ἔνθεν ἀκηχεμένοισι βαρυνόμεναι βλεφάροισι
πολλάκις ὑπνώουσιν, ὅτε κλαίουσι, γυναῖκες.
ἡ μὲν ἀλητεύουσα δολοφροσύνῃσιν ὀνείρων
μητέρα παπταίνειν ὠίσατο, τοῖα δὲ κούρη
ἴαχε θαμβήσασα καὶ ἀχνυμένη περ ἐοῦσα·
χθιζὸν ὀδυρομένην με δόμων ἔκτοσθε φυγοῦσα
κάλλιπες ὑπνώουσαν ὑπὲρ λεχέων γενετῆρος.
ποῖον ὄρος μεθέηκα; τίνας προλέλοιπα κολώνας;
οὕτω καλλικόμοιο μεθ' ἁρμονίην Ἀφροδίτης;
τοῖα δὲ φωνήσασα προσέννεπε Τυνδαρεώνη·
τέκνον ἀκηχεμένη, μὴ μέμφεο δεινὰ παθούσῃ·
ὁ χθιζός με μολὼν ἀπατήλιος ἥρπασεν ἀνήρ.
ἔννεπεν. ἡ δ' ἀνόρουσε καὶ οὐχ ὁρόωσα τιθήνην
ὀξυτέρῃ πολὺ μᾶλλον ἀνεβρυχήσατο φωνῇ·
ἠερίης, ὄρνιθες, ἐύπτερα τέκνα γενέθλης,
εἴπατε νοστήσαντες ἐπὶ Κρήτην Μενελάῳ·
χθιζὸν ἐπὶ Σπάρτην τις ἀνὴρ ἀθεμίστιος ἐλθὼν
ἀγλαΐην ξύμπασαν ἑῶν ἀλάπαξε μελάθρων.
Ὣς ἡ μὲν πολύδακρυς ἐς ἠέρα φωνήσασα,
μητέρα μαστεύουσα, μάτην ἐπλάζετο κούρη.
καὶ Κικόνων πτολίεθρα καὶ Αἰολίδος πόρον Ἕλλης

[a] Sherburne renders:

Sleep is death's twin, and as the younger brother,
In every thing does imitate the other.

not blame. Have the smooth waters covered thee in the depths, swimming in the wet streams of murmuring Eurotas? but even in the rivers and in the depths of the sea the Naiads live and do not slay women."

Thus she wailed, and leaning back her neck breathed Sleep who walks with Death; for verily it was ordained that both should have all things in common and pursue the works of the elder brother:[a] hence women, weighed down with sorrowing eyes, oft-times, while they weep, fall asleep. And wandering amid the deceits of dreams she fancied that she saw her mother; and, amazed, the maiden, in her grief cried out:

"Yesterday to my sorrow thou didst fly from me out of the house and left me sleeping on my father's bed. What mountain have I left alone? What hill have I neglected? Followest thou thus the love of fair-tressed Aphrodite?

Then the daughter of Tyndareus[b] spake to her and said:

"My sorrowful child, blame me not, who have suffered terrible things. The deceitful man who came yesterday hath carried me away!"

So she spake. And the maiden leapt up, and seeing not her mother, uttered a yet more piercing cry and wailed:

"Birds, winged children of the brood of air, go ye to Crete and say to Menelaus: 'Yesterday a lawless man came to Sparta and hath laid waste all the glory of thy halls!'"

So spake she with many tears to the air, and seeking for her mother wandered in vain. And to the towns of the Cicones[c] and the straits of

[b] Helen. [c] Hom. *Od.* ix. 39; a people of Thrace.

Δαρδανίης λιμένεσσιν ὁ νυμφίος ἤγαγε νύμφην.
πυκνὰ δὲ τίλλε κόμην, χρυσέην δ' ἔρριψε καλύπτρην
Κασσάνδρη νεόφοιτον ἀπ' ἀκροπόληος ἰδοῦσα.
Τροίη δ' ὑψιδόμων πυλέων κληῖδας ἀνεῖσα
δέξατο νοστήσαντα τὸν ἀρχέκακον πολιήτην.

---

[a] Athamas, father of Helle, was son of Aeolus.

Aeolian[a] Helle, into the havens of Dardania the bridegroom brought his bride. And Cassandra on the acropolis, when she beheld the new-comer, tore her hair amain and flung away her golden veil. But Troy unbarred the bolts of her high-built gates and received on his return her citizen that was the source of her woe.

TRYPHIODORUS

INTRODUCTION

1. The Life of Tryphiodorus

For the life of Tryphiodorus we have a notice in Suidas *s.v.* Τρυφιόδωρος "of Egypt, grammarian and epic poet; wrote *Marathoniaca, Capture of Ilios* (Ἰλίου ἅλωσις), *The Story of Hippodameia* (τὰ καθ' Ἱπποδάμειαν), an *Odyssey leipogrammatos*—this being a poem on the labours (κάματοι) of Odysseus and myths concerning him and other things."

A second entry in Suidas under the name of Tryphiodorus merely says that he "wrote various things in epic verse; a paraphrase of the similes (παραβολαί) of Homer; and very many other things."

As to the nature of the lipogrammatic *Odyssey* we have two notes:

(1) Suidas *s.v.* Νέστωρ of Laranda in Lycia, epic poet; . . . Ἰλιάδα γράψας λειπογράμματον ἤτοι ἀστοιχείωτον; in similar fashion Tryphiodorus wrote an *Odyssey*; for in the First Book (α') the letter α is not found; and so in each rhapsody its (denoting) letter is wanting."

(2) Eustathius, Hom. *Od.* prooem. 1379, in referring to freak variations on Homer mentions that one Timolaos "of Larissa or Macedon or both," wrote a *Troica*, which he composed by inserting a line of his own alternately with a line of Homer's *Iliad* (παρενέβαλε τῇ Ἰλιάδι στίχον πρὸς στίχον), and he goes on say: "it is said that Tryphiodorus wrote an Ὀδύσσεια λειπογράμματος, from which he banished sigma."

Similarly we are told by Suidas *s.v.* Ἰδαῖος Ῥόδιος that Idaios παρεμβαλὼν στίχον στίχῳ ἐδίπλασε τὴν ποίησιν Ὁμήρου, and *s.v.* Πίγρης that Pigres of Halicarnassus, brother of the famous Artemisia, τῇ Ἰλιάδι παρενέβαλε κατὰ στίχον ἐλεγεῖον, οὕτω γράψας· Μῆνιν ἄειδε, θεά, Πηληϊάδεω Ἀχιλῆος, Μοῦσα, σὺ γὰρ πάσης πεῖρατ' ἔχεις σοφίης. *Cf.* K. Lehrs, *Kleine Schriften*, p. 2, who mentions that Joshua Barnes published at London in 1679 a Greek poem entitled *Susias*, containing the story of Esther in hexameters "presse ad Iliadis exemplar factis," thus: Μῆνιν ἄειδε, θεά, Ἀμαληχιάδεω Ἀμανῆος | οὐλομένην, ἣ μυρί' Ἑβραίοις ἄλγε' ἔθηκε | Περσέων δ' ἰφθίμους κεφαλὰς Ἄϊδι προΐαψεν. See Sandys, *H.C.S.* ii. p. 357 f. for this and Bentley's verdict that "Barnes had as much Greek, and understood it about as well, as an Athenian blacksmith."

The above is the sum of our meagre information about Tryphiodorus. For the rest it is inferred from the fact that Tryphiodorus imitates Nonnus (*circ.* A.D. 400?), and is himself imitated by Colluthus, that he lived about the middle of the 5th century.

It has been inferred that he was a Christian on the very insufficient ground that in v. 604 f. he uses the phrase καὶ οὐ νοέοντα τοκήων ἀμπλακίας ἀπέτινον. But there is nothing specifically Christian about this language.

From the occurrence of the name of the Egyptian goddess Triphis or Thriphis only in a couple of inscriptions (one of the time of Tiberius, the other of the time of Trajan) from the district Athribis it has been argued by Letronne that he belonged to that district and that the correct spelling of his name is Triphiodorus.

2. The MSS.

1. The best MS. is F = Laurentianus xxxii. 16, written in A.D. 1280, which once belonged to Franciscus Philelfus who bought it in Constantinople on 4th January A.D. 1423 from the wife of Johannes Chrysoloras. It contains, among other things, Nonni *Dionysiaca*, Apollonius Rhodius, Theocritus, Hesiod, Oppian, Moschus, Nicander, Tryphiodorus, Gregorius Nazianzenus.

2. Inferior MSS. (fifteenth-sixteenth cent.) are:
Ambrosianus Q 5 *sup.*
Hauniensis 60 (= Reimerianus = Putschianus)
Laurentianus xxxi. 27.
Neapolitanus ii. F 17.
Parisinus 2600.
Parisinus suppl. 109.

3. Bibliography

Editio Princeps: Aldine, Venice (no date, 1521? with Colluth. and Q. Smyrn.). Renatus Perdrierius, Basel, 1555 (Lat. trans.). F. Jamotius, Paris, 1557, 1578. H. Stephanus (in Poet. Gr. princ. heroici carminis), Paris, 1566. Sixtus Henricpetri, Basel, 1569. Michael Neander in Part II. of his Opus Aureum, Leipzig, 1577. W. H. Xylander, Basel, 1578 (Lat. verse trans. in his Lat. trans. of Diodorus Siculus). Nicodemus Frischlin, Frankfort, 1588. Lectius, in Corpus Poet. Gr., Collon. Allobr. 1606. Claud. Dausqueius, Annot. in T., Frankfort, 1614.

J. Merrick, Oxford, 1739 (English trans. in rhymed verse), Oxford 1741 (notes and Frischlin's Lat. verse trans.).

T. Northmore, London, 1791, 1804. G. H. Schaefer, Leipzig, 1808. Wernicke, Leipzig, 1819.

W. Weinberger, Leipzig, 1896 (text and crit. notes).

Translations:—(Besides those mentioned above): Trifiodoro "Lo Sterminio di Troia" by Carlo Lanza (in Atti dell' Accademia Pontaniana 14), Naples, 1881.

Trojas Intagning. En sang af Tryfiodoros i svensk öfversättning af Carl A. Melander, Progr. Umea, 1894.

Other Literature:—H. Koechley, Beiträge zur Kritik u. Erklärung des Tryphiodor, Opusc. Philol. 2, Leipzig, 1882.

H. v. Herwerden, Ad Poetas graecos, Mnemosyne xiv. (1886). Jo. Petersen, Tryphiod. Exc. Tr. 2 in Genethliacon Gottingense, Halle, 1888. F. Noack,

Die Quellen des Tryphiod., Hermes xxvii. (1892).
A. Ludwich, Tryphiodorea, Progr. acad. Regimontii, 1895.
W. Weinberger, Studien zu Tryphiodor u. Kolluth., Wiener Studien xviii. (1896).

THE TAKING OF ILIOS

ΤΡΥΦΙΟΔΩΡΟΥ ΑΛΩΣΙΣ ΙΛΙΟΥ

Τέρμα πολυκμήτοιο μεταχρόνιον πολέμοιο
καὶ λόχον Ἀργείης ἱππήλατον ἔργον Ἀθήνης,
αὐτικα μοι σπεύδοντι πολὺν διὰ μῦθον ἀνεῖσα
ἔννεπε, Καλλιόπεια, καὶ ἀρχαίην ἔριν ἀνδρῶν
κεκριμένου πολέμοιο ταχείῃ λῦσον ἀοιδῇ.
ἤδη μὲν δεκάτοιο κυλινδομένου λυκάβαντος
γηραλέη τετάνυστο φόνων ἀκόρητος Ἐνυὼ
Τρωσί τε καὶ Δαναοῖσιν· ἐναιρομένων δ' ἄρα φωτῶν
δούρατα κεκμήκει, ξιφέων δ' ἔθνῃσκον ἀπειλαί,
σβέννυτο θωρήκων ἐνοπή, μινύθεσκε δ' ἑλικτὴ
ἁρμονίη ῥηχθεῖσα φερεσσακέων τελαμώνων,
ἀσπίδες οὐκ ἀνέχοντο μένειν ἔτι δοῦπον ἀκόντων,
λύετο καμπύλα τόξα, κατέρρεον ὠκέες ἰοί.
ἵπποι δ' οἱ μὲν ἄνευθεν ἀεργηλῆς ἐπὶ φάτνης
οἰκτρὰ κάτω μύοντες ὁμόζυγας ἔστενον ἵππους,
οἱ δ' αὐτοὺς ποθέοντες ὀλωλότας ἡνιοχῆας.
κεῖτο δὲ Πηλείδης μὲν ἔχων ἅμα νεκρὸν ἑταῖρον,
Ἀντιλόχῳ δ' ἐπὶ παιδὶ γέρων ὠδύρετο Νέστωρ,
Αἴας δ' αὐτοφόνῳ βριαρὸν δέμας ἕλκεϊ λύσας
φάσγανον ἐχθρὸν ἔλουσε μεμηνότος αἵματος ὄμβρῳ.

---

[a] The wooden horse built by Epeius with help of Athena; Eur. *Tr.* 534 calls it the "polished ambush of the Argives," ξεστὸν λόχον Ἀργείων.

[b] Patroclus.

THE TAKING OF ILIOS

Of the long delayed end of the laborious war and of the ambush, even the horse[a] fashioned of Argive Athena, straightway to me in my haste do thou tell, O Calliopeia, remitting copious speech; and the ancient strife of men, in that war now decided, do thou resolve with speedy song.

Already the tenth year was rolling on and old had grown the strain of war, insatiate of blood, for Trojans and Danaans. With slaying of men the spears were weary, the menace of the swords died, quenched was the din of breastplate, rent and perishing the coiled fabric of shield-carrying baldricks; the shield endured no more to abide the hurtling of javelins, unstrung was the bent bow, the swift arrows decayed. And the horses—some apart at the idle manger, with heads bowed piteously, bewailed their fellow horses, some mourned to miss their perished charioteers.

Low lay the son of Peleus and with him his comrade[b] dead: over his young son Antilochus old Nestor mourned: Aias with self-dealt wound had unstrung his mighty form, and bathed his foeman's sword[c] in the rain of frenzied blood. The Trojans,

[c] In *Iliad* vii. Aias and Hector fight an indecisive duel and on parting exchange gifts, Aias giving his belt and receiving Hector's sword (*l.c.* 303), with which he afterwards slew himself: Pind. *I.* iii. (iv.), Soph. *Aj.* 815 f.

Τρωσὶ δὲ λωβητῆρσιν ἐφ' Ἕκτορος ἑλκυθμοῖσι
μυρομένοις οὐ μοῦνον ἔην ἐπιδήμιον ἄλγος,
ἀλλὰ καὶ ἀλλοθρόοις ἐπὶ πένθεσι κωκύοντες
δάκρυσιν ἠμείβοντο πολυγλώσσων ἐπικούρων.
κλαῖον μὲν Λύκιοι Σαρπηδόνα, τόν ποτε μήτηρ
ἐς Τροίην μὲν ἔπεμψεν ἀγαλλομένη Διὸς εὐνῇ,
δουρὶ δὲ Πατρόκλοιο Μενοιτιάδαο πεσόντα
αἵματι δακρύσας ἐχύθη πατρώιος ἀήρ.
καὶ δολίην ὑπὸ νύκτα κακῷ πεπεδημένον ὕπνῳ
Ῥῆσον μὲν Θρήικες ἐκώκυον· ἡ δ' ἐπὶ πότμῳ
Μέμνονος οὐρανίην νεφέλην ἀνεδήσατο μήτηρ
φέγγος ὑποκλέψασα κατηφέος ἤματος Ἠώς.
αἱ δ' ἀπὸ Θερμώδοντος ἀρηιφίλοιο γυναῖκες
κοπτόμεναι περίκυκλον ἀθηλέος ὄμφακα μαζοῦ
παρθένον ὠδύροντο δαΐφρονα Πενθεσίλειαν,
ἥτε πολυξείνοιο χορὸν πολέμοιο μολοῦσα
θηλείης ὑπὸ χειρὸς ἀπεσκέδασεν νέφος ἀνδρῶν
νῆας ἐς ἀγχιάλους· μελίῃ δέ ἑ μοῦνος ὑποστὰς
καὶ κτάνε καὶ σύλησε καὶ ἐκτερέιξεν Ἀχιλλεύς.
　εἱστήκει δ' ἔτι πᾶσα θεοδμήτων ὑπὸ πύργων
Ἴλιος ἀκλινέεσσιν ἐπεμβεβαυῖα θεμέθλοις,
ἀμβολίῃ δ' ἤσχαλλε δυσαχθέι λαὸς Ἀχαιῶν.

---

[a] *Iliad* xvi. 490. Patroclus slays Sarpedon, son of Zeus and Laodamia (*Il.* vi. 198 f.). Zeus caused a miraculous darkness to fall upon the battle (*Il.* xvi. 567), the body of Sarpedon was taken up by Apollo and attended by Sleep and Death to Lycia (*ibid.* 676 ff.).

[b] *Iliad* x. 435 ff. Rhesus was killed in his sleep by Odysseus and Diomedes.

[c] Memnon, son of Tithonus and Eos (Dawn), is unknown to the *Iliad*: in *Od.* iv. 188 he is mentioned as slayer of Antilochus and xi. 522 as the most beautiful of those who fought at Troy. His death at the hands of Achilles was

lamenting over the shameful dragging of Hector, had not only their domestic pain, but groaning for the woes of men of alien speech they wept in turn for their many-tongued allies. The Lycians wept for Sarpedon [a] whom his mother, glorying in the bed of Zeus, had sent to Troy; howbeit he fell by the spear of Patroclus, son of Menoetius, and there was shed about him by his sire a mist that wept tears of blood. The Thracians wailed for Rhesus [b] that in the guileful night was fettered by an evil sleep. And for the fate of Memnon [c] Eos, his mother, hung aloft a cloud in heaven and stole away the light of shamefast day. The women from Thermodon [d] dear to Ares, beating the unripe, unsucked circle of their breasts, mourned the warlike maiden Penthesileia, who came unto the dance of war, that war of many guests, and with her woman's hand scattered the cloud of men back to their ships beside the sea; only Achilles withstood her with his ashen spear and slew and despoiled her and gave her funeral.

And still all Ilios stood, by reason of her god-built towers, established upon unshaken foundations, and at the tedious delay the people of the Achaeans chafed.

told in the *Aethiopis* of Arctinus, and is described in Qu. Smyrnaeus ii. 542 f., as also the miraculous darkness which enabled his friends to recover his body, 550 f.

[d] The Amazons, a race of warrior women, whose chief home was Themiscyra on the Thermodon in Pontus. They were reputed to mutilate one or both breasts to enable them better to draw the bow and throw the spear; hence they got their name (α + μαζός) "without breasts." (Here Tryph. seems to take the word to mean "not giving suck." Philostr. *Her.* xx. 42 makes it "unsuckled.") They were in art represented usually with right breast bare. Their queen Penthesileia was slain at Troy by Achilles, who was smitten with love for her as she died and gave her honourable burial.

καί νύ κεν ὑστατίοισιν ἐποκνήσασα πόνοισιν
ἀκάματός περ ἐοῦσα μάτην ἵδρωσεν Ἀθήνη,
εἰ μὴ Δηιφόβοιο γαμοκλόπον ὕβριν ἐάσας
Ἰλιόθεν Δαναοῖσιν ἐπὶ ξένος ἤλυθε μάντις,
οἷα δέ που μογέοντι χαριζόμενος Μενελάῳ
ὀψιτέλεστον ὄλεθρον ἑῇ μαντεύσατο πάτρῃ.
οἱ δὲ βαρυζήλοιο θεοπροπίῃς Ἑλένοιο
αὐτίκα μηκεδανοῖο μόθου τέλος ἠρτύναντο.
καὶ Σκῦρον μὲν ἔβαινε λιπὼν εὐπάρθενον ἄστυ
υἱὸς Ἀχιλλῆος καὶ ἐπαινῆς Δηιδαμείης·
μήπω δ' εὐφυέεσσιν ἰουλίζων κροτάφοισιν
ἀλκὴν πατρὸς ἔφαινε νέος περ ἐὼν πολεμιστής.
ἦλθε δὲ καὶ Δαναοῖσιν ἑὸν βρέτας ἁγνὸν ἄγουσα
ληιστὴ μὲν ἐοῦσα, φίλοις δ' ἐπίκουρος Ἀθήνη.
ἤδη καὶ βουλῇσι θεῆς ὑποεργὸς Ἐπειὸς
Τροίης ἐχθρὸν ἄγαλμα πελώριον ἵππον ἐποίει.
καὶ δὴ τέμνετο δοῦρα καὶ ἐς πεδίον κατέβαινεν
Ἴδης ἐξ αὐτῆς, ὁπόθεν καὶ πρόσθε Φέρεκλος
νῆας Ἀλεξάνδρῳ τεκτήνατο, πήματος ἀρχήν.
ποίει δ' εὐρυτάτης μὲν ἐπὶ πλευρῇς ἀραρυῖαν
γαστέρα κοιλήνας, ὁπόσον νεὸς ἀμφιελίσσης
ὀρθὸν ἐπὶ στάθμην μέγεθος τορνώσατο τέκτων.

---

[a] Helenus, son of Priam and Hecuba, had the gift of prophecy. After the death of Paris he and Deiphobus, his brother, were rivals for the hand of Helen. Deiphobus being preferred, Helenus retired to Ida, where he was by the advice of Calchas seized and brought to the Greek camp. He advised the Greeks to build the wooden horse and to carry off the Palladium.

[b] Neoptolemus, son of Achilles, by Deidamia, daughter of Lycomedes, king of Scyros. His original name was Pyrrhus, and he was called Neoptolemus because he went to war when young, or because his father did so (Paus. x. 26. 4). Helenus prophesied that Troy would not be taken without Neoptolemus and the arrows of Heracles—then in the

And now Athena, unwearying though she be, would have shrunk from her latest labour and all her sweat had been in vain, had not the seer[a] turned from the bride-stealing lust of Deiphobus and come from Ilios as guest of the Danaans, and, as doing a favour to Menelaus in his travail, prophesied the late-fulfilled ruin of his own fatherland. And at the prophesying of jealous Helenus they straightway prepared an end of their long toil. From Scyros, too, leaving that city of fair maidens, came the son[b] of Achilles and august Deidameia; who, albeit he mantled not yet on his goodly temples the down of manhood, showed the prowess of his sire, young warrior though he was. Came, too, Athena to the Danaans with her holy image[c]; the prey of war but a helper to her friends.

Now, too, by the counsel of the goddess her servant Epeius[d] wrought the image that was the foe of Troy, even the giant horse. And wood was cut and came down to the plain from Ida, even Ida whence formerly Phereclus built the ships for Alexander[e] that were the beginning of woe. Fitted to broadest sides he made its hollow belly, in size as a curved ship which the carpenter turns true to the

possession of Philoctetes. So Neoptolemus was brought from Scyrus by Odysseus alone, or with Phoenix (Soph. *Ph.* 343, *cf.* Philostr. *Imag.* ii.), or with Diomedes (Quint. Smyrn. vii. 169 ff.).

[c] The Palladium, the ancient image of Athena, said to have been given by Zeus to Dardanus, on the possession of which the safety of Troy depended. It was stolen by Odysseus and Diomedes.

[d] Epeius, son of Panopeus, built the Wooden Horse by means of which Troy was taken. *Od.* viii. 493, xi. 523, Verg. *A.* ii. 264.

[e] Paris.

αὐχένα δὲ γλαφυροῖσιν ἐπὶ στήθεσσιν ἔπηξε
ξανθῷ πορφυρόπεζαν ἐπιρρήνας τρίχα χρυσῷ·
ἡ δ' ἐπικυμαίνουσα μετήορος αὐχένι κυρτῷ
ἐκ κορυφῆς λοφόεντι κατεσφρηγίζετο δεσμῷ.
ὀφθαλμοὺς δ' ἐνέθηκε λιθώπεας ἐν δυσὶ κύκλοις
γλαυκῆς βηρύλλοιο καὶ αἱμαλέης ἀμεθύσσου·
τῶν δ' ἐπιμισγομένων διδύμης ἀμαρύγματι χροιῆς
γλαυκῶν φοινίσσοντο λίθων ἑλίκεσσιν ὀπωπαί.
ἀργυφέους δ' ἐχάραξεν ἐπὶ γναθμοῖσιν ὀδόντας
ἄκρα δακεῖν σπεύδοντας ἐυστρέπτοιο χαλινοῦ·
καὶ στόματος μεγάλοιο λαθὼν ἀνέῳξε κελεύθους
ἀνδράσι κευθομένοισι παλίρροον ἆσθμα φυλάσσων,
καὶ διὰ μυκτήρων φυσίζοος ἔρρεεν ἀήρ.
οὔατα δ' ἀκροτάτοισιν ἐπὶ κροτάφοισιν ἄρηρεν
ὀρθὰ μάλ', αἰὲν ἑτοῖμα μένειν σάλπιγγος ἀκουήν.
νῶτα δ' ὁμοῦ λαγόνεσσι συνήρμοσε καὶ ῥάχιν ὑγρήν,
ἰσχία δὲ γλουτοῖσιν ὀλισθηροῖσι συνῆψε.
σύρετο δὲ πρυμνοῖσιν ἐπ' ἴχνεσιν ἔκλυτος οὐρὴ
ἄμπελος ὣς γναμπτοῖσι καθελκομένη θυσάνοισιν.
οἱ δὲ πόδες βαλίοισιν ἐπερχόμενοι γονάτεσσιν
εὔπτερον ὥσπερ ἔμελλον ἐπὶ δρόμον ὁπλίζεσθαι,
οὕτως ἠπείγοντο· μένειν δ' ἐκέλευεν ἀνάγκη.
οὐ μὲν ὑπὸ κνήμησιν ἀχαλκέες ἔξεχον ὁπλαί,
μαρμαρέης δ' ἑλίκεσσι κατεσφήκωντο χελώνης
ἁπτόμεναι πεδίοιο μόγις κρατερώνυχι χαλκῷ.
κληιστὴν δ' ἐνέθηκε θύρην καὶ κλίμακα τυκτήν,
ἡ μὲν ὅπως ἀίδηλος ἐπὶ πλευρῆς ἀραρυῖα
ἔνθα καὶ ἔνθα φέρησι λόχον κλυτόπωλον Ἀχαιῶν,
ἡ δ' ἵνα λυομένη τε καὶ ἔμπεδον εἰς ἓν ἰοῦσα
εἴη σφιν καθύπερθεν ὁδὸς καὶ νέρθεν ὀροῦσαι.
ἀμφὶ δέ μιν λευκοῖο κατ' αὐχένος ἠδὲ γενείων
ἄνθεσι πορφυρέοισι πέριξ ἔζωσεν ἱμάντων

line. And the neck he fixed to carven breast and bespangled the purple-fringed mane with yellow gold; and the mane, waving aloft on the arched neck, was sealed on the head with crested band. In two circles he set the gem-like eyes of sea-green beryl and blood-red amethyst: and in the mingling of them a double colour flashed; the eyes were red and ringed with the green gems. In the jaws he set white rows of jagged teeth, eager to champ the ends of the well-twisted bit. And he opened secret paths in the mighty mouth to preserve the tide of breath for the men in hiding, and through the nostrils flowed the life-giving air. Ears were fixed on the top of its temples, pricked up, ever ready to await the sound of the trumpet. And back and flanks he fitted together and supple backbone, and joined hip-joint to smooth hip. Unto the heels of the feet trailed the flowing tail, even as vine weighed down with twisted tassels. And the feet that moved with the dappled knees—even as if they were about to set them to the winged race, so were they eager, yet constraint bade them bide. Not without bronze were the hooves that stood below the legs, but they were bound with spirals of shining tortoise and hardly touched the ground with the strong-hoofed bronze. Also he set therein a barred door and a fashioned ladder: the one that unseen, fitted to the sides, it might carry the Achaean company of the famous horse this way and that; the other that, unfolded and firmly put together, it might be for them a path whereby to speed upward or downward. And he girt the horse about on white neck and cheeks with purple-flowered straps and coiling spirals of compelling

καὶ σκολιῇς ἑλίκεσσιν ἀναγκαίοιο χαλινοῦ
κολλήσας ἐλέφαντι καὶ ἀργυροδίνεϊ χαλκῷ.
αὐτὰρ ἐπειδὴ πάντα κάμεν μενεδήιον ἵππον,
κύκλον ἐυκνήμιδα ποδῶν ὑπέθηκεν ἑκάστῳ,
ἑλκόμενος πεδίοισιν ὅπως πειθήνιος εἴη
μηδὲ βιαζομένοισι δυσέμβατον οἶμον ὁδεύῃ.
ὣς ὁ μὲν ἐξήστραπτε φόβῳ καὶ κάλλεϊ πολλῷ
εὐρύς θ' ὑψηλός τε· τὸν οὐδέ κεν ἀρνήσαιτο,
εἴ μιν ζωὸν ἔτετμεν, ἐλαυνέμεν ἵππιος Ἄρης.
ἀμφὶ δέ μιν μέγα τεῖχος ἐλήλατο, μή τις Ἀχαιῶν
πρίν μιν ἐσαθρήσειε, δόλον δ' ἀνάπυστον ἀνάψῃ.
οἱ δὲ Μυκηναίης Ἀγαμέμνονος ἐγγύθι νηὸς
λαῶν ὀρνυμένων ὅμαδον καὶ κῦμα φυγόντες
ἐς βουλὴν βασιλῆες ἀολλίσθησαν Ἀχαιῶν.
ἡ δὲ τανυφθόγγοιο δέμας κήρυκος ἑλοῦσα
συμφράδμων Ὀδυσῆι παρίστατο θοῦρις Ἀθήνη
ἀνδρὸς ἐπιχρίουσα μελίχροϊ νέκταρι φωνήν.
αὐτὰρ ὁ δαιμονίῃσι νόον βουλῇσιν ἑλίσσων
πρῶτα μὲν εἱστήκει κενεόφρονι φωτὶ ἐοικὼς
ὄμματος ἀτρέπτοιο βολὴν ἐπὶ γαῖαν ἐρείσας,
ἄφνω δ' ἀενάων ἐπέων ὠδῖνας ἀνοίξας
δεινὸν ἀνεβρόντησε καὶ ἠερίης ἅτε πηγῆς
ἐξέχεεν μέγα λαῖτμα μελισταγέος νιφετοῖο·
ὦ φίλοι, ἤδη μὲν κρύφιος λόχος ἐκτετέλεσται
χερσὶ μὲν ἀνδρομέῃσιν, ἀτὰρ βουλῇσιν Ἀθήνης.
ὑμεῖς δ', οἵ τε μάλιστα πεποίθατε κάρτεϊ χειρῶν,
πρόφρονες ἀλκήεντι νόῳ καὶ τλήμονι θυμῷ
σπέσθε μοι· οὐ γὰρ ἔοικε πολὺν χρόνον ἐνθάδ' ἐόντας

---

[a] ἵππιος, an unusual title for Ares. *Cf.* βρισάρματος Hes. *Sc.* 441.

[b] *Iliad* iii. 216 Antenor says, "When Odysseus of many

bridle inlaid with ivory and silver-flashing bronze. And when he had wrought all the warlike horse, he set a well-spoked wheel under each of its feet that when dragged over the plain it might be obedient to the rein, and not travel a difficult path under stress of hands.

So the horse flashed with terror and great beauty, wide and high; not even Ares, lord of horses,[a] would have refused to drive it, had he found it alive. And a great wall was driven about it, lest any of the Achaeans should behold it beforehand and fire the snare revealed. And beside the ship of Agamemnon from Mycenae the kings of the Achaeans gathered to council, avoiding the din and tumult of the stirring hosts. Then impetuous Athena took the likeness of a clear-voiced herald and stood by Odysseus to counsel him, daubing a man's voice with honeyed nectar. And, revolving his mind in godlike counsels, at first he stood like a man of empty wits[b] fixing on the ground the gaze of his unturning eye; but suddenly he opened his lips and delivered him of everflowing speech and thundered terribly, and poured, as from an airy spring, a great torrent of honey-dropping snow.

"O friends, now is the secret ambush prepared, by human hands but by the counsels of Athena. Do ye which have most trust in the might of your hands, heartily follow me with valiant mind and enduring soul; for it is not seemly that we should

wiles arose, he would stand and look downward, fixing his eyes upon the ground, and his staff he moved neither back nor fore, but held it steadfast; thou wouldst have deemed him simply sulky and silly. But when he uttered his great voice from his breast, and words like snowflakes in winter, then could no other mortal vie with Odysseus."

μοχθίζειν ἀτέλεστα καὶ ἀχρέα γηράσκοντας,
ἀλλὰ χρὴ ζώοντας ἀοίδιμον ἔργον ἀνύσσαι
ἢ θανάτῳ βροτόεντι κακοκλεὲς αἶσχος ἀλύξαι.
ἡμῖν θαλπωραὶ προφερέστεραι ἤπερ ἐκείνοις,
εἰ μήπω στρουθοῖο καὶ ἀρχαίοιο δράκοντος
καὶ καλῆς πλατάνοιο καὶ ὠκυμόροις ἐπὶ τέκνοις
μητέρος ἑλκομένης ἁπαλῶν τ' ἐλάθεσθε νεοσσῶν.
εἰ δὲ θεοπροπίῃσι γέρων ἀνεβάλλετο Κάλχας,
ἀλλὰ καὶ ὣς Ἑλένοιο μετήλυδος ὀμφητῆρος
μαντοσύναι καλέουσιν ἑτοιμοτάτην ἐπὶ νίκην.
τοὔνεκά μοι πείθεσθε, καὶ ἱππείην ἐπὶ νηδὺν
θαρσαλέοι σπεύδωμεν, ὅπως αὐτάγρετον ἄλγος
Τρῶες ἀταρβήτοιο θεῆς ἀπατήνορα τέχνην
Ἴλιον εἰσανάγωσιν ἑὸν κακὸν ἀμφαγαπῶντες.
οἱ δ' ἄλλοι πρυμναῖα μεθίετε πείσματα νηῶν
πῦρ ἴδιον πλεκτῇσιν ἐνὶ κλισίῃσι βαλόντες·
Ἰλιάδος δὲ λιπόντες ἐρημαίην χθονὸς ἀκτὴν
πλώετε πασσυδίῃ ψευδώνυμον οἴκαδε νόστον,
εἰσόκεν εὐόρμου τετανυσμένον ἐκ περιωπῆς
ὔμμι συναγρομένοις ἐπὶ γείτονος αἰγιαλοῖο
σημαίνῃ παλίνορσον ἐπὶ πλόον ἑσπέριον πῦρ.
καὶ τότε μήτε τις ὄκνος ἐπειγομένων ἐρετάων
γινέσθω μήτ' ἄλλο φόβου νέφος, οἷά τε νύκτες
ἀνθρώποισι φέρουσιν ἐλαφροῦ δείματα θυμοῦ.
ἔστω δὲ προτέρης ἀρετῆς ἐμφύλιος αἰδώς,

[a] When the Greek expedition against Troy lay at Aulis, as the Greeks were sacrificing, a snake came from under the altar and ascended a plane-tree overhead where was a sparrow with eight young ones. The snake devoured them all. Calchas, son of Thestor, the seer of the Greeks, prophesied that the war would last for nine years and that Troy would be taken in the tenth. (Hom. *Il.* ii. 308 ff.; Qu. Smyrn. vi. 61, viii. 475; Ov. *M.* xii. 11 ff.)

abide here a long time labouring and growing old without accomplishment or profit. Rather should we, while yet we live, do some deed worthy to be sung, or by bloody death escape the shameful reproach of cowardice. We have better comfort than they—if ye have not forgotten the sparrow [a] and the ancient serpent and the fair plane-tree and the mother devoured with her swiftly perishing young, and her tender nestlings.

"And if old Calchas in his soothsaying deferred the day of fulfilment, yet even so the prophecies of Helenus,[b] the alien seer, call us to a right speedy victory. Therefore hearken ye to me and let us hasten with good courage into the belly of the horse, that the Trojans may lead up into Ilios the guileful craft of the dauntless goddess, a self-taken woe, embracing their own doom.[c]

"And do ye others loose the stern cables of the ships and yourselves cast fire upon the plaited tents, and leaving desolate the shore of the land of Ilios, sail ye all together on your pretended homeward way, until the hour that to you, gathered on the neighbouring beach, a beacon at eventide, stretched from a fair-anchoring place of outlook, shall give the signal to sail back again. And then let there be no hesitation of hurrying oarsmen nor other cloud of fear, such as the nights bring to men to terrify the mobile soul. But let each clan respect its former valour, and

[b] Helenus, son of Priam and Hecuba, twin-brother of Cassandra. He was taken prisoner by the Greeks on the advice of Calchas, and he advised the building of the Wooden Horse and the stealing of the Palladium.

[c] A reminiscence of Hesiod, *W.* 58 (of the creation of Woman).

μηδέ τις αἰσχύνειεν ἐὸν κλέος, ὥς κεν ἕκαστος
ἄξιον ὧν ἐμόγησε λάβῃ γέρας ἱπποσυνάων.
ὣς φάμενος βουλῆς ἐξήρχετο· τοῖο δὲ μύθοις
πρῶτος ἐφωμάρτησε Νεοπτόλεμος θεοειδής,
πῶλος ἅτε δροσόεντος ἐπειγόμενος πεδίοιο,
ὅστε νεοζυγέεσσιν ἀγαλλόμενος φαλάροισιν
ἔφθασε καὶ μάστιγα καὶ ἡνιοχῆος ἀπειλήν.
Τυδείδης δ' ἐπόρουσε Νεοπτολέμῳ Διομήδης
θαυμάζων, ὅτι τοῖος ἔην καὶ πρόσθεν Ἀχιλλεύς.
ἕσπετο καὶ Κυάνιππος, ὃν εὐπατέρεια Κομαιθὼ
Τυδηὶς θαλάμοιο μινυνθαδίοιο τυχοῦσα
ὠκυμόρῳ τέκε παῖδα σακεσπάλῳ Αἰγιαλῆι.
ἔστη καὶ Μενέλαος· ἄγεν δέ μιν ἄγριος ὁρμὴ
Δηιφόβου ποτὶ δῆριν, ἀπηνέι δ' ἔζεε θυμῷ
δεύτερον ἁρπακτῆρα γάμου λελιημένος εὑρεῖν.
τῷ δ' ἐπὶ Λοκρὸς ὄρουσεν Ὀιλῆος ταχὺς Αἴας,
εἰσέτι θυμὸν ἔχων πεπνυμένον οὐδ' ἐπὶ κούραις
μαργαίνων ἀθέμιστον· ἀνέστησεν δὲ καὶ ἄλλον,
Κρητῶν Ἰδομενῆα μεσαιπόλιον βασιλῆα.
Νεστορίδης δ' ἅμα τοῖσιν ἔβη κρατερὸς Θρασυμήδης,
καὶ Τελαμώνιος υἱὸς ἑκηβόλος ἤιε Τεῦκρος·
τοῖσι δ' ἐπ' Ἀδμήτοιο πάις πολύιππος ἀνέστη
Εὔμηλος· μετὰ τὸν δὲ θεοπρόπος ἔσσυτο Κάλχας
εὖ εἰδώς, ὅτι μόχθον ἀμήχανον ἐκτελέσαντες
ἤδη Τρώιον ἄστυ καθιππεύσουσιν Ἀχαιοί.
οὐδὲ μὲν οὐδ' οἳ ἔλειφθεν ἀποστρεφθέντες ἀρωγῆς
Εὐρύπυλός τ' Εὐαιμονίδης ἀγαθός τε Λεοντεύς,
Δημοφόων τ' Ἀκάμας τε, δύω Θησήια τέκνα,
Ὀρτυγίδης τ' Ἄντικλος, ὃν αὐτόθι τεθνειῶτα
ἵππῳ δακρύσαντες ἐνεκτερέιξαν Ἀχαιοί,

---

[a] *i.e.* marvelling at the likeness of N. to his father Achilles.
[b] Aegialeus, son of Adrastus and Demonassa, was the

let no man put to shame his fame, so that each may win a recompense for chivalry worthy of his toils."

So he spake, leading them in counsel. And first godlike Neoptolemus followed his advising, even as a colt hastening over the dewy plain, which glories in his trappings of new harness and outruns both the lash and the threat of his driver. And after Neoptolemus rose up Diomedes, the son of Tydeus, marvelling for that even such aforetime was Achilles.[a] Followed also Cyanippus, whom Comaetho, daughter of a goodly sire, even Tydeus, in brief wedlock bare to shield-bearing Aegialeus[b] whose doom was swift. Rose, too, Menelaus; he was driven by a fierce impulse to strife with Deiphobus, and his stern heart boiled with eagerness to find him who a second time stole away his bride. After him rose Locrian Aias, the swift son of Oileus, still prudent of mind and not filled with lawless passion for women.[c] And he roused up another, even Idomeneus, the grizzled king of the Cretans. And with these went the son of Nestor, strong Thrasymedes, and Teucer went, the archer son of Telamon. After them rose up the son of Admetus, even Eumelus of many horses. And after him hasted the seer Calchas, well knowing that accomplishing their difficult labour the Achaeans should now at last ride down the city of Troy. Nor remained behind, turning from the fray, Eurypylus, son of Euaemon, and goodly Leonteus, and Demophoon and Acamas, the two sons of Theseus, and Anticlus, son of Ortyx—who died there and the Achaeans wept for him and buried

only one of the Epigoni who was killed at Thebes (Pind. *P.* viii. 60 f.; Paus. ix. 5. 7).

[c] Aias assaulted Cassandra in the temple of Athena (*E.G.F.*, Kinkel, p. 49). See ll. 647 ff.

Πηνέλεώς τε Μέγης τε καὶ Ἀντιφάτης ἀγαπήνωρ
Ἰφιδάμας τε καὶ Εὐρυδάμας, Πελίαο γενέθλη,
τόξῳ δ' Ἀμφιδάμας κεκορυθμένος· ὕστατος αὖτε
τέχνης ἀγλαόμητις ἑῆς ἐπέβαινεν Ἐπειός.
εὐξάμενοι δὴ ἔπειτα Διὸς γλαυκώπιδι κούρῃ
ἱππείην ἔσπευδον ἐς ὁλκάδα· τοῖσι δ' Ἀθήνη
ἀμβροσίῃ κεράσασα θεῶν ἐκόμισσεν ἐδωδὴν
δεῖπνον ἔχειν, ἵνα μή τι πανημέριοι λοχόωντες
τειρόμενοι βαρύθοιεν ἀτερπέι γούνατα λιμῷ.
ὣς δ' ὁπότε κρυμοῖσιν ἀελλοπόδων νεφελάων
ἠέρα παχνώσασα χιὼν ἐπάλυνεν ἀρούρας,
τηκομένη δ' ἀνέηκε πολὺν ῥόον· οἱ δ' ἀπὸ πέτρης
ὀξὺ καταθρῴσκοντα κυβιστητῆρι κυδοιμῷ
δοῦπον ὑποπτήξαντες ὀριτρεφέος ποταμοῖο
θῆρες ἐρωήσαντες ὑπὸ πτύχα κοιλάδος εὐνῆς
σιγῇ φρικαλέῃσιν ἐπὶ πλευρῇσι μένουσι,
πικρὰ δὲ πεινάοντες ὀιζυρῆς ὑπ' ἀνάγκης
τλήμονες ἐκδέχαται, πότε παύεται ὄβριμον ὕδωρ·
ὣς οἵγε γλαφυροῖο διὰ ξυλόχοιο θορόντες
ἀτλήτους ἀνέχοντο πόνους ἀκμῆτες Ἀχαιοί.
τοῖσι δ' ἐπεκλήισσε θύρην ἐγκύμονος ἵππου
πιστὸς ἀτεκμάρτοιο δόλου πυλαωρὸς Ὀδυσσεύς.
αὐτὸς δ' ἐν κεφαλῇ σκοπὸς ἕζετο· τὼ δέ οἱ ἄμφω
ὀφθαλμὼ ποθέοντες ἐλάνθανον ἐκτὸς ἐόντας.[1]
Ἀτρείδης δ' ἐκέλευσεν ὑποδρηστῆρας Ἀχαιοὺς
λῦσαι λάινον ἕρκος ἐυγνάμπτοισι μακέλλαις,
ἵππος ὅπερ κεκάλυπτο· θέλεν δέ ἑ γυμνὸν ἐᾶσαι,
τηλεφανὴς ἵνα πᾶσιν ἑὴν χάριν ἀνδράσι πέμποι.
καὶ τὸ μὲν ἐξελάχαινον ἐφημοσύνῃ βασιλῆος.
ἠέλιος δ' ὅτε νύκτα παλίνσκιον ἀνδράσιν ἕλκων
ἐς δύσιν ἀχλυόπεζαν ἐκηβόλον ἔτραπεν ἠῶ,

[1] v.l. ἐόντες.

him in the horse; and Peneleus and Meges and valiant Antiphates, and Iphidamas and Eurydamas, offspring of Pelias, and Amphidamas armed with a bow. Last Epeius of glorious craft set foot in the thing he had himself contrived.

Then they prayed unto the grey-eyed daughter of Zeus and hasted into their vessel of the horse. And Athena mixed ambrosia and brought them the food of the gods to eat, that in their ambush all day long they might not be afflicted and their knees weighed down by unpleasant hunger. And as when with the frosts of the storm-footed clouds the snow freezes the air and besprinkles the fields and melting sends forth a great stream; and the wild beasts, cowering from the din of the mountain-cradled river, as it leaps swiftly down from a rock in headlong tumult, withdraw beneath the shelter of their hollow lair and abide there silently with shivering flanks, and, bitterly anhungered, by grievous constraint patiently await the ceasing of the rain: even so the unwearied Achaeans leapt through the carven wood and supported travail beyond enduring. And for them Odysseus, the faithful warder of the unguessed snare, closed the door of the pregnant horse, and sat himself in the head as scout; and both his yearning eyes escaped the notice of those without. And the son of Atreus bade the Achaean servants undo with well-bent mattocks the fence of stone wherewith the horse was hidden. He wished to let it be uncovered that, shining afar, it might send the message of its beauty unto all men. And at the bidding of their king they dug it up.

But when the sun, drawing on shadowy night for men, turned far-shooting dawn to the dusky-

δὴ τότε κηρύκων ἀπεκίδνατο λαὸν ἀυτὴ
φεύγειν ἀγγελέουσα καὶ ἑλκέμεν εἰς ἅλα κοίλην
νῆας ἐυκραίρους ἀνά τε πρυμνήσια λῦσαι.
ἔνθα δὲ πευκήεντος ἀνασχόμενοι πυρὸς ὁρμὴν
ἕρκεά τε πρήσαντες ἐυσταθέων κλισιάων
νηυσὶν ἀνεπλώεσκον ἀπὸ Ῥοιτειάδος ἀκτῆς
ὅρμον ἐς ἀντιπέραιον ἐυστεφάνου Τενέδοιο
γλαυκὸν ἀναπτύσσοντες ὕδωρ Ἀθαμαντίδος Ἕλλης.
μοῦνος δὲ πληγῇσιν ἑκούσια γυῖα χαραχθεὶς
Αἰσιμίδης ἐλέλειπτο Σίνων, ἀπατήλιος ἥρως,
κρυπτὸν ἐπὶ Τρώεσσι δόλον καὶ πήματα κεύθων.
ὡς δ' ὁπότε σταλίκεσσι λίνον περικυκλώσαντες
θηρσὶν ὀριπλανέεσσι λόχον πολυωπὸν ἔπηξαν
ἀνέρες ἀγρευτῆρες· ὁ δ' ἐκκριδὸν οἶος ἀπ' ἄλλων,
λαθρίδιος πυκινοῖσιν ὑπὸ πτόρθοισι δεδυκώς,
δίκτυα παπταίνων ἔλαθεν θηροσκόπος ἀνήρ·
ὣς τότε λωβητοῖσι περίστικτος μελέεσσι
Τροίῃ λυγρὸν ὄλεθρον ἐμήδετο. κὰδ δέ οἱ ὤμους
ἕλκεσι ποιητοῖσι κατέρρεε νήχυτον αἷμα.
ἡ δὲ περὶ κλισίῃσιν ἐμαίνετο παννυχίη φλὸξ
καπνὸν ἐρευγομένη περιδινέα φοιτάδι ῥιπῇ·
Ἥφαιστος δ' ἐκέλευεν ἐρίβρομος· ἐκ δὲ θυέλλας
παντοίας ἐτίνασσεν ἐπιπνείουσα καὶ αὐτή,

[a] Sinon (short form for Sinopos, Maass, *Hermes* xxiii. (1888)) son of Aesimus, who, as son of Autolycus and Amphithea, is brother of Anticleia, mother of Odysseus, was left behind when the Greeks sailed to Tenedos, in order that he might light a beacon as a signal for them to return, and that he might induce the Trojans to drag the wooden horse within the walls. There is some variation in the accounts of Sinon's performance, *cf.* Apollodor. *Epitom.* v. 14 ff. ; Verg. *A.* ii. 57 ff. ; Qu. Smyrn. xii. 243 ff. ; Lycophr. 340 ff. who connects the business with the treason of Antenor.

footed setting, then spread abroad the voice of the heralds, telling the people to flee and launch in the hollow sea their fair-peaked ships and loose the cables. Then raising the rush of pinewood fire and burning the fences of their well-stablished tents they sailed away in their ships from the Rhoeteian shore to a haven over the sea in fair-crowned Tenedos, ploughing the grey waters of Helle, daughter of Athamas. Only Sinon [a] remained behind, the son of Aesimus, his limbs voluntarily scarred with stripes, a deceitful hero, concealing a hidden snare and sorrow for the Trojans. And even as when hunter men cast a net about the stakes and set a meshed ambush for the wild beasts that roam the hills, and one chosen apart from the others secretly creeps beneath the thick branches, a hidden scout of the hunt to watch the nets [b]: even so, his marred limbs marked about with stripes, he devised grievous destruction for Troy; and the streaming blood flowed over his shoulders from wounds purposely made. All night long the flame raged about the tents, belching forth smoke that curled in wandering eddy, and loud-roaring Hephaestus urged it on. Yea, and Hera herself, that gives light to men,[c] the mother

[b] The λινόπτης was the person who watched the nets to see what entered them. Pollux v. 17, Hesych. *s.v.* λινόπτης; *cf.* Aristoph. *Peace* 1178 *ἐγὼ δ' ἕστηκα λινοπτώμενος* and schol. there.

[c] Hera as "bringer of light" is attested by the fact that Phosphoros (the Morning Star or Venus) was sometimes regarded as the star of Hera: Aristot. *De mundo* 2 *ὁ τοῦ Φωσφόρου ὃν Ἀφροδίτης, οἱ δὲ Ἥρας προσαγορεύουσιν.* Pliny, *N.H.* ii. 37 speaking of the "sidus appellatum Veneris" says "in magno nominum ambitu est. Alii enim Iunonis, alii Isidis, alii Matris Deum appellavere."

μήτηρ ἀθανάτοιο πυρός, φαεσίμβροτος Ἥρη.
ἤδη δὲ Τρώεσσι καὶ Ἰλιάδεσσι γυναιξὶν
ὄρθρον ὑπὸ σκιόεντα πολύθροος ἤλυθε φήμη
δήιον ἀγγέλλουσα φόβον σημάντορι καπνῷ.
αὐτίκα δ' ἐξέθορον πυλέων πετάσαντες ὀχῆας
πεζοί θ' ἱππῆές τε καὶ ἐς πεδίον προχέοντο
διζόμενοι, μή πού τις ἔην δόλος ἄλλος Ἀχαιῶν.
οἱ δὲ θοοὺς οὐρῆας ὑποζεύξαντες ἀπήναις
ἐκ πόλιος κατέβαινον ἅμα Πριάμῳ βασιλῆι
ἄλλοι δημογέροντες· ἐλαφρότατοι δ' ἐγένοντο
θαλπόμενοι περὶ παισίν, ὅσους λίπε φοίνιος Ἄρης,
ὀσσόμενοι καὶ γῆρας ἐλεύθερον· οὐ μὲν ἔμελλον
γηθήσειν ἐπὶ δηρόν, ἐπεὶ Διὸς ἤθελε βουλή.
οἱ δ' ὅτε τεχνήεντος ἴδον δέμας αἰόλον ἵππου,
θαύμασαν ἀμφιχυθέντες, ἅτ' ἠχήεντες ἰδόντες
αἰετὸν ἀλκήεντα περικλάζουσι κολοιοί.
τοῖσι δὲ τετρηχυῖα καὶ ἄκριτος ἔμπεσε βουλή·
οἱ μὲν γὰρ πολέμῳ βαρυπενθέι κεκμηῶτες,
ἵππον ἀπεχθήραντες, ἐπεὶ πέλεν ἔργον Ἀχαιῶν,
ἤθελον ἢ δολιχοῖσιν ἐπὶ κρημνοῖσιν ἀράξαι
ἠὲ καὶ ἀμφιτόμοισι διαρρῆξαι πελέκεσσιν·
οἱ δὲ νεοξέστοιο πεποιθότες ἔργμασι τέχνης
ἀθανάτοις ἐκέλευον ἀρήιον ἵππον ἀνάψαι,
ὕστερον Ἀργείοιο μόθου σημήιον εἶναι.
φραζομένοις δ' ἐπὶ τοῖσι παναίολα γυῖα κομίζων
γυμνὸς ὑπὲρ πεδίοιο φάνη κεκακωμένος ἀνήρ·

---

[a] Tryphiodorus here imitates Hom. *Il.* ii. 95 τετρήχει δ' ἀγορή, vii. 345 f. ἀγορὴ . . . δεινὴ τετρηχυῖα. "Confused" is perhaps enough as a rendering in Tryphiodorus, but the associations of the expression, which cannot be discussed here, go much further than that.

[b] According to Tryphiodorus Sinon wounded himself and appeals to Priam as a suppliant and willingly tells about

of immortal fire, breathed thereon and stirred up all manner of gusts. And now in the shadowy dawn there came to Trojans and to the women of Ilios a rumour spoken by many tongues, announcing the flight of the foe by signal of smoke. Straightway they flung open the bars of the gates and rushed forth, foot and horse, and poured into the plain, seeking whether this were some fresh guile of the Danaans. And yoking swift mules to wagons there came down from the city with King Priam the other elders of the people; and most light of heart were they, being comforted for their children whom bloody Ares had spared, and boding of an old age of freedom: but not long were they to rejoice, since the counsel of Zeus willed it so. And when they saw the flashing form of the skilfully fashioned horse, they thronged about it marvelling, even as chattering jackdaws scream about when they see the valiant eagle. And confused [a] and uncertain counsel fell among them. Some wearied with dolorous war and hating the horse, because it was the work of the Achaeans, wished either to dash it on the long precipices or to break it up with two-edged hatchets. But others, trusting in the new polished work of art, bade dedicate the warlike horse to the immortals, to be in after days a memorial of the Argive war. And as they debated, there appeared unto them, dragging his motley limbs over the plain, a naked man in sorry case.[b]

the wooden horse. So Tzetz. schol. Lycophr. p. 134. 12 *αἰκισάμενος ἑαυτὸν πλησίον τοῦ δουρείου ἵππου ἐκάθητο.* In Verg. *A.* ii. 57 ff. he has allowed himself to be captured by the Trojans and is brought before Priam as a prisoner in fetters. In Qu. Smyrn. xii. 360 ff. he is found by the Trojans beside the wooden horse and only speaks after torture, when his nose and ears have been cut off.

αἵματι δὲ σμώδιγγες ἀεικέϊ βεβριθυῖαι
ἴχνια λωβήεντα θοῶν ἀνέφαινον ἱμάντων.
αὐτίκα δὲ Πριάμοιο ποδῶν προπάροιθεν ἐλυσθεὶς
ἱκεσίαις παλάμῃσι παλαιῶν ἥψατο γούνων,
λισσόμενος δὲ γέροντα δολοπλόκον ἴαχε μῦθον·
  ἄνδρα μὲν Ἀργείοισιν ὁμόπλοον εἴ μ' ἐλεαίρεις,
Τρώων δὲ ῥυστῆρα καὶ ἄστεος εἴ με σαώσεις,
Δαρδανίδη σκηπτοῦχε, καὶ ὕστατον ἐχθρὸν Ἀχαιῶν—
οἷά με λωβήσαντο θεῶν ὄπιν οὐκ ἀλέγοντες
οὐδὲν ἀλιτραίνοντα, κακοὶ καὶ ἀπηνέες αἰεί·
ὧς μὲν Ἀχιλλῆος γέρας ἥρπασαν Αἰακίδαο,
ὧς δὲ Φιλοκτήτην ἔλιπον πεπεδημένον ὕδρῳ,
ἔκτειναν δὲ καὶ αὐτὸν ἀγασσάμενοι Παλαμήδην.
καὶ νῦν οἷά μ' ἔρεξαν ἀτάσθαλοι, οὕνεκα φεύγειν
οὐκ ἔθελον σὺν τοῖσι, μένειν δ' ἐκέλευον ἑταίρους·
οἱ δὲ νοοπλήγεσσιν ἀτασθαλίῃσι δαμέντες
εἵματα μέν μ' ἀπέδυσαν, ἀεικελίῃσι δ' ἱμάσθλαις
πᾶν δέμας οὐτήσαντες ἐπὶ ξείνῃ λίπον ἀκτῇ.
ἀλλά, μάκαρ, πεφύλαξο Διὸς σέβας ἱκεσίοιο·
χάρμα γὰρ Ἀργείοισι γενήσομαι, εἴ κεν ἐάσῃς
χερσὶν ὕπο Τρώων ἱκέτην καὶ ξεῖνον ὀλέσθαι.
αὐτὰρ ἐγὼ πάντεσσιν ἐπάρκιος ἔσσομαι ὑμῖν
μηκέτι δειμαίνειν πόλεμον παλίνορσον Ἀχαιῶν.
  ὧς φάτο· τὸν δ' ὁ γέρων ἀγανῇ μειλίξατο φωνῇ·
ξεῖνε, σὲ μὲν Τρώεσσι μεμιγμένον οὐκέτ' ἔοικε

[a] Philoctetes, son of Poeas, king of Malis, having on the voyage to Troy been bitten by a water snake and his wound having become noisome, was left by the Greeks in Lemnos. Afterwards they learned that Troy could not be taken without Philoctetes and the arrows which he had received from Heracles. So he was brought to Troy by Odysseus, and his wound being healed by Machaon he slew Paris.

His weals laden with unseemly blood showed the ruinous track of the swift lash. Straightway he grovelled before the feet of Priam, and touched his ancient knees with suppliant hands; and entreating the old man he uttered his craftily woven tale:

"Sceptred King, son of Dardanus, behold me the fellow voyager of the Argives, if thou pitiest me, and deliverer of the Trojans and their city, if thou wilt save me, and lastly foe of the Achaeans: behold how they evilly entreated me who had done no wrong, heeding not the regard of the gods, evil and unkind always. Even so they snatched away his reward from Achilles, son of Peleus, and even so they left Philoctetes,[a] fettered by the bite of the water snake, and slew in wrath Palamedes[b] himself. And behold now what they have done to me in their wicked folly, for that I would not flee with them, but bade my comrades stay. Overcome by frenzied foolishness they stripped me of my raiment and wounded all my body with unseemly stripes and left me on an alien shore. But, blessed one, do thou have regard unto the majesty of Zeus, the god of suppliants. For I shall be a joy to the Argives, if thou lettest a suppliant and a stranger perish at the hands of the Trojans. But I shall be surety unto all of you that ye no more dread returning war of the Achaeans."

So he spake, and the old man comforted him with gentle voice: "Stranger, it befits thee not to be afraid any more since thou hast mingled with the

[b] Palamedes, son of Nauplius, king of Euboea, exposed the ruse by which Odysseus tried to avoid the expedition to Troy. In revenge Odysseus contrived to bury a quantity of gold in the tent of Palamedes and forged a letter from Priam offering bribes for the betrayal of the Greek army. Palamedes was found guilty of treason and stoned to death.

τάρβος ἔχειν· ἔφυγες γὰρ ἀνάρσιον ὕβριν Ἀχαιῶν.
αἰεὶ δ᾽ ἡμέτερος φίλος ἔσσεαι, οὐδέ σε πάτρης
οὐδὲ πολυκτεάνων θαλάμων γλυκὺς ἵμερος αἱρεῖ.
ἀλλ᾽ ἄγε καὶ σύ μοι εἰπέ, τί τοι τόδε θαῦμα τέτυκται,
ἵππος, ἀμειλίκτοιο φόβου τέρας· εἰπὲ δὲ σεῖο
οὔνομα καὶ γενεήν, ὁπόθεν δέ σε νῆες ἔνεικαν.
τὸν δ᾽ ἐπιθαρσήσας προσέφη πολυμήχανος ἥρως·
ἐξερέω καὶ ταῦτα· σὺ γάρ μ᾽ ἐθέλοντα κελεύεις.
Ἄργός μοι πόλις ἐστί, Σίνων δέ μοι οὔνομα κεῖται·
Αἴσιμον αὖ καλέουσιν ἐμὸν πολιὸν γενετῆρα·
ἵππον δ᾽ Ἀργείοισι παλαίφατον εὗρεν Ἐπειός·
εἰ μὲν γάρ μιν ἐᾶτε μένειν αὐτοῦ ἐνὶ χώρῃ,
Τροίην θέσφατόν ἐστιν ἑλεῖν πόλιν ἔγχος Ἀχαιῶν·
εἰ δέ μιν ἁγνὸν ἄγαλμα λάβῃ νηοῖσιν Ἀθήνη,
φεύξονται προφυγόντες ἀνηνύστοις ἐπ᾽ ἀέθλοις.
ἀλλ᾽ ἄγε δὴ σειρῇσι περίπλοκον ἀμφιβαλόντες
ἕλκετ᾽ ἐς ἀκρόπολιν μεγάλην χρυσήνιον ἵππον·
ἄμμι δ᾽ Ἀθηναίη ἐρυσίπτολις ἡγεμονεύοι
δαιδάλεον σπεύδουσα λαβεῖν ἀνάθημα καὶ αὐτή.
ὣς ἄρ᾽ ἔφη· καὶ τὸν μὲν ἄναξ ἐκέλευσε λαβόντα
ἕσσασθαι χλαῖνάν τε χιτῶνά τε, τοὶ δέ, βοείαις
δησάμενοι σειρῇσιν, ἐυπλέκτοισι κάλωσιν
εἷλκον ὑπὲρ πεδίοιο, θοῶν ἐπιβήτορα κύκλων,
ἵππον ἀριστήεσσι βεβυσμένον· οἱ δὲ πάροιθεν
αὐλοὶ καὶ φόρμιγγες ὁμὴν ἐλίγαινον ἀοιδήν.
σχέτλιον ἀφραδέων μερόπων γένος, οἷσιν ὁμίχλη
ἄσκοπος ἐσσομένων· κενεῷ δ᾽ ὑπὸ χάρματι πολλοὶ
πολλάκις ἀγνώσσουσι περιπταίοντες ὀλέθρῳ.
οἵη καὶ Τρώεσσι τότε φθισίμβροτος ἄτη

Trojans; for thou hast escaped the unkindly violence of the Achaeans. Evermore thou shalt be our friend nor shall sweet desire seize thee for thy fatherland or for thy halls of many possessions. But come, declare thou to me what marvel is this, the horse, a portent of unappeasable terror. And declare thy name and lineage and whence the ships brought thee."

Then the hero of many devices took heart and said: "These things also will I declare; thou biddest me who am myself willing. Argos is my city and the name given to me is Sinon, and my grey-haired sire they call Aesimus; and the famous horse was invented for the Argives by Epeius. If you allow it to abide here in its place, it is decreed that the spear of the Achaeans shall capture Troy; but if Athena receive it a holy offering in her shrine, then they shall flee away with their task unaccomplished. But come, cast it about with entwining chains and draw to the great acropolis the horse of golden reins, and Athena, guardian of the city, be our guide, eager to win the carven offering, even she!"

So he spake, and the king bade him take and do on a cloak and a tunic.[a] And they bound the horse with chains of oxhide and drew it with well-plaited ropes over the plain, mounted on its swift wheels and filled with chieftains; and before it flutes and lyres made shrill minstrelsy together. Wretched generation of heedless mortals! for whom a mist which they cannot pierce enwraps the future. By reason of empty joy many men many times stumble unwittingly on destruction: even as at that time ruinous doom for the Trojans rioted on its own way

[a] *Cf.* Hesiod, *W.* 536 f.

ἐς πόλιν αὐτοκέλευθος ἐκώμασεν· οὐδέ τις ἀνδρῶν
ᾔδεεν, οὕνεκα λάβρον ἐφέλκετο πένθος ἄλαστον.
ἄνθεα δὲ δροσόεντος ἀμησάμενοι ποταμοῖο
ἔστεφον αὐχενίους πλοκάμους σφετέροιο φονῆος.
γαῖα δὲ χαλκείοισιν ἐρεικομένη περὶ κύκλοις
δεινὸν ὑπεβρυχᾶτο, σιδήρειοι δὲ δι' αὐτῶν
τριβόμενοι τρηχεῖαν ἀνέστενον ἄξονες ἠχήν·
τετρίγει δὲ κάλων ξυνοχή, καὶ πᾶσα ταθεῖσα
λιγνὺν αἰθαλόεσσαν ἕλιξ ἀνεκήκιε σειρή.
πολλὴ δ' ἑλκόντων ἐνοπὴ καὶ κόμπος ὀρώρει·
ἔβρεμε νυμφαίῃσιν ἅμα δρυσὶ δάσκιος Ἴδη,
ἴαχε καὶ Ξάνθου ποταμοῦ κυκλούμενον ὕδωρ,
καὶ στόμα κεκλήγει Σιμοείσιον· οὐρανίη δὲ
ἐκ Διὸς ἑλκόμενον πόλεμον μαντεύετο σάλπιγξ.
οἱ δ' ἦγον προπάροιθεν· ὁδὸς δ' ἐβαρύνετο μακρὴ
σχιζομένη ποταμοῖσι καὶ οὐ πεδίοισιν ὁμοίη.
εἵπετο δ' αἰόλος ἵππος ἀρηιφίλους ἐπὶ βωμοὺς
κυδιόων ὑπέροπλα, βίην δ' ἐπέρεισεν Ἀθήνη
χεῖρας ἐπιβρίσασα νεογλυφέων ἐπὶ μηρῶν.
ὧδε θέων ἀκίχητος ἐπέδραμε θᾶσσον ὀιστοῦ
Τρῶας ἐυσκάρθμοισιν ὁδοιπορίῃσι διώκων,
εἰσόκε δὴ πυλέων ἐπεβήσατο Δαρδανιάων.
αἱ δέ οἱ ἐρχομένῳ θυρέων πτύχες ἐστείνοντο·
ἀλλ' Ἥρη μὲν ἔλυσεν ἐπὶ δρόμον αὖθις ὁδοῖο
πρόσθεν ἀναστέλλουσα, Ποσειδάων δ' ἀπὸ πύργων
σταθμὸν ἀνοιγομένων πυλέων ἀνέκοπτε τριαίνῃ.
Τρωιάδες δὲ γυναῖκες ἀνὰ πτόλιν ἄλλοθεν ἄλλαι,
νύμφαι τε πρόγαμοί τε καὶ ἴδμονες Εἰλειθυίης,
μολπῇ τ' ὀρχηθμῷ τε περὶ βρέτας εἱλίσσοντο·

---

[a] All this is closely imitated from the launching of the Argo in Apoll. Rh. i. 388 ff., "The rollers groaned as they

into the city, and none knew that it was fierce sorrow unforgettable that they drew. And gathering flowers from the dewy river they wreathed the tresses on the neck of their slayer. The earth torn about the brazen wheels moaned terribly, and the axles of iron, grinding in them, groaned with harsh noise. The joining of knit ropes creaked and all the taut coiling chain sent up a fiery smoke.[a] And as they haled, loud rose the din and the vaunting. Groaned shady Ida together with her nymph-haunted oaks: the eddying waters of the river Xanthus shrieked, and the mouth of Simois rang aloud: and in the heaven the trumpet of Zeus prophesied of the war they drew. But they haled forward; and the long way waxed heavy, torn with rivers and not like plain lands. And the flashing horse followed them unto the altars dear to Ares, glorying exceedingly; and Athena set her might thereto, laying her heavy hands on the newly carven thighs of the horse. So it sped beyond overtaking, and ran on swifter than an arrow, following the Trojans with lightly prancing feet, until it reached the Dardan gates. And for its coming the folding doors were straitened. But Hera set it free once more to run its course, withdrawing the doors before it, while from the towers Poseidon with his trident drave back the posts of the opening gates. And the Trojan women throughout the city, some here, some there, brides and maidens unwed[b] and mothers experienced of Eileithyia[c] circled about the image with song and dance.

were ground under the heavy keel, and round them the dark smoky flame (λιγνύς) spurted under the weight."

[b] Verg. *A*. ii. 238 "pueri circum innuptaeque puellae Sacra canunt funemque manu contingere gaudent."

[c] Eileithyia, goddess of birth.

ἄλλαι δὲ χνοόωσαν ἀμελγόμεναι χάριν ὄμβρου
ὁλκῷ δουρατέῳ ῥοδέους στορέσαντο τάπητας.
αἱ δὲ θαλασσαίης ἐπιμάζια νήματα μίτρης
λυσάμεναι κλωστοῖσι κατέπλεκον ἄνθεσιν ἵππον.
καί τις ἀπειρεσίοιο πίθου κρήδεμνον ἀνεῖσα
χρυσείῳ προχέουσα κρόκῳ κεκερασμένον οἶνον
γαῖαν ἀνεκνίσσωσε χυτὴν εὐώδεϊ πηλῷ.
ἀνδρομέῃ δὲ βοῇ συνεβάλλετο θῆλυς ἰωή,
καὶ παίδων ἀλαλητὸς ἐμίσγετο γήραος ἠχῇ·
οἷαι δ' ἀφνειοῖο μετήλυδες Ὠκεανοῖο,
χείματος ἀμφίπολοι, γεράνων στίχες ἠεροφώνων,
κύκλον ἐπογμεύουσιν ἀλήμονος ὀρχηθμοῖο
γειοπόνοις ἀρότῃσιν ἀπεχθέα κεκληγυῖαι·
ὣς οἵγε κλαγγῇ τε δι' ἄστεος ἠδὲ κυδοιμῷ
ἦγον ἐς ἀκρόπολιν βεβαρημένον ἔνδοθεν ἵππον.
κούρη δὲ Πριάμοιο θεήλατος οὐκέτι μίμνειν
ἤθελεν ἐν θαλάμοισι· διαρρήξασα δ' ὀχῆας
ἔδραμεν ἠύτε πόρτις ἀήσυρος, ἥντε τυπεῖσαν
κέντρον ἀνεπτοίησε βοορραίσταο μύωπος·
ἡ δ' οὐκ εἰς ἀγέλην ποτιδέρκεται οὐδὲ βοτῆρι
πείθεται οὐδὲ νομοῖο λιλαίεται, ἀλλὰ βελέμνῳ
ὀξέι θηγομένη βοέων ἐξήλυθε θεσμῶν·
τοίη μαντιπόλοιο βολῆς ὑπὸ νύγματι κούρη
πλαζομένη κραδίην ἱερὴν ἀνεσείετο δάφνην.
πάντῃ δ' ἐβρυχᾶτο κατὰ πτόλιν· οὐδὲ τοκήων
οὐδὲ φίλων ἀλέγιζε· λίπεν δέ ἑ παρθένος αἰδώς.

[a] The γέρανος, or crane-dance, is described by Pollux iv. 101, "The crane-dance they danced in a body, one behind the other in line, the extremities being occupied by the leaders, Theseus and his party having first imitated so, round the altar in Delos, their escape from the labyrinth." *Cf.* Plutarch, *Thes.* 21, Lucian, *De salt.* 34. A similar dance called κανδιωτής is still danced in Greece. It seems likely

Others culling the fresh bounty of the rain strewed a rosy carpet for the wooden trail. Others undid the spun girdles of sea-purple about their breasts and with woven garlands wreathed the horse. Some broaching the seal of a great jar poured forth wine mixed with golden saffron and made the piled earth odorous with fragrant mud. With the shouting of men was mingled the cry of women, the huzza of boys was joined with the voice of age. And even as the denizens of rich Ocean, the attendants of winter, the ranks of the cranes [a] crying in air, align the circle of their wandering dance, uttering their notes abhorred by the ploughmen who labour the earth: even so with crying and with tumult they led to the acropolis the horse laden within. And the god-driven daughter [b] of Priam would not abide any more in her chamber. Tearing apart the bars she ran, like restless heifer whom the sting of the ox-tormenting gadfly has smitten and stung to frenzy: which looks no more to the herd nor obeys the herdsman nor yearns for the pasture, but whetted by the sharp dart she passes beyond the range of oxen: in such wise, her heart distraught by the pricking of the shafts of prophecy, the maiden shook the holy laurel wreath and cried everywhere throughout the city. She heeded nor parents nor friends, and maiden shame forsook her. Not so doth the pleasant flute of

enough that Tryphiodorus has in mind also the orderly flight of the cranes (Aristotle, *H.A.* ix. 10; Eurip. *Hel.* 1478 ff.). In Greece the bird was a migrant and its passage from its nesting-places in the north (Macedonia, etc.) to the south (Africa, etc., Hom. *Il.* iii. 2 ff.) which took place about October was the signal for ploughing, Hesiod, *W.* 448 ff.

[b] Cassandra.

οὐχ οὕτω Θρήισσαν ἐνὶ δρυμοῖσι γυναῖκα
νήδυμος αὐλὸς ἔτυψεν ὀρειμανέος Διονύσου,
ἥτε θεῷ πληγεῖσα παρήορον ὄμμα τιταίνει
γυμνὸν ἐπισσείουσα κάρη κυανάμπυκι κισσῷ,
ὡς ἥγε πτερόεντος ἀναΐξασα νόοιο
Κασσάνδρη θεόφοιτος ἐμαίνετο· πυκνὰ δὲ χαίτην
κοπτομένη καὶ στέρνον ἀνίαχε μαινάδι φωνῇ·
ὦ μέλεοι, τίνα τοῦτον ἀνάρσιον ἵππον ἄγοντες
δαιμόνιοι μαίνεσθε καὶ ὑστατίην ἐπὶ νύκτα
σπεύδετε καὶ πολέμοιο πέρας καὶ νήγρετον ὕπνον;
δυσμενέων ὅδε κῶμος ἀρήιος· αἱ δέ που ἤδη
τίκτουσιν μογερῆς Ἑκάβης ὠδῖνες ὀνείρων,
λήγει δ' ἀμβολιεργὸν ἔτος πολέμοιο λυθέντος.
τοῖος ἀριστήων λόχος ἔρχεται, οὓς ἐπὶ χάρμην
τεύχεσιν ἀστράπτοντας ἀμαυροτάτην ὑπὸ νύκτα
τέξεται ὄβριμος ἵππος· ἐπὶ χθόνα δ' ἄρτι θορόντες
ἐς μόθον ὁρμήσουσι τελειότατοι πολεμισταί.
οὐ γὰρ ἐπ' ὠδίνεσσι μογοστόκον ἵππον ἀνεῖσαι
ἀνδράσι τικτομένοισιν ἐπισχήσουσι γυναῖκες,
αὐτὴ δ' Εἰλείθυια γενήσεται, ἥ μιν ἔτευξε·
γαστέρα δὲ πλήθουσαν ἀνακλίνασα βοήσει
μαῖα πολυκλαύτοιο τόκου πτολίπορθος Ἀθήνη.
καὶ δὴ πορφύρεον μὲν ἑλίσσεται ἔνδοθι πύργων
αἵματος ἐκχυμένου πέλαγος καὶ κῦμα φόνοιο,
δεσμά τε συμπαθέων πλέκεται περὶ χερσὶ γυναικῶν
νυμφία, φωλεύει δ' ὑπὸ δούρασι κευθόμενον πῦρ.
ὤμοι ἐμῶν ἀχέων, ὤμοι σέο, πάτριον ἄστυ,
αὐτίκα λεπταλέη κόνις ἔσσεαι, οἴχεται ἔργον
ἀθανάτων, προθέλυμνα θεμείλια Λαομέδοντος.

---

[a] Bacchant.

[b] Before she gave birth to Paris, Hecabe dreamed that

Dionysus raging on the hills strike the Thracian woman[a] amid the thickets: who, smitten by the god, strains a wild eye and shakes her naked head dark-garlanded with ivy. So Cassandra, starting from her winged wits, raged god-maddened; and, beating ever and again hair and breast, she cried with frenzied voice:

"O wretched men! why rage ye possessed, dragging this unfriendly horse, hasting to your last night and the end of war and the sleep that knows no waking? This warlike rout comes from the foemen. Surely now the travail of the dreams of poor Hecabe[b] bears fruit. The long deferred year comes to an end with the resolving of the war. Such a company of chieftains comes, whom the mighty horse shall bring forth in the darkest night, flashing in their armour for battle; now shall warriors most perfect leap to earth and rush to the fray. For not women shall deliver the labouring steed in its travail and attend the birth of men, but she that wrought it shall herself be its Lady of Deliverance; Athena, sacker of cities, midwife of a dolorous birth, shall herself undo the pregnant belly and utter her cry. Lo! now there is rolled within the towers a purple sea of blood outpoured, a wave of death; about the hands of women, sharing the common doom, the bonds of bridal are twined: beneath the wooden planks lurks hidden fire. Alas! for my woes, alas! for thee, city of my fathers, soon shalt thou be fine dust: gone is the handiwork of the immortals, gone utterly the foundations of Laomedon. And

she had borne a firebrand. The seers interpreted this to mean that her child would be fatal to Troy and advised that it should be put to death (Hyginus, *Fab.* 91 and 249; Apollod. iii. 12. 5; Eur. *Troad.* 922; Verg. *Aen.* vii. 320, etc.).

καὶ σέ, πάτερ, καὶ μῆτερ, ὀδύρομαι, οἷά μοι ἤδη
ἀμφότεροι πείσεσθε· σὺ μέν, πάτερ, οἰκτρὰ δεδουπὼς
κείσεαι Ἑρκείοιο Διὸς μεγάλου παρὰ βωμῷ·
μῆτερ ἀριστοτόκεια, σὲ δὲ βροτέης ἀπὸ μορφῆς
λυσσαλέην ἐπὶ παισὶ θεοὶ κύνα ποιήσουσι.
δῖα Πολυξείνη, σὲ δὲ πατρίδος ἐγγύθι γαίης
κεκλιμένην ὀλίγον δακρύσομαι· ὡς ὄφελέν τις
Ἀργείων ἐπὶ σοῖσι γόοις ὀλέσαι με καὶ αὐτήν.
τίς γάρ μοι χρειὼ βιότου πλέον, εἴ με φυλάσσει
οἰκτροτάτῳ θανάτῳ, ξείνη δέ με γαῖα καλύψει;
τοιάδε μοι δέσποινα καὶ αὐτῷ δῶρον ἄνακτι
ἀντὶ τόσων καμάτων Ἀγαμέμνονι πότμον ὑφαίνει.
ἀλλ' ἤδη φράζεσθε—τὰ δὲ γνώσεσθε παθόντες—
καὶ νεφέλην ἀπόθεσθε, φίλοι, βλαψίφρονος ἄτης.
ῥηγνύσθω πελέκεσσι δέμας πολυχανδέος ἵππου
ἢ πυρὶ καιέσθω· δολόεντα δὲ σώματα κεῦθον
ὀλλύσθω, μεγάλη δὲ ποθὴ Δαναοῖσι γενέσθω.
καὶ τότε μοι δαίνυσθε καὶ ἐς χορὸν ὀτρύνεσθε
στησάμενοι κρητῆρας ἐλευθερίης ἐρατεινῆς.
ἣ μὲν ἔφη· τῇ δ' οὔτις ἐπείθετο· τὴν γὰρ Ἀπόλλων
ἀμφότερον μάντιν τ' ἀγαθὴν καὶ ἄπιστον ἔθηκεν.
τὴν δὲ πατὴρ ἐνένιπεν ὁμοκλήσας ἐπέεσσι·

---

[a] Priam. [b] Hecabe.

[c] Priam was slain by Neoptolemus at the altar of Zeus Herceios (Verg. *Aen.* ii. 506 ff. See ll. 634 ff.).

[d] Hecabe was turned into a hound (Eur. *Hec.* 1259 ff.).

[e] Polyxena, daughter of Priam and Hecabe, was loved by Achilles and after the capture of Troy was sacrificed by the Greeks at the tomb of Achilles (*Epic. Gr. Frag.* p. 50 Kinkel; Apollod. *Epitom.* v. 23). The name of Neoptolemus was given as the sacrificer by Stesichorus, Ibycus, and later by Euripides; *cf.* schol. Eur. *Hec.* 41.

for thee, my father,[a] and for thee, my mother,[b] I weep to think what manner of things ye both shall suffer. Thou, my father, piteously fallen shalt lie beside the altar of mighty Zeus of the Court.[c] Mother of the best of children, thee from human shape the gods shall turn into a hound[d] maddened over thy children. Fair Polyxena,[e] for thee lying low near to thy fatherland I shall weep but little: would that someone of the Argives had slain me too with thy lamented fate! For what profit have I in life any more, if life but keep me for a most pitiful death, and an alien soil shall cover me? Such things for me and such a doom for King Agamemnon himself doth my mistress[f] weave, his reward for all his labours. But now take ye heed—in suffering shall ye learn the truth of my words—and put away, my friends, the cloud of infatuate folly. Let the body of the capacious horse be rent with hatchets or burnt with fire. And hiding crafty persons as it does, let it perish and be greatly regretted by the Danaans. And then feast ye and array you for the dance, setting up mixing-bowls in honour of dear liberty."[g]

So she spake; but no one hearkened to her; for Apollo made her at once a good prophet and unbelieved.[h] And her father spake and rebuked her:

[f] *i.e.* Clytemnestra who treats Cassandra as a slave. *Cf.* Aesch. *Ag.* 1035 ff.

[g] Hom. *Il.* vi. 526, "if Zeus grant us to set up in our halls the mixing-bowl of liberty to the everlasting gods."

[h] Cassandra, daughter of Priam, obtained from Apollo the gift of prophecy. But afterwards she refused to fulfil the promise by which she had obtained it. Apollo avenged himself by causing her prophecies not to be believed (Aesch. *Ag.* 1208 ff.).

τίς σε πάλιν, κακόμαντι, δυσώνυμος ἤγαγε δαίμων,
θαρσαλέη κυνόμυια; μάτην ὑλάουσ᾿ ἀπερύκεις.
οὔπω σοι κέκμηκε νόος λυσσώδεϊ νούσῳ,
οὐδὲ παλιμφήμων ἐκορέσσαο λαβροσυνάων;
ἀλλὰ καὶ ἡμετέρῃσιν ἐπαχνυμένη θαλίῃσιν
ἤλυθες, ὁππότε πᾶσιν ἐλεύθερον ἦμαρ ἀνῆψεν
ἡμῖν Ζεὺς Κρονίδης, ἐκέδασσε δὲ νῆας Ἀχαιῶν.
οὐδ᾿ ἔτι δούρατα μακρὰ τινάσσεται, οὐδ᾿ ἔτι τόξα
ἕλκεται, οὐ ξιφέων σελαγή, σιγῶσι δ᾿ ὀιστοί,
ἀλλὰ χοροὶ καὶ μοῦσα μελίπνοος, οὐδ᾿ ἔτι νείκη,
οὐ μήτηρ ἐπὶ παιδὶ κινύρεται, οὐδ᾿ ἐπὶ δῆριν
ἄνδρα γυνὴ πέμψασα νέκυν δακρύσατο χήρη·
ἵππον ἀνελκόμενον δέχεται πολιοῦχος Ἀθήνη.
παρθένε τολμήεσσα, σὺ δὲ πρὸ δόμοιο θοροῦσα
ψεύδεα θεσπίζουσα καὶ ἄγρια μαργαίνουσα
μοχθίζεις ἀτέλεστα καὶ ἱερὸν ἄστυ μιαίνεις.
ἔρρ᾿ οὕτως· ἡμῖν δὲ χοροὶ θαλίαι τε μέλονται.
οὐ γὰρ ἔτι Τροίης ὑπὸ τείχεσι δεῖμα λέλειπται,
οὐδ᾿ ἔτι μαντιπόλοιο τεῆς κεχρήμεθα φωνῆς.
  ὣς εἰπὼν ἐκέλευσεν ἄγειν ἑτερόφρονα κούρην
κεύθων ἐν θαλάμοισι· μόγις δ᾿ ἀέκουσα τοκῆι
πείθετο, παρθενίῳ δὲ περὶ κλιντῆρι πεσοῦσα
κλαῖεν ἐπισταμένη τὸν ἑὸν μόρον· ἔβλεπε δ᾿ ἤδη
πατρίδος αἰθομένης ἐπὶ τείχεσι μαρνάμενον πῦρ.
οἱ δὲ πολισσούχοιο θεῆς ὑπὸ νηὸν Ἀθήνης
ἵππον ἀναστήσαντες ἐυξέστων ἐπὶ βάθρων
ἔφλεγον ἱερὰ καλὰ πολυκνίσσων ἐπὶ βωμῶν·
ἀθάνατοι δ᾿ ἀνένευον ἀνηνύστους ἑκατόμβας.
εἰλαπίνη δ᾿ ἐπίδημος ἔην καὶ ἀμήχανος ὕβρις,
ὕβρις ἐλαφρίζουσα μέθην λυσήνορος οἴνου.
ἀφραδίῃ τε βέβυστο, μεθημοσύνῃ τε κεχήνει

"What spirit of ill name hath brought thee again, prophetess of evil, bold dog-fly? Vainly dost thou try to stay us with thy barking. Is thy mind not yet weary of its plague of madness, and hast thou not had thy fill of ill-omened ravings, but thou hast come in vexation at our mirth, when Zeus, the son of Cronus, hath lighted for us all the day of freedom and scattered the ships of the Achaeans? And no longer are the long spears brandished, no longer are the bows drawn, no longer flash the swords, the arrows are silent. But dances and honey-breathing music is ours and no more strife: no more wails the mother over the child, nor doth the wife send her husband to the fray and weep, a widow, over his corpse. Athena, guardian of the city, welcomes the horse which is drawn along. But thou, bold maiden, rushing before the house with false prophecies and wild raving, labourest to no purpose and pollutest the holy city. Go to! but our care is dance and mirth. For no longer is terror left under the walls of Troy, and no longer have we need of thy prophetic voice."

So he spake, and bade lead away the frenzied maiden, hiding her in her chamber. And hardly and against her will she obeyed her parent, and throwing herself upon her maiden bed she wept, knowing her own doom: already she beheld the fire raging on the walls of her burning fatherland. But the others at the temple of the goddess Athena, guardian of the city, set up the horse on well-polished pedestal, and burned fair offerings on savoury altars; but the immortals refused their vain hecatombs. And there was festival in the town and infinite lust, lust uplifting the drunkenness of wine that unmans. And all the city was filled with foolishness and gaped

πᾶσα πόλις, πυλέων δ' ὀλίγοις φυλάκεσσι μεμήλει·
ἤδη γὰρ καὶ φέγγος ἐδύετο, δαιμονίη δὲ
Ἴλιον αἰπεινὴν ὀλεσίπτολις ἀμφέβαλεν νύξ.
Ἀργείη δ' Ἑλένῃ πολιὸν δέμας ἀσκήσασα
ἦλθε δολοφρονέουσα πολυφράδμων Ἀφροδίτη,
ἐκ δὲ καλεσσαμένη προσέφη πειθήμονι φωνῇ·
  νύμφα φίλη, καλέει σε πόσις Μενέλαος ἀγήνωρ
ἵππῳ δουρατέῳ κεκαλυμμένος, ἀμφὶ δ' Ἀχαιῶν
ἡγεμόνες λοχόωσι τεῶν μνηστῆρες ἀέθλων.
ἀλλ' ἴθι, μηδ' ἔτι τοι μελέτω Πριάμοιο γέροντος
μήτ' ἄλλων Τρώων μήτ' αὐτοῦ Δηιφόβοιο·
ἤδη γάρ σε δίδωμι πολυτλήτῳ Μενελάῳ.
  ὣς φαμένη θεὸς αὖθις ἀνέδραμεν· ἡ δὲ δόλοισι
θελγομένη κραδίην θάλαμον λίπε κηώεντα,
καί οἱ Δηίφοβος πόσις εἵπετο· τὴν δὲ κιοῦσαν
Τρῳάδες ἑλκεχίτωνες ἐθηήσαντο γυναῖκες.
ἡ δ' ὁπόθ' ὑψιμέλαθρον ἐς ἱερὸν ἦλθεν Ἀθήνης,
ἔστη παπταίνουσα φυὴν εὐήνορος ἵππου.
τρὶς δὲ περιστείχουσα καὶ Ἀργείους ἐρέθουσα
πάσας ἠυκόμους ἀλόχους ὀνόμαζεν Ἀχαιῶν
φωνῇ λεπταλέῃ· τοὶ δ' ἔνδοθι θυμὸν ἄμυσσον
ἀλγεινοὶ κατέχοντες ἐεργμένα δάκρυα σιγῇ.
ἔστενε μὲν Μενέλαος, ἐπεὶ κλύε Τυνδαρεώνης,
κλαῖε δὲ Τυδείδης μεμνημένος Αἰγιαλείης,
οὔνομα δ' ἐπτοίησεν Ὀδυσσέα Πηνελοπείης·
Ἄντικλος δ' ὅτε κέντρον ἐδέξατο Λαοδαμείης,

[a] Lit. "received the sting (goad) of Laodameia." The ordinary and natural interpretation is that the wife of Anticlus was called Laodameia. She is otherwise unknown, and as the famous Laodameia, wife of Protesilaus, is the type of the love of husband and wife ("the wife of Protesilaus loved him even after death and made a likeness of him . . . and the gods pitied her and Hermes brought him back from

with heedlessness, and few warders watched the gates; for now the light of day was sinking and fateful night wrapped steep Ilios for destruction. And Aphrodite of many counsels, putting on the likeness of hoary age, came to Argive Helen with crafty intent and called her forth and spake to her with persuasive voice:

"Dear lady, thy valiant husband Menelaus calls thee. He is hidden in the wooden horse, and round him lie ambushed the leaders of the Achaeans, wooers of war in thy cause. But come and heed no longer ancient Priam nor the other Trojans nor Deiphobus himself. For now I give thee to much enduring Menelaus."

So spake the goddess and ran away again. But Helen, her heart beguiled by the craft, left her fragrant chamber, and her husband Deiphobus followed her. And as she went, the Trojan women of trailing tunics gazed upon her. And when she came to the high-roofed temple of Athena, she stood and scanned the form of the well-manned horse. Three times she walked round it and provoked the Argives, naming all the fair-tressed wives of the Achaeans with her clear voice. And their hearts were torn within them with grief and they restrained their pent up tears in silence. Groaned Menelaus when he heard the daughter of Tyndareus: wept the son of Tydeus remembering Aegialeia: the name of Penelope stirred the heart of Odysseus: but only Anticlus, stung by the name of Laodameia,[a]

Hades. And when she beheld him and thought he had returned from Troy she rejoiced; but when he was carried back to Hades she killed herself" Apollod. *epit.* iii. 30), it seems possible that the meaning here is "the goad that pricked Laodameia," *i.e.* desire for the absent spouse.

μοῦνος ἀμοιβαίην ἀνεβάλλετο γῆρυν ἀνοίξας·
ἀλλ' Ὀδυσεὺς κατέπαλτο καὶ ἀμφοτέρῃς παλάμῃσιν
ἀμφιπεσὼν ἐπίεζεν ἐπειγόμενον στόμα λῦσαι.
μάστακα δ' ἀρρήκτοισιν ἀλυκτοπέδῃσι μεμαρπὼς
εἶχεν ἐπικρατέως· ὁ δ' ἐπάλλετο χερσὶ πιεσθείς,
φεύγων ἀνδροφόνοιο πελώρια δεσμὰ σιωπῆς.
καὶ τὸν μὲν λίπεν ἆσθμα φερέσβιον· οἱ δέ μιν ἄλλοι
δάκρυσι λαθριδίοισι κατακλαύσαντες Ἀχαιοὶ
κοῖλον ἀποκρύψαντες ἐς ἰσχίον ἔνθεσαν ἵππου
καὶ χλαῖναν μελέεσσιν ἐπὶ ψυχροῖσι βαλόντες.
καί νύ κεν ἄλλον ἔθελγε γυνὴ δολόμητις Ἀχαιῶν,
εἰ μή οἱ βλοσυρῶπις ἀπ' αἰθέρος ἀντήσασα
Παλλὰς ἐπηπείλησε, φίλου δ' ἐξήγαγε νηοῦ
μούνῃ φαινομένη, στερεῇ δ' ἀπεπέμψατο φωνῇ·
δειλαίη, τέο μέχρις ἀλιτροσύναι σε φέρουσι
καὶ πόθος ἀλλοτρίων λεχέων καὶ Κύπριδος ἄτη;
οὔποτε δ' οἰκτείρεις πρότερον πόσιν οὐδὲ θύγατρα
Ἑρμιόνην ποθέεις; ἔτι δὲ Τρώεσσιν ἀρήγεις;
χάζεο καὶ θαλάμων ὑπερώιον εἰσαναβᾶσα
σὺν πυρὶ μειλιχίῳ ποτιδέχνυσο νῆας Ἀχαιῶν.
ὣς φαμένη κενεὴν ἀπάτην ἐκέδασσε γυναικός.
καὶ τὴν μὲν θαλαμόνδε πόδες φέρον· οἱ δὲ χοροῖο
παυσάμενοι καμάτῳ ἀδδηκότες ἤριπον ὕπνῳ.
καὶ δή που φόρμιγξ ἀνεπαύσατο, κεῖτο δὲ κάμνων
αὐλὸς ἐπὶ κρητῆρι, κύπελλα δὲ πολλὰ χυθέντα
αὐτομάτως ῥείεσκε καθελκομένων ἀπὸ χειρῶν.
ἡσυχίη δὲ πόλιν κατεβόσκετο, νυκτὸς ἑταίρη,
οὐδ' ὑλακὴ σκυλάκων ἠκούετο, πᾶσα δὲ σιγὴ
εἱστήκει καλέουσα φόνον πνείουσαν αὐτήν.

opened his lips and essayed answering speech. But Odysseus leapt upon him and fell about him with both his hands and restrained him while he strove to open his lips, and, seizing his mouth in escapeless fetters unbreakable, held him masterfully. And he writhed under the pressure of his hands, essaying to escape the giant bonds of murderous silence. And breath that gives men life forsook him; and the other Achaeans wept for him with secret tears and hid him away in the hollow flank of the horse, and cast a coverlet over his chilly limbs. And now would the crafty woman have beguiled another of the Achaeans, had not fierce-eyed Pallas met her from the sky and threatened her and led her forth from her dear temple, appearing unto her alone,[a] and sent her away with stern voice:

"Wretch, how far shall thy sinfulness carry thee and thy passion for alien wedlock and the infatuation of Cypris[b]? And thou hast never any pity for thy former husband nor any yearning for thy daughter Hermione, but helpest still the Trojans? Withdraw and go up into thy upper room in the house and with kindly fire welcome the ships of the Achaeans."

So she spake and shattered the woman's empty deceit. And Helen passed to her chamber, while they ceased from the dance, filled with weariness, and fell on sleep. The lyre rested, the weary flute lay beside the mixing-bowl, and many a cup fell from the drooping hand and flowed of itself. Peace, the companion of night, browsed about the city; and no baying of dogs was heard but perfect silence reigned, inviting slaughter-breathing battle. And now Zeus,

[a] *Cf.* Hom. *Il.* i. 198.

[b] Aphrodite.

ἤδη δὲ Τρώεσσιν ὀλέθριον εἷλκε τάλαντον
Ζεὺς ταμίης πολέμοιο, μόγις[1] δ' ἐλέλιξεν Ἀχαιούς·
χάζετο δ' Ἰλιόθεν Λυκίης ἐπὶ πίονα νηὸν
ἀχνύμενος μεγάλοις ἐπὶ τείχεσι Φοῖβος Ἀπόλλων.
αὐτίκα δ Ἀργείοισιν Ἀχιλλῆος παρὰ τύμβον
ἀγγελίην ἀνέφαινε Σίνων εὐφεγγέι δαλῷ.
παννυχίη δ' ἑτάροισιν ὑπὲρ θαλάμοιο καὶ αὐτὴ
εὐειδὴς Ἑλένη χρυσέην ἐπεδείκνυτο πεύκην.
ὡς δ' ὁπότε πλήθουσα πυρὸς γλαυκοῖο σελήνη
οὐρανὸν αἰγλήεντα κατεχρύσωσε προσώπῳ·
οὐχ ὅτε που γλωχῖνας ἀποξύνουσα κεραίης
πρωτοφαὴς ὑπὸ μηνὸς ἀνίσταται ἄσκιον ἀχλύν,
ἀλλ' ὅτε κυκλώσασα περίτροχον ὄμματος αὐγὴν
ἀντιτύπους ἀκτῖνας ἐφέλκεται ἠελίοιο·
τοίη μαρμαίρουσα Θεραπναίη τότε νύμφη
οἴνοπα πῆχυν ἀνεῖλκε, φίλου πυρὸς ἡνιοχῆα.
οἱ δὲ σέλας πυρσοῖο μετήορον ἀθρήσαντες
νῆας ἀνεκρούσαντο παλιγγνάμπτοισι κελεύθοις
Ἀργεῖοι σπεύδοντες, ἅπας δ' ἠπείγετο ναύτης
δηναιοῦ πολέμοιο τέλος διζήμενος εὑρεῖν.
οἱ δ' αὐτοὶ πλωτῆρες ἔσαν κρατεροί τε μαχηταὶ
ἀλλήλοις τ' ἐκέλευον ἐλαυνέμεν· αἱ δ' ἄρα νῆες
ὠκύτεραι κραιπνῶν ἀνέμων ταχυπειθέι ῥιπῇ
Ἴλιον εἰσανάγοντο Ποσειδάωνος ἀρωγῇ.

[1] μόλις F.

---

[a] For the Balance of Zeus *cf.* Hom. *Il.* viii. 69, xxii. 209, Milton, *Paradise Lost*, iv. *ad fin.*

> The Eternal, to prevent such horrid fray,
> Hung forth in Heaven his golden scales, etc.

[b] Here (1) both Sinon and Helen give the beacon, (2) Sinon gives it from the grave of Achilles. In Apollodor. *epitom.* v. 19 only Sinon gives it and from the grave of Achilles, *i.e.* from outside the city. Arctinus, in the *Iliu-*

dispenser of war, weighed the Balance[a] of destruction for the Trojans, and hardly and at last rallied the Achaeans. Phoebus Apollo withdrew from Ilios to his rich shrine in Lycia, grieving over his mighty walls. And straightway beside the tomb of Achilles Sinon[b] showed his message to the Argives with his shining brand. And all night long fair Helen herself also displayed from her chamber to her friends her golden torch. And even as when the moon, full with grey fire, gilds with her face the gleaming heaven: not when, sharpening her pointed horns, she first shines, rising in the shadowless[c] dusk of the month, but when, orbing the rounded radiance of her eye, she draws to herself the reflected rays of the sun: even so did the lady of Therapne on that night in her radiance lift up her wine-hued arm, directing the friendly fire. And when they beheld the gleam of the beacon on high, the Argives speedily set back their ships on the path of return, and every mariner made haste, seeking to find an end of the long war. They were at once sailors and stout warriors and called each on the other to row. So the ships, swifter than the speedy winds, with obedient rush sailed unto Ilios by the help of

persis (Procl. p. 244, *Myth. Gr.* i. Wagner) says Sinon gave the signal πρότερον εἰσεληλυθὼς προσποιητός, *i.e.* apparently inside the city. In Vergil, *A.* vi. 517 ff. the signal is given by Helen. No signal is given by Sinon, but *ib.* 256 a signal is sent by the Greeks to Sinon who then opens the door of the horse. In Quint. Smyrn. xiii. 23 ff. Sinon gives the signal and *ib.* 30 ff. he also opens the door of the horse.

[c] Aratus says (736) that the moon first casts a shadow when she "is going to the fourth day." Fest. Avien. *Progn.* v. ff.

> namque facem quarti sibimet profitebitur ignis,
> corpora cum primo perfundens lumine nostra
> in subiecta soli tenuem porrexerit umbram.

ἐνθάδε δὴ πεζοὶ πρότεροι κίον, οἱ δ᾽ ἐπέλειφθεν
ἱππῆες κατόπισθεν, ὅπως μὴ Τρώιον ἵπποι
λαὸν ἀναστήσωσιν ἀειρομένῳ χρεμετισμῷ.
οἱ δ᾽ ἕτεροι γλαφυρῆς ἀπὸ γαστέρος ἔρρεον ἵππου,
τευχησταὶ βασιλῆες, ἀπὸ δρυὸς οἷα μέλισσαι,
αἵτ᾽ ἐπεὶ οὖν ἔκαμον πολυχανδέος ἔνδοθι σίμβλου
κηρὸν ὑφαίνουσαι μελιηδέα ποικιλοτέχναι,
ἐς νομὸν εὐγυάλοιο κατ᾽ ἄγγεος ἀμφιχυθεῖσαι
νύγμασι πημαίνουσι παραστείχοντας ὁδίτας·
ὣς Δαναοὶ κρυφίοιο λόχου κληῖδας ἀνέντες
θρῷσκον ἐπὶ Τρώεσσι καὶ εἰσέτι κοῖτον ἔχοντας
χαλκείου θανάτοιο κακοῖς ἐκάλυψαν ὀνείροις.
νήχετο δ᾽ αἵματι γαῖα, βοὴ δ᾽ ἄλληκτος ὀρώρει
Τρώων φευγόντων, ἐστείνετο δ᾽ Ἴλιος ἱρὴ
πιπτόντων νεκύων, οἱ δ᾽ ἀνδροφόνῳ κολοσυρτῷ
<ἔζεον>[1] ἔνθα καὶ ἔνθα μεμηνότες οἷα λέοντες
σώμασιν ἀρτιφάτοισι γεφυρώσαντες ἀγυιάς.
Τρωιάδες δὲ γυναῖκες ὑπὲρ τεγέων ἀίουσαι
αἱ μὲν ἐλευθερίης ἐρατῆς ἔτι διψώουσαι
αὐχένας ἐς θάνατον δειλοῖς ὑπέβαλλον ἀκοίταις,
αἱ δὲ φίλοις ἐπὶ παισί, χελιδόνες οἷάτε κοῦφαι,
μητέρες ὠδύροντο· νέη δέ τις ἀσπαίροντα
ἠίθεον κλαύσασα θανεῖν ἔσπευδε καὶ αὐτὴ
οὐδὲ δορυκτήτοισιν ὁμοῦ δεσμοῖσιν ἕπεσθαι
ἤθελεν, ἀλλ᾽ ἐχόλωσε καὶ οὐκ ἐθέλοντα φονῆα
καὶ ξυνὸν λέχος ἔσχεν ὀφειλόμενον παρακοίτῃ.
πολλαὶ δ᾽ ἠλιτόμηνα καὶ ἄπνοα τέκνα φέρουσαι
γαστέρος ὠμοτόκοιο χύδην ὠδῖνα μεθεῖσαι
ῥιγεδανῶς σὺν παισὶν ἀπεψύχοντο καὶ αὐταί.
παννυχίη δ᾽ ἐχόρευσεν ἀνὰ πτόλιν, οἷα θύελλα,
κύμασι παφλάζουσα πολυφλοίσβου πολέμοιο

[1] om. F; ἔζεον Rhodoman.

Poseidon. And there the foot soldiers went in front, while the horsemen fell behind, in order that the horses might not rouse the people of Troy by their loud neighing. And those others poured from the carven belly of the horse, armed princes, even as bees from an oak: which when they have laboured within the capacious hive, weaving the sweet honeycomb with cunning art, pour from their vaulted nest to the pasture and vex the passing wayfarers with their stings: even so the Danaans undid the bolts of their secret ambush and leapt upon the Trojans and, while they still slept, shrouded them in evil dreams of brazen death. The earth swam with blood, and a cry unceasing arose from the fleeing Trojans, and sacred Ilios was straitened with falling corpses, while those others with murderous tumult raged this way and that, like mad lions, bridging the streets with new-slain bodies. And the Trojan women heard from their roofs and some, still thirsting for beloved liberty, submitted their necks to their wretched husbands for slaughter: mothers over their dear children, like light swallows, made lament: and many a young bride wept for her young husband quivering in his death struggle and was fain to die herself, and willed not to follow in the chains of captivity, but roused to anger her unwilling slayer and won to share the death-bed that was owing to her spouse. And many who bare within them breathless children whose months were not yet fulfilled, shed untimely the travail of the womb and died a chilly death, themselves too, with their children. And Enyo,[a] revelling in the drunkenness of unmixed blood, danced all night throughout the

[a] Goddess of War.

αἵματος ἀκρήτοιο μέθης ἐπίκωμος Ἐνυώ.
σὺν δ' Ἔρις οὐρανόμηκες ἀναστήσασα κάρηνον
Ἀργείους ὀρόθυνεν, ἐπεὶ καὶ φοίνιος Ἄρης
ὀψὲ μὲν ἀλλὰ καὶ ὧς πολέμων ἑτεραλκέα νίκην
ἦλθε φέρων Δαναοῖσι καὶ ἀλλοπρόσαλλον ἀρωγήν.
ἴαχε δὲ γλαυκῶπις ἐπ' ἀκροπόληος Ἀθήνη
αἰγίδα κινήσασα, Διὸς σάκος, ἔτρεμε δ' αἰθὴρ
Ἥρης σπερχομένης, ἐπὶ δ' ἔβραχε γαῖα βαρεῖα
παλλομένη τριόδοντι Ποσειδάωνος ἀκωκῇ,
ἔφριξεν δ' Ἀΐδης, χθονίων δ' ἐξέδρακε θώκων
ταρβήσας, μή πού τι Διὸς μέγα χωσαμένοιο
πᾶν γένος ἀνθρώπων κατάγοι ψυχοστόλος Ἑρμῆς.
πάντα δ' ὁμοῦ κεκύκητο, φόνος δέ τις ἄκριτος ἦεν·
τοὺς μὲν γὰρ φεύγοντας ἐπὶ Σκαιῇσι πύλῃσι
κτεῖνον ἐφεστηῶτες, ὁ δ' ἐξ εὐνῆς ἀνορούσας
τεύχεα μαστεύων δνοφερῇ περικάππεσεν αἰχμῇ.
καί τις ὑπὸ σκιόεντι δόμῳ κεκρυμμένος ἀνήρ,
ξεῖνος ἐών, ἐκάλεσσεν ὀιόμενος φίλον εἶναι·
νήπιος, οὐ μὲν ἔμελλεν ἐνηέι φωτὶ μιγῆναι,
ξείνια δ' ἐχθρὰ κόμισσεν· ὑπὲρ τέγεος δέ τις ἄλλος
μήπω παπταίνων τι θοῷ διέπιπτεν ὀιστῷ.
καί τινες ἀλγεινῷ κραδίην βεβαρηότες οἴνῳ,
ἐκπλαγέες ποτὶ δοῦπον, ἐπειγόμενοι καταβῆναι,
κλίμακος ἐξελάθοντο καθ' ὑψηλῶν τε μελάθρων
ἔκπεσον ἀγνώσσοντες, ἐπαυχενίους δὲ λυθέντες

---

[a] The trident; *cf.* Pind. *O.* ix. 30, *Isth.* viii. 35.

[b] φόνος ἄκριτος is not easy to translate adequately, though the sense is clear enough. We write "without discretion" as a reminiscence of Cuddie Headrigg's remark (Scott, *Old Mortality*, chap. xvii.), "The Whigamore bullets ken unco little discretion, and will just as sune knock out the harns o' a psalm-singing auld wife as a swearing dragoon"; *cf.* Bacchylid. v. 129 οὐ γὰρ καρτερόθυμος Ἄρης κρίνει φίλον ἐν

city, like a hurricane, turbulent with the waves of surging war. And therewithal Strife lifted her head high as heaven and stirred up the Argives; since even bloody Ares, late but even so, came and brought to the Danaans the changeful victory in war and his help that is now for these and anon for those. And on the acropolis grey-eyed Athena uttered her voice and shook her aegis, the shield of Zeus; and the sky trembled as Hera bestirred her, and the heavy earth rang as it was shaken by the three-toothed spear [a] of Poseidon. And Hades shuddered and looked forth from his seat under earth, afraid lest in the great anger of Zeus Hermes, conductor of souls, should bring down all the race of men. And all things were confounded together and there was slaughter without discretion.[b] For some in flight they slew standing by the Scaean [c] gates: one leapt from his bed and, seeking his arms, fell upon a darkling spear; one hidden in his shadowy house invited as his guest one whom he deemed to be a friend: fool! no friendly man was he to meet but got hateful gifts of his hospitality; another over his roof, while yet he looked not, fell by the swift arrow. And some, their hearts weighed down with grievous wine, in terror at the din, hasting to come down, forgot the ladder [d] and fell unwitting from the lofty roofs and luxed and brake the bones of their necks,

πολέμῳ· τυφλὰ δ' ἐκ χειρῶν βέλη ψυχαῖς ἔπι δυσμενέων φοιτᾷ θάνατόν τε φέρει τοῖσιν ἂν δαίμων θέλῃ, Appian p. 76 (Bekker), an elephant ran amuck and *ἀνῄρει τὸν ἐν ποσίν, οὐ διακρίνων ἔτι φίλιον ἢ πολέμιον*, and Byron's "friend, foe, in one red burial blent" (*Ch. Har.* iii. 28. 9).

[c] For a discussion of the gates of Troy see W. Leaf, *Troy*, pp. 151 ff.

[d] Like Elpenor in Hom. *Od.* x. 552 ff.

ἀστραγάλους ἐάγησαν, ὁμοῦ δ᾽ ἐξήρυγον οἶνον.
πολλοὶ δ᾽ εἰς ἕνα χῶρον ἀολλέες ἐκτείνοντο
μαρνάμενοι, πολλοὶ δὲ διωκόμενοι κατὰ πύργων
ἤριπον εἰς Ἀίδαο πανύστατον ἅλμα θορόντες.
παῦροι δὲ στεινῆς διὰ κοιλάδος, οἷάτε φῶρες,
πατρίδος ὀλλυμένης ἔλαθον χειμῶνα φυγόντες.
οἱ δ᾽ ἔνδον πολέμῳ τε καὶ ἀχλύι κυμαίνοντες,
ἀνδράσιν οἰχομένοισι καὶ οὐ φεύγουσιν ὁμοῖοι,
πίπτον ἐπ᾽ ἀλλήλοισι· πόλις δ᾽ οὐ χάνδανε λύθρον
ἀνδρῶν χηρεύουσα, περιπλήθουσα δὲ νεκρῶν.
οὐδέ τι φειδωλή τις ἐγίνετο· φοιταλέῃ δὲ
σπερχόμενοι μάστιγι φιλαγρύπνοιο κυδοιμοῦ
οὐδὲ θεῶν ὄπιν εἶχον, ἀθεσμοτάτης δ᾽ ὑπὸ ῥιπῆς
ἀθανάτων ἔχραινον ἀπενθέας αἵματι βωμούς.
οἰκτρότατοι δὲ γέροντες ἀτιμοτάτοισι φόνοισιν
οὐδ᾽ ὀρθοὶ κτείνοντο, χαμαὶ δ᾽ ἱκετήσια γυῖα
τεινάμενοι πολιοῖσι κατεκλίνοντο καρήνοις.
πολλὰ δὲ νήπια τέκνα μινυνθαδίων ἀπὸ μαζῶν
μητέρος ἡρπάζοντο καὶ οὐ νοέοντα τοκήων
ἀμπλακίας ἀπέτινον, ἀνημέλκτου δὲ γάλακτος
παιδὶ μάτην ὀρέγουσα χοὰς ἐκόμισσε τιθήνη.
οἰωνοί τε κύνες τε κατὰ πτόλιν ἄλλοθεν ἄλλοι,
ἠέριοι πεζοί τε συνέστιοι εἰλαπινασταί,
αἷμα μέλαν πίνοντες ἀμείλιχον εἶχον ἐδωδήν,
καὶ τῶν μὲν κλαγγὴ φόνον ἔπνεεν, οἱ δ᾽ ὑλάοντες
ἄγρια κοπτομένοισιν ἐπ᾽ ἀνδράσιν ὠρύοντο,
νηλέες, οὐδ᾽ ἀλέγιζον ἑοὺς ἐρύοντες ἄνακτας.

τὼ δὲ γυναιμανέος ποτὶ δώματα Δηιφόβοιο
στελλέσθην Ὀδυσεύς τε καὶ εὐχαίτης Μενέλαος

and therewithal spewed forth wine. And many gathered together in one place were slain as they fought and many, as they were pursued, fell from the towers into the house of Hades, leaping their latest leap. And a few through a narrow hollow, like thieves, escaped unnoticed from the storm of their perishing fatherland. Others within, in the surge of war and darkness, like to men gone rather than to men fleeing, fell one above the other. And the city could not contain the filth, desolate of men but over-full of dead. And there was no sparing. Driven by the frenzied lash of sleepless turmoil they had no regard even to the gods, but with most lawless onset they defiled with blood the innocent altars of the immortals. And old men most piteous were slain in most unworthy slaughter: slain not on their feet, but, stretching on the ground their suppliant limbs, they had their grey heads laid low. And many infant children were snatched from the mother's breast that had suckled them but a little while and, understanding not, paid for the sins of their parents, while she that nursed it, offered the child the breast in vain, and brought offering of milk it might not suck.[a] And birds and dogs, here and there throughout the city, the fowls of air and the beasts that walk the earth, feasted in company and drank the black blood and made a savage meal. The crying of the birds breathed slaughter, while the barking dogs bayed wildly over torn corpses of men, pitiless and heeding not that they were rending their own masters.

And Odysseus and Menelaus of the goodly hair set out for the house of woman-mad Deiphobus, like

[a] Pliny, *N.H.* xxxv. 98.

καρχαλέοισι λύκοισιν ἐοικότες, οἵθ' ὑπὸ νύκτα
χειμερίην φονόωντες ἀσημάντοις ἐπὶ μήλοις
οἴχονται, κάματον δὲ κατατρύχουσι νομήων.
ἔνθα δύω περ ἐόντες ἀπειρεσίοισιν ἔμιχθεν
ἀνδράσι δυσμενέεσσι· νέη δ' ἠγείρετο χάρμη
τῶν μὲν ἐπορνυμένων, τῶν δ' ὑψόθεν ἐκ θαλάμοιο
βαλλόντων λιθάκεσσι καὶ ὠκυμόροισιν ὀιστοῖς.
ἀλλὰ καὶ ὣς ὑπέροπλα καρήατα πυργώσαντες
ἀρρήκτοις κορύθεσσι καὶ ἀσπίσι κυκλώσαντες
εἰσέθορον μέγα δῶμα· καὶ ἀντίβιον μὲν ὅμιλον,
θῆρας δειμαλέους, ἐλάων ἐδάιξεν Ὀδυσσεύς,
Ἀτρείδης δ' ἑτέρωθεν ὑποπτήξαντα διώξας
Δηίφοβον κατέμαρψε, μέσην κατὰ γαστέρα τύψας
ἧπαρ ὀλισθηρῇσι συνεξέχεεν χολάδεσσιν.
ὣς ὁ μὲν αὐτόθι κεῖτο λελασμένος ἱπποσυνάων,
τῷ δ' ἕπετο τρομέουσα δορυκτήτη παράκοιτις
ἄλλοτε μὲν χαίρουσα κακῶν ἐπὶ τέρματι μόχθων,
ἄλλοτε δ' αἰδομένη, τοτὲ δ' ὀψέ περ ὡς ἐν ὀνείρῳ
λαθρίδιον στενάχουσα φίλης μιμνῄσκετο πάτρης.
Αἰακίδης δὲ γέροντα Νεοπτόλεμος βασιλῆα
πήμασι κεκμηῶτα παρ' Ἑρκείῳ κτάνε βωμῷ
οἶκτον ἀπωσάμενος πατρώιον· οὐδὲ λιτάων
ἔκλυεν, οὐ Πηλῆος ὁρώμενος ἥλικα χαίτην
ᾐδέσαθ', ἧς ὕπο θυμὸν ἀπέκλασεν ἠδὲ γέροντος
καίπερ ἐὼν βαρύμηνις ἐφείσατο τὸ πρὶν Ἀχιλλεύς.
σχέτλιος, ἦ μὲν ἔμελλε καὶ αὐτῷ πότμος ὁμοῖος
ἑσπέσθαι παρὰ βωμὸν ἀληθέος Ἀπόλλωνος

unto wolves of jagged teeth, which in a stormy night, lusting for blood, go to attack unshepherded flocks and waste the labour of the herdsmen. There, though they were but two, they engaged foemen beyond numbering. And a new battle arose, as these attacked and those from a chamber overhead hurled stones and arrows which bring speedy death. Yet even so, fencing their giant heads with helmets unbreakable and encircling themselves with shields, they leapt into the great house. And Odysseus drave and slaughtered the crowd that opposed him, even as wild beasts affrighted. And the son of Atreus on the other hand pursued Deiphobus who skulked away, and overtook and smote him in the midst of the belly and poured forth his liver and slippery guts. So he lay there and forgot his chivalry. And with Menelaus followed, trembling, his spear-won spouse, now rejoicing in the end of dire woes, and now ashamed, and then again, though late, as in a dream, secretly groaning, she remembered her dear fatherland. But Neoptolemus, scion of Aeacus, slew beside the altar of Zeus of the Court-yard the aged king out-worn with woe. He put from him such pity as his father had shown, and hearkened not to his prayers, nor had compassion when he looked on his hair grey even as the hair of Peleus: the hair at which of old Achilles softened his heart and, despite his grievous anger, spared the old man.[a] Hard of heart! verily a like fate was destined afterward to come to him by the altar of truthful Apollo, when, as he sought to

[a] Hom. *Il.* xxiv. 515 ff.

ὕστερον, ὁππότε μιν ζαθέου δηλήμονα νηοῦ
Δελφὸς ἀνὴρ ἐλάσας ἱερῇ κατέπεφνε μαχαίρῃ.
ἡ δὲ κυβιστήσαντα διηερίων ἀπὸ πύργων —
χειρὸς Ὀδυσσείης ὀλοὸν βέλος — ἀθρήσασα
Ἀνδρομάχη μινύωρον ἐκώκυεν Ἀστυάνακτα.
Κασσάνδρην δ' ᾔσχυνεν Ὀιλῆος ταχὺς Αἴας
Παλλάδος ἀχράντοιο θεῆς ὑπὸ γοῦνα πεσοῦσαν·
ἡ δὲ βίην ἀνένευσε θεή, τὸ πρόσθεν ἀρηγὼν
ἀνθ' ἑνὸς Ἀργείοισιν ἐχώσατο πᾶσιν Ἀθήνη.
Αἰνείαν δ' ἔκλεψε καὶ Ἀγχίσην Ἀφροδίτη
οἰκτείρουσα γέροντα καὶ υἱέα, τῆλε δὲ πάτρης
Αὐσονίην ἀπένασσε· θεῶν δ' ἐτελείετο βουλὴ
Ζηνὸς ἐπαινήσαντος, ἵνα κράτος ἄφθιτον εἴη
παισὶ καὶ υἱωνοῖσιν ἀρηιφίλης Ἀφροδίτης.
τέκνα δὲ καὶ γενεὴν Ἀντήνορος ἀντιθέοιο
Ἀτρείδης ἐφύλαξε, φιλοξείνοιο γέροντος,
μειλιχίης προτέρης <τίνων> χάριν ἠδὲ τραπέζης
κείνης, ᾗ μιν ἔδεκτο γυνὴ πρηεῖα Θεανώ.
δειλὴ Λαοδίκη, σὲ δὲ πατρίδος ἐγγύθι γαίης
γαῖα περιπτύξασα κεχηνότι δέξατο κόλπῳ·

---

[a] There are several versions of the death of Neoptolemus at Delphi. (1) According to one story he came to plunder the temple of Apollo (Paus. x. 7. 1), and was slain at the instance of the Pythian priestess by the Delphians (Paus. i. 13. 9) or by Apollo's priest himself (Paus. x. 24. 4). (2) According to another version he came to offer to Apollo the first-fruits of the spoil of Troy, "and there in a quarrel over meats a man slew him with a knife" (Pindar, *Nem.* vii. 40 f.). After his death he was buried in the precincts of Apollo's temple, and yearly offerings were made to him as a hero by the Delphians (Paus. x. 24. 6).

[b] The fate of Astyanax, son of Hector and Andromache, who was hurled headlong from the wall of Troy, is foreshadowed in Hom. *Il.* xxiv. 735.

harm the divine shrine, a Delphian man smote and slew him with a holy knife.[a]

And Andromache bewailed short-lived Astyanax,[b] whom she saw dive headlong from the airy towers, hurled to death by the hand of Odysseus. Swift Aias, son of Oileus, assaulted Cassandra when she took shelter at the knees of the stainless goddess Pallas; and the goddess rejected his violence, and, helper though she had been aforetime, for one man's sake Athena was angered against all the Argives. Aeneias and Anchises did Aphrodite steal away, taking pity on the old man and his son, and far from their fatherland established them in Ausonia.[c] So the counsel of the gods was fulfilled with approval of Zeus, so that imperishable sovereignty should be the lot of the children and the grandchildren[d] of Aphrodite dear to Ares. The children and race of godlike Antenor,[e] that hospitable old man, the son of Atreus saved, in gratitude for his former kindness and that table wherewith his gentle wife Theano had welcomed him. Poor Laodice[f]! thee by thy native land the enfolding earth took to her yawning bosom,

[c] Italy. [d] The Romans.

[e] Antenor and his wife Theano, sister of Hecabe, had entertained Odysseus and Menelaus when they came to Troy to ask the restoration of Helen before the war (Hom. *Il.* iii. 205), and subsequently he advised the surrender of Helen (Hom. *Il.* vii. 347 ff.). His friendly attitude to the Greeks ("Troianae suasorem Antenora pacis," Ovid, *F.* iv. 75) led later to charges of treachery; *cf.* Lycophr. 340.

[f] Daughter of Priam and Hecabe, mother of Munitus by Acamas, son of Theseus, was, at the taking of Troy, swallowed up by the earth; *cf.* Lycophr. 314, 497.

οὐδέ σε Θησείδης Ἀκάμας οὐδ' ἄλλος Ἀχαιῶν
ἤγαγε ληιδίην, ἔθανες δ' ἅμα πατρίδι γαίῃ.
πᾶσαν δ' οὐκ ἂν ἔγωγε μόθου χύσιν ἀείσαιμι
κρινάμενος τὰ ἕκαστα καὶ ἄλγεα νυκτὸς ἐκείνης·
Μουσάων ὅδε μόχθος, ἐγὼ δ' ἅπερ ἵππον ἐλάσσω
τέρματος ἀμφιέλισσαν ἐπιψαύουσαν ἀοιδήν.
ἄρτι γὰρ ἀντολίηθεν ἀπόσσυτος Ὠκεανοῖο
ἠρέμα λευκαίνουσα κατέγραφεν ἠέρα πολλήν,
νύκτα διαρρήξασα μιαιφόνον ἱππότις Ἠώς·
οἱ δ' ἐπαγαλλόμενοι πολέμων ὑπεραυχέι νίκῃ
πάντοσε παπταίνεσκον ἀνὰ πτόλιν, εἴ τινες ἄλλοι
κλεπτόμενοι φεύγουσι φόνου πάνδημον ἀυτήν.
ἀλλ' οἱ μὲν δέδμηντο λίνῳ θανάτοιο πανάγρῳ,
ἰχθύες ὡς ἁλίῃσιν ἐπὶ ψαμάθοισι χυθέντες,
Ἀργεῖοι δ' ἀπὸ μὲν μεγάρων νεοτευχέα κόσμον
ἐξέφερον, νηῶν ἀναθήματα, πολλὰ δ' ἐρήμων
ἥρπαζον θαλάμων κειμήλια· σὺν δὲ γυναῖκας
ληιδίας σὺν παισὶν ἄγον ποτὶ νῆας ἀνάγκῃ.
τείχεσι δὲ πτολίπορθον ἐπὶ φλόγα θωρήξαντες
ἔργα Ποσειδάωνος ἰῇ συνέχευον ἀυτμῇ.
αὐτοῦ καὶ μέγα σῆμα φίλοις ἀστοῖσιν ἐτύχθη
Ἴλιος αἰθαλόεσσα· πυρὸς δ' ὀλεσίπτολιν ἄτην
Ξάνθος ἰδὼν ἔκλαυσε γόων ἁλιμυρέι πηγῇ,
Ἡφαίστῳ δ' ὑπόεικεν ἀτυζόμενος χόλον Ἥρης.

---

[a] For this metaphor *cf.* Lucret. vi. 90 ff. "Tu mihi supremae praescripta ad candida calcis Currenti spatium praemonstra, callida Musa Calliope." We take the sense to be: I cannot go into detail (Eur. *Ph.* 751 ὄνομα δ' ἑκάστου διατριβὴν πολλὴν ἔχει). This is poetry. As the charioteer tries to graze the turning-post ("metaque fervidis evitata rotis," Hor. *C.* i. 1. 4) and not to run wide, so my song will be as brief as may be: βαιὰ δ' ἐν μακροῖσι ποικίλλειν ἀκοὰ σοφοῖς, Pind. *P.* ix. 77.

and neither Acamas, son of Theseus, nor any other of the Achaeans led thee captive, but thou didst perish with thy fatherland.

All the multitude of strife and the sorrows of that night I could not sing, distinguishing each event. This is the Muses' task; and I shall drive, as it were a horse,[a] a song which, wheeling about, grazes the turning-post.

Dawn in her car was just speeding back from Ocean in the East and marking great space of sky with slowly brightening light, dispelling slaughterous night; and they, exulting in their proud victory in war, looked everywhere throughout the city to find if any others were concealed and avoiding the murderous warfare that embraced all the people. But they were overcome by the all-capturing net of death, as fishes poured forth on the shores of the sea. And the Argives carried from the halls their new bravery to deck their ships and many treasured heirlooms did they seize from the desolate chambers. And with them they carried off by force captive wives and children together unto the ships. And having arrayed city-sacking fire against the walls, in one flame they confounded all the works of Poseidon.[b] And even there was smoking Ilios made a great monument to her dear citizens. And Xanthus, beholding the fiery doom of the city, wept with seaward flowing fountain of lamentation, and, terrified by the anger of Hera, yielded to Hephaestus.

[b] In reference to the building of the walls by Poseidon and Apollo. So Verg. *A.* iii. 3 "Ilium et omnis humo fumat Neptunia Troia"; *cf.* *A.* ii. 622.

οἱ δὲ Πολυξείνης ἐπιτύμβιον αἷμα χέαντες,
μῆνιν ἱλασσάμενοι τεθνειότος Αἰακίδαο
Τρωιάδας τε γυναῖκας ἐλάγχανον, ἄλλα τε πάντα
χρυσὸν ἐμοιρήσαντο καὶ ἄργυρον· οἷσι βαθείας
νῆας ἐπαχθήσαντες ἐριγδούπου διὰ πόντου
ἐκ Τροίης ἀνάγοντο μόθον τελέσαντες Ἀχαιοί.

---

[a] Polyxena, daughter of Priam, was loved by Achilles, and it was when he had gone to meet her in the temple of

The Achaeans poured the blood of Polyxena [a] over the tomb of dead Achilles to propitiate his wrath, and took each his lot of Trojan women and divided all their other spoil, both gold and silver: wherewith they loaded their deep ships and through the booming sea set sail from Troy, having made an end of the war.

Thymbraean Apollo that he was slain by Paris. On the capture of Troy Neoptolemus sacrificed her at the tomb of Achilles; schol. Lycophr. 323; Eur. *Tr.* 261 ff.

INDEX OF PROPER NAMES IN COLLUTHUS AND TRYPHIODORUS

[C. = Colluthus. T. = Tryphiodorus.]

INDEX OF PROPER NAMES